Praise for *A Companion to Folklore*

"*A Companion to Folklore* is nothing if not international, and this quality alone distinguishes it from most earlier reference works and makes it an important resource for the field."

Western Folklore

"Nearly all college and university libraries will want this book. Summing Up: Essential."

Choice

"This book presents challenging and inspiring essays about a field that is often misconceived as the harbor of tradition. The volume succeeds in representing folklore as a vital component of human existence and folkloristics as an indispensable discipline within the humanities."

Ulrich Marzolph, Enzyklopädie des Märchens, Göttingen;
President of the International Society for Folk Narrative Research

"Magisterial, engaging, smart, and always thought-provoking, *A Companion to Folklore* both reflects and will help shape the broad and increasingly interdisciplinary ambit – and promise – of the field."

Don Brenneis, University of California, Santa Cruz

"This comprehensive companion to folklore represents the best recent work and an exciting vision of what folklore can offer other disciplines."

Barbara Kirshenblatt Gimblett, New York University

"Magisterial in its scope at bursting at every seam with information, Bendix and Hasan-Rokem's *A Companion to Folklore* will spark a rich transnational conversation regarding future directions for folkloristics."

Charles L. Briggs, co-author of Voices of Modernity

The *Blackwell Companions to Anthropology* offers a series of comprehensive syntheses of the traditional subdisciplines, primary subjects, and geographic areas of inquiry for the field. Taken together, the series represents both a contemporary survey of anthropology and a cutting edge guide to the emerging research and intellectual trends in the field as a whole.

Forthcoming

A Companion to Folklore

Edited by
Regina F. Bendix
and Galit Hasan-Rokem

WILEY Blackwell

This paperback edition first published 2014
© 2012 John Wiley & Sons, Ltd
Edition history: Blackwell Publishing Ltd (hardback, 2012)

Registered Office
John Wiley & Sons, Ltd, The Atrium, Southern Gate, Chichester, West Sussex, PO19 8SQ, UK

Editorial Offices
350 Main Street, Malden, MA 02148-5020, USA
9600 Garsington Road, Oxford, OX4 2DQ, UK
The Atrium, Southern Gate, Chichester, West Sussex, PO19 8SQ, UK

For details of our global editorial offices, for customer services, and for information about how to apply for permission to reuse the copyright material in this book please see our website at www.wiley.com/wiley-blackwell.

Library of Congress Cataloging-in-Publication Data

A companion to folklore / edited by Regina F. Bendix and Galit Hasan-Rokem.
    p.   cm. – (Blackwell Companions to Anthropology)
  Includes bibliographical references and index.
  ISBN 978-1-4051-9499-0 (hardcover : alk. paper) –
  ISBN 978-1-118-86314-5 (paperback : alk. paper)
1. Folklore–Study and teaching.   2. Folklore–Cross-cultural studies.   I. Bendix, Regina.
II. Hasan-Rokem, Galit.
  GR45.C64 2012
  398.2–dc23

                                        2011036434

A catalogue record for this book is available from the British Library.

Cover image: From top: Frank Proffitt sings and plays for Anne Warner, Pick Britches Valley, North Carolina, 1941. Photo by Frank Warner. Frank and Anne Warner Collection (AFC 1950/002, p04), American Folklife Center, Library of Congress; Shadow puppets, Thailand, photo (c) Robert Harding Picture Library Ltd / Alamy; Graffiti photo (c) Core Images – Urban / Alamy.

Set in 10/12.5pt Galliard by SPi Publisher Services, Pondicherry, India
Printed in Singapore by C.O.S. Printers Pte Ltd

1   2014

CONTENTS

NOTES ON CONTRIBUTORS

Cristina Bacchilega is Professor of English at the University of Hawai'i at Mānoa, where she teaches folklore and literature, fairy tales and their adaptations, and cultural studies. She has published *Legendary Hawai'i and the Politics of Place: Tradition, Translation, and Tourism* (2007) and *Postmodern Fairy Tales: Gender and Narrative Strategies* (1997), and she is the review editor of *Marvels and Tales: Journal of Fairy-Tale Studies*. Recent essays include "Generic Complexity in Early 21st-Century Fairy-Tale Film" with John Rieder (2010) and work on nineteenth-century translations of *The Arabian Nights* into Hawai'ian with historian Noelani Arista and translator Sahoa Fukushima (2007). With Donatella Izzo and Bryan Kamaoli Kuwada, she co-edited "Sustaining Hawai'ian Sovereignty," a special issue of *Anglistica*, an online journal of international interdisciplinary studies (2011). Her current book project focuses on the poetics and politics of twenty-first-century fairy-tale adaptations.

Richard Bauman is Distinguished Professor Emeritus of Folklore and Ethnomusicology, Communication and Culture, and Anthropology at Indiana University, Bloomington. The principal foci of his research include narrative, oral poetics, performance, genre, and language ideologies. He has done fieldwork in Scotland, Nova Scotia, Texas, and Mexico, historical research on early Quakers and medieval Iceland, and is currently engaged in research on the metapragmatics of early commercial sound recordings. He has served as President of the Society for Linguistic Anthropology and the Semiotic Society of America, and as Editor of the *Journal of American Folklore*. Among his publications are *Verbal Art as Performance* (1977), *Story, Performance, and Event* (1986), *Voices of Modernity* (with Charles L. Briggs, 2003), which won the Edward Sapir Prize of the Society for Linguistic Anthropology, and *A World of Others' Words* (2004). In 2008, he received the Lifetime Scholarly Achievement Award of the American Folklore Society.

Ursula Baumgardt is Professor of Orality and African Literature at the Institut National des Langues et Civilisations Orientales (INALCO) in Paris. She is also member of the council on Langage, Langues et Cultures d'Afrique Noire (LLACAN) and a member of the council of the International Society for Oral Literature in Africa (ISOLA). Her publications include *Littératures orales africaines. Perspectives théoriques et méthodologiques* (with Jean Derive, Ed., 2008), *Autour de la performance, Cahiers de Littérature orale* (Sandra Bornand, Ed., 2009), and *L'expression de l'espace dans les langues africaines I, Journal des Africanistes* (Paulette Roulon-Doko, Ed., 2010).

Regina F. Bendix has been Professor of Cultural Anthropology/European Ethnology at Georg-August-University in Göttingen, Germany, since 2001; before then she taught folklore and anthropology at the University of Pennsylvania, Philadelphia. She studied folklore and *Volkskunde* in Switzerland and the United States and has throughout her career enjoyed the challenge of linking European and American research traditions. Among her major research interests at present is the interface of culture, economics and politics as it manifests itself in questions of heritage and cultural property as well as productions for tourists. She has also worked extensively on matters pertaining to the history of the discipline, including in her monograph *In Search of Authenticity* (1997), and has contributed to research in narrative and the ethnography of communication as well as the ethnography of the senses.

Fernando Fischman teaches at the University of Buenos Aires, Argentina. He is a researcher for CONICET (Consejo Nacional de Investigaciones Científicas y Técnicas). His main research interests are verbal art, performance theory, Jewish-Argentine folklore, and social memory. He edited *Donos da Palavra: autoria, performance e experiência em narrativas orais na América do Sul* (2007) (with Luciana Hartmann) and *Dime cómo cuentas ... Narradores folklóricos y narradores urbanos profesionales* (2009) (with Maria Inés Palleiro).

Harvey E. Goldberg held the Sarah Allen Shaine Chair in Sociology and Anthropology at the Hebrew University of Jerusalem. He has focused on the cultural history of the Jews in North Africa, on religious and ethnic identities in Israel, and on the interfaces between anthropology and Jewish Studies. He has been a Visiting Professor at the University of California, Berkeley, and at Boğaziçi University, Istanbul, a Visiting Lecturer at the École des Hautes Études en Science Sociale, Paris, and a Fellow at the Center for Advanced Judaic Studies at the University of Pennsylvania. His books include *Jewish Life in Muslim Libya: Rivals and Relatives* (University of Chicago Press, 1990) and *Jewish Passages: Cycles of Jewish Life* (University of California Press, 2003). He has recently co-edited *Perspectives on Israeli Anthropology* with Esther Hertzog, Orit Abuhav, and Emanuel Marx (Wayne State University Press, 2010).

Pauline Greenhill has been Professor of Women's and Gender Studies at the University of Winnipeg since 1996. Her most recent books are *Make The Night Hideous: Four English-Canadian Charivaris* (University of Toronto Press, 2010) and with Sidney Eve Matrix, co-editor, *Fairy Tale Films: Visions of Ambiguity* (Utah State University Press, 2010). With Liz Locke, primary editor, and Theresa Vaughan, she is co-editor of the *Encyclopedia of Women's Folklore and Folklife* (Greenwood Press, 2 vols., 2008). She has published in *Signs: Journal of Women in Culture* *and Society*; *parallax*; *Jeunesse: Young People, Texts, Cultures*; *Acadiensis*; *Resources for Feminist Research/Documentation sur la Recherche Feministe*; *Marvels and Tales*; *Ethnologies*; *Canadian Journal of Women and the Law*; *Manitoba History*; *Türkbilig: Türkoloji Arastirmalari*; and the *Journal of American Folklore,* among other journals. She is currently working with Kay Turner on a collection tentatively entitled *Transgressive Tales: Queering the Fairy Tale* for Wayne State University Press.

Valdimar T. Hafstein is an Associate Professor of Folkloristics/Ethnology in the School of Social Sciences at the University of Iceland, and a Visting Professor at Gothenburg University. He completed his PhD at the University of California, Berkeley, in 2004. His publications in recent years have focused on cultural heritage as a concept, category, and social dynamic and on intellectual property in traditional expressions. His book on the making of intangible cultural heritage in UNESCO is forthcoming from the University of Illinois Press and he is presently involved in a European collaborative research project on "Copyrighting Creativity."

Lee Haring is Professor Emeritus of English at Brooklyn College of the City University of New York. He has conducted folklore fieldwork in Kenya, Madagascar (as Fulbright Senior Lecturer), and Mauritius (as Fulbright researcher). He has published *Malagasy Tale Index*, a comprehensive analysis of folktales, the English translation of *Ibonia, Epic of Madagascar*, available at http://xroads.virginia.edu/~public/ Ibonia/frames.html, and *Verbal Arts in Madagascar*, a study of four genres of oral literature. His book *Stars and Keys: Folktales and Creolization in the Indian Ocean* shows the cultural interrelations of the Southwest Indian Ocean islands, through translating and commenting on a hundred stories from Madagascar, Mauritius, Réunion, the Comoros, and Seychelles. He also published the bilingual field manual *Collecting Folklore in Mauritius*, in English and Kreol, and two collections of tales. He has taught in graduate folklore programs at the University of California at Berkeley, the University of Pennsylvania, and the University of Connecticut.

Lauri Harvilahti, Director of the Folklore Archives of the Finnish Literature Society, has, as a result of fieldwork carried out over 20 years, become familiar with a number of traditional cultures. His theoretical interests lie in ethnocultural processes and ethnic identity, computer folkloristics, and currently questions of archiving oral tradition. He is currently directing a project for the Academy of Finland and the Chinese Academy of Social Sciences on "Documenting and Archiving Oral Tradition: Research and Interdisciplinary Approaches" (2009–2011), and he is in charge of the digital archive projects of the Finnish Literature Society's Folklore Archives. He has published a number of monographs in Finnish and his publications in English include "The Holy Mountain. Studies of Upper Altay Oral Poetry."

Galit Hasan-Rokem is Max and Margarethe Grunwald Professor of Folklore at the Mandel Institute of Jewish Studies at the Hebrew University of Jerusalem and Director of the Folklore Research Center there. Her publications include: *Proverbs in Israeli Folk Narratives: A Structural Semantic Analysis of Folklore. FFC 232* (1982); *The Wandering Jew: Interpretations of a Christian Legend* (1986, co-edited with A. Dundes); *Untying the Knot: On Riddles and Other Enigmatic Modes* (1996, co-edited with D. Shulman); *Web of Life: Folklore and Midrash in Rabbinic Literature* (2000); *Tales of the*

Neighborhood: Jewish Narrative Dialogues in Late Antiquity (Berkeley 2003); "Dialogue as Ethical Conduct: The Folk Festival that Was Not," *Research Ethics in Studies of Culture and Social Life. FFC 292* (2007), eds. B. G. Alver *et al.*, pp. 192–208; "Jews as Postcards, or Postcards as Jews: Mobility in a Modern Genre," *Jewish Quarterly Review* 99/4 (2009): 505–546. She has served as President of the International Society for Folk Narrative Research (1998–2005), and as Head of the Mandel Institute of Jewish Studies at the Hebrew University (2001–2004), as Visiting Professor – among other institutions – at the University of California, Berkeley, the University of Pennsylvania, and the University of Chicago, and has been Fellow at the Wissenschaftskolleg zu Berlin, at the Institute for Advanced Studies, and at Scholion – Interdisciplinary Research Center in Jewish Studies at the Hebrew University.

Gertraud Koch is a Professor at the Department of Communication and Cultural Management at Zeppelin University, a private university in Friedrichshafen, Germany. She studied European Ethnology/Empirical Culture Research in Frankfurt am Main and Tübingen. She has a doctorate in European Ethnology from Humboldt University in Berlin and wrote her dissertation on the culture of artificial intelligence. Her research fields include working cultures, diversity and migration, urban and regional studies as well as virtual communities. Recent publications discuss how the digital media augment and enhance life worlds and how these media can be approached ethnographically.

Debora Kodish is the founding director of the Philadelphia Folklore Project (PFP), where she has worked since 1987. After receiving a PhD in folklore from the University of Texas, she worked on emerging public folklore projects in Oregon and Maine, and taught before focusing primarily on developing public interest folklore practice in Philadelphia (see www.folkloreproject.org). There, she has participated in dozens of long-term collaborative efforts with local activists, artists, and community members (and raised a family). In between responsibilities for the day-to-day management of PFP, she is working on a book on public interest folklore.

Lydia H. Liu is a theorist of language, media, and translingual practices. She teaches at Columbia University as W. T. Tam Professor in the Humanities in the Department of East Asian Languages and Cultures and the Institute of Comparative Literature and Society. She directs the Center for Translingual and Transculture Studies at Tsinghua University in Beijing. Her work has focused on cross-cultural exchange in recent history, the movement of words, theories, and artifacts across national boundaries, and the evolution of writing and technology. She is the author of *Translingual Practice: Literature, National Culture, and Translated Modernity* (1995), *The Clash of Empires: The Invention of China in Modern World Making* (2004), and the editor of *Tokens of Exchange: The Problem of Translation in Global Circulations* (1999). Her new book, entitled *The Freudian Robot: Digital Media and the Future of the Unconscious* was published by the University of Chicago Press in 2010.

Orvar Löfgren is an Emeritus Professor of European Ethnology at Lund University, Sweden. The cultural analysis of everyday life has been an ongoing focus in his research; see for example *The Secret World of Doing Nothing* (together with Billy Ehn, 2010) and *Off the Edge: Experiments in Cultural Analysis* (edited with Richard Wilk

2006). Other central research fields have been studies of national identity and transnational mobility, as in tourism and travel, see, for example, *On Holiday. A History of Vacationing* (1999).

Sabina Magliocco is Professor of Anthropology at California State University, Northridge. She grew up in Italy and the United States. She received her AB from Brown University in 1980 and her PhD from Indiana University in 1988. As recipient of Guggenheim, National Endowment for the Humanities, Fulbright, and Hewlett fellowships, and an honorary Fellow of the American Folklore Society, she has published on religion, folklore, foodways, festival, and witchcraft in Europe and the United States. Her books include *The Two Madonnas: The Politics of Festival in a Sardinian Community* (1993 and 2005), *Neo-Pagan Sacred Art and Altars: Making Things Whole* (2001), and *Witching Culture: Folklore and Neo-Paganism in America* (2004). Along with documentary film maker John M. Bishop, she produced and directed a set of documentary films entitled *Oss Tales* (2007), on a May Day custom in Cornwall and California. Her hobbies include music (she plays guitar and banjo), gardening, and animal welfare. She is a Gardnerian priestess and has a small, eclectic coven in the Los Angeles area. For more information, visit her website at http://www.csun.edu/~sm32646.

Phillip H. McArthur is Professor of International Cultural Studies at Brigham Young University Hawai'i, and an Affiliated Faculty to the Jonathan Napela Center for Hawai'ian and Pacific Islands Studies. He presently serves as the Dean to the College of Language, Culture, and Arts. He is also the current editor of the journal *Pacific Studies*. His research and publications concentrate on social theoretical and semiotic approaches to oral narrative, cultural performance, history, cosmology, nationalism, and globalization in Oceania, with special attention to the Marshall Islands. His publications include, "Narrative, Cosmos, and Nation: Intertextuality and Power in the Marshall Islands" in the *Journal of American Folklore*, "Ambivalent Fantasies: Local Prehistories and Global Dramas in the Marshall Islands" in the *Journal of Folklore Research*, and "Modernism and Pacific Ways of Knowing: An Uneasy Dialogue in Micronesia" in *Pacific Rim Studies*.

Akiko Mori is currently Professor of Cultural Anthropology and Ethnographical Research of Central Europe at the National Museum of Ethnology, Osaka, Japan. She has carried out ethnographical research in Carinthia and Berlin since the mid-1980s. Her recent theme is "Anthropological Descriptions and their Social Context," and in this framework, she worked on "A Comparative Study on the Historical Process of Folklore Studies since the 1950s in Germany and Japan: Academic Interests and Society" (2007–2010). This project includes three folklorists, M. Iwamot, Y. Shigenobu, and H. Hokkyo, and one media study scholar, T. Sato. The contribution in this volume reflects a part of this project. Her works include "German Volkskunde and Cultural Anthropology" (*Bulletin of the National Museum of Ethnology*, 2009) (in Japanese) and "Grab, Epitaph und Friedhof. Neue Zugänge: ethnologischer Familienforschung am Beispiel einer Kärntner Landgemeinde" (*Historische Anthropologie*, 1995) (in German).

Sadhana Naithani teaches literature and folklore at the Centre of German Studies, Jawaharlal Nehru University, New Delhi. She is the author of *In Quest of Indian*

Folktales (2006) and of *The Story-Time of the British Empire* (2010). Her current research interests are German folklore theory since 1945 and Indian folk performers since 1947.

Dorothy Noyes is Associate Professor of English and Comparative Studies at Ohio State University, where she directs the Center for Folklore Studies and is a research associate of the Mershon Center for International Security Studies. She is the author of *Fire in the Plaça: Catalan Festival Politics After Franco* (University of Pennsylvania Press, 2003). Her interests include the traditional public sphere in Romance-speaking Europe, the social organization of vernacular creativity, the careers of culture concepts, and the role of cultural performance in international relations.

Diarmuid Ó Giolláin is Professor in the Department of Irish Language and Literature and Concurrent Professor in the Department of Anthropology at the University of Notre Dame. He previously worked in and headed the Department of Folklore and Ethnology in University College Cork, Ireland. His publications include *Locating Irish Folklore. Tradition, Modernity, Identity* (Cork: Cork University Press, 2000) and *An Dúchas agus an Domhan* (The Native/Vernacular and the World) (Cork: Cork University Press, 2005). He recently was guest editor for a special issue of *Ethnologie française* (2011/2) devoted to Irish ethnology. His research interests include the history of folklore and ethnology; ethnomuseology and heritage; and popular religion.

Arzu Öztürkmen is a professor of Folklore and History at Boğaziçi University, Istanbul. She received a doctorate from the University of Pennsylvania and is the author of *Türkiye'de Folklor ve Milliyetçilik* (Istanbul: Iletism Yayınları, 1998) in addition to numerous articles on folklore, oral history, and cultural history in the Turkish and Ottoman world.

Alexander A. Panchenko is Director of the Research Center for Literary Theory and Interdisciplinary Studies at the Institute of Russian Literature, Russian Academy of Sciences (St Petersburg, Russia), a Professor of Social Anthropology at St Petersburg State University (College of Liberal Arts and Sciences), and the director of the Center for Anthropology of Religion at the European University at St Petersburg. His research interests include religious folklore and vernacular religion in Russia and Europe, theory and history of folklore research, contemporary folklore and popular culture, and anthropological approaches in the study of Russian literature. He published more than 100 research works (including two books) in Russian and other European languages on vernacular religion in rural Russia, various religious movements in modern Russia, the political use of folklore in the Soviet Union, and comparative studies in folklore and anthropology of religion.

Alison Dundes Renteln is a Professor of Political Science and Anthropology at the University of Southern California where she teaches Law and Public Policy with an emphasis on international law and human rights. A graduate of Harvard (History and Literature), she has a PhD in Jurisprudence and Social Policy from the University of California, Berkeley and a JD from the USC Law School. Her publications focus on the conflicts between state law and folk law including *The Cultural Defense* (Oxford, 2004), *Folk Law* (University of Wisconsin, 1995), *Multicultural Jurisprudence:*

Comparative Perspectives on the Cultural Defense (Hart, 2009), and *Cultural Law: International, National, and Indigenous* (Cambridge, 2010). She has taught seminars on cultural rights for judges, lawyers, court interpreters, jury consultants, and police officers at meetings of the American Bar Association, the National Association of Women Judges, North American South Asian Bar Association, American Society of Trial Consultants, and others.

Bjarne Rogan is Professor of Culture History (formerly European ethnology) in the Department of Culture History and Oriental Languages, University of Oslo. He is presently director of the French-Norwegian Center for Social Sciences and Humanities in Paris. He has published extensively in the following fields: Material culture and consumption studies, especially on collecting; transport history and tourism; littoral culture and fisheries; language, culture and communication; museology and the historiography of European ethnology, with a special focus on its organizations. His most recent edited books are on the history, politics, and ideologies of museums (Oslo, 2010) and on material culture and the materiality of culture (Oslo, 2011). He is presently working on a book on the history of ethnology and folklore in Norway. For further information, see http://www.hf.uio.no/ikos/english/people/aca/bjarner/index.html.

Hagar Salamon is the head of the Jewish and Comparative Folklore Program and the Africa Unit at the Harry S. Truman Research Institute for the Advancement of Peace, both at the Hebrew University of Jerusalem, Israel. Her research focuses on cultural perceptions of the Ethiopian Jews both in Ethiopia and Israel, women's expressive culture and life stories, as well as present-day Israeli folklore. She is the author of *The Hyena People: Ethiopian Jews in Christian Ethiopia* (University of California Press, 1999), editor of *Ethiopia: Jewish Communities in the East in The Nineteenth and Twentieth Centuries* (Jerusalem: Ben-Zvi, 2007), and is a co-editor of the journal *Jerusalem Studies in Jewish Folklore*. She lives in Jerusalem with her husband and four daughters.

Dani Schrire is based at the Jewish and Comparative Program at the Hebrew University of Jerusalem. His dissertation, "Collecting the Pieces of Exile: A Critical view of Folklore Research in Israel in the 1940s–1950s" is under evaluation. It is based on an ethnographical-history of folklore studies in Israel in the context of the history of Jewish folkloristics in Europe and it employs an Actor-Network-Theory approach. Currently, he is a Minerva post-doctoral fellow at the Institute for Cultural Anthropology/European Ethnology at the University of Göttingen. His latest publication "Raphael Patai, Jewish Folklore, Comparative Folkloristics, and American Anthropology" appeared recently in the *Journal of Folklore Research*.

Brigitta Schmidt-Lauber is Professor of European Ethnology at the University of Vienna. She studied *Volkskunde,* ethnology (*Völkerkunde*), and social and economic history at the universities of Hamburg and Cologne and gained her PhD in 1997 ("Ethnicity as social practice"). After completing post-doctoral qualifications at the University of Hamburg ("Gemütlichkeit," 2003) and becoming a Visiting Lecturer at the universities of Vienna, Basel, and Zurich she was appointed professor at the Georg-August University in Göttingen in 2006. In 2009 she accepted a full professorship at the University of Vienna. In addition to ethnographic methods and methodology, ethnicity, and migration, she is an expert in the area of cultural urban study. Her empirical research has included fieldwork on the ethnicity of German-speaking people in Namibia, on the St Pauli district soccer club, and soccer as an urban phenomenon. She is also leading a research project on everyday life in middletowns as urban life beyond the metropolis.

Peter Seitel retired from the Smithsonian Institution in 2004 as Senior Folklorist Emeritus. He has written about several folklore genres, about genre itself, and about social practices that make use of folklore genres.

Amy Shuman is Professor of Folklore, English, Women's Studies, and Anthropology at Ohio State University. She is the author of three books: *Storytelling Rights: The Uses of Oral and Written Texts Among Urban Adolescents*, *Other People's Stories: Entitlement Claims and the Critique of Empathy*, and, with Carol Bohmer, *Rejecting Refugees: Political Asylum in the 21st Century*. Her current projects include a study of the life history narratives related by artisan stonecarvers in Pietrasanta, Italy, research on narratives told by the parents of children with disabilities, and community narrative projects at the intersection of collective memory and public policy.

Francisco Vaz da Silva teaches anthropology and folklore at Instituto Universitário de Lisboa (ISCTE-IUL), Lisbon, Portugal. His research interests include symbolic codes in mythology, ritual, wondertales, and the arts; and intertextual techniques for narrative analysis. His most recent book is *Archeology of Intangible Heritage* (New York: Lang, 2008).

Martin Skrydstrup is a Postdoctoral Fellow in the Department of Anthropology, University of Copenhagen. He holds a doctorate in Cultural Anthropology from Columbia University, New York, supported by Fulbright and the Danish Research Academy (FUR). His dissertation project, entitled "Once Ours: The Making and Unmaking of Claims to Cultural Property," cut through a lateral anthropology of exchange with postcolonial theory, arguing for a new theory of topology. For this research, he conducted ethnographies in Hawai'i, Ghana, Iceland, and Greenland, exploring various repatriation cases on a comparative scale, supported by grants from Wenner-Gren and the National Science Foundation. In the field of cultural resource management, he has worked as an expert consultant for the Nordic Africa Institute and the UN World Intellectual Property Organization. He has served on the Board of the International Committee for Museums and Collections of Ethnography (ICME) as a correspondent for repatriation and was appointed a special advisor to the Ethics Committee of the International Council of Museums (ICOM).

Stephen D. Winick is a folklorist, writer and editor at the American Folklife Center at the Library of Congress. He obtained a PhD in folklore and folklife from the University of Pennsylvania, and has taught folklore courses both there and at George Mason University. For over 20 years, he was a columnist and contributing editor at *Dirty Linen, the Magazine of Folk and World Music*, and has published on folk music in many academic and popular venues. He is also a singer of traditional folksongs and performs with several groups in the Washington DC area.

INTRODUCTION

Regina F. Bendix and
Galit Hasan-Rokem

Once, a number of blind men encountered an elephant. Every one of them touched one of the parts of its body with his hand and imagined the animal in his mind. Then they turned away. The one who had touched the leg said that the shape of the elephant was long and round like the trunk of a tree or a palm tree. The one who had touched the back thought that its shape was similar to that of a high mountain or a hill. The one who had touched its trunk described it as something smooth without any bones. And the one who had touched its ear thought it to be of a large size, thin, and constantly moving. In that manner, each of the blind men described that part of the animal that he himself had sensed. At the same time, each of them said something different from the others and accused them of misjudgment and inaccuracy in relation to the elephants shape as sensed by himself.[1]

What do people in general think of when they hear the word folklore: stories, festivals, open air museums, holiday greetings and party games? Masks, riddles, lullabies, and fortune cookies? Crafts and knowledge of healing plants? All of these and much more is comprised in the term folklore and much as in the ancient parable about the wondrous elephant, the field of folklore research unfolds as a multifaceted array of learning, best understood when many views, perspectives, and experiences are combined. This book is meant to introduce its readers to folklore studies by illustrating how folklore has stimulated imaginations and sent individuals to places near and far, to forgotten books and internet blogs – all to study folklore where it lived and lives. Becoming a folklore scholar involves questions about the things that people in general call folklore. Some of the answers may grow out of looking at a number of phenomena that are called folklore or, as in some international contexts, traditional cultural expressions. Yet another set of questions deals with the context and the circumstances in which a thing, an event or a creative expression conceived of as folklore unfolds or materializes. Documenting such phenomena in the here and now, comparing them or

A Companion to Folklore, First Edition. Edited by Regina F. Bendix and Galit Hasan-Rokem.
© 2012 John Wiley & Sons, Ltd. Published 2012 John Wiley & Sons, Ltd.

following their transformations through time and space are all approaches to begin understanding how individuals and groups create and transform expressive forms.

The *Companion to Folklore Studies* seeks to represent the state of the art for readers intrigued with the field's theoretical potential and international scope. The volume has grown out of our conviction that there is not one unambiguous way of defining what folklore is and what its study comprises. For although folkloristics has always been international in aspiration, the field is also closely tied to the politics of groups and states and hence its flourishing has depended on the vagaries of state institutions. The best approach to unveil this elephant appeared thus to be an assembling of answers from colleagues engaged in the subject, its study and history around the globe: to comprehend an elephant, it is necessary to consult as many experts as possible who are situated at diverging angles in relation to the object of our investigation. As our object is not really a humongous mammal but rather a complex, multi-layered and fascinating cultural phenomenon and the equally complex intellectual engagement with it, the discourses unfolding in this book will tell more intricate tales than the leg, the tail or the trunk of the elephant.

This volume is rooted in the awareness that in the present, academic folklore studies find themselves situated among a number of other fields and sharing large portions of discourse with them. With its inconclusive situation between the humanities and the social sciences, folkloristics has lost its maverick status by being joined in this hybridity by many other fields such as large elements of, for instance, geography, psychology, archeology, and even history. The rise of inter-disciplinarity itself – in some places growing into a veritable norm of good research – has renewed the vision of folklore studies in the eyes of its practitioners and others.

Politically, the rise of folklore and its study has been associated with the grand transformations entailed in democratization and industrialization, in short, the powers of (Western) modernity (Bauman and Briggs 2003). Modernist thinking rejected the traditional – long perceived as the seedbed of folklore. In tandem with such rejection, the documentation and preservation of folklore began to flourish as a testimony to a given society's recognition of its movement forward. Yet in the present era, we acknowledge multiple modernities unfolding at different rates within the cultural poly-systems of the world. Detraditionalization and retraditionalization have often gone hand in hand, and the state of folklore research in history and in the present has been intertwined with this dynamic, while simultaneously offering a reflexive accompaniment to it.

As a subject, folklore is vast, for there is hardly a facet of cultural practice that is not in some way shaped by expressive forces. "Folklore is everything" may sometimes be a sour judgment of those who marvel at a field that may stretch from interpreting Homeric texts to investigating immigrant gardening in a Scandinavian capital, to name just some concrete examples of the variation everyone who has been at a folklore studies conference instantly recognizes. Folkloristics comprises the study of many phenomena and areas that are studied by other disciplines. Scholars are engaged in a continuous search for the coordinates which may provide for a common ground for a disciplinary discourse of folkloristics on the one hand, and may shape a graspable entity of knowledge that can be fitted into the existing academic structures on the other hand. The history and sociology of knowledge teaches us that institutionalized forms of transmitting a collectively accumulated set of concepts and a shared methodology and terminology reifies the existence of fields. The congregation of a scholarly collective, albeit on the pages of an edited volume, marks a stance in the persistence of a disciplinary biography. Or, using our own disciplinary tool, a compendium such as this represents one possible incarnation within the field's ethnography. This is also an opportunity for claiming, in addition to genealogy, the charting of new terrain.

We might propose that the striking consciousness about "Uprootings/ Regroundings" (as in the title of a contemporary volume, Ahmed *et al.* 2003) has actualized the kinds of discourse that folklore scholars have developed in their disciplinary dialogues. Terms and concepts such as actors, creative subjects, and locality in performance have been made usable for and by folklorists themselves but also facilitate communication with other fields as a result of new geo-political and geo-cultural configurations. Fresh streams of theory and thought rejuvenate the discussion of the subjects and processes that have been at the center of folklore studies. So, rather than feeling that by composing this reader we are sending out a voice in the wilderness, we instead sense that we are in the midst of a vivid blend of voices and ideas that we can only represent here in part, but hope to stimulate even more.

In putting together this volume, we have chosen the terms "concepts and phenomena," "location," "reflection," and "practice" as organizing principles for bodies of knowledge comprising the field. While we do not consider this order as constitutive or deterministic, we rather saw in sections thus named an opportunity for effective communication with the reader. Approaching folklore through its phenomena allows for an engagement at once with expressive practices and forms and theoretical approaches developed in an effort to circumscribe and understand them. Thanks to the fact that the disciplinary bookshelf is populated by works introducing folklore's subject matter[2] as well as by reference works offering detailed work on folklore genres and folklore in specific geographic regions and groups,[3] we are privileged here to concentrate on overarching concepts that problematize the field rather than describe it. Our format also refers to the history of concepts launched by Reinhart Koselleck (2002), focusing on the historicity of concepts and their socially interactive power, while also throwing light on the time bound ontology and epistemology of phenomena.

Whereas the section on phenomena situates the concepts discussed in a timeframe, our next section pays full tribute to the weight of local specificity and "local knowledge" (Geertz 1983) in the field of folklore studies. Notably the terminology of folklore seems to have been particularly context-sensitive: early on there has been a tension between the need for a universally applicable term, such as "physics" or "philosophy" or even "geography" on the one hand, and on the other an emically recognizable category intelligibly referencing the subject matter and its producers, such as "Volkskunde" (German), "folklivsforskning" (Swedish), "kansanrunoudentutkimus" (Finnish) or "minsuxue" (Chinese).[4] Each of these terms also demarcates clearly the focus of the field in particular linguistic contexts, so that, for instance, the Finnish term that has now been largely replaced by the universalizing "folkloristiikka," reveals the preponderance of the research of epic poetry in the formative stages of the discipline there. It may be suggested that the prevailing sentiment among folklorists to deal with something of "our own" intensified the need to forge a local term in the local language. The blatant absence of a pre-existing term in classical antiquity – which provided the terminology for sciences and disciplines established much earlier – is another reason for the diversified emergence of names for our discipline, the Greek effort to revitalize "laographia" notwithstanding. This terminological multiplicity has far-reaching epistemological consequences for instance on the level of genre, so that despite efforts being made to translate ethnic genres into analytically comparable categories (Ben-Amos 1969), the overlap very often shows discernable gaps.

The "discovery" of the expressive power of group cultures has almost always occurred at moments of political transformation in territorial histories. Such discovery has been a part of firming and defining identities, often vis-à-vis other groups vying for space and control. It is not just during the often mentioned period of Romantic nationalism that this can be observed; liberation movements, especially in postcolonial situations, but also other subaltern assertions such as ethnic or social minority group rights' struggles, show this propensity to mobilize via taking recourse to expressive traditions (Gramsci 1985: 189–195; Scott 1990). Folklore studies could thus take shape in what one might term revolutionary or transformational moments of history, with each of these situations differing in terms of the sociopolitical goals sought and – not always – achieved. Once successful, folklore studies often found themselves in a position of assisting in the preservation of the materials that had contributed to a new political matrix, turning from a revolutionary force to a guarantor of stability and continuity. Folklore thus evolves in peculiar cycles of innovation and conservatism, which also fed into the evolving discipline and is reflected in some of the institutions established both to preserve folklore and to ensure the continuity of the field devoted to its study. Inherent to folklore is, however, the power of subversion and parallel to sanctified forms of folkloric expression, new forms constantly evolve, evading the centralizing cultural institutions responsible for canonization and similar processes. Despite such consistencies observable in the tandem workings of folklore and folklore studies (a phrase that will recur many times in this volume), every location will generate particular situations marked not just by the specificity of the political systems within which actors are engaged, but by the composition of groups present or migrating in and out of a given territory, the legitimacy they are endowed with, and, among other considerations, the languages and religions that have to come into negotiation with one another. Another continuity observable even in the selection of locations assembled here is the dialectics between academic folkloristics and public folklore practice. This is a tenuous relationship which awaits further analysis, as the political contingency of folklore and/ or folklore studies within a given type of political system is far from predictable.

In addition to what we have presented as concepts and phenomena, folklore's versatility in the cultural arena is expressed in reflexive modes that make folklore perform cultural work in the context of other registers and an array of media. We would not necessarily claim a linear order of primary-secondary on an ontological level between what we have categorized as phenomena and reflections, but the analytical procedure of observing them is easiest accomplished by positing such a relationship. Thus the respective status of source and elaboration between folklore and other media with which it is brought to interact constantly oscillates in diachronic sequences, destabilizing any hierarchical order that one might attempt to introduce into the complex. Reification and codification are thus, to an extent, brief moments of stability in a continuously and dynamically unfolding process.

Under the heading of practice, we have assembled contributions that look at the work of folklorists themselves in various arenas of professional life. What do folklorists actually do? From among the many possible answers, this section affords insights into three realms of activity: folklorists' approach to conducting research in the field, folklorists engaged in work with and for the public sector, and folklorists building institutions to promote the endurance of the field and its subject matter.

To pay tribute to the foundational internationalism of folkloristics and to honor the profoundly different research histories and current perspectives of the field in different places around the globe, we approached both authors who were intimately familiar with (their) national research traditions and authors who have by training and fieldwork gained deep knowledge of a region or a central phenomenon. We were as pleased to win the participation of authors deeply grounded in an area as to convince scholars to tackle a subject they had thus far never considered assessing in the handbook format required here. As life takes unexpected turns, not everyone who initially committed to participate in this endeavor could ultimately complete the task in time for the present publication. Readers will undoubtedly note what appear to be glaring omissions. As editors, we have our sights firmly set on a future second edition where we would hope to include further contributions on Africa and the Middle East, ancient and historical folklore issues, theoretical aspects that have not been specifically treated here such as embodiment, gender, ecology and place-making, as well as the interfaces between folklore and other fields of expressive culture such as sports, politics, medicine, painting and sculpture, and so forth.

Finally, it is a great pleasure to thank a number of people without whom this endeavor would not have seen completion. First, we want to express our appreciation and admiration to the contributors; as we realized ourselves, compiling any one of the chapters enclosed proved to be a challenge so as to find an acceptable balance between choosing the most essential aspects of a given corner of disciplinary practice and representing adequately what may be most important to knowledgeable readers. From the cooperation with our authors, we have not only learned a great deal but have also enjoyed their intellectual patience and generosity. Further, we owe thanks to our mentors, colleagues and students who all have enriched and widened our view of the field that we share. Our thanks also go to Rosalie Robertson who approached us to take on this task and to Julia Kirk who has devotedly accompanied our toil. We place this volume into the hands of hopefully many interested readers whose criticism, reflection, and perhaps also some approval, we are expecting with some trepidation. Finally, we thank each other.

NOTES

1 Translated by Ulrich Marzolph from the oldest Arabic version in Abu Hayyan al-Tawhidi's *al-Muqabasat* (cf. Marzolph 2010, 180).

2 We would like to refer the reader here to a small selection of introductory works, largely in English, that have to our knowledge been widely used over years or even decades: Bausinger (1980 and 1999), Brednich (2001), Dorson (1972), Dundes (1967), Oring (1986), and Toelken (1996). We would expect that there exists a range of introductory works in all languages in which folklore is taught, though given the heterogeneity of the field, producing introductory texts is also one of the most difficult tasks confronted by educators working in the field.

3 The encyclopedia on folk narrative, in German, is perhaps the major ongoing reference endeavor in the field (Brednich 1975–); the following is a selection of more concise, recent encyclopedic and handbook efforts: Brown and Rosenberg (1998), Brunvand (1996), Claus *et al.* (2003), Clements (2005), Green (1997), Haase (2008), Korom (2006), Prahlad (2006), Peek and Yankah (2004).

4 For the emergence of the term "folklore" itself which has become the most, if not totally accepted term, see Dundes 1967; cf. also Dundes 1999 for a collection of classic contributions on folklore spanning two centuries which may serve as a companion to the present volume.

REFERENCES

Ahmed, Sara, Claudia Castañeda, Anne-Marie Fortier, and Mimi Sheller. 2003. *Uprootings/Regroundings: Questions of Home and Migration.* Oxford: Berg.

Bauman, Richard and Charles Briggs. 2003. *Voices of Modernity: Language Ideologies and the Politics of Inequality.* Cambridge: Cambridge University Press.

Bausinger, Hermann. 1980. *Formen der Volkspoesie.* 2nd, enlarged edition. Berlin: Erich Schmidt Verlag.

Bausinger, Hermann. 1999. Volkskunde. *Von der Altertumswissenschaft zur Kulturanalyse.* 2nd enlarged edition. Tübingen: Tübinger Vereinigung für Volkskunde.

Ben-Amos, Dan. 1969. "Analytical Categories and Ethnic Genres." *Genre* 2(3): 275–301.

Brednich, Rolf W., Ed. 2001. *Grundriss der Volkskunde.* 3rd, enlarged edition. Berlin: Reimer.

Brednich, Rolf W. *et al.*, Eds. 1975–. *Enzyklopädie des Märchens. Handwörterbuch zur historischen und vergleichenden Erzähl-forschung.* Berlin: De Gruyter.

Brown, Mary Ellen and Bruce Rosenberg, Eds. 1998. *Encyclopedia of Folklore and Literature.* Santa Barbara: ABC-Clio.

Brunvand, Jan Harold, Ed. 1996. *American Folklore: An Encyclopedia.* New York: Garland.

Claus, Peter J., Sarah Diamond, and Margaret A. Mills, Eds. 2003. *South Asian Folklore: An Encyclopedia: Afghanistan, Bangladesh, India, Nepal, Pakistan, Sri Lanka.* New York: Routledge.

Clements, William M., Ed. 2005. *Greenwood Encyclopedia of World Folklore.* Santa Barbara: ABC-CLIO.

Dorson, Richard M., Ed. 1972. *Folklore and Folklife. An Introduction.* Chicago: University of Chicago Press.

Dundes, Alan, Ed. 1967. *The Study of Folklore.* Engelwood Cliffs, NJ: Prentice Hall.

Dundes, Alan. 1999. *International Folkloristics. Classic Contributions by the Founders of the Field.* Oxford: Rowman and Littlefield.

Geertz, Clifford. 1983. *Local Knowledge. Further Essays in Interpretive Anthropology.* New York: Basic Books.

Green, Thomas A., Ed. 1997. *Folklore: An Encyclopedia of Beliefs, Customs, Tales, Music, and Art.* New York: Garland.

Gramsci, Antonio. 1985. *Selections from Cultural Writings.* Trans. William Boelhower, David Forgacs, and Geoffrey Nowell-Smith. Cambridge, MA: Harvard University Press.

Haase, Donald. 2008. *The Greenwood Encyclopedia of Folktales and Fairy Tales.* Westport, CT: Greenwood Press.

Korom, Frank, Ed. 2006. *South Asian Folklore. A Handbook.* Santa Barbara: ABC-CLIO.

Koselleck, Reinhart. 2002. *The Practice of Conceptual History: Timing, History, Spacing Concepts. (Cultural Memory in the Present).* Stanford: Stanford University Press.

Marzolph, Ulrich. 2010. "The Migration of Didactic Narratives across Religious Boundaries" in R. Forster and R. Günthart, Eds. *Didaktisches Erzählen.* Bern: Peter Lang, pp. 173–188.

Oring, Elliott, Ed. 1986. *Folk Groups and Folklore Genres. An Introduction.* Logan: Utah State University Press.

Peek, Philipp and Kwesi Yankah, Eds. 2004. *African Folklore: An Encyclopedia.* New York: Routledge.

Prahlad, Asand. 2006. *The Greenwood Encyclopedia of African American Folklore.* Westport, CT: Greenwood Press.

Scott, James C. 1990. *Domination and the Arts of Resistance. Hidden Transcripts.* New Haven: Yale University Press.

Toelken, Barre. 1996. *The Dynamics of Folklore.* Revised and expanded edition. Logan: Utah State University Press.

PART I

CONCEPTS AND PHENOMENA

INTRODUCTION TO PART I
Concepts and Phenomena

Regina F. Bendix and
Galit Hasan-Rokem

In our initial chapters we would like to introduce folklore as it is dialectically and hermeneutically processed by its practitioners as well as by those who study it. As revealed by the frequent appearance in our writing of the twin expression "folklore and folkloristics," much of folklore studies is invested in the negotiation of the field's epistemology between the production of folklore in communities and the definition of it as a distinct field of academic research. This peculiar interrelationship also accounts for much of the sociological reality which is perhaps unique for this field, i.e. the intense communication between the creators of folklore, on the various levels of its production, and its scientific researchers.

Investigating the social base of folklore is thus the logical point of departure of our exposition. Class, gender, age, occupation; local, linguistic, ethnic or national identity – all these are defining features of the phenomena of folklore. However, only occupation receives separate treatment among the chapters here presented, whereas the presence of the others is interlaced in the other phenomena discussed, especially in the first chapter of this section.

Tradition has always been a major term in the definition of folklore (except for pronouncedly present-oriented definitions). Tradition is of course defined relative to the culture from which the particular definition grows. What is common, however, to all definitions known is their dialogic and dialectical relationship to modernity, to which it most often serves as a foil. Post-modern thought may present some alternative configurations in which tradition becomes intertwined in the contemporary world, due to both inherent theoretical development, but perhaps even more so due to the emphatic mobility of our time where societies earlier conceptualized as traditional become in various modes suffused with characteristics of modernity (technologies, social modes of behavior, etc.). On the other hand, many societies that have been conceptualized as modern are hosts to populations stemming from less modernized contexts.

One of the first and major areas of folklore collection and study was narrative, later termed verbal art so as to include the full span of oral expressive culture. During the initial phase of building the discipline, collecting and sorting the materials in a variety of archival modalities was a major preoccupation, linked not least to the nation build-ing enterprise with which folklore studies was implicitly or explicitly involved. Once sizable amounts of particularly narrative and related materials (such as songs, riddles, proverbs, etc.) had been collected and published, attention increasingly turned to theoretical concerns about classification, origin, and distribution, while communities and individuals engaged in narration and transmission were largely ignored. The top-ics chosen to address phenomena in the realm of verbal art in the present volume represent approaches that amplified this early fascination with the materials' existence and spread in folklore scholarship with new theoretical interests. These also reflect a new engagement with modes of producing folklore and, eventually, with actors. With poetics, orality/textuality, and performance, we direct attention to concepts that allow for the tracing of theoretical transformations which also had profound meth-odological consequences.

The relevance of the concept of poetics may initially be rooted in the early focus on texts and consequently in the theoretical engagement with textual disciplines, mainly literary scholarship. However, with the emergence of semiotics and its borrowing of theoretical models from verbal expressive modes, poetics has become available for the study of folklore in all its manifestations. Through the lens of poetics, genre emerges as a diagnostic, organizing, and interpretive principle, and new ways of considering issues of subjectivity, ethnicity, and universality become discernible.

Fieldwork within oral societies enabled scholars to experience narrative within set-tings not taking recourse to literacy and attendant canons of evaluation. Communicating such experience within the realm of folklore scholarship brought into focus orality's creative universe, and allowed for the recognition of an emic aesthetics in counterdis-tinction to the analytic or etic perspective brought into the field by researchers. Scholars were challenged to evaluate and subsequently modify their own textualiza-tion practices analogously to later moves in anthropological ethnographies reflecting on "writing culture." Performance, in turn, augmented such field experience with trajectories emanating from linguistics and rhetoric. Aided by ever more precise and mobile recording devices, scholars were able to study aspects of folkloric performance in finely grained detail, and could confirm the sophisticated behavioral repertoire and practiced skill constitutive of every instance of folklore production.

Thinking together symbol, myth and ritual is a statement on the interrelatedness of expressive media in folklore. The connection of cognitive, narrative and performative categories underlines the circulation of aesthetic as well as existential and social norms in genres that strongly emphasize the collective manifestations of folklore, often in socially privileged and revered contexts. This triad brings into the discussion estab-lished theoretical and terminological traditions that have long held sway in folklore studies and in neighboring disciplines, emphasizing the phenomenology of all three across divides of register and cultural value.

Similarly, religion as conceptualized in folkloristics today, has left behind a division into faith versus superstition and affords a holistic view of the span of devotional practices actors engage in within established or institutionalized global religions, within the multitude of religious groupings deriving their legitimacy from localized authorities and texts, as well as within syncretistic expressions of belief. Here, as in the realm of narrative, participant observation has opened theoretically challenging vistas; in religion and its corollaries, this pertains particularly to embodied experiences of the numinous.

Work, another activity that has patterned human life most profoundly aside from religious devotion, stands out in its elementary, economic necessity. In the twenty-first century, leisure might appear to absorb creative energies even more, yet work encompasses the span from the routinized to invention, and is a domain within which human capacity for improvisation and traditionalization manifest in tandem. Work produces value in tangible ways and is thus deeply connected to another major field of folkloristic research, material culture.

Much as archives housed collected items of verbal art, museums were the home of collected material items amassed in a manner reminiscent of the accumulation of material goods through work. As sites of display and categorization, museums were the realm within which material culture studies were, for a long time, situated. Attention to processes of crafting and shaping on the one hand and the world of consumption on the other oriented folklorists to new ways of engaging with materiality intellectually while also leading to reflection of exhibitionary practice in museums.

CHAPTER 1

THE SOCIAL BASE OF FOLKLORE

Dorothy Noyes

When the English antiquarian William Thoms coined the word "Folk-Lore" in 1846, he proposed it as a "good Saxon compound" to delineate the field then known as "popular antiquities, or popular literature" (Thoms 1999 [1846]: 11). Most readers have noticed the nationalism implicit in this substitution of words derived from Latin. Less attention has been given to the fact of the compound. To be sure, it mimics Germanic word-formation. But it also suggests a tighter semantic cluster than the previous English phrases might have implied. The hyphen between "folk" and "lore" anticipates key questions for the discipline. What commonsense relationships exist between bodies of knowledge and groups of people? What relationship should scholars posit between cultural forms and social structures?

Do such linkages dissolve over time? Cultural expressions persist and move independently of their creators: stories and songs are heard and retold; craft knowledge is passed on in apprenticeships; proverbs are remembered and invoked in new settings. Literacy and other systems of recording facilitate the detachability of forms from contexts. Today the circulation of both people and cultural goods is so rapid and multidirectional that the very idea of a folk organically connected to a set of customs and expressions seems like a nostalgic fantasy. To be sure, the fantasy has enormous currency. Politicians, both national and local, project it upon the territories they propose to govern. Innumerable industries reproduce it through tourist attractions, restaurants and packaged foods, music, books, clothes and home décor. And an academic discipline exists that seeks to examine the compound term both empirically and theoretically.

Folklorists have always been conscious of their own role in creating the category of folklore. Although "folks" have been objectified in a variety of institutions and representations (including the nation-state as a political entity), such publications as

A Companion to Folklore, First Edition. Edited by Regina F. Bendix and Galit Hasan-Rokem.
© 2012 John Wiley & Sons, Ltd. Published 2012 John Wiley & Sons, Ltd.

the Grimms' *Deutsche Sagen* confer the further dignity of academic objectivity upon the Germans as a people, legends as a kind of thing in the world, and German legends as a distinct corpus (1816–1818). Nationalist, populist, revolutionary, and colonialist scholars around the world have continued to produce cultural objects in the hope of modeling social futures.

The futures occasionally come back to haunt them. In the 1960s, German scholars querying their responsibility for the Nazi myth of the Aryan *Volk* engaged in a thorough critique of the disciplinary past; they laid out a reflexive approach to the afterlife of those concepts in the present (Bendix, this volume). Young folklorists in the United States, seeing the prevailing comparative method as Eurocentric and irrelevant to current civil rights struggles, set out more bluntly to slay the old fathers and reformulate the field on new scientific foundations. To this end, they posited a different kind of relationship between folk and lore. Dan Ben-Amos provocatively redefined folklore as "artistic communication in small groups": tradition and variation were no longer considered essential (1972: 13). In the same forum, published in book form as *Toward New Perspectives in Folklore*, Richard Bauman proposed a new approach to what he termed the "social base" of folklore.

The old European textual scholarship, Bauman explained, took for granted the location of folklore "among peasants and primitives." Postwar American work was instead explicitly concerned with social groups, defined not by their place in the hierarchy but by their communal identity. In this approach the deeper layer of nation-state ideology had been operationalized in functionalist social theory. Bauman argued for a third way. Folklore lives in a "social matrix" (1972: 35) of actors seeking to accomplish their ends not as components of a system but as individuals in competition and conflict. People were connected to folklore not through the abstract linkage of group to tradition but through empirically traceable instances of performance. To be sure, folklore often thematized communal identity, but rather than expressing a pre-existent identity among insiders, it more often constructed one, aggressively or humorously, at social boundaries. Communication of differential identity to outsiders nonetheless required a code held in common. Generated in ongoing social interaction, shared forms rather than shared identity were the *sine qua non* of folklore. Scholarship needed therefore to investigate the "social base" of particular forms empirically, case by case.

Bauman does not define this new phrase, used at that time to refer to the class, ethnic, and occupational makeup of political parties and social movements. The word "base" has, to be sure, an objectivist and perhaps Marxist tinge (cf. Williams 1973). It implies the dependence of cultural forms on societal structures, in contrast to later theorists such as Michel Foucault who treated discourse as constitutive of society itself. This debate would become fruitful for folklorists. For Bauman's immediate purposes, however, the primary value of the phrase "social base" lay in allowing researchers to seek a "direct and empirical" connection between folk and lore (1972: 33).

In this overview, I follow Bauman in tracing the interlocking development of three dominant approaches. Each of them situates the social base of folklore at the nether pole of one of the core binary oppositions of Western modernity: old and new, particular and universal, fluid and fixed. The first takes folklore to be the cultural forms proper to the deepest stratum of social life, flattened and superseded by the historical, hierarchical, or institutional overlay of modernity. The second views folklore holistically as the expressive bonds of community, which assert or maintain its differential being against external pressures. The third turns from stratum and bonds to performance, finding the social base of folklore in the contingencies of a situation it seeks to transform. That very contingency, however, has destabilized the institutional base of the field of folkloristics: is there truly an isolable object to justify an autonomous discipline? I conclude by looking at some folkloristic reactions to the present tension between the visibility of the cultural and the elusiveness of the social.

These formulations pose historical responses to one another. The emphasis on community reacted against the idea of stratum, and the formulation of performance set out to correct a restrictive idea of community. But they are also ongoing parallel strands in the web of the field, each salient in the design at given times and places. Viewed synchronically, they offer complementary points of entry into any given case study.

It is not easy to generalize about a body of scholarship that, more than that of many disciplines with theoretical aspirations, is distributed internationally, ideologically, and institutionally.[1] The social base of folkloristics emulates that of its subject matter insofar as most folklorists are closely engaged with particular situations, populations, and cultural forms. In the wake of civil rights movements, anticolonial movements, and the breakup of the Soviet Union, folklorists around the world challenged the dominance of the comparative "Finnish" method, and the field now has multiple centers and paradigms as well as a healthy suspicion of totalizing assertions. By the same token, the field has rejected canonicity in either its subject matter or its interpretive authorities, remaining open on principle to examining any kind of cultural production and considering knowledge from any source on its merits. This exceptional framework presents challenges for disciplinary self-presentation within the hierarchical knowledge structure of universities. It is not devoid of status anxiety: folklorists take on the tinge of their engagements, which can leave them politically compromised or stigmatized by association with the low, local, or ephemeral. And folklorists are frequently involved with their research at a personal level, particularly if they do ethnographic fieldwork. Studying live cultural forms, they are caught up in performance and aesthetic evaluation, and the performers often criticize or make use of their interpretations. Participating in powerful collective experiences, necessarily accepting hospitality, folklorists develop emotional attachments and ethical responsibilities in relation to an often subaltern and vulnerable "social base." Like many of my colleagues, I feel occasional impulses to valorize myself, my discipline, or my subject matter, and I rarely find it possible to detach the reading of a particular situation from the larger question, "What is to be done?" (Chernyshevsky 1989 [1863]). Such concerns can cloud scholarship, but they also have heuristic value. Folklorists do not find it easy to claim objective scholarly authority over an unproblematic domain of reality. The social base of folklore research itself encourages a useful humility before the task.

The Vernacular Layer

The concept of folklore took shape as Western thinkers began to contrast tradition with modernity. As modernity itself grew older, the sociotemporal location of folklore shifted. In the nineteenth century, most scholars understood folklore as a historical stratum within general culture, a residue surviving chiefly in the lowest layers of society. Today the layers have reversed: folklore is seen as emergent, rising up from the interstices of institutions and the new platforms of digital culture. In between came a Marxist conception of folklore as the culture of the dominated classes and the American liberal idea of folklore as the shared vernacular of everyday life, underlying formal institutions. Borrowed from linguistics, the very word "vernacular" exemplifies the ambiguities of this view of folklore as partial and submerged. Used primarily to contrast a native tongue to a language of power or learning, "vernacular" derives from the Latin word for a native-born house slave (Howard 2005).

Focused attention to vernacular culture began in the wake of Renaissance enthusiasm for vernacular languages, with a burst of political and scholarly attention to "popular antiquities" across Europe. Latin Christianity condemned popular belief as super-stitious awe born of ignorance or surviving from the pagan past of the countryside. But it also valued certain local objects, with their attendant settings and narratives, as "relics" of sacred history. Humanist scholarship secularized this interest in popular culture as historical evidence, documenting oral language and beliefs. Provincial elites seeking to maintain their power against centralizing states celebrated not just their legal privileges but their communal rites and performances as treasures from a prestigious antiquity. Rulers from Philip II to Napoleon sent questionnaires across their empires to identify customs and practices that interfered with governance or, conversely, might be taxed or harnessed for economic development (Abrahams 1993; Bauman and Briggs 2003).

Thus by the early nineteenth century there was already a long history of attention to peasant and provincial expressions in Europe, treating them for the most part as requiring to be recorded in text but eradicated from practice. Of course this history moved in tandem with the discovery of the "primitive" in the process of European overseas exploration and imperialism (De Certeau 1988). But while the imagined primitive is radically alien, the imagined folk is the intimate Other. It lives within the border of the nation state; it lives within the emotional memory of modern Western man. In 1697 Charles Perrault described his fairy tales as learned from peasant nursemaids. More than a century later, the lullaby learned at the breast would remain the metonymy of oral tradition for Herder and the German Romantics (Wellbery 1999: 190). The folk is all that is close and yet estranged: the servant class, the feminine, the domestic, the rural. Close enough both to arouse and to defile the right-thinking bourgeois individual, it excites simultaneous nostalgia and repudiation. The associated late nineteenth-century conception of unschooled beliefs and customs as cultural "survivals" raised similar anxiety, implying both historical anomaly and a certain vigor in persistence.

Marxist theory made the anxiety explicit. Writing in the early 1930s from Fascist Italy, where the southern peasantry lived in quasi-servitude and extreme regional diversity hindered the advance of modernity, Antonio Gramsci began to understand folklore as a foundation for revolution. In an influential few pages, he defined folklore as inchoate philosophy, pieced together from the cultural detritus that made its way to the subaltern strata of society (1985). In the view of Gramsci and the Italian school founded by Ernesto De Martino in the 1950s, the archaism of folklore was objectively, though not consciously, resistant to dominant ideologies

(Lombardi-Satriani 1974). Latin American and US Latino folklorists, writing from the tensions between indigenes and colonizers, produced a more contemporaneous model of cultural contestation. Américo Paredes demonstrated that the heroic history of Texas took very different shape in Anglo-American literary treatments and the oral memory of Mexicanos, with the material evidence largely supporting the latter representations (1958). Attached to union movements, the Federal Writers Project, and the Library of Congress, left-wing populist folklorists in the United States documented work songs, the narratives of former slaves, and other evidence of progressive strains in oral tradition (Green 2001; Hirsch 2010). Young white male scholars in their wake, coming of age in the folksong revival and the Civil Rights era, celebrated the transgressive performances of African American male street culture (Abrahams 2006 [1964]; Jackson 2004 [1974]).

The mainstream of US folkloristics took a different line out of the theory of folklore as survival of earlier stages of civilization. William Wells Newell, founder of the American Folklore Society in 1888, grafted the survivalist anthropology of the Englishman E.B. Tylor onto the new psychology of the American William James. Newell identified supernatural belief as the property not only of children and country people but a common propensity to epistemological error corrected in some cases by the self-conscious rationality acquired through schooling (1904). The psychoanalytic interpretations of Alan Dundes also owe something to this American concern with common foundations. Dundes understood much folklore as the symbolic precipitate of unconscious processes that takes collective shape in such shared forms as the cockfight or the football game (2007). More often, American scholars revised Newell to defend the rationality, self-consciousness, and thereby the full citizenship of the folk: David Hufford's account of supernatural belief shares Newell's emphasis on common perceptual experience as the source of tradition, but documents the self-critical monitoring of the experiencer (1982). Only in the 1990s did many US folklorists become comfortable again with the old European idea of custom as second nature (Kelley 1990), acknowledging the layer of inattention and habit in which much cultural practice is transmitted and reproduced (Cantwell 1993).

Newell's broader approach responded to the American situation. As a settler nation on top of an indigenous population, with a huge population of formerly enslaved forced migrants and a diverse influx of new voluntary immigrants, rapidly urbanizing and industrializing, the United States could not conceive of the folk either as a stable lower social layer or in terms of common ethnic origins. In opposition to the evolutionary anthropology dominating the Bureau of Indian Affairs, which administered Native American populations, Newell argued for the historicist conception of lore espoused by Franz Boas: situational rather than racial particularities accounted for expressive differences (1888). The regional and professional diversity of the American Folklore Society's own early membership imposed a working conception of folklore as something that everyone has, but taking a multiplicity of forms in a multiplicity of groups underneath a national intellectual culture.

This conception of the lower stratum as everyday and familiar had an important afterlife in US folklore studies. Some, influenced by the Chicago school of sociology, saw folklore in localist terms as the "little tradition" coexisting with a shared "great tradition" (Redfield 1956). Implicitly, a strong research emphasis on domestic sociability as the context of folk performance and women as tradition-bearers understood folklore in the framework of liberal politics as the private sphere (e.g. Goldstein 1964). Most explicit theorizing resorted to technological criteria, invoking the oral or, later, the face-to-face stratum of culture (e.g. Thompson 1977 [1946], and still Ben-Amos 1972). This formulation provoked quarrels, with successive cases being made for writing, print, the telephone, the copy machine, and ultimately the Internet as genuine conduits of tradition: in practice folklorists have followed the folk themselves to explore expressive interaction in the favored medium of the moment.

In the "new perspectives" turn of the 1970s, US scholars seeking to revitalize the Boasian tradition in the field began to replace "folk" with "vernacular." Rediscovered by sociolinguists, architects, and cultural critics, this adjective was used to claim the autonomy, coherence, validity, and contemporaneity of practices hitherto defined in terms of lack (Brunskill 1963; Labov 2006 [1966]; Illich 1980). The vernacular was the everyday order of culture, developed in person-to-person interaction without the mediation of institutional codes or controls. "Vernacular" remained a contrastive term to "standard," but now it was seen as dynamically engaged with the upper layer, as folklorists synthesized the Western Marxist, postcolonial, and liberal traditions. Ill at ease with the disdain for popular culture in some of the US literary establishment (e.g. Macdonald 1962) and with what they knew of the Frankfurt school's critique of mass culture as ideological mystification (Benjamin 1968 [1936]; Horkheimer and Adorno 2002 [1947]), most American folklorists emphasized creative adaptation and critique by consumers (e.g. Sutton-Smith *et al.* 1995; Santino 1995). Revising the Italian conception of subaltern cultures as unconscious resistance, the students of Paredes argued that minority expressions explicitly challenged the dominant discourse (Limón 1983).

To be sure, the insistence on synchronic meaning found in Ben-Amos's redefinition of folklore threatened to erase history just as the concern with historical reconstruction had once caused scholars to ignore the communicative present. Several lines of research corrected this tendency. By the late 1960s a preponderance of folklorists rejected the Anglo-American scholarly orthodoxy that enslaved Africans had lost their native cultures on the boat: there was ample evidence of African forms persisting in diasporic expressions (Vlach 1978; Abrahams and Szwed 1983; Thompson 1983). In the 1980s, as creole forms became central to theories of language origins, folkloristic interest in the creole also intensified, encouraging a revisiting of earlier accounts of oral transmission. So did Mikhail Bakhtin's account of verbal utterance as intrinsically dialogic (drawing on previous utterances), subsequently framed in French literary theory as intertextuality (the making and reading of texts through other texts) (Bakhtin 1981; Kristeva 1980). Still determined to demonstrate the active role of the people once deemed mere "tradition-bearers" (Von Sydow 1948), folklorists now argued that creativity entailed the reworking and shaping of available materials – an argument especially favored in feminist revisions of ex nihilo mythologies (Babcock 1986; Weigle 1989). Any given practice was thus likely to have not a single straightforward social base but historical layers, hybrid sources, and complex authorship. Folk art scholars traced social exchanges in women's ritual arts (Turner 1999) and unearthed the social roots of works deemed by the art world to be the spontaneous expression of uneducated "outsiders" (Ward and Posen 1985; Kirshenblatt-Gimblett 1989). In both cases, though, the social was no longer simply the "context" for the cultural expression: rather, it was the very subject of the art.

In Primiano's influential formulation of "vernacular religion" (1995, cf. Magliocco, this volume) and a large body of work on vernacular healing systems (e.g. Brady 2001), the idea of the vernacular is inflected by this work on assemblage to become a more self-conscious version of Gramsci's "common sense." Rather than a stable layer, the vernacular is now described as the immediate sphere of engagement in which actors negotiate between the tradition, professional, and alternative discourses available to them, drawing on multiple resources to create a practical repertoire. We see here some influence of an American tendency to equate agency with consumer choice, but also a sense that actors' space of maneuver is shrinking as institutional procedures and commercial products colonize ever more everyday activities. Parody and poaching necessarily replace autonomous creation in a world so dense with prior discourse (Dorst 1990; M. Hufford 1999). We might now imagine the strata as reversed, with the vernacular growing up from the cracks in the institutional layer.

But if actors are constrained by such a world, their practices proliferate. Modernity's acceleration, breaking up the social base into ever more fields and domains, fosters a fissiparous vernacular. As populations become more mobile and urbanized, recording technologies improve and multiply, commercial incentives intensify, attractive traditions are apt to be professionalized. Professionals who can devote themselves full time to a musical, dramatic, or culinary genre are likely to develop formal elaborations, technical refinements, and variations; the audience may expand in consequence. Meanings will become less context-dependent and influences grow more complex. Performers and audiences will begin to diversify and cluster according to taste and economic possibilities, so that a practice will often develop mass-market and avant-garde variants, followed typically by a reaction seeking to resurrect the authentic version as cultural heritage or to create a classical canon, in either case curated by specialists or specialist amateurs (Kaplan in press). American jazz, for example, has repeatedly undergone this cycle, while continuing to influence new vernacular forms on the ground such as hip-hop – which has itself now undergone a few such cycles. And the phenomenon of social relocation is not unique to arts with commercial potential. Customary practices such as gleaning and trash-picking, once accepted elements of a communal repertoire of subsistence, later even celebrated as folklore in nostalgic cultural representations, became relegated to the social margins of an increasingly affluent consumer society (Varda 2000). Today these now repressed "outsider" practices are returning to the mainstream out of environmental concerns and growing economic necessity, in institutional practices of recycling, civic practices of charitable redistribution, and such "alternative" variants as dumpster diving. Vernacular repertoires are maintained over time as resources for future use by flowing into new social spaces as they are squeezed out of others.

THE SOCIAL BOND

In tandem with the conception of folklore as a lower cultural stratum there evolved a compensatory holistic view. In modernizing mood, nineteenth-century thinkers might see the practices and dispositions of the past as impediments to progress. But in moments of distress with change, they looked back with regret at the apparent cultural coherence and social cohesion of their childhoods; they might also draw on the social knowledge arising from pre-modern constraints to imagine alternatives to the social violence of industrial expansion. Early nationalist work channeling the streams of tradition into forward-moving cultural projects was followed by a concern with the dynamics of small groups, giving way in turn to a discovery of folklore in every conceivable kind of social assembly. In arguing over what might constitute a folk community and examining their own investments in that argument, folklorists produced a variety of insights into the role of cultural form in social bonding: the role of performance in making bounded groups seem like objective realities; the transmission of cultural form in the creation of social networks; and the creation of a sense of communal belonging in individuals.

Folklore research begins to take shape as an autonomous discipline with Romantic nationalism and more specifically in the writings of Johann Gottfried von Herder, who wrote in the 1770s of oral traditions as vital organic processes grounded in place. Herder did not consign traditions to the past, though he judged them vulnerable to external influences. Under normal circumstances, individuals would continue to assimilate their traditions, contribute to them, and develop them as the lifestream of the nation. After the Napoleonic invasions, German thinkers systematized Herder's ideas into a prescription for nation-building. Channeling the flow of poetry into the procedures of philology, Jakob Grimm and others reconstructed a posited cultural community of the past with a view to its future realization. They created the shared cultural currency and pedagogic frameworks that, circulated within the imagined national boundary, would thicken interaction and quicken group consciousness for ensuing political struggles (Anderson 1991; Bendix, this volume).

The Grimms' international network of correspondents shared strategies as well as texts, creating replicable forms that could be filled with national content. They hunted down words, stories, songs, and old texts for anthologies and assembled epics such as the Finnish Kalevala, soon followed by the Estonian Kalevipoeg. New nation-states found resources for large-scale collection projects, creating archives and atlases of folk tradition and open-air museums bringing the architecture and material cultures of the region into a central assembly (Rogan, this volume). In general, a first stage of amassing the national "treasury" (a frequent metaphor for early vernacular dictionaries and folklore collections) was followed by a second stage of winnowing and disciplining the national cultural wealth. The second stage produced standardized abridgments suitable for bourgeois domestic consumption, as in the well-known case of Wilhelm Grimm's reworking of the *Kinder- und Hausmärchen* (Bauman and Briggs 2003).

Seeking to wrest free of powerful neighbors, small would-be nations at the European periphery embraced the new apparatus with special enthusiasm, and small countries such as Finland, Estonia, and Hungary continue to exercise major international influence in the field. But larger polities seeking to retain their hold on diverse populations also produced folkloric documentation for public consumption and created institutions of folklore scholarship. Folklore proved politically labile: the same forms might be made to serve nationalist or separatist, imperial or anticolonial, fascist or socialist agendas. To be sure, most successful political projects, whether revolutionary or reactionary, were led by small elites or soon coopted by them, and the showiest genres of folk performance were often mobilized, sometimes coercively, to signify popular consent to their doings. Thus colorful costumes and rhythmic dances have come to connote collective passivity to many people, and the word "folklore" is tainted by association in Spanish and some other languages.

The village community became the privileged image of the folk group, embodying the national essence while the cosmopolitan cities governed the state and managed its economy. Peripheral outsiders such as the Celtic bard, the African slave, or the Roma "gypsy" became the boundary figures that both colored and confirmed the "normal" citizen; rural communities of the dominant ethnic group mediated between this local difference and the metropolis (Abrahams 1993). Furthermore, as both rural Europe and its colonies were incorporated into an industrializing market economy torn by labor conflict, the owner class conscripted local traditions into the service of a paternalist social order consciously evoking the feudal estate (Noyes 2000). Both statesmen and capitalists turned the rural Gemeinschaft into a conservative icon of the ideal social order. Rural elites and entrepreneurs quickly understood the advantages of playing up to the image.

In the twentieth century, the culture concept rooted in Boas' transplantation of the German Romantic tradition encouraged most American folklorists to maintain their focus on rural communities or their immigrant descendants, with the nation-state taken for granted as backdrop. The idea of culture as a holistic way of life was popularized in mid-century in widely read ethnographies by Margaret Mead, Ruth Benedict, and others; it was also operationalized by social scientists working for the US government during Word War II and after, both in efforts to understand enemy psychology and in campaigns to win the cooperation of local ethnic groups in war and counterinsurgency operations (Price 2008). Functionalist social theory turned nationalist ideology into science by positing that the world was naturally divided into organic self-maintaining collectivities (Parsons 1951).

The culture concept assumed the seamless mutual implication of a bounded group of people, a way of life, a mental framework, and discrete aesthetic expressions. Some US folklorists came to embrace cultural relativism even at the national level, with Alan Dundes writing about American folk ideas as "units of worldview" (1972). More often, because the new ethnographic methods lent themselves to studying small homogeneous populations and because the country's size and diversity impeded generalization, US scholars sought visibly distinct, visibly "cultural" small groups to study: African-American sharecroppers, Anglo-American mountaineers, Ashkenazi Jewish immigrants. But unlike in anthropology or sociology, where the community itself was the usual ethnographic object, folklorists retained their focus on form and genre. Some used the methods of structuralism or psychoanalysis to extrapolate a community worldview from a single domain such as architecture or legend or festival (Glassie 1975a; Dundes and Falassi 1975). A few produced an accumulation of articles on diverse genres in a single setting through the course of a lifelong field engagement, as in Don Yoder's work on the Pennsylvania Germans (1990). More theoretically inclined scholars of verbal art pushed to read genres not just against "culture" but against other genres in a broader "ethnography of communication" that would identify an "expressive economy" of complementary and competing formulations of group experience (Hymes 1964; Ben-Amos 1976; Falassi 1980). This move did not directly challenge the concept of homogeneous community but began to treat cultural forms as flexible and rhetorical, restoring attention to social process.

Common descent or history ceased to be a criterion of folkness for many scholars. The methodological turn to context and participant observation, the political preoccupations of the civil rights era, and professional anxiety about the dwindling population of ballad-singers and fairytale-tellers all prompted a search for a contemporary folk, defined increasingly in sociological rather than anthropological terms as "small groups" without reference to a prior tradition (Ben-Amos 1972). Dundes claimed that any group developed traditions, or what Ben-Amos called artistic communication: "The term 'folk' can refer to any group of people whatsoever who share at least one common factor" (1977). Folklorists argued at meetings over whether lovers, owner-pet dyads, and individuals might constitute folk groups, while pushing earlier lines of research to expand in obvious social directions: from immigrant folklore to family folklore, from urban folklore to suburban folklore, from old sects to new religious movements and even mainline Protestants, from secret societies to college fraternities. Groups acquiring public identities as communities through civil rights struggles followed, with work on gay folklore and the folklore of the deaf (Goodwin 1989; Hall 1991). Pop-cultural publics became objects of folklore research when they thickened into fan communities such as Deadheads and Trekkies (Bacon-Smith 1992). Folklore theory began to reflect explicitly on identity (Dundes 1993; Oring 1994), and personal identity emerged as a new focus, in studies both of traditional performers (Sawin 2004) and of self-formation through consumption, with a special interrogation of women's appropriation of exotic traditions (Lau 2000; Shukla 2008; Bock and Borland 2011).

At the same time as new groups were identified, folklorists increasingly recognized that much folklore is about boundary maintenance rather than group vertebration or even self-integration. The University of Texas folklore program, diverse in its composition and situated in an epicenter of the Chicano movement, pursued this agenda with special vigor, studying the "shouting match at the border" and the exchange of slurring "neighborly names" not as an exception to the rule of coherence but rather as the normal organization of expressive life (Bauman and Abrahams 1981).

New studies of festival and "display events" puzzled out the dialectics of group-making and differentiation. In contrast to anthropological accounts of collective liminality, Abrahams and Bauman addressed conflict not as a temporary ritual break but as structural, arguing for multiple organizing principles and co-existing social positions in a single community (1978). Stoeltje and Bauman identified festivals as key ethnographic sites of modernity, the product of commerce, mediation, and ethnic coexistence (1989). Abrahams explored the expressive repertoire of large-scale events, particularly the nonverbal modalities that could compel a common attention among strangers: noise and explosions, rhythm, gigantized décor, smell, and especially food (1982). There followed studies of ethnic foodways as the medium of intergroup sociability (Brown and Mussell 1984), the aesthetics of marketplace pitches and county fairs (Prosterman 1995; Kapchan 1996), and the gendered construction of embodied experience (Young 1995).

In the face of a growing disciplinary emphasis on communal identities, Noyes argued for the need to make an analytical distinction between group, network, and community: the institutionalized entity, the empirical pattern of social interactions, and the imagined collectivity to which individuals claim belonging (2003 [1995]). Each thread of the earlier research has received ongoing attention.

Institutions generate their own folklore, much of which is not resistant to but supportive of organizational goals (cf. Koch, this volume). Professional authority and identities are sustained by group-specific belief systems and expressive patterns (O'Connor 1995; Schrager 2000). Military units foster cohesion through hazing rituals that submit the individual to the group while often violently excluding others, generating a characteristic dynamic of secrecy, scandal, codification, and reform fostered by modern expectations of institutional transparency (Bronner 2006).

In the course of recognizing their own historical role in objectifying political communities, folklorists observed that the "folk" also objectify themselves in institutions and monuments. African American and Latino folklorists pointed out that the minorities usually studied by white scholars in their transgressive moments spent most of their time in the same struggle to create order as that of the dominant population, under more challenging circumstances (Davis 1992). The performance of respect and organizational hierarchy in Caribbean "tea meetings," African American women's clubs, and Native American ceremonies confirms the aspiration to stable social being (Abrahams 1993; McGregory 1997; Jackson 2003). Like new nations, new religious groups construct lineages, rituals, and bodies of scholarship, linking claims of antiquity to present mechanisms of bonding (Magliocco 2004). In the burgeoning of inter- and intra-national tourism, communities construct themselves for the eyes of outsiders, in text, museum, and performance (Dorst 1989); producing these activities for strangers, however, creates social interaction among members that may become an end in itself (Bendix 1989). More aggressive performances of communal identity, such as initiating a foreign researcher into a local ritual or stuffing a visiting politician with local specialties, force powerful outsiders to acknowledge the group's existence and importance as well as to own an obligation to it (Fenske 2010).

In these last examples we can see that the making and witnessing of objective signs of identity also entails the forging of interpersonal social bonds, sometimes among member-performers, sometimes between performer and audience. This takes us to the network. Folklorists have long studied the diffusion of oral tradition across wide geographic and social distances. The implicit network approach of the historic-geographic method became explicit in work on the "legend conduit" (Dégh and Vaszonyi 1975): still more than the song or the fairy tale, rumor and contemporary legend circulate between strangers, between mouth and media, across racial boundaries (Fine and Turner 2004). Working at a more intimate level, studies of jokes and riddles showed how traditions could regulate social boundaries but also bridge them, the dyadic question-and-answer form establishing complicity and provisional solidarities (Hasan-Rokem and Shulman 1996; Oring 2008). Folklorists interested in patterns of social reciprocity have observed that they are thematized in oral tradition itself. In the Irish tale of "The Man Who has no Story," a guest in a strange house who declines to make the effort of contributing to the evening's entertainment is sent out on the road to be buffeted with supernatural punishments, after which he has indeed a story to tell (Glassie 1997: 319–324). The same requirement of performance in return for hospitality can be found today at Chinese urban banquets: a potential new business partner earns the trust of others by singing a song or telling a joke that attests to grace under pressure, self-mastery while drinking, and a concern for the general well-being (Shepherd 2005).

The word "tradition" comes from a Latin legal term (*traditio*) for a hand-to-hand transfer of property; it is worth considering this handover in terms of the gift exchange first described by Marcel Mauss (1923–1924). Vernacular performances are typically offered and valued knowledge passed on in the context of ongoing social relationships. Where no such relationship exists, the gift creates one: even if giver and receiver never meet again, there is an obligation to remember the giver and context of giving. To be sure, folklore is no stranger to commercial exchange, not only in its recent commodification but in many of its earliest documented manifestations in fairs, marketplaces, and among itinerant peddlers. Nonetheless, there is always a social supplement to the monetary transaction, an expressive "gift." The personhood and social identity of the seller expose themselves to the gaze, perhaps in expressive patter and costume, perhaps in a narrative authenticating the product sold. Sustenance may be shared: ethnic restaurants, with their mimesis of domestic hospitality, are privileged mediators for new immigrant groups in establishing provisional social solidarities, reversing the larger host-guest relationship. In festival and tourist settings, embodied participation is offered through the invitation to join in dance. Although much of folkloristic performance works to objectify and naturalize group shibboleths, the shibboleth can thereby become the invited point of entry for outsiders (Michael 1998), creating social bonds vital to the circulation of information and resources, the restructuring of collective action, and the maintenance of existential solidarities that may be mobilized in time of need.

Just as folklore's rethinking of its keywords found a useful external irritant in Hobsbawm and Ranger's "invention of tradition" in the 1980s (1983; cf. Briggs 1996), so Benedict Anderson's "imagined community," discovered somewhat later by folklorists, provoked both appropriation and contrastive reflection (1991 [1983]). Many scholars argued that not just nations but all communities were imagined. Some, however, were more imagined than others, requiring a greater effort to construct persuasive symbols and narratives that could not be supplied by prior common experience. Imagination, in turn, did not imply unreality. Recurrent exposure to community-marked narratives and images instills compelling memories into individuals; recurrent participation in communal performance incorporates the community into the body such that individuals identify with it not of choice but from a sense of inevitability: they feel connected, responsible, bound in history or bound in fate to those who have shared the powerful experience (Noyes 2003). This naturalized belonging gives rise to its own metafolklore: *blason populaire* and ethnic slurs against outsiders, inside jokes and restricted codes, self-mockery, and even the covert performances of shared experience denied in the public presentation of the group (Herzfeld 1997).

The imaginary that bonds communities may be freely chosen, as in the rituals carefully negotiated and designed by neo-Pagan congregations, with their voluntary membership (Magliocco 2004). It may be imposed from above, as in the state rituals of fascist and communist regimes. It may be imposed from outside, through discrimination and stereotyping, even though imprisonment, expulsion, or genocide. Mobile moderns tend to idealize communal attachments, but belonging is ambivalent in practice, a source of both comfort and tension. Where belonging is thick, with a rich imaginary reinforced by dense interaction among community members or strong external pressures, individuals are likely to feel an almost sacramental strength of meaning in everyday actions that is not free of claustrophobia. Community can be a painful inheritance and it restricts individual freedoms: Glassie has suggested in lectures that the formal intricacy of arts like Turkish rugs and Irish fiddling is the product of personal frustration, the great folk artists being talented individuals who lack other channels for their energies. Folklorists often remain attached to communitarian imaginings nonetheless, in part because of this aesthetic payoff, in part to find redemption from a violent social history, and in part from ethical and practical concern for the future, given that institutional modes of belonging, however consensual and democratic in principle, seem insufficient in practice to create a sense of mutual responsibility or energize commitment to the general good against the prevailing economic pressures to individualism.

PERFORMANCE IN CONTEXT

If the idea of community resisted that of layer, the idea of performance disputed that of community in turn. As folkloristic examinations of community found it to be more an effect than a cause of folk performance, scholars began to look to material circumstances and contingent situations to understand how and why performance might arise. The American concern with self-making, favoring a Boasian folkloristics that emphasized the accidents of history, had already fostered an open-ended approach to the "social base."

European scholarship anticipated a concern with location not as reified homeland but in network terms as a particular juncture of circumstances, actors, and resources. While the nineteenth-century creators of the comparative method often traced the global movement of traditions only in order to make a case for particular origins, later scholars like Carl Wilhelm von Sydow cared more for the migratory process itself. Von Sydow and his followers noticed folktale "ecotypes" that developed in response to local peculiarities and concerns, the obstacles and channels governing the flow of tradition, the differences among "active" and "passive" tradition-bearers, and the migratory characters who moved tradition with themselves: peddlers, soldiers, and immigrants (Von Sydow 1948; Honko and Löfgren 1981; Hasan-Rokem 2000). While folksong scholars such as Kenneth S. Goldstein followed up these concerns with the social shaping of oral tradition (1971), students of dialect, belief, and material culture devoted themselves to mapping projects – an interest renewed today through the availability of GIS technologies allowing scholars to plot not only the movement of repertoire but the geographical consciousness and implied circulation of narrators themselves (Tangherlini 2010). Specialists in vernacular architecture and folk technologies later looked more closely at the interaction of environment, purpose, and aesthetics, and eventually at place-making itself as a discursive practice (M. Hufford 1992).

Scholars of oral tradition focused instead on the human juxtapositions in shared space. Responding to national, ethnic, and immigration conflicts in the present, Mediterraneanist scholars re-examined the cultural evidence of urban coexistence across millenia (Herzfeld 1997; Bromberger and Durand 2001; Hasan-Rokem 2003) and the sharing of performance forms and narratives among apparent enemies (Marzolph 1996; Colović 2002). Sociability among rural neighbors as a counterweight to sectarian performance has similarly interested scholars of Northern Ireland (Glassie 1975b; Cashman 2008), and Jackson has demonstrated that patterns of ceremonial intertribal visiting among Native Americans in Oklahoma invoke a past of vigorous exchange among Native nations prior to their forced relocation (2003).

Because the Americanness of American folklore had to be found not in remote common ancestry but in new common situations, Anglo-American folklore studies caught up comparativism's implicit interest in mobility and contingency (Abrahams 1978). Folksong was collected in prisons and mining camps and from union organizers. Along with new contexts, scholars sought out the new genres generated therein: new forms of worksong, like the chants of the "gandy dancers" who laid out railway lines; new forms of play, like the logrolling competitions of lumbermen; and new forms of religious practice, like the evangelical camp meeting. Particularly prominent in mid-twentieth-century American folklore studies were new kinds of hero celebrated in song and tall tale for their extreme bravery, strength, mobility, independence, appetite, work dedication, and general audacity: figures such as Daniel Boone, Davy Crockett, Pecos Bill, Casey Jones, Paul Bunyan, and (with a racially marked tragic inflection) John Henry, who were associated with the opening up of particular regions or the expansion of particular trades and industries (Clark 1986). (Only later did scholars notice the extent to which these figures were enhanced by regional boosterism.) Their negative counterparts, the con man and the outlaw, received similar attention as realizations of the potentialities of American individualism, and regional variants were explored in innumerable studies of such types as the trickster-like oil promoter (Boatright 1963) or more specific "local character anecdotes," a genre uniting personality, ecology, and history (Stahl 1975).

The Americanist interest in situated action was theorized in the mid-1970s as "performance," defined by Bauman as "the assumption of responsibility to an audience for a display of communicative competence" (1977: 11). Folklorists were to study the creativity mediating between genre and performance, tradition and situation (Hymes 1975; cf. Bauman, this volume). The transformation was felt in every subfield of folklore studies. Early work on urban folklore had given primary attention to the residual lore of migrant groups as they adapted to the new setting (cf. Paredes and Stekert 1971). Now folklorists sought to identify a genuinely urban lore born out of the local environment: street vendor performance, subway customs, and crime legends (Warshaver 1986). After the nineteenth-century view of children as conservative primitives reproducing old English pagan rituals, new research saw children's lore as ribald critique of parents, schooling, media, and other constitutive elements of their lives in the present (Sutton-Smith et al. 1995). From the guardians of group tradition in the intimate sphere, women became recognized as performing tales or songs that subverted the repertoires of men and, in seemingly trivial gendered genres such as the lullaby, expressing frequently violent criticism of their position (Jordan and Kalcik 1985).

The idea of performance redounding back on its social base posed a dynamic contrast to the postwar culture concept. Inspired by Kenneth Burke, Abrahams argued that folklore was rhetorical, seeking to name situations and so transform them (1968). Genres began to be seen as reified intentionality, collectively designed over time to address recurrent situations (cf. Shuman and Hasan-Rokem. this volume). Bauman urged attention to "emergence," the unplanned dimension of performance that arises from contingencies and interaction effects (1977). The vocabulary of folklorists increasingly emphasized the active role of performance and performers: tradition became traditionalization, context contextualization. Performance did not grow inevitably from either a generic or a social base, but declared its own ancestry and pointed to its own sphere of relevance. Emphasizing the conscious application of folklore to situation in performance, scholars also were able to look at the intertextual relations among performances and the effects of textual appropriation, showing how a religious hymn might hearten protesters at risk of arrest, a politician's use of proverbs authenticate him as a member of the people, or a personal narrative in a mass-mailed charitable appeal excite the empathy and open the checkbook of the reader (Mieder 1997; Shuman 2005).

Recent research has taken the performance turn's concern with agency to its extremes. At one end, folklorists study voluntary engagements in ludic, subsistence, religious, and professional activities: quilting, hunting, Scouting, gaming, dancing. They have been interested in the sociological question of how such activities build civil society (Fine 2010), the psychological question of how they build masculinity (Mechling 2004), the folkloristic question of how they build community (Feintuch 2001), and even in the phenomenological question of how they build parallel worlds of experience (M. Hufford 1992). Here performance is performative, in J.L. Austin's sense (1962), creating realities both intentionally and incidentally.

At the other pole lies a growing body of work on folklore as a seizing of agency in situations not of one's own making. The long-term stresses of social change and racial discrimination are known to generate rumor and legend; epidemics like HIV and social disasters such as Hurricane Katrina, September 11, or the occupation of Afghanistan also call forth sense-making efforts when trustworthy information is not available (Goldstein 2004; Lindahl forthcoming; Mills forthcoming). The "spontaneous shrines" marking a roadside death or the site of the Madrid train bombings (Santino 2005) seek to sew up the wounds of community with ritual. The play and memory arts of refugees, even among children torn not only from their homes but from their parents and the normal rites of passage into adulthood, work to process trauma and let life go forward (Slyomovics 1998; Westerman 2006; McMahon 2007).

In pursuing the performance approach to its logical conclusion, folklorists began to undermine their own differential identity. If everything is performance – as scholars coming from theatre, rhetoric, anthropology, and elsewhere were also concluding – then why draw boundaries? This dissolution of disciplines was explicit in the program of the early 1970s, a unified approach grounded in philological method. Addressing the vernacular layer, folklore studies could become the foundation of the human sciences. Institutionally, however, the intellectual convergence made it possible during the 1980s for the most theoretically adept American folklorists to "pass" into better-positioned fields with less historical baggage: cultural theory, American studies, linguistic anthropology, and the new performance studies. (Less theoretically inclined ones did not pass but perhaps melted into departments of art, literature, music, area studies, and even history.) Kirshenblatt-Gimblett, while acknowledging her folkloristic roots, argued that reconfiguration was intrinsic to the natural history of disciplines (1998a).

But most folklorists would not or could not follow, and for years the annual meetings of the American Folklore Society bore witness to general anxiety, often objectified as argument over the name of the field. In the search for theoretical revitalization and a "truly contemporary … subject" (Kirshenblatt-Gimblett 1998a: 283), a field already fragmented by institutional frameworks and ethnographic foci began to disintegrate in the US academy: in the early 1990s some of the most important university programs reconfigured themselves or closed down entirely.

In the same period, however, an accommodation between old and new approaches was created by "public folklorists," those creating public programming in nonprofit organizations and state and federal agencies. The most ambitious organizations carefully transformed their mission from the celebration of identity to the critique of situations, typically in collaboration with the grassroots actors once defined only as informants. An exhibition on New York City street play noted the pressures on communal sociability created by real estate development and zoning laws (Dargan and Zeitlin 1990); a project on West Virginian sense of place produced early evidence of the impact of mountaintop removal coal mining (M. Hufford 2003); a long-term study of Cambodian refugee arts in Philadelphia revealed discursive inequalities in the city's criminal justice system (Westerman 1994a); a conference on Italian-American hip-hop opened up heated community debate on the whiteness of "white ethnics" (Sciorra 2000). Just as subaltern actors have always shaped their social criticisms into symbolic entertainments, so these projects drew broader attention to social issues through the apparent safety of folklore, and revealed the pretty forms to be modes of social action.

Most folklorists did not follow some of the new roads through the performance turn to the social base. Warner's influential notion of "publics" imagined and assembled by a text (2002) went a step too far for many nurtured on an idea of tradition shaped in long-term interaction. More useful was the concept of "scene," appropriated by ethnomusicologists from their informants to describe a site of ongoing encounter around an artistic practice (Straw 1991). In these two conceptions, performance calls its own social base into being. But even the scene has not crossed the disciplinary line to any great extent, though it frees us from the conceptual burdens implied by such words as "folk" or even "subculture." Many folklorists are suspicious of too pure an analytical reliance on performance: the grounding of artistic form in everyday life and the material constraint implied by the formulation of "social base" feel right despite their limitations.

Why should this be? The social base of folkloristics itself must be part of the the answer. In throwing aside their own history of concepts, genres, and practices, folklorists would throw aside a communal identity they have long performed and therefore feel to be real and binding. They would also throw aside a body of insights into cultural creation under conditions of social constraint that have not lost their relevance to most of the world's population. Many folklore scholars feel an obligation to the communities among whom they have lived, from whom they sometimes hail, and to whom they owe their professional advancement. The only humanistic field calling explicitly for comparative attention to subaltern forms and therefore to subaltern people, folklore seems necessarily distinct from broader cultural or performance studies, however close the approaches in practice. If not theorized into a crystalline rationale for disciplinary existence, this folkloristic common sense nonetheless carried the day, and the crisis of US programs in the 1990s was reversed at the turn of the millennium with the expansion and revitalization of university folklore programs. (As this volume makes clear, the international picture is varied, with continuity, renewal, precarity, and proliferation all part of the present scene.)

EMBLEM AND STIGMA

The performance turn brought the field to a difficult question. Might folklorists themselves constitute the social base of folklore? At any rate, many suggest, "folklore" exists insofar as it is identified, entextualized, or created outright by the larger universe of literati, government officials, and entrepreneurs who have an interest in demonstrating the existence of a vibrant popular tradition. Suspicious Anglo-American critics have long looked for falsification in folklore, from Samuel Johnson's ridicule of the putative Gaelic bard Ossian in 1775 to Richard Dorson's 1950 denunciation of the legendary American lumberman Paul Bunyan as "fakelore" (see Dundes 1985). Central European scholars more calmly recognized "folklorismus" as the self-conscious creation of new works of art or commodities drawing on popular traditional models (Voigt 1980). Kirshenblatt-Gimblett eventually declared that there is no authentic tradition against which to weigh the derived. Once objectified in institutions, folklore becomes "a mode of cultural production" that must continue to generate new content to sustain national identities, heritage industries, and the academic discipline of folklore itself (1998a, 284).

This critique of the concept of authenticity was a central preoccupation of folklore studies in the 1980s and 1990s. The idea of a folk tradition streaming unsullied from a pure social source, unclouded by mediation and unpolluted by self-conscious manipulation or foreign influences was not only romantically naive but socially exclusionary, and geared to the creation of differential economic value as well as specious political unity (Bendix 1997). The biographies of folklorists were critically revisited with a view to their ideological compromises. Field engagements and textual practices including folksong collecting, text editing, interviewing, ethnographic writing, and archiving became the object of both historical reexamination and present-day prescription (e.g. Kodish 1987; Lawless 1991; Briggs 1993; Bendix 2010; Fenske and Davidović-Walther 2010). Critiques of misrepresentation in tourism, museums, and folk festivals gave way to a more positive interest in them as sites of cultural production (Kirshenblatt-Gimblett 1998b).

In the US, the prominence of "public folklore," the emergence of collaborative norms in fieldwork and the turning of the scholarly lens back on the scholar began to elide the distinctions between folklorist, "folk," and professional cultural producer (Bendix and Welz 1999). The theorists of verbal art saw that all of these actors were involved in the transmission of texts across performances and contexts; all had to devise routines for making texts speak within one situation while still remaining extractable for re-creation in the next one (Bauman and Briggs 1990). Scholars of festival saw that folklorists and heritage producers live in the same kind of desiring bodies that dancers and musicians do. Regardless of the institutional setting, when these bodies meet in social interaction they cannot help being caught up in the conscious and unconscious play of imitation that Cantwell called "ethnomimesis" (1993).

Styles are by definition imitable through attention and practice. Oral ballad style invigorated English romantic and Spanish modernist poetry. Hip-hop graffiti, clothing, rap and turntable styles have been adapted globally. There is also a generic folk style. Indigenous communities trying to open up tourism know the recipe for creating "traditional crafts" suitable as souvenirs. Global subaltern populations seeking the sympathy of Western audiences for a politically inconvenient cause learn how to construct both oral testimony and sellable crafts in a nonthreatening "folk" register: bright colors, simple shapes, the marks of production by hand, and a thematics of family life, spirituality, and proximity to nature (e.g. Westerman 1994b; Peterson 1998; Adams 2005). Even so new a medium as the Web has an identifiable vernacular style, imitated by designers of corporate sites in order to make product testimonials or political arguments look consumer-volunteered. Howard notes that Cicero already speaks of the "indescribable vernacular flavor" that brought success to a certain Roman orator (2005), and we can compare the current stylistic imitation of popular social movements by American political action committees and lobbyists, recognized by critics as "astroturf" rather than "grassroots" activism. In such cases, the style is purely the emblem of the social base.

The intrinsic detachability of text, generativity of genre, and appropriability of style create vulnerabilities for producers and anxiety for consumers. Culture is designed to spread, commodity form reduces friction, and commercial incentives have greatly accelerated the process. Cultural resources are extracted like mineral resources from poor countries, with multinational corporations reaping the profits. Enthusiasts for traditional musics or therapies look for at least "traceability," if not authenticity (Morisset and Dieudonné 2006). The communities identifying traditions as theirs and the scholars and policymakers interested in the welfare of such communities look to two kinds of remedy (cf. Hafstein, this volume). Cultural heritage initiatives seek to protect traditions from the vicissitude of circulation, by fixing the authentic form to its social base in time and space. Intellectual property initiatives seek to enable circulation by establishing ownership to which profits can be returned. Both strategies necessitate at least some objectification of the social base as a group and some occlusion of the tradition's prior history of circulation and reworking.

A theoretical question is also raised. Does it still make sense to talk of the social base of folklore in a world of flexible networks and mobile traditions? Folklorists recognize themselves as creating fixity out of flux; they recognize their habit of pointing to their own documents as evidence that a world of stable working classes and integrated communities once existed or might still be recoverable. In this, scholars build upon the strategies of those they study. Communities in a state of dispersal compress old lifeways into containable form: a professionalized genre like bluegrass that travels along with migrants, or a festival for which migrants return home once a year (Cantwell 1984; Magliocco 2005). They secure in representation what they can no longer maintain in practice. Entire regions, such as Appalachia in the United States, and entire populations, such as the Roma in Eastern Europe, have moved into an uncanny double reality. Their cultural production, notably music, is mobile, powerful, omnipresent: celebrated as national identity and world heritage, immortal in archives and cyberspace, profitable as commodity form. Their social base is increasingly spectral, subject in the Appalachian case to environmental transformation that is making old communities uninhabitable and in the Roma case to more forthright dehumanization and denial of citizenship. Cultural visibility in both cases seems to work in inverse proportion to social visibility and human rights generally (see Noyes and Silverman in Kapchan forthcoming). The gentrification that comes with touristic development follows a similar logic, multiplying the signs of the Other while expelling the Other's body (Welz 1996).

Some folklorists argue that the body cannot so easily be expelled. Commodity fetishes do not always compel devotion. The conspicuous markers of folk style can more easily be reproduced than their generative logic: attentive audiences can tell the difference between grassroots and astroturf protest, between fast-food sushi and the "real thing." The "real thing," in contemporary appraisals, is less likely to imply authenticity of origins than integrity of style, attention in the workmanship – and these entail the presence of a maker. In turn, the makers of complex forms – jazz musicians, cooks, quilters, preachers, community organizers – tend to be highly conscious of their own lineage, readily describing their apprenticeship and how they reworked their master's teaching. If we take seriously the idea of tradition as gift exchange and the inevitability of ethnomimesis, we may be more optimistic about the persistence of the social meanings attached to cultural forms and the consequent agency of their originators, even as tradition crosses social divides.

Two recent formulations, resonating respectively with the academic and the applied poles of folklore work, have traced back an arc from the performance turn to the field's beginnings. The more matter-of-fact comes from Richard Bauman, summing up the "prevailing theory" of folkloristics as "the philology of the vernacular" (2008). The methods are those of the performance approach, now extended diachronically into textual study reproducing the scope of the older philology. The object is the vernacular, which he now describes as one of two competing communicative modalities: "If the vernacular pulls toward the informal, immediate, locally grounded, proximal side of the [communicative] field, the cosmopolitan pulls toward the rationalized, standardized, mediated, wide-reaching, distal side" (2008: 33). He notes changing sociologies of textual circulation and changing "social bases" of interest to folklorists at different historical stages, instead finding folklore's continuity in the nature of communicative process itself: the informal, immediate, local, and proximal have always been part of its quality space.

The subaltern body returns in the other definition, coined by Diane Goldstein in 2007 and used by Goldstein and Amy Shuman in a series of conference panels and papers since then: "the stigmatized vernacular." In this formulation, the anxiety of folklore research is explicitly problematized, both the ethical commitment to social justice and the desire for disciplinary respectability. The stigma is the conspicuous visibility of something normally kept out of sight, in this case the marked term of modernity's binary oppositions: the traditional, the non-standard, the low, the poor, the collective. Folklore – a word uniting the performances of subalterns with the scholarly framings and institutional packagings thereof – might then be seen as euphemism, the screen that simultaneously conceals and calls attention to an anomalous presence inside the modern nation state or global order. Folklore valorizes rubbish and turns pollution into sacrality. Addressing what is liminal, it cannot escape the instability of its subject; in receiving traditions, it assumes the trace of the subaltern body.

The delineation of folklore as a distinct academic field may ultimately become untenable not for its assumptions about the folk but rather for its presumption of global order and bourgeois subjects: its conception of what is *not* folklore. The communicative field laid out by Bauman already sounds too tidy. As he himself has demonstrated, the rational cosmopolitan is as much an ideal type as the singing member of the folk, and the proliferation of media, vernaculars, and publics has made it difficult to declare any new utterance mainstream, unmarked, or transparent. As environmental and economic pressures close in on the global order, moreover, Western urbanites are no less subject to transformation over the long term than the people once called folk. The expressions marked as folklore hail back to a social base, as the performance scholars have demonstrated: they do not transparently reflect the social world but call our attention to aspects of it. By virtue of their exclusion, they may bring us insights not hitherto attained in mainstream debates. Even idealized or altogether fabricated commodity representations, by the very fact of labeling themselves folklore, point to something recalcitrant to incorporation in dominant narratives. Now that those dominant narratives are as vulnerable to conflicts of value as folklore itself, folklorists' continuing interest in the base is looking wiser.

NOTE

1 For the sake of limiting the discussion to manageable complexity, I concentrate on the field as it has developed in the United States. This is one provincial view among others. As the chapters in this book make clear, the United States has never been the field's center of gravity.

REFERENCES

Abrahams, Roger D. 1968. "Introductory Remarks to a Rhetorical Theory of Folklore." *Journal of American Folklore* 81: 143–158.

Abrahams, Roger D. 1978. "Moving in America." *Prospects* 3: 63–82.

Abrahams, Roger D. 1982. "The Language of Festivals" in Victor W. Turner, Ed. *Celebration: A World of Art and Ritual.* Washington, DC: Smithsonian Institution, pp. 161–177.

Abrahams, Roger D. 1993. "Phantoms of Romantic Nationalism in Folkloristics." *Journal of American Folklore* 106: 3–37.

Abrahams, Roger D. 2006 [1964]. *Deep Down in the Jungle: Negro Narrative Folklore from the Streets of Philadelphia.* New Brunswick: Transaction Publishers.

Abrahams, Roger D. and Richard Bauman. 1978. "Ranges of Festival Behavior" in Barbara Babcock, Ed. *The Reversible World*. Ithaca: Cornell University Press, pp. 193–208.

Abrahams, Roger D. and John F. Szwed. 1983. *After Africa*. New Haven: Yale University Press.

Adams, Jacqueline. 2005. "When Art Loses its Sting: The Evolution of Protest Art in Authoritarian Contexts." *Sociological Perspectives* 48: 531–558.

Anderson, Benedict. 1991 [1983]. *Imagined Communities. Reflections on the Origin and Spread of Nationalism*. 2nd edition. London: Verso.

Austin, J.L. 1962. *How to do Things with Words*. Oxford: Clarendon Press.

Babcock, Barbara A. 1986. *The Pueblo Storyteller: Development of a Figurative Ceramic Tradition*. Tucson: University of Arizona Press.

Bacon-Smith, Camille. 1992. *Enterprising Women: Television Fandom and the Creation of Popular Myth*. Philadelphia: University of Pennsylvania Press.

Bakhtin, M.M. 1981. *The Dialogic Imagination: Four Essays*. Michael Holquist, Ed. Trans. Caryl Emerson and Michael Holquist. Austin: University of Texas Press.

Bauman, Richard. 1972. "Differential Identity and the Social Base of Folklore" in Américo Paredes and Richard Bauman, Eds. *Toward New Perspectives in Folklore*. Austin: University of Texas Press, pp. 31–41.

Bauman, Richard. 1977. *Verbal Art as Performance*. Prospect Heights, IL: Waveland Press.

Bauman, Richard. 2008. "The Philology of the Vernacular." *Journal of Folklore Research* 45: 29–36.

Bauman, Richard and Roger D. Abrahams, Eds. 1981. *And Other Neighborly Names: Social Process and Cultural Image in Texas Folklore*. Austin: University of Texas Press.

Bauman, Richard and Charles L. Briggs. 1990. "Poetics and Performance as Critical Perspectives on Language and Social Life." *Annual Review of Anthropology* 19: 59–88.

Bauman, Richard, and Charles L. Briggs. 2003. *Voices of Modernity: Language Ideologies and the Politics of Inequality*. Cambridge: Cambridge University Press.

Ben-Amos, Dan. 1972. "Toward a Definition of Folklore in Context" in Américo Paredes and Richard Bauman, Eds. *Toward New Perspectives in Folklore*. Austin: University of Texas Press, pp. 3–15.

Ben-Amos, Dan, Ed. 1976. *Folklore Genres*. Austin: University of Texas Press.

Bendix, Regina. 1989. *Backstage Domains: Playing "William Tell" in Two Swiss Communities*. Bern: Peter Lang.

Bendix, Regina. 1997. *In Search of Authenticity: The Formation of Folklore Studies*. Madison: University of Wisconsin Press.

Bendix, Regina. 2010. "Property and Propriety: Reflections on Archived and Archival Cultures" in *Culture Archives and the State: Between Nationalism, Socialism, and the Global Market*. Columbus, OH: The Ohio State University Knowledge Bank. https://kb.osu.edu/dspace/handle/1811/4689. (accessed October 16, 2011).

Bendix, Regina and Gisela Welz, Eds. 1999. *Cultural Brokerage and Public Folklore: Forms of Intellectual Practice in Society*. Special issue, *Journal of Folklore Research* 36 (2/3).

Benjamin, Walter. 1968 [1936]. "The Work of Art in the Age of Mechanical Reproduction" in Hannah Arendt, Ed. Trans. Harry Zohn. *Walter Benjamin, Illuminations*. New York: Schocken, pp. 217–251.

Boatright, Mody C. 1963. *Folklore of the Oil Industry*. Dallas: Southern Methodist University Press.

Bock, Sheila and Katherine Borland. 2011. "Exotic Identities: Dance, Difference, and Self-Fashioning." *Journal of Folklore Research* 48: 1–36.

Brady, Erika, Ed. 2001. *Healing Logics: Culture and Medicine in Modern Health Belief Systems*. Logan: Utah State University Press.

Briggs, Charles L. 1993. "Metadiscursive Practices and Scholarly Authority in Folkloristics." *Journal of American Folklore* 106: 387–434.

Briggs, Charles L. 1996. "The Politics of Discursive Authority in Research on the Invention of Tradition." *Cultural Anthropology* 11: 435–469.

Bromberger, Christian and Jean-Yves Durand. 2001. "Faut-il jeter la Méditerranée avec du bain?" in Anton Blok, Christian Bromberger, and Dionigi Albera, Eds. *L'anthropologie de la Méditerranée*. Paris: Maison Méditerranéenne des Sciences de l'Homme, pp. 733–756.

Bronner, Simon J. 2006. *Crossing the Line: Violence, Play, and Drama in Naval Equator Traditions*. Amsterdam: Amsterdam University Press-Meertens Ethnology Lectures.

Brown, Linda Keller and Kay Mussell, Eds. 1984. *Ethnic and Regional Foodways in the United States: The Performance of Group Identity*. Knoxville: University of Tennessee Press.

Brunskill, R.W. 1963. *Vernacular Architecture: An Account of the Studies in Traditional Domestic Architecture and Applied Subjects Undertaken in the School of Architecture of the University of Manchester*. Manchester: University of Manchester.

Cantwell, Robert. 1984. *Bluegrass Breakdown*. Urbana: University of Illinois Press.

Cantwell, Robert. 1993. *Ethnomimesis: Folklife and the Representation of Culture*. Chapel Hill: University of North Carolina Press.

Cashman, Ray. 2008. *Storytelling on the Northern Irish Border: Characters and Community*. Bloomington: Indiana University Press.

Chernyshevsky Nikolay Gavrilovich. 1989 [1863]. *What is to Be Done?* Trans. Michael R. Katz. Ithaca: Cornell University Press.

Clark, Thomas D. 1986. "The Westward Movement" in Richard M. Dorson, Ed. *Handbook of American Folklore*. Bloomington: Indiana University Press, pp. 32–38.

Colović, Ivan. 2002. "Who Owns the Gusle? A Contribution to Research on the Political History of a Balkan Musical Instrument" in Sanimir Resić and Barbara Törnquist-Plewa, Eds. *The Balkans in Focus: Cultural Boundaries in Europe*. Lund: Nordic Academic Press, pp. 59–81.

Dargan, Amanda and Steven Zeitlin. 1990. *City Play*. New Brunswick: Rutgers University Press.

Davis, Gerald. 1992. "'So Correct for the Photograph': Fixing the Ineffable, Ineluctable African American" in Nicholas Spitzer and Robert Baron, Eds. *Public Folklore*. Washington, DC: Smithsonian Institution Press, pp. 105–118.

de Certeau, Michel. 1988. "Ethno-Graphy – Speech, or the Space of the Other: Jean de Lery." Trans. Tom Conley. *The Writing of History*. New York: Columbia University Press, pp. 209–241.

Dégh, Linda and Andrew Vászonyi. 1975. "The Hypothesis of Multi-Conduit Transmission in Folklore" in Dan Ben-Amos and Kenneth S. Goldstein, Eds. *Folklore: Performance and Communication*. The Hague: Mouton, pp. 207–252.

Dorst, John D. 1989. *The Written Suburb: An American Site, An Ethnographic Dilemma*. Philadelphia: University of Pennsylvania Press.

Dorst, John. 1990. "Tags and Burners, Cycles and Networks: Folklore in the Telectronic Age." *Journal of Folklore Research* 27: 179–190.

Dundes, Alan. 1972. "Folk Ideas as Units of Worldview" in Américo Paredes and Richard Bauman, Eds. *Toward New Perspectives in Folklore*. Austin: University of Texas Press, pp. 93–103.

Dundes, Alan. 1977. "Who Are the Folk?" in William R. Bascom, Ed. *Frontiers of Folklore*. Boulder: Westview Press, pp. 17–35.

Dundes, Alan. 1985. "Nationalistic Inferiority Complexes and the Fabrication of Fakelore: A Reconsideration of Ossian, the Kinder- und Hausmärchen, the Kalevala, and Paul Bunyan." *Journal of Folklore Research* 22: 5–18.

Dundes, Alan. 1993. "Defining Identity Through Folklore" in *Folklore Matters*. Knoxville: University of Tennessee Press, pp. 1–40.

Dundes, Alan. 2007. *The Meaning of Folklore: The Analytical Essays of Alan Dundes*. Simon J. Bronner, Ed. Logan: Utah State University Press.

Dundes, Alan and Alessandro Falassi. 1975. *La Terra in Piazza: An Interpretation of the Palio of Siena*. Berkeley: University of California Press.

Falassi, Alessandro. 1980. *Folklore By the Fireside*. Austin: University of Texas Press.

Feintuch, Burt. 2001. "Longing for Community." *Western Folklore* 60: 149–161.

Fenske, Michaela. 2010. "Grünkohl mit Pinkel. Alltagskost als politisches Instrument" in Michaela Fenske, Ed. *Alltag als Politik – Politik im Alltag. Dimensionen des Politischen in Vergangenheit und Gegenwart.* Berlin: Lit Verlag, pp. 261–280.

Fenske, Michaela and Antonia Davidović-Walther. 2010. *Exploring Ethnological Knowledges.* Special issue of the *Journal of Folklore Research* 47 (1/2).

Fine, Gary Alan. 2010. "The Sociology of the Local: Action and Its Publics." *Sociological Theory* 28: 355–376.

Fine, Gary Alan and Patricia A. Turner. 2004. *Whispers on the Color Line: Rumor and Race in America.* Berkeley: University of California Press.

Glassie, Henry. 1975a. *Folk Housing in Middle Virginia: A Structural Analysis of Historic Artifacts.* Knoxville: University of Tennessee Press.

Glassie, Henry. 1975b. *All Silver and No Brass: An Irish Christmas Mumming.* Philadelphia: University of Pennsylvania Press.

Glassie, Henry, Ed. 1997. *Irish Folktales.* New York: Pantheon Books.

Goldstein, Diane. 2004. *Once Upon A Virus.* Logan: Utah State University Press.

Goldstein, Diane. 2007. Health and the Stigmatized Vernacular. Panel chair at the Annual Meeting of the American Folklore Society, Quebec, October.

Goldstein, Kenneth S. 1964. *A Guide for Field Workers in Folklore.* Hatboro, PA: Folklore Associates.

Goldstein, Kenneth S. 1971. "On the Application of the Concepts of Active and Inactive Traditions to the Study of Repertory." *Journal of American Folklore* 84: 62–67.

Goodwin, Joseph P. 1989. *"More Man Than You'll Ever Be": Gay Folklore and Acculturation in Middle America.* Bloomington: Indiana University Press.

Gramsci, Antonio. 1985. "Osservazioni sul folklore" in *Quaderni dal carcere.* Vol. 3. Turin: Einaudi, pp. 2309–2317.

Green, Archie. 2001. *Torching the Fink Books and Other Essays on Vernacular Culture.* Chapel Hill: University of North Carolina Press.

Grimm, Jakob and Wilhelm Grimm. 1816–1818. *Deutsche Sagen.* 2 Vols. Berlin: Nicolaische Buchhandlung.

Hall, Stephanie A. 1991. "Door into Deaf Culture: Folklore in an American Deaf Social Club." *Sign Language Studies* 73: 421–429.

Hasan-Rokem, Galit. 2000. "Ökotyp" in *Enzyklopädie des Märchens.* Vol.10. Berlin: Walter de Gruyter, pp. 258–263.

Hasan-Rokem, Galit. 2003. *Tales of the Neighborhood: Jewish Narrative Dialogues in Late Antiquity.* Berkeley and Los Angeles: University of California Press.

Hasan-Rokem, Galit and David Shulman. 1996. *Untying the Knot: On Riddles and Other Enigmatic Modes.* Oxford: Oxford University Press.

Herzfeld, Michael. 1997. *Cultural Intimacy: Social Poetics in the Nation-State.* New York: Routledge.

Hirsch, Jerrold. 2010. *America's Folklorist: B.A. Botkin and American Culture.* Norman: University of Oklahoma Press.

Hobsbawm, Eric and Terence Ranger, Eds. 1983. *The Invention of Tradition.* Cambridge: Cambridge University Press.

Honko, Lauri and Orvar Löfgren. 1981. *Tradition och miljö.* Lund: Nordic Institute of Folklore (NIF) Publication 11.

Horkheimer, Max and Theodor W. Adorno. 2002 (1947). *Dialectic of Enlightenment.* Gunzelin Schmid Noerr, Ed. Trans. Edmund Jephcott. Palo Alto: Stanford University Press.

Howard, Robert Glenn. 2005. "Toward a Theory of the World Wide Web Vernacular: The Case for Pet Cloning." *Journal of Folklore Research* 42: 323–360.

Hufford, David J. 1982. *The Terror that Comes in the Night: An Experience-Centered Study of Supernatural Assault Traditions.* Philadelphia: University of Pennsylvania Press.

Hufford, Mary. 1992. *Chaseworld: Foxhunting and Storytelling in New Jersey's Pine Barrens.* Philadelphia: University of Pennsylvania Press.

Hufford, Mary. 1999. "Working in the Cracks: Public Space, Ecological Crisis, and the Folklorist." *Journal of Folklore Research* 36: 157–167.

Hufford, Mary. 2003. "Reclaiming the Commons: Narratives of Progress, Preservation, and Ginseng" in Benita J. Howell, Ed. *Culture, Environment, and Conservation in the Appalachian South.* Urbana: University of Illinois Press, pp. 100–120.

Hymes, Dell. 1964. "Introduction: Toward Ethnographies of Communication." *American Anthropologist* 66: 1–34.

Hymes, Dell. 1975. "Folklore's Nature and the Sun's Myth." *Journal of American Folklore* 88: 345–369.

Illich, Ivan. 1980. "Vernacular Values." *CoEvolution Quarterly* 26.

Jackson, Bruce. 2004 [1974]. *Get Your Ass in the Water and Swim Like Me.* London: Routledge.

Jackson, Jason Baird. 2003. *Yuchi Ceremonial Life: Performance, Meaning and Tradition in a Contemporary American Indian Community.* Lincoln: University of Nebraska Press.

Jordan, Rosan A. and Susan Kalcik, Eds. 1985. *Women's Folklore, Women's Culture.* Philadelphia: University of Pennsylvania.

Kapchan, Deborah A. 1996. *Gender on the Market: Moroccan Women and the Revoicing of Tradition.* Philadelphia: University of Pennsylvania Press.

Kapchan, Deborah A. Ed. Forthcoming. *Intangible Rights: Cultural Heritage and Human Rights.*

Kaplan, Merrill. Forthcoming. "Tradition and Curation on Web 2.0" in Robert Glenn Howard and Trevor Blank, Eds. *Tradition in the Twenty-First Century.* Logan: Utah State University Press.

Kelley, Donald. 1990. "'Second Nature': The Idea of Custom in European Law, Society, and Culture" in Anthony Grafton and Ann Blair, Eds. *The Transmission of Culture in Early Modern Europe.* Philadelphia: University of Pennsylvania Press, pp. 131–172.

Kirshenblatt-Gimblett, Barbara. 1989. "Objects of Memory: Material Culture as Life Review" in Elliott Oring, Ed. *Folk Groups and Folklore Genres: A Reader.* Logan: Utah State University Press, pp. 329–338.

Kirshenblatt-Gimblett, Barbara. 1998a. "Folklore's Crisis." *Journal of American Folklore* 111: 281–327.

Kirshenblatt-Gimblett, Barbara. 1998b. *Destination Culture: Tourism, Museums, and Heritage.* Berkeley and Los Angeles: University of California Press.

Kodish, Debora. 1987. "Absent Gender, Silent Encounter." *Journal of American Folklore* 100: 573–578.

Kristeva, Julia. 1980. *Desire in Language: A Semiotic Approach to Literature and Art.* New York: Columbia University Press.

Labov, William. 2006 [1966]. *The Social Stratification of English in New York City.* Cambridge: Cambridge University Press.

Lau, Kimberly. 2000. *New Age Capitalism: Making Money East of Eden.* Philadelphia: University of Pennsylvania Press.

Lawless, Elaine J. 1991. "Women's Life Stories and Reciprocal Ethnography as Feminist and Emergent." *Journal of Folklore Research* 28: 35–60.

Limón, José E. 1983. "Western Marxism and Folklore: A Critical Introduction." *Journal of American Folklore* 96: 34–52.

Lindahl, Carl. Forthcoming. "Katrina Stories, the David Effect, and the Right to be Wrong." *Journal of American Folklore.*

Lombardi-Satriani, Luigi M. 1974. *Antropologia culturale e analisi della cultura subalterna.* Rimini: Guaraldi.

Macdonald, Dwight. 1962. "Masscult and Midcult" in *Against the American Grain.* New York: Random House, pp. 3–78.

Magliocco, Sabina. 2004. *Witching Culture: Folklore and Neo-Paganism in America.* Philadelphia: University of Pennsylvania Press, pp. 3–75.

Magliocco, Sabina. 2005. *The Two Madonnas: the Politics of Festival in a Sardinian Community.* 2nd edition. Long Grove, IL: Waveland Press.

Marzolph, Ulrich. 1996. "The UNESCO Sponsored 'International Nasreddin Hodja Year.'" *Middle East and South Asia Folklore Bulletin* 13: 11–13.

Mauss, Marcel. 1923–1924. "Essai sur le don. Forme et raison de l'échange dans les sociétés archaïques." *L'Année Sociologique,* seconde série, pp. 30–186.

McGregory, Jerrilyn. 1997. "'May the Work I've Done Speak for Me': African American Women as Community" in Tad Tuleja, Ed. *Usable Pasts*. Logan: Utah State University Press, pp. 96–119.

McMahon, Felicia. 2007. *Not Just Child's Play: Emerging Tradition and the Lost Boys of Sudan*. Jackson: University Press of Mississippi.

Mechling, Jay. 2004. *On My Honor: Boy Scouts and the Making of American Youth*. Chicago: University of Chicago Press.

Michael, Jennifer. 1998. "(Ad)Dressing Shibboleths: Costume and Community in the South of France." *Journal of American Folklore* 111: 146–172.

Mieder, Wolfgang. 1997. *The Politics of Proverbs: From Traditional Wisdom to Proverbial Stereotypes*. Madison: University of Wisconsin Press.

Mills, Margaret A. Forthcoming. "Gnomics: Proverbs, Aphorisms, Metaphors, Key Words and Epithets in Afghan Discourses of War and Instability" in Nile Green and Nushin Arbabzadeh, Eds. *Afghanistan in Ink*. Berkeley and Los Angeles: University of California Press.

Morisset, Lucie K. and Patrick Dieudonné. 2006. "Introduction." *Patrimoines pour le XXIe siècle. Regards du Québec et de la Bretagne*. Québec: Nota Bene.

Newell, William Wells. 1888. "On the Field and Work of a Journal of American Folk-Lore." *Journal of American Folklore* 1: 3–7.

Newell, William Wells. 1904. "The Ignis Fatuus, its Character and Legendary Origin." *Journal of American Folklore* 17: 39–60.

Noyes, Dorothy. 2000. "Breaking the Social Contract: El Comte Arnau, Violence and Production in the Catalan Mountains at the Turn of the Century." *Catalan Review* 14: 129–158.

Noyes, Dorothy. 2003 (1995). "Group" in Burt Feintuch, Ed. *Eight Words for the Study of Expressive Culture*. Urbana: University of Illinois Press, pp. 7–41.

Noyes, Dorothy. 2003. *Fire in the Plaça: Catalan Festival Politics after Franco*. Philadelphia: University of Pennsylvania Press.

O'Connor, Bonnie Blair. 1995. *Healing Traditions: Alternative Medicine and the Health Professions*. Philadelphia: University of Pennsylvania Press.

Oring, Elliott. 1994. "The Arts, Artifacts, and Artifices of Identity." *Journal of American Folklore* 107: 211–233.

Oring, Elliott. 2008. *Engaging Humor*. Urbana: University of Illinois Press.

Paredes, Américo. 1958. *With His Pistol in His Hand: A Border Ballad and its Hero*. Austin: University of Texas Press.

Paredes, Américo and Ellen J. Stekert, Eds. 1971. *The Urban Experience and Folk Tradition*. Austin: University of Texas Press.

Parsons, Talcott. 1951. *The Social System*. Glencoe, IL: Free Press.

Peterson, Sally. 1998. "Translating Experience and the Reading of a Story Cloth." *Journal of American Folklore* 101: 6–22.

Price, David H. 2008. *Anthropological Intelligence: The Deployment and Neglect of American Anthropology in the Second World War*. Durham, NC: Duke University Press.

Primiano, Leonard Norman. 1995. "Vernacular Religion and the Search for Method in Religious Folklife." *Western Folklore* 54: 37–56.

Prosterman, Leslie M. 1995. *Ordinary Life, Festival Days: Aesthetics in the Midwestern County Fair*. Washington, DC: Smithsonian Institution Press.

Redfield, Robert. 1956. *Peasant Society and Culture*. Chicago: University of Chicago Press.

Santino, Jack. 1995. *All Around the Year: Holidays and Celebrations in American Life*. Urbana: University of Illinois Press.

Santino, Jack, Ed. 2005. *Spontaneous Shrines and the Public Memorialization of Death*. New York: Palgrave Macmillan.

Sawin, Patricia. 2004. *Listening for a Life: A Dialogic Ethnography of Bessie Eldreth through her Songs and Stories*. Logan: Utah State University Press.

Schrager, Sam. 2000. *The Trial Lawyer's Art*. Philadelphia: Temple University Press.

Sciorra, Joseph. 2000. Hip-Hop from the Italian Diaspora. Workshop held at the John D. Calandra Italian-American Institute, Queens College, City University of New York, June.

Shepherd, Eric T. 2005. *Eat Shandong: From Personal Experience to a Pedagogy of a*

Second Culture. Columbus, OH: National East Asian Languages Resource Center, Ohio State University.

Shukla, Pravina. 2008. *The Grace of Four Moons: Dress, Adornment, and the Art of the Body in Modern India*. Bloomington: Indiana University Press.

Shuman, Amy. 2005. *Other People's Stories: Entitlement Claims and the Critique of Empathy*. Urbana: University of Illinois Press.

Slyomovics, Susan. 1998. *The Object of Memory: Arab and Jew Narrate the Palestinian Village*. Philadelphia: University of Pennsylvania Press.

Stahl, Sandra K.D. 1975. "The Local Character Anecdote." *Genre* 8: 283–302.

Stoeltje, Beverly J. and Richard Bauman. 1989. "Community Festival and the Enactment of Modernity" in Robert E. Walls and George H. Schoemaker, Eds. *The Old Traditional Way of Life: Essays in Honor of Warren E. Roberts*. Bloomington: Trickster Press, pp. 159–171.

Straw, Will. 1991. "Systems of Articulation, Logics of Change: Communities and Scenes in Popular Music." *Cultural Studies* 5: 368–388.

Sutton-Smith, Brian, Jay Mechling, Thomas W. Johnson, and Felicia R. McMahon, Eds. 1995. *Children's Folklore: A Source Book*. London: Taylor and Francis.

Tangherlini, Timothy. 2010. "Legendary Performances. Folklore, Repertoire, and Mapping." *Ethnologia Europaea* 40: 103–115.

Thompson, Robert Farris. 1983. *Flash of the Spirit: African and Afro-American Art and Philosophy*. New York: Vintage Books.

Thompson, Stith. 1977 [1946]. *The Folktale*. Berkeley and Los Angeles: University of California Press.

Thoms, William. 1999 [1846]. "Folk-Lore and the Origins of the Word" in Alan Dundes, Ed. *International Folkloristics: Classic Contributions by the Founders of Folklore*. Lanham, MD: Rowman and Littlefield, pp. 9–14.

Turner, Kay. 1999. *Beautiful Necessity: The Art and Meaning of Women's Altars*. New York: Thames and Hudson.

Varda, Agnès. 2000. *Les glaneurs et la glaneuse* (film).

Vlach, John Michael. 1978. *The Afro-American Tradition in Decorative Arts*. Cleveland: Cleveland Museum of Art.

Voigt, Vilmos. 1980. "Folklore and Folklorism Today" in Venetia Newall, Ed. *Folklore Studies in the 20th Century*. Woodbridge, UK: D.S. Brewer, pp. 419–424.

Von Sydow, C.W. 1948. *Selected Papers on Folklore*. Copenhagen: Rosenkilde and Bagger.

Ward, Daniel Franklin and I. Sheldon Posen. 1985. "Watts Towers and the Giglio Tradition" in *Folklife Annual 1985*. Washington, DC: Library of Congress, pp. 142–157.

Warner, Michael. 2002. "Publics and Counterpublics." *Public Culture* 14: 49–90.

Warshaver, Gerald. 1986. "Urban Folklore" in Richard M. Dorson, Ed. *Handbook of American Folklore*. Bloomington: Indiana University Press, pp. 162–171.

Weigle, Marta. 1989. *Creation and Procreation: Feminist Reflections on Mythologies of Cosmogony and Parturition*. Philadelphia: University of Pennsylvania Press.

Wellbery, David. 1999. *The Specular Moment*. Palo Alto: Stanford University Press.

Welz, Gisela. 1996. *Inszenierung kultureller Vielfalt. Frankfurt am Main und New York City*. Berlin: Akademie Verlag.

Westerman, William. 1994a. *Cultural Barriers to Justice in Greater Philadelphia: Background, Bias, and the Law*. Philadelphia: Working Papers of the Philadelphia Folklore Project.

Westerman, William. 1994b. "Central American Refugee Testimonies and Performed Life Histories in the Sanctuary Movement" in Rina Benmayor and Andor Skotnes, Eds. *Migration and Identity*. Oxford: Oxford University Press, pp. 167–181.

Westerman, William. 2006. "Wild Grasses and New Arks: Transformative Potential in Applied and Public Folklore." *Journal of American Folklore* 119: 111–128.

Williams, Raymond. 1973. "Base and Superstructure in Marxist Cultural Theory." *New Left Review* 87: 3–16.

Yoder, Don. 1990. *Discovering American Folklife: Studies in Ethnic, Religious, and Regional Culture*. Ann Arbor: UMI Research Press.

Young, Katharine. 1995. *Bodylore*. Knoxville: University of Tennessee Press.

FURTHER READING

Abrahams, Roger D. 1983. *The Man-of-Words in the West Indies: Performance and the Emergence of Creole Culture*. Baltimore: Johns Hopkins.

CHAPTER 2

TRADITION WITHOUT END

Francisco Vaz da Silva

The tradition of talking about tradition has yielded a vast *corpus inscriptionum* (see Noyes 2009). This discussion addresses a particular aspect of the problem. While focusing on narrative traditions, the argument follows the etymological clue and envisions tradition as a dynamic process of transmission. This entails laying out three major ideas.

First, the popular view of tradition as a static, past state of things is arguably a fable. Over the last few decades, in a trend initiated by a collection of essays edited by Eric Hobsbawm and Terence Ranger (1983), a number of studies have provided examples of venerable traditions being actively recreated, or "invented," for present-day purposes.

Second, when examining the dynamics of traditional processes, it is advisable to consider the matter of symbolic equivalences (see Dundes 1987: 167–177). In the realm of oral narrative traditions, as folklorists are well aware, a few hundred stable tale plots are retold over and over in myriad individual variations (see Aarne and Thompson 1961, revised in Uther 2004). Arguably, superficially different tales can only convey the same overarching theme (or stable plot, designated "tale type" by folklorists) if the homologous motifs in parallel versions are, somehow, symbolic equivalents. In other words, understanding the thematic stability of traditional materials requires mapping transformational patterns – gauging how old themes persist and evolve as they are transmitted by means of quasi-equivalent motifs.

Third, once transformational patterns are taken into account it becomes clear that folklore themes often have a longer reach than meets the eye. Oral story patterns frequently persist under new guises, migrate into literature and scholarship, and discreetly percolate into contemporary thought processes. In this sense, tradition is an ongoing process reaching into the future.

A Companion to Folklore, First Edition. Edited by Regina F. Bendix and Galit Hasan-Rokem.
© 2012 John Wiley & Sons, Ltd. Published 2012 John Wiley & Sons, Ltd.

Overall, this essay addresses traditions as open-ended processes shaped by the interplay between individually-generated variations and community-enacted selection mechanisms. It examines some things narrative scholars have to say on tradition, and it submits that tradition pervades some of the things scholars have to say.

TRADITIONALIZATION

"Tradition" derives from Lat. *traditio*, the action of handing over, of delivering. The word refers primarily to the transmission of information, by word of mouth and example, from one generation to the next. By extension, it denotes states of received opinion, inherited patterns of thought and behavior, and bodies of customary lore. So the sense of continuity in time is crucial. All over the world, inquiring folklorists and ethnographers have been treated to justifications of customs and so-called beliefs along the lines of, "We do (or say) it this way because it is the way our forefathers did (or said) it before us." One obvious implication is that the authoritativeness of tradition derives from its (supposed) unbroken connection with the past.

But how do you empirically recognize traditional traits in a given culture? Anthropologist Pascal Boyer proposes to look for memorized and repeated gestures and utterances that are treated as relevant and authoritative by people (Boyer 1987: 58–59, 64). Now, memorized and repeated actions bring the past into the present (which is why they are authoritative) according to prevailing criteria of relevance. In other words, the "traditionalization" of parts of the cultural heritage is a selective process – the process whereby the quality of the traditional is attributed to past cultural traits on the basis of correspondence with contemporary values and goals (Ben-Amos 1984: 115–116; Hymes 1975: 353–354). Of course, to acknowledge that the reception of tradition involves the projection of a contemporary canon into the past entails accepting that tradition is always being created anew – that it reinvents itself traditionally, so to speak, since it produces the ancestors it claims descent from (Lenclud 1994: 32–34). Thus framed, tradition appears as volitional, temporal action by means of which people shape their future (and justify their present) out of the past (Glassie 1995: 395, 399, 409).

But there may be more than volitional action involved. The validation of the status quo by reference to a past state of things implies the projection of tacit cultural assumptions, and (by definition) implicit axioms elude conscious thought. Also, note that the validation of the status quo by reference to a past state of things is a well-recognized function of myth. Relevant to this discussion, Western societies venturing into the age of industrialization have engaged in traditionalization in this mythic, self-reflexive sense by means of the emerging disciplines of folklore and anthropology.

William Thoms, the proponent (in 1846) of the term "Folk-Lore" to name the field of inquiry of the English nineteenth-century antiquarians, defined this field as the study of those "manners, customs, observances, superstitions, ballads, proverbs, and so on, of the olden time" that "may yet be rescued by timely exertion" (Thoms 1999 [1909]: 11). Jacob Grimm had already recommended "salvaging" the remains of *Volkspoesie* by collecting it in the most secluded villages and among peripheral occupations (Grimm 1999 [1815]: 7; cf. Nicolaisen 1995). Generally, nineteenth-century English-speaking folklorists used the terms "lore" and "tradition" to designate the waning ways of life of so-called savage peoples and of the European peasantry (Ben-Amos 1984: 100–105).

Just as exotic peoples were being described as *Naturvölker* or savages (from Lat. *silvaticus*, of the woods), so were European peasants idealized by means of nature metaphors. The Grimms suggested that folk poetry was unspoiled, like children and like nature itself, and was comparable to the last remains of Eden's bounty (Bendix 1992: 109). Since both the "primitive" peoples and the European "unprogressive" classes supposedly represented past stages in the evolution of the "civilized" peoples, folklorists and anthropologists believed they beheld reflections of their own past – of a time of purity and innocence. Anthropologists have produced scores of accounts of the leitmotiv of "the fall from grace of romanticised primitives" (Thomas 1990: 152), and folklorists in the wake of the Grimms have posited that a venerable rural past of intimacy with mother nature receding fast before their gaze (Abrahams 1993: 5–12). Many anthropologists have taken it for granted that "when we change it's called progress ... but when they do it's a kind of adulteration, a loss of their culture" (Sahlins 1999: 2); likewise, the folklorists' pervasive sense of the devolution of traditions has been the flip side of the modern belief in the progress of reason and civilization (Dundes 1969: 10–12).

In short, pioneering folklorists and anthropologists have built a set of variations on the theme of paradise lost for the benefit of an age that embraced industrial civilization with a sense of fall from grace. Their traditionalization of "tradition" has yielded a mythic image of the past mirroring their own conflicting feelings about the present (see Kuper 2005: 10–12).

Traditor

So far I have suggested that traditions are dynamic processes whereby the past is selectively reshaped in light of present needs (the word "traditionalization" felicitously captures this dynamic aspect), and I have noted that the notion of tradition as stasis moored in the past is itself a typical product of traditionalization. Now I propose to tentatively relate the dynamic nature of traditional processes to an interesting etymological twist. Latin *tradere* means "to betray" as well as "to transmit"; thus, *traditor* designates the teacher, the person who hands over something or someone, and ... the traitor. In order to grasp the underlying rationale, consider that in oral traditions any given story exists in multiple versions, so that neighboring groups will shape shared themes in their own ways. Predictably the choices of each group will sound wrong to others, for the treason hint of *traditio* hinges on matters of *quid pro quo*, namely on semantic transpositions. Note that Lat. *transfero* has yielded both "translation" and "transfer," and Lat. *traducere* means to convey across as well as to translate linguistically. Oral transmission involves semantic translations, and the betrayal nuance of *traditio* matches the *traduttore, traditore* adage.

This point is important because to acknowledge that new versions arise out of semantic transpositions entails that variations on a given theme are built on equivalent motifs rather than on arbitrary substitutions. Take a simple example. Alan Dundes noticed that different variants of contemporary limericks and *blasons populaires* use the nose and the phallus interchangeably. He inferred that noses and phalluses are somehow equivalent; and he found independent confirmation of this in an "old joke" that presents a young bride in her wedding night who manages to buy the right size of contraceptive for her husband because she describes the size of his nose to the pharmacist (Dundes 1987: 168–172). Dundes could have mentioned other instances of this symbolic equivalence. For instance, a traveler in Arabia in the 1940s reports, "Bedu say to anyone whose parts are showing, 'Your nose'; I had this said to me once or twice.... The first time I wiped my nose thinking that there was a drip on the end of it" (Thesiger 1991 [1959]: 64). More generally, Freud mentions the "common" comparison between the two appendages as he discusses symbolical transpositions from the lower to the upper part of the body (Freud 1991: 509), and semiologists have endeavored to explain why the nose is "able to metaphorize penis" (Eco and Paci 1983: 231). The point is that, when a given *traditor* replaces a phallus by a nose (or vice-versa), he or she is following a shared (and, in this case, widespread) symbolic equivalence. As Dundes (1987: 168) designated the term "allomotifs" for such sets of equivalent motifs, he stressed that the investigation of allomotifs can materially advance our knowledge of unselfconscious folk symbolism (see also Dundes 2007: 319–324). Insofar as taletellers draw on shared meanings to retell stories – insofar as they use allomotifs to build new versions – the overall tradition is likely to remain stable even while individual narratives vary endlessly.

Let us presently have a closer look at this matter. Folklorists have noticed the "incredible stability of folk narrative" (Krohn 1971 [1926]: 122), "the remarkable stability of the essential story in the midst of continually shifting details" (Thompson 1977 [1946]: 437). Perhaps the best-known effort to explain this phenomenon has been Walter Anderson's description of a law of self-correction in oral traditions. Anderson noted that taletellers usually hear a given story several times and from several sources, thus being able to discard atypical variations and to abide by the normative version of the tale. So, according to Anderson, the stability of tales in the midst of variations does not hinge on verbatim repetition; rather, taletellers construct a composite narrative from a number of variants they heard from various sources, and they manage to keep the "correct" tale going with the help of active criticism from members of the audience (Anderson 1923: 399–406). This empirical description of traditional processes is valuable, and I will return to it in a moment. But, unfortunately, it leaves unanswered the basic question: how exactly do taletellers and their audiences manage to keep correcting the "gaps" and "errors" arising in tradition so as to keep the "correct" tale going?

Arguably, Anderson fails to explain how "self-correction" works because this notion assumes that there is such thing as a "correct" version. This is a distinctly unhelpful assumption. In oral settings, given the absence of recorded texts, stories exist in multiple versions. There is no canonical version; all versions appear as permutations on one another, and so the very notion of an original, "correct" text is quite foreign to this realm. Rather, this notion is the hapless projection of scholars accustomed to dealing with literary texts. As Carl von Sydow (1965 [1948]) pointed out, when philologically-oriented scholars turned to the examination of written texts taken down from oral traditions – a tricky set of hybrid narratives – they transposed old habits of thought into the new realm of studies. The literary gaze created the hybrid notion of "oral *literature*" – a professional fantasy of preset, fixed texts orally transmitted by rote. Given the conspicuous variability of oral materials and the known limitations of human memory, these scholars took for granted that oral tradition is perforce marred by textual corruption due to forgetfulness (Thompson 1977 [1946]: 430–436). Therefore, their professed aim was the reconstitution of Ur-tales expunged of all the "accidental" variations incurred in the course of oral transmission (Taylor 1980 [1927]: 4–6). Ironically, this effort reduces the oral variations to written fixity and thus obliterates tradition itself.

Although Anderson failed to explain how tradition achieves stability because he held on to the "correct version" misconception, he was on the right track as he forcefully remarked that rote memorization is not characteristic of oral traditions. This insight has been confirmed by more recent research suggesting that the cultivation of exact memorization is rather a function of the availability of written texts, which provide a benchmark for correctness (Goody 1977: 36–38, 40–42, 48–49; Goody and Watt 1963: 308–311; Lord 2000: 13–29). If so, it is necessary to step out of the mental habits associated with literacy and ask: what are the principles at work in the realm of *traditio* – that shifting realm where the *traditor* is both transmitter and traitor, and, therefore, themes are stable although no two variants are ever alike?

THEME AND VARIATIONS

We have three clues so far: (i) Oral taletellers tend to perform a creative synthesis of various versions rather than to reproduce verbatim only one text; (ii) taletellers may empirically change a story and still faithfully convey its core theme (the canvas of the shared plot, if you will) by making use of allomotifs; and (iii) audiences have an active role in ensuring that taletellers keep to familiar story patterns. These clues indicate a crucial feature of oral traditions, which was first formulated by Roman Jakobson and Petr Bogatyrev (1982 [1929]: 35–37). These authors argued that in oral settings an individual creation only becomes a fact of folklore after it has been adopted by a given community, and only to the extent that the community has accepted it. By taking into the traditional chain only those aspects of a given story that make sense in the light of shared values and norms, the community keeps individual variations subordinated to the extant canvas of accepted conventions. Jakobson and Bogatyrev called this process the preventive censorship of the community.

But do let not the notion of "censorship" mislead you, for the process is best viewed as a cumulative mechanism of selective appropriations rather than a conscious process. To describe the automatic and unconscious process of selection at stake, Claude Lévi-Strauss, in the wake of Jakobson and Bogatyrev, distinguishes a stable core of shared assumptions from the variable traits contributed by individual tellers. These labile traits will rub against one another and vanish in the course of transmission, he proposes, and so only the "crystalline parts" of each theme persist in the long run (Lévi-Strauss 1971: 560). But take with a pinch of salt this dichotomy between irrelevant individual traits and relevant collective representations. Granted that individual innovations are often idiosyncratic, the relevant question is whether they qualify as allomotifs. The foregoing discussion suggests that, insofar as taletellers follow recognized symbolic patterns, their innovations belong in the "crystalline" nexus of tradition.

Although I have proposed that tradition works by means of symbolic transpositions rather than by attempting to reproduce original texts by rote, there is no denying that memory processes determine how individuals transmit shared materials – again, the relevant point is that memory processes involve semantic equivalences. Frederic C. Bartlett carried out a remarkable series of experiments that left aside the social dimension of traditional processes (see Dundes 1965: 243–245) and instead focused on the workings of individual memory. In a nutshell, Bartlett's experiments show that subjects tend to transpose unfamiliar elements into familiar terms, and to omit whatever data remains meaningless (Bartlett 1920: 36–43). Bartlett describes the cognitive processes he examined as expressions of some fundamental "effort after meaning," which he broadly defines as "simply the attempt to connect something that is given with something other than itself." Overall, he asserts, remembering is "only one special form of the general problem of meaning" (Bartlett 1995 [1932]: 227, 237).

Let us pause for a moment and look back. I have argued that there is nothing mysterious about the stability of oral traditions if we allow that thematic variations follow allomotific lines. On the one hand, as Bartlett shows, taletellers adapt received stories into a personally meaningful composition; on the other, as Jakobson and Bogatyrev suggest, audiences select those variations that fit prevalent values and conventions. The bottom line, then, is that both individual memorization and social tradition are selective processes hinging on the reckoning of meanings.

Symbolic Efficacy

If so, an important question arises. What is the reach of thought patterns embedded in traditional chains? So far I have focused on oral traditions, for writing seems like an obvious dividing line between folkloric creativity and literary modes of thought (Goody 1987 [1977]: 1–18, 52–73; Jakobson and Bogatyrev 1982 [1929]: 38–39). Consider the divide between folklore and the academic study of it. Whilst the oral storyteller is concerned with making the tale live in the minds of the audience, the folklorist is concerned with recording this storytelling faithfully. Whereas storytellers are at liberty to change their stories, folklorists become the guardians of fixed texts (Philip 2006: 45). But, in fact, this dividing line is quite porous. We have seen that philologically-minded scholars have transposed literary criteria onto folklore. Conversely, some folklorists have been influenced by the workings of oral creativity. The Brothers Grimm collected their Märchen for scholarly purposes but then they felt free to change the texts – as though they regarded themselves as links in a chain of storytellers, each having a right to recreate the stories (Neumann 1993: 31–32). Likewise, the nineteenth-century folklorist Joseph Jacobs claimed "the same privilege as any other storyteller" to rewrite orally collected fairy tales (Philip 2006: 45–46). One step ahead, the British writer Angela Carter emulated the workings of tradition as she rewrote a fairy-tale theme as a set of different variants (see Vaz da Silva 2008: 984–986).

And, of course, a wide range of writers – including Plato, Shakespeare, and Freud – have avowedly drawn traditional imagery into their literary works. This prompts the question of whether such crossovers of orally conveyed themes into the literary realm are to be understood as traditional imagery replicating through transformations – as, in other words, showcases of the long reach of traditional processes. Lévi-Strauss makes an interesting point in this regard. Reminiscing on his massive examination of Native American oral narratives while writing his magnum opus, *Mythologiques*, he describes the slow "incubation" of tale variants in his mind while it unconsciously grasped the underlying patterns. He depicts *Mythologiques* as the result of the interplay between native thought processes and his own. And Lévi-Strauss portrays his myth-analysis work as "the myth of mythology," of which he was not so much the author as he was the unwitting executant. These statements suppose the key notion that mythical (or analogical, or symbolic) thinking is dynamic – that, driven by transformations, symbolic thinking continuously generates new variants. This entails that scholarly and other interpretations of a theme are bound to become new versions of it (Lévi-Strauss 1964: 20–21; 1971: 560–565). Indeed, Lévi-Strauss's statement that he was not so much the author as he was the unsuspecting executant of *Mythologiques* is a special case of his general proposition that traditional themes ("myths" in Lévi-Straussian parlance) "get thought in man unbeknownst to him" (Lévi-Strauss 1995 [1978]: 3). Elsewhere, Lévi-Strauss (1974 [1958]: 222–223) describes the underlying driving force as "symbolic efficacy" – the ability of narrative patterns to affect unconscious mechanisms, and organic processes, in individuals – and he associates it with the therapeutic dimension of both shamanism and psychoanalysis. The same understanding of symbolic efficacy tacitly underlies his allusion to the "very dangerous game" scholars play in mythology for "placing one's own intellectual mechanisms in the service of the traditional scheme, allowing it to live and to operate that same mysterious alchemy that afforded it solidity and endurance throughout continents and millenaries" (Lévi-Strauss 1954: 134).

Although these remarks have been shrugged off as bizarre *états d'âme,* some puzzling features of the oeuvre of Lévi-Strauss suggest it is indeed suffused with mythical patterns of thought, quite beyond the awareness of its author. The demonstration is complex and I will not rehearse it here (see Vaz da Silva 2002; 2007: 9–16). But the notion that contemporary scholars and writers may, as a matter of course, inadvertently transform old tales into new guises should give pause to folklorists. The notion of symbolic efficacy suggests that patterns of thought often outlive oral traditions – and I do not mean simply that the "'keys to performance' ... described by Richard Bauman and others, as well as the ethnopoetic features ... delineated by Dell Hymes and his colleagues, can transfer from performance to text, albeit in modified form" (Foley 1996: 25). Rather, I am suggesting that traditional schemes may endure in contemporary scholarly and literary works beyond the awareness of individual authors.

SARAMAGO TRADITOR

In the foregoing discussion I have focused on traditions as dynamic processes that involve thematic transformations; I have noted that such transformations often cross over into the literary realm; and I have speculated that Lévi-Strauss's notion of symbolic efficacy may help explain the long reach of traditional themes. Before following up on this idea, consider the following example of symbolic efficacy at work.

The late Portuguese Nobel Prize-winning author José Saramago published a novel called *O Evangelho Segundo Jesus Cristo* (The Gospel According to Jesus Christ), which mounts a scathing attack on the Judeo-Christian religious tradition. It stirred up a heated polemic in the Portuguese media, and the government demanded its withdrawal from the list of candidates for the European Prize for Literature in 1992 on the grounds that the novel attacks "principles pertaining to the religious heritage of the Portuguese people" (Frier 2005: 367–368).

In his Nobel Lecture, Saramago defines his "heretical Gospel" as not "one more edifying legend of blessed beings and gods, but instead the story of a few human beings subjected to a power they fight but cannot defeat" (Saramago 1999: 9). At the outset of the novel Mary, sleeping in her marriage bed, trembles like water rippling in the breeze as the divine power hovers over her; then Joseph sexually takes her. Thus Jesus has two fathers. He chooses to follow the footsteps of his earthly father, but this is a tricky path. Joseph, forewarned about the massacre of the innocent children of Bethlehem, did nothing to save them. For this "crime" he experiences lifelong guilt and nightmares that ultimately lead him to die crucified by the Romans (in the context of an ongoing "intifada") at the age of 33. Jesus inherits his father's nightmares and guilt. He wishes to atone for the loss of innocent lives associated with his birth, and also dies crucified at 33.

But even while Jesus followed his earthly father he was the plaything of the heavenly Lord. The sacrifice of Jesus, the lamb of God, is part of a divine plan. God is tired of being the parochial divinity of a tiny group of people and wants a universal church. The ghastly death of Jesus is crucial to the plan because martyrdom moves believers to devotion. If the universal church is to be solid, its foundations must be dug in flesh and its walls built with the cement of renunciation, tears, agony, anguish, and every conceivable form of death. And so Jesus learns that his impending death will be but the beginning of an infinite sea of sorrow and tears.

Jesus reasons that if he cannot undo the killing of the innocent children who died because of his birth, he can at least try to spare the lives of the innumerable people fated to die as a consequence of his own impending death. Therefore, he decides to outwit God's appalling plan for the world by dying as a man – as the son of Joseph, not the son of God, and as a would-be king of the Jews, not the Savior. He asks the apostles to denounce him as a political agitator, but only Judas agrees to denounce him; then Jesus himself asks Pilate to put an inscription on the cross that identifies him as the king of the Jews. But when Jesus is dying on the cross God proclaims that this is his beloved son. Then Jesus realizes, alas too late, that he has been tricked as a lamb led to sacrifice is tricked. Even as he is dying like his earthly father he realizes that his hope of redeeming Joseph's sin was in vain, because the heavenly father had preordained his fate. And Jesus calls out to the open sky, "Men, forgive Him, for He knows not what He has done" (Saramago 1994: 377).

Note that Saramago's "heretical Gospel" perpetuates, willy-nilly, the core ideas of the tradition he calls into question. Saramago deems "heretical" his presentation of Christ as a man intent on following his earthly father's path rather than on fulfilling God's plan – but then, the casting of this idea in terms of Jesus's attempt to redeem the transmissible sin of Joseph reads like an echo of the scriptural mission of redeeming the original sin. And, although to cast Judas as the emissary of Jesus likewise appears to subvert the received wisdom of Christian traditions, this authorial choice in fact expresses the inescapable logic of the Christian credo – since Christ was incarnated to die on the cross, the delivery of Jesus to his slayers helps to fulfill the divine plan. Thomas Aquinas, although he upholds the Church's infamous policy of casting Judas and the Jews as reviled scapegoats, unambiguously states in the Question 47 of his *Summa Theologica* that God preordained Christ's Passion for the redemption of humankind and delivered up Jesus to the Passion. Even though Aquinas adduces petty psychological motivations for the betrayal (Judas betrayed from greed, and the Jews from envy…) in order to avoid granting the teleological point that Judas was instrumental to the divine plan, this point is hinted in the gospel of John (Jn 13: 18, 26–31) and it is laid bare in the late antique Gnostic *Gospel of Judas* 56 (see Ehrman 2008). In short, although Saramago casts Jesus as a down-to-earth man, the theological cause for the Incarnation still directs his story, and even when he subverts the received wisdom about Judas, Saramago conveys an unimpeachable strain of Christian theology. His story, intended as subversive, in fact relays in *sotto voce* crucial Christian ideas.

To talk like Lévi-Strauss, Saramago played the dangerous game of placing his intellectual mechanisms in the service of the traditional scheme. Inadvertently, he produced a new variant that transmits the deepest theological strata of the Christian tradition he would dismiss. And this brings us back to the matter of symbolic efficacy.

MEMETIC SELECTION

Lévi-Strauss's vision of ideas playing themselves out in the minds of people may be placed in a wider context. As philosopher Daniel Dennett (1996: 347) notes, "[r]are is the novelist who *doesn't* claim characters who 'take on a life of their own'; artists are rather fond of confessing that their paintings take over and paint themselves; and poets humbly submit that they are the servants or even slaves of the ideas that teem in their heads." To account for such phenomena, biologist Richard Dawkins proposed a viewpoint that is strikingly convergent (and contemporaneous) with that of Lévi-Strauss. Just as, he argues, in the biological realm it is correct to state that evolution is driven by the competition between basic units of replication – genes – that often ride organisms in order to increase their chance of transmission, so in the cultural realm there are units of imitation – "mimemes," which Dawkins shortens to "memes" to rhyme with "genes" – that use their hosts' brainpower to survive, jumping from brain to brain in order to get themselves copied (Dawkins 2006 [1976]:189–201, 234–266). This viewpoint requires that we "make a gigantic flip in our minds," as psychologist Susan Blackmore puts it, because it represents our ideas as not our own creations but rather as autonomous replicators that use human hosts to reproduce themselves (Blackmore 2000: 7–8).

The practical import of Dawkins's proposition, that we think about our own minds as hubs where preexisting ideas renew themselves before going forth into other people's minds, may sound distinctly unappealing. But try putting this idea into perspective. As Freud once remarked (in "A Difficulty in the Path of Psycho-Analysis," 1917), it took the Copernican revolution to make us acknowledge that the Earth is not the center of the universe, not even the center of the solar system, and it took the

Darwinian revolution to make us grant that humanity is not the center of creation, and not its purpose either. The third blow to human narcissism, and probably the most wounding – or so Freud claimed – was his own point that mental processes are unconscious. Dawkins's memetic proposition likewise suggests that the ideas we use are less "ours" than we would like to think. It is a rather prosaic fact of life that people borrow the ideas they pass on, more or less changed, throughout their lives. This is perhaps most obvious in the case of scholars, who are required to punctiliously disclose the sources of the ideas they use for elaborating whatever propositions they pass on to others. There are, of course, stunningly original pieces of scholarship – but, as the saying goes, great scholars stand on the shoulders of giants. In this perspective, every scholar (and every taleteller, and every gossip monger...) qualifies as a link in a traditional chain. Even as Dawkins's memetic perspective cuts to size the illusion of individual uniqueness, it calls attention to the pervasiveness of traditional mechanisms in all walks of cultural life.

It is not surprising, then, that the "meme" meme has already hit narrative studies (Zipes 2006). Although this is hardly the place to enter the wider debate on meme theory (see Aunger 2000 for a sample), let us briefly consider the intriguing theoretical convergence between Dawkins and Lévi-Strauss in regard to traditional processes. The gene/meme analogy applies evolutionary thinking to culture because it relies on the assumption that evolution is a substrate-neutral process bound to happen in any system, biological or cultural, in which there is replication, variation, and selection. In other words, whenever replicators undergo variations as they reproduce, and some fare better than others, an evolutionary process is bound to happen (see Dennett 1996: 40–51, 343). Now take a minimalist definition of tradition as the transmission of a set of thematic variations. As the variations unfold, some will fare better than others due to what Jakobson and Bogatyrev called the preventive censorship of the community. So I am suggesting that the shaping of allomotific variations by the preventive censorship of the community qualifies as an evolutionary process. Indeed, this is where the different perspectives of Dawkins and Lévi-Strauss meet. Whereas Dawkins's notion of memetic evolution stresses the selective pressures on thematic variation, Lévi-Strauss's concept of symbolic efficacy emphasizes the continuity of the transmitted themes. The two perspectives play well together insofar as both allow that traditional themes undergo transformations shaped by selective pressures happening quite beyond the pale of conscious thought. This common ground suggests that changes in cultural settings, shifting selective pressures, if you will, shape the transformations of old themes into new guises matching (in agreement, or otherwise) contemporary standards.

THE LONG REACH OF TRADITION

From this perspective one would expect to see traditional chains spanning the divide between folklore and folkloristics, myth and science, as long as writers and scholars engage in the Lévi-Straussian "very dangerous game" of allowing traditional schemes to operate in their intellectual mechanisms. Let me provide a short example, among many possible cases, of the continuity between oral and scholarly traditions.

The so-called Star Husband cycle of Native American tales has been the object of early studies by anthropologist Gladys Reichard (1921) and folklorist Stith Thompson (1965 [1953]), who focused (from different standpoints) on breaking down the tale into its constituent units and assessing their geographical dissemination. Given the nature of these studies, meaning was never an issue for either author. Likewise, Alan Dundes's morphological analysis of Star Husband (Dundes 1980 [1964]: 87–91) did not broach semantic problems because, by design, the Proppian model discards thematic variations.

However, when Lévi-Strauss (1968: 161–224) proposed an alternative to Thompson's handling of the Star Husband cycle, he did focus on the transformations between homologous motifs in different subplots. This procedure yielded a conceptual scheme that hinges on a set of analogical transitions between winter and springtime, dark and full moon, night and day, and the cyclical phases of feminine physiology. Within this conceptual framework, Lévi-Strauss pays special attention to an Arapaho tale called "Little Star," which he labels M_{428}, *Les épouses des astres* (The Wives of the Sun and the Moon). He notes that this story blends etiological matters pertaining to cosmology, cultural techniques, social rules, and feminine physiology. This tale cycle assumes that the order of the world hinges on the regular succession of days and nights, months, and seasons, and that the physiological functions of women partake of both cosmological and social rhythms; therefore, this etiological story takes the precise ordering of feminine cycles as a token of the cosmic and social organization (Lévi-Strauss 1968: 172–183; compare Dorsey 1903: 177–178, 212–228).

One step ahead, anthropologist Chris Knight (1997: 140–151) – taking up where Lévi-Strauss left off – argued that "Little Star" depicts a primordial situation in which women used to alternate between a spell of menstrual seclusion among their blood relations and a "resurrected" phase of marital life with their husbands, before the establishment of patrilocal marriage broke this alternate rhythm. Indeed, Knight submits that this story depicts the origin of patrilocal marriage and of the domestic power of husbands over wives; for he assumes that mythical tales provide clues regarding an archaic elementary social structure, dating back to the origins of humankind, which he strove to describe in a wide-ranging book (Knight 1995 [1991]).

Knight expects the "time-resistant syntax" of the primal symbolic system characteristic of that elementary social structure, which he finds in "Little Star," to operate in ritual and myth across all cultures and all historical periods. That primal symbolic system associates flowing blood, the dark moon, and kin solidarity on one hand, and cooked meat, the full moon, and marital life on the other (Knight *et al.* 1995: 77–84, 91–92; Knight 1997: 135–136). Interestingly, both the "Little Star" etiological story and Knight's model of the origins of humankind comply with this syntax. It is hard to avoid the inference that Knight's model of social origins, built according to a time-resistant mythical syntax, is itself a mythical construct. Knight does acknowledge that his model has developed according to "its own mythic logic" until it became a satisfactory "myth as pure myth, almost entirely independent of any modern data." But he adds that, having endeavored to learn the scientific protocols for effectively transmitting his origins tale to his peers, he found it was rather common among evolutionary scholars to "transpose the modern world's constructs on to other cultures, on to nature and on to our own most distant past." The game of scientific discourse, Knight claims, lays out ground rules according to which "scientific storytellers" vie to have their own particular myths canonized as science (Knight 1995 [1991]: 4–5, 20–27, 35, 37).

Knight's stance is hardly surprising ever since historian of science Donna Haraway submitted that "scientific practice is above all a story-telling practice in the sense of historically specific practices of interpretation and testimony." Of course, this does not mean that there are no scientific facts; rather, the implication is that "facts" are sets of testimony to experience put together according to prevailing rules, not unlike "a story-telling practice – a rule-governed, constrained, historically changing craft of narrating the history of nature," as she put it. Haraway added that looking at primatology – a discipline concerned with "primal stories" about human origins and human nature – as a story-telling craft may be particularly appropriate (Haraway 1992 [1989]: 4, 9). She noted that there are many claims on the complex and protean narratives of paleoanthropology and primatology, and "each claim can become part of a new version of the stories. The stories taken together constitute a story field, with axes of organization and rules for producing transformations" (1992: 188). Overall, she proposes, this scholarly tradition of primal stories has engaged in constructing the Western self from the raw material of the other – a display of the Western imagination of the origin of sociality itself (1992: 11). In other words, to summarize Haraway in the terms of this discussion, primatology and paleoanthropology rank among the Western disciplines engaged in traditionalization.

But let us return to Knight. Driven by what he calls the time-resistant syntax of ritual and myth, even while playing by the rules of scientific discourse, this author has transposed the themes Lévi-Strauss recognized in "Little Star" (and related tales) into the realm of contemporary inquiries on human origins. The mythic framework of his paleoanthropological model does not bother Knight, who claims that myths reflect archaic facts. Alternatively, I point out that symbolic efficacy pervades his model through and through. Whatever happened at the dawn of humankind, Knight's story of origins is ultimately a variation on a traditional story of aboriginal feminine power appropriated by men – a brilliant transformation of the so-called myth of matriarchy (Knight 1995 [1991]: 40–41, 421–433; cf. Bamberger 1974).

CONCLUDING THOUGHTS

In the foregoing discussion I have portrayed traditions as open-ended processes shaped by the interplay between individually-generated variations, on the one hand, and selection criteria upheld by historically changing communities, on the other. As regards variations, I have suggested that – palimpsest-like, and quite beyond the awareness of taletellers – narratives tend to contain the predecessors they are transcending. Thus, we glimpsed unacknowledged aspects of Christian theology in Saramago's self-professed "heretical" tale. Regarding the matter of selection, I have suggested that Jakobson and Bogatyrev's notion of the censorship of the community is relevant whenever individual innovations must be selectively incorporated into a given transmission medium in order to survive. For instance, beyond oral transmission, peer-reviewing among scientific storytellers plays a role not unlike that of the preventive censorship of the community. We may therefore speak of scholarly traditions, just as one speaks of oral traditions, to designate story fields where – as Haraway (1992 [1989]: 188) put it – "the stories can only be generated, told, and retold in relation to each other. But not any story can be accommodated in the field, and some stories can no longer be told."

To conclude, let me briefly return to Freud's point that Copernicus, Darwin, and he himself delivered three decisive blows to humankind's narcissism. Converging pieces of research suggest that the paradigm-shifting models of Johannes Kepler (who, in the wake of Copernicus, first proposed the heliocentric theory), Darwin, and Freud were steeped in mythological notions (Beer 2009 [1983]; Simon 1979; Vaz da Silva 2007). If so, then a number of assumptions we take more or less for granted in the post-Darwinian and post-Freudian world – such as the slow metamorphosis of species in the tree of life, instinctual drives poised between Eros and Thanatos, Oedipal trials and tribulations – convey archaic resonances into contemporary thought processes. Recent trends in memetics and the epidemiology of representations raise the question of why certain memes spread more than others (Blackmore 2000; Sperber 1996). The foregoing discussion suggests, as one possible answer, that a number of successful ideas are variations on potent traditional themes. And the bottom line is that traditions are vivacious processes to be studied in the present, and into the future.

REFERENCES

Aarne, Antti, and Stith Thompson. 1961. *The Types of the Folktale: A Classification and Bibliography.* 3rd edition. *FF Communications* 184. Helsinki: Academia Scientiarum Fennica.

Abrahams, Roger D. 1993. "Phantoms of Romantic Nationalism in Folkloristics." *The Journal of American Folklore* 106(419): 3–37.

Anderson, Walter. 1923. *Kaiser und Abt: Die Geschichte eines Schwanks. FF Communications* 42. Helsinki: Suomalainen Tiedeakatemia.

Aunger, Robert, Ed. 2000. *Darwinizing Culture: The Status of Memetics as a Science.* New York: Oxford University Press.

Bamberger, Joan. 1974. "The Myth of Matriarchy: Why Men Rule in Primitive Society" in Michelle Zimbalist Rosaldo, and Louise Lamphere, Eds. *Woman, Culture and Society.* Palo Alto: Stanford University Press, pp. 263–280.

Bartlett, Frederic C. 1920. "Some Experiments on the Reproduction of Folk-Stories." *Folklore* 31(1): 30–47.

Bartlett, Frederic C. 1995 [1932]. *Remembering: A Study in Experimental and Social Psychology.* Cambridge: Cambridge University Press.

Beer, Gillian 2009 [1983]. *Darwin's Plots: Evolutionary Narrative in Darwin, George Eliot and Nineteenth-Century Fiction.* 3rd edition. Cambridge: Cambridge University Press.

Ben-Amos, Dan. 1984. "The Seven Strands of Tradition: Varieties in Its Meaning in American Folklore Studies." *Journal of Folklore Research* 21(2/3): 97–131.

Bendix, Regina. 1992. "Diverging Paths in the Scientific Search for Authenticity." *Journal of Folklore Research* 29(2): 103–132.

Blackmore, Susan. 2000. *The Meme Machine.* New York: Oxford University Press.

Boyer, Pascal. 1987. "The Stuff 'Traditions' Are Made of: On the Implicit Ontology of an Ethngraphic Category." *Philosophy of the Social Sciences* 17: 49–65.

Dawkins, Richard. 2006 [1976]. *The Selfish Gene.* Thirtieth anniversary edition. Oxford: Oxford University Press.

Dennett, Daniel C. 1996. *Darwin's Dangerous Idea: Evolution and the Meanings of Life*. New York: Simon and Schuster.

Dorsey, George A. 1903. *The Arapaho Sun Dance: The Ceremony of the Offerings Lodge*. Chicago: Field Columbian Museum.

Dundes, Alan, Ed. 1965. *The Study of Folklore*. Englewood Cliffs, NJ: Prentice-Hall.

Dundes, Alan. 1969. "The Devolutionary Premise in Folklore Theory." *Journal of the Folklore Institute* 6(1): 5–19.

Dundes, Alan. 1980 [1964]. *The Morphology of North American Indian Folktales. FF Communications* 195. Helsinki: Academia Scientiarum Fennica.

Dundes, Alan. 1987. *Parsing Through Customs: Essays By a Freudian Folklorist*. Madison, WI: University of Wisconsin Press.

Dundes, Alan. 2007. *The Meaning of Folklore: The Analytical Essays of Alan Dundes*. Simon J. Bronner, Ed. Logan, UT: Utah State University Press.

Eco, Umberto and Christopher Paci. 1983. "The Scandal of Metaphor: Metaphorology and Semiotics." *Poetics Today* 4(2): 217–257.

Ehrman, Bart D. 2008. "The Alternative Vision of the Gospel of Judas" in Rodolphe Kasser, Marvin Meyer, and Gregor Wurst, Eds. *The Gospel of Judas*. 2nd edition. Washington, DC: National Geographic Society, pp. 79–102.

Foley, John Miles. 1996. "Signs, Texts, and Oral Tradition." *Journal of Folklore Research* 33(1): 21–29.

Freud, Sigmund. 1976 [1991]. *The Interpretation of Dreams*. Angela Richards, Ed. and trans. James Strachey. Harmondsworth: Penguin Books.

Frier, David G. 2005. "José Saramago's 'O Evangelho Segundo Jesus Cristo': Outline of a Newer Testament." *The Modern Language Review* 100(2): 367–382.

Glassie, Henry. 1995. "Tradition." *Journal of American Folklore* 108(430): 395–412.

Goody, Jack. 1977. "Mémoire et apprentissage dans les sociétés avec et sans écriture: La transmission du Bagre." *L'Homme* 17(1): 29–52.

Goody, Jack. 1987 [1977]. *The Domestication of the Savage Mind*. Cambridge: Cambridge University Press.

Goody, Jack and Ian Watt. 1963. "The Consequences of Literacy." *Comparative Studies in Society and History* 5(3): 304–345.

Grimm, Jacob. 1999 [1815]. "Circular Concerning the Collecting of Folk Poetry" in Alan Dundes, Ed. *International Folkloristics: Classic Contributions by the Founders of Folklore*. Lanham, MD: Rowman and Littlefield, pp. 1–7.

Haraway, Donna. 1992 [1989]. *Primate Visions: Gender, Race and Nature in the World of Modern Science*. London: Verso.

Hobsbawm, Eric and Terence Ranger, Eds. 1983. *The Invention of Tradition*. Cambridge: Cambridge University Press.

Hymes, Dell. 1975. "Folklore's Nature and the Sun's Myth." *The Journal of American Folklore*. 88(350): 345–369.

Jakobson, Roman and Petr Bogatyrev. 1982 [1929]. "Folklore as a Special Form of Creativity" in Peter Steiner, Ed. *The Prague School. Selected Writings, 1929–1946*. Austin: University of Texas Press, pp. 32–46.

Knight, Chris. 1995 [1991]. *Blood Relations: Menstruation and the Origins of Culture*. New Haven: Yale University Press.

Knight, Chris. 1997. "The Wives of the Sun and Moon." *The Journal of the Royal Anthropological Institute* 3(1): 133–153.

Knight, Chris, Camilla Power, and Ian Watts. 1995. "The Human Symbolic Revolution: A Darwinian Account." *Cambridge Archaeological Journal* 5(1): 75–114.

Krohn, Kaarle. 1971 [1926]. *Folklore Methodology*. Trans. Roger L. Welsch. Austin: University of Texas Press.

Kuper, Adam. 2005. *The Reinvention of Primitive Society: Transformations of a Myth*. New York: Routledge.

Lenclud, Gérard. 1994. "Qu'est-ce que la tradition?" in Marcel Detienne, Ed. *Transcrire les mythologies*. Paris: Albin Michel, pp. 25–44.

Lévi-Strauss, Claude. 1954. "L'art de déchiffrer les symboles en quatre leçons (à suivre ou à ne pas suivre)." *Diogène* 5: 128–135.

Lévi-Strauss, Claude. 1964. *Le cru et le cuit.* Mythologiques, Vol. 1. Paris: Plon.

Lévi-Strauss, Claude. 1968. *L'origine des manières de table.* Mythologiques, Vol. 3. Paris: Plon.

Lévi-Strauss, Claude. 1971. *L'homme nu.* Mythologiques, Vol. 4. Paris: Plon.

Lévi-Strauss, Claude. 1974 [1958]. *Anthropologie structurale.* 2nd edition. Paris: Plon.

Lévi-Strauss, Claude. 1995 [1978]. *Myth and Meaning.* New York: Schocken Books.

Lord, Albert B. 2000. *The Singer of Tales.* Stephen Mitchell and Gregory Nagy, Eds. 2nd edition. Harvard Studies in Comparative Literature 24. Cambridge, MA, and London: Harvard University Press.

Neumann, Siegfried. 1993. "The Brothers Grimm as Collectors and Editors of German Folktales" in Donald Haase, Ed. *The Reception of Grimms' Fairy Tales: Responses, Reactions, Revisions.* Detroit: Wayne State University Press, pp. 24–40.

Nicolaisen, W.F.H. 1995. "A Gleaner's Vision." *Folklore* 106: 71–76.

Noyes, Dorothy. 2009. "Tradition: Three Traditions." *Journal of Folklore Research* 46(3): 233–268.

Philip, Neil. 2006. "Creativity and Tradition in the Fairy Tale" in Hilda Ellis Davidson and Anna Chaudhri, Eds. *A Companion to the Fairy Tale.* Cambridge, MA: Brewer, pp. 39–55.

Reichard, Gladys A. 1921. "Literary Types and Dissemination of Myths." *The Journal of American Folklore* 34(133): 269–307.

Sahlins, Marshall. 1999. "What is Anthropological Enlightenment? Some Lessons of the Twentieth Century." *Annual Review of Anthropology* 28: i–xxiii.

Saramago, José. 1994. *The Gospel According to Jesus Christ.* Trans. Giovanni Pontiero. Orlando, FL: Harvest Books.

Saramago, José. 1999. "The 1998 Nobel Lecture." *World Literature Today* 73(1): 4–10.

Sperber, Dan. 1996. *Explaining Culture: A Naturalistic Approach.* Oxford: Blackwell.

Simon, Gérard. 1979. *Kepler astronome astrologue.* Paris: Galimard.

Taylor, Archer. 1980 [1927]. *The Black Ox.* New York: Arno Press.

Thesiger, Wilfred. 1991 [1959]. *Arabian Sands.* London: Penguin.

Thomas, Nicholas. 1990. "Partial Texts: Representation, Colonialism and Agency in Pacific History." *The Journal of Pacific History* 25(2): 139–158.

Thompson, Stith. 1965 [1953]. "The Star Husband Tale" in Alan Dundes, Ed. *The Study of Folklore.* Englewood Cliffs, NJ: Prentice-Hall, pp. 414–474.

Thompson, Stith. 1977 [1946]. *The Folktale.* Berkeley: University of California Press.

Thoms, William. 1999 [1909]. "Folk-Lore and the Origin of the Word" in Alan Dundes, Ed. *International Folkloristics: Classic Contributions By the Founders of Folklore.* Lanham, MD: Rowman and Littlefield, pp. 9–14.

Uther, Hans-Jörg. 2004. *The Types of International Folktales: A Classification and Bibliography, Based on the System of Antti Aarne and Stith Thompson.* 3 vols. FF Communications 284–286. Helsinki: Academia Scientiarum Fennica.

Vaz da Silva, Francisco. 2002. "Claude Lévi-Strauss en énigme." *Gradhiva* 32: 1–11.

Vaz da Silva, Francisco. 2007. "Folklore Into Theory: Freud and Lévi-Strauss on Incest and Marriage." *Journal of Folklore Research* 44(1): 1–19.

Vaz da Silva, Francisco. 2008. "Transformation" in Donald Haase, Ed. *The Greenwood Encyclopedia of Folktales and Fairy Tales.* Westport, CT: Greenwood Press, pp. 982–986.

von Sydow, Carl Wilhelm. 1965 [1948]. "Folktale Studies and Philology: Some Points of View" in Alan Dundes, Ed. *The Study of Folklore.* Englewood Cliffs, NJ: Prentice-Hall, pp. 219–242.

Zipes, Jack. 2006. *Why Fairy Tales Stick: the Evolution and Relevance of a Genre.* New York: Routledge.

CHAPTER **3**

THE POETICS OF FOLKLORE

Amy Shuman and
Galit Hasan-Rokem

The topic of poetics in folklore research calls attention to the artistic creativity invested in each instance of folklore. Unlike the poetics of canonical modes of cultural creativity in which poetics often appear as consciously formulated credos and manifests, the poetics of folklore emerges implied and embedded in the presentation and performance of folklore itself. Scholars are thus in a position to infer the poetics of folklore by studying the empirical materials available on the one hand and analyzing various theoretical approaches that have addressed the poetics of folklore on the other.

The topic of poetics is itself a historical discourse; it is the site of intersecting conversations among the disciplines. In our essay we are both referring to those ongoing conversations and also suggesting new areas that, through a shared interest in poetics, might be in conversation with each other. Historically, the field of folklore marks several significant shifts in the study of poetics in general. These shifts are, however, more recursive than linear, with old patterns reconfigured in new paradigms. The study of poetics in folklore works at multiple levels, from philosophical discussions of differences between science/rationality/logic and magic/mythology to textual analyses of communicative practices.

Poetics is famously related to the concept of beauty and it is thus relevant to ask who is entitled to decide on the aesthetic value of folkloristic creativity. There are two possible sources of information for answering this question: practitioners and audiences of folkloristic creativity reflecting on a social value system and theory-based value systems of aesthetic judgment (Hasan-Rokem 1978; Smith 1988).

A Companion to Folklore, First Edition. Edited by Regina F. Bendix and Galit Hasan-Rokem.
© 2012 John Wiley & Sons, Ltd. Published 2012 John Wiley & Sons, Ltd.

HISTORICAL ROOTS FOR A POETICS OF FOLKLORE

Poetics is a term that has historically been applied mainly to the verbal arts and literature in particular. Folklore studies began historically partly in the context of literary and
philological studies. It is thus natural that poetics has been one of the conceptual
frameworks that has inspired theoretical discussions of folklore. The gradual configuration of folklore studies to encompass nonverbal aspects of verbal performance (see
articles by Bauman and Seitel in the present volume) has necessitated the widening of
the concept of poetics with regard to folklore. In conjunction with other cultural developments, it has prompted a theoretical innovation that contrary to the classical purely
literary poetics of Aristotle, Quintilian and Longinus, the medieval poetics inspired by
Augustine and the Enlightenment poetics of Lessing with its specific separation of verbal and visual art, suggests a cross-medial and cross-generic approach to poetics in
general. The discourse of poetics in folklore has developed since the emergence of the
discipline of folklore research, since the beginning of the nineteenth century, with
explicit reference to the contemporary discourse of poetics in literature and the arts.

Poetics as derived from the act of *poiesis*, creating in the artistic sense of the word,
opens the theory of folklore studies to a particular range of concepts and terms closely
associated with artistic creativity. Epistemologically the move aligns with the post-
Enlightenment, or more precisely post-Vico perception of culture as engaged in the
human subject's interpretation of objects of knowledge humanly created. It is thus a
basically contingent theory of folklore that will be revealed in our discussion rather
than any idealist perception of poetics. Poetics will be understood as the total body of
values predicating expressive modes of culture created in various media by individual
authors, artists and performers interacting with values and norms collectively accepted
and processually shaped through shared forms of transmission.

Including the term "poetics" among the concepts pertinent to the study of folklore
is important because of the way it contributes to the mediating and blurring of
particular binary oppositions that have emerged in the sphere of the discipline. The
term "the poetics of folklore" points to an approach that consciously softens the
boundaries between canonical and non-canonical, between written and oral, between
elite and popular. It implies recognition of regularity as well as a set value system on
both sides of the above mentioned dialectic. It implies aesthetic norms as an active
factor in the shaping of folklore (Mukařovský 1970).

The authors of this essay are both primarily scholars of verbal and textual folklore.
This determines our emphasis on forms of folklore from our areas of expertise. We
shall, however, attempt to include in our discussion those elements of the poetics of
folklore that are common to the various media in which folklore emerges and is
created, namely in material, ritual as well as verbal media. Moreover, we argue that the
interrelationship between the various media is not merely conducive for the creation
of folklore but to a certain degree defines the specific character of folklore.

Our discussion of the poetics of folklore also takes into consideration that much of
folkloric poetics is not specifically or exclusively folkloristic, but may be subsumed in
the more inclusive category of "cultural poetics." This also suggests the centrality of
the methodology of "semiotics of culture" for the field of folklore studies. By that the
inseparability and constant interaction of folklore with other modes of cultural

expression will be emphasized. Consequently many elements of the poetics of folklore are common to folklore and other modes of cultural expression.

Following our suggestions above, and focusing now on verbal – especially literary – folklore, poetics from a folkloric perspective combines formal features (style, structure, and genre) and interactional features (performance, framing, turn-taking, tellability, and entitlement) as well as the implications on all the above mentioned on folklore's contents. The history of poetics in folklore is, in part, a history of how scholars have understood the formal and interactional features to overlap and intersect, for example through intertextuality, metacommunicative devices, and dialogism. The key here is that although each of these elements can be defined and discussed separately, the study of poetics in folklore requires that they be studied together.

In *The New Science,* Giambattista Vico defines the poetic as a sphere of knowledge that brings together myth and science in an exploration of the foundations of humanity. From this early modern discussion of poetics through the work of Johann Gottfried von Herder and the nineteenth-century philologists, poetics was already a social poetics, interested not only in questions of form but also of how forms provided resources for negotiating social meanings.

Some major contributions to the study of folklore provide terminologies and concepts for the discussion of poetics. Herder's thought and writings are often considered a decisive impetus on the disciplinary formation of folklore studies, especially as they were adopted by Jacob and Wilhelm Grimm. Herder not only created the modern concept of *Volk,* which may be the most problematic of his legacies perpetuated in folklore studies, positing collective identities of a national character as the subject of folkloristic creativity. But under the influence of Johann Georg Hamann he also developed a theory of knowledge and ultimately of poetics that views language in its social contexts in ways that became very meaningful in folklore research. Herder posited genre as a basic concept for discussing literature as well as the arts. Hence in the Grimm Brothers' historical reconstruction of folk literature, the tripartite genre distinction –*Mythus* (myth), *Sage* (legend), *Märchen* (folktale) – served as the basis for the various internal transformations of the system, such as the "sinking" of myth to the form of the folktale with the disappearance of the belief system that had earlier supported its normative and religious status. Later functionalist study of folk literature has, in the wake of Bronislaw Malinowski's work (1976 [1926]), corroborated the tripartite division and added stylistic and functional characteristics to each of the genres, such as the higher level of stylization of the folktale in comparison to legend (Lüthi 1975), and the supposedly more ritual context of the performance of myth. But especially the latter trait has been questioned in correlation with the more diversified definition of the ritual that has emerged in the wake of the work of Erving Goffman (1967) and others and Kirshenblatt-Gimblett (1975).

The neo-functionalist development in American folklore research in the late 1960s was influenced by the ethno-linguistic work of Franz Boas, one of the main carriers of the Herderian legacy to the Western hemisphere, and his (indirect) disciple Dell Hymes (1972a, b, 1974). It held sway to the early 1990s and questioned the universality of genre suggested by the Grimms and their followers (Ben-Amos 1969) and shifted the poetic interests of research toward performative aspects rather than genre (Bauman 1982); at times, though, attempts were made to correlate both genre and performance (Briggs 1989; Shuman and Briggs 1993).

The poetics of performance may be interpreted as indirectly intimated already in earlier research, as in the approach focusing on the poetics of folk literature which was demonstrated in the 1910 work of Danish folklorist Axel Olrik (Olrik 1965 [1919]. Based on his findings in Scandinavian epic poetry, he claimed an empirical basis for what he called "the epic laws of folk narrative" (Dundes 1965). By their author as well as later folklorists, these laws were understood as fundamentally "super-organic" (Dundes 1965, 1999). Now they are more interestingly explicable as motivated by a number of contingent circumstances, especially those rooted in the texts' embeddedness in performative contexts at some stage of their creation, either originally oral and then recorded in writing, or as written, performed orally. The laws themselves address elements of style as well as structure: opening and closure; repetition; dialogue, "two on the scene"; contrast; "law of three"; linearity of the plot; importance of the first and the last position; the emphasis on the protagonist. Whereas we may today dismiss the super-organic epistemology of these laws, they are all conveniently explainable by the performance paradigm of folklore studies. Thus the laws of opening and closure construct the "framing" as understood by Goffman (1974) and his folklorist followers. For folkloristic creativity it is especially important to emphasize the fact that framing serves "to highlight the integrity of the artistic performance within the continuous spoken language. In Jakobsonian terms its function is – in addition to the poetic, referring to the structure of the message itself – also phatic, ascertaining the conditions of [effective] communication" (Hasan-Rokem 2000a: 271). The other laws of Olrik, too, gain a contextual motivation by interpreting them as ensuring effective communication. Thus the law of repetition compensates for the lack of possibility to "turn back pages" to reconfirm certain details; the law of dialogue, not introducing more than two voices at the time, enhanced by the law of contrast in characterization (male/female; child/adult; human/giant, etc.) enables the audience to distinguish the source of a speech act; and the law of three introduces three-dimensional volume into the two-dimensional medium of speech.

Having hinted at the possibility to maintain Olrik's work's relevance for the poetics of folklore by reinterpreting his "epic laws" in the light of performance and of Roman Jakobson's revolutionary work in the fields of poetics and folklore, separately as well as in conjunction (Hasan-Rokem 2000a: 270–272), we now turn to Jakobson's own major contribution to the study of poetics in general and the poetics of folklore in particular.

In the 1920s, Russian formalism provided a new paradigm for the study of poetics, interested in form and structure rather than in origins and patterns of circulation. Russian formalism remained committed to the study of national languages and poetics and offered methods for identifying patterns within a corpus of texts. Folklore played a prominent role in the study of formalism.

Vladimir Propp's project of mapping and analyzing the morphology of the Russian folktale (Propp 1968 [1928]) resulted in a systematic proposal of a grammar of genre, especially when his method was transported some 30 to 40 years later into other cultural spheres (Italy, France, and later the United States) as well as to other genres (Dundes 1963; Jason 1972). It eventually constituted the main theoretical basis for a whole branch of analytical discourse, namely narratology (Bremond 1980 [1966]; Greimas 1971; Eco 1966). Genre grammars do not necessarily express a view of genre as stable, as the more transformational elaborations of the method may show. Propp's own idea was to provide, with his analysis, a more systematic and exact mode of description of what the geographical-historical scholars had delineated in larger brush strokes, though their main purpose was the investigation of original forms, and original contents in particular (1984). Propp described his work as particularly motivated by a critique of the historic-geographic approach, which he regarded as lacking empirical evidence and insufficiently accounting for questions of form and genre (1984: 48–63). His later work on the history of folklore (Propp 1984) and the transformation of narrative elements (Propp 1972) reveal his deep interest in the historical contextualization of analytical categories in general and genre in particular.

Jakobson, a leading personality in the Petersburg constituency of the Russian Formalists, became a central figure among the Prague Structuralists before his migration to the United States (Erlich 1981). Together with Petr Bogatyrev, he authored the perhaps most fundamental essay ever defining folklore as a specific form of creativity (1966 [1929]). Jakobson and Bogatyrev took as their point of departure literary poetics. However, they widened the scope to material folklore forms such as traditional embroidery. In this they effectively laid the basis of an inter-medial poetics of folklore. Jakobson and Bogatyrev (1966 [1929]) adopted Ferdinand de Saussure's structural analysis of language, a dialectic system in which the abstract level of *langue* materializes on the concrete level of *parole*, and predicated folklore on process rather than product. They further highlighted the continuous interaction between individual and community in this process, in an ongoing "dialectic between tradition and innovation."

THE POETICS OF FOLKLORE AS CREATIVE COMMUNICATION

It is, however, yet another trail-blazing essay of Jakobson that will serve us both in highlighting his contribution to the cultivation of a poetics of folklore and more particularly in the reinterpretation of Olrik's "laws." In his singularly influential essay "Closing Statement: Poetics and Linguistics," Jakobson addressed the function of language in communication with special reference to poetical expression, both canonical and folkloristic (Jakobson 1960). Jakobson identifies six components in every communicative event: sender, addressee, channel, context, message and code. The functions of language may then be analyzed as respectively emotive, conative, phatic, referential, poetic and meta-linguistic – according to the dominant component of the analyzed communicative event (relating to the concept of "dominant" discussed in Jakobson 1987). Jakobson's model is especially devised to identify the dominant role of the poetic function in literary texts, but can by further elaboration be adapted to various forms of creativity. Thus a diversified adaptation of the model may in the case of folk literature reveal legend as a genre in which second to the poetic function, and possibly sometimes even prior to it, a dominant role is also allotted to the referential function; in the proverb genre the second dominant function of the model is quite clearly the conative, teaching lessons and educating about ways of life; and the genres of lyrical folk songs, both love songs and lullabies reveal a secondary dominance of the emotive function. The genre in which the poetic function may have the strongest dominance is perhaps the folktale, although as has been shown in many psychoanalytical studies of the genre (of both Freudian and Jungian persuasions), the emotive as well as the referential (referring perhaps to inner realities) constitute important factors in their communication.

Like formalism, emerging structural analysis relied extensively on the analysis of folk material in the attempts to produce analytical models for the analysis of wider cultural phenomena, including language. However, formalism as well as structuralism extended the analysis significantly beyond poetic language. Structural analysis has addressed literature but also theater, ritual, film, costume, and crafts, and thus contributed to a folkloric concept of the poetic. Claude Lévi-Strauss's enterprise was to unearth the fundamental levels of conceptual thinking in a wide human perspective, bridging cultures until then marked as "primitive" and cultures understood as "civilizations." For this he suggested the universal category of *ésprit* (unsuccessfully translated into "mind") as the abstracted realm where this kind of thinking was rooted and processed the emergent cultural forms of verbal, ritual, material and institutional genres (1966). The mode of communication most relevant to traditional folklore studies that was selected by Lévi-Strauss for cultural analysis was "myth." His treatment of myth radically revolutionized the conceptualization of this category in the study of culture (Lévi-Strauss 1955; 1966; 1967; 1983a; 1983b; 1990a; 1990b). Followed by Roland Barthes's (Barthes 1972) transposition from the tribal societies which remained Lévi-Strauss's "laboratory" forever, to contemporary cultural and political realities, the concept of myth was transformed from its status as literary genre as in the above-mentioned, long-lived, genre system of the Brothers Grimm, into a basic, constitutive, underlying cognitive structure of culture, all cultures, shaping all communicative and creative fields in them. The structural elements, identified by Lévi-Strauss as dialectical pairs, could be seen in a constant dynamics of transformation, generating the multiple forms of cultures (Hasan-Rokem, unpublished).

Lévi-Strauss also differentiated between myth and poetry for certain purposes: "Poetry is a kind of speech which cannot be translated at the cost of serious distortions; whereas the mythical value of the myth is preserved even through the worst translation" (Douglas 1967: 210). The critique of his work is especially useful for understanding the complexity of the relationship between formal and other poetic elements. For example, in a discussion of Lévi-Strauss's analysis of myth as reductive, Mary Douglas writes: "He falls into the trap of claiming to discover the real underlying meaning of myths because he never separates the particular artistic structure of a particular set of myths from their general or purely formal structure" (1967: 64). In general Lévi-Strauss saw myth and poetry as the dialectical poles of linguistic expression, one of the coordinates of genre being the placing of a discursive unit on this particular continuum: "Myth should be placed in the gamut of linguistic expressions at the end opposite to that of poetry" (Douglas 1967: 62).[1]

Dell Hymes shifted the focus of studies of the poetic to be a dimension of what he called "communicative competence" (1972a, b). Inspired by the ethnographic work of Franz Boas, and building on the work of rhetoricians such as Kenneth Burke, linguists (such as Émile Benveniste) interested in *parole* rather than *langue*, and the formalist/structuralist Roman Jakobson, Hymes outlined a method for the study of the ethnography of communication. For Hymes, poetics "encompasses how people shape and interpret aspects of their worlds. He discusses cognitive styles in both the lexicon and grammar of a language and in its use" (Duranti 2001: 187–189). For Hymes, the study of poetics is one part of the larger study of speech situations and speech communities. Building on Hymes, and further developing the paradigm of the study of folklore and poetics as part of what he came to call "the ethnography of performance" (1982: 10), Bauman identified three elements of the folkloric approach to poetics:

1   exploration of the repertoire of a given community;
2   exploration of unified structure – intrerrelationship of "scene, social structure, communicative codes, and genres" (Bauman and Sherzer 1974: 13);
3   exploration of verbal communication as a form of social action (goes further than others).

In addition to the ways that repertoire has been understood in terms of the patterns of poetic communication described by Olrik and others, we suggest addressing Bauman's first category, by stressing its processual character as formulated by Bloomaert: "the nature and structure of repertoires cannot be taken for granted; they need to be established empirically – that is, ethnographically" (2008: 438).

The Permanence/Instability of Form

Questions of the permanence or instability of form are central to folkloristic approaches to the study of tradition and invention. Dan Ben-Amos points to the range of possibilities for considering stability in his proposed four meanings of the term genre for folklorists: "classificatory categories, permanent form, evolving form, and form of discourse" (1976: xv). Through the first half of the twentieth century, many folklorists regarded folk forms as natural and relatively stable, in comparison with literary forms, and although they recognized cultural differences, folklorists considered the forms to share some universal characteristics (Krohn 1971 [1926]: 109, 121; Jolles 1965). Although most folklorists today reject the idea of universal forms, they approach the questions of instability in different ways. The instability of genre occurs at all levels and as John Dorst points out, any discussion of the stability of generic categories points to their instability (1983: 413). Late twentieth-century scholarship has focused more on this instability than on the stabilities of particular genres (Geertz 1983); in fact one might find that Alan Dundes's pronouncement that not even one genre of folklore had been defined (1964: 252) could be understood as a dimension of instability of the phenomenon rather than a failing of the discipline.

First, folklorists offer a critique of the idea of natural, romanticized folk genres. The designation of some genres as "natural" references Romantic claims for the "primitive origins of poetry" (Finnegan 1992 [1977]: 33). In European folkloristics and literature, the concept of native taxonomies was, as Susan Stewart points out, invented as natural in the eighteenth and nineteenth centuries. Stewart writes, "The cultural reproduction of value works by attaching itself to particular forms" (1991: 73). She uses the term "distressed genres" to describe forms that were deliberately "antiqued" to create the appearance of belonging to an earlier period, thus giving them value. "Already in the Heroic Age of Greece, the epic bards are credited with being able, by special inspiration, to transcend the limitations of sense and to rescue the past from oblivion" (1991: 75). Far from transcending history, Stewart details how several genres (epic, fable, proverb, fairy-tale, ballad) are the products of particular historical and ideological configurations of subjectivity, voice, and pastness. Stewart's examples include not only forgeries, literary productions designed to appear as if they were antiquities, but also parodies, such as mock epics, which, she points out, call attention to the nostalgic desire for the antique. "Because of the shadow of parody, the gesture made in distressing genres is an ambivalent one: it implies defamation as well as veneration" (1991: 89).

Like Stewart, Galit Hasan-Rokem integrates historical research on genres with the sociological study of genres in their cultural contexts. In particular, Hasan-Rokem addresses genre not for classificatory purposes but to show how genre is engaged in interpretation (2003: 98). This approach insists on genre as inter-textual, dialogic, and therefore, of necessity, unstable, even as it reveals conventions for interpretation.

Second, folklorists consider questions of the permanence of form to be intertwined with questions of interaction, producing an understanding of genre in terms of a dialectic of stability and fluidity in folklore. In literary studies and in some art history scholarship, genre is sometimes viewed as fixed, in contrast to the innovation found in particular literary or artistic works. In folklore studies, the relationship between fixed and fluid is configured quite differently. Lauri Honko writes, "The 'potentiality' of an oral work leads to a fluidity of its manifest form, a far cry from the fixity of the literary work" (Honko 2000: 5). The fluidity or flexibility of folklore genres is also a dimension of oral forms, in contrast to written literature (Finnegan 1992).

In the wake of formalism and other modernist and postmodern schools of literary theory inspired by it, the permanence of form has become a negative quality, in opposition to creativity and invention. The conventional requirements of genre have been described in terms of reader expectations and authorial production. Authors who play with and sometimes reject genre conventions are preferred. These preferences are historically doubly motivated by the Romantics' emphasis on individual genius as well as the Formalists' emphasis on paradigmatic innovation as a progressive element in style, genre and other formal traits of texts. From the folkloristic perspective all performers destabilize genre conventions, whether in oral or written literature. Some literary scholars account for genres as constitutive as well as conventional. For example, Adena Rosmarin argues, "The use of genre, then, entails contradiction. It is a way of talking about something in terms of what it is not. It is what Burke calls a terministic screen, a way of selecting our topic or text" (1984: 35). Rosmarin considers genre identification to be the role of the critic. Many folklorists recognize genre as always constitutive and as always the work of both performer and scholar, if not always in agreement.

THE POETICS OF FOLKLORE GENRES

Genre theory has been one of the central sites for considering the complex relationships between formal and interactive poetics. Genre categories are marked in a variety of ways, including as textual styles, as metadiscursive elements of a text, or as frames in an interaction. Jacques Derrida argues that as soon as a text (we could add material object, performance) announces itself as belonging to a particular category, it makes a poetic statement. He argues for the reverse as well: poetic texts, performances and objects cannot be "genre-less" (1980: 65). However, not all texts announce themselves as belonging to a particular category; instead, in many cases, references to genre are extra-textual or contextual, as part of a performance, as a way of differentiating between one kind of text and another, or as part of the larger cultural expectations that are used for interpretation and determining meaning.

From an ethnographic perspective, we can observe that many groups differentiate between poetic and other sorts of genres; for example, in modern Western bureaucracies, the poetic can sometimes be differentiated from informational genres such as, for example, parking tickets, maps, and guides. Genre classification is embedded in other cultural systems, therefore a universal system will not only be insufficient to account for how people differentiate among poetic forms, but may also often be inaccurate. The comparison of different classification systems provides a rich resource for understanding the variety of ways that groups utilize genre for interpreting cultural performances (Hanks 1987).

Genre markers can occur both within the text and in multiple contexts and at any level: in the social context, in a frame articulated in a performance, object or text, or in more subtle cues, including out of the consciousness of the performer/writer or audience/reader. Within the text, genre is identifiable through kinds of repetition (Finnegan 1992: 90).

Some theories of genre, for example creolization, begin with the recognition of the inherently dialogic character of genre classification, which is one source of its flexibility. A dialogic theory of genre addresses questions of hierarchy, status, privilege, and value, and it is this dialogism that makes genre categories most unstable.

The most useful examinations of genre take into account all levels of analysis from the stylistic expectations of what a form should look like to the way that a particular form is positioned in relation to other forms in a cultural situation and in the larger repertoire of performers and cultural groups. The failure of generic categories as an orderly system that might account for a culture's communicative resources is actually what makes genre research significant. Genre studies point us to the contradictions, gaps, and excesses, where the categories do not match the performances, rather than to integrated fixed systems. Whereas the concept of genre addresses the poetics of folklore with reference to the bigger constituents of its forms, other concepts such as style may address particular works as determined by given value systems in particular cultural contexts. The particularity of language that defines stylistic discussion in verbal arts limits the urge to intercultural comparison on one hand. On the other hand the development of recording methods has enabled the application of exact modes of measuring and evaluation of the phonological, tonal and other dimensions of texts and their performances, suggesting again the possibility of intercultural comparison (Fine 1984; Tedlock 1983; Seitel 1999; Honko 2000).

Each generation of scholars seems to discover yet again that formal and interactive elements of poetics are integrated. Far from being a repetitive exercise, each of these efforts has generated different configurations for the study of poetics. For some scholars, the conversation begins with a proposed differentiation between folk forms and other, usually high literary forms. M.M. Bakhtin's famous treatise on the epic and the novel is one of the most important and influential of these (1981). Bakhtin contrasts "high" epic (which he regards as dead, an issue we take up below) with "popular laughter" or "folklore":

> It is precisely laughter that destroys the epic, and in general destroys any hierarchical (distancing and valorized) distance ... The plane of comic (humorous) representation is a specific plane in its spatial as well as its temporal aspect. Here the role of memory is minimal; in the comic world there is nothing for memory and tradition to do. One ridicules in order to forget. (1981: 33)

Similarly his study of the carnival as a relevant frame of reference for the reading of the works of Rabelais reveals the realm of folk ritual as a sphere where central norms and institutions of European medieval civilizations are both subverted and reiterated (1984). The aspect of poetics in Bakhtin's analysis points at the stylistic and content elements of the carnival focusing on the "low" rather than the "high," the "corporeal" rather than the "spiritual" and the "ridiculous" and the "amusing" rather than the "uplifting." Consequently ritual as well as verbal performances of folklore abound in elements of surprise, sudden fallings, and other changes, tricks, dirt and debasement. The presence of the carnevalesque in various formations of culture is one of the expressions of the impossibility to fully separate folkloric and other areas of cultural creativity.

One of the reasons for Bakhtin's works' ongoing usefulness for the study of poetics is that they lend themselves to recognizing that the interactive dimensions are themselves formal (1986). Poetics in context can be studied as a structural ritual, whether in highly performed occasions and contexts or in the most minimally performed interactions of everyday life.

Some genres have more formal constraints, for example requirements of rhyme or meter, than others. Sometimes genre is restricted by content, and in other cases, the same content can appear in different genres. Contemporary folkloristic genre theory offers a dialogic approach to understanding what might otherwise be seen as binary oppositions between fixed and changing forms; tradition and invention; classification/ typology and process. In addition, genre classification systems invoke other areas of differentiation, such as literary and everyday, poetic and historical, authentic/ traditional and invented. None of these differentiations holds consistently, and the lack of stability of genre classification systems, combined with efforts to create rigid categories, has created a productive tension in genre scholarship (Harris 1995). Tzvetan Todorov and others propose a distinction between the literary and the historical genres, based on the idea that the literary genres transcend any one particular period (1970).[2]

Third, Dan Ben-Amos proposed that a differentiation between analytic categories and ethnic genres provides one means of addressing the inadequacy of universal (analytic) categories (1969). Analytic categories refer to the scholars' genre classifications; the categorization systems used by particular groups are ethnic genres. However the instability of genre categories is not only a problem of analytic categories but also of the inevitability of "internally" competing genre systems, whether among scholars or cultural groups. As Marie-Laure Ryan points out, "There is no such thing as *the* native taxonomy" (1981: 114).

In folklore scholarship, genre analysis belongs as much to the scholars interested in identifying kinds of texts, objects, and performances as it does to the participants who rely on local cultural classification systems (also called folk taxonomies) to differentiate among and evaluate their cultural practices. Gary Gossen suggests "a model that allows a specific oral tradition to speak for itself, in its own categories of meaning, without ignoring the general social character of all oral symbolic media" (1974: x). He argues against Charles Frake's observation that genres used most frequently, in the most variable contexts, are more important and are more differentiated (1974: 55).

The turn to ethnic or emic genres utilized poetic questions in new ways, calling greater attention to forms as cultural productions. The critique of analytic practices was extended to include ethnography itself. For example, in his essay in his co-edited book *Writing Culture: The Poetics and Politics of Ethnography*, James Clifford described ethnography as governed by six constraints: context, rhetoric, institution, genre, politics, and history (Clifford and Marcus 1986: 6). Ethnography was recognized as a genre shaped by formal, social, and interactive/performative dimensions.

Fourth, by attending to poetry as a performance, both oral-formulaic theory and ethnopoetics offer models for understanding how relatively stable forms are part of ongoing processes of creativity. Ruth Finnegan defines oral poetry as "both an expressive and a socially significant aspect of human action, a form in which human beings use and develop artistically-marked conventions to formulate and manipulate and actively create their own human existence and the world around them" (1992: xvi). Her model was intended to encompass the variety of methods of studying oral poetry.

Oral-formulaic theory, developed by Milman Parry and his student, Albert Lord, demonstrated that oral epics are composed of formulaic phrases that provide guides for oral composition (Lord 1960). Their work refuted the idea that tradition and originality need to be opposed and substantiated their claim that the long epic poems were composed in performance rather than memorized. John Miles Foley's continued research on oral-formulaic theory and provided significant elaborations regarding the ways that oral performances are emergent (Foley 1995).

Dell Hymes characterizes his ethnopoetic research and Foley's work as sharing an interest in "composition in the course of performance" (1994: 330). Hymes carefully reexamined Native American texts that were archived and published in prose form by non-Native researchers, and using a process he describes as "repatriation," Hymes demonstrates that the organizing principle of the narratives is the line. He proposes three principles to analyze the "measured verse" of these narratives. First, he identifies the line breaks. Second, following Jakobson, he identifies sequences of equivalence, often marked by intonation in oral performance, but also marked by the use of particular words that can be used to identify line-breaks when the intonation information is not available. Hymes describes the third principle as succession, groupings of sequences that "give shape to action" (1994: 332). Dennis Tedlock's discussion of ethnopoetics is similarly attentive to the sounds of poetry. In addition to discussing the problem of making the audible visible in translation and transcription (1983: 5), his close examinations of poetic performances includes description of many poetic features, from verisimilitude to questions of which texts are expected to be heard by others. Both oral-formulaic theory and ethnopoetics are not merely ways of understanding how oral poetry works; in both cases, understanding the composition, the poetic dimension of the work, is crucial for understanding it. Hymes showed that in the prose version, a text might seem to have what looks to the non-native collector like either nonsensical portions or fragments of a lost whole. Instead, the version that recognizes the line breaks, sequences, and successions demonstrate, through attention to structural units, the meaning of each part of a narrative. In other words, understanding oral poetry as a composed performance rather than as a fixed text is crucial for interpretation.

Fifth, a different perspective on the stability and instability of genres follows from understanding genre classification as part of the process of interpretation, on the part of both performers/speakers and listeners/audiences/readers. Along these lines, as we have demonstrated above, Dell Hymes, building on Burke's work, understood genre to be part of the ethnography of communication. As such, genres are one way that participants in a communicative event recognize shared forms. Inserting genre within the larger rubric of the ethnography of communication recasts questions of the stability or instability of particular forms in terms of the position of genre in relation to other dimensions of the communicative event. In particular, Hymes argued, "Genres often coincide with speech events, but must be treated as analytically independent of them. They may occur in (or as) different events" (1974: 61).

Following Hymes, many scholars have conceptualized genre as a dimension of communication. In some sociolinguistic discussions, genre becomes a way of differentiating between poetic and non-poetic cultural practices. For example, John Swales writes, "The principal criterial feature that turns a collection of communicative events into a genre is some shared set of communicative purposes" (1990: 46). Swales specifically acknowledges that this definition excludes the poetic, which he says "makes an appeal to the reader or listener so complex as to allow no easy or useful categorization of purpose" (1990: 47). The question here is *who* is doing the categorizing and how. In this statement, Swales implies that purpose is observable as a dimension of context, although complicated by speaker/reader; writer/reader expectations.

Genre is a system of classification based on differences. However, not only is there no universal agreement or consistency in what counts as a difference, such a consistency is not possible because, as Dell Hymes points out, communicative systems do not share the same constituent parts. "Languages differ as to material base. True, it is difficult to say what a language cannot be made to do. But if it has no tones, tone is out" (2000: 192).

Folklorists bring together literary, sociolinguistic, anthropological, historical, and sociological approaches to genre. Rather than divide questions of poetic form and use, genre theory today is a means of understanding, for example, how forms display and reproduce social relationships. Each of the disciplinary approaches brings not only different emphases but also different conceptions of some of the key issues in genre scholarship.

Folklorists today integrate the study of genre as classification, as description of form, and as socially produced category. At its simplest, classification is the recognition of patterns of similarity and difference. This practice turns out to be not so simple, however, and is complicated by thinking about how similarity works, at the level of structure, content, or both and as repetition, as citation, or as allusion, for example. Folklore forms rarely exist as fixed but to some extent, folklorists have endeavored to identify shared dimensions. However, Ben-Amos points to recurrent universal differentiations between fact and fiction, rhyme and prose, and figurative and non-figurative language.

Sixth, Derrida reconceptualizes the controversy of stability and instability in discussions of genre as a problem of an inevitable contamination due to mixing. We could understand Mary Douglas's work on the danger of impure categories as interested in the same problem, although Derrida additionally insists on the mark of genre as an interruption (eruption) of *techne* (often used to distinguish either from the episteme or from the poetic, or from both) by the poetic, thus positing genre and the poetic as a kind of disturbance. Derrida's argument is slightly different from Jakobson's though they bear similarity in the observation of how one function can have emphasis. Jakobson might agree with Derrida that genre is more than emphasis, that genre can act as the assertion, the insistence, of the poetic. Although not characterizing the relationship between *techne* and the poetic as eruption or interruption, Henry Glassie's understanding of the role of genre in material culture is consistent with this position. In his discussion of genres, whether of material culture or verbal arts, Glassie describes genre in terms of a performer's repertory of forms. Glassie, like many other folklorists, resists genre classification when it refers to the scholar's presumption to know more about genres than the performers themselves (2001: 47). Instead, he understands genre as part of form and repertory.

Genre is not only a resource for communication; it is also one way that categories are imposed on people to restrict or obligate their communication. In this dimension of genre scholarship, the edges and boundaries tell us more about the negotiation of categories than do the centers (Shuman 1993: 71). In Derrida's terms, "The law of genre also has a controlling influence and is binding on that which draws the genre into engendering, generations, genealogy, and degenerescence" (1980: 74). These controls and restrictions are as evident in material culture as they are in verbal arts (Babcock 1988). In material culture, what Derrida describes as the "mixing" of genres manifests itself as the mixing and remixing of the aesthetic (poetic) and functional, defining the "contaminations" that define what counts and does not count as a legitimate member of a genre.

Peter Seitel's formulation of the components of genre takes into account many if not all of the above considerations. Seitel proposes that genres (i) refer to a social world; (ii) do particular kinds of work; and (iii) contain frameworks of expectation. In addition, building on Bakhtin's work, Seitel points out that each speech genre (this is probably also true of nonverbal genres) "has characteristic ways of achieving its form, of becoming complete, of what Bakhtin calls attaining 'finalization' along three dimensions – style, composition and theme" (2003: 278).

Heda Jason understands the reference to a social world in terms of the internal elements of particular genres. She writes, "Each genre of oral literature has its own world. The world of the fairy tale, for instance, is populated by golden castles and glass mountains, talking animals and flying carpets. The world of legend contains ghostly dark ruins, hidden treasures and curiously formed stones which are in reality sinners who have been petrified for punishment" (1977: 199–200; cf. Meletinsky *et al.* 1974). This concept of the story world as determining a whole system of signs turning into genre markers has from a different perspective informed the work of Max Lüthi, addressing especially the folktale (*Märchen*) genre, its distinguished phenomenology alongside (Lüthi 1984), in correlation and also in counter-distinction from the genre of legend (*Sage*) (Lüthi 1975) as well as canonical belletristic literature (Lüthi 1970).

Building on the work of Bakhtin, Bauman, and Seitel, Ray Cashman argues that "genres not only accomplish different social tasks, they also accommodate and perhaps inculcate different ideological positions" (2007: 14). Expanding on Morson and Emerson's (1990) idea that genre is a "form-shaping ideology," he suggests that genre is "an ideology-shaping form" (2007: 14). Cashman regards genre as an "extra-personal determinant of ideology" (2007: 25).

As Dorst proposes, in addition to asking the ethnographic questions about "who owns what genres, when they are used, how they are perceived by those who use them, how they are marked, and so on, we need a *dialectics* that considers the relationship between genres and the larger social forces at work in concrete historical circumstances." (1983: 425).

Current folklore scholarship has critiqued the idea of universal fixed typologies as both inaccurate when applied to particular cultural texts or performances as well as insufficient to account for the complex, multi-leveled interactive use of genres. Discussions of genre can be a means for understanding, for example, how forms display and reproduce social relationships, how multiple genres are combined in a single event, or how forms (whether verbal or material) are related to social, political, and historical change. The strong investment in genre in folkloristics may be in fact due to the non-canonical and often fluid character of the material. Genre perceived as a system thus provides an alternative mode of stability and accounts for the conceptualization of continuity and coherence in an otherwise un-systematized universe of discourse.

The past decades have seen a shift from the study of classification or typology to a more integrated approach to genre as the intersection of multiple levels of analysis, including poetic form, structure, context/interaction, and ideological dimensions. In Richard Bauman's terms, research today is "oriented more toward communicative practice than typology, viewing genre as an orienting framework for the production and interpretation of discourse" (1992: 53).

INTERACTIVE, DIALOGIC APPROACHES TO GENRE

In contemporary folklore scholarship, genre is studied both as form and as social practice. Bauman writes, "As elements of social practice, genres are both grounded in and constitutive of structures of social relations, implicating a range of conceptions of speaker and audience and defining a range of possible social meanings. Understood in these terms, generic expectations are flexible communicative resources that may be mobilized in different ways for different communicative ends, though the quotient of flexibility may vary from one genre to another" (1992: 58).

In his famous treatise on the epic and the novel, Bakhtin describes the epic as dead and the novel as dialogic. Bakhtin is describing the literary "high" epic (not epic performance), which is dead because it is distant from personal experience. Bakhtin's pronouncement can be understood as another recasting of the stability/instability discussion. Like other literary scholars, Bakhtin privileges the unstable, but importantly, for Bakhtin, the contrast to the dead epic is folklore, which he describes as "popular laughter" (1981: 23).

Critics of genre, especially Bakhtin and later Jacques Derrida, begin by pointing out the inadequacy of a theory of genre as a bundle of traits. Or rather, as Dorst puts it, a "stabilized grouping of a ready stock of device" (Dorst 1983: 414). Bakhtin undestands genres as chronotopes, orientations in space and time. Genres are produced and recognized in particular social and temporal contexts.

Genre is dialogic at multiple levels. Bakhtin writes, "Dialogic relationships, therefore, are extralinguistic. But at the same time they must not be separated from the realm of *discourse* that is from language as a concrete integral phenomenon. Language lives only in the dialogic interaction of those who make use of it" (1981: 183).

INTERTEXTUALITY

In their essay "Genre, Intertextuality, Social Power" Briggs and Bauman caution that although the performance approach has shifted genre study from a focus on objects to a focus on processes of production, it "runs the risk" of failing to question "the equation of poetics with immanent features of particular discursive acts" (1992: 146). The alternative, they suggest, is an intertextual approach that recognizes the relationship between texts/performances and prior discourse. Intertextuality provides a means for recognizing a particular performance's similarity to other performances of the same genre and for identifying and producing social and historical value without dependence on the stagnating effects of classificatory systems perceived as stable.

Folklorists today generally agree that genre scholarship requires an intertextual approach. As Abrahams (1975), Bauman and Briggs (1990), Honko (2000), Bausinger (1980), Dan Ben-Amos (1976), Jason (1977), Kirshenblatt-Gimblett (1975) and others have pointed out, genres are always relational. Intertextuality is not a matter of the properties of texts but of proximities and distances among texts: "Strategies for maximizing and minimizing intertextual gaps can coexist even more intimately as they enter dialogically into constituting the same text or performance" (Briggs and Bauman 1992: 152). Further, the relations among genres implicate not only different forms but also the values accorded those forms. The intertextual perspective of genres emphasizes their position in "hierarchies of value and taste" (Bauman 2004: 8).

Susan Stewart writes, "The concept of intertextuality relies upon two basic assumptions: first that various domains of meaning are contingent upon one another, and second, that the common-sense world may be considered as a base from which other provinces of meaning are formed" (1978: 16–17). Further, "the intertextual nature of universes of discourse enables us to move from one domain to another. These processes are 'inter' in the sense of interaction. They do not 'stand outside' or 'between' their subjects so much as they are emergent in their subjects. The model here is metacommunication, a gesture that is both reflexive and transforming... The ongoingness of tradition – as a social process – makes a 'finite' province of meaning impossible, for the boundaries of universes of discourse are constantly merging into one another and reemerging as transformed fields of meaning" (1978: 48).

The concept of intertextuality, then, serves as a corrective to the idea that the problem with genre is simply a matter of fit. As Bauman points out "the fit between any given text and a genre category is never perfect" (1992: 80). Building on Susan Stewart's comments, we can observe that it is never only a matter of the fit between text and category but among merging universes of discourse, intersecting performances, and emergent social processes (Kristeva 1986 [1974]).

FRAME AND RITUAL GENRES

Frame is a metacommunicative strategy for making a claim that a text or performance belongs to a particular category. It is one means for understanding how forms are positioned within communicative interaction. Frames are always intertextual, indexing other, presumably already familiar, performances/texts and categories. The poetic can be considered a frame just as there is a poetics of framing. The concept of frame is often attributed either to Gregory Bateson's understanding of the psychological frames that make it possible to have something denote something else (the message "this is play"), or to Erving Goffman's understanding of how people frame, bracket, laminate, interpret, and misinterpret the category of an event. In this sense, a genre is very much like a frame, but Goffman's frame analysis (1974), rather than referring to stable categories, calls attention to the multiple, complex, unarticulated processes people use in everyday life to categorize their experiences. According to Goffman, although frames may not necessarily be articulated, they do constitute an available repertoire for a community.

Bauman's discussion of the interpretive frames of performances similarly refers to occasions and the verbal arts associated with them. He writes, "The first major task, then, is to suggest what kind of interpretive frame performance establishes or represents" (1977: 11).

Scholars of festival or material culture sometimes consider poetics as a sub-category of play and ritual. As Victor Turner claims, the ludic dimension of culture is no less obligatory than other formalized genres, although sometimes people play symbolically inverted roles (1978: 278). On the contrary, the integrated investigation of the realms of the poetic, the ludic, and the symbolic is crucial for consolidating, renegotiating, restabilizing, and changing social systems. Jakobson's understanding of the heightened or subordinate role that the poetic dimension can play in the communication of messages applies also to festival, folk drama, and material culture. However, the research on festival, especially, calls our attention to the additional work of subversion that the poetic/playful can do. The poetic function (as cited from Jakobson 1960 above) is often set at the intersection of significant divisions between modes of expression, such as sacred/secular; work/play; science/magic or tradition/invention.

Although developed from a linguistics-based model for understanding communication, semiotics provides a conception of poetics designed for interpreting the material world as well as language.

CONCLUSION

We opened with tracing the early sources for addressing questions of poetics with regard to folkloristic creativity in early Enlightenment and Romanticism. We then suggested that the study of the poetics of folklore widens the concept of poetics to encompass communication in its processual and interactive aspects. We have identified and highlighted genre and the scholarly discussion of folkloristic genres as a central locus for articulating the poetics of folklore. In addition to the above-mentioned proposal that systematic genre definitions compensate for the canonized forms lacking in folklore to create another mode of stability, rooted in the recurrence of modal expressions articulated structurally as *langue* – genre and genre theory also situates folkloristic creativity in historically and culturally identifiable contexts.

NOTES

1 See, however, Jakobson and Levi-Strauss's (1962) classic analysis of Charles Baudelaire's poem "Les Chats," where the gap is at least partly suspended. This is quite different from the Grimms' view according to which the folktale is poetic and the legend historic, thus essentially separated in each historical instance, although both connected in historical evolution with the myth.
2 There are many discussions of historical poetics with reference to folk narratives in ancient texts; for example, Jan M. Ziolkowski (2007) and Galit Hasan-Rokem (2000b; 2003).

REFERENCES

Abrahams, Roger. 1975. "The Complex Relations of Simple Forms" in Dan Ben-Amos, Ed. *Folklore Genres*. Austin: University of Texas Press.

Babcock, Barbara. 1988. "At Home, No Women Are Storytellers: Potteries, Stories, and Politics in Cochiti Pueblo." *Journal of the Southwest* 30(3) (Autumn): 356–389.

Bakhtin, M.M. 1981. *The Dialogic Imagination: Four Essays*. Trans. Caryl Emerson and Michael Holquist. Austin: University of Texas Press.

Bakhtin, M.M. 1984. *Rabelais and His World*. Trans. Helene Iswolsky. Bloomington: Indiana University Press.

Bakhtin, M.M. 1986. *Speech Genres and Other Late Essays*. Trans. V. McGee. M. Holquist and C. Emerson, Eds. Austin: University of Texas Press.

Barthes, Roland. 1972. *Mythologies*. Trans. Annette Lavers. New York: Hill and Wang.

Bateson, Gregory. 1972. *Steps to an Ecology of Mind*. New York: Ballantine Books.

Bauman, Richard. 1977. *Verbal Art as Performance*. Prospect Heights, IL: Waveland Press.

Bauman, Richard. 1982. "Conceptions of Folklore in the Development of Literary Semiotics." *Semiotica* 39(1/2): 1–20.

Bauman, Richard. 1992. "Genre" in R. Bauman, Ed. *Folklore, Cultural Performances, and Popular Entertainments*. Oxford: Oxford University Press, pp. 53–59.

Bauman, Richard. 2004. *A World of Others' Words: Cross-Cultural Perspectives on Intertextuality*. Oxford: Blackwell.

Bauman, Richard and Charles L. Briggs. 1990. "Poetics and Performance as Critical Perspectives on Language and Social Life." *Annual Review of Anthropology* 19: 59–88.

Bauman, Richard and Joel Sherzer, Eds. 1974. *Explorations in the Ethnography of Speaking*. Cambridge: Cambridge University of Press.

Bausinger, Hermann. 1980 [1968]. *Formen der Volkspoesie*. Berlin: E. Schmidt Verlag.

Ben-Amos, Dan. 1969. "Analytic Categories and Ethnic Genres." *Genre* 2: 275–301.

Ben-Amos, Dan. 1976. "Introduction" in his *Folklore Genres*. Austin: University of Texas Press, pp. ix–xlv.

Bloomaert, Jan. 2008. "Bernstein and Poetics Revisited: Voice, Globalization and Education." *Discourse and Society* 19(4): 425–451.

Bremond, Claude. 1980 [1966]. "The Logic of Narrative Possibilities." *New Literary History* 11(3): 387–411.

Briggs, Charles. L. 1989. *Competence in Performance: The Creativity of Tradition in Mexicano Verbal Art*. Philadelphia: University of Pennsylvania Press.

Briggs, Charles L. and Richard Bauman. 1992. "Genre, Intertextuality, and Social Power." *Journal of Linguistic Anthropology* 2(2): 131–172.

Burke, Kenneth. 1966. *Language as Symbolic Action: Essays on Life, Literature, and Method.* Berkeley: University of California Press.

Cashman, Ray. 2007. "Genre and Ideology in Northern Ireland." *Midwestern Folklore* 33: 3–27.

Clifford, James and George Marcus. 1986. *Writing Culture: The Poetics and Politics of Ethnography.* Berkeley: University of California Press.

Derrida, Jacques. 1980. "The Law of Genre." Trans. Avital Ronell. *Critical Inquiry* 7(1): On Narrative, 55–81.

De Saussure, Ferdinand. 1983 [1972]. *Course in General Linguistics.* Trans. Roy Harris. New York: Open Court.

Dorst, John. 1983. "Neck-Riddle as a Dialogue of Genres: Applying Bakhtin's Genre Theory." *Journal of American Folklore* 96(382): pp. 413–433.

Douglas, Mary. 1967. "The Meaning of Myth, With Special Reference to 'La Geste d'Asdiwal' in Edmund Leach, Ed. *The Structural Study of Myth and Totemism.* London: Routledge, pp. 49–69.

Dundes, Alan. 1963. "Structural Typology in North American Indian Folktales." *Southwestern Journal of Anthropology* 19(1): 121–130.

Dundes, Alan. 1964. "Texture, Text, and Context." *Southern Folklore Quarterly* 28: 251–265.

Dundes, Alan, Ed. 1965. *The Study of Folklore.* Englewood Cliffs, NJ: Prentice Hall.

Dundes, Alan. 1999. *International Folkloristics.* Lanham, MD: Rowman and Littlefield.

Duranti, Alessandro. 2001. *Key Terms in Language and Culture.* Oxford: Blackwell.

Eco, Umberto. 1966. "James Bond: Une combinatoire narrative." *Communications* 8: 77–93.

Erlich, Victor. 1981. *Russian Formalism: History, Doctrine.* New Haven: Yale University Press.

Fine, Elizabeth C. 1984. *The Folklore Text: From Performance to Print.* Bloomington: Indiana University Press.

Finnegan, Ruth. 1992 [1977]. *Oral Poetry: Its Nature, Significance, and Social Context.* Cambridge: Cambridge University Press.

Foley, John Miles. 1995. *The Singer of Tales in Performance.* Bloomington, IN: Indiana University Press.

Geertz, Clifford. 1983. "Blurred Genres" in *Local Knowledge: The Reconfiguration of Social Thought.* New York: Basic Books.

Geertz, Clifford. 2001. "Performance Theory and the Documentary Act." *Indiana Folklife* 1(5): 43–48.

Glassie, Henry. 2001. "Performance Theory and the Documentary Act." *Indian Folklife* 1(5): 43–48.

Goffman, Erving. 1967. *Interaction Ritual: Essays in Face-to-Face Behavior.* Chicago: Aldine.

Goffman, Erving. 1974. *Frame Analysis: An Essay on the Organization of Experience.* Boston: Northeastern University Press.

Gossen, Gary. 1974. *Chamulas in the World of the Sun.* Prospect Heights, IL: Waveland Press.

Greimas, A. Julien. 1971. "The Interpretation of Myth: Theory and Practice" in Pierre Maranda and Elli Köngäs-Maranda, Eds. *The Structural Analysis of Oral Tradition.* Philadelphia: University of Pennsylvania Press.

Hanks, William. 1987. "Discourse Genres in a Theory of Practice." *American Ethnologist* 14(4): 668–692.

Harris, Trudier. 1995. "Common Ground: Keywords for the Study of Expressive Culture Genre." *Journal of American Folklore* 108(430): 509–527.

Hasan-Rokem, Galit. 1978. "Cognition in the Folk-Tale: Aesthetic Judgement and Symbolic Structures." *Scripta Hierosolymitana* 27: 192–204.

Hasan-Rokem, Galit. 2000a. "Aurora Borealis: Trans-formations of Classical Nordic Folklore Theories," in Bjarne Rogan and Bente G. Alver, Eds. *Norden og Europa.* Oslo: Novus, pp. 269–285.

Hasan-Rokem, Galit. 2000b. *Web of Life: Folklore and Midrash in Rabbinic Literature.* Berkeley: University of California Press.

Hasan-Rokem, Galit. 2003. *Tales of the Neighborhood: Jewish Narrative Dialogues in Late Antiquity.* Berkeley: University of California Press.

Hasan-Rokem, Galit. (unpublished) "Transformation: Lévi-Strauss in the Rabbis' Academy." Paper presented at: After 100: the Legacy of Claude Lévi-Strauss's Work in the 21st Century in Arts and Humanities. A Cross-Disciplinary Symposium, Indiana University, Bloomington, October 22–23, 2010.

Honko, Lauri. 2000. "Text as Process and Practice: The Textualization of Oral Epics" in L. Honko, Ed. *The Textualization of Oral Epics*. The Hague: Mouton, pp. 3–56.

Hymes, Dell. 1972a. "Models of Interaction of Language and Social Life" in J. Gumperz and D. Hymes, Eds. *Directions in Sociolinguistics: The Ethnography of Communication*. New York: Holt, Rinehart and Winston, pp. 35–71.

Hymes, Dell. 1972b. "On Communicative Competence" in J.B. Pride and J. Holmes, Eds. *Sociolinguistics. Selected Readings*. Harmondsworth: Penguin, pp. 269–293.

Hymes, Dell. 1974. *Foundations in Sociolinguistics: An Ethnographic Perspective*. Philadelphia: University of Pennsylvania Press.

Hymes, Dell. 1994. "Ethnopoetics, Oral-Formulaic Theory, and Editing Texts." *Oral Tradition* 9(2): 330–370.

Hymes, Dell. 2000. "Poetry." *Journal of Linguistic Anthropology* 9 (1–2): 191–193.

Jakobson, Roman. 1960. "Closing Statement: Linguistics and Poetics" in T.A. Sebeok, Ed. *Style in Language*. Cambridge, MA: MIT Press, pp. 350–377.

Jakobson, Roman. 1987. "The Dominant" in Krystyna Pomorska and Stephan Rudy, Eds. *Language in Literature*. Cambridge, MA: Harvard University Press, pp. 41–46.

Jakobson, Roman and Petr Bogatyrev. 1966 [1929]. "Folklore as a Special Form of Creation" in Roman Jakobson, Ed. *Selected Writings*. Trans. John M. O'Hara. The Hague: Mouton, pp. 1–15.

Jakobson, Roman and Claude Lévi-Strauss. 1962. "'Les Chats' de Charles Baudelaire." *L'Homme* 2(1): 5–21.

Jason, Heda. 1972. "Jewish Near Eastern Numskull Tales: An Attempt at Interpretation." *Asian Folklore Studies* 31(1): 1–39.

Jason, Heda. 1977. *Ethnopoetry: Form, Content, Function*. Bonn: Linguistica Biblica.

Jolles, André. 1965. *Einfache Formen*. (Simple Forms). Tübingen: M. Niemeyer.

Kirshenblatt-Gimblett, Barbara. 1975. "A Parable in Context: A Social Interactional Analysis of Storytelling Performance" in Dan Ben-Amos and Kenneth Goldstein, Eds. *Folklore, Performance, and Communication*. The Hague: Mouton, pp. 105–130.

Kristeva, J. 1986 [1974]. "Revolution in Poetic Language" in Toril Moi, Ed. *The Kristeva Reader*. New York: Columbia University Press, pp. 89–136.

Krohn, Kaarle, 1971 [1926]. *Folklore Methodology: Formulated by Julius Krohn*. Trans. Roger L. Welsch. Austin: University of Texas Press.

Lévi-Strauss, Claude. 1955. "The Structural Study of Myth." *Journal of American Folklore* 68: 428–444 (reprinted as: Claude Lévi-Strauss. 1967. "The Structural Study of Myth" in *Structural Anthropology*. Trans. Claire Jacobson. Garden City, NY: Doubleday Anchor, pp. 202–228).

Lévi-Strauss, Claude. 1966. *The Savage Mind*. Chicago: University of Chicago Press.

Lévi-Strauss, Claude. 1967. "The Myth of Asdiwal" in Edmund Leach, Ed. *The Structural Study of Myth and Totemism*. London: Tavistock, pp. 1–48.

Lévi-Strauss, Claude. 1983a. *The Raw and the Cooked* (Mythologiques, Vol. I). Trans. Doreen and John Weightman. Chicago: University of Chicago Press.

Lévi-Strauss, Claude. 1983b. *From Honey to Ashes* (Mythologiques, Vol. II). Trans. Doreen and John Weightman. Chicago: University of Chicago Press.

Lévi-Strauss, Claude. 1990a. *The Origin of Table Manners* (Mythologiques, Vol. III). Trans. Doreen and John Weightman. Chicago: University of Chicago Press.

Lévi-Strauss, Claude. 1990b. *The Naked Man* (Mythologiques, Vol. IV). Trans. Doreen and John Weightman. Chicago: University of Chicago Press.

Lord, Albert B. 1960. *The Singer of Tales*. Cambridge, MA: Harvard University Press.

Lüthi, Max. 1970. *Volksliteratur und Hochliteratur. Menschenbild, Thematik, Formstreben*. München: Francke.

Lüthi, Max. 1975. *Volksmärchen und Volkssage: Zwei Grundformen erzählender Dichtung*. Bern: Francke.

Lüthi, Max. 1984. *The Fairytale as Art Form and Portrait of Man*. Trans. Jon Erickson. Bloomington: Indiana University Press.

Malinowski, Bronislaw. 1959 [1923]. "The Problem of Meaning in Primitive Languages" in C.K. Ogden and I. A. Richards, Eds. *The Meaning of Meaning*. New York: Harcourt, Brace, & World, pp. 296–336.

Malinowski, Bronislaw. 1976 [1926]. *Myth in Primitive Psychology*. Westport, CT: Negro Universities Press.

Meletinsky, Eleazar, S. Nekludov, E. Novik, and D. Segal. 1974. "Problems of the Structural Analysis of Fairytales" in Pierre Maranda, Ed. *Soviet Structural Folkloristics*. The Hague: Mouton, pp. 73–139.

Melia, Daniel. 2003. *Orality and Aristotle's Aesthetics and Methods*. Boston: Brill.

Morson, Gary Saul and Caryl Emerson 1990. *Mihkail Bakhtin: Creation of a Prosaics*. Palo Alto: Stanford University Press.

Mukařovský, Jan. 1970. *Aesthetic Function, Norm and Value as Social Facts*. Trans. Mark E. Suino. Ann Arbor: Dept. of Slavic Languages and Literature, University of Michigan.

Olrik, Axel. 1965 [1919]. "Epic Laws of Folk Narrative" in Alan Dundes, Ed. *The Study of Folklore*. Englewood Cliffs, NJ: Prentice-Hall.

Parry, Milman and Albert Lord. 1954. *Serbocroation Heroic Songs. I Novi Pazar: English Translations*. Cambridge, MA: Harvard University Press.

Propp, Vladimir. 1968 [1928]. *Morphology of the Folktale*. Trans. Laurence Scott. Austin: University of Texas Press.

Propp, Vladimir. 1972. "Transformations in Fairy Tales" in Pierre Maranda, Ed. *Mythology*. Harmondsworth: Penguin.

Propp, Vladimir. 1984. *Theory and History of Folklore*. Trans. Ariadna Y. Martin and Richard P. Martin. Minneapolis: University of Minnesota Press.

Rosmarin, Adena. 1984. "Theory and Practice: From Ideally Separate to Pragmatically Joined Theory and Practice." *The Journal of Aesthetics and Art Criticism* 43(1): 31–40.

Ryan, Marie-Laure 1981. "On the Why, What, and How of Generic Taxonomy." Introduction to a special issue on genre. *Poetics* 10(2/3): 109–126.

Seitel, Peter. 1999. *The Powers of Genre: Interpreting Haya Oral Literature*. New York: Oxford University Press.

Seitel, Peter. 2003. "Theorizing Genres: Interpreting Works." *New Literary History* 34(2): 275–297.

Shuman, Amy. 1993. "Gender and Genre" in Susan Tower Hollis, Linda Pershing, and M. Jane Young, Eds. *Feminist Theory and the Study of Folklore*. Urbana: University of Illinois Press, pp. 71–85.

Shuman, Amy and Charles L. Briggs. 1993. "Introduction" in Theorizing Folklore: Toward New Perspectives on the Politics of Culture, special issue of *Western Folklore* 52(2, 3, 4): 109–134.

Smith, Barbara Herrnstein. 1988. *Contingencies of Value: Alternative Perspectives for Critical Theory*. Cambridge: Harvard University Press.

Stewart, Susan. 1978. *Nonsense: Aspects of Intertextuality in Folklore and Literature*. Baltimore: Johns Hopkins University Press.

Stewart, Susan. 1991. "Notes on Distressed Genres" in her *Crimes of Writing*. Oxford: Oxford University Press, pp. 66–101.

Swales, John M. 1990. *Genre Analysis: English in Academic and Research Settings*. Cambridge: Cambridge University Press.

Tedlock, Dennis. 1983. *The Spoken Word and the Work of Interpretation*. Philadelphia: University of Pennsylvania Press.

Todorov, Tzvetan. 1970. *The Fantastic: A Structural Approach to a Literary Genre*. Trans. Richard Howard. Ithaca: Cornell University Press.

Turner, Victor. 1978. "Comments and Conclusions" in Barbara Babcock, Ed. *The Reversible World: Symbolic Inversion in Art and Society*. Ithaca: Cornell University Press.

Vico, Giambattista. 1968 [1744]. *The New Science of Giambatista Vico*. Trans. Thomas Goddard Bergin and Max Harold Fisch. Ithaca: Cornell University Press.

Ziolkowski, Jan M. 2009. *Fairy Tales from Before Fairy Tales*. Ann Arbor: University of Michigan Press.

CHAPTER 4

THREE ASPECTS OF ORAL TEXTUALITY

Peter Seitel

Over the past four decades, one might argue that the object of folklore studies has shifted from the "version" to the "text." While in many cases the physical object presented for analysis and interpretation is a similar string of words on a page, the perspective in which they are viewed has markedly changed. A version is an empirical instance of an ideal form whose alternate expression has been observed in at least one other time and place. A perfect example, although drawn from a non-folkloric realm, would be a particular staging of a Shakespeare play, which is to be compared with other productions over its 400-year history, each a version of the original script. Another example would be versions of the "Cinderella story" recorded among Native Americans or Africans.

A text, however, which may refer to an instance of the very same Hamlet or the "Cinderella story," is viewed through a perspective that, on the one hand, sees it composed of complex symbols woven together to form multifaceted relationships ("text," from Latin *texere*, "to weave"); and on the other hand, as a linguistic device used within, and to help create, a web of particular socio-historical associations and effects. In this latter sense, the study of texts has gathered a family of related terms like context, textuality, and intertextuality, which will be useful in the present essay.

In the same four-decade period that, roughly speaking, saw the replacement of version with text in folkloristics, literary criticism arose that focused on textuality, "text-ness," the ontology, or the conditions of existence, of texts. In particular, two such schools of thought sought to use the idea of textuality to demonstrate the non-autonomy both of a printed text in conveying meaning and of a text's author in determining thematic content. To this way of thinking, the non-autonomous text is crucially dependent on a reader's interpretation to achieve coherent meaning, while

A Companion to Folklore, First Edition. Edited by Regina F. Bendix and Galit Hasan-Rokem.

the non-autonomous author's powers of creation are bound to broad institutional forms of power and knowledge. Both of these viewpoints challenged a dominant perspective in which autonomous authors created transcendent works whose self-sufficient meanings are available for discovery by discerning critics.

Having neither the same historical progression of critical paradigms as literary studies nor a sufficient critical mass to create a chain-reaction, folklore studies has remained relatively quiet on the question of textuality. In addition, challenges to the autonomy of texts and authors is simply not as iconoclastic when the traditions in question are oral rather than written. Most folklorists have long understood that performers depend on audiences to enable their art. And folkloristic emphasis on the idea of tradition itself makes authorial non-autonomy a relatively familiar idea.

Nevertheless, I believe that the perspective brought by literary studies of textuality is useful to understanding folklore as an oral phenomenon. In this essay, therefore, I will show that a concern for textuality can define a productive, integrated approach to both the materials of folklore and the crucial interactions that are the social matrix of their production and reproduction – between performer and audience, on one hand, and between performer and tradition, on the other. Studies of textuality comprehend these relationships in ways that preserve their centrality to artistic creativity and situational meaning, and adduce powerful theoretical frameworks and analytic concepts to explore and elucidate them.

In this essay I will show: how the application of this literary theory to folklore envisions a productive relationship between versions and texts; how it sharpens conceptual tools such as context, coherence and intertextuality; and how it helps specify characteristics of authorial autonomy and non-autonomy. Most significantly, a concern for textuality demonstrates the usefulness of the concept of speech genre in understanding folklore both in performance and in its historical situation.

This essay will apply the idea of textuality to folklore by focusing on three aspects of oral textuality: audience participation in the creation of coherent oral texts (i.e., the non-autonomy of texts), strategic relationships between texts and institutional practices (i.e., the non-autonomy of author/performers), and individual creativity in the creation/performance of texts (i.e., a complementary counter-statement, addressing the autonomy of author/performers). Obviously, there are more than three aspects or dimensions of oral textuality. I have chosen the first two because of their usefulness and their historic importance in studies of literary textuality and the third to address analytically many folklorists' experience of extraordinary community-based performers.

Examples of oral literature, chosen to illustrate aspects of textuality and to leaven the analytic discussion, are drawn from my fieldwork among Haya people in northwestern Tanzania, which began in 1968.[1] One of the Interlacustrine Bantu peoples in east-central Africa, Haya (with a population of about two million) still practice patrilineal kinship, intensive agriculture, cattle herding, and fishing on Lake Victoria, and in pre-independence times they had centralized kingships akin to those in Rwanda, Burundi, and Uganda.

Readers who have a Microsoft Windows-equipped computer with broadband access to the Internet can hear field recordings of the examples presented in a synchronized media format powered by Synchrotext software, which simultaneously presents audio recordings of narrative performances together with scrolling transcripts in the Haya language, translations into English, and line-by-line commentaries.[2]

On the Non-autonomy of Texts

In his excellent summary of anthropological linguistic approaches to textuality, W. F. Hanks initially writes:

> Textuality, on a first reading, is the quality of coherence or connectivity that characterizes text. ... I take the position that whereas the formal and functional properties of sign complexes can aid in the establishment of textuality, it is the fit between the sign form and some larger context that determines its ultimate coherence. (Hanks 1989)

Folklorist Lauri Honko agrees that coherence is the principal condition of textuality and that it is achieved through contextual information supplied by an audience (Honko 2000).

As these scholars imply, there are multiple kinds of coherence, and the ultimate or most important one is meaning, which is fully dependent on context. An oral (or a written) text becomes meaningful within the particular situation of its use. Without context (a condition that exists solely as an analytic abstraction) a text has only potential meaning. Contextual information elicited through references in the text to various forms of cultural knowledge, including other texts, enables an audience to model and comprehend a speaker's ethical and aesthetic intentions.

If meaning is the ultimate, what are the other dimensions of coherence? And are they also actuated by performance context? I believe Michael Bakhtin's framework for analyzing speech genres, or indigenously perceived sets of texts, is useful in exploring this question within a folkloristic perspective. Bakhtin understands the same necessary connection between context and meaning, designating as "theme" the abstract, potential significance a text may have in absence of a context. Themes are generated within the text through relationships between symbols, which are juxtaposed and interact according to the logic of particular genres: e.g. in temporal, causal relationships in narrative genres; in axiomatic statements that imply their opposite in speaking proverbs; in dialectic oppositions to be synthesized in riddling, and so on. These progressing, developing symbolic relationships in the text are conveyed through stylistic forms of language and gesture that pertain to the genre in question. In this perspective, the ultimate coherence of a text, its meaning, is achieved by a combination of logical, stylistic, and thematic relationships specific to a particular time and place.

If abstract themes (in always non-autonomous texts) achieve concrete meanings in living social contexts through audience participation, how do the other dimensions of coherence – style and logic – support this achievement? Linguistic and performance style indicate to an audience a variety of ways it can transform presented themes into situational meanings. Such indicative stylistic elements may include a narrator's wink to an audience member as a mark of particular relevance, as well as more usual metalinguistic markers. As we shall see, these stylistic elements evoke common generic frames to shape audience interpretation.

In many speech genres, the generic logic that indicates to an audience how themes in a text are to become meanings in context takes the form of obligatory elements. The "showdown" scene in Hollywood western movies is such an element, in which characters contend who have come to be identified with particular ethical principles. On a more mundane plane, the obligatory headings on an office memo convey thematic hierarchies that signal interpretation, especially the "To:" heading (which specifies whether the missive is addressed to a wide audience, a narrow one, or to a single employee).

In folklore texts, establishing a framing logic is usually more subtle, but it is equally dependent on the audience's cultural knowledge. In proverb speaking, for example, the text might be so familiar that, even when only partially articulated, it itself establishes the full generic logic – the obligatory elements, the symbols juxtaposed through them, and the themes thereby articulated – and thus achieves contextual meaning. For example, one might try to conclude a somewhat heated discussion about scheduling priorities with one's social equal or junior who can't seem to find time to arrange a particular repair by saying only, "Well, 'A stitch in time.'" This well-known phrase becomes its own metalinguistic invocation of proverb logic, enabling the addressee to transform theme into meaning: Just as taking "a stitch in time saves nine [stitches]," the full proverb text, but not taking a stitch in time does not save nine (or anything), so arranging the repair will avoid multiple troubles in the future, but not arranging the repair will not. Therefore, given this binary choice, one should take the correct option: "take a stitch" – arrange the repair. Proverb speaking is an especially powerful example of the non-autonomy of texts and the necessary role of the audience in establishing coherence.

A storytelling audience also deploys its knowledge of genre so a text can achieve thematic coherence in its own cultural milieu. This process can be entertainingly explored, I hope, in a tale told by Mrs. Laulelia Mukajuna, an accomplished storyteller, in her own house in 1970 to an audience composed of her female neighbor and Sheila Dauer, who recorded the performance. Represented in printed translation below, the recorded oral text, along with synchronized transcript, translation, and commentary, can be heard at http://www.performedwords.org/synchrotext.htm within the Haya folktale library of works under its title, "Crested Crane and Dove."

> Now long ago,
> A man had married two wives:
> A crested crane and a ring-necked dove.
> Now you've seen that little short one.
>
> [the story resumes after an interruption]
> Now his wives are two: both crested crane and little gray dove.   5
> Now they dwell, and they dwell, and they dwell there.
> The husband leaves, and he goes to seek fortune.
>
> When he left,
> the ensenene grasshoppers fall.
> Now when they have fallen,   10
> the dove goes with her basket.
> She strikes and puts them in,
>   Strikes and puts them in,
>   Strikes and puts them in.
> Crested crane shoos them out, Sh – sh and swallows them   15
>   Sh – sh and swallows them
>   Sh- – sh and swallows them.
> The dove brings her ensenene,
>   cooks them

dries them   20
wraps them
and stores them.

Now their husband returned from his journey.
"Welcome, husband. Welcome, husband. Welcome, husband."
　　They bring him inside.   25
　　They salute him.
　　They prepare food.

The dove brings out her bundle of ensenene and cuts it open.
She sets out a plate,
　　She sets out a banana-leaf placemat,   30
　　She sets out a papyrus napkin,
All before her husband's eyes.

Crested crane casts down its eyes. [Narrator and audience laugh.]
It looks into its little feather beard.
"Crested crane, where are yours?   35
Yours – where are they?"

At dawn, the crane was already awake and out there in the fields.
There aren't any. They've stopped falling.
It shoos them sh – nothing.
It shoos them sh – nothing.   40

Now that dove, the little bobbing one,
Exults in triumph over that crane, going on like this:
"The short one is the wife.
The short one is the wife.
The short one is the wife."   45

That tall crane with the long neck
Now looked like a slow dimwit out in the fields.
It sh –
It she –
It she –   50
And to this day she has not returned.
But the short one dwelled where she was wed.

Now then, this is to say,
A beautiful appearance
is not the same as heart.   55
Don't think that the dove is ugly,
And the crested crane is beautiful,
For the dove surpassed her in the knowledge of marriage.

It's done!

　　Understanding the textuality of this non-autonomous text simply as coherence may
be somewhat misleading, for it appears that, even to a non-knowing audience, the

story is already fairly coherent. The storyteller deftly overcomes a small interruption at the beginning to establish a narrative conflict, then to depict with dramatic flourishes how that conflict was resolved, and, finally, to draw a comprehensible moral that seems reasonably supported by the depicted action. If the reader assumes that Hayas, like the ancient Jews in Leviticus (and Yemeni Jews in our times), enjoy eating grasshoppers of a certain sort, then the story along with its moral "makes sense." That is, it achieves ultimate (thematic) coherence based upon information supplied by a reader.

This observation, I think, demonstrates the importance of Hanks' concept of "centeredness," a refinement of coherence, as the crucial feature of textuality. According to Hanks, a text "is centered insofar as it is grounded in a locally defined social context, which functions as the source of information an author and reader draw on to flesh out the interpretation of the textual artifact (itself incomplete)"(Hanks 1989). A text is not merely coherent; it is coherent in a particular, localized way.

Thus, a folklorist looks for gaps in this text filled with the unspoken knowledge of a Haya audience, which completes and "centers" the text, creating a locally informed, locally situated coherence. Initially, there are three obvious gaps, all of which can be grouped under Hanks' category of "indexical grounding" – that is, concepts in a local cultural universe pointed to by elements in the text. The three are the ensenene grasshoppers, the dove, and the crested crane.

Ensenene are edible grasshoppers, which fly into Hayaland from somewhere on Lake Victoria, coming once a year with the beginning of the small rainy season. They land in great clouds in fields where traditionally women and children captured them. (Now men also bring them in large plastic bags to market to sell.) Stored in baskets, the live ensenene are brought home, "peeled" (wings and legs removed), boiled, then fried, and served as a relish with a meal or as a bit of food to share with a guest. Alternately, they can be preserved by smoking them over a fire, as the dove does in the tale. Hayas traditionally have called them "the laughter of guests" for the happy feeling they engender, and today they praise the delicacy as "the shrimp of Hayaland." But eating ensenene – and this is crucial to the story – was traditionally forbidden to women. The prohibition probably was informally broken in the past, as is in the present.

Crested crane's fabled beauty graces the national flag of Uganda and her willowy figure and undulating walk are a perceived reflection of the stereotypic body type of the traditional cattle-owning, state-building rulers. Her feathered crest reflects a new bride's hairstyle. Dove's physique, on the other hand, is a perceived reflection of the stereotypic body type of the traditional farming underclass: short, with solid, powerful legs and a vigorous style of movement. Note that after the interruption at the beginning of the performance, the narrator remembers and changes dove's species from *ekiiba*, the ring-necked dove, to *akaiba*, the small grey dove. The latter name is a pun on the word for "the jealousy among co-wives."

This knowledge alters the thematic coherence in the text by redefining the key concepts of beauty and knowledge using local Haya symbols. It replaces our own assumptions about beauty and knowledge with which we initially constructed a non-centered, semantically less rich, coherence. But thematic coherence based in indexical grounding is only one dimension of the rich textuality created by performer and audience.

The way into the other dimensions of textuality is illuminated, in a sense, by crested crane, who is not only an international beauty but, by virtue of the role she plays in this tale, a familiar character in the canon of Haya stories – the gluttonous bride. Told, in part, to shape women's behavior in virilocal marriages, such tales include the following titles found on the Performed Words web site: "Blocking the Wind," "I Ate Minnows," "Kyusi, Kyusi Good Dog," and "The Bride's Relish," with interesting transformations of the concept in "Kibwana," "Have You Not Seen Luhundu?" "The Legend of Lake Ikimba," and "It Was Haste That Killed Her." Crested crane's behavior makes sense because it has a familiar feel to it and its resemblance to and resonance with that of similar characters in the Haya storytelling genre. This kind of unspoken, intertextual reference is as crucial to creating the centered coherence of oral textuality as the underlying cultural knowledge that enables indexical grounding.

But intertextual reference is not always unspoken. The first two lines of the text, "Now long ago,/ A man had married two wives," are sufficient to evoke the genre of Haya stories as a whole. This opening is a shorter variant of the more formal, call-and-response type ("I give you a story." "*I give you another.*" "The news of long ago. I went and I saw." "*See so that we may see.*" "I went and I saw ... A man had married two wives. ..."). But its adverbials "now" and "long ago" and the distant-past tense in the second line serve quite well to frame the action and create the expectations associated with the genre. The only other instance of the distant-past tense in the text is in the bracketing, penultimate line of the performance, "For the dove surpassed her in the knowledge of marriage."

At the beginning, after a brief interruption, the story frame needs to be reestablished, and the narrator achieves this with two lines that begin with "Now." These adverbials were sufficient for her, as the distant past was in a sense already in place.

The "now" adverb, in fact, is the initial word of each of the lines in the text that begin the constituent parts of the story: 1 and 5–6, the initial domestic situation and its reestablishment after the interruption; 10, compounded with "when" here and on line 8, the gathering of grasshoppers; 23, the return of the husband and the revelation of wifely knowledge; 41, punishment and reward; and 53, the moral. Note that, while their use is consistent enough to bear clear meaning, adverbs in oral texts are not as rigidly applied, say, as Roman numerals in a written outline. There is a relaxed, playful variation possible.

Patterned use of these linguistic markers both evokes and structures a world of Haya stories, a generic world – just like, for example, that of fairy tales, or Hollywood westerns, or hard-boiled detective stories – with a characteristic set of protagonists and with a characteristic logic to its unfolding action. Evoked by patterned verbal usages, the expectation of this logic integrates stylistic and thematic coherences within a larger performance frame created by an audience's knowing participation and a performer's art.

The logic that underlies the narrative and unifies the style and theme in "Crested Crane and Dove" is shared by all traditional Haya stories that include a human protagonist. The latter thematic feature differentiates the stories from the animal fables, also present in Hayaland, that are common to most of Sub-Saharan Africa. Like proverb speaking and other speech genres, these Haya narratives have a mandatory element, a type of episode often but not always marked by a song – an extreme and aesthetically pleasing form of stylistic embellishment. Even in stories like the present one that do not have a song, the mandatory element is usually stylistically embellished.

In traditional Haya stories (excluding animal fables) the mandatory element is a dramatically central, paradigmatic action in which a significant boundary is crossed. This forms the primary action of the narrative and also structures secondary, associated actions. The boundary itself is usually a physical border or contrast between value-laden areas in the envisioned landscape – the doorways into or within a traditional round-style house, the gate of a cattle kraal, the outlying fields as opposed to the homestead, the wilderness as opposed to human habitation, the king's palace contrasted with the family hearth. But it may also be a more abstract boundary, especially, but not always, in secondary actions: human bodies that contain irrepressible secrets or antisocial appetites; communications whose external features obscure hidden meanings, and, as in the present story, contrasts between outward appearance and inward knowledge. In this dramatic setting are familiar protagonists, recognized motivations, and devices for controlling and violating borders.

The generically obligatory action for Haya stories is the central part of a narrative sequence that (in its simplest form) begins with an entity displaced inside or outside a border and ends with a reward and/or punishment to the border crosser or controller for establishing or reestablishing the final configuration. Action is usually complexly conceived, involving more than one border at a time. (Only one story I know depicts simple action on a single border – the first one told to the fieldworker by the present narrator, "Have You Not Seen Luhundu?") In "Crested Crane and Dove" there are two border-oriented progressions, and they are related: a household contains two wives, one of whom is to be put outside permanently; and ensenene grasshoppers out in the fields are put inside in different ways by the two wives and then are taken out, inside the house, in a way that resolves both border issues.

This inside-outside way of understanding the progression of episodes is a generic logic that integrates two aspects of textuality – the coherence of style and the coherence of theme. The narrator marks episodic boundaries with adverbials and then embellishes actions in the episodes that embody the obligatory progression, using (in the present case) repetition, rhythmic intonation, and syntactic parallelism.

The first stylistic ornamentations in "Crested Crane and Dove" are thrice-repeated words intoned in a way that captures dove's pulsating, determined energy (lines 12–14), quickly followed by a thrice-repeated description-mimicry of crested crane's longer, swooping moves (lines 15–17). The episode concludes with a four-part parallelism that describes dove's careful preparation of the food (lines 19–22).

The following episode continues with two three-part parallelisms that describe the wives' welcome (lines 25–27) and dove's presentation of food (lines 29–31) and concludes with an echo of crested crane's swooping but now ineffective movements. These two central episodes embody the obligatory plot development of a traditional folktale. The episodes present a mildly complex amalgam of inward and outward trajectories of grasshoppers and wives across several significant spaces and borders – fields, house, food storage vessels, and an individual body. Each stylistic embellishment in the episodes artfully embodies a passage across a domestic boundary and emphasizes the wifely virtue needed for its successful traverse.

Moreover, the latter episode, which resolves the drama, is marked by two unique narrative flourishes. The first envisions a poignant thematic detail – the beautiful crane's casting her eyes downward to acknowledge the shame she feels before her husband. Narrator and audience break into laughter when they picture this. The second is a commentary, a Greek-chorus-like rhetorical question to crane, "crested-crane, where are yours?" (lines 35–36), which explicates the observed shame. These words are spoken by an observer of the scene, not by one of the protagonists. The quoted lines are attributed to no one, unlike the only other direct speech in the text (lines 42–45) but use the marked rising-falling intonation sometimes used in this genre to comment on the depicted events to the audience, as does its other occurrence in the tale on line 54, which proclaims the beginning of the tale's moral. Narrator Kelezensia Kahamba uses the intonation frequently to indicate the excitement and wonder in tales she tells her children (e.g. "I Shall Be Drinking From Them," line 64; "Little Leper" lines 47, 54, 58, 65, 67, etc.; "Teaser" lines 14, 56, 64, etc.; all are online).

The style in the final episode of the sequence, reward/punishment, is also adorned, but not to the same degree as that in the key episodes. The narrator voices dove's rejoicing with thrice-repeated self-praise (lines 43–45) and concludes the narrative action with a final, thrice-repeated echo of crane's swooping motion (lines 48–50). This degree of elaboration maintains both the high performance values of the narrator and the logic of the tale, which winds to conclusion at this point, as an audience that knows other stories in the genre expects.

The moral of this tale, as most morals do when present, calls attention to the virtue, the motivation, or the mistake of one protagonist in crossing or protecting a border. Dove's knowledge of marriage here enabled her to move both the ensenene grasshoppers and the crane in and out of the places that matter.

Mrs. Mukajuna chose an unconventional way to end her performance, a loud "It's done!" which is unlike any formulaic closing. She may have playfully tried to startle a member of the audience whose responsiveness, expressed in eye contact, head nods, and um-humming, was not up to her standard, but that is only conjecture.

In sum, then, our first aspect of oral textuality presents itself as a locally centered coherence that is created through understandings shared by performer and audience. These shared understandings consist of, among other things, indexical grounding, or references to the local cultural universe, and intertextuality, or references to related texts in that universe. Among related texts, those of the same genre are an especially rich source of understandings that inform coherence.

There are several kinds of centered coherence achieved by performers and audiences. Most important from a folkloristic perspective are thematic coherence, through which an audience reaches locally valid interpretations, and stylistic coherence, which is created by a performer's studied art. In texts locally recognized as belonging to particular genres, thematic and stylistic coherences are integrated according to a particular logic. This specifies how juxtaposed symbols are to be combined so as to articulate themes; it also creates opportunities for stylistic elaboration to support the thematic development. In narrative the obligatory logical form is often a particular episode type, but in non-narrative genres like proverbs, the logic may include a particular configuration of elements in the context of performance.

Before shifting focus from the aspect of oral textuality inherent in a non-autonomous text to that which is inherent in a non-autonomous author/performer, I would like to comment briefly on the terminology of coherence and centeredness. Both terms seem to suggest a simple binary discrimination: a text is coherent or it is incoherent; it is centered or it is off-center. But texts that are both centered and coherent may bear different meanings for different audience members. Even with agreement on indexical groundings and intertextual references, individual life experiences may affect perceived thematic emphases. When one confronts the analysis of actual performances, coherence and centeredness, like logic, theme, and style, become heuristic tools rather than axiomatic principles.

On the Non-autonomy of Author/Performers

The textuality of a folklore text – the properties of its existence – results from a practice composed of two parts: creation/re-creation by a performer and reception by an audience. In the last section, we explored the nature of the audience's reception of the (always incomplete) text. In this section, we explore the performer's creation/re-creation of the text in a social setting in which other texts and other social practices always already exist. This shift of focus from reception to production of texts coincides with shifting our analytic perspective on context: from the immediate performance situation, in which a knowing audience "centers" an incomplete text, we shift to the broader historical context, in which prevailing social practices influence author/performers as they compose (or re-compose) and then perform. In this broader perspective, intertextual associations likewise shift: from generic references that key an audience's interpretation, to thematic consistencies between genres and practices, which illuminate the social forces at work on a (non-autonomous) author/performer.

In "The Problem of Textuality: Two Exemplary Positions" the eminent literary critic Edward Said presents a primary example of textuality whose sheer scale challenges the interpretive projects of both Derrida and Foucault:

> One can very well ask – as I have tried to [in *Orientalism*] – what makes it possible for Marx, Carlyle, Disraeli, Flaubert, Nerval, Renan, Quinet, Schlegel, Hugo, Rickert, Cuvier, and Bopp all to employ the word "Oriental" in order to designate essentially the same corporate phenomenon, despite the enormous ideological and political differences between them. The principal reason for this was the constitution of a geographical entity – which, were it not for the Europeans who spoke for it and represented it in their discourse, was otherwise merely passive, decadent, obscure – called the Orient, and its study called Orientalism, that realized a very important component of the European will to domination over the non-European world and made it possible to create not only an orderly discipline of study but a set of institutions, a latent vocabulary (or a set of enunciative possibilities), a subject matter, and finally – as it emerges in Hobson's and Cromer's writing at the end of the nineteenth century – subject races. (Said 1978)

The enormous textuality described – a non-autonomous production of texts that share crucial thematic elements – encompasses genres, disciplines, political orientations, nations, and historical epochs. Said's answer to his posed question "what makes it possible …" – the strategic invention of a unifying concept, the Orient, which helps to build institutions, create textual content, and ascribe social identities, all within an overall imperialist project – shares with Foucault's approach to textuality certain key features that I believe are useful in understanding oral textuality as well.

Using aspects of Said's and Foucault's insights into textuality, this section explores strategic relationships that affect the production of oral texts. We explore the way thematic content shared across texts and genres embodies ethical knowledge and rhetorical power that help to validate social identities and to build and maintain social institutions. Oral performances strategically relate to each other and to broader institutional processes that wield more direct forms of political and economic power. Author/performers in these contexts produce texts non-autonomously to the extent that the thematic content they create is shaped and limited by institutional goals. As in the previous section, I illustrate this aspect of textuality with examples drawn from Haya oral tradition and demonstrate the utility of speech genre as a critical tool in this interpretive project.

Analogous, on a much smaller scale, to European imperialism in the Orientalist example, is the broad historical context for two Haya literary genres to be discussed – heroic ballads (*enanga*) and self-praise poetry (*ebyebugo*): the building of centralized royal states in Hayaland, which began more than three centuries ago. Like other societies in the Interlacustrine region of east-central Africa, Hayas experienced an immigration (peaceful and otherwise) of cattle-herding state-builders who used the value of their livestock and their knowledge of statecraft to create centralized administrations with which they ruled the indigenous agriculturalists and fishermen. This form of state, in which cattle-owners ruled agriculturalists, was common to the region and was one of the enabling conditions of the recent tragic events in Rwanda and Burundi. But in Hayaland and elsewhere, conflict between traditional rulers and those they ruled never reached that cataclysmic scale.

Armed challenges to ruling administrations did occur, however, and one of the devices of statecraft common to the region was the creation and maintenance of a warrior class. Part of warrior practice, and also common to the region, was the recitation of self-praise poetry.[3] In Hayaland, thematic content of the verses alluded symbolically to the integration of patrilineal, agriculturalist clans into the institutions of the state. One source of symbolism was the system of animals (called *balumuna* "brothers" and sometimes referred to as "secondary totems") associated with particular clans by virtue of clan members' occupational responsibilities at the king's court. Another source was allusions to feats of valor done in the past by the speaker and his relatives. The poem was intended to identify an individual through a particular combination of associations. One's geographical origins were also proper sources of identity.

A warrior recited his praise poem while in the king's service, before going out to battle, and again, on returning from the fray. The following example occurred during a performance of the heroic ballad *King Kaitaba* by the bard Abdallah Feza. After hearing Feza sing of Kaitaba's victory over a neighboring king, a member of the audience participated in the depiction of the scene by spontaneously chanting his praise poem, thus enacting the role of a warrior in Kaitaba's victorious legion.

I am the weakened one who stirs things about.   490
  Thunder said, "I'll strike you!" I said, "You strike me?
  I am the grower of sharpened points.
  Iron hammers like a spirit medium's."
When I reached Uganda they refused me space in a canoe.
  So I went by hanging on the stern piece.
  They brought me to Uganda, then bent me over.
  They found hair filled my anus.

I climb a tree but have no fingers or claws.
  They jog the fence chimes and I ring.
  I am a throwing stick. I pass through cracks in shields.
  I am a wooden crook and lie among tree branches.
I come from Bugabo Kingdom, Kabale village of Katwange.
I am a child of the Balwani clan of Mahugulu village.
I am of Byanjweli river of Mashaija.
  I am of Mikimba and Ntule.
  And Kantema Kashamba and Kantundu of Mabiga.
I am the Gatherer.   495
I trust in the snake, the Agitated one, the White spot.
Conquer, Provider! These spears are yours. [That is, Be successful, O King! Your
warriors stand before you]

The first four lines (numbered 490–490.3 by a convention that reserves integers and the left margin for lines preceded by a pause) refer symbolically to the chicken, whose mythical power can challenge that of thunder and whose leg spurs resemble metal tools. The chicken is the clan brother and sometime occupational implement of the Basaizi clan, whose duties at court included augury and sorcery. The speaker claims a relationship to the Basaizi through his mother's great grandmother. The next four lines (491–491.3) refer to the leopard, the clan brother of the Balwani clan, that of the speaker's own mother (493). The following four lines (492–492.3) as well as line 496 symbolically evoke the python, clan brother of the Bajubu clan, according to the speaker. These symbolic clan associations varied across the seven kingdoms of Hayaland, and, even when they were current, more than half a century ago, were probably appreciated more for the flow of recited images than for the exact nature of the semantic ties they created between clan and king. The pragmatic value of the recitation was to create and colorfully mark a distinctive, individual warrior identity, symbolically bound to the king and worthy of his royal notice and reward.[4]

As a speech genre, self-praise recitation, like proverb speaking, depended on the configuration of the performance context for its ultimate coherence. The king must be present, and the occasion must be one where material reward and/or personal prestige can be accorded – that is, before or after a military encounter. But unlike proverb speaking, its thematic coherence does not necessarily depend on indexical (here, metaphorical) grounding.

In self-praise poetry can be seen the non-autonomy of authors as an aspect of oral textuality. When an author/reciter chooses to create a poem of this sort, the thematic content will necessarily be of certain types, but more significantly, his performance will be part of a particular institutional project to build and maintain the kingship and, as part of this, will validate particular social identities, namely his own as a warrior and the king's as the source of political power and economic beneficence. The non-autonomous author's text is shaped by institutional practice in the themes it articulates, in the social identities it confirms, and in the very logic of its performance.

Among present-day Hayas, the recitation of self-praise poetry is an obligatory performance by a bridegroom as part of a wedding celebration. The widespread existence of the form in the Interlaustrine region as a royal-court related genre suggests that its use in weddings derives from warrior practice rather than vice versa. In its kin-related context, the poem is clearly praise for the family or families involved in the marriage.

Heroic ballads, a genre also performed both at the royal court and at weddings, seem to have arrived in Hayaland later than the state-building praise poems, probably between one and two centuries ago. As an example of non-autonomous authorship, the ballads – like self-praise poetry – share a particular range of thematic content, strategically support the institution of the royal state, and affirm particular social identities. But unlike self-praise poetry they use narrative means to accomplish these ends.[5]

In contrast to the situational strategy characteristic of self-praise poetry, it is the thematic content of ballad texts that most conveys their intent. As a narrative speech genre, heroic ballads depict a world in which events unfold according to a particular logic. And like many other narrative genres, heroic ballads have an obligatory type of episode that juxtaposes principal symbols and indicates how they articulate themes.

The following characterization of heroic ballads applies to texts that might be termed "classic" – the older, more widely known stories. The bards who work in the ballad tradition are professional singers who now perform principally at private weddings and places of public entertainment. Their repertoire includes a wide variety of narrative songs. It is to the older stories, including the nine presented on the Performed Words web site, that this description applies.

The obligatory episode type in heroic ballads can be termed "the call." In this episode, a character who represents a social identity associated with the Haya royal state is summoned, directly or indirectly, to act according to the ethical principles specific to his or her social standing. As noted with respect to the folktales, the key episode is rarely a single occurrence in a simple plot. Rather it usually appears in complexly subordinated chains of action, each of which begins with a call and concludes with an equilibrium that supersedes a previous disequilibrium and leads to another call. I have described the shape of this logic in Haya ballads previously (Seitel 1999). A summary the principal calls of nine ballads follows:

Kachwenyanja: a warrior hears and honors the royal war drums that summon him to
   battle.
King Kitekere: the king hears from his distraught cattle herder that the royal cattle have
   been raided, and he mounts a counterattack.
King Kaitaba: the king is made to believe he has been insulted by a neighboring king
   and decides to exact revenge.
Rukiza: (two princpal calls) in an epoch before the state monopolized cattle ownership, the
   king receives a report that a magically protected clan leader has acted with disrespect
   towards his cattle. The king's warriors surround his compound and call him out to fight.
Mugasha: the indigenous lake spirit, whose worship was co-opted to become a royal state
   practice, is insulted by the daughter of his adversary, Wamara, king of the spirits and
   lead figure in a pre-state religious practice. Mugasha vows to marry the daughter, and
   a war ensues.
The Tree Mwata: a towering tree sacred to Wamara and a place of sacrifice to him
   magically speaks and defies warriors of the legendary king who established state
   worship of Mugasha. The king requests the help of Mugasha, who, with his warrior
   minions, attacks the tree.
Kajango: a wife who previously verbally mistreated her husband receives word that he
   has fallen into a deadly faint. She undertakes a journey to the royal court of Wamara
   in the spirit world to save him.

In two ballads, *Kaiyula* and *The Place You Come From*, the calls are verbally elaborate seductions of newly wed brides.

The determining themes in the first six ballads evoke and validate the identities and the practices of the royal state. Kings, warriors, cattle, and spirits are portrayed in a manner that supports the values and alliances that bind them together and increase their efficacy.

The themes in the final three ballads, however, do not seem related particularly to the social roles and political practices of the royal state. They seem more appropriate to a performance context in which beer encourages a contemplative atmosphere for enjoying the pleasures of a long, sung, poetic narrative. Beer was apparently a central feature of life at the royal court – brewed by state labor or contributed to affirm alliances and shared with those whose regular attendance at court attested to their loyalty. Desisting from beer is part of King Kitekere's response to the call to action issued at his court (*King Kitekere* 262–263). The ballad about his son, Kaitaba, begins with a state crisis whose mysterious cause is ultimately revealed to be a shortage of beer (*King Kaitaba* 1–89). And the royal extraction of beer from a kingdom's agricultural laborers may be chillingly symbolized in a spirit-world tableau depicted in *Kajango* (lines 400–416).

But as much as "wine, women, and song" were part of courtly life, there is another dimension of practice evident in the call episodes that speaks directly to oral textuality. The elaborate verbal seductions that constitute the call episodes of *Kaiyula* and *The Place You Come From* at least partly embody, represent, and amuse an audience with the rhetorical power of speech itself. And in light of this, one can see that the other call episodes in the genre also share this thematic dimension. Insults, slander, taunting, requests for help, vows, as well as authoritative reports precede and motivate definitive actions in narratives. Heroic ballads refer to and validate the practices of the royal state, but just as significantly, I believe, they refer to the power of words practiced by the bards themselves. Although allied with the royal court, bards were an independent practice and might also entertain at wedding celebrations sponsored by patrilineal clans. To be sure, themes articulated in and shared by the call episodes mark the ballads as authorial creations within the institutional context of the royal court. But they also assert and celebrate the rhetorical power of the bards.

The non-autonomy of Haya heroic ballad author/performers is evident in the strategic validation in their performances of the identities and practices of the royal state. This prompts a related inquiry. What about Haya folktales? Can the same be said of them? In what sense is storytelling the product of non-autonomous author/performers?

Viewing folktale texts in this light, one sees not only strategic support for the practices of a powerful institution but also a rich narrative elaboration of concepts useful in thinking about that long-lived organization, the patrilineal clan, from the inside, so to speak. From this perspective, the logic of many clan-regulated practices – land tenure, marriage and reproduction, kin and household relationships, food production and consumption – can be productively thought about with the generic narrative contrast inside/outside. This binary discrimination is the core of a household's management of private and public affairs. It is a measure of collaterality in kinship according to which solidarity is expected and inheritance is calculated. It is useful in thinking about human reproduction and food production and the role of self control – or as Hayas phrase it, "self knowledge" – in each domain. Inside/outside is at once simple and capable of almost infinite conceptual and narrative elaboration. Evolved over many centuries, the strategic fit between folktales and the institutional practices of the clan system they support is both rich and elegant.[6]

On the Autonomy of Author/Performers

Texts that depict and validate identities, ethics, and practices of powerful institutions like clans and states also exhibit, of course, an autonomy of creative choices. Author/performers artfully choose – according to their interests and talents – thematic and stylistic elements so as to develop narrative rhythms, punctuate transitions, deepen significance, and create other literary and rhetorical effects. This form of authorial autonomy is ubiquitous in texts and can be seen in the achievement of poignant and complexly interwoven representations. It is clear evidence of the work tellers do on texts in between performances.

Another aspect of autonomous-author textuality also indicates an individual storyteller's preparation to perform – the selecting of particular texts to become part of his or her active repertoire. The stories narrators select from among those they have heard seem to resonate thematically with their experience and with the other tales already in their repertoires. Performers apparently modify these tales according to their individual interest, perspective, and talent. When asked for a storytelling – as might happen in a number of situations, including an episode of folkloristic fieldwork – these are the ones they choose, a thematic sub-genre they have created. My evidence for this aspect of oral textuality – a narrator-centered intertextuality – is not extensive, for I have been able to identify it, in the Haya context, in only a few narrators. However, it is an aspect of oral textuality that is interesting both intrinsically for the artistic achievement it embodies and analytically for the relationships between texts, genres, and versions it entails.

The most extensive example of this form of textuality is provided by the storytelling of Laulelia Mukajuna, a woman in her mid- to late thirties in 1970 when she was recorded. The tales she performed for recording, always before an audience that included native speakers, are almost all about the personal relationships within a household. "Crested Crane and Dove" discussed above is hers. The themes she depicts range from the simple, undifferentiated love of a newly wed couple ("Have You Not Seen Luhundu"), to humorous treatments of a henpecked young man ("Blocking the Wind") and of a marriage magically with and without sex ("Kibwana"). The insight that informs her narrative art is fed by her ability to envision episodes from each character's perspective as she improvises quoted speech, imagines details that build thematic coherence, and draws lessons that emerge organically from depicted action.

Laulelia Mukajuna's telling of "The Legend of Lake Ikimba" recounts the widely known story of how the little lake to the west of the giant Lake Victoria was first formed. Apparently not fully a folktale, the narrative lacks generic opening and closing phrases, but it does unfold according to a familiar logic.

> Now an old woman had caught that lake Ikimba.
> She had closed it up inside,
> in a water jar, inside there.
> There were also fish (*samaki* – Swahili) in there.
> – *enfulu* (fish): let me speak Haya: fish (*enfulu*) –
>
> Now she would take them out and cook.
> She reaches in like this with her hand,
> She takes out fish and cooks.

Now eventually her son came to wed
a bride.

Now the bride,
her family escorts her to her new home.
The old woman, the mother-in-law, took out fish
and cooked for the guests.
She refused the bride something to send home for her mother.
She refused the bride something to send home for her mother.

Now then, the bride became angry.
She thought:
"Even though she cooked for my people, and they ate,
she could have taken out a few more fish
so I could wrap them
and send them for my mother.

Now when the old woman went around back to the banana plants,
(to relieve herself)
the bride said, "Just let me reach in there.
I'll draw out fish to send my mother."
She reached in.

When she had reached all the way inside,
the water boiled over.
She had nothing to stop it.

It poured out of the jar a lake,
Wo wo wo.
Bride! Run! Run! Run!
Wo wo wo wo.
The mother-in-law, from where she stands,
sees the bride.
The water has already driven her away.
"Help! Help! Help!"

The old woman raised her hoe to the water.
"Ikimba, Ikimba," she said,
"Kill one village,
But leave another.
Kill one village,
But leave another."
On the lake:
weh weh weh weh weh.

Bride and mother-in-law
the water swallowed them.

The place they fell
is where the lake subsided.
That's why it doesn't resemble the other one – Lake Victoria.
It stayed a little marsh.

Now, what does this matter point out to us?
It points out to us – I, for example –

If [my son] Lauliani would marry
I would have a bride (in bridal seclusion) in the inner room.
I wouldn't refuse her things to send to her people.
I'd wrap her gift to send her mother.
That's when she'd be happy.

That little lake points out to us:
Don't refuse your son's wife
something to send her people.

Traditionally, when a bride changed residence, the wedding party that accompanied her did not include her mother. According to clan practice, mother and daughter would not see each other until the ceremonial visit occasioned by the daughter's giving birth. (Clandestine visits sometimes occurred, however). The narrator envisions the emotional strength of the mother-daughter tie and the power that gifts have to acknowledge and care for such relationships, especially at a distance. The mother-in-law's refusal to send a gift (she is under no obligation to send one) and the bride's anger at the refusal motivate events. They are unique to the narrator's version, to my knowledge. Other versions rely on the stock figure of the gluttonous bride to set the disastrous events in motion. Laulelia Mukajuna's telling does not suggest that the bride's use of her husband's clan's property was not a violation of social (i.e., clan) ethics. But she does envision a more sympathetic way that a mother-in-law might act so as to remove the motivation for such transgressions.

Here, then, is a text that exhibits (as many oral texts do):

- textuality of the non-autonomous text, observable in the need for audience-supplied centering through cultural references and through the generic logic of its narrative representation, which places opportunities for stylistic elaboration and locates the articulation of principal themes;
- textuality of the non-autonomous author, observable in the portrayed practices and identities of a dominant social institution (the patrilineal clan) and (violations of) its ethics;
- textuality of the autonomous author, observable in the stylization of the telling, the thematic configuration of narrative detail, and explicit interpretation, all of which voice the narrator's interest as an individual creator/performer.

In this perspective, differences between versions of a particular story found in the same community can probably be understood – after their centeredness within performance and historical contexts has been established – with intertextual references to the respective repertoires of the author/performers. Dissimilar elements in the versions may articulate a divergent but overlapping set of themes that express the experience and predilections of a particular narrator or, perhaps, a chain of narrators. But versions found in different communities could only be compared – as texts conveying meaning – in light of the different centering to be seen in the performance and historical contexts of each, especially with respect to their relevant intertextualities.

Ma Laulelia's active repertoire also included stories that do not focus on intimate domestic relationships. She told some stories in which clever speech and contrived situations dramatize the difference between intelligent and not-so-intelligent characters. (One of these is available on the Performed Words site as "Leopard and Sheep.") Ma Laulelia also told a tale ("Blocking the Wind") with a trajectory so comically convoluted by her art that it becomes difficult analytically to differentiate stylistic and thematic dimensions unequivocally. This is to say that textuality, intertextuality, and genre clearly describe aspects of the world of texts but are to be used heuristically to explore rather than to categorically delimit and define.

The preceding analysis adopts the central theoretical insight of the literary criticism that engages textuality of texts – the non-autonomy of texts and authors. I do not engage that movement's styles of literary analysis or its various conclusions. By applying, rather, what the above-cited scholars agree are the movement's central ideas to the textuality of oral texts, one achieves, I believe, a useful perspective for understanding folklore performances. Attention to the ontology of texts as creators of meanings defines a perspective that can integrate, conceptually and operationally, the multidimensional analytic tools of context, intertextuality, and speech genre. As noted at the beginning, textuality is, thus, not a paradigm-busting notion for folklore – conceptualizations of performance and tradition are strengthened rather than weakened by considerations of textuality. Rather, oral textuality provides a useful, constructive base on which to assemble the insights that grow from careful listening and critical comparison.

NOTES

1   Monographs resulting from this work are: "Proverbs and the Structure of Metaphor among the Haya of Tanzania," PhD dissertation, University of Pennsylvania, 1972; *See So That We May See. Translations and Interpretations from Haya Oral Traditions,* Bloomington: Indiana University Press, 1980; and *The Powers of Genre: Interpreting Haya Oral Literature,* New York: Oxford University Press, 1999.

2   In its present state, Synchrotext requires a PC that uses Microsoft Windows operating system (sadly, no Macintosh). It also requires two freely available helper programs: QuickTime, which is probably already installed on your PC, and Adobe Shockwave, which is possibly not. For your first visit to the Haya libraries on the Performed Words site, use Microsoft's Internet Explorer web browser and go to http://www.performedwords.org/synchrotext. htm. You will be automatically directed to the Adobe Shockwave site and asked to download Shockwave. Do so, I suggest, being careful to consider before agreeing to accept any other software from Adobe as part of the package. After installing Shockwave, return to the above-noted web address. You will be prompted to accept the installation of three Shockwave "xtras." Having done that, you may freely explore and experience the Haya libraries. The entire installation process requires less than five minutes and is only necessary on one's first visit. The site is fully functional in most Internet browsers. Mirosoft Internet Explorer is the easiest one with which to manage the initial installation. If you experience difficulties or would like a free copy of the Synchrotext publisher to format your own recordings, transcriptions, translations, and annotations, email me at seitelp@si.edu or peterseitel@yahoo. com.

3   Haya self-praise poetry has been the subject of two monographs, one by Merchades Method Rutechura (2009) and one by Y.I. Rubanza (1994).

4   Other examples of self-praise recited during the performance of a heroic ballad can be heard on the Performed Words web site in *King Kitekere,* beginning at lines 326, 366, 423, 431, and 542.

5 Heroic (epic) ballads, or *enanga*, are extensively described in Mulokozi (2002) and Seitel (1999).

6 This view of the relationship between folktale performance and clan practice differs from functionalist interpretations of traditional narrative. By understanding folktale performance as a practice which develops its own ethical knowledge and rhetorical power and which *usually* provides strategic support for the discursive practices of clans – practices that rationalize and govern marriage, inheritance, land tenure, and so on – one leaves open the possibility that the strategic intent of a particular folktale may be to *oppose* the ethics of clans and of other social institutions. This is relatively rare in my data, but it can be identified. A verbal art performance occurs in a social world governed in part by various discursive practices, and it often situates itself as a point of support or opposition with them. This view of the strategic relationships among discursive practices is most helpful in understanding the role of the independent heroic-ballad bards, which is discussed in Seitel 1999; a concise statement of the discourse-based socio-historical model itself can be found in Foucault 1980.

REFERENCES

Foucault, Michel. 1980. *The History of Sexuality.* Vol. I. *An Introduction.* Trans. Robert Hurly. New York: Random House.

Hanks, W.F. 1989. "Text and Textuality." *Annual Review of Anthropology* 18: 95–127.

Honko, Lauri, Ed. 2000. *Thick Corpus, Organic Variation And Textuality in Oral Translation.* Helsinki: Finnish Literature Society.

Mulokozi, Mugyabuso M. 2002. *The African Epic Controversy: Historical, Philosophical, and Aesthetic Perspectives on Epic Poetry and Performances.* Dar es Salaam: Mkuki na Nyota Publishers.

Rubanza, Y.I. 1994. *Fasihi Simulizi: Majigambo (Ebyebugo).* Dar es Salaam: University of Dar es Salaam Press.

Rutechura, Merchades Method. 2009. *The Ebyebugo Tradition among the Haya: From Pre-Colonial Times to the Present.* Saarbrücken: VDM Verlag.

Said, Edward W. 1978. "The Problem of Textuality: Two Exemplary Positions." *Critical Inquiry* 4: 673–714.

Said, Edward W. 1979. *Orientalism.* New York: Random House.

Seitel, Peter. 1999. *The Powers of Genre: Interpreting Haya Oral Literature.* New York: Oxford University Press.

CHAPTER 5   PERFORMANCE

Richard Bauman

Introduction

Sailing southward off the Pacific coast of North America after an unsuccessful attempt to discover the Northwest Passage, and seeking a sheltered harbor to repair his ship, Sir Francis Drake anchored the *Golden Hinde* off what is now Point Reyes, California in June of 1579. As recorded by Francis Fletcher, a priest on board Drake's ship,

> The next day, after our coming to anchor in the aforesaid harbour, the people of the country showed themselves, sending off a man with great expedition to us in a canoe. Who being yet but a little from the shore, and a great way from our ship, spoke to us continually as he came rowing on. And at last at a reasonable distance staying himself, he began more solemnly a long and tedious oration, after his manner: using in the delivery thereof many gestures and signs, moving his hands, turning his head and body many ways; and after his oration ended, with great show of reverence and submission returned back to shore again. (Fletcher 1854: 119; spelling modernized)

Some days later, the native inhabitants of the area – whom we now know to have been Coastal Miwok – approached a shore party from the *Golden Hinde*, whereupon

> one (appointed as their chief speaker) wearied both his hearers, and himself too, with a long and tedious oration; delivered with strange and violent gestures, his voice being extended to the uttermost strength of nature, and his words falling so thick one in the neck of another, that he could hardly fetch his breath again: as soon as he had concluded, all the rest, with a reverent bowing of their bodies (in a dreaming manner, and long producing of the same) cried *Oh*: thereby giving their consents that all was very true which he had spoken, and that they had uttered their mind by his mouth unto us … (Fletcher 1854: 122–123; spelling modernized)

This intercultural encounter, replete with imperialist resonances, has long been the focus of extended commentary by historians, both because of the early glimpses it

A Companion to Folklore, First Edition. Edited by Regina F. Bendix and Galit Hasan-Rokem.
© 2012 John Wiley & Sons, Ltd. Published 2012 John Wiley & Sons, Ltd.

affords of the indigenous inhabitants of Northern California and because of its role in shaping European imaginings of the imperial mission. Not the least interesting aspects of this fateful encounter, however, are the communicative dynamics of the initial contact with the Miwok, as seen through British eyes. First, while the European visitors had no clue *what* the Miwok speakers were talking about, they were close observers of *how* they were talking about it, perhaps all the more so because they could not understand what the speakers were saying. Of the initial visit, Fletcher remarks on the solemn key, extended length, and strange manner of delivery of the speaker's oration, marked by many physical gestures. That is to say, Fletcher and his shipmates considered that what they were witnessing was a special, marked, stylized verbal display, opaque though its referential content may have been to them. The later speech, like the first, also involved an extended disquisition and conspicuous fluency by the "chief speaker," likewise accompanied by "strange and violent gestures." This time, however, Fletcher also noted the exaggerated volume and rapid pace of the speaker's delivery, the deportment of the native audience, and their stylized evaluative response at the end of the speech. What is more, he inferred from their response a particular kind of participation structure in which the chief speaker "uttered their mind by his mouth to us," calling for ratification on their part to signal that they too were principals in an utterance they had not themselves produced.

As Fletcher and his fellows observed the Miwok speakers, then, it is the formal features, mode of delivery, and participant structure of the speeches that captured their attention, as strange, marked, unusual, the province of specially designated speakers in a species of verbal display and subject to a particular kind of evaluative response by the native audience but also open to evaluation by the British explorers themselves. All this, again, quite apart from whatever it was that the orators were talking about. In a word, Fletcher and the other British observers recognize that they are witnessing a *performance*. It is this special mode of communicative display that I will examine in this chapter.

FOUNDATIONS

The foundations of performance-oriented perspectives in folklore lie in the observations primarily of folktale scholars who departed from the library- and archive-based philological investigations that dominated folk narrative research to venture into the field to document folktales as recounted in the communities in which they were still current. These scholars were drawn understandably to the individuals who had the largest repertoires and were reputed to be the most virtuosic storytellers in their communities. In the course of their efforts, these "field collectors" were strongly impressed by the artistic skills of their star informants in recounting their stories, especially the dramaturgical devices and histrionic flourishes – the mimetic qualities – that the storytellers employed in telling their stories and that their audiences valued in listening to them. Thus, from the late nineteenth century onwards, we find in the framing matter – introductions, notes, appendices – of text collections published by field-oriented scholars vivid descriptions of the theatricality that characterized the performances of their star informants, often tinged with romantic stereotypes about how peasants or members of particular racial or ethnic groups are "natural performers," more expressive than "modern," "cultivated," urban people (Briggs and Bauman 2003).

Of the Roma storyteller, Taikon, from whom he collected approximately 250 *Märchen* plus a large number of legends and other folklore forms, the Swedish folklorist Carl-Herman Tillhagen observed, "he performs [*er spielt*] the tale more than he narrates it" (Tillhagen 1948: 260),[1] thus highlighting the mimetic (as opposed to diegetic) qualities of Taikon's performance. Enumerating the stylistic devices that Taikon employed in his "dramatic accentuation" (Tillhagen 1948: 259), Tillhagen mentions his "special liking for direct discourse," one of the most defining features of mimetic presentation, and the "abrupt chages of tense" that are characteristic of a shift into quoted speech (Tillhagen 1948: 259–260). Tillhagen's description of Taikon's repertoire of dramaturgical devices is worth quoting in full:

> For Taikon, as for most true tale tellers, the word is only *one* of the means of expression with which he shapes his tale. He narrates with gesture and with intonational modulation, with dramatic pauses and effervescent verbosity, with pantomime and solemn preaching, with laugher and with tears. In his voice the sun appears when he portrays the young Princess. Joyful images are reflected in his eyes, and his hands form airy dancing rhythms. And what a lovable old man is the King! The voice sounds like a smile, the hands stroke through the imaginary beard, the eye seizes on a majestic sovereign vision, the movements become a little bit decrepit and thus dignified. The Prince, by contrast, is young and strong. His voice is like the peal of a trumpet, his movement like spring steel. He sits erect in his tent. He swings his sword lightning-fast. He stands derisively before his worst enemy with his hands on his hips, thrusts his sword in the ground, and casts the head from the neck. And how diabolical is the witch! She is hateful, she is malicious, with the subterranean coldness of the evil and the incredible surrounding her … The voice of the storyteller slips into shrill falsetto, his eyes become nearly green with rage. (Tillhagen 1948: 262–263)

To this evocative inventory of Taikon's histrionic techniques, Tillhagen adds other formal devices that mark his artistry, as in his "choice of words. He enjoys a beautiful expressive style, alliteration is his joy, and for the musical euphony of language, he has an alert, sensitive ear" (Tillhagen 1948: 265). Still further, Tillhagen picks out the introductory formulae (e.g., "It was, and it was not. If it hadn't happened, one would not recount it"), narrative formulae (e.g., "He went one day, he went two, and on the third he arrived"), and closing formulae (e.g., "And if they haven't died, they are still living today") that Taikon employed in marking off and fashioning his narrative texts (Tillhagen 1948: 281–283). All in all, Tillhagen's account of Taikon's storytelling style, in all its histrionic and poetic richness, gives us a vivid portrait of his remarkable virtuosity as a performer (see also Lundgren and Taikon 2003). To be sure, the identification of Roma people as especially given to performance has a long history in European racial and performance ideologies (Lemon 2000).

Like Taikon, Richard M. Dorson's "number one informant," James Douglas Suggs, "did not simply tell the story but acted it out and dressed it up with sounds, gestures, and tumbling words," taking on the distinctive voices of characters in his tales and employing various forms of sound symbolism to enrich his narration (Dorson 1956: 21–22, 126; 1958: 155–156). While Suggs is the best of Dorson's narrators, both in terms of the number of tales in his repertoire and his skills as a raconteur, he is not unique among Dorson's African-American sources. Dorson notes of them all that they "not only fully utilize their oral resources but also gesticulate and even act out parts in exciting narratives. …These histrionics build up to a small performance, the tale verging onto drama or farce, and the audience rolling with laughter, exclaiming, commenting, and otherwise appreciated the efforts of the star" (Dorson 1956: 24). Here, the idiom of theatricality serves Dorson not only as a means of capturing the artistry of his sources, but also as a framework for comprehending the enhanced experience and evaluative responses of the storytellers' audience. And of course, it too accords with long-standing stereotypes of African-Americans as "natural performers" (Abrahams 1992).

THEORIZING PERFORMANCE

Evocative and suggestive thought they are, the descriptions of virtuosic storytelling in the metaphorical idiom of theatricality remain impressionistic and ancillary to the collectors' sense of their primary task, which was to publish collections of texts. Missing from the performance-oriented accounts of Tillhagen, Dorson, and their fellows is any effort at conceptual synthesis. The first systematic efforts to articulate a more synthetic notion of performance in folklore began to coalesce in the late 1960s and early 1970s as part of a more general shift of perspective beginning to take hold among ethnographically oriented folklorists from folklore as "an aggregate of things" to folklore as a "communicative process," to use the terms of one influential early formulation (Ben-Amos 1972: 9). Certainly, there were important precursors that energized and helped to shape this emergent concern with performance. To suggest only a few of the most prominent shaping influences:

- Bronislaw Malinowski's insistence on *context of situation* as an essential frame of reference for the comprehension of "narrative speech as … a mode of social action" (Malinowski 1923: 306, 313; 1965 [1935]: 4–8) and his direction of attention to indigenous genre systems as organizing frameworks for verbal performance (Malinowski 1948 [1926]);
- Milton Singer's neo-Durkheimian conception of *cultural performances* as scheduled, bounded, crafted, heightened, and participatory occasions in which culture is put on display for the reflexive contemplation of members and outsiders (Singer 1955, 1958);
- Roman Jakobson's model of a *communicative event*, a synthesis and elaboration of prewar Prague School frameworks for comprehending the multifunctionality of verbal expression and the place of poetic language among those multiple functions (Jakobson 1960);
- Melville Jacobs' conception of *style*, in the Boasian tradition, as a system of formal features that make up the "aesthetic design" of folklore forms in use, comprehending both compositional and performative aspects of cultural expression (Jacobs 1959);
- Milman Parry and Albert Lord's theory of *oral-formulaic composition* as a means of comprehending the radical integration of cultural tradition and individual creativity in the recognition of "Singing, performing, composing [as] facets of the same act" (Lord 1960: 13);

◙   William Hugh Jansen's direction of folklorists' attention to "that dual but inseparable process of *performance* and *reception*" in the recognition that any item of
folklore depends for its very existence on someone "to 'do' that piece of folklore"
for "an auditor" or "a group of auditors" (Jansen 1957: 112, emphasis added).

The conception of performance as the "doing" of folklore gained currency in the
early 1970s as part of the nascent turn to performance I mentioned above. In the
Introduction to *Toward New Perspectives in Folklore* (Paredes and Bauman 1972), a
collection of essays often credited as establishing the framework for the turn to
performance in folklore (Brenneis 1993; Shuman and Briggs 1993), I identified as
one of the principal thrusts of the volume "a full-scale and highly self-conscious
reorientation from the traditional focus upon folklore as "item", the things of folklore,
to a conceptualization of folklore as "event" – the doing of folklore. In particular,
there is an emphasis upon performance as an organizing principle" (Bauman 1972a: v).
While the idiom of "doing" in this charter statement might seem to echo Jansen's
framing of performance as "doing," the larger thrust of the argument marks a major
shift. Where Jansen still assigns primacy to the folklore items that make up the
aggregate textual corpus of folklore, with performance as a secondary supplement,
the contributors to this new collection (especially Dan Ben-Amos, Roger D. Abrahams,
Richard Bauman, Dell Hymes, Dennis Tedlock) were advocating a wholesale
reconceptualization of the field, with performance, as a species of situated
communicative practice, as the organizing focus.

   This conception of performance was shaped most immediately by two convergent
intellectual currents, one literary, the other anthropological. Kenneth Burke's highly
productive notion of "literature as equipment for living," his "dramatistic pentad"
(act, scene, agent, agency, purpose), and his penetrating insight into the power of
significant form to elicit the participative engagement of audiences had, and continues
to have, an energizing influence on folklorists attuned to the poetics of verbal folklore
while recognizing at the same time the profoundly social nature and rhetorical efficacy
of poetic forms in use (Burke 1941, 1968, 1969). Burke's magisterial intellectual
synthesis also had a formative influence on the ethnography of speaking, a subfield of
linguistic anthropology that took shape in the period from the early 1960s to the mid-
1970s with the active participation of anthropologically oriented folklorists (Bauman
and Sherzer 1989 [1974]; Hymes 1972). The ethnography of speaking centers on the
premise that social life is discursively constituted, produced and reproduced by
situated acts of communication that are cross-culturally variable and to be discovered
through ethnographic investigation. Ethnographers of speaking seek to elucidate the
relationships linking the communal and individual repertoires of discursive means, the
formal, functional, contextual, and ideological orienting frameworks for discursive
practice, and the goals and competencies of participants in the production, reception,
and circulation of discourse.

   In some charter formulations of the ethnography of speaking, performance serves
as one of the master terms. For example, after outlining the constituent elements of
the program, as above, the editors of an influential stocktaking volume of case studies
in the ethnography of speaking suggest that "The nexus of all the factors we have
outlined is performance," and go on to urge that "The task of the ethnographer of
speaking ... is to identify and analyze the dynamic interrelationships among the

elements that go to make up performance" (Bauman and Sherzer 1989: 7). *Mutatis mutandis,* this sense of performance as situated discursive practice – for folklorists, the situated use of folklore in the conduct and accomplishment of social life and the production of cultural meaning – retains its currency and productivity to this day.

At the same time that the general conception of performance as practice was gaining traction in the shared territory between folklore and linguistic anthropology, a more restricted sense of the term began to take shape as well. The broad purview of the ethnography of speaking extended to all verbal discourse, from the most routinized and quotidian to the most elaborated and complex, and the ethnography of communication, a more semiotically comprehensive perspective founded on an overarching understanding of society and culture as communicatively constituted, encompassed an even more global domain. For folklorists motivated by the long-standing interest within the broader field in oral poetics, whether under the rubric of "oral literature," "verbal art," "folk literature," or any other, part of the attraction of performance as a concept lay in its implication of artfulness, virtuosity, affecting power, and the intensification and enhancement of experience. Accordingly, some folklorists who were energized by the intellectual program of the ethnography of speaking turned their efforts toward articulating a conception of verbal performance as a special, artful way of speaking, recognizing both its continuities and discontinuities with all other ways of speaking (Abrahams 1972; Bauman 1972b, 1977; Ben-Amos 1972). The line of inquiry that developed out of those efforts has proven to be a durable and productive intellectual enterprise, not only in folklore and linguistic anthropology but in a number of adjacent disciplines as well: history, religious studies, literature, speech communication, media studies, education, and more.

What does this approach to performance as a special, marked mode of communicative practice look like? There are many possible points of entry into the problem, but the brief examples with which I opened this chapter will serve well as a point of departure. Consider again the features that captured the attention of Drake's crew in their encounters with the "chief speakers" of the Miwok, or those that impressed Tillhagen and Dorson in the presentational style of their star informants. The capacity of these various features and devices to capture the attention of the onlookers, to be perceived as uncommon or unusual, to foreground the way in which the act of expression is accomplished, allows them to serve, in effect, as indicators that whatever other communicative business is being accomplished, the speaker is engaged in a special mode of communicative display, a *performance.* That is to say, these attention-getting elements serve a metapragmatic function. In linguistic analysis, pragmatics focuses attention on the situated use of language, that is, on discourse. Metapragmatics, in turn, pertains to those aspects of any given discursive act that refer reflexively, either explicitly or indirectly, to the pragmatic functioning of that act (Silverstein 1993). The features that draw the attention of our observers, then, serve as metapragmatic signals that alert co-participants that the speaker, as performer, is taking responsibility for a display of communicative competence, subject to evaluation for the virtuosic skill, communicative efficacy, and affecting power with which the act of expression is carried out. By invoking this interpretive frame, the performer is at the same time eliciting the participative engagement of co-participants, casting them as an audience, with license to regard the act of display with heightened intensity and inviting them to evaluate how skillfully and effectively it is accomplished.

Consider, for example, the "orations" delivered to the crew of the *Golden Hinde*. Fletcher notes the conspicuous length of these performances and the hyperfluency that marks their delivery. Extended, monologic holding of the floor and rapid, continuous, unbroken delivery both serve well to set off the performer from other participants and to differentiate the performance from a less foregrounded, more turn-taking mode of speech exchange. The extended length and hyperfluent delivery of these orations are further augmented by loud volume and "strange gestures" that distinguish Miwok oratory from their other ways of speaking. By the time the English visitors encounter the Miwok at "a great assembly" on shore, they are able to distinguish the role of the "chief speaker," that is, the incumbent of a special speaking role singled out for his skill in the production of oratory as a genre, marked by the formal features that Fletcher describes. Moreover, the performance role of chief speaker is bound up in a structure of participation that includes the Miwok members of the audience, who offer in unison a ritualized evaluative response to the speech, affirming at the same time their own commitment to the speaker's message. Fletcher's brief descriptions, then, present us with an associational cluster of pragmatic and metapragmatic features – event structure, formal devices, genre, participant roles and relationships – any one of which may serve conventionally to invoke the performance frame in a particular community, but whose co-occurrence makes it abundantly clear that Fletcher and his shipmates are witnessing a performance.

Tillhagen's and Dorson's accounts of the theatricality that mark the storytelling of their star informants offer a complementary inventory of keys to performance, those metasignals that alert co-participants to interpret the act of expression as performance (Bauman 1977: 15–24; Goffman 1974: 43–44). Like the Miwok orators, Taikon's "effervescent verbosity" and Suggs's "tumbling words" display degrees of hyperfluency that display the virtuosity of skilled performers. Likewise, the gestures, bodily orientations, and facial expressions call attention to themselves and heighten the affective intensity of their performances. These embodied aspects of performance commonly work in tandem with a range of oral devices to enhance the storytellers' characterization of the dramatis personae that populate their tales: direct discourse, the taking on of voices by means of the manipulation of pitch, intonation, timbre, and other suprasegmental features. Suggs further ornaments his narration with ideophones and other forms of sound symbolism, Taikon with alliteration and grammatical parallelism, as in "It was and it was not" or "He went one day, he went two ..." (Tillhagen 1948: 281, 284). The former, one of Taikon's introductory formulae employed to open the narration of a *Märchen*, is a functional complement to other formulae that indicate the end of the story. Special formulae of this kind may themselves serve as keys to performance, signaling to the audience that a performance is about to commence or has been brought to a close, bounding off, in effect, that stretch of generically organized discourse for which the speaker assumes responsibility for a virtuosic display.

Our brief set of examples – Coastal Miwok, Swedish Roma, African American – thus reveal a diverse inventory of formal devices, generic features, and pragmatic factors that may serve to key the performance frame. Some, like hyperfluency or vivid gestures, occur in all three cases, suggesting the possibility that certain metapragmatic means of invoking the performance frame may find widespread use among the world's peoples (others might include a high quotient of figurative language, special registers, or appeals to tradition, for example (Bauman 1977: 15–24), while others, such as ideophones, appear to be of more limited distribution (Webster 2008: 343–346). It must be emphasized, though, as explicitly and emphatically as possible, that there can be no universal checklist of keys to performance. Rather, the specific inventories of communicative means that may serve as keys to performance in a given community are to be discovered ethnographically, not assumed a priori. Each community will have its own metapragmatic orienting frameworks by which an individual may signal to an audience, "This is performance. I'm on! I invite you to watch and listen closely and I will impress you, entertain you, move you. I invite you as well to judge just how skillful, effective, and moving a display I can accomplish."

The engagement of an audience is a necessary constituent of performance. Indeed, performance must be viewed as a joint achievement of performer and audience (Barber 1997; Duranti and Brenneis 1986). From the vantage point of the audience, the keying of the performance frame is an invitation to regard the act of expression with special intensity and to evaluate it for the relative skill, correctness, appropriateness, or effectiveness with which it is accomplished. The standards and terms of evaluation will vary from community to community, person to person, situation to situation. They may be explicit ("That's a good one!" or "tedious"), or implicit ("the audience rolling with laughter") in the responses of audience members. At times, the performer himself or herself may offer an evaluation, in an effort to sway the audience (Coplan 1994: 201–202).

Performance is an act of stancetaking, in the parlance of sociolinguistics (Jaffe 2009). That is, the performer, by invoking the performance frame, takes up a particular position, or alignment, to his or her act of expression, the assumption of responsibility for a display of communicative skill and efficacy. Stancetaking, though, is a reciprocal act. By entering into performance, the performer inevitably invokes the complementary stance of audience member, inviting co-participants to assume an alignment to the performance that demands an evaluative response and perhaps more, such as verbal acknowledgment, commentary, encouragement, or ratification (Basso 1985: 15–18; Finnegan 1967: 68–69; Finnegan 2007: 45; Urban 1986), in what amounts to co-construction of the performance. Performance is in this respect heavily stance-saturated: in its fullest manifestations, it makes positioning all but obligatory. I say "in its *fullest* sense" and "all *but* obligatory," though, because performance is not an all-or-nothing phenomenon. Like any other frame, performance is labile, susceptible to being re-keyed, hedged, or otherwise rendered ambiguous, raising the tacit question, "is this performance?"

As I noted earlier in the chapter, not every "doing" of an item of folklore is necessarily a performance in the more marked sense of the term we are now exploring. Although the expectation of performance may be high for a particular item or genre or event or individual, other potential frames may provide for alternative stances, or what Goffman would call different footings (1981: 128). A *Märchen*, for example, or an oration, or any other type of utterance that carries a high expectation for performance, may alternatively be reported, demonstrated, imitated, rehearsed, relayed, translated, quoted, or summarized as opposed to performed (Bauman 2004: 128–158; Goffman 1974: 40–82; Hymes 1975a; Sherzer 1983: 18–20). Likewise, it may be hedged, as when a narrator or public speaker is willing to narrate a story or give a speech for which performance is the normative presentational mode, but without feeling able, qualified, authorized, or willing to assume responsibility for full, unqualified performance (Bauman 2004: 109–127). Note also that a speaker can oscillate in an out of performance, "breaking through" (Hymes 1975a) into performance for stretches of a story, say, that he feels competent to perform, but retreating into report, for example, when he does not feel sufficiently knowledgeable, able, or confident to manage a performance. By the same token, a participant impelled toward the stance of audience member might wish to decline the honor, either by withdrawing from the interaction or by taking on the alternative participant role of mere observer or onlooker, free of demands of evaluation.

Reluctance to assume – or to appear to assume – the mantle of the performer should not be surprising, as performance is by its very nature fraught with risk (Yankah 1985): of failure, of being adjudged incompetent, inauthentic, ineligible, or inappropriately forward. The range of "faultables" (Goffman 1981: 203–225) attendant upon performance will vary from one community to another, but there will always be a potential of failure. On the one hand, to perform is to seek the limelight, to claim special skill, to elicit the participative energies of other participants. In some of the world's societies, especially those with an egalitarian ethos, putting oneself forward is a moral transgression, which might induce some to avoid performance and others to issue a ritualized disclaimer of performance before actually performing (Darnell 1989: 325). Or consider the widespread problem that shadows female performers in many societies, cast simultaneously as objects of desire and as morally compromised (Kapchan 1996; Sawin 2002), and thus at risk of unwanted sexual attention or moral condemnation if they dare to perform. Still further, performances, especially in ritual settings, risk failure insofar as they may not achieve the social ends for which they are undertaken, such as the successful negotiation of bride-price or the curing of an ailing patient (Keane 1997; Keenan 1973; Schieffelin 1985, 1996).

These dynamics of stance-taking, risk, ideology, access to participation, and the like alert us to the politics as well as the poetics of performance. For heuristic purposes, we may identify three principal dimensions of power in performance: control over the organization and production of performance; control over the meaning and interpretation of performance; and control over the ends or outcomes of performance. The politics of performance, then, pertains to the ways in which these aspects of power are claimed, allocated, authorized, negotiated, contested. A concern with power in performance has been part of performance-oriented approaches from their inception (Abrahams 1972; Bauman 2002; Paredes 1993 [1971]) and will re-surface at salient points in what follows.

TEXT AND CONTEXT IN PERFORMANCE

The philological foundations of folklore and the text-historical orientation of its historically most prominent method have made the folklore text the dominant unit of analysis within the field (Fine 1984). Strikingly, however, text and textuality, as concepts, have seldom been the focus of theoretical or critical attention on the part of folklorists, until very recently. The folklore text has been a given, an objectified token of a generic or thematic type that is recognized a priori as part of the folklore canon – Märchen, legend, myth, Schwank, epic, ballad, riddle, proverb, charm, and so on – according to criteria of traditionality, anonymity, social distribution, or some other non-textual factor. The closest the field has come to considerations of textuality lies in the enumeration of formal features that define or characterize particular genres, such as the specification of meter, verse length, internal segmentation, and rhyme schemes of the *décima* or the metrical structure of the Serbo-Croatian epic line.

In the development of performance-oriented perspectives, however, the recognition that many of the same formal devices and patterning principles that enter into certain genre definitions also commonly serve as keys to performance has encouraged the development of a new perspective on the text, not as an autonomous, traditional, literary artifact but as the emergent product of situated communicative practice, a discursive achievement. The communicative resources that key performance, that is, that frame the performer's display of virtuosity, also give form to the performer's act of expression and shape it as a text: bounded off to a degree from its discursive surround, internally cohesive, semantically meaningful.

Certainly, given the predisposition of folklorists toward traditionality, much of the compositional process by which items of folklore are endowed with their shape as texts may occur long before a given iteration of it in performance. Nevertheless, from the vantage point of performance as a mode of communicative practice, each performer must give shape to the utterance anew and mark it as performance in the real-time unfolding of actual events. Textuality thus becomes not merely the a priori packaging of an oft-repeated piece of oral literature, but a discursive accomplishment, the practical process of rendering, even if reproducing, the utterance as a text. This is the process of *entextualization* (Barber 2003; Bauman and Briggs 1990; Silverstein and Urban 1996a).

One of the most salient formative influences in the process of entextualization is *genre*, part of the conceptual bedrock of folklore. Viewed in performance-centered terms, genre becomes a socially constituted orienting framework for the production, reception, and circulation of particular orders of texts (Bauman 2004: 3–8; Briggs and Bauman 1992; Hanks 1987). As such, genres represent schemata that guide the formal regimentation of utterances, routinized constellations of systemically related co-occurrent formal features and structures. At the same time, however, genres have pragmatic and thematic correlates as well, providing conventionalized guidelines for dealing with recurrent communicative exigencies (Luckmann 1995), sets of roles and relationships by which participants are aligned to one another (Hanks 1996; Irvine 1996), vehicles for encoding and expressing particular orders of knowledge and experience. Entextualization is the process by which these formal, thematic, and pragmatic relations are called into play in the formation of texts. When a text is aligned to a given genre, the process by which it is produced and interpreted is mediated through its intertextual relationship with prior texts. The invocation of generic framing devices such as "*Voy a cantar estos versos*" or "Bunday!" carry with them sets of expectations concerning the further unfolding of the text, indexing other texts initiated by such opening formulae. "*Voy a cantar estos versos*" anticipates the singing of a *corrido*, the ballad form of Greater Mexico (Paredes 1976: 83); "Bunday!" marks the opening of a Bahamian "old-story" performance (Crowley 1966: 19–22). These expectations thus constitute a framework for entextualization.

We may observe the process of entextualization at work in the sales pitch, or *pregón*, of a patent-medicine vendor I recorded (January 14, 1986) in a weekly open-air market in San Miguel de Allende, Gto., Mexico. The artfulness of commercial talkers like pitchmen, auctioneers, street-vendors, carnival barkers, and the like is widely recognized, and their talk is often enjoyed as much for its own sake as for its practical role in the sale of commodities (Bauman 2004: 58–81; Dargan and Zeitlin 1983; Kapchan 1996). This vendor was unquestionably engaged in such a display of verbal virtuosity in the service of promoting and selling his remedies. To begin his pitch, he mounted a small wooden platform, faced the space along which shoppers were passing, and began to speak in a loud, declamatory fashion, effecting a marked shift in the prevailing discursive organization of the market-space he occupied. I was among those passing by, and the vendor's performance captured me and others, quickly forming a small crowd, an audience, some of us interested in his medicine, others simply stopping for a bit to enjoy the show. The vendor's hyperfluent speech was clearly not fixed, but a few minutes' listening revealed its emergent textuality, the ways in which he knit his pitch together. The following is an excerpt from the extended whole. I have formatted the transcript to foreground certain formal features of the text. This mode of transcription, designed to lay bare on the printed page significant aspects of formal organization that regiment the performance, follows the core principal of ethnopoetics that the editing of oral performances for publication should take into account the poetic organization of the performed text (Blommaert 2006; Hymes 1981; Sherzer and Woodbury 1987; Tedlock 1983).

1 Para que saque, expulse los parásitos, señor,	Because it draws out, expels the parasites, sir,
2 para las lombrices,	for threadworms,
3 para la solitaria, las amibas, los oxiuros,	for the tapeworm, the amoebas, the pinworms,
4 cuando duele el estómago,	when you have a stomach ache,
5 cuando haya vómito o diarrea	when there is vomiting or diarrhea
6 hervido y tomadito,	boiled and drunk in a small amount
7 llega a sacar precisamente gas estomacales	it suffices to draw out precisely stomach gas,
8 quitar agruras	relieve acidity,
9 asedías la mala digestión.	sieges of indigestion.
10 Para que limpie el estómago,	Because it cleanses the stomach,
11 lave los intestinos,	washes the intestines,
12 ayude al crecimiento,	aids in growth,
13 al desarrollo.	in development.
14 Lombrices, solitarias, amibas,	Threadworms, tapeworms, amoebas,
15 oxiuros, alfilerillo,	pinworms, tobacco borers,
16 tenia, bicho, gusanillo.	tapeworm, bug, small worm.
17 Señoras, señor,	Ladies, sir,
18 esto le sirve para que expulse las lombrices.	this will help you because it expels the threadworms.
19 Le regalo tantito, ándele.	I give you a small bit, come on.
20 En una tacita de agua,	In a small cup of water,
21 taza de agua,	cup of water,
22 póngalo a hervir,	set it to boil,
23 ya hirvió lo cuela lo endulza	once it has boiled strain it, sweeten it,
24 y lo da a tomar en ayunas.	and give it to drink on an empty stomach.
25 Huélalo.	Smell it.
26 Huele a menta como anís.	It smells like mint, like anise.

The transcript reveals a number of additional keys to performance, beyond the raised platform, the continuous, extended holding of the floor, the spatial organization of participation. The devices to which I would call attention include the segmentation of the utterance into measured, cadenced lines marked by breath pauses and syntactic structures, grammatical parallelism, and alliteration (both present, for example, in *Para que limpie el estomago/lave los intestinos* (lines 10–11)). As I suggested earlier, however, these and other formal features and devices serve to knit the utterance together into a tightly cohesive network of interrelationships. Lexical repetition, including grammatical variants of the same word (as in the replaying of the catalog of internal parasites (lines 2–3, 14–16) or *saque/sacar* (lines 1, 7)), grammatical parallelism (e.g., *cuando duele el estómago/cuando haya vómito o diarrea* (lines 4–5); *En una tacita de agua/taza de agua* (lines 20–21)), the cumulation of measured lines, all serve to bind the passage together into a formally cohesive and semantically coherent textual package. These formal patterns, as Kenneth Burke has suggested (Burke 1968 (1931): 124, 140–141), set up patterns of anticipation and fulfillment that elicit the participatory engagement of the vendor's audience, catching them up in the formal regimentation of his sales pitch. What is especially significant about Burke's insight is that it establishes a functional linkage between poetic form and rhetorical or perlocutionary efficacy. That is to say, as the consumer in the market is caught up in the poetic patterning of the calls, he or she becomes receptive to the sales pitch of the vendor and is that much more likely to buy. This nexus of form and function represents a significant aspect of the power of performance.

A look at a second passage, produced about 15 minutes after the first, reveals further dimensions of interrelationship:

1 Le limpia el estómago,	It will cleanse your stomach,
2 y le lava los intestinos.	and wash your intestines.
3 Le regalo,	I give it to you,
4 para qué saque y expulse las lombrices,	because it draws out and expels the threadworms,
5 la solitaria,	the tapeworm,
6 las amibas,	the amoebas,
7 los oxiuros.	the pinworms.
8 Le limpia el estómago,	It will cleanse the stomach,
9 le lava los intestinos,	and wash the intestines,
10 y le ayuda al crecimiento.	and aid you in growth.
11 Arrímese, señorita, para acá.	Come closer, ma'am, over here.
12 Cuando llegue a haber un vómito,	When vomiting begins,
13 una diarrea,	diarrhea,
14 un cólico,	colic,
15 un dolor de estómgao.	stomach ache.
16 Huélalo.	Smell it.
17 Huele coma a menta,	Smells like mint,
18 a anís,	like anise,
19 no amarga,	it isn't bitter,
20 no sabe feo.	it doesn't taste bad.
21 Le va a limpiar el estómago,	It will cleanse your stomach.
22 le ayuda al crecimiento,	aid you with growth,
23 al desarrollo,	with development,
24 matando los animales.	killing the animals.

This passage continues to key the vendor's pitch as performance, and it also exhibits similar mechanisms of internal cohesion to those we perceived in the first excerpt. In addition, however, it displays strong ties of cohesion with the earlier passage, utilizing the same lexical sets (again, see the catalog of parasites (lines 4–7)), closely parallel lines (*Le limpia el estómago/y le lava los intestinos* (lines 8–9); *le ayuda al crecimiento/ al desarrollo* (lines 22–23); *Huele coma a menta/a anís* (lines 17–18)), and so on. These correspondences extend the web of textuality across considerably larger stretches of the vendor's pitch. And indeed, these are only two of many such interrelated passages. The construction of these unifying links that knit the pitchman's extended performance together is the emergent process of entextualization.

Now, at the same time that our vendor was engaged in entextualizing his pitch, he was also *contextualizing* it, aligning it, as part of the entextualization process, to salient features of the phenomenal world. Context has been identified as a core concern of performance-oriented perspectives from their inception, as witness Richard Dorson's early application of the label "contextual" to the then-nascent approach (Dorson 1972: 45–47). To be sure, folklore has always been a contexualist enterprise, insofar as folklorists have viewed folklore texts in relation to something else, though to *what* else has varied: cognate texts, particular social formations, the *Volksgeist* of a people, a stage of evolutionary development, and so on. What was new about the contextual concerns of performance-oriented folklorists was a concentrated focus on *situational contexts of use*, the locally defined situations, events, scenes in which folklore forms and practices serve as "equipment for living" (Burke 1941: 293–304) resources for the conduct of social life. Initially, the constituents and dynamics of such communicative events, as in Jakobson's influential model (Jakobson 1960), were conceived as exerting a formative influence on the texts for which they were construed as context, an approach, in effect, from the outside in, in which the occurrence of the events – scenes of male or female sociability, ceremonial occasions, children's play events, and the like – was presupposed, as part of the cultural way of life that shaped the texts. This approach had – and continues to have – a certain descriptive utility. In a full description, one might well want to know about the location, configuration, political economy, social organization, and lots of other things concerning the weekly open-air market in which our medicine vendor hawks his remedies.

From the vantage point of communicative practice, however, such an approach has a major shortcoming: it fails to take direct account of which of the myriad elements in the contextual surround are salient to the performer, as points of orientation in the emergent fashioning of the performance (Bauman 1986; Bauman and Briggs 1990; Briggs 1988, 1993). How does the performer anchor his or her performance in the world, tying the emergent text, in its process of production, to other salient phenomena? To ask this question is to shift one's attention from context as presupposed to *contextualization* as an aspect of communicative practice, rather than as "digression" from what is construed as the essential text, the perduring traditional narrative that can be abstracted from any anchoring in specific situations of performance (Başgöz 1986; Georges 1981). In the classical philological tradition of folklore, contextualization cues were systematically eliminated from published texts, as extraneous to the traditional core of a narrative, whereas they are absolutely central to performance-oriented conceptions of text and textuality. Returning to our pitchman in the San

Miguel Tuesday market, we may discern the contextualizing work that he undertakes in the course of selling his wares. I will draw examples from three of the many orders of contextualization that emerge in the course of his performance.

Recalling the various keying devices by which the vendor signals to his audience "this is performance," consider the following two brief passages from the beginning of his pitch:

1 Le regalo, señora.	I give it to you, ma'am.
2 Mire.	Look.
3 Venga güerita,	Come, blondie,
4 venga señor,	come, sir,
5 camine, le regalo,	go, I give it to you,
6 ándele.	come on.
7 Ustedes que van al campo.	You who go to the countryside.
8 Venga, señor.	Come, sir.

1 Venga, por favor.	Come, please.
2 Venga para acá.	Come over here.
3 Venga para acá, mire.	Come over here, look.
4 Andele,	Come on.
5 arrímese.	move closer.

In the first excerpt, the vendor is calling out to passers-by in the market to come over to his space, to join, actually, to constitute, his audience. A performer needs an audience, as a vendor needs customers. Here, our pitchman calls both into being, actively recruiting his audience and his potential customers. In the second excerpt, still in the service of these ends, the pitchman holds up a small packet of his medicine and offers it as a gift, a free sample, that establishes a relationship of exchange, and attempts to entice specific individuals with whom he has made eye contact to approach his space. But he also employs a more broadcast strategy, calling in all those within earshot who go out into the countryside where they might pick up the parasites his remedy counteracts. The Tuesday market in San Miguel is heavily frequented by agricultural workers and their families from the farms and ranches in the surrounding area, so this aspect of the vendor's address casts a wide net. Our vendor is thus creating, by means of his pitch, the very situational context in which his performance unfolds, its interpersonal and spatial alignments, its participant roles, its dual exchange relationships of goods and words. The situational context is as much a discursive accomplishment as the text that calls it into play – entextualization and contextualization are part of an integrated, unified process (Bauman and Briggs 1990; Silverstein and Urban 1996a).

The process of contextualization need not be confined to the scene immediately at hand. Indeed, the dynamics of contextualization open up to us the ways in which performances can transcend the boundaries of the individual performance event. At the same time that our pitchman works to produce the situational context of his sales pitch and to locate himself at center stage, he is also at pains to separate himself from the San Miguel Tuesday market and align himself to a world that is outside the here and now of his performance. At numerous points in the course of his pitch, he invokes the distant context of the botanical laboratory in Mexico City that produces his miraculous remedies and of which he is an agent. For example, pointing to a printed sign propped up before him with the name and address of the botanical center, he says,

1 Yo vengo de aquí:	I come from here:
2 Centro Botánico Azteca,	Aztec Botanical Center
3 en México Distrito Federal.	in the Federal District of Mexico.
4 Voy de paso,	I am passing through,
5 no estoy cada ocho días.	I'm not here every week.
6 Soy agente vendedor	I am sales agent
7 del centro botánico más grande	of the largest botanical center
8 de la ciudad de México.	in Mexico City.

By aligning himself to a (quasi-)scientific laboratory in the distant, modern, national capital, the source of prestige and authority, he accrues that prestige and authority to himself, all the more so in a provincial, old-fashioned, open market with a predominantly working-class and peasant clientele. He goes on to imply that he is but loosely coupled to the provincial market that is the immediate site of his performance, but which is overshadowed by the broader context to which he has just connected himself. He does so not only to claim authority for his medical and pharmaceutical knowledge and control the audience's interpretation of his claims, but also as part of a sales strategy to counter the hesitation of those who might persuade themselves that they can put off purchasing his remedy until the next weekly market. "I'm just passing through," he says, in effect, "and may not be here next week. I operate in a bigger world, far from this peripheral place in which we find ourselves. So you'd better buy now."

A third dimension of contextualization – there are many more – involves the pitchman's alignment of his artful words to the words of others, both present and absent. At a number of points in his sales pitch, the vendor commandeers the voices of virtual interlocutors in order to give voice to possible points of resistance to his claims so that he can contain and refute them on his own terms. If, in his personations (Coleman 2004; Tannen 2007:102–132), he can come close to voicing whatever doubts or reservations his potential customers may harbor, he has preempted the grounds of their resistance and asserted his own control over the situation. This rhetorical strategy is, in fact, a generic feature of the *pregón*, at least in Central Mexico. Interestingly, most such constructed dialogues are built around a generic, typified other who represents an amalgam of doubters merged into one articulating voice to which our pitchman can respond. For instance, to counter the hypothetical argument against using his remedy that the internal parasites will be eliminated anyway, in the natural course of things, he says,

1 Hay personas que andan echando así,	There are people who go along expelling [the parasites] like this,
2 pedacito por pedacito,	piece by piece,
3 y sabe qué dicen?	and you know what they say?
4 "Ya pa que me curo,	"So why should I doctor myself,
5 ah solito los echo."	ah, they are eliminated by themselves."
6 Dice un dicho, y dice bien:	A proverb says, and says well:
7 "Cómo estarán los infiernos	"What must hell be like
8 que hasta los diablos se salen."	that even the devils are leaving?"

In this passage, note, the vendor has added to the voice of his constructed interlocutor and his own framing words a third, collective voice in the form of the traditional proverb, "What must hell be like that even the devils are leaving?" By drawing on the traditional authority encoded in the proverb, and by adding his own approving metacommentary – "*y dice bien*" – he counters effectively the argument raised by his virtual interlocutor. To apply a proverb to a situation is a powerful means of controlling what it means, why it matters, and what to do about it.

The vendor's artful incorporation of the proverb into his sales pitch establishes an intertextual relationship between them, a dialogue of genres (Bauman 2004; Stoeltje 2009). The overall sales pitch, or *pregón*, is an extended, improvised, cohesive argument for the efficacy of the vendor's remedy, drawing its authority from rational appeals to science. The proverb is a highly condensed, ready-made metaphorical expression, carrying the traditional authority of collective wisdom. By contextualizing his own words vis-à-vis the collective expression of the proverb, a process that includes naming and evaluating the "*dicho*" in the quotative frame and thus priming the audience for the shape and weight of the argument to come, our vendor skillfully enhances the rhetorical power of his performance.

In broader scope, the comparative analysis of folkloric performance reveals traditionalization, the drawing of explicit or implicit links in the course of performance to antecedent performances, like our vendor's proverb, to be a common mode of contextualizing – and, of course, recontextualizing – practice (Bauman 2004: 25–28; 146–149; Foley 1995; Hymes 1975b: 354; Jackson 2003: 114, 278–279; Jackson 2008). One motivation for a performer to forge traditionalizing links to past performances is to establish an authoritative claim to a particular expressive form. Jón Norðmann, an Icelandic storyteller, closes a performance of a legend concerning Páll Skaldi, a nineteenth-century poet whose verses had magical powers, with the assertion "Now Gudrun, his daughter, told my father this story." By invoking this authorizing chain of transmission, Mr Norðmann constructed for himself a kind of expressive genealogy that ties his ongoing performance directly to the source of the story in Páll's improvisation of a magical poem and subsequent narrative performances by Páll's daughter and his own father. His warrant to perform the story himself is thus secured (Bauman 2004: 25–28).

Or consider the common contextualizing practice among the Limba people of Sierra Leone of framing the performance of a *mbɔrɔ* ('story'; lit. 'old thing') as a reiteration of a tale that was earlier recounted to the teller, heard, perhaps "from the old people" (Finnegan 1967: 124, 240). Here is a sampling of the ways such a relational orientation may be expressed: "Since I heard that story, I told it" (Finnegan 1967: 137); "Since I heard that story... I had to tell it to you" (Finnegan 1967: 183); "Since I heard that story ... I tell it this morning" (Finnegan 1967: 244). Such intertextual alignment of a performance to antecedent instances of production and reception acknowledges a dimension of accountability in Limba storytelling performance: to hear a story is to incur the responsibility of telling it yourself. Each traditionalizing performance, then, "carries it forward" (Finnegan 1967: 102) to projected retellings as well as backward to antecedent ones. Indeed, all performances do so. If performance rests on an assumption of responsibility to an audience for a display of communicative skill and efficacy, it may also include other dimensions of responsibility as well. In the process, for the Limba, acknowledgment of this responsibility becomes one of the keys to the performance of the *mbɔrɔ* as a genre.

A more implicit form of traditionalization consists in the use in performance of a linguistic register that is culturally identified as the speech of the ancestors. In Indonesia, for example, this register is a ritual style that is marked by canonical parallelism (Bowen 1991; Fox 1989; Keane 1997; Kuipers 1990). A similar traditionalizing effect may be accomplished through the use of one of a set of genres classified as "the talk of the elders of bygone days," as in the Mexicano communities of Northern New Mexico (Briggs 1988: 59).

I close with one more excerpt from a sales pitch at the San Miguel Tuesday market, this time from the performance of a vendor selling Cannon Mills pantyhose (December 24, 1985), a bit of an upscale item for the predominantly working-class clientele of this market and thus requiring especially engaging and persuasive talk (Bauman 2004: 67–74). This vendor is a prototypical *merolico*, a market vendor who can sell anything that comes to hand; his wares will vary from market to market and week to week (Haviland 2009: 22–24). Pantyhose is simply what he got hold of to sell on the Tuesday that I recorded him.

1 Vale la pena.	It's worth it.
2 Vea usted las medias de categoria.	Examine the classy stockings.
3 Cannon Mills,	Cannon Mills,
4 Cannon Mills.	Cannon Mills.
5 How many? I got it.	[How many? I got it.
6 Too muche, too muche.	Too much, too much.
7 Panty hose,	Panty hose,]
8 la Cannon Mills,	the Cannon Mills,
9 Cannon Mills,	Cannon Mills,
10 para la calidad Cannon,	for the Cannon quality,
11 calidad Cannon Mills.	Cannon Mills quality.
12 Sabemos de antemano	We know to begin with
13 que una mujer sin medias	that a woman without stockings
14 es como un hombre sin calzones.	is like a man without underpants.
15 Vea usted las medias de Cannon.	Examine the Cannon stockings.
16 [Customer]: Y esto?	[Customer]:And this?
17 Mil pesos, nada mas, señora.	A thousand pesos, no more, ma'am.
18 Cannon Mills,	Cannon Mills,
19 la Cannon Mills.	the Cannon Mills.
20 Señora, vea usted,	Ma'am, examine,
21 que se atoro con la canasta,	whether it got snagged by the basket,
22 con la bolsa, no importa.	by the bag, it doesn't matter.
23 Fibra de vidrio Galilei,	Galileo fiberglass,
24 la versatil magia de la nueva ola,	the versatile magic of the new wave,
25 vea usted.	examine.
26 Más elástica y más resistente	More elastic and more resistant
27 que qualquier media.	than any stocking.
28 Vale la pena.	It's worth it.

First, if we examine this brief excerpt from a much longer, continuous pitch against the earlier passages from our medicine vendor, we can discern more clearly the defining features of the sales pitch as a genre. In formal terms, it is *continuous*, extendable for as long as there are potential customers to buy; *measured*, that is, segmeted into relatively short lines by breath pauses and syntactic structures;

formulaic, insofar as it depends heavily upon ready-made verbal units that recur frequently in the course of the utterance; *repetitive*, not only with regard to the recycling of formulas, but also in its frequent recourse to grammatical parallelism (repetition with systematic variation); and *incorporative*, encapsulating within the overall pitch other voices and other genres, such as *dichos* (proverbs and other aphoristic sayings: "*Sabemos de antemano/que una mujer sin medias/es como un hombre sin calzones*"). Thematically, the sales pitch revolves around the description of the product(s) for sale and their salient, desirable qualities. And pragmatically, the sales pitch is designed to enhance fluency, elicit the participative engagement of the audience/customers through the appeal of form and the forging of ties of identification with the product based on one or another of its purportedly desirable qualities (here durability, cachet of prestige, leading-edge materials, etc.). Our pantyhose vendor, selling what for him is a novel item, creates his performance on the moment by aligning it to the discursive orienting framework provided by the broader genre of the market pitch. The genre is capacious, adaptable to the selling of any wares that demand an extended effort of persuasion, as against a routine purchase, as of eggs or vegetables. It allows the *merolico* to sell merchadise he has not sold before fluently, continuously, persuasively, and with virtuosic skill. And the creative entextualization of his sales pitch, as with the medicine vendor, involves also the creative, on-the-moment contextualization of his performance: in lines 5–7, the vendor's code-switch from Spanish to English was occasioned by my approach. Spotting me as someone from the United States (there are many American tourists and expatriates in San Miguel de Allende), he shifted playfully into my language, and enacted a little send up of those Americans in Mexican markets who seem to believe that they have to bargain and commonly respond to the seller's quotation of an initial price by saying "too much." In other words, he was personating me and my kind, appropriating and speaking in our voice. As we know, aligning your discourse to the discourse of others is itself a generic feature of the market pitch, but the particular act of personation (Coleman 2004) that our vendor fashions on the moment is an emergent, creative actualization of the generic device that is a conventional feature of market performance.

CONCLUSION

I have endeavored in this chapter to chart the trajectory of folklorists' interest in performance from an ancillary, unanalytical attraction to the theatricality of their star informants' delivery of classic folklore texts to a broadly synthetic, comprehensive conceptual and analytical framework for the investigation of artfulness in communicative practice. The systematic development of performance theory has amounted to a full-scale reorientation from text-historical philological perspectives to practice-centered understandings of folklore as "equipment for living," a set of resources for the enhancement of experience in the accomplishment of social life. At the same time, I have wanted to make clear that the turn to performance has provided highly productive vantage points on fundamental and enduring concerns that are part of the bedrock of folklore as a field of inquiry: textuality; the web of contextual relationships within which folklore is bound as a social, cultural, and discursive phenomenon; the generic regimentation of folklore texts; the dynamic tension between the socially given, collective aspects of folklore and the situationally emergent, contingent elements that shape the production and reception of folklore in use.

But to address these considerations is merely to make a beginning. Performance-oriented analysis has enriched folklorists' understanding of a widening range of other factors in the social life of folklore. One fruitful line of inquiry, again continuous with the concerns of earlier scholars like Tillhagen and Dorson, centers on the expressive styles, performance careers, and social lives of individual performers, virtuosic singers and storytellers like the Ozark singer Almeda Riddle (Abrahams 1970), the Texas Gulf Coast fisherman Ed Bell (Bauman 1986: 78–111; Bauman 2004: 82–108; Mullen 1976, 1978, 1981), the North Carolina singer and storyteller Bessie Eldreth (Sawin 2004); the Indian teacher Swamiji (Narayan 1989), the Finnish sexton Juho Oksanen (Kaivola-Bregenhøj 1996) or the whole cast of "stars" in Ballymenone (Glassie 2006). This renewed turn to the individual performer and "master speakers" (Haviland 2009:48) includes also, in a number of studies, the close analysis of reperformances by the same performer, for example multiple iterations on separate occasions and under different circumstances of "the same" narrative. Viewed both as reentextualizations and recontextualizations, such retelling offer an especially illuminating vantage point on the classic problem of variation in folklore, taking account of such variable factors as the co-textual environment of the performed text, participant roles and structures, power dynamics, the information states of participants, obligatory versus variable elements in generic schemata, the dynamics of memory, and other selective forces (Bauman 1986; Briggs 1993; Hymes 1985; Kaivola-Bregenhøj 1996).

Another very productive focus of investigation, enriched by the refinement of semiotic perspectives in folklore, is the analysis of the interplay of expressive means, not limited to verbal language, in folkloric performance. Examples might include the interrelationship between verbal forms and material objects in ritual performance (Keane 1997), the integration of spoken words and bodily movement in storytelling (Farnell 1995; Farnell and Graham 1998; Haviland 1993), or the multisemiotic texture of ritual curing (Briggs 1996). The multisemiotic density of many performances appears in turn to be one of the factors that contributes to the intensification of experience that attends the display of virtuosity. This heightening of affective engagement has emerged as yet another focus of interest in performance, generally involving close attention to the integrated and cumulative effects of formal means and devices in the unfolding of performances (Brenneis 1985, 1987; Feld 1990; Urban 1986; Wilce 2009). The same close attention to form-function interrelationships characterizes the nascent line of investigation exploring the re-mediation of performance, as oral/aural folklore forms are adapted to new media technologies such as sound recording, film, or digital media (Bauman 2010; Bauman and Feaster 2005; Goodman 2005; Silvio 2007).

Finally, I would direct attention to the ways in which a close understanding of performance provides a critical vantage point on the ethnographic encounter between the folklore fieldworker and his or her interlocutors (Briggs 1986; Haring 1972; Hymes 1975a; Paredes 1993 [1977]; Silverstein 1996). How the getting and giving of information is framed and co-constructed in ethnographic practice – as pedagogical exchange, as performance, as interview, or as any other interactional exchange – has profound epistemological implications for our discipline.

In a chapter on performance, it is also important to acknowledge that there is a complementary line of performance-oriented analysis, centered in anthropology and theater studies, that folklorists have found productive in their analyses of collective, public, participatory, reflexive enactments. I refer to the theoretical framework that extends from Durkheim through Singer (1955, 1958), Turner (1982), Schechner (1985), and Geertz (1973) and centers on cultural performances as affording a privileged vantage point on society and culture (Bauman 1992). Folklorists and anthropologists, in their studies of festivals, fairs, markets, ceremonies, folk dramas, and the like, have been actively engaged in this line of inquiry (Abrahams 1981, 2005: 149–174; Bauman 1996; Bauman and Ritch 1994; Bendix 1985, 1989; Beeman 1993; Fabian 1990; Falassi 1987; Glassie 1975; Nájera-Ramírez 1997; Noyes 2003; Seizer 2005; Stoeltje 1993, 1996; Stoeltje and Bauman 1988), interested especially in the reflexive dynamics of these cultural forms about culture.

Over the four decades of its development, then, the close study of performance has developed from a vigorous, sometimes hortatory reform movement in folklore, offering a critical corrective to long-entrenched, even canonical approaches in the discipline, to a mature, broad-based, and well-established vantage point on what have remained core concerns of the discipline since the concept of folklore first took shape in the late eighteenth and early nineteenth centuries. Performance draws our attention to the most highly valued, engaging, persuasive, memorable, replicable, and durable expressive forms and practices in human social life. The more we know of performance, the deeper our understanding of the most meaningful and affecting aspects of human experience.

ACKNOWLEDGMENTS

I thank Charles L. Briggs and the members of the Michicagoan Seminar in Linguistic Anthropology for valuable comments on an earlier draft of this chapter.

NOTE

1   All translations from German are the author's.

REFERENCES

Abrahams, Roger D., Ed. 1970.   *A Singer and Her Songs: Almeda Riddle's Book of Ballads*. Baton Rouge: Louisiana University Press.

Abrahams, Roger D. 1972.   "Personal Power and Social Restraint in the Definition of Folklore" in Américo Paredes and Richard Bauman, Eds. *Toward New Perspectives in Folklore*. Austin: University of Texas Press, pp. 16–30.

Abrahams, Roger D. 1981.   "Shouting Match at the Border: The Folklore of Display events" in Richard Bauman and Roger D. Abrahams, Eds. *"And Other Neighborly Names": Social Image and Cultural Process in Texas Folklore*. Austin: University of Texas Press, pp. 303–321.

Abrahams, Roger D. 1992.   *Singing the Master: The Emergence of African-American Culture in the Plantation South*. New York: Penguin Books.

Abrahams, Roger D. 2005.   *Everyday Life: A Poetics of Vernacular Practice*. Philadelphia: University of Pennsylvania Press.

Barber, Karin. 1997.   "Preliminary Notes on Audiences in Africa." *Africa* 67(3): 347–362.

Barber, Karin. 2003.   "Text and Performance in Africa." *Bulletin of the School of Oriental and African Studies* 66(3): 324–333.

Başgöz, Ilhan. 1986. "Digression in Oral Narrative: A Case of Individual Remarks by Turkish Romance tellers." *Journal of American Folklore* 99(391): 5–23.

Basso, Ellen B. 1985. *A Musical View of the Universe.* Philadelphia: University of Pennsylvania Press.

Bauman, Richard. 1972a. "Introduction" in Richard Bauman and Roger D. Abrahams, Eds. *"And Other Neighborly Names": Social Image and Cultural Process in Texas Folklore.* Austin: University of Texas Press, pp. v–ix.

Bauman, Richard. 1972b. "Differential Identity and the Social Base of Folklore" in Richard Bauman and Roger D. Abrahams, Eds. *"And Other Neighborly Names": Social Image and Cultural Process in Texas Folklore.* Austin: University of Texas Press, pp. 31–41.

Bauman, Richard. 1977. *Verbal Art as Performance.* Prospect Heights, IL: Waveland Press.

Bauman, Richard. 1986. *Story, Performance, and Event: Contextual Studies of Oral Narrative.* Cambridge: Cambridge University Press.

Bauman, Richard. 1992. "Performance" in Richard Bauman, Ed. *Folklore, Cultural Performances, and Popular Entertainments.* New York: Oxford University Press, pp. 41–49.

Bauman, Richard. 1996. "Transformations of the Word in the Production of Mexican Festival Drama" in Michael Silverstein and Greg Urban, Eds. *Natural Histories of Discourse.* Chicago: University of Chicago Press, pp. 301–327.

Bauman, Richard. 2002. "Disciplinarity, Reflexivity, and Power in Verbal Art as Performance." *Journal of American Folklore* 115: 92–98.

Bauman, Richard. 2004. *A World of Others' Words: Cross-Cultural Perspectives on Intertextuality.* Malden, MA: Blackwell.

Bauman, Richard. 2010. "The Remediation of Storytelling: Narrative Performance on Early Commercial Sound Recordings" in Anna De Fina and Deborah Schiffrin, Eds. *Telling Stories: Building Bridges among Language, Narrative, Identity, Interaction, Society and Culture.* Report of the Georgetown University Round Table Discussion on Languages and Linguistics, 2008. Washington, DC: Georgetown University Press, pp. 23–43.

Bauman, Richard and Charles L. Briggs. 1990. "Poetics and Performance as Critical Perspectives on Language and Social Life." *Annual Review of Anthropology* 19: 59–88.

Bauman, Richard and Charles L. Briggs. 2003. *Voices of Modernity: Language Ideologies and the Politics of Inequality.* Cambridge: Cambridge University Press.

Bauman, Richard and Patrick Feaster. 2005. "'Fellow Townsmen and My Noble Constituents!': Representations of Oratory on Early Commercial Recordings." *Oral Tradition* 20(1): 35–57.

Bauman, Richard and Pamela Ritch. 1994. "Informing Performance: Producing the *Coloquio* in Tierra Blanca." *Oral Tradition* 9(2): 255–280.

Bauman, Richard and Joel Sherzer, Eds. 1989. *Explorations in the Ethnography of Speaking.* 2nd edition. Cambridge: Cambridge University Press.

Beeman, William O. 1993. "Anthropology of Theater and Spectacle." *Annual Review of Anthropology* 22: 369–393.

Ben-Amos, Dan. 1972. "Toward a Definition of Folklore in Context", in Richard Bauman and Roger D. Abrahams, Eds. *"And Other Neighborly Names": Social Image and Cultural Process in Texas Folklore.* Austin: University of Texas Press, pp. 3–15.

Bendix, Regina. 1985. *Progress and Nostalgia: Silvesterklausen in Urnäsch, Switzerland.* Berkeley and Los Angeles: University of California Press.

Bendix, Regina. 1989. *Backstage Domains: Playing "William Tell" in Two Swiss Communities.* Bern: Peter Lang.

Blommaert, Jan. 2006. "Ethnopoetics as Functional Reconstruction: Dell Hymes' Narrative View of the World." *Functions of Language* 13(2): 229–249.

Bowen, John R. 1991. *Sumatran Politics and Poetics: Gayo History, 1900–1989.* New Haven: Yale University Press.

Brenneis, Donald L. 1985. "Passion and Performance in Fiji Indian Vernacular Song." *Ethnomusicology* 29: 397–408.

Brenneis, Donald L. 1987. "Performing Passions: Aesthetics and Politics in An Occasionally Egalitarian Community." *American Ethnologist* 14: 236–250.

Brenneis, Donald L. 1993. "Some Contributions of Folklore to Social Theory: Aesthetics and Politics in a Translocal World." *Western Folklore* 52: 291–302.

Briggs, Charles L. 1986. *Learning How to Ask: A Sociolinguistic Appraisal of the Role of the Interview in Social Science Research.* Cambridge: Cambridge University Press.

Briggs, Charles L. 1988. *Competence in Performance: The Creativity of Tradition in Mexicano Verbal Art.* Philadelphia: University of Pennsylvania Press.

Briggs, Charles L. 1993. "Generic Versus Metapragmatic Dimensions of Warao Narratives: Who Regiments Performance?" in John Lucy, Ed. *Reflexive Language: Reported Speech and Metapragmatics.* Cambridge: Cambridge University Press, pp. 179–212.

Briggs, Charles L. 1996. "The Meaning of Nonsense, The Poetics of Embodiment, and The Production of Power in Warao Healing" in Carol Laderman and Marina Roseman, Eds. *The Performance of Healing.* New York: Routledge, pp. 185–232.

Briggs, Charles L. and Richard Bauman. 1992. "Genre, Intertextuality, and Social Power." *Journal of Linguistic Anthropology* 2: 131–172.

Burke, Kenneth. 1941. *The Philosophy of Literary Form.* Baton Rouge: Louisiana State University Press.

Burke, Kenneth. 1968 [1931]. *Counter-Statement.* Berkeley and Los Angeles: University of California Press

Burke, Kenneth. 1969 [1945]. "Introduction: The Five Key Terms of Dramatism" in *A Grammar of Motives.* Berkeley and Los Angeles: University of California Press, pp. xv–xxiii.

Coleman, Steve. 2004. "The Nation, the State, and the Neighbors: Personation in Irish- language Discourse." *Language and Communication* 24(4): 381–411.

Coplan, David B. 1994. *In the Time of Cannibals: The Word Music of South Africa's Basotho Migrants.* Chicago: University of Chicago Press.

Crowley, Daniel J. 1966. *I Could Talk Old-Story Good: Creativity in Bahamian Folklore.* Berkeley and Los Angeles: University of California Press.

Dargan, Amanda and Steven Zeitlin. 1983. "American Talkers: Expressive Styles and Occupational Choice." *Journal of American Folklore* 96: 3–33.

Darnell, Regna. 1989. "Correlates of Cree Narrative Performance" in Richard Bauman and Joel Sherzer, Eds. 1989. *Explorations in the Ethnography of Speaking.* 2nd edition. Cambridge: Cambridge University Press, pp. 315–336.

Dorson, Richard M. 1956. *Negro Folktales in Michigan.* Harvard: Harvard University Press.

Dorson, Richard M. 1958. *Negro Tales from Pine Bluff, Arkansas, and Calvin, Michigan.* Bloomington: Indiana University Press.

Dorson, Richard M. 1972. "Introduction" in Richard M. Dorson, Ed. *Folklore and Folklife: An Introduction.* Chicago: University of Chicago Press, pp. 1–50.

Duranti, Alessandro and Donald Brenneis, Eds. 1986 *The Audience as Co-Author.* Special issue. *Text* 6(3).

Fabian, Johannes. 1990. *Power and Performance: Ethnographic Explorations through Proverbial Wisdom and Theater in Shaba, Zaire.* Madison: University of Wisconsin Press.

Falassi, Alessandro, Ed. 1987. *Time Out of Time: Essays on the Festival.* Albuquerque: University of New Mexico Press.

Farnell, Brenda. 1995. *Do You See What I Mean? Plains Indian Sign Talk and the Embodiment of Action.* Austin: University of Texas Press.

Farnell, Brenda and Laura Graham. 1998. "Discourse-Centered Methods" in H. Russell Bernard, Ed. *Handbook of Methods in Cultural Anthropology.* Walnut Creek, CA: AltaMira Press, pp. 411–457.

Feld, Steven. 1990. "Wept Thoughts: The Voicing of Kaluli Memories." *Oral Tradition* 5(2–3): 241–66.

Fine, Elizabeth C. 1984. *The Folklore Text: From Performance to Print.* Bloomington: Indiana University Press.

Finnegan, Ruth. 1967. *Limba Stories and Story-telling.* Oxford: Clarendon Press.

Finnegan, Ruth. 2007. *The Oral and Beyond: Doing Things with Words in Africa.* Chicago: University of Chicago Press.

Fletcher, Francis. 1854. *The World Encompassed by Sir Francis Drake ... Collated* with an Unpublished Manuscript of Francis Fletcher, Chaplain to the Expedition. W. S. W. Vaux, Ed. London: The Hakluyt Society.

Foley, John Miles. 1995. *The Singer of Tales in Performance.* Bloomington: Indiana University Press.

Fox, James F. 1989. "'Our Ancestors Spoke in Pairs': Rotinese Views of Language, Dialect, and Code" in Richard Bauman and Joel Sherzer, Eds. 1989. *Explorations in the Ethnography of Speaking.* 2nd edition. Cambridge: Cambridge University Press, pp. 65–85.

Geertz, Clifford. 1973. "Deep Play: Notes on the Balinese Cockfight" in *The Interpretation of Cultures.* New York: Basic Books, pp. 412–453.

Georges, Robert A. 1981. "Do Narrators Really Digress? A Reconsideration of 'Audience Asides' in Narrating." *Western Folklore* 40(3): 245–251.

Glassie, Henry. 1975. *All Silver and No Brass: An Irish Christmas Mumming.* Bloomington: Indiana University Press.

Glassie, Henry. 2006. *The Stars of Ballymenone.* Bloomington: Indiana University Press.

Goffman, Erving. 1974. *Frame Analysis.* New York: Harper and Row.

Goffman, Erving. 1981. *Forms of Talk.* Philadelphia: University of Pennsylvania Press.

Goodman, Jane. 2005. *Berber Culture on the World Stage: From Village to Video.* Bloomington: Indiana University Press.

Hanks, William. 1987. "Discourse Genres in a Theory of Practice." *American Ethnologist* 14(4): 666–692.

Hanks, William F. 1996. "Exorcism and The Description of Participant Roles" in Silverstein, Michael and Greg Urban, Eds. *Natural Histories of Discourse.* Chicago: University of Chicago Press, pp. 160–200.

Haring, Lee. 1972. "Performing for The Interviewer: A Study of The Structure of Context." *Southern Folklore Quarterly* 36: 383–398.

Haviland, John B. 1993. "Anchoring, Iconicity, and Orientation in Guugu Yimithirr Pointing Gestures." *Journal of Linguistic Anthropology* 3(1): 3–45.

Haviland, John B. 2009. "Little Rituals" in Gunter Senft and Ellen B. Basso, Eds.

Ritual Communication. Oxford: Berg, pp. 21–49.

Hymes, Dell. 1972. "The Contribution of Folklore to Sociolinguistic Research" in Américo Paredes and Richard Bauman, Eds. 1972. *Toward New Perspectives in Folklore.* Austin: University of Texas Press, pp. 42–50.

Hymes, Dell. 1975a. "Breakthrough Into Performance" in Dan Ben-Amos and Kenneth S. Goldstein, Eds. *Folklore: Performance and Communication.* pp. 11–74.

Hymes, Dell. 1975b. "Folklore's Nature and the Sun's Myth." *Journal of American Folklore* 88: 345–369.

Hymes, Dell. 1981. *"In Vain I Tried to Tell You": Essays in Native American Ethnopoetics.* Philadelphia: University of Pennsylvania Press.

Hymes, Dell. 1985. "Language, Memory, and Selective Performance: Cultee's 'Salmon's' Myth' as Twice Told to Boas." *Journal of American Folklore* 98(389): 391–434.

Irvine, Judith T. 1996. "Shadow Conversations: The Indeterminacy of Participant Roles" in Michael Silverstein and Greg Urban, Eds. *Natural Histories of Discourse.* Chicago: University of Chicago Press, pp. 131–159.

Jackson, Jason B. 2003. *Yuchi Ceremonial Life: Performance, Meaning and Tradition in a Contemporary American Indian Community. Studies in the Anthropology of North American Indians.* Lincoln: University of Nebraska Press.

Jackson, Jason B. 2008. "Traditionalization in Ceremonial Ground Oratory: Native American Speechmaking in Eastern Oklahoma." *Midwestern Folklore* 34(2): 3–16.

Jacobs, Melville. 1959. *The Content and Style of an Oral Literature: Clackamas Chinook Myths and Tales.* Chicago: University of Chicago Press.

Jaffe, Alexandra. 2009. "The Sociolinguistics of Stance" in Alexandra Jaffe, Ed. *Stance: Sociolinguistic Perspectives.* New York: Oxford University Press, pp. pp. 2–28.

Jakobson, Roman. 1960. "Linguistics and Poetics" in Thomas A. Sebeok, Ed. *Style in Language.* Cambridge, MA: MIT Press, pp. 350–377.

Jansen, William Hugh. 1957. "Classifying Performance in the Study of Verbal Folklore" in W. Edson Richmond, Ed. *Studies in Folklore, in Honor of Distinguished Service Professor Stith Thompson.* Bloomington: Indiana University Press, pp. 110–118.

Kaivola-Bregenhøj, Annikki. 1996. *Narrative and Narrating: Variation in Juho Oksanen's Storytelling. FF Communications* 261. Helsinki: Suomalainen Tiedeakatemia.

Kapchan, Deborah. 1996. *Gender on the Market: Moroccan Women and the Revoicing of Tradition.* Philadelphia: University of Pennsylvania Press.

Keane, Webb. 1997. *Signs of Recognition: Powers and Hazards of Representation in an Indonesian Society.* Berkeley and Los Angeles: University of California Press.

Keenan, Elinor O. 1973. "A Sliding Sense of Obligatoriness: The Poly-Structure of Malagasy Oratory." *Language in Society* 2: 225–243.

Kuipers, Joel. 1990. *Power in Performance: The Creation of Textual Authority in Weyewa Ritual Speech.* Philadelphia: University of Pennsylvania Press.

Lemon, Alaina. 2000. *Between Two Fires: Gypsy Performance and Romani Memory from Pushkin to Postsocialism.* Durham, NC: Duke University Press.

Lord, Albert B. 1960. *The Singer of Tales.* Cambridge, MA: Harvard University Press.

Luckmann, Thomas. 1995. "Interaction Planning and Intersubjective Adjustment of Perspectives by Communicative Genres" in Esther N. Goody, Ed. *Social Intelligence and Interaction:Expressions and Implications of the Social Bias in Human Intelligence.* Cambridge: Cambridge University Press, pp. 175–189.

Lundgren, Gunilla and Alyosha Taikon. 2003. *From Coppersmith to Nurse: Alyosha, the Son of a Gypsy Chief.* Hatfield: University of Hertfordshire Press.

Malinowski, Bronislaw. 1923. "The Problem of Meaning in Primitive Languages" in C.K. Ogden and I.A. Richards *The Meaning of Meaning.* New York: Harcourt, Brace and World, pp. 296–336.

Malinowski, Bronislaw. 1948. *Magic, Science and Religion.* New York: Doubleday.

Malinowski, Bronislaw. 1965 [1935]. *The Language of Magic and Gardening.* Bloomington: Indiana University Press.

Mullen, Patrick. 1976. "The Tall Tales of a Texas Raconteur" in Juha Pentikäinen and Tuula Juurikka, Eds. *Folk Narrative Research.* Helsinki: Finnish Literature Society, pp. 302–311.

Mullen, Patrick. 1978. *I Heard the Old Fisherman Say: Folklore of the Texas Gulf Coast.* Austin: University of Texas Press.

Mullen, Patrick. 1981. "A Traditional Storyteller in Changing Contexts" in Richard Bauman and Roger D. Abrahams, Eds. *"And Other Neighborly Names": Social Process and Cultural Image in Texas Folklore.* Austin: University of Texas Press, pp. 266–279.

Nájera-Ramírez, Olga. 1997. *La Fiesta de los Tastoanes: Critical Encounters in Mexican Festival Performance.* Albuquerque: University of New Mexico Press.

Narayan, Kirin. 1989. *Storytellers, Saints, and Scoundrels: Folk Narrative in Hindu Religious Teaching.* Philadelphia: University of Pennsylvania Press.

Noyes, Dorothy. 2003. *Fire in the Plaça: Catalan Festival Politics After Franco.* Philadelphia: University of Pennsylvania Press.

Paredes, Américo. 1976. *A Texas-Mexican Cancionero: Folklsongs of the Lower Border.* Urbana: University of Illinois Press.

Paredes, Américo. 1993 [1971]. "The United States, Mexico, and *Machismo*" in Américo Paredes and Richard Bauman, Ed. *Folklore and Culture on the Texas-Mexican Border.* Austin: CMAS Books, pp. 215–234.

Paredes, Américo. 1993 [1977]. On Ethnographic Work Among Minority Groups: A Folklorist's Perspective" in Américo Paredes and Richard Bauman, Ed. *Folklore and Culture on the Texas-Mexican Border.* Austin: CMAS Books, pp. 73–110.

Paredes, Américo and Richard Bauman, Eds. 1972. *Toward New Perspectives in Folklore.* Austin: University of Texas Press.

Sawin, Patricia. 2002. "Performance at the Nexus of Gender, Power, and Desire: Reconsidering Bauman's *Verbal Art* From the Perspective of Gendered Subjectivity as Performance." *Journal of American Folkore* 115(455): 28–61.

Sawin, Patricia. 2004. *Listening for a Life: A Dialogic Ethnography of Bessie Eldreth*

Through Her Songs and Stories. Logan: Utah State University Press.

Schechner, Richard. 1985. *Between Theater and Anthropology.* Philadelphia: University of Pennsylvania Press.

Schiefflein, Edward L. 1985 "Performance and The Cultural Construction of Reality." *American Ethnologist* 12(4): 707–724.

Schieffelin, Edward L. 1996. "On Failure and Performance: Throwing the Medium out of The Séance" in Carol Laderman and Marina Roseman, Eds. *The Performance of Healing.* New York: Routledge, pp. 59–89.

Seizer, Susan. 2005. *Stigmas of the Tamil Stage: An Ethnography of Special Drama Artists in South India.* Durham, NC: Duke University Press.

Sherzer, Joel. 1983. *Kuna Ways of Speaking: An Ethnographic Perspective.* Austin: University of Texas Press.

Sherzer, Joel and Anthony C. Woodbury, Eds. 1987. *Native American Discourse: Poetics and Rhetoric.* Cambridge: Cambridge University Press.

Shuman, Amy and Charles L. Briggs. 1993. Introduction. *Western Folklore* 52: 109–134.

Silverstein, Michael. 1993. "Metapragmatic Discourse and Metapragmatic Function" in John A. Lucy, Ed. *Reflexive Language: Reported Speech and Metapragmatics.* Cambridge: Cambridge University Press, pp. 33–58.

Silverstein, Michael. 1996. "The Secret Life of Texts" in Michael Silverstein and Greg Urban, Eds. *Natural Histories of Discourse.* Chicago: University of Chicago, pp. 81–105.

Silverstein, Michael and Greg Urban. 1996a. "The Natural History of Discourse" in Michael Silverstein and Greg Urban, Eds. *Natural Histories of Discourse.* Chicago: University of Chicago, pp. 1–17.

Silverstein, Michael and Greg Urban, Eds. 1996b. *Natural Histories of Discourse.* Chicago: University of Chicago Press.

Silvio, Teri. 2007. "Remediation and Local Globalization: How Taiwan's 'Digital Video Knights-errant Puppetry' Writes the History of the New Media in Chinese." *Cultural Anthropology* 22(2): 285–313.

Singer, Milton. 1955. "The Cultural Pattern of Indian Civilization: A Preliminary Report of a Methodological Field Study." *Far Eastern Quarterly* 15(1): 23–36.

Singer, Milton. 1958. "From the Guest Editor." *Journal of American Folklore* 71(281): 191–204.

Stoeltje, Beverly J. 1993. "Power and The Ritual Genres: American Rodeo." *Western Folklore* 52: 135–156.

Stoeltje, Beverly J. 1996. "The Snake-Charmer Queen: Ritual, Competition, and Signification in American Festivals" in Colleen Ballerino Cohen, Richard Wilk, and Beverly J. Stoeltje, Eds. *Beauty Queens on the Global Stage.* New York: Routledge, pp. 13–30.

Stoeltje, Beverly J. 2009. "Asante Traditions and Female Self-assertion: Sister Abena's Narrative." *Research in African Literatures* 40(1): 27–41.

Stoeltje, Beverly J. and Richard Bauman. 1988. "The Semiotics of Folkloric Performance" in Thomas A. Sebeok and Jean Umiker-Sebeok, Eds. *The Semiotic Web 1987.* Berlin: Mouton.

Tannen, Deborah. 2007. *Talking Voices: Repetition, Dialogue, and Imagery in Conversational Discourse.* 2nd edition. Cambridge: Cambridge University Press.

Tedlock, Dennis. 1983. *The Spoken Word and the Work of Interpretation.* Philadelphia: University of Pennsylvania Press.

Tillhagen, Carl-Herman. 1948. "Nachwort" in *Taikon Erzählt: Zigeunermärchen und -Geschichten.* Zürich: Artemis-Verlag.

Turner, Victor. 1982. *From Ritual to Theatre.* New York: PAJ Publications.

Urban, Greg. 1986. "Ceremonial Dialogues in South America." *American Anthropologist* 88(2): 371–386.

Urban, Greg. 1988. "Ritual Wailing in Amerindian Brazil." *American Anthropologist* 90(2): 385–400.

Webster, Anthony K. 2008. "'To Give an Imagination to the Listeners': The Neglected Poetics of Navajo Ideophony." *Semiotica* 171(1/4): 343–365.

Wilce, James M. 2009. *Language and Emotion.* Cambridge: Cambridge University Press.

Yankah, Kwesi. 1985. "Risks in Verbal Art Performance." *Journal of Folklore Research* 22(2): 133–153.

CHAPTER 6

MYTH-RITUAL-SYMBOL

Hagar Salamon and Harvey E. Goldberg

An examination of basic concepts within and between disciplines brings forth their substance, illuminates the ideas and dialectics that lie at their core, and reveals the dynamics of their evolution. In this chapter we utilize this approach in exploring the key concepts "myth," "ritual," and "symbol" in the field of folklore. These three analytic concepts stand at the pinnacle of a collective research program that seeks to reach barely visible and untapped regions that lie beyond "the taken for granted" within social life and folk expression. They thus stand at the center of the discipline on the one hand, but also have been positioned for years at the crossroads of folklore with other disciplines. Thus, by following these three concepts and connections among them we also examine an ongoing network of links that have existed between folklore and related fields.

As Galit Hasan-Rokem has pointed out, folklore is created through a mutual movement involving the talents and cognizance of singers and audience alike, of storytellers and listeners – in a manner that blurs the distinction between them (Hasan-Rokem 1997: 12). This blurring, typical to folklore expression, also reflects the give-and-take between folkloristics and other disciplines, and testifies to the field's openness and an avoidance of a strict disciplinary "patriotism."

In order to fully appreciate the richness of the concepts of myth, ritual, and symbol, and the manner in which contemporary folkloristic understandings of them have emerged, we begin with a brief discussion of their development both within and alongside the field of folklore studies. As we shall demonstrate, shared ideas and interdisciplinary interactions were present in folk research from its outset, but have came into fuller expression in recent years.

A clear example of how myth, ritual and symbol have been central concepts in disciplines close to, and indeed overlapping with, folklore is found in anthropology

A Companion to Folklore, First Edition. Edited by Regina F. Bendix and Galit Hasan-Rokem.
© 2012 John Wiley & Sons, Ltd. Published 2012 John Wiley & Sons, Ltd.

and ethnology. These intertwined fields, parallel with folklore, emerged in the late nineteenth century as recognized academic disciplines in several European locales and in the United States. Figures like James Frazer (England), Arnold Van Gennep (France), Edward Westermarck (Finland and England), and Franz Boas (born in Germany and prominent in American anthropology), were leading scholars dealing with the concepts of our concern, and are recognized as belonging to both fields. Cross-disciplinary perspectives continue to be important and have grown more elaborate over time.

For example, the concept of a "symbol" has its roots in the study of literature and religion, and became central in contemporary approaches to culture as defined within ethnology and folklore. Intertwined with this development has been the impact of linguistics in the latter two fields, particularly its role in social and cultural life as explored in semiotics and in the study of communication. This can be traced to the emergence of modern linguistics that assumed the universality of systemic structuring in all human languages (Sapir 1921; Jakobson and Halle 1956; Saussure 1966). Languages around the world that had never been written, and "dialects" of national languages in Europe, exhibited stable principles of phonetic organization, syntax that was capable of systematic analysis, and an ever-expanding storehouse of semantic content reflecting the complexities of material, social and spiritual life. This demonstrated a shared basis of human cognition and performance that must have far preceded the relegation of speech to written forms, and the expression of myths in formats that presume literacy. Just as "simple societies" were shown to be cognitively complex, so it came to be accepted that the "emotional," non-rational, and "archaic" are part and parcel of contemporary cultural expression. The abstract quality of all languages evident in the arbitrariness of linguistic representation (see below), the effort to methodically decode symbols undertaken by Sigmund Freud (1915 [1900]), with regard to dreams, or Ernst Cassirer's demonstration of the place of symbolism within human consciousness (Cassirer 1944, 1953–1957) all pointed to the relevance of symbols, rituals, and myths to any general schema of human action.

The relevance of these efforts and insights for the contemporary human sciences was made clear by the formulation, around the turn of the twentieth-century, of notions like "culture" and "symbol" as central components of human action. The assumption that modern societies were essentially different from "primitive" or "traditional" societies was challenged at a number of levels. One level has been the expansion of the notion of folk culture beyond the rural settings that nineteenth-century researchers saw as its "natural" home, to apply it to a range of cultural expressions in contemporary urban and industrial society. Consequently, fields such as "ritual studies" (Grimes 1982; Bell 1992) and "cultural studies" emerged, as it became clear that ritual behavior is no less prevalent in contemporary situations than it was in traditional societies, and that myths, often perceived as "inferior" forms of knowledge, continue to be produced even when they are not labeled as such.

Modern life has not eliminated the importance of these notions. While contemporary societies usually do not possess formally canonized myths, mythmaking proceeds apace, and rituals, both modest and bombastic and both old and new, continue to be threaded through social life. Both the humanities and the social sciences now recognize the irrational and a-rational dimensions of industrial society where symbolic expression plays a critical role whether within defined realms like "religion" or "the arts," or interlaced within economic and political processes. Myth and ritual, as general analytic categories, are no longer viewed as confined to societies once designated as "primitive," "folk," "traditional" or "pre-modern." Taking on new configurations, they are linked to deeply held ideas, key symbols, and existential dilemmas within contemporary societies (Barthes 1972).

This expanded view of folk culture, along with its more classic concerns, entails a variety of disciplinary and methodological emphases. Symbols that give shape to cultural worlds, and myths that convey bundles of knowledge that are absorbed by members of a society, are continually reconnected to the reality within which participants in a given society function. Rituals not only "reflect" society, but constitute a powerful transformative mechanism that makes and remakes these linkages (Handelman 1990). It is therefore necessary to examine these concepts at the level of performance as well as within the planes of meaning and significance (Tambiah 1985).

Observing the actual recitation or performance of a myth yields different insights from analyzing it as a written text, and the cross-fertilization of methods is an ongoing process. Folklore increasingly has paid attention to "context" (Ben-Amos 1993), and a term like "inter-textual" is now applied to various realms of culture whether or not an actual written document is involved. Today, the internet provides a setting for both the transmission or creation of myths and even the performance of rituals. The widespread use of a term like "icon" indicates that an awareness of the symbolic dimension of contemporary culture has become a staple of present-day discourse. This vocabulary allows comparative discussion across contemporary cultures and situations while simultaneously plumbing the symbolic depths of particular myths and rituals.

The three vehicles of expression – symbol, myth and ritual – are linked to one another, at the level of aesthetics as well as being regulatory and communicative elements in what may be grasped as an expanded "language of culture." They store and transmit cultural knowledge, which may be transposed into both universalizing and highly particular registers. We do not suggest a strict analogy between language along with its analytic components and aspects of culture, but use the comparison as an orienting device that highlights the communicative dimensions of symbol, myth, and ritual. They all succeed in carrying meaning by virtue of systematic internal structuring, while at the same time demand attention to context in grasping their significance in particular situations. In expounding these points, we first relate to each concept individually and then highlight their communicative aspects by stressing the links among them. Finally, in order to concretize some of the concepts and their dynamic interlacing in lived situations, we illustrate the formulations and processes discussed by reference to the festival of Passover outlined in the Hebrew Bible. This case allows attention both to its elaboration within Jewish tradition and to other cultural developments and formations emerging from within it.

RITUAL

The study of ritual, including the very definition of the phenomenon, has been one of the most complex challenges of the humanities and the social sciences. The richness and multidimensional quality of ritual performance have invited theories from many perspectives. In the same year, 1912, Sigmund Freud published the first essay of *Totem und Taboo*, offering a psychoanalytic view of rituals (Freud 1927), and Émile Durkheim, in *Les formes élémentaires de la vie religeuse*, placed the understanding of rituals firmly within the sociological discipline that he was advocating (Durkheim 1915). Today it is clear that ritual behavior encapsulates many dimensions of social and cultural life, while also resonating powerfully within the life of the individual. Thus, it always has been a challenge to unravel these dimensions without losing a sense of the centrality and vigor of rituals when viewed as a total phenomenon.

One avenue that has been taken is to view ritual action as a kind of language (Leach 1964). Students of language, or more generally of semiotics – the study of signs – distinguish between three levels at which a system may be analyzed: the semantic, the syntactic, and the pragmatic. Precise formulation varies between theoreticians and schools of thought – for example, how they distinguish between the terms "sign" and "symbol" (Peirce 1931–1935; Morris 1946; Saussure 1966; Barthes 1968; Rappaport 1999: 58–68). Differences in terminology aside, separating the three levels is a useful first step in most approaches. "Semantic" deals with cultural content: the meanings or the messages that rituals carry. "Syntactics" recognizes that rituals are made up of a series of acts, whose structure – the ordering of the elements and the relation of each part to the whole – is critical to how rituals are put together and "work." "Pragmatics" explores the relationship between rituals and those who use them and are exposed to them, whether on the communal or personal level. These broad distinctions will guide our discussion, but we first turn to the question of defining rituals, or making explicit the criteria by which we recognize ritual behavior.

One characteristic defining behavior as ritual, or "a ritual," is its standard form and repetitiveness. Repetitiveness is relative, however, for some rituals may take place only once a year, or once every several years (inauguration of a head of state), or at much longer intervals (the coronation of a monarch). These examples point to another side of the standardization of behavior, namely the existence of norms that define rituals in a detailed and strict manner and establish public expectations of correct performance. Although the exact way a ritual is performed may vary from one situation or another, there is always a sense that a ritual carries forward an imperative formulated outside and prior to any specific enactment (Rappaport 1999: 24).

Other forms of behavior are expected to be performed correctly of course, in particular technical activities aimed at specific material goals. This comparison leads to another distinguishing element of ritual; it is "non-utilitarian," or, at least, whatever concrete effects it has are not the major reasons for its existence and practice. Even if forms of magic aimed at specific results (whether baneful or benign) are included under ritual behavior, we call them "magic" because there is no demonstrable means-end connection between the actual behavior and the hoped-for outcome. So the basis for ritual appearing in the repertoire of all societies, albeit to varying degrees, does not stem from its ability to produce tangible "results." Other dimensions of human existence are engaged in motivating ritual behavior.

While seeking for general characteristics of ritual behavior, it is clear that there is a wide range of actions to which the notion of "ritual" may be applied. On the one hand are activities clearly recognized as rituals, such as the Catholic Mass, which is set off from the routine flow of economic and social life. This example also highlights that when ritual behavior is embedded in an elaborate set of beliefs and symbols its status as a separate "kind" of behavior is underscored. Such separation may entail framing by words, dress, time, location, and paraphernalia, all of which convey to the participant: "this is a ritual." On the other hand, there are ritual behaviors that quickly enter into and "disappear from" quotidian behavior such as greetings (a handshake or kissing on the cheeks), standard phrases ("Thank God"), or reading the morning paper (Firth 1973; Anderson 1983). This view of ritual leads us in the direction of deciphering the significance and messages of acts and gestures that are not necessarily flagged as "rituals."

Given the diversity of experiences to which ritual relates, it may be asked how, in spite of its being in some ways like a language, it may play a role different from what we usually associate with language-based messages. A basic feature of language is its capability to infinitely extend the cognitive capacity inhering in the human brain. Much of language has to do with "knowledge": information about the world with its myriad manifestations (material, social, or imagined). Certain experiences, however, challenge or stretch the boundaries of language. Some events seem so sublime that they are "ineffable," incapable of being reduced to language. The description of God speaking to Moses through a burning bush (Exodus 3:14), and presenting his name as "I will be what I will be," may be one attempt to express the inexpressible.

Other experiences may defy common definitions made available by everyday language, or contain contradictory elements according to accepted understandings. The Book of Psalms (2:11) calls upon worshippers to "rejoice in trembling." Still other occasions may overwhelm the emotions (both positive and negative), so that language seems inadequate to convey them. Chaos is a situation, at once social and personal, that paralyzes conventional action or thought, and ritual is often mobilized to help process it, and ward off, even provisionally, the ambivalence and anxiety that it engenders. In all these instances ritual may come into play, sometimes offering an alternative avenue of communication and at times even reworking the categories and units of knowledge that members of a society take for granted. The ability of ritual to meet these challenges is linked to the diversity and flexibility of its structure.

As communicative strings, rituals have principles of combination. Some of them are simple, but capable of having persuasive impact. James Frazer (1922) identified two principles with reference to magic: similarity and contagion. Magic could be worked at a distance based on similarity of form, such as between a physical object being manipulated and the target of the act. Another way of exerting magical influence was based on actual contact between the magician, or the objects with which he or she worked, and the intended goal. The notion of "laying on of hands," based on the Hebrew Bible and continuing into some early Christian as well as rabbinic practices, is another illustration of that logic. In religious traditions around the world, people seek physical closeness to persons and objects that are imbued with sanctity.

To the principles of similarity and contagion, Claude Lévi-Strauss added the relations of opposition and contrast (Lévi-Strauss 1955). Both the colors black and white, often grasped as "opposite" to one another, can conjure up images of death. We frequently imagine the "angel of death" as dressed in a black cloak, while shrouds are white in Jewish, Christian, and Muslim traditions. A common feeling is that good fortune will be followed by bad luck, and in many cultures, it is standard practice to wish a person a "long life" upon hearing them report a frightening dream. At another level, an object, site, or person deemed sacred may be perceived as a source of blessing on the one hand, or danger and harm on the other.

Contrast is also central to a more elaborate structure analyzed by Lévi-Strauss, that of "totemism" (Lévi-Strauss 1963). This term was used by nineteenth-century ethnologists to depict what they saw as an early "primitive" stage of religious evolution based on a systematic ritual relationship between animal species and human groups. Lévi-Strauss suggested that the key element of a set of totemic symbols and rituals was that of a set of differences: just as natural species are distinct, so human groups can be distinguished and categorized as clearly separate from one another. A parallel emphasis was introduced by Mary Douglas (1966) in her discussion of the list of forbidden animals appearing in the biblical Book of Leviticus (Chapter 11). These seem to reflect the cosmological order established in the Book of Genesis, and, taken together, yielded a set of food restrictions that set apart Israelites from other nations.

In addition to the categorical logic implicit in rituals, Arnold Van Gennep (1909) pointed to dynamic structural relationships with his formulation of the notion of "rites of passage." He applied this notion both to the movement of individuals through life stages defined by society, and with regard to the passing of seasons. Van Gennep showed how many rituals could be viewed as reflecting three stages: separation from a previous social status, liminality – or being "on the margins " – within which transformation can take place, and re-aggregation or re-connection to the collective with a new social definition. Both axes discussed in his *Rites de passage*, took place on the background of natural changes, the maturing (and later declining) human body and the change of seasons, while his analysis stressed how rituals did not simply reflect these physical transitions but structured them. Rituals thus "mirrored" the natural world but also shaped and transformed it (Handelman 1990). Van Gennep's notions were later elaborated upon in the work of Victor Turner who, in particular, explored the dynamics of the liminal phase of ritual syntax in greater depth (Turner 1967).

There also are combinatory principles that rituals share with aesthetics such as symmetry, or with the dramatic rhythm of beginning gradually, reaching a crescendo somewhere "in the middle," and then tapering off. As an example of symmetry, the Jewish Sabbath begins and ends with candle-lighting rites, even though the textual and historical basis for the initial and the concluding acts are quite different. In the elaborate *seder* – the celebratory meal on the first night of Passover that will be discussed later – the key textually-defined elements of eating unleavened bread and other symbolic acts take place at the center of the evening, while more light-hearted activities in which children have a role are found both at the beginning and toward the end of the ceremonial sequence. Current analysts of ritual turn to concepts from music, art, literature, and drama to illuminate the inner logic of ritual sequences.

Victor Turner suggested the term "social drama" when studying how rituals among the Ndembu in Central Africa fit into an evolving social context. While the classic view of Durkheim (1915) had linked rituals to the representation and reinforcement of social solidarity, Turner (1957) showed that they could play a key role in expressing and channeling social conflict as well, and even result in a split within a group. While aspects of rituals, such as the symbols they employed, might be assigned some general agreed upon "meaning," their concrete significance as they were performed in actual situations heavily depended on the contexts within which they were enacted. Similarly, a given ritual might convey different messages to different participants. As in languages, the "syntax" of ritual could bear a range of messages, in which both the features internal to the ritual and the complexities of its setting had to be invoked to understand a specific "utterance." More recently, the interpenetration of ritual discipline and relations of power has received attention (Asad 1993).

Turner also laid out a method for unraveling the significance of rituals. He pointed to three dimensions that needed attention: the interpretive, the performative, and the locational or positional (1967). The first, also called the exegetic dimension, refers to the explanation of rituals and their symbols as put forth by participants in a culture in terms of their tradition and their contemporary situation. The second, the performative dimension, emphasizes what people actually do and how this fits into the physical, temporal, and interactional contexts of a society. The locational takes into account that any symbol occurring in a ritual must be viewed in the matrix of other interconnected symbols that are significant within a given society and its web of cultural associations. In outlining this scheme, particularly with reference to the exegetic dimension, Turner moved beyond what was accepted by scholars before him when he attached importance to explanations offered by members of a society themselves. This step leads us to a discussion of myth, and, eventually, to a consideration of the links between myth, ritual, and symbol.

MYTH

A definition of myth that fits our purpose is offered by Finnish folklorist Lauri Honko:

> Myth, a story of the gods, a religious account of the beginning of the world, the creation, fundamental events, the exemplary deeds of the gods as a result of which the world, nature and culture were created together with all parts thereof and given their order, which still obtains. A myth expresses and confirms society's religious values and norms, it provides patterns of behaviour to be imitated, testifies to the efficacy of ritual with its practical ends and establishes the sanctity of cult. (Honko 1984: 49)

Myth is thus a sacred story that seeks answers to the great questions of origins: how was the world created, and what is the basis of sex and fertility; what explains the diversity of living things including human beings; and what the source of the hierarchies is, such as gender, notions of nobility through descent, or practices of caste in which humans are enmeshed. Other basic matters addressed are more abstract, relating to emotions or to notions of good and evil, ethics and justice. Myths also provide the cultural building blocks and knowledge that shape perceptions of time, space and causality, pointing to a correct ordering of the cosmos as well as to the social order and human practice.

The sanctified dimension of myth makes it distinct from other genres of narrative such as folktales or legends that are not perceived as sacred, even though in some instances these forms of expression may overlap. Their correctness is spun by narrative means throughout the concerns of individuals and the institutions of society. Bronislaw Malinowski (1926) saw myths as outlining a charter for social life, providing both ideal models for behavior as well as serving as interfaces against which specific acts and historical events may be assessed. Elaborate myths succeed in weaving threads that link large questions of the origins of the cosmos with concrete social norms and practices.

Even though, or perhaps precisely because, myths make assertions about the absolute, both specific myths and the very notion of myth have been matters of contestation since antiquity. With regard to the cultural traditions that are viewed as standing at the base of what we now deem to be Western civilization, both in ancient Greece and in the writings of the Hebrew Bible, received myths and the entire realm of myth were challenged. This might have stemmed from the rendering of myths in written form, and perhaps, in particular, the development of alphabets that enabled literacy to spread more widely than previously. This technology of "mind" may have provided the opportunity for frequent reviewing and also re-assessment of the content of myths, while the critique of myth that developed in these two traditions reflected different cultural emphases.

In ancient Greece, systematic reflection and speculation began to challenge existing myths as inadequate to explain the universe, how it came about, or the principles according to which it functioned. Myths, sometimes defined as "stories about gods," were thus demoted in relation to rational philosophy, aspects of which included what today we would call "science" (Doty 1986). At the same time, the power and attractiveness of mythic narratives were evident in their persistence, so that interpretations of their place in culture were offered, such as viewing them as distortions of events that had actually taken place. This ambivalent attitude has continued up to the present. The development of modern science constituted an additional challenge to the contents and relevance of ancient myths, but, as we discuss shortly, principles of myth still are at work in contemporary culture.

The Hebrew Bible is often presented as devoid of myth. It does not contain earthly stories of "gods," but of a single omnipotent God who, while described as acting on and within the world, is presented in anthropomorphic imagery that is greatly muted in comparison to the myths of Greece or of the Ancient Near East. At the same time, conceptually, the early parts of the book of Genesis clearly fit our definition of myth in outlining a sacred cosmology of the physical universe and the broad strokes of a blueprint for human existence (Leach 1969). Viewing the text of Genesis theoretically also highlights another analytic dimension of myth: that is pervaded by a non-mundane sense of time.

A contrast that has arisen in challenging the "truth" of myth is the opposition between myth and actual history. Myths in many cultures distinguish between the present time of "ordinary" people and actions and the time of mythic events, when, for example, gods interacted with people, animals conversed with humans, and indeed beings of one existential status readily transformed into another. In Genesis, by contrast, the text seems to acknowledge such a distinction, but also to submerge it in a flow of continuity. Adam and his descendants live hundreds of years, and eventually human longevity is limited to "one hundred and twenty years" (Genesis 6:3), but we are not presented with an explicit existential divide separating mythical from ongoing human existence. This example highlights the importance of analytic distinctions regarding time and other features of myth that enable one to identify parallels in a range of cultural settings while also appreciating differences that distinguish them.

Lévi-Strauss formulated an approach to myth based on analytic properties that are not dependent on whether a person is a "believer" or not; the "suppression of time" is one of those properties (1963). He advocated first understanding the structure of myth itself, before relating myths to other cultural expressions or social contexts.

Seeing myths as built upon expanded linguistic principles, they are constituted by a coherent system of signs with an internal structure that remains constant and may be transposed from one situation to another, over space and time, and still be recognized as "the same." Thus, a sense of eternity appears to inhere within them.

It is precisely this suspension of time that enables myths to bridge space and time, and become a means for the representation of sacred space and time on earth (Eliade 1963). Individuals and groups who are actively engaged in myths, by reciting, reading, or listening to them, may be moved back to mythical time, or more precisely to enter a dialogue moving to and fro between the hoary past and their present situation. Rather than linear movement, the way that we typically understand chronological progress, myth creates a temporal spiral that contains both forward and cyclical thrusts (Eliade 1954, 1963).

In this manner, myths transmit central cultural messages. Through repetition, key categories of the cosmos and society are identified and established, and the relations among them are internalized. Binary oppositions are vital in this process, as in many rituals, and some symbolic pairs like day and night, woman and man, culture and nature, appear in many cultures. At the same time, myths contain figures and images that do not fit established oppositions and that simultaneously reinforce categories, challenge them, and mediate between them (Lévi-Strauss 1967). A close reading of myths shows that they themselves encode the arbitrariness of the categories that they put forth and celebrate. While addressing and appearing to respond to the existential dilemmas of human existence, and the built-in strains and contradictions of specific social structures, they also signal that there are no lasting solutions to them. Rehearsal and repetition of the narratives with their images and structures provide intervals of belief and a sense of relief that solutions exist, while the movement of prosaic life and of history intervene to shatter their persuasive, but ultimately fragile, representations.

SYMBOL

The notion of symbol was introduced into the discourse on culture and behavior to stress the centrality of communication and language in human activities, to emphasize how thought and mental life are based upon social processes, and to underline the place of social learning in the transmission of culture rather than it being biologically based or instinctual in origin. A symbol, or – more generally – a sign, is something that represents (or "re-presents") something else. To a great degree, symbols are arbitrary in form, particularly linguistic symbols. The idea of a dwelling structure is represented by the word *house* in English, *maison* in French, and *bayit* in Hebrew. None of these, in spoken or written form, bears material resemblance to an actual house, even with the range of physical forms that houses may take. Once linguistic tradition combined with the force of social convention has established a link between a linguistic symbol and what it represents, it is transmitted "automatically" and learned anew in each generation, sometimes even producing a sense that the link between the symbol and what it stands for is "natural."

Highlighting the arbitrariness of symbolic forms was an important step in demonstrating that social and cultural processes could not be reduced to simpler explanations such as individual psychology (the "brain"), or to group proclivities (such as "national character"). Now, however, it is appreciated that other modes of signification coexist, and indeed complement, representation through "pure" symbols. Mary Douglas (1970) introduced the notion of "natural symbols," based on the claim that biological processes common to all humans often entered in the symbolism of ritual, thereby limiting its arbitrariness. At the same period, Victor Turner suggested that the basic colors of black, white, and red, which are named in languages around the world, might carry roughly similar if not culturally identical meanings (1966). For example, experience with human and animal feces is common to all societies, and it is notable that the association of blackness with fertility (earth or dung as fertilizer) appears in many of them. Along with these insights, it was appreciated that symbols, or signs more generally, could not be approached like a list of entries in a dictionary assigning "a meaning," or even several meanings, to each symbol as an individual item. Symbols took on significance within fields made up of other symbols, of realms of cultural production such as myths and especially rituals, and of wider social contexts.

Language was thus helpful, but also limited, in serving as a general model for communication via symbols. Myths and rituals as channels of communication may engage all human senses and motor capabilities, such as sound (music as well as language), sight, touch, motion (e.g., dance), smell and taste. Some of these might entail iconic representation along with the symbolic. An icon may be defined as a sign whose form suggests its meaning. An inherent link between form and what it represents does not mean that icons take on specific cultural meanings independent of societal learning. Their meanings are based upon "built-in" resemblances of form, but also on cultural convention and interpretation. For example, a single internationally recognized traffic sign, bearing a house with a sloping roof, indicates a residential area, while that specific type of house roofing is by no means universal. Here we have a single standardized representation of a variety of physical objects. An "opposite" example, in which "the same" natural base leads to a variety of cultural forms, may be seen in the realm of "greeting." Physical touch between individuals is widespread in creating and acknowledging relationships, but takes diverse forms such as shaking hands, cheek-kissing (the number of times varies among societies), or rubbing noses. In all these instances both iconic relations and social tradition shape the process of signification.

In addition to icons, another kind of sign coexisting with symbols is the "index" (Silverstein 1976). In this case, a sign "points to" the referent that it re-presents. Indexical relationships may be partially "natural," as when people widely accept "smoke" as standing for "fire." This link, for example, appears in a well-known English proverb (and in proverbs in other languages), and at times receives visual expression as well. Indexical relationships may also become established on the basis of culturally specific associations such as a flag coming to "stand for" a nation. When rituals, and their paraphernalia, relate to grand religious concepts that are numinous or have sense of mystery, they may not carry an easily defined and specific meaning, but serve as "pointers" to sublime realms of significance. After the revelation to Moses at the burning bush (above), God provides Moses with the ability to carry out miraculous acts as "signs" to the Children of Israel (Exodus 4). Nothing in the substance of these signs relates to the content of God's message, but is intended to direct the attention of those witnessing them. Interpreting the signs becomes complex when Moses has to compete with Pharaoh's magicians who can perform similar wondrous feats (Exodus 7). This example of indexical relations also underlines the importance of *context* in grasping how symbols and signs work within concrete cultural frames and social fields.

Symbols, along with both iconic and indexical signs, are woven through both myths and rituals and contribute to their close association. They effectuate the storing of cultural information and enable its transmission in concentrated messages carrying practical implications along with emotional and spiritual denotations. Through them, interrelated cultural themes are articulated at the levels of both cosmology and its specifications in a range of realms: nature and the supernatural, political orientations, aesthetic taste, law and justice, and other matters of the mundane world.

This web of interrelations is partially enabled by the mechanisms of metaphor and metonymy. These formal terms bear some resemblance to the different forms of magic mentioned earlier, based on similarity of form in the first case and "contagion" or contiguity in the latter (Jakobson and Halle 1956). Raised to a general analytic level, both metaphor and metonymy operate in narrative forms including myths, and also in ritual structures and processes (Lévi-Strauss 1966; Barthes 1968). Metaphor is a move by which a term (or action, or object) is symbolically enriched by referring to another object that is different and separate from the original, but with which it shares some quality allowing a meaningful linkage. Metonymy enhances symbolic value through contiguity: being connected in a verbal string, or being closely linked within physical space or time.

The celebration of Passover, to be depicted shortly, provides illustrations of both concepts. The ritual meal on the night of Passover (the *seder*), involves eating bitter herbs that are said to partake of the bitterness of oppression experienced by the Hebrew slaves in Egypt. Both in the ritual acts described in the Bible at the time of the Exodus (12:8), and in the standard ritual consumption during the *seder* that eventually evolved, bitter herbs are put in close physical connection with *matzah* – the unleavened bread later associated with "affliction." The second, metonymic, link thus reinforces the initial metaphoric assertion. Such associative mechanisms enable the internal elaboration of systems of symbols as well as their ability to both reflect and penetrate the social contexts surrounding them. They move back and forth between circumscribed settings of condensed cultural expression in language and in performance, and the ongoing, shifting, and open-ended challenges of everyday life.

Such to-and-fro movement between ritual-mythic and quotidian contexts allows individuals and groups to address the large questions of human existence that entail ambivalence and lack of clarity. Ritual settings, creating what has been called "time out of time" (cf. Leach 1961), permit approaching these issues with a diminished sense of danger, and with the subsequent return to routine activity. Ambivalence and anxiety, which may be at once cultural and personal, are made available for symbolic mediation. Cultural themes are dramatized and thereby internalized within individuals and threaded through interaction in a manner more powerful than when they appear sporadically in daily activities. In this manner they serve to inform and re-energize routine scenes and enactments.

According to Victor Turner, a feature of symbols that accounts for such flow of "energy," is that they often are built around two poles, one ideological and the other sensory (Turner 1967: 28–29, 50–55). The linking of the two imbues ritual symbols with compelling meaning for participants. Turner's well-known example from the Ndembu in Zambia was a forest shrub called *mudyi* that exuded milky sap, and featured in both girls' and boys' initiations ceremonies. The matrilineal character of the Ndembu descent system emphasized the bond of breast feeding; thus, the *mudyi* represented the matrilineage itself, the virtues of good family living, and the warmth of close attachment to the mother. "Milk" was the sensory pole of the tree's symbolic valence, hinting at the satisfactions of mother's milk and energizing the ideological poles of goodness and matrilineal norms.

Turner, as indicated, argued that understanding symbols entailed the exegesis of local experts, close attention to performance, and locating symbols within wider fields. This led him to stress their *multivocality* (alternately, their *polysemic* quality). A single symbol could carry different and even opposite meanings. It might have differential significance among the participants of a ritual, and could take on distinct associations when performed on a variety of ritual occasions. White, among the Ndmbu in other ritual contexts, could stand for male semen. Red also took on a range of meanings both positive and negative. Red earth might be used in a curing ceremony to heal the ailments of a menstruating woman, while generally the blood of menstruation was considered bad and harmful in comparison to blood associated with men and hunting that was viewed as life-giving. Some members of a society might process meaning in an explicit manner while others might intuit them. An account of symbols must take into account a range of contexts in which they appear.

One set of contexts falls under Van Gennep's rubric of rites of passage (above, 1909), associated with different life stages and the change of seasons. Symbols could appear prominently with regard to a specific life transition, or could link together different "passages" and thereby spin a web of symbols that had dominant significance within a society. Other sorts of rituals were distributed over the years; in each performance certain aspects of a dominant symbolic theme might be highlighted. By attending to a series of contexts, however, the range of symbolic associations becomes both clarified and "naturalized." Members of a society come to feel that the meanings are part of themselves.

The same mechanisms, it should be emphasized, come into play not only when perpetuating the culture and structure of societies, but may reflect and participate in shaping transformations. As technological, socioeconomic, and political shifts proceed apace, societies "manage" them by holding on to precious myths and self-images. The simultaneous sustaining and revision of symbolic motifs are expressed most palpably in ritual moments, both modest and grandiose. These interrelated processes allow individuals and groups to perceive and feel that they remain "themselves" and true to "tradition," even when set in motion by both endogenous and exogenous historical gyrations. In the following discussion, we call upon an example where such a sense of continuity has been maintained over centuries of major historical shifts.

HISTORICAL CHANGE AND COMPARISON: PASSOVER AS AN EXAMPLE

The relationships among the phenomena discussed may be illustrated by the Jewish festival of Passover whose textual and cultural roots are in the Hebrew Bible. In that set of sources, Passover is constituted by mythic narrative and ritual action, and also invites various symbolic readings. This example can be studied with great historical depth and provides the opportunity of adding the vector of change over time to the discussion, along with the perspective of comparative study.

The second book of the Hebrew Bible, to which the name Exodus was given at the time of its translation into Greek in the third century BCE, is built around the theme of the enslavement of the Children of Israel in Egypt, and their successful escape from bondage. This escape, led by Moses who was the recipient of divine inspiration and instruction, evolves in a series of dramatic episodes leading to a special bond between God (YHWH) and the Israelites. Savants have wondered why this account of the "birth of a nation," is preceded by the book of Genesis whose opening chapters more closely correspond to the cosmology-establishing purpose of myth that we have stressed. The biblical text, however, hints at links between the two birth epics. For example, there is resonance between the image of Noah's ark in Genesis, that allows humans and beasts to survive the primeval flood, and the small "ark" in Egypt's river, that ensures the survival of Moses. The same Hebrew word – *tevah* – is used in both episodes (Genesis 6:14; Exodus 2:3). In later times, rabbinic culture applied the term *tevah* to the "holy ark" in synagogues that house the scrolls of the Five Books of Moses. Through repetition, including manifest and subtle redundancies, mythological threads beginning with the creation are drawn into the contours of a specific society and its practices.

The mythic account in the Exodus highlights certain themes that reverberate both at the level of Israel's earthly evolution and regarding its relation with the divine. The miraculous 10 plagues highlight the separation of the Israelites from the wider and dominant Egyptian society within which they have been enmeshed. The month of departure, called Aviv (that later became the Hebrew term for "spring"), was designated the first month of the year, endowing the escaping slaves with a new calendar (Zerubavel 1982). The miraculous crossing of the "Red Sea" (called the "Sea of Reeds" in the text), marks the final physical separation of the Israelites from Egypt and the Egyptians. Next, the purpose and destination of the escape is brought into focus: the revelation of God on Mount Sinai to Moses and the Children of Israel climaxing in their receipt of the "Ten Commandments." Taken together, these adventures comprise a mythical sequence depicting how the Israelites "became a people" in relation to God (Deuteronomy 27:9).

Woven through the mythical tropes of the escape are directives for ritual action, both at the time of the events and for future generations. The first plague involved the Nile turning to blood, and the final blow was the death of the Egyptian first-born. Prior to this destruction, the Children of Israel are commanded to organize in family groups, slaughter lambs selected at the beginning of the month, and "take some of the blood and put it on the sides and tops of the doorframes of the houses where they eat the lambs" (Exodus 12:7). Consequently when the "destroyer" (Exodus 12:13) sets out upon Egypt and smites the first-born male in each household, the homes of the Israelites will be marked with blood and the first-born within them spared. The Hebrew term *pesah*, later translated as "pass over," is presented as reflecting this "skipping over" of the Israelite homes (Exodus 12:27). That night, just before the actual exodus, the lamb meat is to be eaten with unleavened bread and bitter herbs (Exodus 12:8).

In the midst of this drama, God instructs the Israelites to get ready for departure, baking bread (called *matzah*) even before the dough has a chance to rise. At the moment of this hasty escape, Moses, commanded by God, still takes time to announce the implication of these founding events for the future. Each year, in a family gathering, a sheep is to be slaughtered, roasted, and eaten. These acts are explicitly assigned an educative function: "And when your children ask you, 'What does this ceremony mean to you?', then tell them, 'It is the Passover sacrifice to YHWH, who passed over the houses of the Israelites in Egypt and spared our homes when he struck down the Egyptians'" (Exodus 12:26–27).

Along with the specification of rituals to be carried out are a number of prohibitions especially regarding food. Passover is defined as a seven-day festival with a cessation of work on the first and last days, and during the whole period leavened bread, or any food undergoing leavening, must be avoided. As for participation in the Paschal sacrifice, only males who are circumcised (as commanded to Abraham in Genesis 17) may partake of the paschal meal. Outsiders attached to Israelite families may participate if they undergo circumcision (Exodus 12:48). It is notable that precisely at the peak of symbolic acts that define and distinguish the collectivity, rules are laid out regarding the inclusion or exclusion of non-Israelites.

The narrative and ritual acts thus engender a number of symbols, some immediately apparent and others elaborated over the course of time. The *matzah* prescribed both for those leaving Egypt and for future generations, is glossed in Deuteronomy (17:3) as the "bread of affliction," reminiscent of the oppression suffered in Egypt. The "bitter herbs" prescribed at the time of the exodus carry a similar connotation. The "flip side" of eating *matzah* – the prohibition of eating leavened food – has had, over the generations, the pragmatic connotation of separating Jews from Gentiles. Today, *matzah* has become a symbol of Passover *par excellence*, recognized by Jews and many non-Jews as well.

Blood is a salient element of the biblical narrative, while following it as a symbol yields a complex story. It figures in the story of Moses reluctantly taking on God's mission for him (Exodus 4), and later appears as the first plague and in the ritual protecting Israelites from "the destroyer" on the night of the escape. In Talmudic texts, however, blood is not given a place within the repertoire of ritual performance. Wine, which in many cultures is associated with blood (there are two poetic examples in the Hebrew Bible – Genesis 49:11, Deuteronomy 32:14), is central to the Passover ritual, and later became symbolically linked to blood in at least one *seder* practice entailing the recitation of the ten plagues. It is quite possible that this development reflects, in particular, Jewish life in a Christian environment (cf. Yuval 2006), where the symbolic link between blood and wine is prominent (see below).

Within the Hebrew Bible itself, Passover is integrated into an annual ritual cycle that involves three pilgrimage visits to the "place that God will choose" (Deuteronomy 12 – later appearing in the Bible as Jerusalem and the site of the Temple built by Solomon). The other two pilgrimage festivals are *Shavuot* (Pentecost), fifty days after Passover and called the holiday of the first fruits (*bikkurim*), and *Sukkot* (Tabernacles), marking the end of the harvest season and assigned to the fifteenth day of the seventh month (and corresponding to the onset of the rainy season). Tabernacles – actually temporary hut dwellings – also are to remind the Israelites of their sojourn in the desert (Leviticus 23:42), so Passover, as well as its two companion festivals, is enveloped in seasonal – agricultural symbolism along with the historical signification imprinted in the founding myths of the Israelite people.

Passover, as celebrated and understood today, does not stem from biblical sources alone but reflects historical development of both its narrative and ritual elements. With the destruction of the Jerusalem Temple during Roman rule (70 CE), Jewish ritual underwent reorganization at several levels allowing ancient practices to continue in new constellations within decentralized communal and family settings. The performance of the Passover celebration was still anchored in a family gathering featuring a meal structured around foods and rituals concretizing the commandment to "tell your children" in reference to specific texts (cf. Sutton 2001). This came to be called the Passover *seder*, from the Hebrew word for "order" (cf. the term "order" with reference to monastic life). In particular, a condensed summary of Israelite history originally formulated for recitation at the temple on the *bikkurim* festival (Deuteronomy 26:5–9), was transferred to the family feast on the first night of Passover (Bokser 1984). This text, and subsequent elaborations, came to be called the Passover *Haggadah* or "(re)telling."

The *Haggadah* provided the framework for performance, and opportunity of rehearsing, mythic elements in the Passover *seder*, even while absorbing additional influences and symbolic associations as Jewish life spread and diversified during the Middle Ages within Christian and Muslim realms. On *seder*-night, a sense of return to the mythic time of the exodus overwrote what might be considered strict "history." This temporal return may be envisioned in terms of a spiral: mythic events keyed to a series of performed rituals infuse the present while current circumstances are represented in the recitation of ancient texts, and both index a future charged with symbols of redemption. In historical terms, the symbolic webs engendered and engaged in this process, were spread beyond the boundaries of any one specific Jewish community.

A comparative view of Passover entails attention to the variety of historical Jewish communities and also sensitivity to the interaction between Judaism and neighboring religions. Such a view exemplifies how myths, rituals, and symbols undergo transformation and reinterpretation, and also may enter into contestation. The "last supper" in the accounts of the life of Jesus is widely regarded to have been a Passover *seder* (although scholarly opinion on the matter varies), and the image of him as a "sacrificial lamb," becomes a foundational element for central myths and rituals within Christianity. The symbolism and mystical understanding of bread and wine as the body and the blood of Christ, are radically different from the significance of unleavened bread and wine at the *seder*, whatever the historical relationship between them may be (Feeley-Harnik 1994). The case of Jews living in Ethiopia provides an example of how both ancient symbols and recent ethnography illuminate such processes.

Ethiopian Christians likened Beta Israel's (Ethiopian Jews) Passover slaughter to the murder of Jesus. In their view, the Beta Israel, being the progeny of Christ-killers, carry "in their blood" inherited traits of the murderers of God. In concrete practice, the Beta Israel always slaughtered the animals outside, where all could see. The slaughtered beast was then hung on a tree in order to drain its blood. For the local Christians, this act evoked Jesus's crucifixion on a cross of wood. In a similar way, the Christians grasped the ancient crucifixion as a Paschal sacrifice, similar to the Beta Israel's Passover slaughter. This conceptual circle reflects a mutual projection between a myth-based doctrine (the crucifixion of Jesus by Jews), and a reaction to observable praxis.

In another historical arena, the Great Festival of Islam, known alternatively as the Festival of Sacrifice – *'id al adha*, is similar to Passover and entails the slaughter of a victim in a family setting and often a joint meal. One of the Arabic terms for sacrifice – *qorban* – comes from a cognate of a similar term in biblical Hebrew. At the same time, mythical themes of this occasion in Islam hark back to images of Abraham (Ibrahim) and the near-sacrifice of his son, rather than to the national redemption of Exodus. This "shared" mythic theme is also a matter of disagreement. Muslims generally understand Abraham's almost-slaughtered son to have been Ishmael, while Jews follow the biblical text which names the son as Isaac. A practice reported for some rural areas in Libya, regarding the Festival of Sacrifice, was for Muslim notables to invite leaders of a local Jewish community to skin the slaughtered beasts, as if to symbolically elicit their acquiescence, through deeds, to the Muslim understanding of the myth. Jews reported that they acceded to this request, partly out of respect, and partly out of fear.

Each of these settings reflects ethnographic work among the groups cited, carried out by the authors of this chapter. Each instance, placed in the context of ancient oral and textual traditions, provides examples of the processes we have underlined. Concrete performances, placed in the context of ancient narratives, exhibit both constancy and change, accommodation conjoined with appropriation, and resistance along with resilience, emerging out of the dynamic interplay of ritual, myth and symbol.

REFERENCES

Anderson, Benedict. 1983. *Imagined Communities: Reflections on The Origin and Spread of Nationalism*. London: Verso.

Asad, Talal. 1993. *Genealogies of Religion: Discipline and Reasons of Power in Christianity and Islam*. Baltimore: Johns Hopkins University Press.

Barthes, Roland. 1968. *Elements of Semiology*. Trans. Annette Lavers and Colin Smith. New York: Hill and Wang.

Barthes, Roland. 1972. *Mythologies*. Trans. Annette Lavers. New York: Hill and Wang.

Bell, Catherine M. 1992. *Ritual Theory, Ritual Practice*. Oxford and New York: Oxford University Press.

Ben-Amos, Dan. 1993. "Context." *Western Folklore* 52, pp: 209–226.

Bokser, Baruch. 1984. *The Origins of the Seder: The Passover Rite and Early Rabbinic Judaism*. Berkeley: University of California Press.

Cassirer, Ernst. 1944. *An Essay on Man: An Introduction to a Philosophy of Human Culture*. New Haven: Yale University Press.

Cassirer, Ernst. 1953–1957. *Philosophy of Symbolic Forms*. Trans. Ralph Mannheim. New Haven: Yale University Press.

Doty, William G. 1986. *Mythography: The Study of Myths and Rituals*. Tuscaloosa: University of Alabama Press.

Douglas, Mary. 1966. *Purity and Danger: An Analysis of Concepts of Pollution and Taboo*. London: Routledge and Kegan Paul.

Douglas, Mary. 1970. *Natural Symbols: Explorations in Cosmology*. New York: Random House.

Durkheim, Émile. 1915 [1912]. *The Elementary Forms of The Religious Life, A Study in Religious Sociology*. Trans. Joseph Ward Swain. London: G. Allen and Unwin.

Eliade, Mircea. 1954. *Cosmos and History: The Myth of the Eternal Return*. Trans. Willard R. Trask. Princeton: Princeton University Press.

Eliade, Mircea. 1963. *Myth and Reality*. Trans. Willard R. Trask. New York: Harper and Row.

Feeley-Harnik, Gillian. 1994. *The Lord's Table: The Meaning of Food in Early Judaism and Christianity*. Washington, DC: Smithsonian Institution Press.

Firth, Raymond. 1973. *Symbols: Public and Private*. Ithaca: Cornell University Press.

Freud, Sigmund. 1915 [1900]. *The Interpretation of Dreams*. Introduction by

A.A. Brill. Trans. A.A. Brill. London: G. Allen and Unwin.

Freud, Sigmund. 1927 [1912]. *Totem and Taboo: Resemblances Between the Psychic Lives of Savages and Neurotics*. Trans. A.A. Brill. New York: New Republic.

Frazer, James G. 1922. *The Golden Bough*. Abridged edition. London: Macmillan.

Grimes, Ronald. 1982. *Beginnings in Ritual Studies*. Lanham, MD: University Press of America.

Handelman, Don. 1990. *Models and Mirrors: Towards an Anthropology of Public Events*. Cambridge: Cambridge University Press.

Hasan-Rokem, Galit. 1997. "Studying Folk Culture and Popular Culture." *Teoriyah uvikoret* 10: 5–13 (Hebrew).

Honko, Lauri. 1984. "The Problem of Defining Myth" in Alan Dundes, Ed. *Sacred Narrative: Readings in the Theory of Myth*. Berkeley, Los Angeles and London: University of California Press, pp. 41–52.

Jakobson, Roman and Morris Halle. 1956. *Fundamentals of Language*. 's-Gravenhage: Mouton.

Leach, Edmund R. 1961. "Two Essays Concerning the Symbolic Representation of Time" in *Rethinking Anthropology*. London: Athlone Press, pp. 132–136.

Leach, Edmund R. 1964. *Political Systems of Highland Burma*. 2nd edition. Boston: Beacon Press.

Leach, Edmund. R. 1969. *Genesis as Myth and Other Essays*. London: Jonathan Cape.

Lévi-Strauss, Claude. 1955. "The Structural Study of Myths." *Journal of American Folklore* 68: 428–444.

Lévi-Strauss, Claude. 1963. *Totemism*. Trans. Rodney Needham. Harmondsworth: Penguin.

Lévi-Strauss, Claude. 1966. *The Savage Mind*. Chicago: University of Chicago Press.

Lévi-Strauss, Claude. 1967. "The Story of Asdiwal" in Edmund R. Leach, Ed. *The Structural Study of Myth and Totemism*. London: Tavistock, pp. 1–47.

Malinowski, Bronislaw. 1926. "The Role of Myth in Life." *Psyche* 24: 29–39.

Morris, Charles W. 1946. *Signs, Language and Behavior*. New York: Prentice-Hall.

Peirce, Charles S. 1931–1935. *Collected Papers of Charles Sanders Peirce*. Vols. 1–6. Charles Hartshorne and Paul Weiss, Eds. Cambridge, MA: Harvard University Press and Belknap Press.

Rappaport, Roy A. 1999. *Ritual and Religion in the Making of Humanity*. Cambridge: Cambridge University Press.

Sapir, Edward. 1921. *Language: An Introduction to the Study of Speech*. New York: Harcourt.

Saussure, Ferdinand de. 1966. *Course in General Linguistics*. Charles Bally and Albert Sechehaye, Eds., in collaboration with Albert Reidlinger. Trans. Wade Baskin. New York: McGraw-Hill.

Silverstein, Michael. 1976. "Shifters, Linguistic Categories, and Cultural Description" in K. Basso and H.A. Selby, Eds. *Meaning in Anthropology*. Albuquerque: School of American Research/University of New Mexico Press, pp. 11–56.

Sutton, David E. 2001. *Remembrances of Repasts*. Oxford: Berg.

Tambiah, Stanley J. 1985. *Culture, Thought, and Social Action: An Anthropological Perspective*. Cambridge, MA: Harvard University Press.

Turner, Victor W. 1957. *Schism and Continuity in an African Society*. Manchester: Manchester University Press.

Turner, Victor W. 1966. "Color Classification in Ndembu Ritual: A Problem in Primitive Classification" in Michael Banton, Ed. *Anthropological Approaches to the Study of Religion*. London: Tavistock, pp. 47–84.

Turner, Victor W. 1967. *The Forest of Symbols. Aspects of Ndembu Ritual*. Ithaca: Cornell University Press.

Van Gennep, Arnold. 1909. *Les rites de passage*. Paris: Nourry.

Yuval, Israel J. 2006. *Two Nations in Your Womb: Perceptions of Jews and Christians in Late Antiquity and the Middle Ages*. Berkeley and Los Angeles: University of California Press.

Zerubavel, Eviatar. 1982. "Easter and Passover: On Calendars and Group Identity." *American Sociological Review* 47: 284–289.

RELIGIOUS PRACTICE

CHAPTER 7

Sabina Magliocco

Religious practice has been at the center of folklorists' concerns since the inception of the discipline in the late eighteenth century. This very broad category of cultural practice includes phenomena as diverse as saints' day celebrations and cults, calendar customs and seasonal festivities, the construction and maintenance of domestic shrines, cures and health practices that make reference to spiritual or religious notions, non-mainstream spiritual beliefs, and "superstitions." How these expressions all came to be situated under a single rubric despite their obvious divergence is a product of the crucible of cultural forces which brought forth the ethnological sciences in the late eighteenth and early nineteenth centuries.

The study of folklore and anthropology emerged from a confluence of Enlightenment principles, colonialism and Romanticism that led to various modes through which European and American intellectuals strove to separate themselves from those they deemed culturally alien (Bendix 1997). These disciplines constituted dividing practices that served to distinguish expert from lay knowledge, colonizer from colonized, powerful from subdominant. The Other could be situated historically, as inhabiting the past, or geographically, as inhabiting colonies or the rural European landscape. Peasants, the focus of early folklorists' scrutiny, were othered both in space, as rural dwellers in contrast with the urban intellectuals who wrote about them, and in time, as carriers of traditions which were surmised to have survived from ancient times with little or no change. Scholars viewed both colonized peoples and European peasants as having religious practices beyond which urbanized Europeans had progressed. Much of the early study of religious practice among these groups was aimed at bringing to light and ultimately extinguishing erroneous, false or "pagan" customs and traditions (Dorson 1968: 1–43). Thus much of what has constituted "religious practice" for the ethnological sciences encompasses customs and traditions that differ from those of the urban, educated elite who set the discourse of mainstream culture.

A Companion to Folklore, First Edition. Edited by Regina F. Bendix and Galit Hasan-Rokem.
© 2012 John Wiley & Sons, Ltd. Published 2012 John Wiley & Sons, Ltd.

Even when scholars were part of the same complex society as the people whose religious practices they were examining, there was a presupposition that they did not share their customs, traditions and beliefs. While the majority of ethnologists came from a Judeo-Christian religious background (in other words, they were at least nominally Christian or Jewish), their religiosity was inevitably more learned and literary than that of the people whose traditions they documented. This gave them a certain social distance from their objects of study, as well as a significant bias, especially in the study of non-Western religious practices. Nonetheless, the accepted scholarly stance towards the spiritual and supernatural in the ethnological disciplines was at best one of agnosticism, if not outright rejection, creating another layer of separation between scholars and the people they studied.

While this chapter will endeavor to give readers enough historical background to understand the development of more recent approaches, emphasis will be placed on more current schools of theory and interpretation, especially those of the latter quarter of the twentieth century and the first decade of the twenty-first. It will concentrate on Western analytical constructs, and confine itself to reviewing only a few examples of the study of religious practice by scholars from other parts of the globe. Finally, it will focus on the ethnological sciences, which include folkloristics, anthropology and to some degree sociology – all disciplines that rely upon direct observation of cultural phenomena, rather than concentrating solely on the study of religious texts and liturgy.

Ethnological understandings of religious practice have shifted with the rise and fall of theoretical paradigms over the last 200 years. The study of religious practice reflects a number of issues in the studies of folklore and religion themselves, as well as broader issues in the allied disciplines of anthropology and ethnology. Among the most salient are the difficulty in defining religion and the lack of general agreement among scholars about what constitutes religion; the influence of Christianity, as the dominant religion in the West, in the definition and understanding of what constitutes religion; the effects of positivism and scientism on the study of religious practice; the position of the researcher vis-à-vis the studied communities, particularly the fact that scholars generally have not shared the same belief systems as those they have studied; and the phenomenology of religious experience. These issues in turn have been shaped by the historical movements of romanticism, nationalism, colonialism, post-colonialism, and the post-modern critique of academic disciplines as discourses of power that emerged in the late twentieth century. Appreciating ethnological approaches to religious practice means understanding the various influences that have shaped the field of study from the outset.

A number of early folklore scholars turned their attentions to religious texts, often in an attempt to prove that they contained survivals of pagan theological concepts rooted in seasonal or celestial cycles. However, with some exceptions, notably among scholars of folk narrative, ethnological approaches have tended to study religious practice holistically. Folklorists, ethnologists and anthropologists seek to understand religious practice in context, against the backdrop of larger social, economic, political, historical and environmental forces. In fact, most scholars in these disciplines argue that religious practice cannot be understood apart from these larger contexts. Ethnological approaches to religious practice have shared a focus on human behavior and belief, rather than the sacred texts and liturgies which were the province of theological approaches to religion in seminaries and departments of religious studies. The incipient disciplines of folkloristics, ethnology and anthropology concentrated their attentions on the religious practices of peasants, the working classes and colonized peoples, leading to a focus on religious practices designated as "unofficial" or "informal." This inherent power differential between the scholars and the people whose traditions were being studied is another issue that permeates the study of religious practice, and will be further examined below. Another factor uniting folkloristic approaches to religious practice today is their grounding in fieldwork, long-term, face-to-face contact with religious practitioners, usually not limited strictly to religious contexts, but encompassing participant-observation of their entire society.

PROBLEMS IN DEFINING RELIGION

In *Making Magic: Religion, Magic and Science in the Modern World* (2004), Randall Styers argues that the emergence of religion as an analytical category begins in the sixteenth century, when in various accounts of non-Western societies, "religion" is used to refer to ritual practices which observers recognize as a "cross-cultural and potentially universal phenomenon" (Styers 2004: 4). By the eighteenth century, however, the sense of this term had changed considerably as a result of issues brought to the fore by the Reformation and Counter-Reformation, both of which shifted the emphasis from outward forms of religiosity – religious practice, in other words – to an inward state of faith or belief essentially unknowable by anyone outside the believer (Styers 2004: 5). This tendency to define religion on the basis of belief, rather than practice, became so predominant among the European intellectual classes that it served as a lens through which the religions of other cultures, as well as those of the lower classes, were understood. However, this view of orthodoxy poses particular problems for non-Christian religions (for example, Judaism, in which practices such as keeping Kosher, observing the Sabbath, and dress codes define faith) as well as for the practices of non- or semi-literate classes within Western societies. In these cases, orthopraxy may be more important than orthodox belief in determining religious affiliation. Many non-Western indigenous religions both lack texts that codify beliefs, and do not consider faith to be a pillar of religious identity in the way that Christianity does. For non- or semi-literate peasants within Western cultures, religious texts codifying beliefs were inaccessible; much more important were traditional understandings of cosmology rooted in pre-Christian practices, upon which Christian material had been layered. A classic study of these processes was done by historian Carlo Ginzburg, who, by examining witch trial records in sixteenth and seventeenth century Friuli in northern Italy, demonstrated how pre-Christian narratives about certain townspeople journeying in spirit to battle evil sorcerers for the fertility of the fields were overlaid with, and eventually entirely supplanted by, elite notions of demonological witchcraft (Ginzburg 1966). In both indigenous and peasant forms of religiosity, encounters with the divine could take very different forms from what was expected in Christian traditions. Too, the hierarchical organizational model common to many Christian faiths has often been taken to be the standard by which religions are defined, and those lacking centers of worship, holy writs, trained clergy and an established liturgy have been seen as less legitimate, or even deficient in the characteristics that define religion.

It is customary for discussions of the study of religion to begin by calling attention to the fact that there is no shared definition of religion common to all scholars who study religious phenomena, and that there is considerable disagreement among them as to what constitutes a religion. Rather than attempting to provide a synthetic definition, this chapter will outline how a series of key scholars defined religion, and thus shaped the kinds of materials and approaches studied by the ethnological sciences.

Edward B. Tylor, the nineteenth-century scholar often credited as the father of anthropology and the evolutionist "doctrine of survivals," defined religion simply as belief in spirits (Tylor, 1871). The second volume of his magnum opus, *Primitive Culture*, entitled "Religion in Primitive Culture," attempted to explain the development of religion as a natural outgrowth of primitive humans' endeavors to explain the world around them. Tylor's definition must be understood against the backdrop of his theory of cultural evolution, according to which cultures developed over time from simple to more complex forms. All cultures, according to Tylor, began at the "primitive" stage of development, characterized by animistic beliefs in which natural phenomena and inanimate objects were thought to possess souls and respond as individuals to human interaction. A further stage of development, "barbarism," was characterized by polytheistic beliefs, while the apotheosis of religious development was represented by monotheistic religions. Tylor wrongly perceived primitive religions as less complex than those of more "advanced" stages of cultural evolution. Inevitably, his scheme reflected contemporary power relations between Western and non-Western cultures, such that the indigenous religions of colonized peoples were categorized as "primitive," those of non-Western civilizations, including ancient Greek and Roman religions, were "barbarian," and only Western monotheistic Christianity (and Protestantism, at that) qualified as "civilized." Those aspects of earlier belief systems that persisted in a higher stage of cultural evolution were considered to be "survivals," and destined to disappear. It was these so-called cultural leftovers that fascinated early European scholars of religious practice. Late nineteenth- and early twentieth-century folklorists in particular applied Tylor's paradigm to a variety of peasant and indigenous religious practices, interpreting them as survivals of ancient pagan customs (see Dorson 1968). A strong anti-religious bias runs through Tylor's work, as he postulated that eventually all religion would be replaced by science as progress brought education and enlightenment to the world's peoples. Tylor considered belief in God itself to be a survival from a time in which scientific explanations for natural phenomena had not yet been developed.

Tylor's disciple Sir James Frazer elaborated on this system, developing a similar evolutionary scheme for religion. In Frazer's scheme, magic represented the earliest form of religious practice, in that it was a human attempt to both understand and control the workings of the natural world. Religion, a more systematized attempt to relate to the surrounding world through rituals and prayers appealing to deities, was the next development in human perception. But it was Western science that stood at the apex of the system, representing the only true and valid means for understanding natural laws and developing means to subdue nature and control its forces. Frazer's system had an advantage over Tylor's, in that it took magic seriously as a human attempt to understand and control the world – an early, if mistaken, form of science before scientific principles could be articulated by primitive humans. Frazer argued for an underlying logic of magic, the principle of "sympathy," which could further be categorized into homeopathy (the idea that like causes like) and contagion (the principle that two things once in contact continue to influence one another even after separation). All magic, according to Frazer, could be understood according to these underlying principles. Frazer's encyclopedic study of religious traditions, *The Golden Bough*, first published in 1860 in two volumes, enlarged to 12 in the third edition (1906-15), and then abridged in 1922 into a single-volume work, examined rituals from cultures the world over, including those of ancient times as reported by classical writers, in an attempt to isolate their underlying pattern. He argued that all seasonal rites essentially enacted a pattern based upon the life cycle of a dying and reborn deity – one that presaged the development of the Christian mythos. This interpretive structure was so influential that until the middle of the twentieth century, many folklorists interpreted seasonal celebrations almost exclusively as symbolic expressions of death and regeneration whose purpose was to stimulate fertility in the agricultural cycle. This interpretation in turn greatly influenced the development of modern Pagan religions in the mid-twentieth century, which have become one of the foci of early twenty-first-century academic interest.

The French sociologist Émile Durkheim established key parameters attempting to define religion and human relationships to the sacred. These concepts included the distinction between sacred and profane, the belief in souls, spirits, and mythical personages, the belief in deities, some form of asceticism or deprivation within the religion itself, and rituals as the primary expression of religiosity (Durkheim 1965 [1915]). While he argued that these characteristics could be found in religions at all levels of cultural evolution, he did not stray from the evolutionary tendencies of his predecessors, postulating that totemism, the worship of an animal or plant associated with the identity of a social group, constituted the earliest form of religion. Durkheim's definition of religion was very much based on the model of Western complex societies: "a unified system of beliefs and practices related to sacred things – namely things set apart and forbidden – beliefs and practices which unite in one single moral community called a Church, all those who adhere to them" (Durkheim 1965: 55). He saw religion as having an important unifying function for society, and took pains to distinguish it from magic, which he saw as anti-social and focused upon individualistic gains. While Durkheim's approach is more nuanced than either that of Tylor or Frazer, we can still see within it the strong influence of social evolutionism and Christian normativity. In particular, his separation of magic from religion continues the pattern of earlier scholars, ignoring the many magical aspects present within complex religions such as Christianity, and relegating magic to a marginal status with few redemptive social qualities. Durkheim uses magic as a foil against which to define religion, perpetuating a pattern that undergirds Western approaches to religion and magic from ancient times onwards (Hutton 2003: 107).

The anthropologist Ruth Benedict suggested in the 1930s that a more useful approach to magic and religion would be to view them as existing along a continuum of human relationships to the supernatural world, rather than in an evolutionary relationship to one another (Benedict 1933: 39–43). The basic distinction between magic and religion was nevertheless preserved, and reflected in the contributions of Bronislaw Malinowski: magic constituted human attempts to control and manipulate the supernatural for specific aims, and was generally characterized by relationships between individuals and specialized practitioners, while religion was both more broadly concerned with worship and devotion, and more social in nature (Malinowski 1955).

In the 1960s, a number of anthropologists began to challenge the nature of these distinctions, calling attention to the fact that indigenous categories of behavior seldom matched the ones Western scholars had developed. Both E. E. Evans-Pritchard (1965) and Mary Douglas (1966) made this argument, but it was taken to its logical extreme by Murray and Rosalie Wax, who argued the term "magic" was so problematic that either anthropologists ought to dispense with it completely, or that its range of meanings should be expanded to include many indigenous ways of understanding what Westerners would call cosmology, philosophy or even science (Wax and Wax 1963). Dorothy Hammond proposed that rather than abandoning the category of magic completely, it should be understood as part of religious practice – one that imagined a more equal and cooperative relationship between humans and deities, in contrast to worship and prayer (Hammond 1970:1355). By the 1980s, the accepted position within anthropology was that distinctions between magic and religion were products of Western category-making, rather than intrinsic to the organization of human culture and behavior.

In contrast, European folklorists working during the first half of the twentieth century were relatively untroubled by this debate, for two reasons. First, they worked mostly within their own societies, in which the traditional distinctions between magic and religion mirrored those in use by ethnologists of all stripes. The concept underlying their work was necessarily that of an organized, dominant religion, to which the phenomena that they studied were contrasted. Folklorists were well aware of the difficulty in separating magic from religion, as a number of vernacular religious practices were magical in nature, but understood by practitioners as part of religious expression. For example, in many Catholic countries, the palms and olive fronds blessed by the priest during Palm Sunday ceremonies are believed to have apotropaic qualities. These are often woven into crosses or objects resembling flowers, and are placed in the home or other locations (e.g., the byre, or hung from the rear view mirror of a car) for protection. Here the religious and the magical intersect: the palms and olive leaves are believed to offer magical protection and they are thought to derive their power from a publicly performed religious ritual. This coexistence of magic and religion was generally framed in the scholarly discourse as an index of lack of privilege; the presumption was that as practitioners became better-educated, the magical aspects of their religiosity would eventually disappear and be replaced either with normative religious expression, or with non-belief.

The work of Italian ethnologist Ernesto de Martino was emblematic of this approach. Strongly influenced by the Marxism of Antonio Gramsci, who saw folklore both as an expression of peasant resistance and as part of a worldview that ultimately perpetuated social inequality, de Martino sought to understand the popular supernatural beliefs of Italian peasants in the *mezzogiorno*, the unindustrialized, largely agricultural southern half of the peninsula. His approach blended ethnological and psychological concerns with historical ones, but went well beyond the survivalism of some folklorists, as he sought to situate religious practices and beliefs within a context that included a historical dimension. His best-known book, *La terra del rimorso* (1961; translated into English as *The Land of Remorse* 2005), examines *tarantismo*, a cultural complex of behaviors and beliefs linked to the alleged bite of a tarantula and the rituals to cure it. De Martino's contributions are ethnographically thick, theoretically complex and reflexive, foreshadowing many theoretical developments of late twentieth-century ethnography and folkloristics.

RELIGION AS A CULTURAL SYSTEM: GEERTZ AND HIS CRITICS

One of the most significant contributors to debates over the definition of religion in late twentieth-century ethnology was the American anthropologist Clifford Geertz. In his essay "Religion as a Cultural System," he presents his definition of religion as:

> (1) a system of symbols which acts to (2) establish powerful, pervasive and long-lasting moods and motivations in men by (3) formulating conceptions of a general order of existence and (4) clothing these conceptions with such an aura of factuality that (5) the moods and motivations seem uniquely realistic. (Geertz 1973: 90)

He further characterizes religious symbols as addressing three types of existential questions that are fundamental to the human condition: those that strain analytic capabilities; those that strain emotional endurance; and those that challenge the limits of moral insight (Geertz 1973: 108). Geertz attributes to symbols the power to order chaos, impose meaning, and create a cosmos that is ultimately interpretable from a human perspective.

Geertz's definition of religion differs from earlier ones in important ways. First, it completely bypasses evolutionary schemes, being applicable to any type of society, from any historical period or part of the world. It likewise avoids defining religion in contrast to other cultural constructs such as magic or science. Finally, it reflects Geertz's interpretive views of culture as consisting of symbols that operate in the mind of each culture-bearer to both interpret the surrounding world and impel behavior. For Geertz, religious practice is ideology made manifest; its performance creates the text ethnologists observe and describe in order to get at the underlying symbolic constructs. The task of the ethnologist, therefore, is two-fold: to analyze the meaning of religious symbols, and to relate these to the larger structures, both social and psychological, within the particular culture.

Even among interpretive anthropologists, Geertz was not without his critics. Perhaps the most significant among them is Talal Asad. While recognizing that no single definition of religion can be universally viable (1983: 238), Asad points out numerous weaknesses inherent in Geertz's approach. He lays bare the specifically Christian history of the whole idea of religion as a human universal, and shows that by insisting on the centrality of symbolic meanings in his definition of religion, Geertz inadvertently takes what could be interpreted as a theological stance – that is, he places belief before practice, thought before action, and privileges ideas above customs and traditions. This reflects uniquely Western Protestant notions about the importance of faith and belief in religion, but is ill-suited to the definition of non-Western religions or, for that matter, even medieval Christianity, which differed markedly from that of the post-Reformation. For Asad, Geertz's definition is problematic because it removes symbols from any kind of embeddedness in larger discursive processes through which meanings are created – processes that involve practice and behavior rather than thought alone. While Geertz rightly sees the link between religious ideology and religious practice, Asad criticizes him for failing to identify that link as power, and for investigating exactly how power creates religion by identifying spiritually authentic truths, practices and speech (1983: 246). So while Geertz's definition of religion is valuable because it overcomes the shortcomings of earlier ones and draws ethnological attention to the meaning of symbols in performance, it nevertheless reflects a particular kind of notion of religion still based on Western models. Furthermore, it does not adequately explore relationships between religion and power that authenticate certain practices as "religious" by excluding others, and establish links between religion and political ideologies.

The question of power and religion returns to the forefront through the influence of the French scholars Pierre Bourdieu, an anthropologist, and Michel Foucault, a historian. While neither wrote specifically about religion, nor intended to critique the work of Geertz, the effects of their ideas on ethnological approaches are so pervasive that they warrant mention here. Both authors were deeply influenced by Marxism, one of the central paradigms of post-war European scholarship, as well as the experience of French decolonization following World War II, especially the Algerian War (1958–1962). As a result, they turned their attention to structures of power and domination, each examining in his own terms how social domination is imposed on individuals and groups. While retaining a strong interest in symbols, Bourdieu sought to ground his analytical theories in practice – people's ordinary behavior in everyday life. Expanding on Karl Marx's idea of capital, he articulated how social status goes beyond mere economic means and also involves social, cultural and symbolic capital, all of which are mobilized to reproduce inequality. Thus elements of expressive culture, including religion, mark individuals as members of particular social groups, impeding or aiding their social mobility. Bourdieu also drew attention to the ways social status and dominant ideology are deeply embedded in the daily routines of practitioners through bodily practices he terms "habitus," which also reproduce social distinctions. Like Bourdieu, Foucault also studied the effects of domination on the body, particularly through practices that attempt to discipline individuals into compliance and punish deviation from the norm. He explored how dominant ideologies sought to create and control knowledge by determining what constituted accepted truth. He called this conjunction "power/ knowledge." Both Bourdieu and Foucault ultimately influenced the study of religion away from the intellectual and symbolic forms favored by Geertz and his followers, and towards the study of how social domination takes place through embodied practices. As a result, the study of religion shifted in the late twentieth century to focus less on beliefs and more on praxis, with a special emphasis on the body and embodied traditions such as religious ecstasy and possession. New understandings of the processes of knowledge creation and social domination pushed scholars to turn the critical lens towards their own disciplines and the ways they constructed their objects of study, and to reflect upon their own social, cultural, and economic positions vis-à-vis those of the people they studied. Late twentieth-century developments in the ethnological study of religion reflect the influence of these important concepts.

AMERICAN APPROACHES TO THE STUDY OF FOLKLORE AND RELIGION

In the early part of the twentieth century, there was little distinction in the United States between folkloristic and anthropological approaches to the study of religion. Between 1908 and 1940, the *Journal of American Folklore* was edited by anthropologist Franz Boas and his students Ruth Benedict and Gladys Reicherd, who published numerous studies of Native American mythology, religion, and worldview. Boas' students were deeply interested in religious practice: Benedict published *Zuni Mythology* (1935), Reicherd authored *Prayer: the Compulsive Word* (1944) and *Navajo Religion: a Study of Symbolism* (1950). Zora Neal Hurston, another student of Boas, was among the first to systematically study Afro-Caribbean religions in her first-person ethnographic account, *Tell My Horse* (1938). Boas' legacy extends to the Africanists Melville Herskovitz and his student William Bascom. Herskovitz studied the survivals of African cultures in the practices of African Americans, including their spiritual traditions, while Bascom conducted a detailed study of Yoruba religion, as well as conducting research among the Gullah people of the Georgia Sea Islands, emphasizing the importance of understanding the socio-cultural context of religious practices (Primiano 2010).

Other folkloristic approaches to religious practice during the mid-twentieth century centered on the collection, classification, and analysis of oral folklore genres associated with religious practice. The work of Wayland Debbs Hand was typical in this regard. A professor at UCLA, and founder of the Folklore and Mythology Program there, Hand amassed an enormous number of folk beliefs, mostly from literary and written sources, which came to constitute the backbone of the UCLA Archive of Popular Beliefs and Superstitions. Hand was interested in the cross-cultural similarities and differences among various beliefs, and concentrated his attention on factors of content, transmission and variation. However, he gave little attention to the value of these expressions as creative, evocative elements of individual or community religious communication, and continued to view them as characteristic of groups that were uneducated, misinformed, or marginal. Many early folklorists continued to interpret folklore as survivals; it was not until the 1960s that the value of this paradigm began to be questioned as folklorists turned their attention towards the individuals who performed folklore and the context in which it emerged, rather than towards items of folklore as historical relics.

By the early 1980s, American folklorists' approaches to the study of folklore and religion had crystallized around two different constructions: "folk religion" and "religious folklore" (Danielson 1986). Don Yoder, writing in the early 1970s, defined "folk religion" as "the totality of all those views and practices of religion that exist among the people apart from and alongside the strictly theological and liturgical forms of the official religion" (Yoder 1974: 2). Yoder's definition encompasses both unofficial practices associated with mainstream religions, also referred to as "religious folklore," and religions that exhibited a less formal, structured organization than established religions, and often existed among marginal populations or in the margins of mainstream society. Examples of religious folklore could be commonly found in any religious denomination. In his chapter on religious folklore for a major undergraduate textbook used in the United States during the 1980s and 1990s, Larry Danielson cites as an example a common legend told among Catholic school children about to receive their first communion, that if they were to bite down upon the host, their mouths would fill with blood (1986: 50). Pentecostal Holiness churches, with their extensive reliance on oral tradition, lay ministers, unorthodox yet literal interpretation of biblical passages, informal, participatory and ecstatic services, and non-adherence to a liturgical calendar common to other strains of Protestant Christianity, could be taken as examples of "folk religions" (Danielson 1986: 49).

In contrast, scholars interested in belief in the supernatural outside a religious context generally studied legends, focusing issues such as the process of legend formation, the transmission of legends, the worldview and creative interpretation of individual narrators. The work of Linda Dégh is typical of this latter group (see Dégh 1995 and 2001). Dégh criticized earlier folklorists in Europe and the United States for their simplistic and arrogant approaches to folk belief as an archaic survival. In contrast, she saw the authenticating qualities of legend as part of the genre's performative style, asking questions about the nature of reality rather than making statements based on faith. She accurately described the variable nature of belief, both within communities (within every community, there are both believers and skeptics) and over the life course of the individual. She studied legend narration and belief among Hungarian peasants and American university professors alike, also calling attention to its presence in the mass media. At the same time, her work was characterized by a view of supernatural belief as ultimately irrational – an aberrant or mistaken understanding of reality. While an improvement on earlier constructs that relegated folk belief to lower social classes and marginalized groups, or viewed it as a relic of an earlier historical period, these approaches nevertheless presented their own problems. Chief among them were a lack of connection between belief scholarship and legend scholarship, and the stance of the researcher in regards to the individuals being studied.

This orthodoxy began to be challenged in a series of papers published in 1995 in a special issue of *Western Folklore* devoted to the role of reflexivity in the folkloristic study of religion and belief. The term "reflexivity" emerged from scholarly debates of the 1980s on issues of power/ knowledge within the academy, and on the positional bias of the researcher vis-à-vis the studied community. It referred to the need for researchers to turn their analytic lens upon themselves in relation to the communities they studied, reflecting on issues of power, gender, ethnicity, race, sexual orientation, and other factors of positionality that influenced their relationship with their field communities, the kinds of data they were able to gather, and their interpretive structures. Before the latter part of the twentieth century, it was taken for granted that folklore researchers, like anthropologists, were in a position of privilege vis-à-vis their field communities, which were usually drawn from the lower classes in their own complex societies. The normative attitude of ethnologists towards the religious material they studied was one of distance and disbelief. However, in the mid-twentieth century, this began to change as more women and members of under-represented groups entered the academy. By the late twentieth century, many folklorists who studied "folk religions" or "religious folklore" were in fact members of the very groups whose traditions they were documenting. That placed them in a very different position in regard to the materials and communities they studied than earlier folklorists, who may have had little personal connection to them.

As articulated by David J. Hufford, the guest editor of the special issue, "the central point of reflexivity [is that] all knowing is subjective" (Hufford 1995a: 57). Hufford argued that while scholarship generally required a neutral stance in order to be able to evaluate evidence, when it came to spiritual and religious matters, impartiality was impossible (1995a: 61). Further, in the study of religious practice, the scholarly presupposition was that the best methodological stance was an attitude of disbelief towards spiritual and religious phenomena. This presumption put the truth-claims of scholars of religion in direct conflict with those of the populations they studied (1995a: 64). Hufford suggested that reflexivity in the study of folk beliefs and religion was a necessary corrective to this problem, in that "a reflexive analysis of our scholarship enables us to distinguish among the beliefs of our informants, our scholarly knowledge, our personal beliefs and our occupational ideology" (1995a: 71), leading to a greater clarity and cohesiveness of argument.

In his essay "Vernacular Religion and the Search for Method in Religious Folklife" (1995), Leonard Norman Primiano challenged the terms "folk religion" and "religious folklore" as they were commonly used by folklorists, arguing that words such as "folk," "unofficial" and "popular," when applied to religious practice and juxtaposed with "official" religion, were inherently derisive and marginalizing (1995: 38). He maintained that this contrast implied the existence of a "pure" religious normativity uncontaminated by human practice, with its individualistic and idiosyncratic variance. Using a line of reasoning parallel to Asad's critique of Geertz, he asserted that this duality belied an underlying, albeit unconscious, theological orientation on the part of scholars, in that it reified the authority of religious institutions by residualizing the lived religion of practitioners (1995: 39). Instead, he introduced an alternative term, "vernacular religion," as a necessary corrective to what he saw as a history of misrepresentation. Primiano intended vernacular religion as a challenge to both terminology and methodology. As a descriptive term, vernacular religion is meant to encompass a range of religious behavior, practice, and belief that cross-cuts traditional divisions of power, gender, race, ethnicity, and social class by focusing on "the individual as the creator and processor of a single folkloric worldview, who constantly interprets and negotiates his or her own beliefs" (1995: 48). In other words, vernacular religion addresses the personal and private aspects of religious belief and behavior with special attention to the creativity and artistry individuals express as they communicate their religiosity. As a methodology and theoretical orientation, vernacular religion is both reflexive and inductive. It is based on taking the experiences and perceptions of individual believers seriously while balancing them with an empathic scholarly perspective that situates them within their cultural and performative context. Primiano's article successfully shifted the terminology used by many folklorists in reference to religious practice away from earlier constructs, and ushered in a spate of studies focused more closely on individual religious practice and experience. However, his methodological and theoretical exhortations largely reflected trends that were already occurring in ethnological disciplines as a result of the post-modern critique.

A parallel argument was made by Marilyn Motz in her article "The Practice of Belief" (1998). Here, she traces how traditional ways of knowing that were the province of the lower social classes, women and stigmatized minority groups, "folk beliefs," in an earlier parlance, were gradually banished from intellectual discussion as a result of the Enlightenment and the emergence of the scientific paradigm as the dominant discourse. Through this process, the discipline of folklore created its object: the lore, beliefs and practices of marginal peoples which were no longer part of the discourse of the educated elite. She urges folklorists to examine "the practice of belief", the individual ways in which people believe and creatively express those beliefs through praxis.

An additional challenge to the orthodoxy of American approaches to religious practice was offered by David J. Hufford in his 1982 study *The Terror that Comes in the Night: An Experience-Centered Study of Supernatural Assault Traditions,* as well as in numerous subsequent articles. Hufford studied the "Mara" or "Old Hag" tradition in Newfoundland: a physical sensation of being awake and aware, but unable to move, feeling pressed down into the bed or even suffocated, frequently accompanied by fear and the sensation of a malign presence. This cross-cultural phenomenon is experienced by roughly 20% of any random population group (Hufford 1995b: 13), and is rooted in the physiological phenomenon of sleep paralysis. Hufford discovered that various cultures have developed explanations for this experience that make reference to supernatural agents as its cause. Based on this research, he developed the "experiential source hypothesis:" the idea that some folk beliefs are rooted in real, somatic experiences, and represent logical attempts to understand the experience (Hufford 1995b). The experiential source hypothesis differs from the usual "belief source hypothesis" favored by many social scientists: that people have supernatural or spiritual experiences as a result of their belief in supernatural or spiritual agents (1995b: 28). While not all folk beliefs can be explained according to the experiential source hypothesis, those that can, which he calls "core beliefs," derive from what he calls "core experiences:" those occurring cross-culturally regardless of pre-existing beliefs, having a stable perceptual core, and referring intuitively to spirits. Examples of core experiences include the "Old Hag" or "Mara" experience, explained above, and near-death experience, reported by some patients who briefly die while receiving medical treatment, and are subsequently revived. Some of these individuals report experiences of being drawn towards a bright light, reunion with deceased loved ones, seeing the afterlife, and being sent back to the world of the living after being told that their time has not yet come. Associated core beliefs are the existence of threatening spirits and the idea that the soul survives death (1995b: 29). Hufford calls his focus on the phenomenology of spiritual experience the experience centered approach. Based on this method, he argues that some spiritual beliefs are similar cross-culturally because they are based on similar somatic experiences that are part of the human condition. His theory neither argues that spirits are real, nor does it go beyond attempting to explain the origins and persistence of certain beliefs. However, it poses a powerful challenge to the theories of belief which dominated the twentieth century – those based on assumptions that religious beliefs were essentially delusional in nature.

As a result of the critiques of reflexivity and the experience-centered approach, the way American folklorists studied religious practice shifted dramatically in the late twentieth century and the first decade of the twentieth. The distinction between scholars of religion and scholars of legend and belief began to break down. More scholars began to take a phenomenological approach to religious and spiritual belief, searching for underlying core experiences. Closer attention was paid to individual religious practice, interpretation and creativity, including to religious materiality and embodied practice.

Numerous studies in the late 1990s and 2000s reflect these changing orientations in American folkloristics. The essays in *Out of the Ordinary: Folklore and the Supernatural,* edited by Barbara Walker (1995), exemplify many of the changes outlined above, examining "the supernatural" as part of the everyday, lived experiences of individuals, and exploring the phenomenological and experiential basis of belief. Daniel Wojcik explored a variety of prophecies of impending apocalypse in American culture in *The End of the World as We Know It: Faith, Fatalism and Apocalypse in*

America (1997). My own work on neo-pagan Witches investigated both their sacred art and altars as material expressions of religious ideology (2001) and the phenomenological basis of their ecstatic rituals (2004). In the discipline of anthropology, Hufford's movement towards a phenomenology of religious experience was paralleled by Thomas Csordas, whose works *The Sacred Self* (1994) and *Body/Meaning/Healing* (2002) seek to deconstruct the duality between mind and body that has dominated much ethnological research on religious healing.

The consideration of gender in relation to religious expression was one of the chief imperatives to come out of the reflexive critique of the ethnological disciplines. A number of scholarly works from the 1990s and early 2000s explore these dimensions. Kay Turner's work examined the intersections of faith, gender, and materiality in contexts ranging from Mexican American home altars, to the practice of building an altar to St Joseph among Italian Americans in New Orleans, to the way women create altars to express their spiritual worldviews (Turner and Seriff 1987, Turner 1999, 2002). Elaine Lawless studied how women preachers in Pentecostal religions situated themselves vis-à-vis a male-dominated ideology in *Handmaidens of the Lord: Pentecostal Women Preachers and Traditional Religion* (1988), and reflexively explored the life stories of women ministers in *Holy Women, Wholly Women: Sharing Ministries of Wholeness through Life Stories and Reciprocal Ethnography* (1993). Nor were feminist and practice-based perspectives limited to North American folklorists; they were part of a tide of grounded ethnographies from a variety of disciplines that examined religious practice from the point of view of the practitioners. Anthropologist Karen McCarthy Brown gave a vivid portrayal of the everyday practice and family history of a Haitian Vodou priestess in *Mama Lola: A Vodou Priestess in Brooklyn* (1991). Religious historian Robert Orsi examined an Italian American Marian feast in Harlem during the early twentieth century, highlighting women's roles in popular devotion, in *The Madonna of 115th Street* (1995). Both Norwegian ethnologist Jone Salomonsen (2002) and American religious studies scholar Cynthia Eller (1995) examined women's spirituality movements in North America from the perspective of the women's own life stories and experiences. Laura Stark[1] has worked extensively with materials in the Finnish folklore archives to reconstruct the role of magic and ritual in women's negotiation of gender in rural Finland (1998). She subsequently expanded her historical ethnography to explore the performance and narration of magic not as mere reflection of peasant reality but as practices constituting Finnish rural life of the late nineteenth and early twentieth century (2002, 2006).

RELIGIOUS PRACTICE IN A GLOBAL CONTEXT

The North American examples at the center of this overview should be seen as part of greater intellectual currents in the study of religious practice that encompass scholarship across the globe. A few examples of recent works will illustrate current trends in the study of religious practice in a global context.

The movement of peoples across the globe as a result of decolonization, political upheaval, and economic collapse has given rise to a growing interest in the effects of migration upon religious practice. The essays in Gertrud Hüwelmeier's *Traveling Spirits: Migrants, Markets and Mobilities* (2010) seek to understand the reciprocal influences of religion and globalization upon one another: how religions transform, are reinforced or re-invented as a result of transnational networks, migration, and the influence of the marketplace. Among the topics treated in this book are the global spread of Pentecostalism, Hindu nationalism, Islamic radicalism and the increasing popularity of spirit possession cults. The authors situate these practices within the social, cultural, economic and political context of a globalizing world, while at the same time seeing each manifestation of religious practice as a unique expression of vernacular religiosity. A similar trend is evident in the work of Israeli ethnologist Yoram Bilu, *The Saints' Impresarios: Dreaming, Healing and Holy Men in Israel's Urban Periphery* (2009), which examines how the revival of four saints' shrines in contemporary Israel was fueled by the religious practices and traditions of Moroccan Jewish migrants.

The opening of Eastern Europe after the collapse of the Berlin Wall in 1989 created an opportunity for new explorations of religious practice in the former Soviet satellite states. Bulgarian ethnologist and folklorist Milena Benovska Sabkova examined the revival of religion in post-Soviet settings, focusing on the memorialization of the martyrs and heroes in both secular and religious contexts (2010). Another scholar who has treated practices surrounding death is Gabriela Kilianova, whose research found surprising continuities between pre- and post-Soviet death customs (1995). Anthropologist Chris Hann, working at the Max Planck Institute in Halle, Germany, has gathered together a number of scholarly essays in *The Postsocialist Religious Question: Faith and Power in Central Asia and East-Central Europe* (2007). The revival of pre-Christian religions in post-Soviet Europe, especially its racialist political bent, has drawn the attention of a number of scholars, notably Viktor Schnirelman (2002), Adrian Ivakhiv (2005), and Michael F. Strmiska (2005).

A number of European and American ethnologists have manifested an interest in civil religious practice, particularly as it is expressed in secular pilgrimages to locations such as Graceland or Jim Morrison's grave, as well as through the construction of shrines and public memorializations of the type that follow a roadway accident or the death of a celebrity. Two important publications examining these trends are Peter Jan Margry's *Shrines and Pilgrimage in the Modern World: New Itineraries into the Sacred* (2008) and Jack Santino's *Spontaneous Shrines and the Public Memorialization of Death* (2006). These works illustrate how religious idiom can provide a global language of memory and loss that transcends cultural and religious difference. Hungarian scholar Gábor Barna has undertaken similar research on pilgrimage in Hungary, looking at the importance of the yearning for a return to nature in both secular and specialized religious journeys (2005). In Britain, Marion Bowman has studied the global phenomenon of pilgrimage to Glastonbury, a site that attracts both secular and religious visitors from a variety of traditions (1993). Another compelling trend is the collaboration between ethnologists and archaeologists in the study of religious practice. Ethnologists offer complex understandings of everyday interactions with the sacred that can illuminate interpretations of recent excavations as well as heritage sites. In Finland, Vesa-Pekka Herva and Timo Ylimaunu challenge traditional notions of folk beliefs and their relationship to religion, arguing that in early modern Finland, beliefs in trolls and spirits may have been expressions of everyday human relationships with the environment through the material world (Herva and Ylimaunu 2009). In the United Kingdom, cultural anthropologist Jenny Blain and archaeologist

Robert Wallis conducted a five-year intensive research study using participant-observation and reflexive ethnography to understand how modern Pagans relate to "sacred sites," pre-historic stone circles and similar monuments that dot the British landscape (Blain and Wallis 2007). They specifically examine how personal narratives and local legends combine to form emergent folklore about these sites, which in turn influences religious behavior and perception. American folklorist Tok Thompson has also explored the interstices between archaeology and ethnology in his study of traditions surrounding *sí*, pre-historic Irish stone monuments (2004). Thompson argues that a deep knowledge of local traditions surrounding these sites can be helpful to archaeologists attempting to understand the meanings associated with them historically.

Finally, a number of scholars are applying contemporary ethnological insights on vernacular religion and cultural hybridity to historical materials. Hungarian folklorists Gabor Kalinczay and Eva Pócs examine East European traditions of spirit communication and divination in conjunction with the early modern witchcraft persecutions (1998, 2005). British scholar Emma Wilby has applied similar analytical perspectives to trial records from Britain (2005, 2010), arguing for the existence of a uniquely European vernacular tradition of spirit communication that may have persisted well into the nineteenth century.

In sum, early twenty-first-century ethnological scholarship on religious practice encompasses a number of trends. It has incorporated the late twentieth-century postmodern critique to produce works that are reflexive, grounded in practice and phenomenology, concentrated on the individual as a creative interpreter or religious experience, and sensitive to the unique interplay between historical, political, economic and cultural forces in a globalizing world. It does not reject historicism or diachronic approaches, but works to integrate them into broader discussions and interpretations that shed light on both past and present. Deeply grounded in the methodology of participant-observation, it continues a centuries-long tradition of concern with lived religiosity.

NOTE

1   Laura Stark, Finland, has worked a lot with the Finnish Folklore Archives and sought to contextualize textual material with a view toward reconstructing gender, religion/ritual, magic practice, body, as well as how these factors interact within a modernizing Finland; her work is perhaps the most recent within Finnish folklore concerned with religion; Anna Leena Siikala has of course worked with Shamanism (see above under post-socialist suggestions).

REFERENCES

Asad, Talal. 1983. "Anthropological Conceptions of Religion: Reflections on Geertz." *Man* 18(2): 237–259.

Bárna, Gabor. 2005. "Searching for God, Ourselves, or Outing to Nature ..." *Acta Etnographica Hungarica* 50(1–3): 127–134.

Bendix, Regina F. 1997. *In Search of Authenticity.* Madison: University of Wisconsin Press.

Benedict, Ruth. 1933. "Magic" in *Encyclopedia of the Social Sciences* 10: 39–41.

Bilu, Yoran. 2009. *The Saints' Impresarios: Dreaming, Healing and Holy Men in Israel's*

Urban Periphery. Brighton, MA: Academic Studies Press.

Blain, Jenny and Robert Wallis. 2007. *Sacred Sites, Contested Rites/Rights: Pagan Engagements with Archaeological Monuments.* Eastbourne: Sussex Academic Press.

Bourdieu, Pierre. 1977. *Outline of a Theory of Practice.* Cambridge: Cambridge University Press.

Bowman, Marion. 1993. "Drawn to Glastonbury" in Ian Reader and Tony Walter, Eds. *Pilgrimage in Popular Culture.* Basingstoke: Macmillan, pp. 29–62.

Brown, Karen McCarthy. 1991. *Mama Lola: A Vodou Priestess in Brooklyn.* Berkeley: University of California Press.

Csordas, Thomas. 1994. *The Sacred Self: A Cultural Phenomenology of Charismatic Healing.* Berkeley: University of California Press.

Csordas, Thomas. 2002. *Body/Meaning/Healing.* Basingstoke: Palgrave Macmillan.

Danielson, Larry. 1986. "Religious Folklore" in Elliott Oring, Ed. *Folk Groups and Folklore Genres.* Logan: Utah State University Press, pp. 45–69.

Dégh, Linda. 1995. *Narratives in Society: A Performer-Centered Study of Narration.* Helsinki: Academia Scientiarum Fennica.

Dégh, Linda. 2001. *Legend and Belief.* Bloomington: Indiana University Press.

De Martino, Ernesto. 2005. *The Land of Remorse: A Study of Southern Italian Tarantism.* Trans. and annotated by Dorothy Louise Zinn, with a foreword by Vincent Crapanzano. London: Free Association Books.

Dorson, Richard M. 1968. *Peasant Customs and Savage Myths.* Chicago: University of Chicago Press.

Douglas, Mary. 1966. *Purity and Danger.* London: Routledge and Kegan Paul.

Durkheim, Émile. 1965 [1915]. *The Elementary Forms of the Religious Life.* New York: Free Press.

Eller, Cynthia. 1995. *Living in the Lap of the Goddess: The Feminist Spirituality Movement in America.* Boston: Beacon Press.

Evans-Pritchard, E.E. 1965. *Theories of Primitive Religion.* Oxford: Oxford University Press.

Frazer, James G. 1922. *The Golden Bough.* New York: Macmillan.

Foucault, Michel. 1982. "The Subject and Power." *Critical Inquiry* 8(4): 777–795.

Geertz, Clifford. 1973. "Religion as a Cultural System," in *The Interpretation of Cultures.* New York: Basic Books, pp. 87–125.

Ginzburg, Carlo. 1966. *I benandanti.* Torino: Einaudi.

Hammond, Dorothy. 1970. "Magic: A Problem in Semantics." *American Anthropologist* 72: 1349–1356.

Hann, Chris. 2007. *The Postsocialist Religious Question: Faith and Power in Central Asia and East-Central Europe.* Münster: Lit Verlag.

Herva, Vesa-Peka and Timo Ylimaunu. 2009. "Folk Beliefs, Special Deposits and Engagement with the Environment in Early Modern Finland." *Journal of Anthropological Archaeology* 28: 234–243.

Hufford, David J. 1982. *The Terror that Comes in the Night: An Experience-Centered Study of Supernatural Assault Traditions.* Philadelphia: University of Pennsylvania Press.

Hufford, David J. 1995a. "The Scholarly Voice and the Personal Voice: Reflexivity in Belief Studies." *Western Folklore* 54(1): 57–76.

Hufford, David J. 1995b. "Beings Without Bodies: An Experience-Centered Theory of Belief in Spirits" in Barbara Walker, Ed. *Out of the Ordinary: Folklore and the Supernatural.* Logan: Utah State University Press, pp. 11–45.

Hutton, Ronald. 2003. "The New Old Paganism" in *Witches, Druids and King Arthur.* London: Hambledon and London, pp. 87–135.

Hüwelmeier, Gertrud. 2010. *Traveling Spirits: Migrants, Markets and Mobilities.* London and New York: Routledge.

Ivakhiv, Adrian. 2005. "The Revival of Ukrainian Native Faith" in Michael F. Strmiska, Ed., *Modern Paganism in World Cultures.* Santa Barbara: ABC-Clio, pp. 209–240.

Kalinczay, Gabor and Eva Pócs. 2005. *Communicating with the Spirits.*

Budapest: Central European University Press.

Kilianova, Gabriela. 1995. "Old Theme in the Present Time. Narratives about Death in Modern Society." *Slovenský národopis* 43(2):197–204.

Lawless, Elaine. 1988. *Handmaidens of the Lord: Pentecostal Women Preachers and Traditional Religion.* Philadelphia: University of Pennsylvania Press.

Lawless, Elaine. 1993. *Holy Women, Wholly Women: Sharing Ministries of Wholeness through Life Stories and Reciprocal Ethnography.* Philadelphia: University of Pennsylvania Press.

Malinowski, Bronislaw. 1955. *Magic, Science and Religion.* New York: Doubleday.

Margry, Peter Jan. 2008. *Shrines and Pilgrimage in the Modern World: New Itineraries into the Sacred.* Amsterdam: Amsterdam University Press.

Motz, Marilyn. 1998. "The Practice of Belief." *Journal of American Folklore* 111(441): 339–355.

Orsi, Robert. 1995. *The Madonna of 115th Street. Faith and Community in Italian Harlem, 1880–1950.* New Haven: Yale University Press.

Pócs, Eva. 1998. *Between the Living and the Dead: A Perspective on Witches and Seers in the Early Modern Age.* Budapest: Central European University Press.

Primiano, Leonard Norman. 1995. "Vernacular Religion and the Search for Method in Religious Folklife." *Western Folklore* 54/1: 37–56.

Primiano, Leonard Norman. 2010. "Folklore" in Charles Lippy and Peter W. Williams, Eds. *Encyclopedia of Religion in America.* Vol. 2, pp. 845–852. City: CQ Press.

Sabkova, Milena Benovska. 2010. "Martyrs and Heroes. The Religious and Secular Worship of the Dead in Post-Soviet Russia." *Ethnologia Europaea* 40(2): 42–57.

Salomonsen, Jone. 2002. *Enchanted Feminism: the Reclaiming Witches of San Francisco.* London and New York: Routledge.

Santino, Jack. 2006. *Spontaneous Shrines and the Public Memorialization of Death.* New York: Palgrave Macmillan.

Shnirlman, Viktor. 2002. "Christians! Go home? A Revival of Neo-Paganism between the Baltic Sea and Transcaucasia (an overview)." *Journal of Contemporary Religions* 17(2): 197–211.

Stark, Laura. 1998. *Magic, Body and Social Order: The Constsruction of Gender Through Women's Private Rituals. Studia Fennica Folkloristica* 5. Helsinki: Finnish Literature Society.

Stark, Laura. 2002. *Peasants, Pilgrims, and Sacred Promises: Ritual and the Supernatural in Orthodox Karelian Folk Religion. Studia Fennica Folkloristica* 11. Helsinki: Finnish Literature Society.

Stark, Laura. 2006. *The Magical Self: Body, Society and the Supernatural in Early Modern Rural Finland. FFC* 290. Helsinki: Academia Scientiarum Fennica.

Strmiska, Michael F. and B.A. Sigurvinsson. 2005. "Asatru: Nordic Paganism in Iceland and America" in Michael F. Strmiska, Ed., *Modern Paganism in World Cultures.* Santa Barbara, CA: ABC-Clio, pp. 127–180.

Styers, Randall. 2004. *Making Magic. Religion, Magic and Science in the Modern World.* Oxford: Oxford University Press.

Thompson, Tok. 2004. "The Irish *Sí* Traditions, Connectionss Between Disciplines, and What's In A Word?" *Journal of Archaeological Method and Theory* 11(4): 335–368.

Turner, Kay. 1999. *Beautiful Necessity: the Art and Meaning of Women's Altars.* New York: Thames and Hudson.

Turner, Kay. 2002. "Mexican American Home Altars: Towards Their Interpretation." *Aztlan* 25: 327–346.

Turner, Kay and Suzanne Seriff. 1987. "Giving an Altar: The Ideology of Reproduction in a St Joseph's Day Feast. *Journal of American Folklore* 100(398): 446–460.

Tylor, Edward B. 2010 [1871]. *Primitive Culture: Religion in Primitive Culture.* Cambridge: Cambridge University Press.

Walker, Barbara, Ed. 1995. *Out of the Ordinary: Folklore and the Supernatural.* Logan, Utah State University Press.

Wax, Murray and Rosalie Wax. 1963. "The Notion of Magic." *Current Anthropology* 4: 495–503.

Wilby, Emma. 2005. *Cunning Folk and Familiar Spirits.* Brighton, UK and Toronto: Sussex Academic Press.

Wilby, Emma. 2010. *The Visions of Isobel Gowdie: Magic, Witchcraft and Dark Shamanism in Seventeenth Century Scotland.* Brighton, UK and Toronto: Sussex Academic Press.

Wojcik, Daniel. 1997. *The End of the World as We Know It: Faith, Fatalism and Apocalypse in America.* New York: New York University Press.

Yoder, Don. 1974. "Towards a Definition of Folk Religion." *Western Folklore* 33(1): 1–15.

FURTHER READING

Magliocco, Sabina. 2001. *Neo-Pagan Sacred Art and Altars: Making Things Whole.* Jackson: University Press of Mississippi.

Magliocco, Sabina. 2004. *Witching Culture: Folklore and Neopaganism in America.* Philadelphia: University of Pennsylvania Press.

Strmiska, Michael F. and V.R. Dundzila. 2005. "Lithuanian Paganism in Lithuania and America" in Michael F. Strmiska, Ed., *Modern Paganism in World Cultures.* Santa Barbara, CA: ABC-Clio, pp. 241–298.

CHAPTER 8

WORK AND PROFESSIONS[1]

Gertraud Koch

THE MEANING OF WORK

Human life, as well as the existence of communities, is unthinkable without work. In their stories, *Märchen* and myths, many cultures create an image of a blithe life freed from the toils of working. Yet, as in the biblical depictions of paradise, or the *Märchen* of the land of milk and honey, these are images whose reality is not nearly as paradisiacal as is hoped. Idleness, or a life without essential or indispensable tasks, these tales say, is incompatible with human nature, and such a lack ineluctably leads to undesirable social and individual consequences. Work is hence interpreted as a necessity and it is inscribed into cultural systems of meaning. Work is necessary to ensure human survival, and it utilizes as well as shapes the environment.

Unlike any other species, humans have had a transformative effect on their material environment. They have, through work, shaped their living conditions and developmental possibilities to such a degree that anthropologist Jonathan Kingdon speaks of humans having created themselves. Humans have molded ecological conditions in their environment with such vigor that it has affected their own evolution. This productive incorporation of the environment, which is generally understood as work, needs to be understood as going beyond a securing of immediate basic needs, and be seen as playing a substantial role in shaping the understanding of the self and of the world.

If work shapes humans, as individuals and as a species, so fundamentally, then work itself can be regarded as a life sphere that is characteristic of each community, one that reflects its fundamental elements and developmental principles. How people live, and what knowledge, both informal and formal, they have of the world, of themselves and of their community, with its avowals, shared cultural traditions and forms of expression, and how this knowledge is brought forth, transmitted and implemented (see Sims and

A Companion to Folklore, First Edition. Edited by Regina F. Bendix and Galit Hasan-Rokem.
© 2012 John Wiley & Sons, Ltd. Published 2012 John Wiley & Sons, Ltd.

Stephens 2005: 8), is fundamentally determined by the contexts of work in which they move. In this sense, work can be regarded as a key area for researching culture and lifestyle, not least because work occupies a not insignificant part of everyday life. At the same time, the term work is multifaceted. As Hannah Arendt set out in *The Human Condition* (1998), in the Aristotelian tradition, work fundamentally has three different aspects. First, it is trouble and effort, as in the case of labor performed by slaves. Second, work can be understood as producing and creating (*poiesis*). Third, work is a central dimension of acting and interacting with others to create a community.

In terms of cultural history, how work has been experienced and how it has been regarded has changed repeatedly. Work also differs by society and social stratum. In late modern ways of living, work has become of such central importance that one can speak of a "laborization" of all of life. That is, lifestyle and biographical choice have become wholly oriented to the demands of the working world. The universalizing tendency has inscribed itself to such an extent into interpretive contexts that nearly all spheres of life are described in terms of work: family work, relationship work, emotional work (Liessmann 2000). In late modernity, systems of meanings thus become joined to the social meanings attached to work.

Work is the central domain in or by which participation in society is made possible, so in consequence, work also serves to organize or negotiate over social inclusion(s) and exclusion(s). This means it is also integrally involved in the cultural production of the "social body," as has been demonstrated by theorists of culture and society including E.P. Thompson (1963) for Great Britain, Max Weber (1905) for Germany, and Pierre Bourdieu (1977, 1984) for France, though each examined different epochs. A long-term lack of work, now made possible due to the existence of social security systems that permit a certain degree of decoupling (e.g., survival is not wholly dependent on work), has been shown to endanger human creative capacities (Jahoda *et al.* 2002 [1933]). To some degree, this provides empirical foundations for the mythology-based warnings noted at the outset.

Work and Professions as a Topic in Folkloristics

Folkloric research is primarily interested in informal articulation, that is, in the stories, songs, skills, rituals, views, terms used in professions, everyday objects and everyday life, as they are found among the "ordinary folk." In the early days of work studies, the interest was in the work of peasant and craft occupational groups, the day-laborers, farmworkers, and smallholders. Later, mineworkers were the subjects of ethnographic study, as were feminized areas of work such as housekeeping, washing, and weaving, both examined in their regional and local life contexts. If research on work initially focused on rural groups and occupations, it was primarily because folklore was thought to be located there (McCarl 1996; Siuts 1988). At best, workers' culture was perceived as a degenerate form of peasant and craft culture, one that had emerged in the course of industrialization since most industrial workers were recruited from rural milieus. Workers' culture was long seen as a deficient, rudimentary way of life (Assion 2001).

One profession shaped by industrial practices that became of interest to folkloric research early on, largely without being tarred by pejorative comparisons drawn from peasant and craft traditions, was mining. It is an area of research that became, and remained, of international interest for a comparatively long time. George Korson, an American folklorist, drew parallels already in 1927 between mines, as a place where workers lived under semi-primitive conditions that were largely isolated from developments in wider society, and the living circumstances of smallholders. Wayland Hand (1969) called for the comparative study of miner's culture as part of research on industrially-oriented work. Both craft dimensions and the worldviews of miners played equal roles here, for in his view their folklore needed to be understood as an expression of, but also a reflection on, their experience of work. That was reflected in the division of knowledge in this occupation, but it was also a means for miners to distance themselves from the worldviews of managers and mine owners (Green 1972). By now, mining is no longer a significant employer or economic sector, in part due to global competition, so that research interest today focuses on the transformative processes in former mining regions (Moser 2002).

It took time after World War II for workers' culture to become established as a research topic in folkloristics (Korff 1971; Nickerson 1974), though the interest in it was expressed much earlier (Peuckert 1931). However, at that time and for various reasons, the call to work on it went unheeded. Since the 1970s, more extensive research has been carried out on workers' culture. It took into account that workers had become the largest part of the population, and were the decisive economic factor in industrialized nations (Assion 2001).

Disciplinary research on work and professions usually emerged in conjunction with other areas of research, including folk music or folk belief, or research on tools, families, urban culture, women and gender, regions or migration. What repeatedly gave impetus to folkloric research have been upheavals in society and in the world of work. The period since the late nineteenth century has been rich in such changes to the world and society, whether one means by it the two World Wars, the creation and then dissolution of antagonistic socialist and capitalist political blocks, or decolonization and democratization. Without a doubt, these changes affected the forms work took and the organization of labor, but by the same token these geopolitical changes were also influenced by developments in the world of work.

Changes to the world of work were also numerous, and no less serious than those to society and politics. They included shifts in production from peasant and artisanal modes to industrial or factory production which themselves have shifted from the Fordist assembly line to more flexible, post-Fordist, forms of work. Manual and physical labor has declined, owing to technological changes and rationalization, some of which were accelerated by wartime production and the needs of the armaments industry. The need for so-called "knowledge work" to be provided by engineers, managers, and scientists has increased. Computerization and the "virtualization" of work through networked organizational forms have gone hand-in-hand with an increasingly globalized division of labor. The shift to a service sector economy, the "culturalization" of the economy in the wake of the New Economy, and still further changes succeed one another increasingly rapidly, accompanied by the obsolescence of occupations and an increasing differentiation in the forms work takes and in work cultures.

The analysis, documentation and "museumification" of disappearing craft and peasant traditions (as well as of work techniques, cultural forms of expression, and lifestyles) has correspondingly long been an important concern of research in folkloristics – though it is not infrequently colored by a certain nostalgia (Siuts 1988).

Beyond "writing histories of what has been lost," such research on work and occupation is increasingly interested in understanding existing traditions and habitual forms as they have emerged and developed under specific historical circumstances. These traditions and forms are to be understood as resources for dealing with the demands that arise as a result of transformative processes and can be traced through their specific (sub-) cultural forms of expression (Warneken 2006).

WHO ARE THE FOLK WHO WORK AND ARE TO BE RESEARCHED?

When folkloric research began to focus on mining, it had to be justified by showing how miners as a group resembled isolated rural populations that lived, largely cut off from civilization, under semi-primitive conditions. That made miners a relevant group for folkloric study (Korson 1927). The issue is one repeatedly raised in folkloric studies that focus on work. Who should be regarded as the research-relevant population, and where are they to be found? The question the American scholar Bruce Nickerson posed in 1974 in a JAF article ("Is There a Folk in the Factory?") was not at all meant rhetorically. Rather, it was a response to the fact that a growing number of rural "ordinary folk" who were once the subjects of research had now migrated into factory work. A large proportion of the lower-class groups now earned their living by working in industry, so a new orientation and paradigm was necessary, if not an entirely new research area. To this end, it was necessary to show both how industrial work contexts could be conjoined to models and questions in folkloristic research, and that the connection existed.

Other national research traditions have also repeatedly asked the question "who are the folk?" studies of work and folklore can focus on. Hence, research studies that focus on work must often address the question which group is relevant to research, which is complicated by the rapid social changes often reflected in work contexts. Is it the peasants, the workers, or the petty bourgeois who stand at the brink of social decline? Which differentiations are necessary within the group – between large landowners and smallholders, between journeymen, craftsmen, and factory owners, between miners and industrial workers? Do immigrants who intend to remain, either briefly or longer, also belong?

Collective terms given to the particular group being researched are also significant. If they change over time, it signals that it is necessary to reformulate who is the focus of study in the research on work, both with respect to the general population and with respect to socio-demographic developments (Warneken 2006: 331–338). The collective terms used to summarize research about peasant, craftsman, or worker cultures, formulated in an effort to make the characteristic vantage point of the discipline clear (if not binding), have varied over the course of the discipline's history, from "folk" to "lower-class strata" to "popular cultures," the commonly-used term today.

There are also nationally-specific connotations, with the corresponding translation difficulties. For example, in German-speaking Europe, there is a common but untranslatable differentiation made between popular and *popular*. The connotation of the German term *Volksleben* and the US term folklife also differ. Germany has been using *Volksleben* less and less (see Bausinger's 1970 book of that title) and now calls its endeavors "empirical cultural sciences." But "folklife" in US research is now a term that designates a paradigmatic expansion of perspective that goes beyond forms of narrative, literary, and artistic expression to also designate objects and the material culture of the working world. As McCarl notes, "The study of occupational folklore in the United States parallels the evolution of folklore methodology in general, from the desire of the early ballad collectors to rescue surviving ballads and songs, to the impact of European-inspired interest in skill and material expression, to the more recent interest in the intersection between work culture, class, ethnicity, and gender" (1996, 522ff.). McCarl decisively shaped American occupational folklore and what he describes about the relationship between research on work and the development of the field more generally is hardly confined to the United States, inasmuch as the social changes that are relevant to research are articulated earlier and more clearly in the world of work than in many other areas.

THE CONCERNS AND LEITMOTIFS OF RESEARCH ON WORK

There are common central concerns in research on work that are independent of national research traditions. One is to make the expertise, independence, or achievements of certain occupational groups visible. Botkin (1954), from the US perspective, invokes the pathos of the occupational experience of engineers, taxi drivers, steelworkers, policemen, and those in other occupations, and describes them in exemplary terms, or in terms of a generally desirable developmental principle for the entire nation. In the context of the Smithsonian Folklife Festival, and with the broad support of unions, industrial workers, and folklorists, a large-scale presentation of occupations took place which, in its intensity, made clear the necessity for further research on occupational folklore (Byington 1978). The category "Working Americans" was featured every year from 1973 to 1977 at the Folklife Festival. In 1976 (the Bicentennial Year) the Festival was noteworthy largely because the emphasis shifted from individual occupations to broad functionalist categories: Workers Who Feed Us, Workers Who Extract and Shape, Workers Who Build, Workers in Technical and Professional Skills, Workers Who Clothe Us, Workers in Communications, Arts and Recreation.[2]

An important leitmotif in research on ways of working life is to correct the widespread view that workers and peasants are a deficient, if not maladjusted, social group that tends to hold primitive if not anti-modern attitudes (Rosenbaum 1992). Thus, for example, the Tübingen empirical culture studies specialist Bernd Jürgen Warneken (1986), in a historical study of the cultural patterns of peaceful mass demonstrators, was able to show that the masses were able to exert "self-control." The case he examined was that of Social Democratic workers during the political struggle over granting universal manhood suffrage in Prussia in 1908–1910. Warneken argued that what took place on the streets was a dramaturgic blueprint of an alternate political and social order, not a chaotic uprising but instead an ostentatiously ordered and peaceful demonstration – moving progressively forward in both senses of the word, with workers showing their ability to maintain self-control.

With this, Warneken critiqued a classification, largely from socio-philosophical quarters, that these masses were unreflective, epidemic-like confluences of "black blocks" on the brink of exploding, and not individuals acting in a reflective and enlightened manner. The "blackness" of these demonstrating masses, according to Warneken, did not stem from dark or malevolent powers but rather from the black cloth of the Sunday suits the workers had donned to symbolize they were reputable and proper (Warneken 2006: 145).

This very detailed historical study of workers' culture in Germany critiques an apparently widespread image of workers as morally dubious figures who act irresponsibly. That image, independent of the specific national development of the workers' movement, can be found in both public and academic discourse in various European countries. As the Swedish cultural anthropologist Brigitta Skarin Frykman (1990) notes, that image has persisted into the last decades of the twentieth century, and has now devolved on to immigrants. This, too, has been noticed and commented on in various relevant studies in folklore (Hergesell 1994; Schiffauer 1991). Thus it is often the case in folklore studies concerned with work or workers that there is an effort to rehabilitate the social practices of the simple folk, using a perspective on research whose interest is to provide cultural empowerment or to point to the equivalence of all cultural forms of expression, as is the case in some Scandinavian studies of worker history (see Hemmersam 1996). However, studies with such empathetic and emancipatory agendas, often arguing from a historical perspective, always run the danger of concentrating on aspects of worker culture that, at least from the point of view of the researcher, display interesting behavioral alternatives to the dominant social forms oriented to middle-class values. These studies run the risk of idealizing and romanticizing both the ways of life and the daily life of the lower social strata (Warneken 1996).

These political dimensions of worker's lives are often approached in folklore research through studying folkloric songs, which both shape and reflect the occupational lives and world views of occupational communities like fishermen, farmers, miners, factory workers and, craftsmen. The song lore shows an enormous bandwidth of work-life expressions from protest, overcoming disaster, and hardship to celebrating comradeship or expressing success and luck. With the increasing spread of mass media the occupational folkloric songs become a more popular format that is now often consumed rather than performed by the occupational folks themselves (see for example Green 1972). However, through this commercialization the occupational music traditions (shanties, yodeling, country, miners' songs, etc.), which are mostly locally situated, thus become known and spread by larger populations. With this popularization, folklore research thus faces new questions in the study of the song lore such as the adaptation processes on broader audiences or the effects of this commodification of folk songs on local music traditions and folk artists (McCarl 1996).

WORK RESEARCH IN FLUX: FROM "WORK AND OCCUPATIONS" TO "WORK AND ORGANIZATIONS"

The reorientation in studies of work and occupations which began to emerge in the 1970s and which was more strongly articulated by the 1990s (Jones 1991), expanded the research perspective from emphasizing "organizational cultures" to a more broadly understood focus on work cultures (Götz and Moosmüller 1992) – though this reorientation in paradigm has been disputed (see Jones 1991; McCarl 1992). Research on work that goes beyond the organization perspective continues to try to place the work experiences of the "little guy" into broader political and social contexts or worldviews. Beyond that, such studies make increasing efforts to conduct research on organizations as a whole. In doing so, they go beyond the cultural articulations of specific occupations and the examination of informal behavioral patterns in the specific work context to now include an examination of organizational and management practices. That makes further occupational groups relevant and interesting to folklore researchers, and includes white-collar workers (Lauterbach 1998), civil servants (Köhle-Hezinger 1997), and even executive levels (Alvesson 2002). If one does not take them into consideration, it is not understandable how existing theoretical models might be expanded to include entrepreneurial culture.

However, as before, research is largely focused on the lower wage groups. Of particular interest is how they deal with work instructions and company rules, the explanation of or the meaning they ascribe to the work process, and their interactions with management. A good example is Irene Götz's ethnography of a large commercial bakery in Munich which shows how employees perceive of the work rules and working hours, the system of remuneration and the company mission, and how they imbue them with coherent meaning, both individually and with respect to the company's sub-culture. In so doing, market and legal frameworks for work and the organization of work also play a role (Götz 1997). Even the studies of work culture that encompass the entire organization adhere to the long-established empathetic style, supportive of workers' cultural competence (if not empowerment), that is characteristic of folkloristic research on workers' culture.

More than in the past, however, they shift perspective between the various levels in the hierarchy, moving between top and bottom. This expansion in the disciplinary perspective to include research on organizational or business culture is not least to be understood as a response, or demarcate a line, vis-à-vis the growing interest management research has in folklore studies concepts. It is also a reflexive response to the understanding of business culture as it is formulated in management studies.

From the folkloric vantage point, the economic concepts are all too oriented toward managerial interests in finding steering mechanisms (Jones 1991), a focus that cannot be readily brought in line with the differentiated understanding of culture that guides folklore studies. This is starkly illustrated in Andreas Wittel's ethnography of an IT enterprise, in which his cultural analysis differentiates between employee culture and company ideology. There is a discrepancy between the reality and the appearances, the latter of which are set out in the company's guiding principles which state the official value orientations and norms of the enterprise (Wittel 1997).

The inner life of organizations, the title of a conference the DGV's Work Cultures section held in Berlin in 2001, as well as Wittel's study, recently made visible a significant area of research that included management strategies and techniques, since through them one gains access to workers in their working contexts. The perspective extends far beyond it, though, when shift work or flextime or on-call services are introduced to satisfy company or firm interests, it has an effect that reaches deeply into everyday and family life. The research approach that needs to be developed to investigate such dependencies and connections now also needs to be organized transnationally (Garsten 1994).

The extension of research to encompass additional occupational groups allows the unexpected to emerge. For example, research departments staffed by engineers and developers, once thought immune from performance measurement and managerial direction, are now also subject to goal attainment agreements and performance-oriented wage systems. The professional culture and professional ethos of the engineers, in particular, is thereby put in question (Vester 2009).

Along with an intensified observation of organizations as a whole, research on work has been extended beyond wage work (yet again). There are newer studies of family enterprises and small businesses (Lemberger 2007), of the new entrepreneurialism of the self-employed, whether in the creative and innovative parts of the economy (McRobbie 2004), or as a suggestion for transcending unemployment (Hessler 1994), or of enterprises run by migrants. This is not least during times of economic upheaval, which in Europe often involves the termination of permanent jobs. This is often followed by the co-existence of newer (old) forms of work which exist alongside, or in place of, permanent employment.

Given their perceived characteristics as social renewal, these new forms are of particular interest to researchers. Thus, increased attention is now devoted to those forms of work regarded as expressions of a neoliberal economic order, even if they have an oblique connection to wage work. For example, the "self-work" that compensates for missing wage work, the "citizenry-oriented" work that is often tied to particular ideals, the multiple employment taken up to compensate for underpaid jobs, family work that in this context is regarded as a newly recognized area of labor, or unemployment as a realm complementary to gainful employment: all have received increased attention in the cultural-analytic research on work (Herlyn *et al.* 2009).

This "bricolage of activity" (*Tätigkeitsbricolage*, see Warneken 2006) is seen as a means for combining different forms of gainful employment that ensure survival. It is regarded as a recurrent concept, though one that in historical terms takes on ever-new forms and combinations (Hauser 2009). This perspective also reveals the limits to the commodification of work. Given the upheavals in the working life, the "bricolage" perspective often merges into speculation on how work will look in the future, and how, in an organizational sense, societies will be able to ensure that people have a livelihood that is not based exclusively on gainful employment or on entrepreneurialism (Williams 2007).

THE CULTURES OF A GLOBALIZED, NEOLIBERAL REGIME OF WORK

At the beginning of the twenty-first century, it is seldom that peasant, artisan, or worker occupational groups are still the subjects of folkloric studies of work, or at least not in their specific, everyday work and life contexts. The variety of occupations and types of work has grown too large, and the changes occur with such rapidity that it is not possible to research the nature of work – at least not in the older sense of trying to preserve occupational folkways or knowledge of work before they vanish. Instead, the more general upheavals in the world of work associated with globalization, technological developments, and new economic regimes, such as the changes associated with a shift to a service sector society, are what guide folkloristic research, and the chosen focus, on work.

The orientation to the cultural dimensions of new organizational forms, in part brought about by technology (Star and Strauss 1999), and the political economy of work, meaning the distribution of societal resources among the various social groups as well as the conditions of their accumulation, moves folkloristic research on work closer to sociological perspectives. Notable figures here include Richard Sennett (2006) on the culture of the new capitalism or Yann Moulier Boutang (2007) on *capitalisme cognitive*. Such studies may also stand in the tradition (for example, in Boltanski and Chiapello 2003) of Pierre Bourdieu's analyses of work.

The ability to connect to research in economic anthropology to that undertaken in folkloristic studies of work is made clearer with their common orientation to the cultural mode of economic production. Economic production regimes and the changes to workplaces that go with them are considered in the same breath. A study of the development of the Øresund region, conducted by Orvar Löfgren (2000) and others, which saw it as a transnational innovation region shows the diversity and intensity with which the new economy uses "culturalization" as an economic means. This "economization" generates fashions and reputations, creates images of enterprises, and aestheticizes workplaces if not work itself. Work is taken as play, as a cool life in a world full of staged images and auras (Löfgren 2003). Stories and myths, rituals and events, hymns and images thus become part of the managerial repertoire and part of the conduct of economic activity. Informal communication and cultural forms that once served as key entry points for folkloric research on work and occupations now also play a considerable official role in organizations as well. Cultural studies concepts and competencies in folkloristics promise increasing yields within and for economic fields, so that the expertise available from folkloristic research is increasingly in demand in the form of consultancies or employment possibilities.

In examining the results of folkloristic research on the new cultures of work, now bound more closely to the influence of the economic regime of work, one notes some interesting results that are increasingly evident with the establishment of neoliberalism. Still, despite globalization, these remain dependent on what are persistently nationally-colored political economies.

Important insights here include the effects of more flexible employment relationships on everyday lifestyles as well as on work and employment biographies (Schönberger 2007), in particular as found in the service sector. Barbara Ehrenreich (2001) showed that it is difficult or impossible to make ends meet in the United States in the service sector, even when fully employed, if one is given "serving, scrubbing and selling" jobs. These supposedly unskilled jobs are by no means without requirements for abilities and knowledge. Rather, they rely on cultural capital acquired elsewhere. They also demand special competencies, in the face of long, unregulated working hours, the most minimal of income, and the constant threat of being fired, to even find lodgings, health care, and social relations as minimal conditions to maintain a lifestyle. Such jobs in the service sector can hardly be managed without impairment to health or without psycho-social consequences. The difficulties Ehrenreich describes of organizing a living and an everyday life outside work, which would in turn be necessary to guarantee an ability to be employed (or employable), are, in how she depicts it, peculiarly American. But in its basic aspects, what she shows is hardly confined to the United States. Studies in European countries have shown quite comparable problems exist there, as well for those who work in the service sector society, for securing one's own employability, and in sketching out what living in precarious circumstances means.

Ethnographic research into the new realms of work the neoliberal working world has created, focused on service employment and on the new economy, are thereby able to provide differentiated insights into what the culture of the new capitalism specifically means in terms of everyday life and working life relative to mobility, virtual forms of work, and flexibility (Hess and Moser 2003; Kaschnig-Fasch 2003). With their orientation to contextuality and complexity, they are repeatedly able to indicate when things are being glossed over, when empty promises are being made or myths are being promulgated.

Thus, for example, studies of "knowledge work" have made clear that the forms of work often taken to be prototypical for the future of work as a whole, and epitomized by work in the so-called creative industries occur in highly insecure employment and wage relationships. They may be accompanied by precarious living conditions brought about by high demands on work flexibility and working hours, as well as little room left for a private life outside gainful employment, and despite a creative "bricolage of activity," such work relations not infrequently imply wholly unclear occupational futures (McRobbie 2004). Unlike in those service sector occupations that call for lower qualifications and skills, the decisions of highly qualified knowledge workers to engage in working in such insecure circumstances were often knowingly taken, because such workers were in pursuit of self-determined "living work" (Gorz 2003).

An important topic in research on the cultures of the neoliberal world of work is the division of labor, both globally created (Burawoy 2001; Castrée et al. 2004) and gender-specific. In this, gender-specific work hierarchies are not specific of the neoliberal new order, but have long been the object of cultural analysis and research. Research on typically female areas of work, such as that performed by midwives (Benoit 1991), have documented – over long historical periods and beyond purely local circumstances – the underprivileging of female work, its relation to male realms of work, the limitations placed on "female" occupations, and the effects this has on gender-oriented socialization. The studies, which in part argue from international perspectives, cannot help but show the historically ongoing lower social status, poorer remuneration, and reserved character of female work relative to male work, and as it is manifested in gender-specific as well as ethnically segregated labor markets. Gender perspectives have created the awareness that these persisting inequalities are embedded in the persistence of meaning systems that attribute male activities closer to culture and female activities closer to nature (Haug 1991; Ortner 1974). Their presumed closeness to nature thus becomes the main argument for ascribing women still into reproductive occupations or services. Accordingly, folklore studies for a long time mainly described the cultural experiences and expressions in the traditional female areas of the household and in community life thereby focusing the aesthetic dimensions of female crafts like embroidery and quilting instead of its value as work. However, it has been ethnographic research in the intersection of folklore studies and cultural anthropology that have made women's work and its specifics visible.

Women are in demand round the clock, both in gainful employment and family work (Marburg 1988). The work they perform after their paid working hours are over has been called the second shift (Russell Hochschild and Machung 1990). Work at home then takes place without pay, though with specific expectations on the part of the husband as well as from the social environment, with respect to how the household is run and the children raised.

In helping to secure a family's income, women are often en route as labor migrants employed in households, providing care services, in cleaning or in agriculture. With differing intensity, they are repeatedly exposed to sexual molestation, or are even forced to become sex workers. The education, often accompanied by completed diplomas, obtained in the home country can, as a rule, not be put to appropriate use in the foreign labor markets. It is only when female migrants take on reproductive tasks in households, often under restrictive residence permits to work as au pairs or caregivers that the academically-trained (but foreign) women can organize their own gainful employment alongside the work done in and for the family. The access to female wage work these analyses chart, the large proportion of unpaid service work, the comparatively low value of reproductive activity, the demand to constantly be ready to work, the ethnicization of the labor market and the diffusion of work demands into the realm of leisure and the realm of family, have analogies to the practices of neoliberal labor markets.

RESEARCHING WORK

An important principle in the folkloric investigation of work and occupations is the contextualization in time and space of the objects under study. Beyond this, a significant perspective in the folkloristic approach is provided by the historicization of contemporary issues and questions, something often taken up in research on work. Though history does not repeat itself, it is precisely in research on worker culture that one sees how historical analysis can deepen the understanding of contemporary phenomena (Messenger 1975).

It is only through this that a differentiated estimate of its significance is made possible. In particular, a detailed analysis oriented to the contextualization of daily life, with its symbolic and material forms of expression, contributes (Kramer 1987). Some of what appears to be a new tendency, however, such as Ehrenreich's "ethnographicized" study of the working poor in the service sector or what Warneken calls a "bricolage of activities" can be shown to be conceptualizations that already existed in the past. Knowledge of historical precursors or connections permits, or even requires, the specificities of the contemporary developments to be analyzed with greater precision.

Under the larger category of ethnography in organizations (Schwartzman 1993), research now looks at company culture and organizations in their entirety. It is not just industrial workers but management and other occupational groups as well that come under (what is in part new) scrutiny in folkloristics. In the process, researchers need to justify, if not represent, their research direction, questions, and paradigms in a new way.

However, at the upper levels in companies, those under scrutiny tend to argue that they are at the same level as the researchers – or may even feel superior when it is a question of the appropriate perspective to be taken. Such subjects of research may also not have much free time to take part in research (Warneken and Wittel 1997). A further challenge in researching the interior life of organizations using ethnographic means is provided by an increasing medialization, and thereby the spatially networked but translocal organization of work processes. This can only to be countered to a limited extent by a multi-sited ethnography, as for example when one and the same communicative situation is simultaneously transmitted to different places on the globe.

Access to the economic realms that now come increasingly into view becomes increasingly difficult to organize, particularly for an ethnography that stands in a tradition of being critical of power and empathetic towards the underprivileged. Ethnography is not absolutely necessary to depict realistically these economic perspectives, but its capacity to reveal the inside of what is going on (Warneken 2006: 124) has in recent times gained in attractiveness. In the process, the question is raised ever more keenly for whom and in whose interest cultural-analytic knowledge is being produced (Koch 2010). For, hand-in-hand with the culturalization of management and product development is an increased interest in the market in knowledge produced ethnographically or through cultural analysis – including for market research and marketing itself.

In light of the "culturalized" marketplace, there is even increasing demand and interest by companies in their own history, one which may be served by the ability folkloristics has to engage in historical research. The discipline's experience in and with museums has come to the fore in new structures erected precisely for the purpose of "museumifying" a company's history. Folkloristics, once exclusively directed at lower-class research subjects, often conducted with an approach that was community-oriented and collaborative, if not even deliberately action-oriented (McCarl 1992), is now, given its new fields of investigation and questions, faced with a variety of questions that in the end are also ethical. In this sense, the perspectives taken in folkloristic research on work will be able to continue to contribute substantially both to the challenges and to the general development of the discipline.

NOTES

1 Translation by John Bendix.
2 Compare "Smithsonian Folklife Festival" http://www.festival.si.edu/past_festivals/year.aspx (accessed March 14, 2011)

REFERENCES

Alvesson, Mats. 2002. *Understanding Organizational Culture*. London: Sage.

Arendt, Hannah. 1998. *The Human Condition*. Chicago: University of Chicago Press. (Originally published in 1981 as *Vita activa oder vom tätigen Leben*. München: Piper.)

Assion, Peter. 2001. "Arbeiterforschung" in R.W. Brednich, Ed. *Grundriss der Volkskunde. Einführung in die Forschungsfelder der Europäischen Ethnologie*. Berlin: Reimer.

Bausinger, Hermann, Ed. 1970. *Abschied vom Volksleben*. Tübingen: Tübinger Vereinigung für Volkskunde.

Benoit, Cecilia. 1991. *Midwives in Passage. The Modernisation of Maternity Care*. St John's Institute of Social and Economic Research.

Boltanski, Luc and Ève Chiapello, Eds. 2003. *Le nouvel esprit du capitalisme*. Paris: Gallimard.

Botkin, Benjamin Albert. 1954. *Sidewalks of America. Folklore, Legends, Sagas, Traditions,*

Customs, Songs, Stories and Sayings of City Folk. Indianapolis: Bobbs-Merrill.

Bourdieu, Pierre. 1977. *Algérie 60. Structures économiques et structures temporelles*. Paris: Les Éditions de Minuit.

Bourdieu, Pierre. 1984. *Distinction: A Social Critique of the Judgment of Taste*. Cambridge, MA: Harvard University Press.

Burawoy, Michael. 2001. *Global Ethnography. Forces, Connections, and Imaginations in a Postmodern World*. Berkeley: University of California Press.

Byington, Robert H. 1978. *Working Americans. Contemporary Approaches to Occupational Folklife*. Special issue. *Western Folklore* 3. Washington, DC: Smithsonian Folklife Studies.

Castree, Noel, *et al.* 2004. *Spaces of Work: Global Capitalism and the Geographies of Labour*. London, New York: Sage.

Ehrenreich, Barbara. 2001. *Nickel and Dimed. On (not) Getting by in America*. New York: Henry Holt Owl Book.

Garsten, Christina. 1994. *Apple World. Core and Periphery in a Transnational Organizational Culture*. Stockholm: Studies in Social Anthropology.

Gorz, André. 2003. *L'Immatériel. Connaissance, valeur et capital*. Paris: Galilée.

Götz, Irene. 1997. *Unternehmenskultur. Die Arbeitswelt einer Großstadtbäckerei aus kulturwissenschaftlicher Sicht*. Münster, München, Berlin, New York: Waxmann.

Götz, Irene and Alois Moosmüller. 1992. "Zur ethnologischen Erforschung von Unternehmenskultur. Industriebetriebe als Forschungsfeld der Völker-und Volkskunde." *Schweizerisches Archiv für Volkskunde* 88: 1–30.

Green, Archie. 1972. *Only a Miner. Studies in the Recorded Coal-mining Songs*. Urbana, Chicago, London: University of Illinois Press.

Hand, Wayland D. 1969. "American Occupational and Industrial Folklore. The Miner" in H. Foltin, Ed. *Kontakte und Grenzen. Probleme der Volks-, Kultur- und Sozialforschung*. Göttingen: Otto Schwartz, pp. 453–460.

Haug, Frigga. 1991. "Arbeitskultur und Geschlechterverhältnisse" in W. Kaschuba, G. Korff, and B.J. Warneken, Eds. *Arbeitskulturen seit 1945. Ende oder Veränderung?* Tübingen: Tübinger Vereinigung für Volkskunde, pp. 223–241.

Hauser, Andrea. 2009. "Prekäre Subsistenz. Eine historische Rückschau auf dörfliche Bewältigungsstrategien im Umbruch der Industralisierung" in I. Götz and B. Lemberger, Eds. Prekär arbeiten, prekär leben. *Kulturwissenschaftliche Perspektiven auf ein gesellschaftliches Phänomen*. Frankfurt, New York: Campus Verlag, pp. 263–287.

Hemmersam, Flemming, Ed. 1996. "To work, to life or to death." *Studies in Working Class Lore*. Vol. 37. Copenhagen: Society for Research in the History of the Labour Movement in Denmark.

Hergesell, Burkhard. 1994. *Arbeiterkulturen im Betrieb. Interethnische Beziehungen zwischen Produktionsarbeitern. Eine empirische Studie*. Frankfurt: IKO Verlag für Interkulturelle Kommunikation.

Herlyn, Gerrit, *et al.*, Eds. 2009. *Arbeit und Nicht-Arbeit. Entgrenzungen und Begrenzungen von Lebensbereichen und Praxen*. München, Mering: Rainer Hampp Verlag.

Hess, Sabine and Johannes Moser, Eds. 2003. *Kultur der Arbeit – Kultur der neuen Ökonomie. Kulturwissenschaftliche Beiträge zu neoliberalen Arbeits- und Lebenswelten*. Graz: Institut für Volkskunde und Kulturanthropologie.

Hessler, Alexandra. 1994. *Existenzgründer als Leitbild. Zum Umgang mit einem Erfolgsmodell der modernen Arbeitswelt*. Münster, München, Berlin, New York: Waxmann.

Jahoda, Marie and Paul Felix Lazarsfeld. 2002 [1933]. *Marienthal. The Sociography of an Unemployed Community*. Piscataway: Transaction Publishers.

Jones, Michael Owen. 1991. "Why Folklore and Organization(s)?" *Western Folklore* 50(1): 29–40.

Kaschnig-Fasch, Elisabeth. 2003. *Das ganz alltägliche Elend. Begegnungen im Schatten des Neoliberalismus*. Wien: Löcker.

Koch, Gertraud. 2010. "Volkskundliche Wissensproduktion im Unternehmenskontext. Erfahrungen aus einem

Lehrforschungsprojekt" in I. Wandel, B. Götz, B. Lemberger, K. Lehnert, and S. Schondelmayer, Eds. *Mobilität und Mobilisierung. Arbeit im sozioökonomischen, politischen und kulturellen Arbeit und Alltag. Beiträge zur ethnografischen Arbeitskulturenforschung.* Frankfurt, New York: Campus Verlag, pp. 445–453.

Köhle-Hezinger, Christel. 1997. "Die Beamten der Maschinenfabrik Esslingen" in S. Esslingen, Ed. *Zugkraft. 150 Jahre Maschinenfabrik Esslingen.* Esslingen.

Korff, Gottfried. 1971. "Bemerkungen zur Arbeitervolkskunde." *Tübinger Korrespondenzblatt* 2: 3–8.

Korson, George. 1927. *Songs and Ballads of the Anthracite Miners.* New York: Grafton.

Kramer, Dieter. 1987. *Theorien zur historischen Arbeiterkultur.* Vol. 57. Marburg: Arbeiterbewegung und Gesellschaftswissenschaft.

Lauterbach, Burkhart. 1998. *Angestelltenkultur. "Beamten"-Vereine in deutschen Industrieunternehmen vor 1933.* Münster: Waxmann.

Lemberger, Barbara. 2007. *Alles für's Geschäft. Ethnologische Einblicke in die Unternehmenskultur eines kleinen Familienunternehmens.* Vol. 14. Münster: Lit Verlag.

Liessmann, Konrad Paul. 2000. "Im Schweiße deines Angesichts" in U. Beck, Ed. *Die Zukunft von Arbeit und Demokratie.* Frankfurt: Suhrkamp, pp. 85–107.

Löfgren, Orvar. 2000. "Moving Metaphors" in P.O. Berg, A. Linde-Laursen, and O. Löfgren, Eds. *Invoking a Transantional Metropolis. The Making of the Öresund Region.* Lund: Studentenlitteratur, pp. 27–54.

Marburg, AG Frauenforschung in der Volkskunde. 1988. "Rund um die Uhr. Frauenalltag in Stadt und Land zwischen Erwerbsarbeit, Erwerbslosigkeit und Hausarbeit" in *3. Tagung der Kommission Frauenforschung in der Deutschen Gesellschaft für Volkskunde I.f.E.E. Marburg,* Marburg: Jonas Verlag.

McCarl, Robert. 1992. "Response to Michael Owen Jones's Article 'Why Folklore and Organizations?'" *Western Folklore* 51(2): 187–189.

McCarl, Robert S. 1996. "Occupational Folklore" in J.H. Brunvand, Ed. *American Folklore. An Encyclopedia.* New York: Garland.

McRobbie, Angela. 2004. "Making a living as a visual artist in London's small scale creative economy" in D. Power and A.J. Scott, Eds. *Cultural Industries and the Production of Culture.* London, New York: Routledge, pp. 130–145.

Messenger, Betty. 1975. *Picking-up the Linen Threads. A Study in Industrial Folklore.* San Francisco: Bolerium Books.

Moser, Johannes. 2002. "Strategies and Tactics of Economic Survival: De-industrialization, Work and Change in an Alpine Mining Community" in Ullrich Kockel, Ed. *Culture and Economy. Contemporary Perspectives.* Burlington: Ashgate, pp. 60–71.

Moulier Boutang, Yann. 2007. *Le capitalisme cognitif. La nouvelle grande transformation.* Paris: Editions Amsterdam.

Nickerson, Bruce. 1974. "Is There a Folk in the Factory?" *The Journal of American Folklore* 87(344): 133–139.

Ortner, Sherry. 1974. "Is Female to Male as Nature is to Culture?" in M. Rosaldo and L. Lamphere, Eds. *Woman, Culture and Society.* Palo Alto: Stanford University Press, pp. 67–87.

Peuckert, Will Erich. 1931. *Volkskunde des Proletariats.* Frankfurt: Neuer Frankfurter Verlag.

Rosenbaum, Heidi. 1992. *Proletarische Familien. Arbeiterfamilien und Arbeiterväter im frühen 20. Jahrhundert zwischen traditioneller, sozialdemokratischer und kleinbürgerlicher Orientierung.* Frankfurt: Suhrkamp.

Russell Hochschild, Arlie and Anne Machung, Eds. 1990. *The Second Shift. Working Parents and the Revolution at Home.* New York: Avon Books.

Schiffauer, Werner. 1991. *Die Migranten aus Subay. Türken in Deutschland. Eine Ethnographie.* Stuttgart: Klett-Cotta.

Schönberger, Klaus. 2007. "Widerständigkeit der Biografie. Zu den Grenzen der Entgrenzung neuer Konzepte alltäglicher Lebensführung im Übergang vom fordistischen zum postfordistischen Arbeitsparadigma" in M. Seifert, I. Götz, and B. Huber, Eds. *Flexible Biografien? Horizonte und Brüche im Arbeitsleben der Gegenwart.* Frankfurt, New York: Campus Verlag, pp. 63–94.

Schwartzman, Helen B. 1993. *Ethnography in Organizations.* Newbury Park, CA: Sage.

Sennett, Richard. 2006. *The Culture of the New Capitalism.* New Haven: Yale University Press.

Sims, Martha C. and Martine Stephens. 2005. *Living Folklore. An Introduction to The Study of People and Their Traditions.* Logan: Utah State University Press.

Siuts, Hinrich. 1988. "Geräteforschung" in R.W. Brednich, Ed. *Grundriss der Volkskunde. Einführung in die Forschungsfelder der Europäischen Ethnologie.* Berlin: Reimer, pp. 155–167.

Skarin Frykman, Brigitta. 1990. *Arbetarkultur. Göteborg 1890.* Göteborg: Göteborg Universitet Press.

Star, Susan L. and Anselm Strauss. 1999. "Layers of Silence, Arenas of Voice. The Ecology of Visible and Invisible Work." *Computer Supported Cooperative Work* 8: 9–30.

Thompson, Edward P. 1963. *The Making of the English Working Class.* New York: Pantheon.

Vester, Michael. 2009. "Arbeitsteilung, Arbeitsethos und die Ideologie der Entgrenzung" in G. Herlyn, J. Müske, K. Schönberger, and O. Sutter, Eds. *Arbeit und Nicht-Arbeit. Entgrenzungen und Begrenzungen von Lebensbereichen und Praxen.* München, Mering: Rainer Hampp Verlag.

Warneken, Bernd Jürgen. 1986. *Als die Deutschen demonstrieren lernten. Das Kulturmuster "friedliche Straßendemonstration" im preußischen Wahlrechtsdemons-*trationen *1908–1910.* Tübingen: Tübinger Vereinigung für Volkskunde.

Warneken, Bernd Jürgen. 1996. "Zur Motivationskrise der ethnographischen Arbeiterforschung" in I. Dietrich, D. Mühlberg, and K. e.V., Eds. *Vorwärts und nicht vergessen – nach dem Ende der Gewissheit.* Berlin: Kulturwissenschaftliches Institut.

Warneken, Bernd Jürgen. 2006. *Ethnographien popularer Kulturen. Eine Einführung.* Wien, Köln, Weimar: Böhlau UTB.

Warneken, Bernd-Jürgen and Andreas Wittel. 1997. "Die neue Angst vor dem Feld. Ethnographisches research up am Beispiel der Unternehmensforschung." *Zeitschrift für Volkskunde* 93(1): 1–16.

Weber, Max. 1905. *The Protestant Ethic and the Spirit of Capitalism.* New York: Scribner.

Williams, Colin C. 2007. *Rethinking the Future of Work.* New York: Palgrave Macmillan.

Wittel, Andreas. 1997. *Belegschaftskultur im Schatten der Firmenideologie. Eine ethnographische Fallstudie.* Berlin: Ed Sigma.

FURTHER READING

Chapple, E.D. 1953. "Applied Anthropology in Industry" in A.S. Kroeber, Ed. *Anthropology Today.* Chicago: University of Chicago Press, pp. 819–831.

Heilfurth, Gerhard. 1981. *Der Bergbau und seine Kultur. Eine Welt zwischen Dunkel und Licht.* Zürich, Freiburg: Buchclub Ex Libris.

Kaschuba, Wolfgang. 1990. *Lebenswelt und Kultur der unterbürgerlichen Schichten im 19. und 20. Jahrhundert.* München: Oldenbourg.

Willis, Paul. 1977. *Learning to Labour. How Working Class Kids Get Working Class Jobs.* Farnborough: Saxon House.

CHAPTER 9 MATERIAL CULTURE

Orvar Löfgren

How will we live in the twenty-first century? This was a classic theme in the future-gazing genres of the 1950s and 1960s. Most of the commentators could agree on one thing: modern technology and virtuality would make people less dependent upon the cumbersome materialities of everyday life. A simpler and more friction-free – almost cyber-light – existence was forecast. Today we know better. The average Western home houses more things than ever before. Households are veritable jungles of awkward objects and gadgets, utensils and tools crammed into every available space. The cupboards and wardrobes may be bursting, and cellars and attics cluttered. Small gadgets emit red or green bleeps in the kitchen and electric cables create jungles under the tables. People devote a large amount of energy and resources to handling this abundance. Things are shuffled back and forth, rearranged, recycled. Every day, new objects enter people's homes and old ones are lost, forgotten, or left by the back door.

This everyday interaction with objects has been a classic theme for folklorists, folklife researchers, and European ethnologists, but the ways that this interaction has been approached, theorized and sometimes ignored mirror important shifts in research paradigm and scholarly interests. Material objects have been studied in terms of everyday technologies, crafts, and aesthetics, as identity markers, objects of consumption, tracing elements or collectors' items.

Originally the term material culture was coined as a category to contrast immaterial, "mental" culture, like oral traditions and folk beliefs in the study of pre-industrial societies. As Henry Glassie has pointed out, this is not a workable division – material culture is also very much a culture of the mind:

> Material culture is culture made material; it is the inner wit at work in the world. Beginning necessarily with things, but not ending with them, the study of material culture uses objects to approach human thought and action. (Glassie 1999: 41)

A Companion to Folklore, First Edition. Edited by Regina F. Bendix and Galit Hasan-Rokem.
© 2012 John Wiley & Sons, Ltd. Published 2012 John Wiley & Sons, Ltd.

The popularity of the concept material culture has varied. It has had periods of being unfashionable as too awkward a term only to return as a handy label, with varying national styles: *Sachkultur* in German (Heidrich 2000 and König 2005), *culture materiélle* in French (Julien and Rosselin 2005), *material culture studies* in the British tradition, linked to *The Journal of Material Culture Studies* (see Tilley 2006 and Miller 2005). During recent years the concept of *materiality* has been used more widely as it describes an open dimension in cultural processes rather than delineating a category of objects (see the debate in Ingold 2007).

The perspectives of material culture studies thus vary with the local contexts and the ways in which research traditions have been positioned in national academic landscapes. I shall start by a sketching of my own background in Scandinavia and Sweden and then move on to compare that experience with academic contexts. My examples will be derived mainly from European and North American contexts (for a global overview, see Tilley 2006).

GUARDIANS OF FOLK CULTURE

In 1918 Nils Lithberg was appointed to Sweden's first chair in folklife studies. He began by declaring that the discipline should focus on the everyday and should not "neglect a single tiny thing, no matter how commonplace it may seem, among all the many things that belong to the everyday surroundings of the people" (1918: 19–20). His statement reveals an engaging concern for the small, seemingly trivial and valueless objects. Folklife scholars and folklorists had been entrusted with the task of collecting and preserving objects which were no longer used, such as baking shovels, cow bells, milking stools, as well as taking care of folk literature and beliefs neglected by other disciplines. This ambition could easily seem comical or trivial for established scholars in the old humanistic disciplines of Art, History, and Literature, but there was a strong interest in the forgotten or seemingly important. It produced insights into the cultural and social organization of craftsmanship, everyday technologies, the handling of raw material, and the making of everyday aesthetics. The concern with everyday objects also meant that folklife scholars became interested in the processes of learning. How are carpentry or weaving skills acquired? This was a cultural process of learning that often worked without words, based upon imitation and apprenticeship. This traditional study of material culture thus came to be linked to the world of pre-industrial work, as well as the aesthetics of "the folk."

Fieldwork was often organized in terms of salvage operations. There was so much of the material culture that had to be saved from decay, destruction, or oblivion. Documentation in text, drawings, and later photographs became an important skill and museum storage facilities were filled with objects. Today we can see how these collections mirror a selective framework, because Lithberg's admonition not to ignore the commonplace was not easy to follow. In retrospect we can see what was regarded as important to collect and preserve for future generations, and what was ignored or overlooked and what could be categorized as folk art and what could not As in any similar heritage projects we find hierarchies and priorities developing and the result today is that there several examples of the same object in some museums and none or very few in others.

There are, however, a number of classic studies of the material world of peasants that have avoided this selective gaze and also brought in a social dimension by looking at tools and artifacts "at work." A good example is Edit Fél's and Tamás Hofer's study of the material world of the Hungarian village of Atany. Atany is one of the best documented villages in the world. The two scholars studied the community for decades and published extensively on how the material culture of buildings, tools, and utensils functioned in the social life of the villagers (Fél and Hofer 1969, 1974).

For Lithberg and the generations following up to the 1960s, material culture was also a tracing device. Materials were gathered to build further theories on processes of evolution and diffusion. In many European settings, the project of creating atlases of the distribution of items of culture like objects, buildings, and customs channeled a lot of energy and resources (see Rooijakkers and Meurkens 2000). The mapping projects meant pooling resources and also creating transnational research strategies, but in the end the enormous resources put into these projects turned out to have limited dividends. The research paradigm also resulted in a tendency to see objects as agents, plows moving through Europe, a farmhouse structure spreading north. In the 1960s, the atlas projects came under heavy criticism. For younger generations of scholars they were sometimes likened to old steamers with dead engines but still moving ahead. The reaction against the research paradigm was strong and in many cases led to a marked lack of interest in the material. Farm implements, household appliances, and folk art became unfashionable, while social theory and social relations in contemporary society came into the fore as the disciplines of folklife studies and folklore reorganized themselves. This farewell to material culture studies was noticeable in many European settings (see the discussion in Löfgren 1997), but perhaps most so in Scandinavia and especially in Sweden, where the influence of a British social anthropology that almost totally had abandoned an earlier interest in material culture was very strong. In the German-speaking settings of *Volkskunde*, this paradigm shift was also marked (see Bausinger 1990 and for a more recent appraisal Leimgruber 2007), although the traditional cultural history approach survived better and closer ties were maintained with museums. For a discussion of the French transition, see Bromberger and Segalen (1996), but also Martine Segalen's study of the birth and death of a national folk museum, the Musée des Arts et Traditions Populaires, in Paris. Here she puts the problems traditional material culture studies had in re-inventing themselves in a situation where new generations of folklorists and folk-life researchers increasingly turned to the contemporary world or new theoretical approaches in a French context (Segalen 2005).

In the United States the situation was different. Here folklore studies of material culture were part of a quite different academic landscape, often with strong ties to American studies, research on popular culture, and vernacular architecture as well as American social history and the more historically oriented American cultural anthropology. One only has to look at some classic books on American material culture to see the difference (Bronner 1985, 1986 and St George 1988). There is a stronger continuity here, for example, a focus on folk art as well as craftsmanship. What is also notable is an earlier and different interdisciplinary tradition with ties to history and cultural anthropology. The same divide in American studies of material culture is not obvious during the 1960s, compared with many European settings. See for example the discussion in Glassie (1986).

THE RETURN OF THE MATERIAL

A renewed interest in the materiality of everyday life was evident in European ethnology and folklore as well as in anthropology, sociology, and cultural studies in the 1980s, mainly through a new interest in the study of consumption as an active, creative process. This meant that the world of goods was mostly approached in terms of the semiotic and symbolic. How were objects charged with cultural meaning, how did they function as symbols or identity markers? This new interest produced new themes in the field of materiality. Again, we need to ask how certain analytical traditions shape the research landscape of looking and overlooking, selecting some topics, ignoring others. It has been argued that the moratorium on material studies was beneficial in many ways because it fostered a rethinking of the field, but there was also a clear advantage for ethnologists and folklorists returning to the field in that they were able to draw on an older research tradition that was not present in sociology or cultural studies.

So what kinds of fields developed and what were their specific ethnological profiles? First of all, the 1990s saw a massive ethnological contribution to the study of consumption. The ethnological tradition of focusing on everyday practices turned out to be helpful here (Welz 1996), but also the interest in historical comparison, problematizing present-day styles of consumption with that of earlier periods (see for example Fredriksson 1997 and König 2009).

Gender aspects are often important here, especially in studies on the making of the modern consumer in the new material dreamworld of advertising campaigns. The making of the modern consumer was a project that often focused on women. Class and gender entered the discussion of the new dreamworld of department stores (see Williams 1982, for example, in the heated debates about a new character, the kleptomaniac, a person with an irresistible desire to steal). Kleptomania was linked to stealing not out of material need but of desire. The critics argued that it was like impulse buying. Open display cases and easily accessible goods were temptations and acquisition became a form of fulfillment in itself, regardless of the utility of the object. After all, were department stores trying to sell these women what they did not need? Women were overwhelmed by the presence of goods displayed in the vast halls of the new department stores, and disoriented in the dazzling brightness of the new electric lamps. The kleptomaniac was problematic was because the thief was often a woman, and worse, a middle-class one.

The department stores were accused of exploiting "the weaker sex," playing on the supposed emotionality of women, but the world of new department stores also illustrated the empowerment of women, who developed the skills of the sophisticated shopper, knowledgeable about prices, fabrics, models, and bargains. In this way the department store also became a training ground for the critical consumer.

In a study of new discount departments stores of the 1930s the ethnologist Cecilia Fredriksson (1998: 97) has shown how this consumer space also became a free zone. Women could walk along the counters and seem busy shopping, when what they actually wanted was a moment of day-dreaming in private. "Passing through the glass doors was like entering a new world, all these wonderful objects that set your imagination moving," a woman remembered. This was a safe public space where one's right to be there was not questioned.

Another research path was found in studies of material objects and consumer trends as part of identity formation and self-expression. It could be specific fields like clothing and fashion or food (Lysaght and Burckhardt-Seebass 2004). In these fields, ethnologists could fall back on an older research tradition and deepen the historical perspective. How did fashion work in traditional peasant culture as compared with later developments (Gradén and Pettersson 2009)? There is the possibility of drawing here on an older research tradition that followed individual objects or styles over longer time-spans, for example in the classic ethnological tradition of using estate inventories to follow the diffusion of objects through different social strata or a rural-urban continuum (Kramer 2000).

The old interest in folk art became fashionable again, but often within the framework of everyday aesthetics (Klein and Widbom 1994), as for example in studies of interior decoration and vernacular buildings. A special field concerning the aesthetics of youth subcultures, with a focus on clothing, music, body language and other expressive fields also developed (Christensen 1999).

THE NON-MATERIALITY OF MATERIAL STUDIES –
THE PHENOMENOLOGICAL CRITIQUE

However, many of the new cultural studies of consumption of teenagers, home-makers, and shoppers gave the sensation of drifting through a symbolic forest of meanings and messages. There was often very little body work in these discussions of cultural creativity, that tended to read objects and bodies as "cultural texts." The critique came from several directions, first of all from phenomenological research traditions that stressed the importance of studying embodiment as well as the constant work of all the senses (see Poverzanović-Frykman 2003; Bendix and Brenneis 2005).

As Jojada Verrips (2005), among others, has pointed out, there has been a total dominance of one of the five senses in this kind of cultural analysis. It is an ocular-centric type of research, often over-emphasizing the dominance of sight as *the* medium through which people experience the world. In their relations with the material world, people are often described in terms of flaneurs and tourists, as a breed of observers and onlookers. We are not *in* the world, but just looking (or gazing) at it. This tendency overshadows the fact that our senses always work together; we are, of course, never just looking. In his plea for an analytical focus on *aisthesis*, the ways in which all the senses interact and must be studied in relationship to each other, Verrips also underlined how the haptic dimension (touching) is often ignored. The ways in which people feel their way through the world give the haptic a double dimension. In all three concepts of feeling, touching, and emotion there is a link between reaching out (as in the Latin root of emotion, *e-movere*) as well as reacting to the world. People are feeling their way through the environment and at the same time are registering feelings. They are touching and being touched. This double dimension makes the haptic a rewarding element in the analysis of people's interaction with the material world. Like Verrips, many ethnologists argue that the interest in looking at all the senses at work – not just the visual dimension – means not only studying what people do to objects, but also what objects do to people. A good example of this approach is Hjemdahl-Mathiessen's (2003) phenomenological study of the materiality of theme parks.

Another research tradition that also emerged as a critique of the lack of materiality in social analysis came from the loosely organized school that usually is labeled actor-network-theory (ANT). It evolved out of studies of science and technology (Law and Hassard 1999) and gives the material world much stronger agency, analyzing how objects and technologies in constant interaction with humans create dynamic networks. It is in these open relations between different actors – human and non-human – that cultural forms and institutions are shaped. Ethnologists have taken the ANT-approach into studies of everyday life. A good example is a collection of essays, where the materiality of a McDonald's restaurant, a box of wedding keepsakes as well as paper model building kits, among others are analyzed as assemblages of objects and humans interacting (see Brembeck *et al.* 2007).

THE LIFE HISTORY APPROACH

The return of an interest in the material aspects of everyday life has resulted in a number of new or revived fields of study. One is the use of the well-established ethnological tool of life histories. There are different subgenres here, like the biography of things (Kopytoff 1992) and the ways people narrate their own biography through the help of their lives with objects (Kirshenblatt-Gimblett 1989; König 2000; Löfgren 1998; Miller 2008; Otto and Pedersen 1998).

When people narrate their lives with objects during the twentieth century there is often a focus on processes of learning and de-learning. The interviews often start with the early memories of learning how to construct a Christmas list, becoming a collector of Barbie dolls or Smurf figures, or negotiating pocket money. These childhood memories often have a certain freshness. They are memories of the first confrontations with novel styles and scenes of consumption. They often express the exhilarating feeling of entering a world of abundance and desire. For older generations with a rural background, these memories may evoke the first trip to the market or the advent of the mail-order catalogue. For later generations of consumers, new entrances to the world of goods developed. Here, the early memories may deal with the first visit to a department store or a real supermarket.

Consumption as a laboratory for experimentation and identity formation comes out even more strongly when people talk about their teenage years. There are memories of the endless hours spent in front of the mirror, trying out styles, clothes, and poses in order to find forms of self-expression. Teenage memories also emphasize the degree to which the battle with parents and the attempts to secure adult freedom are enacted within the field of consumption. Another dominating theme in teenage consumer life to do with learning the fine social distinctions and questions of gender and class becomes visible here.

During later stages of life, home-making is a central metaphor for narrating consumer life and there is an important generational change here. The idea of home improvement as a family project, uniting wife, husband, and children, became important for the working class during the postwar boom years in ways that would have been unthinkable in 1900 or 1930. Home became a place where one actively tried out different sides of the self, and an important site of cultural production.

A new space for creativity and anesthetization emerged, an opportunity to develop talents and interests among people who had previously lacked the time, money, and energy to invest in their own home. The life histories illustrate how this family project called the home is never finished. People are busy redecorating, mending, planning, day-dreaming, making new sofa cushions, putting in new floors, ripping out old ones, changing wallpaper, driving to the hardware store, leafing through furniture catalogues, moving things around, and moving the family on. (For a discussion of later stages in the life-cycle, see Rogan 1998.)

What are the lessons of this material? One concerns the moral dimension of consumption (Gullestad 1995). The material often underlines the ways in which most discussions about consumption tend to have a moral element. Narrating your life can take the form of an argument about a "now" versus a "then." It becomes important for some to stress how one learned how to make do with little, and this is often meant as an indirect critique of the youngsters of today "who get everything for nothing" and who never learn to forsake desires or think twice about consumption. Such moral lessons can also be condensed into situations or objects, which also may take on rather stable narrative forms, turning into genres of nostalgia or dystopia.

Another lesson is how a personal history of consumption is organized around watershed ideas or turning points in life. A new consumer habit or commodity comes to symbolize an important change. The first bathroom with running hot water, the first ride in the family car, or the first family holiday stand out as utopias which suddenly have come within reach. There are striking gender differences here. In the life histories of many women of earlier generations, it is the memories of the move to the first modern apartment that stand out. In many cases, the expressions used were: "it was like a dream" or "just like paradise." It is remembered as taking a step into the future, being a modern family on the move.

Turning to the genre called "the biography of things" the focus has often been on processes of ageing and cultural wear and tear, following the trajectories of objects from station to station and the ways that may change function and meaning on this journey, moving from the parlor into the kitchen or up in the attic, turning for example into second-hand trading objects, trash, kitsch, or antiques. There are a growing number of studies on the cultural and physical wear and tear of objects, on waste and wasting (Åkesson 2006), as well as on the history of second-hand buying and auctions (Mohrmann 2005), and so on.

ROUTINES, HABITS, AND PRACTICES

The focus on learning in people's interaction with things also gives us a chance to understand how everyday competences are developed. Narratives of my life as a home-builder, car-owner, or teenage consumer highlight the ways people have over the years acquired skills which later have often been naturalized into habits, reflexes, and routines and thus become hard to notice. The slow naturalization of these skills comes out, for example in the material on life with media technologies, from the telephone to the television. Early radio listening or television viewing was surrounded by an almost sacred aura. People remember the solemn atmosphere and the intense concentration in early radio listening, or the ways in which you dressed up for television evenings, telling the children to keep quiet. Both the radio and the television set were given a prominent position in the living room, rather like home altars. Gradually the media became routine. People learned how to listen with half an ear to the radio or how to have the television on as a background for conversation, zapping between channels. Typical of this gradual mastery of new home technologies is the capacity to do several things at the same time: read a newspaper while listening to the radio, have a meal while watching the television news, and so on. There is a long history of multi-tasking here (Löfgren 2007) as well as understandings of the ways in which new technologies and media are domesticated (Bausinger 1984; Beck 2000).

These aspects of life-histories show underdeveloped aspects of material lives: those of handling objects and technologies. There is a growing interest in the analysis of routines, and habits (see for example the collection by Shove *et al.* 2009), an interest that reframes the analysis. Take for example domestic routines that make other aspects visible. Open the door to any home, and what will you be stumbling over as you enter? Furniture, personal belongings, of course, but you will also get entangled in all the routines for organizing domestic consumption inside. The home is above all a web of rules, routines, and rhythms, of silent agreements and ingrained reflexes about "the ways we do things here." You learn how to survive a stressful morning, how to store the food in the fridge, sort the laundry, and much, much more.

This kind of learning goes on everywhere, but in different forms and again it is often highly gendered. Sarah Kjær (2009) has looked at the ways young Copenhagen couples organize their homes, creating patterns of division of labor and running into conflict about consumer priorities. It is in the trivial everyday consumer routines and interaction with the material world that homes are made, challenged, transformed, or broken (see for example Kaufmann 2005). A focus on routines also gives insights into questions of order and ordering, trying to live with an overflow of objects, gadgets, machines and activities (see for example Filiod 2003), that sometimes can turn into a feeling that things take over everyday life, a kind of modern animism Jojada Verrips (1994) has explored in his essay "The Thing Didn't 'Do' What I Wanted."

Discussions of life-history approaches as well as the learning of skills again show an interesting continuity in studies of material culture, which perhaps can best be illustrated by looking at a few important fields in the tradition of folklore, folklife, and European ethnology, fields that illustrate how national styles in analysis have developed and been transformed over time, but also the richness of different approaches, that perhaps all too seldom have come into dialogue. (The national scholarly traditions have been strong, often promoting an inward rather than outward academic gaze, a fact that has been supported by the tendency to publish in native languages.)

HOME AND WORK

Traditionally vernacular architecture had a key position in material culture studies, where local building traditions were documented and compared. Along with this went an interest in traditions of furnishing and interior decoration: the layout of rooms, the uses of furniture, and domestic aesthetics. As this tradition was taken into ethnographies of modern society the focus shifted, away from building techniques and forms, to an emphasis on interior decoration and home-making – a shift that mirrors technological and economic as well as cultural changes in everyday life. We have already met this shift in the material of modern life-histories as well as in the discussions of the importance of domestic routines and rituals above.

In shifting from a study of traditional building and interior decoration, some interesting links were made between the study of pre-industrial and industrial life-modes – and in different national ways. One good example of this is in the work of Henry Glassie. In the years of a disintegrating diffusionist approach in Europe, Glassie sought to re-theorize the material field by bringing in a structural approach, most notably in his study of folk housing in West Virginia (Glassie 1976). Later on he worked with the Ulster village of Ballymenone, where his interest shifted from the male domain of building to the female one of interior decoration (see also Pocius 1991 and the discussion in St George 2006). There is also a strong French tradition of studying traditional and modern homemaking (see for example Segalen and Le Wita 1993). In Germany there is also the tradition of studying home interiors and furniture over longer historical periods, mainly with the help of estate inventories (Mohrmann 1990).

If domestic life has remained a strong field in material culture studies, the same cannot be said of work. Looking at older dissertations from the 1950s and 1960s, a striking feature is the dominance of work, with studies of agricultural implements, fishing methods, textile skills, and artisan traditions. In the comprehensive *Handbook of Material Culture* (Tilley *et al* 2006), there are sections for art, architecture, food, clothing and consumption, but not one for work and work settings, apart from a short and narrow discussion of some aspects of technology.

The return of an interest in material culture meant above all a focus on consumption rather than production and above all a scant interest in working skills. Again, the American situation is different. Here, the traditional interest in craftsmanship had been kept alive, but then mainly focusing on the survival of more exclusive traditional crafts. There are a number of detailed ethnographic studies in US folklore that give an understanding of the everyday life of craftsmanship, such as Charles Briggs's study of the wood carvers in New Mexico (1980), Simon J. Bronner's book on chain carvers (1985), or Glassie's studies of potters and rug weavers (see also the extensive bibliography in Glassie 1999). With reawakened interest in these skills, such classics take on a new life, with the actualization of such questions as, "How is knowledge organized and transmitted and how do the senses work together in producing a chair or a basket?" Studies of craftsmanship traditionally tended to emphasize male worlds. There are hierarchies of gender at work here. Many female crafts were regarded as "less artistic" or interesting – from textile production to cooking. One of the first works trying to redress this imbalance was the collection of essays *Women's Folklore, Women's Culture* (Jordan and Kalcik 1985). For a more recent collection focusing on the history up to the 1950s, see Goggin and Tobin (2010).

There has also been less interest in work skills and the handling of material elements in contemporary urban work settings, although there are a growing number of studies focusing on work technologies, such as the high-tech settings of modern medicine and information technology (see for example Garsten and Wulff 2003). One can speculate about everyday life in academia, a work environment where the strong impact of materiality is constantly downplayed and the focus is on the production of lofty ideas and small footnotes. In that context, for example, what would the material culture of folklore studies look like? A very special perspective on that takes us to Holland.

An old building on the bank of Amsterdam's Kaisergracht canal housed a small research department specializing in the study of dialects and Dutch folk culture up to 1988. Excerpts, records, photographs, and drawings were collected in these run-down premises. When one of the researchers, J.J. Voskuil, retired after 30 years of working there, he energetically and secretly set his hand to writing a *roman à clef* of seven volumes of more than 5,000 pages over five years. His writings were based on an infinitesimal number of diary notes. Neither he nor the publishing company ever imagined that this would be a marketable product, and certainly never a best-seller.

When the first volume of *Het Bureau* (The Office) came out in 1996, it proved to be a sensation. Circulation quickly reached 35,000 copies and readers impatiently waited for the sequel. In total, several hundred thousands of volumes have been sold (see Rooijakkers and Meurkens 2000). What makes Voskuil interesting in this context was that he managed to capture all the minor tasks, rituals, and the use of tools, from maps, index cards, typewriters, and filing systems at this folklore institute. Although nothing much seems to happen, people are fully occupied handling material.

Voskuil had an axe to grind in producing this ironic image of his old work environment, but in taking his revenge and ridiculing many of his former colleagues and international contacts, he gives us at the same time a fascinating ethnography of the materiality of a folklore institute. A similar ethnography could be made even in the most high-tech and cyber-light academic surroundings, in a soundscape of buzzing printers, scraping seminar chairs, hissing coffee machines, and scribbling pencils.

Although there have been attempts to capture the materiality of work places like these, there are not many. Perhaps the only exception is the world of museums. The skills and everyday problems of collecting, selecting, sorting, maintaining, and exhibiting is a rich subgenre in the field.

A special field here is the recycling of old workplaces as heritage parks or event-spaces. Robert Willim (2005) has analyzed what he terms "industrial cool," the new uses of old industrial buildings in "the experience economy," and in a similar perspective, Tom O'Dell (2010) has studied what happens when old spa environments are transformed into modern spas and temples of well-being. He describes how the stage is set, what props are used to create a new ambience, and what goes on backstage in all the less spectacular work life of service providers in such settings.

THE TECHNOLOGIES OF BELONGING

In a similar manner, a material perspective brings new insights or aspects to classic fields, like the study of national or ethnic identity and belonging. Three studies of Danishness illustrate this. The first, by Anders Linde-Laursen, looks at what he calls "the nationalization of trivialities," where he studies how two peoples, the Danes and the Swedes, learned to wash dishes differently, in ways that affected both kitchen design and evening rituals (1993). The second, by Richard Jenkins, explores how the national flag has colonized all kinds of situations in Danish lives, in ways that often make it invisible (2007). The third, by Tine Damsholt (2007), looks at citizenship ceremonies among Danish immigrants and explores the ways in which minor material details come to color the situation. All three studies look at national identity at work, the ways in which it is acted out and emotionalized with the help of everyday objects and materialized rituals.

Other scholars have pointed out that the material perspective may help us get out of obsessions with discourses about ethnicity and identity. For example, Maja Poverzanović-Frykman (2008) has argued that it instead may be helpful to look at the ways different kinds of migrants come to share common experiences through consumer practices and life with objects. This is an approach used in Hilje van der Holst's (2007) study of identity and conceptions of modernity among female Turkish immigrants in Holland. She takes a detail like the use of lace in interior decoration and fashion as her starting point.

Another field where the material approach has renewed cultural analysis is mobility which became a central concern during the 1990s in what has sometimes been called "the nomadic turn." However, in the urge to capture old and new mobilities, there was a striking absence of how the materialities of movement shaped people's experiences. Mobility was often seen as frictionless, more of a mental than a physical process, as Rebecca Solnit has pointed out. The body in motion remained, on the whole, a highly theoretical entity rather than provoking an actual discussion of bodily sensations and practices:

> ...we seem to be reading about the postmodern body shuttled around by airplanes and hurtling cars, or even moving around by no apparent means, muscular, mechanical, economic or ecological. The body is nothing more than a parcel in transit, a chess piece dropped on another square, it does not move but is moved. (Solnit 2001: 28)

Among ethnologists and folklorists there has been a long tradition of interest in the materialities and micro-physics of movement and transport technologies. It is worth mentioning a few examples, like Fredrik Nilsson's (1997) study how new steamboat technology shaped both the poetics and politics of a Pan-Scandinavian student movement in the 1840s, or how conceptions of speed changed with the railways (Kaschuba 2004). Tourism as well as owning two homes is also a form of mobility where material aspects often have been surprisingly scarce (see the discussion in Moser and Seidl 2009 and Bendix and Löfgren 2008).

CONCLUSION

In *The Handbook of Material Culture* (Tilley 2006), the interdisciplinary richness of the field is demonstrated, but also the risk of getting stuck in traditional categories like primitive art, architecture, clothing, food. A handbook like this also clarifies what the specific ethnological and folkloristic contributions to the field are. First of all, there is the tradition of using the historical perspective as a way of problematizing or contrasting the present and to shed light on the processes of cultural learning that are hidden in the often taken-for-grantedness of contemporary interactions with the material world, such as driving a car, handling a fork, listening to the radio, or organizing the kitchen cupboards. A special resource here is the rich historical source materials collected in folklore archives and museums, that in often surprising ways may be brought into new life, as for example Anne-Li Palmsköld (2007) has demonstrated in her discussions of new perspectives on the large and often unused textile collections in museums – a material often seen as "dead" and uninteresting. Again, there is a gender aspect in this disinterest in domestic female worlds.

Second, there is the ethnological tradition of transcending categories like "folk art," "foodways," or identity, mixing aspects and materials in often surprising ways. In this process materialities become a dimension in the analysis, whether it is about household organization, youth subcultures, tourism, or heritage politics.

The challenge ahead is to bring this material dimension into play in new fields and arenas. A lesson to be learned from this research history is that to start with the material everyday world often produces different and sometimes surprising insights, focusing more on what people do than what they say, with more attention to skills and competences than to the rhetoric of identity or symbolism. Handling such issues often calls for new and experimental methods and ethnographies in order to capture processes that are hard to verbalize or activities that have been naturalized into invisiblility.

REFERENCES

Åkesson, Lynn. 2006. "Wasting" in Orvar Löfgren and Richard Wilk, Eds. *Off the Edge: Experiments in Cultural Analysis.* Copenhagen: Museum Tusculanum Press, pp. 39–46. (Also a special issue of *Ethnologia Europaea* 2005: 1–2.)

Bausinger, Hermann. 1984. "Media, Technology and Daily Life." *Media, Culture and Society* 6(4): 343–352.

Bausinger, Hermann. 1990. *Folk Culture in a World of Technology.* Bloomington: Indiana University Pres.

Beck, Stefan, Ed. 2000. *Technogene Nähe. Ethnographische Studien zur Mediennutzung im Alltag.* Berlin: Ethnographische und Ethnologische Studien 3, Institut für Europäische Ethnologie der Humboldt-Universität.

Bendix, Regina and Donald Brenneis, Eds. 2005. *Senses.* Berlin: Lit Verlag.

Bendix, Regina and Orvar Löfgren, Eds. 2008. *Double Homes, Double Lives?* Special issue. *Ethnologia Europaea* 37.

Brembeck, Helene, Karin M. Ekström, and Magnus Mörck, Eds. 2007. *Little Monsters. (De)coupling Assemblages Of Consumption.* Berlin: Lit Verlag.

Bromberger, Christian and Martien Segalen, Eds. 1996. *Culture matérielle et modernité.* Special issue. *Ethnologie française* 1996/1.

Bronner, Simon J. 1985. *Chain Carvers: Old Men Crafting Meaning.* Lexington: University Press of Kentucky.

Bronner, Simon J. 1986. *Grasping Things: Folk Material Culture and Mass Society in America.* Lexington: Kentucky University Press.

Bronner, Simon J., Ed. 1985. *American Material Culture and Folklife. A Prologue and Dialogue.* Ann Arbor: UMI Research Press.

Christensen, Olav. 1999. "The Playing Collective. Snowboarding, Youth Culture and the Desire for Excitement." *Ethnologia Scandinavica* 29(1999):106–119.

Damsholt, Tine. 2007. "The Sound of Citizenship." *Ethnologia Europaea* 38(1): 56–65.

Fél, Edit and Tamás Hofer. 1969. *Proper Peasants. Traditional Life in a Hungarian Village.* Chicago: Aldine.

Fél, Edit and Tamás Hofer. 1974. *Geräte der Atanyer Bauern.* Budapest: Akadémiai Kiadó.

Filiod, Jean Paul. 2003. *Le désordre domestique. Essai d'anthropologie.* Paris: L'Harmattan.

Fredriksson, Cecilia. 1997. "The Making of a Swedish Department Store Culture" in Colin Campbell and Paasi Falk, Eds. *The Shopping Experience.* London: Sage, pp.111–135.

Garsten, Christina and Helena Wulff, Eds. 2003. *New Technologies at Work: People, Screens and Social Virtuality.* Oxford: Berg.

Glassie, Henry. 1986. *Patterns in the Material Folk Culture of the Eastern United States.* Bloomington: Indiana University Press.

Glassie, Henry. 1976. *Folk Housing in Middle Virginia: A Structural Analysis of Historical Artefacts.* Knoxville: University of Tennessee Press.

Glassie, Henry. 1999. *Material Culture.* Bloomington: Indiana University Press.

Gradén, Lizette and Magdalena Petersson McIntyre, Eds. 2009. *Modets metamorfoser: den klädda kroppens identiteter och förvandlingar.* Stockholm: Carlsson.

Gullestad, Marianne. 1995. "The Morality of Consumption." *Ethnologia Scandinavica* 1995: 97–107.

Heidrich, Hermann, Ed. 2000. *SachKultur Forschung.* Bad Windsheim: DGV (Tagung der Arbeitsgruppe Sachkulturforschung).

Hjemdahl Mathiesen, Kirsti. 2003. "When Theme Parks Happen" in Jonas Poverzanović-Frykman and Nils Gilje, Eds. *Being There: New Perspectives on Phenomenology and the Analysis of Culture.* Lund: Academic Press, pp. 149–168.

Horst, Hilje van der. 2007. "Turkish Lace. Constructing Modernities and Authenticities." *Ethnologia Europaea* 36(1): 32–44.

Ingold, Tim. 2007. "Materials Against Materiality." *Archaeological Dialogues* 14(1): 1–16.

Jenkins, Richard. 2007. "Inarticulate Speech of the Heart. Nation, Flag and Emotion in Denmark" in Thomas Hylland Eriksen and Richard Jenkins, Eds. *Flag, Nation and Symbolism in Europe and America.* New York: Routledge, pp. 115–135.

Jordan, Rosan A. and Susan Kalcik, Eds. 1985. *Women's Folklore, Women's Culture.* Philadelphia: University of Pennsylvania Press.

Julien, Marie-Pierre and Céline Rosselin. 2005. *La Culture Materielle.* Paris: La Découverte.

Kaschuba, Wolfgang. 2004. *Die überwindung der Distanz: Zeit und Raum in der europäischen Moderne.* Frankfurt: Fischer.

Kaufmann, Jean Claude. 2005. *Casseroles, amours et crises. Ce que cuisiner veut dire.* Paris: Armand Colin.

Kirshenblatt-Gimblett, Barbara. 1989. "Objects of Memory: Material Culture as Life Review" in Elliott Oring, Ed. *Folk Groups and Folklore Genres: A Reader.* Logan: Utah State University Press, pp. 329–338.

Kirshenblatt-Gimblett, Barbara. 1998. *Destination Culture: Tourism, Museums, and Heritage.* Berkeley: University of California Press.

Kjær, Sarah Holst. 2009. *Sådan er det at elske.* Copenhagen: Museum Tusculanum Press.

Klein, Barbro and Mats Widbom, Eds. 1994. *Swedish Folk Art. All Tradition is Change.* New York: Harry Abrahams.

König, Gudrun. 2000. "Zum Lebenslauf der Dinge. Autobiographisches Erinnern und materielle Kultur" in Hermann Heidrich, Ed. *SachKulturForschung*, pp. 72–85.

König, Gudrun. 2005. *Alltagsdinge. Erkundungen der materiellen Kultur.* Tübingen: Ludwig-Uhland-Institut.

König, Gudrun. 2009. *Konsumkultur. Inszenierte Warenwelt um 1900.* Wien: Böhlau.

Kopytoff, Igor. 1988. "The Cultural Biography of Things. Commodification as a Process" in Arjun Appadurai, Ed. *The Social Life of Things.* Cambridge: Cambridge University Press, pp. 64–94.

Kramer, Karl S. 2000. "'Dinge und Namen.' Probleme der Sachforschung mit historischen Wort- und Bildquellen" in Hermann Heidrich, Ed., *SachKulturForschung*, pp. 117–129.

Law, John and John Hassard, Eds. 1999. *Actor Network Theory and After.* Oxford: Blackwell.

Leimgruber, Walter. 2007. "Woody, Buzz Lightyear und Co.: Vom Umgang mit

Sachen." *Schweizerische Zeitschrift für Volkskunde* 2007: 177–189.

Linde-Laursen, Anders. 1993. "The Nationalization of Trivialities: How Cleaning Becomes an Identity Marker in the Encounter of Swedes and Danes." *Ethnos* 1993(3–4): 275–293.

Lithberg, Nils, 1918 "Mortlar och pepparkrossare hos svensk allmoge." *Fataburen* 1918: 37–53.

Löfgren, Orvar. 1997. "Scenes from a Troubled Marriage: Swedish Ethnology and Material Culture Studies." *Journal of Material Culture* 1997(2): 95 – 113.

Löfgren, Orvar. 1998. "My Life as Consumer" in Mary Chamberlain and Paul Thompson, Eds. *Narrative and Genre*. London: Routledge, pp. 114–125.

Löfgren, Orvar. 2007. "Excessive Living." *Culture and Organization* 13(2): 131–144.

Lysaght, Patricia and Christine Burckhardt-Seebass, Eds. 2004. *Changing Tastes. Food Culture and The Processes of Industrialization*. Basle: SGV.

Miller, Daniel, Ed. 2005. *Materiality*. Durham, NC: Duke University Press.

Miller, Daniel. 2008. *The Comfort of Things*. Cambridge: Polity Press.

Mohrmann, Ruth E. 1990. *Alltagswelt im Land Braunschweig: Städtische und ländliche Wohnkultur vom 16. bis zum frühen 20. Jahrhundert*. 2 Vols. Münster: Waxmann.

Mohrmann, Ruth. E. 2005. "Auctions as Multifunctional Systems in the Rhine Valley, Germany, in the Nineteenth Century." *Folklore* 116: 315–324.

Moser, Johannes and Daniella Seidl, Eds. 2009. *Dinge auf Reisen. Materielle Kultur und Tourismus*. Berlin: Waxmann.

Nilsson, Fredrik. 1997. "'The Floating Republic': On Performance and Technology in Early Nineteenth-Century Scandinavian Politics." *Journal of Folklore Research* 34(2): 85–103.

O'Dell, Tom. 2010. *Spas and the Cultural Economy of Sensuous Magic and Hospitality*. Lund: Nordic Academic Press.

Otto, Lene and Lykke Pedersen. 1998. "Life Stories and Objects of Memories." *Ethnologia Scandinavica* 28(1998): 77–92.

Pocius, Gerald L. 1991. *A Place to Belong: Community Order and Everyday Space in Calvert, Newfoundland*. Athens, GA: University of Georgia Press.

Poverzanović-Frykman, Jonas and Nils Gilje, Eds. 2003. *Being There. New Perspectives on Phenomenology and the Analysis of Culture*. Lund: Nordic Academic Press.

Povrzanovic'-Frykman, Maja. 2008. "Beyond Culture and Identity. Places, Practices, Experiences." *Ethnologia Europaea* 38(1): 13–22.

Rogan, Bjarne. 1998. "Things With a History – and Other Possessions. Some Notes on Public and Private Aspects of Possession among Elderly People." *Ethnologia Scandinavica* 28 (1998): 93–107.

Rooijakkers, Gerard and Peter Meurkens. 2000. "Struggling with the European Atlas. Voskuil's Portrait of European Ethnology." *Ethnologia Europaea* 30(1): 75–95.

Segalen, Martine. 2005. *Vie d'un musée*. Paris: Stock.

Segalen, Martine and Béatrix Le Wita, Eds. 1993. "Chez soi. Objets et décors: des créations familiales?" *Autrement*, série Mutations 137.

Shove, Elizabeth, Frank Trentman, and Richard Wilk, Eds. 2009. *Time, Consumption and Everyday Life*. Oxford: Berg.

Solnit, Rebecca. 2001. *Wanderlust: A History of Walking*. London: Penguin.

St George, Robert. 2006. "Home Furnishing and Domestic Interiors" in Chris Tilley, Webb Keane, Susanne Küchler, Mike Rowlands and Patricia Spyer, Eds. *Handbook of Material Culture*. London: Sage, pp. 221–229.

Tilley, Chris, Webb Keane, Susanne Küchler, Mike Rowlands, and Patricia Spyer, Eds. 2006. *Handbook of Material Culture*. London: Sage.

Verrips, Jojada. 1994. "The Thing Didn't 'Do' What I Wanted: Some Notes on Modern Forms of Animism in Western Societies" in Jojada Verrips, Ed. *Transactions: Essays in Honour of Jeremy Boissevain*. Amsterdam: Het Spinhuis, pp. 35–52.

Verrips, Jojada. 2005. "Aisthesis and An-aesthesia." *Ethnologia Europaea* 35(1): 29–36.

Welz, Gisela, Ed. 1996. *Einkaufen: Ethnographische Skizzen, Konsumenten kulturen in der Region Tübingen. Tübingen.* Tübingen: Ludwig Uhland-Institut.

Williams, Rosalind, H. 1982. *Dream Worlds. Mass Consumption in Late 19th Century France.* Berkeley: University of California Press.

Willim, Robert. 2005. "It's in The Mix. Configuring Industrial Cool" in Orvar Löfgren and Robert Willim, Eds. *Magic, Culture and The New Economy.* Oxford: Berg, pp. 97–104.

FURTHER READING

Briggs, Charles L. 1980. *The Wood Carvers of Córdova, New Mexico: Social Dimensions of an Artistic Revival.* Knoxville: University of Tennessee Press.

Glassie, Henry. 1982. *Passing the Time in Ballymenone: Culture and History of an Ulster Community.* Philadelphia: University of Pennsylvania Press.

Rogan, Bjarne. 2001. "Consuming Passion and Erudite Consumption: Approaches to a Consumption Phenomenon" in Pirjo Korkiakangas and Elina Kiuru, Eds. *An Adventurer in European Ethnology.* Jyväskylä: Atena Kustannus Oy, pp. 85–109.

PART II LOCATION

INTRODUCTION TO PART II
Location

Regina F. Bendix and Galit Hasan-Rokem

While this section of the book naturally will not cover the entire world, we have striven to include most continents, attempting to represent a selection of the variety of languages and cultures within them. The result is far from perfect and we would have preferred a wider representation from everywhere. One of the achievements that the book may claim is a great variety of political and cultural histories which the selected chapters display. It may not be a mere coincidence that by presenting the various histories of folklore studies in different countries, the political and cultural history of those countries is put into relief as a constitutive factor. Folklore's embeddedness in matters of state and policy as well as the ways that various political, academic, and general intellectual powers have related or rejected the potential of folklore, its study as well as production, powerfully reflect some of the most burning issues in each of the communities here described. The same circumstance also contributed to the ultimate selection of the contributors available to the editors to research the histories and ethnographies of folklore and folkloristics everywhere.

The rich selection of chapters bringing into focus both the ancient traditions and the modern state of the art in China, Japan, and India constitute a point of departure that highlights the global span of our enterprise. Moreover, being privileged to include contributions by authors themselves of the culture marks our approach as one that attempts to emphasize the subject of folklore and culture in general as locally situated. In addition to its ideological substance, this approach also communicates something important regarding our view of folklore and folkloristics as intrinsically intertwined with local contexts.

A Companion to Folklore, First Edition. Edited by Regina F. Bendix and Galit Hasan-Rokem.

Some important areas have been included despite being traditionally regarded as the objects of classical anthropological research. Oceania is our prime example for demonstrating that new ways of thinking in folklore studies have enabled the embracing of a region geographically so loosely connected in the same universe of discourse as traditionally included regions.

The diversity of South America is captured here through the lens of one of its post-colonial nations, Argentina, whereas we naturally acknowledge the linguistic, histori-cal, and cultural particularities of other communities on the continent. It is important to remember that especially the interplay between indigenous and immigrant and colonial subjects of the culture have evolved in greatly divergent ways.

Our initial plan was to also devote an inclusive chapter on North America. However we have ended up with a focus on the United States. While some similarities and con-nections in the development of Canadian folklore and folkloristics may be suggested, the differences derived from the origins of the immigrants and especially from radi-cally different post-colonial policies vis-à-vis indigenous populations would warrant separate treatment. The same can be stated for Mexico, which may be considered more akin to Latin America, both linguistically and in its cultural make-up; here, too, a separate treatment honoring the theoretical thrust of Mexican folklore scholars would be desirable, though the border exchanges typical of aspects of US-folkloristics have found reflection in the chapter.

The ancient heritages around the Mediterranean and the entire Middle Eastern region cannot be said to be even metonymically represented here. The absence of the folklore study of classical ancient cultures is especially critical. The relevant chapters have opted for highlighting the modern and the contemporary with some reference to historical circumstance. The chapter on Turkey opens a window especially on the dynamics of the entangled emergence of folklore research and organized folklore production in the context of the establishment of a secularized nation state after the fall of the Ottoman empire. The chapter on Israel introduces the complexity of iden-tities involved in the study of folklore in a nation state carrying on the one hand the heritage of a dispersed community and on the other being involved in various mecha-nisms of constructing a relationship to its contested terrain.

The folklore of the African continent is compressed into the chapter on Fulani oral literature by which only a hint of the continent's linguistic and cultural diversity is demonstrated. It is thus important to remind ourselves of the autonomous theory building of African scholars in defining the characteristics of oral literature ("ora-ture") and the understanding of oral literature by scholars outside Africa based on the continent's rich cultures. The chapter included may be considered a representation of the classic French school of oral literatures in Africa.

The selection of chapters on Europe was restricted to a few cases. The guiding interest was a demonstration of different political histories and involvements of the field on a relatively small terrain. Finland has been extensively studied as a paradig-matic example of folklore's and folkloristics' role in building the nation state, with subsequent scholarship honoring especially the genres revered by the founding schol-ars, in this case epic poetry. Much as in Finland, Irish folklorists have produced mas-sive folklore archives to bolster the field, serving as examples for many other countries. Irish folklore studies have celebrated the linguistic heritage of Celtic culture and built a foundation from which to foster independence and nation building.

German speaking countries are included here not primarily for their historical role during the romantic beginnings of the discipline. Rather, the instrumentalization and deep implication of German folklore studies during the period of National Socialism and the long shadow this has cast on subsequent generations of scholars are the focus of the chapter. Written from a post-communist perspective, the chapter on Russia examines how Russian folkloristics was colored, during most of the twentieth century, by the communist elite's interest in deploying folklore to shape and represent a mentality consistent with their ideology.

Other chapters in this volume illustrate, through the phenomena they explore, further cultural and territorial regions.

Viewed collectively the chapters display the multiple configurations between academic folklore studies and the presence of folklore in other public spheres. In addition to the role folklore and folkloristics can play and have played in political transformations, the place of folklore in addressing cultural diversity, or in denying it, seems consistent across the globe. Folklore studies may be unique among the humanities in occupying a scene where academic and lay scholars together negotiate the profile of the field and the methods to study and represent it.

CHAPTER 10 TRANSLINGUAL FOLKLORE AND FOLKLORICS IN CHINA

Lydia H. Liu

Folklore can mean different things to different people and even become different things as it travels from place to place across the various technological media of transmission: writing, print, gramophone, radio, film, television, and so on. This ontological instability – which troubles the study of folklore, past and present – may confront the analyst with some sobering truths about her own sense of time, place, history, tradition, and the social imaginary. If we agree that modern political structures and national institutions of learning have inaugurated themselves by staking a claim on the voice of the people and its authenticity, it should not be difficult to identify a shared idiom of folk, ethnicity, community and society across the living languages of the world and situate it in the emergence of nationalism, capitalism, and colonial modernity. The problem is how to interpret that idiom. Is folklore always in translation? We may begin by acknowledging that the study of folklore – which is the coming to self-consciousness of that historical movement – is as much about the folk and their voices as about the story of political authority and historical forces that struggle to make the people legible as such.

This struggle over the legibility of the people and their cultural productions is what will concern us as we turn to the situation of folklore and modern folklore studies in China. The focus on legibility indicates that we will be attentive to the traces and nuances of discursive struggles and grant all reiterated acts of statement or translation a degree of openness to contingency, appropriation, and contestation. This approach also raises an interesting question: Does the idea of legibility – commonly associated with writing and literacy – imply a paradox whenever folklore is taken to be orally

A Companion to Folklore, First Edition. Edited by Regina F. Bendix and Galit Hasan-Rokem.
© 2012 John Wiley & Sons, Ltd. Published 2012 John Wiley & Sons, Ltd.

produced? If there is indeed a paradox here – though "historical tension" is the preferred term here to that of "paradox" in logic – the paradox would then be intrinsic to the history and historiography of folklore itself. Oral literature and folklore need not be opposed to writing and literacy and have never been insofar as the collecting and transcription processes are concerned.[1] As we take a longer historical view – for instance, the collecting of folksong in ancient imperial China – we may discover a strong, reiterated pattern of dialectical entanglement between writing and oral literature which spans more than 2,000 years. And as we begin to articulate this temporality to modern folklore, the old debate on orality and literacy in folklore studies and elsewhere would seem less interesting and productive than if we were to focus our attention on the entanglement itself.

In imperial China, it was the political authority associated with the power of writing that made folklore legible to the imperial eye and available to posterity; and likewise, members of the literati would time after time draw on folksong and folk legends from the diverse languages and dialects of that vast land to contest the imperial authority using their own writing. This millennia-long struggle over the voice of the common folk was still operative when modern folklore studies arrived in China from Europe and Japan; but the manner of its operation began to show some distinctly new features. And how could it have been otherwise? As discussed below, Chinese folklorists had no choice but plunge themselves into the politics of colonial mimicry, social reform, nationalism, class struggle, or the world revolution in the fast-changing moments of social transformation in the twentieth century. This chapter is devoted to analyzing such moments and will demonstrate how the work of Chinese folklorists participated in a collective struggle to restage themselves and their country in the modern world.

The Birth of Modern Folklore Studies in China

In the early twentieth century, a number of Chinese intellectuals and scholars began to adopt the neologism *minsuxue* 民俗學 – *min* as "folk," *su* as "popular customs," *xue* as "studies" – to launch a new discipline and to create a modern national literature in the vernacular language. By coining this term in 1922, they were essentially borrowing back the same Kanji characters – read *minzokugaku* in Japanese – that Japanese folklorists had earlier borrowed from the repertoire of existing Chinese characters to translate "folklore studies" into Japanese. This is what I have elsewhere termed as "roundtrip" translingual practice in modern China (Liu 1995). Some of the Chinese enthusiasts of folklore studied in Japan and were well acquainted with the work of influential Japanese folklorists. It was the halcyon days of Japanese folklore gathering, imperial expansion, and ethnological fieldwork. Japanese folklorists and ethnologists conducted systematic fieldwork in rural Japanese villages as well as in the newly colonized societies including Okinawa (1874), Taiwan (1895), and Korea (1910) and would soon extend this work to Micronesia (1919), Manchuria (1931), and elsewhere (Nakao 2005: 19–35).

Zhou Zuoren (1885–1967) became fascinated by the work of Yanagita Kunio (1875–1962), Kobayashi Issa (1763–1827), and Takano Tatsuyuki (1876–1947) when he was a student in Japan in 1905–1911. His attention was drawn primarily toward the literary value of these authors' published writing rather than their ethnography or method. Upon his return to China in 1911, Zhou began to collect and publish folksongs and children's songs from his native Chaoxing in Zhejiang province (Hung 1985: 44–45). Within one year of joining the literature faculty of Peking University in 1917, he began to champion the cause of folklore studies and created a center to begin folksong collection and research. His colleague Liu Bannong started a new column in the *Peking University Daily* (Beida rikan) in 1918 called "Folksong Selection" where one ballad or folksong was printed each day for a total of 148 folksongs. Along with Liu and a scholar named Shen Yinmo, Zhou initiated an institution-building effort that would lead to the formation of the discipline of folklore studies at the Sun Yat-Sen University several years later. By 1920, Zhou, Gu Jiegang, Shen Jianshi, and others founded the Society for Folk Customs Survey and successfully extended their folksong collecting and research activities to as many as 22 provinces in China (Rong 1928: 15–16: 1).

The *Folksong Weekly* – the official publication of the Society for Folk Customs Survey – was launched by Zhou Zuoren and his colleagues in December 1922. This journal issued guidelines for folksong research and made a concerted effort to attract the attention of writers and scholars. The editors' "Foreword" to the inaugural number of *Folksong Weekly* identified the collecting and study of folksongs as part of *minsuxue* or "folklore studies" and treated it as a central task in the rebuilding of Chinese national culture.[2] When the exodus of left-leaning intellectuals to the south occurred under the pressures of warlord tyranny in 1926–1927, some of them, including historian and folklorist Gu Jiegang, were recruited by the Sun Yat-Sen University in the city of Guangzhou where they established a new Society for Folklore Studies, founded a seminal journal in Chinese folklore studies called *Folklore* (Minsu 1927–1943), and started an influential monograph series in folklore studies.

Folklore became the regular publication of the Society for Folklore Studies and made a significant contribution to the consolidation of folklore studies as a discipline in China. The journal published a total of 123 weekly and quarterly numbers and even persisted through the difficult wartime years until 1943. Gu Jiegang (1893–1980), a co-editor of *Folklore*, brought out some of his most influential studies in *Folklore*. Zhong Jingwen (1903–2002), another central figure in early folklore studies and co-founder of *Folklore*, published his first research there. Besides publishing the journal, the Society for Folklore Studies at the Sun Yat-Sen University organized numerous pedagogical and fieldwork activities, including setting up an exhibition hall for ethnological artifacts, organizing regular lecture series in folklore studies, and so on. These academic programs trained the first generation of Chinese folklorists and were responsible for disseminating the theories and practices of folklore studies in the mainstream discourse of urban society (Zhong 1982, 1: 174–175). And what were the theories and practices they helped disseminate to Chinese society at large?

Zhong Jingwen's *Collected Lectures on Folk Arts* was among the first systematic treatments of folklore in what one might call the professionalization of Chinese folklore studies. Published in 1928 by the Society for Folklore Studies, this slim volume provides a comparative study of documented folk legends gathered from selected ethnic minority groups in China. His approach focuses on the formulaic patterns and variations of individual folksongs to establish them as the oral productions of ethnic minorities, such as the Zhuang, whom he describes as simple-minded primitives who love singing and embellishments (Zhong 1928: 95). For example, the story of Liu Sanjie – an immortal female singer from the lore of the Zhuang of Guangxi and Guangdong provinces – is given detailed attention by the author.[3] In his view, the question of whether Liu Sanjie actually existed or not is irrelevant, for the task of the folklorist is to figure out why those simple-minded people invented the stories they did and how they invented them.

Notwithstanding their professional commitment to oral literature and fieldwork, Zhong Jingwen and his fellow folklorists did not shun the use of extant *printed sources* from the past, and there were vast amounts of them stretching from centuries of imperial historiographies to local gazetteers and literary compositions of every single dynasty from the Han (206 BCE–220 CE) through the Qing (1644–1911). Hardly is there a subject of ethnographical interest in China that is not lodged somewhere in the vast bureaucratic print/manuscript machine of the past dynasties. In fact, this has long been a point of contention between Chinese and Euro-American scholars in folklore studies (as well as in archaeology) since the early twentieth century to this very day. Can traditional textual exegesis be credited as evidence to verify ethnographic fieldwork? What is the basis of truth in folklore studies? At stake, of course, has been the scientific standing of the discipline, which requires a professional consensus on what amounts to good and reliable fieldwork and what counts as rigorous analytical methods, and so on.

It is not as if the Chinese folklorists in the early decades of the twentieth century disregarded the centrality of fieldwork in ethnographic research. Their difficulty was of a different sort; namely, what to do with the pervasive impact of writing, literacy, and imperial bureaucracy on peoples and communities and their oral traditions, and what to do with the recorded histories of the past dynasties which have documented this impact continuously over the past 2,000-odd years.[4] To exacerbate the difficulty, the "simple-minded people" in the far south whom the folklorist studied and who practiced so-called oral literature also exhibited a tendency to succumb to writing and literacy. Almost in spite of himself, Zhong's appropriation of textual records demonstrates a profound entanglement of oral and written sources within the ethnographic work itself. In *Collected Lectures on Folk Arts,* for instance, he cites the following passage from a printed work titled *New Stories from Guangdong* (Guangdong xinyu) composed by a well-known seventeenth-century author Qu Dajun (1630–1696):

> The people of Yue [the *Zhuang* ethnic minority] are customarily skilled in singing and, whenever there is an auspicious occasion, they sing in celebration. In ancient times, they used songs to compete for status; the most skilled would be rewarded and be named *gebo* [the song elder]. When seeking a bride and visiting the woman's family, the son-in-law would find a number of men of age and appearance similar to his own and of equal talent and intelligence to serve as his "groom companions." The woman's family would block the gate with verses and songs; the son-in-law would *take up a brush and write* or have the groom-companions make drafts for him. Some of these songs were refined and some unrefined and, in the end, they would improvise, valuing the refined and elegant; [they continued] until the woman's family could not match them any longer, and finally the bride would come forth. (Zhong 1928: 96–98; emphasis added)

Overlooking the presence of writing in the above account, Zhong observes that the exchange of love songs has been an established courtship ritual among the Zhuang people for many centuries (as evidenced from the written record) and that this ritual is rarely found in "civilized" regions across the vast territories inhabited by the Han people. He explains that Guangxi and Guangdong provinces lie to the far south, away from the center of dynastic power, and that the folk customs of the local people necessarily retain elements of primitive society. He speculates further that the psychologists and educators in the West might attribute these people's behavior to their natural desire for knowledge, not unlike that of children and savages. He comments: "the savages exhibit extremely naïve behaviors – all kinds of preposterous myths appear to derive from this natural desire for knowledge – especially the myth of genesis." Zhong concludes that the Zhuang people are "unrefined and uncivilized" and that "the experiences and objects that inform their reasoning are infantile and crude, and they have made up fantastic tales based on their familiar customs and they are steeped in this kind of irrationality" (Zhong 1928: 98).

Zhong's portrayal of Zhuang people as "oral" and "uncivilized" is contradicted by the evidence of literacy within the courtship ritual he cites. Clearly, the men employ the writing brush in the poetry competition and they sing as well as write (using the writing brush of the Han) and seem to prefer "the refined." But how did Zhong manage to overlook this crucial detail even as he drew on the written record to establish the case? Another piece of the puzzle is that Zhong wrote his study in the aftermath of the New Culture movement and the May Fourth movement when many young men and women had rejected arranged marriages to pursue romantic love. The romantic courtship rituals of Zhuang people would have enjoyed affinity with this broad new trend rather than with the traditional arranged marriage practiced predominantly by the Han. Why does Zhong eschew an obvious reading and choose to see "primitive" elements in the cultural practices of the Zhuang? Could it be attributed to his Han chauvinism?

The term Han – named after the Han dynasty – currently designates the largest ethnic group alongside the 55 officially recognized ethnic minority groups in the People's Republic of China. The enunciation of the term Han, however, goes back much further and its meanings fluctuated and transformed through centuries of dynastic cycles of conquest, subjugation, and resistance. That is one of the reasons why we should be careful not to read anachronistically the PRC policies on ethnic minorities back into the dynastic histories of the past and keep in mind that the total or partial subjugation of the Han population by foreigners and ethnic minorities from the north through dynastic regimes – Khitans, Jurchens, Mongols, Manchus – had a long and convoluted history in China.[5] In the seventeenth century, for example, the Manchus – a tribal ethnic society from the north – conquered and subjugated the Han population and established the Qing dynasty following the overthrow of the Ming dynasty. The Manchu minority ruled the Han majority for more than 250 years (1644–1911) (Elliott 2001). Within their own lifetime, not only did the first generation of Chinese folklorists witness the overthrow of the Manchus and the Qing dynasty by Han revolutionaries but they also experienced the birth pangs of the modern nation-state in China in 1912. Memories of the Han submission to the Manchus were still fresh in their minds when they began folksong collecting and ethnographic fieldwork; and the effect, if not the motivation, of their work contributed to a massive structural transformation of Han and minority relations along the directions charted out by Sun Yat-Sen and the other revolutionaries at the dawn of the

Republican Revolution. And as we try to make sense of the place and role of folklore studies in China, this picture of a major dynastic transition may explain some of the fraught issues relating to political rule, civilization, and ethnic identity in the fledgling nation-state. It can also help us understand how the newly gained Han sovereignty over minority groups was consolidated through discursive as well as institutional inventions. However, the consolidation did not happen overnight because the sovereignty of the young nation-state in the Republican era (1912–1949) was fragile and compromised by the presence of European and Japanese colonialism and imperialism.

POLITICAL RULE AND THE VOICE OF THE OTHER

Addressing the fraught relations between the Han and ethnic minorities in China, Stevan Harrell (1995) points to a number of structural similarities exhibited by what he calls the successive civilizing projects of the past and present. He calls them the Confucian project, the Christian project, and the Communist project and argues that each of these projects is conceived of "as emanating from a particular center, as defining civilization (or the desired state) according to a certain set of philosophical principles, as separating groups according to some sort of criterion of 'ethnic identification,' and then giving these groups equal or unequal legal status, while scaling them according to one or another variable" (1995: 17) Although we should not rule out these elements from consideration, the logic of center and periphery is too vague and leaves out too much history to tell us much about the one project or the other. Does the structural similarity exist in the eyes of the beholder? If not, does it suggest a historical linkage, tradition, or internal logic? Let us consider where Confucius and Confucian authority stand with respect to folklore collecting in China.

Confucius's name (552 BCE–479 BCE) is associated with one of the earliest surviving classics known as the *Book of Songs* – an anthology of 300 poems – which he had allegedly selected and compiled. Apparently, a certain portion of these poems belongs to the category of folksong. Although these songs or poems were collected from the eleventh century BCE through the sixth century BCE, we do not know who collected them or how many more works were made available to Confucius in manuscript form or some other form.[6] According to recorded history, the institutionalized collecting of folksong did not begin until the reign of Emperor Wu (141 BCE–86 BCE) of the Han dynasty, though some scholars try to push that date to the reign of the first emperor Qinshihuang (259 BCE–210 BCE) (Allen 1992: 37–43). In any case, Emperor Wu's fame has come down to us as someone who valued creative expressions – poetry, literature, and philosophy flourished in his reign – and he is credited with the establishment (or revival) of the imperial Music Bureau, known as *yuefu*. In a detailed description of how official messengers were sent around collecting folksongs among the people, the *Book of Han* (Han shu, completed in 111 CE) reveals a political motive on the part of Emperor Wu:

> In the early month of spring, those who had huddled together in the winter months were about to venture out. Then came official messengers who stood on the side of the road striking their wooden bells to collect songs. The officials then submitted the songs they

had collected to the Grand Master of Music in the court who regulated them in accordance with the correct notes and tunes before presenting them to the Son of Heaven. It is said that even though the sovereign never looks beyond the window or leaves the door [of his palace], he knows the world very well. (Ban Gu 1964: 1123)[7]

In the above documented instance of imperial folksong collecting, folksong functioned as a kind of intelligence or window that informed the ruler about the sentiments of his subjects. The power of public opinion derived from the anonymous source of folksong, the assumption being that "when the ruler is tyrannical and the subjects are too frightened to air their grievances, then popular songs and ballads will appear to portend evil, and these are called 'poetic omens'" (Liu 1975: 65). Without having to decide how much of that effort was literally driven by a Confucian agenda, there is no doubt that early folksong collecting concerned, first and foremost, political rule and the stability of the state. It was about inventing a set of communication mechanisms whereby the sovereign would get to know his people in order to rule them more effectively. As a result, a good number of transcribed folksongs from the Han dynasty known as *yuefu* poetry have survived the millennia-long cycles of dynastic transitions and evolved into an essential component of the Chinese literary canon. Here, one might observe some interesting resonances and parallels with modern ethnographic work, such as the ways in which German folklorists associated folklore with the *Völkergedanken*, but exactly how does the Han-dynasty Music Bureau compare with the institutions of modern folklore studies in Germany, England, China or elsewhere? What is the ground, if any, for conducting comparisons across the historical divide or across the cultural/linguistic divide?

In her comparative survey of modern German, British, and Chinese folklore studies, Uli Linke (1990) has drawn some interesting conclusions about each tradition. She points out that the German folklorist became "the great advisor and expert in the art of governing, in correcting and improving the social 'body,' as well as maintaining it in a permanent state of order, health, and productivity" (1990: 135). If the institution of German folklore studies reminds us of the Han Music Bureau and their official messengers, the similarity ends about here, because a great deal more is involved in the practices of German *Volkskunde* – the statistical approach to the population, the anxiety about the health of the social body, the national education program, and so on – than does the opening of communication channels between the ruler and the ruled. Linke shows that the German folklorists were directly charged with the task of educating the population and that they also served as counselors to the representatives of power in academies and learned societies.

The linkage between British folklore studies and German *Volkskunde* is suggested through the coinage of the term "folk-lore" by William John Thoms in 1846. Hermann Bausinger has speculated that the English term probably derived from a translation of the older German term *Volks-kunde* (Linke 1990: 136; Bausinger 1969: 50). British folklore studies – in particular, the work of Scottish folklorists – also enjoyed deep ties with popular antiquities and with the desire to advance the cause of romantic nationalism. In contrast to the German statistical accumulation of social information about local populations through comprehensive ethnographic surveys, British folklore research, according to Linke, focused on the reinvention of the national ancient heritage through the study of magic, superstitions, proverbs, legends, and songs. By the nineteenth century, Sir Edward Tylor's work on the development of religion, language, and art began to mark a transition from romantic folklore studies to social anthropology in England. The role that folklore research played in the administration of British colonies abroad – the censuses, surveys, and narratives – seems mitigated in Linke's study, if not made to disappear, whereas it has been shown that the rule of colonized people lay at the heart of the development of British folklore studies and social anthropology.

And how do these developments compare with modern folklore studies in China? Linke suggests that, unlike the German and British schools, the new forms of social knowledge introduced by folklore research in modern China were not initially "an administrative tool of the state; rather, folklore research furnished a means for inciting movements of popular resistance" (1990: 141). This statement captures some aspect of the distinctiveness of early twentieth-century Chinese folklore studies – its political orientation – but overlooks a good number of important developments that the method of "parallel comparison" such as Linke's – German, British, Chinese, and so on – cannot but elide. For instance, what do we make of the interactions, networks, and traveling theories in the making of Chinese folklore studies? Can we ignore the systematic introduction and translation of Herder, Tylor, and other European and British theorists published through the pages of the Chinese journal *Folklore*? How and from where did Zhong Jingwen and his fellow folklorists acquire their evolutionary idea of "primitive culture"? Confucianism could not have been the right answer and, in fact, Confucianism was under attack by radical intellectuals who turned to the voice of the folk and began to promote democracy in modern China. Nor is Han chauvinism a good explanation for the historical reason stated in the above. What ought to concern us, therefore, is not the folklorist's personal biases but a set of discursive developments and social programs that emerged out of the consolidation of modern folklore studies as a discipline in China. To these we now turn.

TRANSLATION AND TRANSLINGUAL PRACTICES

We have learned that Japanese folklore research contributed a new Kanji concept *minzokugaku* or *minsuxue* to the Chinese language by linguistically marking the new discipline as simultaneously foreign and Chinese. Moreover, there is ample research to suggest that the Japanese had turned to German and British folklore studies, anthropology, or primitive law as their primary model. Katsumi Nakao's research has suggested that Okamatsu Sanarō, who was put in charge of ethnological investigations in Taiwan by Japanese colonial authorities in 1901, had studied Civil Code and primitive law in Germany under Josef Kohler. Upon the completion of his studies, he became a law professor at Kyoto Imperial University and was appointed to study the native legal situations in colonized Taiwan. In his investigations, Okamatsu adopted the ethnographic methods he had learned in Germany and published his report on land and kinship in English. According to Nakao (2005), Okamatsu relied on three major sources in his colonial research on Taiwan: "German methodologies developed for the study of primitive law; British methodology employed for the study of colonized indigenous peoples; and the Chinese classics, the intensive and comparative study of which had been greatly developed in the Edo period" (2005: 22). The interconnections among these sources have brought the role of traveling theory and traveling theorists into focus – in this case, colonial anthropology – in the repeated reiteration of the techniques of colonial rule under different circumstances.

Harry Harootunian has linked Japanese folklore studies to the rise of fascism in modern Japan. He argues that Yanagita Kunio and other Japanese folklorists looked to the figure of the folk and the unity of the archaic community it embodied to pursue the colonial space of the East Asia Co-Prosperity Sphere (*Daitōa Kyōeiken*) to be governed by imperial Japan. "Their privileging of the folk," Harootunian (2000) writes, "could not help but supply fascism with its most powerful trope, an object of fantasy and political desire, and thus could not, itself, avoid complicity with the 'gathering' of fascism as it was increasingly articulated in promises to remove both unevenness and conflict and eliminate cultural abstraction in programs proclaiming the establishment of folkism" (2000: 400).

What then was the situation of translingual folklore studies in China, a country that was victimized by Japanese fascism rather than served by it? If the Japanese neologism *minzokugaku* was a Kanji rendering of the German *Volkskunde* and the English "folklore" before completing its roundtrip back in China as *minsuxue*, this interesting trajectory ought to suggest a translingual method or conceptual framework that allows us to put greater emphasis on interaction and mutual entanglement than isolated comparisons or case studies. For how can we continue to make parallel comparisons or observe similar and different practices in folklore studies in different nations when these same theories and practices of folklore studies have been interlinked globally through colonial modernity and capitalism? In other words, we need to pay attention to the traces of translingual, intellectual linkages, and genealogies, as well as their long-distance movement within a relatively short period of time.

How did modern folklore studies metamorphose as it moved from Europe through Japanese imperial expansionism to China? In what ways did a situated understanding of orality, ethnicity, and folk legacies fashion the mainstream cultural imaginary of modern China? One pivotal moment of self-consciousness in the scientific endeavors of Chinese folklore studies can be dated to March 1928 when the editor made the decision to adopt Gu Jiegang's proposal that the journal's name be changed from *Folk Literature and Art* to *Folklore* (also known as *Folklore Weekly*). This change was indicative of a set of broader conceptual shifts from folksong collecting to folklore studies with emphasis on objectivity and social science approaches. The goal was to distinguish professional ethnographic studies as a separate field from the folk arts or "applied folklore" (even if the actual division of labor was difficult to sustain). The fledgling academic discipline accomplished its goal in part by emphasizing field work and, no less important, by producing a wide range of theoretical and technical idioms to justify that work.

Translation became a central task in that endeavor. From the very start, the journal *Folklore* followed the proceedings of international folklore societies closely and began to translate and publish systematically influential theoretical works in folklore studies from Europe, Japan, and United States in almost every issue. Bronislaw Malinowski, Andrew Lang, Lucien Lévy-Bruhl, Franz Boas, and J.G. Frazer were among the first to be introduced to Chinese academia, but an obscure work that seemed to enjoy particular favor amongst Chinese folklorists was *The Handbook of Folklore* written by British folklorist Charlotte Sophia Burne, onetime president of the Folklore Society in

London. In the first number of *Folklore*, a leading folklorist Yang Chengzhi translated and serialized the "Questionary" and "Terminology" sections of Burne's book in twelve continuous installments.

The theoretical positioning of *Folklore* is delineated by He Sijing in an article called "Questions in Folklore Studies" in which he singles England out for praise and emulation, for "just as France is the home of sociology, so is England the home of folklore studies" (1: 1928, 4). What inspiration did English folklore studies offer to its aspiring Chinese counterpart? Drawing on Burne's main line of argument, He Sijing argues that from the time of the Industrial Revolution, the emergence of large-scale industries has led to both the expansion of the metropolis and the enlargement of colonial territories. The extraordinarily rapid developments in these two areas have produced discords of all kinds – relating to morality, belief, thought, emotion, and so on – between urbanites and rural folks in the mother country, and between the rulers and ruled in colonies. Religions such as Christianity can no longer help resolve the contradictions of city and country, of old life and new, or control the thoughts of colonized natives and tame their hostile feelings. Folklore studies has arisen in response to such crises, because the need to know the thoughts and psychology of the natives and the uncivilized through their song and legends is a "deeply felt administrative necessity" for the purpose of achieving political peace and stability. He Sijing continues: "The author of *The Handbook of Folklore* (1894), Madam C.S. Burne, has said that folklore studies cannot overestimate its contribution to the sum of human knowledge and one extremely useful outcome will emerge from studies of this sort; namely, the governing nation will obtain more effective ways of ruling the subject peoples" (1: 1928, 4–5). In the original text of *The Handbook of Folklore*, Charlotte Sophia Burne (1914) has stated the following:

> The conception of man's past history which has resulted from, and now directs, the study of folklore, has already made its impress on modern philosophical thought, and it would be difficult to over-estimate the additions to the sum of human knowledge which may be made in course of years by a continuance of the study on these lines. Meanwhile one very practical result should follow from it, namely, the improved treatment by governing nations of the subject-races under their sway. In the words of Sir Richard Temple, "We cannot understand the latter rightly unless we deeply study them, and it must be remembered that close acquaintance and a right understanding beget sympathy, and sympathy begets good government. (1914: 3–4)

This argument would have made perfect sense to a Chinese folklorist who was acquainted with the imperial tradition of folksong collecting of the past. But the question is where China stood on this map of governing nations and subject-races. What was the position of the Chinese folklorist vis-à-vis their British or Japanese counterparts, and who might the subject-races be as far as the Chinese folklorist was concerned?

Let us consider the larger picture of the social science research of the time and, in particular, how a certain criterion of objectivity was interjected into the requirements of scientific folklore collecting at the turn of the century. In her study of the American Folklore Society (founded in 1888) and the *Journal of American Folklore*, Regina Bendix examines the work of folklorist Otis Mason who did not hesitate to draw parallels between folklore specimens with the minerals or chemicals that the natural scientist studied. After comparing the folk "specimen" with the archaeologist's finds, the paleontologist's fossil, and the anatomist's rare animal, Mason concludes that the folk-cabinet has a distinct advantage, namely, it is like the piles of enumerators' atlases in the Census Office and the material is ever at hand to be considered (Bendix 1997: 127).

To what end? Mason's reference to the Census Office reminds us of Burne's concern with colonial rule and governmentality as quoted in the above. The folklorist's aspirations to objectivity need not contradict the logic of governmentality in this historical framework, because objectivity and colonial governmentality together defined the scientific agendas of the modern empirical social science that came to maturity in the first decades of the twentieth century. The most successful and influential of the new schools of thought was what has come to be called the "functionalist school" of anthropology in Britain whose intellectual progenitor was the Polish émigré Malinowski.[8] Believing that African societies were too fragile, too fragmented, to adapt to rapid change, Malinowski saw the role of anthropology as one that could instruct the government on how to make the best of these delicate social worlds, and coax them into the European-dominated future, without destroying them in the process. This he believed could be achieved through understanding how their worlds operated, and by working through native rules (Cell 2001: 4, 246).

The notion of time became central to this process of modernization. Cultural anthropologist Johannes Fabian (1983) argues that anthropology and folklore studies were erected upon an ethnographic imagining of temporality that pre-establishes the "other" at the primitive end of the long march of history as opposed to the cultural superiority of the modern "us." In effecting temporal distancing from the other, anthropology has produced a "spatialization of time" that physically manifests itself in the trips that anthropologists and folklorists undertake to engage in professional fieldwork outside their own society or community (1983: 30–31). Since the objective situation of the other derives its meaning solely from its translatability or temporal convertibility, the rationale of doing the fieldwork to study them as the past of one's own evolution to humanity attenuates the scholar's responsibility to care about the actual social condition of the other's material existence. That may explain why, after centuries of colonial experience and contact with the non-Western world and the global consequences of that contact, some still believe that the social structures of non-Western societies remain strangely unchanging as if the colonial encounter had never taken place.[9] The evolutionary spatialization of time helps establish the cognitive basis of scholarly objectivity and gives cultural anthropology and folklore studies the authority they assume in the eyes of the lay public. The collecting of the black spirituals, to cite an example from Ronald Radano's study, "enabled white Americans to extract the anonymous sounds of human transcendence from their real-life circumstances, thereby erasing blackness in the name of preservation" (Radano 1996: 530). The possibility of what Fabian calls "co-evalness," or the likelihood of allowing the other to inhabit the same time and space as does the anthropologist and enter into a real-life dialogue or disputation with their work, seems rather remote. It would contradict the logic of ethnographic research and threaten to abolish both the subjectivity and objectivity of the observer.

What happened when the ethnographic gaze turned inward? Elizabeth Mary Wright's book *Rustic Speech and Folk-Lore* (1913) – another well-known source in

China – may shed some light on the question. Wright's work attracted the Chinese folklorists because it demonstrated that British folklorists studied the folk customs of their own society, and not just the subject-races of colonized countries. He Sijing translated Wright's words to say that the key to understanding the seemingly incomprehensible mentality of rural people was to become thoroughly acquainted with their local dialect, because "The country folk's inner secrets are all connected with their traditional speech and rhythms. One has only to master the form of their speech; then the strings of their hearts will be in the palm of your hand" (He 1928: 5).[10] British folklorists regarded both the folk speech of their own society and the folkways of the colonies as raw materials for understanding folk psychology.[11] They were especially interested in the myths, legends, ballads, proverbs, and riddles of the uncivilized, semi-civilized, or uneducated peoples as well as nursery rhymes, children's songs, and so on. Bausinger (1990) has suggested that the rise of comparative and supranational scholarship in folklore studies after its contact and confrontation with ethnology has introduced a generalized concept of *vulgus in populo* but that the "idea of the nation" remained very much alive in the word *Volk* (1990: 2). Did this idea of *Volk* seamlessly translate into minority peoples and dialect groups among the Han population in the work of early Chinese folklorists?[12]

While English and Japanese folklorists were engaged in colonial enterprise abroad, Chinese folklorists directed their attention exclusively to the "primitive cultures" of rural villages and ethnic minorities in their own society. And what other option did they have when both the Han Chinese and all of China's ethnic groups occupied the position of subject-race in the colonial hierarchy dominated by governing imperial nations? While translating European theories of race and ethnicity, the Chinese folklorists took the next step of trying to make China's minority groups *resemble* primitive tribes from other parts of the world. The relation of domination in the classic colonial situation was converted into a structure of domination between the Han majority and minority peoples. By turning the ethnographic gaze upon the ethnic minorities within their own society, the Chinese folklorists could then claim to be the subject of anthropology rather than its object. If this carries the echoes of ethnic tension between the Han, the Manchus, and other ethnic groups from the past, there is something else going on as well, and we need only leaf through the reproduced images of ethnographic photographs in the pages of *Folklore* to get the basic idea (see Figures 10.1 and 10.2).

The reproductions of the photographs, whose sources are not disclosed or acknowledged, provide the incontestable evidence that the Chinese folklorists had a global picture rather than the narrowly defined Han/minority relations in mind. For instead of focusing on the Han and the minorities, they sought to emulate the British folklorists in the representational practices by recasting themselves as the unmarked (white) observer of the ethnographic field. Reproduced on the inside covers of numbers 5 through 15/16 of *Folklore*, for example, are pictures of naked people and savages of the uncivilized races. These photographs were culled from European and American publications, and the images uniformly represent the people of color: ethnic groups from India, Burma, Australia, New Zealand, the Philippines, the South Pacific Melanesian Islands, Northern Africa, Southern Africa, Vietnam, Japan (tattooed figures), and Tibet. Interestingly, these photos were printed side by side with the transcribed versions of mountain songs that the Chinese folklorists had

土 人 的 哀 悼
（ 緬 甸 安 達 曼 島 ）

哀悼的裝飾法是以黃土及青橄欖色泥塗遍了身體，父母們則畫以
垂紋，死者的頭蓋及其他的骨帶着做紀念物的。圖中一個婦人背
後負着的東西卽是頭蓋，坐在中間的一個帶着的頸珠卽手足骨製
成的。至衣服的形式看圖中便可知道了。　　　（志識）

Figure 10.1　Tribal rituals of mourning on a Burmese island, a photographic reproduction in *Folklore Weekly* no. 7, 1928.

collected from Guangxi and Guangdong, or ballads from Taiwanese aborigines, or folksongs from Chaozhou and so forth.

Reflecting on his fieldwork in contemporary China, Dru Gladney has made an observation about similar visual juxtapositions in PRC representations of the Muslim population. He saw a poster featuring men in Turkic and Hui Islamic hats, a veiled woman, and an African or black man with the following caption "I Love the Great Wall." Gladney points out that the black man is on the wall together with the Chinese minorities to demonstrate their ethnic solidarity and "to emphasize their

地　上　畫　圖　騰　的　儀　式
（中　澳　洲　的　北　部　部　族）

這是表明與富剌馬加部族，烏闌店圖騰有關係的最後儀式。演技者把跪坐人們的裝飾脫去。畫圖是代表一種飄流圖騰的祖先（神怪蛇）的。以這種慣俗圖案的痕跡來觀察，可知其代表赤足步行的人了。（志識）

Figure 10.2 Aborigines from northern Australia and their totem figures in *Folklore Weekly* no. 7, 1928.

corporate 'primitivity' (i.e., promoting the idea that China's minorities are like 'primitive' Africans), which is key to understanding the position of the minorities in the Marxist-Maoist evolutionary scheme" (1994: 97). The figuring of minorities in this manner is not so much about the minorities than it is about the subjectivity of the Han majority. Gladney (1994) writes, "the objectified portrayal of minorities as exoticized, and even eroticized, is essential to the construction of the Han Chinese majority, the very formulation of the Chinese "nation" itself. In other words, the representation of the minorities in such colorful, romanticized fashion has more to do with constructing a majority discourse, than it does with the minorities themselves"(1994: 97). Of course, as we have seen, such pictorial representations of ethnic and primitive solidarity go further back than the Marxist-Mao regime, and it would be accurate to say that the mimicking of colonial visuality that marked the inauguration of Chinese folklore studies in the early twentieth century has been perpetuated to a degree by the PRC policies on ethnic minorities.[13]

From the standpoint of Chinese anthropology, the natives are usually not the Han people – certainly, not the educated Han – but the primitive other of civilization. Inasmuch as the Han and white people are virtually absent as the "object" of visual representation in the pages of *Folklore*, they become equivalent, unmarked ethnicities. The cosmopolitan ambitions of *Folklore* were bent on asserting this unmarkedness and equating the (educated) Han with white folklorists – equally unmarked – whom they seek to emulate. But I must hasten to add that colonial mimicry was only part of the story, for the Chinese folklorists had other goals in mind as well, one of which was to bring about a national identity and solidarity through the invention of a new national literature. Many of them participated in the revolutionary struggle to fight imperialism on behalf of the oppressed. This need not, of course, contradict the discursive relation of domination between the Han and ethnic minorities we have just observed but will certainly complicate our understanding of the politics of folklore studies in modern China.

When the architects of folksong studies at Peking University first imagined folklore research in 1922, they stated in the inaugural issue of *Folksong Weekly* that their goal was twofold, one being academic and the other artistic. As folksongs were a major component of folklore, they intended to collect them for disciplined folklore research. The other goal was to accelerate the development of a national poetry to achieve Hu Shi's vision of vernacular literature in the New Culture movement of 1917. Ironically, the inspiration for a new Chinese national poetry with folksong as its foundation came, however, not so much from Hu Shi as from an Italian amateur folklorist in Beijing, Baron Guido Amadeo Vitale (1872–1918).

Vitale lived in Beijing for many years and served as a translator for the Italian embassy. During this time, he collected and published two anthologies of Beijing folksongs and children's songs: *Pekingese Rhymes* (1896), and *Chinese Merry Tales* (1901). Other studies of Chinese folklore by Westerners like Isaac Taylor Headland's (1859–1942) *Chinese Mother Goose Rhymes* (1900) and *The Chinese Boy and Girl* (1901) also came out around this time. Chinese scholars found that the foreigners were well ahead of the game and scrambled to catch up (Hung 1985: 21). The editors of *Folksong Weekly* cite Vitale approvingly: "A new national poetry could perhaps spring up based on these rhythms and on the true feelings of the people" (Hung 1985: 50). Thus, from the very start, the invention of a new national poetry and that of a new academic discipline went hand in hand, sometimes intersecting and sometimes diverging, with each constructing for itself a considerable set of mechanisms – mechanisms inextricably intertwined with the history of China's nation building. We have seen how the modern academic institution responsible for initiating folklore studies helped redefine the relationship between the Han majority and minority cultures. As we turn toward the entanglement of folklore research and social movements as noted by Uli Linke, we enter a rich and vast field of significations where the "masses" and "folk" have become the rallying points of revolutionary struggle and social reform on the left as well as on the right. Here, we may examine further the changing relationships of the state, party politics, the masses and the intelligentsia in modern China.[14]

In *Going to the People*, Chang-tai Hung attempts to identify a discursive tradition in Chinese folklore studies and track down the historical relationship, if any, between what he calls "folk populism" and Maoist populism of the 1940s and after. He argues that "the work initiated by folklorists and the momentum they generated no doubt made the Communist task much easier," but then a "direct link between the minority-culture study initiated by the folk-literature movement in the late 1920s and subsequent Communist interest in minorities is difficult to establish" (Hung 1985: 175). In the next section, we are going to identify a direct linkage between the early folklore studies to Mao's political movement and, specifically, we will see how the folksongs of the Zhuang people we encountered briefly in Zhong Jingwen's earlier work reemerged and metamorphosed in the 1950s. These metamorphoses raise some fascinating issues about the role of broadcast media and mass audiences in the institution of an official popular culture in mainland China after 1949.

FOLKSONG IN OFFICIAL POPULAR CULTURE

The rise of modern folklore studies coincided with the rapid spread of the technologies of gramophone, lithography, photography, film, and news media around the world. In *Yellow Music,* Andrew Jones (2001) has examined the birth of the cultural industry in colonial Shanghai and the ways in which the hybrid musical forms, be it "yellow (pornographic) music" or left-wing mass music, emerged in Chinese popular music. Jones draws our attention to the fact that these hybrid forms were "forged of the discursive, operational, and commercial interaction of new media technologies such as wireless broadcasting, sound cinema, and mass-circulation magazines in urban China." After jazzy "yellow music" was banned in mainland China in the 1950s, "the producers and sing-song girls who had dominated the field (including Pathé-EMI Records and its stable of starlets) were banished to Taiwan and the British Crown Colony of Hong Kong. Throughout the 1950s and 1960s, Hong Kong became a sort of Shanghai manqué – the epicenter of modern song and the Mandarin musical cinema" (2001: 17–18). In China after 1949, state-owned technologies of wireless broadcasting, sound cinema, and mass-circulation magazines began to produce a very different species of mass entertainment which I call "official popular culture."

It is well known that the Communist Party exalted the forms of *minjian wenyi* (folk literature and art) over and above all other forms of popular entertainment (Holm 1990; Gamble 1970). Particularly worth noting is the fact that the work of Chinese folklorists exerted a direct impact on CCP policies and on Mao Zedong's own views on popular art and literature. In spring 1958, Mao launched his own folksong movement and instructed folklore fieldworkers to emulate the ancient practice of *caifeng* (gathering folksongs) and to make the condition of the people known through collected songs. In the Guangxi Autonomous Region of the Zhuang ethnicity, tens of thousands of folksongs and folktales were transcribed, hundreds of folk singers interviewed, several dozen musical tune patterns and a good number of legends and stories about the legendary female singer Liu Sanjie recorded (Zheng 1964: 144). This shows a striking parallel with the ancient Music Bureau I discussed earlier, but with a notable difference: the majority of the fieldworkers hailed from the Zhuang ethnicity rather than from the Han. On the basis of that fieldwork, the Guanxi Folk Musical Drama Troupe created a highly successful musical called *Liu Sanjie* by incorporating some of the folklore and collected folksongs into the play and they were invited to Beijing to give performances in 1960.[15] Mao Zedong watched their performance and praised it highly because "*Liu Sanjie* fights class oppression and is a revolutionary play" whereas drama critics in China viewed it as a milestone in the development of Chinese musical drama (Zhou Zuoqiu *et al.* 1979: 28).

When the Changchun Film Studio adapted *Liu Sanjie* to the screen in 1960, they incorporated as many as 110 Zhuang folksongs into the film, 78 of them taken directly from the musical drama, and subjected them to further modification. Take the riddle verse in the opening scene where Liu Sanjie matches the song with some young men of her village. The fieldworker transcribed the original folksong as follows:

> Who has a mouth but cannot speak?
> Who has no mouth but makes a din?
> Who has feet but cannot walk?
> Who travels far and wide with no feet?
> Bodhisattva has a mouth but cannot speak;
> A copper gong has none but makes a din;
> A stool has feet but cannot walk;
> A boat has no feet but travels far and wide. (*Liu Sanjie* 1961: 11)

The last four lines are modified in the film version thus:

> Bodhisattva has a mouth but cannot speak;
> A copper gong has none but makes a din;
> A rich man has feet but won't walk.
> His money has no feet but travels far. (Loh 1984: 170 with slightly modified translation)

This revision shows the degree of ideological pressure on the use and study of folklore in the early 1960s. Film critics could not, however, agree on the artistic merit or ideological position of the film *Liu Sanjie,* and the judges of the second official Hundred Flowers Film Awards ranked it the fourth place in the Best Feature Film contest. But the film was extremely popular among the Chinese audience. An overwhelming majority of subscribers to the magazine *Popular Cinema,* for instance, voted to give the film three top prizes: best cinematography, best original composition, and best artistic design. When the film *Liu Sanjie* was shown in Hong Kong in the early 1960s, the audience response was no less enthusiastic, and the soundtracks could be heard on the streets of Hong Kong for months. Wai-Fong Loh (1984) informs us that the right-wing film producers of Hong Kong and Taiwan also "imitated the music and songs of *Liu Sanjie* to produce a rightist version called *Shan'ge lian* (folksong love story). This movie was also a financial success and won a prize in Taipei"(1984: 174). The degree of enthusiasm for the film *Liu Sanjie* and its soundtracks across the cold war divide attests to the richness, ambiguity, instability of folksong as form.[16]

CODA

I remember watching *Liu Sanjie* as a child. That experience was primarily associated with the stage because my mother performed in one of the theatrical productions and was cast as Liu Sanjie. Night after night, I sat in an obscure corner backstage watching her perform. To my generation, *Liu Sanjie* – certainly not *Snow White* or *Sleeping Beauty* – was the archetypal fairytale of our girlhood. A talented singer from an ethnic minority group who wielded the magic wand of folksong to protect her people against evil and oppression was absolutely enchanting. There was something about this character and her songs that seemed to lift her above the official discourse of class struggle. Still, I was not prepared for the surprising turn of events concerning the film *Liu Sanjie* in the 1990s.

One of the significant moments of transformation in Chinese society was marked by the introduction of copyright laws and intellectual property rights in 1991. Under the regime of copyright laws, the story of Liu Sanjie underwent further metamorphoses. In January 1996, I learned that the writers of the musical drama script *Liu Sanjie* brought a lawsuit – widely publicized in the media – against the screenplay writer Qiao Yu of the film version for infringement of their copyrights (Hu 1996 and Ren 1996). This lawsuit occurred in the midst of major legal reforms and changing government policies which allowed public properties and collectively owned properties to be transferred or expropriated into private hands.[17] In that spirit, the media coverage of the lawsuit strongly suggested that the musical drama *Liu Sanjie* was an act of original composition when its writers had merely appropriated something collectively owned by the Zhuang. The case was eventually settled outside court after the film director issued an open apology to the playwrights.

Huang Wanqiu – the female actress who starred in the film – came to Qiao Yu's defense and she argued in an interview:

> When the film was completed and approved, Qiao Yu was credited as the screenplay writer, and nobody raised an objection at that time. No matter what, we must not dismiss someone's work if that work bears the fruit of genuine efforts. Had it not been for Qiao Yu, the film *Liu Sanjie* would not have seen the light of day. Guangxi people owe it to him and we should not obliterate his contributions because of some unfortunate circumstances. Many of Liu Sanjie's lyrics in the film are Qiao's compositions, like the tea-picking song and the lyrics in the song matching scene. Whatever one might say after so many years, Qiao's film script has brought fame to Guangxi and made Liu Sanjie known to the country and to the world. Legends of Liu Sanjie had been in existence for nearly a thousand years, but their impact was never so strongly felt as when the film was made. To me and to the people and cadres of Guangxi, it is plain wrong to make the kind of allegations they did against Qiao. Deep down, we cannot accept it. The Third Draft of the musical play and the film script are very different in terms of structure and plot. If there are similarities between them, plagiarism is not the right word because, after all, the material came from the folk to begin with. (Bo 1996)

The playwrights who initiated the lawsuit would not have found Huang's defense palatable especially when her own stardom in the 1960s was dependent on the success of the film. But their allegation of plagiarism on the ground of copyright and intellectual property becomes groundless as soon as the history of folksong collecting, folklore studies, and official popular culture enters into the picture.

Indeed, there are many angles to the picture I have tried to assemble here, and I cannot possibly exhaust all the richness within limited space. In this chapter, I have reflected on the ontological instability of folklore and tried to raise some questions about the legibility of the folk, ethnicity, race, community, and nation, for these questions are centrally related to the rise of modern folklore studies in China, the invention of an official popular culture, and their profound entanglement with the political life of the elite and the common people, home and abroad. The larger picture that emerges is not just about one nation or one people and their folklore but also about an interconnected history of translingual practices in modern times.

One might say that this is a shared and broadly contested history of colonial mimicry, ethnographic imagining, intellectual crosscurrents, revolutionary struggles, and postsocialism.

NOTES

1   Moreover, as Regina Bendix has shown, when folksong and folktale are disembodied from their social contexts and gathered in books, they may turn into something else, such as commodities, to be consumed by bourgeois society in modern times (1997: 48).

2   From December 1922 to June 1925, the *Folksong Weekly* published a total of 97 issues and the Society for Folksong Research gathered about 13,000 folksongs. See *Geyao zhoukan,* nos. 69–76 (1924–1925).

3   The *Zhuang* ethnic minority is China's largest minority group, whose population currently stands at 16 million. The majority of them live in southwest China or the Guangxi *Zhuang* Autonomous Region.

4   The entanglement of orality and writing in the production of literary texts is by no means unique to the ancient civilization of China. Galit Hasan-Rokem's study of the aggadic Midrash in Late Antiquity shows the complex ways in which orality and folk narrative can be incorporated into rabbinic texts. See Hasan-Rokem (2000), *Web of life: Folklore and Midrash in Rabbinic Literature.* What I try to highlight with respect to the Chinese situation is the enduring interplay of literacy and the imperial bureaucratic machine and the sheer amount of millennia-long documented history which seems unique to China.

5   For the Manchu-Han ethnic conflict in the Qing and its long-lasting impact on modern politics, see Liu (2004: 75–90).

6   In his study of the *Book of Songs,* Zhi Chen (2007: 13–29) combines the paleographic-philological method with the archaeo-musicologist approach and argues that the *Book of Songs* was not a synchronically formed collection of songs and hymns in ancient China but the fruits of a long process of evolution and exchanges amongst multiple ethnic groups in China and, in particular, between those of the Shang (1723 BCE–1046 BCE) and Zhou peoples (1034 BCE–246 BCE).

7   Ban Gu (32 CE–92 CE) wrote the history of the Han dynasty to cover the period of 206 BCE to 25 CE. The book was completed with the assistance of his family members and is also known as the *Book of Former Han.*

8   Malinowski trained the first generation of Chinese social scientists, including Fei Xiaotong who is considered the father of Chinese sociology and anthropology.

9   Paul Rabinow (1977) was among the first to critique the field in *Reflections on Fieldwork in Morocco.* For other influential critics, see James Clifford and George Marcus (1986).

10   In her introduction to the original English edition, Wright (1913) merely states "If this book succeeds in pointing out a few of the many ways in which the study of our English dialects may not only contribute to the advancement of knowledge, but also give us a clearer insight into the life and character of the British peasant and artisan, it will have achieved the aim and object of its existence."(xx).

11   For the British treatment of their urban poor as "many savage tribes" in the empire, see Mayhew 1985.

12   Hu Shi argued in 1918 that to create a new national literature, every possible dialectal source must be explored because local dialects provide an inexhaustible supply of what he calls "new blood" to national literature. The Dialect Survey Society at Peking University was founded in January 1924 (Hung 1985: 63).

13   Jay Dautcher's (2000) fieldwork among the Uyghur community in contemporary China shows that the tradition of folksong is very much alive among the people there. His case

study does not tell us how much of that tradition has been appropriated by Chinese folk-lorics and become the mark of Uyghur otherness with respect to the Han.

14 In the 1920s through the 1930s, American-style social sciences as represented by Li Jinghan (Franklin Lee) and others continued to assimilate the problems of folklore studies into the general program of social reform (Chiang 2001).

15 An English version of the musical drama *Third Sister Liu: An Opera in Eight Scenes* was made available by Hsien-yi Yang and Gladys Yang (1962).

16 See Clark (1987: 61–62) for a study of box-office performance and film audiences in China from the mid-1950s through the early 1960s.

17 I analyzed this situation in an earlier study of popular culture and post-socialist ideology in the 1990s Culture" (Liu 1999).

REFERENCES

Allen, Joseph R. 1992. *In The Voice of Others: Chinese Music Bureau Poetry*. Ann Arbor: Center for Chinese Studies at the University of Michigan.

Ban Gu. 1964. *Han Shu* (Book of Han). Beijing: Zhonghua Shuju.

Bausinger, Hermann. 1969. *Volkskunde: Von der Altertumsforschung zur Kulturanalyse*. Berlin: Carl Habel Verslagsbuchhandlung.

Bausinger, Hermann. 1990. *Folk Culture in a World of Technology*. Trans. Elke Dettmer. Bloomington: Indiana University Press.

Bendix, Regina. 1997. *In Search of Authenticity: the Formation of Folklore Studies*. Madison: University of Wisconsin Press.

Bo Qing. 1996. "'Liu Sanjie' Huang Wangqiu shuo: *Liu Sanjie* bu shi piaoqie zhi zuo" ("Third Sister Liu" Huang Wangqiu Claims that the Film *Liu Sanjie* is Not a Case of Plagiarism). *Qianjiang wanbao* (Qianjiang Evening News), April 23.

Burne, Charlotte Sophia. 1914. *The Handbook of Folklore*. London: Sidgwick and Jackson.

Cell, John W. 1999. "Colonial Rule" in Judith M. Brown and William Roger Louis, Eds. *The Oxford History of the British Empire*. Vol. 4. *The Twentieth Century*. Oxford: Oxford University Press, pp. 232–254.

Chen Zhi. 2007. *The Shaping of the Book of Songs: From Ritualization to Secularization*. Sankt Augustin, Germany: Institut Monumenta Serica.

Chiang Yung-Chen. 2001. *Social Engineering and the Social Sciences in China*, 1919–1949. Cambridge: Cambridge University Press.

Clark, Paul. 1987. *Chinese Cinema: Culture and Politics Since 1949*. Berkeley: University of California Press.

Clifford, James and George Marcus, Eds. 1986. *Writing Culture*. Berkeley: University of California Press.

Dautcher, Jay. 2000. "Reading Out-of-Print: Popular Culture and Protest on China's Western Frontier" in Timothy B. Weston and Lionel M. Jensen, Eds. *China Beyond the Headlines*. Oxford: Rowman and Littlefield Publishers, pp. 273–294.

Elliott, Mark. 2001. *The Manchu Way: The Eight Banners and Ethnic Identity in Late Imperial China*. Palo Alto: Stanford University Press.

Fabian, Johannes. 1983. *Time and the Other: How Anthropology Makes its Object*. New York: Columbia University Press.

Gamble, Sidney D. 1970. *Chinese Village Plays from the Ting Hsien Region*. Amsterdam: Philo Press.

Gladney, Dru. 1994. "Representing Nationality in China: Refiguring Majority/Minority Identities." *Journal of Asian Studies* 53(1): 92–123.

Harootunian, Harry. 2000. *Overcome by Modernity: History, Culture, and Community in Interwar Japan*. Princeton: Princeton University Press.

Harrell, Stevan, Ed. 1995. *Cultural Encounters on China's Ethnic Frontiers*. Seattle: University of Washington Press.

Hasan-Rokem, Galit. 2000. *Web of Life: Folklore and Midrash in Rabbinic Literature*. Palo Alto: Stanford University Press.

He Sijing. 1928. "Minsuxue de wenti" (Questions in Folklore Studies), *Minsu* 1–3.

Holm, David. 1990. *Art and Ideology in Revolutionary China*. Oxford: Clarendon Press.

Hu Tiege. 1996. "*Liu Sanjie* banquan shu shei?" (To Whom do the Rights of *Liu Sanjie* Belong?). *Wenhui zhoukan* (US edition), January 20.

Hung, Chang-tai. 1985. *Going to the People: Chinese Intellectuals and Folk Literature, 1918–1937*. Cambridge, MA: Harvard University Press.

Jones, Andrew. 2001. *Yellow Music: Media Culture and Colonial Modernity in the Chinese Jazz Age*. Durham, NC: Duke University Press.

Linke, Uli. 1990. "Folklore, Anthropology, and the Government of Social Life." *Comparative Studies in Society and History* 32(1): 117–148.

Liu, James J.Y. 1975. *Chinese Theories of Literature*. Chicago: University of Chicago Press.

Liu, Lydia H. 1995. *Translingual Practice: Literature, National Culture, and Translated Modernity – China 1900–1937*. Palo Alto: Stanford University Press.

Liu, Lydia H. 1999. "*Beijing Sojourners in New York*: Postsocialism and the Question of Ideology in Global Media Culture." *Positions: East Asia Cultures Critique* 7(3) (Winter): 763–797.

Liu, Lydia H. 2004. *The Clash of Empires: The Invention of China in Modern World Making*. Cambridge, MA: Harvard University Press.

Loh, Wai-Fong. 1984. "From Romantic Love to Class Struggle: Reflections on the Film Liu Sanjie" in Bonnie S. McDougall, Ed. *Popular Chinese Literature and Performing Arts in the People's Republic of China, 1949–1979*. Berkeley: University of California Press, pp. 165–176.

Mayhew, Henry. 1985. *London Labour and London Poor, 1851*. New York: Penguin.

Nakao, Katsumi. 2005. "The Imperial Past of Anthropology in Japan" in Jennifer Ellen Robertson, Ed. *A Companion to the Anthropology of Japan*. Oxford: Blackwell.

Rabinow, Paul. 1977. *Reflections on Fieldwork in Morocco*. Berkeley: University of California Press.

Radano, Ronald. 1996. "Denoting Difference: The Writing of Slave Spirituals." *Critical Inquiry* 22: 506–544.

Ren Xuelu. 1996. "Qunian, yingshi guansi buduan" (Proliferation of Film and Television Lawsuits Over the Past Year). *Wenhui zhoukan* (US edition), March 16.

Rong Zhaozu. 1928. "Beida geyao yanjiuhui ji fengsu diaochahui de jingguo" (How The Society for Folksong Research and the Society for Folk Custom Survey at Peking University Came into Existence). *Minsu* 15(16): 1–10 and 17(18): 14–31.

Wright, Elizabeth Mary. 1913. *Rustic Speech and Folk-Lore*. Oxford: Oxford University Press.

Yang Hsien-yi and Gladys Yang, Trans. 1962. *Third Sister Liu: An Opera in Eight Scenes*. Beijing: Foreign Languages Press.

Zheng Tianjian. 1964. "Guanyu *Liu Sanjie* de chuangzuo" (About the Creation of *Liu Sanjie*) in *Liu Sanjie: bachang gewu ju* (*Liu Sanjie*: a Musical Drama in Eight Acts). Beijing: Zhongguo xiju chubanshe.

Zhong Jingwen. 1928. *Minjian wenyi conghua* (Collected Lectures on Folk Arts). Guangzhou: Institute of Language and History at the National Sun Yat-sen University.

Zhong Jingwen. 1982. *Zhong Jingwen minjian wenxue lunji* (Essays on Folk Literature by Zhong Jingwen), 2 Vols. Shanghai: Shanghai wenyi chubanshe.

Zhou Zuoqiu *et al.*, Eds. 1979. *Zhongguo dangdai wenxue yanjiu ziliao: Liu Sanjie zhuanji: Liu Sanjie zhuanji* (Sources of Contemporary Chinese Literature: The *Liu Sanjie* Volume). Guilin: Guangxi Normal University.

CHAPTER 11 JAPAN

Akiko Mori

INTRODUCTION

The study of folklore in Japan has developed within the context of constant social change. Here, I will give an account of this field of study from a historical perspective, as this will bring the characteristics of folklore study in Japan into relief. In the second section, I discuss the history of folklore study throughout six periods and briefly characterize each one so as to sketch the outline of Japanese folklore studies within their social context.

The third section introduces three issues that have had an important impact on Japanese folkloristics. The first is the development of the field in relation to history and ethnology. The second concerns the context of folklore and introduces the notion of comparison. The third issue consists of the major research topics and the ways in which research is conducted within the modern and postmodern eras. In the final section, I will list some recent works of Japanese folklore, while touching on future prospects.

Beforehand, I should say that the Japanese word encompassing the study of folklore and ethnology is pronounced *minzokugaku*, though it is written ideographically in another form of Kanji. This is something I shall mention when it arises in this chapter.

HISTORICAL DEVELOPMENT

A little less than 100 years have passed since the dawn of the study of Japanese folklore. Here, I try to explain this history as a development that can be divided into six periods: pre-1935, pre-1950, pre-1960, pre-1975, pre-1990, and post-1990.

A Companion to Folklore, First Edition. Edited by Regina F. Bendix and Galit Hasan-Rokem.
© 2012 John Wiley & Sons, Ltd. Published 2012 John Wiley & Sons, Ltd.

The Formative Period (Until the Mid-1930s)

First, I shall look at the political, economic, and social life of Japan in the late nineteenth century. After 1867, Japan launched itself into building a modern nation (the Meiji Restoration), and the extreme westernization of Japanese culture followed with Western goods, ideas, and institutions flowing into the country. National policy at large regarded these Western ways as new and enriching, while Japanese ones were considered to be old and impoverished. However, in the countryside, a rich folk tradition continued to be handed down by each generation to the next.

Against this backdrop, Kunio Yanagita (1875–1962) began studying folklore, the name of which was yet to be coined. Yanagita is considered to be the most important researcher of Japanese folklore, and many researchers have since followed him, contributing to the development of Japanese folklore. Yanagita's work is still sought after even though his work was widely published. However, some of his writings were not very clear, which led to a great deal of discussion and interpretation from later researchers trying to understand just exactly what he was saying. Additionally, there are some works in English on Yanagita and Japanese folklore studies that were written from the standpoint of intellectual history (Koschmann *et al.* 1985; Morse 1990; Kawada 1993; Ivy 1995).

After graduating from university, Yanagita was employed as a civil servant in the Ministry of Agriculture and Commerce. He often traveled around the country and observed local people and their lifestyles. He was interested in the folk traditions of each generation, holding them in very high esteem. He associated with his intellectual contemporaries and organized study groups, which compiled journals of their activities, such as *Kyodo-Kenkyu* (published 1913–1917) and *Minzoku* (published 1925–1929). These groups were interdisciplinary and included scholars of mythology, history, sociology, and ethnology, many of whom later became well known. Intellectuals in those days were interested in Western thoughts and ideas, and had easy access to Western books. After resigning from the civil service, Yanagita was dispatched to Europe as a governmental envoy (in 1921 and 1922), and there he was able to associate with Western scholars.

From the 1910s to the 1920s, Yanagita was interested in the field of agricultural economics; he studied common people and farmers in order to improve their living conditions in the future. His purpose was clear – he hoped to be able to help poor farmers. From the beginning, Yanagita was aware of issues concerning the lives of ordinary people, as well as the ways in which Japan differed from the West.

Kyodo-Kenkyu and *Minzoku* are still regarded as good quality journals, and they include important articles. Yanagita was a key member of the editorial staff of these journals, and clarified his ideas on Japanese folklore through this position.

The "Minkan-Denshô-No-Kai" Period (From the Mid-1930s to the End of the 1940s)

Farming villages in Japan were extremely impoverished during the recession caused by the worldwide financial crisis in the 1930s, while the military became more and more powerful. Thus the seeds were sown for Japan's involvement in World War II.

In 1935, friends of Yanagita gathered to celebrate his sixtieth birthday and established the "Minkan-Denshô-No-Kai" (The Society for Folklore Research). The society's office was situated in Yanagita's own home, and there they held monthly study meetings. The society's journal, *Minkan-Denshô* (1935–1952), was published monthly, except during World War II. Throughout this period, many researchers from all over the country visited Yanagita in order to study folklore.

Present-day researchers agree that Yanagita's study of folklore was firmly established in the mid-1930s. In 1934, ethnologists had established the Nihon-Minzoku-Gakkai (later the Japanese Society of Ethnology) as the first society for ethnologists, and also founded *Minzokugaku-Kenkyu* as the official journal of the society. As ethnologists often felt superior to those studying folklore, Yanagita might have indeed been at odds with ethnology. He published three books in the mid-1930s: *Minkan-Denshô-Ron* in 1934 (Yanagita 1934a), *Kyodo-Seikatsu-No-Kenkyu-Ho* in 1935 (Yanagita 1935a), and *Kokushi-To-Minzokugaku* (Meaning and Folklore) in 1935 (Yanagita 1935b). These books provide an outline of Yanagita's field of research, which he named Minkan-Denshô, derived from the French phrase *traditions populaires*. He then formulated a plan for national folklore (*Ikkoku-Minzokugaku*). From a diffusionist's point of view, he presented his method as a way to explain the origins and the changing process of folk traditions. This method strongly influenced the study of folklore in Japan over a long period.

Then, as a result Japan's involvement in World War II, people's lives, as well as the political, economical, and social system of the time, were destroyed. During the war, Yanagita was not very active, and some of his pupils were sent to Japanese military colonies as researchers. After the war, Japan adopted a way of life and thinking similar to the United States, which gave rise to a new beginning in folklore research as well other areas.

The Establishment the Folklore Society of Japan (From the End of the 1940s to the End of the 1950s)

Minzokugaku-Kenkyû-Sho was established as an institute for specialized folklore research one year before the founding of the Folklore Society of Japan. The Minzokugaku-Kenkyû-Sho had been the driving force behind the Folklore Society of Japan for 10 years and, under the leadership of Yanagita, experienced researchers debated the study of folklore as a discipline and a field of research, and the results were published in successive issues of *Minkan-Denshô*. Articles covered topics studied and the methods of collecting and analyzing data. In 1951, the institute published a lexicon of folklore study entitled *Minzokugaku – Jiten*, (Minzokugaku-Kenkyû-Sho 1951). The institute was dissolved in 1957. While it lasted, it strove to transform Yanagita's study of folklore into an academic discipline.

The Folklore Society of Japan was established in 1949. Its predecessor was the Minkan-Denshô-No-Kai (The Society for Folklore Research), and the *Minkan-Denshô*, the society's journal, continued as the monthly journal of the new society until 1953. After that, the *Nihon-Minzokugaku* (the journal of the Folklore Society of Japan) was published quarterly.

The new name of the society included an academic connotation. Yanagita disliked this name at first; however, the younger researchers persuaded him to accept it in order to improve communication with neighboring disciplines because then, there were large interdisciplinary joint projects consisting of several disciplines. The first interdisciplinary project began in 1947, and from the early 1950s to 1988, 10 big research projects, seven regional ones, and three comparative ones, were carried out. The main members were nine learned societies representing the following disciplines: ethnology, sociology, anthropology, religion, geography, linguistics, psychology, Asian music, and folklore. The results of these joint research projects were published in several volumes (under the editorship of Kyû-Gakkai-Rengô (theUnion of Nine Societies), and so on, 1954–1989).

The Period of Institutionalization 1 (From the Early 1960s to the Mid-1970s)

Yanagita died in 1963, and the publication of his complete work, the *Teihon-Yanagita-Kunio-Shu*, was completed in 36 volumes, starting in 1962. There was much demand for Yanagita's works, and folklore studies became very fashionable during the 1960s, a decade of prosperity for Japan. Since the end of the 1950s, Japan experienced high economic growth, and agricultural machinery flowed into farm villages. As for political issues, people campaigned fiercely between 1959 and 1960 against the Japan-United States Security Treaty with little effect, and since then became gradually inactive. The student movement in the late 1960s, which criticized the social conditions resulting from overextended economic growth worldwide, was popular among younger generations but did not have much of a following in Japan. There was also an increased interest in travel at that time which lauded the virtues of the Japanese countryside.

From the 1960s to the 1970s, important works on Japanese folklore were published and university programs were organized, which finally set the field of folklore studies into their own framework. The word *minzokugaku* (folklore) finally became widely known in the public sphere.

One of the most important of these volumes is the *Nihon-Minzokugaku-Taikei* (Outline of Folklore Studies in Japan), which ran to 13 volumes and was published from 1958 to 1960. The editors were Tokuzo Omachi, Keigo Seki, Masao Oka, Takayoshi Mogami, and Katsunori Sakurada Omachi *et al*. 1958–1960). Most of these editors were researchers at the Minzokugaku-Kenkyû-Sho, which was dissolved in 1957, having achieved its intended objectives. Oka was a prominent figure in the Nihon-Minzoku-Gakkai (The Japanese Ethnology Society). These volumes were compiled by a number of authors, excluding Yanagita, and they summarized the results of folklore studies between 1910 and 1960, aiming to present a profile of Japanese folklore after Yanagita, and constituted the basic literature on folklore study in Japan.

The euphoria concerning folklore studies might also have helped it to form its own standardized way of research. The contents of the *Nihon-Minzokugaku-Taikei* provided a solid framework for Japanese folklore. In the thirteenth volume, a long list of folklore publications is given, and they appear in the following order:

1. General remarks
2. Social organization
3. Livelihood
4. Material culture
5. Life courses

6. Traditional events and folk beliefs
7. Performing arts
8. Oral traditions
9. Regional ethnography
10. Periodicals

It is noteworthy that the first 12 volumes of the *Nihon-Minzokugaku-Taikei* were organized and ordered in the same way. Sections such as "General remarks," "Social organization," "Livelihood," and "Regional ethnography" extend for more than one volume. In the thirteenth volume, there is a chapter on "Methodology of Investigation," as well as a list of publications. The above-mentioned categories, appear as "Investigation Topics" in the same order, and are then sub-classified in detail as a 50-page list of "Investigation Items."

Here, folklore studies was described as being constructed from other subjects, and practical research was also organized in the same subject order, and there was also a list of investigation items. Using a common list of investigation items made it possible for a number of researchers, who were not academically trained experts, to engage in collecting data from every corner of the country, and the results were then gathered together to form a whole.

The idea of using investigation items originated with Yanagita. He first published his ideas concerning the list of investigation items in the *Kyôdo-Seikatsu-No-Kenkyû-Hô* in 1935, and the second phase of his findings in the *Nihon-Minzokugaku-Nyûmon* (Introduction to Japanese Folklore) in 1942 (Yanagita and Seki 1942). This approach formed the basis of his *Shûken-Ron* and *Jûshutsu-Risshô-Hô* (which will be discussed later) and had a great impact. These items also became the standard of "classic folklore" and were referred to repeatedly, especially within a higher-education context. Students had to learn this list before they undertook research trips. However, these items had the disadvantage of misleading them into thinking that the purpose of folklore study was to collect, classify, and record folk customs according to this list.

In spite of some criticism concerning the methodology (Yamaguchi 1939), folklore studies is based on this list of investigation items and subject classification. We also regard this classification as an ordered category of current folklore studies. The *Journal of the Folklore Society of Japan* has published current research trends in the same classification order since 1975 and it continues to this day with few alterations. Meanwhile, the Agency for Cultural Affairs undertook urgent research of local folklore in 1962, with the results compiled and published as the *Atlas of Japanese Folklore* in 1969, modeled on the German publication *Atlas der deutschen Volkskunde*.

During this period, many universities established folklore courses. In 1958, Seijo University set up a special course focusing on cultural history, and the Tokyo University of Education set up a special historical methodology class. In both universities, students began to study folklore as their major, whereas earlier, folklore could only be studied at Kokugakuin University, where Shinobu Orikuchi taught courses in Japanese literature and history. Orikuchi, the most influential among Yanagita's many pupils, specialized not only in folklore, but also in Japanese classics and Shintôology, and was able to explain an ancient Japanese culture deductively from his original viewpoint.

The Tokyo University of Education made a significant contribution to the institutionalization of folklore studies, and formed, so to speak, a "platform for folklore." At the Tokyo University of Education, later renamed the University of Tsukuba in 1974, some of Yanagita's pupils became teachers. These included Taro Wakamori and Hiroji Naoe, who founded the Otsuka-Minzoku-Gakukai (The Otsuka Folklore Society) and published the *Minzoku-Gaku Hyôron* (Review of Japanese Folklore Studies) as its journal in 1967. They also compiled the *Nihon-Minzoku-Jiten* (Lexicon of Japanese Folklore) in 1972. In the introduction to this lexicon, folklore study is characterized as a reflexive discipline that questions the nature of Japan. Here, we do not see any concern for the situation of poor farmers, which had been the big social problem that Yanagita had concentrated on in the 1920s.

Seijo University also had long-standing relations with Yanagita, and after his death, the university founded the *Yanagita-Bunko* from Yanagita's collection of books. At other universities, many students were able to study folklore as a subsidiary course, but never as their major. This situation has not changed much, even in the present day. During this period, Japanese folk tales edited by Keigo Seki were published in United States (Seki 1963). Seki was the first scholar who was interested in the comparative study of folk tales, and classified Japanese folk tales by means of the Aarne-Tompson classification system. Toshio Ozawa, a well-known Japanese scholar in Europe, had similar interests. Japanese folk narrative research is well-known abroad, compared with other fields of folklore studies, but social and economic life is more popular in Japan. This might result from the international comparative perspective of folk narrative research. Ozawa later established a private institute for folk narrative research, and was engaged in publishing a series of public lectures.

The Period of Institutionalization 2 (From the Mid-1970s to the End of the 1980s)

Since the second half of the 1970s, after the oil crisis, a transformation in industrial structures took place around the world. In those days, the majority of Japan's population lived in cities, and local folk traditions came to be spoken of only with nostalgia. When high economic growth had slowed down, Japanese culture was revalued, and the specifications of cultural properties and conservation increased. Against this backdrop, the National Museum of Ethnology was established in 1974 and the National Museum of Japanese History was established in 1981. Both were inter-university research institutes, and were affiliated to national museums and graduate schools. The former is a comprehensive research museum with about 60 academic researchers specializing in ethnology and related fields, and the latter has about 40 academic researchers specializing in Japanese history, archaeology, and folklore studies. Japanese folklore was recognized as a subsidiary subject to national history, and since then, cooperation between folklore, history and archeology advanced quickly. The National Museum of Japanese History became one of the most important institutes specializing in Japanese folklore. In 1982, the Institute for the Study of Japanese Folk Culture, established in 1921 by Keizo Shibusawa, a banker, scholar, and patron of ethnological studies, was transferred to Kanagawa University, and its institute for folklore study and education became highly regarded.

One of the most successful results of cooperation with historians in those days was the publication of the *Nihon-Minzoku-Bunka-Taikei* (Outline of Japanese Folk Cultures), which was completed in 15 volumes and published from 1983 to 1987.

The team of editors consisted of seven scholars, four folklorists (Noboru Miyata, Masao Takatori, Kenichi Tanigawa, and Hirofumi Tsuboi), one historian (Yoshihiko Amino), one archeologist (Koichi Mori), and one ethnologist (Taryo Obayashi). Here, scholars synthesized results of folklore studies with those of archeological and ethnological studies from the perspective of social and cultural history. Folklore was an intellectual trend in the 1970s, and a new perspective on the cultures of the Japanese archipelago was constructed (Amino *et al.* 1983–1987).

Two publications must also be cited as keeping up the tradition of folklore study after Yanagita. The first is the *Current Research of Japanese Folklore*, a special issue of the *Journal of the Folklore Society of Japan* Vol. 100, published in 1975. Here, research trends from 1960 onward were reviewed (after the publication of the *Nihon-Minzokugaku-Taikei*), casting a bright spotlight on the study of folklore after Yanagita. From 1975 up to the present day, the journal detailed current research trends once every few years. The second is a two-volume publication, known as the *Gendai-Nihon-Minzokugaku* (Modern Japanese Folklore Studies), which was compiled by three younger researchers, Takenori Noguchi, Noboru Miyata, and Ajio Fukuta in 1974 and 1975 (Noguchi *et al.* 1974, 1975). This publication consisted of important articles and editorials, setting them in their academic context and it aimed to encourage debate abouot the study of folklore after Yanagita.

In this period, several ethnographies and historiographies were commissioned by municipal governments. These projects were inspired by the general public's interest in local culture, while the researchers' publications were often influenced by structural functionalism. There was a significant increase in membership of the Folklore Society of Japan.

Confronting the Problems of the Present (Since the End of the 1980s)

The 1990s started with a wave of globalization; products from all over the world became central to people's lives, which were characterized by consumerism. At the same time, new ways of thinking and concern for the environment began to have important political implications.

The study of folklore since the end of the 1980s confronted a new problem: how should the study of folklore reflect the life of actual people? The contempt of the younger researchers for the stagnant nature of folklore studies can be discerned, and research and debate on this topic is steadily increasing. The growing debate at present is how research in the study of folklore should be approached. Classical folklore study focused on vernacular traditions passed down by generations of farmers, hunters, and fishermen. At present, when the relative importance of city dwellers is growing, the study of folklore must be relevant to the present-day situation. Researchers are currently looking at urban culture, the environment and nature, tourism, and cultural heritage, as well as discrimination. Although they have tackled such issues, they have not yet decided how to place them within the framework of folklore studies. While these issues are also taken up by neighboring fields, the difference between them and the unique contribution that folklore studies can make has yet to be defined. The study of folklore is expanding, but the theoretical considerations of the discipline have not yet caught up.

The present situation can then be summarized as follows. After Yanagita, the study of folklore continued to define itself, with *Minkan-Denshô* (vernacular tradition) as its key concept. Here, the carriers of the tradition are ordinary people, restricted neither by social class nor time. Their tradition is transmitted by the group collectively, and the group is assumed to be a matrix of tradition. The problem now is that the present-day situation makes it impossible to look at this group.

Under these circumstances, researchers bring into question how the study of folklore should define its own field of research and the sphere within which research unfolds. Recent publications show that there are a growing number of younger scholars interested in debate, reviewing a discipline's history, rethinking a familiar subject, or taking up a new subject. Scott Schnell and Hiroyuki Hashimoto, as guest editors of *Asian Folklore Studies* 62, published "Revitalizing Japanese Folklore" with the intention of promoting a new direction in Japanese folklore-oriented research. Five articles were compiled, including one where Shimamura deals with a multicultural situation, which was never adopted as a subject of folklore studies (Schnell and Hashimoto 2003; Shimamura 2003; Hashimoto 2003; Kawamori 2003; Kawamura 2003; Sensui 2003). Hashimoto reviewed research on the performance of folk arts in a volume and argued in favor of the methods used (Hashimoto 2006). Junichi Koike and 12 younger scholars investigated the discipline's history and proposed new perspectives (Koike 2009).

The Intellectual Context of Japanese Folklore Studies

Discussions Concerning the Character of Folklore Studies

This section takes up the key issues for understanding Japanese folklore studies. Just after the foundation of the Folklore Society of Japan, researchers such as Taro Wakamori, Toshijiro Hirayama, Shigeru Makita, and Ichiro Hori, discussed the characteristics peculiar to folklore studies of Japan in *Minkan-Denshô*, the journal of the society. In those days, it was these discussions that constituted the shape of the discipline, and researchers from later generations adoped these arguments and continued refining them. From these discussions, two themes are selected, each of which concerns the outline of the discipline.

The Study of Folklore and History

One of the central issues here is the relationship between the study of folklore and history, which produces the following questions. Do folklore studies fall under the study of history? If not, what is the difference between the two? Is the study of folklore an independent discipline?

Yanagita mentioned from the beginning that his kind of folklore study (at that time, the Minkan-Denshô) was in a broad sense a historical science, while at the same time, it had to be carried out with the goal of helping society in some way. A lecture he gave just after the establishment of the Folklore Society of Japan in 1949 focused on this topic. Taro Wakamori, a pupil of Yanagita, stated that the goal of the study of folklore was to contribute to the construction of a national history by studying local folklore. He explained further this idea in his book, published in 1947 (Wakamori 1947). On the basis of this premise, he placed the study of folklore as one kind of methodology under the discipline of history. As a professor at Tokyo University of Education and founder of the Otsuka Folklore Society, he was very influential in academic circles. As his popularity increased, his argument changed, stating that the aim of the study of folklore was to explain the historical character and meaning of Japanese folklore.

However, his contemporary, Keigo Seki, took the opposite stance, stating that the purpose of the study of folklore was to investigate contemporary life. Arguing that folklore is a real social phenomenon, he insisted that researchers must be aware of how folklore is related to an organic whole.

Shigeru Makita thought that the study of folklore should follow its course based on the following questions: "What is Japanese?" or, "What is Japanese culture?" The real aim of folklore study, to his way of thinking, was not to try and explain how folklore changes, but to find a way of answering these questions (Makita 1951).

Discussions concerning the relationship between folklore and history in the early 1950s can be summarized thus: (i) folklore aimed to explain national character and national culture; (ii) folklore research dealt with oral data, while history dealt with written data; and (iii) folklore research dealt with repetitive and patterned phenomena, while historical research dealt with unique temporal events.

Up to the present, these points were generally acceptable, and the two disciplines, folklore studies and history, were not considered exclusive but overlapped each other. Furthermore, as already mentioned, in the 1980s, folklore studies became a subsidiary subject of national history, and there was an increase in cooperative works regarding history during that decade. Scholarly focus now seems to be shifting to the contemporary. In 1998, Ajio Fukuta wrote an article entitled, "The Aim and Method of the Study of Folklore" where he stated that the study of folklore is a discipline that aims to clarify the contemporary, and for this purpose, it also traces issues back into the past, in order to discover the factors that have accumulated in the present (Fukuta 1998). Recently, Miyamoto stated that "the study of folklore is a present-day study" (Miyamoto 2006).

It would also be prudent in my thinking to consider the relationship between the study of folklore and the study of cultural and social science. At present, more and more folklore researchers have become more interested in the study of culture. Drastic social and economic changes have contributed to this. At the same time, we have to keep in mind that social organization and the economic systems of local societies have always been important themes in the study of Japanese folklore, and they are now undergoing a drastic change.

Folklore and Ethnological Studies

During the 1910s and 1920s, before the study of folklore began to take shape, Yanagita and his associates did not make any distinction between folklore and ethnological studies. In the mid-1930s, the Nihon-Minzoku-Gakkai (later The Japanese Society of Ethnology), and the Minkan-Denshô-No-Kai (The Society for Folklore Research), were established, and the study of folklore and ethnology began to take their own courses. Since then, the difference between the two has been often examined. First, there are the geographical differences of the study. Folklore study focuses on Japan, while ethnology is concerned with foreign countries. This is not necessarily a satisfactory definition as Japanese ethnology includes Japan in its field of research, and the study of folklore can be undertaken in foreign countries.

Second, the attitude toward Japanese culture delineates the difference between folklore and ethnology. Noteworthy is the fact that Yanagita's attitude to Japanese culture was developed before World War II. While Yanagita's early works included essays on the "mountain people" (Yanagita 1911–1912, 1913a), covering wandering religious practitioners and discriminated villagers (Yanagita 1913–1914, 1914–1915, 1913b), his major interests around the 1930s shifted to people who resided permanently in one place and engaged in rice cultivation. Several scholars have tried to explain why Yanagita leaned toward "rice cultivation monism," but did not reach a consensus (Murai 1992; Fukuta 2000; cf., Shimamura 2003). Yanagita's early interest in mountain people was later taken up by Hirofumi Tsuboi. He explored taro cultivator culture and set the latter against the culture of rice cultivators, and furthermore argued for the existence of plural cultures in Japan (Tsuboi 1979).

Masao Oka and Eiichiro Ishida stood at the crossroads of folklore and ethnology. In the beginning, both Oka and Ishida maintained close relationships with Yanagita. Oka edited the journal *Minzoku* (1925–1929) with Yanagita, and as a younger scholar, lived in the same house as Yanagita for a while. Meanwhile, Oka studied ethnology in Vienna (Völkerkunde), graduating in 1933. Later, he was invited to Vienna to be the Director of the Institute of Japanology at Vienna University (1938–1940). Ishida studied in Vienna for two years (1937–1939). Oka and Ishida regarded Japanese people as the offspring of a mixture of several ethnic groups, viewing Japanese culture as an amalgamation of cultures.

The study of folklore after World War II began with the assumption that Japan was a racially homogeneous nation. Yanagita worked on folk beliefs regarding rice cultivation, and his research was based on the assumption that the Japanese were homogeneous rice cultivators. In strong contrast to this, Oka and Ishida's research was based on the premise that, besides being rice cultivators, the Japanese were also fishermen, hunters, and gatherers. They explained the local variety of social organizational customs, such as kinship relations, as an indication of heterogeneous cultures in Japan, and organized interviews and round-table talks between ethnologists and scholars in other disciplines, publishing their findings in the journal of the Japanese Society of Ethnology (Oka *et al.* 1948). Yanagita and Orikuchi were also invited to these discussions (Yanagita and Orikuchi 1950).

Third, the inclination toward theories from abroad also stands in striking contrast to present-day folklore and ethnology. While ethnology aggressively introduces new theories and methodologies from abroad, Japanese folklore study has focused its research on Japan, referring to the works of earlier researchers such as Yanagita and Orikuchi. However, the approach to scholarship was quite different at the beginning. Yanagita often read Western books published originally in the United Kingdom, Germany, France, and Scandinavia. Some of Yanagita's pupils, Seki, Tokuzo Omachi, and Tokihiko Oto, in particular, actively introduced Western theories and published translated books. Here, only a few examples will be mentioned. Oka's translation of the early *Handbook of Folk-Lore*, by Burne, was published in 1927 (Burne 1927), and in 1930 and 1932, *A Book of Folklore*, by Baring-Gould (Baring-Gould 1930), and *Le Folklore* by van Gennep, were also translated (van Gennep 1932). Meanwhile, in 1940, Seki translated *Die folkloristische Arbeitsmethode*, by Krohn, which was published by the most authoritative publisher in Japan, as a volume in a widely known series (Iwanami-Bunko) (Krohn 1940).

After World War II, as the institutionalization of Japanese folklore moved forward, fewer Western theories were introduced. Yanagita and his pupils gradually became less interested in folklore studies from abroad and simultaneously taught their own courses, parting company with ethnology in the process. The big project published in 1960, the *Nihon-Minzokugaku-Taikei,* was the last instance where the interrelationship between folklore and ethnology was richly reflected. These volumes also introduced overseas research trends. Oka was one of the editors and contributors to this project.

Some researchers were personally involved in both disciplines, and there was a belief in the 1970s that interdisciplinary dialogue between the two would develop (Noguchi 1975). The topic is taken up repeatedly. Twenty years later, observing that the two disciplines were engaged in the same subjects, Masataka Suzuki recommended that folklore studies should look for the accumluation of folk knowledge as a unified whole, instead of employing a theory of causality in pursuing correlative analyses, while expecting to get a viewpoint unrelated to ethnology that was tended to to rely on outside theory (Suzuki 1994).

Recent research has been carried out more and more on an interdisciplinary basis, and in this context, a new movement attracts our attention. Several Japanese folklorists have recently been undertaking research in East Asian countries. There, they compare the folklore of each East Asian country based on the assumption that China, Korea, and Taiwan share cultural traits with Japan. Some scholars in these countries previously studied in Japan, and were currently collaborating with Japanese researchers both in their home countries and in Japan. Additionally, such research groups often include scholars who studied in other countries. Another consequence of this collaboration was that Japanese folklorists encountered Japanese ethnologists undertaking similar research in East Asia, and became colleagues. Here, a new network of researchers was taking shape. Whether these relationships developed into dialogue concerning theories and methodologies depended on how the research progressed.

A Theory of Diffusion and Comparison: "Shûkenron" and "Jûshutsu-Risshô-Hô"

One of the most famous aspects of Japanese folklore studies is "shûkenron," which is a proposition devised by Yanagita to compare local customs. Yanagita thought that cities set new trends one after another, which spread to the countryside as time went on. Therefore, customs in the countryside were older than those in urban areas. According to this rule, the distribution pattern of Japanese customs can be explained, and, since the Japanese archipelago extends from north to south, customs in the far north and the far south of Japan are the same, while in the central urban areas, this similarity is almost non-existent.

Yanagita formed this theory, focusing on the distribution pattern of phenomena using a concentric circles as a model. His thinking was influenced significantly by Western publications on the following topics: (i) Economic geography, particularly the works of Johann Heinrich von Thünen; (ii) Dialectology; (iii) Finnish folklore studies, in particular, those of Kaarle Leopold Krohn; and (iv) British folklore, particularly that of G.L. Gomme (Gomme 1890). Based on the idea that local varieties of folk customs represented historical variety (the geographical-historical school), "shûkenron" suggested that, in a series of concentric circles representing the geographical distribution of a specific folk phenomenon around its point of origin, if the folk phenomenon is further from centre, it tends to retain older forms (Sano 2000, according to Shimamura 2003).

The first application of this proposition was *Sanson-Seikatsu-No-Kenkyu*, which was a study of people in mountain hamlets published in 1937 (Yanagita 1937). In this book, Yanagita enumerated local folk data collected from all parts of Japan. He took these apart and categorized them according to the previously mentioned list of investigation items, and recorded them in that order.

However, this procedure spoiled the unity of each hamlet, and hamlet names only reflected topographical points. As the first critic, Asataro Yamaguchi wrote: "Here, each event of life is treated separate from hamlet life, and the value of historical material is determined without any regard for the character of the hamlet. Each event is as if it was pulled apart from the base by an examiner in a research laboratory and placed side by side." Furthermore, Yamaguchi advocated the idea of "area folklore," insisting that vernacular traditions be taken up first as a unit of the tradition of life phenomenon and then be considered in their own social and economical context (Yamaguchi 1939).

Thanks to Taro Wakamori, this type of comparative study dependent on the theory of diffusion became widely known after World War II, and Wakamori mentioned it in *Jûshutsu-Risshô-Hô* (Wakamori 1947). Keigo Seki severely criticized the approach as an easy comparison maintaining that it was nothing but a schema of evolutionism. Wakamori insisted that *Jûshutsu-Risshô-Hô* permitted vernacular traditions to explain their own transition, but were used simply to apply Japanese culture to a basic stratum in the schema of evolutionary folklorist Gomme (Seki 1958). Moreover, Tokuji Chiba considered that the distribution pattern of a concentric circle model around folklore events reflected the regional organization of national territory by the state. He was also of the opinion that considered the mutual relationship between the centralized distribution of folklore events and the power of the state (Chiba 1963).

In the process of the critique, an interest in the concept of the region took shape, opening the door to a new theme of ethnography within the study of folklore. Two trends in the study of folklore led to this development. The first is "shûkenron" and *Jûshutsu-Risshô-Hô* itself, which is related to both evolutionism and diffusionism. The second is structural functionalism, which severely criticized evolutionism and diffusionism. The latter became mainstream in the 1970s, and was put forward by the generation who continued the study of folklore after the death of Yanagita. Above all, Ajio Fukuta led an animated debate (Fukuta 1982, 1998).

Subjects of Folklore Studies: Cities and Modernity
Recent thematic issues in Japanese folklore can best be illustrated with the themes of "cities" and "modernity." What is of interest here is how cities are regarded as a subject in the study of folklore, how they are approached, and what theory informs this focus.

Cities have long been ignored by those involved in the study of folklore. Around 1970, Japanese folklorists began to regard the city as one area of their field of study, and they named this field "urban folklore" (Miyata 1982). We can divide the research of the 1970s into three types. The first would be the studies of the early 1970s, which were characterized by the "village-city-continuum model." Research focused on former country dwellers who had since sought an urban way of life, living in modern apartments. Consulting Yanagita's work about the social conditions of the city (Yanagita 1929), researchers found among these subjects that the folklore of rural communities was reproduced in urban areas (Kuraishi 1981).

In contrast, the second type looked at people living in towns and found the city to be a field of study in modern history, Edo (Tokyo) being the most typical example. This gave researchers a wealth of data. Their discussions then concerned symbolic space, which was analyzed by drawing on structuralism (Miyata 1981).

The third focus was a trend still common since the late 1970s. Researchers carried out fieldwork in the major historical cities. A typical example would be a garrison town that inherited traditions from 300 years or more ago (Kobayashi 1981).

These studies in the 1970s had in common their pursuit of historical tradition, believed to be handed down from before the nineteenth century, either in the city or in the countryside and in the past or in the present. This posed the following question. If the continuity of tradition from before the nineteenth century is necessary for there to be folklore, is the world of the present with its modern technology not an object of folklore? Here, the argument concerning the character of the study of folklore re-emerged.

As already mentioned previously, "the investigation items" of the *Nihon-Minzokugaku-Taikei* in 1960 had contributed to solidifying the scope of investigation. This "elementalism" fostered by the items of investigation was opposed by some researchers who advocated an "ethnographic study" because they regarded an "area" as a hotbed of the tradition. Both groups of researchers were able to construct a framework for the study of folklore up to the present day, despite being critical of one another. Furthermore, the research work carried out within this framework had certain limitations. For instance, contemporary modernity cannot be defined by "the investigation items" or "the study of ethnography" because contemporary life is borderless, and therefore, the concept of an "area" does not make sense.

The researchers interested in contemporary cities came to express more and more doubts and impatience after 1990. They asked the following question, "What is the study of folklore?" They wanted to focus on the contemporary city and investigate what had never been regarded as tradition, and their research blazed a trail in the field of folklore study. Gradually, their topics moved to the urban realm, and scholars began to discuss contemporary culture. A phrase clarifies this point: "The study of folklore must not be the study *of* folklore, but must be study *through* folklore" (Iwamoto 1998).

Kiyoshi Kawamura reviewed the development of the study of folklore since the 1980s by comparing two publications from 1989 and 2003 (Kawamura 2009; Iwamoto *et al.* 1989; the Folklore Society of Japan 2003). The publication of 1989 consists of two volumes and includes 27 articles on urban folklore, but does not include an introductory article. Here contemporary phenomena were confronted without any theoretical framework. On the other hand, the publication of 2003 was a special issue of the *Bulletin of the Folklore Society of Japan* on the theme of "Folklorism." Both studies opened up a new area at that time, one in the late 1980s and the other in the early 2000s.

Kawamura pointed out three characteristics of urban folklore in the publication of 1989: (i) continuity with classic folklore study; (ii) interest in contemporary phenomena; and (iii) the traditional major city since before modernization.

The contributors were not bound together by common theory, but were all aware of Yanagita's *Meiji-Taishô-Shi Sesôhen,* published in 1931 as a prior example (Yanagita 1931). They took up subjects such as oral literature, folk beliefs, and annual events, which were known as typical subjects in the study of folklore, as they were on the list of "the investigation items" since 1960. However, there were also some subjects that did not correspond to classic investigation items. Intricate media developments and the drift of market economies in the modern world came to the fore, and such themes as comic books involving schoolgirls emerged (Otsuka 1989). Although urban folklore was very popular in the late 1980s, it did not enter the mainstream of the discipline.

The special issue of 2003 dealt with a variety of themes, such as food, exhibitions, oral literature, annual events, rites of passage, material culture, cultural heritage, tourism, and media representation. However, what mattered most was the context in which these themes were set. As events in the contemporary world were not located in a limited geographical space, not a single discussion dealing with a restricted area like a village appeared in this special issue. Here, the idea of unity of tradition breaks down, in other words, as globalization moves forward. The system of a local community is articulated within other systems, and in this process, folk culture is to be reproduced and supplied.

While the publication of 1989 emphasized continuity with previous notions of modernization, the publication of 2003 dealt with phenomena after modernization, particularly after World War II. Furthermore, the latter preferred to refer to international and interdisciplinary theories rather than to the framework of Yanagita. The theories drawn upon concerned culture as articulated in cultural anthropology, constructionism from sociology, and folklorism from German and US folklore.

The study of folklore was founded at a time when society was changing in the face of modernization, focusing on oral and local traditions. Before the study of folklore matured, society changed its course. At the beginning of the twenty-first century, globalization accelerated, and the study of folklore is now searching for its own theory and methodology in order to catch up with a changing society.

RECENT WORKS AND A PROSPECT FOR FOLKLORE STUDIES

Some selected works from recent Japanese folklore studies will now follow, conforming to the order of categories in the current *Journal of the Folklore Society of Japan,* which closely corresponds to the categorization of the *Nihon-Minzokugaku-Taikei* in 1960.

General Remarks

I shall mention here only a few examples of literature. One book entitled "Toward a New Study of Folklore" contains 26 lessons concerning 26 keywords which date from the early days of the discipline (Komatsu and Seki 2002). A practical research textbook which was first published 1974 and revised in 1987 is still in print (Ueno *et al.* 1987). On the subject of nationalism and folklore studies, Kokuni explored the history of school education and clarified that newly discovered "folklore" was linked to the creation of a national identity in schools before and after World War II (Kokuni 2001).

Economics

Economics today embraces works concerning the environment and nature (Torigoe 1994; Shinohara 2005; Suga 2006; Yama *et al.* 2008). Yasumuro argued that traditional occupations, such as farming, fishing, and hunting, needed to be reconsidered (Yasumuro 1992). Noji was able to explain the relaxed lifestyle of fishermen, therefore presenting another view Japanese life.

Society

Much research has been carried out on the family, agricultural, and commercial households, as well as friendships (Aruga 1939; Nakane 1970; Nakano 1964; Hara *et al.* 1979), and some of this is well known abroad. Ethnographical studies of a more complicated modern world are now fashionable. Examples of these include Sato who researched young bikers in the city from a sociological angle, Umeya *et al.*, on superstition s in rural areas, and Sugimoto, on election campaigns (Sato 1984; Umeya *et al.* 2001; Sugimoto 2007).

Life Events, Rites of Passage, Events, and Customs

As far as life events were concerned, Miyamoto wrote the first classical work on upbringing and Hara and Wagatsuma worked on the same subject (Miyamoto 1943; Hara and Wagatsuma 1974). Recently, life history studies throw light on the lives of people engaged in various occupations, such as a racehorse-trainers, Tokyo taxi drivers, and conventional rural occupations (Ôtsuki 1990; Shigenobu 1999; Nomoto 2000). Some recent life history studies deal with welfare (Oka 2004; Goodman 2006; Kondo and Komatsu 2008).

As for rites of passage, scholars have focused on death and burial rituals (Maeda 2010; Shintani 1991; Fujii 1993; Mori 2000). Takahashi described a memorial service for an aborted baby's soul, and Yamada took up the mortician's role (Takahashi 1999; Yamada 2007). Instead of traditional vernacular customs, Ishii carried out research on Christmas and St Valentine's Day as modern urban annual customs (Ishii 1994), and Shintani *et al.* described how people today pass the time of day (Shintani *et al.* (eds) 2003).

Religion and Belief

Hori's classic work dealt with narrative and religious history, and Miyata's well-known work concentrated on relief among the populace (Hori 1953; Miyata 1970). Komatsu described the world of dark emotion through the phenomenon of being possessed, while Miyake tried to systematize the field of religious folklore and Takatori explored the historical formation of secular Shintoism (Komatsu 1982; Miyake 1989; Takatori 1993). Miyata and Komatsu have published several books on Japanese ghosts and monsters from the 1980s up to the present day, and this has had considerable appeal to lay people interested in mysterious phenomena in the modern world. These publications supported a general interest toward folklore studies up to the present day (Miyata 1985; Komatsu 2003). Among younger scholars, Azuma researched narratives concerning folk medicine, and Kadota focused on a pilgrim's narrative (Azuma 2006; Kadota 2007).

Oral Traditions

Miyamoto's well-known work described older villagers and their life histories (Miyamoto 1960) while Shigenobu argued in favor of research of *sekenbanashi* (an anecdotic genre) from a theoretical point of view, stating that it was an oral conversational performance rather than folk narrative literature (Shigenobu 1989, 1994). Tsunemitsu explained ghost stories staged in schools and deeds with magical significance (Tsunemitsu 1993 2006). Furthermore the Society for Folk Narrative Research published a book on the world of words consisting of legend, small talk, and modern legend (Society for Folk Narrative Research 2007).

The Performing Arts

In this active field, most scholars challenged physical techniques used in the performing arts (Oishi 2007; Fukushima 1995; Sako 2003; Sugawara *et al.* 2005). With a view of changing procedures in the performing arts, Hashimoto questioned the research method being used (Hashimoto 2006).

Material Cultures

Several recent works deal with the changing aspects of material life during the period of high economic growth after World War II, and these works shed light on the pre-consumer society (Aoki 2001; Kondo 2003; Amano and Sakurai 1992; Yano 2007; National Museum of Japanese History 2010).

Active Topics

Cultural Properties and Heritage

Heritage is currently one of the most active topics, and scholars deal with folk culture by transforming it into tourist attractions (Iwamoto 2007; Adachi 2010). Kikuchi argued for a transformation of folk culture based on the folklorist's description (Kikuchi 2001).

East Asian Study and Comparative Approach

Recently, folklorists began to study Korea, China, and Taiwan from a comparative point of view. Takeda published a comparative study of ancestor worship between Japan and Korea (Takeda 1995). Ito concentrated on characters in Japanese folklore from ancient times to the present day from an anthropological angle, and compared them with those in East Asian countries (Ito 2007). Manabe analyzed how death is dealt with in Korean society and obtained insight into Korean social structure and Shimamura researched the ethnography of the Korean Japanese (Shimamura 2010).

War and Memory

Commemoration has been an important topic of historical research since the 1990s, and in Japanese folklore studies, this is connected with memorial services for fallen soldiers. During World War II, under the military government, it was believed that the fallen soldier's soul would be transformed into *eirei* (heroic soul), and was worshiped as a god. Scholars have been tracing the process (Tanakamaru 2002;

Kawamura 2003; Imai 2005; Yano 2006) and have considered that a mutual relationship between the state and the people has added a realistic tone to this idea. Analyzing the records of nineteenth-century domestic warfare, Chiba clarified the practical reasons why wars were lost, and investigated people's attitudes to wars themselves (Chiba 1994).

Now, looking back at a very rough sketch of the history of Japanese folklore, it can be said that it took shape in the mid-1930s and experienced active theoretical debate around 1950. In the 1970s and 1980s, folklore flourished in the social context of those days, while discussions among researchers themselves remained rather tame. In the 1990s, without focusing on the common critical points of discussions, research seemed to fall apart, and younger researchers began to rethink what constituted folklore and the methodologies of the study of folklore itself. Some were eager to learn about international and interdisciplinary discussions.

In this context, scholars tried to cast new light on Yanagita. Ajio Fukuta encouraged younger researchers to debate and criticize Yanagita's *Jûshutsu-Risshô-Hô*. In contrast, Iwamoto criticized the fixed course of the study of folklore which came into being after Yanagita. Iwamoto advocated Yanagita's flexible way of thinking rather than criticizing his inconsistencies (Iwamoto 2006). Some younger scholars reading Yanagita's work with a new perspective initiated debates that led to a rethinking of the outline of Japanese folklore studies (Kikuchi 2001; Muroi 2010). *Yanagita-Kunio-Den* should perhaps also be mentioned when considering a review of Yanagita. This was the product of a long established research group, and was based on a mass of concrete materials (Yanagita-Kunio-Kenkyû-Kai 1988).

In conclusion, I would like to mention the relationship between nationalism and Japanese folklore studies. In its early days the study of folklore harbored the seeds of modern nationalism, and this was of prime significance while Yanagita was alive. There were several nationalist movements in Japan in the run up to World War II, but they did not guarantee victory. Japan suffered a crushing defeat in 1945 and the study of folklore was blamed. However, this needs consideration.

As mentioned previously, Japanese folklore was institutionalized after World War II. The "Minzokugaku-Kenkyû-Sho," was established in 1948 as an institute of folklore research, and operated in Yanagita's private house. After 10 years of intensive activity, the study of folklore became a recognized discipline, and the institute was dissolved. The Nihon-Minzoku-Gakkai (the Folklore Society of Japan) was established in 1949. A lexicon of folklore study was published in 1951, and special university courses in folklore education began at Seijo University and at the Tokyo University of Education in 1958. All of these activities were carried out just after World War II, thanks to US General Headquarters. The GHQ believed that Yanagita's folklore was effective as a vanguard in order to implant the US brand of democracy in Japan. That is why Yanagita's Western-style private house was not requisitioned and was used as a folklore research institute. In those days, Yanagita was on familiar terms with the executives of the Civil Information and Educational Section, and this led to him producing school textbooks in his later years.

We can see how Yanagita's idea of "one-nation folklore" (*Ikkoku-Minzokugaku*) penetrated through these activities. He explained that the purpose of folklore study was to look at one's own culture with one's own language and knowledge. He wrote that it would be ideal if "world folklore" could be based on folklore studies of each ethnic group in the world, and each researcher would come from his or her own ethnic group. The aim of Yanagita's folklore was to study Japanese culture as passed down from generation to generation, examine how this affected people's daily lives, and how it motivated and encouraged Japanese people (Yanagita 1934b).

Yanagita was conscious of the Japanese nation and was very much a nationalist. However, since nationalism gained momentum after World War II, there is no obvious break between pre- and post-World War II folklore study.

However, pre-World War II folklore did have something to do with military nationalism. As some scholars argued, some pupils of Yanagita were dispatched to colonial universities as teachers (see Kawamura 1996; Oguma 2002), and membership of Minkan-Densho-No-Kai (The Society for Folklore Research) increased dramatically during the war. When it began in 1935 membership was only 140 strong, but increased to 2,138 in 1944 (Kokuni 2001). This indicated that folklore unearthed by the authorities was of great service to the country, rather than a frivolous pastime.

Japanese folklore and nationalism are intertwined, with strong connections between the history of folklore and the socio-political situation in Japan. Additionally, national concepts of a certain discipline concerned not only wartime militarism but also the postwar world order. From this point of view, I believe that a new debate could be opened up, and some studies are now under way.

REFERENCES

Adachi, S. 2010. *Gujo-Hachiman Dentô Wo Ikiru: Chiiki-Shakai No Katari To Reality.* Tokyo: Shin-Yô-Sha.

Akata, M. *et al.*, Eds. 1998. *Kôza Nihon No Minzokugaku* 1. Tokyo: Yûzankaku.

Amano, M. and A. Sakurai. 1992. *"Mono To Onna" No Sengo-Shi.* Tokyo: Yûshindô-Kôbunsha.

Amino, Y. *et al.*, Eds. 1983–1987. *Nihon Minzoku Bunka Taikei*, 1–15. Tokyo: Shôgakukan.

Aoki, T. 2001. *Danchi 2DK No Kurashi: Saigen, Shôwa 30 Nendai.* Tokyo: Kawade-Shobô-Shinsha.

Aruga, K. 1939. *Nanbu-Ninohe-Gun Ishigami-Mura Ni Okeru Dai-Kazoku-Seido To Nago-Seido.* Tokyo: Attic Museum.

Azuma, M. 2006. "Healing and the Generation of Narrative Tales: Examples from the Folk Medicine of 'A' Village, Irabu Island, Miyako Archipelago." *Nihon-Minzokugaku (Bulletin of the Folklore Society of Japan)* 248 (in Japanese).

Baring-Gould, S. 1930. *Minzokugaku No Hanashi.* Trans. from *A Book of Folklore.* Tokyo: Ôokayama-Shoten.

Burne, C. 1927. *Minzokugaku Gairon.* Trans. from *Handbook of Folklore.* Tokyo: Oka-Shoin.

Chiba, T. 1963. "An Opinion on the Theory of Concentricity of Folklore Diffusion." *Nihon-Minzokugaku-Kaiho (Bulletin of the Folklore Society of Japan)* 27 (in Japanese).

Chiba, T. 1994. *Make-Ikusa No Kôzô: Nihon-Jin No Sensô-Kan.* Tokyo: Heibon-Sha.

Folklore Society of Japan (The). 1975. *Special Edition: Current Researches of Japanese Folklore, Nihon-Minzokugaku (Bulletin of The Folklore Society of Japan)* 100 (in Japanese).

——— 2003. *A Special Issue: Folklorism, Nihon-Minzokugaku (Bulletin of the Folklore Society of Japan)* 236 (in Japanese).

Fujii, M. 1993. *Sosen Saishi No Girei Kôzô To Minzoku.* Tokyo: Kôbundô.

Fukushima, M., Ed. 1995. *Shintai No Kôchiku-Gaku: Shakai-Teki Gakushû Katei To Shite No Shintai-Gihô.* Tokyo: Hituji-Shobô.

Fukuta, A. 1982. *Nihon Sonraku No Minzoku-Teki Kôzô.* Tokyo: Kôbundô.

Fukuta, A. 1998. "Minzokugaku No Mokuteki To Hôhô" in M. Akata *et al.*, Eds. *Kôza Nihon No Minzokugaku* 1. Tokyo: Yûzankaku.

Fukuta, A. 2000. "Minzoku-Gakusha Yanagita Kunio." *Kanagawa Daigaku Hyôron Booklet* 12. Tokyo: Ochanomizu-Shobô.

Gomme, G.L. 1890. *The Handbook of Folklore*. London: Folklore Society.

Goodman, R. 2006. *Children of the Japanese State: The Changing Role of Child Protection Institutions in Contemporary Japan*. Tokyo: Akashi-Shoten (in Japanese).

Hara, H. and H. Wagatsuma. 1974. *Shitsuke*. Tokyo: Kôbundô.

Hara, T. *et al.*, 1979. *Nakama*. Tokyo: Kôbundô.

Hashimoto, H. 2003. "Between Preservation and Tourism: Folk Performing Arts in Contemporary Japan." *Asian Folklore Studies*, 62.

Hashimoto, H. 2006. *Minzoku-Geinô Kenkyû To Iu Shinwa*. Tokyo: Shinwa-Sha.

Hori, I. 1953. *Waga-Kuni Minkan-Shinkô-Shi No Kenkyû* 1, 2. Tokyo: Tokyô-Sôgen-Sha.

Ishii, K. 1994. *Toshi No Nenjû-Gyôji*. Tokyo: Shunjû-Sha.

Ito, A. 2007. *Anthropological Introduction to Japanese Folk Society*. Tokyo: Yûhikaku (in Japanese).

Ivy, M. 1995. *Discourses of the Vanishing: Modernity, Phantasm, Japan*. Chicago: University of Chicago Press.

Imai, A. 2005. *Kindai-Nihon To Senshisha Saishi*. Tokyo: Tôyô-Shorin.

Iwamoto, M. 1998 "Because Its Objective Is 'Folklore' Is It Folklore Studies? Why Has Folklore Studies Lost Its Ability to Deal with 'The Modern Age'?" *Nihon-Minzokugaku (Bulletin of the Folklore Society of Japan)* 215 (in Japanese).

Iwamoto, M. 2006. "The Epistemological Transformation of Post War Folklore and the Theory of Japan's Underlying Culture." *Kokuritsu Rekishi Minzoku Hakubutsukan Kenkyû Hôkoku (Bulletin of the National Museum of Japanese History)* 132 (in Japanese).

Iwamoto, M., Ed. 2007. *Furusato Shigen-Ka To Minzokugaku*. Tokyo: Yoshikawa-Kôbunkan.

Iwamoto, M. *et al.* Eds. 1989. *Toshi-Minzokugaku E No Izanai* 1 and 2. Tokyo: Yûzankaku.

Kadota, T. 2007. "Dialogue and Belief: An Analysis of Pilgrim Narratives, Focusing on Self, Others and Society." *Nihon-Minzokugaku (Bulletin of the Folklore Society of Japan)* 251 (in Japanese).

Kawada, M. 1993. *The Origin of Ethnography in Japan: Yanagita Kunio and His Times*. London: Kegan Paul International.

Kawamori, H. 2003. "Folktale Research after Yanagita: Development and Related Issues." *Asian Folklore Studies* 62.

Kawamura, Kiyoshi 2009. "Toshimin-zokugaku Kara Folklorism E" in J. Koike, Ed. *Minzokugaku-Teki Sôzôryoku*. Tokyo: Serika-Shobô.

Kawamura, Kunimitsu. 2003a. "A Female Shaman's Mind and Body, and Possession." *Asian Folklore Studies*, 62.

Kawamura, Kunimitsu, Ed. 2003b. *Senshisha No Yukue: Katari To Hyôshô Kara*. Tokyo: Seikyû-Sha.

Kawamura, M. 1996. *Dai-Tôa Minzokugaku No Kyojitsu*. Tokyo: Kôdansha.

Kikuchi, A. 2001. *Yanagita Kunio To Minzokugaku No Kindai: Oku-Noto No Aenokoto No. 20 Seiki*. Tokyo: Yoshikawa-Kôbunkan.

Kobayashi, T. 1981. "Structure of the Folklore in the Traditional City of Kanazawa." *Nihon-Minzokugaku (Bulletin of the Folklore Society of Japan)* 134 (in Japanese).

Koike, J., Ed. 2009. *Minzokugaku-Teki Sôzôryoku*. Tokyo: Serika-Shobô.

Kokuni, Y. 2001. *The Folklore Studies Movement and School Education: The Discovery of Folk Customs and Their Nationalization*. Tokyo: University of Tokyo Press (in Japanese).

Komatsu, K. 1982. *Hyôrei Shinkô-Ron: Yôkai Kenkyû E No Kokoromi*. Tokyo: Dentô-To-Gendai-Sha.

Komatsu, K., Ed. 2003. *Nihon Yôkaigaku Taizen*. Tokyo: Shôgakukan.

Komatsu, K. and K. Seki, Eds. 2002. *Atarashii Minzokugaku E: Ya No Gakumon No Tame No Lesson 26*. Tokyo: Serika-Shobô.

Kondo, M. 2003. *Nichiyôhin No Nijû-Seiki: Nijû-Seiki Ni Okeru Shominzoku-Bunka No Dentô To Henyô* 8. Tokyo: Domesu Publishers Inc.

Kondo, N. and K. Komatsu. 2008. *Shi No Gihô: Zaitaku-Shi Ni Miru Sô No Reisetsu, Shiseikan.* Kyoto: Minerva-Shobo.

Koschmann, V. *et al.*, Eds. 1985. *International Perspectives on Yanagita Kunio and Japanese Folklore Studies.* Ithaca: Cornell China-Japan Program.

Krohn, K. 1940. *Minzokugaku Hôhô-Ron.* Trans. from *Die folkloristische Arbeitsmethode.* Tokyo: Iwanami-Shoten.

Kuraishi, T. 1981. "Folklore and Folklore Studies in Urban Areas." *Nihon-Minzokugaku (Bulletin of the Folklore Society of Japan)* 134 (in Japanese).

Kyûgakkai-Rengô Amami Chôsa Iinkai, Ed. 1980. *Amami: Shizen, Bunka, Shakai.* Tokyo: Kôbundô.

Kyûgakkai-Rengô Chiiki-Bunka No Kinshitsu-Ka Henshû Iinkai, Ed. 1994. *Chiiki-Bunka No Kinshitsu-Ka.* Tokyo: Heibon-Sha.

Kyûgakkai-Rengô Nihon No Engan Bunka Chôsa Iinkai, Ed. 1989. *Nihon No Engan Bunka.* Tokyo: Kokon-Shoin.

Kyûgakkai-Rengô Nihon No Fûdo Chôsa Iinkai, Ed. 1985. *Nihon No Fûdo.* Tokyo: Kôbundô.

Kyûgakkai-Rengô Noto Chôsa Iinkai, Ed. 1989. *Noto: Shizen, Bunka, Shakai.* Tokyo: Heibon-Sha.

Kyûgakkai-Rengô Okinawa Chôsa Iinkai, Ed. 1976. *Okinawa: Shizen, Bunka, Shakai.* Tokyo: Kôbundô.

Kyûgakkai-Rengô Sado Chôsa Iinkai, Ed. 1989. *Sado: Shizen, Bunka, Shakai.* Tokyo: Heibon-Sha.

Kyûgakkai-Rengô Shimokita Chôsa Iinkai, Ed. 1967. *Shimokita: Shizen, Bunka, Shakai.* Tokyo: Heibon-Sha.

Kyûgakkai-Rengô Tonegawa Ryûiki Chôsa Iinkai, Ed. 1971. *Tonegawa: Shizen, Bunka, Shakai.* Tokyo: Kôbundô.

Kyûgakkai-Rengô Tsushima Kyôdô Chôsa Iinkai, Ed. 1954. *Tsushima No Shizen To Bunka.* Tokyo: Kokon-Shoin.

Maeda, S. 2010. *Bosei No Minzokugaku: Shisha Girei No Kindai.* Tokyo: Iwata-Shoin.

Makita, S. 1951. "Minzokugaku No Jidai-Sei To Gendai-Sei." *Minkan-Denshô* 15(6).

Minzokugaku-Kenkyu-Sho. 1951. *Minzokugaku-Jiten.* Tokyo: Tôkyô-Dô.

Maeda, S. 1951. *Minzokugaku-Jiten.* Tokyo: Tôkyô-Dô.

Miyake, H. 1989. *Shûkyô Minzokugaku.* Tokyo: University of Tokyo Press.

Miyamoto, K. 2006. "Keynote Essay: Modern Society and Folklore Studies." *Nihon-Minzokugaku (Bulletin of the Folklore Society of Japan)* 247 (in Japanese).

Miyamoto, T. 1943. *Kakyô No Oshie.* Tokyo: Mikuni-Shobô.

Miyamoto, T. 1960. *Wasurerareta Nihon-Jin.* Tokyo: Mirai-Sha.

Miyata, N. 1970. *A Study on the Miroku Belief.* Tokyo: Mirai-Sha (in Japanese).

Miyata, N. 1981. *Edo-Saijiki: Toshi-Minzokushi No Kokoromi.* Tokyo: Yoshikawa-Kôbunkan.

Miyata, N. 1982. *Toshi Minzoku-Ron No Kadai.* Tokyo: Mirai-Sha.

Miyata, N. 1985. *Yôkai No Minzokugaku: Nihon No Mienai Kûkan.* Tokyo: Iwanami-Shoten.

Mori, K. 2000. *Haka To Sôsô No Genzai: Sosen Saishi Kara Sôsô No Jiyu E.* Tokyo: Tôkyô-Dô-Shuppan.

Morse, R. 1990. *Yanagita Kunio and the Folklore Movement: The Search for Japan's National Character and Distinctiveness.* New York: Garland.

Murai, O. 1992. *Nantô Ideology No Hassei: Yanagita Kunio To Shokuminchi-Shugi.* Tokyo: Fukutake-Shoten.

Muroi, K. 2010. *Yanagita Kunio No Minzokugaku Kôsô.* Tokyo: Shinwa-Sha.

Nakane, C. 1970. *Family Structure: Analysis of Social Anthropology.* Tokyo: University of Tokyo Press (in Japanese).

Nakano, T. 1964. *A Study of Merchant Dôzoku: Research on Federations of Ie Units Having Noren and on Networks of Ie Units.* Tokyo: Mirai-Sha (in Japanese).

National Museum of Japanese History, Ed. 2010. *Kôdo-Keizai-Seichô To Seikatsu Kakumei: Minzokugaku To Keizaishi-Gaku To No Taiwa Kara.* Tokyo: Yoshikawa-Kôbunkan.

Noguchi, T. 1974. "Kaisetsu: Minzokugaku To Minzokugaku" in T. Noguchi *et al.*, Eds. *Gendai-Nihon-Minzokugaku* 1. Tokyo: San-Ichi-Shobô.

Noguchi, T. *et al.*, Eds. 1974, 1975. *Gendai-Nihon-Minzokugaku* 1 and 2. Tokyo: San-Ichi-Shobô.

Nomoto, K. 2000. *Shomin Retsuden: Minzoku No Kokoro Wo Motomete.* Tokyo: Hakusui-Sha.

Oguma, E. 2002. *A Genealogy of "Japanese" Self-Images."* Melbourne: Trans Pacific Press.

Oishi, Y. 2007. *Geinô No "Denshô Genba" Ron: Wakamono-Tachi No Minzoku-Teki Manabi No Kyôdôtai.* Tokyo: Hituji-Shobô.

Oka, M. *et al.*, 1948. "Origin of the Japanese People and Culture and Formation of the Japanese State: Round-Table and Discussion." *The Japanese Journal of Ethnology* 13(3) (in Japanese).

Omachi, T. *et al.*, Eds. 1958–1960. *Nihon-Minzokugaku-Taikei*, 1–13 Volumes. Tokyo: Heibon-Sha.

Otsuka, E. 1989. "Omajinai To Shôjo-Manga No Isô" in M. Iwamoto *et al.* Eds. *Toshi-Minzokugaku E No Izanai* 1 and 2. Tokyo: Yûzankaku.

Otsuka Folklore Society. 1972. *Nihon-Minzoku-Jiten.* Tokyo: Kôbundô.

Ôtsuki, T. 1990. *Kyûsha Monogatari.* Tokyo: Nihon Editor School Shuppan-Bu.

Sako, T. 2003. "Geihoku-Kagura Ni Okeru Flow" in H. Imamura and K. Asakawa, Eds. *Flow-Riron No Tenkai.* Kyoto: Sekai-Shisôsha.

Sano, K. 2000. "Shûkenron" in A. Fukuta *et al.*, Eds. *Nihon Minzoku Daijiten* 2. Tokyo: Yoshikawa-Kôbunkan.

Sato, I. 1984. *Bôsô-Zoku No Ethnography: Mode No Hanran To Bunka No Jubaku.* Tokyo: Shin-Yô-Sha.

Schnell, S. and H. Hashimoto. 2003. "Guest Editors' Introduction: Revitalizing Japanese Folklore." *Asian Folklore Studies* 62.

Seki, K. 1958. "Nihon-Minzokugaku No Rekishi" in T. Omachi *et al.*, Eds. *Nihon-Minzokugaku-Taikei.* Vol. 2. Tokyo: Heibon-Sha.

Seki, K., Ed. 1963. *Folktales of Japan.* Chicago: University of Chicago Press.

Sensui, H. 2003. "On Cognitive Aspects of Rhetorical Time Reckoning: Metaphor and Image-Schema in Calendrical Divination in Okinawa." *Asian Folklore Studies* 62.

Shigenobu, Y. 1989. "Reconsidering 'Sekenbanashi' as a Research Method." *Nihon-Minzokugaku (Bulletin of the Folklore Society of Japan)* 180 (in Japanese).

Shigenobu, Y. 1994. "Toward a Study of Discourse on Our Everyday Life." *Kôshô-Bungei-Kenkyû* 17 (in Japanese).

Shigenobu, Y. 1999. *Taxi, Modern Tôkyô Minzokushi.* Tokyo: Nihon Editor School Shuppan-Bu.

Shimamura, T. 2003. "Cultural Diversity and Folklore Studies in Japan: A Multiculturalist Approach." *Asian Folklore Studies* 62.

Shimamura, T. 2010. *"Ikiru Hôhô" No Minzokushi: Chôsen-Kei Jûmin Shûjû Chiiki No Minzokugaku-Teki Kenkyû.* Nishinomiya: Kwansei Gakuin University Shuppan-Kai.

Shinohara, T. 2005. *Shizen Wo Ikiru Gijutsu: Kurashi No Minzoku Shizen-Shi.* Tokyo: Yoshikawa-Kôbunkan.

Shintani, T. 1991. *Ryôbo-Sei To Takai-Kan.* Tokyo: Yoshikawa-Kôbunkan.

Shintani, T. *et al.*, Eds. 2003. *Kurashi No Naka No Minzokugaku* 1. Tokyo: Yoshikawa-Kôbunkan.

Society for Folk Narrative Research. 2007. *Series Kotoba No Sekai 3 Hanasu.* Tokyo: Miyai-Shoten.

Suga, Y. 2006. *Kawa Wa Dare No Mono Ka: Hito To Kankyô No Minzokugaku.* Tokyo: Yoshikawa-Kôbunkan.

Sugawara, K. *et al.*, 2005. "Redistribution of Body Resources in the Succession of a Traditional Folk Dance: An Attempt to Understand the Transformation of Nishiura Dengaku in Central Japan." *Bunka-Jinruigaku* 70–72 (in Japanese).

Sugimoto, J. 2007. *Senkyo No Minzokushi: Nihon-Teki Seiji Fûdo No Kisô.* Tokyo: Fukuro-Sha.

Suzuki, M. 1994. "Minzokugaku To Minzokugaku." *Nihon-Minzokugaku (Bulletin of the Folklore Society of Japan)* 200 (in Japanese).

Takahashi, S. 1999. *Mizuko-Kuyô: Gendai-Shakai No Fuan To Iyashi.* Kyoto: Gyôro-Sha.

Takatori, M. 1993. *Shintô No Seiritsu.* Tokyo: Heibon-Sha.

Takeda, A. 1995. *Sosen-Sûhai No Hikaku-Minzokugaku: Nikkan Ryôkoku Ni Okeru Sosen Saishi To Shakai.* Tokyo: Yoshikawa-Kôbunkan.

Tanakamaru, K. 2002. *Samayoeru Eirei-Tachi: Kuni No Mitama, Ie No Hotoke.* Tokyo: Kashiwa-Shobô.

Torigoe, H. 1994. *Kokoromi To Shite No Kankyô-Minzokugaku: Biwako No Field Kara.* Tokyo: Yûzankaku.

Tsuboi, H. 1979. *Imo To Nihon-Jin: Minzoku Bunka-Ron No Kadai.* Tokyo: Mirai-Sha.

Tsunemitsu, T. 1993. *Gakkô No Kaidan: Kôshô-Bungei No Tenkai To Shosô.* Kyoto: Minerva Shobô.

Tsunemitsu, T. 2006. *Shigusa No Minzokugaku: Jujutsu-Teki Sekai To Shinshô.* Kyoto: Minerva Shobô.

Ueno, K. *et al.*, Eds. 1987. *Minzoku-Chôsa Handbook.* Tokyo: Yoshikawa-Kôbunkan.

Umeya, K. *et al.*, 2001. *Hyôi To Noroi No Ethnography.* Tokyo: Iwata-Shoin.

van Gennep, A. 1932. *Minzokugaku Nyûmon.* Trans. from *Le Folklore.* Tokyo: Kyôdo-Kenkyû-Sha.

Wakamori, T. 1947. *Nihon-Minzokugaku Gaisetsu.* Tokyo: Tôkai-Shobô.

Yama, Y. *et al.*, 2008. *Environmental Folklore.* Kyoto: Shôwadô.

Yamada, S. 2007. *Death and Funeral Ritual in Contemporary Japan: Developing the Funeral Industry and Changing the Cultural Concept of Death.* Tokyo: University of Tokyo Press (in Japanese).

Yamaguchi, A. 1939. "Minzoku-Shiryô To Mura No Seikaku." *Minkan-Denshô* 4(9).

Yanagita, K. 1911. "Itaka Oyobi Sanka." *Jinruigaku Zasshi*, September 1911.

Yanagita, K. 1913a. "Sanjin Gaiden Shiryô." *Kyôdo Kenkyû*, March 1913.

Yanagita, K. 1913b. "Iwayuru Tokushu Buraku No Shurui." *Kokka-Gakkai-Zasshi* 27–25.

Yanagita, K. 1913–1914. "Fujo Kô." *Kyôdo Kenkyû*, March 1913–February 1914.

Yanagita, K. 1914–1915. "Kebôzu Kô." *Kyôdo Kenkyû*, March, April, July, August and September 1914, January and February 1915.

Yanagita, K. 1929. *Toshi To Nôson.* Tokyo: Asahi-Shinbun-Sha.

Yanagita, K. 1931. *Meiji-Taishô-Shi Sesôhen.* Tokyo: Asahi-Shinbun-Sha.

Yanagita, K. 1934a. *Minkan-Denshô-Ron.* Tokyo: Kyôritsu-Sha.

Yanagita, K. 1934b. "Ikkoku-Minzokugaku" in K. Yanagita, *Minkan-Denshô-Ron.* Tokyo: Kyôritsu-Sha.

Yanagita, K. 1935a. *Kyôdo-Seikatsu No Kenkyû-Hô.* Tokyo: Tôkô-Shoin.

Yanagita, K. 1935b. *Kokushi To Minzokugaku.* Tokyo: Rokunin-Sha.

Yanagita, K., Ed. 1937. *Sanson Seikatsu No Kenkyû.* Tokyo: Minkan-Denshô No Kai.

Yanagita, K. and Orikuchi, S. 1950. "From Folklore to Ethnology: Looking Back the Way of Japanese Folklore." *The Japanese Journal of Ethnology* 14(3) (in Japanese).

Yanagita, K. and Seki, K. 1942. *Nihon-Minzokugaku Nyûmon.* Tokyo: Kaizô-Sha.

Yanagita-Kunio-Kenkyû-Kai, Ed. 1988. *Yanagita-Kunio-Den.* Tokyo: Tokyo: San-Ichi-Shobô.

Yano, K. 2006. *Irei, Tsuitô, Kenshô No Kindai.* Tokyo: Yoshikawa-Kôbunkan.

Yano, K. 2007. *"Katei No Aji" No Sengo Minzokushi: Shufu To Danran No Jidai.* Tokyo: Seikyû-Sha.

Yasumuro, S. 1992. "The Future of Vocational Research Lacking a Sense of Being: Integrated Vocational Studies as Methodology." *Nihon-Minzokugaku (Bulletin of the Folklore Society of Japan)* 190 (in Japanese).

FURTHER READING

Ooka, Y. 2004. *Why Care for the Elderly?* Tokyo: Keiso-Shobô (in Japanese).

IMPORTANT JOURNALS (IN JAPANESE)

Bulletin of the National Museum of Japanese History. Sakura: National Museum of National History, 1982–.

Denshô-Bunka. Tokyo: Seijo University, 1960–1976.

Kyodo-Kenkyu. Tokyo: Kyodo-Kenkyu-Sha, 1913–1917.

Mingu Monthly. Yokohama: Kanagawa University, Institute for the Study of Japanese Folk Culture, 1968–.

Minkan-Denshô (Bulletin of the Society for Folklore Research). Tokyo: Minkan-Denshô No Kai, 1935–1952.

Minzoku. Tokyo: Minzoku-Hakko-Sho, 1925–1929.

Minzoku-gaku Hyôron (a Review of Japanese Folklore Studies). Tokyo: Otsuka Folklore Society, 1967–1993.

Nihon-Minzokugaku (Bulletin of the Folklore Society of Japan). Tokyo: Folklore Society of Japan, 1953–57, 1970–.

Nihon-Minzokugaku-Kaiho (Bulletin of the Folklore Society of Japan). Tokyo: Folklore Society of Japan, 1958–1969.

Rekishi To Minzoku. Yokohama: Kanagawa University, Institute for the Study of Japanese Folk Culture, 1986–.

Seijo-Daigaku-Minzokugaku-Kenkyusho-Kiyo. Tokyo: Seijo University, Institute of Folklore Studies, 1977–.

IMPORTANT WEB SITES IN ENGLISH

The Folklore Society of Japan http://wwwsoc.nii.ac.jp/fsjnet/en/index_e.html (accessed October 16, 2011).

The Japanese Society of Cultural Anthropology http://wwwsoc.nii.ac.jp/jse/index-e.html (accessed October 16, 2011).

International Research Center for Japanese Studies http://www.nichibun.ac.jp/welcome_e.htm (accessed October 16, 2011).

National Museum of Ethnology http://www.minpaku.ac.jp/english/ (accessed October 16, 2011).

National Museum of Japanese History http://www.rekihaku.ac.jp/english/index.html (accessed October 16, 2011).

CHAPTER 12 INDIA

Sadhana Naithani

CULTURE ZONE INDIA

The republic of India enjoys not only the most central location in South Asia, it is also the biggest country in terms of its size and population. South Asia comprises the independent nations of Afghanistan, Bangladesh, Bhutan, India, Myanamar (Burma), Nepal, Pakistan and Sri Lanka. Bangladesh, on India's eastern side and Pakistan on the west have common histories stretching back into the ancient times up to 1947. They emerged as a "nation," in the modern European sense of the word, under British colonial rule and until 1947 were regarded as "India." As such, the past and present of folklore genres and performers in these regions have been intensely inter-linked in terms of people, practices, and philosophies. Nepal and Bhutan are to the north of India and in spite of a two-way relationship with India through history, both have distinct cultural identities and geographical separateness from the plains of India. Myanamar is further to the east of India and has been connected to India and South East Asia more generally. That country is currently not open to the rest of the world. Sri Lanka, on the southern side of the Indian peninsula is an island nation in the Indian Ocean. Though technically not connected by land to India, the short distance across the sea has fostered a connection since ancient times.

This geographical situation of India has obviously been invested with the socio-cultural practices of the region. There are differences and the variety is visible right away, but there are also philosophical undercurrents that have defined the inter-connectedness of South Asia. Every scholar writing on the subject has expressed this difficulty, even impossibility, of representing the diverse empirical realities of folklore in India and of the available scholarly sources. There are three religious-philosophical strains that run across the region in an intertwined manner: that of Hinduism, Buddhism, and Islam. The influence of Christianity is embedded in colonial contexts of British India and Portuguese Goa. Hinduism and Buddhism are native to the Indian sub-continent. Nepal is a Hindu nation, Bhutan is officially a Buddhist nation

A Companion to Folklore, First Edition. Edited by Regina F. Bendix and Galit Hasan-Rokem.
© 2012 John Wiley & Sons, Ltd. Published 2012 John Wiley & Sons, Ltd.

and the majority of Sri Lanka's population is Buddhist. Islam came to the subcontinent around the tenth century CE from Western Asia, and became part of Indian society and culture. In the process, Islam gained a distinct "Indian" identity in the international world of Islam – some aspects of which will be evident in the folklore practices discussed in this chapter.

Scholarly Resources for Folklore in India in Historical Perspective

The study of Indian folklore, in the post-romantic sense of the word, started around the middle of the nineteenth century through the theoretical propositions of German philologists, and collections of Indian folklore were compiled by British colonial collectors. The accessible and widely known resources of Indian folklore, produced since the middle of the nineteenth century and up to the early twentieth century evolved in the context of British colonial rule in India. The theoretical debates in this period revolved around the identification of *Panchatantra* and *Jataka* stories, as the oldest folktales of the world, by German indologist Theodor Benfey in 1856. Benfey's proposition that India was the original homeland of European folktales charged debates then and remains uncontested to the present (Stith Thompson 1946), although folklore scholarship has given up its concern with establishing the age of folktales. The famous colonial collectors were Mary Frere (1868 [2002]), Flora Anne Steel, Georgiana Kingscote, Richard Carnac Temple (1962), Charles Swynnerton (1892), and William Crooke. These collections presented to the world folktales from different regions of India, as well as from vastly different communities and tribes. Their voluminous collections and translations have inspired awe for one and a half centuries and had a hold over international readers far into the twentieth century, as in the seminal work of Richard M. Dorson (1968). Postcolonial perspectives in scholarship have problematized these works with reference to their association with actual colonial cultural politics, and also with reference to the contribution of Indian scholars in the making of these voluminous collections (Blackburn 2003; Naithani 2002; Blackburn 2003, Prasad *et al.* 2007).

Postcolonial folklorists have pointed to the role of Indian scholars in the making of colonial collections. Leela Prasad and Stuart Blackburn have highlighted the contributions of Pandit Natesa Sastri in the study of South Indian folklore. The emergence of the unpublished manuscripts of William Crooke's collection of North Indian folktales revealed the role played by his associate Pandit Ram Gharib Chaube. Chaube's example shows that native associates may not actually have been assistants, but scholars and co-authors of colonial collections and that credit may have been denied to them. The processes in which the Crooke-Chaube collection was compiled let Naithani propose that "colonial folkloristics" was a different model from European romantic folkloristics (Naithani 2006).

This hectic phase of colonial folklore scholarship lasted until 1930 and then became dissipated by the historical changes in India and elsewhere. In 1947 India gained independence from British rule and the British administrators, military officers, and missionaries who had been interested in the study of Indian folklore could not pursue this any further, though they had already established Indian folklore in international folkloristics. The number of interested British persons had declined sharply in the 1920s as India's struggle for freedom gained momentum. Simultaneously the number of interested Indian folklorists grew.

Nobel Laureate Rabindranath Tagore had himself popularized folklore by creating folksongs and by promoting folklore in many ways (Dimock 1959: 33). One of these ways was to provide space for a Baul Mela. Baul refers both to a form of mystical devotional music and to its wandering performers. The Mela (fair) continues to be an annual event where Bauls come, camp and perform.

From 1947 the field of Indian folklore had been explored and analyzed by Indian and international scholars, as also by public and private agencies. In 1950s, the need for a bibliography of publications on Indian folklore seemed to have been a major concern for Indian and international scholars, which is evident in the works of K.D. Upadhyaya (1960–1961) and Edwin C. Kirkland (1964). Upadhyaya's bibliography of publications on Indian folklore was organized along the lines of Indian federal states and provided the names of authors/collectors and titles of the works for all regions of India. He neither differentiates between colonial and postcolonial collections, nor between Indian and foreign scholars. Generally, he appreciates every cited work. Another Indian folklorist of the same generation, Ved Prakash Vatuk, felt that this uncritical attitude was the defining characteristic of Indian scholars (Vatuk 2007: 4). Kirkland made an extensive bibliography of Indian folklore publications and wrote an article about the process in which he made various decisions for it (1961). He also mentioned that Upadhyaya handed over his bibliography to Kirkland. Kirkland listed the large number of considerations he had before him while making the bibliography and how he resolved them. Some of the problems of Indian publications, particularly vernacular publications, remain the same: for example, that large numbers of vernacular publications do not have the year of publication and generally no preface or introduction, rendering annotation and analysis difficult. Like Upadhyaya, Kirkland also did not distinguish between colonial and postcolonial publications.

The decades of 1970s and 1980s are distinguished by the contributions of some individuals. In scholarship the works and personality of A.K. Ramanujan drew the attention of international scholars to Indian folklore once again. Ramanujan, based in the United States, was known as a poet, and his retelling of folktales from India placed the subject somewhat outside the anthropological concerns and closer to those of literary studies. Ramanujan did not collect the majority of the tales he retold, but took them from well-known colonial collections (Ramanujan 1991 and 1997; Handoo 2000: 175). Within India, Vijay Dan Detha collected folktales of Rajasthan and retold them in Hindi in fine literary style. Komal Kothari in Rajasthan brought the Langa and Manganiar, and B.V. Karanth in Karnataka brought Yakshagana performers from rural areas into the urban public domain. All three communities of performers gained new popularity with this support and now became directly responsible for the revival and popularity of their art. They perform worldwide. Kothari became a nodal point also for international anthropologists like John Smith and Ann Grodzins Gold (2004) who came to research in Rajasthan. I will shortly return to the present state of his folksong collection.

The Ford Foundation planned a concerted effort in 1980s whereby five folklore collection and research centres were initiated: in Udupi, Chennai, Jodhpur, Tezpur, and in Shillong. All are and have been independent units under of different individuals. The first of these in Udupi, Karnataka is called Regional Research Centre and is part of Mahatma Gandhi College in Udupi. Initially headed by Professor K.S. Haridas Bhat, who was a scholar of Sanskrit, this center commenced its activities by organizing folklore workshops conducted by American folklorist Peter Claus in 1988–1989. Subsequently it focused on oral epics and collaborated on an Indo-Finnish project with Lauri Honko to document the oral epics in the Tulu speaking areas of Karnataka. Lauri Honko's bilingual publication of the Siri Epic was based on this collaboration. The unit in Chennai, called the National Folklore Support Centre, headed by M.D. Muthukumaraswamy is the most visible of all through its series of publications. NFSC has constantly reinvented itself even after the Ford Foundation grant was not renewed, and distributed its newsletter *Indian Folklife* internationally. NFSC has now started making its audio-visual documents freely available through YouTube. The centre in Jodhpur has not really taken off. It was allocated to the elderly independent and public folklorist Komal Kothari in 1995 to organize hundreds of hours of written and audio-recorded folksongs he had collected over three decades. Kothari died soon after, and his descendants have not got beyond getting a rudimentary handwritten catalogue prepared. They have housed the audio materials in an air-conditioned room, and are able to make materials available upon request.[1] The project in the North East of India was based at Tezpur University in Tezpur and in North East Hill University (NEHU) in Shillong. They functioned for a short time and closed due to the withdrawal of the grant by Ford Foundation. Desmond Kharmawphlang, who administered it at NEHU, was told that Ford Foundation's priorities had moved away from folklore.[2]

One of the new institutions in the field of publishing and promoting folklore in a serious and studied manner is the Indira Gandhi National Centre for the Arts in New Delhi. One of its four departments, the Janpada Sampada, headed by folklorist Molly Kaushal, does in-house collection and documentation of various performative, musical and narrative folklore genres. IGNCA staff document in writing as well as in audio-visual formats. Given the ample resources of this privileged institution, collections are increasing at a fast pace and a very limited but committed platform for viewing performances in Delhi is emerging in the IGNCA.

More recently, data on the entire South Asian region has been admirably presented in the most expansive new source for this vast subject: *South Asian Folklore, An Encyclopedia* (2003) edited by Margaret A. Mills, Peter J. Claus, and Sarah Diamond. In many ways, this is the first postcolonial compendium of South Asian Folklore and places a huge amount of previously dispersed as well as new data in perspective. This encyclopedia provides updated information on various folklore and some folk-life practices of the diverse peoples in diverse geographical regions of South Asia. The details of genres, texts, and performance forms have allowed us to have a comprehensive view of this diversity, which can not be easily covered by a single author. The encyclopedia has contributions by experts of different regions, genres, texts and performance and contains valuable information and analysis. Another recent publication on the subject is *South Asian Folklore, A Handbook* (2006), a volume edited by Frank J. Korom. This work, focused mainly on India, is far smaller and limited in its scope and manages to touch upon major folklore genres, texts and performance. Therefore, details of texts, genres, and performative traditions can be referenced from these two encyclopedic sources, among a number of other sources.

Currently a National Mission for Manuscripts, established in 2003 by the central government of India, is in progress. Hundreds of thousands of manuscripts have been located and collected and these might bring to light hitherto unknown and inaccessible sources for Indian folklore.[3]

Yet other sources that have not been systematically studied are the popular and scholarly publications in the vernacular since the nineteenth century. *Folklore of India* is distributed across the country in inexpensive volumes.[4] The most popular of all folktale collections have been various volumes of *Amar Chitra Katha*[5] comics for children. The title of the series can be translated as "immortal picture stories." It was established in 1967 by Ananat Pai precisely to acquaint children with stories from the Indian epics, history, and folklore. Millions of copies are sold every year in about 20 Indian languages, including English. The National Book Trust, a public organization, also publishes small books of folktales from different regions of the country, translated into English and intended for general readers. However, both kinds of publications suffer from the problems cited by Kirkland in 1961. Better books are produced by the Sahitya Akademi (Academy of Letters) and the Sangeet Natak Akademi (Academy of Dance-Drama), but these publications are few and far between and are not distributed vigorously. Both the academies house commendable libraries. Scholarly collections are also produced in different regional languages of India and a study of these would be the best clue to contemporary Indian folkloristics.

Some of the Indian folklorists who have published their works in English are Jawaharlal Handoo, Kishore Bhattacharjee, Puliakonda Subbachary (2002), Guru Rao Bapat (2006) and Soumen Sen, among others. Handoo has written on a number of subjects and promoted the study of folklore during his tenure as folklorist in the Central Institute of Indian Languages, Mysore. Bhattacharjee writes about Assam legends and Sen has concentrated on folktales. Subbachary studies the caste myths of southern India, and Rao Bapat has researched the transformation in the performance of Yakshagana.

Valuable analytical perspectives on Indian folklore have been offered by Arjun Appadurai, Frank Korom, Margaret Mills and their associates in *Gender and Genre in South Asia* (1991). Prominent among the international scholars of Indian folklore in the last quarter of the twentieth century are Stuart Blackburn, Kirin Narayan, Frank Korom, and Leela Prasad, among others. Through various case studies by folklorists, contemporary forms of narratives and songs have become available for research. While Blackburn has studied professional folk performances, Narayan has brought forth the use of folk narratives in the discourse of a religious mendicant (1989) and also documented a woman narrator in the Himalayas (1997). Korom's work is located in Bengal and deals with the scroll painters and narrators of stories depicted. Prasad has documented women's narratives (2006) and continues to investigate issues of ethics in religious discourses.

The collectors have also mentioned, portrayed, and presented the people they collected their narratives from (Narayan, Burckhalter Flueckiger, Blackburn, Wadley). Narayan's (1989) work on a religious mendicant and his discourse give us a glimpse of a type of storyteller that is not only common throughout India, but gaining increasing popularity among urban and international audiences. In yet another work, she portrays a woman storyteller from the Himalayas who is also representative of many others like her. Burckhalter Flueckiger (2006) has profiled a Muslim woman healer and the role of folk narratives in the act of healing. Blackburn lets us see fragments of the lives of the shadow puppet theatre performers. Wadley's study (2004) is based on three decades of interaction with one particular performer of the oral epic Dhola. It lets us visualize not only the performer and his context, but also the complex structure of narrative and verse performance. These studies profile different kinds of narrators and show how diverse the concept of folk performer/ narrator is. One feature that differentiates these works is that Narayan and Burckhalter Flueckiger profile narrators who are fulfilling "another" role (Narayan's *Swamiji* is a religious personality; Burckhalter Flueckiger's *Amma* is a healer) apart from that of being a narrator and performer, while Blackburn and Wadley profile narrators who are "seen" as performers and entertainers (Blackburn's professional puppeteers and Wadley's professional singer of an epic).

MAJOR TEXTS OF INDIAN FOLKLORE

Running across the length and breadth of India are certain story-ideas. In spite of the diversity and differences, the stories of *Panchatantra* and *Jataka* continue to be told by ordinary people as everyday tales. One can say that the overall moral orientation of the Indian folklore is rooted in *Panchatantra* and *Jataka*. The two epics *Ramayana* and *Mahabharata* have innumerable folk and oral versions. The stories of the two epics are performed in all narrative, musical and dance-drama genres, in household and professional performances. One of the features of Indian folklore noted by many scholars is that there is a folk version of almost every classical and mythological story (Thompson 1994: 5, 15). Philosophically, the mystical ideas of the Bhakti movement and of Sufism have influenced folklore overwhelmingly.

Oral epics of India have attracted considerable attention of scholars (Blackburn and Claus 1989). Some of the oral epics are: "Khamba and Toibi" in Manipur, "Madeswara" in Karnataka, "Epic of Kalamariju" in Andhra Pradesh, and the "Pandun ka Kada" sung by Jogis of Mewat, Rajasthan, among others.

Two famous cycles of folktales are Vetal Pachisi, consisting of 25 stories revolving around issues of justice and ethics, and the second, particularly popular in South India, the stories about Tenali Raman – a wise, witty villager and jester.

In the secular realm there are versified legends, as documented by Richard Carnac Temple (1883) in Punjab. These differ from region to region, but the genre is well known. Etiological tales about natural phenomena abound everywhere, but are particularly prominent in the folktales of the North East of India. The North East of India is a distinctive region for folklore. "There are twenty six major tribes and a number of sub-tribes have distinct characteristics in languages and customs" (Barman 2008: 3). In addition to the distinctive tribal cultures and languages there is the presence of all major religious communities. Different tribes have accepted either Hinduism or Christianity as their declared faith, but also integrated it with their tribal identity. Their folklore therefore dates back to their pre-Hindu or pre-Christian identities and tells stories about the origin of the tribes. These myths of origin continue to be believed in, as is the case among the Mizos (Khiangte 2006). Interestingly, the Mizos believe that the oral story is based on a written document which was lost, and along with the story, their script was lost too. The inter-mingling of orality and modernity in the region and the subsequent transformations need to be studied in greater detail for clarity, but the publications continue to be focused on the tribal identity. The region is home to the oldest and the most recent of folklore departments: the University of Guwahati and in the North Eastern Hill University, Shillong, respectively. The first major scholar of the culture of the region was the anthropologist Verrier Elwin.

In the northernmost regions of India the situation of folklore is significantly different from that of the northern, eastern, and southern regions. Laddakh is situated on the eastern side of the northernmost territory and is exclusively Buddhist in faith and Indo-Tibetan in language. From the western side of the northernmost territory to Punjab in the west, the influence of Islam and Sikhism is unmistakable. The songs and stories of medieval Sufi poets are performed in a variety of genres. The region bordered on Afghanistan and Iran and was the route along which Islam and early Muslim rulers of India came. Folklore of the region reflects in performative practices, caste and class relationships, and philosophical ideas as to how people of a multi-religious society accommodate and integrate difference. Famous medieval folk poets like Bulle Shah have commanded the respect and faith of Hindu, Muslim, and Sikh peasantry for hundreds of years and continue to be performed in India, Pakistan, and Bangladesh.

FOLKLORE AND FOLK PERFORMERS IN CONTEMPORARY INDIA

The three issues, in my observation, that concern all professional folk performers today are caste, education, and mobility. These issues are rooted in the contemporary reality of India and did not have any comparable significance, say 50 years ago. Since 1947, India has been a centralized stage and therefore linguistically and aesthetically diverse performers are faced with similar situations across the country. These three issues are inter-linked with reference to the new possibilities and perspectives offered by democratic norms.

Caste

Given the fact that Hinduism is the oldest religion in the region and has impacted on social structures throughout, all professional groups are placed in a certain vertical hierarchy defined as "caste." The "caste" of an individual is determined by birth and cannot be changed. As such, folk performers, too, were placed in the caste hierarchy and assigned definite identification as performers, including obligations to perform and the right to receive patronage. Almost all folk performers belong to lower castes, which coincide with their class status as well. The social injustice embedded in this system is apparent, but that is not the subject of discussion at this point. I will focus my attention on how this system influenced the development of folklore practices in India, and what role it plays today when the Constitution of independent India commits the state not only to removing caste-based discrimination, but also directs it to practice positive discrimination for the development of the lower castes.

For the sake of building an understanding, one can observe how Hindu folk performers are placed in the social structure, how Muslim performers function, and how the religious identities of the folk performers are operating in contemporary secular India. Within Hindu society, folk performers were placed on the lowest rungs of the caste ladder. Yet, as a caste it was their right and duty to continue with their caste profession, complemented by the right of other castes to receive their service and duty to pay for it. In the case of folklore, this meant generations and centuries of a community's professional and social identity. The performance often gained the status of a non-religious ritual. For example, it was necessary to invite the performers to rites of passage, harvests, and visits by important guests. Their performance came in the category of not only entertainment, but was marked as an auspicious event. All this ensured a certain number of performances throughout the year, and consequent remuneration for the folk performers. In certain cases, as throughout the state of Rajasthan, performers were tied in this two-way obligatory relationship, called the *jajmani* system, sometimes at the village level, at other times at the level of a certain set of villages, and at other times they were connected with certain upper caste groups and would perform for them alone. The folk performers themselves could not invade the performance territory of other performers. As such, a definite role, status, and livelihood were ensured for the communities of folk performers.

Professional folk performers have generally been from the "lower castes." Each community of performers has a different caste name, but there are also generic terms for many castes of performers. For example, in northern India *Mirasi* is a common term signifying folk performers, but there is also "one" community which is called "mirasi" that has spread from Haryana in northern India to Pakistan on the west. Linguistically, *Mirasi* is a Persian word,[6] meaning hereditary performer. In a documentary on folk performers of Rajasthan (Sudheer Gupta 2006) I have heard a "mirasi" say that they are so called because their ancestors came from a place called Mirasnagar in Arabia. Police and administrative authorities view "mirasis" with suspicion, a perception that was expressed by colonial folklorist Richard Carnac Temple in 1883. However, there is no doubt that the main occupation of mirasis was that of performers.

If a caste is known for a certain form of performance, then there will be individuals who are known for their talent. It is important to note that a caste of performers does not mean that everyone performs. Individual talent is certainly taken note of by the elders and nurtured, and presented. And yet, this is not the only important task. There will be musical accompaniment from other members. In genres where polyphonic narration is the art there will be more than one narrator on stage. Members of the group will perform all roles from teachers to stage managers. Others not necessarily attending the performance contribute in other ways, for example, by making and maintaining costumes and musical instruments, travel planning, cooking, rearing children, and so on. These roles, however, do not divide the community into differently skilled individuals, because they all see themselves as members of a particular community of performers and can substitute for each other. The popular notions, or even biases, about communities of folk performers would therefore, apply to all in equal measure.

The pre-British infrastructure of support had already become weak by 1947 and continued to disintegrate in independent India. The disintegration is to an extent an essential part and consequence of the making of a democratic and civic society, such as the shift from caste identity to identity as a citizen. The folklore practices have as a result been under severe stress. Loss and extinction of many performative forms cannot be denied. For example, the performance of Nautanki (operatic dance drama in northern states of Uttar Pradesh and Bihar) has almost completely disappeared (Hansen 1992). And yet, there are many other forms that have gained new kinds of performance spaces and revival on new planes of existence, for example Yakshagana (dance drama) in the southern state of Karnataka (Bapat),[7] or Tamasha in Maharashtra (Gargi 1991 [1966]; Zelliot 2003).

One of the factors that played a key role in the transformation was the independence of India and the making of a civic society. As this new nation decided that independence had to be followed by social justice, it took the injustice embedded in the caste system as one point of departure. Henceforth there was to be no discrimination based on caste and no compulsion to follow caste-based professions. In the "secular socialist republic" of India people are free to move into professions according to the rules of the civic society. Having said this, let us now see what it has meant for folk performers who are also lower caste.

The implication of this for folk performers is the same as for all other castes, namely the possibility of choosing one's profession and not have it determined by birth. A large number of people from performers' castes have already taken this step. In July 2009 I witnessed a meeting of the Jogi community in Jodhpur, Rajasthan wherein the overwhelming majority was not practicing the caste-based profession of singing, even though they collectively maintained their caste identity for reasons of social interaction.

"Caste" is not a static category today, but a means of negotiating new identities through the use of a democratic legal framework. One may well ask whether moving out of the village and the new constitution of the country can free the folk performers from their caste status. Caste is something which cannot be changed, and the history of modern India shows that it continues to exist even when its connection with profession is broken up. It even continues to exist in Muslim, Christian, and Sikh communities. The state has attempted to redeem the situation by granting legal equality and opportunities in government employment for the lower castes. While this situation may be made use of unreservedly by other lower castes associated with menial labor, it is different for folk performers because it implies breaking away from their skilled art, that is, from being independent professional artists to accepting the lowest levels of employment. Therefore, many continue to perform. Indeed, the "castes" of performers deserve special consideration if the complexity of their situation is to be addressed.

Education
In pre-colonial and pre-democratic systems the lower castes were denied access to formal education. Today education is one of the most commonly available means of improving one's social status. Except when prevented by abject poverty, folk performers do send their children to school. This is a desirable norm in contemporary society, but presents an unintended contradiction, the creation of other aspirations, for example, that of higher education or other professions. "Increased school-based literacy, with its concomitant expectations for appropriate status behavior (....) compete[s] with older traditions of public performance" (Appadurai 1991: 13).

That education provides the means to choose an identity away from the one given by birth is a democratic phenomenon. Education can also help the folk performers become independent of middlemen and be able to once again control their professional lives, this time in the world of the literate and urbane.

The problem of education is on the other side of the coin. The "education" that is provided by schools and universities does not sensitize students towards the folk performers and their knowledge of poetry, music, dance, religion, region, and so on. A folk performer's child would find no representation of his community or ancestors in school textbooks. At university level, too, the study of folklore in India takes place in less than a dozen departments, and for the majority of the students entering the university system the study of folklore is the most invisible option. Within Indian academia, folklore studies are on the margins.

While researching the subject of folklore in pedagogy, Mallikarjun (2003) came to the conclusion that folklore is used only minimally in school-level teaching and that the stories that are included remain the same over many generations and are used primarily for moral instruction. Mallikarjun also found that the training of teachers for schools did not any include training to use folklore materials. Within the Indian education system folklore, and folk performers, are yet to be considered seriously.

Mobility

The social and economic mobility of folk performers is linked to the above two issues. Moving out of caste-based professions into secular professions implies both social and economic mobility, but what concerns us here is the mobility of those who remain folk performers.

Although the works of the scholars are often balanced in their representation and do not underline the real conditions of the lives of performers, occasional reports in the media tell heart-rending stories about the plight of folk performers in India. For example, there is the well-publicized case of a Tamasha performer, Vithabai Bhau Mang Narayangaonkar (1932–2002). Tamasha is one of the traditions that was able to gain increased popularity in the twentieth century. Women are the major performers of an acrobatic dance form in this musical dance-drama which plays on sexual double entendre. Vithabai gained fame, awards, and was photographed receiving certificates and decorations from national and international dignitaries. And yet, at 70 she was reported to be ill, penniless, and neglected by all (http://openspaceindia.org). Women performers have been subject to sexual exploitation by their upper-caste, upper-class patrons. A revealing autobiographical account of this has been presented by the son of a Tamasha artist, translated as *Against All Odds*. Ironically, Kishore Shantabai Kale was disowned by his mother, as Tamasha women always vowed never to reveal the name of their secret lovers, whose social status was at risk. Such stories in today's India abound and most of the folklorists have come across amazingly talented and widely recognized artists spending their last days in penury and loneliness. These images do not form part of the picture of Indian folklore given in encyclopedias and works focused on collection, translation, and compilation of texts.

Folk performers have experienced social and spatial mobility in the last few decades. Some of them have had international exposure, while others have experienced an expansion of performance contexts in urban centers. Yet, it does not seem to have been seconded by upward economic mobility. In earlier times, folk performers often practiced a second profession. For example, Jhusiya Damai, whom I documented in 2000 on the border of India and Nepal, was not only a performer of heroic legends, but was also a tailor at other times of the year when farmers were busy sowing and tending to their fields and it was not the folklore performance season. In the southern state of Andhra Pradesh the *Ogukatha* performers whom I met in February 2010 in Kuppam, Karnataka, were shepherds. Through these alternating means of livelihood, the communities would have had the time and the obligation to refine their art and perhaps for this reason we find in India highly accomplished folk artists who are also poor and illiterate. The breaking up of caste structures has implied that the possibility of a second profession has vanished or become undesirable. Many of the performers work occasionally for the promotion of state welfare policies, like literacy campaigns, polio vaccinations, rural development, and so on.

So the issue of mobility is complicated. If we look at it from the point of view of the caste system, we may be able to see some mobility, if not upward, then certainly farther away from the confines of the caste. If we evaluate it in terms of performance context, we might see expansion in that arena. From the point of view of the economic situation of the folk artists, mobility may even be downward and the major cause of people giving up the practice of their art.

The role of the independent Indian state is also an issue that is connected with the lives of the folk performers in India. Time and again educated individuals have sensitized various governments to the situation of folk performers and they have responded in a variety of ways. In 1950s the then government decided to allow nomadic folk performers to settle in the outskirts of Delhi. This settlement is called "Kathputli (puppet) Colony" after the first settlers – the puppeteers – and continues to house hundreds of folk performers, albeit in very poor living conditions. In 1980s the state provided international exposure to folk performers by exhibiting their arts in Festivals of India across the world. This became, for many performers, like the Langa and Manganiar communities of Rajasthani performers, a source of regular invitations to perform abroad and earn an additional income. In the same decade, the central government also instituted Zonal Cultural Centres in different parts of the country which are supposed to promote regional cultural activities. The work of these centers has not really been appreciated in the public domain, but at closer investigation it is evident that they provide minimal support to folk artists. Whatever the state has provided is, needless to say, far from consistent and sufficient, but not insignificant.

Another form of mobility is that of the form and texts of folklore, which have remained almost completely out of the international scholarship on Indian folklore. Transformations in form and value of folklore were created by communist cultural activists since 1943 at the beginning of the last phase of the freedom struggle against British colonial rule. Organized under the Indian Peoples' Theatre Association, communist activists established bases in rural areas and small towns across the country with the intention of expressing a new consciousness in the language and artistic forms of the downtrodden (Ramakrishna 2006). Forms of folk narratives, theatre, song and music were transformed to express people's lives and struggles. The influence of this movement was definitive on the struggle for freedom, as the popularity of IPTA productions cut across various social and creative divides. The influence of IPTA on the Hindi film industry (Bollywood) in 1940s and 1950s was not only indirect, but was actually affected by the participation of members in the making of many films.

Although the Communist Party of India faced its first division in 1956, and then again in the 1960s, the engagement of communist activists with performative and narrative folklore forms has continued. One of its most important figures today is Ghaddar in Andhra Pradesh, who has been championing the cause of impoverished tribal members and other sections of the populace in the state of Andhra Pradesh. He has come to be seen as an enemy of the state. His performances have been banned and he has been shot at by the police several times. Ghaddar was the son of a construction worker father and an agricultural laborer mother who was also a village singer and abandoned his degree course in Engineering to sing of peoples' struggle for survival. He observes, researches, listens and meditates upon various performative folklore genres to present his own transformations of them, but the link with specific folklore forms is unmistakable and explicit. Today, his performances and songs have influenced not only the regional film industry, but even his political opponents parody his songs to suit their own purposes (Rao 2006). However, I saw the highest level of Ghaddar's influence when I recently heard OGU Katha performers proudly elaborate upon how Ghaddar's form of performance is essentially their own. This is not a relationship of resentment which folk performers have vis-à-vis commercial film makers and the music industry. Ghaddar has "returned" to the community what he received, with more power (Rao 2006: 102–103).

CONCLUSION

The huge variety of folklore in India has charmed folklorists just as it has kept the people of India enchanted with themselves. Even though it is not possible to encompass this variety in an article, it is still evident that many elements of this variety have been studied and documented in print and audio-visual media. Many others remain undocumented.

Indian folklore today also presents new challenges for researchers because its performers are responding to current realities by transforming their "traditional" practice and, in certain cases, gaining a new lease of life for themselves and their art.

Indian folklore is also being documented, and promoted by a wide variety of agencies – from governmental to radical political, from local to international, and from scholarly to philanthropic. As before, it continues to present interesting texts and contexts for study.

Contemporary folk performers in India are also becoming self-reflective and trying to change their situation by introducing changes in their performative tradition and by adopting various civil society measures. Some of them have established NGOs and brought many groups of artists under them. They are also beginning to forge new solidarities with other performers' groups and castes. As such, they are also transforming the nature of Indian folklore studies, from the study of constant traditional practices to that of innovations and transformations.

NOTES

1 This information was given by Kuldeep Kothari, son of Komal Kothari and current manager of Rupayan Sansthan and Arna Jharna Museum. I visited both institutions in May 2010.
2 As told to me by Desmond Kharmawphlang in an email. I am thankful to Desmond Kharmawphlang for the information and the permission to use it in this chapter.
3 All information relating to the project is available at www.namami.org.
4 A sample of these books can be found at http://www.infibeam.com. Typically the books have no introductions.
5 Titles of the volumes and other details can be found at www.amarchitrakatha.com. A critical study of the publications is: Nandini Chandra (2008) *The Classic Popular. Amar Chitra Katha 1967–2007*, New Delhi, Yoda Press.
6 For a detailed discussion on this term, see: Horace Arthur Rose (1911) *A Glossary of the Tribes and Castes of the Punjab and North-West Frontier Provinces* 1(3). Reprint 1990 Delhi: Asian Educational Services, 108–110.
7 Bapat's PhD thesis "The Semiotics of Yakshagana" is available online at http://despace.vidyanidhi.org.in.

REFERENCES

Bapat, Guru Rao. 2006. "Performance as Discourse" in M.D. Muthukumaraswamy, Ed., *Folklore as Discourse*. Chennai: National Folklore Support Centre.

Barman, Bhaskar Roy. 2008. *Folktales of Northeast India*. Delhi: Gnosis.

Benfey, Theodor. 1859. *Pantschtantra: Fünf Bücher indischer Fabeln, Märchen und Erzählungen*. Göttingen.

Blackburn, Stuart. 1996. *Inside the Drama House*. Berkeley: University of California Press.

Blackburn, Stuart. 2003. *Print, Folklore, and Nationalism in Colonial India*. Delhi: Permanent Black.

Blackburn, Stuart and Peter J. Claus. 1989. *Oral Epics in India*. Berkeley: University of California Press.

Burckhalter Flueckiger, Joyce. 2006. *In Amma's Healing Room. Gender and Vernacular Islam in South Asia*. Bloomington: Indiana University Press.

Dorson, Richard M. 1968. *The British Folklorists: A History*. Chicago: University of Chicago Press.

Frere, Mary. 1868 [2002]. *Old Deccan Days*. Introduction by Kirin Narayan, Ed. Santa Barbara: ABC-CLIO.

Gargi, Balwant. 1966 [1991]. *Folk Theatre of India*. Calcutta: Rupa and Company, pp. 73–88.

Grodzins Gold, Ann. 2004. "Original Tales: Komalda, Goddess Shrines, Breathing Space." Keynote address delivered May 20, 2004 at Columbia University, NYC, for a conference entitled "Remembering Komal Kothari. A Conference on Intellectual Contributions to Scholarship on Rajasthan and Folklore." www.arnajharna.org/English/Komal_Kothari_Writings_on.aspx (accessed October 16, 2011).

Handoo, Jawaharlal. 2000. *Theoretical Essays in Indian Folklore*. Mysore: Zooni Publications.

Hansen, Kathryn. 1992. *Grounds for Play: The Nautanki Thatre of North India*. Berkeley: University of California Press.

Khiangte, Laltluangliana. 2006. "The Discourse in Oral Society of the Mizos" in M.D. Muthukumaraswamy, Ed. *Folklore as Discourse*. Chennai: National Folklore Support Centre.

Kirkland, Edwin. 1961. "A Bibliography of South Asian Folklore." *Journal of American Folklore* 74: 413–418.

Mills, Margaret, Peter Claus and Sarah Diamond. 2003. *South Asian Folklore: An Encyclopedia.* New York, London: Routledge.

Narayan, Kirin. 1989. *Storytellers, Saints and Scoundrels. Folk Narrative in Hindu Religious Teaching.* Philadelphia: University of Pennsylvania Press.

Narayan, Kirin, in collaboration with Urmila Devi Sood. 1997. *Mondays on the Dark Night of the Moon. Himalayan Foothills Folktales.* New York: Oxford University Press.

Naithani, Sadhana. 2002. "Prefaced Space" in Luisa del Guidice and Gerald Porter, Eds. *Imagined States. Nationalism, Utopia and Longing in Oral Cultures.* Logan: Utah University Press.

Naithani, Sadhana. 2006. *In Quest of Indian Folktales.* Bloomington: Indiana University Press.

Naithani, Sadhana. 2010. *The Story-Time of the British Empire. Colonial and Postcolonial Folkloristics.* Jackson: Mississippi University Press.

Prasad, Leela, Ruth B. Bottigheimer, and Lalita Handoo. 2007. *Gender and Story in South India.* Albany: SUNY Press.

Rao, D. Venkat. 2006. "Risking Spaces: The Politics and the Pain of Singing" in Simon Charsley and Laxmi Narain Kadekar, Eds. *Performers and their Arts. Folk, Popular and Classical Genres in a Changing India.* New Delhi: Routledge.

Subbachary, Pulikonda. 2006. "Caste Myth: A Multi Voice Discourse" in M.D. Muthukumaraswamy, Ed. *Folklore as Discourse.* Chennai: National Folklore Support Centre.

Swynnerton, Charles. 1892. *Indian Nights Entertainment. Folk Tales from Upper Indus. With Numerous Illustrations by Native Hands.* London: Elliot Stock.

Temple, Richard Carnac. 1883–1985 [1962]. *Legends of Punjab.* Vols. 1–3. Patiala: Punjabi University Press.

Thompson, Stith. 1946. *The Folktale.* Berkeley: University of California Press.

Vatuk, Ved Prakash. 1966 [2007]. "Method and Interpretation in the Study of Folklore in India. A Comment." *Journal of the Indian Anthropological Society* 1: 156–166 (reprinted in Kira Hall, Ed. *Essays in Indian Folk Tradition. Collected Writings by Ved Prakash Vatuk*). Meerut: Archana Publications.

Wadley, Susan. 2004. *Raja Nal and the Goddess. The North Indian Epic Dhola in Performance.* Bloomington: Indiana University Press.

Zelliot, Eleanor. 2003. "Tamasha" in Margaret Mills, Peter Claus, and Sarah Diamond, Eds. *South Asian Folklore. An Encyclopedia.* New York, London: Routledge.

FURTHER READING

Islam, Makbul. 2006. "Shifting Identity of Performing Artists: The Patuas of Bengal" in Simon Charsley and Laxmi Narain Kadekar, Eds. *Performers and their Arts. Folk, Popular and Classical Genres in a Changing India.* New Delhi: Routledge.

Mayaram, Shail, 2004. "On Komal Kothari." *Indian Folklife* 3, 3(16): 8–10.

Nair, Venugopal. 2006. "Jagar as Discourse" in M.D. Muthukumaraswamy, Ed. *Folklore as Discourse.* Chennai: National Folklore Support Centre.

FILM

Gupta, Sudheer. 1996. *Ananat Kalakar*, a documentary film about an Indian folk performer.

CHAPTER 13 OCEANIA

Phillip H. McArthur

For a place that has received much unwanted attention for its exotic appeal, and for a place situated at the center of some of the grandest anthropological debates, Oceania receives very little attention from European and American folklorists. Indeed, its near absence from many global anthologies and most discussions within the discipline remains stark. One will need to search long and hard to find how folklore materials or ethnographies from Oceania have informed the prevailing theories or discussions fostered in the Western world within the discipline the past 50 years. Because disciplinary objectives have long followed national interests (Abrahams 1993), folklorists most often attend to traditions in close proximity, either the dominant tradition of the nation or "otherness" lingering in the cracks of the modern state. Accordingly, groups defined by class, occupation, location, religion or ethnicity become the locus of investigation, whereas those in "far-away-places" typically belong to the purview of anthropologists and a few historians. If anthropology went out on the coattails of the colonial project, then folklore has found its purpose within the context of modern nationalism. Of course folklorists have researched beyond Euro-America, and yet the distant "other" in Oceania has escaped much of the discipline's attention, all the while it has captured the romantic imagination of novelists, travel writers, and anthropologists.

Oceania is burdened by the "noble savage" portrayal that captured the imagination of the West at least since the eighteenth-century voyages of Captains Cook and Bougainville, and reports of these "happy people" living carefree in "paradise." This exotic image was paradoxically both a longed for fantasy and simultaneously held up with a degree of disdain by both Enlightenment thinkers and Victorian apologists. The island savage, albeit "noble," was nonetheless positioned on the lower end of the social evolutionary scale. This romantic spin on a social inferior was no more positive than the view that the islanders were debased heathens in need of conversion and civilization. The romantics wanted to keep the islanders in their place, as relics of an

A Companion to Folklore, First Edition. Edited by Regina F. Bendix and Galit Hasan-Rokem.
© 2012 John Wiley & Sons, Ltd. Published 2012 John Wiley & Sons, Ltd.

idealized past, while the missionaries saw in them a capacity for change, to "be like us." Even so, island peoples offered an ideal target for study with their clearly demarcated populations, seemingly culturally static traditions, and lack of civilized respectability – just so much bacchanalia and stories of cannibalism. Even with this condescending posture, the islanders stood for something admirable; they were the descendants of ancient navigators who sparked imaginations about dangerous prehistoric expeditions, erotic liaisons, and the bloodlust of the xenophobic. How could a backward people achieve such impressive sailing feats? Admired and look down upon at the same time, the Pacific Islander has always occupied an ambivalent position in the Western imagination.

In contrast to folklore studies, within anthropology Oceania retains a charmed position even if the actual number of scholars pales in comparison to other world areas. Thanks to the great theoretical impact of Malinowski and his researches in the Trobriand Islands (1922, 1926), Oceania lays claim to the first longitudinal ethnography and a secure place in the theoretical genealogy of the discipline. From magic coral gardens and *kula* rings to the sex life of savages, Malinowski's work retains its place among the standard readings in anthropology. His psychological functionalism did infiltrate some discussions in folklore at mid-century (e.g., Bascom 1954, but as such arguments waned, so did most ethnographic examples from Oceania. Malinowski gave ample attention to traditional narratives and vernacular forms, in many ways his influence on the tripartite generic designations of myth, legend and folktale continue their import. But perhaps even more consequential was his emphasis on the significance of folklore as an active and immediate resource in the conduct of social life. Long ago he recognized that narratives do not merely reflect culture and social structure, but function in times of social strain and where profound historical changes have taken place. But today Malinowski is known for his confessional journals full of libidinal strain, and the angry, disdainful attitude toward the natives resulting from his own culture shock (Clifford 1988; Torgovnick 1990). His legacy has also taken other critical hits; he just got his primitive economic theory wrong and missed the point for how gender plays out in the exchanges of a matrilineal society (Weiner 1996), and he overemphasized the principle of exchange as a tangible display commodity and missed how the Kula ring comprises a "total sensory fact" that engages the oral and aural social norms more than the visual (Howes 2003).

While this anthropological ancestor has been the recipient of an aggressive deconstruction, the Margaret Mead and Derrick Freeman debate has garnered even more attention. Commentators have spilled enough ink now by taking sides between these two American and Australian luminaries respectively to rival what either one of them originally produced. At the heart of the controversy remains Mead's representation of female adolescent sexuality (1928) and Freeman's claim (1983, 1999) that she not only lacked the language skills and got the ethnography wrong, but the Samoan girls she interviewed duped her. Motivated by a Boasian relativism, Mead wished to document socialization and the cultural formation of personality. Her work gained immense notoriety when it spoke to an emerging sexual liberation in America in the 1920s and 1930s and challenged its middle-class sensibilities. Campaigning for a cultural ecological model, Freeman made a career out of challenging one of American Anthropology's darlings and disciplinary popularizers. His attacks were aggressive with the intent to smear her character as much as academically challenge her scholarship. After a generation of "Thrashing Margaret Mead" by scholars and indigenous writers, more recent commentary presents Freeman as riddled with his own pathological resentments and fear of this dominant female figure (Shankman 2009). Whatever position one takes, this controversy makes for a good story and has drawn a great deal of attention to Oceania, but regrettably, it reconfirms and perpetuates its exotic status. Very little folkloristic value can be found in either Mead's or Freeman's pages, but they do remind us how scholarship itself is narrative making, and that variation, an inevitable result of positioning, reveals how stories come into conflict.

A more recent debate within anthropology and centered in Oceania speaks more directly to folklore and raises thorny questions with which folklorists continually grapple. Marshall Sahlins' classic description (1981) of the death of Captain Cook at Kealakakua Bay by the hands of Hawaiians in 1779 served to illustrate his structural history. Simply put, Sahlins argued that Cook's positive reception by the Hawaiians, and then subsequent killing, resulted from the captain inadvertently stepping right into a mythological and ritual cycle of the Hawaiians. Cook's arrival corresponded to the annual return of the God *Lono* (the deity of fertility, crops and rain). With such propitious timing, natives welcomed him with all the pomp and treatment of divinity. After several days of the most extraordinary and lavish treatment, Cook departs, confident in his status as a dominant Englishman respected and admired by the islanders. His unfortunate return a few days later in order to repair a broken mast results in a very different reception. This time the Hawaiians are hostile, agitated, and become aggressive, ultimately dispatching the captain, confiscating his body, removing his flesh, then archiving his bones at sacred *heiau* (temples). Sahlins proposes that the abrupt shift in Hawaiian disposition turned because Cook's return disrupted the mythological cycle, forcing the Hawaiians to reconcile the incongruence. The alternative provided by the narrative was to sacrifice the god and acquire his *mana*.

Sahlins does recognize the complex political machinations on the ground in Hawai'i at the time of Cook's arrival and that played out in the captain's death, but he chooses to emphasize how the Hawaiian response enacted and reenacted a story, and that such histories are made and structured by narratives that have deep salience and meaning. Mythic narratives provide a sense-making resource for history. Gananath Obeyesekere (1992), a Sri Lanka-born anthropologist, challenges Sahlins with a polemical attack; if anyone has fallen into myth-making it was not the Hawaiians but Sahlins. Obeyesekere puts forward that Sahlins represents a long line of Euro-Americans who have fashioned an apotheosis of Captain Cook to justify their colonial ambitions and rationalize their dominance. The real interest was not the events that took place at Kealakekua Bay that day, but how people like Sahlins perpetuate the myth of their own privilege. In this case an American anthropologist has fallen into a trap by mischaracterizing the "other" and assuming he can look through the lens of their narratives and represent their thinking. He claims that Sahlins misunderstood the Hawaiian response; they did not really kill him as a god but attempted to protect themselves from an invader who would not go away when offered gifts and a friendly greeting.

As with all good debates people take sides, and again, much effort has gone into the defense of either Sahlins or Obeyesekere, most notably by themselves. Folklorists will quickly detect that the intertextual relationship that developed within this debate comes to rival the interest in the substance of each argument. Here narrative texts are recentered into publications by these two non-islanders, resulting in continual text-making, all the while relegating Hawaiian voices into an obscure in-between location. Sahlins' aggressive response to Obeyesekere came in the form of a book (1995) longer and more thoroughly presented than his initial publications that sparked the controversy. Obeyesekere for his part replied to Sahlin's response with a significantly extended "Afterward" (nearly 60 pages) in the subsequent printing of his book. The barbs were sharp, and clever diminutives hurled back and forth. Obeyesekere continued to represent Sahlins as a colonial perpetuator and a smug theoretician. Sahlins countered with a vitriolic questioning of Obeyesekere's paucity of ethnographic justification and questioning his own position as an outsider who presumptuously feels privileged to represent the voice of the native. These attacks and counter-attacks bordered on racism. Within this grand debate a folklorist cannot help but see how both anthropologists appropriate cultural property to spin their respective narratives for and about the Hawaiians. The textual interplay becomes dizzying and opens wide the door to the politics of representation; it provides a cautionary tale to the practice of folklore research.

These celebrated debates have reverberated throughout the discipline of anthropology and demonstrate that Oceania remains a contested ground for theory. Ironically, they also perpetuate the peripheralization of the region by reconfirming its strange and alien status; it represents more a playground for tourists and scholars alike than a serious location for consideration of the people who live there. Much in these debates centers more on academic discourse than understanding Pacific Islanders, and the folklore of Oceania has too often proven a resource more for outsider invectives with each other than understanding it within the cultural and historical contexts of the islanders. I do not put forward here a diatribe on theory, far from it, but simply a recognition that folklore research characterizes a practice in text-making that includes the appropriation of the texts of cultural others, and that it behooves us to be cautious about becoming territorial over our representations of the "other" that minimize their presence. For this reason, folklore scholarship may offer a corrective in Oceania by supplying a renewed focus on the text-making by the islanders and their representations of themselves, even within the complex context of ethnographer and subject (cf. Seitel this volume). Despite the absence of folklorists in the larger Pacific debates, indigenous activists and scholars equally may welcome the bottom-up approach to a folklore method.

A difficulty with discussing folklore in Oceania is that the three regional designations (Melanesia, Polynesia, Micronesia) are themselves a product of colonial impress. Native and scholar alike now bring these sub-regions into question. At one end of the challenge are those who argue that the boundaries have never been fixed, that cultural flows, outliers, and population continuities have always been the reality in Oceania, and any hard and fast designation obscures more than it reveals (Hanlon 1989; Mahina 1999; Kirch 2000). Regional lines drawn on a map are nothing more than Western impositions that have served colonial administrations, but do not reflect real cultural identifiers and cultural groupings (Hereniko 1999). The indigenous scholar Epelui Hau'ofa championed this position most elegantly. He sought to undermine the colonial gaze and reposition the whole argument about these far flung islands when he redrew Oceania into an inclusive whole, "Our Sea of Islands" (1993). He contended that a re-envisioning of the region in terms of the islander experience leads to a different metaphor; instead of viewing the ocean as something that divides and separates, it has always provided a link and a "highway" of communication and exchange. While the historical movement of people and culture across the whole of Oceania is clearly substantiated, others remain less willing to quickly abandon the regional designations, especially linguists who highlight language continuities and discontinuities. Whereas Polynesia, the largest region covering 180 million square kilometers, shows immense continuity among core cognate words and grammatical structures, Melanesia may represent the most linguistically diverse location on the planet, some counting from 600 to 800 distinct languages. Others have also recently countered the wish to abandon the sub-regions (e.g., Petersen 2009). They argue that environmental and historical factors (e.g., the breadfruit revolution and trade among matrilineal groups in Micronesia) have indeed generated clearly identifiable continuities within each respective region.

The absence of folklorists in Oceania in some measure is unexpected since much of the research in the region has centered on migration and diffusion. During the heyday of the historic-geographic method Oceania may have offered a paradigmatic testing ground for this folkloristic objective. Arguments about the origins of the islanders of Oceania have enjoyed a long history (see Howe 2003; Kirch 2000). The range of propositions is too vast and varied to go into here. In any case, the general arguments have either proposed a migratory departure from South America and a westward migration (least supported), or an eastern migration out of South Asia in a sequence of starts and stops until all of Oceania was colonized (most supported). Still others now provide compelling evidence for an Asian point of origin out of Taiwan. The peoples of Oceania, known as Austronesians (with the much older Papuans in Highland New Guinea), cover the largest language area in the world from Madagascar in the west of the Indian Ocean, to Hawai'i in the north Pacific, and Rapanui in the southeast. Prehistoric studies on origins and dispersions include archeology, historical linguistics, genetics, geography, and even extraterrestrial explanations. A migration theory has not only been the obsession of academics, but questions of origin and inter-island travel have led to bold contemporary seafaring projects (Finney 1994) that contribute to cultural renaissance movements, efforts at regional solidarity, and post-colonial resistance. The struggle has also generated indigenous counter narratives to the positivist claims – the islanders resist being told about who they are by outsiders (e.g., Hereniko 2000). The absence of folklorists in these efforts, whether scientific or romantic, reveals the discipline's minimal consequence to the region. Those few folklorists who have made a foray into the region have left an uneven influence on subsequent scholarship, either in the discipline or the culture area.

And indeed, the seemingly esoteric effort by the folklorist Bacil Kirtley, a student of Stith Thompson, characterized a clearly marked attempt to make the case for the historic-geographic method most suited to the large-scale migratory studies. Using the same categorization and identification scheme laid out by Thompson in the *Motif-Index of Folk Literature*, Kirtley created first an Oceania-wide index ("A Motif Index of Polynesian, Micronesian, and Melanesian Folktales," 1955) for his dissertation, and then published the geographically more limited, *A Motif-Index of Traditional Polynesian Narratives* (1971). Nothing indicates that this index enjoyed much service within folklore studies and only a smattering of nods from Pacific scholars. Only recently have some scholars revisited Kirtley's indexes to situate their collections within the larger region, but motif identifications are relegated to footnotes and do not provide any real point of departure for discussions about historical or cultural significance. This is inopportune, since Kirtley provided carefully crafted indexes that drew upon the extant sources of his time. The real challenge for the whole legacy of motif indeces remains, however; their utility has been limited to cross-referencing without informing theory or the trajectory of folklore studies. So Kirtley's work remains obscure within folklore and among Pacific scholars, resulting in a negligible impress on migration and diffusion studies.

The most well-known folklorist to work in Oceania was the incomparable Martha Beckwith, the first scholar to hold an academic chair of folklore in the United States, and a former President of the American Folklore Society. Beckwith had a long and noteworthy career at Vassar College and her work in Hawai'i served as the foundation to much of her subsequent scholarship. Her method and objectives followed from Franz Boas, her mentor at Columbia University, and reflect both nostalgia for the Hawaiian materials and the fastidious attempt to salvage the folklore of a highly colonized and changing culture. Her collection of *Hawaiian Mythology* (1940) remains to this day one of the most comprehensive presentations of the archipelago's narratives and a bestseller both in bookstores and mega-department store outlets. Not only is the breadth of narratives impressive and the translation absorbing, but without the aid of indeces she provided comparative versions to other parts of Polynesia. And despite the pretense to a simple offering of an unmediated collection of stories, her politic still comes through; these narratives provide a counter to the intense colonization by the United States after the illegal overthrow in 1898 of Queen Lilokalani by US businessmen. While not overt, Beckwith reminds the English-speaking world that these stories belong to another language and have their life in a deeply rooted culture struggling for survival.

This work has received mixed reception from the indigenous Hawaiian population. Some hail it a great contribution to the preservation of oral traditions by one who cared deeply about them, while others see in it a devious form of appropriation and an unwelcome voice of advocacy. Nonetheless, Beckwith is still read, much more outside the academy than in it. Despite the recognition generated by the narrative collection, her most complete contribution to Hawaiian folklore specifically and Oceania generally was her translation of *The Kumulipo: A Hawaiian Creation Chant* (1951), and her commentary on this sophisticated oral tradition. In this work she contextualized the social and historical background of the chant within the setting of Hawaiian religious values, cosmology, and sacred genealogies. Most impressively, she recognized that the chant was not a product from the immemorial past but represented an undertaking for very distinct purposes in the more recent development of Hawaiian polity and the ascendency of the Kamehameha dynasty. Her presentation of the chant also foreshadowed the priorities of ethnopoetics long before they entered folklore research by rendering the chant in verse lines using parallelism, meter and pause, and other poetics devices so essential to the elaborate multiplication of vowel sounds in the Hawaiian language. Her commentary is both descriptive and interpretive about culture and the production of the chant, and again similar to her mythology collection, she links the form and content of the chant to other parts of Polynesia. These publications situate Beckwith within folklore's grand legacy of advocacy work. Unfortunately, outside her popular success among Hawai'i readers, her specific work in the islands has mostly remained unrecognized in folklore scholarship, albeit her career as a folklorist who worked in Oceania is sometimes noted.

Trained under the tutelage of Alfred Kroeber and Robert Lowie at University of California, Berkeley, the folklorist Katherine Luomala joined Beckwith's efforts. Concentrating again on Hawai'i, she worked for many years at the Bishop Museum in Honolulu and taught courses at the University of Hawai'i. Her scholarship ranged from Hawaiian puppetry to Polynesian myth and chant (1955). Using the myth of "Snaring the Sun," a widely distributed narrative motif throughout Oceania, she also drew comparisons to similar Native American and African versions (1940). Perhaps the most widely read work that bears her name included a set of essays, *Directions in Pacific Traditional Literature: Essays in Honor of Katherine Luomala* (Kaeppler and Nimmo 1976), published to credit her contribution to folklore studies in the Pacific. While this publication seemed to launch a renewed interest in folklore in Oceania, progress seemed to stall and the study of oral traditions remains with anthology popularizers, anthropologists, and an occasional historian.

Drawing hard boundaries between disciplines often proves counter-productive, yet the general point of departure of both anthropology and history signal dissimilarities with folklore. Anthropologists, usually less sensitive to performance texts and textual histories, most often condense a corpus of renderings into a generic or composite text on their way to using it to enter into further discussions on religion and belief, social structure, or culture history. Folklore is more often viewed as a reflection of culture and society rather than constitutive of it. Historians on the other hand, uncomfortable with variation and the dynamism of folklore performances, situate oral traditions, not within their own textual history, but as additional sources to flesh out local histories when they corroborate with written documents (e.g., Mercer 1979). Neither discipline typically addresses intertextuality or performance in situated contexts. Nonetheless, practitioners from all these disciplines, including folklore studies, have compiled collections of folklore without often recognizing how such an undertaking is embedded in ideological contexts; how, when, and by whom the collections are made reveal a sociology of control over the words of others. Even translations manifest ideological decisions. A copious abundance of folklore collections on the three regions of Oceania and most island groups within have been published by popularizers, all the same any careful contextualization and folkloristic analysis is left wanting. While these collections afford resources to texts and cultures, their greater import lies in how they supply information about the text-making project itself, riddled with political intent, usually for national purposes, or promoted as popular commodity.

One folklorist who dabbled in Oceania and then left was Indiana University-trained Roger Mitchell who contributed a corpus of folklore with his collection of *Micronesia Folktales* (1973). This title alone reveals his folkloristic background. While most collections in Oceania either use the myth, legend, or oral tradition genre labels (e.g. Andersen 1928), Mitchell felt confident using this etic designation for fiction. But this approach lacks purpose and does not attend to how islanders think about their own narrative forms. Some of the most engaging scholarship, too, often stays hidden in obscure journal articles, and this appears the case for Mitchell. His most discerning piece, "Oral Tradition and Micronesia History: a Microcosmic Approach" (1970) represents an exemplary folkloristic effort in Oceania. In this little known publication Mitchell demonstrates how a seemingly insignificant scuffle in the late nineteenth-century between two islands within the Chuuk archipelago resulted in a long-term stereotype about the "hospitable" women of one of the islands because of their role in procuring a visiting German ship captain's aide that turned the course of battle. In this compelling piece Mitchell outlines how, within a "micro-history" (clearly playing upon the term for the region) the legend corroborates with the written documents and can be checked for dates. But more importantly, it reveals how people keep oral traditions alive when they continue to bear on contemporary social affairs. In this case the strain between the two islands remains a point of contention. These legends give flesh to the barebones descriptions of historical events to illuminate how the islanders perceive the past and make it meaningful in the present. Most tellingly, the written source in this case demonstrates as much bias and self-censorship as the oral account, since the German's log carefully avoids anything about the "hospitality" of the native women, while the oral account accentuates this key historical variable.

Despite the fact that folklorists are largely absent in Oceanic research, a few representative scholars have shown a nuanced understanding of the folklore process. Three illustrative works from each of the regions demonstrate a careful attention to oral traditions. From Micronesia, the work by the American anthropologist Richard Parmentier, *The Sacred Remains: Myth, History, and Polity in Belau* (1987), provides a complex semiotic analysis of the verbal and nonverbal signs (e.g., landscapes and stone figures) through which the islanders transmitted historical knowledge and transformed Belauan traditional politics. He mixes historical, linguistic, and ethnographic methods to present the place of oral traditions in pre-contact social relations and the coding of historical consciousness. Stories and other signs of history on the landscape that were recorded, transmitted, and manipulated set in course a complex history of matrilineal authority and ranked island districts, villages, and houses, all part of a sacred history that reproduces political hierarchy through a series of changing events.

From Polynesia, a book by the Finnish scholars Anna-Leena and Jukka Siikala, *Return to Culture: Oral Tradition and Society in The Southern Cook Islands* (2005) integrates a folkloristic analysis with social anthropology to present a well-rounded study that brings to parity attention to textual traditions, repertoires, and genres with sociological considerations of the Cook Islander social politics and the cosmological underpinnings of historical relations. They follow the social base of folklore from the local to modern state structures, and beyond. Their study provides a laudable work on both how folklore, in part, generates social life, and how society reciprocally animates traditional discourses. Cook Islander voices are not obscured by theory here, but become foregrounded through texts and ethnographic descriptions of specific social settings.

From Melanesia, a most engaging work was completed by neither anthropologist nor historian, but the French geographer, Joel Bonnemaison, *The Tree and the Canoe: History and Ethnogeography of Tanna* (1986). In this treatise he contextualizes one of the so called cargo cults named the "John Frum Movement" in a small island of Vanuatu. He concentrates especially on the historical contact records and mythological narratives about space and place, and how the Tanna Islanders imagine current colonial events within the context of their mythical landscape. The islanders draw upon this story to create a cultural identity that flows from memories and stories anchored in the land. It provides a logic for integrating Christianity with their own "Kastom," each granting a different way of knowing about the past and even the future. Research on the John Frum participants continues with the support of the Vanuatu Cultural Center which collaborates with scholars to document this movement. As with many emerging Pacific nations, the interplay of indigenous expressions, scholarship, and government objectives contribute to novel formations of identity underpinned with political interests.

Regardless of the dearth of folklore scholarship on Oceania, some recent research trends provide optimism for new considerations of folklore in the region. The following directions and representative scholarship present promising possibilities for folklore research in Oceania.

Folklore and Philosophy – Scholars such as Gregory Schrempp (1992) and a group of Melanesianists have charted new territory by placing folklore materials into conversation with philosophical considerations. Much of this work attends to indigenous cosmologies that correspond to deep Western concerns with ontology, epistemology, and phenomenology. These scholars demonstrate how much of the Western philosophical tradition may find a home in the cultures of Oceania; the two traditions simply represent alternative discursive strategies for arriving at the same point. While Western philosophy uses the individually produced written text and the tools of logic, philosophical ruminations in Oceania are embedded in traditional narratives, the result of a deep historical collective undertaking. For instance, Schrempp illuminates how the Maori myth of *Papa* and *Rangi*, or the separation of earth and sky by their children locked within the primordial embrace, speaks directly to Kant's antimonies, and those narratives of the "Great Race" recapitulate Zeno's classic paradoxes. Several Melanesianists (Goldman and Ballard 1998) revisit myths and rituals to highlight how groups from the highlands of Papua New Guinea grapple with fundamental questions about the nature of the universe, especially problems of being, self, and substance, each age old deliberations in Western thought. In contrast, some indigenous scholars (Meyer 1998, Helu 1999a, Moutu 2008 seek to illustrate a philosophy and world view distinct from the West. These presentations resist universal arguments that over-read and impose Western constructs on to indigenous formulations. This often proves a challenge since in an effort to elevate indigenous philosophy they cannot help but draw upon philosophical terminology and postulates familiar to Western arguments. The source for both islander and non-islander philosophical treatises is always the traditional narrative, mostly drawn from collections and anthologies.

Folklore and Diffusion – no question issues of cultural and folklore diffusion have gone out of fashion within the discipline. Perhaps with the rapidity of global flows and the movement of cultural property via new technologies of communication we may see a return to problematizing the movement of folklore through time and space. This is more than simply following threads of folklore migration and making copious charts; it is to recognize that this new medium profoundly implicates issues of control, both for purposes of domination and resistance. The diffusion of folklore has always been about power – the authority to transmit it, receive it, and interpret it. And when we consider the contexts of performance and exchange, social relationships become clearly conspicuous. So interests in the movement of folklore are not for some arcane plotting of tale types and motifs, but a concerted revisiting of the transmission process as a social practice, one with significant political consequence. The popular migration studies in Oceania dominated by archaeologists, linguists, and now geneticists, could use Kirtley's motif indexes to identify potential cultural routes and the lines of pre-historical imperial power relationships in the region. Even more importantly, diffusion research itself characterizes a political act of control now resisted by indigenous populations who reject the Western scientific narrative to provide alternative stories of origin and migration. Some scholars would like to seek a consilience between the two narrative representations, but many indigenous scholars grow tired of the imposed narratives and find biological appropriation a new form of theft and imperialism. Interestingly, Kirtley's indexes may prove effectual for indigenous purposes and counter-narratives.

Folklore and Performance in History – the interest in using folklore for a historical source is well established in Pacific research (e.g., Helu 1999b), but other scholars, working outside folklore's ethnographically informed performance perspective, turn to both written and oral texts to ground the performative and theatrical dimensions of encounters between outsiders and islanders. For instance, Greg Dening (1981, 1996) addresses how beaches on Pacific islands served symbolically and literally for the space or crossroad where local and outsider narratives encounter each other, and that the conflicting intercultural performances that resulted generated new histories and narratives, both on the land and by the discoverers who either moved on or sought to im-place themselves on the land. At such moments narratives met head on and offered scripts by which the social actors performed. These performances sometimes led to violence (e.g., Death of William Gooch at Waimea Bay Hawai'i) and at other times new occasions for mutual exploitation and self-interested alignments (1981). For Dening, historical texts and local traditional narratives may be read for the historical performances they capture.

Folklore and the Politics of Culture – increasingly Pacific scholars have come to recognize that in the nationalist and post-colonial movements, folklore often serves up the primary symbolic resource for resistance and revolution (Otto and Thomas 1997). This kind of work identifies familiar ground among folklorists attentive to the role of folklore in the creation of nationalism and ethnic identity. More recent scholarship has cast disapproving attention upon the representation and appropriation of the folklore imaginary and how oral traditions get resituated into a range of media and the tourism industry. A critical gaze deconstructs the fantasy of the exotic islanders. Such works by Nicholas Thomas *In Oceania: Visions, Artifacts Histories* (1997), Rod Edmond, *Representing the Pacific: Colonial Discourse from Cook to Gauguin* (1997) and Patty O'Brien, *The Pacific Muse: Exotic Femininity and the Colonial Pacific* (2006) survey the forms through which the Western representation has eroticized, minimized, and sought to control and capitalize on the region and its people. Rooted in post-colonial theory, these critiques challenge the narrative constructions of the West and the mythmaking that has empowered the imperial project. A most cogent critique of these representations comes from the folklorist Cristina Bacchilega whose careful analysis in *Legendary Hawai'i and the Politics of Place: Tradition, Translation, and Tourism* (2007), illuminates how folklore materials, even the anthologies, are themselves instruments in the creation of a popular imagination about Hawai'i and that their intended audience has always been non-Hawaiians and their purposes. Her critique even takes on the earlier folklorists

Beckwith and Luomala whose translations and collections served more the interests of outsiders than Hawaiians, and perpetuated the image of Hawai'i as a paradisiacal wonderland of primitive authenticity. But Bacchilega recognizes that folklore materials characterize a double-edged sword; they at once may furnish a colonial tool for control and domination, while they also can provide a resource for resistance and liberation. The sovereignty movement in Hawai'i has taken on many shapes, but with each resistance group, activists re-present traditional resources and a folklore of Hawai'i deeply rooted in memories of place.

The Sociology of Folklore – The islands of Oceania are geographically isolated from the centers of global capital and world politics. On occasion, during World War II and the Cold War, they assumed a more prominent role as global powers struggled for dominance, using these small remote locations for points of contestation. But today they hardly draw much attention when new conflicts and scrambles for economic resources take place far away from Oceania. Despite their apparent isolation, the people of Oceania are very aware of recent historical trends, and the way they look out from and position themselves in relation to global realities through traditional resources encourages some rethinking of folklore in social life and identity formation (Hereniko 1999). Most of the studies on folklore in Oceania tend to emphasize a historical trajectory. Still, some scholars have adopted a performance-centered perspective in their ethnographies to analyze the vibrancy and contemporary relevance of *South Pacific Oral Traditions* (Finnegan and Orbell 1995). With emphasis on performance they attend to local level political actions and the complexity of immediate social relations in contemporary contexts. As with the Siikalas, this approach moves us closer to a sociology of folklore and a careful examination of the role of folklore in the constitution of social life. These folkloristically mediated relationships form at local level relations in villages and on islands, and then extend out to the new post-colonial states and ultimately to global relations. The new nation-states in Oceania, like all emerging states, mix old social arrangements, political structures, and ethnic alliances with new state structures and governance models. Drawing upon two examples from the Marshall Islands (McArthur 2004, 2008), I wish to elucidate how first, enactments of a traditional narrative constitute, in part, power within the modern nation, and then second, how a narrative tradition of the trickster repositions the relationship of the local to the global.

Arguably the most well-known mythic narrative known by all living generations in the matrilineal society of the Marshall Islands is the story of the primal matriarch *Lōñtañūr* and her son *Jebro*. This story is found in all local anthologies and education readers, performed by accomplished storytellers in intimate gatherings, referred to often in conversation to make commentary on social behavior, lyrically referenced in popular songs that observe contemporary culture, and used in political speeches by candidates to make claims to cultural legitimacy. In this story *Lōñtañūr* descends from the heavens to her 10 sons on *Ailiñlaplap* Atoll, the oldest is *Tūmur* and the youngest *Jebro*. She tells them that the victor of a paddling canoe race from *Woja* Islet in the west across the lagoon to *Jeh* Islet in the east (about 30 miles) will determine who will receive the first high chief title. As of yet sailing canoes remain un-invented. On the day of the race each son launches his canoe. From the beach their mother calls out to each in turn to take her along. They see her on shore with a large bundle and reject her request fearing they will lose the race. So it goes until the youngest son *Jebro*, who returns to take his mother along because he determines he must obey her. *Jebro* slowly paddles east, anticipating his loss. His mother then unfolds from her bundle a set of ropes, the mast, and the first woven sail. She instructs him how to rig it all up and sail. He quickly catches and passes all his brothers until *Tūmur*, the oldest. The elder brother demands the sailing canoe, and once on board throws his mother off into the sea. But before *Jebro* jumps overboard *Lōñtañūr* instructs him to remove the boom socket so *Tūmur* will not be able to tack into the winds. *Tūmur* drifts off struggling with the sailing canoe. When *Lōñtañūr* and *Jebro* reach *Jeh* Islet in *Tūmur*'s paddling canoe it is low tide, and they carry the canoe into the center of the islet. *Tūmur* finally arrives but at high tide, and seeing no footprints proclaims brashly that he is chief. At this point *Lōñtañūr* escorts *Jebro* from the center of the islet, after anointing and clothing him in the chiefly investiture. All the people chant,

> Jebro rises in the East.
> He makes the surface calm.
> He loves people.
> He is Chief Jebro oooo.
> He is Chief Jebro.
> Jebro is chief.

Tūmur is so furious he refuses to look at this brother forever more. Each character eventually returns to the heavens to become a star constellation (*Jebro* is Pleiades and *Tūmur* Antares). When *Jebro* sets *Tūmur* will rise to bring bad weather, drought, rough seas, and poor fishing. When *Jebro* returns annually, with his mother as escort, he calms the seas, brings good rains, and returns bounty to land and sea. "*Jebro*," they say, "is kind, he feeds his people."

Encoded in this narrative of usurpation of the older brother by the younger includes all the islanders identify as most valuable in Marshallese culture: matrilinearity, obedience and respect for one's mother from whom titles, status, and most land derives, a man achieving heroic deeds after being granted cosmological power from a woman, the institutionalization of chiefs, a chief who continues to feed his people, the origin of sailing, and a cosmological explanation of stars and their relation to the seasons. All Marshallese recognize its significance. As such, it may serve a powerful resource within the modern nation-state.

In 1991 the Republic of the Marshall Islands finally gained independence from the United States after years of semi-independence and submission during the Trust Territory arrangement. In that year the first national election since independence was held. From the inception of the country one key figure, *Amata Kabua*, had led the way, serving as the nation's only president to that point. His traditional power as holder of the highest chiefly title in the islands reinforced his political supremacy in the state. With this dual power he was a formidable politician. Nonetheless, as he and his party sought re-election he was challenged by a group of young American educated entrepreneurs who lacked his matrilineally ascribed rank. Because they could not just ignore cultural values in this campaign, they used the *Lōñtañūr* and *Jebro* narrative in political display events to emphasize nostalgia for a romantic past of sailing, navigation, folk crafts and food, and the principle of kindness, without acknowledging any links to chiefly significance. *Amata* countered these upstarts with his own use of the narrative, but instead he emphasized chiefly matrilineal authority imbued with cosmological significance. And that he, like the god *Jebro* in the primordial past, would bring a promising and abundant future (after the *Tūmur*-like years under the United States). He made this association often in his political speeches. His most subtle, but poignant self-reference to the narrative came in the form of a giant feast in which he served more than 4,000 individuals great quantities of food. The most notable food was the meat of 22 large pigs killed and prepared for the feast. Pig epitomizes a high-status meat and usually only one pig is killed at ceremonies and brings prestige to those who offer it. Even to this day people comment about the number of pigs *Amata* provided that night. The most prominent symbols, however, were his mother and sister displayed prominently on the stand where the chief was seen feeding his people. These women stood for that great matriarchical escort who helps her son win the race that led to the institution of a worthy chief. In this political theater the institutions of state power and chiefly authority become overlapping images. The many people who I heard comment about this performance, saying "*Amata* is kind. He loves his people. He feeds his people," echoed the chant of the narrative. Just as *Jebro* won the race with the aid of his mother, *Amata* easily won the political race. His rhetorical use of the narrative at that historical juncture resonated more with the people than his opponents' folklorization of the past. This example from Oceania puts forward a demonstration of folklore's powerful role in the constitution of social life, particularly during the formation of an emerging post-colonial nation-state.

While the nation remains a vital social space for identity formation and the exercise of social power, the global and local often operate independent of old nationalisms. In the Marshall Islands, the international relationships derived from colonialism and imperial occupation predate the formation of the state. Folklore addressed these imbalances in social power before it was used in the struggles for nationhood and the political differences within. Since these global relationships are ongoing, folklore continues to provide local considerations of these far reaching transnational relationships. A narrative episode about the Marshallese trickster that developed after World War II continues to emerge and dramatizes local conceptualizations of global power. Like all good tricksters, the Marshallese version mediates between apparent oppositions, in this case, the relationship between the local and the global and the relations of power upon which the dichotomy rests.

After years of colonial subjugation by Germany and then Japan, the United States entered the islands after World War II with a mandate from the League of Nations. The US military incursion into the Marshall Islands left an indelible impression on the Marshallese with their decisive attacks and victories over the Japanese. Following the war, the US military also forcibly relocated the islanders of *Enewetak* and *Bikini* for atomic bomb testing that decimated entire islets, and made some atolls uninhabitable for years. The nuclear radiation continues to bear adverse consequences including cancer, still births, and deformations. The history of cover-up and attempts to absolve responsibility by the United States represents a story of deception and international intrigue. The United States also continues to occupy Kwajalein Atoll as a missile tracking station. Inactive warheads are shot from California and use the lagoon as target practice. Despite these clear abuses of exploitation and control, the attitude of the Marshallese toward the United States is marked more by ambivalence than angry resistance.

In part the Americans have been seen to enact the dualistic image of traditional chiefs; at once they are viewed as distant and untouchable warriors with great knowledge, while also they are populist leaders who maintain their power by taking care of people, mainly in how they feed them similar to *Jebro*. After showing their warrior prowess during the war, the Americans then enacted the populist image by providing the Marshallese with abundant clothes and food. While the Americans performed these chiefly images unaware, they have also proven unpredictable and a bit sly in their subsequent behaviors. Consequently, the Marshallese continue to address US occupation and atomic tests with a story about their trickster that playfully dramatizes this ambivalent history.

A most ubiquitous story told throughout the islands explains how *Letao* the trickster, whose name means, "the sly one", moves on south from the Marshall Islands after tricking all the high chiefs. When he arrives at *Kiribati* they are experiencing a famine. Because he desires the chief's wives, he willingly resolves the famine by creating an earth oven then jumping inside. He instructs the locals to cover him with leaves and sand. He miraculously appears from the oven, and when they uncover it, a cornucopia of food is revealed and he feeds the starving population. He does this on several occasions, and then one day tells the chief he will be leaving. The chief asks to be taught the trick so he may take care of his people. *Letao* instructs him to lie down in the hot earth oven, and when the chief screams out, the trickster commands the villagers to cover him quickly with leaves and sand, assuring them all will be right. After several hours, he still has not appeared and the people grow concerned. *Letao* directs them to uncover the oven and to expect an abundance of food. Instead, they expose a very well-done, cooked chief. *Letao* then spends the night with the traumatized wives of the chief. Eventually the people of *Kiribati* chase him off. He continues to the south where he encounters an American ship. He covets their apparent wealth, and they recognize his sly powers. They make a deal with him, that if he will go to America and teach them what he knows they will make him rich. Many generations later, during Japanese occupation, American ships appear, and with their guns, aircraft, and soldiers attack and destroy the Japanese defenses. A few years later the Americans build a bomb so powerful it can destroy the entire earth. At the end of performing this episode of the trickster a storyteller will often ask, "Where did the Americans get their power?" And then they will rehearse how *Letao* is the embodiment of all extremes: he is at once good and bad, possesses all knowledge and all stupidity, all love and all hate, all kindness and all meanness, all truth and all lies, and then rhetorically asks, "Isn't that just like the Americans?"

Through all the negotiations and reparations since the nuclear tests the Americans have come to be seen as deceptive tricksters who, after feeding the Marshallese like a powerful populist chief should, eventually "burned us – cooked us," just as *Letao* did to the *Kiribati* chief. The Americans parallel the extremes of the trickster, and in doing so, the source of their ambivalent power derives from the Marshallese trickster. With this episode that enlarges the trickster tale cycle, the islanders have narrated themselves to the center of contemporary global power. They forge a link between their ancient origins and a modern social life that becomes increasingly global. Any attempts to fix the Marshallese as a peripheral and bounded oceanic people imposed upon by a world power misses their vision of themselves; they see the slipperiness and pourousness of boundaries and explore possibilities within the interstices of the local and the global. This example suggests that long before the West began to theorize the forces of globalization, indigenous people had already been considering the global for some time, and their theorizing is often manifest in narratives that dramatize these forces. This case in the Marshall Islands illustrates a sociology of folklore within ever-increasing and complex transnational and global relations, but the point of departure to understand it starts at the location of the "folk," or a local culture who continually invest meaning and significance into their histories and lives through folklore.

The folklore traditions of Oceania remain vibrant, adaptive, and meaningful to the people who create and use them. Good folklore study in the region will continue to be pursued with energy and insight by many from a variety of disciplines and interests. But the tools folklorists bring to the table, sensitivity to time and place, tradition and creativity, issues of representation, power and control, and a methodology that is attuned both to the performance and social history of texts, have much to contribute. Conversely, the folklore of Oceania has much to offer reconsiderations of old interests in cultural flows and identity, and new considerations of the relationship between local communities and global forces.

REFERENCES

Abrahams, Roger. 1993. "Phantoms of Romantic Nationalism in Folkoristics." *Journal of American Folklore* 106(419): 3–37.

Andersen, Johannes C. 1928 [1995]. *Myths and Legends of the Polynesians*. New York: Dover Publications.

Bacchilega, Cristina. 2007. *Legendary Hawai'i and the Politics of Place: Tradition, Translation, and Tourism*. Philadelphia: University of Pennsylvania Press.

Bascom, William. 1954. "Four Functions of Folklore." *Journal of American Folklore* 67: 333–340.

Beckwith, Martha. 1940 [1970]. *Hawaiian Mythology*. Honolulu: University of Hawai'i Press.

Beckwith, Martha. 1951. *The Kumulipo: A Hawaiian Creation Chant*. Honolulu: University of Hawai'i Press.

Bonnemaison, Joel. 1986. *The Tree and the Canoe: History and Ethnogeography of Tanna*. Honolulu: University of Hawai'i Press.

Clifford, James. 1988. *The Predicament of Culture: Twentieth-Century Ethnography, Literature, and Art*. Cambridge, MA: Harvard University Press.

Dening, Greg. 1981. *Islands and Beaches: Discourse on a Silent Land: Marquesas, 1774–1880*. Honolulu: University Press of Hawai'i.

Dening, Greg. 1996. *Performances*. Chicago: Chicago University Press.

Edmond, Rod. 1997. *Representing the South Pacific: Colonial Discourses from Cook to Gauguin*. Cambridge: Cambridge University Press.

Finnegan, Ruth and Margaret Orbell, Eds. 1995. *South Pacific Oral Traditions*. Bloomington: Indiana University Press.

Finney, Ben. 1994. *Voyage of Rediscovery: A Cultural Odyssey through Polynesia*. Berkeley: University of California Press.

Freeman, Derek. 1983. *Margaret Mead and Samoa: The Making and Unmaking of an Anthropological Myth*. Cambridge, MA: Harvard University Press.

Freeman, Derek. 1999. *The Fateful Hoaxing of Margaret Mead: A Historical Analysis of Her Samoan Research*. Boulder: Westview Press.

Goldman, L.R. and C. Ballard. 1998. *Fluid Ontologies: Myth, Ritual and Philosophy in the Highlands of Papua New Guinea*. Westport, CT: Bergin and Garvey.

Hanlon, David. 1989. "Micronesia: Writing and Rewriting the History of a Non-entity." *Pacific Studies* 121: 1–21.

Hau'ofa, Epeli. 1993 [2008]. "Our Sea of Islands" in *We are the Ocean: Selected Works*. Honolulu: University of Hawai'i Press.

Helu, I. Futa. 1999a. *Critical Essays: Cultural Perspectives from the South Seas*. Canberra: Journal of Pacific History.

Helu, I. Futa. 1999b. "South Pacific Mythology" in Alex Calder, Jonathan Lamb, and Bridget Orr, Eds. *Voyages and Beaches: Pacific Encounters, 1769–1840*. Honolulu: University of Hawai'i Press.

Hereniko, Vilsoni. 1999. "Representations of Cultural Identities" in Vilsoni Hereniko and Rob Wilson, Eds. *Inside Out: Literature, Cultural Politics, and Identity in the New Pacific*. New York: Rowman and Littlefield Publishers, Inc.

Hereniko, Vilsoni. 2000. "Indigenous Knowledge and Academic Imperialism" in Robert Borofsky, Ed. *Remembrance of Pacific Pasts: An Invitation to Remake History*. Honolulu: University of Hawai'i Press.

Howe, K.R. 2003. *The Quest for Origins: Who First Discovered and Settled the Pacific Islands?* Honolulu: University of Hawai'i Press.

Howes, David. 2003. *Sensual Relations: Engaging the Senses in Cultural and Social Theory*. Ann Arbor: University of Michigan Press.

Kaeppler, Adrienne L. and H. Arlo Nimmo. 1976. *Directions in Pacific Traditional Literature: Essays in Honor of Katherine Luomala*. Honolulu: Bishop Museum Press.

Kirch, Patrick V. 2000. *On the Road of the Winds: An Archaeological History of the Pacific Islands before European Contact*. Berkeley: University of California Press.

Kirtley, Bacil F. 1955. "A Motif Index of Polynesian, Micronesian, and Melanesian Folktales." PhD Dissertation, 2 Vols. Indiana University.

Kirtley, Bacil F. 1971. *A Motif-Index of Traditional Polynesian Narratives*. Honolulu: University of Hawai'i Press.

Luomala, Katherine. 1940. *Oceanic, American Indian, and African Myths of Snaring the Sun*. Honolulu: The Museum.

Luomala, Katherine. 1955. *Voices of the Wind: Polynesian Myths and Chants*. Honolulu: Bishop Museum Press.

Mahina, Okusitino. 1999. "Theory and Practice in Anthropology: Pacific Anthropology and Pacific Islanders." *Social Analysis* 43(2): 44–69.

Malinowski, Bronislaw. 1922. *Argonauts of the Western Pacific*. New York: Dutton.

Malinowski, Bronislaw. 1926. *Myth in Primitive Psychology*. London: Kegan Paul.

McArthur, Phillip H. 2004. "Narrative, Cosmos, and Nation: Intertextuality and Power in the Marshall Islands." *Journal of American Folklore* 117(463): 55–80.

McArthur, Phillip H. 2008. "Ambivalent Fantasies: Local Prehistories and Global Dramas in the Marshall Islands." *Journal of Folklore Research* 45(3): 263–298.

Mead, Margaret. 1928. *Coming of Age in Samoa: A Psychological Study of Primitive Youth for Western Civilization*. New York: William Morrow and Company.

Mercer, P.M. 1979. "Oral Tradition in the Pacific: Problems of Interpretation." *Journal of Pacific History* 14(3): 130–153.

Mitchell, Roger. 1970. "Oral Tradition and Micronesian History: A Microcosmic Approach." *Journal of Pacific History* 5: 33–41.

Mitchell, Roger. 1973. *Micronesian Folktales*. Nagoya: Asian Folklore Institute.

Meyer, Manu A. 1998. *Native Hawaiian Epistemology: Exploring Hawaiian Views of Knowledge*. Cambridge, MA: Cultural Survival, Inc.

Moutu, Andrew. 2008. Review Essay, "James F. Weiner, 'Tree Leaf Talk: A Heideggerian Anthropology.'" *Pacific Studies* 31(1): 105–120

Obeyesekere, Gananath. 1992. *The Apotheosis of Captain Cook: European Mythmaking in the Pacific*. Princeton: Princeton University Press.

O'Brien, Patty. 2006. *The Pacific Muse: Exotic Femininity and the Colonial Pacific*. Seattle: University of Washington Press.

Otto, Ton and Nicholas Thomas, Eds. 1997. *Narratives of Nation in the South Pacific*. Amsterdam: Harwood Academic Publishers.

Parmentier, Richard J. 1987. *The Sacred Remains: Myth, History, and Polity in Belau*. Chicago: University of Chicago Press.

Petersen, Glenn. 2009. *Traditional Micronesian Societies: Adaptation, Integration, and Political Organization*. Honolulu: University of Hawai'i Press.

Sahlins, Marshall. 1981. *Historical Metaphors and Mythical Realities: Structure in the Early History of the Sandwich Islands Kingdom*. Ann Arbor: University of Michigan Press.

Sahlins, Marshall. 1995. *How "Natives" Think: About Captain Cook for Example*. Chicago: University of Chicago Press.

Schrempp, Gregory. 1992. *Magical Arrows: the Maori, the Greeks, and the Folklore of the Universe*. Madison: University of Wisconsin Press.

Shankman, Paul. 2009. *The Thrashing of Margaret Mead: Anatomy of an Anthropological Controversy*. Madison: University of Wisconsin Press.

Siikala, Anna-Leena and Jukka Siikala. 2005. *Return to Culture: Oral Tradition and Society in the Southern Cook Islands*. Helsinki: Suomalainen Tiedeakatemaia, Academia Scientiarum Fennica.

Thomas, Nicholas. 1997. *In Oceania: Visions, Artifacts, Histories*. Durham, NC: Duke University Press.

Torgovnick, Marianna. 1990. *Gone Primitive: Savage Intellects, Modern Lives*. Chicago: University of Chicago Press.

Weiner, Annette. 1976. *Women of Value, Men of Renown: New Perspectives in Trobriand Exchange*. Austin: University of Texas Press.

CHAPTER 14

FOLKLORE AND FOLKLORE STUDIES IN LATIN AMERICA[1,2]

Fernando Fischman

The word "folklore" is of widespread use in Latin America. The usages and understandings of the term coined by William Thoms that were incorporated into the Spanish and Portuguese languages as "folklore" or "folclore" have been the outcome of historically grounded and naturalized processes of conceptualization. The establishment of folklore studies as a field of intellectual inquiry and political application since the last decades of the nineteenth century involved the development of practices of collection, transcription, archiving, classification, publication, dissemination, and recreation. All those tasks were undertaken by an array of actors: academic scholars, public sector officials, independent collectors, and members of the cultural industries (writers, journalists, musicians, singers, dancers). Hence, the perceptual phenomena that fall under the rubric of "folklore" in Latin America at present have that quality as a result of the works carried out in the eclectically constituted field of folklore studies. The multiple mediations of the diverse actors involved in the field have shaped the past and present understandings of the term "folklore" in different directions. At certain levels – in the educational discourse, the media, commonplace speech – the term "folklore" evolved with a remarkable semantic consistency throughout the decades. Therefore, in those contexts of use "folklore" currently encompasses expressive forms tied to regional, national, or continental identities as in the formative years of the field. In that understanding, a complex formed by music, songs, dances, food, legends, and costumes, among other expressions, are considered to be "folklore" because they are "ours," "authentic," "telluric," and a seemingly endless set of essentialist associations. At other levels, in the controversies within the academy and between the academics

A Companion to Folklore, First Edition. Edited by Regina F. Bendix and Galit Hasan-Rokem.
© 2012 John Wiley & Sons, Ltd. Published 2012 John Wiley & Sons, Ltd.

and the non-academic scholars, the term "folklore" has been (and still is) polysemic. In those quarters, there is a constant unsettled disagreement about the term's scope. That disagreement expresses ideological as well as conceptual contradictions with regard as to how to define this field of study and practice and how to characterize its sociological constituency.

Is it possible to speak of Latin American folklore studies as a unified field in view of the multiplicity of nation-states that comprise the continent, their specific social and political histories and the disciplinary developments within each country? Latin American countries share a colonial heritage, the almost simultaneous achievement of independence from the Spanish or Portuguese rule in the second and third decades of the nineteenth century, and the consequent construction of nation-states in a concurrent period in similar historical processes. Likewise, the local elites that carried out nation-building processes that extended well into the twentieth century tackled the political goal of establishing conflict-free societies. That involved dealing with the presence of diverse social subjects: indigenous peoples, criollo populations, European immigrants, and rural migrants to the cities who joined the urban working classes, in contexts that became more and more complex as a result of the transformation of socioeconomic structures that took place in every country. Folklore studies provided a shaping force for the construction of those "imagined communities" (Anderson 1983) that the romantic notions that were its basis generously supplied. In later years, folklore studies were instrumental for the so-called "populist" movements, in order to make visible the cultural creations of the groups that were their constituency. In those respects, folklore studies followed similar routes in every Latin American country. This chapter focuses on some common denominators the field acquired in the continent. Therefore, it centers on the general shared processes brought about as a result of common directions. At some points in this chapter, I individualize certain countries in order to situate specifically where a given development took place. At others, I provide the nationality of some relevant scholars. These localizations index the wide reach of folklore studies in Latin America and they give an indication of the sites where the most relevant developments happened, particularly in the southern cone. Those developments, although they took place in specific countries, have had a bearing on the field of folklore studies in the entire continent, given that scholars met and exchanged ideas in formal and informal venues on quite a regular basis.

As I mention above, in Latin America, folklore studies is a field that has been established by the conjunction of cultural policies, academic work, and by the labor of writers, journalists, poets, musicians and amateur collectors. The effort of all these actors in combination has shaped a more or less specific cutout of culture that came to be called "folklore," which turned out to be easier to recognize than to explain. Simultaneously, it configured a field of inquiry that dealt with such a cutout that, as I will point out later, never acquired a definite name or a conceptual unity. In this respect, the development of folklore studies is similar to what Ana María Ochoa-Gautier claims for the field of ethnomusicology, when she refers to "dispersed textualities embodied in different practices of writing about music from journalism to fiction, to written compositions, to formal academic forms of writing" (2006: 809). A significant example of the heterogeneous textual and textural materials that were considered to be relevant for the field is the collection of folklore materials published by Argentine scholar Félix Coluccio in 1948. The anthology, which he called *Folklore de las Américas* (folklore of the Americas) included a multifarious array of legends, couplets, myths, and festivals, collected by a diverse set of amateur and skilled collectors and professional writers. Most of the materials had been published earlier in other formats. Coluccio reframed them as folklore forms and grouped them together by country. He thus established a crystallized link between the expressions reported and national identities.

FOLKLORE STUDIES IN LATIN AMERICA: FROM THE LATE NINETEENTH-CENTURY PRECURSORS TO THE PRESENT

The history of folklore studies in Latin America can be divided into three stages.[3] The first one dates from the last decades of the nineteenth century, when the term folklore begins to be used, the first collections are made and the first folklore associations are founded, to the 1920s. The second one, from the 1920s to the 1970s, marks the official establishment of the field. In those years, folklore studies enters the academy, but it is principally in the public sector where it finds a niche. Folklore scholars partake of academic life and of the establishment of public sector institutions. Some work for both, but the majority establish themselves in governmental organizations. In this period the field thrives both as a result of the politics of culture of the nation-states, strongly influenced by the political needs of the ruling elites, and of some of the scholars' relentless activity. The former aimed at selecting expressions representative of the national identities. The latter intended to shape an epistemology that would provide folklore studies with academic legitimacy among the social sciences and the humanities while trying to keep a balance with the ideological expectations of those that sponsored their work. Those decades cover the period of institutionalization of the field. The third period encompasses the 1970s to the present. In it, alternatives to the earlier notions predominant in the field surface in academic settings concurrently with the developments that take place in other parts of the world, particularly the United States. During this phase, the basic tenets of folklore studies in Latin America begin to be systematically questioned and theoretical challenges are formulated. Such a problematization, which takes place in the academy, does not reach the public sector where folklore as an independent area has been well established. In those quarters, it remains tied to its original views.

Folklore studies has evolved with national particularities in each of the Latin American countries. However, although each of the first two stages had different dominant tenets, there was a shared general orientation in all the countries in every one of them. Beyond the larger, shared, sociohistorical issues mentioned earlier, the common directions were shaped by scholarly networks. In the first stage, those networks were established by the common national origin and interests of the practitioners, and were cultivated mainly through correspondence among them. In the second stage, the set of connections was established mainly through conferences. Among the most important of such meetings were the Brazilian Folklore Congresses that took place in the 1950s, and the International Folklore Congresses that met in São Paulo in 1954 and in Buenos Aires in 1960. The network of scholars developed in this stage (some of them academics, some independent researchers, and many amateur collectors) facilitated constant dialogue and provided a strong, shaping force in the history of folklore studies in Latin America. This set of connections comprised such an eclectic composition of scholars from diverse backgrounds, institutional affiliations, training and experience that is inconceivable in other fields.[4] This heterogeneity left an imprint that lasts to this very day. Several specific folkloristic conferences take place regularly in Latin America at present. They usually involve the participation of researchers from different walks of scholarly life, together with amateur collectors and artists. The range of papers presented in those venues goes from very elementary descriptive case studies to highly articulate theoretical elaborations. Such diversity underscores the disciplinary heterogeneity of its practitioners as one of the field's more stable patterns.

THE FIRST STAGE: THE PRECURSORS

During the first stage, folklore comes into view in Latin American discourse. The concern for the collection and safeguarding of materials had already started in the late nineteenth century and continued through the first decades of the twentieth century with the constitution of the first folklore associations. The common pattern is that although some of the first collectors were philologists, most of them had scientific backgrounds, including botany, medicine, archaeology, and zoology. As part of their academic interests, these scientists collected legends and folktales, and wrote descriptions of local customs like festivals and celebrations. In Venezuela, collectors Adolfo Ernst and Aristides Rojas started the publication of the first theoretical formulations on folklore in the 1880s and 1890s. In Argentina the first ones who ventured to collect folklore materials were archeologists. The most prominent were Samuel Lafone Quevedo and Juan B. Ambrosetti (Carrizo 1953). Lafone Quevedo, who had a doctorate from Cambridge University, was the first in using the term "folklore" in 1888 to designate an anthology of customs and legends that he had compiled in the province of Catamarca, in northwest Argentina. Ambrosetti, who was the first director of the Ethnographic Museum of the University of Buenos Aires, collected materials in several regions of the country (the northwest, the northeast and the Pampas). He was not only concerned with folklore materials per se, but used them as sources of data for his archeological interpretations (Ambrosetti 1963).

Besides the work done by scientists in their academic settings as part of enterprises related to their own disciplinary interests, this stage also sees the founding of the first associations devoted solely to the collection and study of folklore materials. The allegedly first folklore association in Latin America was founded in Chile. It was the *Sociedad de Folklore Chileno*, established in 1909. In 1910 this association began to publish a newsletter, the *Revista de Folklore Chileno*. In 1911 a *Sociedad de Folklore* was promoted in Panama in order to study dialect speech (Moreno 2007), and similar associations in Brazil and Venezuela followed suit.

Many of the precursors were European – German, Swedish, English – scholars. Others were native to the Latin American countries but had been educated in Europe. A strong influence on the development of folklore studies at this stage was provided by a network of mostly German scholars. They carried out fieldwork throughout the Americas among indigenous groups, focusing particularly on the collection of texts. Among them were Franz Boas, Carl von den Steinen, Theodor Koch-Grünberg, Konrad Theodor Preuss, Rodolfo Lenz, and Roberto Lehmann-Nitsche

(Malvestitti forthcoming). The founder of the *Sociedad de Folklore Chileno*, German philologist Rodolfo Lenz, published his work *Estudios Araucanos* in 1895–1897. In this volume, he states his methodological chart for the study of the Mapuche language, which includes the collection of a wide variety of genres. He highlights the relevance of the compilation of personal narratives, tales, descriptions of ceremonies and festivals, and songs, "no matter how stupid and dull they may seem to us" (Lenz 1895–1897: viii–ix). Another relevant individual for the advancement of folklore studies was German ethnologist, Roberto Lehmann-Nitsche, a researcher at the Museum of Natural Sciences at the University of La Plata, who carried out far-reaching studies of indigenous languages, and also put together and classified an extensive compilation of riddles that he collected among non-indigenous people, specifically urban university students (Blache 1991). In his linguistic studies, Lehmann-Nitsche, who emphasized the collection of texts, considered that methodologically, the materials collected in indigenous languages should not be considered to be completely separate from the ones that could be collected in Spanish (Malvestitti 2005).

The orientation outlined by the precursors was not followed in the subsequent years. The study of indigenous cultural productions was left in the domain of ethnology, and the study of ethnolinguistic data was not considered to be of interest for folklore studies.

The Second Stage: The Formative Years of Folklore Studies

The second stage encompasses the decades between the 1920s and the 1970s, when folklore studies entered both the academy, where it evolved as an independent area of study with relative success, and the public sector institutions, where it thrived. This stage was a period of solid discipline building. The task was carried out on different planes. The intellectual foundation was provided by the formulation of a theoretical framework and the ensuing work of systematization. The political foundation was the creation of institutions devoted to the collection of folklore materials and the dissemination of folklore studies.

In dealing with the history of folklore studies in Latin America, assessing its relationship to nationalist movements is, as it is for the field in general, unavoidable. The use of folklore studies by nationalist ideologues was not only a part of a process of gluing different groups together in the course of nation building, but also a practice that continued in well-established nation-states.

In an early piece published in pamphlet form in the late 1930s, Argentine scholar Augusto Raúl Cortazar, who would eventually become one of the leading figures in the field, argued that the "science" of folklore was fundamental in the fight against "cosmopolitanism," which he contended lacked a "soul, a physiognomy and a flag" (1939: 10). According to Cortazar, one of folklore studies' goals should be to "identify the popular that is *diluted* in the totality of the national culture" (my emphasis). These statements are relevant because Cortazar went on to develop in the 1940s the most influential Latin American conceptualization of folklore, which lasted in certain circles, the populist rhetoric and governmental cultural institutions, until today, with a steady, unmodified meaning.

By the middle of the twentieth century governments had further reasons to support the development of folklore studies, like strengthening the social foundations of the political movements that were evolving at the time and were their constituency. The advancement of these movements required the valuation of social subjects that had been disregarded until then and linking them to a national heritage. Therefore, in the discourse of cultural institutions devoted to the study or dissemination of folklore, and in the field's scholarly works, references to the nation and to national cultures were extensive.

The following pronouncement by Juan Alfonso Carrizo, who was the first director of the Argentine *Instituto Nacional de la Tradición* (National Institute of Tradition), founded in 1943 and devoted to the collection of folklore materials and the promotion of folklore studies, is quite indicative of the rhetoric that was at the field's foundation:

> It is a duty to study the national tradition in Argentina because we must create a common emotional source that draws us together in the remembrance, the way they are united by spiritual ties, with the solidness of a diamond, the English, the German, the Russians, the Jews, and so on. (1953: 8)

According to Carrizo, a *national* Argentine tradition already existed. The task of folklore studies was to study its artistic manifestations in order to contribute to the project of amalgamating them and thus furthering the national cohesion. All the Latin American folklore endeavors shared a similar paradigm. The main creed of this paradigm consisted of the notion that folklore forms carried within them the essence of nationality, but all of these expressions were either diluted, as Cortazar suggested, or about to be lost because of the processes of industrialization and urbanization that Latin American societies were going through. Then, folklore scholars' main task was to collect and classify those manifestations in order to preserve them. Therefore, two principles construed this paradigm: the nationalistic and the rescuing enterprise. These two conceptual stances have generally gone together as major guidelines.[5]

Nationalist ideologues have been successful in fixing a meaning for the term "folklore" that poses a strict correlation between folklore and nation. Thus, the pronunciation of the word "folklore" in commonplace use evokes a straight association with the homeland in practically every speaker uttering the word. The Colombian musicologist Carlos Miñana Blasco (2000) paints a quite precise portrait when he argues that the idea of "folklore" has become untouchable, and tied to the national identity to such a degree that anyone who dares put it into question runs the risk of being accused of lack of patriotism and lynched or at least excluded.

In all the Latin American countries, a large number of folklore scholars established themselves primarily outside the academy in the public sector. They were influential in the support of cultural policies that emphasized and promoted the appraisal of the forms and practices that fell into the category of folklore. In Brazil, the influence of folklore scholars was decisive in training the first generation of social scientists and they were instrumental in academic development of those fields. Later, however, they were relegated to a peripheral role because of their decision to work for governmental cultural institutions (Vilhena 1997).

Inserting itself in the public sector was at once the field's strength and its weakness. Individuals located within institutions generating and applying cultural policies were able to reach a great part of the populations. Here, practitioners of folklore studies could strongly establish the idea that "folklore" was something intrinsically valuable, as folklore was seen as expressing national and regional identities. Folklore represented the *peoples's culture*. Governmental positions, however, weakened the disciplinary core, as they promoted theoretical stagnation and scholars who held them lacked the opportunity to do research and train new scholars. A governmental organization is the place where policies are applied and not a site to think of new concepts. Consequently, and together with its power and its influence in the national imaginaries and its concomitant semantic permanence, the concept of "folklore" and, by extension of "folklore studies" was subject to denigration by academic scholars.

Augusto Raúl Cortazar, who was one of the most influential figures in this stage, offered the first formulations of what he himself called a "functional and dynamic" theory in his seminal books *Bosquejo de una introducción al folklore* (An Outline of an Introduction to Folklore) (1942) and El *carnaval en el folklore calchaquí* (Carnival in Calchaqui Folklore) (1949). He kept publishing along the same lines in his long and productive career until the 1970s. According to Cortazar, folk culture, the culture of the folk community, an idea based on Robert Redfield's folk-urban continuum, was constituted by a set of tributaries: a superior (sic) cultural tradition (e.g., medieval Spanish songs that survive in folksongs); urban transculturations assimilated by the "folk" (e.g., goods from urban settings and industrial innovations that were incorporated by the "folk" after an adaptive process, such as the use of nylon to make clothing); autochthonous survivals (e.g., from cultures that reached a high (sic) level like the Aztecs, Mayas, Incas); passages from "folk" to "folk" (which were less frequent but that could still be found, for instance, in speech forms). This view proposed that folklore materials proceeded from a higher social stratum, that they had been discarded, and once they had lost currency and efficacy, they were relegated and confined to lower strata. Such a standpoint implicitly admitted that the "folk" could imitate the folklore phenomenon but they could not create it. They could only assimilate it, and transmit it from generation to generation among the members of the community through a process in which a given behavior became "folkloric." This formulation is similar to the *gesunkenes Kulturgut* theory proposed by Eduard Hoffman-Krayer. Cortazar does not cite him, though, in any of his works.[6] He explicitly acknowledges the inspiration for his own developments to the idea of "latency" put forward by Spanish philologist Ramón Menéndez Pidal. He rephrases it as "latent fluidity," which refers to a universal substratum of culture that springs up, in variants, in folk communities. Cortazar metaphorically describes this latent fluidity as "an eternal flow that runs under the ground throughout the world during the history of civilization, unacknowledged by literate society and by the urban intellectual centers because it does not express itself in written documents and it evolves in isolated, remote, rustic places" (1975: 49). In that respect, Cortazar credits old Spanish traditions that he holds in high regard for a great number of current Latin American folklore expressions. However he also quotes autochthonous cultures as a relevant base for rural folklore. As well, he takes into consideration as a source of folklore forms the translocations from folk community to folk community.

There are several key concepts in Cortazar's work that shape his formulation and that have had a lasting influence in Latin American folklore studies. One of them is that of folk community, the rural, isolated society, as the locus where folklore is to be found. This concept is particularly relevant because it serves as an indicator of the locations where the items that he considers to be "folk" have to be looked for, and consequently of the disciplines entitled to study them. For Cortazar, a legend told in an urban society should fall under the purview of sociology and a legend told in an indigenous group should be analyzed by ethnography.[7]

Another key concept is that of "process of folklorization," which is closely tied to the idea of "function." According to Cortazar, an item acquires a folkloric quality after a process of adaptation in which it is incorporated by a folk community because it covers a social function.[8] Cortazar outlined eight traits that had to be present in order to consider that a given cultural phenomenon was folklore:

> A folklore item is popular, collective, traditional, oral, anonymous, empirical, functional and regional. (1975: 53)

Those eight traits were so naturalized and widespread in the Latin American folklore studies literature, that in several treatises it is common to find that two or three of those characteristics are named, followed by an "and so on," that accounts for the other traits that thus do not even need to be mentioned. Scholars who made efforts to establish links between folklore studies and other disciplines that were also flourishing at the time, did not consider it necessary to put into question the basic traits that circumscribed the folklore expressions according to Cortazar's formulations. A case in point is that of Brazilian scholar Paulo de Carvalho Neto. When he attempted to provide psychoanalytical explanations for folklore materials following the teachings of his mentor, Arthur Ramos, he never contested the fundamental premises that defined folklore. It was a given that folklore was popular, anonymous, and traditional, and he felt no need to explain what he meant by each of those terms.

Carvalho Neto proposed a challenging psychoanalytic interpretation of folklore. He argued that psychoanalysis "helps folklore understand the folkloric cultural fact in itself, that is, the reason of being of such a fact, the reason of its existence, and its hidden and true signification" (1953: 282). In his conception, folklore materials had meanings that could only be explained through psychoanalytical insights. He saw folklore, at least in this stage of his productive intellectual life, as a normative social science that, following the psychoanalytical leaning, could have liberating effects. In explaining the hidden reasons for superstitions, witchcraft, and popular medicine, he claimed that the discipline of folklore had a pedagogic goal. Once the truth of those behaviors was revealed, people would not resort to them and would adapt to better forms of life. Carvalho Neto summarized it this way: "folklore kills folklore" (1953: 283), meaning that the discipline that studies irrational folklore expressions, by unmasking their true signification, would make those manifestations fade away. Carvalho Neto's innovative developments did not achieve currency and there is hardly any contemporary reference to his psychoanalytical interpretations. However, they are quite indicative of two facts:

1. By the mid-twentieth century there was a well-established and widely shared definition of the forms that constituted folklore in Latin American scholarship.
2. There were explanations that attempted to go beyond the essentialist association between expressive forms and national or regional identities. They were put forward but not widely accepted. Ideas that parted from the predominant paradigm

and had the potential of subverting some of its tenets were rarely echoed and mostly forsaken.[9] Folklore studies remained strictly focused on the link between expressive forms and popular, eventually national, identities. Hence, the predominant perspective asserted that the "folk" were the country people, the "peasants," those who lived in isolated and homogeneous communities that were self sufficient, tied into ancestral traditions, relied on simple technologies and had little division of labor.[10]

The developments in Latin American folklore studies during this stage presented endless discussions around the terms that best described the discipline and its practitioners. This terminological inconclusiveness was at the field's core, considering that there had always been a wide range of practitioners working within the discipline in different capacities: as academic researchers, officials of cultural institutions, independent amateur collectors, artists, or entrepreneurs within the cultural industries. A division of labor was at the heart of these discussions. The peasants were the producers of the genuine folklore expressions, the folklorists the elite intellectuals that studied them, and the artists that recreated the genuine expressions for the non-folk people. Although there was an agreement as to who the "folk" were, the role of the scholars and the recreators was a source of discrepancy. Studies of some of the materials encompassed by the early definitions of the field (folktales, legends, superstitions) were undertaken by academics as well as by amateur researchers. Musicians and dancers who started to be called "folklorists" (folkloristas) performed other materials, like songs and dances in urban settings. This situation posed a dilemma for folklore scholars who were working to establish a legitimate field of inquiry that was expressed in the following question. How are academic scholars to be called and identified as such, considering that amateur collectors call themselves "folkloristas" and the same is true for the artists that recreate the folkloric forms? A definite criterion to draw distinctions was never established, at least not one that attained widespread use.

With respect to the field's name, in Latin American usage, the Spanish term for "folkloristics" (folklorística) never attained prevalence. "Folklore" as a name for both the field and the object had wide currency. Alfredo Poviña (1954) put forward the name "folklorologist" for the "scientist" as opposed to "folklorist," which he left to designate the artists that performed allegedly folk expressions. The term "folklorologist" did not gain predominance either. "Folklorists" did, and it is now generally used to call the artists devoted to the recreation of dances or songs outside their original context for urban audiences and also for the independent scholars and amateur collectors who both collect materials and perform them.

In the struggle to attain intellectual legitimacy, the debates over what to call scholars, "folkloristas" or "folklorólogos" went beyond a mere terminological difference. Being the former meant being a practitioner of folk expressions or an amateur researcher, and being the latter meant being a "scientist" (i.e., a true scholar). The following paragraph by the Panamanian author Dora P. de Zárate hints at several interesting points relevant to this issue. She writes:

> Folklorologists are very few, folklorists are many. The folklorologist does not need to know how to dance, does not need to dress with typical costumes, nor does he need to be an artist. He is just a scientist. His work goes in other directions, looks for other horizons. (P. de Zárate1975: 148–149)

P. de Zárate does not explain what horizons the folklorologist looks for, but she makes a clear distinction between the "artists" and the "scientists." The latter are not expected to dance or to wear any specific "folk" attire. They are the experts who study and illustrate the literate about the vernacular traditions. Being a performer of folklore expressions, a folklorist, and a researcher on the practice of what were considered to be folklore expressions, a folklorologist, a folklore scholar, were two categories that could be easily blurred in commonplace language and views. It is evident that academic scholars saw early on the need to establish a rhetoric that would set them apart from the artists in public consideration, but they did not always attain that distance. Among the academic practitioners, there is even contemporarily a frequent complaint against the use given by non-academic scholars to the term. They claim that the word has been appropriated by nativistic or nationalistic groups to such a degree that there is a "semantic corrosion":

> [There is] … the well known weathering of the word "folklore" because of its bad use by the institutional dance troupes inspired in the tradition. Those troupes have called themselves "folkloric" and their promoters and performers folklorists. Such an irregular absorption of a term that among us (Latin) Americans was untainted during the first half of the century brought about, little by little its semantic corrosion to the point of generating in the hearts and minds of many specialists an ostensive shame of being called "folklorists" because it was the dancers who were "folklorists" and not the scientists, (Carvalho Neto 1990: 53)

In spite of his argument about the purity of the term in the first half of the twentieth century, Carvalho Neto cites sources from that time, such as a statement by scholar Arthur Ramos, who said in 1942 (during the allegedly "untainted" times) that "folklore fell in discredit" (Carvalho Neto 1990: 54) indicating a rift between scholars and recreators, or it may be more accurate to say between some scholars and recreators as a constitutive feature of the folklore field. In 1951, during the First Brazilian Congress of Folklore, Raúl Lima stated that "there is nothing more lamentable and intolerable than the deformations of something as serious, beautiful and important as the reproduction of customs and traditional manifestations of the spontaneous art of the people" (Lima in Carvalho Neto 1990: 54). Uruguayan scholar Lauro Ayestarán also tackles the issue of the appropriation of folklore by artists who are not "folk" themselves. In his discussion of the use of folk music by composers of classical music, he states that "folklore is a closed and non-transferable world." He traces a line that starts with "the inaccurately called 'folklorists'" and ends with "the supreme uses of a Manuel de Falla or Bela Bartók" (Ayestarán 1968: 44). Thus, Ayestarán presents a negative characterization of "folklorists," that is, the artists that perform folklore forms in non-folk contexts for massive audiences. According to him they go against grain of the classical music composers who make "supreme" (sic) uses of folklore when they incorporate it into their compositions.

The common orientation of Latin American folklore studies in its formative years is best expressed in a book published in 1975 called *Teorías del Folklore en América Latina* (Theories of Folklore in Latin America) edited by the Chilean scholar Manuel Dannemann and published in Venezuela. This book attempted to piece together a consistent disciplinary body from developments that had been carried out in different countries. The volume features essays by Manuel Dannemann (Chile), Augusto Raúl Cortazar (Argentina), Darío Guevara (Ecuador), Luis da Cámara Cascudo (Brazil),

Renato Almeida (Brazil), Dora P. de Zárate (Panama), Ildefonso Pereda Valdés (Uruguay), Guillermo Abadía Morales (Colombia) and Isabel Aretz (Venezuela). The volume intended to offer a comprehensive survey of Latin American folklore scholarship, something that it largely accomplished, as there were several countries with a history of disciplinary development represented. One of the book's main goals was to show the advancement that had taken place in each country. The essays show a great deal of shared notions, influenced by the ideas of Cortazar, who was also present in the book with a posthumous work (he died in 1974). The volume was a consequence of the interaction between Latin American and US folklore scholars mediated by Américo Paredes, himself an intellectual who lived "in between" two worlds. Paredes sought to promote a dialogue between Latin American and US folklore scholars. For American folkloristics, the eventual outcome was the acclaimed volume *Toward New Perspectives in Folklore* (1972), a book that Paredes edited together with Richard Bauman and which became a milestone in the field of Folkloristics in general.[11]

Of all the works published in the Latin American volume, it is Dannemann's that stands out as proposing an alternative approach to folklore studies. In the first part of his essay, he surveys and criticizes different approaches to folklore, both in Latin America and in the United States. In the second part, he makes an effort to depart both from the approaches he surveys and from what the other essays published in the volume propose by outlining his "fundamental concepts of folkloric culture" (1975: 23).

Toward New Perspectives in Folklore presented innovative approaches that were still in the process of being formulated. In his essay "Differential Identity and the Social Base of Folklore" Bauman asserted that a common identity was not necessary for the sharing of folklore expressions. He thus initiated an approach that he developed further in later works and that in Latin America came to be called "Nuevas perspectivas" echoing the book title that he had edited with Paredes. The Latin American counterpart, *Teorías del Folklore en América Latina,* presented elaborations that had been in the making since the 1940s. They all stressed the common identity as a basic feature of folklore, either as a given extant trait (contra Bauman, see above), or as something that had to be programatically construed. Most of the scholars who participated in this volume expressed ideas that were a culmination of their scholarly production more than a beginning. In that respect, the two books are asynchronous. The volume that collects the works of mostly US scholars is a harbinger of upcoming developments in the field; the Latin American volume represents more of an end of a stage in folklore studies' development. Certainly, Paredes's was a valuable attempt. However, the conditions for a fruitful dialogue were not given at the time. While the scholars that Paredes and Bauman invited to take part in *Toward New Perspectives in Folklore* belonged to the upcoming generation, the scholars that partook in the Latin American counterpart, with the sole exception of Dannemann, were older researchers tied to the principles they had espoused in their long careers. In the late 1970s, the advent of a younger generation began something that came close to a dialogue. I say "close to a dialogue" because a dialogue would have entailed communication going both ways. The years following the publication of both volumes saw a quite systematic translation of scholarly works originally published in English and translated into Spanish, which has been very beneficial for the academic development of the field in Latin America (in those places where folklore studies found a site within the academic system). There have not been any substantial translations the other way.

THE THIRD STAGE: NEW LATIN AMERICAN PERSPECTIVES FROM THE 1970s TO THE PRESENT

Up until the 1970s, the general orientation of folklore studies in Latin America evolved along similar lines. Folklore studies dealt with phenomena that were "traditional," "popular," "anonymous," and "oral." As mentioned earlier, those traits were not questioned, and the terms were used rather uncritically. In the 1970s, a younger generation of folklore scholars attempted a rupture from earlier conceptions. They got acquainted with the new developments in US Folkloristics, arguably an outcome of the efforts of Américo Paredes and his connections to both worlds, and they embraced other fields, such as communication studies and semiotics, as ways of furthering the interpretative scope of folkloristics. Thus, the Latin American academic study of folklore after the 1970s developed new theoretical and methodological approaches. One of the key issues newly addressed was that of folklore's social base. Scholars proposed a different way of conceptualizing the "folk." The "folk" was no longer defined by the belonging to any social group in particular but rather by the behavior itself and by the quality of membership that the behavior accomplished.

Manuel Dannemann (1976), who based his ideas on the postwar works of Swiss scholar Richard Weiss, headed the rupture. Opposing the idea of the isolated rural community as the single locus of folk culture, he argued that no group of people was folk in itself; rather, every human being could be a bearer of folklore notwithstanding his or her social condition or geographic location. He asserted that folklore was a kind of behavior in which each person participated in terms of the particulars of a given context. Dannemann also did not judge that those who were members of a folk communities were stable groups, lasting over time, or that they all shared the same traits. Rather, there were situations more or less conducive for a person to behave vernacularly. This could happen in a permanent group, like a peasant community, in which people got together for a festival; but folk behavior could also be manifest in situations where participation was contingent on an event or a site and not the joint membership of a group. In his understanding, drivers who stopped at a religious shrine by a road could belong to different social classes, ethnic groups, region, but they became members of a particular folk group the moment they left their offering at the shrine.

Following Dannemann's lead of breaking with the approaches that postulated an aprioristic definition of the folk group was Argentine scholar Martha Blache. Blache was a graduate student at Indiana University's Folklore Institute in the 1960s and defended her dissertation in the 1970s. Although she carried out her first studies in Argentina in the previous stage, her stay in the United States, at the time when folklore studies were reformulated, exerted great influence on her views of the discipline. In 1980 Blache put forward a novel definition of folklore. Together with semiotician Juan Ángel Magariños de Morentin, she delivered a groundbreaking paper at the Congreso de Folklore Iberoamericano that took place in Santiago del Estero, Argentina. That work *Enunciados fundamentales tentativos para la definición del concepto de folklore* (Tentative Basic Statements for the Definition of the Concept of Folklore) (1980) set the foundation for a series of papers and articles that endeavored to establish a new agenda for the study of folklore. In their initial paper, Blache and Magariños de Morentin defined folklore as "a social message that simultaneously identifies and differentiates groups through recourse to a non-institutional metacode in force in the group of substitutive successors of those who generated it" (1980: 15). With this formulation, they attempted several tasks at once:

- to conceptualize folklore as a social discourse. They therefore stressed that folklore studies should move the focus from the study of "things" in themselves to the analysis of behaviors.
- to show that the "folk" could be an encompassing and flexible category, those who shared a particular code, or as they put it a "non-institutional metacode," that is, not a language, but a distinct way of speaking that language; not an established ritual, but a singular way of practicing it, which had to be proven by the researchers by following rigorous methodological steps;
- to address the traditionality of folklore forms by dealing with the issue of the "substitutive successors," that is, those who learned to carry out a certain behavior from others, not necessarily belonging to an older generation. This was an alternative to the ideas of intergenerational transmission and time depth as a defining trait of folklore;
- most and foremost, to develop an analytical framework for a field that they perceived as merely descriptive.

In order to accomplish those goals, both scholars coauthored, and also published separately, a number of conceptual and methodological works, throughout the 1980s and 1990s. The initial charter, issued in 1980, was followed by a series of articles that refined it. Blache and Magariños de Morentin thus tackled the definition of "folk group" (1986), put forward a methodological outline for the analysis of folk narrative (Magariños de Morentin 1987; Magariños de Morentin 1994), revised their initial definition of folklore (Blache and Magariños de Morentin 1992), and addressed the concept of context (Magariños de Morentin 1993; Blache and Magariños de Morentin 1993).

The two scholars were pivotal among different actors in the Latin American scene. They carried out a critique of the romantic descriptive folkloristic studies done by a plethora of scholars who worked for cultural institutions or independently, or even those in academic settings who upheld older viewpoints. They were blatantly explicit in their criticism, both by promoting their approach and by emphasizing, against the romantic creed, that "love for the stuff is not enough" (1980: 6). They argued that the discourse about the scientific nature of the field that had been an important part of the rhetoric in the earlier phase was not accompanied by equal efforts to support who claim, such as the use of rigorous methodological tools (Blache and Magariños de Morentin 1980).

At the same time, they defended the field against other Latin American academics who put into question the existence of folklore studies as a legitimate discipline. The following statement is quite indicative of their position in this dialogue with different interlocutors:

> The system of relationships that folklore allows, tells us about the social transcendence of this discipline, even when anecdotal studies that limited themselves to the description of tales, myths or ponchos, did not inform about that transcendence. To leave aside the

analysis of such manifestations, as some would suggest, would not contribute to clearing up the criticism of these approaches. One should change the perspective and pay heed to the system of relationships that folklore puts into play. (Blache and Magariños de Morentin 1986: 7)

The exemplification with the listing of "tales, myths or ponchos" is crucial to understand who their major interlocutors were. On the one hand, the scholars who worked for cultural institutions, the amateur collectors, and the "folkloristas," that is, artists who performed the allegedly "folk" expressions in settings such as festivals and theaters. On the other, the academics that criticized the essentialist notions and whom they wanted to present with alternative ways of researching the materials that had historically been studied by folklore studies. The "poncho" is one of the main diacritics of "folklore" in commonplace discourse, associated with a nationalist rhetoric and the idea that folklore is something to be found in rural society; both notions complement one another and relate to the way in which the Latin American concept of folklore was constructed in the previous stage. The poncho stands metonymically for the gaucho, a figure that through the persistent work of folklore scholars, but also of other intellectuals that embraced criollismo, like writers, playwrights, and journalists, came to symbolize the Argentine nation (Prieto 1988). In this respect, Blache and Magariños de Morentin were linked to the field as practiced in the earlier stage. Yet they became a hinge for its future developments by addressing the other interlocutors, that is, the academic scholars who dismissed the study of folklore. Thus, they argued that it was not necessarily the type of materials historically undertaken by folklore studies that had to be abandoned, but rather the old ways of approaching them. Blache and Magariños de Morentin's work intended to be in connection with the international developments in folklore studies. They took up the notions put forward by contemporary US scholars like Richard Bauman and Dan Ben-Amos, to establish analogies and set up differences. They thus aimed at the ambitious task of relating their rigorous methodological approach for the study of folklore materials based on cognitive semiotics with the approaches derived from the ethnography of speaking. Unfortunately, though they found a venue for the dissemination of these ideas in the *Revista de Investigaciones Folklóricas*, which Blache herself founded and directed for 20 years, these scholars did not put together all those works in a representative volume that would have placed this new conceptualization of folklore in dialogue with contemporary trends in folklore studies.

From its inception, Blache and Magariños de Morentin's formulation of folklore that broke away from essentialist conceptions met with resistance by Latin American folklore scholars, and was not known by the non-Spanish reading academic folklore community in the rest of the world. Consequently, it never reached beyond the small academic circles that had embraced folklore as a legitimate field in Latin America. Nor did it reach the cultural policies organizations, which continued abiding by the older way of approaching folklore. For those organizations, adopting or simply thinking over this formulation would have involved questioning the foundations of their work. Their mission was the collection and promotion of the cultural production of groups perceived as about to wane or unable to give continuity to their own culture. This formulation was not taken up by the Latin American academic community devoted to the critical studies of culture either. Basing themselves on what had been the history of folklore studies and its static conceptions of culture throughout the twentieth century, they rejected Folkloristics altogether. Latin American scholars of culture did not bother to ponder that the ruptures within the field itself involved a distancing from the established essentialist ideas.

As a consequence of that disregard, at present, in spite of the problematization of the concept of folklore carried out by some of the most prominent scholars, many Latin American academics as well as independent scholars see the field of "folklore" negatively. It appears to them as transparent and uniform, serving an acritical, reactionary agenda. These scholars only take into consideration the fixed meaning of the term tied to an essentialist view of culture and do not contemplate its polysemic side, the one in which definitions and analysis are provisional and subject to contestation.

One of the most prominent Latin American scholars of culture, Néstor García Canclini, regards folklore as a means through which large sectors of the population have been constituted as isolated components of the modern nation and at the same time a reservoir of a seemingly uncontaminated national culture. García Canclini argues that

> (...) Folklore Studies (el folklore) most of the time acts with a melancholic intent to remove the traditional from the industrial reordering of the symbolic market and to put it under custody as an imaginary reserve of nationalist political discourses. (1988: 9)

García Canclini contends that in spite of the abundance of "descriptions," folklore scholars presented decontextualized facts, hence they gave very few explanations of "the popular" (1992: 198). He thus fails to differentiate between "folklore" as an ideological tool and "folklore" as a scholarly discipline.

Articulating a negative view of the field of folklore studies as an endeavor offering picturesque descriptions of customs devoid of the social relations of which they are part, critical works on the field have been influential in establishing the notion of "popular culture" instead of "folklore" as the appropriate one to use. The concept of "popular culture" is thus frequently applied in academic writing instead of folklore. Governmental and non-governmental organizations dealing with the materials that folklore studies was historically preoccupied with have also made the decision of using this term. In spite of their rhetoric against folklore and folklore studies, the renaming as "popular culture" of what had previously fallen under the rubric of "folklore" has not necessarily meant a real conceptual shift from the shortcomings of the word that it replaces. Some of the concepts that have received the sharpest criticism within the field of folklore studies are often used acritically. Even though the academic study of folklore departed from the essentialist notions, its old concepts come back when cultural policies are implemented, regardless of allegedly critical standpoints.[12]

REAPPRAISING LATIN AMERICAN FOLKLORE STUDIES

Although the practice of collecting and the use of the term "folklore" can be traced back to the last decades of the nineteenth century, the field of folklore studies in Latin America was shaped between the 1920s and the 1970s. The guiding principles of that time persist to this day through the inclusion of the field in cultural institutions and in schools devoted to the teaching of artistic expressions like "folk" dance and music. They are as well apparent in the current formulation of cultural policies devoted to "folk culture" and in the endurance of commonplace ideas about folklore and its qualities (traditional, authentic, genuine, pertaining to the "people"), which are expressed in a multiplicity of venues from mass media to everyday conversation.

In spite of what has been established as a standard notion in critical appraisals of folklore studies, namely, that they only served nationalist ends, the conceptual foundations of the field and the actual praxis of its scholars paint a more complex, nuanced portrait. Affirming this does not mean denying the strong relationship between folklore studies and nationalist ideologies. That link that has been well proven for European scholarship had a counterpart in Latin America. Nationalism and the rescuing enterprise have been two basic tenets of the field, which persist in some circles to this day. However, folklore studies, understood in that same way, also allowed for an insight into folk culture that undermined the nationalistic principle. The practice itself of the collection of folklore materials made by cultural institutions and independent amateur scholars, and the teaching of "folk arts," despite the nationalist rhetoric that they may have used, paved the way for a positive assessment of otherwise disregarded cultural productions. This assessment was based on an explicit valuation of those materials, independent of how they were perceived, whether as relics, survivals, or stuff to be rescued before it was gone. The work of folklore scholars, even of those that held essentialist views provided the basis for the recognition of cultural diversity and the agentive power of the groups whose lore was collected and eventually recreated. Therefore, the effect has been paradoxical. Even when done from a reactionary perspective, the recovery of the so called "saberes populares" (popular lore) has contributed to the positive valuation of cultural expressions of social collectives that elite intellectuals did not judge as producers of culture. Isabel Aretz, the renowned Argentine musicologist who carried out the most productive part of her career in Venezuela, argued, echoing Cortazar's ideas, that it was necessary to "safeguard the traditional oral culture amassed by generations in the most remote corners while the elites consumed first, European, and then North American cultural productions" (1975: 8). Hence, albeit from a paternalistic standpoint, the recovery of certain forms of knowledge was considered worthwhile. Expressions produced in remote areas by isolated peoples were thus worth collecting, preserving and promoting. I would argue that this way of carrying out folkloristic work has brought about positive unplanned outcomes. Even critics of the works done following this paradigm acknowledge their positive influence. Carlos Miñana Blasco (2000) relates that he himself, together with many other young idealists, went on field trips in the 1960s inspired by the works done by such collectors in order to record, experience, and learn traditional music. In addition to the creative and mind-opening effects of folklore studies done in the "traditional" manner, the field proved to be engaging and challenging and drew in people to carry out research on expressive forms previously overlooked by elite intellectuals. In this respect, the semantic stability of the term "folklore" (with all its associations) has been the basis of intellectual and artistic reelaborations that undermined its conservative principles. A positive example in the artistic sphere is the Nuevo Cancionero movement which originated in the 1960s, in which poets and singers recreated folk expressions and contextualized them in revolutionary political discourse.

If one considers the general orientation established with the institutionalization of folklore studies in the public sector, one is faced with a field with a static perception of society. Still, it should be noticed that:

First, folklore scholars themselves (not all of them, but several) after the 1970s reformulated some of its tenets. They put forward alternate ways of conceptualizing the field that are in use to this day. Some of those different ways proceed not only from new formulations in other areas like communication studies and semiotics, but also from a reassessment of the disciplinary charts of the first-stage precursors. For instance, in the context of the University of Buenos Aires, Blache's work led to the formation of a research team that studied expressions previously ignored by the field practitioners, like those performed in urban areas. It also advanced the translation of works by European and US scholars into Spanish. The space of folklore studies, though peripheral in the academic milieu, was preserved. To this day, folklore has preserved a space in the Argentine academic context and her disciples have found ways of carrying forward her work. Current research in folklore studies is undergoing a revision of the terms proposed by Blache's work, in an ongoing dialogue with international approaches like performance theory.

Second, the materials recorded by the folklorists from the second stage, even under the romantic nationalistic paradigm, also provided the basis for the recognition of certain, previously disregarded social groups as producers of valuable culture. This established the basis for later reappraisals of their culture, and to creative reelaborations by contemporary artists.

While the establishment in cultural institutions has led to stagnation, the academic study of folklore, which, although peripherally, has endured, has allowed for the restatement of earlier essentialist concepts. To this day, the disagreements about its scope and the constant need to redefine it have been productive. Paradoxically, some of the old essentialist notions have reappeared under new guises, such as some of the formulations in heritage studies, a growing field of inquiry and application in the 1990s. The concept of intangible or immaterial heritage is a case in point (Bialogorski and Fischman, 2001). Those old notions provided the basis for the founding of associations that undertake tasks of protection and preservation, in the same way that the early folklore scholars attempted to safeguard the expressive forms that supposedly were about to wane. The difference is that folklore studies evolved in recent decades through the criticism of its initial foundations (Fischman 2004), while heritage policies still uphold the goal of preserving the "authentic legacy from our past," the one that "speaks about our roots" and is threatened, if not anymore by industrialization and modernity, by globalization. Such current reframing of the old concepts and rhetoric should lead to a reappraisal of folklore studies as a field that has provided insightful means to analyze cultural expressions and that has been able to submit its basic premises to criticism. Latin American folklore studies, for all its contradictions and opposing theoretical developments, which come from the early stages of the field and that have endured and coexist with the recent formulations in a constant and lasting debate, has an unquestionable say when it comes to thinking critically about creative cultural expressions in their social and historical contexts.

NOTES

1 The term Latin America in this chapter encompasses all the nations in the American continent that were part of the Spanish and Portuguese empires from the conquest until they achieved their independence from colonial rule.

2 In this chapter, all translations are by the author.

3 I am aware of the arbitrariness of periodizations. The one I propose here combines conceptual and institutional turning points. As I show throughout the chapter, old and new ideas coexist in what appears to be an endless continuum, from early days to the present. However, certain shifts that mark reorientations can also be noted. Then, marking three stages allows for an enhanced consideration of nuances in the field's history.

4 Some of the most prominent Folklore Studies scholars in Latin America, who developed their careers in the second stage of the field, had degrees in the following disciplines: law, literature, history, geography, sociology, dentistry and medicine (Blache 1983).

5 Renato Ortiz (1992) on discussing the relationship between the development of Folklore Studies and the establishment of the nation-states for the Brazilian case notes a correlation between the construction of the field and the emergence of a regional consciousness that opposes the centralizing character of the state. He considers the studies of folklore as a resource that the elites used in order to confront the centralization of the state.

6 It could be hypothesized that Hoffman-Krayer's concept got to Cortazar via the works of the Italian fascist ethnologist José Imbelloni, who moved to Argentina in the 1920s, and whom he credits in some of his books (1944, 1959). Imbelloni's concept of folklore and the "folk" can be read in the following statements: "As far as the music, the songs, and dances of Argentine folklore are concerned, it is not possible to ignore that they are cultural goods of the highest lineage for the fact that they proceed from the musical culture and poetry of the Spanish Golden Age" (…) "all the folklore forms, even the ones that seem to be more rustic were one day property and ornament of the chiefs, courtiers, priests, caciques, wealthy merchants, teachers and artists" (1959: 46). Although the volume where these quotes appear was published in 1959, the chapters were, according to a footnote by Imbelloni, from a symposium that met in 1942. I would like to stress that acknowledging Imbelloni´s influence on Cortazar's works by no means implies attributing fascist ideas to Cortazar.

7 He relativized these ideas when he sketched out his "deslindes conceptuales"(conceptual demarcations) as a way of broadening his framework's scope. He thus included within the purview of Folklore Studies what he termed "transplantes" (transplants) – that is, the expressions that were originally performed in "folk" communities and are performed in urban contexts when their inhabitants move to the cities, "elementos folklóricos transculturados" (transculturated folkloric elements), expressions that were originally folk, but are currently performed by urban dwellers, like proverbs, sayings, and superstitions, and "proyecciones" (projections), expressions produced outside the folk community and transmitted by mechanical and institutional means.

8 Malinowski's thoughts were also an influence on Cortazar. He translated *A Scientific Theory of Culture and Other Essays* into Spanish (1948).

9 The same was going to happen later with the new formulations that were put forward in the late 1970s and early 1980s.

10 In academic circles, there was in addition another view, influenced by the works of Antonio Gramsci and the elaborations of Luigi Lombardi Satriani, which had, however, fewer adherents. This group contended that the "folk" were the working classes (Blache 1983). According to this position, folklore was the possession of the social class that did not own the means of production or as Peruvian scholar Efraín Morote Best called them, they were,

the "bereft producers" (1991: 85) who used their cultural expressions in their struggle against hegemony.

In spite of the different understandings on *who* the "folk" were, isolated peasants or well integrated subaltern groups, both views shared the notion that it was possible to determine a priori who would be the carriers of folklore. Belonging to a folk community as the most widespread conception proposed or to a particular location in the social structure defined who could partake of particular cultural forms. In this way, folklore was delimited socially by locating it in the lower strata of the social structure, and physically by situating it in rural areas or in the poor areas of the big cities. Once the folk were circumscribed in this way, scholars could delimit the "lore" or type of knowledge that this segment of the population could produce. This became the object of study of this discipline.

11   Toward New Perspectives in Folklore was published first as a special issue of the *Journal of American Folklore* 84: 331 (1971). Compare the chapter on North American folklore studies (Bendix and Haring, in this volume).

12   In a recent compilation done in Ecuador by the Centro Interamericano de Artesanías y Artes Populares (CIDAP), the word "folklore" is explicitly removed from the study and replaced by the term "popular culture" with the argument that the former has acquired "odd and demeaning connotations" (Naranjo Villavicencio 2002: 20). The author uses the term "folklore" with negative overtones when he explains that "certain social sectors of Manabí society consider popular celebrations like the Fiesta de San Pedro y San Pablo as folkloric in the worst possible meaning of the term (sic)" ("en el peor sentido del término (sic)" (2002: 20). The author goes on to state that "it should not be forgotten that in this province, in spite of all processes of modernization, its rural population is still in the majority, and it is there, in the Manabita rural areas where popular culture acquires its most *authentic, purest* identitary expression" (2002: 26, my emphasis). This statement brings us once again to the persistence of romantic notions that have remained in governmental institutions and cultural agencies.

REFERENCES

Ambrosetti, Juan Bautista. 1963. *Los argentinos y su folklore*. Edición a cargo de Augusto Raúl Cortazar. Buenos Aires: Centurión.

Anderson, Benedict. 1983. *Imagined Communities: Reflections on the Origin and Spread of Nationalism*. London: Verso.

Aretz, Isabel. 1975. "Palabras liminares" in *Teorías del Folklore en América Latina*. Caracas: INIDEF.

Ayestarán, Lauro. 1968. *Teoría y práctica del folklore*. Montevideo: Arca.

Bialogorski, Mirta and Fernando Fischman. 2001. "Folklore y patrimonio intangible: viejas y nuevas conceptualizaciones." *Revista de Investigaciones Folclóricas* 16: 99–102.

Blache, Martha. 1983. "El concepto de folklore en Hispanoamérica." *Latin American Research Review* XVIII(3): 135–148.

Blache, Martha. 1991. "Folklore y nacionalismo en la Argentina: su vinculación de origen y su desvinculación actual." *Revista de Investigaciones Folklóricas* 6: 56–66.

Blache, Martha and Juan A. Magariños de Morentin. 1980a. *Síntesis crítica de la teoría del folklore en Hispanoamérica*. Buenos Aires: Tekné.

Blache, Martha and Juan A. Magariños de Morentin. 1980b. "Enunciados fundamentales tentativos para la definición del concepto de folklore." *Cuadernos* 3. Buenos Aires: Centro de Investigaciones Antropológicas, pp. 6–15.

Blache, Martha and Juan A. Magariños de Morentin. 1986. "Criterios para la delimi-

284   FERNANDO FISCHMAN

tación del grupo folklórico." *Revista de Investigaciones Folklóricas* 1: 5–8.

Blache, Martha and Juan A. Magariños de Morentin. 1987. "Lineamientos metodológicos para el estudio de la narrativa folklórica." *Revista de Investigaciones Folklóricas* 2: 16–19.

Blache, Martha and Juan A. Magariños de Morentin. 1992. "Enunciados fundamentales tentativos para la definición del concepto de folklore: 12 años después." *Revista de Investigaciones Folklóricas* 7: 29–34.

Blache, Martha and Juan A. Magariños de Morentin. 1993. "El contexto de la actuación en la narrativa folklórica." *Revista de Investigaciones Folklóricas* 8: 23–28.

Carrizo, Juan Antonio. 1953. *Historia del folklore argentino.* Buenos Aires: Ministerio de Educación. Instituto Nacional de la Tradición.

Carvalho-Neto, Paulo de. 1953. *Folklore y psicoanálisis.* Buenos Aires: Psique.

Carvalho-Neto, Paulo de. 1990. "Valor de la palabra 'folklore'." *Revista de Investigaciones Folklóricas* 5: 53–56.

Cortazar, Augusto Raúl. 1939. *El folklore y el concepto de nacionalidad.* Buenos Aires.

Cortazar, Augusto Raúl. 1942. *Bosquejo de una introducción al folklore.* Tucumán: Universidad Nacional de Tucumán.

Cortazar, Augusto Raúl. 1944. *Confluencias culturales en el folklore argentino.* Buenos Aires: Artes Gráficas Sebastián de Amorrortu.

Cortazar, Augusto Raúl. 1949. *El carnaval en el folklore calchaquí.* Buenos Aires: Sudamericana.

Cortazar, Augusto Raúl. 1959. *Esquema del folklore.* Buenos Aires: Editorial Columba.

Cortazar, Augusto Raúl. 1975. "Los fenómenos folklóricos y su contexto humano y cultural" in *Teorías del Folklore en América Latina.* Caracas: INIDEF, pp. 45–86.

Dannemann R. Manuel. 1975. "Teoría folklórica. Planteamientos críticos y proposiciones básicas" in *Teorías del Folklore en América Latina.* Caracas: INIDEF, pp. 13–43.

Dannemann, Manuel. 1976. "Nuevas reflexiones en torno al concepto de folklore." *Folklore Americano* 22: 121–129.

Fischman, Fernando. 2004. "La competencia del folklore para el estudio de procesos sociales. Actuación y (re)tradicionalización" in María Inés Palleiro, Ed. *Arte, comunicación y tradición.* Buenos Aires: Dunken, pp. 167–180.

García Canclini, Néstor. 1988. "¿Reconstruir lo popular?" *Revista de Investigaciones Folklóricas* 3: 7–21.

García Canclini, Néstor. 1992. *Culturas híbridas. Estrategias para entrar y salir de la modernidad.* Buenos Aires: Sudamericana.

Imbelloni, José. 1959. "Introito. Concepto y praxis del folklore." *Folklore Argentino.* Buenos Aires: Editorial Nova, pp. 7–83.

Lenz, Rodolfo. 1895–1897. *Estudios Araucanos.* Santiago: Imprenta Cervantes.

Magariños de Morentin, Juan A. 1993. "El contexto de interpretación de los fenómenos folklóricos." *Revista de Investigaciones Folklóricas* 8: 19–22.

Magariños de Morentin, Juan A. 1994. "El código folklórico en la narrativa oral." *Revista de Investigaciones Folklóricas* 9: 14–17.

Malinowski, Bronislaw. 1948. *Una teoría científica de la cultura y otros ensayos.* Buenos Aires: Sudamericana.

Malvestitti, Marisa. 2005. "'Descubriendo' los textos araucanos de Lehmann-Nitsche." *Anuario de la Facultad de Ciencias Humanas de la UNLPam,* Santa Rosa 7: 299–303.

Malvestitti, Marisa. Forthcoming. *Mongeleluchi Sunga. Los Textos Araucanos documentados por Roberto Lehmann-Nitsche.*

Mañana Blasco, Carlos. 2000. "Entre el folklore y la etnomusicóloga. 60 años de estudios sobre la música popular tradicional en Colombia." *A Contratiempo. Revista de música en la cultura,* Bogotá (11): 36–49.

Moreno, Arosemena Julio. 2007. "El siglo XX y los estudios folklóricas en Panamá." *Diversidad* 1(1): 10–23.

Morote Best, Efraín. 1991. "Acerca del folklore" in *Folklore: bases teóricas y metodológicas.* Lima: Lluvia Editores, pp. 80–91.

Naranjo Villavicencio, Marcelo. 2002. *Manabí/Colección La Cultura Popular en el Ecuador.* Tomo IX. Cuenca: Cidap.

Ochoa-Gautier, Ana María. 2006. "Sonic Transculturation, Epistemologies of Purification and the Aural Public Sphere in Latin America." *Social Identities* 12(6): 803–825.

Ortiz, Renato. 1992. *Românticos e folcloristas: cultura popular.* São Paulo: Olho D'água.

Paredes, Américo and Richard Bauman, Eds. 1972 [2000]. *Toward New Perspectives in Folklore.* Bloomington: Trickster Press.

Poviña, Alfredo. 1954. *Teoría del folklore.* Córdoba: Imprenta de la Universidad.

Prieto, Adolfo. 1988. *El discurso criollista en la formación de la Argentina moderna.* Buenos Aires: Sudamericana.

Vilhena, Luís Rodolfo. 1997. *Projeto e missão: o movimento folclórico brasileiro.* Rio de Janeiro: Funarte/Fundação Getulio Vargas.

Zárate, Dora P. de. 1975. "Nuestra posición frente a las teorías folklóricas" in *Teorías del Folklore en América Latina.* Caracas: INIDEF, pp. 131–150.

CHAPTER 15

FOLKLORE STUDIES IN THE UNITED STATES

Lee Haring and Regina F. Bendix

The history of North American folklore studies shows successive modes of thinking about the folk ("natives," immigrants, oppressed) and their lores. Changing conceptions of *folk* (not "us") and *lore* ("their" expressions) facilitated the invention of an identity for an emerging American bourgeoisie. On the settler continent that would eventually bring forth the states of Canada, the United States, and Mexico, relations between indigenous groups and successive waves of immigrants followed a different, often violent course. The negotiation of group relations is ever-present as the inescapable surrounding for folklore.

The continent became a space of settler nations; long before anyone was called a folklorist, it was settlers who took an interest in vernacular expression. Great thinkers among them, like Madison and Jefferson, disdained the culture of those not yet touched by the Enlightenment. But after the American Civil War, a consciousness emerged to mark off myths, legends, tales, proverbs, riddles, and folksongs as folklore. Westward expansion, nationalism, industrialism, ethnocentrism, commerce, conflicts, and competition created the history of folklore studies in the United States. Folkloristics made its special contribution by articulating multiple points of view and demonstrating how various folk groups see reality.

The chapter is organized in three parts. After sketching what is known about pre-contact and first contact modes of folklore, or what the twentieth century would define as "artistic communication in small groups" (Ben-Amos 1971), the second part turns to the emergence of folklore as a category of public interest. The final part discusses the unfolding of folkloristics in the United States from World War II to the present. Such a rapid survey limits the representation of the voluminous work carried out by American

A Companion to Folklore, First Edition. Edited by Regina F. Bendix and Galit Hasan-Rokem.

colleagues. Fortunately, however, several studies and compendia provide more comprehensive insights and materials, which supplement the references in this chapter.[1]

FROM THE COLONIAL PERIOD TO INDEPENDENCE

Ten thousand years before Europeans named the place "North America," and before an Englishman thought up the word "Folk-lore," men, women, and children participated in networks of in-group and external communication. Most of those years had to elapse before the Jesuits began recording the stories being told by the "Indians" they met. Early observers saw them only through European lenses. At first contact, Columbus refused to admit the Indians were even speaking language. He promised Ferdinand and Isabella "to take from this place six of them to Your Highnesses, so that they may learn to speak" (Todorov 1984: 30). Three centuries after the Jesuits, the anthropologist Franz Boas gave his fellow Americans a reliable way of telling Indian tribes apart: their languages. Only in the nineteenth and twentieth centuries did systematic, painstaking research make North American Indians the best-documented indigenous people in the world. By that time, their folklore underwent many transformations. Their myth cycles they treated conservatively, but normal, fluent, variable folkloric communication went on all the time, unobserved by government, censured by the condescension of Christian missionaries. Some Indian groups, such as Cherokees, have been described and studied for three centuries and more; observation of others, such as the Iroquois, was born at the same time as anthropology itself (Morgan 1851). Now, groups like the tradition-minded Hopi of Arizona, teach the world themselves about their traditions through the Internet.

After Europeans arrived and began to settle, the colonization of North America was followed by the opening of the American West. Settlers brought their inherited systems of thought to bear upon the strangeness of their new life. Among the settlers of New England, the prevailing system was Puritanism; Puritans knew "bloody ballads, old wives' cures, pithy proverbs, children's pastimes, sailor superstitions" (Dorson 1959: 38). Their system of thought, imported from Britain, became their most powerful boundary marker. With it, they could identify themselves against supposed, folkloric threats, like Thomas Morton's Maypole celebration at Mount Wollaston in 1627 (romanticized two centuries later in a story by Nathaniel Hawthorne). Morton imported English countryside festivity into a New World evocation of the pagan past, colorfully challenging the somber decor of the colony. Puritans read it clearly: it was a successful, hence unacceptable attempt to set up an alternative political and social order. Morton was deported. Protest folklore and the authoritarian system had found their conflictful way to New England.

Puritans nourished a belief in supernatural happenings, which to them were anything but folklore. As they were specially favored and specially chosen, what happened to them always carried a message. Every event was deployed by God directly, to punish sinners and warn his saints. Accordingly, Mary Rowlandson's account of her captivity among the Indians is cast for her fellow Puritans in the rhetoric of a testimony of her faithfulness under hardship. It was an in-group message, often anthologized for its literary quality. It resembles later examples of "personal experience narrative" (Stahl 1989): withdrawal is followed by marginality, then by final reincorporation into her society. Rowlandson continually reminds her Christian readers that she is not giving them a piece of fiction, but attesting in her title to *The Sovereignty [sic] and Goodness of God*. Her plot is inherently dramatic; her inclusion of vivid detail links her account to the best of oral legend style. So the Puritan system of thought subsumed the oral genre of legend and disseminated it through writing.

Puritan folklore had one preeminent genre – the "providence," which was an occurrence conveying a message, perhaps an indecipherable one. When anything wild or unexpected happened, Puritans had to examine it closely for God's intention in it. Any strange happening was a providence carrying a message. To this genre classification, motivated by Puritan ethnocentrism, is owed the first systematic collection of North American verbal art, Increase Mather's *Essay for the Recording of Illustrious Providences* (1684). According to a modern scholar, this prominent divine "employed a conceptual approach for his collecting project; he faithfully garnered accurate texts from living informants as well as from other fieldworkers …; and he carefully prepared a typology and analysis of his collected materials" (Narvaez 1995: 198). The hand of God was evident to Increase Mather in incidents like this one:

> I have good information that on August 28, 1683, a man there (viz., Samuel Wilson), having caused his dog to mischief his neighbor's cattle, was blamed for his so doing. He denied the fact with imprecations, wishing that he might never stir from that place if he had so done. His neighbor, being troubled at his denying the truth, reproved him, and told him he did very ill to deny what his conscience knew to be truth. The atheist thereupon used the name of God in his imprecations, saying, "He wished to God he might never stir out of that place, if he had done that which he was charged with." The words were scarce out of his mouth before he sunk down dead and never stirred more, a son-in-law of his standing by and catching him as he fell to the ground. (Dorson 1950: 124)

Mather's diligent criteria for collecting and his clear conception of the genre were important forerunners of the scientific standards that were to come along two centuries later. Rowlandson's narrative reinforced the community boundary by addressing the unspeakable atrocities of the "Indians"; Mather's collection reinforced it by arraying remarkable in-group occurrences.

More inter-ethnic folklore developed when the colonists began importing slaves from Africa. Though there was no systematic recording of African American folklore until shortly before the Civil War, the state of things in the slaveholding South was keenly observed by Frances Trollope (mother of the novelist).

> We were much pleased by the chant with which the Negro boatmen regulate and beguile their labour on the river; it consists of but very few notes, but they are sweetly harmonious, and the Negro voice is almost always rich and powerful. (Trollope 1832, 1:28)

Half a dozen years later, that other keen British observer Fanny Kemble heard that voice.

> Their voices seem oftener tenor than any other quality, and the tune and time they keep something quite wonderful; such truth of intonation and accent would make almost any music agreeable.

She even discerned the mélange of styles that always characterized African American expressiveness.

That which I have heard these people sing is often plaintive and pretty, but almost always
has some resemblance to tunes with which they must have become acquainted through
the instrumentality of white men. (Kemble 1863: 127)

So was born the long-lived American stereotype of African Americans as a musical but
imitative people.

After independence was won, settlers generated new forms of folklore to confirm
or challenge the rising bourgeois order. Most flagrant, in the early national period,
was the "anti-rent war," a protest uprising in New York State (1839–1845), in
which tenants disguised themselves as "savages," namely Indians, to harass landlord
agents and sheriffs. The mode of land ownership, imported from feudal Europe,
dictated that every tenant owed both money and goods to his landlord. Troupes of
young men had fun teasing Indians with pistols and tomahawks, but their tarring
and feathering of the landlords' deputies led to the longest rent strike in American
history. Protest folklore was cheered on by the spectators.[2] In the early national
period, when the American economy was so unstandardized that Andrew Jackson
could destroy the Bank of the United States, the backwoodsman Davy Crockett and
the keelboatman Mike Fink were emerging as folk heroes of the period (Dorson
1973: 57–92).

To write the history of folklore in the colonial and early national periods, modern
folklorists have had to do without orality and rely on written sources. Only when the
study of American Indians was launched in the nineteenth century was folklore
recorded from oral performances. Then unseen differences began to emerge. Indian
societies always had their own ways, genres, and categories for their verbal arts. But
the New England Puritans knew only how to draw battle lines between themselves
and the savages. Then when the extensive collecting of the nineteenth century began,
translators of verbal art often obscured the content and pattern of the original material.
For example, they would omit what in their own unreflective aesthetic were repetitions,
which in the Indian aesthetic served poetic purposes. What appeared to be nonsense
syllables in a poem were actually mirroring the patterned content of the rest, summing
up the poem as a whole. Such omissions and failures of understanding reflect the
prevalent mode of nineteenth-century thinking about Indians, even amongst scholars
who were sympathetic to them.[3] With their reliance on written sources, modern
folklorists have tested the successive modes of thought engendered by cultural novelty
and ethnic difference. They find that the Puritans' providences conform to the
requirements of folklore and that heroes like Davy Crockett embodied the traits and
values of their time (Dorson 1959: 24–33, 203–214). These modern tests, and a new
discipline called folklore, were derived from the earlier systems of thought which
settlers had brought with them.

THE INVENTION OF FOLKLORE: FROM THE CIVIL WAR
TO WORLD WAR II

The nineteenth century in North America brought to the rising bourgeoisie a new
way of thinking about the "primitive" (Indians) and a new class consciousness that
engendered the "folk" (immigrants, workers). In Europe, folklore – both concept and

study – was being born in and of industrial societies, as a response to modernization and as a foundation for nation-states built on language groups rather than monarchies. Colonial expansion had already enriched the European public sphere with reports of living human beings who personified the racial, cultural, and religious Other. The self-other dichotomy continually wove itself through folklore's history. Having rationalized technology as far as possible, those societies had distanced themselves most from nature, whereas North America presented itself to the settlers as the world's supreme example of a state of nature. The concept of folklore implied social critique, pointing to class differences, even to older forms of agriculture, against which the best-regulated, most orderly societies then began to think and reflect about themselves. European collecting on the scientific model responded to the sense that old forms as being threatened, on the verge of disappearance. When the British antiquarian W.J. Thoms coined the term "Folk-lore" in 1846, he was recognizing the vitality inherent in those forms (Thoms 1965). In America such recognition, fueled by the sense of loss inherent to any modernizing society, asked whose lore was in most need of salvaging. Continuing hostility between colonials and Native American populations, coupled with the westward settlement, generated, at least initially, contrasting priorities and ethnic slurs. If the "folk" were to be a distinct segment of a developed society, could the "natives" – savages by the definitions of the time – be a folk? Only after the American Civil War did the concept of "lore" expand enough to take them in. By that time, American society had developed so much technology that the emerging bourgeoisie had to create an ideology which would invent ways of handling the social realities. As they learned to celebrate cultural uniqueness, they latently invoked the cultural difference of various others. Divisions between rich and poor, slave and master, black and white, woman and man were displacing the Enlightenment dream of an impossible democracy.

"Culture" belonged to the rich and the masters. The great observer of democracy in America, Alexis de Tocqueville, could not imagine any literary culture outside a ruling class. In America, he knew, literary style was bound to be "fantastic, incorrect, overburdened, and loose" – a reasonably accurate characterization (Tocqueville 1901: 544) of much folklore he never heard or read, such as the tall tales and legends of the early national period. Intuiting the importance of orality, Tocqueville also called for attention to spoken rather than written language. His time, for the United States, was the period of romantic nationalism. The novels of Fenimore Cooper, such as *The Last of the Mohicans*, set in 1757 but published in 1826 as one of the "Leatherstocking Tales," as much as Henry Wadsworth Longfellow's 1855 poem "The Song of Hiawatha," can be seen to be groping, through dressing up "Indian" stories, for an ancient cultural foundation. Thought and reflection determined that the treasure trove of expressive culture or folklore – the heritage of song, the epic that must surely exist, the "native" costume, the tales and legends – could all be gathered, cleaned up, and brought to the public. So was foreshadowed the theme park of the twentieth century and later.

Politically, the re-presentation of folklore confirmed one of the gravest of America's problems. How, in this new land of settlers, could there be a shared culture, which would make for a shared polity? Only by carefully selecting which groups would be mined and which ignored. Intellectually, however, the selection of materials and the resultant mode of thinking about them are the seeds of systematic folklore study, which quickly imported to America its inherently political critique. There if nowhere else, one social base of folklore could be not a shared, but a differential identity, which would be theorized a century later (Bauman 1971). The invention of the study of folklore could then take place, always within the constraints of the classificatory categories and interpretations then available. The conversation would be on bourgeois terms. Rebellion and open conflict could be averted by containing possibly threatening groups through exploiting them culturally. So African-American narratives emerged into white culture through the mediation of the Atlanta journalist Joel Chandler Harris; so religious songs composed by slaves, with the strongest of rebellious undertones, were daintily presented on stage by Hampton Institute and Fisk University students on tour.

At the same time, Americans displayed a fascination with their own national character. In folklore as in literature, the Yankee and the Southern planter-aristocrat emerged as personifications of American traits. The fascination hardly lessened when American industrialization came of age, during the same era as post-Civil War Reconstruction. Both called out a new sort of labor force and dislocated a great many people from their rural homes. Workers were alienated from the products they contributed to but no longer had control over. The work day, with its rigorously structured time, and the opening of the West, with its dangers and fatalities, created the new kind of time called leisure. The loss of one's home context – be this literal or figurative – and the melting away of earlier modes of production contributed to a yearning for the home and the past, no matter how wholesome or toxic that past might actually have been. The newly gained leisure time became a space within which people, amongst many other activities, began to practice the remnants of their old culture. Community singing clubs, costume associations, and amateur scholar circles were another seedbed for a scientific field. Their persistence up to the present confirms the enduring ambivalence of folklore's position between academic inquiry and community-interest-plus-activism.

The later national period, in which the pursuit of happiness became the pursuit of riches, was the formative period for American thought at all social levels. Intellectual leaders like Oliver Wendell Holmes, C.S. Peirce, William James, and John Dewey paid no attention to popular or folk culture, but were obliged to attend to difference, personified in the new presence of European immigrants. Creating and celebrating the cultural uniqueness of the new nation, these leaders implied the cultural difference of various Others; the strength they drew from such celebration had equal potential for the weakness of divisiveness. Awareness of race and class differences spawned a scientific discipline of cultural pluralism.

After the Civil War, as American science began to professionalize, cultural or humanities disciplines began to define themselves. A professional study of folklore had to be inscribed in previously existing scientific discourses. So at first, it accepted the prevailing assumptions about evolution. Establishing a folklore society, and later a university discipline, required creating a specific rationale. There was a subject, the folk, who produced an object, the lore – tales, riddles, songs, and so on; there were folklorists, who produced collections and analyses. Phenomena of expressive culture were newly classified or reclassified, in an emerging terminology claimed and created by the nonfolk. Somehow in 1889 Henry Adams, as much a product of a true American elite as Holmes or William James, envisioned the future of folklore studies in his country: "A few customs, more or less local; a few prejudices, more or less popular; a few traits of thought, suggesting habits of mind, – must form the entire material for a study more important than that of politics or economics" (Adams and Harbert 1986: 31). Did Adams, discerning another level of culture, also intuit the issues of class and race division? Anyway the folk were far less important than the lore. The arrival of Franz Boas (1858–1942) from Germany, the ballad studies of Francis James Child (1825–1896), and the founding of the American Folklore Society (1888) by William Wells Newell (1839–1907) marked the inauguration of folklore as not merely a scholarly and intellectual undertaking, but a moral one as well.

The cultural economy made room for intellectual entrepreneurs like anthropologist Franz Boas (1858–1942), whose Jewish background – unlike what it threatened to do in his native Germany – did not prevent his becoming in the cultural sphere the same sort of agent as Andrew Carnegie or John D. Rockefeller in the economic one. For him, folklore was always part of the emerging discipline of anthropology, which required the collecting of folkloric data as both linguistic and cultural evidence. His early training in physics and geography, followed by extensive fieldwork in British Columbia, led to a new professionalization of anthropology, and hence of folklore studies (though he never taught a university course titled "Folklore"). Through microscopic attention to what he called elements of folk narratives (plots, incidents) in North America, Boas opposed the prevailing evolutionist view of human history, which sought the origin and development of humankind through patterns found in narrative shape and distribution. He successfully disproved the assumption that culture was the result of evolution away from savagery to civilization, and that differences among cultures were caused by race. Culture, including folklore, was what people learned in the sociohistorical circumstances around them. Boas's painstaking attention to folklore among Northwest Coast Indians laid a foundation for an emphasis on the local and specific, which shaped folklore studies ever after in the United States and Canada. Like his colleagues Child and Newell, Boas conceived of American folklore as specimens to be gathered, not rewritten as their predecessors had done. Even when analyzing Tsimshian mythology, Boas searched out "ideas" as objects to study.

> It is obvious that in the tales of a people those incidents of everyday life that are of importance to them will appear either incidentally or as the basis of a plot. Most of the references to the mode of life of a people will be an accurate reflection of their habits. The development of the plot of the story, furthermore, will, on the whole, exhibit clearly what is considered right and wrong. From these points of view it seemed worthwhile to review connectedly those ideas which are either implied or described in detail. Material of this kind does not represent a systematic description of the ethnology of a people, but it has the merit of bringing out those points which are of interest to the people themselves. They present in a way the autobiography of a tribe. (Boas 1916)

The North American Indians Boas studied were only observable in a reduced state of culture, which increased the distance between researcher and researched. The distinctness of the Indian tribes impelled him to invent, and introduce into folklore studies, the concept (though not the term) of cultural pluralism. Under his influence, the *Journal of American Folklore*, founded in 1888, favored publishing verbal materials, leaving material culture to the anthropologists.

The model of Boas' field expeditions directed his students and subsequent folklorists toward "historical particularism"; their accounts tended to attribute uniqueness to every local folk group. The method was soon bolstered by Bronislaw Malinowski's "participant observation."[4] Boas' students were the following: Alfred Kroeber teaching comparative mythology; Robert Lowie writing a dissertation on Plains Indian oral literature; Melville Jacobs inventing a performance-oriented view of folklore; Melville Herskovits placing African American folklore back into African American history; William Bascom collecting Yoruba proverbs and divination practices; Elsie Clews Parsons amassing the details of black and American Indian folklore (Zumwalt 1992); Ruth Benedict teaching folklore while putting anthropology on the popular map (Benedict 1934) – and others maintained folklore studies' roots in anthropology. Nearly a century after his death, Franz Boas continued to be the progenitor of North American folkloristics.

There were conflicts and divisions, because folklore studies already crossed disciplinary borders. Boas the anthropologist made common cause with the philosophy professor-schoolteacher William Wells Newell to move folklore studies towards professionalization. Thereafter, conflict between anthropological and literary folklorists impeded the creation of a unified discipline, until after World War II (Zumwalt 1988). The towering literary folklorist was Francis James Child, who pioneered the American appropriation of British literary materials. His orientation, entirely to the past, and his reliance on written sources influenced many to envisage folklore as comprising the obsolescent and archaic. Child's huge, decades-long amassing of English and Scottish popular ballads was a defining moment in the history of North American folklore studies (Child 1883–1898). It confirmed the old evolutionist master narrative: folklore was by definition a conglomeration of survivals of past stages of the evolution of civilization from lower to higher. Part of Child's motivation, as a Chaucer and Spenser scholar turning away from his native land, was to restore the body of purely oral balladry as a window into late medieval society. Thenceforward to many minds, the essence of American folklore was imported old songs. Those found in the New World would have to be in a decayed and inferior state. Thus the collecting of ballad texts became urgent, because these survivals were a window into history. What was surviving was a system of thought both literary and survivalist.

Yet Child, Boas, and Newell worked together long enough to found the *Journal of American Folklore* (which Boas suggested ought to be named the *American Journal of Folklore* so as to reveal its international scope). Newell, the first editor, discovered that American children were singing songs and playing games that reminded him of Child's English and Scottish ballads (Newell 1883). Thus his orientation to the performance of folklore in the country around him contrasted, solidly but collaboratively, with Boas' dedication to dying Indian languages and Child's medievalism. The three founded a society that would "encourage the collection of the fast-vanishing remains of folk-lore in America … relics of Old English Folk-Lore (ballads, tales, superstitions, etc.) … Lore of Negroes in the Southern States … Lore of the Indian Tribes in North America (myths, tales, etc.) [and the] Lore of French Canada, Mexico, and so on" (Newell 1888: 3). The ballads and children's games in the Journal, being survivals, seemed to say nothing about social tensions, which began to show in the folksongs published by John and Alan Lomax (Lomax, J.A. 1910; Lomax and Lomax 1934). In one of their songs, from the Spanish-American war, American soldiers voiced a typical racism, which would recur among their successors in future wars: "Damn, damn, damn the Filipinos" (Lomax et al. 1934: 547–548). Folkloristics would have to take up a new mode of thinking.

BREAKTHROUGH INTO DISCIPLINARITY

Before World War II, the most productive American folklorists were self-trained. Disoriented from anthropological research, literary studies, or any theory of folklore, they had a commitment to vernacular culture. John Lomax (1867–1948) "started his work in the Southwest very simply because he thought that the artistic products and the basic points of view of the people who worked the cattle ranges of his day deserved wide attention" (Baron and Spitzer 1992: 70). So recalled his daughter Bess Lomax Hawes (1921–2009), who later directed the new Folk Arts Program of the National Endowment for the Arts (1977–1992). The populist vision was shared by others, whose devotion to their folk moved them towards paying attention to the contexts in which items were communicated. They began to notice features of folklife, the regional ethnology European scholars had been studying for decades.

In the New Deal period (1931–1941), American folk traditions began to draw more attention in books and magazines. The Lomaxes and the poet Carl Sandburg published collections of American folk songs, transcribed so as to facilitate performing them at home (Sandburg 1927). As part of the Federal Writers' Project, B.A. Botkin (1901–1975) and Herbert Halpert (1911–2000) conducted folklore fieldwork which saw government-sponsored publication. Botkin's *Lay My Burden Down* was an especially affecting anthology of oral testimony from ex-slaves (Botkin 1945). Botkin followed his well-received *Treasury of American Folklore* (Botkin 1944) with several regional treasuries, voicing a wide, Whitmanesque vision of American culture not shared by all his academic contemporaries. Also addressing a popular, nonscholarly audience were Alan Lomax's record albums of 1947, *Listen to Our Story* and *Mountain Frolic*. Lomax, personifying interdisciplinarity through a long career as pioneering folksong collector, radio, television and record producer, writer, and conceiver of gigantic research projects, anticipated the broad attention to contexts of performance which his academic colleagues would later take up. His later ambitious work on world musical styles was less well received by ethnomusicologists, partly because of comparative assumptions they found reductionist, partly because he stayed outside their university milieu (Lomax, A. 1968).

In the post-World War II years the folk were changing and new lore was being created. Postwar novels – James Jones's *From Here to Eternity*, Joseph Heller's *Catch-22*, and Norman Mailer's *The Naked and the Dead* – were full of GI folklore.[5] Beside the populist love for ordinary people and their arts existed the academic aspiration to establishing a discipline distinct from anthropology and literature. By 1940, four United States universities were offering a concentration in folklore; by 1970, one of them could boast of training 110 graduate students. In subsequent decades, Stith Thompson at Indiana established summer institutes of folklore, to which he invited people outside the academy. At his 1946 institute, when urban folklore in Detroit was presented to an audience of nurses and teachers, their interest in folklore foretold a new mode of thinking soon to develop. The presentation of people's traditions and cultural products to new audiences outside their native heath came to be called "public folklore."[6] New advocates emerged, the first public folklorists. In both university and public settings, folklore and the study of it were a tool for critiquing the concerns of the time: race, ethnicity, and gender.

Race came first. What replaced foreign immigration as a source of tension after World War II was the migration of some 4.5 million African Americans, including many folk artists, from the South to the North. Despite Lomax's extraordinary collecting for the Archive of American Folk Song at the Library of Congress, African American expressive culture was still treated as secondary; the conception of folklore dominating American scholarship was Eurocentric. The "folk" were Europeans; African Americans were denied the status of folk much as American Indians had always been. Few white observers saw in black folklore the resentments, the anger, the memories of slavery, the daily humiliation, which were to surface in the black power movement of the 1960s. Zora Neale Hurston (1891–1960), who studied with Boas, brought anthropological attention to African American folklore (Hurston 1935). A generation later, folklorist Roger D. Abrahams documented "the dozens," a poetic genre performed by black urban youth (Abrahams 1970). Studies of blues songs (Evans 1982) and folk preaching (Rosenberg 1988) revealed that African Americans had invented vernacular forms of the oral formulaic composition found by classicists Parry and Lord in Yugoslavia (Lord 1960). Both folklorists and linguists participated in the struggle for recognition of black culture and language, asserting the coherence of black vernacular language, black expressive culture, and eventually black material culture. Folkloristic scholarship was clearly countering white assertions about the derivativeness of slave culture and voicing its criticism of American racism. Abrahams subsequently uncovered the arts of African American resistance in earlier periods of history (Abrahams 1992). The paradox of folklore studies began to emerge: the effort to unify a broadening field coexisted with its increasing attention to difference and the microscopics of expressivity.

Ethnicity drew more attention than before, first in a revival of the xenophobia of the 1920s. The Cold War was surely not outside consciousness when some folklorists began to abandon the search for individual items of verbal folklore – tales, ballads, proverbs – and to think more attentively about the lives of the minority populations and the individual bearers of tradition within them. Within the university, the impulse to contain difference within the national was urged by the Indiana University professor Richard Mercer Dorson (1916–1981). Trained in American Civilization at Harvard, Dorson conceived folklore as a university discipline; he cast the professional folklorist in the role of a custodian of folklore, which he saw as a possession of the nation. Charged with training those custodians in theory and field methods, he took seriously the duties of department head and thesis supervisor. As book review editor, then as head editor of the *Journal of American Folklore*, he strove to realize a vision of rigorous scholarship. He founded a new *Journal of the Folklore Institute* (later *Journal of Folklore Research*) to strengthen folklore's claim as a discipline. He presided over the American Folklore Society, staged numerous conferences, and built up international connections for North American folklore. Out of his progress-oriented vision Dorson forged a regional folkloristics he proclaimed as genuinely American – which meant keeping American Indians and African Americans on the sidelines. The immigrant Other could be inspected through his nationalist lens, but that lens distorted a folkloristic understanding of North America's plural societies. Despite a textbook that declared the coming-of-age of American folkloristics (Dorson 1972), Dorson's untiring ambition to establish an authoritative discipline with scientific rigor did not succeed in shifting folklore from the university's margin to its center. Yet he persisted in wanting to belong to a community of scholars like the one connecting Andrew Lang, Max Müller, and the other Victorian folklorists (Dorson 1968), and like what he saw in Finland (which had its own history of nurturing nationalism through folklore (Wilson 1976)). Only after Dorson's death did that community arise and flourish, as the American Folklore Society continued to meet year after year in ever-expanding numbers. In the mid-1960s, the AFS had sufficiently gained in membership and momentum to begin meeting separately from other professional societies. With the passing of the American Folklife Preservation Act and the launching of the Smithsonian Folklife Festival, an urban setting for professional folklorists further developed, alongside the regionalism Dorson emphasized.

One of Dorson's most influential students led the university world into the next mode of academic thinking, again attending more to the lore than to the folk. Alan Dundes (1934–2005), in a widely used anthology (Dundes 1965) and in several score articles and books, embraced an unprecedented number of scholarly and critical methods. Among them, comparatism, of both lore and scholarship, stood out. The breadth of folklore, as he conceived it, called for testing theories and importing methods from linguistics, Russian formalism, psychoanalysis, anthropology, literary criticism, myth studies, and structuralism. His call was timely; he made it practical by taking up and demonstrating method after method, applying each one to folklore data. Freud's psychoanalysis was brought to bear on tales, customs, and the very practices of folklorists themselves. Russian formalism was imposed on non-European materials in his analysis of American Indian tales. Indeed, for Dundes the morphological approach to verbal folklore promised to define every genre, thereby rectifying an egregious lack in his discipline. If Dorson had defended a national base for American folklore, Dundes proclaimed the international foundations of the field in his teaching and his editorial work, as well as in building and maintaining scholarly contacts around the globe. Bringing international scholars to teach in the folklore program at the University of California at Berkeley, compiling casebooks on tales, beliefs, and myths to demonstrate a spread of theoretical approaches (Dundes 1988), Dundes fostered a view of folkloristics as an international, cooperative endeavor, united in the fascination with both the specifics of folklore materials and theoretically convincing interpretations (Dundes 1980). Most influential was Dundes' proposal for a synthetic approach embracing three aspects of folklore: the "texture" (phonemes and morphemes of language), the "text" (a single version or performance, as transcribed), and the "context" (the social situation in which a tale might be told or a proverb spoken) (Dundes 1964). The three prongs became standard equipment for US folklorists for the next decades.

In the same years, from a convergence of anthropology, sociolinguistics and folklore arose a new mode of thinking about folk and lore in which folklore figured prominently. Reconceiving linguistic anthropology, Dell Hymes (1927–2009) delineated a sphere of work which insisted on keeping actual performance in the foreground. He named it ethnography of speaking. It would study "the situations and uses, the patterns and functions, of speaking as an activity in its own right" (Hymes 1962: 45). Thus the object of folkloristic study was enlarged to embrace Dundes's three aspects. The boundary between linguistics and ethnography would dissolve, and vernacular verbal art would become a central concern. Hymes's followers quickly turned ethnography of speaking to account. Complexifying the concept of performance, they systematically observed it in Mesoamerica and Africa (Seitel 1980; Sherzer 1983). Rather than set off storytelling and ritual performances as particularly noteworthy sorts of human behavior, ethnography of speaking tended to find artistry in all uses of language, if not to assimilate all language to poetry. A literary movement, "ethnopoetics," the study of nonwestern poetic systems (Tedlock 1972), demanded the integration of oral literatures into the world's literary canon, as a political protest against confining literature to the works of named individual authors. The appeal of ethnography of speaking and ethnopoetics attracted new scholars into the field, and ethnography of speaking became the matrix for the performance-based study of folklore.

In mid-century, American pluralism fostered a new regionalism, in the upper Midwest for example: by the end of the twentieth century, the University of Wisconsin offered a strong folklore concentration. Another flourishing region was the Texas-Mexico border, with a folklore program arising at the University of Texas. Doyen of this flowering was the Mexican-American Américo Paredes (1915–1999), who pioneered the study of minority cultures on the border. Thereby he anticipated later research into the convergence of languages and cultures in other regions, and in non-western societies. Under Paredes's influence, Texas folklorists began to ask to what extent and in what ways the artistic product is related not only to the artist's personality, but also to his or her sociocultural context and the political surroundings. At Texas, Richard Bauman (following up on Hymes, as well as on earlier personality-based studies, for instance by the Hungarian American Linda Dégh), devised a "performance approach" to folklore. Cultural comparatism was conjoined with its logical complement, an attention to the specific character of a performer's individuality; the approach paid so much attention to one of Dundes's aspects that context expanded into the matrix of the folklorist's study (Bauman 1977). Bauman later called this approach the philology of the vernacular; it became the dominant mode of thinking about folklore in United States universities from the 1980s. Descriptive poetics of performance and attention to border cultures opened the way to future studies in bilingual and bicultural communities. It lent a political sensitivity to the study of immigrant and ethnic folklore, which had grown throughout the 1970s at Indiana University (Dégh 1975; Georges 1982; Stern and Cicala 1991). Both directions afforded, to immigrant and the hyphenated Americans from all over the world, a status as "folk" that an earlier, more nationally oriented concept of American folklore had not conceived. Outside the academy, in another kind of in-group pluralism, arose a folksong movement housing a conservative dedication to tradition and a progressive advocacy of a politics of change. Some young people followed Pete Seeger (1919–) in welcoming the rewriting of traditional songs into quasi-propagandistic proclamations; others, like his brother Mike (1933–2009), plunged into tradition and reproduced traditional performance styles (Allen 2010).

At last gender demanded to be recognized. Movements for civil rights and ethnic awareness mobilized members of that group that makes up at least half of any population, women. Folklore studies long attracted women, but only in the 1970s did American women folklorists begin to challenge aspects of the disciplinary heritage and insist on gender as a necessary component of folkloristic understanding. The ethnography of speaking and the performance-centered approach offered them a new way to think about both folk and lore. With few exceptions, particularly in international narrative research, the creative difference and power of women's expressive culture had thus far found little attention. Even the few prominent women folklorists in the history of the field, such as Hurston and Elsie Clews Parsons (1875–1941), had often relied on men as their informants. Studies thus reproduced the gender biases of American culture, until feminist theory began asking what symbols and expressive behavior might have been provided to women by the socially sanctioned circumscribing of their activities. The worldwide women's movement of the 1970s led United States folklorists to discover distinct genres and styles among women. The first women's symposium within the annual AFS conference became a book (Farrer 1975). The 1979 AFS meeting saw an entire women's day, subsequently edited into another book (Jordan and Kalcik 1985). Women's craft and material culture were reframed in terms of women's biography and female life experience. The performance framework also facilitated seeing the intermeshing of genres (Abrahams 1976). So women's narrative genres could be seen as situated performances within craft circles, such as a quilting bee. Women's conversational genres and styles could now be theorized as gendered preferences of artistic production. Nearly a decade later, as attention to women's lore matured into work with feminist theory, Jo Radner edited *Feminist Messages* (Radner 1993), and Margaret Mills connected attention to gender to both folklore practice and academic theorizing (Mills 1993). Questions about the body and embodiment had received little attention; now with a collection of case studies (Young 1993), folklorists formulated their own, empirically-founded contributions to an intellectual realm charted by gender theorists like Judith Butler or Hélène Cixous. Gender perspectives and attention to the cultural patterning of bodily experience would henceforth figure increasingly in work on performance and ritual (Kapchan 1993; Magliocco 2004; Noyes 2003). The body, as a site of aesthetic work and experience, became the furthest development of the aesthetics of material culture.

During the same decades, American material culture studies developed significantly, attesting to the creative powers and aesthetic politics of various American folk groups, and focusing attention on the materialization of folk thought in artifacts and landscapes. Henry Glassie, beginning from an initial morphology of genres of material expression (Glassie 1968), developed a theoretically sophisticated reading of the mental transformations encoded in folk housing (Glassie 1975). His attention to individuals and their craft eventually led him to a profoundly humanist, holistic approach to understanding folk aesthetic legacies (Glassie 1982; Glassie 1999). Simon Bronner focused both on craft and individual biography (Bronner, S.J. 1996) and on the broader convergence of material life and cultural meaning (Bronner, S.J. 1986). Echoing William Bascom's insistence, a generation earlier, on the African roots of African American folk narrative, John Vlach found evidence of African origins in both African American folk housing and the entire material expressive repertoire (Vlach 1991, 1993). The intertwined understanding of material culture and verbal arts within a folk community was emphasized in Charles Briggs' ethnolinguistic approach to folklore (Briggs 1980, 1988).

Among these intellectual developments of the last third of the twentieth century, the ethnography of speaking and performance studies were most empowering, bringing forth both the new perspective that folklorists had pushed for (Paredes and Bauman 1972) and an actor-centered view of folklore. Scholarly rigor entailed a new mode of thinking about *folk* – a commitment to the people being studied. Folklorists began to develop space within the public sphere for such groups to represent themselves. Disciplinary conflict between folklorists working in universities and those working in the public sphere began to smolder, despite efforts to transform the tension of a "mistaken dichotomy" into a productive engagement with processes of representation (Kirshenblatt-Gimblett 1988), which had become an issue in literary studies.

The conflict could be recognized soon after World War II. Richard Dorson, defending university custodianship, issued diatribes against the work of popularizers, who published folklore collections for a broad reading public. He also castigated commercial interventions and inventions making use of the American folklore imaginary, branding them "fakelore." Yet parallel to his call, for the first time since Roosevelt's New Deal, some folklorists took responsibility for authenticating folk traditions, as the federal government involved itself in sponsoring presentations of folklore to the public; more degree-holding scholars became public folklorists. Though some voices discouraged such stepping outside the scholarly role, many others declared it was desirable to make folklore available to the public. The second generation saw major innovations. The Smithsonian Institution's annual Festival of American Folklife, on the National Mall in the nation's capital, was launched in 1967, anticipating bicentennial celebrations in 1976. Then the National Endowment for the Arts created a Folk Arts Program in 1974. Finally, after a decade of lobbying (most of it by a single folklorist, Archie Green, 1917–2009), the government adopted the American Folklife Preservation Act (1976), which would "provide for the establishment of an American Folklife Center in the Library of Congress." These Washington-based programs brought about decentralization, as state and municipal governments set up their own folk arts programs. Thus outside the university new posts were created for a new breed of scholar, the public folklorist.

The conflict continued when, in the 1980s, the concept of heritage entered the public sphere, promulgated by UNESCO's successive conventions for creating lists of monumental and intangible world cultural heritage. Within the United States, state heritage awards, ethnic apprenticeships and other honors to practitioners of folk traditions were instituted, many administered with the assistance of public folklorists. The problematic term also figured within cultural tourism. *Heritage* and what it stood for in public discourse received incisive critique from scholars: for one thing, heritage can never be a totality, and folkloristics emphatically declares it can only be an inventory (Kirshenblatt-Gimblett 2007: 164). The next step was conceiving heritage and heritage productions as a new area of research. The most prominent public folklore event of the United States, the Smithsonian Folklife Festival, turned into a realm of joint inspection and an object of the ethnographic gaze. Conceiving exhibition practices and traditions as something of special value began to be understood as itself a cultural practice (Bauman and Sawin 1991; Cantwell 1993). The role of the culture broker was theorized (Kurin 1997). A broad framework characterized Barbara Kirshenblatt-Gimblett's observations, beginning from the old practice of exhibiting cultures in worlds' fairs and museums, and arriving at a provocative and explanatory characterization of heritage: "a new mode of cultural production in the present that has recourse to the past" (Kirshenblatt-Gimblett 1995, 369). Her formulation furnished legitimation for folklorists who, almost from the inception of the field, had been walking the line between academic training and public practice. To embrace public folkloristics as a mode of production required training, as much as academic knowledge production. University folklore programs began to offer training by teaching public practice within their curricula and in cooperation with public programs, institutions and organizations.[7]

Public folklore also brought a new mode of thinking about the lore. Academic folklorists were already documenting the ceaseless changes in texture, text, and context which characterize folklore in a globalizing world. What was public presentation but another such change, of actors, settings, audiences? The frequent relocation of populations since World War II forced to an agonizingly painful extreme awareness of the constant movement of people, money, images, and expectations. Collaboration between academic and public folklorists promised to heal the old breach between the public sector and the university. Both groups could analyze the components involved in constructing a piece of heritage and readying it for the marketplace. It fell to the discipline of folklore to show how American vernacular culture is canonized, and to decry the reduction of the vitality of local culture into a mere assertion that people are different.

In the twenty-first century, ethnographic and folkloric research took in the subjectivity of the researcher as a factor requiring acknowledgment. Researchers had to rethink their relationship to the folk. A poignant instance erupted out of lifelong work with a Navajo community by the folklorist Barre Toelken. Having accumulated an archive of his field recordings and transcripts, he came to understand and respect the request from the families he knew to have recorded voices destroyed: a voice must not outlive a deceased community member (Toelken 1976, 1998). Folklorists began to see that the criterion of accuracy they inherited from Boas raised questions of ethics, fidelity, and loyalty. From the evocation of tradition as monolithic, which facilitated concepts like imitation and "fakelore," American folkloristics began to proclaim (out of that long-ago pluralism) that voicings are many and genres are blurred or leaky.

After the 1990s, self-examination was a constant burr in the side of American folkloristics. If the celebration and documentation of difference, in the hands of disparate specialists, was the goal, how could American folklore call itself a unified field? As the tension between public and university folklorists found a productive resolution, the academic status of folkloristics was becoming unstable. University programs were reduced or eliminated, evidently under the impression that a discipline dedicated to the obsolescence of trivia could afford to wither. Yet at the same time, the discipline, like its often subversive materials and processes, called for recognition of folk and lore that were forgotten in the commercial domination of popular culture (for example "world music"). Folklorists began to take account more of the larger forces surrounding them: the culture of computers, the deluge of information, the fascination with media, the never ending material acquisitiveness of Americans. While texture and text were still the focus, context began to mean the global growth of capitalism and the world system. In the twenty-first-century university, American folkloristics retained the vitality of its methods when combined with other concentrations, such as performance studies, but public folklore too formed part of a larger association of interests labeled "culture and communication," which would exhibit the innumerable ways in which the folk express the heteronomy of postmodernism.

NOTES

1 Chapters in the present volume by Bauman, Seitel, and Kodish treat crucial components of American folklore studies in more detail. Handbooks and encyclopedic works, themselves demonstrating the maturity of folkloristics, introduce the field as practiced in the United States (Bronner, S.J. 2006; Dorson 1983; McCormick and White 2010) and its varieties (Herrera-Sobek 2006; Mood 2004; Locke *et al.* 2008; Tucker 2008), as well as the intertwining of folklore materials, American civilization, and folklore studies (Dorson 1959). The disciplinary formation of the field in the nineteenth and twentieth centuries is treated in (Zumwalt 1988).

2 On "playing Indian" within white American associational and public life, see (Abrahams 2006).

3 Further reading on comparative views of genre will be found in the chapter by Hasan-Rokem and Shuman in this volume. Issues of oral textuality are treated in the chapter by Seitel.

4 On the development and nature of fieldwork methods, see the chapter by Schmidt-Lauber in this volume.

5 During World War II, "GI" was military folk speech for "government issue," labeling all things in use by the United States armed forces. Quickly it became the colloquial word for soldiers, who called themselves "GIs."

6 The development of public folklore is treated in the article by Kodish in this volume.

7 Current information on folklore training, folklore-related institutions and events is found on the web site of the American Folklore Society (www.afsnet.org).

REFERENCES

Abrahams, Roger D. 1970 [1963)]. *Deep Down in the Jungle: Negro Narrative Folklore from the Streets of Philadelphia*. Revised edition. Chicago: Aldine Press.

Abrahams, Roger D. 1992. *Singing the Master: The Emergence of African American Culture in the Plantation South*. New York: Pantheon Books.

Abrahams, Roger D. 2006. "Calico Indians: Festive Play in Acts of Resistance." *Voices* 32.

Adams, Henry and Earl N. Harbert, Eds. 1986. *History of the United States of America During the Administrations of Thomas Jefferson*. New York: Library of America.

Allen, Ray. 2010. *Gone to the Country: The New Lost City Ramblers and the Folk Music Revival*. Urbana: University of Illinois Press.

Baron, Robert and Nicholas R. Spitzer, Eds. 1992. *Public Folklore. Publications of the American Folklore Society*. New series. Washington: Smithsonian Institution Press.

Bauman, Richard. 1971. "Differential Identity and the Social Base of Folklore." *Journal of American Folklore* 84(331 January–March): 31–41.

Bauman, Richard. 1977. *Verbal Art as Performance*. Prospect Heights, IL: Waveland Press.

Bauman, Richard and Patricia Sawin. 1991. *The Politics of Participation in the Folklife Festival. Special publications of the Folklore Institute*. Bloomington: Folklore Institute.

Ben-Amos, Dan. 1971. "Toward a Definition of Folklore in Context." *Journal of American Folklore* 84(331 January–March): 3–15.

Benedict, Ruth. 1934. *Patterns of Culture*. Boston and New York: Houghton Mifflin Company.

Boas, Franz. 1916. *Tsimshian Mythology*. Reports. Washington, DC: Bureau of American Ethnology, pp. 29–1037.

Botkin, Benjamin A., Ed. 1944. *A Treasury of American Folklore.* Foreword by Carl Sandburg. New York: Crown Publishers.

Botkin, Benjamin A. 1945. *Lay My Burden Down: A Folk History of Slavery.* Chicago: University of Chicago Press.

Briggs, Charles L. 1980. *The Wood Carvers of Córdova, New Mexico: Social Dimensions of an Artistic "Revival."* Knoxville: University of Tennessee Press.

Briggs, Charles L. 1988. *Competence in Performance: The Creativity of Tradition in Mexicano Verbal Art.* University of Pennsylvania Press Conduct and communication Series. Philadelphia: University of Pennsylvania Press.

Bronner, Simon J. 1986. *Grasping Things: Folk Material Culture and Mass Society in America.* Lexington: University Press of Kentucky.

Bronner, Simon J. 1996. *The Carver's Art: Crafting Meaning from Wood.* Lexington: University Press of Kentucky.

Bronner, Simon J., Ed. 2006. *Encyclopedia of American Folklife.* Armonk, NY: M.E. Sharpe.

Cantwell, Robert. 1993. *Ethnomimesis: Folklife and the Representation of Culture.* Chapel Hill, NC: University of North Carolina Press.

Child, Francis James. 1883–1998. *The English and Scottish Popular Ballads.* Boston and New York: Houghton, Mifflin and Company.

Dégh, Linda. 1975. "People in the Tobacco Belt: Four Lives." *Mercury Series Paper – Canadian Centre for Folk Culture Studies* 13. Ottawa: National Museums of Canada.

Dorson, Richard M. 1950. *America Begins: Early American Writing.* New York: Pantheon.

Dorson, Richard M. 1959. *American Folklore. The Chicago History of American Civilization.* Chicago: University of Chicago Press.

Dorson, Richard M. 1968. *The British Folklorists, A History.* Chicago: University of Chicago Press.

Dorson, Richard M., Ed. 1972. *Folklore and Folklife, An Introduction.* Chicago: University of Chicago Press.

Dorson, Richard M. 1973. *America in Legend: Folklore from the Colonial Period to the Present.* New York: Pantheon Books.

Dorson, Richard M. 1983. *Handbook of American Folklore.* Associate Ed. Inta Gale Carpenter. Assisted by Elizabeth Peterson and Angela Maniak. Bloomington: Indiana University Press.

Dundes, Alan. 1964. "Texture, Text and Context." *Southern Folklore Quarterly* 28: 251–265.

Dundes, Alan, Ed. 1965. *The Study of Folklore.* Englewood Cliffs, NJ: Prentice-Hall.

Dundes, Alan. 1980. *Interpreting Folklore.* Bloomington: Indiana University Press.

Dundes, Alan, Ed. 1988 [1982]. *Cinderella, A Casebook.* Madison, WI: University of Wisconsin Press.

Evans, David. 1982. *Big Road Blues: Tradition and Creativity in the Folk Blues.* Berkeley: University of California Press.

Farrer, Claire R., Ed. 1975. *Women in Folklore.* Austin: University of Texas Press.

Georges, Robert A. 1982. *American and Canadian Immigrant and Ethnic Folklore: An Annotated Bibliography.* Compiled by Robert A. Georges and Stephen Stern. Garland Folklore Bibliographies. New York: Garland.

Glassie, Henry. 1968. *Pattern in the Material Folk Culture of the Eastern United States.* University of Pennsylvania Monographs in Folklore and Folklife 1. Philadelphia: University of Pennsylvania Press.

Glassie, Henry. 1975. *Folk Housing in Middle Virginia: A Structural Analysis of Historic Artifacts.* Drawings by the author. Knoxville: University of Tennessee Press.

Glassie, Henry. 1982. *Passing the Time in Ballymenone: Culture and History of an Ulster Community.* Philadelphia: University of Pennsylvania Press.

Glassie, Henry. 1999. *Material Culture.* Bloomington: Indiana University Press.

Herrera-Sobek, Maria. 2006. *Chicano Folklore, A Handbook.* Santa Barbara: ABC-CLIO/Greenwood.

Hurston, Zora Neale. 1935. *Mules and Men.* Introduction by Franz Boas. Miguel

Covarrubias, Illustrator. Philadelphia: J.B. Lippincott Co.

Hymes, Dell. 1962. "The Ethnography of Speaking" in Thomas Gladwin and William C. Sturtevant, Eds. *Anthropology and Human Behavior.* Washington, DC: Anthropological Society of Washington, pp. 13–53.

Jordan, Rosan A. and Susan J. Kalcik, Eds. 1985. *Women's Folklore, Women's Culture.* Philadelphia: University of Pennsylvania Press.

Kapchan, Deborah A. 1993. *Gender on the Market: Moroccan Women and the Revoicing of Tradition.* Philadelphia: University of Pennsylvania Press.

Kemble, Frances Anne. 1863. *Journal of a Residence on a Georgian Plantation in 1838–1839.* New York: Harper and Brothers.

Kirshenblatt-Gimblett, Barbara. 1988. "Mistaken Dichotomies." *Journal of American Folklore* 101(400 April–June): 140–155.

Kirshenblatt-Gimblett, Barbara. 1995. "Theorizing Heritage." *Ethnomusicology* 39: 367–380.

Kirshenblatt-Gimblett, Barbara. 2007. "World Heritage and Cultural Economics" in Ivan Karp and Corinne Kratz, Eds. *Museum Frictions: Public Cultures/Global Transformations.* Durham, NC: Duke University Press, pp. 161–206.

Kurin, Richard. 1997. *Reflections of a Culture Broker: A View from the Smithsonian.* Washington, DC: Smithsonian Institution Press.

Locke, Liz, Theresa A. Vaughan, and Pauline Greenhill, Eds. 2008. *Encyclopedia of Women's Folklore and Folklife.* Santa Barbara: ABC-CLIO/Greenwood.

Lomax, Alan, with Edwin E. Erickson. 1968. *Folk Song Style and Culture.* AAAS Publication 88. Washington: American Association for the Advancement of Science.

Lomax, John A. 1910. *Cowboy Songs and Other Frontier Ballads.* New York: Sturgis and Walton Co.

Lomax, John A. and Alan Lomax, Collected and compiled by. 1934. *American Ballads and Folk Songs.* New York: Macmillan Co.

Lord, Albert B. 1960. *The Singer of Tales.* Cambridge, MA: Harvard University Press.

Magliocco, Sabina. 2004. *Witching Culture: Folklore and Neo-Paganism in America. Contemporary Ethnography.* Philadelphia: University of Pennsylvania Press.

McCormick, Charlie T. and Kim Kennedy White, Eds. 2010. *Folklore: An Encyclopedia of Beliefs, Customs, Tales, Music, and Art.* Second edition. Santa Barbara: ABC-CLIO/Greenwood.

Mills, Margaret A. 1993. "Feminist Theory and the Study of Folklore: A Twenty-Year Trajectory Toward Theory." *Western Folklore* 52(2–3–4): 173–192.

Mood, Terry Ann. 2004. *American Regional Folklore, A Sourcebook and Research Guide.* Santa Barbara: ABC-CLIO/Greenwood.

Morgan, Lewis Henry. 1851. *League of the Ho-Dé-No-Sau-Nee, or Iroquois.* Rochester: Sage and Brother.

Narvaez, Peter. 1995. "Increase Mather's Illustrious Providences, the First American Folklore Collection" in Roger D. Abrahams, Ed. *Fields of Folklore: Essays in Honor of Kenneth S. Goldstein.* Bloomington: Trickster Press, pp. 198–213.

Newell, William Wells. 1883. *Games and Songs of American Children.* New York: Harper and Brothers.

Newell, William Wells. 1888. "On the Field and Work of a Journal of American Folk-Lore." *Journal of American Folklore* 1: 3–7.

Noyes, Dorothy. 2003. *Fire in the Plaça: Catalan Festival Politics After Franco.* Philadelphia: University of Pennsylvania.

Paredes, Américo and Richard Bauman, Eds. 1972. *Toward New Perspectives in Folklore.* Austin: University of Texas Press.

Radner, Joan Newlon, Ed. 1993. *Feminist Messages: Coding in Women's Folk Culture.* Publications of the American Folklore Society. New Series. Urbana: University of Illinois Press.

Rosenberg, Bruce A. 1988. *Can These Bones Live? The Art of the American Folk Preacher.* Urbana: University of Illinois Press.

Sandburg, Carl. 1927. *The American Songbag.* New York: Harcourt, Brace.

Seitel, Peter, with Sheila Dauer. 1980. *See So That We May See: Performances and*

Interpretations of Traditional Tales from Tanzania. Bloomington: Indiana University Press.

Sherzer, Joel. 1983. *Kuna Ways of Speaking, an Ethnographic Perspective*. Austin: University of Texas Press.

Stahl, Sandra Dolby. 1989. *Literary Folkloristics and the Personal Narrative*. Bloomington: Indiana University Press.

Stern, Stephen and John Allan Cicala, Eds. 1991. *Creative Ethnicity: Symbols and Strategies of Contemporary Ethnic Life*. Logan: Utah State University Press.

Tedlock, Dennis, in collaboration with Andrew Peynetsa and Walter Sanchez. 1972. *Finding the Center: Narrative Poetry of the Zuni Indians*. New York: The Dial Press.

Thoms, William. 1965. "Folklore" in Alan Dundes, Ed. *The Study of Folklore*. Englewood Cliffs, NJ: Prentice-Hall, pp. 4–6.

Tocqueville, Alexis de. 1901. *Democracy in America*. Vol. 2. Trans. Henry Reeve. New York: D. Appleton.

Todorov, Tzvetan. 1984. *The Conquest of America: The Question of the Other*. Trans. from the French by Richard Howard. New York: Harper and Row.

Toelken, Barre. 1976. "The 'Pretty Languages' of Yellowman: Genre, Mode, and Texture in Navaho Coyote Narratives" in Dan Ben-Amos, Eds. *Folklore Genres*. Austin: University of Texas Press, pp. 145–170.

Toelken, Barre. 1998. "The Yellowman Tapes, 1966–1997." *Journal of American Folklore* 111(442 Fall): 381–391.

Trollope, Frances Milton. 1832. *Domestic Manners of the Americans*. London: Whittaker, Treacher and Co.

Tucker, Elizabeth, Ed. 2008. *Children's Folklore, a Handbook*. Santa Barbara: ABC-CLIO/Greenwood.

Vlach, John Michael, with a foreword by Lawrence Levine. 1991. *By the Work of Their Hands: Studies in Afro-American Folklife*. Charlottesville: University Press of Virginia.

Vlach, John Michael. 1993. *Back of the Big House: The Architecture of Plantation Slavery*. The Fred W. Morrison Series in Southern Studies. Chapel Hill: University of North Carolina Press.

Wilson, William A. 1976. *Folklore and Nationalism in Modern Finland*. Bloomington: Indiana University Press.

Young, Katharine, Ed. 1993. *Bodylore*. Knoxville: University of Tennessee Press.

Zumwalt, Rosemary Lévy. 1988. *American Folklore Scholarship: A Dialogue of Dissent*. *Folkloristics*. Bloomington: Indiana University Press.

Zumwalt, Rosemary Lévy. 1992. *Wealth and Rebellion: Elsie Clews Parsons, Anthropologist and Folklorist*. Foreword by Roger D. Abrahams. Publication of the American Folklore Society. New Series. Urbana: University of Illinois Press.

16

DANCING AROUND FOLKLORE
Constructing a National Culture in Turkey

Arzu Öztürkmen

Chief among Turkish folklore genres that can give us an idea of the religious, ethnic, and linguistic diversity of the Ottoman Empire is the *Karagöz* shadow theater, which derived its humor mainly from the linguistic and communicative failures among the different ethnic groups – Turks, Greeks, Bulgarians, Armenians, Albanians, Arabs, Kurds, Laz, and others. Most of these groups once formed "Ottoman society"; they gave way to new national states during the nineteenth and twentieth centuries in the Balkans and the Middle East.[1] When the republic of Turkey was founded in 1923, it declared itself "Turkish," distancing itself from its multi-cultural Ottoman past, and focusing more on its Central Asian roots and on Anatolia as the new "Turkish" motherland with its folklore, language and material heritage. This chapter reviews the historical process during which Ottoman-Turkish intellectuals discovered folklore as a new field of study in the age of nationalism and follows how their ideas were pursued during the republican era with a new generation of researchers and institutions. A historical analysis of how Turkish folkloristics were shaped during the republican period requires a closer look at central institutions like the Turkish Hearths (1911–1931), the People's Houses (1932–1951), the challenge to establish academic folklore (1947–1950), and private enterprises, where folk dance long dominated folklore-related activities and discourses (1960–1990s).

A Companion to Folklore, First Edition. Edited by Regina F. Bendix and Galit Hasan-Rokem.

OTTOMAN-TURKISH INTEREST IN FOLKLORE

Ottoman intellectuals on the margins of a decaying empire engaged in folklore research long before the foundation of the Turkish republic. Their primary concern was to formulate new ways to make their multi-ethnic society survive the challenges of surrounding nationalisms. In the aftermath of the Turco-Russian and Balkan wars, but also closely aware of the ideas of European Enlightenment, they began to explore such concepts as "national language," "motherland," "folk," "culture" and "civilization."

During the *Tanzimat* period[2] many intellectuals stressed the need to simplify Ottoman Turkish in order to propagate more effectively the newly formed political and social ideas. Prominent figures were Namık Kemal (1840–1888), Şinasi (1826–1871), and Ziya Paşa (1829–1888), the so-called "Young Ottomans," who had not particularly mentioned folklore per se, but touched upon its diverse aspects (Mardin 1962). As agents of Ottoman enlightenment, and although referring to it from different angles, these intellectuals were not always fond of folklore. Namık Kemal for instance, promoted the importance of the "folk" and a sense of "motherland" as a nest of culture and identity, advocated the cleansing of Ottoman Turkish language from its ornamental style, but always remained skeptical towards folk literature, which included "supernatural" elements. There were, however, other Tanzimat writers like Şinasi or Ziya Paşa who regarded folk literature as "valuable material." While Şinasi had published a collection of proverbs, Ziya Paşa had drawn attention to the *aşık* minstrel tradition as a source of the "pure language" (Başgöz 1972; Boratav 1982). There was also interest in the display of material cultural assets, like folk costumes, handicrafts, and architectural designs particularly at the Ottoman pavilions in World Fairs (Zeynep Çelik 1992). The first Ottoman museum, opened in Istanbul in 1846, also included samples of handcrafts. Interest in Ottoman culture was not confined to world exhibitions, as foreign scholars also visited and observed Ottoman lands, and collected folklore during the nineteenth century. One should mention particularly the works of Hungarian folklorist Ignácz Kúnos (1862–1945) who collected folk tales and folk songs in 1899, German scholar George Jacob who wrote about *Karagöz* shadow theater tradition, and French researcher Henry Carnoy who published books related to Ottoman folk customs and legends about Istanbul (Kunos 1969; Jacob 1925; Carnoy 1889; 1892; 1894).

The nineteenth-century Ottoman state experienced much political reform, suppression, and revolution in. First, there had been a short-lived Constitutional Era (1876–1878), followed by Sultan Abdülhamid II's (1876–1909) oppressive rule for three decades. His policies paved the way for an underground opposition movement leading in 1908 to the "Young Turk Revolution." Young Turks showed a growing interest in Turkism, as Ottomanism and Islamism collapsed with the rising nationalisms among the subject peoples of the empire. Based on an original cultural myth rooted in the Central Asian past, Turkism conformed to an imperial imagination uniting all Turkic communities not only in Anatolia, but also in the Caucasus and Central Asia. Turkism aroused interest not only in Turkish language but in the foundations of Turkish culture as well. Among institutions which clearly pursued Turkist goals, *Türk Ocakları* (Turkish Hearths, 1911) was the most effective.[3] It was not, however, until the 1910s that leading intellectuals of the Young Turk movement began to write articles where they introduced folklore as a new and important field of study. The most important among them were Ziya Gökalp's "Preface to Folk Civilisation," Rıza Tevfik's "Folklore," Fuat Köprülü's "A New Science; Folklore," Selim Sırrı Tarcan's "Among the Educators: Folklore," and a transcribed lecture on folklore and Turkish folklore history by Yusuf Akçura.[4]

Many of these writers acknowledged the political dimension of the idea of folklore, referring particularly to the use of folklore in constructing a nation. Ziya Gökalp believed that folklore was akin to a storehouse where the original culture of the Turkish nation was collected without having been spoiled. Fuad Köprülü drew attention to the instructive and even "informing" role folklore plays in the administration of a nation and state. Selim Sırrı emphasized the representational aspect of folklore, situating a nation within the larger international community. For the majority of these writers, comparison with Europe was a key point. They referred to several researchers and intellectuals like Herder, Thoms, the Grimm Brothers, and Van Gennep in their discussion of folklore.[5]

These intellectuals also commented on the content and types of folklore in Ottoman Turkish culture. Gökalp divided *halkiyat* (folklore) into eight parts: folk institutions, folk philosophy, folk morals, folk law, folk aesthetics, folk language, folk economy, and ethnography. While not exactly a classification of folklore genres, Gökalp's categories reflected his ideas on the scope of folklore research. Rıza Tevfik focused more on the range of genres that could be studied in Turkish folklore, embracing proverbs, folk fables, riddles, legends, stories, folk songs, and plays. In another earlier article entitled "About Folk Dances" he focused on folk dances around the empire. Both Fuad Köprülü and Selim Sırrı also listed a broad range of genres including folk songs, fables, proverbs, customs, beliefs, stories, myths, epics, and legends as areas for future folklore research. Like Rıza Tevfik, Selim Sırrı also had a particular interest in folk dance, an area he later pursued as a choreographer (Tarcan 1948). One common aspect of these pioneer writers lay in the fact that they did not confine their approach to folklore only to oral genres, and included belief systems and dramatic forms as well.

FROM TURKISH HEARTHS TO PEOPLE'S HOUSES: THE MAKING OF "TURKISH FOLKLORE"

When the republic of Turkey was officially founded in 1923, some of the late Ottoman institutions like the Turkish Hearths made their way into the new regime. Rooted in the trauma of the late Ottoman world, however, they were not in a position to implement the republican reforms, nor bond with a displaced population after years of war. The 1920s were a transitional decade where other cultural institutions took initiatives regarding folk research. The Music Conservatory (*Darülelhan*) in Istanbul, for instance, initiated questionnaire-based research to collect folk songs in 1924. In 1927, a group of intellectuals founded the Anatolian Folklore Society (*Anadolu Halk Bilgisi Derneği*), the first folklore society. In 1928, it was renamed Turkish Folklore Society (*Türk Halk Bilgisi Derneği*).

The primary aim of the Turkish Folklore Society was to mobilize local lay people to collect folklore, opening agencies in different towns, issuing publications, and organizing field-trips and conferences. One of their primary publications was a guide for fieldworkers, inspired by the works of Arnold Van Gennep, Achille Millien, and Eduard

Hoffmann-Krayer, which provided information about different folklore genres. The society also began its own publications to document new collections. These publications introduced international definitions of folklore from the *Grande Encyclopédie* and the *Encyclopedia Britannica*, translations of Van Gennep's ideas on folklore genres, and samples of folk songs, proverbs, and folk poetry. The Turkish Folklore Society organized four field trips between 1929 and 1932 to the Black Sea, the Marmara region, Southern and Eastern Anatolia, where folk songs, beliefs, and customs had been collected (Ülkütaşır 1973; Ay 1990; İpekkan 1978).

The new republican regime in the 1920s needed a more forceful and centralized organizational network to promote its reforms but also to conduct more systematic research within the new national borders. The debates in the Turkish Hearths circles proved how Ottoman Turkism was no longer relevant to new national policies. The new regime was also challenged by the increasing number of new institutions such as the Turkish Workers' Union (1923), the Turkish Women's Union (1924), and the Turkish Folklore Society (1927–1928). Giving them a "national" title was one way to control them. In other cases, the state asked independent culture organizations to join a new network of cultural organization, the "People's Houses" (*Halkevleri*).

Following the closing of the Turkish Hearths in 1931, People's Houses were founded in 1932 as the semi-official cultural organs of the ruling single party, the Republican People's Party (RPP). People's Houses were designed to disseminate the republican reforms in the fields of education, Western art, and women's emancipation and to conduct regional research for the construction of a national culture. People's Houses offered a perfect ground for the nation-building process, as perhaps a good example of Benedict Anderson's concept of "imagined communities," using their publications and cultural performances of all kinds. The Houses were often criticized for their elitism and small size, but they had a considerable impact even though they could not mobilize big masses. Their journals circulated in small numbers, but they were marketed together with all other publications, while the annual festivals organized in Ankara gathered different regional groups on a national platform.

The People's Houses were organized around nine activity sections: (1) Language, History and Literature, (2) Fine Arts, (3) Theater, (4) Sports, (5) Social Help, (6) Public Classes and Courses, (7) Library and Publishing, (8) Village Development, and (9) Museum and Exhibition. Most sections conducted a folklore-related activity. Members of People's Houses took the first steps in undertaking fieldwork in their own towns and the surrounding regions. They both legitimized folklore in the eyes of the public, and helped in the construction of a "national genre repertoire," publishing the results of their work in periodicals and books. Turkish folklore genres today follow to a great extent the genre categorization laid out by the People's Houses in the 1930s and 1940s. To give a few examples, traditional folk theaters *Karagöz* and *Ortaoyunu* were promoted under the "Theater" section. The "Language and Literature" sections compiled pioneering collections of local dialects, proverbs, and narratives, working in cooperation with, and under the guidance of the Turkish Language Society.[6] The "Fine Arts" section collected folk songs; the "Sports" section supported the practice of traditional sports like wrestling or *cirit* (traditional polo). Folk costumes and local material culture were collected and displayed under the "Museum and Exhibition" sections. Historical studies focused on local history, and encouraged the establishment of folklore archives in cooperation with the "Library and Publishing" sections. And finally, visits to villages organized by the "Village Development" sections, however naive and positivist they were, generated the first village monographs.

In 1943, Radio Ankara started a program called "People's Houses, Art and Folklore," which became a platform for the presentation of original collections of folk music to a larger audience. Similarly, choirs founded in Ankara, Izmir, and Istanbul began to broadcast on national radio. The so-called "Choir of Tunes from Homeland" (*Yurttan Sesler Korosu*) played an important part in the building of a national repertoire, which "gentrified" folk songs of different regions by turning local dialects into Istanbulite Turkish, translating non-Turkish lyrics, and inventing an orchestra of multiple traditional instruments.[7] This was a period where nation building required rejection of the commonalities between shared repertoires. Translation of the lyrics was a dominant characteristic of the nation-building processes, in the quest for immunity from the influence of "the others" (Poladian 1978; Silverman 1989; Pennanen 2004). This trend of exclusion long continued not only for Greek or Armenian songs and dances, but also for Kurdish and Laz repertoires (Açıkdeniz 2009; Yıldız 2009; Öner 2008, Kolivar 2007).

National repertoires were formulated in other fields as well. A "National Costume Exhibition" had opened in Ankara in 1943, displaying materials sent by different local branches (Çeçen 1990). Local efforts to collect folklore were also documented in the People's Houses Journals, which were the most influential tool for the Houses to communicate their achievements. Published by the "Library and Publishing" section and circulated between different branches, these journals helped to establish a common understanding of what kind of folklore material was available throughout the Anatolian and Thracian peninsulas.

The cultural topics undertaken in the People's Houses' journals were not limited to local folklore. Reference to Central Asian roots was still important, and it was frequently used to characterize "national culture," especially when the article wanted to emphasize that modern Turkish identity had a "genuine" language, a society less bound to Islam, and was more supportive of active roles for women. Numerous articles thus explored the history of Central Asian Turks, their traditions, philosophy, belief, and arts (Öztürkmen 1998a: 118). A 1935 article in *Fikirler* emphasized, for instance, the fact that ancient Turkish women had neither worn veils nor lived in harems, and that they shared the same social and administrative roles with men until the Turks adopted Islam (Fikirler-a). Another article in *Aksu* suggested that the idea of a republican regime existed among ancient Turks (Selçuk 1934a).

People's Houses' journals also manifested the prevailing dilemma of the republic, hesitating between two cultures waiting to be legitimized within the new Turkish identity – the Central Asian and the Anatolian. Therefore, quite often journals would also publish articles on the ancient Anatolian civilizations, linking their origins to Central Asia as well.[8] Although relatively rare, there were also references to the non-Muslim Turkish-speaking Anatolian groups (Fehmi 1934) but never to non-Turkish speaking minorities.[9]

But when it came to discovering new sources for the making of a national culture, People's Houses were more trustful of those embedded in the Anatolian present than in the Central Asian past. Local research was promoted in a spirit of contribution to the national project, and the official discourse integrated these various samples of local data into a single national culture in which variety and diversity were now credited with making it "rich" rather than "dissimilar." This consolidated a sense of regionalism or locality not in opposition to nationalism but as an obligatory component of it.[10] Invention of a historical consciousness of belonging to a certain part of the country was very significant for a post-Ottoman population unsettled by wars and migrations. This new sense of regionalism, defined within the limits of a new territory, was reinforced by original and translated articles on the history of the press or of sports, on the old social and economic life based on historical documents, on the naming of towns and villages, and on the tourist assets of a region (Öztürkmen 1998a:120; Kaynak-a 1937: 248–249). Life stories of local figures offered another way of consolidating this new historical consciousness. Personal narratives of local men and women, who had survived the War of Independence, or the commemoration of those who died as unknown war heroes, helped to build a certain local pride (Cemal 1933; Alper 1938; Aksu-a 1934: 48–49).

Although interest in Central Asian culture and in local history were both related to folklore in one way or another, People's Houses' journals also explicitly devoted space to the study of folklore. In general terms, one could group the folklore-related topics into four categories: (i) articles on folklore theory and method, (ii) village monographs, (iii) collections of folk poetry, riddles, trickster tales, jokes, folk songs, and (iv) studies on theatrical and dance genres.

Articles on Folklore Theory and Method

Folklore research during the republic was seen as a concrete means to redefine national culture. In this respect, the articles published in the People's Houses' journals not only stated directly "what folklore was" but also "how to do it." Scholars of folklore contributed translations of foreign works on folklore theory and methods, including studies by Arnold Van Gennep and Ruth Benedict (Gennep 1939a; Berkes 1941). One could even come across a review surveying the contents of the *Journal of the International Association for Folklore and Ethnology* and reporting on the folklore archives of Germany, Sweden, Denmark and Norway (Fevziye 1938).

To give a few examples, one can refer to Enver Behnan Şapolyo's article on the definition and history of "ethnography" in *Ün,* which made a distinction between folklore and ethnography, the former dealing with oral genres and the latter with material culture (Şapolyo 1935). Pertev Naili Boratav published an article in *Ülkü* in 1939 on how to pursue folklore research under the People's Houses. Emphasizing the benefits of having People's Houses already established throughout the country, Boratav suggested that the elementary and high school teachers could contribute useful data if they were well advised. Boratav also proposed the establishment of a national archive, citing examples from European countries (Boratav 1939). In 1940, Osman Turgut Pamirli published a series of articles in *Aksu,* where he discussed issues like the comparative history of the discipline (Pamirli 1940a), fieldwork method, "objectivity" and respect for peasants (Pamirli 1940b), and finally, the representation of folklore on "stage" (Pamirli 1941). All these writers believed that the People's Houses would play a central role in collecting, circulating, and staging folkloric material.

Izmir's People's House journal *Fikirler* also published articles on folklore. Based on Pertev Naili Boratav's class notes, one essay emphasized that folklore "reflected" spontaneous and symbolic characteristics of a society within the boundaries of a particular historical and geographical context (Z.S. 1943). Another focused on the Brothers Grimm and underlined the importance of women and old people in collecting such materials (Akyol 1945). Besides these articles on theory and methodology, the journals fastidiously reported numerical accounts of their "folklore inventory." And finally, essays on other topics, such as tourism or village education, also made reference to folklore (Saffet 1933a; Saffet 1933b; Nusret 1933).

Village Monographs

As one of the founding principles of the republic, the spirit of "villagism" was the driving force behind numerous amateur fieldwork projects conducted by local researchers, who included doctors, engineers and teachers.[11] In 1933, *Ülkü* published guidelines on how to conduct research in villages. This undoubtedly encouraged many inquisitive people to make journeys to villages, mostly under the "Village Development" sections of the People's Houses, but some independently. These reports were published as "village monographs" in the journals, some closely following the questionnaire provided by *Ülkü* (Süreyya 1934, *Ülkü-a* 1933: 151–158) and others, who followed more of an impressionistic style (Yalgın 1941; Akpınar 1945; H.C. 1934). Village monographs mainly consisted of reports on the customs, beliefs, and material culture of a particular village. However, their ethnographic data remained superficial in most cases, lacking information about the interviewees.[12] Their tone was mainly romantic but at times revealed a discourse which marked their different status vis-à-vis the villagers. This became more explicit in those sections of the monographs reporting on the villages' religious conservatism or loyalty to the republic's reforms.[13]

Collections of Verbal Folklore Genres

Verbal genres represented the core of the folklore-related material published in the People's Houses' journals, partly because of the republic's sensitivity to consolidating its language reform, but also because of the enthusiasm of local people to promote their vernacular literature nationally. People's Houses were also regarded as an important means of publicizing the reforms of Turkish Language Society (Ülkü-b 1935: 85–87). In the context of language reform, folk literature had gained prestige and began to be promoted by People's Houses' journals. Many researchers discovered *cönk*s and *risale*s, manuscripts giving biographical information and anthologies of folk poets and transcribed them using the new alphabet in their People's Houses' journals.[14] This gave way to the popularization of several folk poets and literary works which soon made their way into school textbooks as pieces of "Turkish folk literature." Folk poets like Karacaoğlan, Köroğlu, Yunus Emre, and Dadaloğlu were first recognized as pillars of "Turkish folk literature" through these journals (Refet 1933; Elçin 1938; Gürkaynak 1939; Halit Bayrı 1941).

Nafi Atuf Kansu's speech on the ninth anniversary of the People's Houses illustrated how such folk artists had become national figures:

> ... Ottoman Empire were all influenced by ancient Turkic traditions. But as the borders expanded ... old Turkish traditions and customs slowly disappeared from palaces and big

centers; they took refuge in the people. People were trying to satisfy themselves with stories of the Oğuzname, Hamzaname, Battalgazi, Köroğlu's epic and with works of the poets like Karacaoğlan, Aşk Ömer, Emrah ... While the Palace was being represented by its own music, literature, world view and science, people deviated from it with their own folk songs, their own musical instruments, their own poetry and their own masters like Nasreddin Hoca. (Kansu 1941)

There were also attempts to report on other oral forms of folklore besides the minstrel tradition. Local sayings, proverbs, *manis*, riddles, folk tales, legends, and folk songs made their way into the People's Houses' journals.[15]

Representational Performances: Folk Music, Drama, and Dance Research

Representational performances were central to the People's Houses' activities. Their journals often included news, reports and reviews about music, dance, and theater performances and national holiday celebrations. In most towns, these performances were the initial attempts to adopt Western artistic styles. In that respect they showed the public how to appreciate an indoor theater show. Waiting in line for tickets, not eating while watching, or sitting quietly during the performance were part of this "modern experience," which differed from traditional ways of singing, dancing, and drama. Folk performances also received attention and were soon transported to the stage. People's Houses' articles supported local research in this area, including articles on traditional sports, dances, drama, and games. *Uludağ* and *Fikirler* published articles on the history of the *Karagöz* shadow theater (Şapolyo 1936; Aktaş 1946) emphasizing the multiple dimensions of *Karagöz* plays – text, songs, beliefs, material like sticks, costumes, and the curtain – and criticizing the obsession for locating *Karagöz* in an individual. Some journals gave accounts of *Karagöz* performances, while some others urged the need for their revival (Fikirler-b 1938: 16). In a speech published in *Aksu*, B. Kaya stated that the shadow theater could be used as an effective mode of education and suggested reviving it, especially for children's education (Aksu-b 1937: 3–10). Traditional plays and games were also reported on from time to time. Traditional sports, adult leisure activities like camel wrestling, or examples of children's games were published.[16] People's Houses' journals also published collections of folk songs, which, with a few exceptions, consisted of song lyrics rather than musical notation (Çoruh-a 1938: 8–9; Çoruh-b 1938: 37; Fikirler-c 1939: 12; Fikirler-d 1942: 6; Uludağ-a 1940: 35; Uludağ-b 1940: 25). These collections derived from different regional traditions served as appreciation of local music, which was seen as a source for developing a national music genre. The journals also discussed theoretical issues concerning music in Turkey, commenting Bela Bartók's ideas and on how a national music genre could be created (Tarcan 1935; Salcı 1938). One article published in *Ülkü* is extremely significant is it shows disdain for the Ottoman rooted, classical Turkish music, the *fasıl* genre. The article urged the People's Houses not to teach Turkish classical music accompanied by instruments such as the *ud, tambur,* and *kanun,* but only folk music and Western classical music (Ülkü-d 1941: 468–469). Some other writings explored local musical traditions and compared Turkey's musical achievements with those in other countries. M.R. Kösemihal saw the People's Houses as local conservatoires, also stressing the importance of broadcasting and music competitions (Kösemihal 1938a, b). Occasionally, journals also published musicians' life stories or introduced local folk song collection committees to the general public (Demirdal 1937, 1943).

The journals also engaged in material culture research. Articles on folk architecture appeared in journals such as *Ülkü, Uludağ*, and *Aksu*. Abdullah Ziya's article in *Ülkü* praised the village architect as follows:

> The village architect is nameless. But he is an artist as famous and worthy of applause as an unknown soldier is when he competes with his commander in the path of heroism ... The peasant's school is his experience ... The village architect is a peasant artist, an architect, master-builder and material-producer at the same time... A village's architecture and architect are born out of necessity from within the village. Its construction can only be done with the village's own rock, soil and tree. (Ziya 1933)

Ziya's article was significant in providing sketches of different types of village houses in different regions of the country. In most village monographs, one could also find descriptions of vernacular architecture, neighborhood maps, home decorations and similar (Öğütçü 1940; Erenel 1940a and b).

Village monographs were most illuminating in their accounts of folk costume. Although each monograph usually focused on a specific aspect of the costume, one could ultimately learn how summer clothes differed from those worn in winter, how long they were used, and what kind of material they were made of (Nuri 1933; Arif 1934). Folk costumes also attracted the attention of groups interested in founding museums. Articles on the history of museums emphasized their importance in reviving national culture (Şapolyo 1934), and artifacts discovered during trips to villages with "Village Development" sections were put under the protection of the relevant People's House (Kaynak-b 1935: 491–500). Quite often, People's Houses organized costume parties to attract audiences and encourage local people to "modernize" their traditional costumes (Fikirler-e 1938: 73–75; Kaynak-c 1937: 272).

The monographs published in the People's Houses' journals also gave information on local dance traditions. These accounts were usually very short, listing only the names of the dances and giving information related to the gender of the performers or to the occasions and places where these dances were performed.[17] But People's Houses had a more fundamental role in popularizing folk dances by staging them during anniversary celebrations called the People's Houses Festivals. By the end of the 1930s, leading local dancers would travel to Ankara to perform their dances. It was critical that they manifested order rather than chaos, and grace and refinement rather than over-excitement. Uniformity and self-control, which were the most important factors in putting on a *spectacular* performance,[18] also remained a great concern for collectors of these dances (Ortaç 1941).

These local dances were named after their town of origin, for example, Erzurum dances, Sivas dances, Artvin dances. This, of course, was a national construction at another level. Towns and villages, which did not have direct access to one another under Ottoman rule, began to get to know each other for the first time. Yet while some towns played a leading role in organizing their local dance groups for presentation on a national platform, it took a few decades for others to start collecting theirs for national exposre. The issue of "national belonging" was a sensitive concept for some regions heavily populated by migrants from the Balkans or the Caucasus. Şerif Baykurt, a Balkan migrant himself, was interested in the 1940s in collecting Thracian dances for performance on national platforms. Baykurt wanted Thrace to be acknowledged instead of lying in in the shadow of "Anatolian" dances. He also wanted to change the assumption that Thrace only had "gypsy" dances, and as such could not be part of the national repertoire. Baykurt began to search for dance performances at weddings and other dance events. As an active member of Kırklareli People's House, he began to invite elderly dancers and musicians to perform there. At first, most of these performers were reluctant to perform in the People's House in front of the town's mayor and high-ranking officials. According to Baykurt, they were basically afraid of the mayor's presence, an attitude dating back to the Ottoman times. But they also worried that as dancing *men*, they would be regarded as very low status by these high-ranking officials.[19] Baykurt finally convinced them, complimenting their skills and using his own status as a teacher. A special performance in the Kırklareli People's House legitimized the performance of Kırklareli dances, elevating them to the level of other "national" folk dance representations. Although Baykurt was frequently blamed for promoting migrants' dances (*muhacir oyunları*) or non-Muslim dances (*gavur oyunları*), Kırklareli dances had easily made their way into the national repertoire of folk dances by the 1950s.[20]

When Baykurt commenced his research, People's Houses had already begun to gather different local dance groups to give performances in Ankara. Thus, Baykurt and his friends were integrated into this newly consolidated tradition of "performing folk dances in national events or celebrations." This new tradition flourished under the People's Houses. It offered small towns and villages an institutional framework through which they could be integrated into the newly emerging national culture. In addition, People's Houses also communicated to these provincial areas that all kinds of cultural activities could be approved by the state. Even if only a handful of dancers would have the chance to visit Ankara for the Houses' anniversary celebrations, repercussions from their achievements would go far beyond this. Upon returning to their native town, they would receive a heroe's welcome, enhancing the belief that their dances – something that as natives of that culture they always took for granted – were what made the biggest impression in the capital city.[21]

PUTTING FOLKLORE ON TRIAL: THE REVIVAL OF TURKISM AND ITS IMPACT ON FOLKLORE STUDIES

By the end of the 1940s, the People's Houses began to lose their original zeal with the growing opposition during World War II. Although Turkey did not take part in the war, the influence of extreme nationalism was strongly felt in the press and various intellectual circles. In fact, Turkism had kept a low profile during the 1930s, as the new regime had de-emphasized all expansionist political aspirations and made certain from the beginning to concentrate its resources on developing of what remained as legitimate territory, the Anatolian and Thracian peninsulas. A few journals were published, but they were mostly confined to cultural aspects of the Turkic world.[22] With the exception of *Atsız Mecmua,* their political tone was prudent. The situation changed when the mainstream press began to adopt a pro-German approach in the early years of the war. There was a visible escalation in Turkist publications between 1939–1944, marking the "golden years" for Turkism under the republican regime. This escalation was not only in terms of numbers but also in terms of a change in the tone of these publications. Journals like *Ergenekon* (1938–1939), *Kopuz* (1939–1940), *Bozkurt* (1939–1942), *Gök-Börü* (1942–1943), and *Çınaraltı* (1941–1944, 1948) became the passionate voices of the Turkist movement. The revival of Turkism had two important dimensions: first, it had a strongly emotional tone rather than a long-term political program or an agenda for academic research. Introducing new literary and political symbols, it emphasized, once again, the dilemma of Turkish national culture, hesitating between its Anatolian and Central Asian legacies. Second, it had an "anti-government" and "pro-war" discourse. Turkists criticized the government for not taking part in the war and missing the opportunity to expand Turkic unity further. They also criticized its socio-economic policies, claiming that it ignored the needs of the rural areas.

The increase and intensification of Turkist publications, along with the consistently pro-German commentaries in the press, stimulated an anti-German, anti-racist, and leftist opposition. Given the context of the war and the antagonism between the Soviet Union and Germany, "anti-Germanness" led directly to a "pro-Soviet" and "communist" association. In between escalating emotional debates, and as the war changed its course after the German defeat at Stalingrad, the government changed its tolerance towards Turkism, closing down its journals. But at the same time, it made sure that the author of an influential leftist brochure was arrested as well. The hope of keeping the balance failed, however, when a series of trials began, based on mutual accusations between Turkists and leftist-leaning intellectuals.

One of these trials concerned folklorist Pertev Naili Boratav, known today as the founding father of Turkish folkloristics. Boratav was a student of early republican intellectuals like Hilmi Ziya Ülken (1901–1974) and Mehmet Fuad Köprülü (1890–1966). Following his interest in folklore, he had joined the Department of Literature at Istanbul University. In 1931, he became a member of the newly established *Türkiyat Enstitüsü* (Institute of Turkish Studies), working as an assistant for Mehmet Fuad Köprülü, a historian known for his pioneering studies in the history of Anatolian folk literature. He was also influenced by Georges Dumézil (1898–1986), an acclaimed French mythologist, who was then a visiting scholar at Istanbul University. Working as a translator for Dumézil's lectures, Boratav accompanied him on field trips in Anatolia (Başgöz 1998). The French school of ethnology had a signficant impact on Boratav, who was able to visit Paris in 1928 with a scholarship. In Paris he learned about the international scholarship developing around folklore. This is probably how he became acquainted with the work of Arnold Van Gennep, whom he would later translate in the leading People's House journal *Ülkü* (Gennep 1939b). Boratav later taught at high schools in Konya, where he developed his skills as a fieldworker and organized his students to collect folk tales in a systematic way, recording essential ethnographic information (name and age of the storyteller, the place and origin of the folk tale) in a questionnaire. During his military service in Anatolian towns like Beyşehir and Kars, Boratav continued to teach as part of his military service and to collect folklore as well. In 1936, he went to Germany on a state scholarship, where he found himself among other Turkish students, who sympathized with the rising

German nationalism and were inspired by it to revive Turkism. The critical stance Boratav took towards extreme nationalism alarmed certain students who reported him to Ankara as an "anti-nationalist." His grant was terminated and he was called back to Turkey. After a follow-up investigation, he was cleared, and as a settlement, he was offered a teaching post in Folk Literature at Ankara University.

In Ankara, Boratav found, in the beginning, a stimulating intellectual milieu, shared by enthusiastic students and inspiring colleagues. He founded an archive with the help of his students and initiated a series of publications for beginners in folklore studies (Boratav 1942). In 1947, he established the Department of Folk Literature, the first academic institution devoted to folklore studies. His early publications discussed the history, theory, and methodology of the discipline of folklore.

Boratav was surrounded by other social scientists, such as Behice Boran, Muzaffer Şerif and Niyazi Berkes, all educated in the United States during the early 1930s, a time when Marxism was an influential ideology in the social sciences. These scholars were gathered under the roofs of several independent journals such as *Yurt ve Dünya* (Country and World), *Adımlar* (Steps) and *Görüşler* (Views). The anti-fascist and anti-racist stance of their journals was not very well received by the newly ascendant Turkist circles of the postwar Turkey.[23] They were soon targeted by extreme nationalist students in the polarized domestic political scene and frequent government reshuffles. As opposition to "leftist" professors escalated with demonstrations, Boratav and his friends found themselves prosecuted for "the provocative information that appeared in the press" (Kabacalı 1992: 112). The new Minister of Education, Reşat Şemsettin Sirer, took an active role in the process, accusing Boratav and his friends of creating polarization among students.

The trial began in June 1948 and ended in February 1950. During the hearing, several students, faculty members, and administrators from Ankara University gave evidence for and against these professors. The press gave serious attention to the trial and adopted a mainly negative stance vis-à-vis the case (Öztürkmen 1998b). Pertev Naili Boratav presented a final defense to the court in 1950, exposing his academic concerns about the status of his discipline during an extremely politicized era. Some of the accusations concerned Boratav's interpretations of Turkish folklore. Both the Minister's petition to the court and other testimonies by former students and colleagues tried to establish an affinity between Marxism and Boratav's approach to folklore.[24] There were, however, a few faculty members and members of the univiersity's staff who testified on Boratav's behalf, targeting mainly Ankara University's administrative staff, who failed to control demonstrations and to stand by their own colleagues.

Boratav's defense overruled all allegations with examples from his own research and publications. His trial finally came to an end. Although he was acquitted, he was stripped of his post at Ankara University all the same. A law was passed to cut off government funding for Boratav's department supported by the Minister of National Education. Thus, although he never officially resigned from the post of "professor of folklore" at Ankara University, Boratav's teaching career was trucated by government intervention. He continued to contribute to Turkish folklore and pursued his career in France.

The Boratav case remained a traumatic memory and marked a fixed point in the periodization of Turkish folklore studies. In the aftermath of the trial, the study of folklore in Turkey shifted from the academy to a state-sponsored enterprise, distancing itself from a social scientific framework – theoretically as well as methodologically – of the type Boratav had imagined in the 1940s. His departure was a true deprivation for the development of academic folklore in Turkey.

During his 60-year-long career, Boratav collected a large variety of genres of Anatolian oral tradition, including folk tales, stories, beliefs, lullabies, and *mani*s (rhymed idioms). His archive includes material dating back to the 1920s and is considered today of invaluable historical importance as it contains one of the earliest written documents of the Turkish oral tradition in the late Ottoman and early republican eras.[25] The archive is particularly important in showing Pertev Naili Boratav's classification system. It consists of a collection of designated Turkish folklore genres, which includes folktales, folk poetry, stories, jingles, jokes, proverbs, folksongs, plays, folk theater, ceremonies, dress, ethnobotanics, folk medicine, and folk astronomy. Boratav paid particular attention to recording the sources of his collections, giving information on the person, time, and place. However, while publishing the results of these collections in the genre of "folk tale books," he combined different ethnographic texts into one single narrative. In *Zaman Zaman İçinde* (Once Upon a Time) and *Az Gittik, Uz Gittik* (Our Road was Short but our Journey Long) one can observe that Boratav was primarily concerned with the idea of "presentation" of the collected material. He wanted the final text of the "folk tale book" to have an "artistic touch." This was indeed a process of transferring ethnographic data into an artistic form so that it could be more comprehensible for the general reader.

Taken as a whole, Boratav's archive brings together important documents related to his own life as well as folklore material that he collected since 1927. In a country like Turkey, which has undergone an enormously rapid transformation in oral culture, such an archive has two important dimensions. The first is literary, comprising the richness and variety of folkloric material representing a period of nearly half a century. Second, the archive is of great historical value. In this respect, Boratav's archive forms one of the rare written sources of the oral culture of the early republican era in Turkey. The legacy of Boratav's archive reveals itself in a corpus of books and articles published in both Turkish and other languages (Öztürkmen 2005c).

FOLKLORE AS POPULAR CULTURE: THE YEARS DOMINATED BY FOLK DANCING

Following the closing of the People's Houses in 1951 and the closing of the Folk Literature Department at Ankara University, the course of folklore studies took a different turn in Turkey. Both events were in fact part of the same political chaos Turkey was undergoing while changing its regime from a single party system to a multi-party democracy (Yılmaz 1997). The oral genres, collected and classified during the People's Houses era, had already made their way into national education curriculum textbooks. Folk songs were broadcast as the mainstay of Turkish folk music, and local museums displayed regional folk art. Nevertheless, folk dancing grew to be the most popular national folklore genre, taking on new representative forms over the years. The historical process through which regional dances turned into ultimate cultural forms of national representation was parallel to the decline of the People's Houses and the end of academic folklore in Turkey. The appeal and functionality of folk dancing therefore deserves a closer look.

Regional dances developed into an urban tradition the People's Houses era. Local folk dance groups traveled from their own towns to national centers like Ankara and Izmir, or to nearby towns, to take part in national holiday celebrations. After the 1950s, when People's Houses ceased to invite these groups to their anniversary celebrations, private institutions, mostly banks, began to sponsor them. These folk dance shows were essential in consolidating an urban audience for staged folk-dance performances. Yet the encounter was not only between the "urban" and the "provincial." The main encounter, however, was being experienced at another level. Local dance troupes had not met each other previously. They were now visually exploring the other dances, observing their differences in steps, costumes, and musical instruments. The real change came during the 1960s when university students founded their own folk dance associations. Folk dancing offered an informal opportunity for the first generation of students coming from the provinces to familiarize themselves with the urban social space. These students began by performing and promoting their own local dances, but they soon developed an interest in learning other dances as well. This process transcended that of a simple visual encounter between different localities celebrating the same national event. The student folk dancers adopted one another's movements, developed choreographies, and created a new dance platform by teaching the dances in schools. During the 1970s and 1980s, a large folk dance repertoire made its way into the extra-curricular activities of national schools, from elementary schools to higher education. As a consequence of such growth, there soon developed an industry around folk dancing, involving teachers, musicians, costume-makers, and organizers. Competitions, year-end shows, national celebrations, all became events where folk dance was the main component of public entertainment. Between 1970 and 1980, different regional dances began to influence one another in terms of movement, musical accompaniment, and costume material, leading eventually to a new hybrid system of movements, popularly called *folklor oynama*, "dancing folklore." Given the rising political conflict between university students during the 1970s, folk dancing bestowed certain social and political benefits. First, both the state and the families saw folk dancing as a more respectable youth activity than leftist or extreme nationalist youth organizations. The situation continued after the 1980 military coup. Folk dancing survived when many youth organizations were closed down. It also provided a social environment where young men and women could meet, flirt, travel, and dance and not offend the conservative Turkish family structure.

University students were also active in promoting folklore at another level. They took the first initiative to open a National Folklore Institute. Their attempts proved to be fruitful as the Institute opened in 1966 under government supervision and in later years was attached to the Ministry of Culture. The academic study of folklore was not revived until after the 1980s, when folklore programs were established at Ankara and Hacettepe Universities, and folk dance departments opened at the State Conservatories of Istanbul and Izmir. However, the universities which gained their autonomy at the end of the 1940s have once more been subject to close government supervision under the new regulations brought in by the 1980 military coup. Thus, in contrast to the late 1940s, contemporary folklore programs and departments have operated within the boundaries determined by the state and its folklore-related agencies.

To conclude, one can emphasize again the different breakthroughs in Turkish folklore studies. Leaving behind the Turkist Turkish Hearths, the nation-builder People's Houses, Boratav's de-nationalizing academic perspective and finally the sweeping popular folk dance movement, interest in folklore as it was defined in the past is not so enthusiastically followed. Following the 1980 military coup, the politics of culture emerged as a new and important research agenda, particularly for a generation of new researchers who wanted to understand the complex nature of their changing society, to interpret the emotional burden of ideologies around them, but also to situate past and present knowledge of culture in a critical framework. The 1990s witnessed an era when a wave of graduate students joined various social science departments abroad, making their way into international debates in folklore, anthropology, and cultural studies programs. Coming from different academic backgrounds and writing their dissertations in the heyday of nationalist studies, they developed new research agendas and merged them with the changing paradigms of Turkish studies. This encounter also coincided with the intensification of the Internet revolution, the rising power of the media, increasing Islamic fundamentalism, and fervent debates on feminism, ethnicity, and human rights.

These developments bring us back to the world of *Karagöz*, encouraging new researchers to rethink the multi-ethnic, multi-lingual heritage of today's Turkey, where folklore emerges as one of the few domains which have preserved the memory of past repertoires. In the complex ethnographic settings, folklore studies offer a unique perspective to read and comment on the complexities of the Turkish social and cultural domains.

NOTES

1 For an analysis of how national culture was constructed in these areas see Herzfeld (1982); Silverman (1989); El-Shamy (2004); Shay (2002).

2 The *Tanzimat* (Regulation) era refers to a period in Ottoman history when the Ottoman state decided to reform its administrative and military structure. The *Tanzimat* program, declared in 1839, had aimed to transform the traditional political and legal institutions of the empire in line with Western ones. Among the new institutions the most important was the principle of "equality before law" for every subject of the empire irrespective of his religion. The impact of the *Tanzimat* was also felt in the fields of education and in particular in the popularization of language.

3 One should also mention other Turkist organizations which preceded the Turkish Hearths, like Türk Derneği (Turkish Association, 1908), Genç Kalemler (Young Pens, 1911), or Türk Yurdu Cemiyeti (Turkish Homeland Society, 1911).

4 Ziya Gökalp's "Preface to Folk Civilisation" was published in 1913 in the periodical *Halka Doğru*; Rıza Tevfik's "Folklore" was published in the literary supplement of the daily *Peyam*; Fuat Köprülü's "A new Science; Folklore" was also published in 1914 in *İkdam*. Selim Sırrı Tarcan's "Among the Educators: Folklore" appeared in the 1922 issue of *Terbiye ve Oyun* (Education and Play) and Yusuf Akçura's lecture was published in 1929 in the magazine *Yeni Muhit*. For the reprints of Gökalp, Rıza Tevfik, and Köprülü in the Roman alphabet see Evliyaoğlu and Baykurt (1988); Tarcan's article in *Oyun ve Terbiye* was transcribed into the modern Turkish alphabet by Mutlu Öztürk. For Akçura, see *Yeni Muhit* 2(13): 975–1153.

5 For a discussion of the European impact on Turkish folklore studies see Öztürkmen 2005b.

6   Established in 1932, the Turkish Language Society conducted linguistic research on Turkish and other Turkic languages. It has acted as the official authority on Turkish language, publishing the official dictionary of the language.

7   For a critical analysis of the "Choir of Tunes from Homeland" (*Yurttan Sesler Korosu*), see Değirmenci (2006); Tekelioğlu (1996); Balkılıç (2009).

8   The Turkish History Society had adopted an official "History Thesis'" in the 1930s, linking Central Asian culture as the most important influence on Ancient Anatolian civilizations. The thesis argued that Central Asia was a cradle of civilization, which through migrations, left an imprint on the prehistoric cultures of Anatolia, Europe, and other parts of the world. See Saffet 1934; Nazım 1935. For a critical analysis of the "'History Thesis'" see Ersanlı (1992).

9   The interest in Central Asian Turkic folklore remained, however, mostly limited to literary genres, traditional sports, and religious beliefs (Elöve 1935; Kepecioğlu 1935; Anahin 1941). One of the most frequently mentioned Central Asian literary genres was the Ergenekon epic, which was used as a metaphor for the founding of the republic and the War of Independence (Arif 1934a, 1933).

10 The discussion of how to define *regionalism* and *locality* in the Turkish context certainly requires more investigation. To put it briefly, regional boundaries of the former regime were not valid anymore and the new boundaries were not yet defined. Journals like *Fikirler, Uludağ,* or *Aksu* would report on neighboring localities as well from time to time, and thus contribute to the integration of a sense of locality. Yet, more often, journals like *Çoruh, Kaynak, Ün*, focused on their own towns and their neighboring villages, which I refer to as *localities* in this chapter. See also Öztürkmen (2005a).

11 Villagism (*köycülük*) was a strong component of the Young Turk revolutionary ideas, in reaction to both imperialism and Ottoman landlord system. Therefore, "the village" emerged as the most important sociological unit among early republican Turkish intellectuals. Villagism also brought together Young Turk intellectuals engaged in the national independance movement. Trained in European social thought, yet at the same time reacting to European imperialism, these intellectuals were committed to the idea of "'development'," acting on their interest in the village by establishing formal institutions like the village sections of the People's Houses or the Village Institutes (Türkdoğan 2006; Üstel 1989; Karaömerlioğlu 1998).

12 As an exception, Adalan (1943).

13 See İbrahim Erenel's account of Şeyhmusa Köyü's "national sentiments" being "in good shape and strong," in Erenel (1940a).

14 Öztürkmen (1998a: 129).

15 See Öztürkmen (1998a: 130–131).

16 See the account on *pehlivan güreşi* during the celebration of the republic's tenth anniversary in Ülkü-c 1935: 430; Kepecioğlu (1935). See also Özay (1944); Bayduhan (1943); Turgut (1940); Duru (1944).

17 Öztürkmen (1998a: 231–241).

18 The review in *Aksu* congratulated the Giresun dancers for "their success in achieving a regularity and maturity which Giresun should be proud of." See Aksu-c (1948: 1).

19 Baykurt also recalls the reluctance of the *zurna* player Kara Ömer (Ömer the Black) to perform outside his conventional performance settings, especially in other towns, because he disliked the image of the Thracian gypsy.

20 Personal interview with Şerif Baykurt on July 25, 1992.

21 The impact of this national platform of folk dancing continued through the 1980s, making its way into national schools and universities and independent folk dance clubs. For a more detailed analysis see Öztürkmen (2002).

22 Turkist journals of this era include *Atsız Mecmua*, (1931–1932), *Azerbaycan Yurt Bilgisi* (1932–1934), *Birlik* (1933–1934), *Doğu* (1933–1934) and *Orhun* (1933–1934).

23 For an analysis of the Turkist journals and the Turkist movement see Özdoğan (1990).

24 A lecture Boratav presented on Köroğlu, the sixteenth-century Anatolian folk poet, regarded as a threat to the Ottoman order, was for instance linked to an "'anti-government'" stance. One student argued that Boratav interpreted Turkish epics as the struggle of the neglected poor classes against the rich classes. Another colleague argued that Boratav was hostile to to notions of family, virtue, history and nationality. This colleague also maintained that Boratev had communist sympathies in that that among the narratives Boratav collected, there were were some which were "against private property'" and which attacked social institutions. There were also allegations that regarded the the Alevi *kızılbaş* poets as important, thus contradicting "'the nationalistic view.'"

25 The original archive was established at the Université Paris 8, Nanterre and a duplicate archive was donated to the History Foundation in Istanbul in 1998.

REFERENCES

Açıkdeniz, Banu. 2009. "Nationalization of Folk Dances in Greece and Turkey: The Case of Zeybek and Zeibekiko" (Unpublished MA Thesis), Istanbul Bilgi University.

Adalan, Malik. 1943. "Fatma Nine Konuşuyor." *Uludağ* 55: 14.

Akçura, Yusuf. 1929. "Folklor Nedir?" *Yeni Muhit* 2(13): 975–1153.

Akpınar, Zeki. 1945. "Köy Odaları." *Uludağ* 68–69: 10–11.

Aktaş, Kemal Kamil. 1946. "Memleketimizin Tiyatro Tarihine Bir Bakış." *Fikirler* 304–305: 7–8.

Aksu-a. 1934. "Babamın Albümü." *Aksu* 1(3, 4, 5, 6): 48–49.

Aksu-b. 1937. "B.Ş. Kayanın Davamızı Teşrih Eden Nutku." *Aksu* March 1937(14): 3–10.

Aksu-c. 1948. "Folklor Ekibimizin Ankara Seyahati." *Aksu* 5(50): 1.

Akyol, Hamit. 1945. "Folklor." *Fikirler* 296–297: 3.

Alper, C. 1938. Havva Bacı. *Çoruh* 1 (3): 11–12.

Anderson, Benedict. 1983 [1991]. *Imagined Communities: Reflections on the Origin and Spread of Nationalism*. London and New York: Verso.

Arif, Ali. 1934. "Giresun Köylüler." *Aksu* 12: 10.

Ay, Göktan. 1990. *Folklora Giriş*. İstanbul: İTÜ Türk Musikisi Devlet Konservatuarı Mezunları Yayınları 1.

Balkılıç, Özgür. 2009. *Cumhuriyet, Halk ve Müzik: Türkiye'de Müzik Reformu, 1922–1952*. Ankara: Tan Yayınları.

Başgöz, İlhan. 1972. "Folklore Studies and Nationalism in Turkey." *Journal of the Folklore Institute* 9: 162–176.

Başgöz, İlhan. 1998. "Pertev Naili Boratav'ın Türk ve Dünya Folklor Araştırmalarındaki Yeri" in Metin Turan, Ed., *Pertev Naili Boratav'a Armağan*. Ankara: T.C. Kültür Bakanlığı Yayınları, pp. 17–32.

Bayduhan, N. 1943. "Milli Halk ve Çocuk Oyunları." *Fikirler* 240–241: 6–7.

Berkes, Mediha. 1941. "Review of 'Patterns of Culture'." *Ülkü* 17(97): 84–90.

Boratav, Pertev Naili. 1939. "Halkevlerinin Folklor Çalışmaları İçin Yaptıkları ve Yapabilecekleri İşler Hakkında Notlar." *Ülkü* 13(73): 195–211 and 13(76): 295–298.

Boratav, Pertev Naili. 1942. *Halk Edebiyatı Dersleri*. Ankara: DTCF Turkish Language and Literature Institute Publications 4.

Boratav, Pertev Naili. 1982. *Folklor ve Edebiyat*. Vol. 1. İstanbul: Adam Yayıncılık.

Carnoy, Henry and Jean Nicolaïdes. 1889. *Traditions populaires de l'Asie Mineure*. Paris: Maisonneuve.

Carnoy, Henry and Jean Nicolaïdes. 1892. *Traditions populaires de Constantinople et de ses environs. Contributions au folklore des Turcs, Chrétiens, Arméniens*. Paris: La Tradition.

Carnoy, Henry and Jean Nicolaïdes. 1894. *Folklore de Constantinople*. Paris: Emile Lechevalier Libraire.

Çeçen, Anıl. 1990. *Halkevleri*. Ankara: Gündoğan Yayınları.

Çelik, Zeynep. 1992. *Displaying the Orient: Architecture of Islam at Nineteenth-Century World's Fairs*. Berkeley: University of California Press.

Çoruh-a. 1938. "Çoruh'un Milli Oyunlarından Sarı Çiçek: Deli Horon." *Çoruh* 1(2): 8–9.

Çoruh-b. 1938. "Ata Barı." *Çoruh* 1(4): 37.

Değirmenci, Koray. 2006. "On the Pursuit of a Nation: The Construction of Folk and Folk Music in the Founding Decades of the Turkish Republic." *International Review of the Aesthetics and Sociology of Music* 37(1): 47–65.

Demirdal, Sait. 1937. "Mahalli Halk Türkülerini Toplama Komitemiz Çalışırken." *Taşpınar* 5(52).

Demirdal, Sait. 1943. "Çopur Ali." *Ün* 106: 1479–1481.

Duru, Gültekin. 1944. "Kıbidik." *Eskişehir Halkevi* 72: 19–20.

Elçin, Murat. 1938. "Köroğlu Hakkında Notlar." *Ülkü* 10: 271 and 326.

El-Shamy, Hasan. 2004. *Types of the Folktale in the Arab World. A Demographically Oriented Tale-Type Index*. Bloomington: Indiana University Press.

Erenel, İbrahim. 1940a. "Bulancak Kazasının (Şeyhmusa) Köyü." *Aksu* 2(21): 3–7.

Erenel, İbrahim. 1940b. "Şeyhmusaköyü." *Aksu* 2(21): 3–7.

Ersanlı, Büşra. 1992. *İktidar ve Tarih, Türkiye'de "Resmi Tarih" Tezinin Oluşumu (1929–1937)*. (Power and History, The Formation of the "Official History Thesis" in Turkey, 1929–1937). Istanbul: AFA.

Evliyaoğlu, Sait and Şerif Baykurt. 1988. *Türk Halkbilimi*. Ankara: Ofset Reprodüksiyon Matbaacılık.

Fehmi, Hasan. 1934. "Anadolu'da Gregoriyen ve Ortodoks Türkler." *Ülkü* 4(21): 173–182.

Fevziye, Abdullah. 1938. "'Folk,' The Journal of the International Association for Folklore and Ethnology (Müşterek Folklor ve Etnoloji Cemiyeti Mecmuası), Ağustos, 1937." *Ülkü* 11(62): 189–192.

Fikirler-a. 1935. "Türk Kadını Saylav." *Fikirler* 5(120): 1.

Fikirler-b. 1938. "Halkevi Haberleri." *Fikirler* 1938(165): 16.

Fikirler-c. 1939(182): 12.

Fikirler-d. 1942(234): 6.

Fikirler-e. 1938. "Kadın Modalarında Türk Zevki." *Fikirler* 1938(166, 167, 168): 73–75.

Gennep, Arnold Van.1939a. "Folklor." *Ülkü* 12(71): 409 and 12(72): 499.

Gennep, Arnold Van. 1939b. *Folklor*. Trans. Pertev Naili Boratav. Ankara: CHP Kılavuz Kitaplar 2. This work was reprinted in 2000 as an appendix to Halk Edebiyatı Dersleri, Istanbul: T.E.T.T.V. Yayınları, pp. 147–204.

Gürkaynak, Murtaza. 1939. "Yunus Emre: Hayatı, Şahsiyeti ve Şiirleri." *Fikirler* 188: 4–5.

H.C. 1934. "Kuyucak." *Eskişehir Halkevi* 1934(21): 28–32.

Halit Bayrı, M. 1941. "Dadaloğlu Hakkında Notlar." *Ülkü* 17(99): 225–234.

Herzfeld, Michael. 1982. *Ours Once More: Folklore, Ideology, and the Making of Modern Greece*. Austin: University of Texas Press.

İpekkan, Levent. 1978. "Türkiye'de Cumhuriyet Döneminde Halkbilim Alanında Çalışma Yapan Kuruluşlar (1927–1977)." *Halkbilimi* 6(52): 17–28.

Irmak, Hüseyin. 2009. *Dinler Arası Sevda Türküleri*. İstanbul: Punto Yayınları.

Jacob, Georg. 1925. *Geschichte des Schattentheaters im Morgen- und Abendland*. Hannover: Lafaire.

Kabacalı, Alpay. 1992. *Türkiye'de Gençlik Hareketleri*. İstanbul: Altın Kitaplar Yayınevi.

Kansu, Natif Ansu. 1941. "Halk Terbiyesi ve Halkevleri." *Ülkü* 17(97): 3–6.

Karaömerlioğlu, Asım. 1998. "The Village Institute Experience in Turkey." *British Journal of Middle Eastern Studies* 25(1): 47–73.

Kaynak-a. 1937. "Eski. Tarihlerde Garbi Anadolu'dan İstanbula Üzüm Nakline Dair Bir Vesika." *Kaynak* 1937(57): 248–249.

Kaynak-b. 1935. "Halkevimizin Beş Yıllık Çalışması." *Kaynak* 5(69): 491–500.

Kaynak-c.1937. "Cumhuriyetin Ondördüncü Yılında Balıkesir Halkevinin yaptığı İşler." *Kaynak* 5(57): 272.

Kösemihal, Mahmut Ragıp. 1938a. "Artvin ve Kars Havalisi Müzik Folkloru Hakkında." *Yeni Türk* 67: 253–255.

Kösemihal, Mahmut Ragıp. 1938b. "Onbeş Yıllık Müzik Çalışmalarımız." *Yeni Türk* 71: 452–455.

Kolivar, Ayşenur. 2007. "60'lardan günümüze Doğu Karadeniz kültürlerinde müzikal normların değişimi." *Halkbilimi* 2007(1): 31–36.

Kunos, Ignácz and Robert Nisbet Bain. 1969. *Turkish Fairy Tales and Folk Tales.* New York: Dover Publications.

Mardin, Şerif. 1962. *The Genesis of Young Ottoman Thought. A Study in the Modernization of Turkish Political Ideas.* Princeton: Princeton University Press.

Nazım. 1935. "Etiler Nasıl Yaşarlardı." *Uludağ* 1(2): 38–40.

Nuri. 1933. "Kütahya'da Alayund Köyü." *Ülkü* 2(8): 156.

Nusret, Kemal. 1933. "Bir Köycülük Projesi Tecrübesi." *Ülkü* 2(8): 123.

Öğütçü, Rahmi K. 1940. "Düzköy." *Aksu* 2(20): 10–12 and 2(22): 11–16.

Öner, Senem. 2008. "Folk Songs, Translation and the Question of (Pseudo-) Originals." *The Translator* 14(2): 229–246.

Ortaç, Hüsnü. 1941. "Bursa'da Halk Raksları." *Uludağ* 45–46: 26–32.

Özay, Mahmut. 1944. Deve Güreşi. *Fikirler* 266–267: 18–19.

Özdoğan, Günay Göksu. 1990. "The Case of Racism-Turanism: Turkism during Single-Party Period, 1931–1944." (Unpublished dissertation), Boğaziçi University.

Öztürkmen, Arzu. 1998a. *Türkiye'de folklor ve Milliyetçilik.* İstanbul: İletişim Yayınları.

Öztürkmen, Arzu. 1998b. *Pertev Naili Boratav Davasına Dair Basın ve Mecliste Yer Alan Tartışmaların Söylemi* (Discourse of the Debates on the Case of Pertev Naili Boratav in Press and in the Parliament). Üniversite'de Cadı Kazanı: 1948 Tasfiyesi ve Pertev Naili Boratav'ın Müdafaası. Istanbul: Tarih Vakfı Yurt Yayınları.

Öztürkmen, Arzu. 2002. "I Dance Folklore" in Deniz Kandiyoti and Ayşe Saktanber, Eds. *Fragments of Culture: The Everyday Life of Turkey.* London and New York: I.B.Taurus, pp.128–146.

Öztürkmen, Arzu. 2005a. "Rethinking Regionalism: Memory of Change in a Turkish Black Sea Town." *East European Quarterly* 39(1): 47–62.

Öztürkmen, Arzu. 2005b. "The European Impact on the Early Turkish Folklore Studies" in Hakan Yılmaz, Ed. *Placing Turkey in the Map of Europe.* Istanbul: Boğaziçi University Press, pp. 134–151.

Öztürkmen, Arzu. 2005c. "Folklore on Trial: Pertev Naili Boratav and the Denationalization of Turkish Folklore." *Journal of Folklore Research* 42(2): 185–216.

Pamirli, Osman Turgut. 1940a. "Folklor-1." *Aksu* 2(19): 9–11.

Pamirli, Osman Turgut. 1940b. "Folklor-3: Kadroları." *Aksu* 2(21): 9–11.

Pamirli, Osman Turgut. 1941. "Folklor ve Sahne." *Aksu* 3(29): 3–5.

Pennanen, Risto Pekka. 2004. "The Nationalization of Ottoman Popular Music in Greece." *Ethnomusicology* 48(1): 1–25.

Poladian, Sirvat. 1978. "Komitas Vartabed and His Contribution to Ethnomusicology: Komitas the Pioneer" in Vrej Nersessian, Ed. *Essays on Armenian Music.* London: Kahn and Averill, pp. 13–28.

Refet, İshak. 1933. "Karacaoğlan." *Ülkü* 1(3): 222–229.

Saffet, Reşit. 1933a. "Turizm." *Ülkü* 1(1): 69.

Saffet, Mehmet. 1933b. "Köycülük Nedir." *Ülkü* 1(6): 430.

Saffet, Mehmet. 1934. "Anadolu'da En Eski Türk Medeniyeti." *Ülkü* 3(16): 263–267.

Salcı, Vahid Lutfi. 1938. "Gizli Halk Musikisi." *Ülkü* 11(62):113–123.

Salih, Cemal. 1933. "İradenin Kuvveti." *Aksu* 1(2): 3.

Şapolyo, Enver Behnan. 1934. "Müzeciliğin Tarihi." *Ülkü* 3(18): 428–431.

Şapolyo, Enver Behnan. 1935. "Etnoğrafya." *Ün* 1935: 273–275.

Şapolyo, Enver Behnan. 1936. "Karagöz Efsanesi." *Uludağ* 5: 42–43 and 6: 30–31.

Selçuk, Orhan. 1934a. "Bayramlar Bayramı." *Aksu* 1(2): 3–4.

Shay, Anthony. 2002. *Choreographic Politics: State Folk Dance Ensembles, Representation and Power.* Middletown: Wesleyan University Press.

Silverman, Carol. 1989. "Reconstructing Folklore: Media and Cultural Policy in

324 ARZU ÖZTÜRKMEN

Eastern Europe." *Communication* 11: 141–160.

Süreyya, Ali. 1934. "Alucra Kazası Gicora Köyü." *Aksu* 1(3, 4, 5, 6): 29–32.

Tarcan, Selim Sırrı. 1935. "Milli Müzik Nasıl Doğdu?" *Ülkü* 5(27): 200–205.

Tarcan, Selim Sırrı. 1948. *Halk Dansları ve Tarcan Zeybeği* (Folk Dances and The Zeybek of Tarcan). İstanbul: Ülkü Basımevi.

Tekelioğlu, Orhan. 1996. "The Rise of a Spontaneous Synthesis: The Historical Background of Turkish Popular Music." *Middle Eastern Studies* 32(2): 194–215.

Turgut, S. 1940. "Giresun Sporunun Geçmiş Zamanlarına Bir Bakış." *Aksu* 2(21): 22–24.

Türkdoğan, Orhan. 2006. *Türkiye'de Köy Sosyolojisi.* İstanbul: IQ Kültür Sanat Yayıncılık.

Ülkü-a. 1933. "Kütahya'da Alayund Köyü." *Ülkü* 2(8): 151–158.

Ülkü-b. 1935. "T.D. Araştırma Kurumunun Bildirisi." *Ülkü* 5(26): 85–87.

Ülkü-c. 1935. "Köyde Bayram." *Ülkü* 1933(11): 430.

Ülkü-d. "Fasıl Musikisi Hakkında Bir Cevap." *Ülkü* 1941(101): 468–469.

Ülkütaşır, M. Şakir. 1973. *Cumhuriyet'le Birlikte Türkiye'de Folklor ve Etnografya Çalışmaları.* Ankara: Başbakanlık Kültür Müsteşarlığı.

Uludağ-a. 1940(27): 35.

Uludağ-b. 1940(28): 25.

Üstel, Füsun. 1989. "Köycüler Cemiyeti." *Tarih ve Toplum* 72: 12–16.

Yalgın, Rıza. 1941. "Çeki Köy." *Uludağ* 42–43: 7–11.

Yıldız, Burcu. 2009. "Türkiye'de Popüler Müzik ve Çokkültürlülük Üzerine Notlar" *Dinler Arası Sevda Türküleri.* İstanbul: Punto Yayınları, pp. 194–201.

Yılmaz, Hakan. 1997. "Democracy and Freedom: The Redefinition of the Ideology of the Turkish Regime in the Postwar Period" in Antonio Marquina, Ed. *Elites and Change in the Mediterranean.* Madrid: FMES, pp. 27–44.

Ziya, Abdullah. 1933. "Köy Mimarisi." *Aksu* 1(5): 370–374.

Ziya Işıtman, Tarık. 1941. "Bolu'da Milli Oyunlar: Meşeli." *Fikirler* 219–120: 19–20.

Z.S. 1943. "Folklor Çalışmalarında İlmin Direktifi ve Bazı Esaslar." *Fikirler* 1943(246–247): 10–11.

CHAPTER 17 FOLKLORE STUDIES IN ISRAEL

Dani Schrire and
Galit Hasan-Rokem

Israel is a state in which territorial and cultural identities are marked by extreme discontinuities and where ideological, indeed utopian and religious motivations play a tremendously significant role in the socio-political reality. We thus have tried to capture the meaning and role of folklore in this chapter by presenting a double perspective. While first trying to sketch a more or less chronological description of the cultural history of the country, the history of folklore research will then be presented – rather than as a historical account from a proposed point of origin in the past – as a discussion of folklore and its study in Israel from the present backwards. Mapping the state of the discipline and its profile here and now, we shall try to look for trajectories leading back to various historical and textual points of departure for its emergence.

WHO? WHERE? WHY? WHEN?

But even before that, a number of broadly contextual circumstances that have determined the profile of folklore and folkloristics in Israel need to be explained by way of introduction.

First, the borders of the state of Israel have been in a process of change since its establishment in 1948 as a part of the 1947 United Nations Partition Plan for the British Mandate of Palestine. As a result of the ensuing war, a considerable Palestinian population was incorporated in the state of Israel, together with what became its Jewish majority. In the aftermath of the war of 1967 Israel remained an occupier of the rest of the former British Mandate of Palestine. The unresolved relations with Palestinians – as a minority in the state, as neighbors beyond an indefinable border, and as enemies under occupation – escape any systematic or unambiguous description.

A Companion to Folklore, First Edition. Edited by Regina F. Bendix and Galit Hasan-Rokem.
© 2012 John Wiley & Sons, Ltd. Published 2012 John Wiley & Sons, Ltd.

Second, the definition of Israel as the state of the Jewish people encompassing a large Palestinian/Arab minority within the borders of the Jewish state proclaimed in 1948 complicates the definition of a subject of folklore as *Israeli*, especially in a historical perspective.[1]

Third, even more than the common instability that characterizes the continuous dwelling of any group in any defined territory, the interrupted residence of Jews in the area of their present state has been characterized as a history of disruption and exile. *Jewish* historiography can traditionally be broken down into periods with regard to residence in the land of Israel. First of all, they were living as Israelites in the Biblical period, etiologically associated with Abraham's journey from Mesopotamia to the Promised Land in the book of Genesis, terminated temporarily by about 200 years of slavery in Egypt, followed by a kingdom, then two kingdoms (Judea and Israel), brought to an end by exile to Babylonia (586 BCE). Then there was a renewed kingdom of Judea and then another loss of independence as a vassal state under the Romans (70 CE). Furthermore, the initially unstable relationship of the Jews with the land of Israel evolved into a predominantly diasporic identity based on a common canonical literature: both the Hebrew Bible and its later elaborations and interpretations, the liturgical and exegetical tradition in Hebrew (and somewhat less in Aramaic), and a commonality of existential conditions as a mobile and rejected minority both in Christian and Muslim countries. During this long period there were Jewish, Christian, and Muslim pilgrimages to the Holy Land as well as small Jewish settlements already there, especially in Jerusalem and the other sacred cities. Finally, the growth of modern European nationalism and expectations of equality fostered by the Enlightenment instigated a number of reactions, which can be divided broadly into three categories: emancipation, assimilation and Jewish nationalism. The latter was manifested in various political programs, notably Zionism, which envisaged national fulfillment in the then Ottoman Palestine, where Jews were encouraged to emigrate.

When writing about the folklore of Israel we thus need to ask ourselves about whose folklore in Israel we are writing. Our pondering stems from the situation where borders construct identity only in a certain sense, as linguistic, ethnic, and even national affiliation are organized spatially in a much more complex way than an "in-out" conceptualization may suggest. Indeed, Jewish life in Israel is relatively new, as most Israeli Jews have arrived there in the twentieth century – several decades after Jewish folklore emerged as a scholarly enterprise. Hence Jewish-Israeli folklore has from its beginning been attributed to places outside of Israel.

As our own academic knowledge is rooted mostly in Jewish folklore, our discussion will focus on some of the transformations between the concepts of Jewish folklore and Israeli folklore. Palestinian folklore, the main non-Jewish folklore in Israel and the one most studied in the Israeli academic context alongside Jewish folklore, will also be addressed here. Our inclusion of the discussion of Palestinian folklore in Israel does not express any kind of entitlement to it or its study, nor a wish to appropriate it or to blur its specificity. However similar dilemmas, although perhaps morally less explicit, arise in several of the cultural interfaces that will be treated throughout this chapter. Our theoretical point of departure emphasizes folklore's and folklore studies' abiding to conditions of cultural contact and intercultural communication. This necessitates the dynamic reading of the shared lives of folklores in a troubled social, political, and cultural reality.

The category of "folklore" arrived in Israel with nineteenth-century travelers who visited what has been referred to as the Holy Land, and "discovered" its inhabitants and their customs (*The Library* 1971) that were some years later introduced into the anthropological canon (Granqvist 1931,1935). In fact, such travel echoes the situation of a land whose folklore has emphatically developed in relationship to other places: The Holy Land has since antiquity been frequented by pilgrims. The Hebrew Bible assigns three main pilgrimages. Depending on accessibility, Jewish pilgrimage has been more or less steady since antiquity. It intensified in the second millennium CE, directed primarily to Jerusalem, but also to the three other sacred cities: Hebron, Tiberias and Tsfat (Safed). Christian pilgrimages have existed from the fourth century CE onwards, with Jerusalem, Bethlehem, Nazareth, and the sites around the Sea of Galilee as their main pilgrimage sites. There were also Islamic pilgrimages to Jerusalem as well as the two main ones to Mecca and Medina in the Arabian Peninsula.

The customs and artifacts associated with pilgrimage have thus remained a long, continuous, multi-cultural, and multi-religious part of the folklore of the country, among its various inhabitants as well as visitors. These customs include the ritual canonization of certain routes according to each confession, the performative reading of certain texts – passages of Scripture, prayers, psalms and songs as well as outright preaching and tourist guiding – ordained by the various traditions, as well as other modes of ritual behavior (bowing, kneeling, collective meals, etc.). The folklore of pilgrimage is also materialized in the commercial and artistic production of artifacts both for ritual use at the pilgrimage itself (head gear for Jewish males; palm branches for Christians, etc.) and for commemorative purposes upon return (water from the Jordan, earth of the Holy Land, and symbolic mementos made from the wood of olive trees – all for both Jews and Christians alike). Like other holy sites of the world, the sites of the Holy Land are according to the believers endowed with curing and restoring powers, a belief in which is reinforced by legendary narratives related to the sacred figures of each of the religions (Coleman and Elsner 2003; Hasan-Rokem 1999a; Limor 2007).

FROM THE PAST TO THE PRESENT – A CULTURAL HISTORICAL BIRD'S EYE VIEW OF THE CONTEXT OF FOLKLORE IN THE HOLY LAND

Looking back in history, under the Roman rule of Palestine the cohabitation of Jews and Pagans, and later Christians, gave rise to a common folklore (popular medicine, dream interpretation, magic) and also a divergent one (especially religious folklore) (Niehoff 1992; Hasan-Rokem 2000: 89–107; 2003: 76–82). From the fourth century CE Christianity became the dominant power in the region followed by the Muslims in the seventh century. Muslim rule was interrupted by the Crusades, but was reinstated throughout the Holy Land by the end of the thirteenth century, and in 1517 the area was integrated into the Ottoman Empire. At about the same time and as a result of the influx of Jews expelled from Catholic Spain in 1492, a relatively large group of them settled in Palestine, especially in the Galilean town of Tsfat (Safed) that developed into a center of an emerging Kabbalah (Patai 1978; Werblowsky 1987; Fine 2003; Garb 2008). The Kabbalah spread among Jews around the world, its repertoire ranging from esoteric modes of mystical meditation and massive mythologizing of earlier Jewish religious motifs such as the creation narrative of Genesis, to concrete forms of everyday magic – all of which persist in contemporary culture and have even experienced a heightened popularity from the 1980s onwards (e.g., Huss 2007).

Syncretism was the name of the cultural game in all of the Eastern part of the Mediterranean, including input from at least as far as Iran and India, especially expressed in the path of migrating narratives, both single and in compilations.[2] In the historical study of folk narratives, the Levant has indeed been considered a major crossroads.

During the nineteenth century – with the crumbling of the Ottoman Empire and as Egypt developed independently from Constantinople – the region of Palestine was under the growing influence of European empires. During that time Jews started emigrating in increasing numbers from various places in Europe and Asia. Indeed, the present Jewish population of Israel is largely composed of members and descendants of waves of immigrants who arrived in growing quantities from the beginning of the nineteenth century, and especially at the end of that century. Under the influence of European national movements that inspired the Jewish national movement known as Zionism and due to growing politically organized animosity against Jewish minorities in Europe, especially in the Russian Empire, Jewish immigration to Palestine changed its character from religious to political and national. West European Jewish philanthropy was instrumental in supporting Jewish settlement in Jerusalem since the nineteenth century as well as in semi-urban agricultural settlements in the coastal region. Pioneering Jewish immigrants mainly from Eastern Europe, who chose to make their living from agriculture and road building, settled in the Galilee and the Jezreel and Jordan valleys in the north of the country. Other immigrants began establishing urban settlements especially in the coastal region, most famously the city of Tel-Aviv that was founded in 1909 more or less at the same time as Deganiah – the first kibbutz to the south of the Sea of Galilee (Kinnereth).

The various type of lifestyles produced various forms of folklore. In the pioneering settlements, consisting mostly of young people, folklore moved, at least to begin with, between radical innovation of family formation and labor distribution with the idealistic purpose of shaping nothing less than the "New Human" and "The Religion of Labor" (associated with the charismatic figure of the Tolstoyan A.D. Gordon). This included memories of the old country, such as Russian songs, the Russian shirts adopted by the Narodnik movement of "going to the people," collective dancing with various European roots such as the Romanian "hora," local practices such as riding unsaddled horses, wearing the traditional Arab headgear "kuffiyeh" and hiking to locally venerated sources, hills and ruins (Salamon 2008). The kibbutz collective settlements developed their independent holiday traditions which were contrary to the religious festival traditions practiced in the Diaspora.

When Ottoman rule was brought to an end in 1917, a growing European influence changed the lives of both the local Arab population as well as the Jewish one. Despite that, the urban folklore of Jews in Jerusalem was more marked by traditions of the countries of origin than in other places since the immigrants who settled there were predominantly, although not solely, more religiously observant and safeguarded their particular expressions that they had brought along from various places in Europe as well as Asia (Hazaz 1956: 1–2). Correspondingly, their folklore also bore many religious traits, such as particular versions of prayers and melodies, but they also persisted in wearing clothing, cooking food, and producing artifacts from their countries of origin. The traditionalist tendencies of the various Jewish groups in Jerusalem – emphasizing their roots in their everyday culture – coalesced with the emphatically touristy culture of the Holy City which created an eager market for marks of particularity to be interpreted as marks of authenticity. Due to Orientalist tendencies (Said 1978) there was a special interest in the cultural production of the groups originating from countries of the Middle East, such as Turkey, Yemen, Iraq, Iran, Kurdistan, Syria, and North Africa (Egypt, Libya, Tunisia, Algeria, and Morocco).

The urban culture of Tel-Aviv, a city that soon developed into a modern metropolis with ambitions to emulate the big centers of fashion in Europe, most explicitly Paris and Vienna, included bohemian folklore associated with the cafés frequented by poets, authors, artists and theater people as well as journalists and politicians (Helman 2002, 2006, 2008, 2010). Public folklore expressed in festival processions flourished in celebration of the emergence of an all-Jewish public arena and a more benevolent climate that permitted outdoor celebrations all the year round. Tel-Aviv's folkloristic scene excelled in the production of festival processions, many of which coincided with traditional Jewish holidays, for example, Hanukkah and Purim, but took on much more worldly and secular traits, some of which had already appeared in celebrations among secularized Jews in Europe. Thus Tel-Aviv's most famous holiday procession, the Purim "Ad-delo-yada" (named after the unconscious state of one who has fully obeyed the command to drink wine on that particular holiday) was possibly modeled on carnivals in Catholic countries which were probably based on Pagan traiditions (Horowitz 2006: 248–250), but also focused strongly on a stylized beauty queen contest concluding in the coronation of the annual "Queen Esther," the heroine of the biblical book of Esther from which stems the etiology of the holiday (Aryeh-Sapir 2006).

Palestinian-Arab independent national identity began developing during the British Mandate. Whereas Jewish folklore varied according to the countries of origin and ideologies that had brought various groups and individuals to Palestine, Palestinian-Arab culture varied greatly by region, social strata and groupings: Jerusalem Palestinian elite culture was influenced by the British and contacts with Europe, and distinct urban cultures also developed in Jaffa and Acre. However, like the culture of peasants (Fellahin), some continuity of life in the Ottoman age remained evident. The semi-nomadic culture of the Bedouin had its own distinct character. After the 1948 War (Israel's War of Independence/Palestinian Naqba) both folk-cultures entered into massive processes of change as a result of the growing pressure of conforming to a nation (Benvenisti 2000). Palestinian nation-building involved folkloristic work, as Salim Tamari has shown (Tamari 2009).

THE CURRENT STATE OF THE STUDY OF FOLKLORE IN ISRAEL

Relative to the size of the population, Israeli folklore research is remarkably well represented in academic institutions, however affected by the worldwide economic crisis of academic institutions and especially the humanities. All major research universities maintain some form of folklore studies, and even some colleges, teaching colleges, and community colleges provide courses in folklore. On the other hand, the presence of folklore enterprises in the public sphere seems to continually decrease. This situation reveals a contrast between the status of folklore until the 1960s and after, and it reflects the institutional efforts carried out first and foremost by Dov Noy and his students.

Multiple disciplinary roots gave rise to twentieth-century folklore studies in Mandatory Palestine and in the state of Israel. Much of it continued along various paths that began in the nineteenth century mostly in Europe. It comprised the engagement of Israeli folklorists with Jewish folklore of diaspora Jews on the one hand and continued many ideas that Jews in Europe developed and that were later used by Zionist folklorists on the other. Hence, although the academic institution-alization of folklore studies in Israeli academia to a great extent developed from the work of Dov Noy, Noy himself as well as his students and other folklorists in Israel continuously attribute the roots of Jewish folklore studies to various works and writ-ers, other ethnographies of the Holy Land as well as other bodies of folkloristic knowledge developed in European and American institutions where the discipline has been fostered. Indeed, in our description of Israeli folklore studies, our point of reference will be the trunk and its branches, but simultaneously we follow other trajectories that enrich the work of the various folklorists that have been active in Israel. These roots extend about a century prior to the successful integration of folklore in Israeli academia, when Jews in Europe found it very hard to integrate in academic faculties (and even harder in folklore). Despite that, the scope of Jewish folklore studies was immense and differed greatly between centers of Jewish learning, serving various ideologies and purposes across Europe and beyond, which we will necessarily mention here only very briefly.

In late nineteenth-century Western Europe, especially Germany, Jews were largely excluded from academic institutions (Hauschild 1997; Kaschuba 1999, 46ff. esp. 56; and in Sweden, Klein 2003). Their position vis-à-vis the budding folklore studies of the time (compare the article on Germany in the present volume) was even more problematic than in other fields since the discipline generally emphasized the national character of the subject of folklore, in which the Jews were viewed as outsiders. It is thus indicative that Jews were strongly represented in the early phases of what was to become cultural studies, emphasizing the discontinuity of modern culture from traditional forms of culture, focusing on urban rather than rural lifestyles, analyzing innovation rather than tradition, as found preeminently in the work of Georg Simmel, and later in the writings of Sigfried Kracauer and Walter Benjamin (cf. Frisby 1986).

Max Grunwald formed the Gesellschaft für jüdische Volkskunde in Hamburg in 1898 – a learned society with a few hundred members. Its main activities were connected to the society's journal that appeared regularly for 30 years (Daxelmüller 1986, 2010; Staudinger 2010). The study of folklore was also part of the activities of the rabbinical seminaries of Breslau, Vienna, and particularly Budapest (Scheiber 1986). At the same time, a Jewish historical and ethnographic society was formed in St Petersburg, launching in 1912–1913 the famous ethnographic expedition to the Jewish pale of settlement, led by the charismatic character of Sh. An-sky (Safran 2010; Safran and Zipperstein 2006). After An-sky's death and after the Russian revolution, similar societies were formed in Warsaw and Vilnius where this legacy continued (Kuznitz 2006). In Poland, folklore studies were undertaken by various groups in Warsaw and especially in Vilnius, where YIVO launched a vast ethnographic activity across the Yiddish-speaking world (Gottesman 2003; Bar-Itzhak 2010). At the same time, Jewish folklore was studied in France (Scheiber 1986), in England (Rabinovitch 2009), and the Mediterranean (Cohen and Stein 2010). Sooner or later much of this activity arrived in Palestine – through the Historical and Ethnographic Society of Jerusalem, many members of which were faculty of the Hebrew University, followed by the Yeda Am society formed in Tel-Aviv in the 1940s (a society that numbered hundreds of members), as well as the Palestine Institute of Folklore and Ethnology in Jerusalem (Schrire 2010).

All of this weighty folkloristic activity performed by societies in Europe and then in Palestine/Israel constituted a sharp contrast to the situation today, when folklore in Israel is set mainly in academic frameworks. Indeed, folklore was only institutionalized academically in Israel in the early 1970s and so it hardly co-existed with most of this non-academic activity. This situation is common among other (academic) fields in Jewish Studies (even when these were established academically in Israel earlier) and so it is not surprising that folklore scholars in Israel refer to a long history of their field by pointing to such non-academic activity as part of their own disciplinary history.

The return of Dov Noy (PhD Indiana University 1952 and a student of Stith Thompson) to Israel in the mid-1950s precipitated this change. Noy spent most of his academic career at the Hebrew University, where he also completed his undergraduate studies in Talmud and Hebrew literature. For almost 20 years, he taught folklore in the department of Hebrew literature, as well as late-antique, Talmudic-midrashic Rabbinic literature. Thanks to his pioneering academic activity, the Hebrew University became, in the early 1970s, the first Israeli university to establish a folklore minor program.

In addition to his teaching and to the formation of the minor program, Noy founded the Folklore Research Center, which issued a series of publications that appeared between 1970 and 1985. The center has developed considerably since its formation. Today it encompasses various projects as well as collections directed by scholars at the Hebrew University, which will be mentioned below.

Noy was the first scholar in the world to be appointed to an endowed chair in folklore, the Max and Margarethe Grunwald Chair of Folklore. This chair, which was established in 1972, reminds us of the roots of the study of folklore in Israel, which despite many ruptures continuously refers to the way Jewish folklore developed in Europe: in this case, Max Grunwald, who moved between the rabbinical seminary of Breslau, and the cities of Hamburg, Vienna and Jerusalem (where he went after Hitler's invasion of Austria). In fact much of Grunwald's legacy is present in Noy's work: Grunwald's drive to investigate Jews of various regions and the view of Jewish culture as a multiple one (this view was derived from Grunwald's view of emancipation and his attempts to combat anti-Semitic racial ethnographies). Although Noy refers to Grunwald in some of his more programmatic work (Noy 1980), nowhere is Grunwald's cultural conception more evident than in Noy's greatest endeavor that took place outside the Hebrew University: the Israeli Folktale Archives (IFA). Founded in 1955, under the auspices of the municipality of Haifa, the IFA is the biggest single folklore archive of Israel (Hasan-Rokem 1998). The IFA, housing today over 24,000 texts, is a fieldwork-based archive of folk narratives encompassing most folk narrative genres from all ethnic groups in Israeli society. The archive materials have been collected by accomplished researchers as well as students, lay people, and even schoolchildren. The narrative texts appear mostly as texts without much context but are complemented by detailed questionnaires including personal details about narrators and recorders. The awareness of the importance of contextual materials for the further study of the texts has grown especially when new generations of scholars and students became educated in other than geographical-historical methods of texts and formalist methods of analysis.

Noy's activities at the Hebrew University led back to other roots that point specifically to various affinities between folklore studies and the Hebrew University prior to his return from the United States. In fact the first doctoral dissertation ever ratified at the Hebrew University (1936) was Raphael Patai's investigation of miracle stories about rain – a central theme in the lives of communities in arid areas – in the Hebrew Bible and the Talmudic-midrashic literature (Patai 1938). Patai's thesis was heavily influenced by James Frazer's theory and method. However, Patai's experiences at the Hebrew University were to a great extent based on institutional rejection. After publishing two more books on ancient Jewish folklore, he formed the Palestine Institute of Folklore and Ethnology, which he directed between 1944 and 1947, editing its journal *Edoth* (Communities) as well as two series of books devoted to Jewish folklore. Eventually Patai tried establishing himself in Israel, hoping to integrate folklore and anthropology into the newly founded Hebrew University Institute of Social Sciences, but this never materialized and Patai's career continued in the United States (Schrire 2010).

Although ethnographic studies were present at the Hebrew University Institute of Jewish Studies when the university was founded in 1925, they slowly fell out of favor under the dominance of a philological-historical research paradigm, inherited from the nineteenth century *Wissenschaft des Judenthums*, privileging the study of Jewish texts rather than other modes of Jewish life and creativity. Despite that, many scholars of the Talmud periodically integrated into their work an ethnographic perspective which to a great extent had been established in the Rabbinical seminaries of Breslau, Budapest, and Vienna. Two of Noy's early teachers at the Hebrew University during his undergraduate studies were Professor Simha Assaf and Professor Victor (Avigdor) Aptowitzer (the latter had been a teacher at the Viennese seminary). Later, one of Noy's supporters at the Hebrew University on his return from the United States was Ephraim E. Urbach, who had been a teacher at the Breslau seminary and was a professor of Talmud at the Hebrew University.

A renewed presence of folklore studies first emerged at the Department of Yiddish that was established only in the early 1950s, personified in Dov Sadan (Stock), a diversified intellectual, author, newspaper editor, member of parliament, literary scholar of both Hebrew and Yiddish literature, and publisher of numerous folklore compilations as well as studies especially of traditional idiomatic language. Sadan was a major agent in bringing Noy to the Hebrew University together with the aforementioned Ephraim E. Urbach. Sadan himself devoted numerous works to Jewish humor (Sadan 1952, 1953), continuing the compilations of East European Jewish humor gathered by Alter Druyanow and Immanuel Olsvanger in the 1920s – the former appearing in Hebrew (Druyanow 1935) and the latter based on Yiddish and gathered among South African Jewry (Olsvanger 1936).

Noy's double folkloristic genealogy, rooted in classical Hebrew tradition and in an ethno-specific Jewish tradition from the Diaspora, largely defined the scope of folklore studies not only at the Hebrew University but in Israel in general. Through his activity at IFA in Haifa, Noy however aggregated yet another universe of discourse that had been present at the Hebrew University at the Institute for Oriental Studies – that of Orientalist ethnography, which was led by scholars trained in Germany. Shlomo Dov (Fritz) Goitein (who later emigrated to the United States), one of the most well-known Orientalists who would become the preeminent scholar of the Geniza (a Cairene cache of medieval Jewish manuscripts), devoted some of his early works to the study of Yemenite Jewish ethnography (Goitein 1934). Parallel to him, Joseph J. Rivlin, who was the first to author a translation of both the *Koran* and of the *Arabian Nights* into Hebrew, studied the folklore and literature of Jews from Kurdistan (Rivlin 1959, cf. Sabar 1982: 3–70). While Goitein and Rivlin joined the academy – both had begun their academic career in Frankfurt before they were incorporated into the Institute at the Hebrew University – other ethnographers active in Jerusalem held temporary positions. Nevertheless, their work had a profound impact on later ethnographic work in Israel: Erich Brauer, who studied ethnology in Leipzig (his dissertation was devoted to the study of the Herero religion), began his ethnographic study among Yemenite Jews in Palestine (Brauer 1934), followed by other studies of Bukharian Jews, Afghani Jews and Jews from Kurdistan (published posthumously by Patai; revised edition – Brauer and Patai 1993). Robert Lachmann, a Berlin-trained comparative musicologist, was active at the Hebrew University in the 1930s. He was a renowned scholar of Arab music, participating in the Cairo Congress of Arab Music (1932) before he arrived in Jerusalem (Katz 2003; Davis 2010). After his death, some of his work was taken on by Edith Gerson-Kiwi who had studied in Germany and Italy, before joining Lachmann's recording studio. In the 1940s she was active in Patai's independent Institute and later in the 1950s she was affiliated to the Institute for Oriental Studies at the Hebrew University, where she continued recording mostly Jewish music from Arab countries.

Much of these pioneering studies were incorporated into Noy's work at the IFA as well as in the work of some of Noy's students who studied the folklore of Jews from Arab countries. Thus the collection efforts of IFA were on the one hand directed to the remnants of European Jewry, a project Noy had already initiated while active as a teacher in Cyprus for Jewish refugees from Europe who were barred from entering Palestine during the last years of the Mandate. On the other hand, IFA collected from Jews of Arab and other Oriental lands, in a gesture embodying the ideology of "in-gathering of the exiles." In fact, the first three comprehensive published volumes were devoted to the narratives collected from the members of three North African Jewish communities: Morocco, Tunisia, and Libya, followed by a volume of Iraqi Jewish narratives, and much later the fourth ethnic volume by Noy, co-edited with Tamar Alexander, of Sephardi (Judeo-Spanish speaking) narratives (the latter was the first to be published in an academic context). The publication project of IFA also encompassed smaller volumes with a professed intention to represent all groups in Israel, Jewish, and non-Jewish. Thus, smaller volumes were dedicated to Druze and Samaritan narrative traditions.

All through Noy's work a far-reaching tension between particularity and unity can be noticed. One could claim that this tension is characteristic of the entire field of folklore in which methods always oscillate between pointing out the specific, for an individual performer or a tradition belonging to a group, and the comparable and sometimes universally shared, structure, motif, tale-type, symbol. This tension is clear in the numerous articles on folk literary matters in rabbinic literature that Noy, as an openly secularized person, published in the journal *Mahanayim* issued by the rabbinate of the Israeli army (Hasan-Rokem 1991–1992). It also penetrated the editorial principles and scholarly annotations of the volumes published by IFA focusing on, for example, Druze narratives, Yemenite Jewish narratives, narratives from a particular town in Austro-Hungarian/Polish Galicia, or narratives told by one Jewish woman from a small Polish town. Ethnic specificities were emphasized. However, operating as a synecdoche of the in-gathering of the exiles, IFA published every year a book in the series "A Tale for Each Month," where 12 ethnically variant tales at the same time materialized the symbolic and ideologically charged idiom of "the twelve tribes of Israel." This tension is also manifest in previous projects of Jewish folklore studies – as in the case of Max Grunwald's *jüdische Volkskunde* (see especially Daxelmüller 2010) and in the case of Patai's work in the 1940s. This tension was somewhat softened in Noy's IFA work by the adoption of the comparative framework that he had acquired studying with Stith Thompson. In fact, already in the 1930s the renowned folklorist Bernhard Heller (who taught in Budapest) discussed Jewish folklore in the context of the historic-geographic folktale school in his comprehensive program for the study of Jewish folklore in Palestine (Hasan-Rokem 2010). Heller was one of the few scholars who contributed to Bolte and Polívka's *Anmerkungen zu den Kinder – und Hausmärchen der Brüder Grimm*, demonstrating the longstanding involvement of Jewish folktale studies in international frameworks. He was also one of the first scholars to emphasize the connection between Jewish folktales and Arab ones, a legacy followed by Noy's contemporary, Haim Schwarzbaum (Schwarzbaum 1959, 1968).

Indeed, the standard format of all IFA publications included systematic tale type and motif indexes in addition to some background material about the relevant ethnic groups and personal details about the narrators and their interviewers. Since its foundation, the IFA was based on a network of enthusiastic collectors fostered by Noy. It is here that Noy's roots in Eastern Europe are particularly evident. Parallel to the foundation of the Hebrew University, Jews in Vilnius formed YIVO (Yidisher Visnshaftlekher Institut), which promoted the study of Yiddish culture – history, philology and folklore. Consequently the folklore and ethnographic section of YIVO established a vast network of collectors across much of Eastern Europe (Biran 1998). This was also carried out in folkloristic circles centered in Warsaw, notably around the figure of Noah Prilutsky who was later murdered by the Nazis (Gottesman 2003). In fact the proliferation of collectors in the Yiddish-speaking world of Eastern Europe originates even a generation before in both Polish endeavors, notably integrated in the *Wisla* journal, edited by Jan Karlowicz (Goldberg-Mulkiewicz 1989) as well as in the Austro-Hungarian Empire, in the journals edited by (Jewish) Friedrich S. Krauss, notably his *der Urquell* (Daxelmüller 1994). Indeed the IFA – as it was formed by Noy – was based on collectors who worked among Jews who emigrated from various lands, speaking different vernacular languages.

On the academic front, even before the formal opening of a folklore program at the Hebrew University, Noy tutored at the department of Hebrew literature a considerable number of folklorists who widened the academic basis of the field in the next generation. The range of topics and the variation of the students who studied with him point to the same urge to express Israeli culture in its complexity through a folkloristic platform. While the inclusive character of the project served the nationally devised "melting pot" policy, its particularistic aspects unabashedly although inconspicuously subverted that tendency.

Heda Jason was Noy's first student to earn a PhD, although she did so at Noy's own alma mater in Bloomington, Indiana. From its beginning, Jason's work emphatically addressed Jews from Arab and Muslim countries (Jason 1965; 1975a). She collected the tales of Jefet Shvili which were the basis for Noy's German volume (Noy 1963); she published a type index of Iraqi Jewish tales (in 1988 in Hebrew, not listed here), and carefully edited the posthumously published type index of Iranian Jewish tales by Sorour Soroudi (Soroudi 2008). In addition to a continuous commitment to the indexing systems of the geographical-historical school (Jason 1965; 1975b; 2000), she adopted a strong theoretical bent based on her reading of the texts of the Russian formalists in their original language while they were still relatively unknown in the West (Jason 1977). Jason's sharp analyses of the formalist classics and her broad synthetic vision of the concept of genre (Jason 2000) are witness to her substantial contribution to Israeli and international folklore studies, although her research was carried out without her assuming an academic position at any Israeli or other university, albeit supported by central research foundations in Israel. Notably, she published some of her work under the auspices of the Israeli Institute of Ethnography (e.g. Jason 1975b), operated by her in apparent resonance of the Patai legacy in Jerusalem.

Another of the earliest students of Noy is Aliza Shenhar (PhD Hebrew University 1975) who established the folklore program of the University of Haifa in 1975 within the Hebrew literature department. She later incorporated IFA at the university where it is still housed, with Haya Bar-Itzhak (PhD Hebrew University 1988) the follower of Shenhar as its academic head (today it is named after Noy, its founder). The long-time administrator and coordinator of IFA, Edna Hechal, was followed by Idit Pintel-Ginzberg (PhD University of Haifa 2001) in 2003. Shenhar herself expanded her field of activity from folklore studies to a successful academic administrative and public career, as the first female university rector in Israel, at the University of Haifa, as Israel's ambassador in Moscow, as deputy mayor of Haifa, and then the president of the Max Stern Academic College of Emek Yezreel. In her research she has focused among other topics on the links between oral narratives and modern written literature as well as on folklore in Israel (Shenhar-Alroy 1986). Her public achievements in addition to the leadership that she and her follower Bar-Itzhak have demonstrated have ensured a relatively good status for folklore studies at the University of Haifa, enhanced by the massive presence of the archival materials of IFA.

Another of the earliest Noy students is Mun'am Haddad whose ethnic, national, and cultural background as a native of the village Buq'aya/Peqi'in in the Upper Galilee (the northernmost part of Israel) determined the theme of his dissertation: Folklore of inter-ethnic relations in Buq'aya/Peqi'in. As mentioned at the beginning of this chapter, the continuity or lack of continuity in residence of any one of the groups of Israel's present population constitutes an issue of legitimacy and, sometimes in most distorted forms, also a territorial claim. The native village of Haddad where the majority of the population is Druze (next in size is the Christian population, Muslims are the third group), also boasted an uninterrupted Jewish population throughout the periods of Roman, Byzantine, Muslim, Frankish, Ottoman and British rule. Although during the twentieth century the Jewish presence has almost totally disappeared, Haddad's work addresses this peculiar inter-ethnic and inter-religious array of traditions within one place.

Haddad was the first scholar in Israeli academia to focus on non-Jewish folklore and specifically to engage with Arab-Palestinian folklore. In fact his inclusion here relates directly to the problems we address here, as Haddad has been instrumental in the development of Palestinian folklore (Haddad 2006). He reminds us of a long-standing engagement with the folklore of the people of the Holy Land, which is only loosely connected to the development of Jewish folklore in Europe. When visitors throughout the nineteenth century confronted the inhabitants of the Holy Land and their peculiar habits and rituals, their discourse constructed "Others" as manifested in Orientalist writings. Some of the European ethnologists and folklorists who arrived in the Holy Land were motivated by theological reasons to research possible survivals from the period of Jesus's life which were found in some cases in the folklife of the Palestinians as in the work of Gustaf Dalman (see Männchen 1993) and Hilma Granqvist (1931).

Orientalist perspectives on the folklore of the Holy Land became much more pronounced when the British arrived in Palestine in 1918. It was then that Orientalist institutions were formed and published works that related also to the folklore of the people of the Land (e.g. the Palestine Oriental Society). Simultaneously Jewish visitors from Europe constructed their discourse as a meeting with their co-religionists who inhabited the Holy Land. Under the umbrella of a colonial super-power, Jews and Palestinian Arabs worked together and separately in presenting traditions of various groups (Tamari 2009). Yet as Jewish nationalism and Palestinian nationalism became more pronounced, such collaboration declined and the study of folklore was demarcated between Palestinian folklore and Jewish folklore.

Other than Haddad, the study of Arab-Palestinian folklore within Israeli academia continued with the work of three of Galit Hasan-Rokem's students at the Hebrew University: Hany Musa, Hannan Karkaby-Jaraisy, and Amer Dahamshe. Outside academic institutions, Yoram Miron has cooperated with Riad Kabaha and other Israeli Palestinians in the publication of annotated folktale collections in Arabic translated into Hebrew.

For the next student of Noy, the late Eliezer Marcus, the study of folklore was always a component of his educational work. Whether a teacher in school, the principal of the first open school in Israel, an educator of teachers or the highest academic authority of the Israeli Ministry of Education (under the title of pedagogical secretary), folklore served him not only as the dialogic mode of communication with diverse populations of students, but also as a thought model for multi-culturality and shared cultural responsibility, due to its inherently anti-hierarchical character. Among his favorite projects, one finds the recording of folk narratives by schoolchildren especially of Arab-Jewish origin, from their parents and grandparents, and the annotated publication of these narratives. His dissertation (1977) addressed the ethnic confrontations of Jews with non-Jews in Jewish folk narratives from Arab countries.

Eli Yassif (PhD Hebrew University 1977, supervised by Joseph Dan and Dov Noy), who initially started folklore studies at the Ben Gurion University of the Negev in the 1980s, later became the incumbent of a chair in Jewish Folk Culture at Tel-Aviv University where he has held a position since 1995. Yassif's folkloristic research has mainly addressed Hebrew folk narratives of the long Jewish Middle Ages in Europe. His monumental work *The Hebrew Folktale* (Yassif 1999) is the most comprehensive attempt to write the long history of folk narratives in the Hebrew language (with some non-Hebrew, Greek exceptions from the Hellenistic period). As Yassif demonstrates, the Hebrew folktale tends to become, especially from the tenth century onwards, mainly a written mode of expression, since Jews in most countries begin to develop Jewish languages strongly based on local languages (Judeo-Arabic, Judeo-Persian) or on languages that reflect earlier domiciles, such as the Germanic Yiddish of East European Jews who had moved in from Central Europe, or the Judeo-Spanish of Jews in the Ottoman Empire as well as in Spanish Morocco, brought along from the Iberian Peninsula after the expulsion of the Jews from Spain in 1492.

Yassif's work bridges the gap between Jewish folkloristics and other fields in Jewish Studies, reaching out to much of the folkloristic exploration of medieval narratives. Thus Yassif draws on scholars who were active in the nineteenth century and the beginning of the twentieth century in Central and Western Europe and who were important in the folkloristic study of ancient Jewish texts: Hermann Gunkel and his study of the Bible, Avraham Berliner, Moritz Güdemann, Moses Gaster, and Arthur Marmorstein in the study of medieval works. In some of his works, Yassif has explicitly demonstrated the wealth of folkloristic work carried out by figures central in the *Wissenschaft des Judenthums* (Yassif 1987, 1988, 2004). His emphasis on Hebrew is somewhat unique in the current folkloristic topography in Israel, reminding us of the centrality of folklore in the work of Hebraists at the turn of the nineteenth to the twentieth century, notably Bialik who together with Rawnitski compiled one of the most canonical works on the Talmud. Indeed Yassif's student, Tsaffi Seba-Elran (PhD Tel-Aviv University 2010) studied Hebrew Aggadic compilations of the late nineteenth century to the beginning of the twentieth century, including Bialik's and Rawnitski's.

Galit Hasan-Rokem (PhD Hebrew University 1978), the Max and Margarethe Grunwald Professor of Folklore at the Hebrew University after Noy's retirement, has since her dissertation embraced Noy's double legacy. In her dissertation (translated as Hasan-Rokem 1982), she analyzes proverbs in folk narratives from IFA and others collected in field work, and includes historical sources in the interpretation of the proverbs as well as the narratives, especially from late antique rabbinic literature. The folkloristic and ethnographic perspective of this historical corpus later became one of her main fields of research (Hasan-Rokem 2000, 2003). The book based on the dissertation reveals her inclination to theory, in this case focusing on one genre, the proverb, inspired by her other mentor, Matti Kuusi of the University of Helsinki. Kuusi, the initiator of the Matti Kuusi International Proverb type system, also founded the journal *Proverbium* of which Hasan-Rokem became assistant editor in 1982 under the editorial leadership of paremiologist Wolfgang Mieder. Although more analytic, Hasan-Rokem's work on proverbs draws on previous works on the same topic initiated by collectors already in the nineteenth century (notably, Bernstein 1908; Tendlau 1860). It is in this context that she formed a proverb archive at the Folklore Research Centre, which is now in the process of digitalization (Hasan-Rokem and Kats 2009).

Beginning with her year of studies with Kuusi and Lauri Honko in her native city of Helsinki, Hasan-Rokem's work has early on been marked by international networking, culminating in her 1998–2005 presidency of the International Society of Folk Narrative Research. Consequently Hasan-Rokem tutored at the Hebrew University, together with folklorist-Africanist Hagar Salamon, Kenyan scholar Mbugua Wa-Mungai (PhD 2005) in his dissertation on the urban folklore of Nairobi, before his return to his home university in Nairobi, as well as with the eminent historian of Japan, Ben-Ami Shillony, their student Fumihiko Kobayashi (PhD Hebrew University 2011) in his work on Japanese folktales.

Hasan-Rokem's work on the rabbinic corpus emphasizes inter-cultural and inter-religious dialogic sharing of narratives as well as a feminist research perspective, viewing the interpretation of the classical corpus as part of a cultural debate about the ownership of traditionally patriarchally transmitted and interpreted texts. Her approach to the study of this corpus was extended to other domains by her students: Dina Stein in her work on Pirke de Rabbi Eliezer, and Haim Weiss whose dissertation on dreams in the Talmud was followed by his work on the incorporation of figures of rabbinic literature in Zionist discourse. Both also partly took up another of Hasan-Rokem's main areas of research, the proverb genre (Hasan-Rokem 1982, 1994).

Hasan-Rokem co-founded in 1981 together with Tamar Alexander the Hebrew journal *Jerusalem Studies in Jewish Folklore* (now co-edited in addition to the two founders also by Shalom Sabar and Hagar Salamon). In addition Alexander and Hasan-Rokem initiated the annual inter-university folklore conferences.

The journal and the annual conferences are the most important nationwide platforms in folklore studies in Israel. They have become an important tool for safeguarding the standard of the field in Israeli academia, demonstrating the change the field has undergone. *Jerusalem Studies in Jewish Folklore* is directed primarily to an academic audience. It was preceded by the *Folklore Research Studies* – publications that Noy edited together with Issachar Ben-Ami between 1970 and 1985, which appeared irregularly. The *Jerusalem Studies in Jewish Folklore* also differs from the *Yeda Am* journal, established in 1948 and has appeared continuously ever since. *Yeda Am* was established by the Yeda Am Society, a group of scholars mostly from Eastern Europe. This journal served one of their key objectives, that of *popularizing* the interest in folklore. Clearly *Jerusalem Studies in Jewish Folklore* set a very different standard with other aims. In a similar vein, the Yeda Am society launched the first Israeli folklore conference (also in 1948) and organized similar conferences from time to time. As a culmination of such efforts, they hosted the first International Israeli Folklore Congress in 1959, attracting 2,000 participants to its opening event in Tel Aviv. This was undoubtedly the peak of the activity of this society, which has dwindled after the death of its leader Yom-Tov Lewinsky in 1972. By then, it was clear that the center of gravity of folklore studies in Israel had shifted to the Hebrew University.

Hasan-Rokem's institution building activity at the Hebrew University has included the broadening of the folklore minor program founded by Noy to a Folklore undergraduate major, and following her mentor in educating a large number of graduate students, many of whom teach folklore at various research universities and academic colleges in Israel. She also served as the academic head of Hebrew University's venerable Institute of Jewish Studies, attempting to emphasize the original double character of Jewish studies from the foundational years, intertwining the historical-philological and the ethnographic paradigms of research.

Tamar Alexander's activities have likewise continued to enhance the position of folklore studies in Israeli academia. Since 1985 she has made a significant impact on folklore studies at Ben Gurion University of the Negev in Be'er Sheva where she has expanded the former minor program established by Yassif to a full-fledged undergraduate major, as well as initiated graduate studies in the field. Her dissertation (1977, published 1991), written at UCLA under the supervision of the folklorist Robert Georges, Hebrew literature scholar Arnold Band and cultural historian Amos Funkenstein, was a folk narrative analysis of a Hebrew pietistic text composed by

German Jews in the twelfth to thirteenth centuries. During her undergraduate studies at the Hebrew University Alexander also came under the influence of Noy. Most of her research after her dissertation has been devoted to the post-1492 Judeo-Spanish folk literary tradition including a comprehensive study of the oral narrative traditions (2008) and two large compilations of proverbs accompanied by theoretical and inter-pretative chapters. Alexander's research has addressed more and more the ethno-spe-cific folklore of Sephardic, Judeo-Spanish speaking Jews, which she has promoted through the founding of the Gaon Center at Ben Gurion University, also publishing a multi-lingual journal *El Presente*. Her activities demonstrate a very important folk-loristic genealogy, that of the continuous engagement with Sephardic folklore. This interest is manifested in Max Grunwald's work which he drew from the Sephardic presence in Hamburg and Vienna (Daxelmüller 2010). In fact the interest in Sephardic poetry had already been central in the work of Meyer Kayserling in the nineteenth century. The interest in Sephardic folklore of Hayim Nachman Bialik – Israel's "national poet" – informed the works of other Zionist Sephardic scholars. Thus in Bialik's folk-loristic collection *Reshumot* – Baruch Uziel's programmatic article of the study of Sephardic folklore – appeared together with the work of Moses Attias, who specialized in the Sephardic Romance. Both Uziel and Attias were natives of Thessalonica. They were part of a network of scholars active in the Eastern Mediterranean, which was also engaged in folkloristic work of Sephardic Jews and of Arabic-speaking Jews (Cohen and Stein 2010). This work was published mostly in Ladino, Hebrew, and French by such scholars as Abraham Galante, Moshe David Ga'on, Avraham Elmaleh, Shmuel Ben-Shabat, Yosef Baran Meyuchas, and others. Much of this work promoted ethnic folklore against the dominance of Zionist Ashkenazi Jews. Such pioneering Sephardic folkloristic works were integrated into Alexander's scholarly work. This was expanded by Alexander's students, including Eliezer Papo (PhD Ben Gurion University 2009), born in Sarajevo, who has also researched such works published before World War II in Serbo-Croatian. Another of her students – Yoel Peretz (PhD Ben Gurion University) investigates connections between his activity as a storyteller and his study of contem-porary storytellers in Israel. He has also studied Bedouin and Sephardic folktales. Hagit Rappel, jointly tutored by Alexander and Yassif, studies the folklore of kibbut-zim in the southern part of Israel, the Negev, the culture of which is emphatically investigated at the Ben Gurion University of the Negev, in the city of Be'er Sheva. Rappel teaches at Sapir college in the town of Sderot.

Thus, Alexander is connected with three institutions at Ben Gurion University: the Gaon Research Center of Sephardic culture, the folklore program, and the Hebrew Literature department, which she has chaired a number of times.

In this context, one should also mention works focusing on contemporary Sephardic folklore that were carried-out by Hasan-Rokem's students at the Hebrew University: Michal Held who has studied contemporary Sephardic storytellers, as well as Nina Pinto-Abecassis who has studied nicknaming practices as well as humor among the Jews of Tetuan (northern Morocco).

The last Noy student to be mentioned here is Haya Bar-Itzhak whose dissertation (Hebrew University 1987) addressed the genre of hagiography in Jewish oral tradi-tions based on IFA texts, as well as independent fieldwork. In her work the double legacy of Noy produces another set of bifurcations: as well as studying some North African Jewish narrative traditions (Bar-Itzhak and Shenhar-Alroy 1993), she has also specialized in local Israeli folklore especially in rural northern Israel (Bar-Itzhak 2005). The latter, focused especially on the kibbutzim, was developed by her student, Ronnie Kochavi-Nahav, who demonstrated the continuation between Zionist memory culture and Jewish memory culture in Eastern Europe. As mentioned above, Bar-Itzhak occupies a central position in Israeli folklore research as the academic head of IFA, whose academic council includes all the figures (alive) that have been mentioned here. Her proximity to the IFA is manifested also in the work of her students, Idit Pintel-Ginsberg, who directs the archive, and Ravit Raufman, who employs psychoanalysis in her interpretation of folktales. In addition Bar-Itzhak has also become an expert on the folklore of the Jews of Poland, including some trail-blazing work on the history of Jewish folklore research in Eastern Europe, where she demonstrates the relevance of some of the pioneers of Jewish folkloristics in Poland (Bar-Itzhak 2010).

The study of Jewish folklore in Poland brings us to the first scholar of folklore in Israel after the founding of the state who was not trained by Noy or his students (except for the ethnologist of Moroccan Jewry, Issachar Ben-Ami, who was trained by Kurt Ranke in Göttingen). Olga Goldberg-Mulkiewicz, who had trained in Poland, joined the Hebrew University as a researcher in 1969 and became a faculty member in 1972. Drawing on such scholars who were active in Poland such as Giza Frankel (Goldberg-Mulkiewicz 1989), Goldberg was the first to introduce the study of folk art to the Israeli folkloristic academic sphere. Her work was developed by her students, for example, Carmela Abdar whose study of Yemenite brides' clothing explored Yemenite Jewish group dynamics after emigration to Israel. Other work supervised by her has been fieldwork conducted in Poland such as that of Rivka Parchak and Rina Ben-Ari. Much of Goldberg's work is undertaken also at the Folklore Research Center where she directs the Giza Frankel paper-cut documentation center, a locus of activity for this unique tradition in Israel.

Shalom Sabar furthered the engagement with Jewish folk art in both the folklore program and the Folklore Research Center at the Hebrew University. Trained in art history at UCLA, Sabar joined the Hebrew University faculty in 1987. He has focused on the Jewish life-cycle and year-cycle and its manifestation in material folk art of Jews from Europe and Islamic countries, notably examining Jewish illuminated marriage contracts, and studying historical aspects of Jewish folk art. He is the director of the Joseph and Margit Hoffman postcard collection, which contains 7,000 postcards which are a unique visual source for Jewish folklife in various places from the end of the nineteenth century onward.

Goldberg and Sabar draw on a rich history that Jewish folklorists and Jewish folk art share. They also continue the long-established affinities between the study of Jewish art and museological practices connected to it. This strong connection was already established by Max Grunwald, who formed the society of Jewish folklore's journal alongside a museum of Jewish folklore. Grunwald's rich contacts with Jewish art collectors and art scholars (Albert Wolf from Dresden, or Cecil Roth) attest to his interest in folk art. Likewise the study of folk art in Israel is closely related to the development of collections and ethnographic activities that relate to them. In fact, Noy formed the IFA as part of the Haifa ethnological museum, which he directed in the 1950s–1960s. It is here that Aviva Muller-Lancet held her first position as a curator of folk art before she formed the ethnographical department in the Israel Museum. Similarly, Ester Juhasz began her scholarly activity in Noy's museum and continued at the Israel Museum in Jerusalem, where she became an expert on material folklore of Jews from the Ottoman Empire, before obtaining a PhD (supervised by Hasan-Rokem and Sabar).

In addition to the integration of folk art in the study of folklore in Israel, the chair of the academic committee of the Folklore Research Center at the Hebrew University today is the ethnomusicologist Edwin Seroussi, himself a graduate of the Folklore Program of the same university. While ethnomusicology and folklore are taught separately in Israel, the disciplines are much better related in research. Jewish folklore and Jewish folk music share a common history, as attested in Grunwald's journal as well as in the shared networks of scholars in St Petersburg before World War I. The connection between the two fields is also reflected in ethnographic work carried out by the aforementioned Edith Gerson-Kiwi as well as other folklorists active in Israel in the 1950s. In fact, it is also reflected in Noy's own family as his late brother, Me'ir Noy, was one of the pioneers in the study of folksongs in Israel and his collection has been integrated in the National Library of Israel.

Although folkdance was studied by one of Noy's students – Zvi Friedhaber – it is not studied in Israel academically (the exception being a sociology/anthropology dissertation in 2006 by Dina Roginsky). This is in contrast to the huge amount of public following and attention that it receives – which owes much to the pioneering work of such figures as Gurit Kadman and the popular folkdance festivals that took place near kibbutz Dalia in the 1940s–1960s. In a similar vein, as much as folk medicine has been part and parcel of Israeli public life, it has not received much attention from folklorists in Israel, with the exception of Hagit Matras – another of Noy's students – whose dissertation focused on eighteenth-century medical books that were published in Hebrew.

Parallel to the inclusion of old and new fields in the study of folklore in Israeli academia, the work of "third generation" folklorists in Israel demonstrates the wide scope of the discipline. Hagar Salamon, devoted her dissertation (supervised by Harvey Goldberg, Galit Hasan-Rokem, and Steve Kaplan) to the folkloristic expression of the relationship between Ethiopian Jews (Beta Israel) and their Christian neighbors (Salamon 1999, 2003). Alongside her continuous ethnographic studies of Jews from Ethiopia (Salamon 2008, 2010, 2011), her work expanded in other directions, such as the study of political stickers in the contemporary Israeli public sphere (Salamon 2001) and other phenomena of Israeli folklore in inter-ethnic contexts. The engagement with the Jews from Ethiopia has a very long history in Jewish folklore. In the first monograph dedicated to Jewish *Volkskunde*, ethnologist-geographer Richard Andre used "racist criteria" to rule out Jews from Ethiopia as essentially non-Jewish (Andree 1881). In Max Grunwald's opening issue of the *Mitteilungen,* he presents a contra-racist formulation of Jewish *Volkskunde,* and deliberately refers to Jews from Ethiopia as Jewish for they share the idea of longing to Zion. Notwithstanding, the Jews from Ethiopia were studied primarily by Jewish ethnologists from the Sorbonne, first by Joseph Halévy and later and most importantly by Jacques Faitlovitch, who emigrated to Palestine in the 1930s (Semi 2007). Thus, in Salamon's teaching and research at the Hebrew University, folklore studies in Israel continue an engagement which was begun by Jewish folklorists and ethnologists in Europe a long time before most of the Jews from Ethiopia emigrated to Israel. Her study of the Ethiopian Jews continues to challenge and problematize ethnic and racial definitions of identity.

Ilana Rosen, another Hasan-Rokem student, focused on life-stories of Shoah survivors from Hungary. Her work on narratives of the Shoah applied folkloristic research to a domain which before was studied mainly by historians and sociologists (Rosen 2004, 2008, 2011). Her work on life-stories continues at Ben Gurion University where she currently is studying life-stories of immigrants to the Southern part of Israel, and continues publishing on the folklore of communities and individuals victimized by the Shoah. Her student Yael Zilberman has furthered this engagement with life stories from a feminist perspective.

While also focusing on life-stories, the work of Nili Aryeh-Sapir, another student of Galit Hasan-Rokem, takes us to a very different setting – an engagement with urban festivals in Tel-Aviv as well as an analysis of early Zionist folklore (Aryeh-Sapir 2006).

Larissa Fialkova is yet another example of the various influences on the development of folklore in Israel. Born in the Ukraine, she studied Russian literature in Kiev and in Tartu (completing her PhD there in 1985). Her folkloristic work engages with contemporary legends, cyber-lore, but especially folklore of immigration which she has carried out in ethnographic work among Russian immigrants in Israel (Fialkova and Yelenevskaya 2007). Fialkova also mediates Israeli folklore in translation to a Ukrainian and Russian readership.

Yuval Harari (PhD 1998, a Hebrew University graduate tutored by Shaul Shaked and Moshe Idel) currently heads the folklore program at Ben Gurion University. He brings folklore in Israel back to one of the central domains that occupied earlier Jewish folkloristics – magic (Harari forthcoming). While the study of Jewish magic has been the focus of numerous studies in the last century, it typically related to a philological-historical approach. Nevertheless one can point to a continuous engagement with magic in Jewish folkloristics in various works of Moses Gaster, Grunwald, Joshua Trachtenberg, Theodore Schrire, Raphael Patai and others.

Finally two of the most recent folklorists from the Hebrew University also complete the circle: Vered Madar's (Hasan-Rokem's student) research on the oral poetry of Yemenite Jewish women while theoretically cutting edge in its feminist, hermeneutic and performative approaches, also links back to Goitein's pioneering studies in the folklore of Yemenite Jews in Jerusalem. Madar, who identifies as a "halfie" (Abu-Lughod 1991), combines the "native" perspective as she was born and raised in a *moshav* founded by (or rather for) Yemenite immigrants in the beginning of the 1950s with a strongly reflexive ethnographic perspective.

Dani Schrire is the first Israeli folklorist to attempt a systematic, strongly archive-based, history of Israeli folklore, focusing on the crucial period of 1942–1959, when the post-traumatic effects of the Shoah and World War II powerfully affected the rise of academic folklore in Israel in a fateful double-bind with Noy's personal history as the only one of his family from Kolomea of then Polish Galicia to escape Europe before the war broke out (his brother Meir, the ethnomusicologist mentioned above, survived Shoah in Europe). Schrire's research (supervised by Hasan-Rokem and Hannan Hever at Hebrew University), informed by critical studies and Latourian analysis of institutional practices and actor-network-theory, provides a new dimension of disciplinary consciousness and reflection for future Israeli folkloristics.

The distribution of Noy's students as the leading folklore scholars in all Israeli research universities where the field is represented in more or less institutionalized frameworks marks his focal and seminal role in the academic development of the field of folklore in

Israel. At the same time the very growth of the field and its penetration into these four schools as well as to a number of academic colleges, teachers' colleges, and community colleges, indicate the relevance of the field at this particular moment in Israeli history. The great number of folklore students graduating continuously raises hopes about the future of the field, while it also causes some concern about the ability of all these accomplished scholars to find suitable jobs in Israeli academia or at all.

We have underlined the inbuilt ambiguity and ideological complexity of folklore studies in a society constantly revising its bases of identity, its territorial boundaries, and its language politics (from uncompromising Hebrew dominance in the 1950s and 1960s, repressing both Yiddish and Judeo-Arabic to a much more lenient approach to immigration languages of the 1980s and 1990s such as English and Russian) and its value system and religious codes. It seems that it is exactly the high level of ambiguity that invites folklore studies to occupy a position in the universities' traditionally hierarchical structure of knowledge shaping, inherently antithetical to the non-hierarchical structure of knowledge shaping in folklore. As a concrete example we may mention the fact that numerous ethnic cultures thriving in Israel have no representation in the university syllabus except in the folklore program. For instance, if a young person from a family of Ethiopian origin wants to learn about her culture rather than about the percentage of delinquents or disease among Ethiopian Israelis, her only chance is with Hagar Salamon at the Folklore program of the Hebrew University.

While the study of folklore in Israel has been greatly influenced by the history of Jewish folkloristics in Europe, since the 1950s it has been informed by its ties with American folklorists. This can be traced first to Noy and his work with Stith Thompson, as well as some of Noy's students who studied in various institutions in the United States. Some of the leading scholars of folklore in the United States have had a profound influence on the way folklore studies have been practiced in Israel. Dan Ben-Amos carried-out his undergraduate studies with Noy before leaving to study in Bloomington. Throughout his career, Ben-Amos has been instrumental in the shaping of the discipline in Israel, as well as continuously publishing works on Jewish folklore in English (Ben-Amos 1991). Ben-Amos also collaborated with Noy in publishing annotated anthologies of Jewish folktales based on the IFA (Ben-Amos 2006). Finally, as the editor of The Raphael Patai Series in Jewish Folklore and Anthropology (named after the series founder), Ben-Amos has made many works of Israeli folklorists available to English readers.

Other folkloristic studies published in the United States have contributed to the folkloristic discourse in Israel, such as the works of Elliot Oring and Yael Zerubavel, both addressing Zionist folklore (Oring 1981; Zerubavel 1995). In their study of Sephardic folklore, Rosemary Zumwalt and Isaac Levy included fieldwork carried out in Israel. The number of people who have done fieldwork in Israel is, however, larger than can be accounted for here, and has not necessarily had an impact on the unfolding of folklore studies and their institutionalization in Israel. Other American folklorists who contributed to the study of Jewish folklore and have continuously informed folklorists and participated in debates in Israel are Alan Dundes and Barbara Kirshenblatt-Gimblett.

Folklore studies not only optimally embody the variation of a culture. They also introduce the very idea of subjective cultural agency for particular cultures in a state, which has at different periods publicly adhered to a policy of obliterating differences and pragmatically still acts to oppress these differences.

It has thus been important to show how the doubleness, complexity, and subversion of folklore studies has been embraced by each of Noy's students and their students in various ways, as none of them has avoided the necessity of coping with and handling them.

NOTES

1   Hasan-Rokem (1999a, 2005) makes an effort to be inclusive, but finds this a challenge.
2   A well-known example is "Kalilah wa-Dimnah," the Persian version of Indian Panchatantra that came to Europe as "Tales of Bidpai." See Steinschneider (1893).

REFERENCES

Abu Lughod, Lila. 1991. "Writing against Culture" in Richard G. Fox, Ed. *Recapturing Anthropology: Working in the Present.* Santa Fe, NM: School of American Research Press, pp. 137–162.

Alexander-Frizer, Tamar. 1991. *The Pious Sinner: Ethics and Aesthetics in the Medieval Hasidic Narrative.* Tübingen: J.C.B. Mohr.

Alexander-Frizer, Tamar. 2008. *The Heart is a Mirror: The Sephardic Folktale.* Detroit: Wayne State University Press.

Andree, Richard. 1881. *Zur Volkskunde der Juden.* Bielefeld und Leipzig: Velhagen and Klasing.

Aryeh-Sapir, Nili. 2006. *The Formation of Urban Culture and Education: Stories of and about Ceremonies and Celebrations in Tel-Aviv in its First Years.* Dor Ledor: Studies in the History of Jewish Education in Israel and the Diaspora. Tel-Aviv: Tel-Aviv University (in Hebrew).

Bar-Itzhak, Haya. 2005. *Israeli Folk Narratives: Settlement, Immigration, Ethnicity.* Detroit: Wayne State University Press.

Bar-Itzhak, Haya. 2010. *Pioneers of Jewish Ethnography and Folkloristics in Eastern Europe.* Ljubljana: Založba ZRC.

Bar-Itzhak, Haya and Aliza Shenhar-Alroy. 1993. *Jewish Moroccan Folk Narratives from Israel.* Detroit: Wayne State University Press.

Ben-Amos, Dan. 1991. "Jewish Folklore Studies." *Modern Judaism* 11(1): 17–66.

Ben-Amos, Dan, Ed. 2006. *Folktales of the Jews.* Philadelphia: Jewish Publication Society 2.

Benvenisti, Meron. 2000. *Sacred Landscape: The Buried History of the Holy Land since 1948.* Berkeley: University of California Press.

Bernstein, Ignatz. 1908. *Jüdische Sprichwörter und Redensarten.* Warsaw: Kaufmann.

Biran, Ronnie. 1998. "L'affaire Berl Verblunsky. Polémique autour du folklore juif entre les deux guerres." *Cahiers de littérature orale* 44.

Brauer, Erich. 1934. *Ethnologie der jemenitischen Juden.* Heidelberg: C. Winter.

Erich. Brauer. 1993. *The Jews of Kurdistan,* Detroit: Wayne State University Press.

Cohen Philips, Julia and Sarah Abrevaya Stein. 2010. "Sephardic Scholarly Worlds: Toward a Novel Geography of Modern Jewish History." *Jewish Quarterly Review* 100(3): 349–384.

Coleman, Simon and John Elsner, Eds. 2003. *Pilgrim Voices: Narrative and Authorship in Christian Pilgrimage.* New York: Berghahn Books.

Davis, Ruth F. 2010. "Ethnomusicology and Political Ideology in Mandatory Palestine: Robert Lachmann's 'Oriental Music' Projects." *Music and Politics* 4(2): 1–15.

Daxelmüller, Christoph. 1986. "Jewish Popular Culture in the Research Perspective of European Ethnology." *Ethnologia Europaea* 16: 97–116.

Daxelmüller, Christoph. 1994. "Friedrich Salomo Krauss (Salomon Friedrich Kraus[s]) (1859–1938)" in Wolfgang Jacobeit, Hannjost Lixfeld, and Olaf Bockhora, Eds. *Völkische Wissenschaft: Gestalten und Tendenzen der deutschen und österreichischen Volkskunde in der ersten Hälfte des 20. Jahrhunderts*. Wien: Böhlau, pp. 87–114.

Daxelmüller, Christoph. 2010. "Hamburg, Wien Jerusalem. Max Grunwald und die entwicklung der jüdische Volkskunde zur Kulturwissenschaft 1898 bis 1938." *Österreichische Zeitschrift für Volkskunde* 113: 375–393.

Druyanow, Alter. 1935. *Sefer Ha-Bediḥah Veha-Ḥidud* (The Book of Humor and Witticisms). Tel Aviv: Dvir (in Hebrew).

Fialkova, Larisa and Maria N. Yelenevskaya. 2007. *Ex-Soviets in Israel: From Personal Narratives to a Group Portrait*. Detroit: Wayne State University Press.

Fine, Lawrence. 2003. *Physician of the Soul, Healer of the Cosmos: Isaac Luria and his Kabbalistic Fellowship*. Palo Alto: Stanford University Press.

Frisby, David. 1986. *Fragments of Modernity: Theories of Modernity in the Work of Simmel, Kracauer and Benjamin*. Cambridge, MA: MIT Press.

Garb, Jonathan. 2008. "The Cult of Saints in Lurianic Kabbalah." *Jewish Quarterly Review* 98: 203–230.

Goitein, Shlomo Dov. 1934. *Jemenica*. Leipzig: Otto Harrassowitz.

Goldberg-Mulkiewicz, Olga. 1989. *Ethnographic Topics Relating to Jews in Polish Studies*. Studies of the Center for Research on the History and Culture of Polish Jews, The Hebrew University of Jerusalem. Jerusalem: Magnes Press.

Gottesman, Itzik Nakhmen. 2003. *Defining the Yiddish Nation: The Jewish Folklorists of Poland*. Detroit: Wayne State University Press.

Granqvist, Hilma. 1931. *Marriage Conditions in a Palestinian Village*. Helsingfors: Centraltryckeri och bokbinderi.

Granqvist, Hilma. 1935. *Marriage Conditions in a Palestinian Village*. Helsingfors: Societas Scientiarum Fennica.

Haddad, Mana'm. 2006. "Palestine" in William. M. Clements, Ed. *The Greenwood Encyclopedia of World Folklore and Folklife*. Vol. 2. Westport, CT: Greenwood Press, pp. 400–411.

Harari, Yuval. Forthcoming. "Jewish Magic in the Ancient Period" in Henk Versnel and David Frankfurter, Eds. *A Guide to the Study of Ancient Magic*. Leiden: Brill.

Hasan-Rokem, Galit. 1982. *Proverbs in Israeli Folk Narratives: A Structural Semantic Analysis*. Folklore Fellows Communications 232. Helsinki: Suomalainen Tiedeakatemia, Academia Scientiarum Fennica.

Hasan-Rokem, Galit. 1991–1992. "Between Unity and Plurality – Dov Noy's Studies of Folklore in Talmudic-Midrashic Literature," *Jerusalem Studies in Jewish Folklore* XI–XII: 19–28 (in Hebrew).

Hasan-Rokem, Galit. 1999a. "Folk Religions in Modern Israel: Sacred Space in the Holy Land." *Diogenes* 187: 83–87.

Hasan-Rokem, Galit. 1998. "The Birth of Scholarship out of the Spirit of Oral Tradition: Folk Narrative Publications and National Identity in Modern Israel." *Fabula* 39(3–4): 277–290.

Hasan-Rokem, Galit. 2000. *Web of Life: Folklore and Midrash in Rabbinic Literature*. Palo Alto: Stanford University Press.

Hasan-Rokem, Galit. 2003. *Tales of the Neighborhood: Jewish Narrative Dialogues in Late Antiquity*. Berkeley: University of California Press.

Hasan-Rokem, Galit. 2010. "Ancient Jewish Folk Literature: The Legends of the Jews and Folklore Research at the Beginning of the Twentieth Century." *Jewish Studies* 47: 57–75 (in Hebrew).

Hasan-Rokem, Galit and Pavel Kats. 2009. "From a Structural Semantic Analysis towards a Computational Classification Framework" in Kevin J. McKenna, Ed. *The Proverbial "Pied Piper": A Festschrift Volume of Essays in Honor of Wolfgang Mieder on the Occasion of His Sixty-Fifth Birthday*. New York: Peter Lang, pp. 111–125.

Hauschild, Thomas. 1997. "Christians, Jews, and the Other in German Anthropology." *American Anthropologist* 4: 746–753.

Hazaz, Haim. 1956. *Mori Sa'id* (Thou That Dwellest in the Gardens). New York: Abelard-Schuman.

Helman, Anat. 2002. "'Even the Dogs in the Streets Bark in Hebrew': National Ideology and Everyday Culture in Tel-Aviv." *Jewish Quarterly Review* XCII(3–4): 359–382.

Helman, Anat. 2006. "Two Urban Celebrations in Jewish Palestine." *Journal of Urban History* 32(3): 380–403.

Helman, Anat. 2008. "Was there anything particularly Jewish about 'The First Hebrew City'?" in Barbara Kirshenblatt-Gimblett and Jonathan Karp, Eds. *The Art of Being Jewish in Modern Times: Essays on Jews and Aesthetic Culture*. Philadelphia: University of Pennsylvania Press, pp. 116–127.

Helman, Anat. 2010. *Young Tel Aviv: A Tale of Two Cities*. Hanover, NH: University Press of New England.

Horowitz, Elliott. 2006. *Reckless Rites: Purim and the Legacy of Jewish Violence*. Princeton: Princeton University Press.

Huss, Boaz. 2007. "The New Age of Kabbalah: Contemporary Kabbalah, the New Age and Postmodern Spirituality." *Journal of Modern Jewish Studies* 6(2): 107–125.

Jason, Heda. 1965. "Types of Jewish Oriental Oral Tales." *Fabula* 7: 115–224.

Jason, Heda. 1975a. *Studies in Jewish Ethnopoetry: Narrating, Art, Content, Message, Genre*. Taipei: Chinese Association for Folklore.

Jason, Heda. 1975b. *Types of Oral Tales in Israel*. Jerusalem: The Israel Ethnographic Society.

Jason, Heda. 1977. *Ethnopoetry: Form, Contents, Function*. Bonn: Linguistica Biblica.

Jason, Heda. 2000. *Motif, Type and Genre: A Manual for Compilation of Indices and a Bibliography of Indices and Indexing*. Helsinki: Academia Scientiarum Fennica, Folklore Fellows Communications 273.

Kaschuba, Wolfgang. 1999. *Einführung in die Europäische Ethnologie*. München: C.H. Beck.

Katz, Ruth. 2003. *The Lachmann Problem: An Unsung Chapter in Comparative Musicology*. Jerusalem: Hebrew University Magnes Press.

Klein, Barbro. 2003. "Silences, Cultural Historical Museums, and Jewish Life in Sweden." *Ethnologia Europaea* 33(2): 121–132.

Kuznitz, Cecile E. 2006. "An-sky's Legacy: the Vilna Historic-Ethnographic Society and the Shaping of Modern Jewish Culture" in Gabriella Safran and Steven J. Zipperstein, Eds. *The Worlds of S. An-sky*. Palo Alto: Stanford University Press, pp. 320–345.

Library of the Palestine Pilgrims' Text Society (The). 1971. New York: AMS Press.

Limor, Ora. 2007. "Sharing Sacred Space: Holy Places in Jerusalem Between Christianity, Judaism and Islam" in Iris Shagrir, Ronnie Ellenblum and Jonathan Riley-Smith, Eds. *In Laudem Hierosolymitani: Studies in Crusades and Medieval Culture in Honour of Benjamin Z. Kedar*. Aldershot: Ashgate, pp. 219–232.

Männchen, Julia. 1993. *Gustaf Dalman als Palästinawissenschaftler in Jerusalem und Greifswald, 1902–1941*. Wiesbaden: Harrassowitz.

Niehoff, Maren. 1992. "A Dream Which Is Not Interpreted Is Like a Letter Which Is Not Read." *Journal of Jewish Studies* 43: 58–84.

Noy, Dov, Ed. 1963. *Jefet Schwili Erzählt; Hundertneunundsechzig jemenitische Volkserzählungen, aufgezeichnet in Israel, 1957–1960*. Berlin: De Gruyter.

Noy, Dov. 1980. "Eighty Years of Jewish Folkloristics. Achievments and Tasks" in Frank Talmage, Ed. *Introduction to Studies in Jewish Folklore: Proceedings of a Regional Conference of the Association for Jewish Studies held at the Spertus College of Judaica, Chicago, May 1–3, 1977*. Cambridge, MA: The Association for Jewish Studies, pp. 1–11.

Olsvanger, Immanuel. 1936. *Rejte Pomeranzen; Ostjüdische Schwänke und Erzählungen*. Berlin: Schocken Verlag.

Oring, Elliott. 1981. *Israeli Humor: The Content and Structure of the Chizbat of the Palmah*. Albany: State University of New York Press.

Patai, Raphael. 1938. "The 'Control of Rain' in Ancient Palestine." *Hebrew Union College Annual* 14: 251–286.

Patai, Raphael. 1978. "Exorcism and Xenoglossia among the Safed Kabbalists." *Journal of American Folklore* 91(361): 823–833.

Rabinovitch, Simon. 2009. "Jews, Englishmen and Folklorists: The Scholarship of Joseph Jacobs and Moses Gaster" in Eitan Bar-Yosef and Nadia Valman, Eds. *The "Jew" in Late-Victorian and Edwardian Culture: Between the East End and East Africa*. New York: Palgrave Macmillan, pp. 113–130.

Rivlin, Joseph J. 1959. *Shirat Yehude Ha-Targum*. Jerusalem: Mossad Bialik (in Hebrew).

Rosen, Ilana. 2004. *Hungarian Jewish Women Survivors Remember the Holocaust: an Anthology of Life Histories*. Lanham, MD: University Press of America.

Rosen, Ilana. 2008. *Sister in Sorrow: Life Histories of Female Holocaust Survivors from Hungary*. Detroit: Wayne State University Press.

Rosen, Ilana. 2011. *Saul of Saul: The Life, Narrative, and Proverbs of a Transylvanian-Israeli Grandfather*. Proverbium Supplement Series 31. Burlington: Vermont University Press.

Sabar, Yona. 1982. *The Folk Literature of the Kurdistani Jews: An Anthology*. New Haven: Yale University Press.

Sadan, D. 1952. *A Bowl of Raisins*. Tel Aviv: M. Neuman (in Hebrew).

Sadan, D. 1953. *A Bowl of Nuts*. Tel Aviv: M. Neuman (in Hebrew).

Safran, Gabriella. 2010. *Wandering Soul: The Dybbuk's Creator, S. An-Sky*. Cambridge, MA. Harvard University Press.

Safran, Gabriella and Steven J. Zipperstein, Eds. 2006. *The Worlds of S. An-sky. A Russian Jewish Intellectual at the Turn of the Century*. Palo Alto: Stanford University Press.

Said, Edward. W. 1978. *Orientalism*. New York: Pantheon Books.

Salamon, Hagar. 2003. "Blackness in Transition: Decoding Racial Constructs through Stories of Ethiopian Jews." *Journal of Folklore Research* 40(1): 3–32.

Salamon, Hagar. 1999. *The Hyena People: Ethiopian Jews in Christian Ethiopia*. Berkeley: University of California Press.

Salamon, Hagar. 2001. "Political Bumper Stickers in Contemporary Israel: Folklore As An Emotional Battleground." *Journal of American Folklore* 114(453): 277–308.

Salamon, Hagar. 2008a. "Cow Tales: Decoding Images of Slavery in the Ethiopian Jewish Community." *Slavery and Abolition* 29(3): 415–435.

Salamon, Hagar. 2008b. "A Woman's Life Story as a Foundation Legend of Local Indentity" in Ruth Kark, Margalit Shilo, and Galit Hasan-Rokem, Eds. *Jewish Women in Pre-state Israel: Life History, Politics and Culture*. Waltham MA and Hanover, NH: Brandeis University Press and University Press of New England, pp. 141–163.

Salamon, Hagar. 2010. "Misplaced Home and Mislaid Meat: Stories Circulating Among Ethiopian Immigrants in Israel." *Callaloo* 33(1): 165–176.

Salamon, Hagar. 2011. "The Floor Falling Away: Dislocated Space and Body in the Humour of Ethiopian Immigrants in Israel." *Folklore* 122: 16–34.

Scheiber, Sandor. 1986. "Jewish Folklore" in Moshe Carmilly-Weinberger, Ed. *The Rabbinical Seminary of Budapest, 1877–1977. A Centennial Volume*. New York: Sepher-Hermon Press, pp. 265–268.

Schrire, Dani. 2010. "Raphael Patai, Jewish Folklore, Comparative Folkloristics, and American Anthropology." *Journal of Folklore Research* 47(1–2): 7–43.

Schwarzbaum, Haim. 1959–1960. "The Jewish and Moslem Versions of Some Theodicy Legends." *Fabula* 3: 119–169.

Schwarzbaum, Haim. 1968. *Studies in Jewish and World Folklore*. Berlin: De Gruyter.

Semi, Emanuela T. 2007. *Jacques Faitlovitch and the Jews of Ethiopia*. London: Vallentine Mitchell.

Shenhar-Alroy, Aliza. 1986. *Jewish and Israeli Folklore*. New Delhi: South Asian Publishers.

Soroudi, Sarah Sorour. 2008. *The Folktale of Jews from Iran, Central Asia and*

Afghanistan: Tale-Types and Genres. Dortmund: Verlag für Orientkunde.

Staudinger, Barbara. 2010. "Der Kategorisierende Blick der 'Jüdischen Volkskunde': Die Volkskundliche Wissenschaft und das 'Jüdische'." *Österreichische Zeitschrift für Volkskunde* 113: 525–541.

Steinschneider, Moritz. 1893. *Die hebräischen Übersetzungen des Mittelalters und die Juden als Dolmetscher: Ein Beitrag zur Literaturgeschichte des Mittelalters, meist nach handschriftlichen Quellen.* Berlin: Kommissionsverlag des bibliographischen Bureaus.

Tamari, Salim. 2009. *Mountain against the Sea: Essays on Palestinian Society and Culture.* Berkeley, CA: University of California Press.

Tendlau, Abraham M. 1860. *Sprichwörter und Redensarten Deutschjüdischer Vorzeit. Als Beitrag zur Volks-, Sprach- und Sprichwörter-Kunde.* Frankfurt: J. Kauffmann.

Werblowsky, Zwi, R.J. 1987. "The Safed Revival and its Aftermath" in Arthur Green, Ed. *Jewish Spirituality II: From the Sixteenth-Century Revival to the Present.* New York: Crossroad, pp. 7–33.

Yassif, Eli. 1987 [1988] "Mehqar ha-folqlor u-mada'ei ya-yahadut: kivunim u-megamot." *Yedion ha-iggud le- mada'ey ha-yahadut* 27(28): 3–26 (in Hebrew).

Yassif, Eli. 1999. *The Hebrew Folktale: History, Genre, Meaning.* Bloomington: Indiana University Press.

Yassif, Eli. 2004. "Moshe Gaster: porets derekh be-folklor u-ve-mada'ei ha-yahadut." *Pe'amim* 100: 113–123 (in Hebrew).

Zerubavel, Yael. 1995. *Recovered Roots: Collective Memory and the Making of Israeli National Tradition.* Chicago: University of Chicago Press.

FURTHER READING

Bendix, Regina. 1997. *In Search of Authenticity. The Formation of Folklore Studies.* Madison: University of Wisconsin Press.

Hasan-Rokem, Galit. 1999b. "Homo Viator et Narrans – Medieval Jewish Voices in the European Narrative of the Wandering Jew" in Ingo Schneider, Ed. *Europäische Ethnologie und Folklore im Internationalen Kontext: Festschrift für Leander Petzoldt zum 65. Geburtstag.* Frankfurt: P. Lang, pp. 93–102.

Hasan-Rokem, Galit 2006. "Israeli Folklore" in William M. Clements and Thomas A. Green, Eds. *Greenwood Encyclopedia of World Folklore.* Vol. 4, Westport, CT: Greenwood Press, pp. 372–383.

Salamon, Hagar and Esther Juhasz. 2011. "Goddesses of Flesh and Metal: Gazes on the Tradition of Fattening Jewish Brides in Tunisia." *Journal of Middle Eastern Women Studies* 7(1): 1–38.

CHAPTER 18

FULANI (PEUL, FULFULDE, PULAAR) LITERATURE[1]

Ursula Baumgardt

This transnational language, sweeping across a score of countries in the Sudan-Sahel region from Senegal to the Nile, is known by several names: Fula or Fulani in English, Peul in French, Ful in German. Speakers themselves call it *pulaar* or *fulfulde*; UNESCO prefers the latter. The language is classified by Greenberg as part of the West Atlantic section (Greenberg 1970: 25). Its sociolinguistic status varies: it can be an in-community language, a regional language, or a vehicular language. At least four groups of dialect variation are usually distinguished, corresponding to four quasi-states that took shape in the eighteenth and nineteenth centuries: *Fuuta Tooro* (in Senegal and Mauritania), *Fuuta Jallon* (in Guinea), *Maasina* (in Mali), and *Aadamaawa* (in northern Nigeria and northern Cameroon).

Beyond an undeniable intrinsic interest, Fulani presents several questions confronting many other African languages, as regards teaching, linguistic planning, standardization, and modernization. First, in the absence of school teaching, what are the means whereby the language and its lore are transmitted? Second, without models to be followed or tools for reference, what is the nature of the many writing practices? Third, how is the problem of orthography of this language handled? Fourth, given the diversity of writing practices, how shall the orthography of the language be harmonized?

As regards literature, the wide expanse of the language again raises questions that go well beyond the single case of Fulani. (1) What is the effect of its many cultural contacts? (2) Is there truly a Fulani literature? (3) In what way is oral literature influenced by social changes such as neo-orality? (4) How do oral and written literatures coexist? First I take up one of the conditions of literary production: the

A Companion to Folklore, First Edition. Edited by Regina F. Bendix and Galit Hasan-Rokem.

contribution to the language by those who speak it. Then I review the findings of research on Fulani language and literature; in the quasi-total absence of independent publications, such research constitutes the fundamental documentation in this domain. Finally I present the oral literature genre by genre and treat Fulani literature written in the Arabic or Latin alphabet.

THE CONTRIBUTION OF SPEAKERS TO THE LANGUAGE

It is well known that the attachment of speakers to the language they speak is a subjective and affective affair. Difficult though it is to measure, their investment seems indispensable; one has to love one's language to have any desire to speak it, to write it, to produce literature. Fulani speakers are quite conscious of their degree of knowledge of their language, and they value those who speak it well. Expressions about appropriateness are often heard, for example these from northern Cameroon: *fulfulde laaßnde,* fine Fulani, *fulfulde welnde,* beautiful Fulani, *o waawi wolde* he/she knows how to speak. Christiane Seydou (1973) suggests that the Fulanis' high investment in language seems to be favored by their way of life. Being of nomadic origin, they had few material media for artistic expression. Under these conditions, verbal art, being non-material, offered itself as a privileged domain; it required no particular equipment save for a light musical instrument, the *hoddu,* a lute, usually with three strings, which accompanies certain verbal productions. Furthermore, given the considerable dialect variation, speaking or creating literature in one dialect is a way of drawing attention to the specificity of a group within a community while underlining one's membership in the latter. Roger Labatut, in his teaching, would explain that this function seems to be one of the factors favoring dialectal differentiation. At the same time it constitutes a brake on attempts to standardize the language into a single form.

This traditionally strong investment of identity in Fulani language is central to the promotion of the language which many intellectuals and militants since the 1970s have pressed (Bourlet 2009). Indeed, in a multilingual context, once French was established as an official language in France's former colonies, the language criterion became an essential factor in defining cultural identity: a Fulani is one who speaks Fulani. Thus language has become a link voicing one's cultural affiliation, beyond dialect variants and the considerable social stratification.

These sociocultural factors help to explain the vitality of Fulani literary production. What is more, being primarily oral, the language lends itself particularly well to playing with sounds across a whole network of recurrent markers. In the noun system, all the elements of a sentence connected to the same noun carry the same inflection as the noun class, as with *ki* in the following example: *lekki mawki kii, b'e coppi ki,* that big tree, they cut it down. Similarly the verb system, in the *pulaar* of *Fuuta Tooro* for example – which is founded on the aspect *done/not done* and the distinction of active, middle, and passive voice – potentially embraces more than 850 inflections (Mohamadou 2016). This function of the language permits a multitude of sound games, rhymes, alliterations, and what Christiane Seydou has named *tuilage:* the construction of an identical sound with an identical vowel or consonant or both, with a gradual movement towards a different sound (Seydou 1977b). Dominique Noye has observed games in northern Cameroon that initiate the young into language by drawing on these kinds of inherent resources and sensitizing children to them (Noye 1971).

Research in Fulani Literature

For a long time, research interest in Fulani literature was an anthropological affair, even more a linguistic one, and far less a literary matter. Hence this problem: the very substance constituting Fulani literature, oral literature or folklore, was not recognized as a distinct or separate scientific domain. A number of linguists have published collections of texts. One was Henri Gaden (1867–1939), an officer in the French army and later a colonial administrator, who published a collection of proverbs (1931) and an edition of a poem composed by Mohammadou Aliou Tyiam modeled on the canons of Arabic poetry, "The Life of El-Hadj Omar" (Gaden 1935). Pierre-François Lacroix (1924–1974), a colonial administrator, then a professor at the National Institute of Oriental Languages and Civilizations (INALCO) in Paris, published two volumes titled *Fulani Poetry from Adamawa* (Lacroix 1965). The missionary Dominique Noye collected and published many folktales (1980, 1981, 1982, 1982). Roger Labatut (1931–1996), also a professor at INALCO, collected songs from the nomadic Fulani of northern Cameroon. More recently, the linguist and Fulani speaker Henri Tourneux, who oversees the publication of texts and analyses of oral literature at Editions Karthala in Paris, awards a preferential place to Fulani literature in his reflections on questions of "Languages, cultures, and development in Africa" (Tourneux 2008). Fulani literature has benefited from work by linguists and historians such as Bernard Salvaing (1985, 2003), but also by researchers more specifically interested in the literary, such as S.M. Ndongo (1986) and M. L Ngaidé (1983), for the western and central part of the Fulani area, and Abdoulaye Oumarou Dalil (1988), Veit Erlmann (1979, 1980), and especially Paul Eguchi, a published poet (1976), who from 1975 on has been collecting texts of Fulani oral literature in Cameroon. Aware of the lack of theorization in folklore recently remarked by Lee Haring (2008), my own research and thesis supervision move towards an approach to orality that is expressly literary, theoretical, and methodological (Baumgardt and Ugochukwu 2005) and that situates oral literature in relation to other forms of literary production (Baumgardt and Derive 2008).

Fulani literature has especially benefited from work by celebrated researchers who have made it known on the international plane. So emblematic a personage as the great sage Amadou Hampâté Bâ has decisively contributed to the influence of African literature in general and Fulani literature in particular. His consequential engagement is recalled by Lilyan Kesteloot.

> Things nearly turned out badly when Hampâté's sympathy for the Hamallists[2] rendered him suspect in the eyes of the French authorities. In 1942, never (he says) having done anything political, he was caught in the hunt for Hamallists and arrested. However Théodore Monod – founder of the Institut Fondamental de l'Afrique Noire (IFAN), a branch of the Dakar Museum, then in various West African capital cities – had met Hampâté and made use of his services during sojourns in Bamako. So Hampâté called on him for aid when the Bamako administration threatened him with imprisonment. Théodore Monod then approached the French West African government with the request that Hampâté Bâ be assigned to IFAN as an interpreter responsible personally to him. Thus instead of rotting in prison or worse, Hampâté became a researcher at IFAN, by the grace of the person he called his "great silent river." Between these two men, who were almost of an age, arose a spiritual current, a fraternity which would endure for several years, Monod all the while playing the elder's role, as some of Hampâté's letters show.

During this period Hampâté Bâ, under Théodore Monod's aegis and within the IFAN framework, collected most of the Fulani initiatic texts that made him famous: *Koumen, Kaïdara, L'éclat de la grande étoile,* the *Lootori* songs, and *Njeddo Dewal Ina Baasi.* The majority of these narratives and poems were entrusted to him by the *Silatigui* Ard'o Dembo Sow, from the Lingère region in Senegal, with whom he probed the depths of Foûta Tôro, as an IFAN researcher but even more as a Fulani in search of esoteric knowledge. (Kesteloot 2005: 17)

Aliou Mohamadou recalls the pioneering work of Alpha Ibrahima Sow (who left us on January 21, 2005), especially in refining the writing and publication of Fulani literature.

Alpha Ibrahima Sow remained for his whole university career at the National Institute of Oriental Languages and Civilizations (INALCO) up to 1992, when he retired. Together with Professor Pierre-François Lacroix, he was one of the initiators of the famous Bamako conference of April–May 1966, organized under UNESCO auspices, on the transcription of African languages, which remains the reference point for Fulani orthography today. His participation in that conference was surely important. But to me, his more important role was played afterward, for as Alpha Ibrahima Sow well knew, recommendations not followed up with actions are a dead letter. He did not rest until the scientists' conclusions found a real application among researchers, who at that time were, with missionaries, the only ones truly dealing with the writing of African languages ....

Alpha Ibrahima Sow's contribution to the orthography of Fulani, as it is practiced today, also was effected through the publishing house Nubia, which he set up, and through his own work, notably the introductory manuals he authored for reading Fulani, which covered the dialectal diversity of the language: *Textes d'étude de fulfulde* (Texts for Studying Fulfulde, 1968–1969) and *Janngen fulfulde* (two volumes, 1970).

Among his scholarly works are *La Femme, la Vache, la Foi* (Woman, Cow, Faith), sacred and secular poetry in the *Ajami*[3] of Foûta-Djalon (1966) and *Le Filon du bonheur éternel* (Vein of Eternal Happiness), religious poems by Tierno Mouhammadou Samba Mombêya (1972). Original texts in *Ajami* appear in the appendix of *Le Filon*, as they do also here and there in his *Chroniques et récits du Foûta-Djalon.* (Sagas and stories from Foûta-Djalon, 1968) (Mohamadou 2005: 13)

Then there is Christiane Seydou, who has produced numerous collections of texts and analyses of Fulani literature.[4] The beginnings of her Fulani literary research were in the Maasina region of Mali, where her first project was an account of the totality of literary genres existing in the region.

I organized my research by genre. At the start I looked especially for epic texts, then for religious texts, because Maasina is very productive in this realm. For secular poetry, I conducted research among sheepherders, and for pastoral poetry, at the same time among *mergôbé* poets. Then too, in every project and in all the families I visited, there were evenings for tales. I was thus able to record many narratives, not by request, but only because the rumor had quickly gone round I was interested in such. For many people, also, curiosity about this visiting *toubab* played a role. (Seydou 2005: 22).

She demonstrated the success of her initial project on a large scale, in publications about epic (Seydou 1972, 1976, 2010a, b), poetry (Seydou 1981a, b, 1991, 2008) and tales (Seydou 1975, 2005). One of the indispensable tools for entering Fulani literature is Christiane Seydou's "General Bibliography of the Fulani World" (Seydou 1977b), which unfortunately has not been systematically brought up to date. Partial bibliographies were published in the *Bulletin de liaison des études peules*, Information Bulletin of Fulani Studies, in 1991 and 1992. The Timtimol (Rainbow) Association, headed by Aliou Mohamadou of INALCO and LLACAN, undertook the publication of a "Selective Bibliography for Fulani Language, Linguistics, and Literature" (*Bibliographie sélective: langue, linguistique et littérature peules*) on its site www. timtimol.com. Beyond these, there are several articles giving an idea of the literature (Arnott 1985; Seydou 1973, 2000; Fagerberg 1995), as well as the work of Aliou Mohamadou (2000), who was the first to present texts by several writers in Fulani language.

Fulani literature – defined as a function of the language as actually used – is characterized by the presence of multiple forms of expression; these may be conceived in terms like "traditional" and "modern" literature, or in the perspective of a transition from the oral to the written, but these notions imply objectionable biases. A more objective criterion is that of the mode of communication being chosen, which allows us first to treat oral and written literatures separately, then examine the various genres and regions of literature, and lastly take up the interrelations of the various expressive forms.

ORAL LITERATURE

Fulani oral literature, by virtue of its wide geographic scope, is unquestionably one of the African literatures with the largest diversity of cultural contacts. Thus arises the question of its unity. Since the language is not taught in school, both language and literature are anchored primarily in a locality or a region. Consequently for Fulani speakers, there is no problem about unity, but rather a problem of access to the various forms of literary expression. In the eyes of researchers, there is no doubt that the literature, like the language, does form a structural unity with considerable regional variations, which are linked to (among other things) the differing social organization of the various regions. In fact the proportion of still-nomadic groups to groups having adopted a sedentary life differs from one region to another. Similarly, there is greater and lesser social stratification; the western region has socioprofessional classifications not found in the eastern. There are certain literary genres which are linked to particular professional functions exercised by their members; this is the case for some of the poetry. Thus one of the most immediately perceptible differences is about genre: certain literary genres are confirmed for the whole of the Fulani area, others are not.

For all that, since Fulani oral literature (like oral literatures generally) is always and everywhere linked to performance, it is through performance that oral texts exercise comparable functions. Thus, to give but one example, the inscribing of texts in referential space always takes account of the space of performance, in one way or another. This has been analyzed for Fulani folktales:

> The referential space is identified by means of indices which may be lexical, such as spatial terms, or deictic, pointing back to the particular geographic space where the text is uttered, viz. the Fulani area. Examination of these indices for two corpora of Fulani tales,

one from Sénégal in the west, one from Cameroon in the east, reveals an identical function, beyond lexical variants in dialect and different degrees of referentialization. (Baumgardt and Bourlet 2010: 263)

Thus at the lexical level, the same term may be used to designate a different referent, or different terms may be used for the same referent, but beyond these differences there is a common lexical stock for fundamental facts, for example inhabited and uninhabited spaces.

Genres

Three genres exist through all regions of the Fulani area: proverbs, riddles, and tales. For the first, in the major collection mentioned above (Gaden 1931), Henri Gaden offered a thematic classification for his proverbs. Pioneering though this work was in its time, it suffers from the reductiveness inherent in this type of classification, which awards only a single meaning to an utterance that in reality is polysemic. A more recent work, *Payka,* is a collection of 1,726 proverbs, with commentary in *pulaar* (Sek and Mohamadou 2008). The data are given in alphabetical order by the first pertinent lexical term. The utterances are explained and commented on in *pulaar.* Most often the context of usage is given, thus facilitating an understanding of the meaning by pointing to the situation of its being said. The lexical terms in the collection are exhaustively inventoried in an index of over 30 pages, showing the numbers of the sentences where they appear.

As to folktales, many have been collected in the eastern region, in Cameroon notably by Paul K. Eguchi (1978a, b, 1980a, b, 1982, 1984a, b), Dominique Noye (1980, 1981, 1982, 1983) and Ursula Baumgardt (2000). Fewer have been collected in Senegal (Gaden 1913; Meyer 1988, 1991), in Guinea (Salvaing 1985), and in Mali (Seydou 1975, 2005). Published documents must not be thought of as the only reliable source: numerous texts have been collected but not published, or show up only in university theses. A dissertation by Mélanie Bourlet (1999), for example, presents 26 Fulani tales collected in Senegal. Published texts are sometimes presented only in the language of translation, but (fortunately) fairly often bilingually. Fulani folktales have been extensively studied. Thematic approaches include representations of the child (Baumgardt 1988), marriage (Seydou 1991; Baumgardt 1991), women (Baumgardt 2000) or the word (Seydou 1987; Baumgardt 2005). Typological approaches are exemplified by analyses of the tale type of the defiant girl, or *fille difficile* (Seydou 2001; Baumgardt 2001). From content analysis of cultural representations arise more theoretical interrogations: under what conditions of performance are tales, and oral literature generally, produced? How do these conditions influence the content? As to collective research on oral and written literatures in African languages, the CNRS team #8135, Language, Languages, and Cultures of Black Africa (LLACAN), has published studies of the representation of space in African languages (Baumgardt and Roulon-Doko 2010), on the notion of performance in theory, over the 40 years since it was defined in France by Geneviève Calame-Griaule (Baumgardt and Bornand 2009), and on otherness (*altérité*) (Baumgardt forthcoming). Work currently in progress concerns the performer, in his or her function as a producer of texts and as a text element. Beyond these, an analysis of Fulani folktales, planned initially as a thematic study of the representation of women, ended as a study of one storyteller's whole repertoire. This notion opened new perspectives, because a repertoire, complemented by a life history or information about the performer, thus opens access to both the complexity of texts and the performer's individual involvement (Baumgardt forthcoming).

As for sacred and secular poetry, collections from all the regions have been published: for the East (Dalil 1988; Haafkens 1983; Labatut 1978; Lacroix 1965; Noye 1976), *Maasina* (Seydou 1981a, b, 1991, 2008), *Fuuta Jallon* (Sow 1966, 1971) and *Fuuta-Tooro* (Ndongo 1986). Also deserving mention is Oumar Ndiaye's thesis (2010) on the fishermen's poetry of that region, *pekaan*.

Fulani texts of historical interest have been published especially for the East (Mohammadou 1980), but also the West (Sow 1968). As for myth, in particular the myth of Tyâmaba – the snake whose secret is divulged by his twin brother, thus causing his departure with a big share of the cattle-herd – it has been observed only in the West (Kesteloot 1985). Finally, initiatic narratives such as *Kaïdara* are known thanks to the rewriting and translation of the texts by Amadou Hampâté Bâ (1968). The literary genre best illustrating the uneven distribution over the various regions of the Fulani area is epic, which is met only in the West (Correra 1992; Meyer 1991; Ngaidé 1983; Sy 1978a, b; Ly 1991; Dieng and Wane 2004), notably in the *Maasina* (Seydou 1972, 1976, 2010a, b). According to Christiane Seydou, the epic in its function as "organising schema" may have been borrowed by the Fulanis from Bambara culture to engender the Fulani epic (Seydou 1976: 37). Its absence from the East probably owes to reasons of function, the affirmation of an identity anchored in pre-Islamic society. After the Fulani Empire of Sokoto was founded by Ousmane Dan Fodio in 1804, any evidence of such traits seems to have been forcefully scrutinized in the name of Islam. In fieldwork in that region, I have many times heard that folktales were not encouraged by religion.

Transmission of Oral Literature

When we come to the movement of oral literature into new contexts, such as the adaptation of folktales in bilingual editions (Diallo 2004), several recent initiatives were presented at a "Day of Fulani Studies" at INALCO in Paris on 17 June 2009. There Mamadou Abdul Sek, *griot* and author of several novels in *pulaar*, explained that he took up writing to transmit more effectively knowledge of the language and literature, by publishing for example *Payka*, his volume of proverbs, that oral genre *par excellence*.[5] Pierre Amiand, the director of the film *Magui, le génie du fleuve*, Magui, the River Genie, brought up two sets of questions from Fulani pastoral poetry. How should performances be filmed, and how should the filmed performances be handled? He opened a new direction for research on the production of Fulani-language audovisual documents. In a presentation titled "Transferring information: preventing AIDS in Fulani, Northern Cameroon," Henri Tourneux shared his thinking about the choice of terms for the virus in Fulani and the means of disseminating information. He presented a song in Fulani which was conceived, recorded, and widely diffused in Cameroon. In last place, the question of transmission in the immigrant context was taken up by Bénédicte Chaîne in *Kulle Ladde* (2009), a multidialectal painter of wild animals, who is inspired by ethnic slurs (*jobbitooje*), a genre of folklore found in the Diamaré department of Northern Cameroon. Each of his animals introduces itself to children and calls up its qualities, but also its defects. The introductory material, several lines in *pulaar*, are adapted and recapitulated in a panel for the Guinean version; the whole is translated into French and English. As for "neo-orality" – the production of oral texts outside the traditional performance context, in the setting of a show or folktale festival – surely that constitutes one way to preserve essential traits of orality, whilst allowing oral genres to be adapted to new conditions of communication.

FULANI WRITTEN LITERATURE

Written Fulani literature, in various historical contexts, relies on two kinds of writing, the Arabic and the Roman alphabets.

One corollary of the spread of Islam was the introduction of Qur'anic teaching, and with it writing in the Arabic alphabet. *Ajami*, which at first was reserved for literati who took it up to compose religious poetry, served to commit to writing works which, while being circulated in manuscripts, were recited and diffused orally. Unfortunately, hardly any of this literature has been published or studied from a literary perspective. Representative examples are *Le Filon du bonheur éternel* (The Vein of Eternal Happiness) (Sow 1971), Christiane Seydou's recent book on mystical poetry (Seydou 2008a, b, and c), and *The Collected Works of Nana Asma'u, Daughter of Usman 'dan Fodiyo* (Boyd and Beverly 1997).

Writing in Roman characters has taken on more importance since a conference organized by UNESCO at Bamako in 1966, that was devoted to the writing of six West African languages including Fulani (Mohamadou 2005). Contemporary literary creation in the Roman alphabet is expanding and engendering monolingual publications, notably from authors from the the Senegal river region. The emergence of this literature has been analyzed by Mélanie Bourlet in a two-part study (2009). The first part deals with the interrelation of history, sociology, and the political context, as well as the status of Fulani language for literary writing in the Roman alphabet. The second bears on literary creation itself. She has gathered some 60 texts of prose and poetry in several field trips to Senegal and Mauritania. In order to illustrate the riches of these writings and refer to well-known authors, she analyzes four novels in detail: Yero Dooro Jallo's *Nidkkiri Joom Moolo*, Ndikiri the Guitar Player (1981); Ibraahiima Dem's *Sahre Goongo*, The World of Truth (1997); Saydu Bah's *Sammba Jallo. Moni fof et feccere mum*, Sammba Jallo, To Each his Destiny (2005); and Mammadu Abdul Sek's *Ngayngu Giɗ li*, Love-Hate (2004). A final section of her dissertation presents detailed summaries of the four novels and biographical information about the authors, as well as surveys of some 15 other authors, their poetic output, and their novels.

The clear conclusion is that among African literatures, Fulani stands out because it offers, all at the same time, very sizable oral production, written literature in various forms of *ajami*, and rich and growing contemporary writing. And some well-known francophone writers deliberately advertise their Fulani origin, such as Bakary Diallo, Cheikh Hamidou Kane, and Thierno Monénembo, an internationally renowned francophone novelist who chose for his novel the title *Fulanis* (Monénembo 2004).

NOTES

1 The author as well as the editors thank Lee Haring for translating this chapter from French.
2 Translator's note: Hamallism (Hamallayya) was an Islamic social protest movement in Mali and Mauritania of the 1930s–1940s.
3 Translator's note: *Ajami* refers to Fulani poetry transcribed in Arabic script.
4 A complete bibliography of Christiane Seydou's work up to 2005 appears in Baumgardt and Derive 2005.
5 See the summary of his remarks on the site timtimol.org.

REFERENCES

Arnott, D.W. 1985. "Literature in Fula" in B.W. Andrzejewski, S. Pilaszewicz, and W. Tyloch, Eds. *Literatures in African Languages: Theoretical Issues and Sample Surveys.* Cambridge and Warsaw: Cambridge University Press and Wiedza Powszechna, pp. 72–96.

Bâ, Amadou Hampâté and Lilyan Kesteloot. 1968. "Kaïdara, récit initiatique peul." *Classiques Africains 7.* Paris: Julliard.

Baumgardt, Ursula. 1988. "L'enfant à travers des contes peuls du Cameroun" in Veronika Görög-Karady and Ursula Baumgardt, Eds. *L'Enfant dans les contes africains.* Paris: CILF, pp. 83–111.

Baumgardt, Ursula. 1991. "Le mariage heureux et le mariage malheureux à travers quatre contes peuls du Nord-Cameroun." *Actes du IVe Colloque Méga-Tchad.* Paris: ORSTOM Éditions, pp. 71–122.

Baumgardt, Ursula. 1994. "La représentation de l'autre: l'exemple du répertoire d'une conteuse peule de Garoua (Cameroun)." *Cahiers d'études africaines* 133–135: 295–331.

Baumgardt, Ursula. 1997. "Littérature orale et récit autobiographique: un exemple peul." *Cahiers de littérature orale* 42: 135–154.

Baumgardt, Ursula. 1999. "Littérature orale et identité" in R. Botte, J. Boutrais, and Jean Schmitz, Eds. *Figures peules.* Paris: Karthala, 323–335.

Baumgardt, Ursula. 2000. *Une conteuse peule et son répertoire. Goggo Addi de Garoua, Cameroun.* Paris: Karthala.

Baumgardt, Ursula. 2005a. "La parole comme engagement: l'exemple d'un répertoire de contes peuls du Cameroun." *Approches littéraires de l'oralité africaine.* Paris: Karthala, pp. 17–42.

Baumgardt, Ursula, Ed. 2005b. *Littérature peule.* Numéro spécial 2005/19 de la revue de l'APELA. *Études littéraires africaines.* Paris: Karthala, pp. 5–54.

Baumgardt, Ursula. 2010. "Mobilité spatiale et contacts culturels à travers les contes peuls du Nord-Cameroun" in Henri Tourneux and N. Woïn, Eds. *Migrations et mobilité dans le bassin du Lac Tchad.* CD-ROM. Marseille: IRD.

Baumgardt, Ursula and Sandra Bornand, Eds. 2009. "Autour de la performance." *Cahiers de littérature orale,* No. 65. Paris: INALCO.

Baumgardt, Ursula and Jean Derive, Eds. 2005. *Paroles nomades. Écrits d'ethnolinguistique africaine.* Paris: Karthala.

Baumgardt, Ursula and Jean Derive, Eds. 2008. *Littératures orales africaines. Perspectives théoriques et méthodologiques.* Paris: Karthala.

Baumgardt, Ursula and Françoise Ugochukwu, Eds. 2005. *Approches littéraires de l'oralité africaine.* Paris: Karthala.

Baumgardt, Ursula and Paulette Roulon-Doko, Eds. 2010. "L'expression de l'espace dans les langues africaines." *Journal des Africanistes* 79: 1–3.

Baumgardt, Ursula and Paulette Roulon-Doko, Eds. Forthcoming a. "Création et répertoire en littérature orale."

Baumgardt, Ursula and Paulette Roulon-Doko, Eds. Forthcoming b. *L'altérité en littérature orale africaine*.

Boyd, J. and B.M. Beverly. 1991 [1992]. *Bulletin de liaison des études peules* 2–3. Paris: INALCO and CNRS URA 1024.

Boyd, J. and B.M. Beverly. 1997. *Collected Works of Nana Asma'u, Daughter of Usman 'dan Fodiyo (1793–1864)*. East Lansing: Michigan State University Press.

Correra, I. 1992. "Samba Guéladio, épopée peule du Fuuta Tooro." *Initiations et études africaines* 36. Dakar: Université de Dakar-IFAN.

Diallo K.Z. 2004a. *Daado l'orpheline et autres contes du Fouta Djallon de Guinée*. Paris: L'Harmattan.

Diallo K.Z. 2004b. *Le Fils du roi de Guémé et autres contes du Fouta-Djallon de Guinée*. Paris: L'Harmattan.

Dieng, B. and Wane, I. 2004. *L'Épopée de Boubou Ardo*. Amiens: Presses du Centre d'Études médiévales.

Eguchi, Paul K. 1976. *Poem of Repentance*. Tokyo: ILCAA.

Eguchi, Paul K. 1978a. "Beeda: a Fulbe Mbooku poem." *Africa 1, Senri Ethnological Studies* 1: 55–88.

Eguchi, Paul K. 1978b. *Fulfulde Tales of North Cameroon*. Vol. I. Tokyo: Institute for the Study of Languages and Cultures of Asia and Africa, (ILCAA), 251 pp.

Eguchi, Paul K. 1980a. "The wood ibises: a Fulbe mbooku poem." *Africa 2, Senri Ethnological Studies* 6: 125–152.

Eguchi, Paul K.1980b. *Fulfulde Tales of Northern Cameroon*. Vol. II. Tokyo: ILCAA.

Eguchi, Paul K. 1982. *Fulfulde Tales of Northern Cameroon*. Vol. III. Tokyo: ILCAA.

Eguchi, Paul K. 1984a. *Fulfulde Tales of Northern Cameroon*. Vol. IV. Tokyo: ILCAA.

Eguchi, Paul K. 1984b. "Let us insult Pella: a Fulbe mbooku poem." *Africa 3, Senri Ethnological Studies* 15: 197–246.

Erlmann, Veit. 1979. *Booku, Eine literarisch-musikalische Gattung der Fulbe des Diamaré (Nord-Kamerun)*. Marburger Studien zur Afrika und Asien Kunde. Berlin: D. Reimer.

Erlmann, Veit. 1991 [1992]. *Bulletin de liaison des études peules* 2–3. Paris: INALCO and CNRS URA 1024.

Erlmann, Veit. 1980. "Die Macht des Wortes: Preisgesang und Berufsmusiker bei den Fulbe des Diamare, Nordkamerun" (Le pouvoir de la parole: chants d'éloge et musiciens professionnels chez les peuls du Diamaré, Nord-Cameroun). *Studien zur Musik Afrikas*. Köln: K. Renner.

Fagerberg-Diallo, S. 1995. "Milk and honey: Developing written literature in Pulaar." *Yearbook of Comparative and General Literature* 43. Indianapolis: Indiana University Press.

Gaden, H. 1913–1914. *Le Poular. Dialecte peul du Fouta sénégalais*. Vol. 1. *Étude morphologique, Textes*. Vol. 2. *Dictionnaire peul-français*. Collection de la Revue du monde musulman. Paris: Leroux.

Gaden, H. 1931. "Proverbes et maximes peuls et toucouleurs traduits, annotés, expliqués." Travaux et *Mémoires de l'Institut d'ethnologie* 16. Paris: l'Institut d'ethnologie.

Görög-Karady, Veronika and Christiane Seydou, Eds. 2001. *La Fille difficile. Un conte-type africain*. Paris: CNRS Éditions.

Greenberg, Joseph H. 1970. *The Languages of Africa*. Bloomington: Indiana University Press.

Haafkens, J. 1983. *Chants musulmans en peul: textes de l'héritage religieux de la communauté musulmane de Maroua, Cameroun*. Leiden: Brill.

Haring, Lee. 2008. "America's Antitheoretical Folkloristics." *Journal of Folklore Research* 45(1): 1–9.

Kesteloot, Lilyan, C. Barbey, *et al.*, Eds. 1985. *Tya-maba, mythe peul et ses rapports avec le rite, l'histoire, la géographie*. Dakar: IFAN, Notes Africaines, pp. 185–186.

Kesteloot, Lilyan, C. Barbey, *et al.*, Eds. 2005. "Amadou Hampâté Bâ: de l'initié peul à l'humaniste œcuménique." *Études littéraires africaines* 13, *"Littérature peule."* Paris: Karthala.

Ly, A. 1991. *L'Épopée de Samba Guéladiégui*. Dakar: IFAN/UNESCO.

Meyer, Gérard. 1988. *Paroles du soir. Contes toucouleurs*. Paris: L'Harmattan.

Meyer, Gérard. 1991. *Récits épiques tou-couleurs. La vache, le livre, la lance.* Paris: Karthala, ACCT.

Mohamadou, Aliou. 2000. "Nouvelles tendances en littérature peule: présentation des textes de quatre auteurs haal-pulaar (Sénégal et Mauritanie)" in A. Bounfour, Ed. *Panorama des littératures africaines.* Paris, L'Harmattan/INALCO, Coll. Bibliothèque des études africaines, pp. 77–92.

Mohamadou, Aliou. 2004. "Stratégie de représentation du générique dans les prover-bes peuls" in A. Bounfour, Ed. *Le Proverbe en Afrique: forme, fonction et sens.* Paris: L'Harmattan/INALCO, pp. 1–12.

Mohamadou, Aliou. 2005a. "Si Bamako m'était conté … À propos de la transcription et de l'orthographe du peul" in Ursula Baumgardt and Jean Derive, Eds. *Paroles nomades. Écrits d'ethnolinguistique africaine* Paris: Karthala, pp. 139–151.

Mohamadou, Aliou. 2005b. "In memoriam Alpha Ibrahima Sow." *Études littéraires africaines* 13. *"Littérature peule."* Paris: Karthala.

Mohamadou, Aliou. 2005[2006]. "*Ndikkiri joom moolo* (Ndikkiri le guitariste) de Yero Dooro Jallo, premier roman peul (1981)" in Xavier Garnier and Alain Ricard, Eds. *L'Effet roman. Arrivée du roman dans les langues d'Afrique.* Paris: L'Harmattan/Université Paris 13, pp. 209–229.

Mohammadou, E. 1969. "Yeerwa: Poème des peuls Yillaga de l'Adamawa." *Camelang* 1: 73–111.

Mohammadou, E. 1980. *Traditions histor-iques des Foulbés de l'Adamaoua.* Paris: CNRS.

Monénembo, Thierno. 2004. *Peuls.* Paris: Seuil.

Ndiaye, Oumar. 2010. "La notion de réper-toire dans l'œuvre de Guellâye, poète épique de pêcheur haalpulaar du Foûta Tôro" (Thesis, INALCO, Paris). 3 Vols.

Ndongo, S.M. 1986. *Le Fantang. Poèmes mythiques des bergers peuls.* Paris: Karthala-IFAN-UNESCO.

Ngaidé, M.L. 1983. *Le Vent de la razzia. Deux récits épiques des peuls du Jolof.* Dakar: FAN.

Noye, Dominique. 1971. *Un Cas d'apprentissage linguistique: acquisition de la langue par les jeunes peuls du Diamaré (Nord-Cameroun).* Paris: P. Geuthner.

Noye, Dominique. 1976. *Blasons peuls: éloges et satires du Nord-Cameroun.* Paris: P. Geuthner.

Noye, Dominique, Ed. 1980. *Le Menuisier et le cobra.* Paris: Luneau-Ascot (reprinted by Karthala in the collection "Contes et légen-des" as *Contes peuls du Nord-Cameroun*).

Noye, Dominique. 1981. *Taali ful'be talaa'di Baaba Zandu* (Les contes peuls de Bâba Zandu). Maroua: Mission Catholique.

Noye, Dominique. 1982. *Contes peuls de Bâba Zandou du Cameroun.* Paris, CILF-EDICEF.

Noye, Dominique. 1983. *Bâba Zandou rac-onte. Contes peuls du Cameroun.* Paris: CILF-EDICEF.

Noye, Dominique. 1999. *Le menuisier et le cobra. Contes peuls du Nord-Cameroun.* Paris: Karthala.

Salvaing, Bernard. 1985. *Contes et récits du Fouta Djalon.* Édition bilingue peul-fran-çais. Paris: Conseil international de la langue française/Edicef.

Salvaing, Bernard. 2003. "Hagiographie et saints au Fouta-Djalon" in B. Hirsch and M. Kropp, Eds. *Saints, Biographies and History in Africa. Saints, biographies et histoire en Afrique. Heilige, Biographien und Geschichte in Afrika.* Frankfurt: Peter Lang, pp. 295–319.

Sek, M.A. and Aliou Mohammadou. 2008. *Payka* (Delicious Words in Pulaar). Paris: Timtimol KJPF.

Seydou, Christiane. 1972. "Silâmaka et Poullôri, Récit épique peule raconté par Tinguidji." *Classiques Africains* 13. Paris: Les Belles Lettres.

Seydou, Christiane. 1973. "Panorama de la littérature Peule." *Bulletin de l'IFAN* XXXV B, (1): 176–218.

Seydou, Christiane. 1975. *Contes et fables des veillées.* Paris: Nubia.

Seydou, Christiane. 1976. "La Geste de Ham-Bodêdio ou Hama le Rouge." *Classiques Africains* 18. Paris: Les Belles Lettres.

Seydou, Christiane. 1977b. "Bibliographie générale du monde peul." *Études Nigériennes* 43 (Niamey).

Seydou, Christiane. 1981a. "'Le Chameau': poème mystique ou … pastoral ?" *Itinérances en pays peul et ailleurs*, Vol. 2. Paris: Mémoires de la Société des Africanistes, pp. 25–52.

Seydou, Christiane. 1981b. "Les 'jammooje na'i', poèmes pastoraux des peuls du Mali." *Bulletin des études africaines de l'INALCO* 1: 133–141.

Seydou, Christiane. 1987. "La notion de parole dans le dialecte peul du Mâssina (Mali)." *Journal des Africanistes* 57(1–2): 45–66.

Seydou, Christiane. 1991. *Bergers des mots. Poésie peule du Massina présentée et traduite par Christiane Seydou*. Classiques Africains 24. Paris: Les Belles Lettres.

Seydou, Christiane. 2000. "Littérature peule" in Ursula Baumgardt and A. Bounfour, Eds. *Panorama des littératures africaines. État des lieux et perspectives*. Paris: L'Harmattan/INALCO, pp. 63–75.

Seydou, Christiane. 2001. "La Fille difficile peule I (du Sénégal … au Nigeria)" in Veronika Görög-Karady and Christiane Seydou, Eds. *La Fille difficile. Un conte-type africain*. Paris: CNRS Éditions, pp. 23–64.

Seydou, Christiane. 2005. *Contes peuls du Mali*. Paris: Karthala.

Seydou, Christiane. 2008. *La Poésie mystique peule du Mali*. Paris: Karthala.

Seydou, Christiane. 2010a. *Profils de femmes dans les récits épiques peuls (Mali-Niger)*. Paris: Karthala.

Seydou, Christiane. 2010b. *L'épopée peule de Boûbou Ardo Galo, héros et rebelle*. Paris: Karthala.

Sow, A.I. 1966. *La Femme, la vache, la foi. Écrivains et poètes du Foûta-Djalon*. Classiques Africains 5. Paris: Julliard.

Sow, A.I. 1968. *Chroniques et récits du Foûta Djalon*. Paris: C. Klincksieck.

Sow, A.I. 1971. *Le Filon du bonheur éternel, par Tierno Mouhamadou Samba Mombêya*. Classiques Africains 10. Paris: A. Colin.

Sy, A.A. 1978a. *Ségoubali, épopée des pêcheurs pulaar*. Dakar: ENDA/IFAN.

Sy, A.A. 1978b. *Seul contre tous. Deux récits épiques des pêcheurs du Fouta Toro*. Dakar-Abidjan: NEA.

Tourneux, Henri, Ed. 2008. *Langues, cultures et développement en Afrique*. Paris: Karthala.

FURTHER READING

Bâ, Amadou Hampâté. *XXXX* "L'Éclat de la grande étoile, suivi du Bain rituel, récits initiatiques peuls." *Classiques Africains* 15. Paris: A. Colin.

Bâ, Amadou Hampâté. 1985. *Njeddo Dewal, Mère de calamité*. Abidjan-Dakar-Lomé: Les Nouvelles Éditions Africaines.

Bâ, Amadou Hampâté and Germaine Dieterlen. 1961."Koumen, texte initiatique des pasteurs peuls." *Cahiers de l'Homme, nouvelle série 1*. Paris-La Haye: Mouton,

Bâ, Alpha Oumarou. 2005. "Communauté et classe sociale: deux notions prégnantes dans les épopées peules du Mâcina (Mali) et du Fouladou (Sénégal)" in Ursula Baumgardt and Jean Derive, Eds. *Paroles nomades. Écrits d'ethnolinguistique africaine*. Paris: Karthala, pp. 193–205.

Bâ, Alpha Oumarou. 2008. "L'initiation du héros dans l'épopée peule du Fouladou: ellipse de l'enfance et conversion" in J.-P. Martin, M.-A. Thirard, and M. White-Le Goff, Eds. *L'Enfance des héros. L'enfance dans les épopées et les traditions orales en Afrique et en Europe. Actes du Quatrième Congrès International du Réseau Euro-Africain de Recherches sur les Épopées*. Artois: Presses Université, pp. 121–129.

Bah, Ibrahima Kaba, and Bernard Salvaing. 1994. "À propos d'un poème en peul du Fouta-Djalon provenant de la collection d'Al-Hadj Omar Diallo (Bambeto)." *Islam et sociétés au sud du Sahara*. Décembre, pp. 123–138.

Bah, Ibrahima Kaba, and Bernard Salvaing. 2005. "Le Commentaire du Coran, texte écrit par Cerno Muhammadu Ludaajo Dalabaa (Guinée)" in Ursula Baumgardt and Jean Derive, Eds. *Paroles nomades. Écrits d'ethnolinguistique africaine*. Paris: Karthala, pp. 153–175.

Baumgardt, Ursula. 2001. "La Fille difficile peule (Cameroun)" in Veronika Görög-Karady and Christiane Seydou, Eds. *La Fille difficile. Un conte-type africain*. Paris: CNRS Éditions, pp. 65–80.

Baumgardt, Ursula. 2002. "De la répétition dans l'épopée peule" *Littérales* 29, Université de Paris X-Nanterre: Centre des Sciences de la littérature, pp. 73–92.

Baumgardt, Ursula. 2003. "Représentations de l'espace dans la littérature orale" in J. Vion-Dury, J.-M. Grassin, and B. Westphal, Eds. *Littérature et espaces*. Limoges: PULIM, pp. 499–506.

Baumgardt, Ursula. 2008a. "La performance" in Ursula Baumgardt and Jean Derive, Eds. *Littératures orales africaines. Perspectives théoriques et méthodologiques*. Paris: Karthala, pp. 49–75.

Baumgardt, Ursula. 2008b. "La littérature orale n'est pas un vase clos" in Ursula Baumgardt and Jean Derive, Eds. *Littératures orales africaines. Perspectives théoriques et méthodologiques*. Paris: Karthala, pp. 243–269.

Baumgardt, Ursula. 2008c. "Pour une théorie de la littérature orale" in Ursula Baumgardt and Jean Derive, Eds. *Littératures orales africaines. Perspectives théoriques et méthodologiques*. Paris: Karthala, pp. 383–431.

Baumgardt, Ursula. 2008d. "Variabilité et création" in Ursula Baumgardt and Jean Derive, Eds. *Littératures orales africaines. Perspectives théoriques et méthodologiques*. Paris: Karthala, pp. 77–101.

Baumgardt, Ursula with Mélanie Bourlet. 2010. "De la référentialisation spatiale en littérature orale: l'exemple des contes peuls du Cameroun et du Sénégal." *Journal des Africanistes* 79(2): 263–284.

Bourlet, Mélanie. 1999. "Les figures féminines dans un corpus de contes *haal-pulaar* du *Fuuta-Tooro* (Sénégal). Vol. 2. *Textes, Mémoire de DREA*. Paris: INALCO.

Bourlet, Mélanie. 2005a. "Entre écriture et oralité. *Silaamaka e Pullooru* de Yero Dooro Jallo" in Ursula Baumgardt and Jean Derive, Eds. *Paroles nomades. Écrits d'ethnolinguistique africaine*. Paris: Karthala, pp. 207–221.

Bourlet, Mélanie. 2005b. "La littérature peule contemporaine: caractéristiques et enjeux." *Études littéraires africaines* 19, Littérature peule. Paris: Karthala, pp. 34–43.

Bourlet, Mélanie. 2007. "Poésie *pulaar* et politique au Sénégal et en Mauritanie dans les années 70 et 80." *Littératures, savoirs et enseignements. Actes du colloque de l'APELA 2004*. Bordeaux: PUB.

Bourlet, Mélanie. 2008a. "L'oralité de la poésie de Bakary Diallo. État d'une recherche en cours." *Études littéraires africaines* 24, *La question de la poésie*. Paris: Karthala, pp. 25–30.

Bourlet, Mélanie. 2008b. "Littératures en langues africaines et développement. L'exemple peul au Sénégal et en France" in Henri Tourneux, Ed. *Langues, cultures et développement*. Paris: Karthala.

Bourlet, Mélanie. 2009. "Émergence d'une littérature écrite dans une langue africaine: l'exemple du poulâr (Sénégal/Mauritanie)" (Dissertation). Paris: INALCO.

Boyd, J. 1989. *The Caliph's Sister: Nana Asma'u 1793–1865, Teacher, Poet and Islamic Leader*. London: Frank Cass.

Dalil, A.O. 1988. *Mbooku, poésie peule du Diamaré*. Paris, L'Harmattan.

Dalil, A.O. 2004a. *Daado l'orpheline et autres contes du Fouta Djallon de Guinée*. Paris: L'Harmattan.

Dalil, A.O. 2004b. *Le Fils du roi de Guémé et autres contes du Fouta-Djallon de Guinée*. Paris: L'Harmattan.

Eguchi, Paul K. 1982. "Daacol: Preisegesänge der Ful'be des Diamaré vorgetragen von Alhaji Buuba Gerdele." *Anthropos* 77(5–6): 775–830.

Eguchi, Paul K. 1983. "Marginal Men, Strangers and Wayfarers: Professional Musicians and Change Among the Peul of Diamaré (North Cameroon)." *Ethnomusicology* 27: 187–225.

Eguchi, Paul K. 1985. "Model, Variation and Performance. Ful'be Praise-song in Northern Cameroon" *Yearbook for Traditional Music*, pp. 88–112.

Eguchi, Paul K. 1994. *Fulfulde Tales of Northern Togo*. Kyoto: Shokado.

Eguchi, Paul K. 1996. *Fulbe Folktales of Northern Cameroon I: Stories Told by Baaba Zandu*. Kyoto: Nakanishi Printing Co.

Eguchi, Paul K. 1997. *Fulbe Folktales of Northern Cameroon II: Stories Told by Baaba Zandu*. Kyoto: Nakanishi Printing Co.

Eguchi, Paul K. 1998. *Fulbe Folktales of Northern Cameroon III: Stories Told by Baaba Zandu*. Kyoto: Nakanishi Printing Co.

Eguchi, Paul K. 2003. *Taali Fulb'e Aadamaawa bee Binuwoy (Contes peuls de l'Adamaoua et de la Bénoué)*. Tokyo:

362   URSULA BAUMGARDT

Institute for the Study of Languages and Cultures of Asia and Africa.

Erlmann, Veit and S. Adama. 1986. "Konu Rabe: A Fulbe mbooku song on Râbih b. Fadlallah." *Africana Marburgensia* 19(2): 79–94.

Gaden, H. 1935. "La vie d'El Hadj Omar, qaçida en poular de Mohammadou Aliou Tyam." *Travaux et mémoires de l'Institut d'Ethnologie* 21. Paris: L'Institut d'Ethnologie.

Humery, M.-E. 1997. "Facteurs et enjeux du développement écrit d'une langue africaine: le cas du mouvement pulaar au Sénégal (1960–1996)." *Mémoire de DEA d'Études africaines*. Paris: Université Paris I.

Jaany, M. 1989 [1986]. "Ngulloori" (The Town Crier). *Série pulaar* 10. Dakar: SIL.

Jah, A. 1998. *Booy Pullo*. Dakar: Ed. Papyrus GIE.

Jallo, Y.D. 2003. *Ndikkiri joom moolo* (Ndikkiri the Guitar Player). Dakar: ARED.

Joob, M.S. 1991. *En caltiima* (We Refuse). Paris: Binndi e jannde.

Joob, M.S. 2002. *Wullaango boolumbal* (Cry of the Kingfisher). Dakar: ARED.

Kulibali, B. 1982a. "Daarol Pennda e Dooro" (Pennda and Dôro's Story). *Binndi e jannde* 7. Paris: Binndi e jannde, pp. 41–59.

Kulibali, B. 1982b. "Koode men ne na nyaara" (Our Stars Are Shining). *Binndi e jannde* 8. Paris: Binndi e jannde, pp. 43–57.

Kulibali, B. 1986–1988. *Luhral* (Discord). Paris: Binndi pulaar 1, 2, 4.

Kulibali, B. 1991. *Nguurndam tumaranke* (An Immigrant's Life). Paris: Binndi e jannde (first edition 1981–1983).

Labatut, Roger. 1978. *Chants de vie et chants de beauté recueillis chez les peuls nomades du Nord-Cameroun*. Paris: Publications Orientalistes de France.

Lacroix, Pierre-François. 1965. "Poésie peule de l'Adamawa." *Classiques Africains* 3 and 4. Paris: Julliard.

Lebeuf, J.-P. and Pierre-François Lacroix. 1972. *Devinettes peules suivies de quelques proverbes et exemples d'argots (Nord-Cameroun)*. Paris: Mouton.

Mbaalo, T. 1982. *Wuuri ko maccu'do, maayi ko tumaranke* (Lived as a Slave, Died as a Runaway). Bordeaux: KJPF.

Ndiaye, Oumar. 2005. "Les Mutations du pékâne, chants épiques des pêcheurs du Foûta-Tôro (Sénégal-Mauritanie)" in Ursula Baumgardt and Jean Derive, Eds. *Paroles nomades. Écrits d'ethnolinguistique africaine*. Paris: Karthala, pp. 221–229.

Njaay, S.N. 1993. *Mbaggu Lenyol* (The People's Drum). Dakar: Publifan.

Njaay, S.N. 2001. "Bakkari Jallo winndiino kadi e pulaar" (Bakary Diallo also wrote in pulaar). *Lasli/Njëlbéen* 26: 4.

Pondopoulo, Anna. 1996. "La construction de l'altérité ethnique peule dans les écrits de Louis Léon César Faidherbe." *Cahiers d'études africaines* 143(XXXVI-3): 421–441.

Pondopoulo, Anna. 2002. "À la recherche d'Henri Gaden (1867–1939)." *Islam et sociétés au sud du Sahara* 16: 7–34.

Saar, I. 1983. "À propos de Dia et de ses lettrés au XIXe siècle." *Annales de l'Université d'Abidjan*, série I (Histoire), Vol. XI: 119–135.

Saar, I. 2000a. *B'okki*. Dakar: Ed. Papyrus GIE.

Saar, I. 2000b. *Kartaali nib'b'e* (Nighttime Sobs). Dakar: Ed. Papyrus GIE.

Sek, M.A. 1992. *B'ii tato* (Child of Three Fathers). Paris: Binndi e jannde.

Sek, M.A. 1995. *Tenngaade* (Straw Hat). Mantes-la-Jolie: KJPF.

Sek, M.A. 2003a. *Dono Wod'aab'e* (Heir of the Wodâbé). Mantes-la-Jolie: KJPF.

Sek, M.A. 2003b. *Nganygu gid'li* (Love and Hate). Mantes-la-Jolie: KJPF.

Seydou, Christiane. 1977a. "La devise dans la culture peule: évocation et invocation de la personne" in Geneviève Calame-Griaule, Ed. *Langage et cultures africaines. Essais d'ethnolinguistique*. Paris: Maspero, pp. 187–264.

Seydou, Christiane. 1982. "Comment définir le genre épique? Un exemple: l'épopée africaine." *Journal of the Anthropological Society of Oxford* 13(1): 84–98.

Seydou, Christiane. 1993. "Unité et diversité du monde peul à travers sa production littéraire: quelques aperçus" (Unity and Diversity of a People: The Search for Fulbe Identity) in Paul K. Eguchi and V. Azarya,

Eds. *Senri Ethnological Studies* 35 (Osaka), pp. 163–179.

Seydou, Christiane. 1994. "Du mariage sauvage au mariage héroïque" in Veronika Görög-Karady, Ed. *Le Mariage dans les contes africains.* Paris: Karthala, 85–134.

Seydou, Christiane. 1999. "Expression poétique et conscience linguistique." *Faits de langue* 13. Oral, écrit: formes et théories. 57–76.

Seydou, Christiane, Geneviève Calame-Griaule, Veronika Görög-Karady, Suzanne Platiel, and Diana Rey-Hulman. 1984. "De la variabilité du sens et du sens de la variabilité" in Veronika Görög-Karady, Ed. *Le Conte. Pourquoi? Comment?* Paris: Éditions du CNRS, pp. 201–226.

Storbeck, F. 1920. "Ful-Sprichwörter aus Adamaua, Nord-Kamerun." *Zeitschrift für Eingeborenen Sprachen* 10: 2106–2122.

CHAPTER 19

FROM *VOLKSKUNDE* TO THE "FIELD OF MANY NAMES"

Folklore Studies in German-Speaking Europe Since 1945

Regina F. Bendix

In the twenty-first century, German-speaking scholars in the field once called *Volkskunde* have come to speak of their discipline as the *Vielnamenfach*, the "field of many names."[1] Looking at academic institute names from the northernmost Department for European Ethnology/*Volkskunde* (Kiel University) straight down to the Institute for Popular Cultures, Popular Literatures and Media (University of Zurich) and the Institute for Cultural Research and European Ethnology (University of Basle), from the easternmost Institute for European Ethnology (University of Vienna) and via the Institute for Empirical Culture Research (Tübingen University) to the westernmost Seminar for *Volkskunde*/European Ethnology and a Masters program in Cultural Anthropology/*Volkskunde* (Münster University), the profusion of names among some 20 degree granting university departments is indeed obvious.[2] One can read this variety as evidence of an intellectually vigorous community of researchers, engaged in their discipline's present with a profoundly reflexive awareness of their field's past. One might also ask what, in this profusion of minor and major differences in the name signals a common academic discipline. A joint history, rich in debate not least about the contours and the name of the discipline, evidence that the precursors of these institutes once were named *Volkskunde*, and being listed on the

A Companion to Folklore, First Edition. Edited by Regina F. Bendix and Galit Hasan-Rokem.
© 2012 John Wiley & Sons, Ltd. Published 2012 John Wiley & Sons, Ltd.

homepage of the *Deutsche Gesellschaft für Volkskunde* (German *Volkskunde* Society) as places offering training in the field are the strongest markers of a disciplinarity that is, however, porous and historically built on interdisciplinary foundations.

German-language folklore studies are practiced in three – or more – countries, and in a number of additional regions.[3] Political events of the twentieth century require that one may speak of more than three political entities to be considered. Rolling time back further, the division into territorial units is still more complex, with *Volkskunde* or at the very least folklore materials playing a considerable role in legitimizing a language and territory based German state emerging out of countless smaller states in the course of the nineteenth century, with scholars such as Johann Gottfried Herder or the Brothers Grimm contributing to the linking of folksong and tales with a common language and territory. Germany came into being as a nation state as late as 1871. During the Nazi régime, *Volkskunde* mutated into a handmaiden of national socialist ideology (Gerndt 1986; Dow and Lixfeld 1994). In 1949, as part of the aftermath of World War II, the country was divided into the Federal Republic of Germany (FRG), occupied by Britain, France, and the United States, and the German Democratic Republic (GRD) occupied by the Soviet Union. After 40 years of separate histories, the two states merged into one Federal Republic in 1990. The memory of what was the GDR, including scholarly achievements and differences to Western practice, asserts itself, if slowly, in the twenty-first century. Austria was, until 1918, the territorially vast, multilingual Austro-Hungarian empire and the emerging discipline of *Volkskunde* at the beginning of the twentieth century was strongly patterned by this geographic reach and linguistic diversity, even though politically, German national sentiment as well as numerous other ethno-nationalist movements in Austro-Hungary contributed strongly to the break-up of this empire and to the outbreak of World War I. After the politically turbulent Weimar Republic, Hitler, himself born in Austria, annexed in 1938 the country whose population was overwhelmingly in favor of germanophile politics. Echoes of this history reverberate in the Second Republic of Austria and hence in the practice of the discipline. Switzerland has maintained its territorial and democratic contours since Napoleonic times. The country maintained neutrality during World War I and II and prides itself for having staved off a much feared German takeover, though economic reasons may well have contributed to this good fortune. German speakers make up the largest part of the population, but the presence of overall four language groups shapes Swiss national identity which in turn has an impact on disciplinary practice.

The chapter will focus on the phases of reflection and deconstruction of knowledge making traditions in German-language *Volkskunde* since the Second World War, thus bypassing the story of the field's emergence, to an extent characteristic of folklore studies worldwide, starting with the pre-romantic fascination with the "Volk."[4] Looking at the postwar developments provides a mirror into the field's divergent formation, the socio-political role it plays in the respective countries, and offers an entry point for understanding the breadth of current preoccupations and the simultaneously diminished interest in the kinds of projects and characteristics of German-language folklore studies before the war.

Though no one has attempted to write this comprehensive history, one can without a doubt speak of a German-language *Volkskunde* going back into the nineteenth century, with adjoining interests in collection and mutual reception of scholarship across the national borders. This led, in 1904, to the foundation of the *Verband der Vereine für Volkskunde* (Alliance of *Volkskunde* Associations) intended to maintain communication between the national and regional *Volkskunde* associations. Re-founded in 1963, the German *Volkskunde* Society (*Deutsche Gesellschaft für Volkskunde* or dgv), serves rather more the profession within Germany, but some of the prewar legacies remained until the early twentieth century, including the effort to elect to the board a representative each from Austria and Switzerland. While Austrian and Swiss scholars flock to the congresses organized by the German association, this is less the case for the Austrian equivalent and the annual Swiss meeting sees practically only Swiss participation. There is a clear numerical dominance of German *Volkskunde* scholars and it is more likely that Germans occupy university chairs and assistantships in Austria or Switzerland than vice-versa. Yet the disciplinary profiles are far from identical and the postwar developments demonstrate the differences with which the discipline was re-established. I begin with Switzerland, turn then to the two Germanies that eventually, after 1989, became one again, and conclude with Austria. The sheer number of individuals working in the German-speaking field since 1945 forces me to limit mention to a few. Furthermore, I concentrate on scholars' engagement with the discipline overall and thus give less space, with few exceptions, to particular research topics.

SWITZERLAND

Though there were supporters of the Nazi regime in various segments of the Swiss population, Swiss folklore scholarship was not beset by the disturbing impact of fascist instrumentalizations of the field.[5] A state with four officially recognized languages – German, French, Italian and Romansh – represented an endorsement of diversity quite alien to the national socialist dogma of a pure race. While Swiss *Volkskunde* scholars such as Eduard Hoffmann-Krayer, co-editor of the problematic *Handbuch des deutschen Aberglaubens,*[6] clearly participated in a border-crossing German intellectual discourse, such vigorous scholarly contacts grew sparse. Nonetheless, German-language scholarship in *Volkskunde* remains dominant in Switzerland, with French language work focused more on folk literature, and ethnology or social anthropology a more strongly developed field and Italian language work represented by but a handful of scholars (who often also studied in the German-speaking north). The Italian part of the country, the Ticino, opened universities (with limited scope) only toward the end of the twentieth century, and there are no universities in the Romansh speaking area. In 1929, German scholars had begun to collect contributions for a territorially embracing Atlas of German *Volkskunde*, but as of 1937, the Swiss endeavored to compile their own Atlas of Swiss *Volkskunde* – with the results published from 1950–1995 – so as to demonstrate "the cultural intermingling" in their country and to show the importance of factors such as ecology, history, religion or economy on the endurance of cultural practices (Weiss 1950; Hugger 1992a: 23). Work on the atlas lead to first discussions of fieldwork methods: eight individuals, selected also for their psychological aptitudes, were trained for "exploration"; until 1942, they amassed answers to 150 questions in 387 places (Gyr 2001: 113).

Neutrality afforded a lasting sense of not sharing in the guilt that the German aggressor to the North had wreaked upon the world. Arguably, a lesser share in the guilt after World War II initially also led to a slower renovation of the disciplinary enterprise. For while chroniclers of the field in Switzerland make reference to the disciplinary revolution of the 1970s occasioned by the deconstruction of Nazi folkloristics, this revolution happened almost exclusively in the Federal Republic of Germany. In Switzerland, the first postwar decades saw a blossoming of archival endeavors and thorough documentation efforts aimed toward encyclopedic coverage, somewhat to the detriment of theoretical engagement and leaving "urgent problems of the time" up to "scholars from other disciplines" (Niederer 1970: 225). The Swiss Society of *Volkskunde*[7] initiated documentary endeavors and continues to act not just as the publisher of the society's journal, the *Schweizerisches Archiv für Volkskunde* (1897–), and an occasional publication series amounting to more than one hundred volumes, but fosters, among other activities, the still ongoing research on vernacular architecture, and, since 1942, the production of documentary films, initially under a title reflecting the salvage ethnography framework, "Dying Crafts."[8] The capacity to do so in such a small country with correspondingly few professional, dues-paying folklorists lies in the membership which since the society's inception has welcomed lay folklorists including medical doctors, lawyers, and other individuals from a generally well educated, urban elite among its ranks who continue to attend annual meetings and provide practical assistance in this scholarly society's endeavors. Marching the tight rope between scholarly rigor and popular interest is – for a field devoted to the understanding of everyday culture – a familiar phenomenon (Noyes 1999).[9] In Switzerland it was solved within the framework of this national society also through the second regular publication *Schweizer Volkskunde* (Swiss *Volkskunde*), published in German, French, and Italian. It offers shorter, topical articles and news of exhibits and events exclusively in Switzerland while the journal seeks international appeal. Such an associational arrangement carries legacies and assets which a recent volume reflects under the title *Vereintes Wissen* – which translates both as "joint" and "associational" knowledge (Schürch, *et al.* 2010). As there are at present only departments for the field at the universities of Zurich and Basle,[10] the society's membership from the non-German-speaking areas hovers around 10%.

Two other institutions maintain(ed) the link between the academic field and the public sphere – museums and education. As in all of German-speaking Europe, many local and regional museums were founded in the late nineteenth century, often under the name *Heimatmuseum* (homeland museum) and led by lay scholars acting at once as curators and promoters. They were and to an extent remain devoted to the safeguarding of traditional material culture, sought to educate younger generations about their cultural past within a rapidly modernizing polity, and offered educational entertainment to tourists. Collections of Swiss folk culture also made up a major part of the historical Swiss National Museum in Zurich, founded in 1897; the European collection of what today is called Museum of Cultures in Basle was initiated in 1904 and houses a big collection of folk material culture and art.[11] Compared to Scandinavian open air folklife museums, German-speaking Europe followed suit later. In Germany Cloppenburg opened in 1934, Detmold in 1971, and the Austrian Stübing near Graz in 1961. The Swiss open air museum in Ballenberg opened only in 1978, and endeavors to combine educational outreach with research. Again as in all of German-speaking Europe, *Heimatkunde* or "knowledge about the homeland" is a subject taught in primary schools through fourth or fifth grade, preparing for geography, history, and social science subjects taught in secondary school (Mitzlaff 1985). In most of Germany and Austria, the name for this subject has changed to *Sachkunde* (lit. "knowledge of things," meaning, however, social studies). In Switzerland, Heimatkunde has remained a colloquially used, non-pejorative term for this school subject. In some areas such as Bavaria and Austria, primary teacher education thus included *Volkskunde* as part of the university curriculum – thus also legitimizing chairs in *Volkskunde* contributing to such training. In Switzerland, university *Volkskundler* were not generally involved in teacher education or the production of general education materials, though teachers in training might take courses in the field as electives.

One reason for the appeal of the field in postwar Switzerland may be found in the first major German-language *Volkskunde* publication after World War II, Richard Weiss' *Volkskunde der Schweiz* (1946) – a work which also evened the path for a quiet paradigm shift. Weiss, installed in the newly established *Volkskunde* chair at the University of Zurich in 1946, has been called the symbolic figurehead of German-language *Volkskunde* for the first postwar decades, penning a work that "in its respectability proved the potential" of a badly damaged discipline and offering a point of reference for a new start away from the fascist abuse of the field for German *Volkskunde* scholars (Hugger 1992a: 24–25; Gyr 2009). In this work, Weiss offered a view of Swiss culture from a "moderate, functionalist perspective" (Niederer 1970:222), tinted by psychological assumptions and not averse to historical dimensions. Trained like many folklorists of the time in German language and literature, Weiss built strongly on his knowledge of Alpine pastoralists. However, he meant his characterization of Swiss folk culture to capture the population in its entirety, not one particular social class. He thus took a position against class-based definitions of the folk established in German *Volkskunde* in the first part of the twentieth century, where folklore was conceptualized, for instance, as "sunken cultural goods" which trickled down from the upper classes (Meier 1906) or as a primitive layer below the more civilized tiers of society (Naumann 1922). His compatriot, Hoffmann-Krayer, with a phonetics chair at Basle University, had been teaching Swiss dialect and *Volkskunde* since 1900, and had valiantly argued against such German positions and suggested, in turn, a concept of folk as *vulgus in populo* and gave space to individuals for shaping and reshaping the folk elements within a population (1902, 1903). Weiss' concept of folk culture embraced individuals of all walks of life whose habits were patterned by their participation in a functioning cultural organism.

Weiss, who died aged 55 in an accident in 1962, had focused on empirical research on Alpine life and economics in the Romansh-speaking Grisons (1941). His students continued an essentially present-day oriented approach free of romanticizing the folk. Arnold Niederer who succeeded Weiss in Zurich in 1964, began his research career with documenting communal labor among pastoral communities in the Valais (1956). He maintained and encouraged what proves a lasting Swiss research interest in Alpine cultures – the Alps are the most dominant geographic feature and hold ideological power: the Swiss locate their semi-mythological beginnings in 1291 in central, Alpine Switzerland, and structured their military defense during World War II in the so-called "reduit" – with strongholds and bunkers built into the Alps and a political rhetoric foregrounding the Alps as an insurmountable stronghold of the Swiss people since time immemorial. The Alps have, of course, also been the major tourist attraction for more than 200 years; most folklore scholarship on the Alps thus explores both the actual and symbolic resource potential of this characteristic geological feature (Leimgruber 2005a and b).

Niederer also emphasized comparative Alpine perspectives (1983), opened theoretically toward Anglo-American social anthropology and fostered interest in work with migrant laborer communities and the realm of non-verbal communication (Gyr 1980). Walter Escher arguably carried out the first fieldwork based study of an annual event with a functionalist perspective (1947), a path that broadened over the years into many case studies combining ethnography with historical analysis, with an ever stronger assertion of a constructivist lens (e.g., Bellwald 1997; Bendix 1985).[12] Some students of Weiss, most notably Rudolf Braun (1965), studied the transformation of folk culture in industrializing areas past and present.

The Basle institute was officially founded in 1961, but the first professor, Hans Trümpy, was appointed only in 1965. Though the Swiss *Volkskunde* society had its seat in Basle since the beginning of the century, and though Eduard Hoffmann-Krayer had given his influential inaugural lecture as a professor of German Studies on the topic of "*Volkskunde* as a Scholarly Discipline" in 1900 (1902), the field had remained in custody, so to speak, of German studies, history and classics. The classicist and folklorist Karl Meuli had resisted the establishment of *Volkskunde* as a separate field; once he relented, the institutionalization could proceed (Burckhardt-Seebass, n.d.). While Trümpy largely emphasized Swiss historical and narrative research topics, Robert Wildhaber as head of Basle's Swiss *Volkskunde* museum was an internationally well connected folklorist who published far more in the field of folk narrative, including a historic-geographic monograph (1955) than in material culture. He also edited the *International Folklore Bibliography* for many years.

Since 1968, folk narrative scholarship had a chair of its own in Zurich, affiliated with the *Volkskunde* department, and created specifically for Max Lüthi whose international renown was founded in his characterization of the European *Märchen* or folktale, published in German in 1947 (1986). He worked on folklore in literature, had reservations vis-à-vis formalism and structuralism and was more intrigued by Jungian psychoanalysis which manifested somewhat in his work on Swiss legends, carried onward by some of his students (e.g., Isler 1992). While Basle-trained Paul Hugger became Niederer's successor in Zurich, known particularly for editing a new handbook on Swiss folk culture[13], the German Rudolf Schenda took over the chair for "European Folk Literature" when Lüthi retired. Schenda's interests in the social, cultural, political and economic dimensions of narration beyond orality and beyond texts brought energy into this realm of research that has not ceased since, even though the chair had been vacant after his retirement in 1995 for 16 years.[14] He opened up questions in the realm of popular print literatures (1977) that have been carried further in particular by Ingrid Tomkowiak who has led the chair-less degree program, now called "Popular Literatures and Media" for more than a decade, followed topics of interest to Schenda (e.g., Tomkowiak 2002) and launched, along with her colleague Brigitte Frizzoni, a research area integrating traditional folk narrative research within the study of forms and media of entertainment at large (Frizzoni and Tomkowiak 2006). Schenda oversaw a comprehensive investigation of Swiss legend tellers and collectors; the work's subtitle – "studies on the production of folkloric history and histories from the sixteenth to the twentieth century" – points to the constructivist perspective he introduced into legend scholarship (Schenda and ten Doornkaat 1988). In another project he collaborated with a foundation for the elderly, collecting and preparing for publication life histories from Swiss individuals of diverse walks of life (Schenda and Böckli 1983).

Swiss *Volkskunde* increased in productivity and opened up toward ever broader topics in the late 1980s to mid 1990s, with Christine Burckhardt-Seebass becoming the first woman professor of *Volkskunde* in Basle and with Ueli Gyr taking the *Volkskunde* chair in Zurich.[15] Gyr contributed extensively to tourism research, continued Niederer's interest in nonverbal communication, broadened folkloristic lenses from folk art to Kitsch and explored urban forms of tradition making (cf. Muri 2010). Burckhardt-Seebass initiated disciplinary history with an eye toward questions of gender; she studied regional Swiss folk costume from the perspective of invented tradition, and reflected and redirected the legacy of the folk song archive and attendant scholarship a young John Meier had left behind in Basle when he returned to Germany in 1910 (e.g., Burckhardt-Seebass 1991; 1993). Walter Leimgruber who took over from Burckhardt-Seebass in 2001, continued this concern (Leimgruber et al. 2009), but also built critical reflection and new initiatives in the area of documentary film, and supported research in migration, and consumer culture. The perhaps most ambitious recent research endeavor in Switzerland headed by Leimgruber was the nationally funded research project "Culture and Politics: 'Volkskultur' between Scholarship, Cultural Practice and (Cultural-)Political Sponsorship." "Volkskultur" along with concepts such as "Volksmusik" remain heavily used within Swiss society such as in voluntary associations devoted to music, traditional dance, and costume but also as a resource in branding particular craft products and, last but not least, in the rhetoric of a powerful, conservative political party. The research team examines the construction and meaning of the term in different regional and local circles of practice as well as in mass mediated and sociopolitical contexts. The *Schweizerische Volkspartei* (Swiss People's Party) has been enjoying rising mass support with its anti-immigration platform and, among other things, its successful political initiative against the building of minarets in 2009. Scrutinizing the term Volkskultur is thus a present-day rather than a post-World War II concern. For the Swiss discipline of *Volkskunde*, the seeming closeness between Volkskunde and right-wing politics also has contributed to the change of institute names in Switzerland, where name-discussions were hardly an issue after World War II. The Volkskultur-project grew alongside Sabine Eggmann's discourse analytic examination of the culture-concept in German-language *Volkskunde* scholarship (2009). In their reflexive grappling with a term, its history, present meaning and popular appeal, Swiss folklorists thus work on their field's own political legacy and its entanglement with sociopolitical interests and milieus, and seek to differentiate between localized aesthetics and mass mediated amplifications labeled with this term. That they do so in cooperation and conversation with the groups, associations, and sponsors under study is, perhaps, still indicative of the closeness between professional and lay scholars characteristic of early *Volkskunde* days in Switzerland, but it also demonstrates an open approach to what has – particularly in Germany – been an uneasy grappling with manifestations of applied or public folklore since World War II (Bendix and Welz 1999).

THE GERMANIES

The end of World War II may have brought a new beginning, but it also entailed a massive clean-up of rubble on the ground and in the mind. During the first postwar years in what was now the Federal Republic of Germany, *Volkskunde* struggled to regain its bearings, not least with the support of the allies who oversaw de-nazification in all realms of German society, including universities. The first *Volkskunde* chair to be reopened in 1946 was at the University of Göttingen. Will Erich Peuckert had lost his university position during the Third Reich; to rebuild the discipline in Göttingen, he set aside his own more esoteric research interests in favor of core areas of study such as material culture and regional folklife (Jacobsen 2007). He argued that during the country's dark years, there had been two branches of *Volkskunde*, one that was tainted and guilty of collaboration, and one consisting of scholars who had steered clear of involvement and who had kept inquiry solid and uncompromised. Peuckert thus helped to prepare the ground for a return to endeavors that had been at the core of scholarly interest, in particular large projects. He himself wanted to continue where the builders of reference works had left off and began to compile an encyclopedia of legend (Fenske and Bendix 2009). Others assembled their energies to return to atlas projects – all under the assumption that mere data, even if gathered under National Socialism, would not be tainted. The only large scale project initiated during those initial decades that would survive was the *Encyclopedia of the Märchen* whose editorship had been offered to Peuckert's successor, folklorist Kurt Ranke, by one of the large, surviving publishing houses. Yet just as narrative research grew to be a more and more marginalized field within Volkskunde in subsequent decades, grand projects for which Germany had once been known internationally lost in luster and, with the exception of the Märchen-endeavor, turned into a burden rather than an intellectual asset. This, at least, was the tenor of a conference reevaluating such projects (Schmitt 2005). A turn toward folkloristic knowledge history has, however, succeeded in drawing insight from deconstructing the nature of knowledge production that led to the constitution of endeavors such as the Atlas of German *Volkskunde* (Schmoll 2009), folkloristic dialectology (Keller-Drescher and Tschofen 2009) and encyclopedic endeavors (Fenske 2010).

Elsewhere, de-Nazification created a vacuum. Some too heavily compromised professors did not return to teaching, and, fortuitous for German folkloristics, such a vacuum existed at the University of Tübingen. Here, a young scholar named Hermann Bausinger returned from the front and in a departmental landscape still in disarray. He wrote a dissertation on everyday narration, followed by a habilitation on folk culture in a world of technology (1986 [1961]) – both works that revealed new directions for German *Volkskunde* that would eventually take hold, despite being heavily embattled at first.[16]

Scholars at other institutes faced yet different conditions; the heterogeneity of viewpoints with regard to disciplinary continuity and change and the occasional deep rifts in disciplinary outlook are a result of the first two postwar decades. Parallel to the student revolts of the 1960s, this led to harsh confrontations about Volkskunde's past. Such disciplinary rebuilding efforts did not make the past vanish; indeed, if one follows research on memory and trauma, the war and the holocaust leave their traces in successive generations. The field of *Volkskunde*, hardly institutionalized before World War II, had been one of the disciplines chosen to shore up national socialist ideology, and Peuckert's two-field hypothesis is hard to maintain. The politics of folklore played a role in the emergence of a German state during the nineteenth century. Declaring German folk songs and tales an authentic testimony to the longevity of a German repertoire and printing them contributed to the transformation and unification of a geographic and political entity which had consisted of many small states (Bendix 1997: 25–44). Early folkloristic thought and vocabulary was thus readily available as were scholarly paradigms fuelling an interest in mythological origins of a nation in search of unity (Bausinger 1965; Kaschuba 2006: 70–78).

A look back at the field's beginning, further explains its ready instrumentalization. Due to its traditions in philology and literature (the lineage of the Brothers Grimm), in early cultural statistics, history, and politics (with Wilhelm Heinrich Riehl a major protagonist) as well as early psychology, classics, and archeology, the field had been taught out of those fields, in particular German language and literature. Focused folkloristic interest had unfolded in the late nineteeenth century, with various organizations and publications. During National Socialism, two institutions, the SS *Ahnenerbe* and *Amt Rosenberg*, were created; they contributed to research seeking to legitimize German cultural supremacy (Dow and Lixfeld 1994; Gerndt 1987). The Verband für deutsche Volkskunde, an umbrella organization for all scholarly associations of *Volkskunde*, founded in 1904 and led by John Meier since 1911, intended to steer clear of political influence, but there is evidence to the contrary.

As is typical of totalitarian states, all fields of German knowledge production were affected, albeit in different ways. *Volkskunde* scholars were, however, earlier by decades than many others in confronting their fascist past. While not the entire field was or is participating in the unrelenting uncovering of compromised projects, publications, and institutional histories of the Third Reich period, there has been a steady stream of works on Nazi *Volkskunde* as well as National Socialist everyday culture and its impact since the mid-1960s. The topic is firmly ensconced in the introductory curriculum and special seminars on the Nazi-involvement of the discipline continue to be offered at most institutes to this date. The discipline's self-scrutiny finds its parallel in German public memorialization of sites of fascist atrocities such as concentration and labor camps, funded by the federal government and private foundations. German folklorists also participate in the research and exhibition work in such initiatives; the bi-annual *Volkskunde* congress of 1989 was devoted to "Remembering and Forgetting" (Bönisch-Brednich and Brendich 1991) and demonstrated an overall commitment of the field to keep this difficult history alive. One might argue, indeed, that of all the countries that lived through totalitarian dictatorships during the twentieth century, Germany is the most thorough in keeping this memory and the guilt associated with it alive in education and the public sphere.

In *Volkskunde*, the confrontation and sense of responsibility and guilt associated with the role of the field during the Nazi reign also fostered what James Dow and Hannjost Lixfeld subtitled "a decade of theoretical confrontation, debate and reorientation" (1986).[17] The "coming to terms with the past" (Stein 1987) began in earnest in the mid-1960s, not least fueled by the specific contours of the student revolts in West Germany.[18] It culminated in a working conference in 1970 where some members of the discipline agreed on a course of research: "*Volkskunde* analyzes the transmission of cultural values (including their causes and the processes which accompany them) in their objective and subjective form. The goal is to contribute to solving sociocultural problems" (cited after Dow and Lixfeld 1986: 2). The meeting and what it stands for are referred to simply as "Falkenstein," after the meeting site; the typescript protocol exists in every department library (Brückner 1971). The sharp disagreements of those days left deep marks in the field as practiced in West Germany. There were defenders of an older canon interested in building on the empirical data compiled for the *Volkskunde* Atlas and developing the field in a predominantly historical direction, seeking insight into historical contours of folk culture through the interpretation of archival records and material culture. This approach was championed by Günter Wiegelmann, at the time president of the dgv, and others keen on defining folk culture as something located in the past and accessible largely through historical methods or else as a field capable of tracing regional cultural variation in preparation for historical interpretation, a central goal of the folk atlas endeavors. Others embraced a more empirically based and present oriented path, leaning at least in the initial years heavily on social science methodologies. Research in folk narrative, once a corner stone of German *Volkskunde* in the lineage of the Brothers Grimm, has not recovered from the increasing marginalization incurred during those decades. There were internationally respected narrative scholars such as Lutz Röhrich in Freiburg who also directed the German Archive of Folksong or Kurt Ranke who succeeded in bringing the Encyclopedia of the *Märchen* to Göttingen, the only grand folklore project successfully established in postwar Germany – a country internationally known for its "grand projects" (Schmitt 2005). Yet the only narrative scholar actively participating in the negotiation of the discipline's new directions during those turbulent years was Hermann Bausinger. He was also the only narrative scholar introducing innovative dimensions into this subfield; with his dissertation (1952), he broadened the lens to include everyday narrating in the generic canon and thus also built a bridge between narrative analysis and fieldwork methods, as "just so" narrating naturally opens perspectives into all kinds of subjects and subcultures of the present. Albrecht Lehmann expanded into the realm of autobiographical narrating (1983) and Bausinger along with his then assistant Rudolf Schenda also expanded narrative research to look at popular and mass literature as well as reading practices. Yet a look across the curriculum taught at the numerous German programs today will reveal that the breadth of approaches to verbal arts are taught at best sporadically and only at very few departments, and if it were not for the popular literature and media division in the above mentioned Zurich department, there would not be any systematic into this realm of everyday life anywhere in the German-language discipline.

The debate in Falkenstein built on a number of smaller meetings and publications whose titles were indicative of the contributors' will for a major paradigm shift. Conference proceedings such as *Populus Revisus* (Bausinger 1966) or *Abschied vom Volksleben* (Farewell to Folklife; Geiger 1970) gathered within them critical reflection of core terms, as did the Festschrift *Kontinuität?* (Continuity? Bausinger and Brückner 1969). This volume was published for Hans Moser, one of the first *Volkskunde* scholars who, along with Karl-Sigismund Kramer, employed source criticism to establish solid historical evidence for various folk traditions and thus set a methodological standard against the vague and mythologizing folk history so typical of the pre-World War II and Nazi *Volkskunde* era. The most powerful disciplinary revision emanated, not surprisingly given the time of his coming of age in scholarship, from Hermann Bausinger whose explanation for the fascist take-over of the field (1965) and critical engagement with disciplinary terminology (e.g., 1969) laid the foundations for what, at his institute in Tübingen, came to be newly called Empirical Culture Research (*Empirische Kulturwissenschaft* or simply EKW). The rift within the discipline emanating from those years has not been completely overcome.

The bi-annual congresses of the *Deutsche Gesellschaft für Volkskunde* (dgv[19]) continued to bring everyone together, and the topics chosen – from "*Heimat* and Identity" to "Children's Culture," "Face-to-Face Communication and Mass Media" to "Pictures, Books, Bytes," "Workers and Folklife" to "The Industrialized Human,"

"Culture Contact, Culture Conflict," "Violence and Culture" and "Borders and Differences" – show a continuity of fields of interest with changing foci of what are generally micro case studies. Trained scholars following different methods and pursuing *Volkskunde* in occupational settings from universities to museums and public practice participate. In the off-years, the society organizes working meetings concerned with issues of particular relevance to disciplinary practice at universities.[20] Falkenstein had, in effect, been the first of these working meetings which have addressed questions of methodology, conceptual questions, and the changing situation of the field within the academy. A look at textbooks published since World War II shows the Tübingen school to be leading in this realm. Directing the course of the Tübingen institute since the late 1950s, Hermann Bausinger had set a new course with his 1961 publication *Folk Culture in a World of Technology* (1986).[21] His introductory text *Volkskunde* (1971) remains unparalleled in narrating the history of the field and unfurling the essential research areas associated with that history.[22] In 1978, Bausinger and his former students Utz Jeggle, Gottfried Korff, and Martin Scharfe offered a further introductory text focused on the four concepts culture, everyday life, historicity, and identity (Bausinger *et al.* 1999 [1978]). Ingeborg Weber-Kellermann had moved from East Berlin to Marburg in 1960 where she became professor in 1968; she published a slender introduction tracing the field's dual emergence from philology and social sciences (1969). In compiling *Grundriss der Volkskunde* (2001), the Göttingen-based Rolf W. Brednich assembled authors from different intellectual corners of the field, asking them to each characterize a particular aspect of the field's canon (2001). Aside from an introductory volume on the different methodological approaches of the field (Göttsch and Lehmann 2007, or. 2001) and various more locally directed entry-level offerings for freshmen, there have been almost only Tübingen based or trained scholars venturing major introductions to the field: Wolfgang Kaschuba's introduction to European Ethnology (2006 [1999]) was also the first post-reunification single-author attempt to capture the field in its entirety. Kaspar Maase and Bernd Jürgen Warneken, both based in Tübingen, assembled an introductory volume with the telling title "Netherworlds of Culture" (2003) which also signaled the field's commitment to marginal populations. Warneken, finally, authored a sophisticated introduction with the title "The Ethnographies of Popular Cultures" (2006) – signaling the selective but by no means full adaptation of Birmingham Cultural Studies into some German folkloristic research. A separate path was walked by Ina-Maria Greverus, who had started as a folk narrative researcher but subsequently instituted an anthropological paradigm at the Frankfurt department which is also evident in her introduction to the field (1978). Her student and successor Gisela Welz has endeavored to intellectually bridge more strongly with the discipline both as practiced in Germany and the United States (Welz 1996; Bendix and Welz 1999).

The Falkenstein revolution occurred roughly 20 years after World War II. A decade and a half later, more conservative voices sought disciplinary self-assessment and assurance, with a conference taking place to trace the discipline's institutional formation (Brückner and Beitl 1983); in the mid-1980s, the discipline's National Socialist past finally took center stage at a German Volkskunde meeting (Gerndt 1987); the topic was no longer owned by the radical Tübingen voices; it had become, in this second wave, everyone's business. By contrast, more than twenty years have passed since German reunification in 1990, but a coming to terms with both the divided disciplinary history and the former East's very speedy incorporation into the West is slow in coming. Reunification had brought a fast evaluation of all fields of science and scholarship in the former GDR through committees largely led by West Germans. While there were initiatives launched to provide junior GDR scholars with opportunities for further qualification, the larger percentage of professorships was given to scholars trained in the West. Much as in the post World War II years, scholars' biographies were scrutinized; however, this time it was not allies but fellow Germans who did the judging. This process may throw a shadow but it could also lead to productive reflexive histories of the process of both political and scholarly unification.[23]

The division into East and West Germany, with military occupation by the Soviet Union in the East and by Britain, France, and the United States in the West, had an impact on how the discipline *Volkskunde* could continue. The initial goals of the occupational powers were the same: denazification and disabling of war time industries. Yet living conditions and scholarly opportunities were far more dire in the, eventually, one-party socialist East under the control of an economically suffering Soviet Union. In the democratic West, as of 1948, more resources and opportunities were available for building up what would become one of the strongest postwar economies. During 40 years of separate statehood, 1949–1989, the scholarly contacts between the two scientific communities were limited, and the foci of research correspondingly differed.[24] There were and remain far more university *Volkskunde* departments in the West than in the East. During the GDR years, academic Volkskunde was concentrated almost completely in Berlin. After 1989, new opportunities were created in the East, most notably at the University of Jena in Thuringia and, as a non-teaching research endeavor, the Institute for the History and Culture of Saxony, founded and funded by the State of Saxony since 1997. At the University of Rostock, finally, space was given to the research archive of Richard Wossidlo, a language and folklore specialist of Mecklenburg, who died in 1939. Yet compared to the profusion of departments in the West and the many specialized sections within the re-founded, at first only West German dgv,[25] the balance between East and West was and remains uneven. And much as Gingrich observes for the case of GDR ethnology (2005: 147), the work carried out in *Volkskunde* during those decades went mostly unnoticed in the pre-1989 FDR and has only recently come to be reconsidered, predominantly by scholars at universities in the former East (Neuland-Kitzerow and Scholze-Irrlitz 2010).

The fact that research had to be conducted within parameters openly outlined as part of a political program contributed to the skeptical view of research done during the GDR period on the part of "West" scholars. After reunification, one West German *Volkskunde* scholar chose to publish a diatribe against the integration of former GDR scholars and their "sympathizers" in the West (Brückner 1990), yet behind this single voice denouncing the proximity of (Western) socialist and (Eastern) communist scholarship, additional layers wait to be unpacked. In the West, there was a broadly shared sentiment concerning the "imprisonment" of fellow-Germans in an authoritarian state, and given the wall, the border guards, and the prohibition on travel to the West for most East Germans, there was a grim, factual basis for it. Yet there were scholars who returned to East Berlin by conviction. Mitchell Ash (2002, 2010) has observed that the relationship between research and politics has been entwined in ever shifting, complex ways all through the twentieth century, with either side constituting a resource for the other, and folkloristics illustrates this in just about every region discussed in the present volume. Though there was a (West) German call for "*Volkskunde* scholarship free of ideological influence" (Heilfurth 1962), such work is *de facto* impossible. All work is ultimately constituted in part through the historically and socially embedded interests of the researcher. Working within the universities of the present, it is business models that govern intellectual productivity; ironically they often demand three to five-year plans as did the much decried communist regimes: the ideology is different, the personal freedom not jeopardized, but the academic freedom remains constrained.

In the turbulent first years after the war, Adolf Spamer, who had held the first German *Volkskunde* chair in 1936 in Berlin, tried to build *Volkskunde* institutions in the Soviet Zone of Germany, both in Dresden and within the Academy of Sciences in East Berlin. There was little attention given to compromising National Socialist allegiances and activities, and Spamer revived the research paradigm of the 1920s and 1930s, seeking continuity with endeavors such as the German Atlas project of which he had been a part. Spamer's intellectual and institutional efforts were of limited success (Brinkel 2009: 146–150; Scholze and Scholze-Irrlitz 2001). In 1946, the Finno-Ugric scholar and folklorist Wolfgang Steinitz returned to East Berlin. Born of Jewish ancestry in Breslau (Wroclaw in what is now Poland) and a member of the communist party, he had fled in 1934, first to Leningrad and later to Stockholm. A party member but not a political hardliner, Steinitz was given a position within the rebuilding of the German Academy of Sciences. He had the capacity to navigate the increasingly complex institutional bureaucracy and under his leadership, a new, though institutionally and numerically not very large, *Volkskunde* could be developed in the GDR. In 1949, the Soviet Occupational Zone turned into the GDR and in 1952, the new state also formulated science policies which asked scholarly institutions to formulate plans of research appropriate to the goals set by the state overall (Brinkel 2010: 147).

Another scholar who moved to East Berlin was Wolfgang Jacobeit. He had trained in Göttingen with Will Erich Peuckert, the first postwar *Volkskunde* chair. In 1956, Jacobeit accepted Steinitz' invitation to develop work in material culture at the German Academy Institute of *Volkskunde*. Jacobeit was intrigued by Steinitz' reconceptualization of the folk as the working classes and tried to contribute to it in his comparative study on shepherding (1961). Steinitz had set a new course in his study and edition of "German Folk Songs of Democratic Character" (1955–1962) – a work that included songs of protest and dissent and continues to find favorable reception up to the present. Due to his position between the two Germanies (and being one of the few allowed to travel West), Jacobeit's voice and work remained heard in the West; in that capacity, he has continually pointed to the intellectual rigor and social contribution of GDR *Volkskunde*, without embellishing the problems of working within the one-party state under Soviet influence (e.g., Jacobeit 2000a and b). His students have contributed to making work conducted during the GDR era known (Scholze and Scholze-Irrlitz 2001). A number of ongoing projects carried out predominantly at the Humboldt University in Berlin but also at the University of Jena likewise seek to shed light on the nature and content of university instruction, museum work (Neuland-Kitzerow and Scholze-Irrlitz 2010). The integration of what was eventually termed the "Ethnography Section" in the History Division of the German Academy of Sciences secured continued work within *Volkskunde*, and the former *Volkskunde* found itself joined with the former Völkerkunde. A collectively conceived multi-volume work on the history and culture of German working peoples was one of the outcomes of this orientation (Weissel 1972; cf. Jacobeit 2000b). Another initiative, attributed to Jacobeit, brought forth an unspoken joint East-West research endeavor focused on village-society. As Kaschuba put it, *Volkskunde* "returned to the village," not with the totalizing romantic gaze in search of a wholesome folk, but rather with the tool kit of social scientific methods and interested in tracing the path of villagers into a capitalist and bourgeois lifeword (*Lebenswelt*). The East German academy of sciences undertook the Magdeburger Börde project, and West German scholars documented the path of Swabian villagers into a civilizing modernity. While planned independently, comparable research interests fueled the endeavor and conversations between Berlin and particularly the Tübingen researchers flowed into the projects (Kaschuba 2003: 20).[26] Correspondingly, these village studies were a quite different endeavor from the community studies that had been instigated elsewhere in West Germany under the auspices of the American allies (Davidović-Walther and Welz 2010).

(East)Berlin remained the major training ground for future GDR scholars and practitioners, yet there was also a correspondence degree course available. University projects were initially very strong in their historical orientation, concentrating on "working people" broadly conceived, rather than either *Volk* or *Ethnos*. The name of the journal *Demos* (from the Greek for "community") signaled this broadened perspective that was international in scope; *Demos* began publication of information on ethnographic research and ended only in 2001. The *Deutsches Jahrbuch für Volkskunde* was published from 1955–1969, yet compared to the abundance of journals and book series in West Germany, the limitations in numbers and possibilities is evident. Similarly, in contrast to scholars in the FRG, opportunities for major museum exhibitions were rare and thus stand out in the recollections of those involved in them (Brinkel 2010). There were, however, initiatives in the realm of what was termed "lay art" (*Laienkunst*) intended to broaden the base of documentation and exhibition of GDR culture in a participatory fashion (Kaschuba 2003:17; Kühn 2007).[27] There were also performing folklore ensembles, the most prominent and enduring one in the Lausitz, an area settled by the Sorbs, one of two official ethnic minorities in Germany (the other being in East Frisia), but to a far less pronounced degree than in many of the other Eastern Bloc countries. The Sorbian Institute, founded by the (East) German Academy of Sciences in 1951 was continued under a new funding structure after reunification and emphasizes research in language and ethnicity (e.g., Tschernokoshewa 2000 Tschernokoshewa and Mischek 2009).

The Berlin institute is the only one where East and West needed to find immediate means to unite and even there coming to terms with the divided disciplinary past took time. Wolfgang Kaschuba held the first chair of European Ethnology after reunification at Berlin's Humboldt University. He has carefully navigated the intellectual as well as human legacy; numerous individuals were in Berlin who trained or were in training at the former GDR Institute for Ethnography. There was staff facing scrutiny over their participation in aspects of GDR politics. In the course of nearly two decades, Kaschuba fostered rapprochement through a number of symposia (e.g., Steinitz and Kaschuba 2006 and research projects recovering some aspects of the GDR *Volkskunde* history (e.g., Kühn 2007), all the while building a new politically engaged and internationally connected Institute for European ethnology.

In his much quoted, early postwar assessment, sociologist Heinz Maus argued for the complete erasure of *Volkskunde* as the field had been so disasterous in its ideological support of German fascism (Maus 1946). Yet *Volkskunde* continued and did so in two countries separated by the iron curtain. German scholarship lost a great deal of its international standing as after World War II, and the German language no longer served as an academic lingua franca in Europe. Though internationalization is a priority item in many of the above mentioned five-year plans, it is still far more likely that new theoretical trends are translated and germanified so as to amplify German intellectual discourse than for German contributions to reach an international audience. A prime example is the German folklorism debate (Bendix 1988): begun in 1962, it presaged components of what would enter international cultural research decades later under the heading of "invention of tradition" and, another two decades onward, "ethnicity incorporated" without ever being cited.

Austria

A look at what the revived *Österreichische Zeitschrift für Volkskunde* published in its first post-World War II volumes shows nary a change from the last issues before the war. Contributions focused on examples from the established canon – customs, folk sayings, folk plays, songs with notation, masks and folk narratives from specific locales or regions. Herbert Nikitsch would name such pieces "folklore in Austria" rather than "Austrian folkloristics" (2005: 80) and establishing the latter has proven a complex undertaking. The leading article in the first postwar issue was written by Viktor Geramb who held the *Volkskunde* chair in Graz from 1931 to 1954 (with a ten year hiatus during the war). His title, "Concerning Our Tasks," was expanded to "Current State and Tasks of Austrian *Volkskunde*" in the lead-contribution in the second volume of the journal that appeared in 1948. Leopold Schmidt wrote this second piece; he would become the most productive Austrian *Volkskunde* scholar in the postwar decades.[28] Schmidt saw the task in cleansing the field of Pan-Germanic and National Socialist premises (Nikitsch 2006: 257). While this appeared to be possible in the first years of the young second republic, the return to university teaching of a number of heavily compromised scholars, such as, at Vienna University, in 1954 Richard Wolfram, a National Socialist of the first hour and stripped of his *venia legendi* in 1945, would indicate a rather gentle cleansing.

As of the mid-1980s, some Austrian scholars contributed to the second phase of laying bare the genesis and workings of Nazi folkloristics (Bockhorn 1988; Jacobeit, *et al.* 1994). Yet while this confrontation with the past led to major paradigm shifts among many German colleagues, most Austrian folklorists "rather endured than brought about" the transformation. Reinhard Johler made this observation while evaluating the general sense of the Austrian field as one of being "the little brother" of German *Volkskunde*, a sense instilled not least by the northern neighbor's own rhetoric.[29] Johler saw in such submission to the German branding of the discipline as practiced in Austria also the danger of neglecting what were characteristics of the Austrian research tradition (Johler 1989: 26).

To understand the development of Austrian *Volkskunde*, one needs to look back beyond World War II.[30] As an outcome of the First World War, the large Austro-Hungarian empire collapsed. The empire, ruled by the Habsburgs, had assembled within its borders a multitude of people and languages. This very multitude was one of the major reasons for the outbreak of the war, as ethno- and linguistic nationalisms had been smoldering for half a century or more. The beginning of Austrian *Volkskunde* reflects this dual, tension laden history. The ethnographic lineage celebrated the *Vielvölkerstaat* ("many peoples' state"). Partially grown from the state-serving cultural statistics, protagonists within this lineage were interested in documenting the cultural difference assembled within the realm and collecting material culture as evidence for the cultural riches of the dual monarchy. There was imperial pride and hope inscribed in this venture: Crown prince Rudolf of Habsburg himself initiated such a documentary, descriptive endeavor a few years before his suicide in 1889, and expressed his hope that ethnography might illustrate just how well the multitudes of peoples coexisted in the Austrian empire (Johler 1998; Bendix 2003; Johler and Fikfak 2008). The First World War would prove him wrong, but in 1894, Michael Haberlandt and Wilhelm Hein founded the Austrian association of Volkskunde, in 1895, a museum and scholarly journal were added, both existing to this day. Until the fall of the dual monarchy, this group enjoyed imperial support and protection and pursued the comparative study of folklore and material culture (Nikitsch 2005: 83).

What traces remain(ed) in Austrian everyday culture of this multi-peoples configuration and its borders with – not only – the Ottoman empire, are but scantily researched.[31] This is attributable, undoubtedly, to the powerful force of the second intellectual lineage of Austrian *Volkskunde*. For, within the university, one can trace a Pan-Germanic nationalism that also shaped the folklore curriculum since the late nineteenth century (Bockhorn 1988). It was this lineage that proffered intellectual fuel for coming political events. Politically, the first Austrian republic, a territorially tiny state compared to what the empire had been, was shaken by political and economic upheaval which lasted until 1933. Then a fascist government established itself and – after a brief civil war – imposed a new order. Though fascist in orientation, the leadership attempted to maintain independence from Germany, but in 1938, Hitler's army entered the country, and National Socialists declared Austria's accession and integration into Germany as the *Ostmark* (Berger 2007: 54–190). There is ample testimony that many Austrians welcomed the annexation and that the new German province participated in the holocaust and other war atrocities. But after World War II, the 1938 military take-over was used as grounds for easing allied measures. Although, like Germany, occupied by the allies, there was no division into two countries, and what is perhaps more troubling, individuals implicated in National Socialist endeavors were pursued with less zeal in Austria.[32]

Some folklorists implicated in National Socialist research achieved reinstatement and even prestige not least due to social networks not broken by war's end. This was the case in academic institutions as well as organizations devoted to folklore documentation, archiving and preservation. Right after the war, the relatively mild inspection of Nazi pasts kept or returned such figures into office, and for less implicated or not at all implicated folklorists, the issue of how to rebuild institutions and projects entailed negotiating social relations with those individuals. Other than Leopold Schmidt in Vienna who saw a need to draw clear boundaries, efforts to avoid conflict and find ways to not dwell on that particular aspect of the past were the rule. This was coupled with the late inspection of disciplinary paradigms and their contribution to ideological perversions. Thus one finds more than one Festschrift for Richard Wolfram who was blessed with a long life and likely contributed, through his unapologetic adherence to research interests not far from those of prewar years, to the delay in Austrians' grappling with *Volkskunde's* entanglement in Nazism. Aside from the Austrian contributions in the massive volume by Jacobeit *et al.* (1994), a conference in Salzburg in 1994 devoted itself to Volkskunde and custom preservation during National Socialism. In the last decade, leadership in confronting aspects of this past has emanated from the Austrian Museum of Folk Culture in Vienna. In 2004, the life and the collection of Eugenie Goldstern, deported and killed in 1942, was honored in a special exhibition (Österreichisches Museum für Volkskunde 2004). In 2009, the museum organized a conference on Jewish *Volkskunde* combining work on the complex history of this focus in the German-language discipline and seeking bridges into the international field of Jewish Studies (Johler and Staudinger 2010).

Compared to the reverberations of the lost empire, the discomfort with the longevity of germanophile and nativist sentiment of the first half of the twentieth century has led to more disciplinary inspection and deconstruction (e.g., Johler *et al.* 1995), including introspection on how Austrians "learned" to be Austrians in the course of the twentieth century (Johler and Tschofen 2001). The empire, though, may ultimately have had a deeper impact on the nature of Austrian scholarly practice and spatial imagination. An analysis of German-language folklorists' use of this language in print would likely reveal that none are as gifted in the use of understatement and irony as are the Austrians. One might venture to see in this an inheritance of the kind of social and linguistic aesthetic typical of what is jocularly referred to as Kakanien – a belletristic label for the old empire.[33] Irony is a means of creating distance, and in the context of Volkskunde scholarship, it may signal a measure of being next rather than a part of the society that one's field is studying.

A 1992 volume on Austrian *Volkskunde* institutions (Beitl 1992) shows a rich landscape of associations, museums and state level research and public service endeavors. In universities, a total of three *Volkskunde* chairs had been reestablished after World War II. The histories of these institutes at the universities of Graz, Innsbruck, and Vienna are unique and intermeshed with local circumstance and the characteristics of individuals shaping the first decade until 1955, when the allies discharged Austria into self-administered statehood (cf. Jacobeit, Lixfeld and Bockhorn 1994: 579–616). The fortunes of the discipline appear nonetheless most strongly shaped by institutions located in the capital Vienna. The Vienna university institute eventually reappointed Richard Wolfram, the only Volkskundler who had had a research post of his own within the *Ahnenerbe*, the scientific branch of Himmler's *Schutzstaffel* or SS. But it was Leopold Schmidt who left the stronger mark on the discipline's development. He directed the Austrian museum of Folk Culture which traditionally is also the seat of the *Wiener Verein für Volkskunde* and holds the editorship of the Austrian *Volkskunde* journal. Schmidt wrote numerous programmatic pieces, specialized works on folk art and folk plays, and a history of the discipline in Austria (1951). Perhaps his most effective move to put distance between an ideologically still compromised *Volkskunde* at the university and research located within the present was the founding of the *Institut für Gegenwartsvolkskunde* (institute for present day *Volkskunde*) in 1973, closed in 1992. Part of the Austrian Academy of Sciences, this institute was also the launching pad for research engaged in working-class and urban culture. Helmut Fielhauer is generally credited with introducing these research fields in both historical and ethnographic dimensions as well as with their introduction in exhibitionary work (Fielhauer 1982), though reference is invariably also made to the influence of Hermann Bausinger in providing the impetus to broaden the field's scope beyond the peasant heritage. As he died relatively young, Fielhauer's line of work was truncated and numerous publications in his honor signal the sense of loss on the part of his colleagues. Yet this sense of loss – echoing that long gone empire – constituted an occasional baseline in Austrian research well into the late twentieth century.

In the last two decades, though, transformations and vigorous intellectual labor are evident in all three institutes. Innsbruck has expanded a profile dedicated to narrative research on legend and the supernatural to include, with Ingo Schneider's work, new communicative media as well as work on tourism and critical heritage studies – fittingly so, given the Alpine location. In Graz, a tradition of political engagement going back to Geramb has taken an entirely different turn with Elisabeth Katschnig-Fasch's research projects, heavily influenced by Pierre Bourdieu, focused on lower classes' living conditions past and present; most recently a new emphasis on mobility studies has been added. In 1994, Konrad Köstlin arrived in Vienna to chair the department; his orientation to the field (Köstlin 1997) brought forth not simply the name change to European Ethnology, but an outlook decidedly European in orientation, with vigorous new ties particularly to East European colleagues, teaching exchanges and conferences grappling not least with the political transformation of 1989 (Köstlin *et al.* 2002).

THE PRESENT AND FUTURE

The Bologna accords in European higher education, with signatories joining since 2001, will without a doubt greatly influence the institutional future of folklore studies and related fields in Europe in general. The Bologna process seeks to replace nationally diverse degree programs with comparable bachelor's and master's degrees and thus improve student mobility Europe-wide and enhance the comparability of qualifications. The structural effects of this political endeavor leave their mark particularly on small fields that have to enter into cooperation with neighboring disciplines so as to be able to offer degree programs at all. Merging with fields such as religious studies, social anthropology, or archaeology in the realm of instruction will, in the long run, most definitely leave an imprint on the further course of the "field of many names." While the implications of this institutional shift can, at this point in time, not be fully seen yet, its dynamics may have an effect on the workings of the discipline – both on the micro level of universities, museums, or research institutes and on the macro level of changing political interests. A successful degree program based on the merging of disciplines may bring forth future scholars grounded in something other than a disciplinary lineage leading straight back to Herder and the Brothers Grimm, a lineage within which the course-setting works of great intellects of the postwar decades flow together with impulses from cultural, religious and media studies, cultural sociology, material culture studies and communications.

How come that in such a time of transformation members of the discipline do not at least make an effort to overcome the surely unique state of practicing a field of many names? After the name discussion during Falkenstein, no agreement could be reached and it appears that, coupled with the lingering discomfort with the label *Volkskunde*, many prefer to accept the differences. A recognizable, joint disciplinary history, three national flag ship journals and three national associations, all with the term *Volkskunde* in them, constitute the ties that bind. But attending to the micro-climate of every institution within which the field is taught and practiced is apparently considered more important than having one shared name.

Yet aside from major institutional transformations and questions of nomenclature, disciplinary development depends to a great extent on individual minds and research interests within specific political contexts, something I have tried to demonstrate with this chapter. Despite shared language, divergent political and spatial histories have brought forth related yet nonetheless particular research trajectories. What is common is that working in folklore-related fields in German-speaking Europe requires the capability to grapple in an engaged and reflexive fashion with a complex disciplinary past and to go forward vigorously into an academic and societal future shaped by an increasing interdisciplinary breadth of cultural research.

ACKNOWLEDGMENTS

Many thanks to the following individuals who provided me with information and recent work not yet broadly available: Ernst Huber, Basel, Reinhard Johler, Tübingen, Wolfgang Kaschuba, Berlin; Walter Leimgruber, Basel; Leonore Scholze-Irrlitz, Berlin and Johann Verhovsek, Graz; Christoph Bock assisted with library research; for comments on earlier drafts I am indebted to Michaela Fenske, Andre Gingrich, and Galit Hasan-Rokem.

NOTES

1   Unless otherwise noted, translations from the German are by the author. The term "Vielnamenfach" was in oral circulation in the 1990s and came first into print in 2001 in Göttsch and Lehmann's method's handbook (2007, 2nd edition).

2   Zimmermann (2005) offers the most up-to-date survey of university institutes; the implementation of the Bologna reform has altered some local structures, but research emphases are relatively stable.

3   Occasional publications as well as museums working with German can be found in the bilingual areas Alsace (France), South Tyrol (Italy) as well as Luxembourg; these will, however, not be further considered in this chapter.

4   Numerous works recount aspects of the history of the study of German folklore, though few are in English. The most apt remains Bausinger (1971); Brednich (2001) contains three chapters covering the unfolding of the field from the Enlightenment to the twentieth century; Kaschuba (2006: 20–111) gives a succinct account of the development. Nikitsch (2006) valuably reconstructed the beginnings of the Austrian Volkskunde society since the late nineteenth century. Brückner and Beitl coordinated a conference with excerpts on institutional foundations of the field in this geographic area up to World War II (1983). Bendix (1997) looks at this history through the very specific lens of authenticity's role in legitimating the field. Other English language work has focused specifically on the Herderian period (e.g., Wilson 1973) or on specific scholars or aspects of scholarship such as the Brothers Grimm and their work (Zipes 2003). There is, however, no account destilling major stages of development as there is for the sister discipline Völkerkunde or social anthropology (Gingrich 2006). Similarly, there exists no comprehensive overview of the many journals and book series. Almost every Volkskunde institute has a book series within which dissertations, excellent master theses as well as occasional conference proceedings are published; many institutes publish, in addition, journals or yearbooks. Via the homepage of the Deutsche Gesellschaft für Volkskunde (http://www.d-g-v.org/, accessed December 2, 2010), the individual institutes can, however, be located and most of them offer links to their publications.

5   The core works concerned with coming to terms with national socialism consistently focus on Germany and Austria exclusively (e.g., Gerndt 1987, Dow and Lixfeld 1994, Jacobeit et al. 1994).

6 Abbreviated as HdA, this reference work (Bächtold-Stäubli and Hoffmann-Krayer 1927–1942) constitutes at once a treasure trove of information on folk belief in German-language areas and beyond, and a testimony to the kind of intellectual fallacies on which Nazi-Volkskunde would build. Despite scholarly criticism of the decontexualized presentation of data unfit for a proper historical and social understanding of belief practices, the renowned publisher Walter de Gruyter opted to reprint the work in 1975, with a new introduction by Christoph Daxelmüller in 1987, again in 2000 and 2002 and as a digital edition in 2006, asserting publisher's privilege to earn an income off popular interest despite deepest scholarly reservations.

7 The *Schweizerische Gesellschaft für Volkskunde* maintains a web site also featuring the society's publications: http://www.volkskunde.ch/ (accessed December 28, 2010).

8 Niederer (1970) offers a detailed assessment of the institutional set-up as well as intellectual achievements of the postwar decades in all language areas.

9 The notion of "lay scholars" cannot be properly explored here, though it should at the very least be clarified that a lay-status more often than not entails also a highly educated status. Medical doctors, for instance, have in many countries been interested participants in folkloristic documentation, and their impact on ethnographic fields along with teachers and lawyers ought to be examined just as carefully as that of missionaries, priests, and pastors.

10 A third professorship of Volkskunde had been created in 1946 at Berne University for the dialect, name and proverb researcher Paul Zinsli, but after his retirement in 1971, the chair was left vacant. In Neuchatel, Pierre Centlivres carried out various field projects within Switzerland, but as in all French-Swiss departments, the ethnological direction was closer to social anthropology (cf. Gyr 2001). Christian Giordano, trained in cultural anthropology (formerly Volkskunde) in Frankfurt, holds an ethnology chair at the bilingual (German and French) university in Fribourg.

11 The museum was founded in the mid-nineteenth century and the European collection blossomed into a separate branch called "Swiss Museum of *Volkskunde*" in 1944–1996; the head of this branch usually taught courses on material culture and folk art at the Basle university institute, thus ensuring some foundational training for future curators at the many small *Heimat*-museums; the whole museum was renamed "Museum of Cultures" in 2001 and amalgamated the Swiss division within the totality of the ethnological collection; cf. "Museum der Kulturen" http://www.mkb.ch/en/museum.html (accessed January 2, 2011).

12 Bendix 1985 and 1989 contain assessments of Swiss postwar scholarship on both annual events and voluntary associations fostering custom and ritual.

13 The three volume work (Hugger 1992b) appeared in German, Italian, and French and was geared to satisfy both scholarly standards and reach a broader interested reading public.

14 With the renaming of the Zurich institute into "Institute of popular cultures," the number of students has increased consideraably. By 2013 there are to be three professorships, with urban Volkskunde and technology expert Thomas Hengartner having taken over the chair of Ueli Gyr in the fall of 2010 and a renewed search for a Schenda succession under way at present.

15 The variety of themes within the publication series *Zürcher Beiträge zur Alltagskultur, Populäre Literaturen und Medien,* and *Culture [kylty:r]. Schweizer Beiträge zur Kulturwissenschaft,* signal the breadth of research carried out in both institutes during the last decades.

16 In Bausinger *et al.* (2006), transcriptions of conversations on Bausinger's career and its relationship with German Volkskunde have been made available.

17 Dow and Lixfeld (1986) selected some 19 articles from that decade for translation into English; many though not all of them represent the transformative direction that German Volkskunde took at the time and their volume can thus be highly recommended as a compendium of original texts that flesh out the brief summaries offered in this survey.

18   Compare Gingrich (2005: 145–6) who observes such a dynamic also for German-language ethnology, though the movement to lay open the Nazi past was clearly far more pronounced in Volkskunde.

19   The Volkskunde society chooses the small letters dgv, so as to mark the difference between itself and the DGV, the scholarly society of the German-language ethnologists, "Deutsche Gesellschaft für Völkerkunde."

20   On the web site of the "Deutsche Gesellschaft für Volkskunde" (http://www.d-g-v.org/, accessed March 1, 2011), the link "Veröffentlichungen" provides publication details on all postwar conferences and working meetings.

21   The most interesting reflection on the postwar building of West German folkloristics is a volume recording conversations with Bausinger at the occasion of his seventy-fifth birthday (Bausinger *et al.* 2006). Bausinger and other scholars, thinking regarding the name changes in the field are recorded in a published sequence of talks (Bendix and Eggeling 2004).

22   Excerpts of this introductory history have been included in the 1986 translation *Folk Culture in a World of Technology.*

23   The Berlin-Brandenburg Academy of Sciences has held occasional talks, workshops, and conferences on the broad topic of scholarship and reunification. Kocka and Mayntz edited a first proceedings (1998), a blog informs about a follow-up event in 2009: "Über das Blog Wissenschaft und Wiedervereinigung" http://www.scienceblogs.de/wissenschaft-und-wiedervereinigung/about.php (accessed March 1, 2011).

24   My summary of East German Volkskunde builds on Kaschuba and Scholze-Irrlitz (2010), Neuland-Kitzerow and Scholze Irrlitz (2010) and Teresa Brinkel's not yet published dissertation (2010), written under the auspices of a German-Israeli grant comparing the emergence of Volkskunde in the new states of the GDR and Israel, directed jointly by Galit Hasan-Rokem and myself. One chapter of Brinkel's dissertation has appeared in English (2009); the dissertation follows the shifting institutional base of the field and outlines areas of research emphasis based on oral history interviews and archive materials.

25   The web site of the dgv (http://www.d-g-v.org/, accessed March 1, 2011), assembles links to all presently existing departments and institutions, the sections or working groups of the dgv, completed and ongoing masters theses and doctoral theses, as well as conference dates.

26   Numerous volumes with the series title *Untersuchungen zur Lebensweise und Kultur der werktätigen Dorfbevölkerung in der Magdeburger Börde* began to be published as of 1978 by Akademie Verlag in Berlin; the Kiebingen studies in Tübingen began with Jeggle (1977) and, perhaps more in dialogue than continuation, Kaschuba and Lipp (1982).

27   There would be a good opportunity here to compare this GDR institution for instance with the folklore and folk music related work of the Public Works Administration during the New Deal in the United States (cf. chapter by Haring and Bendix in this volume).

28   The table of contents of all three incarnations of the main Austrian journal can be viewed on OEZV Index_01.pdf (http://www.volkskundemuseum.at/uploads/pdf/OEZV/OEZV-INDEX_01.pdf, accessed October 26, 2010).

29   Verhovsek (2010), though not using the same metaphor, traces a similarly slow and subdued transformation.

30   Contributors in Jacobeit *et al.* (1994: 397–630) describe Austrian history in more detail than is possible here.

31   Gingrich (1998) has coined the term frontier orientalism for examining everyday traces of the Muslim presence in Austria.

32   Paradigmatic for this less thorough examination of the political past is the case of Kurt Waldheim. He served as fourth secretary general of the United Nations (from 1972–1981) and only during his (successful!) electoral campaign to become Austria's

prime minister in 1985 was he forced to remember aspects of his past as officer within the German *Wehrmacht* (Berger 2007: 379). Similarly, the transformation of the Pan-German Freedom Party into a right-wing populist movement built undoubtedly on continuities in political sentiment. Party leader since 1986, Jörg Haider harnessed anti-immigrant sentiment, and easily recovered from political set-backs involving his positive mention of Nazi policies. When he successfully led his party to a coalition government in 1999, European leaders briefly shunned Austria and froze diplomatic relations, as it was the first though sadly not the last success of a right-wing extremist party into national leadership.

33   In his novel *Der Mann ohne Eigenschaften*, with publication beginning in 1930, Robert Musil coined the name Kakanien with ironic intent from k.and.k. for *kaiserlich-königlich* (imperial-royal), an abbreviation often used in Austrian daily life as an adjective for matters of official relevance to the Habsburg government and administration.

REFERENCES

Ash, Mitchell. 2002. "Wissenschaft und Politik als Ressourcen für einander" in Rüdiger vom Bruch and Brigitte Kaderas, Eds. *Wissenschaften und Wissenschaftspolitik.* Stuttgart: Steiner, pp. 32–51.

Ash, Mitchell. 2010. "Wissenschaft und Politik: eine Beziehungsgeschichte im 20. Jahrhundert." *Archiv für Sozialgeschichte* 50: 11–46.

Bausinger, Hermann. 1952. "Lebendiges Erzählen" (Dissertation), Tübingen University.

Bausinger, Hermann. 1965. "Volksideologie und Volksforschung. Zur nationalsozialistischen Volkskunde." *Zeitschrift für Volkskunde* 61: 177–204.

Bausinger, Hermann, Ed. 1966. "Populus Revisus. Beiträge zur Erforschung der Gegenwart." *Volksleben* 14. Tübingen: Tübinger Vereinigung für Volkskunde.

Bausinger, Hermann. 1969. "Zur Kritik der Tradition. Anmerkungen zur Situation der Volkskunde." *Zeitschrift für Volkskunde* 65: 232–250.

Bausinger, Hermann. 1971. *Volkskunde. Von der Altertumsforschung zur Kulturanalyse.* Darmstadt: Carl Habel.

Bausinger, Hermann. 1986. *Folk Culture in a World of Technology.* Trans. Elke Dettmer. Bloomington: Indiana University Press (German original 1961).

Bausinger, Hermann and Wolfgang Brückner, Eds. 1969. *Kontinuitätä Geschichtlichkeit und Dauer als volkskundliches Problem.* Berlin: Erich Schmidt Verlag.

Bausinger, Hermann, Utz Jeggle, Gottfried Korff, Martin Scharfe, Kaspar Maase. 1999 [1978]. *Grundzüge der Volkskunde.* Darmstadt: Wissenschaftliche Buchgesellschaft.

Bausinger, Hermann, Wolfgang Kaschuba, Gudrun König, Dieter Langewiesche and Bernhard Tschofen. 2006. *Ein Aufklärer des Alltags: Der Kulturwissenschaftler Hermann Bausinger im Gespräch.* Wien: Böhlau.

Beitl, Klaus, Ed. 1992. *Volkskunde Institutionen in Österreich.* Wien: Selbstverlag des Österreichischen Museums für Volkskunde.

Bellwald, Werner. 1997. *Zur Konstruktion von Heimat. Die Entdeckung lokaler "Volkskultur" und ihr Aufstieg in die nationale Symbolkultur. Die Beispiele Hérens und Lötschen (Schweiz).* Sitten: Kantonales Museum für Geschichte und Ethnographie.

Bendix, Regina. 1985. *Progress and Nostalgia. Silvesterklausen in Urnäsch, Switzerland.* Berkeley: University of California Press.

Bendix, Regina. 1988. "Folklorismus: The Challenge of a Concept." *International Folklore Review* 6: 5–15.

Bendix, Regina. 1989. *Backstage Domains: Playing "William Tell" in Two Swiss Communities.* Bern: Peter Lang.

Bendix, Regina. 1997. *In Search of Authenticity.* Madison: University of Wisconsin Press.

Bendix, Regina. 2003. "Ethnology, cultural reification, and the dynamics of difference in the Kronprinzenwerk" in Nancy M. Wingfield, Ed. *Creating the Other: Ethnic Conflict and*

Nationalism in the Habsburg Central Europe. London; Berghahn, pp. 149–165.

Bendix, Regina and Tatjana Eggeling. 2004. "Namen und was sie bedeuten" *Beiträge zur Volkskunde in Niedersachsen* 19. Göttingen: Schmerse.

Bendix, Regina and Gisela Welz. 1999. *Cultural Brokerage and Public Folklore: Forms of Intellectual Practice in Society.* Special issue. *Journal of Folklore Research* 36(2 and 3).

Berger, Peter. 2007. *Kurze Geschichte Österreichs im 20. Jahrhundert.* Wien: Facultas Verlag.

Bockhorn, Olaf. 1988. "Zur Geschichte der Volkskunde an der Universität Wien. Von den Anfängen bis 1939" in Albrecht Lehmann and Andreas Kuntz, Eds. *Sichtweisen der Volkskunde.* Berlin: Reimer, pp. 63–83.

Bönisch-Brednich, Brigitte and Rolf Wilhelm Brednich, Eds. 1991. *Erinnern und Vergessen.* Vorträge des 27. *Deutschen Volkskundekongresses 1989.* Göttingen: Schmerse.

Braun, Rudolf. 1965. *Sozialer und kultureller Wandel in einem ländlichen Industriegebiet (Züricher Oberland) unter Einwirkung des Maschinen- und Fabrikwesens im 19. und 20. Jahrhundert.* Erlenbach: Rentsch.

Brednich, Rolf W., Ed. 2001 [1988]. *Grundriss der Volkskunde. Einführung in die Forschungsfelder der Europäischen Ethnologie.* 3rd revised and enlarged edition. Berlin: Reimer.

Brinkel, Teresa. 2009. "Institutionalizing Volkskunde in Early East Germany." *Journal of Folklore Research* 46: 141–172.

Brinkel, Teresa. 2010. "Volkskundliche Wissensproduktion in der DDR. Zur Geschichte eines Faches und seiner Abwicklung" (Unpublished Dissertation), University of Göttingen, Germany.

Brückner, Wolfgang, Ed. 1971. "Falkensteiner Protokolle" (mimeographed typescript), Frankfurt.

Brückner, Wolfgang. 1990. "Volkskundler in der DDR." *Bayerische Blätter für Volkskunde* 2: 84–111.

Brückner, Wolfgang and Klaus Beitl, Eds. 1983. *Volkskunde als akademische Disziplin. Studien zur Institutionenausbildung.* Wien: Verlag der Österreichischen Akademie der Wissenschaften.

Burckhardt-Seebass, Christine. n.d. "Zur Geschichte des Seminars. Online text on 'Seminar'" http://pages.unibas.ch/kulturwissenschaft/content/Komponenten/Seminar/Sites/Geschichte.html (accessed February, 1 2011).

Burckhardt-Seebass, Christine. 1991. "Spuren weiblicher Volkskunde: ein Beitrag zur schweizerischen Fachgeschichte des frühen 2." *Jahrhunderts. Schweizerisches Archiv für Volkskunde* 87: 202–224.

Burckhardt-Seebass, Christine et al., Eds. 1993. *...im Kreise der Lieben": eine volkskundliche Untersuchung zur populären Liedkultur der Schweiz.* Basel: Helbig und Lichtenhahn.

Davidović-Walther, Antonia and Gisela Welz 2010. "Community Studies as an Ethnographic Knowledge Format." *Journal of Folklore Research* 47: 89–112.

Dow, James and Hannjost Lixfeld, Eds. 1986. *German Volkskunde: A Decade of Theoretical Confrontation, Debate, and Reorientation.* Bloomington: Indiana University Press.

Dow, James and Hannjost Lixfeld. 1994. *The Nazification of an Academic Discipline. Folklore and the Third Reich.* Bloomington: Indiana University Press.

Eggmann, Sabine. 2009. "'Kultur'-Konstruktionen. Die gegenwärtige Gesellschaft im Spiegel volkskundlich-kulturwissenschaftlichen Wissens" (Transcript) Bielefeld.

Eggmann, Sabine and Beatrice Tobler. 2002. "Das Ästhetische in der Alltagskultur. Zur Einführung in die Festschrift für Christine Burckhardt-Seebass." *Schweizerisches Archiv für Volkskunde* 98: 3–5.

Escher, Walter. 1947. "Dorfgemeinschaft und Silvestersingen in St.Antönien. Ein Beitrag zum Problem Gemeinschaft und Brauch." *Schriften der Schweizerischen Gesellschaft für Volkskunde* 31. Basel: Krebs.

Fenske, Michaela. 2010. "The Undoing of an Encyclopedia: Knowledge Practices within German Folklore Studies after World War II." *Journal of Folklore Research* 47: 51–78.

Fenske, Michaela and Regina Bendix. 2009. "Hinter verschlossenen Türen. Akteure und Praxen der Wissensaushandlung am Beispiel des 'Handwörterbuchs der Sage.'" *Berliner Blätter* 50: 27–48.

Fielhauer, Helmut, Ed. 1982. *Die andere Kultur: Volkskunde, Sozialwissenschaften und Arbeiterkultur. Ein Tagungsbericht.* Wien: Europaverlag.

Frizzoni, Brigitte and Igrid Tomkowiak, Eds. 2006. *Unterhaltung: Konzepte – Formen – Wirkungen.* Zürich: Chronos.

Geiger, Paul, Ed. 1970. "Abschied vom Volksleben." *Untersuchungen des Ludwig Uhland Instituts* 27. Tübingen: Tübinger Vereinigung für Volkskunde.

Gerndt, Helge, Ed. 1987. "Volkskunde und Nationalsozialismus." *Münchner Beiträge zur Volkskunde* 7. München: Münchner Vereinigung für Volkskunde.

Gingrich, Andre. 1998. "Frontier Myths of Orientalism: The Muslim World in Public and Popular Cultures of Central Europe" in *Baskar, Bojan and Borut Brumen, Eds. Mediterranean Ethnological Summer School, Piran/Pirano Slovenia 1996. MESS.* Vol. II., Ljubljana, pp. 99–127.

Gingrich, Andre. 2005. "The German Speaking Countries. Raptures, Schools, and Non-traditions. Reassessing the History of Sociocultural Anthropology in Germany" in: F. Barth, A. Gingrich, R. Parkin and S. Silverman, Eds. *One Discipline, Four Ways. British, German, French, and American Anthropology.* Chicago: University of Chicago Press, pp. 59–153.

Göttsch, Silke and Albrecht Lehmann, Eds. 2007 [2001]. *Methoden der Volkskunde: Positionen, Quellen, Arbeitsweisen der europäischen Ethnologie.* Berlin: Reimer.

Greverus, Ina-Maria. 1978. *Kultur und Alltagswelt: eine Einführung in Fragen der Kulturanthorpologie.* München: Beck.

Gyr, Ueli. 1980. "'… mit Bezug auf ….' Einblicke in die Forschungs- und Lehrtätigkeit des Volkskundlers Arnold Niederer. Ein Zwischenbericht zu seinem 65. Geburtstag, zugleich ein Beitrag zum Standort der Zürcher Volkskunde." *Schweizerisches Archiv für Volkskunde* 76: 3–76.

Gyr, Ueli. 2001. "Feldforschung in der Schweizer Volkskunde. Eine forschungsgeschichtliche Skizze" in Prijo Korkiakangas and Elina Kiuru, Eds. *An Adventurer in Ethnology.* Etnografia 4. Publications of Department of Ethnology, University of Jyväskylä. Jyväskylä: Gummerus Printing, pp. 110–128.

Gyr, Ueli. 2009. "Richard Weiss – Standorte und Werk einer volkskundlichen Symbolfigur." *Schweizerisches Archiv für Volkskunde* 105: 65–80.

Heilfurth, Gerhard. 1962. "Volkskunde jenseits der Ideologien." *Hessische Blätter für Volkskunde* 54: 9–28.

Hoffmann-Krayer, Eduard. 1902. *Die Volkskunde als Wissenschaft.* Zürich: Arnberger.

Hoffmann-Krayer, Eduard. 1903. "Naturgesetze im Volksleben?" *Hessische Blätter für Volkskunde* 2: 57–64.

Hugger, Paul. 1992a. "Zu Geschichte und Gegenwart der Volkskunde in der Schweiz" in Hugger, Paul, Ed. *Handbuch der schweizerischen Volkskultur* 1. Basel: Schweizerische Gesellschaft für Volkskunde, pp. 15–33.

Hoffmann-Krayer, Eduard. 1992b. *Handbuch der schweizerischen Volkskultur. Leben zwischen Tradition und Moderne. Ein Panorama des schweizerischen Alltags.* 3 Vols. Basel: Schweizerische Gesellschaft für Volkskunde.

Isler, Gotthilf. 1992. Die Sennenpuppe. *Eine Untersuchung über die religiöse Funktion einiger Alpensagen.* 2nd edition. Basel: Gesellschaft für Volkskunde.

Jacobeit, Wolfgang. 1961. *Schafhaltung und Schäfer in Zentraleuropa bis zum Beginn des 20. Jahrhunderts.* Berlin: Akademie Verlag.

Jacobeit, Wolfgang. 2000a. *Von West nach Ost – und zurück: Autobiographisches eines Grenzgängers zwischen Tradition und Novation.* Münster: Westfälisches Dampfboot.

Jacobeit, Wolfgang. 2000b. "Mehr als ein Questionnaire" in Rüdiger Hohls and Konrad H. Jarausch, Eds. *Versäumte Fragen. Deutsche Historiker im Schatten des Nationalsozialismus.* München: DVA. Also available online under "Review Symposium http://hsozkult.geschichte.hu-berlin.de/rezensio/symposiu/versfrag/sympos.htm (accessed December 22, 2010).

Jacobeit, Wolfgang, Hannjost Lixfeld, and Olaf Bockhorn. 1994. *Völkische Wissenschaft. Gestalten und Tendenzen der deutschen und österreichischen Volkskunde in der ersten Hälfte des 20. Jahrhunderts.* Wien: Böhlau.

Jacobsen, Johanna Micaela. 2007. "Boundary Breaking and Compliance: Will-Erich Peuckert and the 20th Century

German Volkskunde" (PhD Dissertation, University of Pennsylvania).

Jeggle, Utz. 1977. *Kiebingen, eine Heimatgeschichte. Zum Prozess der Ziviliations in einem schwäbischen Dorf.* Tübingen: Tübinger Vereinigung für Volkskunde.

Johler, Birgit and Barbara Staudinger. 2010. "Vorwort: Ist das jüdisch?" *Die Jüdische Volkskunde in historischer Perspektive.* Special issue. *Österreichische Zeitschrift für Volkskunde* LX/V (3+4): 369–274.

Johler, Reinhard. 1989. "Der 'große' und der 'kleine Bruder.' Anmerkungen zum Verhältnis 'österreichischer' und 'deutscher' Volkskunde und umgekehrt." *Kuckuck* 1: 24–26.

Johler, Reinhard. 1998. "… die Lesewelt auffordernd zu einer Wanderung durch weite, weite Lande, zwischen vielsprachigen Nationen, inmitten stets wechselnder Bilder: zur Geschichte des Monumentalwerkes Die österreichisch-ungarische Monarchie in Wort und Bild, dargestellt am Beispiel des 1898 erschienen Bandes Galizien" in Klaus Beitl, Ed. *Galizien. Ethnographische Erkundung bei den Bojken und Huzulen in den Karpaten. Kittseer Schriften zur Volkskunde* 9. Wien: Ethnographisches Museum Schloss Kittsee, pp. 43–55.

Johler, Reinhard, Herbert Nikitsch, and Bernhard Tschofen. 1995. 2Schönes Österreich. Heimatschutz zwischen Ästhetik und Ideologie." *Kataloge des Österreichischen Museums für Volkskunde* 65. Wien: Österreichisches Museum für Volkskunde.

Johler, Reinhard and Jurij Fikfak, Eds. 2008. *Ethnographie in Serie. Zu Produktion und Rezeption der Österreichisch-ungarischen Monarchie in Wort und Bild.* Veröffentlichungen des Instituts für Europäische Ethnologie der Universität Wien 28. Wien: Institut für Europäische Ethnologie.

Johler, Reinhard, Herbert Nikitsch and Bernhard Tschofen. 2001. "'Gelernte Österreicher.' Ethnographisches zum Umgang mit nationalen Symbolen" in Beate Binder, Wolfgang Kaschuba, and Peter Niedermüller, Eds. *Inszenierungen des Nationalen.* Wien: Böhlau, pp. 186–208.

Kaschuba, Wolfgang. 2003. "Splitter, Facetten, Erinnerungen: Versuch einer Subjektiven Bestandesaufnahme." *Berliner Blätter* 31: 15–25.

Kaschuba, Wolfgang. 2006 [1999]. *Einführung in die Europäische Ethnologie.* München: C.H. Beck.

Kaschuba, Wolfgang and Carola Lipp. 1982. *Dörfliches Überleben: Zur Geschichte materieller und sozialer Reproduktion ländlicher Gesellschaften im 19. Und frühen 20. Jahrhundert.* Tübingen: Tübinger Vereinigung für Volkskunde.

Kaschuba, Wolfgang and Leonore Scholze-Irrlitz, Leonore. 2010. "Von der Ethnographie zur Europäischen Ethnologie: Volks- und Völkerkunde in Berlin von 1945–2000" in R. von Bruch and H.-E. Tenorth, Eds. *1810–2010 – 200 Jahre Universität unter den Linden. Geschichte der Universität zu Berlin.* Berlin: Akademie Verlag, pp. 423–438.

Keller-Drescher, Lioba and Bernhard Tschofen, Eds. 2009. "Dialekt und regionale Kulturforschung: Traditionen und Perspektiven einer Alltagssprachforschung in Südwestdeutschland." *Tübinger kulturwissenschaftliche Gespräche* 5. Tübingen: Tübinger Vereinigung für Volkskunde.

Köstlin, Konrad. 1997. "The Passion for the Whole. Interpreted Modernity or Modernity as Interpretation." *Journal of American Folklore* 111: 261–276.

Köstlin, Konrad, Peter Niedermüller, and Herbert Nikitsch, Eds. 2002. *Die Wende als Wende? Orientierungen Europäischer Ethnologien nach 1989.* Wien: Verlag des Instituts für Europäische Ethnologie.

Kühn, Cornelia. 2007. "'… eine neue, mit dem Volk verbundene Kultur entwickeln' – Laienkunst als Ressource für die Etablierung der Volkskunde in der frühen DDR" in Sibylla Nikolow/Arne Schirrmacher, Eds. *Wissenschaft und Öffentlichkeit als Ressourcen füreinander. Studien zur Wissenschaftsgeschichte im 20. Jahrhundert.* Frankfurt/New York: Campus, pp. 197–216.

Lehmann, Albrecht. 1983. *Erzählstruktur und Lebenslauf.* Frankfurt: Campus.

Leimgruber, Walter. 2005a. "Alpine Kultur: Welche Kultur für welchen Raum?" in Beate

Binder, Silke Göttsch, Wolfgang Kaschuba and Konrad Vanja, Eds. *Ort – Arbeit – Körper. Ethnographie Europäischer Modernen.* Münster: Waxmann, pp. 147–155.

Leimgruber, Walter. 2005b. "Heidiland: Vom literarischen Branding einer Landschaft" in Jon Mathieu, Simona Boscani Leone, Eds. *Die Alpen! Les Alpes! Zur europäischen Wahrnehmungsgeschichte seit der Renaissance. Pour une histoire de la perception européenne depuis la Renaissance.* Bern 2005. pp. 429–440.

Leimgruber, Walter, Ed. 2009. *Ewigi Liäbi: Singen bleibt popular.* Basel: Schweizerische Gesellschaft für Volkskunde.

Lüthi, Max. 1986. *The European Folktale. Form and Function.* Trans. John Niles. Bloomington: Indiana University Press.

Maase, Kaspar and Bernd Jürgen Warneken, Eds. 2003. *Unterwelten der Kultur. Themen und Theorien der volkskundlichen Kulturwissenschaft.* Köln: Böhlau.

Maus, Heinz. 1946. "Zur Situation der deutschen Volkskunde." *Die Umschau* 1: 349–359.

Meier, John. 1906. *Kunstlied und Volkslied in Deutschland.* Halle: Max Niemeyer.

Mitzlaff, Hartmut, Ed. 1985. "Heimatkunde und Sachunterricht – Historische und systematische Studien zur Entwicklung des Sachunterrichts – zugleich eine kritische Entwicklungsgeschichte des Heimatideals im deutschen Sprachraum." 3 Vols. (Dissertation), University of Dortmund.

Muri, Gabriela. 2010. "Über Grenzen gehen und zum Eigenen finden. Ueli Gyr zum 65. Geburtstag. Mit einem Verzeichnis seiner Schriften 1973–2010." *Schweizerisches Archiv für Volkskunde* 106: 1–26.

Naumann, Hans. 1922. *Grundzüge der deutschen Volkskunde.* Leipzig: Quelle und Meyer.

Neuland-Kitzerow, Dagmar and Leonore Scholze-Irrlitz, Eds. 2010. "Akteure, Praxen, Theorien: Der Ethnografin Ute Mohrmann zum siebzigsten Geburtstag." *Berliner Blätter – Ethnographische und ethnologische Beiträge* 52.

Niederer, Arnold. 1956. Gemeinwerk im Wallis. *Bäuerliche Gemeinschaftsarbeit in Vergangenheit und Gegenwart.* Basel: Schweizerische Gesellschaft für Volkskunde.

Niederer, Arnold. 1970. "Zur volkskundlichen Forschung in der Schweiz 1955–1970." *Hessische Blätter für Volkskunde* 61: 221–235.

Niederer, Arnold. 1983. "Volkskundliche und völkerkundliche Forschung im Alpenraum" in Heike Nixdorf and Thomas Hauschild, Eds. *Europäische Ethnologie.* Berlin: Reimer, pp. 107–117.

Nikitsch, Herbert. 2005. Volkskunde in Österreich nach 1945. in Institut für sächsische Geschichte und Volkskunde, Ed. *Bausteine aus dem Institut für sächsische Geschichte und Volkskunde 7.* Dresden: Thelem, pp. 67–78.

Nikitsch, Herbert. 2006. *Auf der Bühne früher Wissenschaft. Aus der Geschichte des Vereins für Volkskunde (1894–1945).* Vienna: Selbstverlag des Vereins für Volkskunde.

Noyes, Dorothy. 1999. "Provinces of Knowledge; or, can You Get Out oft he Only Game in Town?" *Journal of Folklore Research* 36: 253–258.

Noyes, Dorothy. 2004. *Ur-Ethnographie: Auf der Suche nach dem Elementaren in der Kultur. Die Sammlung Eugenie Goldstern.* Wien: Österreichisches Museum Für Volkskunde.

Österreichisches Museum für Volkskunde, Ed. 2004. *Ur-Ethnographie: Auf der Suche nach dem Elementaren in der Kultur. Die Sammlung Eugenie Goldstern.* Wien: Österreichisches Museum für Volkskunde.

Schenda, Rudolf. 1977. *Volk ohne Buch. Frankfurt. Studien zur Sozialgeschichte der populären Lesestoffe 1770–1910.* Frankfurt: Klostermann.

Schenda, Rudolf and Ruth Böckli, Eds. 1983. *Lebzeiten: Autobiographien der Pro Senectute-Aktion.* Zürich: Unionsverlag.

Schenda, Rudolf and Hans ten Dornkaat, Eds. 1988. *Sagenerzähler und Sagensammler der Schweiz.* Bern: Haupt.

Schmidt, Leopold. 1951. *Geschichte der Volkskunde in Österreich.* Wien: Österreichische Gesellschaft für Volkskunde.

Schmitt, Christoph, Ed. 2005. *Volkskundliche Grossprojekte: Ihre Geschichte und Zukunft. Hochschultagung der Deutschen Gesellschaft für Volkskunde in Rostock 2002.* Münster: Waxmann.

Schmoll, Friedemann. 2009. *Die Vermessung der Kultur. Der "Atlas der deutschen Volkskunde" und die Deutsche Forschungsgemeinschaft 1928–1980.* Stuttgart: Steiner.

Scholze, Thomas and Leonore Scholze-Irrlitz, Eds. 2001. *Zehn Jahre Gesellschaft für Ethnographie-Europäische Ethnologie in Berlin. Wolfgang Jacobeit zum 80.* Geburtstag. Berlin: LIT-Verlag.

Schürch, Franziska, Sabine Eggmann, and Marius Risi, Eds. 2010. *Vereintes Wissen – Die Volkskunde und ihre gesellschaftliche Verankerung. Ein Buch zum 100. Geburtstag der Sektion Basel der Schweizerischen Gesellschaft für Volkskunde.* Münster: Waxmann.

Stein, Mary Beth. 1987. "Coming to Terms with the Past: The Depiction of 'Volkskunde; in the 'Third Reich' since 1945." *Journal of Folklore Research* 24: 157–185.

Steinitz, Wolfgang. 1955–1962. *Deutsche Volkslieder demokratischen Charakters aus sechs Jahrhunderten.* Berlin: Akademie Verlag.

Steinitz, Klaus and Wolfgang Kaschuba, Eds. 2006. *Wolfgang Steinitz: Ich hatte unwahrscheinliches Glück. Ein Leben zwischen Wissenschaft und Politik.* Berlin: Dietz.

Tomkowiak, Ingrid, Ed. 2002. *Populäre Enzyklopädien: Von der Auswahl, Ordnung und Vermittlung des Wissens.* Zürich: Chronos.

Tschernokoshewa, Elka. 2000. *Das Reine und das Vermischte: die deutschsprachige Presse über Andere und Anderssein am Beispiel der Sorben.* Münster: Waxmann

Tschernokoshewa, Elka and Udo Mischek, Eds. 2009. *Beziehungsgeflecht Minderheit: zum Paradigmenwechsel in der Kulturforschung/Europäischen Ethnologie.* Münster: Waxmann.

Verhovsek, Johann. 2010. "Die stille späte '(R)evolution.' Auf Spurensuche nach dem 'Umbruch' der Volkskunde in Österreich" (Unpublished Paper), dgv-Hochschultagung Marburg, September 25.

Warneken, Bernd Jürgen. 2006. *Die Ethnographie popularer Kulturen. Eine Einführung.* Berlin: Böhlau.

Weber-Kellermann, Ingeborg. 1969. *Deutsche Volkskunde zwischen Germanistik und Sozialwissenschaften.* Stuttgart: Metzler.

Weiss, Richard. 1941. *Das Alpwesen Graubündens. Wirtschaft, Sachkultur, Recht, Aelplerarbeit und Aelplerleben.* Erlenbach: Rentsch.

Weiss, Richard. 1946. *Volkskunde der Schweiz.* Erlenbach: Rentsch.

Weiss, Richard. 1950. *Einführung in den schweizerischen Atlas für Volkskunde.* Basel: Schweizerische Gesellschaft für Volkskunde.

Weissel, Bernhard *et al.* 1972. *Zur Geschichte und Kultur der werktätigen Klassen und Schichten des deutschen Volkses vom 11. Jahrhundert bis 1945.* Berlin: Dt. Historiker-Gesellschaft.

Welz, Gisela. 1996. *Inszenierungen kultureller Vielfalt.* Frankfurt, New York, and Berlin: Akademie Verlag.

Wildhaber, Robert. 1955. "Das Sündenregister auf der Kuhhaut." *Folklore Fellows Communication* 163. Helsinki: Suomalainen Tiedeakatemia.

Wilson, William A. 1973. "Herder, Folklore and Romantic Naionalism." *Journal of Popular Culture* 6: 819–835.

Zimmermann, Harm Peer, Ed. 2005. *Empirische Kulturwissenschaft, europäische Ethnologie, Kulturanthropologie, Volkskunde. Leitfaden für das Studium einer Kulturwissenschaft an deutschsprachigen Universitäten. Deutschland – Österreich – Schweiz.* Marburg: Jonas Verlag.

Zipes, Jack. 2003. *The Brothers Grimm. From Enchanted Forests to the Modern World.* New York: Palgrave Macmillan.

FURTHER READING

Berrisch, Sigmar. 2005. *Adolf Strack: Ein Beitrag zur Volkskunde um 1900.* Giessen: Universitäts–Bibliothek.

Kocka, Jürgen and Renate Mayntz, Eds. 1998. *Wissenschaft und Wiedervereinigung.* Berlin: Akademie Verlag.

CHAPTER 20

FINLAND

Lauri Harvilahti

INTRODUCTION

The present article opens with a glimpse of the process of engaging in mythology and folklore in Northern Europe beginning with the eighteenth century, then the Enlightenment, and Romantic nationalism during the nineteenth century, both being among the most powerful cultural currents that enhanced the history of the studies of folklore. This resulted in the ideologically inspired interpretation of early sources available in the eighteenth century, and the wide-scale collection of folklore that ensued in nineteenth-century Finland. During Romanticism there was a tendency to (re-)construct mythological golden ages and anonymous poets. The idealized *folk* was considered the carrier of religious and artistic traditions. In the waning of Romantic currents, a number of scholars of the twentieth century have pointed out that some Finnish oral poems in Kalevala meter, rather than being autochthonous, were created in medieval Finland under the influence of Scandinavian oral and literary traditions. Kalevala epic poetry, as this chapter will have occasion to demonstrate, is the foundational genre not just of Finnish nation but also of Finnish folkloristics.

In recent times, the focus of Finnish folkloristics has shifted towards a more global orientation in oral tradition and cultural heritage, and new methodological frameworks. The present overview places its focus on oral tradition, as this realm of folklore has arguably given occasion to the most widely discussed Finnish folklore scholarship.

DANIEL JUSLENIUS, HISTORICAL KNOWLEDGE, AND FOLKLORE DOCUMENTS OF EIGHTEENTH-CENTURY FINLAND

The early Finnish historian Daniel Juslenius (1676–1752) made his contributions to research on Finnish culture during the period when Finland was under Swedish rule. He used oral traditions to shed light on what is, from a present point of view, a somewhat imaginary Finnish history. His writings in Latin were created in the spirit of the Baroque rather than that of the Enlightenment. In his *Aboa vetus et nova* (Turku Old and New), Juslenius referred to the Swede Olof Rudbeck's glorious history of the peoples of Scandinavia (Rudbeck 1937–1950 [1679]; compare Wilson 1976: 12–13). Juslenius regarded folk poetry as proof of ancient Finnish civilization and, referring to a ballad text, he maintained that a school for the sons of the nobility had existed in ancient times in Turku. Juslenius writes: *Mihi quidem aliud non succurrit quam vetus quoddam carmen patrio sermonem compositum* ("I had no other source to aid me than an old Finnish poem composed in the domestic dialect"; Juslenius 2005 [1700]: 136–140). This epic poem, called *Anderuksen virsi*, "The Lay of Anderus," is a typical medieval ballad. According to Matti Kuusi, this was the first Finnish ballad ever introduced in a literary form (Kuusi 1963:12), while other scholars have suggested that the text might be of later Swedish origin. Juslenius cites a short chapter from the very beginning of the poem in Finnish, and provides the reader with a Latin translation:

Anderus Pyhäjoelda	Anderus from Pyhäjoki
Pyhäjoen poica pyhä[1]	Pyhäjoki's sacred son
tuli Coulusta cotia:	Came home from school:
mitäs poican cotia tulit?	Why did you come home, my son?
Ongo Coulu cohdallansa	Is the school in its place,
Turcu Uusi toimesansa?	new Turku in its position?
id eſt, Andreas ex Pyhäjoki/	That is, Andreas from Pyhäjoki,
Bothniæ orientalis parœcia,	From Ostrobothnian parish
venerit ex Schola domum;	Came home from school
& interrogatus a matre,	And he was asked by his mother
Cur domum venerit:	Why he came home:
num immota ſit Schola,	Whether the School was in its place,
& Aboa nova vigeat?	And new Turku in its vigour?

On the basis of this short passage, it appears that Juslenius knew the principles of Kalevala poetry. Later in his work, he provides the reader with a description of typical poetic devices like the use of alliteration and assonance, and the verse structure of eight syllables. He also observes that the choice of words and the rhythm of the verse were typical for the poetry of the Finns, and emphasizes that the rustics are as well versed in this art as the learned. The overtones of the emerging Fennophile movement are very clear in the following sentence: "A foreigner might find this unbelievable, but numerous experiences have taught us that in Finland in particular poets are born, not made" (Juslenius 2005 [1700]: 152–155). The six lines cited above are written in a more or less exact Kalevala meter, and even the rules of syntactic parallelism are followed (is the school in its place / new Turku in its position), and all in all the short chapter follows the primary features of Finnish oral poetry. The common feature shared by these verses is the trochaic tetrameter, known as the "Kalevala meter." This meter is also known in Estonian folk poetry. In "Turku Old and New," the rest of the poem is preserved mainly as a short summary of the content in prose.

Apparently the main purpose of citing the poem was the use of oral poetry as a historical source, the only existing form of records testifying to the (supposed) high status of arts and learning of the medieval inhabitants of Turku. The latter part of the poem tells about the wooing of the highborn maiden from Kokemäki by the protagonist. The mother attempted to dissuade her son because the maiden had refused the offers of Swedish nobles, and proposals of rich Ostrobothnians. Anterus leaves, however, for the journey. Juslenius cites two more verses in nearly faultless Kalevala meter and syntactic parallelism. The content of these two verses is very typical of the imagery of medieval epics with a description of the gear of the hero:

Yljän kilpi cullan kiilsi,	The suitor's shield gleamed with gold
caicki muut hopian hohdit	All other gear shone with silver

The end of the ballad is tragic, as was the norm for this genre. After the betrothal, the bride died and Anterus returned home burdened with grief.

As Matti Kuusi notes, there are only two typical or "pure" medieval "chivalric" ballads known from Finland. *The Lay of Anderus* in Juslenius's rendition is the first example, and *the Lay of Inkeri*, a Finnish version of the Danish-Swedish *Lagmansvisa* is the second (Kuusi 1963: 329–331).

Kuusi points out that there are no other close variants of the former ballad known in Finland, only distant, fading hues of the plot. He proposes that the ballad might take its origin in fourteenth-century western Finland (Kuusi 1963: 329–332).

The Pyhäjoki parish north of Ostrobothnia has existed since the sixteenth century. The *Lay of Anderus* seems to refer to the estate of Kokemäki. In medieval Finland, the Kokemäki province comprised the whole Satakunta (see map below), and before the establishment of the royal demesne of Korsholm, it reached to Ostrobothnia. It is possible that the specification of Juslenius in Latin *Andreas ex Pyhäjoki/Bothniæ orientalis paræcia* was purposely written in order to give name to the native place of the ballad, at least according to the knowledge of his time. For this reason, it might have been necessary for him to explain the location of Pyhäjoki ("the sacred river") to his readers as *(ex) Bothniæ orientalis paræcia,* namely "from Ostrobothnian parish," instead of giving the exact translation of the verse according to the Finnish poem: "Pyhäjoki's sacred son."

Unfortunately, Juslenius does not reveal where he has learned the ballad, nor does he mention other sources of oral poetry. In *Aboa vetus et nova* he refers, however, to the killing of the legendary bishop Henry by "a Finnish native nobleman" and adds some information about the legends related to the saint (Juslenius 2005 [1700]: 60–63). This implies that he knew oral traditions of his time as well as liturgical legends of Bishop Henry's life quite well. The sources of oral tradition used by Juslenius have not been preserved to our time. It is known that he had at his disposal a collection of folk poetry. There is no information as to its size and content, except for the few remarks that have been cited in his works. According to J.G. Porthan, this collection was destroyed in a fire in 1711 (see Hautala 1954: 48).

Aboa vetus et nova includes mostly imaginary descriptions, following typical stylistic precepts of his time. According to Juslenius, the Finns arrived at the region of Turku led by Magog, Japheth's son, soon after the Flood, and they quickly built up Turku into a trading centre (Juslenius 2005 [1700]: 46, 154–155; cf. Wilson 1976: 13). Concerning the religion of the ancient Finns, Juslenius writes that Magog provided a heritage of theology and sacred rites, and since that time, the Creator passed into oblivion (in the

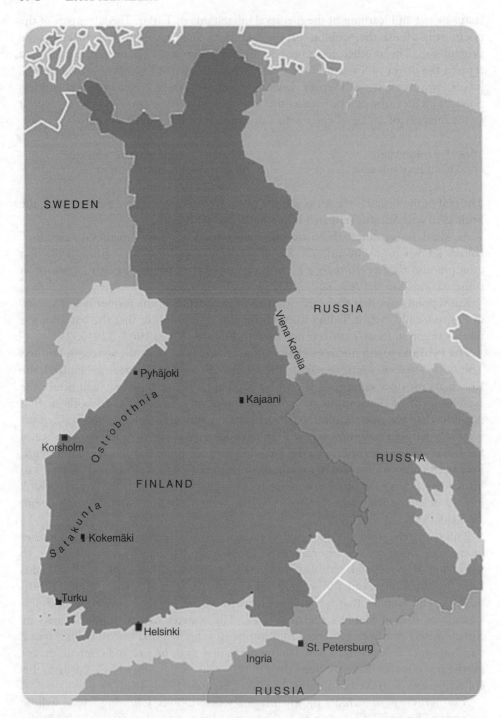

Figure 20.1   Finland in the nineteenth century.

minds of the people) and they created "a palpable idol" and started to worship that idol with great reverence. Juslenius goes on to identify the god of the Finns, *Jumala*, with the Swedish *Thor*, and cites a number of descriptions of various sacrificial rites. He accepted Rudbeck's claims that civilization and learning came to Middle and Southern Europe (and even to the Roman Empire) from Sweden, but claimed that the Swedes were in their turn indebted to the Finns. After the conversion of the Finns to Christianity, the Swedes destroyed all of the Finns' written records in order to annihilate the Finns' pride in their own history (Juslenius 2005 [1700]: 144–147). Another striking example of the eighteenth century as a period of research fostering imaginary tendencies can be taken from Christfrid Ganander's (1741–1790) *Finnish Mythology*. Ganander collected riddles, proverbs, folk poems and incantations and compiled a dictionary of the Finnish language that remained unpublished in his time. It was first printed in the 1930s. His *Finnish Mythology* (published in 1789) was created as an appendix to the dictionary. Ganander gave a quasi-classicist etymology of the Finnish town called *Kajaani* (written *Cajanus* in old scripts). According to him, a picture of the Roman god *Janus* happened to flow downstream along the river and the rapids of *Ämmänkoski* near the town, and the Finns standing on the bank shouted *Ka Janus*, "Look, it's Janus," and hence the name of the town (Ganander 1789; Hautala 1954: 81).

THE ADVENT OF THE ROMANTIC CURRENTS

The growing influence of Romanticism and Romantic nationalism inspired an interest in antiquity, ancient traditions, folk religion and folklore in later eighteenth and (especially) nineteenth-century Europe. The works of thinkers such as Jean Jacques Rousseau, Johann Wolfgang von Goethe, August Wilhelm and Friedrich von Schlegel, Friedrich von Schelling, Johann Gottfried von Herder, and Georg Wilhelm Friedrich Hegel formed part of the ideological background of Romanticism.

National Romanticism emerged, inspired by the Herderian mythologically oriented view on nations. The mythical school was followed by the nationalistic Romantic movement influenced by the Hegelian concept of *Zeitgeist* (the spirit of the times), determining the historical moment for the development of a nation (Kaukonen 1979: 102–106, 163, 166; Branch 1994: 12). This approach emphasized the role of a nation in the mystical collective process of creation of the heroic Golden Age, matured in the right stage of development of the people. The Romantic trends that spread throughout Europe began to be felt more and more strongly in Finland too. At that time Finland was an autonomous grand duchy under the Russian tsar (as of 1809). National Romanticism (in Finnish "kansallisromantiikka") aroused a need for recreating or reconstructing a mythical past with poetic landscapes of a golden age (see Harvilahti 1997b: 740–741). In the latter half of the nineteenth century national Romanticism aimed mostly (as in the case of Finland) at supporting the formation of nation-states.

Jacob and Wilhelm Grimm's work of collecting and publishing folktales served as an epoch-making impulse for the recording and publishing of folklore materials all over Europe. These early projects were used as blueprints, serving as a model for further interpretations in the spirit of Romantic nationalism, and as a guide for selecting and editing materials for the ideological use of traditions.

The organized collection of folklore began in Finland in the first half of the nineteenth century. The major event in the history of collecting and protecting the Finnish traditional heritage was the founding of the Finnish Literature Society in Helsinki in 1831 by members of educated circles. The poems in Kalevala meter were collected mainly thanks to the initiative of the Finnish Literature Society. The Kalevalaic poems were joined at the end of the century by collections of folktales. Elias Lönnrot (the Society's first secretary) compiled the Finnish national epic, the Kalevala, on the basis of traditional Kalevala poetry. The first edition appeared in 1835, the second and greatly enlarged edition in 1849. Lönnrot was, while preparing the first edition of Kalevala (1835), guided by the Herderian view on nations. While preparing the 1849 edition of the New Kalevala he was persuaded to add elements and ideals of a heroic Golden Age of the Finns in accordance with the ideals of philosophers and scholars (especially J.V. Snellman and J.R. Tengström) influenced by the Hegelian concepts of *Zeitgeist*. In addition, Lönnrot was influenced by the European research tradition of literary epics, especially by Friedrich Wolf, who in his *Prolegomena ad Homerum* (1795) had maintained that the Iliad and Odyssey were composed orally in the form of short songs and edited later to obtain the unity an epic embodies. He found in the literary theories and in the national-romantic currents of his time a theoretical and ideological justification for his work. Thus he believed that he knew the method of how the Iliad and the Odyssey were created and how an epic comes into being (Harvilahti 1997a: 509; 2008a: 529–530). Lönnrot also edited lyric poetry, proverbs, riddles and spells for publication.

The Estonian counterpart of the Finnish *Kalevala* was the epos called *Kalevipoeg* (1857–1861) compiled by F.R. Kreutzwald. He used as building material local legends and tales of origin. Similarly, Andrejs Pumpurs, the author of the Latvian national epic *Lāčplēsis* "Bear Slayer" (1888), created his epic poem on the basis of Latvian etiological tales, folktales, local legends, wedding songs, and other items excerpted from folklore (see Harvilahti 1997b: 738).

Important nineteenth-century folklore collections from other parts of the Nordic Countries include such works as *Svenska folksagor och äfventyr* (Swedish Folktales and Fairy Tales) by Gunnar Olof Hyltén-Cavallius and George Stephens (1844–1849), *Norske volkeeventyr* (Norwegian Folktales) by Peter Asbjørnsen and Jørgen Moe (1841), *Danske Folkesang* (Danish Folk Legends) by Just Mathias Thile (1818–1823), *Danske folkeeventyr* (Danish Folktales) by Mathias Winther (1823), *Danmakrs gamle folkeviser* (Danish Ballads) by Svend Grundtvig (1853), and especially Evald Tang Kristensen's large collections of Danish folk narratives (Hult 2008: 832–841).[2]

In Finland, from the mid-nineteenth century onwards a new mode of collecting folklore was initiated, namely publishing requests to collectors in the newspapers, which met with enthusiastic reactions. Towards the end of the century a network of collectors was created, guides to collections written, and folklore collection encouraged in general. Various organizations and educational establishments also took shape in response to this urge to collect. In the 1870s researchers already thought that everything of any importance had been collected. Around 1900 the folklore archive of the Finnish Literature Society had already about 200,000 "items" of folklore.

There are also some 2 million lines of poetry in Kalevala meter in the archives of the Finnish Literature Society, collected mainly in the nineteenth century and the first half of the twentieth century. About two thirds of this material has been published in the 34-volume *Suomen Kansan Vanhat Runot* "Ancient Poems of the Finnish People" (1908–1948, and 1993), and all published materials are available as a digital corpus on the Web since 2007. Kalevala poems are usually divided into four groups: epic poetry, lyric songs, wedding songs and incantations.

Poems vary in length and unity – from short lyric poems and incantations to ballads and other epic songs of several hundred lines. Most of the collected material comes from the northeastern part of the Autonomy of Finland, Viena Karelia (in our days the Archangel Karelia part of the Republic of Karelia belonging to the Russian Federation) and Ingria (an area inhabited by Finnic and Slavic ethnic groups along the southern and eastern shores of the Gulf of Finland near St Petersburg, now part of Russia). In western Finland, just a few Kalevala poetry themes still survived in the nineteenth century, in the period during which most of the material was collected. In the remote villages of the Northern (Karelian) area, solo singing performed by men prevailed. In the southern (Ingrian) areas the singers were usually female and the mode of performance was chorus singing with a lead singer beginning every new chapter or even every new line. The performers were not professionals (it is assumed that in an earlier time there were professional bards), but were usually farmers, fishermen or (in the North) hunters, and singing was part of their everyday life. From earlier times there is some evidence that at least in the Karelian and Ingrian areas some songs were performed by wandering singers, called the *skomoroh* in the Russian tradition (see Zguta 1978: 78, 96, passim).

The Historical-geographic Method and the Folktales

The history of Finnish folklore research has been above all (until the end of 1950s) the history of epic poetry research and of folktale typologies. The so-called Finnish method achieved international repute in the first phase as an approach to the study of folktales. The adherents of the historical-geographical school strove in the beginning of the twentieth century to reconstruct archetypes or invariants of folktales.

The classic example of a type-index is the folktale taxonomy devised by the Finnish scholar Antti Aarne at the beginning of the twentieth century. In Aarne's system (see Aarne 1910), folktales are divided into three main categories: (i) animal tales, (ii) ordinary folktales, and (iii) anecdotes. Ordinary folktales are further divided into four subcategories: tales of magic, religious tales, novella-tales and tales of the foolish devil. Aarne's "types" are in practice different tales, not groups of tales. He numbered each folktale, so that nos. 1–299 were animal tales, nos. 300–1199 ordinary folktales, and so on. For example, the "folktale about a magic ring" is no. 560 and the "folktale about three magic objects and the miraculous fruit" no. 566. The advantage of the type-index is its universality: numerical codes are independent of language. It is, however, necessary to stress that variants given the same type number are not necessarily intrinsically related. Nor can such a taxonomy fully accommodate the constant variation of a living tradition. In practice, numerous codes are needed simultaneously for classifying the majority of folktale variants, and new types to which no existing code applies are always being discovered.

Folktale taxonomies of a number of European and some non-European peoples have been published according to Aarne's system. The method was taken up and further developed by the US scholar Stith Thompson (The Types of Folk-Tale. Helsinki 1927), who later published his monumental life-work, the "Motif-Index of Folk-Literature" I–V (1932–1936). The typology of folktales by Antti Aarne and Stith Thompson was originally based on the assumption that each type had a prehistory and an archetype. As its newest version expanded, focusing on European materials by Hans-Jörg Uther as Aarne-Thompson-Uther or ATU system (Uther 2004), the tale-types are understood to be a flexible type of units, not anymore constant units referring to the past archetypal forms.

THE HISTORICAL-GEOGRAPHIC METHOD AND THE KALEVALA EPICS

Methodological questions of folklore research in Finland during the transition from the nineteenth to the twentieth century were mainly connected with the study of epic folk poetry. The diachronic method established by Julius Krohn (1835–1888) and Kaarle Krohn (1863–1933) attempted the reconstruction of the archetypes of the collected texts from archived poems in Kalevala meter, and the analysis of its "primary" and "secondary" features. The aim was to reconstruct the poem's hypothetical basic form and draw conclusions concerning its time and place of origin, in accordance with their understanding of the principles of textual criticism in a historical-geographic framework. In Finnish folkloristics, this method was connected to an evolutionary idea in the diachronic comparative studies of the laws of geographic distribution. Kaarle Krohn became the first ("extraordinary personal") professor for Finnish and comparative folklore research at the University of Helsinki in 1898. In the early phase of his career, Kaarle Krohn supposed that the Kalevala metric poetry had its roots in Catholic western Finland during the Middle Ages. Krohn proposed that in Karelia, the poems had developed from "primordial cells" into long poems, more developed in form and content, but the historical evidence was very limited. In 1907 he established with his colleagues Axel Olrik (Danish) and Johannes Bolte (German) the organization called Folklore Fellows (Folkminnes-Forskare, Folkeminde-Forskere, Fédération des Folkloristes, Folkloristisches Forscherbund, see Hautala 1954: 121). The aim of the Folklore Fellows was to enhance the international cooperation in the field of comparative studies of folklore by publishing research works, materials, and catalogues of collections. In 1908 Krohn became a permanent professor in Finnish and comparative folkloristics, and in 1910, the folkloristic publications series called *Folklore Fellows' Communications* was established.

A declaration of independence was ratified by the Finnish Parliament on December 6, 1917, while World War I was still raging. In the civil war that followed in 1918, the socialist forces were defeated, and Finland became a parliamentary republic. It has been disputed whether the tumultuous political changes had an influence on the development of Finnish folklore research methodology (see Wilson 1976: x). This might explain why Kaarle Krohn declared in his new two-volume handbook entitled *Kalevalankysymyksiä*, "Kalevala Questions," published in 1918, that he had completely changed his theories on the origin of both Kalevala poems and Finnish folktales. According to his new understanding, poems and folktales did not develop from primordial cells or archetypal original forms. In the past, the collected epic poems had been primarily and originally concise, whole poems and folktales. They had been created during the late iron-age in western Finland and migrated to eastern Finland and Karelia. Along their route, the poems and folktales intermingled with other folklore according to specific laws of variability. According to the new theory, the closest parallel with Finnish ancient poetry was to be found in the Scandinavian ancient poetry of the Viking age (Hautala 1954: 223, 261).

Krohn developed a number of specific "laws" that had influenced the changing or altering of the poem or folktale: the law of mind (forgetting, adding) and the law of variation as in Axel Olrik's "epic laws" (Olrik 1908). Krohn published a further study on folkloristic methodology, based on a series of lectures he gave in Norway (1926). In this book, he once again emphasized the points he had made in *Kalevala Questions*. Referring to the work of J. Bolte and G. Polívka on folktale variants, he added that the new focus was in reconstructing the so called *normal form* on the basis of the complete material of all *variants* collected of a particular poem or folktale. Krohn mentioned the synchronically oriented theories of Arnold van Gennep, a scholar who already in 1924 had called the historical, diachronic research the "maniac disease" of the nineteenth century. Krohn also mentioned the theories of C. W. von Sydow on the "ecology" of folklore. Von Sydow had formulated the concept of "ecotypes," that is the notion that narratives might take on features characteristic or unique to a region and its people (v.Sydow 1934, cf. Cochrane 1987). Krohn himself remained a scholar with a firm diachronic orientation.

THE FINNISH SCHOOL IN THE 1930S AND 1940S

The Finnish or Historical-Geographic Method was very much alive during the 1930s and 1940s. The most ardent proponent of this theory was, after Kaarle Krohn, the academician Martti Haavio. The large-scale collection of oral tradition did not weaken, even though the Romantic national currents began to wane. By 1930, the figure of archived folklore items already stood at more than 500,000. The collection continued in a new ideological setting in the 1930s by focussing on legends, and encompassed gradually all fields of agrarian folklore, proverbs and riddles, the belief tradition, and laments. In 1934 the Society's folklore collections were consolidated into a research institution known as the Folklore Archive. The first director, Martti Haavio, organized a major collection campaign on prose genres. Since then, collecting campaigns have been a productive means for collecting folklore materials.

One literary-based idea was repeatedly emphasized by Haavio, namely the *Poeta anonymus*, the ideal anonymous composer looming behind each epic poem or folktale (Haavio 1952: 38–39; Lehtipuro 1974: 16). One of the tasks of the Finnish school in Haavio's time was to uncover the earlier developmental phases of a particular traditional text (the so-called motif-historical analysis). Haavio and some other scholars also sought to draw conclusions concerning the time and place of the poem's creation as well as the social position, order, sex, age, and even world-view of the supposed original rune-singer. The paragon for this kind of procedure was to be seen in literary analyses aimed at revealing authors of thus far unidentified ancient texts. The validity of this literary analogue has been questioned with regard to folklore texts (Harvilahti 1997a: 512). Martti Haavio and his Swedish colleague C. von Sydow mutually influenced one another. The result of these contacts was an approach that was called traditional-psychological method, a combination of diachronic and synchronic aspects.

From the point of view of the development of Finnish folkloristics, the most important among Haavio's numerous monographs is *Piispa Henrik ja Lalli*, "Bishop

Henry and Lalli." In this book, Haavio compared church legends and folk poetry, making an attempt to create a reliable picture of the performer of the epic folk poem and its background. He concluded that the *poeta anonymus* was well versed in the poetic means of the chivalric ballads and liturgical tradition, and created a folk legend on the killing of the Bishop Henry by the Finnish peasant Lalli in the latter half of the thirteenth century. This folk legend was compiled before the literary liturgical legend was written (Lehtipuro 1974: 12; Hautala 1954: 360, 371).

THE TYPOLOGICAL SCHOOL

According to Matti Kuusi, the method of Haavio had serious shortcomings: the history of folklore motifs cannot be based on imaginary strands between separate (and distant in time and place) associations or imaginary analogies. Instead of focusing on loose motifs, Kuusi pointed out the need to build the comparison of folklore motifs on diachronic relations and structural combinations (Kuusi 1980: 70–71). Kuusi sought, for his part, to approach the problem of the origin of epic poems through a theory of dating stylistic and structural features. Thus, for example, he interpreted some of the Finnish Kalevala metric poems as medieval in origin on the basis of loanwords that were adopted during the medieval period. Likewise, he discovered hints of the "pauperistic" ideology of mendicant friars in Kalevala poetry. The poem *Viron orja ja isäntä* "The Slave and the Lord of Estonia" was regarded by Kuusi as a sort of "manifesto of proletarian-Christian ideology" due to several stylistic devices. In the poem, the slave had dropped dead along the road due to fatigue; he was given a tankard made of silver, full of mead and spirits, when he arrived in Heaven, but his mean and miserly lord got a mug "containing fire and tar." *Mataleenan virsi* "The Lay of Mataleena" distantly refers to the biblical story of Mary Magdalene. The poem relates that a woman (Mataleena) has killed her three sons. She meets the shepherd Jesus on the waterway, begs him for forgiveness, and promises to accomplish whatever Jesus asks her to do, and in some manuscripts washes his feet. In this poem, Kuusi sees features of the Dominican mendicant ideology, and finds typical indigenous Finnish poetic "social and national contrasts." *Leino leski* "The Sad Widow" tells about a woman who boasts of her riches and of her three influential sons. She gets a punishment that follows the pattern of *hybris-nemesis*. Death personified hears her boasting and kills all of her sons (Kuusi 1963: 313–314). This is the third poem that Kuusi interprets as a medieval ballad that originates from the influence of the Dominican and Franciscan friars. The ideological pattern behind these folk ballads is, in his opinion, the humiliation of rich and proud people.

Very typical of the typological analyses of Matti Kuusi are the so-called repetitive patterns that according to him were introduced into Finnish folk poetry in medieval times. One of these patterns is the so-called antonymic repetition. The main characters and events of parallel episodes follow the same narrative pattern, but the content of these chapters is antonymic, as for example in the description of the kind treatment of the slave and the rough handling of the lord mentioned above. According to Kuusi, another medieval device is the so-called "overlapping repetition," the repetition of a hemistich in the beginning of subsequent verses: *Pahoin palkka/maksettihin,//,pahoin palkka,/vaivoin vaate* "Bad wage/was paid,//bad wage,/poor clothing"/, or:

"*Mitäs puhut/Suomen sulha,// Suomen sulha,/maiden orja*" "What do you speak, /you Finnish groom,/you Finnish groom,/serf of the soil" (Kuusi 1963: 311–314). One problem of using poetic devices for dating poems might be caused by the fact that the same kind of stylistic and poetic devices might be known in different traditions, and sometimes from a time before the Middle Ages (cf. Harvilahti 1992: 196, n. 150; Foley 1991: 121–122). I admit, however, that the Kalevala metric poems that Kuusi has dated as medieval do correspond to his theoretical assumptions of similarity in form, content and poetic devices. What remains uncertain is the exact dating of the epics.

This research method required that the corpus of text variants should be "complete," taking also into account the time and place in which each text was collected. This was justified on the basis of the assumption that the geographical or typological distribution of the preserved texts would reveal the prehistory of textual forms, and that some texts might work as a unique and "most original" version (usually referred to as *codex unicus*), with key importance. In his article on the religious epic poem *Silta ja kirkko*, "The Bridge and the Church," Matti Kuusi used many methods for textual analysis that belong more to a synchronic than diachronic frame of reference, such as structural analysis and a genre perspective. According to Kuusi, this particular poem belongs to a cluster of songs narrating the escape of *The Virgin Mary and Baby Jesus*. The central element in this short epic poem is the bridge that offers a place of shelter for *Jesus*. Kuusi proposed that the poem was composed by a Dominican mendicant in the mid-fourteenth century in southwestern Finland. After that, the poem was performed in the procession rituals of the mendicants, and it was preserved as transformed redactions in the tradition of the region of Ingria in the Southern area on the Gulf of Finland. The evidence for this dating was, once again, found in the pauperistic world-view and proletarian-Christian influence (Kuusi 1963: 314; 1975: 37–75; 1980).

Ultimately, it became clear that the initial forms can hardly be revealed or reconstructed on the basis of the collected texts or variants. The researchers had to content themselves making hypotheses, selecting one that for the moment offered the most reliable answers.

DID THE HISTORICAL-GEOGRAPHIC SCHOOL PERSIST?

The role that folklore has played in cultural and social processes varies from preliminary efforts in collecting folklore items to diverse uses of folklore in the cultural and national movements. In many cases metadiscursive practices (Briggs 1993: 387–434), that is, dominant, ideologically influenced approaches, have represented the research material in a modified or reconstructed form, according to the prevailing fashions or politic and didactic aims (cf. Briggs 1993: 420; Honko 1998: 156–165). If the purpose is to evaluate the usefulness of sources for research, it is essential to discern the ideological aims looming in the background of the texts.

In the light of this framework I would be ready to support the hypotheses of Martti Haavio and Matti Kuusi regarding the medieval origin of several Finnish ballads and Kalevala metric epic songs. According to Kuusi the Finnish freeholders and noblemen, and noble families built their freehold estates in the surroundings of Turku (Åbo), and their sons received their education and military training in Sweden and Denmark (Kuusi 1963: 329–330). Since the chivalric ballads were flourishing in Scandinavia, it would be probable that the themes known in Scandinavia were already put into the Finnish oral-poetic garment of Kalevala meter during the fourteenth to the sixteenth century. The influence of Scandinavian saint cults is very well documented in Finland, and it may be assumed that Dominican and Franciscan friars had an influence on certain oral lyric-epic songs that were common in medieval coastal Finland and in the southern region of Häme-Tavastland. The existence of a number of lyric-epic songs of Scandinavian origin in coastal Finland seems to imply that there was a well established oral poetry culture shared by all walks of society, not only by freeholders and noblemen.

The main problem of diachronic text research with materials collected from the oral tradition during the nineteenth and twentieth centuries is the fact that the folklore manuscripts are of too recent an origin. The gap between the supposed creators of the thirteenth- or fourteenth-century religious songs and the folklore of the nineteenth century is too great, and any theories on the initial form of the songs remain highly hypothetical. The theories on historical development and distribution of folklore tend to omit synchronic variation in the countless performances of folklore through the centuries. For a contemporary folklorist, finding out who was the "creator" or "poeta anonymus" of a given text is not of value per se. The texts may, however, reflect the social culture and mental model of different times, layers of society and ideological currents, much as held already by Kuusi (cf. Siikala 2002: 339–349). In this sense, we might consider that the religious folklore of the Middle Ages may be reflected in the texts collected during the extensive compilation of collections of the nineteenth century. However, over the years scholars have become increasingly cautious. A scholar cannot reconstruct old "exhibits" or "specimens" of tradition with a sufficient degree of reliability on the basis of the song tradition of just a few generations.

THE METHODOLOGICAL REVOLUTION OF FINNISH FOLKLORISTICS IN THE 1960s

Folkloristics in Finland today has very little in common with the old Finnish method, or the geographic-historical school. There are many reasons for this: first, the methodological revolution of Finnish folkloristics in the 1960s; second, the development of modern fieldwork in the 1960s and 1970s, and a shift from romantic (and nationalistic) understanding of folklore towards a more global comprehension of cultural heritage and oral tradition; third, the new politics of collection of the Finnish Literature Society's Folklore archives from the 1965 onwards, and fourth, a new understanding of the old archived collections.

According to Lauri Honko, an essential shift, and with it a new picture of reality was developed in Finnish folkloristics at the end of the 1950s and the beginning of the 1960s. Finnish folkloristics was from that time onwards supposed to be focussing on context instead of text, on producers of folklore instead of folklore products. The principles of functional analysis and perspectives of ecology of tradition replaced the former geographical-historical orientation of the Finnish school. New research currents built their methods on the functionalistic perspective of folklore, as well as on sociology and social psychology, cultural anthropology, and on the study of folklore genres. Some concepts of these disciplines were used to build new methods of folklore studies in Finland (see Harvilahti 2008a: 458–459, Honko 1998). One of the key-concepts of Lauri Honko's theory, the ecology of tradition, was borrowed from Carl Wilhelm von Sydow (1934), apparently via Martti Haavio, as Honko himself has admitted. However, Haavio remained throughout his life an adherent of the diachronic historical-geographical paradigm, and Lauri Honko took (as he himself wrote) the responsibility of guiding Finnish folkloristics and the study of comparative religion towards new perspectives and goals: functionally oriented folkloristics and tradition ecology, with an emphasis on folkloristic fieldwork (Honko 1962: 8; Lehtipuro 1974: 22–25) rather than a mining of the rich archival records from the nineteenth and the twentieth century up to 1939, after having himself completed some major work based on them (Honko 1959; 1962).

THE DEVELOPMENT OF MODERN FIELDWORK IN THE 1960s AND 1970s

A shift towards field research occurred in 1965 during the first Scandinavian fieldwork seminar organized in Vöyri, Finland (see Lehtipuro 1974: 30). The focus in the 1960s and 1970s turned to storytellers, musicians, and other performers of oral tradition and folk music.

Folklore research in Finland also turned to what von Sydow has called the bearers of the passive tradition (von Sydow 1948: 12–13, 15; Goldstein 1971: 62). Many people in Finland were unable to adapt the folklore they once learned to a changing environment, but they had memories of the feelings of identity associated with folklore. Such memories can be actualized by means of collection. This channel for the expression of tradition became particularly important because new research methods were applied to traditional items, and the mechanisms for recalling and producing folklore were studied by using new fieldwork methods, particularly in the realm of interview techniques strongly diverging from a strict "collection mode," as well as new research tools such as voice and later also video recording (see Pentikäinen 1978).

Many genres of folklore associated with old forms of agrarian culture have vanished with the passing of the last performers familiar with them. Yet there is living folklore all around us: workplace lore, various contemporary tales, legends and anecdotes, rumors, gossip, graffiti, parodies on proverbs and riddles, the rich children's tradition. Folklorist Leea Virtanen dedicated most of her life to research on contemporary tales and children's folklore (Virtanen 1978). The interest in popular culture may be added to this, especially from the 1980s onwards, originated by Matti Kuusi's approach to "idol-analysis," and the fieldwork-oriented study on sub-cultures and ethnic minorities.

THE FINNISH LITERATURE SOCIETY'S FOLKLORE ARCHIVES FROM THE 1965 ONWARDS: LIFE STORIES AND ORAL HISTORY

The Folklore Archives seek to collect oral tradition, personal narratives, and memory lore in a number of different ways. Nowadays, this work is primarily focused on organizing collection campaigns and fieldwork across the country. The archives also actively maintain their own respondent network.

Since the 1960s, various groups have been encouraged to write responses to archive collection campaigns. These have tended to focus on some previously unexplored areas of life. In 1965–1966, a collection of material associated with the events of the civil war of 1918 was organized. This was the beginning of a rapidly growing tendency to gather material related to oral history and autobiographical research, a collecting method that is still, among other methods, used in Finnish archives. The next collection campaign was organized in 1969 on the tradition of the lumberjacks. Both sets of materials were used for Finnish doctoral dissertations by Ulla-Maija Peltonen *Punakapinan muistot* (Memoirs of the Civil War, 1996), and Jyrki Pöysä *Jätkän synty* (The Birth of the Lumberjack, 1997). In the collections of the Folklore Archives there were, in 2010, around 1 million pages of oral history materials.

A few further examples will illustrate the scope of these collection campaigns: construction workers (1970), tuberculosis and rheumatism sanatoria (1971), postmen (1972), trenches during the war (1973), workers in the state alcohol monopoly (1975), the advent of radio and television (1982), engineers (1984), white collar workers (1987), the police (1988), the sauna (1992), women (1990), men (1992), and the advent of computers (1995). The latest collection campaigns include: Who defends your country? (2004–2005), and Politics and power games: oral history on social activism in Finland (2006–2007). Memories of World War II, reconstruction work in Finland after the war and experiences of people from different parts of Finland have been among the most popular themes of the newest collections. This material has been used by students, researchers and enthusiasts representing a large range of scientific fields within the humanities, social sciences, and other disciplines.

A New Understanding of The Old Archived Collections

According to Roger Abrahams, the collection takes away the particularities of the objects collected, stripping them of both history and cultural context (Abrahams 1993: 18). He cites Susan Stewart (1984: 131): "The collection does not displace attention to the past, rather the past is in service of the collection, for whereas the souvenir lends authenticity to the past, the past lends authenticity to the collection." In the light of folkloristic research carried out in many parts of the world during the past 15 years, it seems, however, possible to formulate a new understanding of folklore collections. Records from the past are evidence of cultural diversity, functioning as a materialization of collective memories. If approached in new ways, it is possible for these records to exceed the lifetimes and experiences of the individuals who produced or created them. Even the old archived collections, in spite of deficiencies such as their obvious lack of contextual information, offer a view into the past, a window that can be reopened using new methods.

During the past five decades the integration of various disciplines has yielded very promising results in the study of archived folklore in Finland as well as newly recorded materials, including expertise in gender studies, performance theory, sociolinguistics, psycholinguistics, cognitive sciences, ethnopoetics and, structuralism, oral-formulaic school, oral history, and many other approaches and methodological currents which have been in an interesting global exchange of views on folklore methodology since the beginning of the 1960s.

Annikki Kaivola-Bregenhøj's work on dreams and above all riddles has employed sophisticated structuralist methods in the analysis of archival materials. Kaivola-Bregenhøj's and Anna-Leena Siikala's studies of narration (Siikala 1990; Kaivola-Bregenhøj 1996) have further combined contextual analysis, inspired by American narrative studies (Bauman, Briggs *et al.*) with cognitive models of text production.

In her dissertation on women's magic rituals (1998) Laura Stark used a rich archival corpus of ritual belief legends, incantations in Kalevala meter and descriptions of magic rites. By applying anthropological perspectives she examined the ways in which women constructed and performed gender by using magic and rituals, in their social context in rural Finland. The doctoral thesis by Lotte Tarkka (2005), translated into English under the title *Songs of the Border People. Kalevala-Meter Poetry in Vuokkiniemi Parish 1821–1921* (forthcoming in 2011) is another example of the integration of various disciplines. Tarkka analyzes 2,960 texts collected from Vuokkiniemi, Viena (Archangel) Karelia using notions of intertextuality, dialogue among genres, and contextual strategies that "root the historical reality of the singers and their audiences." New theoretical perspectives on old archived texts are being covered in a large number of future monographs.

Folklore scholarship has changed fundamentally during the past 50 years, and Finnish folkloristics continues in our days in a new, global setting. Thus for instance Pertti Anttonen's critical, historiographic work on the development of folklore studies has traced the development of the discipline as a continuous engagement with modernity and modernization, from the nationalist beginnings to postmodern times (2005, 2008). It is not possible to equate the present situation with the one that prevailed 100 years ago. However, there are still some folkloristic organizations and publication series in Finland that date from the early twentieth century. The Folklore Fellows still exist, and the Folklore Fellows Communications which still has its home at the Finnish Academy of Science and Letters celebrated its one-hundredth anniversary. The field of folkloristic research remains open and expansive.

NOTES

1   The orthography differs to some extent from the current Finnish. Juslenius writes *c* instead of the current *k* before vowels *a*, *o*, and *u̱*: poica vs. poika 'son, boy'.
2   Editor's' note: though the chapter focusses primarily on Finland, the rich folklore research done in Scandinavia since the heyday of folklore collections should not go unnoticed. For an English reading audience, Kvideland and Sehmsdorf's volume of translated articles is a good entry (1989).

REFERENCES

Primary Sources

Ganander, Christfrid. 1789. *Mythologia Fennica, eller förklaring öfver de nomina propria deastrorum, idolorum, locorum, virorum &c. eller afgudar och afgudinnor, forntidens märkelige personer, offer och* *offer-ställen, gamla sedvänjor, jättar, troll, skogs- sjö- och bergs-rån m. m. Som förekomma i de äldre finska troll-runor, synnyt, sanat, sadut, arwotuxet &c. samt än brukas och nämnas i dagligt tal; til deras tjenst, som vela i grund första det finska språket, och hafva smak för finska historien och poesin, af gamla runor samlad och uttydd af Christfrid Ganander, Thomasson philos. mag. & sacell.* Åbo: Frenckellska boktryckeriet.

Juslenius, Daniel. 2005 [1700]. *Aboa vetus et nova: Vanha ja uusi Turku.* Helsinki: Suomalaisen Kirjallisuuden Seura.

Rudbeck, Olof, the Elder. 1937–1950 [1679]. *Olaus Rudbecks Atlantica:* svenska originaltexten på uppdrag av Lärdomshistoriska samfundet utgiven av axel nelson. Uppsala: Almqvist and Wiksell.

Suomen Kansan Vanhat Runot (SKVR).1908–1948, 1993. "The Ancient Poems of the Finnish People," 34 volumes. Helsinki: Suomalaisen Kirjallisuuden Seura http://www.finlit.fi/english/research/digital_skvr.htm, http://www.finlit.fi/skvr/ (accessed October 16, 2011).

Literature

Aarne, Antti. 1910. "Verzeichnis der Märchentypen." *Folklore Fellows' Communications* 3. Helsinki: Academia Scientiarum Fennica.

Abrahams, Roger. 1993. "Phantoms of Romantic Nationalism." *Journal of American Folklore* 106(419): 3–37.

Anttonen, Pertti. 2005. "Tradition through Modernity. Postmodernism and the Nation-State in Folklore Scholarship." *Studia Fennica Folkloristica* 15. Helsinki: Finnish Literature Society.

Anttonen, Pertti. 2008. "Tradition and Heritage in Anthropological Practice and Theory." *Anthropological Journal of European Cultures* 17: 84–97.

Branch, Michael. 1994. "The Invention of a National Epic" in Michael Branch and Celia Hawkesworth, Eds. *The Uses of Tradition. A Comparative Enquiry into the Nature, Uses and Functions of Oral Poetry in the Balkans, the Baltic, and Africa.* University of London: School of Slavonic and East European Studies and Finnish Literature Society, Helsinki.

Briggs, Charles. 1993. "Metadiscursive Practices and Scholarly Authority in Folkloristics." *Journal of American Folklore* 106(422): 387–434.

Cochrane, Timothy. 1987. "The Concept of Ecotypes in American Folklore." *Journal of Folklore Research* 24: 33–55.

Foley, John Miles. 1991. *Immanent Art: From Structure to Meaning in Traditional Oral Epic.* Bloomington: Indiana University Press.

Goldstein, Kenneth S. 1971. "On the Application of the Concepts of Active and Inactive Traditions to the Study of Repertory." *The Journal of American Folklore* 84 (331): 62–67.

Haavio, Martti. 1952. "Väinämöinen. Eternal Sage." *Folklore Fellows' Communications* 144. Helsinki: Academia Scientiarum Fennica.

Harvilahti, Lauri. 1992. *Kertovan runon keinot. Inkeriläisen runoepiikan tuottamisesta.* Helsinki: Suomalaisen Kirjallisuuden Seura.

Harvilahti, Lauri 1997a: "The Literary Method" in T.E. Green, Ed. *Folklore, an Encyclopedia of Beliefs, Customs, Tales, Music, and Art.* Volumes I–II. Santa Barbara, CA: ABC-CLIO.

Harvilahti, Lauri. 1997b. "Romantic Nationalism" in T.E.Green, Ed. *Folklore, An Encyclopedia of Beliefs, Customs, Tales, Music, and Art.* Vols. I–II. Santa Barbara CA: ABC-CLIO.

Harvilahti, Lauri. 2008a. "Kalevala" in Donald Haase, Ed. *The Greenwood Encyclopedia of Folktales and Fairy Tales.* Vol. 2. Westport, CT: Greenwood Press.

Hautala, Jouko. 1954. *Suomalainen kansanrunoudentutkimus.* Helsinki: Suomalaisen kirjallisuuden seura.

Honko, Lauri. 1959. "Krankheitsprojektile. Untersuchung über eine urtümliche Krankheitserklärung." *Folklore Fellows' Communications* 178. Helsinki: Academia Scientiarum Fennica.

Honko, Lauri. 1962. "Geisterglaube in Ingermanland I." *Folklore Fellows' Communications* 185. Helsinki: Academia Scientiarum Fennica.

Honko, Lauri. 1998. "Textualizing the Siri Epic." *Folklore Fellows' Communications* 264. Helsinki: Academia Scientiarum Fennica.

Hult, Marte. 2008. "Scandinavian Tales" in Donald– Haase, Ed. *The Greenwood Encyclopedia of Folktales and Fairy Tales.* Vol. 3. Westport, CT: Greenwood Press.

Kaivola-Bregenhøj, Annikki. 1996. "Narrative and Narrating: Variation in Juho Oksanen's Storytelling." *FF Communications* 261. Helsinki: Suomalainen tiedeakatemia.

Kaukonen, Väinö. 1979. *Lönnrot ja Kalevala.* Helsinki: Suomalaisen Kirjallisuuden Seura.

Kuusi, Matti, Ed. 1963. *Suomen kirjallisuus I. Kirjoittamaton kirjallisuus.* Helsinki: WSOY.

Kuusi, Matti. 1975. "'The Bridge and the Church': An Anti-Church Legend" in Pentti Leino, Annikki Kaivola-Bregenhøj, and Urpo Vento, Eds. *Finnish Folkloristics* 2. *Studia Fennica* 18. Helsinki: Suomalaisen Kirjallisuuden.

Kuusi, Matti. 1980. "Suomalainen tutki-musmenetelmä" in Outi Lehtipuro, Ed. *Perinteentutkimuksen perusteita.* Porvoo: WSOY.

Kvideland, Reimund and Henning K. Sehmsdorf, eds. 1989. *Nordic Folklore. Folklore Studies in Translation.* Bloomington: Indiana University Press.

Lehtipuro, Outi. 1974. "Trends in Finnish Folkloristics" in Pentti Leino, Ed. *Finnish Folkloristics 2. Studia Fennica* 18. Helsinki: Suomalaisen Kirjallisuuden Seura.

Lord, A.B. 1960. *The Singer of Tales.* New York: Harvard University Press.

Olrik, Axel. 1908. "Episke love i folkedigt-ningen." *Danske studier* 5. København: Det schubotheske Forlag.

Peltonen, Ulla-Maija. 1996. *Punakapinan muistot.* Helsinki: Suomalaisen Kirjalli-suuden Seura.

Pentikäinen, Juha. 1978. "Oral Repertoire and World View. An Anthropological Study of Marina Takalo's Life History." *Folklore Fellows' Communications* 219. Helsinki: Academia Scientiarum Fennica.

Pöysä, Jyrki. 1997. *Jätkän synty.* Helsinki: Suomalaisen Kirjallisuuden Seura.

Siikala, Anna-Leena. 1990. "Interpreting Oral Narrative." *Folklore Fellows' Communications* 245. Helsinki: Academia Scientiarum Fennica.

Siikala, Anna-Leena. 2002. "Mythic Images and Shamanism. A Perspective on Kalevala Poetry." *Folklore Fellows' Communications* 280. Helsinki: Academia Scientiarum Fennica.

Stark, Laura. 1998. "Magic, Body and Social Order. The Construction of Gender Through Women's Private Rituals in Traditional Finland." *Studia Fennica Folkloristica* 5. Helsinki: Finnish Literature Society.

Stewart, Susan. 1984. "Notes on Distressed Genres." *Journal of American Folklore* 104(411): 5–31.

von Sydow, C.W. 1934. "Geography and Folk-tale Ecotypes." *Béaloideas* 4: 344–355.

von Sydow, C.W. 1948. "On the Spread of Tradition" in Laurits Bødker, Ed. *Selected Papers on Folklore.* Copenhagen: Rosenkilde and Bagger.

Tarkka, Lotte 2005: *Rajarahvaan laulu. Tutkimus Vuokkiniemen kalevalaisesta kulttuurista.* Helsinki: Suomalaisen Kirjallisuuden Seura.

Tarkka, Lotte. 2011. "Songs of the Border People. Kalevala-Meter Poetry in Vuokkiniemi Parish 1821–1921." *Folklore Fellows' Communications.* Helsinki: Acade-mia Scientiarum Fennica.

Thompson, Stith. 1927. "The Types of the Folk-Tale. A Classification and Bibliography. Antti Aarne's Verzeichnis der Märchentypen" *Folklore Fellows' Communications* 3. Trans. and enlarged. *Folklore Fellows' Communi-cations* 74. Helsinki: Academia Scientiarum Fennica.

Thompson, Stith. 1932–1936. "Motif-Index of Folk-Literature I–VI." *Folklore Fellows' Communications* 106–109, 116–117. Helsinki: Academia Scientiarum Fennica.

Virtanen, Leea. 1978. *Children's Lore. Studia Fennica* 22. Helsinki: Finnish Literature Society.

Uther, Hans-Jörg. 2004. "The Types of International Folktales. A Classification and Bibliography. I–III." *Folklore Fellows' Communications* 284–286. Helsinki: Academia Scientiarum Fennica.

Wilson, William A. 1976. *Folklore and Nationalism in Modern Finland.* Bloomington and Indianapolis: Indiana University Press.

Wolf, Friedrich August. 1795 [1988]. *Prolegomena to Homer 1795*. Princeton, NJ: Princeton University Press.

Zguta, Russell. 1978. *Russian Minstrels. A History of the Skomorokhi*. Oxford: Oxford University Press.

Further Reading

Foley, John Miles. 1995. *The Singer of Tales in Performance*. Bloomington and Indianapolis: Indiana University Press.

Harvilahti, Lauri. 2008b. "Honko, Lauri (1932–2002)" in Donald Haase, Ed. *The Greenwood Encyclopedia of Folktales and Fairy Tales*. Vol. 2. Westport, CT: Greenwood Press.

Holbek, Bengt. 1987. "Interpretation of Fairy Tales. Danish Folklore in a European Perspective." *Folklore Fellows' Communications* 239. Helsinki: Suomalainen Tiedeakatemia.

Kaivola-Bregenhøj, Annikki. 1978. "The Nominativus Absolutus Formula – One Syntactic-semantic Structural Scheme of The Finnish Riddle Genre." *FF Communications* 222. Trans. Susan Sinisalo. Helsinki: Suomalainen tiedeakatemia.

Krohn, Kaarle. 1918. *Kalevalankysymyksiä I–II*. Sust XXXXV–XXXVI. Helsinki: Suomalais-Ugrilainen Seura.

Krohn, Kaarle. 1926. *Die folkloristische Arbeitsmethode, begründet von Julius Krohn und weitergeführt von nordischen Forschern*. Oslo: H. Aschehoug.

Köngäs-Maranda, Elli. 1978. "Review of William A. Wilson. 'Folklore and Nationalism in Modern Finland'." *Western Folklore* 36(1): 63–67.

CHAPTER 21 IRELAND

Diarmuid Ó Giolláin

Ireland (*Éire*) was a culturally unified country with a standardized language and a rich vernacular literature from the early medieval period. While the notion of a national political supremacy existed, in practice the country was divided into competing polities. It became a lordship of the English Crown as a result of the twelfth-century Anglo-Norman invasion (with the title King of Ireland later adopted by English monarchs). An English-speaking population (Irish *Gall*) lived in Ireland since then, distinct from the native Irish (*Gael*), but effective English control was limited to the Pale, the region around Dublin, until the seventeenth century. The indigenous language and culture were seriously threatened only from this time on.

Sixteenth and seventeenth century English accounts compared the Irish to the contemporary American Indians and Elizabethan adventurers were attracted as much by Ireland as they were by America; figures such as Sir Walter Raleigh, notorious in Ireland, were active in both. Formal schemes of Protestant colonization were undertaken in the sixteenth and seventeenth centuries, notably the Plantation of Ulster. The Elizabethan and Cromwellian conquests, in the sixteenth and seventeenth centuries respectively, and the defeat of James II in 1691 led to great losses to Ireland's cultural heritage. Denied patronage with the dispossession of most of the native nobility and the suppression of the Catholic Church, Gaelic high culture was dealt a near fatal blow. Conquest and its aftermath left Catholics, the descendants both of the native Irish and of the Anglo-Norman settlers (the "Old English"), largely deprived of their traditional elites, above all in Ulster, and subject to official discrimination of one kind or another until the late nineteenth century (and until the 1960s in Ulster). Protestant settlers, forming more than a quarter of the population by the end of the seventeenth century, were not a homogenous group. They included the so-called Protestant Ascendancy, which now owned most of the country and monopolized political power, and more humble colonists also mostly of recent English origin who shared with them membership of the Anglican Church of Ireland, the established church (numbering perhaps 12% of the population of Ireland). They were distinguished

A Companion to Folklore, First Edition. Edited by Regina F. Bendix and Galit Hasan-Rokem.
© 2012 John Wiley & Sons, Ltd. Published 2012 John Wiley & Sons, Ltd.

from dissenting Protestants, the most numerous of whom were Presbyterians of Scottish origin, concentrated above all in Ulster.

The Irish language gradually became socially and geographically marginalized, spoken by less than half the population on the eve of the Great Famine of the 1840s. Nearly 50 years later, when the language revival movement began, Irish speakers had been reduced to 14.5% of the population. By then there was little writing in the language, in effect a continuum of peasant dialects. The value of the crumbling Gaelic tradition, literary and oral, came into its own in the age of cultural nationalism as both the evidence of the persistence of an Irish nation and the justification of Ireland's claim for international recognition. Without this cultural argument, the problem would be simply that Ireland, racked by poverty and unrest, needed better government; indeed it was in those terms that Giuseppe Mazzini was to pose the Irish question (Ó Giolláin 2000: 117–118).

NATIONAL OR POPULAR?

The modern Irish word for folklore, *béaloideas*, renders "tradition" in the first English-Irish dictionary, published in Paris in 1732. Printing in Irish began with sixteenth century Protestant texts, part of a state effort to promote the Reformation in Ireland, while early Catholic printing was associated with the continental Irish colleges such as that of Paris, centres for the Counter-Reformation and for a substantial Irish Catholic diaspora. In a survey of the semantics of the word, Dáithí Ó hÓgáin (2002) sees it initially referring to the oral tradition of the Church (*béal-*, "oral," *oideas*, "instruction"), an important question of authority in the light of the Protestant challenge to Rome. The word then shifted semantically to include oral tradition in general. The first record of *béaloideas* is in a religious work by the poet, scholar and Counter-Reformation priest Geoffrey Keating (Seathrún Céitinn (about 1569–1644)). Keating is best known for his history of Ireland, *Foras feasa ar Éirinn* ("a foundation of knowledge about Ireland," c. 1634), in which he asserted that, other than the Bible, the three things by which the truth of history is assured are *béaloideas na sean* ("of the elders"), old writings and those artifacts called in Latin *monumenta*.

Keating's history long remained the outstanding example of Irish literary style. While it did not appear in print in Irish until the scholarly edition of 1902, a rich scribal tradition circulated it widely down to the nineteenth century. *Foras feasa* refuted the supposed barbarism of Ireland and her inhabitants used by English writers to justify conquest and attempts to impose the Reformation. Tracing the history of Ireland from the creation to the twelfth century through its succession of mythical and historical invaders, it concluded with the "Old English," Keating's own ancestors. The old ethnic divide between *Gael* and *Gall* was transcended in this new national narrative: the country's inhabitants were now simply *Éireannaigh*, "Irish," and contrasted with the contemporary Protestant colonists, the "New English."

Seán Ó Conaill's long poem *Tuireamh na hÉireann* ("Ireland's elegy," c. 1655–1659) "has been viewed as the poor person's *Foras feasa*" (Cunningham 2000: 192). Covering similar ground to Keating, it dealt additionally with contemporary events, culminating with the Cromwellian conquest. It outlined the oppression and suffering of the Irish people and affirmed their Irish and Catholic identity. The number of surviving manuscript copies, including nineteenth-century English translations, suggests an extraordinary popularity. Clearly influenced by it and by Keating was a long poem well known from oral tradition, *Seanchas na Sceiche* ("history of the bush"), by the oral poet Raftery (1779–1835), that recounted Ireland's history from the Flood up to the calamities of the seventeenth century (as witnessed by the thorn bush under which the poet was forced to take shelter on a rainy day).

Of great popularity in the Irish-speaking regions of the West, Raftery's songs came to the attention of Douglas Hyde and Lady Gregory, folklorists and luminaries of the late nineteenth-century literary revival. Learned historical traditions were key influences on Raftery, who was illiterate and blind from early childhood. Poems by the leading eighteenth-century poets, whose fame was preserved in folklore, circulated widely in manuscript, but also as songs, to be later recorded by folklore and song collectors. Many of them were political, reflecting continuing loyalty to the Jacobite cause after the defeat and exile of James II. Manuscripts circulated widely down to the nineteenth century and storytellers interviewed in the early twentieth century sometimes recalled hearing them being read aloud in their youth.

The director of the Irish Folklore Commission was to stress the preservation of elements of Gaelic high culture by peasants and referred to himself and his staff as "literary executors of earlier generations" (Ó Duilearga 1943: 13). This points to a key feature of Irish Gaelic culture since the seventeenth century: the symbiotic relationship of the literary and oral traditions. From this derived the implicit argument within the developing field of Irish folklore studies that in transcending popular culture, oral traditions asserted the continuation of a national tradition.

From Antiquarianism to the First Collectors

One of the strands from which folklore studies emerged was antiquarianism, which discovered evidence of national antiquity in peasant culture and thus, for the first time, made it a legitimate object of knowledge. The literary value of folk culture was already clear from the 1760s in the poetry of Macpherson and Bishop Percy and its philosophical value in the writings of Rousseau. Herder understood this in his project to create an authentic German literature and in his opposition to Enlightenment universalism. His literary model was revolutionary in that it gave writers who had no native literary models access to literary resources of their own. Hence "the popular tales collected, edited, reworked, and published by patriotic writers ... became the first quantifiable resource of a nascent literary space," contends Pascale Casanova (2004: 224–225), pointing to the relationship between the founding of a literature and the founding of a nation. Folklore, instead of being the mark of the popular or the provincial, could be both evidence of national history and raw material for the construction of a national culture.

An interest in Ireland's history, literature, and language gradually appealed to Ireland's new Protestant elite, especially when its interests clashed with those of England. Eighteenth-century patriotism, seeking to contribute to the betterment of society, was open to an interest in Irish antiquities, but Anglo-Irish antiquarianism had a colonial relationship with native Gaelic learning, and a colonial perspective informs the work of some of the pioneers of Irish folklore studies *avant la lettre*. Yet the first stirrings of modern Irish nationalism can be seen in the strivings of the eighteenth-century Protestant Patriots for legislative independence in Ireland's colonial parliament, in some ways comparable to the "creole nationalism" of the European colonists in the Americas. If Ireland could be considered a colony before 1800, with the Act of Union it was fully integrated into the United Kingdom.

Charles Vallancey came to Ireland in 1750 as a British army officer and specialist in military fortifications. The most famous antiquary of the day, his writings on the Irish language and on Irish antiquities were important, not so much for their scholarly value (much of his work is patently absurd), but by validating such interests. He communicated with the orientalist Sir William Jones in India, and saw himself emulating Jones' work by studying Irish law. Indeed he saw definite racial and cultural links between Ireland and India. Clare O'Halloran (2004: 48–49) sees "obvious parallels between Vallancey's career as a soldier, engineer and cartographer in Ireland, and the orientalists of the East India Company, all of whom, whether soldiers or not, were engaged directly in the colonial enterprise." Furthermore, the colonial relationship in India between pandit and orientalist was mirrored in that of Vallancey and Maurice O'Gorman, his scribe and teacher of Irish (2004: 51). Vallancey's own journal, *Collectanea de rebus hibernicis* (1770–1804) included two essays on folk festivals and a section of "Queries recommended to the curious" with questions covering other aspects of popular custom and belief.

The political dimension to understanding Ireland's past was clear in late eighteenth- and nineteenth-century debates. Conservative Protestants saw a country saved from barbarism by English intervention. Catholics and liberal Protestants saw an Irish Golden Age prematurely ended by foreign invasions. Gathering the lost or dispersed proof of Ireland's past was thus a necessary task. The pioneering Irish antiquarian societies, the Physico-Historical Society (1744–1752) with its solely Protestant membership, the Select Committee of Antiquities of the Dublin Society (1772–1774) and the Hibernian Antiquarian Society (1779–1783) were short lived and of limited effectiveness. The Dublin Society was an enlightened body founded in 1731 to improve the country by promoting agriculture, arts, industry and science (and it was to be at the origin of later national institutions such as the National Museum and the National Library). Its Select Committee was founded at Vallancey's instigation, to purchase Gaelic manuscripts and to publish translations of them. Vallancey was also a founder member of the prestigious Royal Irish Academy (1785–), one of the concerns of which was antiquities. The first volume of its *Transactions* included a study of Macpherson's Ossian. Theophilus O'Flanagan's short-lived Dublin Gaelic Society (1807) was the first of a series of such societies that was to stretch to the foundation of the Gaelic League in 1892.

Tales of the Fianna were known in Irish literature from the eighth century. Telling of the exploits of a mythical pagan warrior band, they ostensibly passed into the historical era when Oisín, son of the Fianna's leader Fionn, after a sojourn in the Land of Youth (Tír na nÓg), returned to find his comrades long dead and gone and St Patrick in the process of converting the Irish. Until the nineteenth century the tales were copied and circulated in manuscript in Ireland and in Gaelic Scotland (which shared a literary language until the eighteenth century). Folktales and oral lays of the Fianna carried great prestige and were vibrant into the twentieth century in both countries and in the Scottish Gaelic outpost of Cape Breton in Nova Scotia; a few of the oral tales are known to be of literary origin.

The Fianna burst into European consciousness with James Macpherson's *Ossian* (1760–). Ossian (Scottish Gaelic *Oisean*, Irish *Oisín*) appeared when positive ideas of the Celts were already circulating, in Britain as well as in France, and primitivist ideas were influential in literature. Irish opposition to Macpherson's claims for the authenticity of his translations, for Ossian's Scottishness, for the priority of the Scottish literary tradition over the Irish, and to his dismissal of Irish historians such as Keating was almost immediate. Leerssen (1996a: 344) points out that partisans of a noble Irish past profited from the debate, "not only in the literary aspect, which was ... not implicated in Macpherson's eclipse, but also in the historical aspect; moreover Irish antiquaries had from the beginning ranged themselves on the anti-Macpherson side when it came to the historical implications of Ossian." The defence of the Gaelic past became a national Irish concern, thus taken up by Anglo-Irish writers as well; the founding of the Select Committee of the Dublin Society took place in the shadow of the Ossianic debate (Leerssen 1996: 346–347). Gaelic and Anglo-Irish versions of Ireland's past, while differing on many profound issues, began to converge in this particular debate.

Two works in particular showed the clear influence of the Ossianic debate and of the contemporary fashion for primitivism, Joseph Cooper Walker's *Historical Memoirs of the Irish Bards* (1786) and Charlotte Brooke's *Reliques of Irish Poetry* (1789). Walker's work depended on the assistance of more established antiquaries, whose essays were included in the volume; one of his own contributions was an account of the life of the famous blind harper Turlough O'Carolan (1670–1738). Walker also included musical notation of Irish melodies, including folksongs. The translations of Gaelic poetry and song were by Brooke, whose own anthology was informed by her extensive contacts with other scholars and antiquaries, including Maurice O'Gorman, and with Thomas Percy, author of *Reliques of English Poetry* (1765), who had come to Ireland in 1782 as Anglican Bishop of Dromore. It included lays of the Fianna as well as folksongs, translated by her into an ornate English style. *Reliques*, mindful of the Macpherson controversy, also gave the original Irish texts. In both of these Anglo-Irish works, Gaelic learned and oral cultures were treated indistinctly; in contemporary Ireland both were subaltern.

Belfast grew rapidly in the late eighteenth century, its industrial development led by the enlightened Presbyterian bourgeoisie (educated in Scotland since Trinity College Dublin (TCD), Ireland's only university, was Anglican). An interest in native Irish culture, seen as a patriotic endeavour, overlapped with the radical politics of the United Irishmen whose aim, in the words of their chief ideologue Theobold Wolfe Tone, was "to substitute the common name of Irishman in place of the denominations of Catholic, Protestant, and Dissenter." The harp, played with long fingernails on metal strings, had an esteemed place in Gaelic elite culture but had long been in decline. A series of harp festivals culminated with that of Belfast in 1792, by which time the few remaining harpers were wandering musicians playing folk music along with a few compositions of O'Carolan's. The young Edward Bunting was asked by the organizer, Dr James MacDonnell, to transcribe the music at the festival. The first volume of his pioneering work, *A General Collection of the Ancient Music of Ireland*, appeared in 1796, but, Bunting, knowing no Irish, excluded song texts, so after the festival the Gaelic scholar Patrick Lynch was employed to make good this lack in the field.

The previous year a Gaelic magazine, *Bolg an Tsolair* ("miscellany"), had appeared in Belfast, published by the *Northern Star*, the organ of the United Irishmen.

Compiled by Lynch, it contained, besides grammar and vocabulary, a poem of the Fianna and other poems and folksongs, translated by Brooke. There was but a single issue of it; the printing presses of the *Northern Star* were destroyed in 1797 as part of the repressive measure against the United Irishmen, who rose in revolt in 1798. The rebellion convulsed much of the country, brought a belated French military intervention and was savagely repressed, leading directly to the Act of Union of 1800. Anglo-Irish elite patronage of Irish learning did not survive these events and in the early nineteenth century was largely the preserve of Catholic intellectuals. MacDonnell, the Protestant scion of an old Gaelic family, and Robert Shipboy MacAdam founded the Ulster Gaelic Society in 1830. A successful Presbyterian businessman, MacAdam collected Gaelic manuscripts, often taking advantage of business trips for that purpose and hiring Gaelic scribes on to his staff. He wrote down lays and tales of the Fianna from oral tradition, as well as other folktales, and published a collection of 600 proverbs.

State intervention in social affairs in Ireland in the nineteenth century was much greater than in Britain and was "in response to what was seen as acute economic crisis and continuing violence and disorder..." (Ó Ciosáin 1998: 93). The Ordnance Survey, founded in 1791 in order to accurately map Britain in anticipation of the feared French invasion, was extended to Ireland in 1824. Using an unprecedentedly detailed scale, it mapped all 32 counties between 1825 and 1841. At its height its staff numbered 2,000, including noted Irish scholars, and gathered information on antiquities, toponymy, geology, industry, and traditional culture. Stiofán Ó Cadhla (2007: 5) argues for the colonial nature of this engagement with popular culture, articulated in "an almost impervious evolutionary science."

Thomas Crofton Croker (1798–1854), who spent his career as an admiralty clerk in London, is best known for *Fairy Legends and Traditions of the South of Ireland* (1825). This work appeared as *Irische Elfenmärchen* in the Grimm Brothers' version the following year and their introduction was translated for a second volume of Croker's. With Croker and his contemporaries, "[t]he Irish peasantry, until then seen as the pauperized, brutish and sullen dregs of a dead old culture, full of disaffection and hatred for their new rulers, gain cultural interest" (Leerssen 1996b: 162). Croker was a leading antiquary in the England of his day and was a founder member of the Camden Society, the Percy Society and the British Archaeological Society. Like Vallancey and Walker before him, his knowledge of the Irish language was limited. His later works were devoted to song, of which *Keen of the South of Ireland: As Illustrative of Irish Political and Domestic History, Manners, Music, and Superstitions* (1844) is based on folk traditions ("keen" or *caoineadh* is the funeral lament), though it does not, however, give the original texts.

Croker was the first of many Irish folktale collectors and editors. Also London-based, Thomas Keightley (1789–1872) is best known for *The Fairy Mythology* (1828) and *Tales and Popular Fictions* (1834), "the two most mature English studies on comparative folklore in the first half of the century" in Richard Dorson's estimation (Dorson 1968: 52). Patrick Kennedy (1801–1873), of humble Catholic origin, was familiar with contemporary folklore scholarship, mentioning the Grimm Brothers and Asbjørnsen and Moe in the preface to *Legendary Fictions of the Irish Celts* (1866), one of his many collections of reworked tales, and emphasizing the importance of recording disappearing Irish traditions. The interest of the artist and archaeologist

George Petrie (1789–1866), who was in charge of the Topographical Section of the Ordnance Survey, was music. His *The Ancient Music of Ireland* (1855–1882) is one of the key collections: nearly two hundred melodies, song texts in Irish and English as well as notes on the songs and their sources. William Crooke (1848–1923), like Keightley a graduate of TCD, was a civil servant in India who published widely on Indian folklore. In retirement in England, he became president of the Folklore Society and editor of *Folklore*. He was an important example of what Sadhana Naithani has called the "colonizer–folklorist," his work a product of imperial relations, dependent on the largely uncredited contribution of the Indian scholar Pandit Râm Gharîb Chaube (Naithani 2002: xxiii–xlvii).

ETHNOGRAPHIC POPULISM?

The nation-state is usually seen as a response to modernity. In Ernest Gellner's formulation, dynastic states such as France or England developed into modern nation-states under an existing ethnic high culture, gradually eliminating folk traditions along the way. Majority ethnic groups lacking a continuous high culture and dominated by a ruling class of foreign origin – a situation common enough in central and Eastern Europe – had to construct a modern high culture from folklore (1996: 139). Miroslav Hroch (1996: 84) argues that most European national movements long predated industrial society. There were often antecedents for modern nation building in late medieval and early modern times, often in aborted earlier efforts that left resources for a later period: the memory of former independence or statehood, the survival of the medieval written language. In Ireland the majority ethnic group lacked a continuous high culture and was dominated by a ruling class of foreign origin, leaving folklore as an important resource for building a modern national culture. Even more importantly, the memory of a medieval Golden Age and the persistence of an ancient literary language were invoked to give historical depth to a modern Irish nation.

The creation of a national high culture is part of a deeper question: the emergence of a people. Who are the people, and how may the people be formed? Ernesto Laclau (2005: 94) argues that the *populus* is the given in a society, "the ensemble of social relations *as* they actually are." If there is a breach in what he calls the "communitarian space," if the normally legitimate demands of the *plebs* are unfulfilled, the *plebs* "can identify itself with the *populus* conceived as an ideal totality." The demands of the *plebs* are isolated at the beginning, but by recognizing a similarity between the different demands and articulating them together, a barrier can be formed separating the *plebs* from the dominant group in society and a collective agent articulated as the people (2005: 74). Folklore, cultural representations of the *plebs*, helped to clarify this barrier when attributed to the *populus*. This was in fact part of Herder's project: the *Volk* in his *Volkslieder* (1778–1779) were both *plebs* and *populus*. Ethno-linguistic criteria are relevant, especially when they distinguish the *plebs* from the dominant group in society, but the *populus* is not necessarily defined in ethno-linguistic terms.

Folklore thus oscillated between the national and the popular. Claude Grignon and Jean-Claude Passeron (1989: 69) characterize the debate on popular culture in terms of an initial "class ethnocentrism." There are two moves away form this, a cultural relativism that attributes autonomy to popular culture, and a "miserabilism" that slots popular culture into the wider social order: "where the populist marvels at discovering the symbolic treasures in a popular culture ... the bourgeois like the miserabilist sees only penury." Evolutionary folklorists were "miserabilists" and appeared more in metropolitan countries with continuities in cultural and political life; following Tylor's *Primitive Culture* (1867), they saw themselves as working with "survivals" from an earlier and more primitive era. Folklore also appealed to the nostalgia of traditional elites for a harmonious world upset by industrialization and the growth of class politics, but it could not challenge the accumulated prestige of high culture. The "devolutionists" (Dundes 1969: 5–19) saw themselves as recuperating dispersed fragments of an earlier integral and harmonious whole. Their point of departure was the inadequacy of the present, and their perspective was most convincing in countries that had suffered ruptures in cultural and political life. They were "populists": for them, folklore's value was in its resistance to change.

The *Volk* in the science of *Volkskunde* as conceived in late eighteenth-century Germany leaned towards the whole, the *populus*, the "folk" in "folklore" conceptualized in Victorian England towards the part, the *plebs*. Herder saw folksongs as the archives of the German people (*Volk*). In Italy in the 1930s, Gramsci (1991: 44) observed that "the folkloric comes close to the 'provincial' in all senses ..." Folklore was identified with the regional in the work of late nineteenth- and early twentieth-century English, French, and Brazilian folklorists, according to Renato Ortiz (1992: 68). He argues that they were provincial intellectuals marginalized by the consolidation of the modern state and who thus positioned themselves as the privileged interlocutors of regional culture on the metropolitan stage, using folklore as a means to maintain their cultural capital.

The general emergence of an ethnological discourse was thus tempered by specific national or regional contexts. Joan Prat (1991: 13–14) argues for two orientations in the origins of Spanish ethnology, one from the Enlightenment and informed by positivism and evolutionism, leading to an anthropological discourse proper, the other based on Romanticism and associated with regionalist and nationalist movements, leading to a folkloristic discourse. In the United Kingdom, serious consideration was given in the 1890s to the merging of the Royal Anthropological Institute of Great Britain and Ireland and the Folk-Lore Society (Stocking 1996: 104), of which anthropologists such as J.G. Frazer, Tylor and A.C. Haddon were members. But it was anthropology that was institutionalized (both in the United Kingdom and in Spain) while folklore studies remained outside the academy and hence, by definition, the preserve of amateurs. The observation of the Finnish-born folklorist Elli Köngäs-Maranda has to be qualified, but bears more than a grain of truth: "[a]nthropology studies the others, the folklorist studies his or her own ... Colonizing countries have anthropological museums; colonized countries have folklore archives ..." (Köngäs-Maranda [1979]: 166). From initial "miserabilist" and evolutionary perspectives on Irish folklore informed by colonialism, motivated by the ethnocentrism of the Irish elite, a populist and "devolutionary" perspective came to dominate, giving evidence of national antiquity and providing raw material for a national literature. Ireland's secession from the United Kingdom in 1921 was to make the institutionalization of Irish folklore studies possible.

The Young Ireland movement, which staged an abortive rising in 1848, introduced cultural nationalist ideas to Ireland. Politics, nevertheless, was to be dominated until the 1890s by the question of the repeal of the Act of Union, to which most Protestants were opposed, fearing that "Home Rule" would be "Rome Rule." The Great Famine of 1845–1848 was a watershed in Irish history: 1 million deaths, mass evictions and mass emigration. Population censuses give a good illustration of the momentous change that followed: 8.18 million in 1841, 6.55 in 1851, 5.8 in 1861, 5.41 in 1871, 5.18 in 1881, and 4.7 in 1891. Sir William Wilde, in his 1849 introduction to *Irish Popular Superstitions* (1852), wrote

> In this state of things, with depopulation the most terrific which any country ever experienced, on the one hand, and the spread of education, and the introduction of railroads, colleges and industrial and other educational schools, on the other, – together with the rapid decay of our Irish vernacular, in which most of our legends, romantic tales, ballads and bardic annals, the vestiges of Pagan rites, and the relics of fairy charms were preserved, – can superstition, or if superstitious belief, can superstitious practices continue to exist? (Wilde 1979: 10–11)

Wilde (1815–1876) was a noted surgeon, statistician, and antiquary. His wife Jane (1826–1896) was well known as a translator, writer of patriotic verse in *The Nation* (the Young Ireland nationalist paper founded in 1842), and editor of some of the folklore originally gathered by Sir William in *Ancient Legends, Mystic Charms, and Superstitions of Ireland* (1888). They were overshadowed, of course, by their son Oscar, whose literary works include *Kunstmärchen*.

Johann Kaspar Zeuss' *Grammatica Celtica* (1853) was the foundation stone of Celtic philology and greatly encouraged the study of Irish. Zeuss had pioneered the study of the seventh- and eighth-century Irish glosses found in manuscripts in Würzburg, Milan, St Gallen and other centres, and was first in a line – mostly German – of eminent Celticists specializing in Irish. The revelation of the extent and of the importance of medieval Irish literature was an important legitimation for Irish when it was associated with poverty and ignorance at home; Douglas Hyde invoked these scholars in "The Necessity for de-Anglicising Ireland," as did Séamus Ó Duilearga in his editorial in the first issue of the folklore journal *Béaloideas* (1927).

The study of the contemporary language brought Celtic philologists such as the Dane Holger Pedersen (1867–1953) to Irish-speaking parts of Ireland. He visited the Aran Islands in 1896 and worked with a storyteller from whom he made a large collection of tales. This man, Máirtín Neile Ó Conghaile (about 1826–1904), also claimed to have taught Irish to Franz Nikolaus Finck whose *Die araner Mundart* (1896, 1899) was the first study of an Irish dialect, and to have narrated stories that were published by Jeremiah Curtin. The Norwegian Carl Marstrander (1883–1965) visited the Great Blasket Island in Co. Kerry in 1907 and studied Irish with Tomás Ó Criomhthain (1855?–1937), a peasant and fisherman whose encouragement by visiting scholars led to his publication of a memoir, *An tOileánach* (*The Islandman*, 1929), the first of a series of works of great literary – as well as ethnographic – value from the island.

The Irish-American Jeremiah Curtin (1835–1906) studied under Francis James Child in Harvard and from 1883 to 1891 worked for the US Bureau of Ethnology. A prodigious learner of languages, he developed a keen interest in myth, publishing Native American, Russian, Hungarian and Siberian texts. He made three visits to Ireland, beginning in 1887, in search of myths, first consulting scholars in the Royal

Irish Academy. He used interpreters on his fieldwork, but had a reasonable knowledge of Irish. *Myths and Folklore of Ireland* (1890), *Tales of the Fairies and of the Ghost World* (1893) and *Hero Tales of Ireland* (1894), though failing to consistently name informants, were of a high scholarly standard. James Mooney (1861–1921), another Irish-American who worked for the Bureau of Ethnology, published a series of essays on Irish folk medicine, death and calendar customs. His fame rests, of course, on his works on Native American cultures (Ó Siadhail 2009: 1–36). Irish immigrants to the United States were the major source for one of the great collections of Irish folk music. Francis O'Neill (1848–1936) ran away to sea at the age of 17 and eventually settled in Chicago, where he joined the police force, rising in the ranks to eventually become chief of police. His collections of Irish folk music are the largest ever published: *The Music of Ireland* (1903) was his first; *The Dance Music of Ireland* (1907) remains hugely influential among Irish folk musicians.

The literary movement of which W.B. Yeats (1865–1939) was the leading light is usually dated from around 1890. Its origins were in earlier antiquarian study, translations of medieval Irish literature, the popular nationalist literature of Young Ireland, and folklore. In 1891 Yeats and Douglas Hyde (1860–1949) founded the Irish Literary Society in London. A year later, along with John O'Leary, veteran revolutionary and man of letters, they founded the National Literary Society to promote the literature and folklore of Ireland. Hyde's inaugural lecture to the society, "The Necessity for de-Anglicizing Ireland" (1892), argued that Ireland, by rejecting the *Volksgeist* – abandoning its native language and culture, made itself incapable of any worthwhile cultural creation and denied its own claims to recognition as a separate nation.

Though part of the Protestant elite, Hyde's rural childhood brought him close to Irish-speaking peasants. From 1890 he began publishing folksongs with his own striking translations and commentary in the pages of *The Nation*, later collected in the seminal volume, *Love Songs of Connacht* (1893). *Beside the Fire* (1890) gave a scholarly introduction to the folktale and portraits of storytellers with a pioneering historical overview of the collection of Irish folklore; in it Hyde complained of Irish collectors' ignorance of and indifference to the Irish language. These two books were more than scholarly works; as literature they became seminal contributions to the Irish literary revival. Hyde's *Songs ascribed to Raftery* (1903) was largely responsible for that poet's subsequent fame.

Yeats, drawn to folklore by disenchantment with modernity, published two folklore anthologies, as well as *The Celtic Twilight* (1893), a mixture of oral testimony and tradition along with his own commentary and speculation. A poet influenced by Irish mythology, William Larminie (1849–1900) spent much of his career in London as a civil servant in the India Office. He learnt Irish and published faithful translations of the tales he collected in *West Irish Folk-Tales and Romances* (1893). Lady (Augusta) Gregory (1852–1932) was a dramatist, translator, one of the founders of the national theatre, and a folklorist. A member of a Protestant ascendancy family whose husband had been Governor of Ceylon, she became a convert to Irish nationalism through witnessing the revolution in Egypt in 1882. Some of her influential contributions to Irish folklore include *Poets and Dreamers: Studies and Translations from the Irish* (1903), with its essays on Raftery and on Jacobite poetry, and a later collection of legends and memorates, *Visions and Beliefs of the West of Ireland* (1920). Like Hyde,

Yeats and Larminie a graduate of Trinity College Dublin, John Millington Synge (1871–1909) learned Irish and studied contemporary folklore scholarship. Yeats had suggested he travel to the Aran Islands when they met in Paris in 1896, and Synge spent a number of summers there between 1898 and 1901. *The Aran Islands* (1907) is part travelogue, autobiographical memoir, and ethnography (the storyteller Old Mourteen in the book is Máirtín Neile Ó Conghaile). Synge's plays, notably *The Playboy of the Western World* (1907), are strongly influenced by rural life in the west of Ireland.

Hyde represented the coming of age of Irish folklore scholarship, but he was also a bridge between Gaelic scholarship and Anglo-Irish literary tradition. "The Necessity for de-Anglicising Ireland" was a manifesto, which led to the founding of the Gaelic League the following year (1893) with Hyde as president. The League aimed to preserve Irish as a spoken language in Irish-speaking districts, to extend its use beyond them, and to create a modern Gaelic literature. Its aims were in fact foreshadowed by the journal founded in New York in 1881, *An Gaodhal* ("the Gael"), which published Irish lessons, sermons, original literary compositions, learned texts, translations and folklore. It was to be the model for the other journals published by the League, all of which published a considerable amount of folklore until the foundation of the folklore journal *Béaloideas* in 1927.

The conclusion of the debates about reviving Irish as a modern literary language, the proponents of Keating's seventeenth-century prose losing out to supporters of the modern dialects, strengthened the League's links to vernacular culture. Owing to the dearth of books in Irish, folklore was used both as a source of reading materials and as a literary model. In its first 30 years folklore texts were the most common books published by the League, usually edited with contextual information. From 1897 the Oireachtas, the League's annual cultural festival modelled on the Welsh Eisteddfod, and similar events at a local level, held competitions for literary composition, for collecting folklore, for storytelling, for traditional singing, and also hosted arts and crafts exhibitions of the kind that had become common at the national, international, and universal exhibitions of the time.

The connection between world's fairs and folklife is well known, whether through their replicas of vernacular architecture, the use of wax dummies to display folk costume or the exhibition of arts and crafts (Wörner 1999; Stoklund 2003). From the Great Famine, there were philanthropic efforts by upper-class women to alleviate Irish poverty through the development of cottage industries. The Donegal Industrial Fund, founded by an Englishwoman Alice Rowland Hart influenced by John Ruskin and William Morris, and the Irish Industries Association, by Ishbel Countess of Aberdeen, wife of the Viceroy of Ireland, were behind what were perhaps the first ambitious attempts at representation of Irish folklife. For the Irish Exhibition held in London in 1888, Hart had a facsimile village built consisting of 12 thatched houses in which Irish craft workers demonstrated their skills and sold their produce. The two Irish villages erected for Chicago's World's Columbian Exposition of 1893 had replicas of peasant houses in which lace-makers and knitters demonstrated their craft. The two organizations gradually declined in the beginning of the new century and were displaced by projects with a more obviously cultural nationalist orientation (Helland 2007).

The first volume of *Folk-Lore* (1890) included an article by Alfred Cort Haddon, a member of the Folk-Lore Society's council, entitled "Legends from Torres Straits."

Professor of Zoology at the Royal College of Science in Dublin since 1881, Haddon, an Englishman, had made a first trip to the Torres Straits in 1888. The ethnography of the Aran Islands that he carried out with C.R. Browne and published in 1892 (Section V was devoted to "Folk-Lore") was a part of the ethnographic survey of the United Kingdom instituted by the British Association for the Advancement of Science. Haddon's ethnographic work in the Aran Islands was a training ground for the 1898 Torres Straits expedition, a foundational event for British social anthropology, which helped him to gain a position in England, in the University of Cambridge, where he spent the rest of his career.

INSTITUTIONALIZATION

Cultural organizations like the Gaelic League for a long time were a neutral ground where both unionists and nationalists could meet; the assimilation of Ireland's Gaelic past into the modern national narrative was the work of unionists and nationalists, Catholics and Protestants; in fact the Protestant Ascendancy bastion of TCD played a major role. Initially the League grew slowly, but in time its influence permeated national life. A major spur to its growth was the Boer War (1899–1902), which galvanized nationalist opinion in Ireland. The League adopted a formally nationalist position in 1915, which led to the resignation of Hyde.

The independence movement was strongly marked by the Gaelic League. After years of armed conflict the Anglo-Irish Treaty of 1921 recognized an Irish Free State, the 1921 Government of Ireland Act having already unilaterally ensured the separation of the six Ulster counties with a Protestant majority, which henceforth became Northern Ireland. Folklore studies continued to be cultivated by figures such as Hyde, professor of Modern Irish in University College Dublin since 1909 and until his retirement in 1932 (he became first President of Ireland in 1938). A short-lived Society of Irish Tradition (1917–1919) that aimed to advance the study of traditional culture and of which Hyde was a member prefigured more significant developments (Stephens 1999). In 1921 Séamus Ó Duilearga (James Hamilton Delargy (1899–1980)), assistant to Hyde, met Reidar Th. Christiansen in a Dublin bookshop. Christiansen's advice led to the founding of the Folklore of Ireland Society in 1927 with its journal, *Béaloideas*, under Delargy's editorship. The same year, on a visit to Ireland, Carl Wilhelm von Sydow on Hyde's recommendation met Ó Duilearga. Von Sydow had first come to Ireland in 1920 and, like Christiansen, had studied Irish with Marstrander in Oslo. Both considered Ireland to be of great importance to comparative folklore research.

With von Sydow's help, Ó Duilearga was granted leave by University College Dublin in 1928 to visit Sweden, the other Nordic countries, Estonia and Germany to familiarize himself with folklore studies. Among the scholars he met were Kaarle Krohn, Oskar Loorits, and Johannes Bolte, and he was greatly impressed by a visit to Skansen, the open-air folk museum in Stockholm (Briody 2007: 88–91; Ó Catháin 2008). After representations to the government, the Irish Folklore Institute was established in 1930 with Ó Duilearga as its director, to be superseded five years later by the Irish Folklore Commission (IFC), attached to the Department of Education, with Ó Duilearga again as director. Seán Ó Súilleabháin (1903–1996) was appointed archivist and spent three months that same year training at the Landsmåls och folkminnesarkivet of Uppsala University. The IFC's task was collecting, cataloguing and publishing folklore. Its remit covered all of Ireland, but its Pan-Gaelic vocation also saw it sending a recording unit to the Isle of Man in 1948 to record from some of the last speakers of Manx (a language related to Irish), and it employed a collector in Gaelic Scotland, Calum MacLean, from 1946 until his secondment to the new School of Scottish Studies in the University of Edinburgh in 1951 (Briody 2007: 306).

Based on the Uppsala classification system, Ó Súilleabháin's handbooks for folklore collectors, *Láimhleabhar Béaloideasa* (1937) and *A Handbook of Irish Folklore* (1942), were an important aid for the full-time collectors. Numbering at most nine at any given time, and mostly native speakers of Irish, they were generally sent to work in their home districts, using Ediphone recording machines and keeping field diaries. Their work was supplemented by the voluntary contributions eventually of thousands of others, including in 1937–1938 senior pupils from most of the primary schools in the state outside the largest towns (Briody 2007: 227ff.). Folklife studies were part of the brief of the IFC. Kevin Danaher (Caoimhín Ó Danachair 1913–2002), who between 1937 and 1939 had studied folklore under Adolph Spamer in Berlin and Leipzig while on a Humboldt scholarship, was the resident specialist and a gifted photographer.

The intangible nature of folklore lent itself to the national-popular, where traditions recorded from peasants transcended their social condition and were used to assert the continuation of a national tradition. The late recognition of folklife in Ireland was due to the fact that it was irrevocably linked to the peasant condition and to popular culture and, as such, developed as a lower-key research field. From the late 1920s the National Museum of Ireland set about assembling an Irish ethnographic collection under its Austrian director, the archaeologist Adolf Mahr (an active Nazi who was not reinstated after the War). The museum later cooperated with the IFC and with the Irish Countrywomen's Association, which had surveyed craftworkers. Field surveys such as those by the Swedish ethnologists Åke Campbell and Albert Nilsson (Eskeröd) in the 1930s added further documentation. The first major exhibition of folklife material was in 1937, a full-time appointment in folklife was made in 1947, A.T. Lucas (1911–1986), later director of the museum, and there was a permanent exhibition from 1950. The material was part of the Irish Antiquities Division until 1974, when a separate Irish Folklife Division was created.

The museum's collection of some 50,000 artefacts – the largest in Ireland – was neglected and had no permanent home until 2001, when the Museum of Irish Country Life, a branch of the National Museum of Ireland, was opened in Turlough House in Co. Mayo. It is an indoor museum, with a new purpose-built gallery and the lower floor of the Victorian mansion used for the exhibits; the upper floor is used for administration. The fate of the National Museum's substantial non-Irish ethnographic material, seen for long as a British imperial relic, was even greater neglect and the collection remains largely unknown to the general public, though plans are afoot to display it properly.

The important non-European ethnographic collection of the Ulster Museum in Belfast has fared better and is accessible to the public. The Welsh-born Emyr Estyn Evans (1905–1989) was the key figure in folklife studies in Northern Ireland, where he arrived in 1928 to set up a geography department in Queen's University, Belfast.

With a background in geography, anthropology, and archaeology, he was also influenced by Swedish folklife studies and by Skansen, which he had visited as a student. In 1955, he established the journal *Ulster Folklife* and his work was widely read, especially *Irish Folk Ways* (1957). Ireland he understood as a periphery in which prehistoric and medieval relics survived because the country was essentially a peasant society that had escaped the industrial revolution. He saw the province of Ulster as differing both from the rest of Ireland and from Britain in its geography, prehistory, and history.

An Ulster Folk Museum finally emerged as part of a postwar movement in museums of everyday life in the United Kingdom, and was founded in 1958; the act establishing it specified its mission as "illustrating the way of life, past and present, and the traditions of the people of Northern Ireland." Occupying a large site on the former estate of Cultra Manor, on the shores of Belfast Lough, it follows the Skansen model with representative vernacular buildings – furnished and decorated as they would have been around 1900 – and demonstrations of traditional arts and crafts. Its remit covers the whole province of Ulster (i.e., Northern Ireland plus three contiguous counties of the Irish Republic). In 1961 the Ulster Folklife Society was founded and collaborated with the museum. The Ulster Folk Museum was merged with the Belfast Transport Museum in 1967 to form the Ulster Folk and Transport Museum, and in 1998 it was amalgamated in the umbrella grouping of the National Museums of Northern Ireland. Its first two directors, George B. Thompson and Alan Gailey, were both geographers by training and former students of Evans'. With a large staff of curators and researchers, it is the major centre in Ireland for folklife research.

Modern Irish anthropology really began in 1931 with the exploratory visit of Lloyd Warner from Harvard University to Co. Clare in order to find a suitable site for ethnographic research. Ó Duilearga was instrumental in providing the researchers, Conrad Arensberg and Solon Kimball, with letters of introduction and a wide range of contacts in the field. Arensberg and Kimball's *Family and Community in Ireland* (1940), became a benchmark for Irish anthropological research. Anthropologists and folklorists were aware of each other and each privileged the partly Irish-speaking West but the lack of common interest tended to militate against any serious engagement with one another until relatively recently.

Folk music was also part of the brief of the IFC and it made substantial music collections. Under the charismatic Seán Ó Riada (1931–1971), a gifted composer who turned away from art music to folk music, University College Cork's music department became an important centre for Irish folk music. The anthropology department of Queen's University Belfast, under the headship of the eminent English ethnomusicologist John Blacking (1928–1990) attracted researchers from within the field of Irish folk music. One of them was a student of Ó Riada's, Mícheál Ó Súilleabháin, who went on to found the Irish World Music Centre in the University of Limerick in 1994; now known as the Irish World Academy for Music and Dance, it specializes in ethnomusicology and ethnochoreology. The Irish Traditional Music Archive was founded in Dublin in 1987 and holds the largest collection of Irish folk music.

The IFC was abolished in 1970, its staff transferred to the new Department of Irish Folklore in UCD, headed by Bo Almqvist, a former student of Dag Strömbäck's in Uppsala. By that time the archives had at least 2 million pages (the greater part in

Irish), a huge collection of photographs, and thousands of hours of sound recordings. In 2005, the department was abolished and incorporated into a new School of Irish, Celtic Studies, Irish Folklore, and Linguistics while the archival function was separated and established as the National Folklore Collection.

The IFC's collections are extraordinarily rich, though there are gaps and weaknesses that can be explained by the constraints, ideological, social, cultural and financial, under which the IFC worked. Contemporary understandings of folklore led to a philological orientation, a neglect of new cultural forms, the undervaluing of women's traditions – and a certain cultural pessimism associated above all with Ó Duilearga. The enormity of the task the IFC set itself and the precarious situation of the Irish language meant that the recording and cataloguing of materials – clearly understood as an eleventh hour mission – usually took precedence. The IFC itself worked under precarious conditions, of its own continuity, of staff employment and of funding (Briody 2007); under those circumstances its achievements are extraordinary.

Ó Duilearga believed that the IFC's priority was collecting and did not encourage his staff to undertake research. Most articles in *Béaloideas* until the 1970s consisted of texts. Nevertheless, important scholarship on Irish folklore did appear. Ó Duilearga's *Leabhar Sheáin Í Chonaill* (1949; trans. *Seán Ó Conaill's Book* 1981), a collection from the narration of a South Kerry storyteller, set the benchmark for editing and annotating Irish oral texts. The German linguist Hans Hartmann worked for a time with the IFC; his study *Der Totenkult in Irland* appeared in 1952. The result of Reidar Christiansen's engagement with Ireland included *Studies in Irish and Scandinavian Folktales* (1959). Máire MacNeill's *The Festival of Lughnasa* (1962) was the major work of analytical research published by a member of the IFC. Ó Súilleabháin and Christiansen's *The Types of the Irish Folktale* (1963) made the IFC's collection available for comparative folktale research.

The small number of professional folklorists and ethnologists and the widespread ignorance of Irish among the practitioners of other disciplines (of which history is the most influential) have made the collections an under-utilized resource. In University College Cork (UCC), folkloristics was established in 1977 under Gearóid Ó Crualaoich, an anthropologist-folklorist, with a full Department of Folklore and Ethnology dating from 2000. It maintains a close relationship with the Northside Folklore Project (1996–), a community-based folklore and oral history scheme in a largely working-class district of Cork City. In the University of Ulster a chair of ethnology and folklife was established in 2005. The nomenclature of the discipline in both UCC and the University of Ulster consciously identifies it with European ethnology. The folklore programme in University College Dublin (UCD) is taught in English, but students must know Irish. In UCC, there are two programs, one in Irish and one in English. Student numbers are small in both institutions; courses in folklore are also taught in departments of Irish language and literature. Outside Ireland, American folklorists have made major contributions to Irish folkloristics, Henry Glassie of the University of Indiana most of all. The University of Notre Dame, also in Indiana, has recently appointed an Irish folklorist.

Folklore collections have long been published in Irish. There is also a rich genre of peasant autobiography in Irish, some dictated, beginning with the Blasket Island books and some have literary merit. Besides *Béaloideas* and *Ulster Folklife*, there are two bilingual journals edited by graduate students of folkloristics, *Sinsear* (1979–) in

UCD, and *Béascna* (2002–) in UCC. Since the late 1990s a number of analytical works has appeared, of which the following in English give some indication of their depth and range. Angela Bourke's *The Burning of Bridget Cleary: A True Story* (1999) is an interdisciplinary study of a notorious murder in 1895 for which fairy belief was blamed. Gearóid Ó Crualaoich's *The Book of the Cailleach: Stories of the Wise-Woman Healer* (2003) interprets such stories as a traditional hermeneutics of the human predicament. Lillis Ó Laoire's *On a Rock in the Middle of the Ocean* (trans. 2005) is a study of song and singers in the Irish-speaking Tory Island. Anne O'Connor's *The Blessed and the Damned* (2005) looks at gender representation in legends of sinful women and unbaptized children. Henry Glassie's *The Stars of Ballymenone* (2006) looks at the individuals in a rich traditional culture. Stiofán Ó Cadhla's *Civilizing Ireland. Ordnance Survey 1824–1842: Ethnography, Cartography, Translation* (2007) examines ethnography within the imperial project of mapping Ireland. Mícheál Briody's *The Irish Folklore Commission 1935–1970* (2007) is a comprehensively detailed and nuanced institutional history. Historian Guy Beiner's *Remembering the Year of the French: Irish Folk History and Social Memory* (2007) is a local study of the 1798 Rebellion using folklore sources. Ray Cashman's *Storytelling on the Northern Irish Border: Characters and Community* (2008) sees local character anecdotes as appealing to a local identity that at times can transcend sectarian division. Ríonach uí Ógáin's *Going to the Well for Water: The Séamus Ennis Field Diary 1942–1946* (trans. 2009) is more than the edited diary of the famous piper when he was a song collector for the IFC; the author's research among his informants and their descendants and the detailed contextual information she unearths are a richly textured homage to the humanity of the singers.

REFERENCES

Briody, Mícheál. 2007. "The Irish Folklore Commission 1935–1970: History, Ideology, Methodology." *Studia Fennica Folkloristica* 17. Helsinki: Finnish Literature Society.

Casanova, Pascale. 2004. *The World Republic of Letters.* Trans. M.B. DeBevoise. Cambridge, MA and London: Harvard University Press.

Cunningham, Bernadette. 2000. *The World of Geoffrey Keating: History, Myth and Religion in Seventeenth-Century Ireland.* Dublin: Four Courts Press.

Dorson, Richard. 1968. *The British Folklorists.* London: Routledge and Kegan Paul.

Dundes, Alan. 1969. "The Devolutionary Premise in Folklore Theory." *Journal of the Folklore Institute* 6(1): 5–19.

Gellner, Ernest. 1996. "The Coming of Nationalism and Its Interpretation: The Myths of Nation and Class" in Gopal Balakrishnan, Ed. *Mapping the Nation.* London and New York: Verso, pp. 98–145.

Gramsci, Antonio. 1991. *Folclore e senso comune.* Rome: Editori Riuniti.

Grignon, Claude and Passeron, Jean-Claude. 1989. *Le savant et le populaire. Misérabilisme et populisme en sociologie et en littérature.* Paris: Seuil.

Helland, Janice. 2007. *British and Irish Home Arts and Industries 1880–1914: Marketing Craft, Making Fashion.* Dublin and Portland, OR: Irish Academic Press.

Hroch, Miroslav. 1996. "From National Movement to Fully-formed Nation" in Gopal Balakrishnan, Ed. *Mapping the Nation.* London and New York: Verso, pp. 78–97.

Köngäs-Maranda, Elli Kaija. n.d. "Ethnologie, Folklore et l'Indépendance des majorités minoritisées (1979)" in *Travaux et inédits de Elli Kaija Köngäs-Maranda.* Québec: Cahiers du CELAT 1: 164–178.

Laclau, Ernesto. 2005. *On Populist Reason.* London and New York: Verso.

Leerssen, Joep. 1996a [1986]. *Mere Irish and Fíor-Ghael. Studies in the Idea of Irish Nationality, its Development and Literary Expression prior to the Nineteenth Century.* Cork: Cork University Press.

Leerssen, Joep. 1996b. *Remembrance and Imagination.* Cork: Cork University Press.

Naithani, Sadhana, Ed. 2002. *Folktales from Northern India: William Crooke and Pandit Ram Gharib Chaube.* Santa Barbara, CA: ABC-CLIO.

Ó Cadhla, Stiofán. 2007. *Civilizing Ireland Ordnance Survey 1824–1842; Ethnography, Cartography, Translation.* Dublin: Irish Academic Press.

Ó Catháin, Séamas. 2008. *Formation of a Folklorist: The Visit of James Hamilton Delargy (Séamus Ó Duilearga) to Scandinavia, Finland, Estonia and Germany 1 April–29 September 1928.* Dublin: The Folklore of Ireland Council.

Ó Ciosáin, Niall. 1998. "Boccoughs and God's Poor: Deserving and Undeserving Poor in Irish Popular Culture" in Tadhg Foley and Seán Ryder, Eds. *Ideology and Ireland in the Nineteenth Century.* Dublin: Four Courts Press, pp. 93–97.

Ó Duilearga, Séamus. 1943. "Volkskundliche Arbeit in Irland von 1850 bis zur Gegenwart mit besonderer Berücksichtigung der 'Irischen Volkskunde – Kommission'" *Zeitschrift für keltische Philologie und Volksforschung* 23: 1–38.

Ó Giolláin, Diarmuid. 2000. *Locating Irish Folklore: Tradition, Modernity, Identity.* Cork: Cork University Press.

O'Halloran, Clare. 2004. *Golden Ages and Barbarous Nations: Antiquarian Debate and Cultural Politics in Ireland c. 1750–1800.* Cork: Cork University Press.

Ó hÓgáin, Dáithí. 2002. "'Béaloideas': Notes on the History of a Word." *Béaloideas* 70: 83–98.

Ó Siadhail, Pádraig. 2009. "James Mooney, 'The Indian Man,' agus Béaloideas na hÉireann." *Béaloideas* 77: 1–36.

Ortiz, Renato. 1992. *Românticos e folcloristas. Cultura popular.* São Paulo: Olha d'Água.

Prat, Joan. 1991. "Historia" in Joan Prat, Ubaldo Martínez, Jesús Contreras, and Isodoro Moreno, Eds. *Antropología de los Pueblos de España.* Madrid: Taurus Universitaria.

Stephens, Shane. 1999. "The Society of Irish Tradition 1917–1919." *Béaloideas* 67: 139–169.

Stocking, George W., Jr. 1996. *After Tylor: British Social Anthropology 1888–1951.* London: The Athlone Press.

Stoklund, Bjarne. 2003. "Between Scenography and Science. Early Folk Museums and Their Pioneers." *Ethnologia Europaea* 33(1): 21–36.

Wilde, William R. 1979. *Irish Popular Supersitions.* Dublin: Irish Academic Press.

Wörner, Martin. 1999. *Vergnügung und Belehrung: Volkskultur auf den Weltausstellungen 1851–1900.* Münster, New York, München, and Berlin: Waxmann.

CHAPTER 22 RUSSIA

Alexander Panchenko

Introduction: Social Constructionism and the History of Russian Folkloristics

This chapter deals with general trends and paradigmatic patterns that allow an understanding of the development of the discipline and its present state in contemporary Russia. Since it is impossible to even give a brief outline of what was being done or what has been done regarding the collection of texts, publications, and research works on various genres and theories, I will confine myself to certain key figures, concepts and episodes of the history of Russian folkloristics. First of all, however, it is necessary to make some preliminary remarks related to contemporary theoretical approaches to the study of folklore.

In recent decades, "traditional" Russian folkloristics has changed dramatically. The habitual concepts of folklore genres and texts, tradition and authenticity have been challenged and deconstructed by a number of American and European folklorists. The most important aspect of the crisis is related, in my opinion, to the contradiction between essentialism (or "simplistic realism") and social constructionism in understanding the nature of folklore research in particular and key concepts of the humanities in general. Since the publication of the seminal book *The Social Construction of Reality* by Peter Berger and Thomas Luckmann (1966), the theoretical analysis of terminology and disciplinary boundaries in the humanities and social sciences was quite often based upon the idea that key concepts and even the very subjects of scholarship should be viewed as socially constructed and, therefore, dependent not on the "essence" of history and culture, but rather on the socially and politically shaped production of knowledge within a given scholarly convention. Regarding the study of folklore, this idea, in turn, implies the problem of "politics of culture," namely political, ideological, and cultural factors that are involved in the formation and development of folkloristic research. One should not underestimate the impact of

A Companion to Folklore, First Edition. Edited by Regina F. Bendix and Galit Hasan-Rokem.
© 2012 John Wiley & Sons, Ltd. Published 2012 John Wiley & Sons, Ltd.

these factors on scholarly ideas and concepts, since they appear to be quite powerful in the construction of a seemingly "scientific" research agenda.

From this point of view, right from the birth of the term "folklore" (and, particularly, in empires and totalitarian states), there existed "two folklores." The first, which I shall term "folklore 1" (F^1) is oral popular culture that is not controlled or sanctioned by the cultural elite. "Folklore 2" (F^2), on the other hand, consists of texts approved by society, officially and/or conventionally designated as folklore, and recorded in or on special data media, such as wax cylinders, CDs, academic and popular publications of folksongs and folktales, scholarly essays and books, and so on. The irony is, however, that the postulated "folkloric nature" of F^1 stems from the latter's freedom from control exerted on it by an individual or social group, while the actual nature of F^2 is related to the controls imposed on it by professional communities of scholars, writers, and musicians, as well as politicians and cultural workers (and this is the reason why many folklorists in Russia argue bitterly over whether a text or a group of texts can be considered "folklore"). Whereas this dichotomy between non-institutionalized and socially constructed folklore can be observed in the history of folklore research in nearly every European country, it is particularly characteristic to Russia.

The essentialist notion of folklore which was a characteristic feature of Russian folkloristics both in the nineteenth and twentieth centuries, presumes a non-reflexive division of popular praxis and expressive culture into "important" and "unimportant," "artistic" and "non-artistic," "folklore" and "non-folklore" and so on. In fact, the formation and development of Russian and Soviet folkloristics both in the nineteenth and twentieth centuries seem to be determined by two general cultural tendencies, namely "romantic nationalism" and "internal colonialism." Although the Russian Empire did not have external colonies comparable to those possessed, for example, by Britain or France, the very mode of relations between the urban elite and the rural majority in eighteenth- and nineteenth-century Russia seems to be of a colonial type. On the one hand, Russian peasants of that time were directly exploited by the state and the nobility. On the other, this economic exploitation was accompanied by indirect symbolic exploitation which presumed various political and ideological uses of the virtual image of the "folk." The Russian equivalent to the English *folk*, *narod*, possessed, in this sense, many more colonial connotations. When William Thoms suggested describing "popular antiquities" and "popular literature" using "a good Anglo-Saxon compound, Folklore," he emphasized that the term meant "the Lore of the People." In Russia, however, the term *narod* was actually used in reference to the peasants only, and the very idea of folklore was related to the image of peasant culture.

The idea of *narod* was thus used in Russia for constructing and supporting both national and imperial identity. According to actual political, ideological, and aesthetic priorities of the elite, the latter ascribed "wisdom," "poetry," "ideals" and so on to the virtual folk. The ambivalence of the writers', statesmen's and churchmen's attitude to the peasants was reflected in that the life of the latter was seen both as "ignorant," "pagan," "superstitious," "savage" and as "the treasury of national culture," or "the mysterious psyche of the people." At the same time, urban popular culture in nineteenth-century Russia was not considered by the educated elite to be of any particular social or historical value. Anti-bourgeois ideology of the *intelligentsia*, the Russian educated elite, presumed both straight-out rejection of the "vulgar" way of life of a *meschanin* (a term with certain pejorative connotations which was used to describe an urban middle-class man) and ideological manipulations of the image of peasant culture which were often used to legitimize various political and aesthetic doctrines.

In nineteenth-century Russia, the image of peasant culture was used to construct "the Other," both in a negative and a positive sense, both as disgusting and attractive. It seems that such ambivalent attitudes to peasant culture are generally characteristic of societies in the stage of modernization. One of the underlying factors of European folkloristics in general is a dialectic unity of ideology of rationalism and progress, on the one hand, and "existential anxiety" reflected in an irrational desire for antiquity and authenticity on the other. However, the actual social status of the Russian *narod* was much lower than that of the European *folk*. Serfdom existed in Russia until 1861 when Alexander II abolished it. Less known but equally important in the history of Russian agrarian culture of the nineteenth century was the communal possession of land (*pozemel'naia obschina*) that preserved rural communities intact and blocked any private initiatives, either economic or social, by their members. The institution of communal possession of land was at least partly disaffirmed by the legislation of the early 1910s, but it still existed up to the first decade of the Soviet regime. The collectivization from the late 1920s to the early 1930s in fact resulted in reviving both serfdom and communal possession of the land: the latter was now owned by "collective" or "soviet" farms (*kolkhozy* and *sovkhozy*) and their "members" and employees were not able to migrate to urban locations and even other rural regions until the late 1960s and early 1970s. That meant that both serfdom and peasant communes in fact existed in Russia until the 1970s. After the introduction of a new passport system in 1974 the rural population were able to obtain passports and this led to mass migration from villages to cities. According to statistical data, in 1959, 52% of the population of the USSR lived in the countryside. In 1989, that population was 34%. According to the last Russian census of 2002, the rural population comprised only 27%.

All these facts suggest that one should pay particular attention to social, political, and ideological contexts in the formation and development of Russian folklore research. Specifically, the ideology of Russian and Soviet elites in the nineteenth and twentieth centuries always wavered between that of a modern nation-state and that of a colonial empire. Perhaps this peculiar ideological pattern was the most important one in the history of Russian folkloristics.

ROMANTIC BEGINNINGS: RUSSIAN FOLKLORISTICS AND GERMAN MYTHOLOGICAL STUDIES

It is not easy to point to a particular date or publication that could be viewed as a starting point for the discipline of folklore in Russia. The English term "folklore" became discussed and used widely only in the 1920s. Before that, scholars preferred to use terms such as "folk poetry" (*narodnaia poeziia*) or "(oral) folk literature" (*narodnaya slovesnost'*). Historians of Russian folkloristics, such as Mark Azadovskii, sometimes dated the discipline's beginning back to the eighteenth century when the first collections of "folk" songs and tales as well as "dictionaries of superstitions" appeared in print. It seems more reasonable, however, to date the beginning of the discipline to the period when the first explanatory models related to the concept of "folk literature" appeared. In Russia, that was the middle of the nineteenth century, and at that time, Russian folklore research was predominantly influenced by German students of folklore and mythology, from the Grimm brothers to Adalbert Kuhn, Wilhelm Schwartz, Max Müller and Wilhelm Mannhardt.

One of the key figures of that early period of Russian folklore research was Aleksandr Afanas'ev (1826–1871) who graduated from Moscow University as a legal expert but spent most of his life collecting and studying Slavic folklore. He published the first representative collection of Russian folktales (*Russkie narodnye skazki*, 1855–1864) inspired by the *Kinder- und Hausmärchen* of the Grimm brothers and a collection of popular religious narratives entitled *Russian Folk Legends* (*Narodnye russkie legendy*). The first edition of the latter was banned in Russia and printed in London in 1859 but was reprinted in Moscow in 1860. He also published a collection of obscene and erotic folktales entitled *Russian Secret Tales* (*Russkie zavetnye skazki*) that was printed in Geneva in 1872 and published in Russia for the first time only in 1991, since the Imperial as well as Soviet censorship did not tolerate what was thought to be "pornography" in folklore publications.

Besides his collections of Russian folklore, Afanas'ev published a huge research monograph entitled *Poetic Views of Nature by Slavic Peoples* (*Poeticheskie vozzreniya slavian na prirodu*, 3 volumes, 1865–1869), obviously inspired by the *Deutsche Mythologie* (German Mythology, 1835) by Jacob Grimm and *Die poetischen Naturanschauungen der Griechen, Römer und Deutschen in ihrer Beziehung zur Mythologie* (The Poetic View of Nature among the Greeks, Romans, and Germans and their Connection to Mythology, 1864) by Wilhelm Schwartz. In his comparative analysis of Slavic mythology, Afanas'ev followed the key ideas of his German predecessors, namely the concept of a basic Indo-European language that had degenerated over time and given birth to various mythological ideas, "solar" and "meteorological" interpretations of mythological and folklore plots being interpreted as either "naïve" or "poetic" "explanations of natural phenomena" that had been created by "the folk" "in the prehistoric period." Subsequently, nearly all motifs and themes of Slavic folklore were interpreted by Afanas'ev as the remnants or fragments of ancient solar and meteorological Indo-European myths sometimes "distorted" or "corrected" by Christian ideas and symbols. He was one of the first supporters of the "double belief" (*dvoeverie*) concept implying that until modernity Slavic folklore comprised a mixture of "Christian" and "pre-Christian" beliefs and rituals.

The "mythological" explanatory model elaborated by Afanas'ev did not convey any nationalistic ideas. He often argued that since German, Baltic, and Slavic languages have common Indo-European (or "Arian") roots, their folklore and popular culture must possess similar features that are the survivals of ancient mythological heritage. In this respect, Afanas'ev appeared to be quite a liberal scholar sharing in a European scholarly horizon. His romanticism was mainly related to representation of folklore as a sort of "naïve poetry," notwithstanding particular "national" specifics. In his foreword to the second edition of "Russian Folktales" (published after his death in 1873), he argued: "On the prehistoric stage of its development, the folk is necessarily a poet. Deifying the nature, he thinks it to be a living creature that responds to every joy and grief. Contemplating the solemn phenomena of nature, the folk embodies all his ideas, beliefs, and observations in lively poetic concepts that constitute an unceasing poem with an even and quiet view on the whole world."[1]

RUSSIAN HEROIC EPICS (*BYLINY*) AND THE POLITICS OF FOLKLORE

Another key point in Russian folklore research of the nineteenth century was the discovery of heroic epics (*byliny*) as a part of lived oral culture of the Russian North. The very term *byliny* is not related to oral popular culture, but borrowed from "The Lay of Igor's Campaign" (*Slovo o polku Igoreve*), an epic story or poem about Prince Igor' Sviatoslavich that was allegedly composed and written down in the thirteenth century. The authenticity of "The Song," however, is still debatable and the text has no similarities to oral epic songs. The original term for *byliny* in oral culture of the nineteenth century was *stariny* which literally meant "old songs" or "songs about old times." This ethnic term covered a wide range of texts that often were not related to heroic epics. Therefore *byliny* cannot be considered as an "emic genre."

Some texts of Russian *byliny* were recorded in the eighteenth and the first half of the nineteenth century. The earliest representative collection of Russian epic songs is a *Collection by Kirsha Danilov* (*Sbornik Kirshi Danilova*) composed in handwritten form in the mid-eighteenth century and published for the first time in 1804. Both scholarly and public interest in heroic epics was stimulated by recordings and publications by Pavel Rubnikov (four volumes published in 1861–1867) and Alexander Gil'ferding (collection of texts recorded near the lake Onezhskoe in 1871 and published in 1873). On the one hand, epic songs were considered by the educated elite to be a feature of "living antiquity" and "the voice of medieval Russian people." On the other, from the last decades of the nineteenth century onwards, *byliny* were consistently discussed and interpreted in a more or less political mode, that is, in relation to the "Russian national spirit" or the "heroism of Russian people." In this context, discussions of the genesis, evolution, and transmission of *byliny* were often influenced by political ideas and trends. Obviously, "historical" explanatory schemes representing *byliny* as songs about particular events in Russian medieval history were quite popular and influential both in late Imperial and Soviet Russian scholarship. However, from an analytic point of view they are quite dubious, given that they were at least partly inspired by political rather than scholarly reasons. Meanwhile, researchers leaning towards international comparison or "migratory" explanations in relation to the genesis of Russian epics were sometimes accused of being "unpatriotic." Nationalistic representations of Russian folklore in general and *byliny* in particular played quite an important role during the times of so-called "Soviet folklore" (see below).

RUSSIAN FOLKLORISTICS IN THE 1870S–1920S

Russian folklore research of the late Imperial era was neither romantically informed nor politicized. In fact, the independent academic discipline of folklore with all its possible political implications was formed during the early Stalin era. Before that, studies of what is today called folklore were split between history of literature, ethnography, and cultural geography. Consequently, Russian folklore research in the late nineteenth to early twentieth century was quite diverse and multi-faceted. One of the most influential philologically oriented Russian students of folklore between the 1870s and 1890s was Aleksandr Veselovskii (1838–1906) whose research interests covered the history of European literature and folklore. Although theoretical insights by Veselovskii eventually have lost their heuristic value, his contribution to the history of Russian folklore is important. In fact, he was the first to discuss themes of medieval and modern legends, tales and epic songs of the Eastern Slavs in the broad context of European Christian culture. In his comparative analysis of folklore motifs and plots, Veselovskii thoroughly rejected "mythological" interpretations and argued that beliefs and themes of folklore can both emerge independently in a given social context or spread internationally due to particular historical and social conditions. His research on both written and oral culture was often referred to as "historical poetics." The main idea of this approach was that one should always pay particular attention to the immediate social, cultural, and ritual context of a piece of oral culture or a literary text under consideration. In this respect, Veselovskii was one of the first Russian scholars who tried to interpret folklore themes proceeding from well-documented data on their geographical and historical location. The main purpose of his research was, however, the comparative study of the migration of particular folklore themes, an approach that corresponded in a way with the "historic-geographical" or "Finnish" method by Julius Krohn, Kaarle Krohn, and Antti Aarne. At the same time, Veselovskii was obviously influenced by contemporary British and French studies in folklore and anthropology by Edward B. Tylor, Andrew Lang, Gaston Paris, and others whose publications were often cited in his own work.

Research by Veselovskii influenced directly or indirectly the major part of Russian studies of folklore and medieval literature studies of the early twentieth century. Students of Veselovskii produced a number of valuable monographs on the history of particular folklore themes and plots, pre-Christian beliefs of the Eastern Slavs, and popular religious culture in Russia. Generally speaking, Russian philological folkloristics after Veselovskii was mostly oriented towards a comparative approach and historic-geographical aspects of the folklore research. It is noteworthy that one of the most well known adherents of the historic-geographical method, Walter Anderson (1885–1962), often described as an Estonian or German folklorist, started his work in the University of Kazan, where he prepared and published, in Russian, two monographs including the first part of his famous *Kaiser und Abt* (Russian version published in 1916, German in 1923). A student of Anderson, Nikolai Andreev (1892–1942), was the main supporter of the historic-geographical method in Soviet Russia in the 1920s. He prepared the first index of East-Slavic folktales based upon the system of Antti Aarne (published in 1929).

However, there existed another influential group of folklorists in Russia in the late nineteenth to early twentieth century led by Vsevolod Miller (1848–1913) and known as "the historical school." Miller and his followers predominantly analyzed heroic epics. Miller tried to decipher these as poetic representation of particular events and figures of medieval Russian history. These interpretations, however, often seem quite dubious and arbitrary because of the lack of empirical underpinnings. Some scholars of the late Soviet period (for example, the archaeologist Boris Rybakov) tried to reanimate this explanatory model, but to no effect. Meanwhile, as I have already said, "historical" interpretations of the Russian epics were always somewhat politically influenced and related no nationalistic ideology.

Veselovskii's legacy was still tolerated and even popular among some scholars of the first Soviet decades. His name was, however, almost banned in the USSR after the late

Stalinist campaign against "cosmopolitanism" and "groveling before the West" during the late 1940s. Students of comparative literature and folklore were accused of having a "foreign and hostile bourgeois-liberal approach to literature." Some scholars were dismissed from their academic positions. Among them were Victor Zhirmunskii, who had prepared a collection of essays by Veselovskii published in 1940, and Vladimir Shishmarev whose short monograph on Veselovskii appeared in 1946. New research on Veselovskii and his method appeared in print only in the early 1960s.

Besides "philologically" oriented students of folklore, Russian scholarship of the early twentieth century included a number of outstanding ethnologists interested in the study of East-Slavic popular beliefs and oral culture. One of the best-known Russian ethnologists of the period was Dmitrii Zelenin (1878–1954) whose research interests included a broad range of popular belief and practices as well as the material culture of Russian, Byelorussian, and Ukrainian peasants. His book *Russische (Ostslavische) Volkskunde* (Berlin; Leipzig, 1927; Russian translation published for the first time in 1991) was, for that time, the most comprehensive survey of research works and data on East-Slavic popular culture. The leading principle of Zelenin's ethnological studies was synchronous research of a particular belief or ritual that took into account its immediate meaning and functions in contemporary rural culture. Proceeding from this analysis, Zelenin then tried to reconstruct the history of a piece of culture under consideration. Although this retrospective approach did not prove to be successful in a number of cases, Zelenin's research still presented a number of valuable insights in the history of popular beliefs in Russia. Zelenin's most often cited work dealt with the beliefs about "unclean death" in Russian rural culture. Although Zelenin sometimes mistakenly identified various categories of dead and different commemorative traditions of Slavic and Finnish cultures (the very regional term "*zalozhnye*" he used to define "unclean dead" obviously referred to "clean" but "forgotten" dead), the book presented a number of important ideas and hypotheses.

Despite the Bolshevik régime, the 1920s were still a period of, in ideological and intellectual terms, relative freedom in the Russian humanities. Formalist methodology was quite influential in literary scholarship until at least the second half of the decade. Probably it was not without some formalistic influence that the idea of folkloristics as an independent discipline and folklore as a specific domain of culture with its own "laws" started to be discussed by Russian philologists in the late 1920s. At the same time, the essentialist approach to folklore grounded initially in the scholarly efforts to make the study of oral culture more "scientific" and "positivistic" seemed to be quite popular in the early twentieth-century Europe as well. One can remember, for example, the famous theory of "epic laws" proposed by Danish folklorist Axel Olrik. Quite representative for Russian discussions of this matter was the essay *Die Folklore als eine besondere Form des Schaffens* by Petr Bogatyrev and Roman Jakobson (1929). Proceeding from the distinction of *parole* and *langue* by Ferdinand de Saussure, Bogatyrev and Jakobson argued that folklore should never be regarded as individually produced oral forms similar to literary texts but as the result of "preliminary collective censorship," that is as oral repertoire transformed, assorted, and accepted by a certain social group. From this point of view, they suggested looking for functional and structural specifics of folklore. The discipline responsible for this analysis should be, in their opinion, quite independent from the study of literature. Although the basic theoretical model for the essay was borrowed from linguistic works by de Saussure, it is very likely that Bogatyrev and Jakobson were well aware of contemporary French sociology, in particular works by Émile Durkheim and Marcel Mauss. The influence of Durkheim and Mauss's ideas can be also traced in Bogatyrev's *Actes magiques, rites et croyances en Russie subcarpathique*, published in Paris in the same year.

Although Soviet folkloristics soon became a quite independent discipline, its mainstream appeared to be very different from what Bogatyrev and Jakobson as well as some other Russian scholars of the 1920s were talking about. As of the mid-1930s, the study of folklore in Russia underwent most dramatic and exotic transformations.

"Soviet folklore": A New Politics of Culture

The period I am describing now is usually called "the epoch of Soviet folklore" (late 1920s to the 1950s). What was created then was probably symptomatic not only of the culture of the Stalin period, but also of mainstream Russian folklore study as a whole from its emergence to the end of the twentieth century. In fact, the texts of pro-Soviet "invented folklore," which are, one might say, those least "spoiled" by the influence of peasant culture, permit us to see what generic, thematic, and ideological modes, tendencies, and priorities were ascribed to F^2 by its publishers, researchers, and consumers. Obviously, the officially declared ideological need for a Soviet folklore and the high social status of folklore study in the Stalin era were both grounded in cultural models and values formed in the Russian empire in the late nineteenth and early twentieth centuries. On the other hand, political suppression and near total isolation from international scholarship forced post-Stalin and even some post-Soviet Russian folklorists into using and combining, for the most part, both "Soviet" and "pre-Soviet" conceptions of what "a folklore text" should look like, and what its social significance and aesthetic values were. Paradoxically enough, one could say that this Soviet "fakelore" is a distillation of "authentic Russian folklore" (in the F^2 sense).

"Soviet folklore" became a matter of public interest in the mid-1920s and faded away soon after Stalin's death. The end results of this "creative work by the liberated *narod* (folk)" were discussed in the collective volume, *Studies in The Russian Folk Poetry of the Soviet Epoch* (*Ocherki russkogo narodnopoeticheskogo tvorchestva sovetskoi epokhi*), published by the Academy Institute of Russian Literature (Pushkin House) in 1952. It stimulated a lively discussion of what should be considered contemporary folk creative work, what features were characteristic of the "artistic culture of the Soviet people," and so on. The arguments continued in the 1960s, but by the end of the decade both discussions about "Soviet folklore" and publications or republications of examples of it had stopped. However, a number of texts of this nature were republished in readers up to the 1980s.

One can divide the history of "Soviet folklore" in two periods. The first falsified "pro-Soviet" texts, allegedly of folk origin, were all published (and probably fabricated) between 1924 and 1930. They represent the first "Lenin" period in the history of Soviet folklore. In this period, the themes for "creative work by the liberated folk" were restricted to the figure of Lenin and the history of the Civil War in Russia after 1917. The dominant genre was prose narrative, and the texts were called "folktales" or "legends." It is significant that, even then, what was being published included not only falsifications of Russian folklore but some texts allegedly borrowed from other cultural traditions. For example, the collection, *Lenin in Russian Folktale and Oriental Legend*, compiled by the historian N. Piaskovskii in 1930, included a part entitled "Oriental Legends about Lenin," in which readers were to discover three "Uzbek" texts, as well as a "Chinese," a "Kirghiz," an "African," and a "Chukchi" text.

The situation changed radically in the mid-1930s: prose narratives gave way to epic or lyric verse. The dominant form then was the long epic, constructed on the basis of the traditional *byliny*. Labeled "Soviet *byliny*," "*noviny*" (i.e., "new *byliny*"), "*bylina-folktales*" or "poem-tales" (*poemy-skazy*), these works glorified Stalin, Lenin, Kirov, Chapaev, the development of collective farms, the heroes of polar expeditions, the Eighteenth Party Congress and so on. Beyond this, a considerable proportion of the "Soviet folklore" of the late 1930s consisted of funeral orations for Soviet officials and celebrities. Undoubtedly, this "folklore for Stalin" (Miller 1990) was redolent of heroic themes and plots, while novelistic themes and mythological elements were completely excluded from what was called "Soviet folk poetry." The techniques involved in creating "Soviet folklore" also changed. Co-authorship between professional singers (*skaziteli*) and their "supervisors," folklorists or writers, replaced forgeries by specific authors, using disparate elements of peasant narrative tradition in an eclectic manner. Curiously enough, the "new Soviet epic verses" never existed and circulated in oral form; once "recorded," they were published in newspapers or magazines and then republished in academic collections of "Soviet folklore." The singers themselves, however, did not bother to remember or reproduce their own improvisations about the "heroic present." Before World War II, "Soviet folklore" was considered international, with particular attention paid to epic singers from Central Asia and the Caucasus.

What factors determined such a notable change in the dominant ideas about the form and the content of the "oral folk poetry of the Soviet epoch"? It is evident that the development of "Soviet folklore" was a part of the much broader process of creating a Stalinist imperial culture. Of course, both Stalinist and post-Stalinist imperial ideology were based upon heroic and epic themes that were used for the construction and maintenance of national and political identity. At the same time, the transition from the "mythological" to the "heroic" period in the history of Soviet folklore was shaped by specific social and historical circumstances. It is important to remember that these changes took place just after collectivization – a new enslavement of the Russian peasantry, which furnished the urban elite (writers and folklorists included) with an effective means for the economic and ideological exploitation of the rural population. Obviously, "co-authorship" between folklorists and folk singers, as mentioned above, became possible thanks to the administrative mechanisms directly affecting the peasants rediscovered by the elite in the early 1930s. Moreover, the leaders of Soviet folkloristics of that time made no secret of their aspiration for dominance over peasant culture. Thus, the leading Soviet folklorist Yurii Sokolov remarked in 1930 as follows:

> Since we are managing the literature systematically, it would be inconsistent to leave oral creative arts to the mercy of fate: it is necessary for the proletarian consciousness to subdue spontaneous forces in the oral culture as well. It is natural that bourgeois folklorists will be against this "meddling" in the "folk creative work." But I would remind these bourgeois scholars that, in fact, "original" oral arts were always under pressure of

ruling classes. It is strange to declare inviolability of folklore nowadays when deliberate supervision comes not from outside but from the very heart of the working masses. (Sokolov 1931: 92–98).

Soviet folkloristics became an independent academic discipline at this time (the first university departments of folklore were established in Leningrad and Moscow in 1930s), but it was quite far from what Bogatyrev and Jakobson were writing about. Instead of "collective censorship" and "social laws of folklore," folklorists of the late 1930s studied "Soviet oral literature" with particular attention to "creative skills" of individual singers. Since the promotion of folklore and folkloristics in the second half of the 1930s was supervised by the leaders of Soviet literature (Maxim Gorky and Alexey Tolstoy in particular) the main trend of the research during the period was the analysis (and establishment) of normative poetics and the stable hierarchy of genres ascribed to folklore regarded to be a creative art. The most praised genre was, of course, heroic epics, both "old" and "new."

However, one can hardly blame at least some of those scholars who were engaged in the creation of "Soviet folklore." A lot of folklorists and ethnologists were either imprisoned or executed in Russia in the 1930s. Those who managed to survive had to yield to the dictatorship of totalitarian ideology, since they actually had no choice other than 10 or 25 years of gulag or even death.

VLADIMIR PROPP

While discussing the Russian folkloristics of the twentieth century one cannot but mention Vladimir Propp (1895–1970), who is perhaps the best known Russian folklorist in international scholarship due to his first research monograph, *Morphology of the Folktale* (English translation 1968, or *Morfologia skazki*, 1928). Although Propp never belonged to the formalistic school of literary criticism, the influence of Russian formalism upon the *Morphology* is quite obvious. Proceeding from the analysis of Aarne-Thompson tale types 300–749 (Propp largely used the folktale collection published by Afanas'ev and, since he did not regarded the classification by Aarne to be of special importance, he preferred to use the term "wondertales" instead of tale type numbers), he arrived at the concept of overall narrative structure of Russian fairy-tale, that, he argued, consisted of 31 units which Propp himself named "functions" (*funktcii*). In English-speaking folkloristics these units are sometimes called "motifemes" or "narrathemes."[2] According to Propp, functions "serve as stable, constant elements in folktales, independent of who performs them, and how they are fulfilled by the dramatis personae" and the sequence of functions in a folktale is always identical (Propp 1968: 20). This analytical model that presented an alternative analytic system for folktales to the tale-type system by Antti Aarne was later successfully applied to the narrative structure of some genres of literature and cinema in the context of narratology. However, the model required some general historical explanation. It was not clear from the formal analysis by Propp why the particular tale types were based upon this specific narrative structure and how the latter could appear at all. However, Propp himself was not too eager to continue his formalistic research. In the 1930s, it was quite dangerous for a Soviet scholar to be known as formalist, and in 1930–1931

Propp had already spent seven months in prison, suspected to be a member of "illegal German nationalistic organizations." Although some papers by Propp that appeared in print after the 1930s still retained formalistic ideas and methods, his next monograph, *Historical Roots of the Fairy-Tale* (*Istoricheskie korni volshebnoi skazki*), completed in the late 1930s, but published only in 1946, was only slightly related to his "morphological" studies (Propp 1984). Then, he used the theory by French folklorist Pierre Saintyves who argued that at least some folk-tale plots are to be regarded as exegesis of ancient rituals or their survivals. According to Propp, key motifs of fairy-tales (here he only partly followed his own scheme of 31 functions) are closely related the rites of passage, especially initiation and funeral rituals. Such an approach in fact suggested a return to "ritualistic" explanatory models elaborated by British anthropologists of the late nineteenth century and presented, in particular, in research works by James George Frazer, who insisted that mythological and folklore themes are derived from ritual survivals. In his later monograph about "Russian agrarian festivals," published in Russian in 1963, Propp relied heavily on the Frazerian theory of magic as well. At the same time, *Historical Roots* openly proceeded from the scheme of rites of passage presented by French anthropologist Arnold van Gennep at the turn of the twentieth century.

Perhaps the most consistent follower of Propp's "morphological" method was the Israeli scholar Heda Jason (see the chapter on Israel in this volume) and American folklorist Alan Dundes who used it in his doctoral thesis published in 1964 under the title *The Morphology of North American Indian Folktales*. Unlike Propp, Dundes tried to look for "morphological" structures not only in folktale texts but, for example, in rituals and social organization as well. It seemed, however, that eventually he became disappointed with explanatory potential of the "morphological" approach since in the 1970s he concentrated largely on the classic Freudian psychoanalytical model for the explanation of genesis and functions of folklore themes and plots.

The *Morphology of the Folktale* was published in English in 1958 for the first time, three years after the publication of the famous paper "The Structural Study of Myth" by French anthropologist Claude Lévi-Strauss. The structural model proposed by Lévi-Strauss was in many ways similar to Propp's morphological sequence, although the French scholar tried to avoid the pure syntagmatic approach and looked for paradigmatic logical structures beyond archaic mythology and rituals. In 1960, Lévi-Strauss published a review of Propp's *Morphology* where he considered the Russian scholar to be a forerunner of structural analysis but criticized Propp for limiting himself to syntagmatic research of folktales rather than myths that, in Lévi-Strauss's opinion, presented quite "stronger" binary oppositions. Six years later, in the Italian edition of the *Morphology*, Propp published an aggressive rebuttal where he claimed to be an empirical scholar whose work was "based on a study of data" rather than a "philosopher" and argued that the paradigmatic model by Lévi-Strauss did not "correspond to reality." It seems to me, however, that the response by Propp was largely inspired by political rather than scholarly reasons. In fact, one might think (and not unreasonably so) that it would have been quite dangerous for a Soviet folklorist to discuss seriously any theoretical issues beyond the normative "Marxist-Leninist" ideological framework. From this point of view, Lévi-Strauss and Propp were simply not equally free to start a theoretical discussion on the advantages and disadvantages of the "morphological" and "structural" approaches (cf. Dundes 1997).

LIBERAL TURN: TRENDS OF FOLKLORE RESEARCH IN 1960s–1980s

The 1960s, however, were the period of a "liberal turn" not only in the political life of the USSR but in the Soviet humanities as well. Although the structural approach to mythology and folklore could hardly be a matter of broad theoretical discussion in Russia, it nevertheless became quite popular in the practical analysis of the data. One of the most influential trends in the study of folklore that appeared in the USSR during that decade is known as "the structural-semiotic school." It assembled folklorists, ethnologists, linguists and literary critics using quite different methods and approaches. One might say, in this context, that "Russian structuralism" looked more like descriptive discourse rather than analytical method. The key concepts of the discourse (*binary oppositions, word model,* and *categories of culture* rather than *mediation* and *bricolage*) in fact referred to a form of meta-description of structural units that allegedly constituted the "archaic" or "mythological" world view. Perhaps the most consistent use of Western structuralism was presented in works by Eleazar Meletinskii (1918–2005) who tried to combine the approaches by Propp and Lévi-Strauss in the study of myths and folktales but at the same time often applied comparative and historical approaches to his research which were less related to structural anthropology. At the same time, "structural" reconstructions of Slavic and Indo-European mythology presented in a number of research works by Viacheslav Ivanov (born 1929) and Vladimir Toporov (1928–2005) unexpectedly mixed Lévi-Straussian terminology with "mythological" explanatory models dating back to Wilhelm Schwartz and Aleksandr Afanas'ev. Comparing both old and new items of mythology and folklore from East-Slavic and various Indo-European cultures they arrived at the idea of a "principal Indo-European myth" of the battle between the god of thunder and his antagonist (a serpent or some chthonic deity) that allegedly underlay the major part of popular beliefs and folklore plots in Europe, the Middle East and Central Asia. Like their predecessors in the nineteenth century, both scholars were more linguistically than anthropologically oriented, so their approach demonstrated a lot of traits of comparative linguistics. Ivanov and Toporov relied heavily on the idea of "double belief" and tried to discover "pagan survivals" in medieval and modern religious practices and beliefs of East-Slavic peasants. The same method was applied by Boris Uspenskii in his book about Russian cult of St Nicholas published in 1982.

Although in his "Poetics of Myth" Meletinskii discusses "Rabelais and His World" by Mikhail Bakhtin (written in 1930s but published for the first time in 1965) as highly relevant for the studies of mythology and folklore, one can hardly say that the book influenced Russian folkloristics of the late Soviet decades. At the same time, Bakhtin's work was widely used by Soviet historians and philologists studying medieval Russian and European culture in the 1970s and 1980s. However, the neglect of Bakhtin's ideas and findings by folklorists is explicable in the given political and ideological context. It was possible to discuss medieval society and literature in terms of "carnival behavior" and "obscene laughter," but the same terms could not be applied to folklore. Since the 1930s, obscene themes and forms of folklore were not allowed by both official and unofficial censorship to be the matter of research discussions and publications. The collections of Russian "erotic" and "obscene" folklore were republished and revised only after the collapse of the Soviet Union. As to the concepts of "dialogue" and "chronotope" introduced by Bakhtin and used widely by post-structural literary criticism in Europe, they, in fact, did not fit well into the theoretical agenda of both "liberal" and "conservative" folkloristics in the Soviet Union of the 1960s and 1970s.

Another important trend in the study of Slavic popular culture was presented by the so called "ethnoliguistic school" led by Nikita Tolstoi (1923–1996). Although linguistically oriented as well, the members of this research group were not too fond of the "structural" methods in the study of folklore and, in a way, proceeded with the retrospective method of Zelenin and synchronous studies of rituals and beliefs by Bogatyrev. Being largely descriptive, their approach included *arealia* studies of popular culture in various Slavic regions (Eastern, Southern, and Western) and paid particular attention to the relationship between language, folklore, and ritual. Among the principal goals of such ethnoliguistic research was the development of a "cultural dialectology" of the Slavic peoples. One of the main results of these studies was the encyclopedia of "Slavonic antiquities" (*Slavianskie drevnosti: etnolingvisticheskii slovar,'* published in the mid-1990s, the last, fifth volume is still in print) that nowadays presents the most comprehensive overview of Slavic popular culture and folklore.

Finally, it is necessary to mention some outstanding research published between the 1960s and the 1980s by Russian folklorists that stood outside the above-mentioned schools, namely, comparative studies of Slavic epics by Boris Putilov, paremiogical research works by Grigorii Permiakov, and studies of Russian legends and folk narrative theory by Kirill Chistov. Since the early 1860s, the very term "legend" (*legenda*) in Russian folkloristics was commonly used in reference to oral narratives with religious meaning. In the twentieth century, this point of view was promoted by Propp in a number of his papers. However, this particular use of the term generated a number of analytical problems since sometimes it was indeed too complicated to find a borderline between "religious" and "non-religious" meaning of particular texts. On the other hand, the approach allowed the application of the term "legend" to various texts of different forms, functions, and origins. Chistov, in turn, tried to develop a more elaborate and analytically consistent theory of legend. Proceeding from the division of oral narratives into *Chroniknotizen (Sagenbericht), Memorat* and *Fabulat* suggested by Carl von Sydow, Chistov considered "legend" to be a dynamic process of narrative transmission rather than a stable textual form. He argued that every legend should be studied as a dynamic group of "filial" texts somehow related to a certain "core" idea, belief, or plot. From this point of view, Chistov discussed beliefs and narratives about "royal redeemers" and "happy lands" that were predominantly popular among Russian peasants of the eighteenth and nineteenth centuries. The last research work by Chistov dealt with the oral and written culture of the prisoners of World War II. He studied and partly published the so called "Freiburg collection" – a card index of "folkloric" excerpts from the Ostarbeiter letters, made by German war censors in 1942–1944.

DEVELOPMENT OR DECLINE? FOLKLORISTICS IN POST-SOVIET RUSSIA

After the collapse of the Soviet Union, the Russian humanities changed radically; they have become quite diverse and westernized. For the study of folklore, these changes brought a lot of new subjects of research and analytical approaches. In fact, post-Soviet folkloristics in Russia was faced with a choice: either to transform itself into a kind of antiquarian discipline, concerned only with "dead" cultural forms, or to broaden the sphere of its research dramatically and to include the "living," actually functional phenomena of mass culture. Studies of contemporary forms of popular urban culture, both oral and written, were, in fact, unofficially prohibited in the late Soviet decades. Research work on these matters was resumed in the late 1980s and 1990s. One of the most visible attempts to advance studies in that direction was a seminar on urban folklore and a number of subsequent conferences organized by folklorists Sergei Nekliudov and Alexander Belousov in the late 1990s. The papers resulting from this research were published in a volume entitled *Contemporary Urban Folklore* (*Sovremennyi gorodskoi fol'klor*) in 2003. The range of research topics of the seminar was quite broad, ranging from various types of jokes to urban graffiti. However, the work of the seminar did not result in a consistent program of research in contemporary urban culture. Perhaps the most successful and still popular domain of post-Soviet urban folkloristics is the study of so-called "subcultural folklore" or "folklore of subcultures," namely oral and written culture of small "folk groups," professional associations, and particularly, official institutions such as secondary schools, the army or prison camps. One can mention in this relation the collected volume *Russian School Folklore* (*Russkii Shkol'nyi Fol'klor*, 1998) edited by Alexander Belousov.

It is important to remember that mainstream Russian folkloristics since the early years of the discipline was predominantly oriented towards oral peasant culture. Therefore, it is natural that a lot of specialists in Russian folklore were not prepared for the rapid decline of peasant folklore and the simultaneous development of urban popular culture. It is symptomatic that they did not try to extend or modify their notion of folklore but instead invented new terms to protect the borderline between rural and urban culture. Urban folklore in this context was referred to as "post-folklore" (suggested by Sergei Nekliudov) or even "anti-folklore" (suggested by Nikita Tolstoi). However, these terminological innovations seem to be the evidence of theoretical consternation and confusion in the face of changing culture and scholarship. They mean, in fact, that the very idea of folklore and folkloristic research is still associated with a particular social stratum and a historical period rather than with theory and methods of research. It is likely, on the other hand, that many Russian folklorists who insisted on contrasting peasant "folklore" with urban "anti-folklore" were all too aware of the words by Alan Dundes, who had already argued in the 1960s that "the term 'folk' could refer to any group whatsoever who shared at least one common factor" but were not too eager to apply this conception in their own research. The strict opposition between rural and urban popular cultures which underlay the notions of "post-folklore" or "anti-folklore" came not from contemporary folklore theory but from prejudices of the nineteenth-century Russian elite. However, the study of contemporary urban and "post-urban" culture enjoys a rising popularity in contemporary Russian folkloristics. The most recent trend of folklore research is related to the study of the internet, viewed not only as a collection or a database for folklore texts but rather as a particular domain of communication and performance.

Another important trend in post-Soviet folklore research in Russia is related to the study of popular religion and religious folklore. The concept of "double belief" was largely rejected by folklorists and ethnologists in the 1990s. Instead, the idea of "religious practices" or "vernacular religious cultures" as the main subjects of study by folklorists and anthropologists has become rather popular. Research on vernacular religion involved a broad range of themes including both rural and urban forms of so called "popular Orthodoxy," heterodox religious groups of the eighteenth and nineteenth centuries and new religious movements as well.

Theoretical and methodological changes in post-Soviet folkloristics in Russia are no less visible. Perhaps the first book that introduced ideas and methods by Western folklorists of the late twentieth century to the Russian readers was published by Boris Putilov in 1994. Putilov presented a broad overview of American folklore research of the 1960s to 1980s with special attention to the "performance-centered" approach. The monograph *Pragmatics of Folklore* (*Pragmatika Folklora*, 2004) by Svetlana Adon'eva is also related to this theoretical trend. Adon'eva considers folklore to be a "specific form of oral performance" and, at the same time, a "particular institution for control of human behavior," "an instrument of power and control." Subsequently, she tries to discover how particular forms of rural folklore are related to social roles and institutions of power within local communities. Yet, Adon'eva still relies on an essentialist approach to folklore, with the subject matter being treated as an independent domain of culture with its own laws and dynamics. More "postmodern" and "deconstructivist," in this perspective, is the book *Everyday Life and Mythology* (*Povsednevnost' i Mifologija*, 2001) by Konstantin Bogdanov who rejects a number of key concepts of "old-fashioned" folkloristics including "tradition," "authenticity," and "the folk." He suggests that folklorists should look for their research themes and subjects proceeding from social pragmatics of narratives, either oral, written, printed, or transmitted by electronic media, rather than from a vague essentialist idea of "self-sufficient" folklore.

This "loss of subject" in contemporary Russian folkloristics does not necessarily mean, in my opinion, the overall decline of the discipline. In fact, international folklore research today becomes more anthropological than philological and that makes folkloristics even more flexible and viable. It is obvious, at the same time, that contemporary Russian folkloristics is extremely diverse in terms of subjects, methods, and theoretical approaches. The "old-style" folklorists relying on ideological norms and discursive practices of the Soviet time are still quite active, so, in fact, today there are several different scholarly practices in the study of folklore that actually have little in common except the very name of the discipline. Paradoxically, the lack of public and political interest in folklore allows contemporary Russian folkloristics to enjoy a period of maximal intellectual freedom. However, the future of the discipline, as always in Russia, is still uncertain.

NOTES

1 "Narodnye russkie skazki A.N. Afanas'eva." Tom 1. Moscow: Nauka, 1984, p. 8.
2 Editors' note: Alan Dundes (1964) introduced "motifeme" in his application of Proppian morphology to Native American materials so as to avoid the confusion with the use of "function" within anthropological functionalist analysis.

REFERENCES

Dundes, Alan. 1964. "The Morphology of North American Indian Folktales." *Folklore Fellows' Communication* 196. Helsinki: Suomalainen Tiedeakatemia (sold by Akateeminen Kirjakauppa).

Dundes, Alan 1997. "Binary Opposition in Myth: The Propp/Lévi-Strauss Debate in Retrospect." *Western Folklore* 56(1): 39–50.

Jakobson, Roman and Petr Bogatyrev. 1980. "Folklore as a Special Form of Creation." Trans. John M. O'Hara. *Folklore Forum* 13(1): 1–21.

Jason, Heda. 1970. "The Russian Criticism of the 'Finnish School' in Folklore Scholarship." *Norveg* 14: 285–294.

Miller, Frank. 1990. *Folklore for Stalin: Russian Folklore and Pseudofolklore of the Stalin Era*. Armonk, NY: M.E. Sharpe.

Propp, Vladimir. 1963. Russkie agrarnye prazdniki: Opyt istoriko-etnographicheskogo issledovaniya (Russian Agrarian Festivals: A Historic-ethnographic Study). Leningrad: Leningrad State University.

Propp, Vladimir. 1968. *Morphology of the Folktale*. Trans., Laurence Scott. 2nd edition. Austin: University of Texas Press.

Propp, Vladimir. 1984. "Theory and History of Folklore." A. Libermann, Ed. Trans. A.Y. Martin and R.P. Martin. *Theory and History of Literature*. Vol. 5. Minneapolis: University of Minnesota Press.

Sokolov Yu. M. 1931. "Znachenie fol'klora i fol'kloristiki." *Literatura i marksizm* 5: 92–98.

FURTHER READING

Abrahams, Roger. 1993. "Phantoms of Romantic Nationalism in Folkloristics." *The Journal of American Folklore* 106(419): 3–17.

Meletinsky, Eleazar. 1998. *The Poetics of Myth*. London: Routledge.

Oinas, Felix J. 1973. "Folklore and Politics in the Soviet Union." *Slavic Review* 32(1): 45–58.

Panchenko, Alexander. 2005. "The Cult of Lenin and 'Soviet Folklore'." *Folklorica. Journal of the Slavic and East European Folklore Association* 10(1): 18–38.

Roch, Stella. 2009. *Popular Religion in Russia: "Double Belief" and the Making of an Academic Myth*. Abingdon: Routledge.

Sokolov, Yurii. 1950. *Russian Folklore*. Trans. Catherine Ruth Smyth. New York: Macmillan Company.

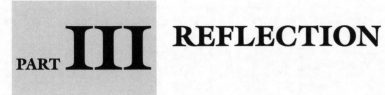

PART **III** REFLECTION

INTRODUCTION TO PART III
Reflection

Regina F. Bendix and
Galit Hasan-Rokem

In this section we look at the social life of folklore, often in reified, codified form, as it becomes a subject of elaboration, adaptation and discussion on a further level of creative agency, and is subject to preservation, as well as institutional, political, and legal power and agency.

Folklore's "second life" in literature has venerable roots in all ancient civilizations known to us. From the Mesopotamian Gilgamesh, through the Egyptian "Tale of the Two Brothers," the tales of Solomon's wisdom or the wedding songs in the Hebrew Bible, the adventures of the Mahabharata, and the Sirens of Homer – all are folk literary creations encapsulated in canonized works transmitted through the ages in written form. The earliest folk literary scholars from Vico and Herder onwards identified folk literature with ancient periods and acknowledged the presence of its genres in those works of old. But literature does not only provide a reservoir to draw narrative or other literary materials from; it rather continues in an interactive relationship with oral tradition throughout the ages. Written documents are transmitted in oral tradition and vice versa in innumerable contexts and formations. In other media, too, the cross transmission between collective and anonymous creativity interacts with individual and/or canonical cultural productions. Music and film are the examples that have been selected for this volume; other visual arts and theatre are further blatant examples.

The desire to preserve cultural manifestations of the past has brought forth an additional realm within which new sets of cultural practices, some have called them meta-cultural, have been developed. Localized and private efforts to safeguard houses and crafts indicative of region or ethnicity led, in the nineteenth century, to associational

A Companion to Folklore, First Edition. Edited by Regina F. Bendix and Galit Hasan-Rokem.
© 2012 John Wiley & Sons, Ltd. Published 2012 John Wiley & Sons, Ltd.

and political initiatives, often in conjunction with political interests to maintain material evidence of an ethnic or national past. Folklorists participated in this endeavour, for instance in the creation of open-air museums and associated curatorial activities, the selection of exemplary tradition bearers skilled in particular ethnic or folk arts, as well as in the staging of representative ethnic and regional folk festivities. In the course of the second half of the twentieth century, a globalized regime safeguarding material and intangible cultural manifestations has emerged under the banner of "heritage." Scholars find themselves in a situation where their expertise contributes to the workings of heritage making on the one hand, while on the other hand, heritage processes and the resulting cultural industries have become a topic of research in their own right, much as has tourism. Similarly lodged between local concerns and international agents and stages, the question of ownership, cultural property, has moved communities as well as folklorists to participate in negotiating the rights of folklore and traditional knowledge bearers and to give of their expertise in questions of restitution. Both cultural property and heritage are new realms of cultural, legal, and economic practice that warrant close documentation and analysis by folklorists as their field has, in harnessing the elusive and often evanescent folklore performance and traditional knowledge, turned into a commodity as much as an ideologically powerful instrument.

The legal realm, finally, is one which, arguably, arose from customary law before it reached normative contours, within the institution of national constitutions and legal realms developed from it. While fields such as cultural property negotiations bring renewed attention to vernacular codices of law, institutionalized law has in recent decades sought ways to address cultural heterogeneity. In the form of "cultural defense" strategies, cultural difference has entered courts of law and is confronting civil societies with the question of whether everyone is the same before the law.

CHAPTER 23

FOLKLORE AND LITERATURE

Cristina Bacchilega

RE-SITUATING THEIR DYNAMICS

As a college-student in Rome, Italy, in the 1970s, I read Antonio Gramsci, and I am still mulling over his analysis of culture, folklore, and literature. In his view, early twentieth-century Italians persisted in "magic" beliefs and "traditional" customs that seemingly deterred economic development, and Italy lacked the "national-popular" literature sustaining the emergence of other European nations as imagined communities. The dynamics between folklore and literature in the schools troubled Gramsci especially. He wrote of Italy in the 1920s and 1930s: "the individual consciousness of the overwhelming majority of children reflects social and cultural relations which are different from and antagonistic to those which are represented in the school curricula." Gramsci objected, "There is no unity between school and life, ... no automatic unity between instruction and education" (1971: 35). "Life," meaning living traditions and beliefs, or folklore, was dismissed as anachronistic within the "modern" education system that instructed children to believe in science as progress and to read a literature whose nationalistic and elitist canon set it apart both from the realities or aspirations and the vernacular languages of many, especially in the South of Italy. Countering this school bureaucracy, Gramsci refused to see folklore as simply residual: because he recognized how expressive culture was actively appropriated to serve the state but could also compete with hegemonic culture, he argued that folklore be taken seriously. In the struggle to undo a folklore vs. literature dichotomy that persists in today's educational Euro-American systems, I find Gramsci's observations useful for the way he vividly situates the expressive practices of folklore and literature in relation to *both* political society (the nation-state) and civil society (especially religion and education); in other words, to both political and social institutions.

A Companion to Folklore, First Edition. Edited by Regina F. Bendix and Galit Hasan-Rokem.
© 2012 John Wiley & Sons, Ltd. Published 2012 John Wiley & Sons, Ltd.

Aspects of Gramsci's approach to folklore and literature inform my own understanding. First, Gramsci directs our attention to dynamics of political power, social struggle, and ideological reproduction in the cultural sphere. He insists on the significance of historical conjunctures (rather than structures alone) and pedagogy, highlighting them as *processes* in which the specifics of human socialization, expression, and agency – that to which folklorists attend – do matter. Second, Gramsci's focus on the institutionalization of education in schools as state apparatus denaturalizes literature, demanding that, with Raymond Williams, we recognize it "as a specializing social and historical category," a specialization "made in terms of social class" (1977: 53), a specialization that since the eighteenth century in Europe no longer coincides with literacy but is realized through the canonization and commodification of select printed books. We know that, in tandem with this narrow conception of literature, folklore emerged in nineteenth-century Europe as another specialized discourse, also differentiated from popular culture. Third, in considering cultural practices and institutions within the nation-state, Gramsci's "notion of subaltern denies the autonomy of the 'folk'" so that folklore must be understood "as the product of a historical process, firmly within the framework of the state and in an unavoidable relationship with a hegemonic culture" (Ó Giolláin 2004: 159). Fourth, Gramsci pointed the way to understanding how specific conjunctures made the "instruction" of literacy and Italian literature *colonial* in Southern Italy. Being aware of these dynamics helps me to recognize, now that I teach at the University of Hawai'i in an occupied and colonized nation, the significance of Hawaiian *mo'olelo* (hi/stories) as "social and political action" (ho'omanawanui 2010) in a continuing struggle to "unwrite" western constructions of Oceania (Winduo 2000).

Gramsci's ideas are not without influence in folkloristics, and neither are Williams's in literary studies. But have they applied to twentieth-century North American and European scholarship on "folklore and literature"? How is this interdisciplinary field of study framed? My view from within is that the interdisciplinarity of folklore and literature as a field of study is still today more an ambition than a practice: valorizing folklore *or* literature remains all too often an unquestioned orientation; formalist or functional approaches to either folklore or literature have tended to foreclose located understandings of their dynamics; the crossover of folklore studies' insights into literary or cultural studies has not been significant; and the conversation between scholars of folk literature and scholars of Native and postcolonial literatures has been limited. Disciplinary prejudice and ethnocentricity are ongoing problems that we as scholars of "folklore and literature" must address.

A survey of the intersections of such vast discursive formations as "folklore" and "literature" was undertaken in the *Encyclopedia of Folklore and Literature* (Brown and Rosenberg 1998). This essay follows the critical tradition of mapping the field as constituted by the analysis of folklore *in* literature, folklore *as* literature, and folklore *and* literature. I aim to identify some of the debates and trajectories that have informed North American, and to some extent European, discourses on folklore in, as, and literature; intervene in discussions of oral vs. print transmission with an eye to re-situating "folklore and literature" within the larger dynamics of cultural politics; foreground the crucial role of intertextuality, commodification, and translation; and provide examples of how scholars of folklore and literature are contending with the legacies of nationalism and colonialism.

RE-VIEWING FOLKLORE IN/AS LITERATURE

We expect to encounter folklore *in* literary texts because "folklore is a pervasive aspect of life" (Brown 1976: 346), and authors as well as literary characters exhibit, encounter, or seek to understand the behaviors and traditions of one or more social group. For instance, literary characters often use proverbial language or participate in festivals. Ghosts appear in William Shakespeare's, Henry James's, Maxine Hong Kingston's, and Toni Morrison's texts as testaments to different and culturally-located beliefs concerning the supernatural. All the way into the 1960s, the most common project for American folklorists who examined literature was to mine texts for ethnographic information; the point (Dorson 1957) was to collect folkloric data from the literature and to corroborate their authenticity and social circulation via comparison. "Folklorists plunge into literary sources and emerge with dry lists of motifs or proverbs lifted from their literary context.... The problem is that for many folklorists identification has become an end in itself instead of a means to the end of interpretation" (Dundes 1965: 136).

Alan Dundes's 1965 essay called for a new critical agenda by proposing that the identification of folklore in literature be only a step towards interpretation: his example built on identifying how a riddle in James Joyce's *Ulysses* draws on "The Robber Bridegroom" tale, in order to further interpret the character Stephen's ambivalence toward his mother. This contextualist approach to folklore in literature encouraged taking folklore seriously, in Gramsci's sense. First, re-centering the folklorist's work on interpretation countered the hegemonic perception that folklore could only be a relic of the past, hardly an active force at play in the cultural dynamics of any text or modern society. Second, considering folklore's "text, texture, and context" in the process of interpretation made room for attending to folklore's verbal artistry. Third, advocating that folklorists apply parallel methods to fieldwork and literature also paved the way for not considering the literary in a sphere of its own. And finally, for Dundes, the focus on context meant recognizing the importance of "metafolklore" and the need for folklorists to "elicit the meaning of folklore from the folk," what he called "oral literary criticism" (2007 [1966]: 81). To arrive at the meaning of folklore in a literary text would then involve paying attention to all aspects of its performance, including the asides that performers and audience members make, their own reflections about the story, proverb, or song and its uses.

While European folklorists like Carl Wilhelm von Sydow, Lauri Honko, and Gyula Ortutay were already focusing on social and performance contexts, the attention in the 1970s to folklore as performance, as event rather than text (Paredes and Bauman 1972), changed the discourse of American folkloristics. This shift had an impact on the study of folklore in literary texts as well (Jones 1984), as seen in Mary Ellen Brown's 1976 analysis of how Nigerian writer Chinua Achebe's fictional representation of material and verbal Igbo folklore enhances "character development and plot motivation" and also functions as "a reminder of identity, as a call to identity, and as a basis for a revitalized nation" (1998: 3). The meanings of folklore, in literature as in the world, are read as specific to textual, social, and political contexts.

Re-Situating Folklore: Folk Contexts and Twentieth-Century Literature and Art lists the most common "uses" of folklore in literature: the creation of "local color" and "remoteness of time and place," the suggestion of "the transcendental and the mystical," and the presentation of "values, perspectives, wisdom – not found in other media" (De Caro and Jordan 2004: 16, 17). These representational practices often point to folklore as residual or anachronistic. To counter the perception that "folklore is not of the modern world, indeed is incompatible with if not antithetical to it" (2004: 19), Frank De Caro and Rosan Augusta Jordan analyze how quilting, storytelling, and riddling contribute to the construction of textual meaning specifically in *twentieth-century* literature. While interpreting uses of folklore in contemporary literature and culture is now a well-established scholarly practice (see Wolfgang Mieder's numerous contributions including 1985 and 2008; also Harris 1991; Wilson 1993; Bacchilega 1997; Barzilai 2009), the association of folklore with old-fashioned rather than postmodern ways or subaltern knowledges persists.

While the popular misapprehension that folklore is simple, and its pleasures childlike, has led to a strong association of folklore with children's literature and to yet another common misconception that folktales were always for children, most of the critical discussion of folklore *as* literature puts folk literature (ballads, folktales, legends, riddles, myths, epics, proverbs) firmly at its center. Lasting analyses abound, and I mention a few here to underscore the range of studies that foreground distinctive matters of style and genre in folk narrative (e.g., Lüthi 1982 [1947]; Nicolaisen 1980; Dégh 2001); address the role of orality in verbal artistry (Lord 2000 [1960]); detail the adaptation (Rölleke 1975) and commodification of Jacob and Wilhelm Grimm's *Kinder- und Hausmärchen* as children's literature (Haase 2003); and compare the textualization of epic traditions (Honko 2000). The study of folklore as literature also intersects with postcolonial and Native poetics, which reject the European Romantic notion of the folk as creators of all poetry but affirm vernacular storytelling traditions as both the foundation of new national literatures and the backbone of literary histories unhinged from a textual, Eurocentric, and elitist tradition.

Within the wide-ranging scholarship on folklore as literature, references to "oral traditions," "folk literature," and "verbal art" can be confusing because, while substantially overlapping, not all oral traditions are folk, not all folk literature is oral, not all verbal art is literary or oral. One could say that "oral traditions" emphasizes the medium of transmission and contrasts their extra-individual dimension to an author-centered literature; "folk literature" identifies narrative traditions and genres as subaltern; "verbal art" recognizes the aesthetics of everyday performance practices and a poetics not strictly literary.

In practice, scholars engaged in ethnography of performance, oral theory, and ethnopoetics address the relationship of "orality" and "literacy" to "literature" in different ways. The ethnographer focuses on oral traditions as performances embedded in and constitutive of social life; critics engaged in oral theory seek to read poetry on the page as oral performance and to read oral performance in cultures across the world as poetry (Foley 2002); and following the approach that Dennis Tedlock, Jerome Rothenberg, and Dell Hymes took to Native American traditions, the concern of ethnopoetics is with the translation into print of cultural and performance-centered specifics, from vocal dynamics to facial expressions and audience responses (McCarthy 1994; de Gerdes *et al.* 2000; Honko 2000). Together, these approaches to orality, literacy, and literature have much in common with late twentieth-century literary theory: a critique of New Critical decontextualizing, considerable attention to audience/reader participation in the narrative event, and acceptance of textual instability (Amodio 1998).

The MLA volume *Teaching Oral Traditions* (1998) made a significant contribution towards undoing the naturalized "predisposition toward the written, textualized word" that so many of us in literature departments share, and towards affirming a new approach to genre and comparative literature (Dimock and Robbins 2007). "From the Sumerian *Gilgamesh* and the ancient Greek *Odyssey* through the medieval European vernacular texts and on to the contemporary, living performance traditions of central Asia, China, Africa, Australia, and the United States, conventionally defined 'literature' is indeed just the iceberg's tip" (Foley 1998: 4). To envision living oral traditions as well as texts that originate in the oral tradition in an oral-literate continuum moves us away from seeing orality vs. literacy as the great divide that Walter Ong and the Parry-Lord theory made it. In the same volume, folklorist Lee Haring provocatively asks "if comparative literature eliminates elitism and periodization, ... [w]hat would a true comparative literature look like?" His response is promising: "Using translations and ethnographies, comparative literature can take as its field both oral and written literatures in literary systems around the world" (1998: 37); not in an imperialist way, but one that shows "how literary and folkloric texts are embedded in their social context" and how "the diversity of artistic systems is an irreplaceable laboratory for an understanding of the nature of verbal art" (1998: 41). Orality is hardly dead, intersecting with internet-based technology (Foley 2008; Cherubini 2008) and remaining crucial to the production and reception of an ancient epic, children's language play, a fairy tale, James Joyce, a contemporary Oceanian novel, or North American slam poetry. Approaching the oral-literate continuum, then, no longer involves matters of origin, but diversified heuristics of interpretation, encoding and decoding.

Ethnography of performance, oral theory, and ethnopoetics dovetail with one another – and with a new comparative literature – each working to subvert frameworks where folk literatures, oral traditions, and Native traditions are held subaltern to print and canonized "literature." Recognizing multiple cultural esthetics, gendered poetics, and genre systems rather than assuming an ethnocentric and elitist print literature as their standard, these approaches crack the transdisciplinary door open. Overall, rather than taking the orality vs. literacy debate as their core, I find it more productive to recognize that what I have been discussing is performance studies, as applied – within the disciplines of literary studies, linguistics, folkloristics, and anthropology – to verbal arts across time and cultures; and that their common orientation is to provide counter-narratives to an elitist and ethnocentric conception of literature. Contributing to this orientation are studies attentive to gender dynamics and gendered traditions (see Langlois 1985; Radner 1993; Hasan-Rokem 2000 and 2003) as well as to place-centered (Hau'ofa 2008; Dupres 2010), aural (Bendix 2000), and visual (Teaiwa 2010) poetics.

In the face of such varied performances and traditions, who decides what is literature and what is not? I learned from performance studies and folkloristics the importance of recognizing discursive genres and their functions *within* localized systems of meanings and communities. It's helpful to have analytical categories from linguistics – emic and etic – to refer to the insiders' and the outsiders' systems of genre classification, but it is distorting and arrogant to impose definitions that assume an outsiders' system as standard. I also learned from indigenous and postcolonial scholars of oral traditions that "folklore" is often seen as a colonizing label that has kept their literatures in captivity, thus their preference for "orature," a term introduced by Ugandan linguist Pio Zirimu (Wa Thiong'o 2007). To approach orature as well as subaltern artistic genres in ways that do not implicitly buttress othering practices remains a challenge, not least because these expressive forms are overwritten by colonizing systems of knowledge. If "[t]he great contribution of oral tradition study to criticism is its insistence on the importance of the actual behavior of oppressed people" (Haring 1994: 16) and their perspectives, it is a worthy challenge that requires, as Gramsci also suggested, learning from the oppressed as intellectuals (Hereniko and Wilson 1999; King 2005; Winduo 2000). "Unwriting" literature from Native and postcolonial perspectives is a *political* project that involves producing narratives that de-center the oral vs. print debate *and* sustain projects of sovereignty, autoethnography as re-writing history, and re-education through the decolonization of methodologies (ho'omanawanui 2010; Teaiwa 2010; Tuhiwai-Smith 1999).

RE-CONTEXTUALIZING FOLKLORE AND LITERATURE

The focus here is not textual interpretation as it is with folklore in literature, or the valorization and disciplinary configuration of folklore as literature, but theorizing how folklore and literature are systematically imbricated with one another, and why this matters. Within the larger "folklore and literature" field of study, then, folklore *and* literature approaches distinctively focus on the dynamic (not inherently hierarchical) and intertextual relations of these two semiotic systems or cultural fields. Overall, such folklore and literature studies have increasingly moved away from universalizing frameworks and become more concerned with context-specific dynamics of genre and performance that connect questions of poetics with those of representation, commercialization, technology, and the politics of culture. Bruce Rosenberg's *Folklore and Literature: Rival Siblings* surveys "the theoretical intersection of the study of folklore and literature" (1991: 1) via a discussion of *Beowulf*, Chaucer, Shakespeare, and Faulkner. In what follows I will foreground how folklore and literature questions have figured prominently in fairy-tale studies, a recently institutionalized critical discourse that aspires to be transdisciplinary (Haase 2008: xxxiii–xxxix).

Folklore and literature approaches are often grounded in semiotics, and their precursors are associated with Russian formalism and structuralism. While Petr Bogatyrev and Roman Jakobson's "Die Volkskunde als eine besondere Form des Schaffens" (1929; "Folklore as a Special Form of Creativity," 1982) portrayed folklore as an anonymous, collective tradition in contrast to literature's individual-centered creativity, this early twentieth-century study also conceptualized the two as systems of communication with different functions and a *dynamic* boundary between them, along the Saussurean lines of *langue* and *parole*. Activating a different understanding of function – not social but narrative – Vladimir Propp's *Morphology of the Folktale* (originally published in Russian in 1928) did not only provide a systematic analysis of the plot of 100 Russian tales, but became foundational to narratology's distinction between story or plot and discourse. And Mikhail Bakhtin's emphasis on dialogism, as intertextual conversation, continues to be especially influential in highlighting how all texts, oral or written, participate in a web of intertextual relations.

Overall, the study of language, and of narrative texts as signs, is the backbone of semiotic perspectives whereby the communicative and social functions of folk narratives are distinctive, but not separate, from those of literature. Further contextualizing folklore and literature in the twentieth-century culture industry, folklorists De Caro and Jordan elaborate:

> As communicative media, literature and folklore obviously have quite different characteristics: written language vs. oral (and even non verbal); silent reading by a 'public' vs. hearing/watching a performance; fixed, printed text vs. a shifting, unwritten one; a physical text vs. memory; a rather complex infrastructure of editors, publishers, and booksellers vs. a simple one of a few people in contact with each other. Yet different media do overlap and interconnect. (2004: 3)

Within this intertextual framework, scholars have sought to understand the process and impact of re-situating folklore not simply in a single literary text but in a literary system (as with folktales and ballads in canonical European literature), or vice versa of folklorizing literature (as with *Harry Potter* slash fan fiction or modern Italian jokes quoting Dante). Calling on Bakhtin, de Caro and Jordan point to how twentieth-century literary writers re-situate folklore and give it new or different meanings: representing folklore mimetically, adopting the conventions and form of a folkloric genre, adapting folkloric plots, or playing out a folk concept (2004: 6–12). Another taxonomy of eight intertextual strategies to situate folklore in postmodern literature includes fabulation, metafiction, and chronotopia (Smith 2007).

Such "re-situating," I emphasize, necessarily involves decontextualizing – the extraction of discourse from a person, group, nation, genre, context – as well as entextualizing – the process that enables turning discourse into extractable units or texts (Bauman and Briggs 2003). By reflecting on these often-naturalized discursive strategies, we can shift our attention from folklore and literature as systems, or "contexts," to their "contextualization," or discursive production. This has consequences for how we think of intertextuality and genre as well as how we inhabit critical authority.

Intertextuality, to gloss Julia Kristeva, is not the dialogue of fixed meanings or texts with one another; it is an intersection of several speech acts and discourses (the writer's, the speaker's, the addressee, earlier writers' and speakers'), whereby meanings emerge in the process of how something is told and valued, where, to whom, and in relation to which other utterances. From this perspective, whether literary or folkloric, genres are not structures or forms, but frameworks of orientation that are dynamic, often hybrid, and emergent so that linking a text with a genre inevitably effects an "intertextual gap" (Briggs and Bauman 1992: 149) and involves not only historicizing, but traditionalizing. In retrospect, this is how I read Angela Carter's collection of short stories, *The Bloody Chamber*, intertextually in my *Postmodern Fairy Tales: Gender and Narrative Strategies* (1997). My analysis foregrounded Carter's re-contextualization of the fairy tale as historically layered and multi-voiced in order to decouple the genre from the stereotypical infantilization, victimization, and witchification of women. I focused on the entextualization of fairy tales and on how the genre's de-contextualization – from oral traditions, women's lives, sexuality, and the politics of othering – is interrogated in Carter's discourse. I pointed to how Carter's fairy tale is co-inhabited by the folktale and the legend. And I marked how Carter's stories maximize intertextual gaps with the fairy tale as socializing literature for children, in order to contest this hegemonic understanding of the genre.

More recent fairy-tale studies have deployed intertextuality to pursue widely divergent intellectual projects that address different folklore and literature questions. Expanding intertextual reading to include theory, Stephen Benson's *Cycles of Influence: Fiction. Folktale. Theory* makes a claim for the cyclical nature of the interplay of these three discursive formations. Postmodern and feminist fictions play out critiques of narrative traditions; folktales continue to spur reflection on narrative and narrativity; theories of narrative and subjectivity are sustained by the idea of orality and the folktale. By representing the folktale "as a significant narrative model and source of material in both the literature and the narrative theory of the past fifty years" (2003: 12), Benson seeks to undo a narrative of progress where folktales only figure as simple or outmoded. Of Angela Carter's and Margaret Atwood's feminist adaptations of "Bluebeard" narratives, Benson writes: "The newly composed tales seek to change the direction of both particular stories and of the genre as it is known, giving a voice to an often passive, silenced presence, a voice that speaks both against the grain of the narrative and through the breaks and gaps in the overlaid moralities of previous generations. This is achieved by pulling submerged stories through these gaps, stories both in the sense of alternative life stories and submerged, parallel folk narratives" (2003: 200). His incisive discussion of intertextuality includes cycles of tales, their staged orality in *The Arabian Nights* and *The Pentameron*, and the difference between fairy tales and "fairy-tale fictions."

Drawing on Tzvetan Todorov and Bakhtin's dialogism, *Textualité et intertextualité des contes* (Heidmann and Adam 2010) explores how a literary fairy-tale text responds to rhetorical, generic, and semantic propositions made by other texts; specifically, how Charles Perrault's tales can be seen to reference and at the same time distance themselves from tales by Apuleius, La Fontaine, Straparola, Basile, and Lhéritier, in order to produce a distinctly modern genre, characterized by a "trompe-l'oeil" and pseudo-naïf character. When Heidmann and Adam hypothesize Perrault's intertextual dialog with Apuleius, it is not to situate the origin of the genre in Latin antiquities (Ziolkowski 2006) but to foreground the generic and rhetorical complexities of Perrault's fairy tales. The literary intertextuality they discuss operates within a multilingual and European-wide network that does not assume the oral tradition to be Perrault pre-text, but does not exclude it either (2006: 24).

Attentive to different aspect of intertextuality in twentieth-century fairy-tale fiction and popular culture, Jessica Tiffin's *Marvelous Geometry: Narrative and Metafiction in Modern Fairy Tale* traces the production of a "folkloric voice" – the "self-aware invocation of oral tradition in the tone and phrasing of the tale" – to an "inherent metafictionality of the literary fairy tale." Constructed upon the awareness of "folk roots" as an "idealized notion of peasant identity" (2009: 138), the folkloric voice signals a desire to recover a presumably trusted and simple teller/listener relation. This "dialog with an artificial notion of oral historicity" (2009: 139) echoes Susan

Stewart's understanding of the fairy tale as a nostalgically "distressed genre" (1991). Tiffin points out how the folkloric voice is particularly problematic in mass-culture productions where folklore is appropriated primarily for commercial profit: the reassuring voice-over at the start of Disney fairy-tale films is one of her examples. But she also observes in late twentieth-century popular literature by Tanith Lee and Terry Pratchett "a movement to reassert and recapture" the fairy tale as a "popular medium" that actually reflects the experiences of a community (2009: 4–5). Either way, for Tiffin, these intertextual marks represent folklore and literature dynamics being re-imagined within the culture industry and within current struggles to re-appropriate popular culture.

Contestation of hegemonic meanings is at stake for Cathy-Lynn Preston, who focuses on how generic intertextuality can rupture the hierarchies of both genre and gender. Preston builds on Amy Shuman's Bakhtinian analysis of how reporting the words of another – especially of a traditional "other" – involves a negotiation of authority. Having noted that in late twentieth-century North America the "stuff" of fairy tales circulates as "free-floating cultural data" (2004: 210), Preston argues that "for many people the accumulated web of feminist critique (created through academic discourse, folk performance, and popular media) may function as an emergent and authoritative – though fragmented and still under negotiation – multivocality that cumulatively is competitive with the surface monovocality" of the dominant Perrault-Grimms-Disney tradition (199). Elizabeth Harries also argues for a multivocality of the genre: "there are in fact *two* genres of fairy tales – one the compact model Perrault and the Grimms favored; one the longer, more complex and more self-referential model" (2001: 16) that aristocratic women writers in seventeenth- and eighteenth-century France preferred; and their narrative strategies and concerns have been adapted by twentieth-century women writers. These two projects are quite different: Preston emphasizes the emergent role that folklore has in the hegemonic and anti-hegemonic dynamics of contemporary North American culture; Harries intervenes in the history of the fairy tale as a literary genre. However, by taking into account not only pre-texts or hypotexts but prospective performances and adaptations that dominant genre definitions may very well seek to exclude, Preston, Harries, and Marina Warner before them (1994) foreground intertextuality to produce a feminist critique of authority that crosses over disciplinary boundaries.

These few examples alone are symptomatic of how folklore and literature questions in this field have shifted from "what defines a folktale, or a fairy tale?" to "how do we read a fairy tale's dialog with the genre and other intertexts?" and to "what is a [folktale or] fairy tale understood to be in the twenty-first century?" (Makinen 2008: 148). These shifts, as one 2009 narrowly literary construction of fairy tale demonstrates (Bottigheimer), are hardly to be understood as simply consecutive to one another, marking some linear progress; rather their ongoing competition suggests that tensions running across folklore and literature approaches are no different from those shaping the larger history and unresolved struggles of Western critical discourses in the late twentieth century. Within folklore and literature and fairy-tale studies, we need to keep grappling with specific questions. For instance, how is relying on the tale type (Dundes 1982), a construct that has been foundational to folklore studies, compatible with taking an intertextual approach? How do we move away, in theorizing the porous boundaries between folklore and literature, from questions of origin without de-historicizing? How do we approach the pervasive invocation of folktale and fairy tale in contemporary culture without reproducing hierarchies that place literature at the top? Such questions interrogate our construction of textuality in relation to social life and our own responsibilities and response-abilities as scholars to the struggles of representation.

In the influential oeuvre of Jack Zipes, folk and fairy tales are represented as fluid texts *and* symbolic acts, versions with wide-ranging aesthetic, educational, and political impact; cultural adaptation is the lifeblood of these tales in *a range of media*; and fairy-tale discourse plays out different power struggles within specific cultural fields as well as socio-historical contexts (2009). What, then, justifies isolating "folklore and literature" from other dynamics of cultural production and social practices? What are the consequences of insulating intertextuality from race-gender-class relations? For Susan Stewart, intertextuality has to do more with the interpretive operations that we employ to frame "common sense" or "realism" in social life than with the dialog among texts; she investigates wordplay in a children's rhyme and Vladimir Nabokov's novels to get at how it transgressively transforms "two major features of common-sense interpretive procedures, context and hierarchy" (1978: 37). Within her intertextual approach, as well as in Zipes's, there is also no isolating "folklore" and "literature" from other forms of cultural production or from dynamics of power.

For me too, the value of a folklore and literature approach – in its multiple shapes – resides in the methodological shifts and ethical considerations that it demands. From folklorists we learn to consider the multiplicity of versions through which a speech act or narrative is experienced; and we foreground the tradition and performance interplay as well as the performative elements that contextualize any telling as a retelling or rewriting, but not as replication. From literary theorists who have turned away from reading literature as autonomous and fixed texts that are the sole product of individual creativity and have meaning per se, we learn to read a text as framed by specific institutions – including that of literature – and as a site of dialog and possibly struggle. We work with multiple versions, whether it's a Shakespeare play or "Cinderella" tales, their print and performed versions, their textual imbrications, their adaptation in different cultures as well as media, and how they confirm, challenge, subvert received understandings of what they mean.

Furthermore, awareness of the dynamics and implications of entextualizing, decontextualizing and recontextualizing *in social life* as well as in literature and in scholarship greatly enriches folklore and literature perspectives on intertextuality. Whether we are focusing on oral and literary fairy tales only, or we are studying fairy-tale discourse in a variety of cultural practices, it matters how the fairy-tale "text" is constructed, who does the defining, in relation to which other definitions, in relations to which other genres and cultural fields, in relation to which social behaviors, in what kind of historical conjunctures, and for whose benefit. And if the text is plural so are knowledges: we learn not only about, but from other communities while remaining anchored in our own. This kind of folklore and literature lens helps to see a social formation as multiple and connected, an individual as a network, a teller as an artist, an artist as a manipulator of received knowledge, and metalanguages (in the plural) as a type of speech that exercises authority and also involves playing with and across traditions.

RE-VALUING TRANSLATION IN FOLKLORE AND LITERATURE

Scholars of folklore and literature seek to recognize a web of intertextuality where folklore is not set apart from literature and, at the same time, their differences are not erased; and some of us are invested in the material and ideological relations that inform the web's links and hierarchies. The practice of translation foregrounds how differences between what we call folklore and what we call literature are not inherent in genres or texts, but *located* in specific systems of textual production and socio-cultural histories as well as in their power dynamics. If we understand both "folklore" and "literature" as products of modernity, the significance of translation for the articulation of folklore *and* literature is not limited to the circulation of stories across language confines or to the intermedial translation from the oral to the written/printed word; it expands further to the roles that translation plays in the commodification, expropriation, and re-appropriation of subaltern cultures. My goal here is to foreground how intervening in and interrogating practices of translation contribute to confronting the legacies of -isms, including sexism and colonialism, in dominant configurations of folklore and literature.

The interlingual and intercultural translation of folktales and fairy tales has naturalized gender and ethnic stereotypes, promoted exoticizing fantasies, and played major roles in colonizing projects. This is particularly clear in the convoluted history of European translations of the *Thousand and One Nights* that contributed much to eighteenth- and nineteenth-century Orientalism and to contemporary vilification in US media of Arabs (Sheehan 2003). A transnational approach has been significant to counter this Euro-American-centered construction of the phenomenon of the *Arabian Nights* (Yamanaka and Nishio 2006; Marzolph 2007). Discussions of translation also impact how we think of the economy of genres as well as cultures: why are *The Arabian Nights*, which have strong ties to multiple folk traditions, commonly marketed in the West as "world literature"? Antoine Galland's French edition in the early eighteenth century highly influenced the modern novel as a Western literary genre, and yet the *Nights* were not held in as much esteem within the literary Arabic cultures from which they originated until they were in turn influenced by Western literary theories and forms, such as the novel, in the nineteenth and twentieth centuries (Makdisi and Nussbaum 2008). New translations are also crucial to denaturalizing stereotypes, as seen in Husain Haddawy's 1990 English-language translation of the *Arabian Nights* and in the 1980s and 1990s abundant production of anthologies of folk and fairy tales that sought to actualize feminist and multicultural agendas. Enabling such interventions are still, however, the notion of translation as simply instrumental and the projection of the translator as invisible (Haase 2004; Hennard and Heidmann 2009).

Two recently translated collections of narratives that, while making ideological interventions in folklore and literature, run counter to this ventriloquizing norm and promote a culture of translation are Jack Zipes's *Beautiful Angiola: The Great Treasury of Sicilian Folk and Fairy Tales, Collected by Laura Gonzenbach* (2004) and the bilingual edition of a Hawaiian epic, *Ka Moʻolelo O Hiʻiakaikapoliopele. The Epic Tale of Hiʻiakaikapoliopele, By Hoʻoulumāhiehie*, edited and translated by Puakea Nogelmeier and his team (2007). Laura Gonzenbach collected stories from lower-class Sicilian women, often in women-only spaces, thus representing localized subaltern perspectives that were marginalized in other European nineteenth-century collections; her collection, originally published in her native German, rather than Sicilian or Italian, was also the product of multiple mediations across languages, class, and genres. Zipes's translation contributes to undermining the construction of folk and fairy tales as inherently sexist or conservative; and its extensive introduction, comparative notes, and translator's notes – the paratext that, in Gérard Genette's terms, the threshold that frames readers' expectations – highlight the various mediations that produced Gonzenbach's text in the first place.

Ho'oulumāhiehie's *Mo'olelo O Hi'iakaikapoliopele* is the most extensive of the many versions of the epic poem that appeared in nineteenth- and twentieth-century Hawaiian newspapers. Its recent bilingual edition showcases how Ho'oulumāhiehie presents his tale as part of a literary tradition that needed to be preserved in print and was also self-consciously adapting to print. Nogelmeier and his team of translators made some bold editing choices, such as using modern spelling and diacritics for the Hawaiian, supplementing missing text with words or lines from other published versions, and commissioning illustrations that incorporate textual detail and offer vivid portraits of the various characters. The elaborate paratextual apparatus seeks to enhance readers' awareness of the translators' choices and aims, but also to valorize Ho'oulumāhiehie's narrative as literature.

What boundaries between "folklore" and "literature," and between non-Western and Western narrative production, are being protected and/or challenged through translation, generic framing, and marketing? While these practices are hardly straightforward and we must resist generalizing about them, several studies point our attention to how, in specific contexts, the blurring of "translation" and "adaptation" has a role to play in the perpetuation and the contestation of a cultural politics of inequality.

In "Framing the Brothers Grimm: Paratexts and Intercultural Transmission in Postwar English-Language Editions of the *Kinder- und Hausmärchen*," Donald Haase takes into account two processes of translation – from oral tradition to printed text and across languages and cultures – to ask about the value of publications "aimed ostensibly at the Anglo-American children's-book market" (2003: 56). Focusing on the "paratextual dimensions" of these translations (frontispiece, prefaces, notes), Haase observes that surprisingly none of these English-language editions reproduce the Grimms' own paratext. And yet these translations exploit the connection the Grimms established with the oral tradition within their prefatory materials. Just as the Grimms "opted to speak, in print, for the folk, ... rather than let the Grimms speak for themselves, translators find it more convenient to re-frame the tales in their own way" (2003: 61). The translators invoke in their own new paratextual materials "the myth of the folk and oral authenticity to lend the translated tales authority," and they "simultaneously erase the German voice by substituting a universal human voice" (2003: 64). One of the conclusions to draw from Haase's analysis is that the English-language translations' erasure of cultural specificity and their ventriloquism enable the exaltation of Grimms' tales into the field of "literature," albeit of children's literature.

My project in *Legendary Hawai'i and the Politics of Place: Tradition, Translation, and Tourism* (2007) also focuses on the marketing of culturally-specific narratives in English-language translations, but to foreground their production of stereotypes and their promotion of Hawai'i as tourist destination for Americans in the early twentieth century. In the process, Hawaiian *moʻolelo*, Native histories and stories centered in place, were transformed into "legends" or "myths," and generally fanciful stories. This rhetorical re-framing of authority, genre, readership, and geosymbols, I argue, operated a violent displacement of Hawaiian knowledge that furthered the dispossession of Hawaiians following the overthrow and the US occupation of their nation in 1893. However, well before this textual production of a "legendary Hawaiʻi," Hawaiians had been translating the *moʻolelo* into print in Hawaiian-language newspapers and also translating foreign narratives, including stories from the *Arabian Nights* and the Grimms' collection, for readers in Hawaiʻi. These intermedial and interlingual translations show how Hawaiians were not only objects of translation, but deployed translation to exercise agency as storymakers in print (Kuwada 2009). Hawaiians were building a national literature, which was for many decades forgotten due to the decline and suppression of Hawaiian language and the dominant colonial mindset following the annexation of Hawaiʻi to the United States, but nevertheless lived on in the traditions of Hawaiian dance, chant, and more recently in print, in both Hawaiian and English. Neither literature nor folklore production in Hawaiʻi can be understood outside historical and present dynamics of political and cultural power.

"An irony embedded in the standard discourse escapes us," writes Sadhana Naithani: "that the history of folkloristics in the United Kingdom can be written without reference to its colonial past, but the history of folkloristics in erstwhile colonized countries must begin in the colonized past." To correct this imbalance, Naithani's work on translation and colonialism forcefully shifts our attention: "colonial folkloristics can only be studied and analyzed beyond national boundaries, because it was not created within a nation" (2010: 4). Within this transnational framework, *The Story-Time of the British Empire* examines how folktales in the British colonies of India and Africa were collected, transcribed, translated, and published for international consumption. Two specific aspects of this groundbreaking book are particularly relevant to a discussion of folklore and literature. First, Naithani documents how in colonial India the collectors were primarily colonial "officials" or their female spouses so that "the infrastructure and authority of the colonial state was involved in the method of folklore collection" (2010: 45). The "creators" of these collections were not motivated by an interest in creativity or poetry – as was often the case in Europe – but in "knowing" the colonized so as to ensure the success of empire. Second, she holds a literary lens to texts that have been mostly read ethnographically: "I am reading colonial texts like *haiku* poems – that is, with an awareness that something is said, not everything, and that that which is not said is actually as important as that which is said" (2010: 28). And, I extrapolate, this is how we should also read postcolonial literatures that, in today's globalized culture industry, translate and adapt a "folklore" that has necessarily been inflected by colonialism and anti-colonial struggles as well.

Silences are just as important as voices in a textual economy of folklore and literature that seeks to resist appropriating other, oral or subaltern, cultures (see Spivak 2003, 11; Bauman 2004). The words of others – groups, individuals, and institutions – inhabit us; we re-inhabit them; and we are responsible for how we exercise these habits because they always require representation, translation, and some exercise of authority over others. In a field of folklore and literature that is shifting away from colonizing paradigms, we confront these responsibilities all the time by listening for voices and silences and by working towards a re-cognition of their always mediated articulations, in an effort – to echo Gramsci with a difference – to move away from "instruction" and towards "education."

REFERENCES

Amodio, Mark C. 1998. "Contemporary Critical Approaches and Studies in Oral Tradition" in John Miles Foley, Ed. *Teaching Oral Traditions*, pp. 95–105.

Bacchilega, Cristina. 1997. *Postmodern Fairy Tales: Gender and Narrative Strategies*. Philadelphia: University of Pennsylvania Press.

Bacchilega, Cristina. 2007. *Legendary Hawai'i and the Politics of Place: Tradition, Translation, and Tourism*. Philadelphia: University of Pennsylvania Press.

Barzilai, Shuli. 2009. *Tales of Bluebeard and His Wives from Late Antiquity to Postmodern Times*. New York and London: Routledge.

Bauman, Richard. 2004. *A World of Others' Words: Cross-Cultural Perspectives on Intertextuality*. Malden, MA: Blackwell Publishing.

Bauman, Richard and Charles L. Briggs. 2003. *Voices of Modernity: Language Ideologies and the Politics of Inequality*. New York: Cambridge University Press.

Bendix, Regina. 2000. "The Pleasures of the Ear: Toward an Ethnography of Listening." *Cultural Analysis* 1: 33–50.

Benson, Stephen. 2003. *Cycles of Influence: Fiction, Folktale, Theory*. Detroit: Wayne State University Press.

Bogatyrev, Petr and Roman Jakobson. 1982. "Folklore as a Special Form of Creativity" in Peter Steiner, Ed. *The Prague School: Selected Writings, 1929–1946*. Austin: University of Texas Press.

Bottigheimer, Ruth B. 2009. *Fairy Tales: A New History*. Albany: State University of New York Press.

Briggs, Charles and Richard Bauman. 1992. "Genre, Intertextuality, and Social Power." *Journal of Linguistic Anthropology* 2.2: 131–172.

Brown, Mary Ellen (Lewis). 1976. "The Study of Folklore in Literature: An Expanded View." *Southern Folklore Quarterly* 40: 343–351.

Brown, Mary Ellen and Bruce A. Rosenberg, Eds. 1998. *Encyclopedia of Folklore and Literature*. Santa Barbara, CA: ABC-Clio.

Cherubini, Lorenzo. 2008. "The Metamorphosis of an Oral Tradition: Dissonance in the Digital Stories of Aboriginal Peoples in Canada" *Oral Tradition* 23(2): 297–314.

Dégh, Linda. 2001. *Legends and Belief: Dialectics of a Folklore Genre*. Bloomington: Indiana University Press.

De Caro, Frank and Rosan Augusta Jordan. 2004. *Re-Situating Folklore: Folk Contexts and Twentieth-Century Literature and Art*. Knoxville: The University of Tennessee Press.

De Gerdes, Marta, Kay Sammons, and Joel Sherzer, Eds. 2000. *Translating Native American Verbal Art: Ethnopoetics and Ethnography of Speaking*. Washington, DC: Smithsonian Institution Press.

Dimock, Wai Chee and Bruce Robbins, Eds. 2007. *Special Topic: Remapping Genre*. *PMLA* 122: 5.

Dorson, Richard M. 1957. "The Identification of Folklore in American Literature." *Journal of American Folklore* 70: 1–8.

Dundes, Alan. 1965. "The Study of Folklore in Literature and Culture: Identification and Interpretation." *Journal of American Folklore* 78: 136–143.

Dundes, Alan. 1982. "'To Love My Father All': A Psychoanalytical Study of the Folktale Source of *King Lear*" in Alan Dundes, Ed. *Cinderella: A Casebook*. Madison: University of Wisconsin Press, pp. 229–244.

Dundes, Alan. 2007 [1966]. "Metafolklore and Oral Literary Criticism" in Simon Bronner, Ed. *The Meaning of Folklore: The Analytical Essays of Alan Dundes*. Logan: Utah State University Press.

Dupres, Christine. 2010. "Landscape and Identity: Continuity of Identity and Attachment to Place in the Cowlitz Indian Tribe." *Fabula* 51: 75–89.

Foley, John Miles. 2002. *How to Read an Oral Poem*. Urbana: University of Illinois Press, http://oraltradition.org/hrop (accessed October 16, 2011).

Foley, John Miles, Ed. 1998. *Teaching Oral Traditions*. New York: The Modern Language Association.

Foley, John Miles. 2008. "Navigating Pathways: Oral Tradition and the Internet." *Academic Intersections* 2 http://pathway-sproject.org/AI-article/1-Abstract.html (accessed October 16, 2011).

Gramsci, Antonio. 1971. *Selections from the Prison Notebooks*. Trans and Ed. Quintin Hoare and Geoffrey Nowell Smith. New York: International Publishers.

Haase, Donald. 2003. "Framing the Brothers Grimm: Paratexts and Intercultural Transmission in Postwar English-Language Editions of the *Kinder- und Hausmärchen*." *Fabula* 44: 55–69.

Haase, Donald, Ed. 2004. *Fairy Tales and Feminism: New Approaches*. Detroit: Wayne State University Press.

Haase, Donald, Ed. 2008. *Greenwood Encyclopedia of Folktales and Fairy Tales*. Santa Barbara: Greenwood.

Haring, Lee. 1994. "Introduction: The Search for Grounds in African Oral Tradition." *Oral Tradition* 9(1): 3–22.

Haring, Lee. 1998. "What Would a True Comparative Literature Look Like?" in John Miles Foley, Ed. *Teaching Oral Traditions*, pp. 34–45.

Harries, Elizabeth W. 2001. *Twice Upon a Time. Women Writers and the History of the Fairy Tale*. Princeton: Princeton University Press.

Harris, Trudier. 1991. *Fiction and Folklore: The Novels of Toni Morrison*. Knoxville: University of Tennessee Press.

Hasan-Rokem, Galit. 2000. *Web of Life: Folklore and Midrash in Rabbinic Literature*. Palo Alto: Stanford University Press.

Hasan-Rokem, Galit. 2003. *Tales of the Neighborhood: Jewish Narrative Dialogues in Late Antiquity*. The Taubman Lectures on Jewish Civilization. Berkeley: University of California Press.

Hauʻofa, Epeli. 2008. *We Are the Ocean: Selected Works*. Honolulu: University of Hawaiʻi Press.

Heidmann, Ute and Jean-Michel Adam. 2010. *Textualité et intertextualité des contes: Perrault, Apulée, La Fontaine, Lhéritier...* Paris: Editions Classiques Garnier.

Hennard Dutheil De La Rochère, Martine Heidemann and Ute Heidmann. 2009. "New Wine in Old Bottles: Angela Carter's Translation of Charles Perrault's 'La Barbe bleue'." *Marvels and Tales* 23(1): 40–58.

Hereniko, Vilsoni and Rob Wilson, Eds. 1999. *Inside Out: Literature, Cultural Politics, and Identity in the New Pacific*. New York: Rowman and Littlefield.

Honko, Lauri, Ed. 2000. *Textualization of Oral Epics*. Berlin and New York: Mouton.

Hoʻoulumāhiehie and Puakea Nogelmeier. 2007. *Ka Moʻolelo O Hiʻiakaikapoliopele. The Epic Tale of Hiʻiakaikapoliopele, By Hoʻoulumāhiehie*. Trans. and ed. Puakea Nogelmeier. Honolulu: Awaiaulu Press.

hoʻomanawanui, kuʻualoha. 2010. "Moʻolelo as Social and Political Action" in hoʻomanawanui, kuʻualoha, Noenoe Silva, Vilsoni Hereniko, and Cristina Bacchilega, Eds. *Folktales and Fairy Tales: Translation, Colonialism, and Cinema*. Mānoa: University of Hawaiʻi at Mānoa Library, http://scholarspace.manoa.hawaii.edu/handle/10125/1560 (accessed October 16, 2011).

Jones, Steven Swann. 1984. *Folklore and Literature in the United States: An Annotated Bibliography of Studies of Folklore in American Literature*. New York: Garland.

King, Thomas. 2005. *The Truth About Stories: A Native Narrative*. Minneapolis: University of Minnesota Press.

Kuwada, Bryan. 2009. "How Blue Is His Beard? An Examination of the 1862 Hawaiian-Language Translation of 'Bluebeard'." *Marvels and Tales* 23(1): 17–39.

Langlois, Janet. 1985. *Belle Gunness. Lady Bluebeard*. Bloomington: Indiana University Press.

462   CRISTINA BACCHILEGA

Lord, Albert B. 2000 [1960]. *The Singer of Tales.* Stephen Mitchell and Gregory Nagy Eds. Cambridge, MA: Harvard University Press.

Lüthi, Max. 1982 [1947]. *The European Folktale: Form and Nature.* Trans. John D. Niles. Bloomington: Indiana University Press.

Makdisi, Saree and Felicity Nussbaum, Eds. 2008. *"The Arabian Nights" in Historical Context: Between East and West.* Oxford: Oxford University Press.

Makinen, Merja. 2008. "Theorizing Fairy-Tale Fiction, Reading Jeanette Winterson" in Stephen Benson, Ed. *Contemporary Fiction and the Fairy Tale.* Detroit: Wayne State University Press, pp. 144–177.

Marzolph, Ulrich, Ed. 2007. *The Arabian Nights in Transnational Perspective.* Detroit: Wayne State University Press.

McCarthy, William Bernard, Ed. 1994. *Jack in Two Worlds: Contemporary North American Tales and Their Tellers.* Winston-Salem: University of North Carolina Press.

Mieder, Wolfgang. 1985. *Disenchantments: An Anthology of Modern Fairy Tale Poetry.* Hanover and London: University Press of New England.

Mieder, Wolfgang. 2008. *"Proverbs Speak Louder than Words": Folk Wisdom in Art, Culture, Folklore, History, Literature, and Mass Media.* Bern and New York: Peter Lang.

Naithani, Sadhana. 2010. *The Story-Time of the British Empire: Colonial and Postcolonial Folkloristics.* Jackson: University Press of Mississippi.

Nicolaisen, W.F.H. 1980. "Space in Folk Narrative" in Nikolai Burlakoff and Carl Lindahl, Eds. *Folklore on Two Continents: Essays in Honor of Linda Dégh.* Bloomington: Trickster Press, pp. 14–18.

Ó Giolláin, Diarmuid. 2004. *Locating Irish Folklore: Tradition, Modernity, Identity.* Cork: Cork University Press.

Paredes, Américo and Richard Bauman, Eds. 1972. *Toward New Perspectives in Folklore.* Austin: University of Texas Press.

Preston, Cathy Lynn. 2004. "Disrupting the Boundaries of Genre and Gender: Postmodernism and the Fairy Tale" in Donald Haase, Ed. *Fairy Tale and Feminism. New Approaches,* pp. 197–212.

Radner, Joan. 1993. *Feminist Messages: Coding in Women's Folk Culture.* Urbana: University of Illinois Press.

Rölleke, Heinz, Ed. 1975. *Rölleke, Heinz, Ed.: Die älteste Märchensammlung der Brüder Grimm: Synopse der handschriftlichen Urfassung von 1810 und der Erstdrucke von 1812.* Cologny-Genève.

Rosenberg, Bruce A. 1991. *Folklore and Literature: Rival Siblings.* Knoxville: The University of Tennessee Press.

Sheehan, Jack. 2003. "Reel Bad Arabs: How Hollywood Vilifies a People." *Annals of the American Academy of Political and Social Science* 588: 171–193.

Smith, Kevin Paul. 2007. *The Postmodern Fairy Tale.* New York: Palgrave Macmillan.

Spivak, Gayatri Chakravorty. 2003. *Death of a Discipline.* New York: Columbia University Press.

Stewart, Susan. 1978. *Nonsense: Aspects of Intertextuality in Folklore and Literature.* Baltimore: Johns Hopkins University Press.

Stewart, Susan. 1991. *Crimes of Writing: Problems in the Containment of Representation.* Oxford: Oxford University Press.

Teaiwa, Teresia. 2010. "What Remains To Be Seen: Reclaiming the Visual Roots of Pacific Literature." *PMLA* 125(3) (May 2010): 730–736.

Tiffin, Jessica. 2009. *Marvelous Geometry: Narrative and Metafiction in Modern Fairy Tale.* Detroit: Wayne State University Press.

Tuhiwai-Smith, Linda. 1999. *Decolonizing Methodologies: Research and Indigenous People.*

Wa Thiong'o, Ngũgĩ. 2007. "Notes Towards a Performance Theory of Orature." *Performance Research* 12(3): 4–7.

Warner, Marina. 1994. *From the Beast to the Blonde: On Fairy Tales and Their Tellers.* London: Chatto and Windus.

Williams, Raymond. 1977. *Marxism and Literature.* Oxford: Oxford University Press.

Wilson, Sharon. 1993. *Margaret Atwood's Fairy-Tale Sexual Politics.* Jackson: University Press of Mississippi.

Winduo, Steven Edmund. 2000.   "Unwriting Oceania: The Repositioning of the Pacific Writer Scholars within a Folk Narrative Space." *New Literary History* 31: 599–613.

Yamanaka, Yuriko and Tetsuo Nishio, Es. 2006. *The Arabian Nights and Orientalism: Perspectives from East and West.* New York: I.B. Tauris.

Ziolkowski, Jan M. 2006.   *Fairy Tales from Before Fairy Tales: The Medieval Latin Past of Wonderful Lies.* Ann Arbor: University of Michigan Press.

Zipes, Jack, Ed. and Trans. 2004.   *The Beautiful Angiola: The Great Treasury of Sicilian Folk and Fairy Tales, Collected by Laura Gonzenbach.* New York: Routledge.

Zipes, Jack. 2009.   *Relentless Progress: The Reconfiguration of Children's Literature, Fairy Tales, and Storytelling.* New York: Routledge.

CHAPTER 24 FOLKLORE AND/ IN MUSIC

Stephen D. Winick

In 1979, the American country-rock group The Charlie Daniels Band released what would become their greatest chart hit, "The Devil Went Down to Georgia." In Daniels's song, the Devil ventures to the southern state to obtain souls, and decides to challenge a local fiddle champion to a contest:

> Now you play a pretty good fiddle, boy, but give the Devil his due:
> I bet a fiddle of gold against your soul, "cause I think I'm better than you."
> The boy said: "My name's Johnny, and it might be a sin,
> But I'll take your bet, you're gonna regret, 'cause I'm the best that's ever been.
> ("The Devil Went Down to Georgia", Charlie Daniels Band)

The song contains two instrumental breaks led by Charlie Daniels on fiddle; each of these represents the playing of one of the contestants. The Devil's tune has no real melody, but an uncanny sound that Daniels achieved by overdubbing several tracks of his own fiddle playing. Johnny instead plays a version of the traditional tune known as "Fire on the Mountain." His tune is introduced in the song by the following cryptic stanza:

> Fire on the mountain, run boys run
> Devil's in the house of the rising sun
> Chicken's in the bread pan pecking out dough
> "Granny, does your dog bite?" "No, child, no."

When each fiddler has played his tune, the Devil has to admit that he has lost. He leaves the golden fiddle for Johnny, and departs in defeat.

In writing this song, Charlie Daniels was clearly influenced by folk legends about the Devil engaging in fiddling contests, which have been current in the United States for over a hundred years. Charles M. Skinner (1896: 74) recorded such a legend, told of an African American fiddler named "Joost," in Brooklyn, New York, probably during the mid-nineteenth century. As in many similar ghost and Devil stories, in Skinner's the Devil is driven away by Joost's piety in playing a hymn tune, and by the arrival of dawn. In other versions of the legend, however, the Devil is simply defeated by superior musicianship. For example, consider a version collected in 1940 by Herbert Halpert from Elven Sweet, in the New Jersey Pine Barrens:

> Old Sammy Giberson, he was playin' to a dance, and after he got done, he said he could beat the devil. So – on his road home, he come to a bridge – he had to cross a bridge. And the Old Man appeared to him right on that bridge – that's the Devil hisself. "I understand," he said, "that you can beat the Devil playin' the fiddle." "Well," Old Sammy says, "that's what I said and that's what I meant." So they went at it, and by God, Sammy played every piece the Devil did, and the Devil played every one that he did, except one, and Old Sammy heard the tune comin' through the air, and that's he beat him. The Devil couldn't play it and Old Sammy could. That's it, that all of it. (Cohen 1983: 34–35)

Based on a traditional story, the Charlie Daniels song is thus an example of folklore being transformed by music. But there are also individual, specific items of folklore embedded within the larger narrative. For example, to explain the seemingly nonsensical stanza that introduces Johnny's tune, let's examine folklorist Alan Jabbour's notes for the fiddle tune "Fire on the Mountain" from the Library of Congress web site *Fiddle Tunes of the Old Frontier*:

> The tune seems to be associated with a cluster of playful rhymes and jingles used in children's songs, play-party songs, and courting songs across the early frontier. The jingles in turn give rise to many of the bewildering array of titles that have turned up for this tune. Some representative examples are ..."Granny Will Your Dog Bite"...[and] "Chicken in the Bread Tray."

From this, we can surmise that three of the four lines of the "Fire on the Mountain" stanza are items of embedded folklore, at the same time snippets of traditional rhymes associated with the tune Johnny plays, and alternate titles for the tune itself. (The second line is the title of an American ballad, "House of the Rising Sun," with the Devil added to it; this cleverly makes the whole stanza thematically relevant to the larger song.) Finally, and not least, "Fire on the Mountain," as a traditional American fiddle tune, is itself an item of folklore, as well as a piece of music.

In this single performance, Charlie Daniels has thus encapsulated many of the ways in which folklore and music interact. By presenting a traditional American fiddle tune, the song highlights folk music – that is, folklore that is also music. By adapting this tune into a larger framework that incorporates elements of commercial country and rock, and by incorporating traditional rhymes and alternate titles, it exemplifies the adaptation of traditional folk forms and folk knowledge into new musical contexts. By presenting a legend already current, about a musical event (a contest between the Devil and a fiddle player), it demonstrates that there is folklore *about* music. And finally, by presenting this legend, which is normally spoken or written in prose, as a song instead, it shows us that narrative folklore can inspire the composition of music; that there is, in other words, music *about* folklore as well.

FOLK MUSIC

In the world of folklore scholarship, folk music has always had a prominent place. Ballads and songs were among the first types of folklore to be systematically collected, and they helped theorists to conceptualize folk culture. In the eighteenth century, songs were among the items that led Johann Gottfried von Herder to begin thinking about "Volkskunde" as a stratum of culture (Cocchiara 1981: 176). Later, when the word "folklore" was coined in English, William John Thoms (1996 [1846]: 187) included ballads among the six genres that he thought most exemplified his new idea.

Most introductions to folk music begin by exploring what makes folk music different from other music; thus, they begin by discussing the idea of folklore as it relates to music. Rarely does a folk music scholar define what is meant by "music," but surely this is crucial as well. A working definition was suggested by Robert Clifton (1983: 1), who noted that music is "an ordered arrangement of sounds and silences whose meaning is presentative rather than denotative." By presentative, Clifton means that there is not a one-to-one correspondence of musical sounds with specific meanings as in language; instead, musical sounds "present to some human being a meaning which he experiences with his body – that is to say, with his mind, his feelings, his senses, his will, and his metabolism" (Clifton 1983: 1). Typical features of music include pitch, rhythm, and texture. A sequence of pitches organized to create meaning is a melody, while several pitches sounding at once to create meaning is a harmony. Rhythms, too, can be purely sequential (a single, patterned, recurring alternation of sound and silence) or can be polyrhythmic, if several such sequences of sounds and silences occur simultaneously.

"Music" and "folklore" are clearly very different ideas. Each has its own history, and there is disagreement and controversy about what constitutes each category. However, "folk music" can be simply defined, based on the two contested ideas of "music" and "folklore": folk music is music that is also folklore.

As noted, most analysts are concerned with distinguishing folk music from other kinds of music: what makes a song a folk song, or a melody a folk tune? Process-oriented definitions cannot answer these questions. If we employ the definition of folklore proposed by Dan Ben Amos (1971: 13), "artistic communication in small groups," then the idea of a "folk song" or a "folk tune" seems to lose all meaning. Any event in which a song is sung with small group of people present, including an operatic aria or the latest pop hit, is a folkloric performance, and thus "folk music." Even more strangely, a rehearsal of a classical string quartet is folk music, but the following night's performance onstage is not, even though the music itself is identical!

For this reason, scholars of folk music genres tend to use item-oriented defintions: specifically, they suggest that folk music items must circulate orally, that is, without the use of writing or notation, and that they must exist in variants. Frequently, the original author of a piece of folk music is unknown, and this has also been an important criterion for some scholars: folk music is thought of as anonymous or communal. In particular, the idea of communal re-creation, discussed below, continues to be widely applied to folk music.

These criteria are also difficult to apply very strictly. For example, classical music sometimes circulates orally; individual musicians sometimes learn by ear. On such occasions, they may either forget some aspect of the music, or embellish some aspect in an unusual way, creating what might be considered a "variant." And many people may know common pop songs or classical pieces without knowing who wrote them. The scholar of folk music then has the same problem as the one using a process-oriented definition: any piece of music, in certain circumstances, becomes "folk music," while in other circumstances the same piece of music is not.

Because of this, it is useful to think of "folk" as a quality that a piece of music may have to a greater or lesser degree. This will allow us also to employ process-oriented definitions as well as item-oriented ones. From this perspective, a piece of music is likely to be "folk music" if it strongly exhibits characteristics associated with folklore. For example, if in its history it has circulated predominantly orally, has been performed predominantly in small-group settings, exists in many variants, and has an unknown author, it would be safe to call a song or tune "folk music." If it has circulated predominantly on a CD, in a book, or as a written score, is typically performed onstage or for TV cameras, exists in few variants, and is known to have been written by a certain composer, it is unlikely to be called "folk music." Most music lies somewhere between these extremes, and thus defining an item as "folk music" is an act of interpretation for which we must accept responsibility.

In English-speaking countries, especially the United States, there is a commercial genre called "folk music," which does not correspond well with the folklorist's idea of folk music. This genre includes singer-songwriters, typically with acoustic guitars or small acoustic ensembles. The historical reasons for which this genre is called "folk" need not concern us here; it is enough to say that, while many of the performers in this style are fine singers, writers, and musicians, most folklorists do not consider their music "folk music," because it is not folklore by most of the criteria discussed above. Bohlman (1988) offers a comprehensive overview of folk music.

TYPES OF FOLK MUSIC

For many years, folklorists paid by far the greatest attention to one type of folk music: the *ballad*. The ballad is most simply defined as a folk song that tells a story; many scholars would further differentiate the ballad from the epic on the grounds that the ballad is memorized word-for-word, while the epic is composed in performance. (We will not dwell on epics, but a classic treatment can be found in Lord 2000.) Partly because its name, "ballad," seems to be related to the Latin root for "dance," early scholarly arguments about ballads focused on whether they were originally composed by an individual, or communally, by a "singing and dancing throng." Scholarly consensus settled on the idea of "communal re-creation," that is, that each ballad was composed by one individual, but that over the course of time many other people added to it and took away from it. Each ballad thus existed in many versions, each of which contained the artistic ideas of many people. While this idea was created as a means of explaining first folk melodies (Barry 1910: 440) and then ballads (Barry 1933), it has since been applied to most of what we call "folklore."

Many of the melodies of ballads use old modal scales, and analysts often use the Greek names of these scales to discuss them. The English folklorist Cecil Sharp (1908: 104–118) maintained that tunes in the Aeolian, Dorian, and Mixolydian modes were common to the folk music of much of Western Europe, and he found the same modes among English and Anglo-American songs. Bertrand Bronson (1969: 61–62) opined, interestingly, that Anglo-American ballad singers were more skilled and creative as musicians than as poets or storytellers, and that therefore, while ballad texts tended to change because the singer forgot, misheard, or misunderstood, the tunes changed due to the singers' creative input. The result is that texts merely got less comprehensible over time, but tunes varied in more complex ways, remaining aesthetically beautiful for longer. One thing upon which all scholars agree is that the text and the tune of any given version of a ballad are necessarily interrelated in complex ways.

Ballad poetry has been studied exhaustively by many scholars with various characteristics elaborated on in detail; these are best considered within the larger folkloristic discussion of poetics and genre (cf. chapters by Hasan-Rokem and Shuman in this volume). A basic definition was put forward by MacEdward Leach (1955: 1): "(1) The ballad tells a story; (2) it tells its story in song, in simple melody; (3) it is a folk story-song, since it has the unmistakable qualities of treatment, of style and of subject-matter that come only from folk culture."

Ballads continue to be composed today, and as was typical for earlier times, they employ the vernacular language and expressions of the present. For example, one version of a ballad written in the 1840s in New York, and collected in 1948 in Virginia, began like this:

Young Charlotte lived on a mountainside
In a wild and lonely spot
There was no other dwelling-place for five miles round
Except her father's cot (Leach 1955: 723)

Apart from the slightly archaic word "cot" for "house," this could have been written today. Indeed, it is not so far from:

The Devil went down to Georgia
He was looking for a soul to steal.
He was in a bind 'cause he was way behind
He was willin' to make a deal.

"The Devil Went Down to Georgia," in fact, tells a folk story in simple melody, as a song, and does so with many of the "unmistakable qualities" of folk culture. It thus fits directly into the tradition of American ballads, and this certainly contributed to its popularity.

Another interesting genre that blends song with story, the *cante-fable*, is essentially a spoken story with short segments of song embedded within it. Cante-fables have been common in various European traditions since medieval times, and while unusual in modern Anglo-American settings, they are not unheard-of; for example, Halpert (1942) found them in New Jersey and Ben Lumpkin (1968) found them in Iowa. Moreover, several scholars, including D.K. Wilgus (1968) and Charles K. Wolfe (1978), have noted the similarity between cante-fable and "talking blues," a style of American song performance in which much of the lyric is chanted, intoned or spoken rather than sung. "The Devil Went Down to Georgia" clearly borrows the talking-blues performance style, in that its verses are more intoned than sung, and this may connect it to the older tradition of cante-fable.

In contrast to songs that tell a story, there are many songs whose primary purpose is to express emotions. These are known as *lyric songs*. Because they do not have the underlying structure of a story to keep them intact, lyric songs gain and lose stanzas with ease in oral tradition; any stanza can be slotted into a song, provided it has a similar meter and a similar emotion to express. As a result, many lyric songs are nothing more than collections of loosely related "floating verses." Lyric songs thus challenge our notions of "type" and "variant," so useful in studying other kinds of folklore; when any lyric song can draw verses from any other, it is frequently impossible to assign any given text to a particular "type." Musically, they are very similar to ballads, and indeed often use the same tunes. Many scholars would include *spirituals* in the category of lyric songs, since their primary purpose is to express and share religious feeling. Other scholars put spirituals in a special category of their own.

In many cultures, laborers use *work songs and work music* in the performance of daily tasks. In this context music serves the function of coordinating the efforts of a group of people who need to do things at the same time or at the same speed. In hauling a heavy yard up the mast of a square-rigged ship, or moving a section of railroad track a quarter-inch to the right, using nine-pound hammers to tap on the rails, a single man would have no effect at all. But a group of men, pulling or tapping at the same time, can get the job done, and music can be used to keep them in time with one another. Music used to coordinate labor takes many forms, including fife-and-drum bands or bagpipes for soldiers on the march, drumming for oarsmen on large galleys, and women singing rhythmic "waulking songs" while they beat on the fibers of newly-woven cloth in order to shrink it.

Probably the most highly developed tradition of labor-coordinating work songs evolved on sailing-ships during a period ranging from the late eighteenth to the early twentieth centuries. This was the tradition of *sea shanties*, in which a song specialist or shanteyman sang the verses of each song, and the laborers together sang the refrains or choruses. Shanties generally fell into several classes, depending on whether the work was, for example, a short drag on a rope, a more sustained but still intense task such as raising a halyard, or an hours-long but low-intensity job such as walking around the capstan to raise the anchor. These different tasks had consequences for the musical form and style of the shanties: short-drag shanties are explosively rhythmic, with short lines and refrains; halyard shanties have slightly longer lines, often with a chorus as well as a refrain; and capstan shanties have long verses and choruses, and slow, steady rhythms. In this case, then, the form of the music is subservient to its primary function.

The second function of the work song is to relieve the tedium of the work. Hearing an amusing or diverting song can make otherwise bored and unenthusiastic workers enjoy themselves, and work more effectively and quickly. In many work song traditions, because it is understood that the songs are necessary for the work to go smoothly, protest was tolerated when expressed in song lyrics, which can be another form of uplift for downtrodden workers. Both harmless diversion and protest in work songs are documented among railroad workers (Holtzberg-Call 1989: 68–70) as well as chanteying sailors (Hugill 1979: 32).

Lullabies are work songs; after all, putting children to bed is one of the traditional jobs of parents in all societies. Like other work songs, lullabies contain an element of protest, in which mothers express consternation with their lives and hostility toward their babies: why else sing about putting your baby in a tree-top, so that "when the bough breaks, the cradle will fall?" In Margaret McDowell's (1977: 214) words, "though the violence in [folk lullabies] is formidable, the energy with which the threats are expressed suggests vigor and defiance." Indeed, in many traditional songs the subversive nature of the lullaby stands out; in both the Irish-language song "Suantraí na Mná Sí" (Ní Uallacháin) (in which the bride is taken by the fairies and forced to nurse their children), and the Arabic-language song "Ughniyah li al-Atfal" (*Florida Folklife*) (in which a Lebanese girl is enslaved by Turks and similarly made into a nursemaid), the resourceful young woman encodes subversive information into her lullabies to help her family rescue her, and allows the songs to be overheard by passers-by.

In many cultures, *music for dancing* plays an important social role. Dances vary from culture to culture: England's most famous form of folk-dance, morris dancing, features teams of men dancing on special occasions; America's are couple-dances such as square dances and contra dances; and in Brittany, in western France, chain dances and circle dances are the most common. These different kinds of dances require different music; for example, simple, hypnotic, repetitive tunes are best for chain and circle dances, while tunes with several parts work well for couple dances, so that couples (who have more freedom of movement than a person in a chain of 50 people) can vary their steps. Each culture thus develops a repertoire of dance music suited to its style of dancing.

Among Anglo-Americans in the United States, by far the most important instrument in dance music is the fiddle. In Europe, one is likely also to encounter bagpipes, flutes, hurdy-gurdies, and accordions, but among Anglo-American communities these are uncommon. The United States is also peculiar (but hardly unique) in its traditional view of dancing as a sin. Because of this view, when performed by children and adolescents, dances are often referred to as "play" and "games," and events at which such "games" are "played" have come to be known as "play-parties." Because instrumental music, especially the fiddle, was associated with sin, at "play-parties" the participants sang as well as danced, providing the music for their own entertainment (cf. Spurgeon 2005).

Given these conditions, it is easy to see how legends of the Devil as a fiddler could thrive. It is partly because of the sinfulness of dancing, Halpert (1995) argues, that the fiddle came to be known as the Devil's instrument. Unsurprisingly, then, legends of the Devil as a good dancer abound. The Devil, it turns out, likes dance tunes best.

In most cultures, there are forms of *social music* whose main purpose is for the musicians themselves to interact. There are no listeners and no dancers; or at least, the music is not made FOR the listeners or the dancers. In America and Europe, such music-making events take the form of *jam sessions, song circles*, and *drum circles*, among others. As in any social gathering, rules of etiquette apply to social music-making; however, these rules are not always clear to people just joining the group. For this reason, there are guides to etiquette for such occasions, both as published books (e.g., Foy 1999) and on the internet (e.g., Cormier).

FOLK MUSIC AND MUSICAL STYLE

All students of folk music grapple with the question of musical style. We ask ourselves not only what is sung and played, but how it is sung and played. Often in individual studies of folk music, comments on style are restricted to general statements, such as: "Southern traditional singers perform in an impersonal or objective style. The singers maintain one tempo, one level of intensity, one timbre throughout the song ..." (McNeil 1987: 28–29).

In other books, the most salient elements of a community's style might be brought to the fore in a chapter; Ó Canainn's (1993: 40–48) discussion of Irish music style, Savoy's (1984: 4–6) interview with Dewey Balfa about Cajun fiddle style, and Sharp's comments on modal melodies in English folksong (Sharp 1907: 54–72) and on English singing techniques (Sharp 1907: 104–118), are useful in describing the most obvious elements of a musical culture, but they are also unsystematic and therefore somewhat subjective. For instance, Balfa's description of Cajun fiddle style does not comment at all on the elements it has in common with other kinds of fiddling.

Bruno Nettl (1973: 17–36) makes an attempt at setting out the elements of style that should be attended to in any analysis of folk music: general sound (including such elements as vocal tension, timbre, sharpness of attack, and ornamentation), form (including whether pieces are audibly divided into sections, whether multiple musicians arrange a piece, and what patterns of repetition can be discerned), polyphony (the rhythmic and harmonic relationships among sounds that occur simultaneously), "rhythm and tempo" (how fast a piece is, and whether it consists of two-beat, three-beat, or five-beat units), and "melody and scale."

One prominent attempt has been made to suggest a thorough and systematic way of documenting style. In the 1968 book *Folk Song Style and Culture*, Alan Lomax presents his "cantometrics" experiment, which enumerated the stylistic elements of music and devised a way to rate a piece of music for each element. Ultimately, his team devised 37 elements of style, including the relationship of the group leader with the chorus, relationships among members of the orchestra, wordiness and coherence of song texts, range of melody, average melodic interval, and nasality and raspiness of the voice. Although it is rarely used by other scholars, it proved to be a useful system of musical analysis for Lomax and his team.

The study of style in folk music is best accomplished as part of a wider ethnographic inquiry. One can, of course, sit in an office, listen to recordings of folk music, and analyze their style in purely formal, statistical terms. However, the question of what that style means to the people who use it would not be answerable by such a method. In his classic study of Kaluli music in Papua New Guinea, for example, Steven Feld (1990: 264–266) found that the principle of *dulugu ganalan*, or "lift-up-over-sounding" was important both to the way in which Kaluli people construct songs, and to the way in which they experience the natural soundscape of the forest in which they live. This suggests a deep connection between the native aesthetics of music and the lived environment, which would have been completely missed had Feld not experienced the forest and conversed with its people. The rich and thriving field of ethnomusicology is devoted to the study of music in culture, and historically it has tended to focus on what folklorists would refer to as "folk music."

FOLK MUSIC, ART MUSIC, POP MUSIC

Folk music has been a great influence on both art music and popular music. The Hungarian composer Béla Bartók, for example, was an important collector, a pioneering ethnomusicologist, and a composer of classical music, some of which was based on folk tunes. Bartók suggested three ways in which a composer might use folk music. In the first, the composer might "take over a peasant melody unchanged or only slightly varied, write an accompaniment to it and possibly some opening and concluding phrases." In the second, "the composer does not make use of a real peasant melody but invents his own imitation of such melodies." And in the third, "neither peasant melodies nor imitations of peasant melodies can be found in his music, but it is pervaded by the atmosphere of peasant music." (Bartók 1976: 341–344.) Similarly, Ralph Vaughan Williams collected many English folk songs and tunes and composed orchestral and chamber music based on them.

For a stirring and well-known example of an orchestral work based on a single folk musician's unusual rendition of a folk melody, listen to the "Hoedown" section of Aaron Copland's ballet *Rodeo*. In 1937, Alan and Elizabeth Lomax recorded a fiddler named William H. Stepp, in Salyersville, Kentucky. One of the tunes he played was a common melody known as "Bonaparte's Retreat." According to folklorist Alan Jabbour, writing in the liner notes to the CD *American Fiddle Tunes*:

> Most traditional renditions of this tune preserve a stately pace in the manner of the old 4/4 marches. W. H. Stepp characteristically plays his tunes at an unusually fast tempo, however, and here he almost doubles the usual tempo of "Bonaparte's Retreat," converting the tune into a breakdown. By a curious combination of circumstances this unusual rendition has been catapulted into national fame. John and Alan Lomax published Ruth Crawford Seeger's transcription of it in [a book entitled] *Our Singing Country* (1941). When Aaron Copland was looking for a suitable musical theme for the "Hoedown" section of his ballet *Rodeo* (first produced in 1942), his eye was caught by the version in the Lomax book, and he adopted it almost note for note as the principal theme.

Readers unfamiliar with ballet may know Copland's arrangement from the American television advertisements for beef, with the slogan "Beef – it's what's for dinner!"

Progressive rock fans, on the other hand, might know the version of "Hoedown" played on electronic keyboards, bass, and drums by Emerson, Lake, and Palmer in the 1970s – this was also based on Copland's arrangement. This leads us to another observation: if folk music has provided grist for the classical composer's mill, it has been even more important in the development of mass-mediated popular music. Indeed, many early popular recordings were almost indistinguishable from field recordings in their presentation of folk music, and a wide range of ethnic music, from Cajun two-steps to German polkas to Irish reels, was recorded by thriving local industries. Media also had an early and lasting effect on Anglo-American folk music: longer ballads were shortened to fit on cylinder and disc recordings, unaccompanied singing and fiddling were discouraged by producers, and ensembles such as string bands consisting of fiddle, banjo, and guitar were encouraged.

The first generation of popular music stars, in genres such as country, jazz, and blues, recorded a good many traditional songs among their hits: Ma Rainey's "Stack O'Lee Blues" (1926) is a traditional African-American ballad; Louis Armstrong's "St.

James Infirmary" Blues (1928) is a lyric lament, ultimately of English origin; The Carter Family's "John Hardy" (1928) is an American folk ballad; and Mississippi John Hurt's "Spike Driver Blues" (1928) is a railroad work song reinterpreted for solo voice and guitar. When rock music developed from blues and country roots, rock musicians continued borrowing traditional songs. Bill Haley and His Comets' "Stop Beatin' Round the Mulberry Bush" (1953) and "Pat-a-Cake" (1953) are both play-party songs; the Animals' "House of the Rising Sun" (1964) is an American ballad; and the Beach Boys' "Sloop John B." (1966) is a lyric folksong from the Bahamas. "Bo Diddley" (1954), by the artist of the same name, is a traditional lyric common to both Anglo- and African American communities, which is used both as a lullaby and as a hand-dancing game known as "hambone." The "Bo Diddley beat," which Diddley introduced into rock music with this song, is simply the "hambone" beat interpreted on rhythm guitar, drums, and maracas – an example of a musical element other than words or melody making the transition from folklore to pop music.

At the same time that rock music was developing, several new styles for performing folk songs emerged in the United States. One was bluegrass, developed by Bill Monroe and several others. These bluegrass pioneers were people of rural, southern background, who adapted old-time country string-band music by adding arrangement ideas from jazz and blues, including instrumental soloing and innovative chord progressions. The typical ensemble involved mandolin, fiddle, banjo, and guitar, with vocals often sung by several singers with pure, piercing, vibrato-free voices in close harmony (cf. Rosenberg 2005).

Another, more urban style also developed; the musicians were aware of rural folk music, but also valued other styles. This music typically used guitars and banjos like bluegrass, but the singing was fuller-throated, lower in the vocal range, and sung with vibrato, and the harmonies were influenced by cabaret music and musical theater. Early proponents of this style included the Weavers; later ones included the Tarriers, the Journeymen, and the Kingston Trio. In 1958, the Kingston Trio had a major pop hit with their version of an American ballad called "Tom Dooley." Soon, other folk groups and folk singers were enjoying chart successes, in a movement that has come to be known as the "Folk Revival," discussed in depth by Cantwell (1996) and Cohen (2002).

In the 1960s and 1970s, pop musicians in both Europe and North America began self-consciously combining traditional folk music with what had by then become the dominant pop music form for young adults, rock and roll. Although the previous generation of rock musicians had already taken folk songs and performed them in a rock style, this new movement blended the stylistic conventions of folk music with those of rock. In America, bands like The Byrds and Simon and Garfunkel, along with individuals like Bob Dylan and Judy Collins, blended traditional songs and sounds with electric guitars and drums. Although this style came to be known as "folk-rock," traditional folk music formed a very small part of the repertoire for most of these bands. Unterberger (2002) has offered a detailed account of folk-rock.

In both Canada and Europe, by contrast, artists began to emerge whose repertoire was largely traditional folk music, played on a combination of acoustic and electric instruments. Garolou from Quebec and Figgy Duff from Newfoundland are the best-known Canadian examples. Fairport Convention and Steeleye Span in the United Kingdom, Malicorne, Alan Stivell, and Tri Yann in France, Horslips in Ireland,

Ougenweide in Germany, and Folk & Rackare in Scandinavia are only a few of the many such groups that emerged all over Europe.

All of these ways of adapting and using traditional folk music survive and thrive today. Bluegrass and folk revival bands can still be found, and folk-rock has kept up with the times, incorporating punk, grunge, hip-hop, and other musical trends. Electronica and dance artists not only use traditional folk music as the basis of their compositions, they use samples of field recordings as the basis of new tracks; one good example is Moby's 1999 album *Play*, which sampled many field recordings made by Alan Lomax. The advent of sampling opens new questions in the field of intellectual and cultural property (cf. Skrydstrup in this volume), but for the artist, the process is much the same as earlier forms of imitation. When Moby went down to Alabama, it wasn't so different from "The Devil Went Down to Georgia;" the result was the adaptation of folk music to a new musical environment.

FOLK, POP, AND GLOBAL CULTURAL FLOW: THE CASE OF "MISIRLOU"

Although I have focused on North America and Western Europe, a folksong from a different region may have been adapted into the widest range of popular musical genres: "Misirlou," a lyric love song common to Greek, Turkish, Jewish, Arabic, and other ethnic groups. The earliest recorded versions are in the Greek rebetika style, and date to the late 1920s. They use a macaronic lyric mostly sung in Greek, but with a title that is a Turkish loan word meaning "Muslim Egyptian woman," and several lines in Arabic.

The rebetika recordings of the 1920s and 1930s were only the beginning of a long history of adaptations of "Misirlou." In the 1930s, Folklorists Alton Morris and Carita Doggett Corse recorded it as an unaccompanied folksong, from the oral tradition of Greek sponge-fishing families in Florida (cf. *Florida Folklife*). In the 1940s, "Misirlou" was arranged, published, and recorded by Nicholas Roubanis, a Greek-American jazz bandleader; it quickly became a standard among American big bands, including those of Woody Herman and Wayne King. A vocal version with big band was recorded by Connie Francis, the most popular American vocalist of the 1950s. In the burgeoning world of Jewish music in 1940s and 1950s New York, "Misirlou" also thrived: Yiddish music pioneer Seymour Rexite wrote new Yiddish words for it, and a field recording made by Harry Smith preserves Rabbi Nuftali Abulafia's use of the Misirlou melody for a Hebrew prayer to Elijah. At the same time, Klezmer musicians in New York had been playing it since the 1920s, and believed it to be an Israeli melody (Sapoznik 1999: 166). In the pop genre of exotica – a blend of easy-listening and world music popular in the 1950s and 1960s – "Misirlou" became a standard, with recordings by Xavier Cugat, Korla Pandit, and Martin Denny. As symphonic "mood music," it was recorded by 101 Strings and other successful orchestras.

In 1961, rock guitarist Dick Dale, a pioneer of the genre known as "surf rock," was issued a challenge by a 10-year-old boy in his audience: could he play a song on only one string of his guitar. According to a 2006 NPR interview, Dale asked the boy to return the following night, and, as he lay in bed later that evening, tried to figure out what he could play on one string. Dale, a Lebanese American, had grown up playing traditional percussion instruments to accompany his uncle, who played the oud, an Arabic lute. He recalled a belly-dance melody his uncle used to play by sliding up and down a single course of strings on the oud. It was "Misirlou." He quickly fetched his guitar. The left-handed guitarist experimented with the tempo of his playing until he reached a feverish, staccato strum, imitating his own Lebanese drumming, and slid his right hand up and down the fingerboard. The following night, Dale made good on his promise, and a rock and roll classic was born.

Some weeks later, Dale recorded "Misirlou" for his first album. The recording was a modest success, and was soon being covered by artists in various traditions; The Beach Boys did another surf version on their album *Surfin' USA* in 1963. Later that year, "Misirlou" was so familiar that Pete Seeger was able to perform it as an audience sing-along at Carnegie Hall. Felix Pappalardi produced a hard-rock version in 1966, and around the same time English folk guitarist Davey Graham recorded it on fingerstyle acoustic guitar. It remained a popular standard in rock, pop, belly-dance, world music, and other styles for decades. In 1994, director Quentin Tarantino featured Dick Dale's version in his hit movie *Pulp Fiction*, and Dale received a platinum record. A new round of covers and releases ensued, including an appearance in the 1998 French film *Taxi*, and a 2004 ska version by the German band Bluekilla. Sampling technology has also affected "Misirlou;" in 2005, Dick Dale's version was sampled by the Black-Eyed Peas for their song "Pump it." These versions can be heard online at the Dinosaur Gardens blog and the ΜΑΓΙΚΗ, ΞΩΤΙΚΗ, ΟΜΟΡΦΙΑ blog.

The history of "Misirlou" highlights an important area in today's musical landscape: the tension between the traditional culture of individual communities on the one hand, and the global nature of popular music on the other. The origin of "Misirlou" cannot be established with certainty; the lyrics are mostly in Greek, the title appears to originate in Turkish, and the lyrics include Arabic words and allude to the Muslim community in Egypt. Nevertheless, some people make passionate claims for their own ethnic community as the true originators and owners of "Misirlou." For example, the song's Wikipedia Talk page features arguments between proponents of Turkish and Greek origins.

The main Wikipedia entry for "Misirlou" (substantially written by a proponent of a Greek origin) states, without evidence, that the melody was most likely composed collaboratively by Michalis Patrinos's group in Athens, and that the lyrics were "almost certainly written by Patrinos." This is another attempt to assert a Greek origin for both melody and lyrics. But there is evidence to the contrary: the standard discography of early Greek recordings (Spottswood 1990) lists an earlier recording made in New York (by a Greek-speaker born in Constantinople). Ethnomusicologist Hankus Netsky writes in the liner notes to The Klezmer Conservatory Band's *Dancing in the Aisles* that the song has been known to klezmer musicians since the 1920s. The melody of "Misirlou" was being used for belly-dancing among Lebanese-Americans in Boston during Dick Dale's youth, and by an Orthodox Jewish Rabbi in New York in 1951. This would suggest to most folklorists that a Greek origin for the melody is far from a certainty. Patrinos, the purported originator of the song, came from Izmir in Turkey, but spoke Greek; even if he did write the Greek lyrics, it is more than likely that he knew the melody from the cosmopolitan environment of the Ottoman state where he was born. This would help explain why Jews and Arabs both seemed to know the tune as well.

Interestingly, Adela Peeva's 2003 documentary, *Whose is this Song?*, makes similar observations concerning another piece of music that probably originated in the Ottoman state, and that went on to be a pop hit in the United States: "Üsküdara Gideriken," which as "Uska Dara (A Turkish Tale)" was a Top 40 hit for Eartha Kitt in 1953. The film shows that Serbians, Greeks, Albanians, Turks, and Bulgarians all claim the melody as their own. It further demonstrates that many people are willing to fight to prove that the song is theirs. As with "Misirlou," the true origins of the song are harder to discover, and ultimately less important, than people's feelings about its origins.

We can see that "Misirlou," and by extension all adaptations of folk music into either classical or mass-mediated popular music, are excellent examples of the global cultural "flows" theorized by Arjun Appadurai (1990). Folk songs can and do go from locally treasured expressions of community values to internationally known embodiments of commodity value. A Greek folksong sung by sponge-fishers in Florida may turn up in a Hollywood blockbuster, and a fiddle tune played by the financially disadvantaged W.H. Stepp may translate into the sale of millions of dollars worth of beef. Appadurai's description of the world as a locus of ethnoscapes, technoscapes, mediascapes, finanscapes, and ideoscapes can be translated into questions that are helpful in framing debates on such topics: by whom, and in what communities, is this music performed? How does technology facilitate its movement from one realm to another? How are media and channels of dissemination implicated in this movement? Who stands to gain and lose, financially and otherwise, from the transactions? And what implications does the cultural flow have to ideological questions, especially those of nationality and identity? The arguments about "Misirlou" exemplify these questions, but for the moment, there are no easy answers.

MUSIC ABOUT FOLKLORE

We have seen that folk music often inspires composers. The same can be said for non-musical folklore. Verbal folklore, custom and belief often inspire composers of music, and the results run the gamut from operas and ballets to pop songs and film scores. Small genres of folklore, such as proverbs, can be absorbed into song, and studies of the blues (Taft 1994), reggae (Prahlad 2001), and German folksongs (Mieder 1978) confirm that proverbs are often the bases for musical works. One could argue that among the bases for "The Devil Went Down to Georgia" are the proverbial phrases "the Devil is in the fiddle" and "the fiddle is the Devil's instrument," both of which have been documented by Herbert Halpert (1995). Even when not the basis for a song, a proverb or proverbial phrase may be included in the lyrics, as is the case with "give the Devil his due," also used by Daniels in his song.

Narrative folklore has also inspired a great deal of music. Some German and Russian composers, such as Engelbert Humperdinck (1854–1921) and César Cui (1835–1918), were particularly known for their fairy-tale operas; the former wrote *Hänsel und Gretel* and the latter *Little Red Riding-Hood*, among others of the same type. Other composers, such as the Italian Giacomo Puccinni (1858–1924) with *Turandot*, the Belgian André Grérty (1741–1813) with *Zémire et Azor*, and the Americans Philip Glass and Robert Moran with *The Juniper Tree*, have also written fairy-tale operas, making them a significant part of the international operatic repertory. Since the

1930s, similar musical productions have more often been created in the form of animated films, most notably by Disney. Examples include "Snow White and the Seven Dwarfs" (1937), "Cinderella" (1950), "Aladdin" (1992), and "The Lion King" (1994). Chinese operas, too, have often been based on folktales, including the legend of "Lady White Snake."

Individual songs can also be inspired by folk stories; "The Devil Went Down to Georgia" is only one prominent example. The well-known legend of "The Vanishing Hitchhiker" is another; it has been turned into a song several times, most notably "Bringing Mary Home" by the bluegrass band The Country Gentlemen. A joke about a kilt-clad Scotsman sleeping in a ditch after a night of drinking was turned into a song by Mike Cross, and a Japanese fairy tale became The Decemberists' award-winning song "The Crane Wife." All of these used music that was both appropriate to the story's theme, and acceptable to the band's audiences: a typical bluegrass arrangement for "Bringing Mary Home," a melody influenced by Scottish ballads for "The Scotsman," and classically-influenced acoustic rock music for "The Crane Wife," which is a 15-minute song divided into three movements like a concerto.

Sometimes, what begins as music about folklore ends up as folklore itself. Consider, for example, the overture to the opera *Guillaume Tell* by Gioachino Rossini (1792–1868). Rossini based this opera on a drama by the playwright Friedrich Schiller (1759–1805). Schiller's play was based, at least in part, on folk dramas and songs about the marksman and freedom fighter Wilhelm Tell, which had existed for at least 200 years in Schiller's day (Bendix 1989). Thus, the opera was itself an adaptation of folklore, filtered through elite intellectual culture, but Rossini's score for it was original music in the classical style.

The overture of *Guillaume Tell* became a standard short piece of orchestral music, far more popular than the opera itself. Because of its popularity, it was repeatedly adapted into various forms of popular culture. As a pop instrumental, it has been played by such musicians and bands as Mike Oldfield, Manowar, and Piltdown Men. As film music, it has appeared in *A Clockwork Orange* and *Brassed Off*. And, most importantly, on radio and TV, the overture's finale was adapted for use as the theme music for *The Lone Ranger*.

It was this last adaptation that allowed the music to "cross over," as it were, into folklore. When I was a child, a popular American riddle-joke posed the question "where does the Lone Ranger take his garbage?" The answer was "to the dump, to the dump, to the dump dump dump," sung to the tune of the *Lone Ranger* theme. Note that Rossini's melody is an integral part of this joke's meaning: the punch line has no verbal association with *The Lone Ranger* at all, and it is only in sharing the melody with the *Lone Ranger* theme that the punch line makes any sense. Thus, this melody, originally "music about folklore," has become "folklore about music." It is thus an integral part of folklore, even if we might hesitate to identify it as a folk tune.

FOLKLORE ABOUT MUSIC

Folklore about music and musicians comes in many forms, from proverbs and beliefs to jokes and riddles, and on to legends and tales. The belief that music is good for mental health is expressed in proverbs such as "music has charms to soothe the savage breast," and "music is the medicine of the mind." On the other hand, there are certain ailments that music cannot help, as we are warned with the proverb "music cannot cure the toothache." Proverbs also tell us that music is as important as food to a good celebration ("the fiddle makes the feast"), and that music is essential to courtship ("music is the key to the female heart.") These ideas are also expressed in the triadic proverbs "wine, women and song," which dates at least to 1775 (cf. Mieder 1993), and its late twentieth-century corollary, "sex, drugs and rock-n-roll." Jokes about music and musicians are many, some involving music in general, and others describing the stereotypical characteristics of players of particular instruments (Groce 1996).

One fascinating area of musical folklore involves stories about well-known musicians. In many cases, such legends seem to reflect popular perceptions of their music. Rod Stewart, who after a 20-year career of thoughtful and topical songs was widely criticized for his mindlessly sexual 1978 disco hit "Da Ya Think I'm Sexy?" was rumored to have developed out-of-control sexual appetites. Frank Zappa, whose lyrics and song titles are bizarre, and include such ideas as eating frozen urine ("Do Not Eat the Yellow Snow") was rumored to have eaten excrement onstage (cf. snopes.com).

Paul McCartney was for a time rumored to have died and been replaced by a double. Beatles fans the world over combed the band's songs and albums for "clues" to the truth behind this story, resulting in a large body of folklore about the Beatles' music, including claims of hidden messages about Paul's death in at least 35 Beatles songs (cf. snopes.com). On the other hand, Elvis Presley is widely rumored either to have survived the 1977 heart attack that supposedly killed him, or to have returned to earth in a spiritual or ghostly form. Given that he was known both for rock-and-roll that epitomized a seemingly boundless youth and vitality, and for gospel songs that discussed the mystery of death and stressed the immortality of the soul (e.g., "You'll Never Walk Alone" and "Farther Along"), these legends are hardly surprising. (cf. Marcus 1991; Rodman 1996.)

Among opera singers, most stories are about incredible acts of nerve; Leo Slezak, for example, is supposed to have hired a man to impersonate the German composer Christoph von Gluck, and to come onstage for a curtain-call after a performance of Gluck's opera *Armide*. Slezak then reportedly told the press that Gluck had told him that he had never heard a more sublime performance of Slezak's role. The newspapers reported the story, only to be ridiculed by readers; the real Gluck had been dead for over a hundred years (Mordden 1988: 167).

More and more, the internet has become important in documenting creative trends in folklore, particularly about a trendy topic such as pop music. The Web abounds with jokes about Kanye West, who in September, 2009, interrupted the acceptance speech of country singer Taylor Swift at the MTV Music Awards, in order to praise another nominee, Beyoncé. West's embarrassing lapse in judgment caused him to become an instant punch line, a situation that persisted for a matter of years. In addition to Daily Comedy's "Kanye West Jokes" site, one could find fan-made collage comic strips of West interrupting everyone from heads of state to walruses, at "imaletyoufinish.com," many months after the events being satirized. Both sites encouraged fan submissions, making them showcases of vernacular creativity in the realm of folklore about music.

Folklore can also develop about individual pieces of music. In traditional Irish music, some tunes are known to be "fairy tunes," and some, such as the five-part jig

"The Gold Ring," have quite involved narratives about the fairies' use of the tune (Wilson 1995: 141–142). An elaborate but apparently baseless story about Phil Collins's 1981 song "In the Air Tonight" claimed that he had composed it after witnessing a drowning, and used it to shame a bystander who had not helped the victim. So many rock songs are supposed to contain veiled references to Satan and Satanism that it's hardly worth detailing them; one of the most famous is the Eagles' "Hotel California."

Finally, there is narrative folklore in which music forms an important part of the plot. In this category, we find two closely related legends about the Devil's relationship to music. In one of these stories, a musician sells his soul to the Devil in exchange for musical talent. This variation on the Faustian bargain or Devil's Contract tale type (AT 756B) exists as a general legend, told of fictional or generic musicians throughout history. In this form, it has become the basis of works of fiction. These include *The Fifth String*, a novel by the famous composer of marching-band music, John Philip Sousa, and the 1849 ballet *Le Violon du Diable*, with music by Cesare Pugni and choreography by Arthur St Leon, who also appeared as principal dancer *and* violinist (!) in the ballet's premiere performances.

As a migratory legend, the same tale has attached itself to real musicians. The classical violin virtuoso Niccolo Paganini, the jazz pianist Ferdinand "Jelly Roll" Morton, and, perhaps most famously, the blues guitarist and singer Robert Johnson, have all had versions of this legend attached to them. To use Carlo Rotella's (2004: 154) summary of the Robert Johnson legend:

> He upgrades his chops by selling his soul to the devil one midnight at a crossroads in the Mississippi Delta. Hellhound on his trail and the open road before him, Johnson pauses just long enough in his rambling to record twenty-nine songs brimming with the aforementioned raw intensity. He dies at twenty-seven, barking like a dog on all fours and/or calling out for the Lord's mercy after being fatally poisoned and/or stabbed and/or struck down by syphilis. Picture all five variants at once for maximum drama.

The second legend, even better known in popular culture, is the one adapted by Charlie Daniels for "The Devil Went Down to Georgia." As we have seen above, traditional versions of this tale typically involve the fiddle, because European and Euro-American tradition has consistently identified the fiddle as the "Devil's instrument" (Halpert 1995). However, in modern film retellings, the instrument tends to be the guitar. Both *Crossroads* (1986) and *Tenacious D in the Pick of Destiny* (2006) feature versions of this legend about a musical duel with the Devil. Clearly, Charlie Daniels was neither the first popular artist nor the last to appreciate this musical folk legend.

CONCLUSION

The twenty-first century is an interesting time for folklore and music. Although the advent of media technologies, from file-sharing to Facebook, has blurred the boundaries of "oral transmission," there will always be traditional folk music undergoing the process of communal re-creation. There will also always be small-group gatherings where music is performed and shared. Alert students of culture will always be able to identify new songs and tunes that fit the category of "folk music." We can also attend to and analyze the ways in which folk songs and tunes are adapted and shaped by new musical and technological trends. We can stay alert for musical adaptations of non-musical folklore, and for folk stories developing about music and musicians. We can do this in oral, face-to-face settings, but also on the internet, through social networks, and through whatever unforeseen technologies develop in the future.

Most importantly, we can attend to the ways in which people play, discuss, and think about music, asking the question, "What does this mean?" As musicians, as folklorists, as scholars, we can ask no better question than that.

REFERENCES

Appadurai, Arjun. 1990. "Disjuncture and Difference in the Global Cultural Economy." *Theory, Culture and Society* 7(2/3): 295–310.

Barry, Phillips. 1910. "The Origin of Folk-Melodies." *The Journal of American Folklore* 23(90): 440–445.

Barry, Phillips. 1933. "Communal Recreation." *Bulletin of the Folk Song Society of the North-East* 5: 4–6.

Bartók, Béla. 1976. *Béla Bartók Essays.* London: Faber and Faber.

Ben-Amos, Dan. 1971. "Toward a Definition of Folklore in Context." *The Journal of American Folklore* 84 (331): 3–15.

Bendix, Regina. 1989. *Backstage Domains: Playing "William Tell" in Two Swiss Communities.* Bern: Peter Lang.

Bohlman, Philip V. 1988. *The Study of Folk Music in the Modern World.* Bloomington: Indiana University Press.

Bronson, Bertrand Harris. 1969. *The Ballad as Song.* Berkeley: University of California Press.

Cantwell, Robert. 1996. *When We Were Good: The Folk Revival.* Cambridge, MA: Harvard University Press.

Clifton, Thomas. 1983. *Music as Heard: a Study in Applied Phenomenology.* New Haven: Yale University Press.

Cocchiara, Giuseppe. 1981. *The History of Folklore in Europe.* Philadelphia: Institute for the Study of Human Issues.

Cohen, David Steven. 1983. *The Folklore and Folklife of New Jersey.* New Brunswick: Rutgers University Press.

Cohen, Ronald D. 2002. *Rainbow Quest: The Folk Music Revival and American Society, 1940–1970.* Amherst: University of Massachusetts Press.

Feld, Steven. 1990. *Sound and Sentiment: Birds, Weeping, Poetics, and Song in Kaluli Expression.* 2nd edition. Philadelphia: University of Pennsylvania Press.

Foy, Barry. 1999. *Field Guide to the Irish Music Session.* Lanham, MD: Roberts Rinehart.

Groce, Nancy. 1996. *The Musician's Joke Book.* New York: Schirmer Books.

Halpert, Herbert. 1942. "The Cante-Fable in New Jersey." *Journal of American Folklore* 55 (217): 133–143.

Halpert, Herbert. 1995. "The Devil, the Fiddle, and Dancing in Fields of Folklore" in *Essays in Honor of Kenneth S. Goldstein.* Roger D. Abrahams *et al.*, Eds. Bloomington: Trickster Press.

Holtzberg-Call, Maggie. 1989. "The Gandy Dancer Speaks: Voices from Southern Black Railroad Gangs in Alabama Folklife" in *Collected Essays.* Stephen Martin, Ed. Birmingham: Alabama Folklife Association.

Hugill, Stan. 1979. *Shanties from the Seven Seas.* London: Routledge and Kegan Paul.

Lomax, Alan. 1968. *Folk Song Style and Culture.* Washington, DC: American Association for the Advancement of Science.

Lord, Albert Bates. 2000. *The Singer of Tales.* 2nd edition. Cambridge, MA: Harvard University Press.

Lumpkin, Ben Gray. 1968. "'Mr. Fox' (Baughman Type 955C): A Cante Fable." *Journal of American Folklore* 81(319): 68–70.

Marcus, Greil. 1991. *Dead Elvis.* New York: Doubleday.

McDowell, Margaret B. 1977. "Folk Lullabies: Songs of Anger, Love, and Fear." *Women's Studies* 5(2): 205–218.

McNeil, W.K. 1987. *Southern Folk Ballads.* Little Rock, AR: August House.

Mieder, Wolfgang. 1978. "Das Sprichwort im Volkslied. Eine Untersuchung des Deutschen Liederhortes von Erk/Böhme." Jahrbuch des österreichischen Volksliedwerkes 27: 44–71.

Mieder, Wolfgang. 1993. *Proverbs are Never Out of Season.* New York: Oxford University Press.

Mordden, Ethan. 1988. *Opera Anecdotes.* New York: Oxford University Press.

Nettl, Bruno. 1973 [1965]. *Folk and Traditional Music of the Western Continents.* 2nd edition. Englewood Cliffs, NJ: Prentice-Hall

Ó Canainn, Tomás. 1993. *Traditional Music in Ireland.* Cork, Ireland: Ossian.

Prahlad, Anand. 2001. *Reggae Wisdom: Proverbs in Jamaican Music.* Jackson: University Press of Mississippi.

Pugni, Cesare, M. Despléchin, M. Thierry, and Arthur Saint-Léon. 1849. *Le violon du diable: ballet fantasique en deux actes et six tableaux de M. Saint-Léon.* Paris: Mme. Jonas, Éditeur-Libraire de L'Opéra.

Rosenberg, Neil V. 1985. *Bluegrass: A History.* Urbana: University of Illinois Press.

Rodman, Gilbert B. 1996. *Elvis After Elvis.* London: Routledge.

Rotella, Carlo. 2004. "Jelly Roll Morton's Parole from Hell." *Raritan* 24(1): 151–165.

Sapoznik, Henry. 1999. *Klezmer! Jewish Music from Old World to Our World.* New York: Schirmer.

Savoy, Ann Allen. 1984. *Cajun Music: A Reflection of a People.* Eunice, LA: Bluebird Press.

Sharp, Cecil James. 1907. *English Folk-Song, Some Conclusions.* London: Simpkin.

Skinner, Charles M. 1896. *Myths and Legends of Our Own Land.* Philadelphia and London: J.B. Lippincott.

Sousa, John Philip. 1902. *The Fifth String.* New York: Bowen-Merrill.

Spottswood, Richard. 1990. *Ethnic Music on Records: A Discography of Ethnic Recordings Produced in the United States, 1893 to 1942.* Urbana and Chicago: University of Illinois Press.

Spurgeon, Alan L. 2005. *Waltz the Hall: The American Play Party.* Jackson: University Press of Mississippi.

Taft, Michael. 1994. "Proverbs in the Blues: How Frequent Is Frequent?" *Proverbium: Yearbook of International Proverb Scholarship* 11: 227.

Thoms, William J. 1996 [1846]. "Folk-Lore." *Journal of Folklore Research* 33(3): 187–189.

Unterberger, Richie. 2002. *Turn! Turn! Turn!: The '60s Folk-Rock Revolution.* San Francisco: Backbeat Books.

Wilgus, D.K. 1968. "Review: From the Record Review Editor: Negro Music." *Journal of American Folklore* 81(319): 89–94.

Wilson, David A. 1995. *Ireland, a Bicycle and a Tin Whistle.* Belfast: McGill-Queen's University Press.

Wolfe, Charles K. 1978. "I'm On My Journey Home: Vocal Styles and Resources in Folk Music." Booklet accompanying New World Records CD 80549.

Discography

Charlie Daniels Band. 2002. *The Ultimate Charlie Daniels Band.* New York: Sony Music Entertainment.

Country Gentlemen (The). 2003. *Can't You Hear Me Callin'.* Rebel Records.

Cross, Mike. 1994. *Crème De La Cross.* Sugarhill.

Decemberists (The). 2006. *The Crane Wife.* Capitol.

Klezmer Conservatory Band. 1997. *Dancing in the Aisles.* Rounder.

Lane, Louis and Atlanta Symphony Orchestra. 1983. *Copland: Fanfare, Rodeo and Appalachian Spring.* Telarc.

Various Artists (American Folklife Center). 2000. *American Fiddle Tunes.* Rounder Select.

Various Artists. 1978. *I'm On My Journey Home: Vocal Styles and Resources in Folk Music*. New World Records.

Web Resources

Cormier, Rick. "Drum Circles: Guidelines and Tips." *http://synthrick.tripod.com/id31.html* (accessed October 16, 2011).

DailyComedy.com "Hot Topic – Kanye West 47 Jokes Fresh daily. Submit Your Own!" http://www.dailycomedy.com/hottopic/Kanye_West (accessed October 16, 2011).

Dinosaur Gardens. "The Mysteries of 'Misirlou'." http://www.dinosaurgardens.com/archives/297 (accessed October 16, 2011).

"Fiddle Tunes of the Old Frontier: The Henry Reed Collection" (American Memory from the Library of Congress). http://memory.loc.gov/ammem/collections/reed/ (accessed October 16, 2011).

"Florida Folklife from the WPA Collections, 1937–1942. (American Memory from the Library of Congress). http://memory.loc.gov/ammem/collections/florida/ (accessed October 16, 2011).

"Kanye West Will Let You Finish – I'ma Let You Finish – Kanye Interrupts." http://imaletyoufinish.com/ (accessed October 16, 2011).

Misirlou Article, Wikipedia, the free encyclopedia http://en.wikipedia.org/wiki/Misirlou (accessed October 16, 2011).

Misirlou Talk Page, Wikipedia, the free encyclopedia. http://en.wikipedia.org/wiki/Talk:Misirlou (accessed October 16, 2011).

"NPR 'Misirlou,' from Klezmer to Surf Guitar (NPR Story)." http://www.npr.org/templates/story/story.php?storyId=5134530 (accessed October 16, 2011).

snopes.com: "Urban Legends Reference Pages" http://www.snopes.com/ (accessed October 16, 2011).

ΜΑΓΙΚΗ, ΞΩΤΙΚΗ, ΟΜΟΡΦΙΑ...: 200. Μανώλης Αγγελόπουλος: Μισιρλού. http://4misirlou.blogspot.com/2010/03/200.html (accessed October 16, 2011).

CHAPTER 25

FOLKLORE AND/ ON FILM

Pauline Greenhill

In the horror film *Little Erin Merryweather* (directed by David Morwick, 2003), a serial killer preys on men on an American college campus, disemboweling victims and filling the cavity with stones. Students working for the campus paper want to know why the murderer chooses this *modus operandi*. Their abnormal psychology professor Dr Paula Sheffield (Elizabeth Callahan) suggests that they seek answers in folklore. Hero Peter Bloom (David Morwick), searches the famous collection of wonder tales collected by the brothers Grimm (see Zipes 2002). He discovers that in the story of "Little Red Cap" (better known as "Little Red Riding Hood"), after the hunter-rescuer cuts Little Red and her grandmother out of the wolf's stomach, the three pile rocks into the wolf's stomach. With this clue, the puzzle is soon solved, and Peter and Paula go on to locate the killer and the reasons behind the murder-mutilations. Basing plot elements on a traditional tale is only one of many modes in which folklore[1] and film intersect, and *Little Erin Merryweather* joins a great number and range of movie types which draw on or relate to folklore.

Folkloristic scholarship concerning intersections of folklore and film has greatly expanded since the beginning of the twenty-first-century. However, films depicting folklore and/or (re)presenting the traditional cultural expressions of groups and communities have been made since the first public film screenings in 1895, when Félix-Louis Regnault "filmed the pottery-making techniques of a Wolof woman at the Exposition Ethnographique de l'Afrique Occidentale in Paris" (MacDougall 1978: 406). Though film could include still images, I will consider only motion pictures, recorded onto physical and/or digital media. Potentially relevant works include short and feature-length movies, animated as well as live action, but I focus on live action examples, including several features. My discussion reflects theory and analysis available in English and French, addresses mainly North American films, and centers on topics within my own scholarly expertise. Thus this chapter dips little more than a

A Companion to Folklore, First Edition. Edited by Regina F. Bendix and Galit Hasan-Rokem.
© 2012 John Wiley & Sons, Ltd. Published 2012 John Wiley & Sons, Ltd.

toe into the vast waters of the topic; I aim to be provocative rather than exhaustive, and to stimulate rather than satiate interest. For those who want more, I offer sources that can begin a reader's search for further information.

In this chapter, I look at four (sometimes overlapping) categories at the cusp of folklore and film. First, I consider documentaries produced as ethnographic records to describe and/or represent a culture or tradition in a realist mode. Second, I look at vernacular films, mostly home movies, produced by amateurs to record significant events in the lives of their families and communities. Third, I examine films incorporating traditional culture as part of a fictional narrative (cinematic folklore), with a special focus upon fairy-tale film adaptations. Finally, I look at fictional films produced by Indigenous individuals and communities, about their traditional and popular culture, often aimed simultaneously at their own groups and at outsiders, usually with implicit political intention to recast and/or correct settlers' and outsiders' too often simplistic and/or stereotypical views.

I draw as much as possible for extended examples upon widely available films, so that readers can screen them and reach their own conclusions. As the four divisions above suggest, I explore films as they exemplify the perspectives of cultural insiders and outsiders, amateurs and professionals; as they concern textual material from the filmmakers' own cultures or those of others; as fiction and fact; and as they take the position of auteur (the creative expression of filmmakers' points of view) or voyeur (the realist representation of activities taking place beyond filmmakers' direct control). Like all such distinctions, the latter sets of oppositions offer abstract constructions rather than direct reflections, but they help to sort out folkloristically significant matters.

I distinguish between the raw footage, often gathered for archiving and research purposes, and a film digested for display and performance using selections from that footage and usually containing additional information such as voice-overs and musical score. My analysis of diegesis refers to actions that take place within the film's represented world. Thus, diegetical music takes place within the story – when a character in a fictional film plays an instrument or turns on a car radio, for example. Extra-diegetical music, among many purposes, can guide the audience's mood, as does the percussive background for frightening scenes in horror movies, for example. Because film is such a rich medium, offering verbal and nonverbal information, and sights as well as sounds, I attend as much as possible to its broadest sensory aspects.

DOCUMENTARIES OF TRADITIONAL CULTURE

In the United States, public sector folklorists have used film extensively to record various aspects of traditional cultures but also to display their work and research results to the public. In Canada, the National Film Board (NFB) has been the primary source for ethnographic film. Pre-dating the NFB, *Nanook of the North* (directed by Robert Flaherty, 1922), a film about the Inuit inhabitants of northern Canada, is generally credited as the first ethnographic documentary film (Sherman 1998:5). *Nanook* has been extensively criticized as a romanticized and generally contrived representation of Inuit life, and writer/director Flaherty "bitterly condemned ... for fudging details in an effort to make life in the Arctic seem more primitive and exotic than realism would admit" (Evans 2008: 140–141, see also Knopf 2009). Folklorist filmmakers aim at a more representational voyeurist perspective, instead of Flaherty's submerged auteurist view.

Recent documentaries follow contemporary urban North American life and can range from films about musical stars and their concerts to gadfly writer/director/producer Michael Moore's denunciations of aspects of American life. While all such films hold potential interest for folklorists, ethnographic films – usually offering Euro-North American renderings of other, marginalized, minority cultures – are the subgenre most often produced *by* folklorists. Folklorist filmmaker Sharon Sherman notes that folklorists have documented texts (like the Blues); artifacts (like the fiddle), communities, regions, processes (like how to make molasses), events and celebrations (like Halloween or Passover), artists, and performers. In general, folklorist filmmakers choose subjects associated with rural locations and/or non-elite groups. Thus, they are unlikely to document the culture of the board of a multinational corporation, but are quite apt to examine a group of quilters in the southern United States. Sherman distinguishes folklorists' ethnographic films from "feminist, minority, and Third World films" (Sherman 1998: 27) in which those from groups representing sociocultural alternatives to the Euro-North American mainstream create their own works expressing aspects of their own cultures to themselves and to others, primarily in a realist mode. Often, though, all that distinguishes a folkloristic ethnographic film is that it is made by someone with formal training in folklore or a related discipline (see e.g., Von Rosen 1992).

The non-profit website service "Folkstreams" offers an indispensable record, archive, and source of films. Its goals are "to build a national preserve of hard-to-find documentary films about American folk or roots cultures … [and] to give them renewed life by streaming them on the internet" (www.folkstreams.net). Among the films, *Grandma's Bottle Village: The Art of Tressa Prisbrey* (directed by Allie Light and Irving Saraf, 1982; http://www.folkstreams.net/film,102), documents Prisbrey's Simi Valley, California, constructions, beginning when she was "55 or 60"[2] in the mid-to-late 1950s. At first, she wanted to house her collection of 17,000 pencils, gathered when she was "in politics" in North Dakota. Finding conventional building materials too expensive, she sought alternatives. By the time of filmmaking, her village had "15 or 16" structures made from discarded items. Prisbrey's building and decorating materials comprise not only the bottles mortared together to form the buildings' walls, but also found objects – dolls, drink can pull tabs, golf tees, intravenous feeding tubes and more. She also incorporated an array of objects into her walkways, including scissors, knives, license plates, guns, keys, and dishes.

The film's many hand-held shots, used even when recording stationary objects, and its 16mm original form, give it a home-made feel. The filmmakers supplement core interviews with Prisbrey with banter with her sister during a shared meal, walks through the village with various visitors, and a visit to the dump where she decisively selects or discards objects, sometimes opening garbage bags to search. When diegetical sound is absent, visuals are punctuated by voice-overs of Prisbrey explaining her methods and telling stories. She sings two risqué songs, talks about life, family, and experiences (good and bad) with visitors, and narrates expeditions to gather construction materials. Prisbrey's voice and person are nearly ubiquitous in the film. No omniscient third person narrator's voice intrudes, and only once does the audience hear the filmmaker's question. The film frequently offers Prisbrey's punctuating questions, "Can you imagine that?" "Ain't that crazy?" "That's alright, isn't it?" The extra-diegetical music – solo or piano-accompanied – retains a light and happy tone, even when Prisbrey discusses the deaths of a son and daughter to cancer, or her annoyance and distress at theft and vandalism against her creation. The film conveys Prisbrey's enormous energy and dedication to her unusual, even self-described "crazy" project.

Métis filmmaker Christine Welsh's *The Story of the Coast Salish Knitters* (2000) offers a telling example of the NFB's ethnographic films. It concerns the Cowichan sweaters and other garments made for nearly a hundred years by the Coast Salish peoples of southern Vancouver Island. Archival footage supplements interviews with three generations of woolworkers. A film primarily about Aboriginal women made by an Aboriginal woman, *Story* takes the objects and their makers from pre-settler times to the present. It covers the changing but ever-present economic significance of wool-working, designs, alterations in processes and materials, and disputes with merchants over prices and racism. It documents Sara Modeste's acquisition of a nineteenth-century carding machine to speed wool production – made more difficult because people like her, living on First Nations, cannot use their homes as collateral for a loan. It shows sweaters commissioned and sold at canoe races (the west-coast equivalent of the powwow), and notes competition in sales from sweaters not made by First Nations people. Brightly colored sweaters, in which greens, blues, purples, reds, and yellows in synthetic yarns replace the earlier whites, beiges, grays, browns, and blacks of sheep's wool, clearly demonstrate makers' changing needs and aesthetics.

Though Welsh has no folkloristics background, her film reflects the discipline's concern with a holistic representation not only of texts (the knitted objects), but also of performers/creators (the women and men who make them); audiences (white merchants and tourists, and other Aboriginal people); performance and presentation contexts (including shops and gatherings of Aboriginal peoples); and the sociocultural surround (economics, colonization, and marginalization). Welsh's understanding of the makers' own views, and obvious wish to represent them as they would want, makes this an exemplary ethnographic documentary.

VERNACULAR FILM

Vernacular films can include raw footage and, more rarely, edited productions. Like documentaries, they demonstrate a realist mode – the intention to reflect rather than to construct the world. Yet they are conventionally limited to a positive view of "togetherness, children, and travel" (Zimmermann 1988: 29). Generally made by amateurs, their purview is limited to life-cycle rituals and family events. Unlike documentaries, they rarely find an audience beyond kin and community (see Chalfen 1986). Hitherto, the expense of equipment and supplies made home movies accessible only to the upper middle classes and above. Recently, however, a range of more reasonably priced, easily portable, and relatively unobtrusive video recording devices have democratized access to the medium. Nevertheless, vernacular film offers an incredibly broad genre, arguably comprising everything from sex videos produced for home consumption (see e.g., Hillyer 2004) to the record of a child's birthday party or a family's vacation.

Though popularly understood as voyeurist rather than auteurist, "home movies do not simply stop time and preserve the past; they might just as well be said to create it. The home movie constitutes one story out of thousands of others possible, a chosen private recollection that excludes all that is outside the frame ... a fictive memory" (Lindström 2003: 21). Visual anthropologist Richard Chalfen analyses white middle-class Euro-North American home movies' cultural work in addressing issues of "stability ... conformity ... generational continuity ... socialization, and the maintenance of ethnocentric value schemes and ideology" (1986: 106). These videos can offer material for analysis in their own right, and their production can also shed light on particular kinds of traditional events.

For example, in my research on mock wedding traditions in Canada (e.g., Greenhill 1988), home videos provided access I could not have at first hand, but also proof for my skeptical students who could not believe that rural Ontarian or rural Manitoban men would ever cross dress in public! Mock weddings, incorporated into wedding showers or milestone (twentieth, twenty-fifth, fiftieth, sixtieth) anniversary parties, travesty the traditional wedding. Including procession of the bridal party and raucous, humorous, and often ribald vows, this folk drama is routinely performed cross dressed. Texts can incorporate personal references to the honored couple's meeting, courtship, and/or idiosyncrasies, as well as socially recognizable stereotypes from the shrewish wife and henpecked husband to the gun-toting father of the bride. Mock weddings break into an ongoing celebration, providing an interlude of humor for performers, subjects (the honored couple), and audience. Although in the families' own documentation, compared to professional work, visual and sound quality may be sacrificed, and despite the fact that they are rarely transformed from raw footage, mock wedding videos, as films for insiders, by insiders, offer a unique window into what the family and community see as significant in this social interaction.

At one such event, not one but two videographers recorded a mock wedding for a twenty-fifth anniversary, held in the mid-1980s in rural Waterloo County, Ontario, Canada. In this literal double vision, one videographer even recorded family members costuming themselves and each other before the presentation. Most home movies record only an event's performative aspects – the child blowing out candles on her birthday cake rather than her mother baking it, for example, though wedding videos are exceptions, often filming the bride putting on her gown. Offering a rarely recorded aspect of a folk dramatic event, this video demonstrates that women served as dramaturges and crew – gathering and placing costumes and props and assisting the male actors in dressing and make-up – where female actors were responsible for their own dressing and make-up. This division of roles is expressive rather than instrumental. That is, a grown man should be perfectly capable of stepping into a skirt or dress, even if it is not a garment he wears every day. However, the backstage video shows women – including some of the actors – working diligently to do up men's front buttons, put on and tie their shoes, and apply their lipstick. The fiction that this "women's stuff" must be so foreign to the male performers that it would be impossible for them to negotiate on their own was rigidly maintained in the backstage.

Both videos of the mock wedding ceremony began with the procession of the bride and groom, following the priest (played by a man, and thus not cross dressed), with the ring bearer, flower girl, father of the bride, and mother of the groom coming after. Despite the best efforts of the ring bearer and groom, the bride (the honored couple's eldest son) and the priest (who doubled as musician) dominated the performance. The cultural truism that men's cross dressing is funnier than women's was supported by the audience's hilarity at the bride's antics, unmatched in responses to any woman's acting. Masculine clothing and behaviors tend to be generic, so women's are socioculturally marked as deviations from a norm. Thus, women dressing and acting as male is far less transgressive than men acting and dressing as female. Cameras focus on the performers for most of the play, but periodically pan or cut to interactions with the assembled friends and family, including recording their reactions to particularly outrageous hamming by the bride, or noting the honored couple's amusement.

These videos also recorded surrounding events. Beginning with the honored couple's surprise when they entered the hall (they had been prepared to expect another community event), the videographers turned their cameras to performative highlights like the speeches, the presentation of the money tree (guests were encouraged to pin bills on a small fake Christmas tree to offer as a communal gift), and the first dance by the honored couple. But the cameras also pan around the gathered friends and family, record a table piled with food, and show dancing and mingling by the honored couple and others. While aspects of such events – like advance preparation and motivation – cannot be divined from the videos, they offer a spectacular window onto an event unlikely to be otherwise documented.

Such movies are not conventionally available to researchers, and raise ethical issues in contemporary academic culture. When university ethics protocols demand that every person audio- or video-recorded give explicit permission to participate in research, a nearly insurmountable obstacle to use arises. (I was fortunate that these films came to me in the late 1980s, before this aspect of informed consent was so stringently observed!) Luckily, home movies, digital videography, and hand-held camcorder footage are increasingly employed in advertising, television, video blogs, YouTube, and even feature film, all public uses that override problems in obtaining first-hand access to such materials, and the ethical concerns that private documents raise. Of course, such secondary footage has an interested quality, since it has been chosen to support the ad, TV, or film creator's notions, rather than as a representation of the family's own view. Nevertheless, such derived use of home movies can be revelatory.

Andrew Jarecki's fascinating, disturbing *Capturing the Friedmans* (2003) makes unusually extensive use of vernacular film. Narrating events leading up to and following the 1987 Thanksgiving Day arrest of Arnold Friedman of Great Neck, New York, and his son Jesse, on charges of pedophilia, this postmodern documentary constantly raises and undermines its own questions around truth, authenticity, accuracy, and memory. Even the title offers a *double entendre*. The Friedmans' "capture" includes the colloquial term for creating the home movie (the folklorist's primary concern) as well as Arnold's and Jesse's incarceration. Sequences from Friedman family home movies include rites of passage like birthday parties; celebrations of Thanksgiving and Passover; the children's piano performances; and vacations. The Friedmans' posing and play before the camera joltingly contrasts with interviews of family, lawyers, police, and an investigative reporter, as well as contemporary news footage about the case.

Home movies' "constructed view regularly includes life affirming and pleasurable characteristics of the human condition, while it simultaneously suppresses life's pain and personal distress. Leisure activities are emphasized at the expense of recording labor related aspects of life. Smiles far outnumber frowns and tears; comfort is preferred to discomfort; and pride takes precedence to embarrassment" (Chalfen 1986: 105). Thus, perhaps even more telling from documentary and folkloristic perspectives alike, because it so clearly diverges from conventional home movies, is eldest son David's video diary. He purchased a video camera around the time of the arrests, and used it to record the family's disintegration. Such material is rarely included in home movies, even when "[l]urking just beneath the smiles is perhaps an upcoming divorce, an alcoholic parent, a depressed child" (Lindström 2003: 20). David's camera literally has a seat at the family dinner table as the members fight over what happened and who should take responsibility. Few would choose to record such difficult material, let alone make it available to a documentary filmmaker, although the current popularity of reality television may change that aesthetic.

The result recalls Japanese director Akira Kurosawa's fictional film *Rashômon* (1950), which presents distinctly different perspectives on the same event. David's footage is usually shown with its own sound, in stark contrast to the family home movies' extra diegetical music and narration. The selective, intentionally positive image of the "normal" family's accomplishments, passages, and play in the Friedmans' home movies is thus demarcated from David's disturbing but equally vernacular documentation of family fights and of Arnold's and Jesse's last nights of freedom before beginning their sentences. Jarecki's manipulations and juxtapositions clearly indicate his sympathy with the family's impossible situation, but also encourages viewers to evaluate some footage, interviews, and perspectives as more real and authentic than the rest. The result is both ethnographically and dramatically telling (see Greenhill and Kohm 2011).

FILMS INCORPORATING TRADITIONAL CULTURE (CINEMATIC FOLKLORE)

A broad range of folkloric texts, forms, and processes can be found in fictional films, from beliefs about menstruation and werewolves in *Ginger Snaps* (directed by John Fawcett, 2000; see e.g., Miller 2005) to the traditionally styled storytelling performance that opens Robert Rodriguez's *Desperado* (1995). Among them are adaptations of traditional fairy tales – the oral narratives of wonders collected and retold since well before the Grimm brothers popularized them in the nineteenth century. Adaptations offer "acknowledged transposition of a recognizable other work or works ... A creative and an interpretive act of appropriation/salvaging ... An extended intertextual engagement with the adapted work" (Hutcheon 2006: 8). Literary theorist Linda Hutcheon points out that "an adaptation is a derivation that is not derivative – a work that is second without being secondary. It is its own palimpsestic thing" (2006: 9). As fairy-tale films show, adaptation can reference ventriloquism (the aim to reproduce an original, usually literary form, as closely as possible, but in a different medium); genetic transfer (the aim to communicate the essence, if not the actual text, of the original to the adaptation); de(re)composing (which incorporates various cultural narratives, not only the original literary form);

incarnation (the shift "from more abstract to less abstract signs" (Elliott 2004: 235)); and trumping (the idea that one form – not necessarily the original – is better than another) (see Elliott 2004).

The continuing appeal of fairy-tale films is perhaps best illustrated by the Disney corporation's many highly successful adaptations, beginning with Walt Disney's own bizarre short animation of *Little Red Riding Hood* (1922), through the company's literary fairy-tale rendition *The Little Mermaid* (see e.g., Bendix 1993), to its reflexive pastiche, *Enchanted* (2007; see e.g., Bacchilega and Rieder 2010), and beyond. Unlike Disney's, however, many recent fairy-tale films do not presume an audience exclusively or even primarily comprising children. Distinctly adult narratives include film versions of and riffs on "Little Red Riding Hood" exploring pedophilia (see Greenhill and Kohm 2009). Some adventurous filmmakers venture beyond standards like "Cinderella" and "Snow White and the Seven Dwarfs," seeking less well-known narratives, including ones that diverge from the stereotypical gender roles found in too many Disney and other popular children's fairy-tale films.

Mutzmag (directed by Tom Davenport, 1993), generally in a mode of genetic transfer, draws on Appalachian versions of international traditional tales "The Brothers and the Ogre" and "The Boy Steals the Ogre's Treasure" (see e.g., Greenhill, Best, and Anderson-Grégoire forthcoming). Though the generic titles suggest male primary characters, many versions have female heroes, after whom they are usually named. Mutsmag, Molly Whuppie, Mally Whuppie, or Muncimeg outsmarts evil figures – ogres, giants, and/or witches; male, female, or both (see Figure 25.1). The tomboyish protagonist defeats dangerous adversaries and solves complicated problems both within and outside her expected domestic context, using her intelligence, knowledge of character, powers of observation, and unlikely tools and materials. In Davenport's film, a dying widow gives her older daughters her house and cabbage patch, but the

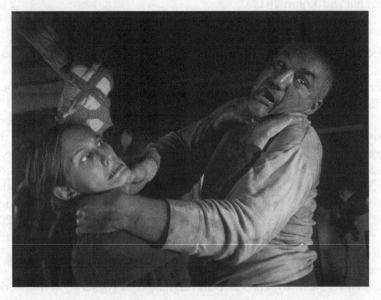

Figure 25.1 The witch (Stephanie Astalos-Jones) and giant (Bart Whiteman) fight after Mutzmag has tricked them. *Mutzmag* 1993. Directed by Tom Davenport. USA: Davenport Films.

youngest, Mutzmag (Robbie Sams), gets only an old pocket knife. Her two sisters, leaving to seek their fortune, try to keep Mutzmag from following them, but eventually give in, allowing her to come if she agrees to act as their hired girl. Seeking food and shelter for the night, the three encounter a witch and giant, who plan to kill them while they sleep. Clever Mutzmag tricks the giant into slaying the witch's three daughters instead. The girls escape to a wealthy home, where the kind couple who feeds and shelters them offer $1,000 rewards for returning their "ten mile stepper" horse and for ridding them of the giant and witch. Mutzmag succeeds, and builds a house where she is seen sitting on the white porch in a white dress, in the final scene.

Mutzmag is only one of several "Appalachian heroines who appear as strong and self-reliant as many of their more familiar male counterparts and European ancestors" (Hanlon 2000: 226). Her German name directly denominates her character – *mut* is "courage" and *magd* is "maid." In Davenport's film, she begins as less feminine than her sisters and less concerned than they are with girly appearances and appurtenances. Though she starts out a tomboy, at the end she is a much feminized but still independent and apparently unmarried woman. Mutzmag comes up in the world without resorting to a heterosexual relationship. Thus, her character certainly diverges from the "innocent persecuted" ingenue heroines of the best-known fairy tales whose primary reward for their suffering is marriage (see Bacchilega 1993). Instead, Mutzmag and others like her "are female counterparts of Jack and other giant killers" (Hanlon 2000: 236).

Davenport's film locates the tale and its primary character in an initially poverty-stricken Appalachian context. Traditional banjo music helps to heighten the sense of the local. While displaying the beautiful hills, woods, and streams of the local countryside, it also represents well the too often marginal existence of its residents and their wish to improve their socioeconomic position by seeking paid labor. Local actors – not the standard prettified bodies and faces of Hollywood stars, nor their generic English – enhance the film's verisimilitude, and make it compelling and striking. Robbie Sams, cast as Mutzmag, had never acted professionally before, and brings both vulnerability and strength to her role.

Adapted from quite a different type of wonder tale, both *The Juniper Tree* (directed by Nietzchka Keene, 1990; see Greenhill and Brydon 2010) and writer/director Micheline Lanctôt's *Le piège d'Issoudun* (*The Issoudun Exit/Trap*; English title *The Juniper Tree*) (2003) de(re)compose and incarnate the Grimm version of this international tale. Tale scholar Hans-Jörg Uther summarizes the traditional narrative:

> A childless couple wishes for a child. A boy is born but his mother dies. The little boy is slain by his cruel stepmother who closes the lid of an apple chest on him … She cooks him and serves him to his father who eats him unwittingly … The boy's stepsister gathers up his bones and puts them under a juniper tree … A bird comes forth and sings about what happened. It brings presents to the father and the sister and drops a millstone on the stepmother, killing her … The boy is resuscitated. (2004, 1: 389)

In Keene's film, sisters Katla (Bryndís Petra Bragadóttir) and Margit (pop singer Björk Guðmundsdóttir in her feature-film debut; see Figure 25.2, Margit [Björk], the main character in Keene's *The Juniper Tree*), flee the region where their mother has been burned for witchcraft. The elder, Katla, plans to find a man to take care of them, intending to bind him with spells. Her choice is a widower, Jóhann (Valdimar Örn Flygenring), whose son, Jónas (Geirlaug Sunna Þormar), is immediately suspicious.

Figure 25.2 *The Juniper Tree*, 1990. Directed by Nietzchka Keene. USA: Wisconsin Center for Film and Theater Research.

But Margit bonds with Jónas over their shared grief. She has regular visions of her mother (Guðrún Gísladóttir) and convinces Jónas that his mother has placed a feather on her own grave as a charm. But all Katla's attempts to get along with Jónas fail. He repeatedly calls her a witch, witnessing her casting a pregnancy spell, and wondering at his father's seeming enchantment. Jónas resists all his stepmother's attempts to gain power in her relationships with him and his father.

Eventually a pregnant Katla taunts Jónas to show how his mother will protect him if he leaps from a cliff. He falls and dies. Katla sews one finger from Jónas's body into his mouth and puts another into a stew. Margit, finding it, eats none, though Jóhann and Katla do. A raven appears on the tree that grows from the mother's grave, where Margit buried Jónas's finger. She tells Jóhann that Katla killed his son. Katla flees, but at the film's end, Jóhann goes in search of her with the apparent intention of resuming their relationship. The final scene focuses on Margit. Her voice-over tells the haunting tale of two children with a bird-mother. Their human father fails to recognize them when they return from the land of the birds. "And so they stayed behind, and they knew what the birds know."

Where Keene's *Juniper* historicizes and localizes the tale in an obviously non-North American venue, Lanctôt's *Issoudun* sets the narrative in contemporary Montreal, Quebec. On a winter day, Esther (Sylvie Drapeau) dresses her two children and herself in warm, constricting clothing and jumps into her backyard pool with her them. They drown, but her suicide fails. In a state of shock, she speeds along a highway – trying again to kill herself. She is stopped by police officer, Laurier (Frédérick De Grandpré), who eventually agrees to drive her home. Their intense interactions en route reveal some of Esther's background, but little about her motivation for the murder/suicide, beyond her extreme fears. She learns that the divorced Laurier has not seen his three boys for five months, and plans to meet them to explain why the marriage ended. His obvious love for children, displayed in his repeated queries about Esther's children (he sees their seats in the back of her car), and his horror when he discovers the murder leads to the film's conclusion.

Issoudun explicitly links to "The Juniper Tree" in a staged presentation of the traditional narrative that punctuates the film. The stark grey scenes of a Canadian winter contrast with the play's bright reds. The only primary characters in the realistic narrative are Esther and Laurier; Drapeau and Grandpré enact their play counterparts, the stepmother and father respectively. However, the staged drama includes several other characters, including the murdered son and his mother, as well as the bird's interlocutors. More ventriloquism and genetic transfer than any other adaptation mode, the play paradoxically offers motivation and psychological detail well beyond that of the realistic scenes.

Comparing Keene's and Lanctôt's versions demonstrates how different interpretations of a fairy tale can be. Yet they also have overlapping elements, including using ravens to mark particularly ominous scenes. Equally successful on their own terms as films, they offer fairy-tale renditions that address the psychological complexities of a culturally tabooed subject – child murder by mothers – that nevertheless retains a perennial fascination.

FICTIONAL FILMS BY INSIDERS ABOUT INSIDERS

As Gerald L. Davis (1992) argues, perspectives by groups marginalized from society's mainstream are often politicized. That is, as well as producing aesthetically satisfying results, insiders often want to correct stereotypes about their group, more accurately reflect their culture, and stimulate reflection for their own and other peoples alike. Joanna Hearne argues that:

> [I]ndigenous media ... involves ... the changed appearance of what is observed when viewed from another position. Many of the texts, images, and footage from earlier ethnographic and Hollywood representations have had a continued half-life as cultural documents ... Such films challenge folklorists to attend to the relationships between film content and film production, to the politicized re-use of films in new group contexts, to the specifically cinematic ways in which folklore is embedded in film content and to the act of filmmaking itself as a powerful form of cultural performance. (2005: 192)

Though such processes may be most obvious in documentary, voyeur media, they are equally present in auteurist works (see e.g., Cham 2005).

One example, *Smoke Signals* (directed by Chris Eyre, 1998) "comments specifically on the human consequences of appropriating and circulating images of Indians as cultural signs. The filmmakers re-frame earlier ethnographic and popular images, disrupting the way such images have been claimed, contextualized, and given meaning by outsiders, and mapping the impact of popular culture representations on tribal identities" (Hearne 2005: 193). It "visually locates native culture in a temporality that is not focused exclusively, and ethnographically, on a vanishing past" (Dickinson 2007: 97–98). A road movie, buddy movie, and comedy/drama, based on a story by Coeur D'Alene writer Sherman Alexie (who also wrote the screenplay), it concerns the developing friendship between handsome, athletic, troubled Thomas Builds-the-Fire (Adam Beach) and cheerful, nerdy Victor Joseph (Evan Adams). Victor's father

Arnold (Gary Farmer) saved baby Thomas from a house fire that killed the boy's parents. But Arnold eventually leaves 12-year-old Victor and his wife Arlene (Tantoo Cardinal). Several years later, having learned the Arnold has died, Victor and Thomas leave their reservation in Idaho for Phoenix, Arizona, to bring his ashes home.

Smoke draws on popular culture, especially movies about "cowboys and Indians." But traditional culture also manifests, from the culinary ritual centrality of frybread to inveterate storyteller Thomas's narration of experiences, legends, and family anecdotes. Both young men sardonically discuss their image as "Indians." The film satirizes Kevin Costner's blockbuster *Dances With Wolves* (1990) and other historicized views that relegate First Nations "authenticity" to the past. After facing racism from fellow bus passengers, Victor and Thomas sing "John Wayne's teeth," which Alexie describes as "a combination of English lyrics and Western musical rhythms along with Indian vocables and Indian traditional drums" (West and West 1998:n.p.): "John Wayne's teeth, heya ... Are they false, are they real? Are they plastic are they steel? Heya ..." Indeed, intertextual references abound in this alternately sarcastic, ironic, funny, and tragic story. For example, the repeated phrase from *Little Big Man* (directed by Arthur Penn, 1970), "It's a good day to die," is parodied multiply, when it becomes a good day to "play basketball," "have breakfast," and so on. Insider jokes about Indians' cars range from references to multiple wrecks and breakdowns to two girls driving around in reverse gear. *Smoke Signals* refuses to leave Aboriginal culture in the historic past, asserting that despite over 500 years of colonial domination, native society and native people retain their stance against assimilation.

A quite different film celebrates Aboriginal language, culture, and history alike. *Atanarjuat: The Fast Runner* (directed by Zacharias Kunuk, 2001), is "the first Inuit-made feature-length film" (Evans 2008: 76). As its web site describes:

> [A] mysterious, unknown shaman enters a small community of nomadic Inuit and... leaves behind a lingering curse of bitterness and discord: after the camp leader Kumaglak [Apayata Kotierk] is murdered, the new leader Sauri [Eric Nutarariaq/Eugene Ipkarnak] drives his old rival Tulimaq [Stephen Qrunnut/Felix Alaralak] down through mistreatment and ridicule ... Tulimaq['s] ... two sons – Amaqjuaq, the Strong One [Pakak Innuksuk], and Atanarjuat, the Fast Runner [Natar Ungalaaq ... the camp's best hunters ..., provoke jealousy and rage in their rival, Oki [Peter-Henry Arnatsiaq], the leader's ill-tempered son. When Atanarjuat wins away Oki's promised wife-to-be, the beautiful Atuat [Sylvia Ivalu], in a head punching competition, Oki vows to get even ... Oki and his friends plot to murder both brothers while they sleep. Amaqjuaq is speared through their tent and killed, but Atanarjuat miraculously escapes, running naked for his life across the spring sea ice. Eluding his pursuers with supernatural help, Atanarjuat is hidden and nursed back to health by an old couple who themselves fled the evil camp years before. After an inner struggle to reclaim his spiritual path, and with the guidance of his elder advisor, Atanarjuat learns to face both natural and supernatural enemies, and heads home to rescue his family. (http://www.isuma.tv/hi/en/atanarjuat/legend-behind-film; for further detail see Evans 2008: 77–99)

Kunuk explains,

> I first heard the story of Atanarjuat from my mother when I was a kid ...
> [O]nce you get that picture into your head of that naked man running for his life across the ice, his hair flying, you never forget it. It had everything ... for a fantastic

movie – love, jealousy, murder and revenge, and at the same time, buried in this ancient Inuit "action thriller," were all these lessons we kids were supposed to learn about how if you break these taboos that kept our ancestors alive, you could be out there running for your life just like him! (2002: 17)

The all-Inuit, Igloolik-resident cast included experienced and first-time actors. Aside from Norman Cohn, New York-born cinematographer and co-founder of Isuma Productions, relatively few southern professionals were involved pre- and post-production.

Kunuk's long-term interest in filming related to recording knowledge about traditional practices: "I noticed when my father and his friends came back from hunting they would always sit down with tea and tell the story of their hunt. And I thought it would be great to film hunting trips so you wouldn't have to tell it, just show it. In 1981 I sold some carvings and bought a video camera" (2002: 18). A folklorist might want to record the oral history/personal experience narratives but Kunuk recognizes the value of the practices and experiences themselves, as great or greater than the storytelling, a philosophy very much reflected in Isuma's filmmaking.

The complex context for filmmaking in Canada's North differs from other locations, but offered unique opportunities both culturally and artistically. Hearne notes that "[t]he production of the film itself … worked to sustain and revive the Inuit skills and social values that the story of Atanarjuat was meant to reinforce" (2006: 322). When shooting on location, cast and crew melded the diegetical hunting camp and the actual location camp; "crew and cast had to go seal and caribou hunting in order to sustain themselves" (Knopf 2009: 207). Objects for the film – tools, weapons, sleds, caribou goggles, sealskin tents, kayaks, clothing, and so on – "were re-created mostly by local artists and elders after traditional models which either belong to cultural knowledge handed down orally from generation to generation" (2009: 207–208) or from historical accounts. Writer Paul Apak developed story concepts while thinking of particular actors, linking their identities to their roles. Inuit naming practices (where people are given names of dead ancestors to whom they are spiritually linked, as the film depicts) acting a character inhabiting the body of another person familiar to and comfortable for Inuit; "[t]he relationship between Inuit naming practices and acting deconstructs the binary opposition between imagined and essential (or blood) identities" (Hearne 2006: 324).

Nearly three hours long, in Inuktitut with subtitles, portraying a culture far removed from most Euro-North Americans' experience and knowledge, *Atanarjuat* may not seem likely to reach a wide audience. But despite its leisurely pace and attention to details of social life and interaction, it grippingly builds inexorably to the murderous climax, with Atanarjuat's dramatic naked run to escape his brother's killers. Though deeply culturally inflected, "demonstrat[ing] its power through the depiction of shamanic communication and reincarnation" (2006: 320), the film's "melodramatic qualities [make it] available for multiple readings" (2006: 321). Remarkably available as a dramatic and compelling narrative, as its win of the 2001 *Camera D'Or* at the Cannes Film Festival and six Genie Awards, including Best Picture, attest, *Atanarjuat* eschews romanticism and nostalgia for a noble people, manifest in *Dances With Wolves* and its ilk, so successfully lampooned in *Smoke Signals*.

Writer/cinematographer Norman Cohn filmed on widescreen digital betacam, transferred to 35mm film. "The goal of Atanarjuat is to make the viewer feel inside the action, looking out, rather than outside looking in. This lets people forget how far away they really are, and to identify with the story and characters as if they were just like us" (http://www.isuma.tv/hi/en/atanarjuat/filmmaking-inuit-style). It succeeds by using close-ups, long landscape views, point-of-view and low angle shots, hand-held and mounted camera work, and long sequences of running and walking, including with "the camera ... positioned on the ground, showing Atanarjuat and his pursuers as tiny little figures moving within the vast Arctic landscape" (Knopf 2009: 217). Taking viewers literally into the present, the film closes with credits accompanied by outtakes of actors and crew in present-day clothing, working with the filming and other modern equipment.

The filmmakers did not strictly follow oral versions of the narrative; "the screenplay is the only variant that ends bloodlessly ... [T]he oral variants all show Atanarjuat as thirsty for revenge" (Evans 2008: 93). This decision was no sop to a Hollywood happy ending. Instead, "Apak, Kunuk, Cohn, and the others at Isuma decided on a positive ending because they wanted to emphasize the importance of working together, a vital Inuit value honed over millennia of cooperation in small bands immersed in a harsh environment" (2008: 94). Norman Cohn says the film is "about how to communicate the right way to behave and live. You learn by being told how to behave through stories ... A community in the sixteenth century goes wrong. There's a moral breakdown. They are trapped by evil and dishonesty. Then it recovers itself. There is a restitution of moral authority by restoring the value of community as superior to the value of the individual. That's an Inuit value" (quoted in ibid.). Indeed, Isuma even worked to sustain non-hierarchical relations among the workers, unlike Hollywood systems (Hearne 2006: 322).

Anthropologists have been nearly univocal in asserting the need for a politicized viewpoint on *Atanarjuat*, recognizing the simultaneous commodification and economic marginalization of Inuit in global capitalism. Some even criticized the filmmakers for not being explicit about their dominated society and culture (see e.g., Siebert 2006). But Isuma members seem satisfied with aesthetic responses and interest in cultural details from outsiders, while simultaneously offering education and entertainment for insiders.

Is That All There Is?

Folklore and film intersect in a myriad of ways, and on a great variety of levels. Filmmakers document traditions from girls' playground games to fox hunting; family folklorists consider home movies in terms of kin and culture; scholars find fairy-tale deep structures in horror films; and Indigenous peoples worldwide see film as a valuable resource as well as an indispensable communicative tool. As yet under-explored areas remain, like the uses of lines from the cinema as quasi-proverbial sayings. For example, it is difficult for Euro-North Americans to say "I'll be back" without referencing Arnold Schwarzenegger's filmic catch phrase. But as folklorists continue to explore these areas, fascinating new material comes to light – camera – and ... action!

ACKNOWLEDGMENTS

Thanks to the Social Sciences and Humanities Research Council of Canada for ongoing support, to Tom Davenport and Davenport Films for permission to include a photograph from *Mutzmag*; to Patrick Moyroud for permission to use a photograph from *The Juniper Tree*; and to Dorinda Hartmann of the Wisconsin Center for Film and Theater Research for access to materials from Nietzchka's Keene's papers and Juliette Loewen for locating relevant materials from M2005-051/WCFTR, boxes 4 and 5. Thanks also to Sidneyeve Matrix for her always helpful comments.

NOTES

1   My Francophone colleagues in Canada generally prefer "ethnology" to refer to work focussing on traditional and popular culture. I follow this volume's use of "folklore," but I intend the inclusion of ethnology, its materials, perspectives, and practitioners.
2   Quotations without sources are from the films under consideration.

REFERENCES

Bacchilega, Cristina. 1993. "An Introduction to the 'Innocent Persecuted Heroine' Fairy Tale." *Western Folklore* 52(1): 1–12.

Bacchilega, Cristina and John Rieder. 2010. "Mixing It Up: Generic Complexity and Gender Ideology in Early 21st-Century Fairy Tale Films" in Pauline Greenhill and Sidney Eve Matrix, Eds. *Fairy Tale Films: Visions of Ambiguity*. Logan: Utah State University Press, pp. 23–41.

Bendix, Regina. 1993. "Seashell Bra and Happy End: Disney's Transformation of 'The Little Mermaid'." *Fabula* 34 (3/4): 280–290.

Chalfen, Richard. 1986. "The Home Movie in a World of Reports: An Anthropological Approach." *Journal of Film and Video* 38(3/4): 102–110.

Cham, Mbye. 2005. "Oral Traditions, Literature, and Cinema in Africa" in Robert Stam and Alessandra Raengo, Eds. *Literature and Film: A Guide to the Theory and Practice of Film Adaptation*. Malden, MA: Wiley-Blackwell, pp. 295–312.

Davis, Gerald L. 1992. "'So Correct for the Photograph:' 'Fixing' the Ineffable, Ineluctable African American" in Robert Baron and Nicholas R. Spitzer, Eds. *Public Folklore*. Washington, DC: Smithsonian Institution Press, pp. 105–118.

Dickinson, Peter. 2007. *Screening Gender, Framing Genre: Canadian Literature into Film*. Toronto: University of Toronto Press.

Elliott, Kamilla. 2004. "Literary Film Adaptation and the Form/Content Dilemma" in Marie-Laure Ryan, Ed. *Narrative Across Media: The Languages of Storytelling*. Lincoln: University of Nebraska Press, pp. 220–243.

Evans, Michael Robert. 2008. *Isuma: Inuit Video Art*. Montreal: McGill-Queen's University Press.

Greenhill, Pauline. 1988. "Folk Drama in Anglo Canada and the Mock Wedding: Transaction, Performance, and Meaning." *Canadian Drama/L'Art dramatique canadien* 14: 169–205.

Greenhill, Pauline, Anita Best, and Emilie Anderson-Grégoire. Forthcoming. "Queering Gender: Transformations in 'Peg Bearskin' and Related Tales" in Kay Turner and Pauline Greenhill, Eds. *Transgressive Tales: Queering the Grimms*. Detroit: Wayne State University Press.

Greenhill, Pauline and Anne Brydon. 2010. "Mourning Mothers and Seeing Siblings: Feminism and Place in The Juniper Tree" in Pauline Greenhill and Sidney Eve Matrix, Eds. *Fairy Tale Films: Visions of*

Ambiguity. Logan: Utah State University Press, pp. 116–136.

Greenhill, Pauline and Steven Kohm. 2009. "Little Red Riding Hood and the Pedophile in Film: 'Freeway,' 'Hard Candy,' and 'The Woodsman'." *Jeunesse: Young People, Texts, Cultures* 1(2): 35–65.

Hanlon, Tina L. 2000. "Strong Women in Appalachian Folktales." *The Lion and the Unicorn* 24(2): 225–246.

Hearne, Joanna. 2005. "John Wayne's Teeth: Speech, Sound and Representation in 'Smoke Signals' and 'Imagining Indians'." *Western Folklore* 64(3/4): 189–208.

Hearne, Joanna. 2006. "Telling and Retelling in the 'Ink of Light': Documentary Cinema, Oral Narratives, and Indigenous Identities." *Screen* 47(3): 307–326.

Hillyer, Minette. 2004. "Sex in the Suburban: Porn, Home Movies, and the Live Action Performance of 'Love in Pam and Tommy Lee: Hardcore and Uncensored'" in Linda Williams, Ed. *Porn Studies*. Durham, NC: Duke University Press.

Hutcheon, Linda. 2006. *A Theory of Adaptation*. New York: Routledge.

Knopf, Kerstin. 2009. "'Atanarjuat' – Fast Running and Electronic Storytelling in the Arctic" in Frank Schulze-Engler and Sissy Helff, Eds. *Transcultural English Studies: Theories, Fictions, Realities*. Amsterdam: Rodolpi, pp. 201–220.

Kohm, Steven and Pauline Greenhill. 2011. "Pedophile Crime Films as Popular Criminology: A Problem of Justice?" *Theoretical Criminology* 15(2): 195–216.

Kunuk, Zacharias. 2002. "I First Heard the Story of Atanarjuat from My Mother." *Brick* 70: 17–18.

Lindström. Mikael. 2003. "Family Fiction." *Film International* 6: 20–21.

MacDougall, David. 1978. "Ethnographic Film: Failure and Promise." *Annual Review of Anthropology* 7: 405–425.

Miller, April. 2005. "'The Hair that Wasn't There Before': Demystifying Monstrosity and Menstruation." *Ginger Snaps* and *Ginger Snaps Unleashed*. Special issue. *Western Folklore* 64 (3/4): 281–303.

Sherman, Sharon R. 1998. *Documenting Ourselves: Film, Video, and Culture*. Lexington: University of Kentucky.

West, Dennis and Joan M. West. 1998. "Sending Cinematic Smoke Signals: An Interview with Sherman Alexie." *Cineaste* 23 (4): 28–32.

Zimmermann, Patricia R. 1988. "Hollywood, Home Movies, and Common Sense: Amateur Film as Aesthetic Dissemination and Social Control, 1950–1962." *Cinema Journal* 27(4): 23–44.

Zipes, Jack, Ed. and trans. 2002. *The Complete Fairy Tales of the Brothers Grimm*. 3rd edition. New York: Bantam Books.

FURTHER READING

Chalfen, Richard. 1986. "The Home Movie in a World of Reports: An Anthropological Approach." *Journal of Film and Video* 38(3/4): 102–110.

Evans, Michael Robert. 2008. *Isuma: Inuit Video Art*. Montreal: McGill-Queen's University Press.

Greenhill, Pauline and Sidney Eve Matrix, Eds. 2010. *Fairy Tale Films: Visions of Ambiguity*. Logan: Utah State University Press.

Ishizuka, Karen L. and Patricia R. Zimmermann, Eds. 2008. *Mining the Home Movie: Excavations in Histories and Memories*. Berkeley: University of California Press.

Koven, Mikel J. 2003. "Folklore Studies and Popular Film and Television: A Necessary Critical Survey." *Journal of American Folklore* 116(460): 176–195.

Koven, Mikel J. and Sharon R. Sherman, Eds. 2007. *Folklore/Cinema: Popular Film as Vernacular Culture*. Logan: Utah State University Press.

MacDougall, David. 1978. "Ethnographic Film: Failure and Promise." *Annual Review of Anthropology* 7: 405–425.

Sherman, Sharon R. 1998. *Documenting Ourselves: Film, Video, and Culture*. Lexington: University of Kentucky.

Sheman, Sharon, R. Ed. 2005. *An Expanded View of Film and Folklore*. Special issue. *Western Folklore* 64(3–4).

Siebert, Monika. 2006. "'Atanarjuat' and the Ideological Work of Contemporary Indigenous Filmmaking." *Public Culture* 18(3): 531–550.

Stone, Melinda and Dan Streible, Eds. 2003. *Small-Gauge and Amateur Film.* Special issue. *Film History* 15(2).

Von Rosen, Franziska. 1992. "'Micmac Storyteller: River of Fire': The Co-Creation of an Ethnographic Video." *Canadian Journal for Traditional Music* 20: article 6.

Zimmermann, Patricia R. 1995. *Reel Families: A Social History of Amateur Film.* Bloomington: Indiana University Press.

Zipes, Jack. 2011. *The Enchanted Screen: A History of Fairy Tales on Film.* New York: Routledge.

FILMOGRAPHY

Atanarjuat. 2001. Directed by Zacharias Kunuk. Canada: Igloolik Isuma/National Film Board.

Capturing the Friedmans. 2003. Directed by Andrew Jarecki. USA: HBO Documentary.

Dances With Wolves. 1990. Directed by Kevin Costner. USA: Tig Productions.

Desperado. 1995. Directed by Robert Rodriguez. USA: Columbia Pictures Corporation.

Enchanted. 2007. Directed by Kevin Lima. USA: Walt Disney Pictures.

Ginger Snaps. 2000. Directed by John Fawcett. Canada: Copperhead Entertainment.

Grandma's Bottle Village: The Art of Tressa Prisbrey. 1982. Directed by Allie Light and Irving Saraf. USA: Light-Saraf Films.

The Juniper Tree. 1990. Directed by Nietzchka Keene. USA: n.p.

Little Big Man. 1970. Directed by Arthur Penn. USA: Cinema Center Films.

Little Erin Merryweather. 2003. Directed by David Morwick. USA: Three Stone Pictures.

The Little Mermaid. 1989. Directed by Ron Clements and John Musker. USA Walt Disney Pictures.

Little Red Riding Hood. 1922. Directed by Walt Disney. USA: Laugh-O-Gram Films.

Mutzmag. 1993. Directed by Tom Davenport. USA: Davenport Films.

Nanook of the North. 1922. Directed by Robert J. Flaherty. USA/France: Les Frères Revillon.

Rashômon. 1950. Directed by Akira Kurosawa. Japan: Daiei Motion Picture Company.

Smoke Signals. 1998. Directed by Chris Eyre. Canada/USA: Shadow Catcher Entertainment.

The Story of the Coast Salish Knitters. 2000. Directed by Christine Welch. Canada: Prairie Girl/National Film Board.

Valdimar T. Hafstein

HERITAGE BY FIRE

On April 18, 2007, fire laid waste to two buildings in the heart of downtown Reykjavik, Iceland. One of them, built in 1801 or 1802, housed a dance club called Pravda. It was the second oldest building still standing in Reykjavik. The other building, from 1852, had a restaurant on the upper floor, Café Romance, and a kebab joint on the ground floor. The fire engines were there within minutes after the fire broke out, followed in short order by reporters and camera crews. Two out of three TV stations interrupted their programming to bring hours of direct footage from the fire. To make television out of the crackling spectacle, reporters lined up interviewees on the main square against a smoking background of fire fighters hosing down the flames: from the fire marshal to the building owners, from historians to patrons of the burning dance club, and from the mayor of Reykjavik to anonymous passers-by, the audience was treated to the live reactions of each. To most of their interlocutors, reporters posed some variation on the question: "are we witnessing the destruction of priceless cultural heritage?" From the fire marshal to the mayor, everyone concurred that, yes, before our very eyes, the cultural heritage of the capital was going up in flames.

I sympathized with the clubbers facing their Disco Inferno, but I was more intrigued by the smoldering heritage; or rather, by the metamorphosis of house to heritage, as yellow flames licked the red Coca-Cola sign on the façade of the kebab shop. Born and raised in the capital, I live and work downtown and I pass by those buildings every day. This was the first time I heard anyone refer to them as cultural heritage. I knew they were old – relative to other buildings in Reykjavik, that is – but to the best of my knowledge, before these two buildings caught fire, no one ever spoke of them in the language of heritage. As smoke engulfed the city center, however, as flames

A Companion to Folklore, First Edition. Edited by Regina F. Bendix and Galit Hasan-Rokem.
© 2012 John Wiley & Sons, Ltd. Published 2012 John Wiley & Sons, Ltd.

burst through the roof and water spouted from red hoses, all of a sudden the language of heritage rolled off everyone's tongues. Before the flames were doused, television audiences witnessed the mayor – in full firefighter's uniform – pledge to rebuild the house from the ground up, exactly as it had stood.

AGE OF HERITAGE

Something in all this was like a siren song for the folklorist in me: since the inception of the field, folklorists have been driving an ambulance from the scene of one cultural disaster to the next. As Barbara Kirshenblatt-Gimblett notes, "the time of our operation is the eleventh hour" (1996: 249). Racing at breakneck speed, we arrive only to find we have come too late – the angel of history has always already wafted by and we are left to pick our way through the landscape of smoldering ruins in his wake (Anttonen 2005; Dundes 1969; Gamboni 2001: 8). With my windows firmly shut to keep the smoke out, I sat glued to the television screen and tried to recall the significance of rebuilding the Temple of Jerusalem. Is it a sign of the end times?

Destruction and preservation are surely two sides of the same coin, so it is no surprise that a fire should trigger a discursive eruption about heritage (Gamboni 2001; Holtorf 2010). In the weeks following the fire, intense debate raged in the papers, on the radio, and on television talk shows about cultural heritage, preservation, restoration, and about objects and buildings that suture the past to the present. Such discursive eruptions are not an everyday occurrence, to be sure, but neither are they particularly unusual. Heritage discourse is not all in the form of eruptions, however. It is not all fire and floods. There is also the steady purr of heritage claims, in and out of the public ear: urgent, melancholic, resigned or resistant, a variety of people regularly claim that this or that constitutes important heritage that we must preserve. Such heritage claims may not make the news, but they certainly make other sections of the paper.

Cultural heritage, it seems, is suddenly at every turn. That is not to say that buildings or practices referred to as heritage are not old. More often than not they are. What is new and remarkable is to speak of them in terms of cultural heritage. Cultural heritage is itself not an old practice. Although the term was coined in the late nineteenth century, it only came into more general usage in the 1970s, and its usage only grew common in the 1990s, growing year by year to the present day (Björgvinsdóttir 2009; Hafstein 2006; Klein 2006a).

PATRIMONIAL RÉGIME

In the last couple of decades a vast number of social actors have seized upon the concept of cultural heritage in hundreds of thousands of scattered places. The success of cultural heritage in this period is nearly without precedent. In a path-breaking work on *The Heritage Crusade and the Spoils of History*, historian and geographer David Lowenthal compares the rise of heritage to a religious movement, proclaiming that "only in our time has heritage become a self-conscious creed, whose shrines and icons daily multiply and whose praise suffuses public discourse" (1998: 1).

Although Lowenthal's book is a classic in the nascent interdisciplinary field of heritage studies, it is perhaps better known for the fire-and-brimstone rhetoric of its critique of "the cult of heritage" than for any analytic concept or theorization that poses interesting problems or open up new avenues for serious research. One blind alley is its fundamental but all-too-easy distinction between history (science, genuine, truth) and heritage (religion, spurious, fabrication), which repeats all the twentieth-century debates about authenticity, all-too-well-known to folklorists (Bendix 1997; Dundes 1985; Handler and Linnekin 1984; Timothy and Boyd 2003). More importantly to my way of thinking, Lowenthal's religious analogy is not terribly useful for understanding what cultural heritage is, how it operates, or how people make use of it.

A more helpful comparison may be drawn to the environmental movement, organized around another powerful concept. A relatively recent invention, the concept of the environment has had a profound (if insufficient) impact on how we conceive of the material world and how we act upon it. There have long been rivers and oceans and atmosphere, of course, but the environment creates a connection between water pollution in a Mexican village and rising sea levels in Amsterdam; it ties together the depletion of cod stocks around Newfoundland and smog in Beijing. Most importantly, the environment creates a common cause for the people affected. There is no question as to whether or not the environment actually exists; it is a category of things, an instrument for classifying the world and therefore also for changing it. Categories of this kind have a performative power. They make themselves real. By acting on the world, molding it in their image, they bring themselves into being.

If the environment is one such category, cultural heritage is another. Much like the environment, cultural heritage is a new category of things, lumped together in novel ways under its rubric; things as motley as buildings, monuments, swords, dances, jewelry, songs, visual patterns, religious paraphernalia, literature, and woodcarving traditions. Again, like the environment, heritage does not seek to describe the world; it changes the world. Just like the environment, the major use of heritage is to mobilize people and resources, to reform discourses, and to transform practices. Like the environment, then, heritage is about change. Don't be fooled by the talk of preservation: all heritage is change.

The magnetic field of heritage is so strong that we constantly risk being pulled in and to critique on its terms instead of critiquing its terms. To pull out of its orbit, it helps to consider heritage as a particular régime of truth: the patrimonial régime, all at once material and ethical, economic and emotional, scientific and sensory (cf. Poulot 2006: 153–181). It is a régime in rapid expansion, both across and within our societies. Although it is deeply implicated in industry and government, its rhetoric is primarily moral; speaking within the patrimonial régime, the moral imperative to conserve is self-evident.

While the patrimonial régime is among other things a formation of knowledge, replete with experts and professionals, journals and conferences, these are largely concerned with means rather than ends: with methods and priorities, or, more often, with particular projects of conservation. They respond to a growing sense of urgency in the face of what are believed to be grave threats of destruction. Rarely is conservation itself questioned or its urgency examined. As French historian Dominique Poulot observes, within the confines of an ethical discourse of heritage, a radical critique is most easily understood as iconoclasm or vandalism (Poulot 2006: 157). In other words, the alternative to conserving is not *not* to conserve; the alternative to conserving is to destroy.

CRITIQUE OF HERITAGE

Yet the very prevalence of the patrimonial régime demands our critical attention. Barbro Klein warns that "a naive, uncritical, unhistorical, and untheorized understanding of cultural heritage" poses a danger in an era in which the modern boundaries between the cultural field, the political field and the market are blurring. "The term heritage is not innocent," Klein continues, and it is easy – but important – to agree that, "we must ponder its role in the ongoing worldwide remapping of ideological, political, economic, disciplinary, and conceptual landscapes" (Klein 2006a: 74).

Many explanations have been put forward to account for the rising tide of heritage. Some say it bears witness to an intensified historical awareness, others associate it with the development of the tourist industry, and others yet see it as part of a nostalgic Zeitgeist, associated with the so-called cultural logic of capitalism. Other explanations include the rise of localisms and patriotisms in the face of globalization; longer life-spans and changing family relations; the mobility of individuals and the dispersion of peoples in a deterritorialized world; the exoticization of the past in film and television; the gradual commodification of culture; and the list goes on (see e.g., Bendix 2000; Björgvinsdóttir 2009; Holtorf 2006, 2010; Huyssen 2000; Klein 1997, 2006a; Löfgren 1997; Lowenthal 1998; Lumley 2005; Mitchell 2002, 179–205; Nora 1989; Poulot 2006; Smith 2006; Turtinen 2006; Yúdice 2004; Žižek 2000). No doubt, there is something to each of these explanations, though no one of them will account for all the various invocations of cultural heritage around the globe.

The rise of cultural heritage is perhaps the chief example of a newfound valuation of cultural practices and objects in terms of their expediency for economic and political purposes. This is culture as a resource: a novel configuration in which culture is now a central expedient in everything from creating jobs to reducing crime, from changing the face of cities through cultural tourism to managing differences and conflicts within the population (Yúdice 2004: 9–13). In this context, heritage provides a strong but flexible language for staking claims to culture and making claims based on culture.

HERITAGE UNDER UNESCO

In an important book on *Uses of Heritage*, archeologist Laurajane Smith has argued that it is "no accident that the very discourses of 'heritage' and concerns about its loss arose in a period perceived to mark major social and cultural changes" (Smith 2006: 100). Vastly increased public access to media has helped foster a public debate "about environmental, political and social issues" and Smith argues that a major factor in the recent prominence of discourse about and concerns for cultural heritage is that it represents "an attempt to deal with, negotiate and regulate change" (Smith 2006).

According to Smith, such concerns and debates are partly channeled into "a self-referential 'authorized heritage discourse,' whose authority rests in part in its ability to 'speak to' and make sense of the aesthetic experiences of its practitioners and policy makers" and in part on "institutionalization within a range of national and international organizations and codes of practices" (Smith 2006: 28). Smith's "authorized heritage discourse" corresponds by and large to what I have here termed the patrimonial régime. Indeed, its strong institutional matrix is a central factor in the rapid expansion of this régime. I have argued elsewhere (Hafstein 2009) that the love affair of cultural administration with the patrimonial régime is due to a considerable degree to the principal instrument through which heritage is administered: the list (or register or inventory or schedule). Heritage lists are a convenient object for administrative logic: listing produces quantifiable results that defy the notorious difficulty of counting culture; and heritage lists are also politically expedient for they allow governments to claim success in the cultural field when monuments and practices are listed on international rosters of merit, like UNESCO's World Heritage List (Schuster 2002; Turtinen 2006).

In fact, no discussion of the patrimonial régime is complete without reference to the United Nations Educational, Scientific, and Cultural Organization (UNESCO), which has been enormously successful in shaping national and local discourses and practices of heritage. Established in 1946, one of UNESCO's first accomplishments was to adopt, in 1954, the Convention for the Protection of Cultural Property in the Event of Armed Conflict, often called the Hague Convention for short (see Skrydstrup, this volume and 2009). In the half century following the adoption of the Hague Convention, UNESCO developed separate legal instruments and bodies for the protection of cultural property and the safeguarding of cultural heritage. The term and discourse of cultural property gained currency worldwide following the adoption of the Hague Convention in 1954, not the other way around. Likewise the ascendancy of cultural heritage in recent decades only gained momentum in the wake of the adoption of the World Heritage Convention in 1972. Conversely, UNESCO is today best known for the World Heritage List associated with that convention (Di Giovine 2009; Turtinen 2006).

In 2003, UNESCO added to its legal arsenal the Convention for the Safeguarding of the Intangible Cultural Heritage, with a Representative List of the Intangible Cultural Heritage of Humanity (Bortolotto 2008; Hafstein 2004; Kapchan 2011; Kirshenblatt-Gimblett 2006; Smith and Akagawa 2009). In spite of its etymological roots in bureaucratese, the term "intangible cultural heritage," concocted in the assembly halls of UNESCO as recently as the 1990s, has rapidly gained acceptance following the adoption of the convention dedicated to safeguarding it. In this, it repeats the international success story of "cultural heritage" itself, propounded by the 1972 convention, not only as a term but as a system of values, a set of practices, a formation of knowledge, a structure of feeling, and a moral code.

HERITAGE AS SOCIAL IMAGINATION

Taken over from probate law, the concept of heritage (or, in Romance languages, patrimony) points to one of the metaphors for the nation: that of the family. Projecting on to the state intergenerational relations, obligations, and succession in the family, the republican nation-state carried over to the cultural sphere a dynastic model that it did away with in other areas of government. At the same time as it evokes an earlier model of the body politic, however, the notion of national patrimony democratizes what previously belonged to elites alone (Bendix 2000). The idea of a common cultural heritage transfers "the goods and rights of princes and prelates, magnates and merchants" (Lowenthal 1998: 60) to the public at large; it throws open the doors of the Louvre to the throng in the streets outside (Poulot 1997).

The simultaneous adulation of material signs of privilege and assertion of universal access reveals an interesting paradox in the patrimonial imagination. On the one hand, those castles, manors, monuments, crown jewels, and courtly fashions that figure most prominently in representations of heritage and which most money is spent on preserving, restoring, and exhibiting, all belonged to the few in a society where the many were downtrodden and destitute. Now as before, it is the many who pay for the maintenance of these outwards signs of class privilege. The difference, however, lies in the patrimonial valuation of these material signs, their consecration as "our" heritage, which urges the general population to identify with the facade of its own historical subordination, the visual markers of its domination. The present accessibility of these signs of privilege, albeit behind rails or in glazed cabinets, underlines and perhaps overstates the difference of contemporary societies from previous eras. Through an act of patrimonial imagination, identification with the symbolic armature of social distinction helps to foster the illusion not so much of classlessness as of universal inclusion in the ruling class, or at least inclusion for the museum-going, heritage-conscious middle classes who have invested most in the cultural field. This facility for fantasies of social climbing is an innovative feature of the patrimonial régime, for, as Regina Bendix has remarked, what distinguishes heritage from other ways of aligning the past with the present "is its capacity to hide the complexities of history and politics" (Bendix 2000: 38).

Extending the scope of heritage to popular, vernacular culture – as the new notion of intangible heritage does – makes this more inclusive and encompassing heritage a matter of even greater public, national concern. In that same act, it helps constitute a national public that identifies as such. The national public may thus be said to constitute itself as a collective subject partly through a curious combination of snobbery and slumming – that is to say, it is partly defined through common investment in and common responsibility for "our palace" and "our folk dance."

According to Pierre Bourdieu's analysis of taste in his magnum opus on *Distinction*, based on French mass surveys from the 1960s, folk dance is "one of the spectacles most characteristic of middle-brow culture (along with the circus, light opera and bull-fights)." The "spectacle of the 'people' making a spectacle of itself, as in folk dancing," Bourdieu hypothesizes, "is an opportunity to experience the relationship of distant proximity, in the form of the idealized vision purveyed by aesthetic realism and populist nostalgia, which is a basic element in the relationship of the petite bourgeoisie to the working or peasant classes and their traditions" (Bourdieu 1984: 58). One of the signature traits of the heritage relationship in the contemporary era is its conflation of distant proximity to peasants (experienced through folklore and folk museums) with a distant proximity to aristocrats (experienced in manors and national museums). Spectacles of sanitized slumming combine with fantasies of social climbing to create a versatile instrument for social identification, one that claims our allegiance and channels our social imagination both upwards and downwards while leaving the impression that social hierarchies are a thing of the past, inciting nostalgia rather than resistance.

NATIONAL CULTURE AND CULTURAL HERITAGE

Whereas cultural heritage obscures class difference, it highlights cultural difference. Formed in all essential respects during the latter half of the twentieth century, the patrimonial régime succeeds and partially supersedes the earlier régime of "national culture," the heyday of which was in the latter half of the nineteenth and the first half of the twentieth century (though to be sure it is still invoked to various extents in various places, now usually in conjunction with cultural heritage). If national culture was a tool for forging cultural differences along state borders while suppressing difference within the borders, cultural heritage is a more resourceful instrument for representing and orchestrating differences within the state as well as between states. The patrimonial régime presents a postmodern strategy for coping with difference as states slowly come to terms with the failure of the modern régime of national culture.

To be sure, heritage continues to be an important instrument for representing the nation, rallying citizens around a common identity and sense of belonging (Anderson 1991; Anttonen 2005; Bendix and Hafstein 2009; Hafstein 2007; Klein 2006a; Mathisen 2009; Hálfdánarson 2001; Löfgren 1989; Thompson 2006). The uses of folklore for this purpose have been documented in a wide range of contexts (see, e.g., Abrahams 1993; Anttonen 2005; Christiansen 2005, 2007; Dundes 1985; Gunnell 2010; Herzfeld 1982; Hobsbawm and Ranger 1983; Leersen 2007; Ó Giolláin 2000). However, it is more difficult now than ever before to imagine national monocultures, with intensified migration, the multiplication of diasporas, and the resurgence of regional identities and indigenous groups. The modern national subject came at a price: it glossed over difference and demanded allegiance to a uniform national culture and history, through selective oblivion, and at the expense of alternative loyalties.

It is no coincidence that it is under circumstances of intensified migration and visible difference that cultural heritage is all at once everywhere (see Klein 1997; Ashworth *et al.* 2007; Littler and Naidoo 2005, esp. Hall 2005 and Khan 2005). Cultural heritage creates a discursive space in which social changes may be discussed and it provides a particular language for discussing them (cf. Klein 2006a; Rastrick 2007). It enables people to represent their own understandings of their histories and identities. Yet at the same time, the terminology of heritage is a mechanism of power: it curtails expression by defining the sort of things that it makes sense to say (Graham *et al.* 2000; Hafstein 2007).

PATRIMONIALITY

It is under these conditions, at the dawn of a new century, that "intangible heritage" has emerged as an instrument in the production of a strong (but not exclusive) sense of belonging for members of cultural communities within (and sometimes across) states. Population groups objectify their practices and expressions as "intangible heritage" and at the same time they subjectify themselves as "communities." Government can then act on the social field through communities and by means of, among other things, heritage policies (Hafstein 2012; Bortolotto 2009; cf. Bennett 2000; and Rose 1999: 167–196).

This parallels recent developments in environmental conservation, where there is now widespread preoccupation with community, and programs proliferate that devolve to communities the responsibility for putting environmental policy into practice. Political scientist Arun Agrawal has coined the term "environmentality" to describe this governmental rationality in which communities are interpellated as "environmental subjects" (Agrawal 2005). Populations learn to conceive of their habitat as "the environment" and to appreciate the need for its conservation, and – through an infusion of expertise and in cooperation with state, non-governmental, and intergovernmental organizations – are charged with administering themselves and their environmental practices (e.g., Agrawal and Gibson 2001; Li 2001; McDermott 2001; cf. Foucault 1991).

Much the same may be said for the safeguarding of heritage and the "patrimoniality" that interpellates individuals and populations as "patrimonial subjects"; that teaches them to conceive of some of their practices and material culture in terms of heritage and to appreciate the need to safeguard these; and, through cooperation with state, non-governmental and intergovernmental organizations and experts, inducts them into the patrimonial régime. In an interview with the *World Heritage Newsletter*, Joseph King of ICCROM (International Centre for the Study of the Preservation and the Restoration of Cultural Property), argues that the "conservation of heritage can be a very important aspect" of development on the African continent. Even in "those places facing more serious problems," he continues, "conservation of cultural heritage can play a part (even if small) in improving the situation" (King 2001: 2). Together with Jukka Jokilehto, chief of ICCROM's architectural conservation program, King explains this in greater detail in their jointly authored "Reflections on the Current State of Understanding" of authenticity and conservation in the African context. Here, they clarify that it may not always "be possible to insist on continuing traditional habitat as a 'frozen entity'" for "it may sometimes be taken as arrogance to insist on conservation of traditional ways of life if the population does not appreciate this." The question then arises, they go on, "of how to control and guide such modifications in life patterns?" In response, they urge that "the present community should be given every opportunity to appreciate and respect what is being inherited from previous generations." "This is a learning process," they explain, "which may require incentives and examples, and which is especially founded in a close collaboration between the population and authorities." The goal, they conclude, is to "identify ways to generate a cultural process that desires such heritage, and therefore takes care of its safeguarding" (Jokilehto and King 2001: 38; cf. Mitchell 2002: 179–205).

These directions are a fine example of how heritage-making and safeguarding serve as instruments for acting on the social field, to "control and guide modifications in life patterns" and to "generate a cultural process." They also underline that heritage is a transformative process. It transforms the relationship of people with their practices and, as a consequence, their relationship with one another (mediated through those practices). It does so by appealing to their civic duty and moral responsibility for maintaining a particular alignment between the past and the present, in which strong emotions and identities are invested. In this sense, heritage is a technology for acting on the social, giving rise to changed behavior (Hafstein 2011; Smith 2006; cf. Bennett 2000 and Foucault 1991).

HERITAGE AS A METACULTURAL PRACTICE

The alignment of the past with the present is central in generating a cultural process "that desires such heritage." As Barbara Kirshenblatt-Gimblett has noted, "the possession of heritage – as opposed to the way of life that heritage safeguards – is an instrument of modernization and mark of modernity" (Kirshenblatt-Gimblett 2006). By cordoning off certain places and practices as sites of continuity with a cultural tradition or an historical past, everything else is in effect severed from that tradition and history. Inheriting marks the passing away of the social relations that heritage objectifies; it signals a radical disjuncture between the past and the present. Hence, to possess heritage is to be modern; it is a modern way of relating to the past. This past, as it is given material form in buildings, sites, and objects, or as it is performed in musical, dramatic, costume, or ritual heritage, is inevitably a product of the present that appoints, organizes, and represents it (Bendix 2009; Berliner 2010; Björgvinsdóttir 2010; Klein 2006a; Rastrick 2007; Smith 2006; Thompson 2006; Tornatore 2010).

Barbara Kirshenblatt-Gimblett's theorization of heritage as a metacultural relationship to cultural practices (1995, 1998, 2006) is one of the more influential accounts of cultural heritage; her work formulates interesting problems and suggests fruitful approaches. In short, as a metacultural practice cultural heritage points beyond itself to a culture it claims to represent. Through this invocation of culture more broadly conceived, heritage practices refer themselves also to the social field: they call into play a collective subject such as family, community, ethnicity, or nation that share the heritage and are defined by it. Such heritage practices are performative: they bring into being what they enact. Thus, heritage practices perform both culture and collectives – they lend substance and reality to social abstractions. Moreover, the performance of cultural heritage has clearly observable effects, tangible for example in the physical world of construction work and urban development, as well as in the cultural, economic, and social fields. It configures particular spaces as privileged zones of contact between the past and the present and as metonyms of the collective – as heritage sites, that is, be they old buildings, museum collections, festivals, dances, costumes, or foods.

Following Kirshenblatt-Gimblett, to recycle "sites, buildings, objects, technologies, or ways of life" as heritage is to give these things a new lease on life, not as what they once were, but as "representations of themselves" (Kirshenblatt-Gimblett 1998: 151). To label a practice or a site as heritage is not so much a description, then, as it is an intervention. In fact, heritage reorders relations between persons and things, and among persons themselves, objectifying and recontextualizing them with reference to other sites and practices designated as heritage. Heritage assembles previously unrelated buildings, rituals, paintings, and songs, and it constitutes these as something to be safeguarded, that is, acted upon through programs, schemes, and strategies carried out and evaluated by experts whose operations connect the calculations of authorities with the desires and ambitions of citizens.

JEMAA EL-FNA, OR VERTICAL INTEGRATION OF VERNACULAR CULTURE

This theorization is perhaps best illustrated through empirical example. One of the more important events that led to the institutionalization of intangible heritage through UNESCO is a meeting that took place in Marrakesh in 1997, referred to as the International Consultation on the Preservation of Popular Cultural Spaces. The meeting was sponsored by UNESCO's division for cultural heritage and the Moroccan national commission for UNESCO, but the initiative came from a group of intellectuals in Morocco spearheaded by the Spanish writer, dissident, and long-term resident of Marrakesh, Juan Goytisolo. Their principal motivation was to protect Jemaa el-Fna square, later proclaimed by UNESCO to be an intangible heritage of humanity (Hafstein 2004; Schmitt 2008; Goytisolo 2000).

Located at the entrance to the Marrakesh Medina (inscribed on the World Heritage List in 1985), UNESCO's publications describe this bustling marketplace as follows:

> The population of the region and from even further afield converges on this square where the frenetic commercial activity and entertainment opportunities attract crowds well into the night. Lined with restaurants, shops, hotels and public buildings, the square itself is a meeting-point and creative hub for languages, music, art and literature. There is a huge range of performances and acts: story-tellers, musicians, dancers, snake-charmers, glass-eaters and performing animals. A wide variety of services are also offered, such as dental care, traditional medicine, fortune-telling, preaching, astrology, henna tattooing, fruit stalls, water carrying and lantern hiring. The cosmopolitan nature of Jemaa el-Fna is reflected in the mix of languages and dialects from across Morocco and Europe. The stories told there, and the manner in which they are relayed to the audience, are based on ancient tradition. (UNESCO 2001: 22)

In the same text, UNESCO also details the dangers that threaten to undo Jemaa el-Fna as living heritage; it cites socio-economic transformations as a "serious obstacle to the preservation and flourishing of this cultural space," compounded by the advance of modernization, urbanization, and the growth of tourism, all of which threaten "the authenticity of the acts and performances." In an interview with Arcadi Espada, however, Juan Goytisolo himself offers a rather different perspective on the menace facing the Marrakesh marketplace:

> The bourgeois "society" of Marrakesh looks at the square with disdain and has on various occasions attempted to do away with it because they think it is a symbol of backwardness and decay. ... The latest ambition of the bourgeoisie was to build a mall here, taller than the mosques. The bourgeois live off the square, off the tourism that the square brings, but they don't realize that tourists don't come here looking for malls. Well, what we are attempting – and UNESCO's decision will help us in this – is to change the way that many of Marrakesh's own inhabitants look at the square. So that they feel a justified sense of pride. (Espada; my translation)

The principal threat to Jemaa el-Fna, it turns out, is not from the outside, and not from the faceless modernization and urbanization that UNESCO would have us believe, nor even the growing number of tourists. The principal threat is from local inhabitants who wield political and economic power. The purpose of reimagining the marketplace as heritage is to transform the relationship of Marrakesh's own inhabitants to what goes on in Jemaa el-Fna.

Goytisolo's explanation of what exactly it is that inclusion on UNESCO's list can help to achieve sheds light on how an international roster of merit provides incentive to national and local governments to preserve particular expressions or spaces of traditional culture. In Marrakesh, a local commission has been created to implement a 10-year protection plan that includes an urban planning study, the creation of a research facility, the identification of traditional knowledge holders, and provisions to strengthen the customary law relevant to the square's management (UNESCO 2001). In addition, an early analysis of the impacts of UNESCO's recognition identifies such measures as the organization of weekly storytelling sessions, the creation of prize competitions for storytelling, and a fund-in-trust for the benefit of old storytellers to encourage them to transmit their skills to young apprentices. Moreover, the Medina governor is reported to have taken the following measures: "destruction of two buildings unsuited to the popular and traditional aspect of the square, removal of illuminated advertising boards, transformation of streets converging on the Square into pedestrian zone, reduction of car traffic" (UNESCO 2002: 7).

The preservation measures that precede and follow from heritage listing amount, then, to a concerting of efforts to guard against change, to ensure the perpetuation of the ways in which the cultural space is orchestrated, and to promote uninterrupted continuity in the associated practices and expressions. This coordination (and the provision of requisite resources) is facilitated by the support of local and national authorities. By changing the way in which the Marrakesh elite looks at the square, by underlining and adding to its value through international recognition, its incorporation into a patrimonial régime solicits the interest of the upper echelons and encourages their active participation in safeguarding this heritage.

This participation may well be a precondition for the success of undertakings such as these, but it comes at a price. That price is the vertical integration of vernacular culture: its incorporation into the administrative structures of official culture and compliance with the logic of policy and bureaucracy. The programs and prize-competitions in Jemaa el-Fna afford an example of particular ways in which administrative structures turn vernacular practices into objects for the government to act on. The actions taken by the Medina governor, destroying buildings "unsuited to the popular and traditional aspect" of Jemaa el-Fna and removing illuminated billboards, demonstrate how this compliance with administrative logic can serve to museify everyday practices, converting habitat and habitus to heritage. The intervention thus retains the association of the square with backwardness, to which Goytisolo objected, but the language of heritage refigures backwardness as authenticity. As a token of authenticity, this "backwardness" needs to be maintained. More than maintained, actually, for in fact it is actively reconstituted – in this case, with bulldozers and dynamite.

Through safeguarding programs, then, local councils, administrators, national bodies, and the international community attempt to act on the social field. Their interventions transform the cultural space into a resource for administering populations, a resource through which communities can police and reform themselves, so they can conduct themselves in accordance with the way they have been, or will be, trained to see the square, that is, with "a justified sense of pride."

THE ALIEN GAZE, OR GOVERNMENT OF HABITUS IN THE NAME OF HERITAGE

In 2008, when presenting the first Representative List of the Intangible Cultural Heritage of Humanity, Koichiro Matsuura, UNESCO's Director-General, declared his confidence that "with time, this List – designed to give more visibility to our living heritage – will contribute to raising awareness of its importance and instill a sense of pride and belonging to custodian communities" (UNESCO 2008). The prestige of international recognition that comes with listing is thus designed to elicit the community's self-recognition as inheritor and guardian of its heritage.

In the interview with Espada, Juan Goytisolo explains that there is in fact nothing unusual about the disdain of the Marrakesh bourgeoisie for Jemaa el-Fna: "Often," he says, "it is the alien gaze that returns beauty and integrity to places. Alhambra, for example, was discovered by English writers and travelers. Borrow recounts that when he asked people from Granada about Alhambra they referred to it as 'these little Moor things.' Something similar is happening in Marrakesh" (Espada; my translation).

Through this "alien gaze," and by means of the measures and policies put in place, Jemaa el-Fna is symbolically reformed from a rogue element – a "liberty" in the early modern sense of a marketplace outside the city walls, and hence outside the sphere of administration (Bakhtin 1984: 145–195; Mullaney 1988) – to a public theater of power and Marrakesh-ness. Existing customs, habits, pastimes, and expressions are transformed, as Kirshenblatt-Gimblett would have it, to representations of themselves, and they become objects of conservation through plans developed by local, national, and international experts with reference to officially sanctioned criteria of excellence.

The great achievement of the UNESCO enterprise, and of those activists who lobby for the recognition of local popular traditions as humanity's heritage, is the successful expansion of official criteria for just what is worth preserving. A newfound polyphony and diversity is introduced into otherwise uniform and elitist criteria. That achievement, however, comes at the price of subjecting to official criteria and the instruments of their administration. It means accepting the insinuation of government into vernacular forms of culture: a government of habitus in the name of heritage.

Lest this last remark be taken for purism or anarchism, I hasten to add that such intervention need not be bad. Much may depend on the particulars of preexisting relations between governments and local communities, including indigenous and cross-border populations whose presence always complicates the narrative of the nation-state and the logic of national borders. Nor would I want to give the impression that the customs, expressions, and spaces in question were previously unaffected by the practices and policies of local and national governments. What is new here is the direct interest taken in the customs and expressions as such and their refiguration as cultural heritage to be safeguarded through government intervention from threats to their continued existence.

The Body of Heritage

Goytisolo's "alien gaze" illustrates another key trait of the patrimonial régime, namely the reflexive distance that the heritage relationship introduces between the subject and object of heritage, between the inheritor and her cultural heritage (cf. Urry 1998). Thus conceived, heritage is transformative. It transforms people's relationship with their own practices, the ways in which they perceive themselves and the things around them. The conscious inheritor understands her practice differently than another who does not pause to consider, for example, how her needle sutures the past

Figure 26.1   Illustration. Cover of the *Reykjavík Grapevine*, June 2004. Cover art by Hörður Sveinsson and Hörður Kristbjörnsson.

to the present and, eventually, to the future, nor how her craftsmanship transmits culture from one generation to the next. Heritage practices create distance between activities that are marked as heritage, on the one hand, and on the other hand everything else the same people do. Everything that is not heritage is therefore modern: in my native Iceland, football is a modern sport, as opposed to *glíma* (a traditional form of wrestling), which is considered a heritage sport, though the first organized competitions in Iceland in football and *glíma* both date from the early twentieth century; Kentucky Fried Chicken and pizza are modern fare, as opposed to heritage foods like singed sheep heads, putrefied shark, and pickled ram's testicles. To have a heritage is to experience a distance from the things you consider to be your heritage; to have a heritage is also to be modern. This transformation is indicative of how the present relates to history. Indeed, heritage says more about us than it does about past generations or what they've left behind.

Many heritage practices take the body as their central objects – they turn the body into a site of performance (Kapchan 2003: 2011). In effect, heritage is very much concerned with the ways in which culture is embodied and the ways in which bodies are cultured. This is plain to see in countless ethnic parades and in immigrant heritage (Klein 2006b; Larsen 2009; Gradén 2009). Indeed, a central problematic in heritage is the relation between social practices, on the one hand, and kinship or heredity, on the other (Bendix 2000). If heritage is innovative, it is partly in so far as it represents a new way of constituting social collectivity around representations of culture and pedigree.

Of course culture and pedigree do not always make a neat fit. Thus, in June 2004, the *Reykjavik Grapevine* – a free English-language weekly – marked Iceland's Independence Day with cover art depicting a young African woman in a traditional Icelandic costume (Figure 26.1). In many places I can think of, such cover art would not have raised an eyebrow, but in Iceland the cover made waves – that was the idea. The editor introduced the issue by recounting how difficult it had been to get a hold of a traditional Icelandic costume for the photo-shoot. Actually, very few people own such costumes, and in order to rent or to borrow one, people usually turn to the Reykjavik Folkdance Association. According to the editor, however, the photographer who went to Folkdance headquarters was turned down. The lady at the costume rental had expressed concern that the planned photo-shoot might be disrespectful to the national costume. The story made headlines. It even made the evening news. It was a public relations disaster for folk dancing. To be fair, I should add that, despite the editorial, there is some doubt as to whether the photographer's request was in fact flat-out refused at the costume rental (Björgvinsdóttir 2009; Hafstein 2006). Regardless, the point I want to make here is that externalizing culture in human bodies invites racist distinctions. In Iceland, it is difficult to get away from the whiteness of heritage.

CULTURAL HERITAGE AND THE IRONIC SUBJECT

The *Grapevine* cover and editorial bring into relief the politics of representation and beg the question of who speaks for heritage. They bring us back, in fact, to the social collectivities invoked by heritage practices. Communities are not monoliths. Whether they are local or diasporic, indigenous or national, communities are tentative attempts to organize social networks and draw boundaries around them (Noyes 2003). If heritage practices are cultural representations of cultural representations, as Kirshenblatt-Gimblett suggests, then it is at this meta-level of representation that individuals and factions jockey for power over who can speak for the community and who decides how it is to represent itself (e.g., Berliner 2010; Bortolotto 2009; Kuutma 2009; Lowthorp 2007; Tauschek 2009; Tornatore 2010). The stakes are not inconsequential; they concern how the collective subject – the *we* – is invoked and how its boundaries are drawn (Noyes 2006). Authority over heritage and political power within the community are thus to some extent mutually translatable.

For that very reason, however, heritage practices are also ideal sites for challenging authority by contesting collective legacies. Thus, cultural heritage is not just a site for establishing and renewing hegemony by winning consent, structuring allegiance, and orchestrating social networks around official metacultural representations. Cultural

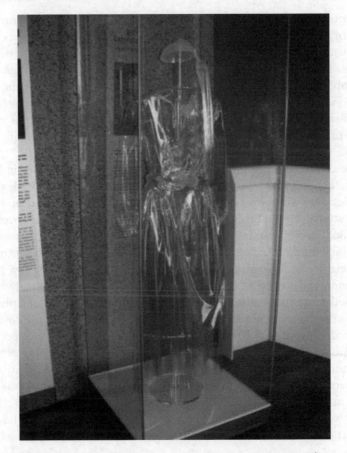

Figure 26.2   Plastic costume in the National Museum of Iceland. Artist: Ásdís Elva Pétursdóttir. Photo: Áslaug Einarsdóttir.

heritage is also a site of contestation, where individuals and groups display dissent, question structures of allegiance, and blur social boundaries. This is accomplished either by offering alternative representations of heritage (of Saami heritage, or gay heritage, or deaf heritage) or else by suggesting alternative metacultural relations to officially sanctioned representations (like the *Grapevine* cover in Iceland or, say, blowing up the Bamiyan Buddhas in Afghanistan). The former is a form of protest, the latter subversion.

Because heritage is a metacultural relationship – a reflexive relation to one's own practices – it sets the stage for its own subversion. The heritage relation is a dialogic process, one that creates a sense of distance by imagining a vista outside one's own self from where one may observe one's own customs and expressions with, as it were, an alien gaze – according to Barbara Kirshenblatt-Gimblett, the hallmark of heritage is "precisely the foreignness of the 'tradition' to its context of presentation" (Kirshenblatt-Gimblett 1998: 157). The distance that this introduces between the subject and itself enables the recognition of the collective subject of cultural heritage: the cultural "we." It enables us to speak reflexively in the first person plural: we Icelanders, we wrestle and we eat putrefied shark (regardless of the fact that many of us do neither), and, implicitly, we are white (though some of us are not).

At the same time, however, this distance allows for detachment; it opens up the prospect that we might imagine ourselves differently, that we might disrupt the official representation of who and what we are and what it is we do. As a reflexive, metacultural relationship to one's own practices, heritage sets the stage for the ironic subject – the self-conscious actor whose ironic stance measures her distance from the culture and collective identity that official representations of heritage attribute to her (e.g., Schram 2009).

Upon leaving the twentieth-century exhibition in the National Museum of Iceland, one is sent off with a work of art that is at once thought-provoking and tongue-in-cheek. It is a traditional Icelandic costume wrought in transparent plastic material, life-size, suspended in a glazed cabinet with the appropriate (plastic) headdress perched above it (Figure 26.2). Like the cover art of the *Reykjavik Grapevine*, the plastic costume experiments with our metacultural relationship to officially sanctioned heritage. For starters, its synthetic medium queries notions of authenticity. Its transparency blurs the boundaries between past and present. More important, however, is its hollow interior. The contours of hollowness open up to scrutiny the ironic subject and the distance that separates her from her heritage; the subject of heritage is, precisely, outside the glass looking in.

REFERENCES

Abrahams, Roger. 1993. "Phantoms of Romantic Nationalism in Folkloristics." *Journal of American Folklore* 106: 1–37.

Agrawal, Arun. 2005. "Environmentality. Community, Intimate Government, and the Making of Environmental Subjects in Kumaon, India." *Current Anthropology* 46(2): 161–190.

Agrawal, Arun and Clark C. Gibson. 2001. "The Role of Community in Natural Resource Conservation" in Arun Agrawal and Clark C. Gibson Eds. *Communities and the Environment. Ethnicity, Gender, and the State in Community-Based Conservation.* New Brunswick: Rutgers University Press, pp. 1–31.

Anderson, Benedict. 1991. *Imagined Communities. Reflections on the Origin and Spread of Nationalism.* 2nd edition. London: Verso.

Anttonen, Pertti. J. 2005. "Tradition through Modernity. Postmodernism and the Nation-State in Folklore Scholarship." *Studia Fennica Folkloristica* 15. Helsinki: Finnish Literature Society.

Ashworth, Gregory J., Brian Graham, and John E. Tunbridge. 2007. *Pluralising Pasts. Heritage, Identity and Place in Multicultural Societies.* London: Pluto Press.

Bakhtin, Mikhail. 1984. *Rabelais and his World.* Bloomington: Indiana University Press.

Bendix, Regina. 1997. *In Search of Authenticity. The Formation of Folklore Studies.* Madison: University of Wisconsin Press.

Bendix, Regina. 2000. "Heredity, Hybridity and Heritage from One Fin-de-Siècle to the Next" in Pertti J. Anttonen, Ed. *Folklore, Heritage Politics and Ethnic Diversity.* Botkyrka: Multicultural Centre, pp. 37–54.

Bendix, Regina. 2009. "Heritage between Economy and Politics. An Assessment from the Perspective of Cultural Anthropology" in Laurajane Smith and Natsuko Akagawa, Eds. *Intangible Heritage.* London: Routledge, pp. 253–269.

Bendix, Regina and Valdimar T. Hafstein. 2009. "Culture and Property. An Introduction." *Ethnologia Europaea: Journal of European Ethnology* 39(2): 5–10.

Bennett, Tony. 2000. "Acting on the Social. Art, Culture and Government." *American Behavioral Scientist* 43: 1412–1428.

Berliner, David. 2010. "Perdre l'esprit du lieu. Les politiques de la transmission à Luang Prabang (Laos)." *Terrain* 55: 90–105.

Björgvinsdóttir, Bryndís. 2009. "Frá melankólíu til mótspyrnu: Menningararfur á Íslandi." (Unpublished MA Thesis), University of Iceland, Faculty of Social and Human Sciences.

Björgvinsdóttir, Bryndís. 2010. "Menningararfur sem ásetningur." *Skírnir: Tímarit hins íslenska bókmenntafélags* 2010(1): 100–120.

Bortolotto, Chiara, Ed. 2008. *Il patrimonio immateriale secondo l'Unesco. Analisi e prospettive.* Rome: Istituto Poligrafico e Zecca dello Stato.

Bortolotto, Chiara. 2009. "The Giant Cola Cola in Gravina. Intangible Cultural Heritage, Property, and Territory between Unesco Discourse and Local Heritage Practice." *Ethnologia Europaea: Journal of European Ethnology* 39(2): 81–94.

Bourdieu, Pierre. 1984. *Distinction. A Social Critique of the Judgement of Taste.* London: Routledge.

Christiansen, Palle Ove. 2005. "Den folkelige kultur. Almuens nye betydning som dansk og national" in Palle Ove Christiansen, Ed. *Veje til danskheden. Bidrag til den moderne nationale selvforståelse.* Copenhagen: C.A. Reitzels forlag.

Christiansen, Palle Ove. 2007. "Folket – både fundet og opfundet. Folkets og folkekulturens rolle i dansk og europæisk nationalitet 1770–1900" in Palle Ove Christiansen and Jens Henrik Koudal, Eds. *Det ombejlede folk. Nation, følelse og social bevægelse.* Copenhagen: C.A. Reitzels forlag.

Dallen J. Timothy, and Stephen Boyd. 2003. *Heritage Tourism.* London: Prentice Hall.

Di Giovine, Michael A. 2009. *The Heritagescape: UNESCO, World Heritage and Tourism.* Lanham, MD: Lexington Books.

Dundes, Alan. 1969. "The Devolutionary Premise in Folklore Theory." *Journal of the Folklore Institute* 6: 5–19.

Dundes, Alan. 1985. "Nationalistic Inferiority Complexes and the Fabrication of Fakelore. A Reconsideration of Ossian, the Kinder- und Hausmärchen, the Kalevala, and Paul Bunyan." *Journal of Folklore Research* 22(1): 5–18.

Espada, Arcadi. Interview with Juan Goytisolo, *La espía del sur.* http://www.geocities.com/laespia/goytisolo2.htm (accessed October 20, 2004).

Foucault, Michel. 1991 [1978]. "Governmentality" in Graham Burchell, Colin Gordon, and Peter Miller, Eds. *The Foucault Effect. Studies in Governmentality,* London: Harvester Wheatsheaf, pp. 87–104.

Gamboni, Dario. 2001. World Heritage: Shield or Target? *Conservation: The Getty Institute Conservation Newsletter* 16(2): 5–11.

Goytisolo, Juan. 2000. "Jemâa-el-Fna's Thousand and One Nights." *UNESCO Courier,* 53 (December): 34–36.

Graham, Brian, Gregory J. Ashworth, and John E. Tunbridge. 2000. *A Geography of Heritage. Power, Culture and Economy.* London: Arnold.

Gradén, Lizette. 2009. "Transatlantic Place Making. The Use of Swedish Bridal Crown as Heritage Performance in the United States." *Arv: Nordic Yearbook of Folklore* 65: 73–92.

Gunnell, Terry. 2010. "Daisies Rise to Become Oaks. The Politics of Early Folktale Collection in Northern Europe." *Folklore* 121(1): 12–37.

Hafstein, Valdimar T. 2004. "The Making of Intangible Cultural Heritage: Tradition and Authenticity, Community and Humanity" (Unpublished PhD dissertation), University of California, Berkeley.

Hafstein, Valdimar T. 2006. "Menningararfur: Sagan í neytendaumbúðum" in Hilma Gunnarsdóttir, Jón Þór Pétursson, and Sigurður Gylfi Magnússon Eds. *Frá endurskoðun til upplausnar. Tvær prófritgerðir, einn formáli, þrjú viðtöl, sjö fræðigreinar, fimm ljósmyndir, einn eftirmáli og nokkrar minningargreinar af vettvangi hugvísinda.* Reykjavik: Center for Microhistorical Studies and the Reykjavik Academy, pp. 313–328.

Hafstein, Valdimar T. 2007. "Claiming Culture: Intangible Heritage Inc., Folklore©, Traditional Knowledge™" in Regina Bendix, Dorothee Hemme, and Markus Tauschek, Eds. *Prädikat "Heritage."*

Wertschöpfungen aus Kulturellen Ressourcen. Münster: Lit Verlag, pp. 75–100.

Hafstein, Valdimar T. 2009. "Intangible Heritage as a List: From Masterpieces to Representation" in Laurajane Smith and Natsuko Akagawa, *Intangible Heritage.* London: Routledge, pp. 93–111.

Hafstein, Valdimar T. 2012. "Protection as Dispossession: Government in the Vernacular" in Deborah Kapchan, Ed. *Intangible Rights: Heritage and Human Rights in Transit.* Philadelphia: University of Pennsylvania Press.

Hálfdánarson, Guðmundur. 2001. *Íslenska þjóðríkið. Uppruni og endimörk.* Reykjavík: Hið íslenska bókmenntafélag and ReykjavíkurAkademían.

Hall, Stuart. 2005. "Whose Heritage? Un-settling 'the Heritage,' Re-Imagining the Post-Nation" in Jo Littler and Roshi Naidoo, Eds. *The Politics of Heritage. The Legacies of "Race."* London: Routledge, pp. 23–35.

Handler, Richard and Jocelyn Linnekin. 1984. "Tradition, Genuine or Spurious." *Journal of American Folklore* 97(385): 273–290.

Herzfeld, Michael. 1982. *Ours Once More. Folklore, Ideology, and the Making of Modern Greece.* Austin: University of Texas Press.

Hobsbawm, Eric and Terence Ranger. 1983. *The Invention of Tradition.* Cambridge: Cambridge University Press.

Holtorf, Cornelius. 2006. "Can Less be More? Heritage in the Age of Terrorism." *Public Archeology* 5: 101–109.

Holtorf, Cornelius. 2010. "Heritage Values in Contemporary Popular Culture" in George S. Smith, Phyllis Mauch Messenger, and Hilary A. Soderland, Eds. *Heritage Values in Contemporary Society.* Walnut Creek: Left Coast Press.

Huyssen, Andreas. 2000. "Present Pasts: Media, Politics, Amnesia." *Public Culture,* 12(1): 21–38.

Jokilehto, Jukka and Joseph King. 2001. "Authenticity and Conservation: Reflections on the Current State of Understanding" in Galia Saouma-Forero, Ed. *Authenticity and Integrity in an African Context.* Paris: UNESCO, pp. 33–39.

Kapchan, Deborah A. 2003. "Performance" in Burt Feintuch, Ed. *Eight Words for the Study of Expressive Culture.* Urbana: University of Illinois Press, pp. 121–145.

Kapchan, Deborah A. 2011. *Intangible Rights. Cultural Heritage and Human Rights.* Pennsylvania Studies in Human Rights. Philadelphia. University of Pennsylvania Press.

Khan, Naseem. 2005. "Taking Root in Britain. The Process of Shaping Heritage" in Jo Littler and Roshi Naidoo, Eds. *The Politics of Heritage. The Legacies of "Race."* London: Routledge, pp. 133–143.

King, Joseph. 2001. "Africa 2009. Interview with Joseph King of ICCROM." *World Heritage Newsletter* 32 (October–November): 2.

Kirshenblatt-Gimblett, Barbara. 1995. "Theorizing Heritage." *Ethnomusicology* 39(3): 367–380.

Kirshenblatt-Gimblett, Barbara. 1996. "Topic Drift: Negotiating the Gap between Our Field and Our Name." *Journal of Folklore Research* 33: 245–254.

Kirshenblatt-Gimblett, Barbara. 1998. *Destination Culture. Tourism, Museums, and Heritage.* Berkeley: University of California Press.

Kirshenblatt-Gimblett, Barbara. 2006. "World Heritage and Cultural Economics" in Ivan Karp, Corinne A. Kratz, Lynn Szwaja, and Tomás Ybarra-Frausto, Eds. *Museum Frictions: Public Cultures/Global Transformations.* Durham, NC: Duke University Press, pp. 161–202.

Klein, Barbro. 1997. "Tillhörighet och utanförskap. Om kulturarvspolitik och folklivsforskning i en multietnisk värld." *Rig* 1–2: 15–32.

Klein, Barbro. 2006a. "Cultural Heritage, the Swedish Folklife Sphere, and the Others." *Cultural Analysis* 5: 57–80.

Klein, Barbro. 2006b. "More Swedish than in Sweden, more Iranian than in Iran. Folk Culture and World Migrations" in Bo Sundin, Ed. *Upholders of Culture: Past and Present.* Stockholm: Royal Swedish Academy of Engineering Sciences, pp. 67–80.

Kuutma, Kristin. 2009. "Who Owns Our Songs? Authority of Heritage and Resources for Restitution." *Ethnologia Europaea: Journal of European Ethnology* 39(2): 26–40.

Larsen, Hanne Pico. 2009. "Danish Maids and Visual Matters. Celebrating Heritage in Solvang, California." *ARV. Nordic Yearbook of Folklore* 65: 93–109.

Leersen, Joep. 2007. *National Thought in Europe. A Cultural History.* Amsterdam: Amsterdam University Press.

Li, Tania Murray. 2001. "Boundary Work. Community, Market, and State Reconsidered" in Arun Agrawal and Clark C. Gibson, Eds. *Communities and the Environment. Ethnicity, Gender, and the State in Community-Based Conservation.* New Brunswick: Rutgers University Press, pp. 157–179.

Littler, Jo and Roshi Naidoo. 2005. *The Politics of Heritage. The Legacies of "Race."* London: Routledge.

Löfgren, Orvar. 1989. "Nationalization of Culture." *Ethnologia Europaea* 19: 5–25.

Löfgren, Orvar. 1997. "Kulturarvets renäs-sans. Landskapsupplevelse mellan marknad och politik." *Rig* 1–2: 3–14.

Lowenthal, David. 1998. *The Heritage Crusade and the Spoils of History.* Cambridge: Cambridge University Press.

Lowthorp, Leah. 2007. "The Cultural Politics of UNESCO's Intangible Cultural Heritage in India: Kutiyattam Sanskrit Theatre." Unpublished paper delivered at the Annual Meeting of the American Folklore Society and the Folklore Studies Association of Canada in Quebec City.

Lumley, Robert. 2005. "The Debate on Heritage Reviewed" in *Heritage, Museums and Galleries. An Introductory Reader.* Abingdon: Routledge, pp. 15–25.

Mathisen, Stein R. 2009. "Narrated Sámi Siedis. Heritage and Ownership in Ambiguous Border Zones." *Ethnologia Europaea. Journal of European Ethnology* 39(2): 11–25.

McDermott, Melanie Hughes. 2001. "Invoking Community. Indigenous People and Ancestral Domain in Palawan, the Philippines" in Arun Agrawal and Clark C. Gibson, Eds. *Communities and the Environment. Ethnicity, Gender, and the State in Community-Based Conservation,* New Brunswick: Rutgers University Press, pp. 32–62.

Mitchell, Timothy. 2002. *Rule of Experts.* Berkeley: University of California Press.

Mullaney, Stephen. 1988. *The Place of the Stage: License, Play, and Power in Renaissance England.* Chicago: University of Chicago Press.

Nora, Pierre. 1989. "Between Memory and History. Les Lieux de Mémoire." *Representations* 26: 7–24.

Noyes, Dorothy. 2003. "Group" in Burt Feintuch, Eds. *Eight Words for the Study of Expressive Culture.* Urbana: University of Illinois Press, pp. 7–41.

Noyes, Dorothy. 2006. "The Judgment of Solomon. Global Protections for Tradition and the Problem of Community Ownership." *Cultural Analysis* 5: 27–56. http://socrates.berkeley.edu/~caforum/ (accessed October 16, 2011).

Ó Giolláin, Diarmuid. 2000. *Locating Irish Folklore. Tradition, Modernity, Identity.* Cork: Cork University Press.

Poulot, Dominique. 1997. *Musée, nation, patrimoine.* Paris: Gallimard-Jeunesse.

Poulot, Dominique. 2006. *Une histoire du patrimoine en Occident.* Paris: Presses Universitaires De France.

Rastrick, Ólafur. 2007. "Menningararfur í fjölmenningarsamfélagi. Einsleitni, fjölhyg-gja, tvíbendni" *Þriðja íslenska söguþingið 18.–21. maí 2006: Ráðstefnurit.* Reykjavík: Sagnfræðingafélag Íslands.

Rose, Nikolas. 1999. *Powers of Freedom. Reframing Political Thought.* Cambridge: Cambridge University Press.

Schmitt, Thomas M. 2008. "The UNESCO Concept of Safeguarding Intangible Cultural Heritage: Its Background and Marrakchi Roots." *International Journal of Heritage Studies* 14: 95–111.

Schram, Kristinn. 2009. "Performing the North. Folk Culture, Exoticism and Irony among Expatriates." *ARV. Nordic Yearbook of Folklore* 65: 49–71.

Schuster, J. Mark. 2002. "Making a List and Checking it Twice: The List as a Tool of Historic Preservation." Working Paper 14, The Cultural Policy Center at the University of Chicago, http://culturalpolicy.uchicago. edu/publications.html (accessed October 16, 2011).

Skrydstrup, Martin. 2009. "Theorizing Repatriation." *Ethnologia Europaea. Journal of European Ethnology* 39(2): 54–66.

Smith, Laurajane. 2006. *Uses of Heritage.* London: Routledge.

Smith, Laurajane and Natsuko Akagawa, Eds. 2009. *Intangible Heritage.* London: Routledge.

Tauschek, Markus. 2009. "Cultural Property as Strategy. The Carnival of Binche, the Creation of Cultural Heritage and Cultural Property." *Ethnologia Europaea. Journal of European Ethnology* 39(2): 67–80.

Thompson, Tok. 2006. "Heritage versus the Past" in Fabio Mugnaini, Pádraig Ó Hélaí, and Tok Thompson, Eds. *The Past in the Present. A Multidisciplinary Approach.* Catania: Edit Press, pp. 197–208.

Tornatore, Jean-Louis and Annick Arnaud. 2011. "Du patrimoine ethnologique au patrimoine immatériel. Suivre la voie politique de l'immatérialité culturelle" in Chiara Bortolotto and Sylvie Grenet, Eds. *Le patrimoine culturel immatériel. Enjeux d'une nouvelle catégorie*, Paris: Maison des sciences de l'homme.

Turtinen, Jan. 2006. "Världsarvets villkor. Intressen, förhandlingar och bruk i internationell politik." *Stockholm Studies in Ethnology* 1. Stockholm: Acta Universitatis Stockholmiensis.

UNESCO. 2001. *Proclamation of Masterpieces of the Oral and Intangible Heritage of Humanity. Guide for the Presentation of Candidature Files.* Paris: Intangible Heritage Section, Division of Cultural Heritage, UNESCO.

UNESCO. 2002. UNESCO RIO/ITH/2002/INF. International Expert Meeting. Intangible Cultural Heritage: Priority Domains for an International Convention. Impacts of the First Proclamation on the Nineteen Masterpieces Proclaimed Oral and Intangible Heritage of Humanity. Rio de Janeiro.

UNESCO. 2008. UNESCOPRESS Press Release No. 112, 511-2008.

Urry, John. 1998. *The Tourist Gaze. Leisure and Travel in Contemporary Society.* Thousand Oaks, CA: Sage Publications.

Yúdice, George. 2004. *The Expediency of Culture. Uses of Culture in the Global Era.* Durham, NC: Duke University Press.

Žižek, Slavoj. 2000. Melancholy and the Act. *Critical Inquiry* 26(4): 657–681.

Martin Skrydstrup

In the mid-1990s, during ethnographic fieldwork in the Crystal Mountains of Gabon, I focused on a rich oral tradition associated with the harp zither *mvett* among an ethnic group known as the *Fang*. In the course of several months, I worked closely with a bard, who reported the principal ideas of the mvett, the performative aspects, the different genres of the epic and the associated initiation rites and sacrifices. The bard performed regularly at the Place d'Indépendance in Oyem for hours, where I recorded and he told tales of the resources of the past. After I had followed this *conteur du mvett* for some months, he confided the outline of an epic about the secret mission of Mvé Ndong set in the war of the worlds between the land of *Okú* and the land of *Engong*. As the bard explained and translated the epic, I jotted down the cast of characters and the narrative in my field notes. At our next meeting, the bard arrived with an entire crew: driver, manager, assistant, and accountant. He told me that he wanted to discuss the copyright conditions of our work and stated that he felt confident that his epic about Mvé Ndong had the potential to make it big in Hollywood: "The mvett epic compares to Star Wars," as the bard's assistant developed the storyline and continued, "a never-ending war between mortals and immortals in an imaginary space, where the force is with the good and against the evil" (Skrydstrup 2000: 63). This was a way of elaborating that the local bearers of this tradition were well aware that the mvett had commercial potential as a blockbuster, which could be exploited far beyond the traditional performative context of the *aba'a*.[1] I knew that the customary codes governing intellectual ownership of songs, lyrics, and epics within the mvett tradition were complex and intricate, but were largely regulated by the personal relationship between master and apprentice. However, if revealed to an outsider, such as an anthropologist, and recorded as field notes, how did this affect intellectual ownership and what ought to happen? Thinking through this question – what *is* and what *ought* "cultural property" to be in any particular context *pre* and *post* acquisition/appropriation – raises fundamental, as well as mundane questions. How useful is the concept of "cultural property" for such an exercise in thinking? Does it merely represent a Western legal artifact? If so, how was it made and what are its current ramifications and effects around the globe? Does "cultural property" hold much sway and application beyond trans-national elite institutions run by bureaucrats? What conceptual repertoires are at our disposal to critically and productively interrogate "cultural property"? I shall try and address some of these broader questions and in the end return to what the mvett troubadour in Oyem ultimately was concerned about and the form of "cultural property" our encounter produced. However, it is important here at the outset to specify that this chapter deals primarily with cultural property as *something tangible*, rather than an all encompassing rubric also comprising intellectual property.

WHAT IS CULTURAL PROPERTY?

In 1976, UNESCO asserted that "cultural property is a basic element of people's identity" (Barkan 2002: 25), and accordingly recognized claims or requests for cultural property which have "a fundamental significance from the point of view of the spiritual values and cultural heritage of the people of a member state ... which they feel are the most vital and whose absence causes them the greatest anguish" (UNESCO 1978; M'Bow 1979). Formally speaking "cultural property" represents a wrap-around term deployed in a range of different national and international codes regulating the circulation, access, and preservation of what Henry Merryman has defined as: "a flexible and continually expanding category that at its core includes the works of art, artists and artisans, manuscripts, archives and libraries, antiquities and historical relics. Any human artifact may come to be valued as cultural property, from scientific and musical instruments to perfume bottles and fruit-box labels" (Merryman 2000). The inclusiveness of the term is clearly registered inside the law itself, where cultural property-related issues are being dispersed across the law of charitable trusts or foundations, private ownership law, the law relating to export controls, planning, preservation, tax breaks for donors (in the United States), and behind much or all of this, the ceaseless impersonal work of bureaucrats at local, national, or trans-national levels building a parlance and a discourse in soft law and ethics around the question. Thus, cultural property looks like an catch-all concept. It has led critics to argue that if defined in too encompassing a manner, we run the risk that it will become meaningless and open the floodgates for absurd claims, such as Italy's claim that pizza is its very own cultural property.

Looking beyond the formal legal inscriptions of the term, institutional mission statements, policy papers and the like, Jordanne Bailkin offers a more analytical definition, arguing that the distinctive features of cultural property is "that it involves duties, rather than rights and that it is an amalgam of all the other property regimes, copying aspects of the law of land, chattel, and intellectual property" (Bailkin 2004). She further argues that the key characteristics of cultural property are "inalienability" and "nonexclusive ownership"; that it is a "finite, irreplaceable, depletable, scarce, and non-renewable resource," like an endangered species; and finally that it is governed by some key doctrines such as "natural right" and a "Benthamite theory of utility" (Bailkin 2004). I would add that all these definitions are highly contested terrain.

Initially, we may say that "cultural property" is both a *discursive register* involving codified rights, enabling and hindering communities and nations to make claims in the name of culture, and an *institution* dedicated to the rights of distribution and allocation of tangibles and intangibles. The question of what "cultural property" might mean in a postcolonial world of 189 nation-states all embedded in a global market economy is to ask important questions about finding legality and morality in the mutually defining nature of culture, capital and colonialism at work in the world today. This is a world where tangible objects have crossed borders as a consequence of warfare, scientific exploration, colonialism and straightforward looting and where knowledge is instantly sampled, transmitted, and downloaded. Given this predicament, perhaps the best place to begin to get a sense of cultural property is through its contemporary contestations.

Setting the Stage: Debates and Debacles

Sampling technologies, both analogue and digital, enables fixation and dissemination of cultural and artistic articulations, far beyond the control of the original performing context. This has produced a number of landmark cases, where ethnographic materials in one form or another have been appropriated, trans-medialized, commercially exploited or "misrepresented" in various ways. The examples are legion, ranging from missionary photographs of Hopi secret-sacred religious ceremonies (Brown 2003) to ethno-musical flute sampling among the Pygmies (Feld 2001), just to name two of the most cited. Within the realm of the Western intellectual property institution, the traditional producers of ethnographic materials are most often not the beneficiaries, due to a number of conceptual and technical issues.

This has led to a policy debate about how best to protect ethnographic materials, or what have been glossed as "traditional cultural expressions" (TCEs), which roughly oscillates between bending existing intellectual property rights to accommodate TCEs or adopt a new *sui generis* form of international instrument intended to provide more adequate protection of TCEs. These debates can be traced back to the conference for revision of the Berne Convention in Stockholm (1967)[2] and continue today in the forum of the WIPO Intergovernmental Committee on Genetic Resources, Traditional Knowledge and Traditional Cultural Expressions/Folklore (2001–). One argument in this debate runs along the lines that the possibilities of existing intellectual property legal systems to accommodate indigenous claims about misappropriations have yet to be fully explored. This line of argument is often made with recourse to Australian case law,[3] where customary laws and fiduciary relationships have been recognized by the courts. The counter-argument claims that intellectual property law is an inherently Western artifact embodying deeply Eurocentric notions of ownership, authorship, and originality, and when put to work on indigenous cultural productions is at best inadequate (Coombe 1998). Many of these critics argue for a *sui generis* system, which fundamentally re-conceives existing concepts of intellectual property such as the public domain, fixation criteria, individual versus collective authorship and the notion of "appropriation" in non-monetary terms.

What underwrites this rather technical policy debate is the often-quoted dictum that the type of cultural products embodied in TCEs is a poor fit for Western intellectual property laws, which was the official reason given for why the revision of the Berne Convention stalled in 1967. Specifically, the criterion of copyrightable subject matter – which generally includes original literary, scientific and artistic works, provided such works are in a permanent tangible expression that can be seen, heard or touched – fits poorly with the nature of TCEs. The four main problems are the following: (i) the criterion of "originality" is often understood in intellectual property law as an independent creation attributable to an identifiable author or authors. This is clearly at odds with TCEs which are often, but not always, expressions of, by, and for collective entities; (ii) the criterion of "permanence" found in many national copyright laws is related to the often-quoted dictum that copyright law does not protect ideas, but the tangible expressions of ideas. TCEs such as dance, ritual performance, oral narrative and other forms of choreographic and verbal art are not intended to be permanent in any tangible medium, thus making a poor fit for those IP laws which require permanence; and (iii) finite duration of protection is a common feature of copyright law. However, with reference to certain sacred and highly sensitive TCEs, protection is sought for in perpetuity; and (iv) conventional copyright law vests the rights with an individual creator, whereas many TCEs are considered to be held by a community, clan, or tribe, without any designated individual ownership. However, thinking through these conundrums between copyright laws and TCEs, one should not forget that intellectual property law often faces similar problems vis-à-vis the subject matter of contemporary conceptual art, where originality, tangibility and authorship are often elusive if not to say evasive.

If we move to the more tangible domain of cultural property, the debacles and conflicts often seem more intractable. Here, a tug-of-war is fought over *location*, along the lines of the inalienability of cultural material from its original context versus comparative contexts in so-called "universal museums." Roughly speaking, the arguments in favor of returning cultural objects to the contemporary descendants of the people who made them run along the lines of what has often been termed "identity politics." The key idea is that many indigenous communities and postcolonial nation-states (often elaborated as "source cultures/first nations" in the debate) have been deprived of a great deal of their culture through imperialism and colonialism. The argument goes that this material needs to be restored to secure cultural memory and ultimately, cultural survival. Running through this justificatory rationale is the assumed inalienability between the original context of the material and contemporary identities, wrongful taking in the acquisition context, and the contemporary need for the material in the name of cultural revitalization and/or the aesthetic integrity of built monuments. This discourse runs jointly with the Herderian idea of the value of particular cultures having "inalienable heritage" and constituting "authentic original contexts." These justificatory rationales resonate with the contemporary discourse on "cultural diversity." At times these justificatory rationales are backed by recourse to fundamental human rights, ideas of distributive justice, "cultural liberation" and the right of diverse societies to observe their own traditional practices and ultimately the survival of cultural identities in a globalized world.

Such claims for culture, writ large, seem to have given birth to a neo-Enlightenment current, boldly phrased in *The Declaration on the Importance and Value of Universal Museums* (2003). Here an argument is made for a very different context from the original *in situ* one, namely a comparative context, where the cultural productions of the whole world are assembled under one roof with public access, allowing all cultures to be represented and placed in meaningful relationships with each other. The key idea is that some 20 "universal museums" in the world – read, in the Occident – with collections considered as "encyclopedic," foster mutual understanding and tolerance between cultures. Or as Anthony Appiah, one of the most cited protagonists of this view, claims: "I like to think of encyclopedic museums as a place in which you can see, say, a Chinese artifact, without being of Chinese origin and think of it for a moment as your own transcending the normal divisions of identity" (Appiah 2006). The justificatory rationale for keeping cultural objects where they reside today in Western metropolises is that here they are held in trust for humankind, enabling the world to think about itself and its diversity in ways not possible elsewhere. This kind of civil space, according to this line of argument, ultimately fosters cultural dialogue and a sense of belonging to the "family of humankind."

Thus, most generally, we may say that the concept and institution of cultural property is highly contested, because cultural property always has something to do with the transgression of borders – be they individual, communal or national. Initially, we may also conclude that physical *location* is paramount in the tangible domain, whereas *reproductions* are tantamount in the intangible realm, which makes intangibles more susceptible to new media technologies.

Four Modes of Thinking Through Cultural Property

If we leave the public debates on cultural property and ask about the conceptual terrain, we primarily encounter topical literatures in folklore, ethnology, anthropology, art history, archeology, legal studies, cultural studies, political science, museology, and so on, more so than bold theoretical attempts to grapple with the issue. The conventional wisdom of topical studies abounds in simple contrasts, such as the ones I have reiterated above for the purpose of introduction and sake of argument: intangible cultural property (IP) versus tangible cultural property (cultural objects/ antiquities), soft law (ethics) versus hard law (codes), historically removed objects versus contemporary illicit trafficking, human remains versus cultural objects, source nations (southern hemisphere) versus market nations (northern hemisphere), cultural property (US) versus cultural heritage (Continental EU), copyright (US) versus *droit d'auteur* (Continental EU), commodification and producers' rights (US) versus public domain/creative commons (Continental EU),[4] and so on. Generally, a closer look into the particulars of each case will reveal that these simple contrasts are much messier, intertwined, and implicated than what is generally held.

Roughly speaking we may identify four major analytical forays to cultural property in the relevant literatures: (i) the first strand draws largely on post-Appadurai inspired material culture studies and hinges on the conceptual register of *reification, objectification*, and *commodification* processes (Miller 2005); (ii) the second approach draws largely on cultural studies and focuses on *the negotiation of ethnic and national identities* coupled with claims for culture writ large; (iii) the third perspective pivots on the conspicuous genealogy of exchange theory in the discipline of anthropology, ultimately aiming at new analytic perspectives on what "property in" persons, things and knowledge might look like from indigenous perspectives; (iv) the fourth is essentially a critical historical perspective on the emergence of "cultural property" as a legal and institutional category in Western liberal democracies and how indigenous/subaltern claims challenges this, drawing on contemporary political theory and postcolonial studies. I shall now briefly present each perspective, although with the caveat that these four perspectives are not clear cut and nicely demarcated in the literature.

Objectifications

Richard Handler's groundbreaking work on cultural property (1985, 1988, 1991, 2004) is one of the most prominent examples offering exhaustive analysis of how things come to represent cultural property, patrimony, or public culture through bureaucratic practice, which he refers to as "objectifying logic." Drawing on folklore, built heritage, and roughly 69 years of cultural property legislation in the province of Quebec (Canada), Handler maps how material artifacts become designated as the nation's "cultural property," linking it to existential legitimacy: "a group's existence as a unique individual is believed to rest upon its undisputed possession of property, and that property often comes in the form of historically significant objects" (Handler 1991: 67). Probing what exactly enables this objectifying logic, Handler argues that the bureaucratic expansion of the culture concept – a concept shaped by modern anthropological notions of culture as bounded, internally homogenous, territorial, and representative of a total way of life is precisely what enables this reification.

How does Handler then understand claims to cultural property? He maintains that disputes come into play when "a self-conscious national or ethnic group will claim possession of cultural properties as both representative and constitutive of cultural identity" (Handler 1985: 211). He reads the response to such claims through the prism of an "objectifying logic" and asserts that the nation will guard its possessions from other collective individuals through bureaucratic practices: "As the Quebec case shows, to do this entails inventory, acquisition, and enclosure" (Handler 1985: 214). Ultimately, he expands his argument about the objectifying logic – the idea that objects represent culture on a one-to-one basis – to encompass the whole world: "Yet despite often bitter disagreements, the disputants in contemporary 'culture wars' share an understanding of what cultural property is; that is, all disputants – current, would-be, and former imperialists, as well as oppressed minorities, ex-colonies, and aspiring new nations – have agreed to a worldview in which culture has come to be represented as and by 'things'" (1985: 215).

Amiria Henare (2005a, b) represents the latest and most congenial attempts to promote Handler's argument about our understanding of material objects in public institutions such as museums. Seeking to understand indigenous cultural property claims, Henare discards such claims as "cultural fundamentalism" or "strategic essentialism" defined as "neo-traditionalization crafting commensurability out of political expedience and instrumentality" (Henare 2006). Instead, she argues that: "all the things claimed in Wai 262, including genetic resources, are claimed as *taonga*, a concept often glossed as 'treasured ancestral possessions,' but which, I suggest, may be understood as particular kinds of objectifications" (Henare 2006). Another key example of post-Appadurai inspired material culture studies of cultural property is Fred Myers' extensive work on the ways in which Pintupi painters' production of acrylic paintings is translated into exchangeable values ("dots for dollars") as these objects move outward from Aboriginal communities through art dealers, governmental art administrators, up-market galleries, auction houses, museums, international traveling exhibitions and the circles of art critics (Myers 2002). Myers' broader question revolves around understanding how acrylic paintings became Aboriginal High Art in more surprising, unexpected, and ethnographic "denser" ways than the one-sided story of commoditization. Within this larger picture, Myers largely understands indigenous cultural property claims in terms of materiality or in his own words: "a renegotiation of the boundaries of indigenous and other identities largely through the materiality [*in which*] the recognition of Aboriginal objects as art is a material practice" (Myers 2005: 106–110). Thus, from the perspective of materiality, claims are largely seen as the effect of the efficacy of objects.

This perspective leads to the key question whether materiality is consequential for transactions in cultural property. Since the late 1980s, Western institutions have much more readily relinquished human remains than cultural objects – a fact which seems to support the argument that the nature of materiality matters.[5] However, there is a wide-ranging debate as to whether human remains fall under the category of "cultural property." In common law, for example, human bones are not recognized as property. Generally, the perspective on materiality and material practices has yielded productive understandings of cultural property through the concepts of appropriations, (in)-alienability, objectification, subjectification, reification, commoditization and the currency and convertibility of value registers; all important in their own right, but also by now perhaps fairly well understood. Moreover, if we, like Henare, understand cultural property claims as particular forms of objectification, we may lose sight of the fact that cultural property claims begin, if anywhere, in the mail. That is, indigenous property claims are also written texts most often addressed to metropolitan property regimes.

Identities

As we have seen, the notion that material objects can be constitutive of cultural identity formation and thus inalienably forms a leitmotif in the policy debate, but also figures in much contemporary academic thinking about cultural property. Among the key examples of this perspective is Moira Simpson who framed the problem of cultural property as an issue of museum management and the politics of representation: "One of the most difficult issues seeking resolution by museums in the postcolonial era is that of repatriation ... As a result, curatorial staff are re-examining museological practices and their rights ... they are having to address questions of ownership, care, display, and interpretation" (Simpson 1996). Simpson's understanding of these issues were based on cultural continuity and essentialisms: "... the cultures did not die: they live and thrive today and their people seek the return of objects which are symbols of cultural identity and survival, potent and necessary ceremonial items and resources for teaching the young and ensuring cultural continuity" (Simpson 1996: 246). Generally, Simpson advocated repatriation as a mean to restore and revitalize cultural identities wounded by colonialism. Through her work with indigenous groups such as the Blackfeet in Canada, she demonstrated the positive effects of repatriation of tangible and intangible culture on the vitality and well-being of an indigenous community.

Thus, she urged institutions to become "context and people-focused museums, instead of object-focused" (Simpson 1996: 266).

This mode of thinking about cultural property as material objects, which are vested with cultural identity whose absence causes loss and anguish in the "source communities" continues to be rehearsed. Christina F. Kreps' work *Liberating Culture* (2003) is more encompassing in geographical scope than Simpson's, but the thrust of her thinking about the problem of cultural property unfolds in the same way: "I have shown how certain forms of cultural property, such as sacred and ceremonial objects, have been essential means of cultural transmission and thus necessary for the perpetuation of cultural traditions, and in turn, cultural heritage preservation. A deeper understanding of the power and meaning certain objects hold for their cultures of origin bolsters native peoples' requests for the repatriation of these materials" (Kreps 2003: 89). Here again, material objects are seen as constitutive of cultural identity, which ultimately brings Kreps to advocate repatriation in the name of humanity: "Indeed, in their struggles for cultural restitution, Native Americans and other indigenous peoples are reclaiming the spirit of culture, not only for themselves but for us all, by helping move a seemingly dispassionate science and society toward a renewed sense of humanity" (Kreps 2003: 113).

The philosopher and cultural studies scholar Elizabeth Burns Coleman subscribes to the same notion of objects as constitutive of cultural identity, set within an explicit normative framework. She does not set out to understand Aboriginal claims. Instead she is interested in the problem of how to evaluate them: "I will explore whether the claims made about identity and intellectual property are ambit claims made with a political agenda of power redistribution in postcolonial Australia, or claims with which we can fully agree as necessary changes to the law in the interests of 'justice'" (Coleman 2005: 9). Her basic argument is that if Aboriginal claims are "true" then "we are faced with a moral dilemma," and it follows that if "we" strengthen cultural property protection through laws then "we undermine our own cultural traditions." On the other hand, if weakened "we would destroy Aboriginal cultures" (Coleman 2005: 12). Coleman's book strongly advocates the first position, which she justifies with a premise about three modalities of the relationship between Aboriginal art and identity: "'essential to', or 'constitutive of' or 'expressive of' the identity of the group" (Coleman 2004). From this premise Coleman deduces that "the appropriation of Aboriginal art will result in the destruction of Aboriginal cultures" which is how she justifies that "copyright should be extended to protect it," taking for granted that common property law always protect Aboriginal interests (Coleman 2005).

What is notable in Simpson's, Kreps's, and Coleman's reasoning about cultural property are the assumptions about the inalienability of things in indigenous contexts and the assumptions about dying cultures if cultural property is alienated. These scholars have simply not addressed the complexities of "cultural property" from the perspective of genuine fieldwork experiences in and from such "cultures" and they have bracketed the predicaments of the culture concept, which Handler labored hard to overcome or reconcile. Moreover, they situate their work explicitly within a normative horizon, which conflates (even collapses) the distinction between *is* and *ought* and between *fact* and *norm*; that is in this case between analytic framework and policy recommendations. This is a larger problem, which no academic inquiry into cultural property can escape. However, these three scholars never seem explicitly to bother about or reflect upon the implications of critical and analytical understandings of cultural property versus evaluative assessments.

The general drift of this mode of thinking about cultural property is the conception of material objects as constitutive of cultural identities, expressive of cultural ethos, and inalienable from their place of origin or "source community." This key idea is nicely epitomized by the archeologist Claire Lyons: "through inexplicable chemistry, artworks, religious icons, monuments, literary manuscripts, traditional myths, and rituals hold the power to create a profound sense of belonging" (Lyons 2002: 187). Consequently, the loss or absence of such "material expressions" causes suffering, trauma, memory loss and prevents the society from flourishing and developing. Thus, this mode of thinking is treating the removal of objects as a kind of identity theft and the notion of "cultural property" which is mobilized depends on "culture" being just the thing the monograph genre in anthropology thought it was: uniform, internally consistent, complete in and by itself. Political philosopher Patchen Markell got this right: "A right to one's own culture, it seems, depends on culture being just the sort of thing Herder and the anthropologists had thought" (Markell 2003).

Transactions

The idea that indigenous notions of "cultural property" might be very different from those inscribed in Euro-American codes and institutions represents an important body of work conducted by a number of British social-anthropologists based at Cambridge University. These scholars have conducted long-term fieldwork on Massim exchange and generally conceive their work on cultural property as being situated "on the periphery of international debate, but at the heart of how people in Papua New Guinea negotiate claims" (Strathern 2004: 85). Along with members of her Papua New Guinea [PNG] research team, *Property, Transactions and Creations*, Strathern primarily addresses the language of international regimes of intellectual property (IPR), challenging the inherent assumptions about creativity as a communal or collective resource in these property regimes. Generally speaking, the drift of her main argument is that the notion of cultural property inherent in this language is conceived as a Euro-American alternative to private property, which does not have any bearing on the forms of property we might find in PNG. That is, the regimes and institutions of IPR amount to a form of *Orientalism*, which does not capture how Melanesians conceive transactions in property. The interests of the PNG research team revolve around social ontologies of property in Melanesia, where "cultural property" is understood as a claim made upon other persons, not material objects: "The genius of Papua New Guinean practice is that, by locking transactions into the values they have for social relationships, people are not constrained by the nature or materiality of the items themselves" (Strathern 2004: 87).

In fact, Strathern's PNG ethnography leaves her to argue that people have no direct relations with material objects and such relations are always socially mediated. This makes the concepts surveyed previously, such as objectification, reification, appropriation or even inalienability are rather alien in her work: "Inalienability signifies the absence of a property relation. Rather than talking about "inalienable property," I prefer to sustain the systemic contrast. Persons simply do not have alienable items, that is, property, at their disposal; they can only dispose of items by binding themselves in relations with others" (Strathern 1988). Thus, objects and knowledge are not alienated, but transacted according to value conversions, which bind social assemblages. This implicates that Strathern's project is about explicating the social ontologies of the ways in which objects and knowledge are held and transacted in PNG, which often seem incommensurable with Euro-American ways. This brings us back to the conundrums sketched at the outset: "The problem remains: how can anthropologists assist in the formation of legal provisions that recognize the fundamentally social basis of cultural property?" (Sykes 2004: 200). Sykes answers this question through an analysis of Malanggan art carvings on display in the Kavieng International Airport (New Ireland, Papua New Guinea): "The protection of cultural property entails living with an apparent contradiction; that is, if you know who you are in relation to the rest of the people who dreamed, carved, painted, enchanted and displayed it, then you are free to gaze at it. When someone looks intelligently at cultural property in New Ireland, they preserve it as a form of social and cultural life" (Sykes 2004: 203). Thus, we do seem to have a perspective "at the margins of the international debates, but at the heart of how Melanesians navigate the issue of 'cultural property'."

To a large extent, this perspective resonates with the cluster of published indigenous narratives of the institution of cultural property, which generally infers that repatriated objects are somehow embedded in social agency: "In earlier days, people were sometimes taken by raiding parties. When they returned to their homes, either through payment of ransom or by retaliatory raid, they were said to have '*u'mista*.' The return of our treasures from distant museums is a form of *u'mista*" (*u'mista* 2006). Thus, the return of objects is here conceived as a form of distributed personhood (collective, ancestral, and essentially political in tone) and *u'mista* becomes a perfect native gloss for cultural property. In conclusion, Strathern's analytic approach seems to lend itself well to the explanation of indigenous modes of understanding "cultural property." However, being excessively preoccupied with socializing the relations between persons understood as social assemblages mediated by exchange, this perspective may be of limited use in understanding the more comprehensive aspects of large-scale cross-cultural phenomena, which stretch far beyond the social-relational matrix in Mount Hagen. For a more comprehensive framework, we need to move from the lateral thinking of ethnography to larger epochal shifts and extend the analysis to meta-narratives of colonialisms and modernities.

Trajectories

When and how did "cultural property" come into being as a textual invention with discursive implications? Such questions interrogate cultural property as a fulcrum for the intersection of law, power, and capital in world historical time – a perspective which invites conjectures about the making of cultural property as a by-product of modernity writ large. Such a perspective is largely entertained in Rosemary Coombe's extensive work (1998). Coombe explores the ways in which "subaltern groups" use texts, celebrity images, trademarks, commercial brands, insignia and logos to produce identities in what she calls "media-saturated consumer societies." Coombe's master stroke is a comprehensive notion of "cultural appropriation" defined as: "the taking from a culture that is not one's own of intellectual property, cultural expressions or artifacts, history and ways of knowledge" (Coombe 1998: 6). She frames the legacies of this "cultural appropriation" within a postcolonial framework, asserting that "the West has created categories of property – intellectual property, cultural property, and real property – that divide peoples and things according to the same colonizing discourses of possessive individualism that historically disentitled and disenfranchised Native peoples in North America" (Coombe 1998: 86). Her argument that colonial residues inform cultural property laws, which orientalize others implicates that Native peoples are forced to articulate their claims in a legal language which separates the oral from the written, the intangible from tangible, and the idea from material expression: "... ripping asunder what many First Nations people view as integrally related, freezing into categories what Native peoples find flowing in relationships" (Coombe 1998: 92–93). Briefly, in mounting claims, native peoples are forced to use categories that are antithetical to their needs and foreign to their aspirations. Thus, Coombe's thinking opens up much broader questions about the legitimacy of the postcolonial state and whether law holds a redemptive status in postcolonial contexts.

The assumption that cultural property is a product of colonialism is challenged and revised in Bailkin's work (2004), which pursues a "prehistory of cultural property, that is, of the legal category of cultural property that emerged at The Hague in 1954 and has shaped the rules of circulation and exchange ever since" (Bailkin 2004: 7). Accordingly, it is anachronistic to describe objects as cultural property before the mid-twentieth century. Drawing on detailed case material from and Britain and Ireland, Bailkin further contends that the institutional practice of repatriation did not emerge as "a method of postcolonial resistance," but "in fact originated as the product of nineteenth- and twentieth-century colonial engagement" (Bailkin 2004: 23–24). Contrary to most scholars, who see the emergence of cultural property and the repatriation movement as an epochal shift, Bailkin argues that "the return of cultural objects cannot always be read as a reversal of colonial relations" (Bailkin 2004: 209), and that acts of repatriation "historically speaking, have been one way of keeping things very much the same" (Bailkin 2004: 77). However, there are some important caveats to this revision. First, Bailkin does admit a conjuncture or a co-presence – not a causality – between cultural property and postcolonialism: "From a global perspective, there has been an explosion of protective cultural property legislation following termination of colonial status and the inauguration of modern sovereignty in Africa, Southeast Asia, South America, and the Pacific" (Bailkin 2004: 32–33). Moreover, in tracking the concept of cultural property behind the Hague Convention of 1954 to the Congress of Vienna in 1815 (which included a special clause devised by Lord Castlereagh to ensure that the art objects looted by Napoleon were returned) Bailkin emphasizes "that these objects were returned not to the source nations that had originally produced them, but to the European museums from which they had been looted most recently." In this sense, Bailkin's perspective is not postcolonial, but develops around different models of British nationalism and post-nationalism (1870s–1914). In fact, Bailkin traces the beginning of the prehistory of cultural property to "the Liberal crisis in Britain [which] produced a new conceptualization of culture and property," where "cultural property represented the meeting point of Liberalism's individualist past and its collectivist future."

Elazar Barkan, Professor of History and Cultural Studies at Columbia's SIPA school, largely concurs with Bailkin's "pre-history" of cultural property, albeit with a couple of modifications. Like Bailkin, Barkan also tracks the emergence of cultural property to post-Napoleonic Europe, where its "national character" and "geographical distribution principle" was being invented in front of Parisian eyes (Barkan 2002). However, Barkan notes that while the Congress of Vienna experimented with restitutions to Prussia, the Vatican, Venice, and the Netherlands, artifacts from the rest of the world were being appropriated, removed, and dislocated as a product of European imperialism and colonialism. Roughly, Barkan argues that the return of cultural objects has two phases: first, in the aftermath of World War II (1946–), and second, in the aftermath of colonialism (1960s–). Generally, Barkan historicizes the concept of cultural property and shows how it swings from universalism to particularism within a broad philosophy of history. According to him, the concept was coined by the universalism of the Hague Convention of 1954, but with the UNESCO 1970 Convention it became increasingly national and its particularistic accent peaked in the 1980s, which marked "a watershed in the international community's attitude to the question of universalism and particularism" (Barkan 2002: 25–26). From the mid-1990s, the legal regime UNIDROIT came to embody "a global view of justice that places objects not with the collector but with the originator" (Barkan 2002: 26). However, the contemporary triumph of particularism over universalism "comes to a halt when faced with the risk of the destruction of world treasures" like the Bamiyan Buddhas in Afghanistan. In this trajectory, Barkan identifies a "neo-Enlightenment global doctrine," which he claims has replaced the "might makes right" of imperial and colonial times with new forms of collective rights (Barkan 2002: 37–38).

What Barkan tracks as a swing from universalism to particularism is registered as a shift from "cultural Darwinism" to "cultural diversity" in Ana Filipa Vrdoljak's major study (2006). As a legal scholar, she seeks to extrapolate from a large case material what the doctrine might look like. She identifies three distinct rationales for restitution: first, the "sacred property" principle; namely the link between territoriality, people, and cultural objects, which was established at the Congress of Vienna (1815), embodied in Lord Castlereagh's referral to the spoliations of Napoleon as the "title deeds of the countries which have been given up" (Vrdoljak 2006); and second, the righting of past wrongs, including the reversal or amelioration of discriminatory and genocidal practices. Vrdoljak tracks this rationale back to the allied restitution program following World War II and specifically post-Holocaust claims, which "has led to a growing appreciation that restitution includes moral restitution that is accomplished by confronting the past honestly and internalizing its lessons" (Vrdoljak 2006: 3). Finally there is the the right of every people to self-determination, which includes the return of land, ancestral remains, traditional knowledge and "cultural objects held by the museums of former metropolitan and national capitals [which constitute] an essential component of a people's ability to maintain, revitalise and develop their collective cultural identity" (Vrdoljak 2006: 300). Vrdoljak argues that this principle emerged from the claims pursued by newly independent states and indigenous peoples during the decolonization period onward, and that it integrates the two former rationales. The common denominator for all three rationales is "the requirement that the holding parties' confront the past honestly" (Vrdoljak 2006: 300) and the unifying purpose of them is to ensure the "continuing contribution of a people and their culture – not cultural objects *per se* – to the cultural heritage of all humankind" (Vrdoljak 2006). The normative question that drives the explanation is why these rationales have not been extended to postcolonial states and indigenous peoples on a broader international scale, when "the removal of these cultural objects represented the dispossession of their [*colonized peoples*] lands, autonomy and identity" (Vrdoljak 2006: 299). Vrdoljak argues that the principle which most importantly has led to the retention of cultural objects by metropolitan powers following decolonization is "the ascendancy of the State as the exclusive subject of international law," and secondary what she calls a "cult of forgetfulness," namely colonial amnesia. Thus, like Barkan, Vrdoljak also argues that the non-recognition of indigenous claims to cultural property in the international arena is a core problem.

More generally, what do we know about the trajectories of cultural property? Historical work has focused on the birth of modern nationalism, cultural property, and patrimony in post-revolutionary France (Furet 1997; Héritier 2003; Merryman 2000; Merryman and Elsen 2002; Savoy 2003). Of central importance here, is Dominique Poulot's analysis of the Louvre as a radical critique of royalist notions of patrimony and the "inconclusive conclusion" (Merryman 2001) reached through the partial restitutions at the Congress of Vienna (1815) and the purchase of the Parthenon sculptures by the British government (1816). We know that the formal legal definition of cultural property came into existence with the 1954 Hague Convention, which differs significantly from the one given at the 1970 UNESCO convention (Merryman 1986). We know that the emergence of postcolonialism in the second part of the twentieth century, implicated the ascendency of new rights holders in the shape of the third and fourth worlds, although national claims from former colonized states have been few and claims by the fourth world are currently not recognized in the international arena. In the intangible domain, Bolivia's official appeal to UNESCO's Director-General in 1973 for an international intellectual property instrument preventing misappropriations of expressions of folklore is generally seen as a postcolonial critique crafted in the aftermath of Simon and Garfunkel's appropriation of the Andean folksong *El Cóndor Pasa* which featured in their album *Bridge over Troubled Waters* (1970). We know that in the 1980s and 1990s a number of "settler nations" such as Canada, the United States, Australia and New Zealand implemented ethical or legislative frameworks for repatriation vis-à-vis their indigenous inhabitants. This is the rough outline of the state of knowledge on the trajectories of cultural property in which of course the local agency has lost sight of.

To sum up the question of how the literatures have understood claims for cultural property and their responses: Handler understood claims for cultural property as expressions of essentialism and reification but Coleman regarded them as either fabricated and instrumental to identity politics or authentic, genuine and primordial. Simpson saw them as revitalizing and healing the "wounds of colonialism" and Kreps conceived them as emancipative and "humane." Kuper (2003) believed they were as articulations of nativism but Coombe suggested thinking through this question in the broad terms of shifting identifications of mimesis and alterity, contributing to understanding claims as indigenous quests for alternative modernities. Stuart Kirsch (2001) and James Weiner (1999) have generally argued that the institutionalization and codification of the forums through which restitution claims for alienated property are forwarded "influence the form and content of the claims that are advanced" (Kirsch 2006: 128). Most generally, contemporary political theory has conceived cultural property claims as challenging the idea of free exchange and access and consequently cast the central question as one of how to accommodate indigenous collective claims without compromising the idea of the public domain constitutive of Western liberal democracies. However, as we have seen, the perspective of transactions has labored to show that this is in fact a pseudo-question, without much ethnographic backing, at least in Melanesia.

I would argue along with Coombes, Weiner, and Kirsch that claims cannot be read independently from the regimes they address. Claimant and keeper represent two sides of a transaction between – in postcolonial contexts – a subaltern and a metropolis. Thus, a more compelling question would be to investigate the links, if any, between subaltern claims and metropolitan regimes. We may ask in what ways metropolitan regimes enable or disenable the emergence and articulation of subaltern claims in particular settings. Are claims forged independently or mimetically of regimes? Do metropolitan regimes enable claims to be realized in resistance to their own discursive field? Or do regimes force claimants to articulate their culture in ways alienable to them, violating their cultural integrity? These are the key questions on the relationship between creative agency and discursive regimes, which remain largely unanswered by the surveyed literatures.

THE CUNNING OF CULTURAL PROPERTY

If we return to the outset and the Crystal Mountains in Gabon, the ownership issues raised by the mvett bard were different from the ones Barre Toelken (1998) set out in his seminal essay on the Yellowman Tapes, although his questions seem pertinent: Would it make sense to ship the mvett recordings back to Gabon? And where is Fang culture after all? Is it in my recordings and transcriptions of the mvett epic or in the performative context of the aba'a? Contrary to Toelken's relationship with the Navaho, the mvett bard had sought the anthropologist out, believing that the mvett epic was a master narrative for what he called "Bantu Africa *en pair* with the Bhagavad Gita (sic), the Koran, the Talmud, or the Bible" (Skrydstrup 2000) which deserved much wider dissemination and recognition. The bard saw the anthropologist as a vehicle to achieve that recognition. However, that is not to say that mvett epics cannot be owned, like some stories can be personal or family property in Tlingit (World 2005; Dauenhauer and Dauenhauer 1987: 24–29; Farrer 1994: 321–322). In fact, according to the bard, a French ethno-musicologist had recorded an mvett epic of his father (ritual initiator) in the 1970s, which had seriously violated Fang rules of intellectual proprietorship. As in Toelken's case, the bard's primary concern was not "ownership, sovereignty, or hegemonic control" of recordings and texts, nor was it "prudent husbandry of potentially dangerous spoken words"; rather, it was a concern about not suffering the same destiny as his father, where an epic of his craft and imagination had been transferred to a different medium, beyond his control. The bard I was working with saw the epic he gave me about the secret mission of Mvé Ndong as a teaser to attract commercial interest and the outcome of our encounter was an entry in my field notes stating that: "the bard had given his personal experiences with the mvett to the anthropologist in good faith and consent."[6] However, if the bard's team had included an attorney, I doubt that this encounter would have produced a similar ad hoc practical result.

NOTES

1   In colonial times these were referred to as the "palaber house," but, in fact, the meeting of the council of men took place in a traditional Fang village.

2   The Diplomatic Conference in Stockholm for the revision of the Berne Convention for the Protection of Literary and Artistic Works was convened in 1967. The Delegates found themselves unable to draft elaborate legal principles for folklore protection, referring to the conceptual and definitional difficulties of this topic. The only legislative trace of their attempt is article 15(4)(a) of the Berne Convention (added in the Stockholm and Paris Acts of 1967 and 1971), which provides a possibility for the international protection of "unpublished works where the identity of the author is unknown, but where there is every reason to presume that he is a national of a country of the Union." In such cases, national legislation may designate the competent authority to represent the unidentified author.

3   In the case *Milpurrurru v. Indofurn Pry Ltd.* (1994), Aboriginal artists sued to prevent the import of carpets with prominent aboriginal designs reproduced without the permission from the artists from Vietnam to Australia. In its decision, the federal court awarded the Aboriginal artists substantial damages for infringement of copyright. Although its wording is strong, this decision ultimately rested on traditional copyright law and compensated only the individual artists, not the larger community. In a similar case, *Bulun Bulun and Anor v. R and T Textiles Pty Ltd.* (1998), the Aboriginal artist John Bulun argued that his painting *Magpie Geese and Waterlilies at the Waterhole* (1980/Natural pigments on bark) represented the principal totem for his clan and that unauthorized reproduction threatened the coherence and survival of his society by interfering with the relationship between the Ganalbingu people, their ancestors, and the land given to them. The court decided that a fiduciary relationship did exist between the plaintiff and the Ganalbingu people, preventing the claimant from exploiting his artistic work contrary to customary laws. However, the Court dismissed the action, ruling that the Ganalbingu people had no "collective rights" under Australian law, but that the claimant had a personal right to enforce his copyright against third party infringers, in which he had already prevailed. This case confirmed the precedent established in *Yumbulul v. Reserve Bank of Australia* (1991), where the claim of communal harm caused by the unauthorized use of sacred images also was rejected.

4   Briefly and very simplified, Anglo-American laws define copyright as a "property right" which can be "freely traded" (the alienability of the copyright interest). In this context, "free trade" means that the transfer of rights is governed only by economic power. Mainland European law, in general, talks about "authors' rights" and "moral rights" – essentially a translation of the French *droit d'auteur* and its subdivision *droit moral* – and see these as personal rights which are to some extent "inalienable." "Authors' rights," that is, present a somewhat different legal philosophy to "copyright."

5   Scores of case studies speak to this, such as Sarah Bartman, Namibia El Negro, and so on.

6   The actual entry goes like this: "Je reconnais avoir travaillé, donné mon experience personelle à Monsieur Martin Skrydstrup afin de reussir dans ses recherches sur le monde du Mvett, je l'ai fait avec ma bonne fois et ma propre volonté" (fieldnotes).

REFERENCES

Appiah, A. 2006. "Whose Culture Is It?" *New York Review of Books* LIII(2) (February 9): 38–41.

Bailkin, J. 2004. *The Culture of Property: The Crisis of Liberalism in Modern Britain.* Chicago: University of Chicago Press.

Barkan, E. 2002. "Amending Historical Injustices: The Restitution of Cultural Property – An Overview" in E. Barkan and R. Bush, Eds. *Claiming the Stones – Naming the Bones: Cultural Property and the Negotiation of National and Ethnic*

Identity. Los Angeles: Getty Publications, pp. 16–46.

Brown, M.F. 2003. *Who Owns Native Culture?* Cambridge, MA: Harvard University Press.

Coleman, E.B. 2004. "Aboriginal Art and Identity: Crossing the Borders of Law's Imagination." *Journal of Political Philosophy* 12(1): 20–40.

Coleman, E.B. 2005. *Aboriginal Art, Identity and Appropriation.* Aldershot, UK: Ashgate.

Coombe, R.J. 1998. *The Cultural Life of Intellectual Properties: Authorship, Appropriation, and the Law.* Durham, NC: Duke University Press.

Dauenhauer, N.M. and R. Dauenhauer. 1987. *Haa Shuka, Our Ancestors: Tlingit Oral Narratives.* Seattle: University of Washington Press.

Farrer, C. 1994. "Who Owns the Words? An Anthropologist's Perspective." *Journal of Arts Management, Law, and Society* 23: 317–326.

Feld, Steven. 1994. "From Schizophonia to Schismogenesis: On the Discourses and Commodification Practices of 'World Music' and 'World Beat'" in Charles Keil and Stephen Feld, Eds. *Music Grooves: Essays and Dialogues.* Chicago: University of Chicago Press.

Furet, F. Ed. 1997. *Patrimoine, temps, espace: patrimoine en place, patrimoine déplacé.* Paris: Fayard.

Handler, R. 1988. *Nationalism and the Politics of Culture in Quebec.* Madison: University of Wisconsin Press.

Handler, R. 2003. "Cultural Property and Culture Theory." *Journal of Social Archaeology* 3(3): 353–365.

Henare, A. 2005a. *Museums, Anthropology and Imperial Exchange.* Cambridge: Cambridge University Press.

Henare. 2005b. "Wai 262: A Maori 'Cultural Property' Claim" in B. Latour and P. Weibel, Eds. *Making Things Public: Atmospheres of Democracy.* Cambridge, MA: MIT Press, pp. 64–69.

Héritier, A. 2003. *Genèse de la notion juridique de patrimoine culturel, 1750–1816.* Paris: L'Harmattan.

Kirsch, S. 2006. *Reverse Anthropology: Indigenous Analysis of Social and Environmental Relations in New Guinea.* Palo Alto: Stanford University Press.

Kirsch, S. 2001. "Lost Worlds: Environmental Disaster, 'Cultural Loss' and the Law." *Current Anthropology* 42(2): 167–198.

Kreps, C. 2003. *Liberating Culture: Cross-cultural Perspectives on Museums, Curation, and Heritage Preservation.* London: Routledge.

Kuper, A. 2003. "The Return of the Native." *Current Anthropology* 44(3): 389–402.

Lyons, C. 2002. "Objects and Identities: Claiming and Reclaiming the Past" in E. Barkan and R. Bush, Eds. *Claiming the Stones/Naming the Bones: Cultural Property and The Negotiation of National and Ethnic Identity.* Los Angeles: Getty Research Institute.

Markell, P. 2003. *Bound by Recognition.* Princeton, NJ: Princeton University Press.

M'Bow, A.-M. 1979. "A Plea for the Return of an Irreplaceable Cultural Heritage to Those Who Created It." *Museum* XXXI: 58.

Merryman, J.H. 1986. "Two Ways of Thinking about Cultural Property." *American Journal of International Law* 80: 831–853.

Merryman, J.H. 2000. *Thinking About the Elgin Marbles: Critical Essays on Cultural Property, Art, and Law.* The Hague: Kluwer Law International.

Merryman, J.H. and A.E. Elsen. 2002. *Law, Ethics, and the Visual Arts.* London: Kluwer Law International.

Miller, D., Eds. 2005. *Materiality.* Durham, NC: Duke University Press.

Myers, F. 2002. *Painting Culture: The Making of an Aboriginal High Art.* Durham, NC: Duke University Press.

Myers, F. 2005. "Some Properties of Art and Culture" in D. Miller, Ed. *Materiality.* Durham, NC: Duke University Press.

Savoy, B. 2003. *Patrimoine annexé: Les biens culturels saisis par la France en Allemagne autour de 1800.* Paris: Maison des sciences de l'homme.

Simpson, M.G. 1996. *Making Representations: Museums in the Post-Colonial Era.* London: Routledge.

Skrydstrup, M. 2000. "The Global Horizon of Local Tradition: The Mwett Harp Zither of the Fang in Gabon." *Thesis series* 178. Copenhagen: Department of Anthropology, University of Copenhagen.

Strathern, M. 1988. *The Gender of the Gift: Problems with Women and Problems with Society in Melanesia.* Berkeley: University of California Press.

Strathern, M. 2004. "Transactions: an Analytical Foray" in E. Hirsch and M. Strathern, Eds. *Transactions and Creations: Property Debates and the Stimulus of Melanesia.* Oxford: Berghahn Books, pp. 85–109.

Sykes, K. 2004. "Negotiating Interests in Culture" in E. Hirsch and M. Strathern, Eds. *Transactions and Creations: Property Debates and the Stimulus of Melanesia.* Oxford: Berghahn Books, pp. 132–148.

Toelken, B. 1998. "The Yellowman Tapes, 1966–1997." *The Journal of American Folklore* 111 (442): 381–391.

U'mista Cultural Society, http://www.umista. org/ (accessed October 16, 2011).

UNESCO. 1978. "Statutes of the Inter-governmental Committee for Promoting the Return of Cultural Property to its Countries of Origin or its Restitution in case of Illicit Appropriation." Resolution 4/7.6/S of the Twentieth Session of the General Conference of UNESCO.

Vrdoljak, A.F. 2006. *International Law, Museums and the Return of Cultural Objects.* Cambridge: Cambridge University Press.

Weiner, J. 1999. "Culture in a Sealed Envelope: The Concealment of Australian Aboriginal Heritage and Tradition in the Hindmarsh Island Bridge affair." *Journal of the Royal Anthropological Institute* 5(2): 199.

FURTHER READING

Coombe, R.J. 2003. "Works in Progress: Traditional Knowledge, Biological Diversity, and Intellectual Property in a Neoliberal Era" in R.W. Perry and B. Maurer, Eds. *Globalization under Construction: Governmentality, Law and Identity.* Minneapolis: University of Minnesota Press, pp. 273–314.

Fforde, C., J. Hubert, and P. Turnbull Eds. 2002. *The Dead and Their Possessions: Repatriation in Principle, Policy, and Practice.* London: Routledge.

Greenfield, J. 1996. *The Return of Cultural Treasures.* 2nd edition. Cambridge: Cambridge University Press.

Skrydstrup, M. 2009. "Theorizing Repatriation." *Ethnologia Europaea. Journal of European Ethnology* 39(2): 54–66.

Skrydstrup, M. 2010. "Once Ours: The Making and Unmaking of Claims to Cultural Property" (Unpublished PhD dissertation), Columbia University.

Tapsell, P. 2000. *Pukaki – A Comet Returns.* Auckland: Reed Books.

Ziff, B.H. and P.V. Rao, Eds. 1997. "Introduction to Cultural Appropriation: A Framework for Analysis" in *Borrowed Power: Essays on Cultural Appropriation.* New Brunswick, NJ: Rutgers University Press, pp. 1–27.

CHAPTER 28

FOLKLORE: LEGAL AND CONSTITUTIONAL POWER

Alison Dundes Renteln

Introduction: The Intersection Between Folklore and Law

Of the hundreds of genres in the field of folkloristics, folk law is one of the most fascinating. It concerns not only the rules by which folk groups operate, but also the rituals, symbols, and disputes that influence their group identities. In this chapter I discuss the status of folk law as a distinct intellectual enterprise, the role of folklorists and folklore in legal processes, and national and international attempts to regulate folklore. Some of the most interesting questions arise when there is tension between folk law systems and the legal systems that operate at the level of the state. The manner in which folk law is adjudicated in national institutions established in accordance with constitutional mandates is often a question of legal pluralism, that is, the existence of multiple legal systems within the same territory (Griffiths 1986; Hooker 1975; Sheleff 1999). The difficulties associated with the simultaneous functioning of multiple legal orders within a single geographical area have important implications for the enduring nature of folk law (Chiba 1989). Ultimately, the stature of folk law as a discipline may depend on the willingness of international institutions to create innovative mechanisms to ensure its continuation.

Distinct Concepts

Before embarking on a consideration of folk law in national and international contexts, a basic definition may be instructive. Folk law refers to the socially defined institutionalized norms by which groups operate. An overview of the field begins with the following formulation: "Folk law is a socially defined group's orally transmitted traditional body of obligations and prohibitions, sanctioned or required by that group, binding upon individuals or subsets of individuals (e.g., families, clans) under pain of punishment or forfeiture" (Renteln and Dundes 1994: xiii). As with all forms of folklore, two requirements must be met: there must be both multiple existence and variation.

Although there is a tendency to treat folk law as though it is necessarily "unwritten" law, this is a somewhat misleading definition because it is ultimately written down, whether by judges in court cases, by jurists in treatises, or by legislatures in statutes when it is permitted or prohibited. Hence, folk law is sometimes found in written form, and there have been famous historical attempts to codify folk law (Renteln and Dundes 1994: 483–597). The desire for certainty in legal standards has led many societies to compile codes incorporating customary law norms, for example, the Assyrian Code of Hammurabi, the Greek Codes of Draco and Solon, the Twelve Tables of Rome, Justinian's Code, and the Napoleonic Code. These codes incorporated customs existing during their respective eras. There are remarkably similar notions reflected in some of them, for example, the various penalties assigned to the owner of a goring ox, namely an ox who killed another ox or a human being (Goetze 1994; Yaron 1966). This scholarship demonstrates that customary law was important in antiquity and other historical eras.

With regard to modern legal systems, some maintain that the common law is itself a form of customary law (Simpson 1994). There is no question that some of the most significant legal principles in Anglo-American jurisprudence such as the right to privacy are not written in the US Constitution and Bill of Rights. Furthermore, the foundation of landmark decisions may be legal maxims. These may take the form of legal proverbs such as "a man's home is his castle" which is cited in landmark United States Supreme Court cases such as *Stanley v. Georgia* (1969) (Taylor 1965–1966). Judicial systems in other countries also invoke proverbs to justify their holdings (Messenger 1994).

Folk law includes common practices such as shaking hands after a bargain has been struck and swearing of oaths to ensure truth-telling, for example, on a Bible. Scholars have documented a range of procedures to ensure truth-telling including the ordeal (Reik 1994). Other types of folk law studies examine the manner in which furniture is arranged in courtrooms in various countries (Hazard 1994), judicial robes as folk custom, symbols such as the gavel, and devices used for punishment, for example, shackles, the rack, the gallows, and so on. Those interested in semiotics will find the study of folk law appealing (Krstic 1994).

For the most part jurists do not consider the manifold aspects of legal systems that represent types of folklore. The folkloristic dimensions of law become evident most often when customary law conflicts with the dominant legal system. In cases where folk law conflicts with state law, judges must grapple with the significance of folklore in their courtrooms. Because they have usually not studied folklore or anthropology, they are ordinarily not well prepared to evaluate the customs that are at the crux of the litigation. The methods for the ascertainment of customary law, about which a great deal has been written, would serve them well.

Custom has influence not only in domestic legal systems but also in international law (Bederman 2010). In international law one of the major sources of norms is customary international law. Here jurists recognize that some norms emerge as important if there is state practice, that is states observe them, and if there is *opinio iuris*, that is, a sense of legal obligation that states must adhere to the norms. Fields such as international environmental law, human rights, and space law are constituted to a large degree by customary norms (see, for example, Vereshchetin and Danilenko 1994).

Sometimes there is a question as to which is a more important source of law – treaties or custom. While lawyers tend to prefer written instruments that delineate the precise nature of rights and duties that states willingly undertake, as a matter of prioritization, custom is arguably more significant. Were it not for the existence of the legal adage *"pacta sunt servanda"*, which means treaties must be followed, states would not feel compelled to fulfill their treaty obligations. Hence, custom appears to be logically prior to treaties as a source of law, and unwritten law is a *sine qua non* for written law. As Rudolf Bernhardt aptly notes: "… all written international law owes its existence to unwritten law and must be supplemented by unwritten law in order to be applied in practice" (1994: 916). International law is derived in large part from custom. The main virtue of customary law is that is it binding on all states in contrast to treaties which are binding only on those states that choose to ratify them.

Not only do states operate so as to generate new legal norms as part of customary international law, but states have also participated in the drafting of international instruments designed to safeguard traditions. The creation of international standards that protect folklore has been complicated by the involvement of multiple international organizations that have failed to harmonize their conflicting approaches to regulation. UNESCO has played a leading role in sponsoring the progressive development of these norms, supplemented by work of the WTO and WIPO (see Hafstein in this volume). In this way not only does folklore become incorporated into international law, but international law, via these global regimes, in turn, influences the status of folklore as well.

THE STATUS OF FOLK LAW IN THEORY AND PRACTICE

How does folk law intersect with the dominant jurisprudential theories of law? In the Western tradition there are three main legal traditions – Natural Law, Legal Positivism, and the Historical School of Jurisprudence, and customary law is only recognized as possessing juridical force in the context of the last of these (Golding 1966). Natural law posits that law must correspond to a conception of universal morality in order to constitute law. Whether one considers the early versions that assumed the law originated in divine inspiration or the secular version in the twentieth century, in order to qualify as law, the law had to correspond to objective criteria by which to determine if law is just. Natural law theorists generally questioned the legitimacy of customary law. This was reflected in the tendency of colonial systems to reject folk law notions to the extent that they conflicted with "natural justice", that is, so-called repugnancy clauses. In doing so, they invoked natural law principles.

By contrast, legal positivists treat law and morality as distinct. In their conception of law, law is whatever the political apparatus chooses to enforce, and consequently the question of the morality or immorality of the legal system does not determine whether it counts as a legal system. Whereas legal positivists assume that law is tied to the apparatus of the state, folk law does not require the state for its existence. Because the positivistic conception is quite narrow insofar as law requires a state to enforce it, legal positivists reject the proposition that customary law constitutes law. For instance, the famous Oxford scholar, H.L.A. Hart wrote in *The Concept of Law* that his theory does not consider ecclesiastical law, "primitive" law, or international law as law (Hart 1961: 3).

Conceptually, folk law falls squarely under the Historical School of Jurisprudence associated with Karl von Savigny,[1] Sir Henry Maine, and Paul Vinogradoff. According to these conceptions of law, the critical factor was whether the law reflected the *Volksgeist* or common consciousness of the people. Other formulations included Eugen Ehrlich's "the living law". The social context of law was highlighted, and social scientists emphasized that what was important for understanding law was not the formal laws on the books, but rather the law in action. This more empirically oriented understanding of law influenced legal studies. While folk law is clearly part of this intellectual development, folklorists have, to date, not played a significant role in the law and society movement. Much of the scholarship on customary law with which law and society scholars are familiar has been written by scholars in disciplines such as anthropology, history, law, and political science. Indeed, major contributions have come from legal anthropology, for example, most notably those of Laura Nader (1997) and Paul Bohannan (1967).

One of the better known debates about the status of folk law is Paul Bohannan's conceptualization of law as being custom "double-institutionalized" (Bohannan 1967). His notion was that custom is the first institution, and that when norms become sufficiently well established that society wishes to emphasize their importance, they "double institutionalize" them; this means designating them as legal institutions. In this framework the phrase customary law seems illogical and confusing. By comparison, the term folk law seems intuitively more clear (Renteln 2002a, b). Bohannan's research influenced legal studies perhaps because it seemed to show the way that folk law norms are incorporated in dominant legal systems.

Another study of folk law that is well known in legal circles is the work of Max Gluckman. In his classic *Judicial Process among the Barotse of Northern Rhodesia* (1967), *Barotse Jurisprudence* (1965), and other monographs Gluckman sought to demonstrate the presence of the "reasonable man standard" in African law. While motivated by a beneficent motive, namely to show that other societies also have legal systems, he may have gone overboard by claiming that precisely the same English legal standards were also found in their African jurisprudence. Consequently, some argue that he projected this conceptual framework on to his data. While it may be true that notions of reasonableness are found around the world, it is unlikely that the Barotse had the identical notion found in Anglo-American tort law. The status of the reasonable person standard has remained a central, contentious issue in legal studies (Saltman 1991).

Folk Law as a Distinct Professional Discipline

Even though legal scholars have, for the most part, tended to overlook the study of folk law, the literature on the subject is vast. Their research spans the globe and is rich and diverse. Because some of these researchers were associated with colonial administrations, some of the studies may be somewhat suspect. Nevertheless, their contributions to the study of the relationship between folklore and law deserve careful consideration.

Some of the most significant research on customary law was undertaken in Africa (Bennett 1985; Elias 1966). For example, Sir Anthony Allott's comprehensive Restatement of African Law represented a serious attempt to document the status of African law (1960). He and his colleagues at the School of Oriental and African Studies undertook a major research project designed to codify all the rules constituting African legal systems. Although this was an ambitious project, some considered it slightly insulting to write down all the rules, as though Africans did not know the inner workings of their own legal systems. The difficulties associated with writing down customary law have received considerable attention in scholarship (Elias 1994; Roberts 1994; and Ndulo 1994).

Seminal work on customary law in Asia also deserves mention (Barton 1969; Bodde 1963; Lee 1978; Taniguchi 1964; and Tsao 1966). Dutch scholars played an important role in establishing the academic study of folk law (Strijbosch 1994). For example C. Van Vollenhoven established the Adat Law School notably creating a classificatory scheme for the study of customary law in Indonesia. These adat law scholars, following his methodological approach, actively documented the powerful influence of customary law in Indonesia (Strijbosh 1994). Pioneering scholarship on folk law in India highlights the manner in which it had to be proved in court (Jain 1994; Sinha 1976; Rankin 1939). The legal system allowed for the different religious communities to be governed by their own customary law, a classic example of legal pluralism.

European scholars opened up the field by showing the wide range of phenomena that is part of folk law (Maunier 1938). For instance, Hermann Baltl explains:

> The instruments of legal life include all objects: not only the instruments of punishment and execution, which stand in the foreground of popular interest, but also the buildings used for legal purposes, e.g., city halls, courthouses, prisons, palaces, castles, and other seats of legal authority. The badges of authority are also included, and here we touch on the realm of symbols such as boundary markers, weights and measures, and the utensils, such as chests and coffers, employed in the guilds. (1994: 399)

His treatment of folk law also includes children's games and dances that reflect prevalent legal notions. Even though he preferred the use of the term "legal archaeology" to folk law, he demonstrated the breadth of the field. Research undertaken by scholars in Eastern Europe provides catalogues of legal symbols that are pervasive in legal systems and yet have not been subject to much scrutiny. Symbols that are part of the everyday life of institutions arguably deserve greater attention.

In the Middle East there are pioneering researchers such as Aharon Layish who studied the status of Arab customary law in Israel (Layish 1980–1982; Stewart 1987). Clinton Bailey wrote a classic monograph on Bedouin customary law (2009).

Despite the remarkable and extensive range of topics folk law encompasses, mainstream legal scholars have largely overlooked this literature. The worldwide study of customary law has received insufficient attention in both folkloristics and legal studies. The existence of the Commission on Folk Law and Legal Pluralism attests to the worldwide, interdisciplinary interest in the study of the subject (see, for example,

Morse and Woodman 1988).[2] Even though the Commission has continued to promote folk law research because of its importance, the Commission dropped "Folk Law" and came to be known simply as the Commission on Legal Pluralism. Despite the politics of nomenclature, the study of the folk law remains an important academic enterprise, and one which has been unjustifiably ignored in many disciplines. For those wishing to investigate this intriguing field, *The Journal of Legal Pluralism and Unofficial Law* has long served as one of the primary outlets for scholarship on folk law.

STATE CONTROL OF FOLK LAW: COLONIAL CONTEXTS

In colonial settings Europeans often tried to regulate customary law to eliminate customs they regarded as abhorrent. They adopted legislation containing what were known as "repugnancy" clauses. If a custom was deemed repugnant to natural justice, it was prohibited. This framework was applied to practices like sati, female circumcision, and killing based on a belief in witchcraft. Despite well-intentioned efforts to abolish these customs, this did not necessarily succeed in halting them and sometimes caused additional problems.

A great deal of scholarship has focused on the problems colonial authorities had regulating "witchcraft" in various parts of the world (see, for example, Hogbin 1935: 27–32; Mutungi 1971, 1977; Howman 1994; Chukkol 1983; Lewis 1958; and Vasdev 1961). The difficulty for Africans who killed based on a belief in witchcraft was that they lost this argument, no matter how the defense was presented. If they claimed that they had killed in self-defense because the individual considered a witch had put a spell on them or on some member of their family, the courts rejected the argument because self -defense requires that the belief be reasonable, and the reasonable person does not believe in witchcraft. If, however, the individual prosecuted for murder raised the insanity defense, that, in turn, was unsuccessful simply because sane Africans believe in witchcraft. Consequently, some commentators criticized the European approach as ethnocentric because it failed to take into consideration the widespread acceptance of belief in the supernatural in the worldview of many African peoples (Aremu 1980; Hund 2000). Killings based on a belief in witchcraft continue in the twenty-first century and demonstrate the persistence of this folk belief (Comaroff and Comaroff 2004; Tebbe 2007).

Some African scholars pointed out the cultural bias in the application of repugnancy clauses (see, for example, Bennett 1985: 81–82). Colonial judges relied on European standards, not culturally neutral ones, to evaluate the customs. Their condemnation of those deemed repugnant to natural justice reflected ethnocentric assessments.

Those critical of the recognition of customary law maintain that it was not a pure system. They emphasize that folk law systems have long been influenced by interaction with the national legal systems. Moreover, those who contend that the colonial systems should be discarded in favor of customary law fail to recognize that this may relegate individuals to antiquated systems that no longer correspond to the worldview of extant groups. Some have gone so far as to argue that the preservation of customary law has been a strategy for subjugating peoples, and excluding them from the mainstream political process (Gordon 1994). On this view, such arguments risk legitimizing the preservation of apartheid-like political systems.

Although the more common practice in colonial legal regimes was to outlaw customary law, in some countries the state law formally authorizes the recognition of folk law. Furthermore, where there might be conflict, the Constitution specified that the folk law would trump the more recent statutes. In Kenya, for instance, this was brought to the world's attention when the High Court handed down the *Otieno* case (Howell 1994). This was a case in which a Westernized Luo attorney died intestate, and there ensued a contentious dispute between his wife, a Kikuyu, who wanted to give her husband a secular burial and the Luo people who wanted to bury him in accordance with customary law. The protracted litigation sparked riots and much criticism and attracted international media coverage. Ultimately the Luo people prevailed because of the priority given to customary law in the constitutional system.

Another colonial context for the adjudication of folk law claims is in North America. In many cases the central issue is what sentence is proportionate given the cultural context of the crime. The judiciary in the dominant legal system must determine whether to take into consideration the folk law of the defendant. In one highly publicized case, the judge delegated the decision-making to the elders. Two teenage Tlingit men assaulted a pizza deliveryman in Washington. Although they might have been incarcerated, the Tlingit elders sentenced them to banishment, a customary form of punishment (Miller 2004). While some protested that the punishment was too lenient, others thought it violated the Eighth Amendment prohibition against cruel and unusual punishment to leave young men in the wilderness to survive on their own (Kim 1995). Despite the various responses of the members of the public, the Washington state judge deserves praise for his courage in recognizing the importance of customary law to the Tlingit community (Renteln 1994). Ultimately, however, the trial judge's ruling was reversed on appeal on the ground that he had abused his discretion by ignoring state policy that clearly mandated sentencing the men to prison (*State of Washington v. Roberts* 1995).

Refusing to take folk law into account may have serious repercussions. For example, if indigenous people impose punishment for a violation of customary law and then the state legal system also incarcerates the defendant, this violates the principle of double jeopardy according to which no one should be subject to punishment twice for the same offense (Australian Law Reform Commission report 1986: 366–367). The failure to recognize the existence of legal pluralism can result in excessive punishment according to the logic of the dominant legal order.

In some instances, legal elites have seen fit to consider customary law practices. For instance, criminologists investigated native use of sentencing circles as an alternate method for handling transgression (Lyon 2006). Sometimes referred to as restorative justice, the tribal technique involves a community-based decision about how best to reintegrate an offender into the society as opposed to taking a punitive, retributive approach. The practice of sentencing circles was in vogue for some time, showing how the creativity of the folk can influence the legal practices of the elites.

FOLK LAW – MIGRATION AND THE CULTURAL DEFENSE

When individuals migrate to new countries, they carry their important folkways with them. Although they usually follow their traditions without any difficulties, on occasion, the practices may clash with the law of the new country (Renteln 2010). If prosecuted, they may seek to raise a cultural defense which, if successful may result in an acquittal or a reduction in the penalty (Renteln 2004). The primary motivation for invoking the defense is to introduce cultural evidence to provide the context within which the defendant acted. As with any defense, it may also be rejected entirely. The key point is that having the cultural defense ensures the consideration of the evidence related to the tradition; it is a separate question how much weight, if any, should be given to it in the ultimate disposition of the case. To ensure that litigants do not raise fraudulent claims, judges could use a cultural defense test (Renteln 2004, 2005. The determination of whether the cultural imperative should influence the outcome in litigation must be made on a case-by-case basis.

Sometimes there is a cognitive difference involved, as when Fumiko Kimura, a Japanese American woman tried to commit *oyako-shinju*, or parent-children suicide, a relatively common occurrence in Japan (Renteln and Valladares 2009; Woo 1989). Distraught after discovering her husband's affair, she walked off the Santa Monica shore into the ocean taking her two young children with her. College students tried to rescue all of them, but the children died. Mrs. Kimura was subsequently charged with first-degree murder with special circumstances which could have brought the death penalty. Her defense was that in Japan it was considered more cruel to leave the children behind without anyone to look after them than to take them with her to the afterlife. Because of this less individualistic worldview, the relationship between parents and children was arguably construed differently. Without an understanding of this practice and the cultural context in which it occurs, the court would not be able to comprehend the cultural motivation for her action. After thousands of members of the Japanese American community signed a petition imploring the court to apply Japanese law, a plea negotiation resulted in a suspended sentence and counseling for Mrs Kimura. While those concerned about the protection of children's rights considered the sentence too light, the disposition of the case showed that the California court had been influenced by Japanese customary norms.

Another cognitive difference concerns the use of folk medicine. For example, when the Vietnamese use a technique known as coining or *cao gio*, some of them have been arrested and prosecuted for child abuse. A coin rub involves first placing mentholated oil on the body after which the rubbing is performed with a coin that has a serrated edge, like a dime or quarter; it results in bruises on the torso. Although there is mild discomfort, many attest to the therapeutic benefits of the folk remedy. Adults who are arrested are astonished to learn that this type of folk medicine is regarded as a crime (Renteln 2004: 57–58). Although the parents realize that child abuse is illegal, they regard the coin massage as a traditional remedy. Hence they are not claiming ignorance of the law, which in any event is no excuse in Anglo-American jurisprudence. Rather they contend that the act in question was not a crime.

In other cases the behavior involves a volitional impairment. This may happen, for instance, when an individual is insulted and is unable to exercise self-control and commits an act of violence. Claiming to have been provoked, a defendant may raise the provocation defense, one of the most ancient defenses in the criminal law, to obtain a reduction from murder to manslaughter (provocation is a partial excuse). In order to prevail, the defendants must meet two requirements by proving: (i) that an individual was provoked (the subjective part), and (ii) the average reasonable person would have been provoked (the objective part). For individuals who were brought up in a different cultural system, what constitutes a provocation will vary.

For example, in one case in Los Angeles, California, a Thai man, Mr Trakulrat was singing on Melrose at a Thai restaurant one evening in the early 1990s (Renteln 2004: 232). Some people in the audience, who did not care for his performance, put their feet up on the table, pointing the soles of their feet at him. Because this is such an egregious insult, Trakulrat pulled out a gun and shot and killed them. While this gesture might not seem particularly offensive to American jurors, it is the worst possible insult in Thai culture. Without an explanation as to the magnitude of the offense in Thai culture, a jury would be unlikely to regard the gesture as a significant provocation. This suggests that individuals from other traditions will not be successful when they raise the provocation defense inasmuch as the insults that provoke them are largely incomprehensible to the so-called average reasonable person. Hence, this arguably constitutes a violation of equal protection of the law.

The question in some cases has been whether words can constitute adequate provocation. The usual common law rule has been that words are not adequate provocation because "sticks and stones can break my bones, but words can never hurt me." Despite this, in some jurisdictions like California, courts have found that ethnic slurs can be provocation. However defendants still lose their cases. For example, in *People v. Giacomo Bonadonna* (1990), Dr Lucia Chiavola Birnbaum, testified as to the significance of the term "cornuto" (cuckold) in Sicilian culture when the defendant raised the provocation defense in a homicide case. Even though the expert was of Sicilian ancestry and a scholar of Italian folklore, the judge was not persuaded that the term was sufficiently offensive as to count as adequate provocation.

Folk law can be important in civil law matters as well. In some cases the rules for marrying may be important to the interpretation of the act in question. For instance a Hmong man prosecuted for rape in Fresno, California in 1986 argued that he had simply followed traditional Hmong customary law for getting married. When he tried to carry off this bride, she protested saying "no, no, no, I'm not ready", as custom required. Later when she and her parents filed kidnapping and rape charges against Mr. Moua, he claimed that her ritualized protest was culturally expected and that he had made a mistake of fact, which is a complete excuse (provided it is objectively reasonable). The question of whether there had been a mistake of fact as to the woman's consent hinged on the presentation of Hmong customs (Evans-Pritchard and Renteln 1994). Because of all the confusion surrounding the facts and the judge's lack of familiarity with Hmong marriage traditions, the case was resolved with Mr Moua pleading guilty to false imprisonment, the lesser included offense under kidnapping. In a legal system based on the presumption of innocence beyond a reasonable doubt, this may not have been a fair result.

In another case Moluccans living in the Netherlands were unable to marry because the man and woman came from clans that were too closely related according to the *pela* rules to which their community adhered (Strijbosh 1985). Because they wanted to obtain permission to marry, they traveled to the place from which their relatives had migrated to request an exception to the customary law. The elders were surprised to learn that there appeared to be so little flexibility in the interpretation of the rules in the Netherlands. This suggests that immigrants may enforce customary law more stringently than in the place of origin. It may be that the law provides a means of reinforcing cultural identity and thus must therefore be strictly followed.

Westerns abroad who are unfamiliar with the folkways of a new country may also encounter difficulty. An English teacher in Sudan allowed her elementary school class to choose the name Mohammed for a teddy bear. Unaware that this was considered blasphemy, she was surprised to receive death threats and also to be incarcerated. Remarkably ignorance of naming customs resulted in legal consequences for the teacher. Similarly Americans and British traveling abroad have been shocked to find that kissing in public was considered an outrage (Renteln 2009). These examples reveal the importance of knowing the folk law when visiting distant lands.

FOLKLORE AND THE LITIGATION OF RELIGIOUS DISPUTES

Folk law arguably includes religious law. Some aspects of Jewish law and Islamic law are customary in nature (El Awa 1973). Insofar as religious law constitutes a subcategory of folk law, one may consider the range of disputes in which religious traditions are on trial. Many of these are concerned with religious garb. The question is whether government regulations prohibiting the attire based on public safety, public health, or some other rationale are sufficiently compelling to justify the limitation on religious freedom. Controversies have involved issues such as whether women may testify in court wearing the niqab, whether governments may impose fines on women who wear the burkha in public places, and whether schools may ban conspicuous religious symbols (Bakht 2009). Whether liberal democracies consistent with principles of secularism can permit the display of religious symbols in public places, like crucifixes, Menorahs, and nativity scenes, is another important issue (Grimm 2009). Folklorists have played a role in determining whether, for example, Christmas is secular or religious. (Samuelson 1982).

Traditions associated with Orthodox Jewish law have generated lawsuits concerning the separation of church and state in the United States and England (Cooper 2004: Metzger 1989). As the Orthodox interpret Jewish law as forbidding 39 types of work on the Sabbath, they have, on occasion, sought public support to facilitate their ability to follow their religion. The litigation sometimes involves a request for accommodation of the *eruv*, or a thread on public property like telephone poles that creates a demarcation of space within which Orthodox Jewish individuals can carry objects on the Sabbath and perform necessary tasks (e.g., *Tenafly Eruv Association, Inc. v. The borough of Tenafly* 2002; Dundes 2005: 45–49) The elaborate system of rules also permits means by which they can be circumvented, a principle known as *shinui* (Dundes 2002: 33). Besides the *eruv*, these may include reliance on the *Shabbes Goy*, or a non-Jewish individual who can do work on the Jewish Sabbath or performing an ordinary task in an unusual way, for stance, by using one's elbow to push on an elevator button.

Devout individuals sometimes seek to have the ability to handle decision-making within their own dispute settlement mechanisms. In the early twenty-first-century controversy surrounded the proposal that Muslim religious arbitral boards be established in Canada and the United Kingdom (Bakht 2006; Shachar 2008; Estin 2009; Poulter 1990 Taher 2008). While some defended the use of the mechanisms for family law matters, others worried that delegation to religious boards would endanger the rights of women. Other objections included a concern regarding whether there could be appeal made to the national judicial institutions.

Possibly in response to these developments, in the United States voters passed initiatives banning the consideration of Sharia law in Oklahoma. In some cases involving family law matters it is difficult to imagine how judges would be able to resolve issues without taking Islamic law into account (Estin 2004, 2009). Efforts to ban the law of other jurisdictions in national legal systems may turn out to be impractical, ineffectual, and unconstitutional.

THE SIGNIFICANCE OF LANDSCAPES: ENVIRONMENT LITIGATION

In litigation to secure title to territory or to protect sacred landscapes from environmental degradation folklore has sometimes played an important role. When development projects are on the horizon, the law often requires the completion of environmental impact reports. If the landscapes have cultural significance for particular peoples, the folk groups are required to demonstrate this by means of evidence that modern legal systems will accept (Orebech et al. 2005). In some cases indigenous people have been required to prove that they have a special relationship to the land in question in order to establish title to territory. This occurred in landmark cases that reached the Supreme Courts of Australia and Canada (Eisenberg 2009: Nettheim 1995). In one Canadian Supreme court decision, the Delgamuuk case (1997), First Nations peoples sought to present the oral histories of elders to document their relationship to the land in question. In order to allow the consideration of this type of evidence, the judge had to make an exception to the ordinary common law rule against hearsay (Culhane 1998: 116–126).

Other jurisprudence reflects the notion that individuals and groups cannot simply feel a connection to particular landscapes. Their perception of the significance of the place is insufficient; they must demonstrate that they use them for special rituals. This requirement reflects an ethnocentric bias about what is necessary in order to prevent development.

In some cases testimony concerning the relationship between indigenous peoples and ancestors is crucial. This is significant in much of the sacred site litigation around the world. For instance, in the Mount Graham litigation, the Apache sought to prevent the building of a telescope that the University of Arizona wanted to erect as part of an international scientific collaboration (Williams 1994). The claim was that the site at which the telescope would be placed was sacred because that was where the Gaans had taught the Apache about traditional medicine. Likewise, in litigation that reached that Supreme Court of Hawai'i, the plaintiffs claimed that the proposed geothermal plant would destroy the Goddess Pele (*Dedman v. Board of Land and Natural Resources* 1987). The Pele practitioners maintained that the construction would rob her of her life's breath. Skepticism about these narratives may have contributed to the judges' decisions to allow the development projects. While this may not seem surprising, it does reflect a double standard insofar as judges would be less inclined to authorize the construction of scientific or energy projects on the cemeteries of their own relatives, regardless of whether they believed the development would affect their ancestors. Moreover, even if they were to win the litigation, requiring that peoples divulge information as to the location of the sacred places itself constitutes a violation of customary law.

In litigation concerning sacred sites, the claim to environmental protection coincides with a claim that the right of a people to their way of life, or more simply their right to culture. In other lawsuits these claims are in opposition. Indigenous peoples seek to hunt animals considered endangered species because they need parts for the performance of ceremonies. In the United States Indians hunt eagles to obtain feathers or panthers for their parts. Some Asians from Korea and Taiwan have been prosecuted for the sale of parts of endangered species that are considered important for medicinal or aphrodisiac purposes. Likewise aboriginal communities have sought a subsistence exemption from policies banning the taking of whales; Japanese and Norwegian whaling communities have claimed they also deserve an exception to support their way of life (Kalland and Moeran 1990: Mathisen 1996). In such disputes as these the legal system has to make a choice between the right to environmental protection or the preservation of the value of biodiversity on the one hand and the right to culture on the other.

To reconcile competing rights claims, some have proposed mechanisms of co-management. These would theoretically involve indigenous peoples in decision making about land use and conservation of wildlife. In practice some think that delegation will only occur insofar as the groups will implement the policies of the dominant legal order. This type of arrangement ultimately constitutes a form of ecocolonialism (Burton 2002).

How International Law Protects Folklore: Cultural Rights and Cultural Heritage

International law affords protection to folklore in various ways. With regard to sacred places and monuments the 1970 UNESCO Convention on Cultural and Natural Heritage provides some protection. In addition, the Convention on Intangible Cultural Heritage is designed to ensure the continuation of various types of folklore including dance, crafts, and knowledge about the medicinal properties of plans (Nafziger *et al.* 2010; Telesetsky 2008), although research suggests that the implementation of this treaty has been somewhat problematic because ownership may be contested.[3] Ironically, it is also unclear whether customary international law exists to ensure the protection of cultural heritage. However insofar as states have fulfilled their treaty obligations and feel compelled to do so, these norms may become part of customary law.

There is also a large literature on the degree to which particular human rights guarantee the right to culture (Stamatopoulou 2007; Renteln 2002a). The scholarship makes reference to several key conventions that deal with the right of minorities and language. To date the most powerful formulation of the right to culture is found in Article 27. It guarantees the right to culture, which is not subject to any restrictions clause as is Article 18 which stipulates that the right to religious freedom may be limited in democratic systems to protect such public goods as health, morality, and safety. Although some claim that the drafters of Article 27 must have expected that the right to culture would be subject to the same limitations, that seems unlikely. The drafters would have included that language in the treaty had they intended them to apply to the right to culture as well.

One of the main problems with the recognition of cultural rights is the failure to develop any conceptual analysis for weighing them against other human rights such as women's rights and children's rights. To the extent that courts privilege cultural claims, there are certainly risks. For example, insofar as honor killings are motivated by customary law, this is devastating to women's rights (Freed 1994). Similarly, racist actions in the United States and caste discrimination in South Asia may have been supported with claims of customary law. This suggests that the state will at times legitimately need to limit the influence of customary law, most obviously when its invocation is connected to killing and acts of violence. Thus, while constitutional systems and international law instruments must protect folklore and culture, they must also take into consideration other important competing rights claims.

There are, of course, potential benefits to the study of folklore for jurists as well. The comparative study of folkways can help establish cross-cultural support for particular norms. The relevance of empirical research for documenting shared values has become an urgent matter in the twenty-first century. Folklorists can play a crucial role by showing specifically how expressive culture encodes and, perhaps more accurately put, negotiates the values of particular societies. By so doing, they can help demonstrate the cross-cultural legitimacy of specific rights codified in human rights instruments (Renteln 1990).

Not only can folklorists assist with the progressive development of international standards, but they can also contribute to the successful enforcement of international human rights. In the landmark case *Filartiga v. Pena-Irala*, a federal appellate court in the United States held that aliens may sue aliens in federal court for a tort involving a violation of the law of nations, in this case the right against torture. The basis for ruling that the right against torture was binding in the United States was customary international law because the United States had not yet ratified the Convention Against Torture or Cruel, Inhuman or Degrading Treatment or Punishment. This highlights the benefit of a customary norm, namely that it is, by definition, binding on all states parties. The landmark *Filartiga* ruling paved the way to hundreds of other cases in which those who suffered gross violations of human rights could seek redress of grievance in court. This has been a profoundly important development.

Customary law has also had a significant impact on the law of war which protects civilians. The Geneva Conventions represent the codification of customary law, and the conventions have helped minimize suffering during armed conflict, whether inter-state or internal conflicts.

CONCLUSION

Even though legal scholars have often overlooked the ubiquitous influence of folk law, there is growing recognition of the importance of this field. For instance, some contend that "...customary norms live as an authentic source of legal obligation" (Bederman 2010: 174). After having existed beneath the radar for quite some time, there is no longer any question about the significance of customary norms for constitutional litigation, regimes, and international trade (Snyder 1999). Folklorists provide an important role as culture brokers showing how concepts must be properly interpreted to ensure legal protection. They can inspire others to study norms that are central in the lives of people in many societies.

Likewise folklorists should pay more attention to the study of legal phenomenona. The protection of cultural rights is too important to be left to lawyers. It is encouraging to see that more folklorists are taking an interest in the systems by which legal standards are established. This bodes well for the future of legal studies and folkloristics.

NOTES

1   Savigny was the teacher of Jacob Grimm (Renteln and Dundes 1994).
2   The commission changed its name to "Commission on Legal Pluralism"; for more informa-
     tion on its work, see www.commission-on-legal-pluralism.com (accessed May 10, 2011).
3   On the complex social, economic, and legal impact of the heritage regime, see Hafstein in
     this volume; on the linkage between heritage matters and issues in cultural property, see
     Skrydstrup in this volume. On the ramifications of propertizing culture in social, legal, and
     economic terms, see the ongoing work of the research group "The Constitution of Cultural
     Property" at Göttingen University, Germany (http://www.uni-goettingen.de/en/86656.
     html, accessed May 10, 2011).

REFERENCES

Allott, Antony. 1960.   *Essays in African Law.* London: Butterworth.

Aremu, L.O. 1980.   "Criminal Responsibility for Homicide in Nigeria and Supernatural Beliefs." *International and Comparative Law Quarterly* 29: 112–131.

Australian Law Reform Commission. 1986. *The Recognition of Aboriginal Customary Laws.* Vol. 1. Report no. 31, 507pp.

Bailey, Clinton. 2009.   *Bedouin Law from Sinai and the Negev: Justice Without Government.* New Haven: Yale University Press.

Bakht, Natasha. 2005. "Were Muslim Barbarians Really Knocking On the Gates of Ontario? The Religious Arbitration Controversy-Another Perspective." *Ottawa Law Review Fortieth anniversary,* pp. 67–82.

Bakht, Natasha. 2010. "Veiled Objections: Facing Public Opposition to the Niqab" in Lori Beason, Ed. *Defining Reasonable Accommodation.* University of British Columbia Press.

Barton, R.F. 1969.   *Ifugao Law.* Berkeley: University of California Press.

Bederman, David. 2010.   *Custom as a Source of Law.* Cambridge: Cambridge University Press.

Bennett, T.W. 1985.   *Application of Customary Law in Southern Africa.* Cape Town: Juta and Co.

Bernhardt, Rudolf. 1994 [1977]. "Unwritten International Law" in Alison Dundes Renteln and Alan Dundes, Eds. *Folk Law: Essays in the Theory and Practice of "Lex Non Scripta."* 2 Vols. New York: Garland, pp. 915–938.

Bodde, Derek. 1963. "Basic Concepts of Chinese Law: the Genesis and Evolution of Legal Thought in Traditional China." *Proceedings of the American Philosophical Society* 107(5): 375–398.

Bohannan, Paul. 1967. "The Differing Realms of the Law" in Paul Bohannan, Ed. *Law and Warfare.* Garden City: New York: The Natural History Press, pp. 43–56.

Burton, Lloyd. 2002. *Worship and Wilderness: Culture, Religion, and Law in Public Lands Management.* Madison: University of Wisconsin Press.

Chiba, Masaji. 1989. *Legal Pluralism: Towards A General Theory Through Japanese Legal Culture.* Tokyo: Tokai University Press.

Chukkol, Kharisu Sufiyan. 1983. "Supernatural Beliefs and Criminal Law in Nigeria." *Journal of the Indian Law Institute:* 444–474.

Comaroff, John and Jean Comaroff. 2004. "Policing Culture, Cultural Policing: Law and Social Order in Postcolonial South Africa." *Law and Social Inquiry* 29(1): 513–546.

Cooper, Davina. 2004. *Challenging Diversity: Rethinking Equality and the Value of Diversity.* Cambridge: Cambridge University Press.

Culhane, Dara. 1998. *The Pleasure of the Crown: Anthropology, Law, and First Nations.* Burnaby: Talonbooks.

Dedman v. Board of Land and Natural Resources (1987). 740 Pacific Reporter (2d) 28.

Dundes, Alan. 2002. *The Shabbat Elevator and Other Sabbath Subterfuges.* Lanham: Rowman and Littlefield.

Eisenberg, Avigail. 2009. *Reasons of Identity: A Normative Guide to the Political and Legal Assessment of Identity Claims.* New York: Oxford University Press.

El-Awa, Mohamed. 1973. "The Place of Custom ('Urf) in Islamic Legal Theory." *The Islamic Quarterly* 17: 177–182.

Elias, T. Olawale. 1956. *The Nature of African Customary Law.* New York: Humanities Press.

Elias, T.O. 1994 [1958]. "The Problem of Reducing Customary Law to Writing" in Alison Dundes Renteln and Alan Dundes, Eds. *Folk Law: Essays in the Theory and Practice of "Lex Non Scripta."* 2 Vols. New York: Garland, pp. 319–330.

Estin, Ann Laquer. 2004. "Embracing Tradition: Pluralism in American Family Law." *Maryland Law Review* 634: 540–604.

Estin, Ann Laquer. 2009. "Unofficial Family Law." *Iowa Law Review* 94: 449–480.

Evans-Pritchard, Deirdre and Alison Dundes Renteln. 1994. "The Interpretation and Distortion of Culture: A Hmong Marriage by Capture Case in Fresno, California." *Southern California Interdisciplinary Law Journal* 4: 1–48.

Freed, Ruth. 1994 [1971]. "The Case of Maya" in Alison Dundes Renteln and Alan Dundes, Eds. *Folk Law: Essays in the Theory and Practice of "Lex Non Scripta."* 2 Vols. New York: Garland, pp. 671–688.

Gluckman, Max. 1965. *The Ideas in Barotse Jurisprudence.* New Haven: Yale University Press.

Gluckman, Max. 1967 [1955]. *Judicial Process among the Barotse of Northern Rhodesia.* 2nd edition. Manchester: Manchester University Press.

Gluckman, Max, Ed. 1969. *Ideas and Procedures in African Customary Law.* Oxford University Press.

Goetze, Albrecht. 1994 [1949]. "Mesopotamian Laws and the Historian" in Alison Dundes Renteln and Alan Dundes, Eds. *Folk Law: Essays in the Theory and Practice of "Lex Non Scripta."* 2 Vols. New York: Garland, pp. 485–494.

Golding, M.P., Ed. 1966. *The Nature of Law: Readings in Legal Philosophy.* New York: Random House.

Gordon, Robert J. 1994 [1989]. "The White Man's Burden: Ersatz Customary Law and Internal Pacification in South Africa" in Alison Dundes Renteln and Alan Dundes, Eds. *Folk Law: Essays in the Theory and Practice of "Lex Non Scripta."* 2 Vols. New York: Garland, pp. 367–394.

Griffiths, John. 1986. "What is Legal Pluralism?" *Journal of Legal Pluralism and Unofficial Law* 24: 1–55.

Grimm, Dieter. 2009. "Conflicts between General Law and Religious Norms." *Cardozo Law Review* 30(6): 2369–2382.

Hart, H.L.A. 1966. *The Concept of Law.* Oxford: Clarendon Press.

Hazard, John N. 1994 [1962]. "Furniture Arrangement as a Symbol of Judicial Roles" in Alison Dundes Renteln and Alan Dundes, Eds. *Folk Law: Essays in the Theory and Practice of "Lex Non Scripta."* 2 Vols. New York: Garland, pp. 459–465.

Hogbin, H. Ian. 1935. "Sorcery and Administration." *Oceania* 6(1): 1–32.

Hooker, M.B. 1975. *Legal Pluralism: An Introduction to Colonial and Neo-Colonial Laws*. Oxford: Clarendon Press.

Howman, Roger. 1994 [1948]. "Witchcraft and the Law" in Alison Dundes Renteln and Alan Dundes, Eds. *Folk Law: Essays in the Theory and Practice of "Lex Non Scripta."* 2 Vols. New York: Garland, pp. 637–654.

Howell, Roy Carleton. 1994 [1989]. "The Otieno Case". African Customary Law Versus Western Jurisprudence" in Alison Dundes Renteln and Alan Dundes, Eds. *Folk Law: Essays in the Theory and Practice of "Lex Non Scripta."* 2 Vols. New York: Garland, pp. 827–844.

Hund, John. 2000. Witchcraft and Accusations of Witchcraft in South Africa: Ontological Denial and the Suppression of African Justice. *Comparative and International Law Journal of South Africa* 33(3): 366–389.

Jain, M.P. 1994 [1963]. "Custom as a Source of Law in India" in Alison Dundes Renteln and Alan Dundes, Eds. *Folk Law: Essays in the Theory and Practice of "Lex Non Scripta."* 2 Vols. New York: Garland, pp. 49–82.

Kalland, Arne and Brian Moeran. 1990. *Endangered Culture: Japanese Whaling in Cultural Perspective*. Copenhagen: Nordic Institute of Asian Studies.

Kim, Stephanie J. 1995. "Sentencing and Cultural Differences: Banishment of the American India Robbers." *John Marshall Law Review* 29: 239–267.

Krstic, Durica 1994 [1981]. "Symbols in Customary Law" in Alison Dundes Renteln and Alan Dundes, Eds. *Folk Law: Essays in the Theory and Practice of "Lex Non Scripta."* 2 Vols. New York: Garland, pp. 439–454.

Layish, Aharon. 1980–1982. "Challenges to Customary Law and Arbitration: The Impact of Islamic Law upon Settled Bedouin in the Judaean Desert." *Tel Aviv University Studies in Law* 5: 206–221.

Lee, Orlan. 1978. *Legal and Moral Systems in Asian Customary Law: The Legacy of the Buddhist Social Ethic and Buddhist Law*. San Francisco: Chinese Materials Center.

Lewis, Justin. 1958. "The Outlook for a Devil in the Colonies." *Criminal Law Review*: 661–675.

Lyon, Clare E. 2006. "Alternative Methods for Sentencing Youthful Offenders: Using Traditional Tribal Methods as a Model." *Ave Maria Law Review* 4: 211–247.

Mathisen, Stein R. 1996. "Real Barbarians Eat Whales: Norwegian Identity and the Whaling Issue" in Pertii J. Anttonen, Ed. *Making Europe in Nordic Contexts* pp. Turku: Publisher?, 105–136.

Maunier, René. 1938. *Introduction au folklore juridique*. Paris: Les Editions d'art et d'histoire.

Messenger, Jr., John C. 1994 [1959]. "The Role of Proverbs in a Nigerian Judicial System" in Alison Dundes Renteln and Alan Dundes, Eds. *Folk Law: Essays in the Theory and Practice of "Lex Non Scripta."* 2 Vols. New York: Garland, pp. 421–431.

Metzger, Joshua. 1989. "The Eruv: Can Government Constitutionally Permit Jews to Build a Fictional Wall Without Breaking the Wall Between Church and State." *National Jewish Law Review* 4: 67–92.

Miller, Colin. 2004. "Banishment from Within and Without: Analyzing Indigenous Sentencing Under International Human Rights Standards." *North Dakota Law Review* 80: 253–288.

Morse, Bradford W. and Gordon R. Woodman, Eds. 1988. *Indigenous Law and the State*. Dordrecht: Foris Publications.

Mutungi, O.K. 1971. "Witchcraft and the Criminal Law in East Africa." *Valparaiso University Law Review* 5: 524–555.

Mutungi, O.K. 1977. *The Legal Aspects of Witchcraft in East Africa with Particular Reference to Kenya*. Nairobi: East African Literature Bureau.

Nafziger, James, Robert Paterson, and Alison Dundes Renteln. 2010. *Cultural Law: International, Comparative, and Indigenous*. Cambridge: Cambridge University Press.

Nader, Laura, Ed. 1997 [1969]. *Law in Culture and Society*. Berkeley: University of California Press.

Nettheim, Garth. 1995. "Mabo and Legal Pluralism: The Australian Aboriginal Justice

Experience" in Kayleen M. Hazlehurst, Ed. *Legal Pluralism and the Colonial Legacy: Indigenous Experiences of Justice in Canada, Australia, and New Zealand.* Aldershot: Avebury, pp. 103–130.

Ndulo, Muna. 1994 [1981]. "Ascertainment of Customary Law: Problems and Perspectives with Special Reference to Zambia" in Alison Dundes Renteln and Alan Dundes, Eds. *Folk Law: Essays in the Theory and Practice of "Lex Non Scripta."* 2 Vols. New York: Garland, pp. 339–349.

Orebech Peter *et al.* 2005. *The Role of Customary Law in Sustainable Development.* Cambridge: Cambridge University Press.

Poulter, Sebastian. 1990. "The Claim to a Separate Islamic System of Personal Law for British Muslims" in Chibli Mallat and Jane Connors, Eds. *Islamic Family Law.* London: Graham and Trotman, pp. 147–166.

Rankin, George. 1939. "Custom and the Muslim Law in British India." *Transactions of the Grotius Society* 24: 89–118.

Reik, Theodor. 1994 [1945]. "The Euro-American Trial as Expiatory Oral Ordeal" in Alison Dundes Renteln and Alan Dundes, Eds. *Folk Law: Essays in the Theory and Practice of "Lex Non Scripta."* 2 Vols. New York: Garland, pp. 473–482.

Renteln, Alison Dundes. 1990. *International Human Rights: Universalism Versus Relativism.* Newbury Park, CA: Sage.

Renteln, Alison Dundes. 1994. September 7. "Local Judge Recognizes Significance of Thlingit Folk Law. *Seattle Post-Intelligencer,* A11.

Renteln, Alison Dundes. 2002a. "Cultural Rights" in Paul Baltes and Neil Smelser, Eds. *International Encyclopedia of Social and Behavioral Sciences.* Oxford: Elsevier.

Renteln, Alison Dundes. 2002b. "Custom" in Kermit Hall, Ed. *The Oxford Companion to American Law.* New York: Oxford University Press.

Renteln, Alison Dundes and Alan Dundes, Eds. 1994. *Folk Law: Essays in the Theory and Practice of "Lex Non Scripta."* 2 Vols. New York: Garland.

Renteln, Alison Dundes and Rene Valladares. 2009. "The Importance of Culture for the Justice System." *Judicature* 92: 193–201.

Renteln, Alison Dundes. 2004. *The Cultural Defense.* New York: Oxford University Press.

Renteln, Alison Dundes. 2005. "The Use and Abuse of the Cultural Defense. Cross-Cultural Jurisprudence." *Culture in the Domain of Law.* Special issue. *Canadian Journal of Law and Society.* 20(1): 47–67.

Renteln, Alison Dundes. 2009. "When Westerners Run Afoul of the Law in Other Countries." *Judicature* 92: 238–242.

Renteln, Alison Dundes. 2010. "Making Room for Culture in Court." *The Judges' Journal* 49(2): 7–15.

Roberts, Simon 1994 [1971]. "The Recording of Customary Laws to Writing" in Alison Dundes Renteln and Alan Dundes, Eds. 1994. *Folk Law: Essays in the Theory and Practice of "Lex Non Scripta."* 2 Vols. New York: Garland, pp. 331–337.

Saltman, Michael. 1991. *The Demise of the "Reasonable Man": A Cross-Cultural Study of a Legal Concept.* New Brunswick: New Jersey: Transaction Publishers.

Samuelson, Sue. 1982. *Christmas: An Annotated Bibliography.* New York: Garland Publishing.

Shachar, Ayelet. 2008. "Privatizing Diversity: A Cautionary Tale from Religious Arbitration in Family Law." *Theoretical Inquiries in Law* 9(2): 573–607.

Sheleff, Leon. 1999. *The Future of Tradition: Customary Law, Common Law, and legal Pluralism.* London: Frank Cass.

Simpson, A.W.B. 1994 [1973]. "The Common Law and Legal Theory" in Alison Dundes Renteln and Alan Dundes, Eds. 1994. *Folk Law: Essays in the Theory and Practice of "Lex Non Scripta."* 2 Vols. New York: Garland, pp. 119–139.

Sinha, B.S. 1976. "Custom and Customary Law in Indian Jurisprudence." *Indian Socio-Legal Journal.* 83–97.

Snyder, Francis. 1999. "Governing Economic Globalisation: Global Legal Pluralism and European Law." *European Law Journal* 5: 334–374.

Stamatopoulou, Elsa. 2007. *Cultural Rights in International Law: Article 27 of the Universal Declaration of Human Rights and Beyond.* Leiden: Martinus Nijhoff.

Stewart, Frank H. 1987. "Tribal Law in the Arab World: A Review of the Literature." *International Journal of Middle East Studies* 19: 473–490.

Strijbosch, Fons. 1985. "The Concept of Pela and Its Social Significance in the Community of Moluccan Immigrants in the Netherlands." *Journal of Legal Pluralism* 23: 177–208.

Strijbosch, A.K.J.M. 1994 [1978]. "Methods and Theories of Dutch Juridical-Ethnological Research in the Period 1900 to 1977" in Alison Dundes Renteln and Alan Dundes, Eds. 1994. *Folk Law: Essays in the Theory and Practice of "Lex Non Scripta."* 2 Vols. New York: Garland, pp. 231–249.

Taher, Abul. 2008. September 14. "Revealed: UK's First Official Sharia Courts." *The Sunday Times.*

Taniguchi, Tomohei. 1964. "La loi et la coutume au Japon" in *Études Juridiques offertes à Leon Juilliot de la Morandière.* Paris: Librairie Dalloz, pp. 571–582.

Taylor, Archer. 1965–1966. "The Road to an 'Englishman's House...'" *Romance Philology* 19: 279–285.

Tebbe, Nelson. 2007. "Witchcraft and Statecraft: Liberal Democracy in Africa." *Georgetown Law Journal* 96: 183–236.

Telesetsky, Anastasia. 2008. in James Nafziger and Tullio Scovazzi, Eds. *The Cultural Heritage of Mankind.* Leiden: Martinus Nijhoff, pp. 297–354.

Tsao, Wen Yen. 1966. "The Chinese Family from Customary Law to Positive Law." *Hastings Law Journal* 17: 727–765.

Vasdev, Krishna. 1961. "Ghosts, Evil Spirits, Witches and the Law of Homicide in Sudan." *Sudan Law and Reports*: 238–244.

Vereshchetin, Vladlen S. and Gennady M. Danilenko. 1994 [1985]." Custom as a Source of International Law of Outer Space" in Alison Dundes Renteln and Alan Dundes, Eds. 1994. *Folk Law: Essays in the Theory and Practice of "Lex Non Scripta."* 2 Vols. New York: Garland,, pp. 1003–1018.

Williams, Robert A. 1994. "Large Binocular Telescopes, Red Squirrel Pinatas, and Apache Sacred Mountains: Decolonizing Environmental Law in a Multicultural World." *West Virginia Law Review* 96: 1133–1164.

Woo, Deborah. 1989. "The People v. Fumiko Kimura: But Which People?" *International Journal of the Sociology of Law* 17: 403–428.

Yaron, Reuven. 1966. "The Goring Ox in Near Eastern Laws." *Israel Law Review* 1: 396–406. *State of Washington v. Roberts* (1995). 894 P.2d 1340.

PART IV PRACTICE

INTRODUCTION TO PART IV
Practice

Regina F. Bendix and
Galit Hasan-Rokem

For this final section, we have chosen three contributions that in turn shed light on how folklorists work professionally. As a representation of folkloristic work to generate bodies of data, we have included a chapter on ethnographic fieldwork authored from within the more recent German research tradition and thus reflecting the Anglo-American, anthropological influence. Folklorists also work with literary sources and with historical materials, as is evident from other contributions in this volume. Those may be archival sources collected by earlier generations of folklorists and/or records about everyday life as they are accessible in state and local repositories as well as church and associational archives. Archiving, new technologies for the preservation of collected materials, and the politics of archival maintenance and access have become important issues of their own.

As the chapters in the section on location have demonstrated, folklorists have always interacted with the public sphere. This interaction has different and often controversial histories depending on the sociopolitical context. For this volume we have chosen to represent American public folklore, as "public folklorist" is an acknowledged professional designation which, in the United States, at this point in time numbers more practitioners than the academy, though most public folklorists are trained within academic university programs. Furthermore, Americans have carried out a debate on the respective roles and responsibilities of folklorists active primarily within academic or public spheres, which has resulted in a high degree of reflection over the nature of folkloristic work in general.

A Companion to Folklore, First Edition. Edited by Regina F. Bendix and Galit Hasan-Rokem.
© 2012 John Wiley & Sons, Ltd. Published 2012 John Wiley & Sons, Ltd.

Ensuring the continuity of the discipline requires, above all, institutions peopled with actors capable of maintaining the place of the subject within the academy and the public sphere. With the last chapter of the volume we hope to demonstrate the variegated ways with which actors representing the interests of folklore studies have sought to establish permanence for their complex field.

CHAPTER **29**

SEEING, HEARING, FEELING, WRITING
Approaches and Methods from the Perspective of Ethnological Analysis of the Present[1]

Brigitta Schmidt-Lauber

EUROPEAN ETHNOLOGY (VOLKSKUNDE) AND ITS METHODOLOGICAL APPROACH

It has become a tradition that scholars of European ethnology try to explain their discipline and reflect critically on its cognitive identity. What is this discipline that calls itself "European ethnology"? The discipline, from the perspective of which I write, is a so-called "small discipline" in German-speaking countries. It came to questionable prominence in the 1930s, when it was still called "Volkskunde," but can also look back on an eventful history with many breaks and changes (cf. Bendix in this volume). It is a disciplinary specificity of the German-speaking countries – a "German special discipline" as the historian Thomas Nipperdey (1983: 522) once described it.

European ethnology must be seen as institutionally and historically distinct from social anthropology (formerly "Völkerkunde"), which has often led to confusion, especially considering that most theories and core discourses in terms of methodology

A Companion to Folklore, First Edition. Edited by Regina F. Bendix and Galit Hasan-Rokem.
© 2012 John Wiley & Sons, Ltd. Published 2012 John Wiley & Sons, Ltd.

and many research fields today strongly overlap. Therefore I will occasionally speak in the plural of the "ethno-disciplines" to stress the increased intermingling of these two disciplines with different traditions and orientations and independent institutions (cf. Rogan in this volume).

The specific German-language distinction is not easily transferable to today's international scholarly scene. European ethnology is closely related to *cultural anthropology* and has significant overlaps with *cultural studies*, but differs from these in its specific history. The field has developed a different perspective, even if the key literature on cultural theory or on methodological issues from these other disciplines provide vital and formative points of reference (among them, for example, the writing culture debate, multi-sited ethnography, "thick description," and texts on the semiotic concept of culture). Still primarily focused on the analysis of *one's own* society and social dynamics on the micro level, European ethnologists study everyday life (especially in Europe) in the past and present and the emergence of contemporary phenomena from an actor-centered perspective. The discipline has at its disposal a wide range of methods that it in part shares with others. I will discuss them in this review with a focus on ethnographic methods.

The methodological approaches can best be explained historically, specifically in the discipline with a tradition in Germany as the country with the largest concentration of professional associations. The discipline was established in connection with the German nation-building process culminating in German unification in 1871. Known at the time as "Volkskunde" it provided knowledge of and legitimation for the "Volk" or "people" as a constructed unity of the nation. This focus on the people (Volk) and on different peoples (Völker) and the concomitant central paradigms had, nevertheless, a long history.

This history explains the initial methodological approaches, an often romantically tinged German philological perspective on specific genres and literary traditions, such as folktales, legends, and folksongs, and a statistical-statist social science perspective on "the land and the people." Both methods of narrative study have a strong focus, in contrast to the American folklore tradition (see Bendix 1995), on texts and stories. This led to an increasing concentration on everyday narrative and biographical narration as consciousness analysis (Lehmann 2007); observation and interviewing techniques can also be traced back to these origins. The focus was on the everyday life of the lower and especially agrarian classes of society. The discipline was characterized for a long time by this interest in the rural and peasant world, and the question of the origin of culture (and cultural phenomena), which intensified its strong political affinity especially to nationalist movements. The ongoing, highly reflexive character of the discipline (the process of positioning the discipline as I am doing here is always present) can be located not least in the problematic political involvement of the field during the National Socialist era and the subsequent coming to terms with this past (cf. Bendix in this volume).

Two significant paradigm shifts have taken place since then, each reflected in new methodological foci, terminologies, and research interests. In the 1970s, sociology emerged as a model for European ethnology. The credo at the time was "farewell to folk life" (Bausinger 1970) and entailed a shift to social issues and problems of the present. With this *sociologization*, methods of empirical social research (both qualitative and quantitative) and, in particular, interview techniques grew in importance. The focus on this ideal of an exact science with "objective" methods can also be understood as a response to the often speculative practices of earlier, Germanocentric-oriented work. A particular focus since the late 1970s has been – most often qualitative – biographical studies (see, among others, Lehmann 1978/80, 1983, 2007; Seifert *et al.* 2007), in which the focus on the everyday actor is manifested. This has contributed to the interdisciplinary dialogue that resulted in new methodological and theoretical impulses for dealing with autobiographical narratives (see Lehmann 2007). Since the 1980s, an *anthropologization* of the discipline also took place in the context of the interdisciplinary "cultural turn," in which interpretive approaches and qualitative ethnographic methods in particular acquired greater relevance (see Jeggle 1984). Fieldwork, participant observation, and different forms of qualitative interviews and discussions are key research methods today. The horizon of issues, fields, and methods has expanded significantly in comparison to earlier periods, marking a shift to becoming an actor-oriented, processual cultural science of everyday life concerned with the lives and thoughts of a broad range of groups within a population, past and present, accessed by means of microanalytical study (cf. Kaschuba 1999).

That said, I come now to the actual issue in hand, namely introducing the methodical means of cultural analysis especially in the present and the ongoing debates and discussions that accompany them. First, I will provide an overview of the range of methodological approaches, then focus on the most important, namely fieldwork and the qualitative interview, and discuss possibilities, problems, and applications. In the second part of the chapter I introduce trends and discussions on current methods relevant to ethnographic practice.

AVENUES OF RESEARCH: (ETHNOGRAPHIC) METHODS AT A GLANCE

A broad range of tools is available for the analysis of culture in European ethnology (see Göttsch and Lehmann 2001). One can distinguish between data or sources that are generally available, and data that must first be generated before they can be analyzed. A good deal of data can already be found in various places and is more or less accessible for analysis. These existing sources include archival materials, images, literary and journalistic texts and material objects. Knowledge of social relationships and individual life-worlds cannot only be acquired by the analysis of administrative and criminal court records, statistics on population or public health, birth and marriage registers. It can also be read in furniture, clothing, or technical appliances. Private photographs taken during holidays, family celebrations, of children, graffiti, comic books and other image forms provide data about everyday life and cultures. Depending on theoretical orientation and research interest, different techniques exist for the analysis of this data (methods of historical-archival research and source criticism, methods of material and image analysis, discourse and content analysis of texts, etc.).

A good part of anthropological source material is such that it must first be created in the research process. This is particularly true for studies of aspects of contemporary everyday culture. In the following I will discuss in general terms this second category of source material and the core methods for its creation. The primary method used for cultural analysis of the present takes the form of a collection of techniques known together as (ethnographic) *fieldwork* and (often subsumed by it) the (mostly qualitative) *interview*.

Fieldwork/Ethnography: Understanding by Means of Experience and Participation

Fieldwork – also called *ethnography*[2] – is of central importance in the range of methods of cultural analysis (cf. Schmidt-Lauber 2007a). It can be defined as direct, participatory access to cultural events and people in their respective spaces. Fieldwork is a specific research process within which different procedures are used flexibly in meeting the relevant research issue and the momentary situation. Characteristic of fieldwork is that the researcher becomes part of the method and is physically present. He or she enters into close contact with the people and milieus that are being studied and engages in the process of understanding and comprehending the (often very disparate) views internal to "the field." The concept of *emic* and *etic* has been borrowed from linguistics (Pike 1967 [1954]) to describe the different types of ethnographic understanding and writing, an "emic cultural description" being a representation based on local perspectives and concepts. One of the most important founders of anthropological fieldwork, Bronislaw Malinowski, said that the purpose of fieldwork was "to grasp the native's point of view" (Malinowski 2007 [1922]: 25). Etic is a representation then where the terminology and perspective taken is from the outside, specifically that of modern academia.

One should not, however, imagine the *field* in fieldwork as being given, or as simply being visited and studied. The idea of closed cultures (or groups) that could be studied in their entirety – even discovered – by means of fieldwork has played a significant role in the history of ethnography, and supposedly limited units such as islands, villages, or specific ethnic groups have been sought out by ethnographers with this ideal in mind. Today, an open, dynamic concept of culture has emerged together with an awareness of the fact that the field is in a constant state of construction, the sense of sighting and siting the field (cf. Welz 2009) on the part of the researcher as well as in the research and interaction process. Cultures do not simply stand still for the ethnographer while he paints a portrait (Clifford 1986: 9). Instead, a constant (re)negotiation and communication process is taking place, in the form the study is conducted as well. Fieldwork is a suitable method for microanalytic case studies and close research of everyday life in specific milieus and dynamics. Fieldwork is often spoken of as a holistic approach. While this characterization has remained controversial – considering that this implies an object of study that is complete or bounded – it does do justice to the multi-perspective, comprehensive, and detailed approach it entails. The exemplary moment of micro-analytical fieldwork is essential both pragmatic and methodological – but I will return to the (contentious) issue of determining the field later.

At the core of fieldwork is the presence at and participation in events on the part of the researcher – the *participant observation*, by means of which "feeling" and empathy for the research field or issue should be achieved (see Hauser-Schäublin 2003). Participant observation combines two inherently contradictory behavioral patterns, namely, absorbed participation and objective distance. The term is indicative of the range of possible interactions, but also the potential risks. "Excessive" empathy and too great an identification with the field can result in "going native," that fabled loss of cultural identity on the part of the researcher, while maintaining too great a distance runs the risk of exoticism or even xenophobia and racism. This also explains the fact that fieldwork as a methodological approach should be particularly (self) reflexive, to the point that professional supervision is appropriate for dealing with the emotional involvement inherent in the research process, with transfer and countertransfer, and for recognizing so-called interferences (Devereux 1967; Lindner 1981; Nadig and Reichmayr 2000). Contact denial or role-playing, for example, because the researcher is thought to be a spy for the management or the government, are initially irritating side-effects on the way into the field, but these phenomena are at the same time indicators of the realities on the ground and people's past experiences. Such side-effects are then less an obstacle to gaining data than they are data in and of themselves.

The fact that fieldwork is an ongoing *process* of understanding that includes a wide variety of encounters, contacts, and situations is an indicator of the intensity and necessary openness of the methodology. The exact course of a field study is far from predictable – the research thesis may often change in the course of the study, which then demands new research strategies. That can sometimes be frustrating, because some inquiries prove to be dead ends and not every approach leads to the expected results. This "failure," while an inseparable aspect of the business, is discussed surprisingly seldom in the literature. But it is, luckily, not just a painful personal experience but also a form of cognition and a tool for intensifying an understanding of methodology. For example, if a woman wanted to examine everyday practice in a mosque and be denied access to the prayer room, which appears to her as a hermetically closed world, she will be forced to find another form for accessing this inner sphere. But above all, this fact is data in and of itself about the cultural imaginations of the scholar and about the gender norms in the field. This "failure" sensitizes the scholar to the possibilities and limits of access and about the importance of insights gained. Helpful for developing the fieldwork and for the evaluation of results, given the dynamics and process-driven nature of this kind of research, are the approaches of *grounded theory* (Glaser and Strauss 1967). Grounded theory seeks to arrive at conclusions and interpretations close to the object of study.

What form of *access* is chosen and how one represents oneself in the field must be well thought out. The literature on the issue is rich in examples on how to do so, with special attention being paid to first encounters and the first days in the field (Agar 1996 [1980]; Whyte 1943; Wolff 2000). Should a field be entered via institutions and "from above," or is it better that key persons in the field, so called *gatekeepers*, provide initial contacts and prepare initial networks that then can be extended? It is in any case vital to reflect on the consequences of the form of access and (the diversity of) roles in the field and to choose them appropriately. It makes a difference whether someone introduces themselves in an embassy or in the drug scene as a "researcher" from a university, as a "folklorist" or "anthropologist" or even as a "student of culture" with an interest in conducting a study of how other people live. Hermann Tertilt, for example, applied various confidence-building techniques, such as tolerating and even concealing criminal acts to establish a viable relationship with his informants in youth subcultures on the fringes of legality (Tertilt 1996). Fieldwork thus sometimes raises ethical and often legal questions where the researcher must position him or herself.

A stance constitutive to any fieldwork is a desire to get to know and understand other people and their life-worlds. This includes respect and recognition for the other, precluding a hierarchical perspective in which informants are seen merely as "providers of data." The ideal of a research partnership has in this regard long been a guiding principle that has found special emphasis in the concept of a "dialogical anthropology" (Tedlock 1999; cf. Greverus 1995, etc.), even if the relationships continue to be less than truly reciprocal in most cases.

A precondition and marker of fieldwork is openness to lively exchange and to the dynamics and characteristics of the field as it unfolds. Fieldwork in ethnology or folklore entails more than a researcher's mere presence during data collection or short, one-time contacts with people. It is a time-intensive method. In European ethnology, however (and sometimes also in related disciplines, such as ethnomusicology), the term is understood so broadly that any time the researcher is in "a field" and any form of contact is defined as fieldwork. Simply meeting someone for an interview, recording it, and making notes on the situation and on the biography of the individual could thus be called "fieldwork." In part this (too) broadly applied definition may be explained with the strong focus on interviews and texts in European ethnology. In part it is because the ideal of fieldwork as it was developed especially by Bronislaw Malinowski early in the twentieth century appeared as a counter-model to the armchair anthropology of the nineteenth century, leading to an empirical turn in anthropological fields. Henceforward, the direct contact between researcher and the field was emphasized as was the personal generation of data, taking this task out of the hands of the missionaries, travelers, or colonial officials who had upheld it previously. In the strict sense, however, the mere presence of the researcher should not be defined as fieldwork, but simply as "empirical research."

Another sticking point on the interpretation of the constitutive methods of participation and observation is in the transfer of fieldwork into virtual space and its definition as "online ethnography" (Correll 1995), as "virtual ethnography" (Hine 2000) or as "netography" (Kozinets 2010). The presence of the ethnographer here is physically, temporally, and spatially disparate and often there are no instances of face-to-face interaction with the field and no visibility on the part of the researcher, so much less participation takes place. Currently, in an age where so many people spend time in virtual interaction, the question of the importance of physical presence is reflected upon and fiercely discussed.

As a rule and in the strictest sense of the term, fieldwork is thus the intensive and ongoing immersion through physical presence and participation in day-to-day life and thereby the experiencing and recording of what is going on. Work without boundaries is a characteristic of fieldwork not only in terms of the study of foreign or unfamiliar phenomena. Even for *anthropology at home*, namely, research carried out at the anthropologist's doorstep, everything is potential data. Thus, in an ethnographic study of a football club in Hamburg, where I lived at the time, daily walks through the city and specifically through the district which was the home of the club were a substantial part of the research. I visited bars frequented by fans, but I also encountered the football club when I went out with friends. Even shopping in the supermarket in and around the city offered again and again points of information about the local and regional significance of the club. In the same vein, my own family and working life in the city of Göttingen were a substantial impetus for an ethnographic project in the city, where I examined, together with students, the everyday worlds and specific urbanities of a medium-sized university town.

For European ethnology the concept of *anthropology at home* is the usual working mode, since everyday cultures in close vicinity and often within the immediate environment continue to be the preferred object of research.[3] This leads then to a specific *research design* in terms of the approach to and duration of the research, assuming that various skills necessary for the research (such as language skills and knowledge of the site) have been acquired. Fieldwork in European ethnology is sometimes spoken of in terms of "short visits," in which repeated, specific insights on the issue of study are gained. The choice of words is somewhat inconvenient as it hides the characteristic intensity and density of the fieldwork. The average *duration* of fieldwork has no doubt changed in recent years, not least in the light of changing working and teaching requirements and funding constraints. But even if fieldwork, which according to the old rule of thumb should last at least a year – justified in view of the annual cycle of so-called "primitives" – cannot be realized in this intensity, and often was not realized even in the days in which the methodology emerged, the obligation to shorten fieldwork periods for financial or structural reasons should be proved.

Fieldwork is thus a specific process of generating knowledge and can ideally be divided into *phases* marked by different roles, growing familiarity with the field and possibly different research methods.

- The *initial phase* is the explorative investigation of what the field is and the first contact with people and situations. In this phase everything must be considered a potential source of data. All the more important is thus the detailed recording of as many details and processes, people, and peculiarities, especially since with increasing familiarity these become less remarkable and tend to no longer make an impression.
- This is followed by an *extensive research phase* – which, depending on the field and working conditions can be divided into numerous fieldwork periods – in which material is collected systematically and by different methods in accordance with the initial research questions and during which one's roles in the field may solidify or change. During this phase, an initial analysis of material (transcriptions of interviews, media analyses, etc.) is highly recommended because data collection and analysis in ethnographic research are intertwined and concrete approaches (interview techniques, sample building) need to be verified and, if necessary, adjusted.
- *Review and evaluation* serve the systematic analysis of the collected material and the (usually written) presentation of the results (often in the form of a monograph) to the professional and interested public. Renewed short visits to the field may be recommended, even necessary. Fieldwork is thus a process and aims at examining culture as a dynamic, processual category, which itself is subject to ongoing revision and change.

In documenting research, different representational techniques are used, which in turn generate different kinds of texts. In the wake of the post-mortem publication of Bronislaw Malinowski's "A Diary in the Strict Sense of the Word" (Malinowski 1967), the question of the subjectivity of the researcher was discussed in detail. The need to consider and record personal sensitivities and feelings about the field, both for letting off steam and as a source of data, has in turn become commonplace. The usual text form used in this context is the *diary*, in which daily impressions, experiences, and moods are noted so that the processes of research can be retraced afterwards. In addition – and often integrated into it – are *field notes* or observation logs that are less subjective than detailed descriptions of specific events, interactions, and environments.

Above, I described fieldwork as a principally multi-methodological approach. In addition to participant observation, *further research methods* are available (Beer 2003; Burgess 1984; Agar 1996 [1980]; Bernard 1995, 2000; De Munck and Sobos 1998; Dewalt and Dewalt 2002; Fetterman 1989; Spradley 1980). Participant observation is clearly the core and constitutive approach, but the intensive, processual approach to fieldwork also requires the use of other means for acquiring data on the topic being studied. These can include, for example, genealogies, cartographic records and census surveys, job descriptions, visual representations of the natural and material environment and so forth; they play an important role especially in traditional anthropological fieldwork in foreign cultures. Other possible instruments include the observational walk, which can take place alone or with an informant, or the completion of *mental maps* (see Lynch 1960). In addition, and generally in the initial period of fieldwork, explorative methods such as *nosing around*, as described in the context of the Chicago School (Park 1915), can be undertaken. The latter connotes a roaming through the field and the initial, broadly cast exploration of the fieldwork environment.

As well as the participation in, and observation of, processes, social dynamics, and the existing environment, talking to people is a central aspect of fieldwork. This is undertaken through different *interview forms* and techniques (Schmidt-Lauber 2007b). In addition to so-called unstructured *informal discussions,* as they take place in everyday life, systematic interviews with selected informants need to be recorded – today mostly digitally – and then transcribed. The available options for doing so will be discussed in the next section.

Fieldwork is then an experience-based means to access social life and cultural events with the goal of developing an understanding of and insights into everyday life and social dynamics. It is a close, microanalytical research practice that acquires its specific form and direction in the course of the research process and in constant negotiation with the relevant actors. Fieldwork is also a special form of interaction and a particular mode of experience. The strong interweaving of the method with the person of the researcher and their subjective experiences and impressions entails that other *senses* beyond those of the eye (seeing what is done) and ear (hearing what is said) have increasingly and consciously been applied as media of perception (Bendix 2006). Smells, tastes and sounds have come into "view," as has research by touch. The whole spectrum of the human senses is applied not only for the purposes of generating data but also as forms of presentation of ethnographic data and insights beyond the medium of the written word. Film and photography are in this regard the most frequently used media (Ruby 2000; Overdick 2010),[4] but occasionally an appeal is made to taste and smell, which is best possible in the form of an exhibit. A developing dialogue between art and fields of cultural research has emerged in recent years that has led to mutual inspiration and to new forms of data analysis and presentation (see Binder *et al.* 2008).

Qualitative Ethnographic Interviews: The Art of Letting Someone Speak

While participant observation provides access to specific traditions and processes, such as a ritual, social etiquette, a subculture, or everyday activities, discussions and interviews provide insights into the subjective perceptions, experiences, and imaginations of people and into how people want to present themselves. An example of the difference between observation and interview and how they complement one another is again my own fieldwork experience in Namibia. It was quite common among German speakers in the late 1980s to speak of black Namibians as "Kaffer" or "Neger" (nigger) and of the domestic staff as "Boy" or "Perle" (pearl), or, at best in the possessive form, namely "mein Johannes." As opposed to daily usage, in interviews these same people struggled to find acceptable words and spoke, for example, of "our black citizens." After all, they were under no illusion that social values and practices in Europe were different from those in what was at the time apartheid South West Africa, with its hermetic legal, political, and practical everyday divisions between the so-called "ethnic groups" and "races." From the perspective of a reflexive (European) ethnology, both ways of speaking, and thus both familiar everyday practice as well as the selective presentation to the outsider European ethnographer, describe relevant dimensions of everyday culture. In any case it is part of ethnographic practice to reflect on the presence of and interaction with the researcher and the (not necessarily disruptive) consequences thereof. After all, every statement and every form of self-representation is made for a specific recipient. This principle is true for the (ethnographic) interview as well. Representations and narratives are always tied to the specific conversation and life situation and need to be analyzed with this in mind.

Another characteristic that has been mentioned above for ethnographic fieldwork applies to the interview situation as well, namely the flexibility and adaptability of the methodology. There is no such thing as "the interview" in the sense of a singular approach that can be applied to all issues. Depending on the topic at hand as well as the theoretical approach, different interview forms and techniques have been developed (see Flick *et al.* 2000). Each must be adapted to the momentary investigation and be open for modification – after all, methods are tools of cognition. In general, (qualitative) interviews are classified in terms of their thematic focus or their interest in (specific) people, such as in "biographical interviews" (Lehmann, 1979/80, 1983; Fuchs-Heinritz 2005) or in "expert interviews," and in terms of the degree to which they are structured (cf. Schmidt-Lauber 2007b). This ranges from "open" to "closed" approaches, from interviews where little more than an opening question is formulated by the interviewer, who leaves the further course of the interview to the interviewee, as in the sub-category of "narrative interviews" (cf. Schütze 1977), to questionnaires on specific issues with a specific set of interrelated questions based on pre-tests, such as the so-called guided interview. Different rules and procedures exist for each of the different types of interviews (which, incidentally, have strikingly different designations). Guided interviews, for example, require the flexible arrangement of the questions based on the specific situation. These run the risk of becoming bureaucratic, as the questions are asked and answered in a rote manner without considering either the position of the interviewee or the situation. The narrative interview theoretically requires a maximum of restraint on the part of the interviewer so as to allow the narrative to take its course and to allow the narrator to potentially reveal information that he or she would not necessarily have said in another context. This is one reason why the role of the interviewer in this situation has been rightly criticized as being that of a mere "narrative animator" (Bude 1985). This interview form also assumes the homology of narrative and experience, which is a problematic assumption from the perspective of cultural research. But more important than an abstract distinction and a complete summary of different interview concepts and techniques with their respective premises and risks is the research practice itself and thus the embedding of interviews in ethnological and folkloristic research.

Earlier interview techniques used in European ethnology were often carried out as written surveys, and for a time used quantitative methods with closed questions (yes/ no, multiple-choice or scales). Today, *qualitative* interviews are preferred, with open questions asked in a direct, face-to-face encounter with individuals, and more rarely in focus groups (Bohnsack 2000). So called E-interviews, that is, interviews completed electronically via the Internet or via e-mail (see Schlehe 2003: 81), have also increased in popularity. Their specific, temporally and spatially displaced form of communication and the fact that they are reduced to the written word require a specific form of research methodology, source criticism, and analysis that has only just begun to be reflected in cultural research.

In general it can be said that qualitative interviews as they have been developed in the qualitative social sciences (cf. Flick et al. 2000; Lamnek 1995) are a flexible practice suitable for cultural research. They can be adapted to the situation and course of the interview as well as the individual interviewee, allowing him or her to develop responses and themes in an appropriate manner in view of the local rules of communication (for the principle, the openness of communication, see Hoffmann-Riem 1980: 343 ff.).[5] Questions must be formulated in ways that open the door for detailed flows of words and not short, monosyllabic answers. The wording of a question needs to be prepared and reflected on critically. Thus, the question "when did you first go to school?" would be better put in terms of "what was it like to begin going to school?" so as to initiate a narrative. Qualitative interviews focus in particular on the perspective and (biographical) experience of the subject. In keeping with the reflexivity, openness, and processuality of these interviews, I will now refer to them as *ethnographic interviews*, which at the same time is a reminder of the epistemological roots of this methodology in fields of cultural research such as cultural anthropology, ethnology, and folklore studies.

Longer discussions have taken place in cultural anthropology and the social sciences on the distribution of roles and the communicative situation during an interview, including some proposals to reduce the so-called "artificial nature" of interviews by means of developing a "less forced" conversational atmosphere (cf. Hoffmann-Riem 1980; Hopf 1978).[6] I am a little skeptical about such proposals because they negate the variety of communication forms and situations that exist in everyday life and reduce a whole range of socially established conversation and relationship types down to two forms of dialogue: a supposedly non-hierarchical, "natural" conversation on the one hand and a professional, "artificial" dialogue with a hierarchical division of labor on the other. It is sufficient to mention such different interview formats as the patient-doctor conversation, the political interview, or the oral exam to show that there are many more interview types and roles in everyday practice. Western media society can be rightly regarded as an "interview society" (Atkinson and Silvermann 1997), in which interviews are a familiar format and a common interaction situation. How to conduct oneself in an interview situation and the roles of the actors present can be considered a given. Thus, the erroneous idea that an interview is an "artificial and unnatural conversation," has long been obsolete. In contrast to the rapid question-answer cycle of (mostly quantitative) social science survey techniques, such as in market research, ethnographic interviews should encourage the interviewees to tell stories and leave much room for them to develop the situation and the course of the conversation while the interviewers should show as much restraint as possible, adjusting their comments to the course of the narrative and to the person of the interviewee, avoiding any clear hierarchical division of labor. Interviewers should define themselves as a person as well, in terms, for example, of their personal interest in the topic, or sometimes their own experiences and impressions. Competent interviewing is thus far more a question of practice and methodological reflection than the simple following of recipes. While many a conversation partner may need to be reminded repeatedly about the actual issue at hand and be held within the scope of their narrative, more often than not, signs and comments of confirmation are necessary, as is patience in order to let the interviewee slowly develop the narrative.

Even if no standard guidelines exist, two basic rules of qualitative-ethnographic interviewing can be noted: first, that an interview should encourage narratives on a specific theme and thus requires preparation both in terms of content and method (always in consideration of the fact that any list of questions should not be checked off in parrot fashion but woven into the situation as reminders or guiding remarks), and second and most importantly, that the interview should communicate an understanding of the life world and perspective of the interviewee that the interviewer wants to comprehend and in which she or he is truly interested. It goes without saying that an interview also requires a willingness to communicate on the part of the interviewee, which also needs to be reflected on (what interests an individual is following when talking about their lives, their day-to-day activities or their experiences). Not only for methodological but also for ethical reasons, the understanding of ethnographic interviewing and fieldwork practice in general has changed to an ideally reflexive relationship between equal partners (cf. Lindner 1981), even if the participants in an interview hardly ever have common interests and the relationship is far from reciprocal.

Ethnographic interviews are usually *recorded* electronically and transcribed. In addition, notes should be made on the interviewees' partners (such as sex, age, marital status, occupation, etc.) and the interview (atmosphere, duration, special situations). It happens again and again that the technology fails, so that the timely verification of the proper functioning of the recording equipment and familiarization with its operation is essential. The process of *transcription* has for a long time, surprisingly enough, been subject to very little reflection in the context of methodology discussions in social research, despite the fact that the transmission of the spoken word into a written text is at the same time an act of interpretation and the construction of a source of data.[7] As for the *analysis* of interview transcripts, various techniques are available depending on the question in hand, (sub-)discipline, and theoretical context (such as content analysis, objective hermeneutics, and so on; cf. Merten, 1995 [1983]; Oevermann 1989; Wernet 2000). The individual stages must be adjusted to the specific research. The aim of cultural analysis is to determine the meaning of what has been said and done and via coding, classification, and interpretation of the material to develop an understanding of cultural processes and relationships. For both the analysis as such and the presentation of the results, it is possible to either single out a typical case or to develop a comparative synopsis of the materials. Characteristic of qualitative-ethnographic analysis is, first, the inductive manner in which the results are achieved. Concepts, theories, and solutions are developed based on the material itself and less in answer to pre-formulated hypotheses that are to be verified or refuted. The second characteristic is the contextualization of the various statements. Conclusions about (parts of) interviews are based on a variety of materials and details and in relation to the context (the interview situation, the interviewee, the relationship between the interview partners). Individual statements are always seen in a question and answer context and interpreted in the context of the whole interview.

The handling of the sources in the *presentation of results,* namely in ethnographic texts, is also dependent on when the text was written and the culture of the scholarly community at a given time. The relatively loose ways of dealing with the presentation of interview material in classical monographs – neither Bronislaw Malinowski nor Clifford Geertz cite specific interviews or a specific passage and often their informants are not even mentioned directly – can be contrasted with the more stringent reference system that has emerged. Today, it is considered usual practice to cite the interview, the specific interviewee, and often even the exact location of the comment within the transcript. The visibility of the research subjects has become a central concern during the last decades. Conversation partners must be provided with a pseudonym, and/or they must agree to being named and to being quoted. It has also become common practice – especially in the United States – to sign an interview agreement. Considering the fact that different disciplinary and national practices (and laws) apply for dealing with research data and material, it is highly recommended to inform oneself about the local practice beforehand.[8]

TRENDS IN AND CURRENT DISCUSSIONS ON ETHNOGRAPHY

Scholarship as a whole and individual disciplines are in constant development. Paradigms change and so do their perspectives and tools of cognition. Methods and theories are often no longer constants of research and must be seen in their historical and social context as well as in relation to contemporary interests and time-bound goals of a discipline. Within the fields of ethnological and folkloristic research, two issues have been discussed vehemently in the last three decades, showing clearly the transformations that also affect methodology. These are, first, the question of defining the field and fieldwork in response to contemporary globalization processes and, second, the critical reappraisal of ethnographic representation and the attempt to find new polyphonic means of representation.

On Defining the Concepts of Place and Field in Field Research – Single and Multi-sited-Ethnography

A societal awareness has emerged for the global interconnectedness and interdependence of systems of every kind, of states and economies. A consciousness of the mobility of people, objects, ideas, and problems on the micro level has become *common sense*. Globalization has thus also advanced to become an issue of analysis for the cultural disciplines traditionally focused on specific localities. It is not only in this context that the concept of culture has become more flexible, dynamic, and processual. It has also been liberated from geographical and especially national constraints. The idea that states encompass cultures or, vice versa, that cultures may be defined in nationally or, more generally, in territorially limited terms may be considered obsolete today. The units studied by (European) ethnology are no longer understood as spatially or socially closed groups or communities (Welz 2009: 200). The concept that a researcher must become a recognized member of a supposedly homogeneous *community* has also been revised. A new, interdisciplinary interest in spaces has emerged in the so-called *spatial turn* (Bachmann-Medick 2006; Löw 2001, 2004; Warf and Arias 2008), and this has also taken hold in cultural theory, inspiring new concepts and, in any case, the connection between culture and space has begun to be understood as far more complex and sophisticated than past cultural theories might have suggested.

Thus the question of fieldwork as a practice of localization and, more concretely, the definition of the respective field of study has been raised. George Marcus presented a proposal that has since then found significant interest and led the debate in the discipline. Considering the mobility and multi-locality of the actors and objects of research, he called for a *multi-sited ethnography*, in which the researcher himself becomes mobile, following the paths of (i) people, (ii) objects, (iii) metaphors, (iv) life stories, (v) plots, and (vi) conflicts (Marcus 1995). This concept is often set against a model of single-sited ethnography in which the stationary researcher (Welz 1998) is ascribed a hermetically outdated, territorialized understanding of culture. It is in turn often argued that "in the past," field research was practiced as single-sited ethnography, while today we have the approach of a multi-sited ethnography. This polarized representation is a simplification both in methodological and in historical terms. Neither did scholars limit themselves to a single site in so-called stationary fieldwork, and even the dean of anthropological fieldwork, Bronislaw Malinowski, moved from one village to another. George Marcus makes explicit reference to the multi-locality of past fieldwork practice; nor does this supposed immobility result in images of closed cultures. Rather, it is the theory-based perspective of research on islands or in clubs that leads (or has led) to closed horizons, the specific research design having been based on the research hypotheses (cf. Schmidt-Lauber 2009).

George Marcus's reflections on multi-sited ethnography are seen, especially in debates within European ethnology, primarily as a question of locality, of research practice under conditions of globalization and the examination of changes in specific cultural ties to specific spaces (Welz 2009: 197). Mobility becomes here the category that is to be observed (Welz 1998: 192). But George Marcus can also be read more generally as a challenge to reexamine the interwoven nature of the field. He is looking to reconsider the process of the constitution of the field and the contextualizing, dynamic practice of research close to the object of study, arguing in terms of the multi-perspective nature and processuality of ethnography that I have described above.

There is no doubt that the current discussions have developed a deep awareness for underlying theoretical concepts. They have made clear that cultures cannot be limited territorially and that their study requires temporally and spatially flexible approaches.

Ethnographic research requires modification, but at the same time runs the risk of abandoning key assumptions of fieldwork: A narrow interpretation of a multi-sited ethnography can lead to a significant reduction in the intensity, density, and duration of immersion into the culture, with the consequence that ever shorter visits are treated as fieldwork.[9] This trend is also critical in terms of university politics and the financial conditions under which ethnographic research is to take place.

The Crisis of Ethnographic Representation and Meta-anthropology

Another issue that continues to preoccupy ethnological and folkloristic research and debate is the question of how (foreign) cultures can be represented. Many events since the 1960s have shaken the credibility and authority of the discipline in this regard. These include the publication of Malinowski's diary, which not only undermined his claim to friendly-benevolent empathy. Various revisions, namely fieldwork at one and the same site at different times and by different researchers, have resulted in completely different interpretations such as Mead (1943) and Freeman (1983) on Samoa or Redfield (1949) and Lewis (1960) on Tepotzlán, casting doubt on the validity of the genre of the ethnographic monograph. And finally, emancipation movements in the context of decolonization and a sensitization for power relationships in anthropological research, not only in the wake of the feminist anthropology (cf. Behar and Gordon 1995; Abu-Lughod 1991), contributed to criticism of the genre of ethnographic realism. Anthropological knowledge as such was put in question, as the predicament of culture of "being in culture while looking at culture" and the fact that there is no neutral observer (Clifford 1988).

Based on papers given at a research seminar, James Clifford and George Marcus published in 1986 the widely acclaimed anthology "Writing Culture," a phrase that has provoked a virulent debate in current ethnographic fields (Clifford and Marcus 1986). In it, anthropological texts were themselves subject to analysis. It was asked, how and by means of which rhetorical devices authors described cultures and their own presence in the field. Clifford Geertz analyzed and classified the writing styles of anthropological classics such as Margaret Mead and Edward E. Evans-Pritchard (Geertz 1988) and James Clifford discussed the issues and strategies of ethnographic authority (Clifford 1988). The fictional character of ethnographic texts came into view, which could as a result only be understood as "partial truths" (Clifford 1986). In addition to this *meta-anthropology*, new rhetorical styles, media, and formats of ethnographic representation have been and continue to be experimented with in an attempt to do justice to the emic perspectives within a given field and the so-called polyphony of voices and cultural events within it. These include new text genres, such as the dialogue in the form of letters (Tedlock 1999), or new forms of representation, such as providing uncommented excerpts from the source material separate and distinct from the scholarly narrative, such as Marjorie Shostak's "Nisa – The Life and Words of a !Kung Woman" (1981). These works, of course, continue to be edited versions (not only in terms of translation and transcription) of the authors' interviews and conversations.

Creative approaches, as for instance collaborations with artists, are not without reason subsumed under the heading *experimental ethnography*. They may not have endured as new rhetorical styles or heralded new forms of ethnographic representation, but they have contributed to a consciousness of the deliberate use of language, image, and sound and a breadth of representational forms. The "writing culture" debate has set in motion an ongoing process of reflection and, given the discipline, an awareness of the constructed nature of knowledge and representation. Today there is no question that the research and writing process should be reflected upon methodologically and that reflection and dialogue shape any representation. [10]

OUTLOOK: ETHNOGRAPHIC TURN

Ethnography and ethnographic methods are in vogue today. I remember from my own time as a student the amusement of many other students from different disciplines who initially associated fieldwork with agricultural studies and, in the truest sense, a down-to-earth form of analysis. Considering this novelty, the current interest in the method is remarkable. Terms such as "ethnography," "fieldwork," and "participant observation" have crept into journalism and literature and a variety of disciplines far beyond the social and cultural disciplines. I am inclined to speak of an "ethnographic turn," a "turn," that is not only associated with methods and terms but also in a change in perspective to one of an empathetic understanding and interest in everyday life.

Within European ethnology, the "redemption of the ethnographic dimension" (Jeggle 1984: 13) claimed necessary in the 1980s, has been broadly realized. Ethnography is so popular that it has found entry even into the study of the history of the everyday, an important field of research of the discipline, as "historical ethnography" or "historical fieldwork." Here is not the place to discuss the point or the viability of these latter concepts (see Schmidt-Lauber 2010). To my mind, the attempt to declare a specific historical research method as "historical ethnography" is also a justification and strategy in a time in which most attention is given to contemporary cultural and social phenomena. There is no doubt that ethnography as a method of contemporary cultural analysis and the ethnographic interpretation of individual methods such as the interview will continue to be a hallmark of a field interested in the study of everyday events in specific places and the facets of the lives of particular actors.

NOTES

1 Translation by Andreas Hemming, MA.
2 The term ethnography is often used synonymously with the particular methodological approach to fieldwork or participant observation. But the term is also a specific form of anthropological writing, a combination of the Greek words *ethnos* and *graphein*, meaning "writing (about) a people." Ethnography as a literary style is often used in the descriptions of particular situations and actors and in Geertzian cultural analysis that has come to be known as "thick description" (Geertz 1973). Finally, the term is also used for identifying a specific form of knowledge and an epistemological approach. Primarily, though, the term is used to identify a particular methodological approach.
3 As opposed to European ethnology, anthropology has only recently discovered the value of researching one's own culture, but has increasingly turned to this possibility, especially since

the process of decolonization and the emergence of so-called indigenous anthropologists have called into question the legitimacy of research by Western scholars in non-Western societies. This relationship is now considered an aspect of authority practices and a ritual of asserting power.

4   Compare the contributions to the conference "Beyond Text: Image; Voice; Sound; Object: Synaesthetic and Sensory Practices in Anthropology" at the Centre for Visual Anthropology of the University of Manchester, June/July 2007.

5   Qualitative research generates and does not verify hypotheses. It is best suited for gaining new insights or making new associations and less for verifying or refuting existing knowledge.

6   In American folkloristics, Kenneth Goldstein suggested the "induced natural context" as a means to solve this methodological issue (Goldstein 1964).

7   Ethnopoetic work, particularly on Native American verbal art, must be mentioned as an early exception: here since the 1980s, the crucial place of transcription as both an act of translation and interpretation brought forth groundbreaking insights bolstering the emergence of performance perspectives. See, for example, Hymes (1981) Tedlock (1983), Toelken and Scott (1981). See also the chapters by Bauman and Seitel in this volume.

8   The practice of citing interview transcripts in German-speaking European ethnology appears to me to be more rigid than in Anglo-American scholarly practice, which may have something to do with a traditional consciousness in the discipline for language and texts as well as specific disciplinary ethics.

9   The duration of fieldwork is of course only one indicator of its intensity. My point is that while fieldwork can also take place in short visits, not every short visit constitutes fieldwork.

10 An important theoretical context in this deconstruction is, moreover, the concept of the *linguistic turn* (cf. Rorty 1967; Bachmann-Medick 2006), which has had a significant impact on the understanding of scholarship across disciplines, the linguistic considerations of which have found entry into cultural analysis. In (European) ethnology it has led to the abandonment of the concept of science as great, true narrative (see Bräunlein and Lauser 1992, Berg and Fuchs 1993).

REFERENCES

Abu-Lughod, Lila. 1991. "Writing against Culture" in Richard G. Fox, Ed. *Recapturing Anthropology: Working in the Present*. Santa Fe: School of American Research Press, pp. 137–162.

Agar, Michael. 1996 [1980]. *The Professional Stranger. An Informal Introduction to Ethnography*. New York: Academic Press.

Atkinson, Paul, and David Silverman. 1997. "Kundera's Immortality: The Interview Society and the Invention of the Self." *Qualitative Inquiry* 3(3): 304–325.

Bachmann-Medick, Doris. 2006. *Cultural Turns. Neuorientierungen in den Kulturwissenschaften*. Reinbek/Hamburg: Rowohlt.

Bausinger, Hermann. 1970. "Abschied vom Volksleben." *Untersuchungen des Ludwig-Uhland-Instituts der Universität Tübingen* 27. Tübingen: TVV.

Beer, Bettina, Ed. 2003. *Methoden und Techniken der Feldforschung*. Berlin: Reimer.

Behar, Ruth and Deborah A. Gordon, Eds. 1995. *Women Writing Culture*. Berkeley: University of California Press.

Bendix, Regina. 1995. *Amerikanische Folkloristik. Eine Einführung*. Berlin: Reimer.

Bendix, Regina. 2006. "Was über das Auge hinausgeht: Zur Rolle der Sinne in der ethnographischen Forschung." *Schweizerisches Archiv für Volkskunde* 102: 71–84.

Berg, Eberhard and Martin Fuchs. 1993. "Phänomenologie der Differenz. Reflexionsstufen ethnographischer Repräsentation" in Eberhard Berg and Martin Fuchs, Eds. *Kultur, soziale Praxis, Text. Die Krise der ethnographischen Repräsentation.* Frankfurt: Suhrkamp, pp. 11–108.

Bernard, Harvey Russel. 1995. *Research Methods in Anthropology: Qualitative and Quantitative Approaches.* Walnut Creek: Alta Mira Press.

Bernard, Harvey Russel. 2000. *Handbook of Methods in Cultural Anthropology.* Walnut Creek: Alta Mira Press.

Binder, Beate, Dagmar Neuland-Kitzerow, and Karoline Noack, Eds. 2008. *Kunst und Ethnographie: Zum Verhältnis von visueller Kultur und ethnographischem Arbeiten.* Berlin: LIT.

Bohnsack, Ralf. 2000. "Gruppendiskussion" in Uwe Flick, Ernst Kardorff, and Ines Steinke, Eds. *Qualitative Forschung. Ein Handbuch.* Reinbek/Hamburg: Rowohlt, pp. 369–384.

Bräunlein, Peter J. and Andrea Lauser, Eds. 1992. "Einleitung." *Kea. Zeitschrift für Kulturwissenschaften* 4: i–iv.

Bude, Heinz. 1985. "Der Sozialforscher als Narrationsanimateur. Kritische Anmerkungen zu einer erzähltheoretischen Fundierung der interpretativen Sozialforschung." *Kölner Zeitschrift für Soziologie und Sozialpsychologie* 37: 310–326.

Burgess, Robert G. 1984. *In the Field: An Introduction to Field Research.* Hemel Hempstead: George Allen and Unwin.

Clifford, James. 1986. "Introduction. Partial Truths" in James Clifford and George E. Marcus, Eds. *Writing Culture. The Poetics and Politics of Ethnography.* Berkeley: University of California Press, pp. 1–26.

Clifford, James. 1988. "On Ethnographic Authority" in James Clifford, Ed. *The Predicament of Culture. Twentieth-Century Ethnography, Literature, and Art.* Cambridge: Harvard University Press, pp. 21–54.

Clifford, James and George E. Marcus, Eds. 1986. *Writing Culture: The Poetics and Politics of Ethnography.* Berkeley: University of California Press.

Correll, Shelley. 1995. "The Ethnography of an Electronic Bar: The Lesbian Café." *Journal of Contemporary Ethnography* 24(3): 270–298.

De Munck, Victor and Elisa J. Sobos, Eds. 1998. *Using Methods in the Field: A Practical Introduction and Casebook.* Walnut Creek: Alta Mira Press.

Devereux, George. 1967. *From Anxiety to Method in the Behavioral Sciences.* The Hague: Mouton.

Dewalt, Kathleen M. and Billie R. Dewalt. 2002. *Participant Observation: A Guide for Fieldworkers.* Walnut Creek: Alta Mira Press.

Fetterman, David M. 1989. *Ethnography Step by Step.* Newbury Park, CA: Sage Publications.

Flick, Uwe, Ernst Kardorff, and Ines Steinke, Eds. 2000. *Qualitative Forschung. Ein Handbuch.* Reinbek/Hamburg: Rowohlt.

Freeman, Derek. 1983. *Margaret Mead and Samoa. The Making and Unmaking of an Anthropological Myth.* Cambridge: Harvard University Press.

Fuchs-Heinritz, Werner. 2005. *Biographische Forschung. Eine Einführung in Praxis und Methoden.* 3rd edition. Wiesbaden: Verlag für Sozialwissenschaften.

Geertz, Clifford. 1973. "Thick Description: Toward an Interpretive Theory of Culture" in *The Interpretation of Cultures. Selected Essays.* New York: Basic Books, pp. 3–30.

Geertz, Clifford. 1988. *Works and Lives: The Anthropologist as Author.* Palo Alto: Stanford University Press.

Glaser, Barney G. and Anselm L. Strauss. 1967. *The Discovery of Grounded Theory: Strategies of Qualitative Research.* Chicago: Aldine.

Goldstein, Kenneth S. 1964. *A Guide for Fieldworkers in Folklore.* Hatboro, PA: Folklore Associates.

Göttsch, Silke and Albrecht Lehmann, Eds. 2001. *Methoden der Volkskunde. Positionen, Quellen, Arbeitsweisen der Europäischen Ethnologie.* Berlin: Reimer.

Greverus, Ina Maria. 1995. *Die Anderen und Ich. Vom Sich Erkennen, Erkannt – und Anerkanntwerden. Kulturanthropologische Texte.* Darmstadt: Wissenschaftliche Buchgesellschaft.

Hauser-Schäublin, Brigitta. 2003. "Teilnehmende Beobachtung" in Bettina Beer, Ed. *Methoden und Techniken der Feldforschung.* Berlin: Reimer, pp. 33–54.

Hine, Christine M. 2000. *Virtual Ethnography.* London: Sage Publications.

Hoffmann-Riem, Christa. 1980. "Die Sozialforschung einer interpretativen Soziologie. Der Datengewinn." *Kölner Zeitschrift für Soziologie und Sozialpsychologie* 32: 339–372.

Hopf, Christel. 1978. "Die Pseudo-Exploration – Überlegungen zur Technik qualitativer Interviews in der Sozialforschung." *Zeitschrift für Soziologie* 7(2): 97–115.

Hymes, Dell. 1981. *In Vain I Tried to Tell you. Essays in North American Indian Poetics.* Philadelphia: University of Pennsylvania Press.

Jeggle, Utz, Ed. 1984. "Feldforschung. Qualitative Methoden in der Kulturanalyse." *Untersuchungen des Ludwig-Uhland-Instituts der Universität Tübingen* 62. Tübingen: TVV.

Kaschuba, Wolfgang. 1999. *Einführung in die Europäische Ethnologie.* München: C.H. Beck.

Kozinets, Robert V. 2010. *Netnography. Doing Ethnographic Research Online.* London: Sage Publications.

Lamnek, Siegfried. 1995 [1988]. *Qualitative Sozialforschung.* 2 Vols. Weinheim: Beltz PVU.

Lehmann, Albrecht. 1979/1980. "Autobiographische Methoden. Verfahren und Möglichkeiten." *Ethnologia Europaea* XI (1): 36–54.

Lehmann, Albrecht. 1983. *Erzählstruktur und Lebenslauf. Autobiographische Untersuchungen.* Frankfurt: Campus.

Lehmann, Albrecht. 2007. *Reden über Erfahrung. Kulturwissenschaftliche Bewusstseinsanalyse des Erzählens.* Berlin: Reimer.

Lewis, Oscar. 1960. *Tepotzlán: Village in Mexico.* New York: Holt, Rinehart and Winston.

Lindner, Rolf. 1981. "Die Angst des Forschers vor dem Feld. Überlegungen zur teilnehmenden Beobachtung als Interaktionsprozess." *Zeitschrift für Volkskunde* 77: 51–66.

Löw, Martina. 2001. *Raumsoziologie.* Frankfurt: Suhrkamp.

Löw, Martina. 2004. "Raum – Die topologischen Dimensionen der Kultur" in

Friedrich Jaeger and Burkhard Liebsch, Eds. *Handbuch der Kulturwissenschaften. Grundlagen und Schlüsselbegriffe.* Stuttgart: Metzler, pp. 46–59.

Lynch, Kevin. 1960. *The Image of the City.* Cambridge, MA: MIT Press.

Malinowski, Bronislaw K. 1967. *A Diary in the Strict Sense of the Term.* London: Routledge.

Malinowski, Bronislaw. 2007 [1922]. *Argonauts of Western Pacific.* Eschborn/Frankfurt: Klotz.

Marcus, George M. 1995. "Ethnography in/of the World: the Emergence of Multi-sited Ethnography." *Annual Review of Anthropology* 24: 95–117.

Mead, Margaret. 1943 [1928]. *Coming of Age in Samoa: A Study of Adolescence and Sex in Primitive Societies.* Harmondsworth: Penguin.

Merten, Klaus. 1995 [1983]. *Inhaltsanalyse: Einführung in Theorie, Methode und Praxis.* Opladen: Westdeutscher Verlag.

Nadig, Maya and Johannes Reichmayr. 2000. "Wie qualitative Forschung gemacht wird. Paul Parin, Fritz Morgenthaler und Goldy Parin-Matthèy" in Uwe Flick, Ernst Kardorff, and Ines Steinke, Eds. *Qualitative Forschung. Ein Handbuch.* Reinbek/Hamburg: Rowohlt, pp. 72–84.

Nipperdey, Thomas. 1983. *Deutsche Geschichte 1800–1866. Bürgerwelt und starker Staat.* München: C.H. Beck.

Oevermann, Ulrich. 1989. *Objektive Hermeneutik – Eine Methodologie soziologischer Strukturanalyse.* Frankfurt: Suhrkamp.

Overdick, Thomas 2010. *Photographing Culture. Anschauung und Anschaulichkeit in der Ethnographie.* Zürich: Chronos Verlag.

Park, Robert E. 1915. "The City: Suggestions for the Investigation of Human Behavior." *American Journal of Sociology* 20: 577–612.

Pike, Kenneth Lee. 1967 [1954]. "Language in Relation to a Unified Theory of Structure of Human Behavior." *Janua Linguarum: Series Maior* 24. The Hague: Mouton.

Redfield, Robert. 1949 [1930]. *Tepotzlán, A Mexican Village: A Study of Folk Life.* Chicago: University of Chicago Press.

Rorty, Richard. 1967. *The Linguistic Turn: Recent Essays in Philosophical Method.* Chicago: University of Chicago Press.

Ruby, Jay. 2000. *Picturing Culture. Explorations of Film and Anthropology.* Chicago: University of Chicago.

Seifert, Manfred, Irene Götz, and Birgit Huber, Eds. 2007. *Flexible Biografien? Horizonte und Brüche im Arbeitsleben der Gegenwart.* Frankfurt: Campus.

Schlehe, Judith. 2003. "Qualitative ethnographische Interviewformen" in Bettina Beer, Ed. *Methoden und Techniken der Feldforschung.* Berlin: Reimer, pp. 71–93.

Schmidt-Lauber, Brigitta. 2007a. "Feldforschung. Kulturanalyse durch teilnehmende Beobachtung" in Silke Göttsch and Albrecht Lehmann, Eds. *Methoden der Volkskunde. Positionen, Quellen, Arbeitsweisen der Europäischen Ethnologie.* 2nd revised and extended edition. Berlin: Reimer, pp. 219–248.

Schmidt-Lauber, Brigitta. 2007b. "Das qualitative Interview oder: Die Kunst des Reden-Lassens" in Silke Göttsch and Albrecht Lehmann, Eds. *Methoden der Volkskunde. Positionen, Quellen, Arbeitsweisen der Europäischen Ethnologie.* 2nd revised and extended edition. Berlin: Reimer, pp. 169–188.

Schmidt-Lauber, Brigitta. 2009. "Orte von Dauer. Der Feldforschungsbegriff der Europäischen Ethnologie in der Kritik" in Sonja Windmüller, Beate Binder, and Thomas Hengartner, Eds. *Kultur – Forschung. Zum Profil einer volkskundlichen Kulturwissenschaft.* Berlin: LIT, pp. 237–259.

Schmidt-Lauber, Brigitta. 2010. "Der Alltag und die Alltagskulturwissenschaft. Einige Gedanken über einen Begriff und ein Fach" in Michaela Fenske, Ed. *Alltag als Politik – Politik im Alltag.* Berlin: LIT, pp. 45–61.

Schütze, Fritz. 1977. *Die Technik des narrativen Interviews in Interaktionsfeldstudien – dargestellt an einem Projekt zur Erforschung von kommunalen Machtstrukturen.* Bielefeld:

Fakultät für Soziologie an der Universität Bielefeld.

Shostak, Marjorie. 1981. *Nisa – The Life and Words of a !Kung Woman.* Cambridge: Harvard University Press.

Spradley, James. 1980. *Participant Observation.* Fort Worth: Harcourt.

Tedlock, Dennis. 1983. *The Spoken Word and the Work of Interpretation.* Philadelphia: University of Pennsylvania Press.

Tedlock, Dennis. 1999 "Fragen zur dialogischen Anthropologie" in Eberhard Berg and Martin Fuchs, Eds. *Kultur, soziale Praxis, Text. Die Krise der ethnographischen Repräsentation.* Frankfurt: Suhrkamp.

Tertilt, Hermann. 1996. *Turkish Power Boys. Ethnographie einer Jugendbande.* Frankfurt: Suhrkamp.

Toelken, Barre and Tacheeni Scott. 1981. "Poetic Retranslation and the 'Pretty Languages' of Yellowman" in Karl Kroeber, Ed. *Traditional Literatures of the American Indian: Texts and Interpretations.* Lincoln: University of Nebraska Press, pp. 61–116.

Warf, Barney and Santa Arias. 2008. *The Spatial Turn: Interdisciplinary Perspectives.* London: Routledge.

Welz, Gisela. 1998. "Moving Targets. Feldforschung unter Mobilitätsdruck." *Zeitschrift für Volkskunde* 94: 177–194.

Welz, Gisela. 2009. "'Sighting/Siting globalization.' Gegenstandskonstruktionen und Feldbegriff einer ethnographischen Globalisierungsforschung" in Sonja Windmüller, Beate Binder, and Thomas Hengartner, Eds. *Kultur–Forschung. Zum Profil einer volkskundlichen Kulturwissenschaft.* Berlin: LIT, pp. 195–210.

Wernet, Andreas. 2000. *Einführung in die Interpretationstechnik der Objektiven Hermeneutik.* Opladen: Leske and Budrich.

Whyte, William. 1943. *Street Corner Society: The Social Structure of an Italian Slum.* Chicago: University of Chicago Press.

Wolff, Stephan. 2000. "Wege ins Feld und ihre Varianten" in Uwe Flick, Ernst Kardorff, and Ines Steinke, Eds. *Qualitative Forschung. Ein Handbuch.* Reinbek/Hamburg: Rowohlt, pp. 334–349.

FURTHER READING

Gerndt, Helge, Ed. 1988. "Fach und Begriff 'Volkskunde' in der Diskussion." *Wege der Forschung* 641. Darmstadt: Wissenschaftliche Buchgesellschaft.

Maase, Kaspar and Bernd Jürgen Warneken. 2003. *Unterwelten der Kultur. Themen und Theorien der volkskundlichen Kulturwissenschaft*. Köln: Böhlau.

Warneken, Bernd Jürgen. 2006. *Die Ethnographie popularer Kulturen. Eine Einführung*. Wien: Böhlau.

CHAPTER 30

IMAGING PUBLIC FOLKLORE

Debora Kodish

What folklore *isn't* public? What folklore isn't, inevitably, about more than private, individual effort? Here I explore public folklore as an occupation committed to broadly democratic cultural participation. Over the last 50 years, increasing numbers of folklorists in the United States have worked as public and applied folklorists, holding the deceptively simple and radical notion that all peoples' experiences, arts, and expressions are worthy of attention, and that we neglect such attention to our certain risk (Davis 1996; Green 2001; Baron 2008). Public folklore is frequently described in terms of job setting (outside the university) and medium (festivals, exhibitions, documentaries): external features defined by their differences from mainstream academic norms. Here, however, I want to focus on practice: what the work is, and what it allows. Among the many threads of public folklore, I distinguish a progressive public interest tradition where labor equitably dedicated towards the flourishing of people's power and capacities, traced in arts and culture, is a critical variety of liberation struggle (Reagon 1990).

Folklorists may agree on folklore's critical role in cultural life; they vary in embracing vernacular practices as means of addressing fundamental social inqualities and inequities (Stewart *et al.* 2000; Graves 2005: 196–220; McCarl 2006a, 2006b; Kirshenblatt and Kirshenblatt-Gimblett 2007; Haring 2008; Ivey 2008: ix; Scott 2009). Some have named these cultural rights issues; the inalienable human right to (and responsibility for) culture, that is to say, to dependable access to excellent and vital folk arts. The emerging field of US public folklore, my focus here, has been slow to explicitly address big-picture questions, large challenges, and visions. When politics are not made explicit or are pictured as a minority concern, radical traditions in folklore are easily buried (Alvarez 2005: 7–17, 89–96; Cocke 2002). But we have developed over the

A Companion to Folklore, First Edition. Edited by Regina F. Bendix and Galit Hasan-Rokem.

last 50 years – reacting against the pernicious impacts of corporate capitalism, trying to avoid well-documented pitfalls, narrowly focused, repudiating nationalist, universalizing, and regressive strains, hampered by a general absence of reference to the accomplishments of significant actors and to shared struggle, yet against the steady background of the African American freedom movement and other liberation struggles that have changed the terrain of our lives. Amidst such forces, separately and against huge odds, straddling the economies that threaten us, great teachers have shaped the practice of public folklore. This chapter is a small payment on large debts.

POLITICS AND PRINCIPLES

For me and many others, one of these great teachers was Archie Green, a man who had enormous impact in shaping a developing discipline nationally through work as a scholar without a long-term academic base, an organizer and public intellectual, an "anarcho-syndicalist with strong libertarian tendencies," a person with diverse friendships (Cantwell 2001: xv–xvi). *Partisan, particular*, and *pluralist* were the terms he often used to characterize public folklore: the practice of folklore in public contexts, for public good (Green 2001: 157). His framework reflects a preoccupation with large social concerns – notably environmental and workers' struggles, and questions of democratic engagement and public responsibility. Robert Cantwell describes the artful reflexivity of Archie's writing: He was "caulking the joints in the discursive hull (to use the figures of Archie's own trade), bolting the rhetorical decking to the argumentative framework, plugging the bolt-holes and applying a protective varnish" (in Green 2001: xxii). Archie was a shipwright before he was a folklorist and his language, well-crafted and well-considered, treats public folklore as a type of everyday labor: particular skill put to necessary task (Green 2001: 199). Here, in his honor and memory, I take liberties in describing *anti-subordination* and *radical pluralism* as politics that elaborate his approach (Matsuda 1996). They animate the following keywords and describe the work that I most admire and to which I aspire.

Here, a *partisan* is committed and accountable, resists draconian forces. Frankly partisan public folklore work develops from long relationships with people to whom we have become responsible. And it comes from everyday confrontation with the inequalities circumscribing our lives. My generation has painfully witnessed the costs of 30 years of neo-liberalism. We continue to be excoriated for owning up to our politics (see Oring 2004). In these contexts, being partisan is a matter of the kinds of questions we learn to ask, the forms of respect we tender, the kinds of contributions we learn to make, and the forms of power that we build (Sheehy 1992: 323–329; McCarl 2006b: 23; Lindahl 2010).

Public folklorists are *particularists*: in our diverse locations; in insisting on the importance of vernacular practices; in our long obsession with high-context expression and attention to the divergent understandings shaped by people's wide and varied experiences; in the close eye we have kept the dynamic and protean nature of culture-making over generations and on people's places in these efforts. But we are also closet collectivists: in friendships and long-term engagement with others as part of the work; in attention to how community authority is inscribed in popular expression and practice; and in cultivating a capacity to see creativity and individuality where they are lodged collectively – one of Roger Abraham's great contributions (1970). An activist mix of particularism and collectivism is close-up work. Notions of fixed identities and authenticities give way to awareness of people's struggles for expanded subjectivities, self-determination, and self-fashioning of arts and community quality of life (Graves 2005; Lear 2006: 7–10, 31, 42–52; Davis 2007; Sheehy 2007; Spitzer 2007). We recognize strategic progressive essentialisms and anti-essentialisms as choices that people make in standing against subordination (Matsuda 1996). Locating folk arts and ourselves in the context of wider struggles and freedom movements allies us with others who resist re-inscribing inequalities (Reagon 1990, 1991; N'Diaye and Bibby 1991; Payne 1995; Bambara 1996; Kelley 2002; Briggs and Mantini-Briggs 2003: 324–331; Freeman 2006; Asian Americans United). These shifts are led by feeling, and marked by character and reputation. The work is *personal*. Another dimension to add to Archie's alliterative trio. And, of course, the personal is *political*.

Few of us are as fully integrated as Archie: clear about guiding ideologies, excellent craftspeople, eloquent speakers and writers. "Write this down," he would bark, until I learned to come prepared. I write as that apprentice. But I know apprenticeships as true lifelong endeavors in terms of the relationships they trace and the work they embrace (Peterson 1996: 24–31; Hawes 2008:154). Guerrilla work, Archie called it. What is this labor? It is harder to say than it might seem. Out here in the US hinterlands – Elko, Middlebury, Austin, Boise, Madison, Fresno, Philadelphia – many of us have operated for decades as sole practitioners or in relatively small shops. We remain severely under-resourced. The field is splintered and disconnected: united in no single movement or moment. Like many of Archie's students and extended kin, I am by now deeply embedded, gratefully accountable to many local teachers – activists, artists, and people with wide ranges of experience – who, like Archie, took time and care in instructing me (Philadelphia Folklore Project website).

We undertake this work together with diverse others, though we lack clear common language that might allow us to articulate our agenda more precisely (Narayan 2008; Lindahl 2010). Situated peripherally within what has been called the art camp, in one local hinterland, I outline here one purpose that may bind us: how it is possible to imagine and cultivate healthy grounds for culture. Tracing features of occupational practice, I look to stories traded, visions embraced, accomplishments recounted and measured. (Learning to value what we trust and love is a lesson long in coming). We have to be as "equally at ease inside barnyards as bureaucracies," wrote Nick Spitzer, and to "strive for eloquence" in cultural conversations (Spitzer 2007: 99). He articulates the creolist awareness that we speak in complex and layered tongues and that we participate in significant dialogues about our fate and future collectively, ethically, and imaginatively. I find public folklore at its best when it answers Toni Cade Bambara's call for (and her example in shaping) a bridge language by which revolutionaries might speak with clairvoyants (1996: 235).

Practitioners writing about the field and addressing themselves to the discipline have taken other directions in describing public folklore. They offer programmatic overviews, surveys of key issues, wide perspectives on such questions as the founding of federal and state folk arts programs, pros and cons of modes and metaphors, case studies, and useful ruminations, far more than I can do justice to here. Collections and special journal issues introduce a range of important voices and perspectives (Collins 1980; Camp 1983; Feintuch 1988; Hufford 1994; Jones 1994; Baron 1999 and 2008; Shuldiner 1993–1995; McDowell and Smith 2004; Wells 2006; Baron and Spitzer 2007; MacDowell and Kozma 2008). Essayists hint at the broad ranges of conversations in which people participated at different stages of their careers, and I recommend these writings as introductions to critical themes in US public folklore. The lifelong labors of leading workers, artists, and people of color (too seldom appearing in such references) offer further examples of principled practice honed over many years into fine craft (Cannon 2000; Peterson 1996; Alliance for California Traditional Arts website, Fund for Folk Culture website). Our kin in community arts have shaped parallel agendas (Tchen 2007; Appalshop and Community Arts Network websites). Ample ground has been laid.

Valuing Multiple Excellences

Bill Westerman observes that the work of public and applied folklore contributed to a revolutionary expansion of what is considered art in the United States (Westerman 2006: 118; Hawes 2008: 128). But this fight continues, against the odds. Folk arts and those committed to them challenge mainstream (elite, universalizing, top-down, bureaucratic) notions of what counts as art, where it occurs, and how it is meaningfully embodied and supported. Here is art, after all, that is participatory, exists in the lives and hearts of common people, is recognizable in repertoire as much as in individual virtuosity. Official structures shove diverse vernacular traditions to the periphery; the commercial sector dwarfs them, although they are abundant in shadow economies, currencies based on alternative values (Ivey 2008). Folk arts struggle for equitable measures of respect. So, consider that Native and Sea Island basket-making, cowboy poetry, Irish music, blues, klezmer, and African American storytelling are just a handful of the significant folk arts said to have enjoyed "revivals" or "renaissances" over the last 50 years. What does this mean? Westerman sees a radical reconfiguration of elite notions of excellence here.

Start with Westerman's optimistic picture, and consider how *excellence* is reckoned in diverse grassroots contexts. Carl Lindahl breaks down this process, distinguishing between interconnected elements of forestory, performance, and understory (2010: 257). One place to begin (both curious and obvious) for glimpsing great *performance* is with individual artists celebrated in prestigious awards. However imperfect and problematic honorific systems are, they recognize some remarkable artists. The National Endowment for the Arts Heritage Awards (the nation's highest honor in folk arts, modeled after Japan's living national treasures program) has since 1982 annually named keepers of significant cultural heritage. Look up the winners: Mary Jackson, Buck Ramsey, Elaine Hoffman Watts, LaVaughn Robinson, and others. Their life stories – part of Lindahl's *forestory* – invoke hosts of others who made their way possible. Attention here has the capacity to widen cultural histories, offering particular detail and vivid context for the birth and cultivation of diverse artistic excellences; their meaning for communities; the challenges they face (since one-time awards are no guarantee of survival); and the signs of health for these parts of our social body (National Endowment for the Arts website; Siporin 1992; Cannon 2000; Freeman 2006; Hawes 2008: 155–168; Mulcahy 2010).

And then, the *understory*: what we take from all of this and hold in mind. The late and great Gerald Davis, a public folklore pioneer in his own right, noted that "we have been slow to plumb our own experiences" (Davis 1989: viii). What is excellence in public folklore practice? Davis offered benchmarks in his plenary address to the American Folklore Society (1996), and earlier, when he described his 1972 encounters with photographer and activist Roland Freeman, then contemplating work among his own people, Baltimore's surviving arabbers (the local name for African American horse-cart vendors). Thirty years later, Freeman would be named an NEA Heritage Award winner. In these early encounters, Davis judged that Roland already had what was needed: passionate conviction, the capacity for "caring documentation," "family history," "active relationships," "a love for the integrity of the tradition," and "professional craft." The requirements for excellent work are clear, simple, and profound: it is envisioned as a practice of guiding attention to what is essential in the human spirit (Davis 1989: viii). Freeman himself observed that the work has been "rewarding, healing and integrating" (1989: ix).

Davis's criteria for good practice and Freeman summary of his life-changing labor are examples of authentic evaluation: trustworthy measures yielding enduring value. Excellence is articulated in terms of artfulness and fine craft; knowledge (personal and collective) on which we can build; integrity of self and work (I will return to this notion of *authenticity* later); ethical, purposeful labor; trust; means of cultivating a vision in which others have a genuine stake; real change. This work offers pathways to freedom (Bambara 1996: 91–92; Atlas and Korza 2005: 162–163). As another late great public interest folklorist, Beverly Robinson, insisted, shifting into African American vernacular: this is not playing.

For many reasons, the African American freedom movement and civil rights struggle remain underacknowledged forces in the development of, and examples of excellence in, public interest folklore. The model of a beloved community and life stories of veterans in this tradition offer many detailed descriptions of excellent engaged work for a just purpose, where people are accountable to others and to larger and widely held freedom dreams, and where folk arts are central to stories of social change and present at critical junctures (Davis 1996; Freeman 1989; Kelley 2002; N'Diaye and Bibby 1991; Reagon 1990, 1991). It is not accidental that Charles Cobb describes African American activists (including folklorists) with a large vision: seeing themselves as part of a tradition in which people are "totally committed to 'the redemption and vindication of the race' – black race or human race, take your pick ... [a] commitment [that] leads straight to culture and tradition." Cobb refers to generations-old traditions of community organizing that sustained enslaved Africans, and still sustain movements for justice (in Freeman 2006: 44; also see Roberts 2000; Payne 1995; Shapiro *et al.* 1976). In the context of meaningful work for social change, such pointed evaluation is certainly debated – a public matter, reflecting collective judgments and deep ideological divisions – but it also articulates vernacular criteria of excellence. The stories people tell about one another hold meaningful folk history and analysis (Lindahl 2010). Character and life story, held and shared among a community, are an important way in which people (including public folklorists) are judged.

So consider a place where such a narrative tradition is elaborated. Consider a celebration documented in a book. In 2005 Roland Freeman organized a tribute to honor Worth Long, "a remarkable person," civil rights activist, cultural and blues historian, interpreter of material culture, organizer of festivals around the country (Freeman 2006: 5). Family and friends contributed appreciations picturing Long.

Doing fieldwork, with family, engaged in the African American freedom struggle as a student activist in Arkansas, as a sit-in protester, as Student Nonviolent Coordinating Committee (SNCC) coordinator in Selma. Who was beaten and bloodied in Selma but would not stop naming himself "Mr. Worth Long" (Charles Bonner in Freeman 2006:35). That same spirit inspired his organizing and his folklore fieldwork, each a matter of "listening" and "making yourself at home" and then as a matter of course treating it like home and paying people just the same respect you would expect to be given. Walking the walk. Long was hard to contact, often in the field or traveling by Greyhound bus. But you could put the word out that you were looking for him and Bernice Johnson Reagon observes that "he always turned up when you needed him" (Freeman 2006: 35). He was where he needed to be, "on the case" (Freeman 2006: 5). Others still on the case clarify the terms.

Accolades describe the community's names for Worth Long. They value the man's artistry and integrity in this work. People describe *virtuosity* (great skill and accomplishment, solid research), *significant relationships* (the many artists he befriended, doors he opened to let others move dreams forward), *vision* (showing us that folk arts are as important an ingredient for freedom movement as voting rights or algebra skills [Moses and Cobb 2001]), and *seriousness of purpose* (a disinclination to mess around). Testimonies filled with love ground this work and secure its future. These are signs of excellence to value and believe in. That Davis, Freeman, and Long portray great work in similar terms is not accidental.

If community development policy had an eye on serious cultural sustainability, it would track the real outcomes of such public interest folk cultural investments and actions. It would find in Worth Long's life a template for cultivating a vital social body and expanding freedom of expression. It would pay attention to significant indicators of the value of Long's work: a generation of African American folklorists, the National Black Arts Festival, the Mississippi Folklife Project, the "Will the Circle Be Unbroken?" radio history of the Civil Rights Movement, films, exhibitions, the Mississippi Blues and Heritage Festival ("the first major music festival in this country to be owned and organized by an African American organization"), the Southeastern Louisiana Zydeco Festival, the blues revival, Penn Center's Heritage Days Celebration and stewardship of Gullah culture, his influence on the Smithsonian Festival of American Folklife, Bess Lomax Hawes and the National Endowment for the Arts, Julie Dash's *Daughters of the Dust* and much more (Freeman 2006). Outcomes, and the community *celebrating* its own / telling Worth Long's true names, aptly illustrate what *excellence* means within a radical vision of folklore (Mills 2008: 20). Plumbing oral tradition for what it says about character, reputation and cultural history fills in the picture with recurring vernacular definitions of power, authority, and authenticity. For example: "He helped me develop 'my voice' and understand the importance of using it" (Crosby in Freeman 2006: 47).

Such community criteria can be useful means of evaluating other public folklore work as well. Consider the Smithsonian Center for Folklife and Cultural Heritage (CFCH) and its Festival, established in 1967 and now in its forty-third year (Smithsonian Center for Folklife and Cultural Heritage website). The Smithsonian Folklife Festival is perhaps the most-documented of US public folklore efforts. It is the subject of six books or book-length collections and countless other essays; many dozens of annual Festival program books, monographs, and recordings; and a score of state / regional / country spin-offs. Hundreds of folklorists initiated programs, were trained, or developed aspects of their practice on a CFCH paycheck. Questions of how to historicize and analyze festivals and display events in general, and the Smithsonian's Festival in particular, have generated a disproportionate amount of scholarly ink (Bauman *et al.* 1992; Cantwell 1993; Price and Price 1994; Sommers 1994; Kurin 1997; Hasan-Rokem 2007; Diamond 2008). Critics have addressed the problematics of representation and reported on gaps between idea and actualization, but their critiques often reflect distance and double standards in analysis – for example, a persistent habit of subordinating vernacular genres and grassroots voices; lack of attention to proportion, time depth and long-term outcomes; inadequate or partial contextualization; failure of sympathy (marking disbelief, bad faith, or limits of engagement).

The examples I draw from African American activist folklorists' work offer a different framework for understanding what the CFCH and the Festival have accomplished. Here is a way to evaluate excellence in public interest folklore by what actually happens on the ground, according to people who are positioned to recognize good work and feel its impact, a habit of documenting histories of exemplary work pursued over many years and with reference to meaningful community opinions. We look to where and how mission and vision are made real and aptly judged (Mills 2008: 20). Where CFCH is concerned, important generative work includes the African Diaspora program that I have alluded to here, and the signal efforts of Bernice Johnson Reagon and others; work that has addressed class and abilities (i.e., occupational folklore and laborlore, family folklore and aging); the development and distribution of media and documentation efforts; the significant flourishings of music and arts with which I began this section; and the lifework of individuals. Here are places where doors have opened, offering ways forward, which returns us to the inspiring example of Worth Long. For histories of the future, we might well measure our celebrations to see who we have become.

Cultivating diverse forms of community-significant excellence is the unfinished revolution that Westerman describes. Attention to this task requires us to rethink where universalisms blind us: where top-down dominant notions squash the possibilities offered by community alternatives. In the face of extreme inequality, a certain kind of *authenticity* is required – and not the problematic notion of authenticity in its reified or universalizing versions, critiques of which dominate the literature. The authenticity I describe reflects vernacular usage: it is often felt as the opposite of a divided/internally oppressed self, the idea of "trusting [your] inner voice," "knowing on the deepest level that who you are to yourself is the same essence you offer to the world in which you move" (Reagon 1990: 2). Here, authenticity – and other categorical tools for measuring quality – are placed in particular, partisan, and personal contexts (Kirshenblatt and Kirshenblatt-Gimblett 2007; Spitzer 2007: 85; Welsch 2011). Vernacular forms of authenticity retain critical weight as experiential and existential processes by which we come to realize our own best excellences in company with others and in the face of draconian forces (Kodish 2011).

This is community-accountable work. The notion of community is often used loosely. By *community* I mean a beloved, self-constituted assemblage: people organized by common visions, committed to regenerating vital and sustainable place. Reid and Taylor talk about this as the conditions for life, the social basis of livability, of healthy body-place-commons (2010: 10–12). Robin D. G. Kelley and Jonathan Lear describe the critical importance of freedom dreams, love, and creative practical reason to constituting such communities. *Communitas* and *solidarity* are other terms. Toni Cade Bambara describes the obligation "to constantly remove any kind of camouflage or any kind of barrier that exists between me and the community that names me" (Bambara 1996: 216).

How can we grapple with, support, and defend diverse authenticities in appropriate ways? This labor might yield a robust theory of sustainable body-space-commons where multiple artistic excellences (and especially folk arts) are signs of cultural health and community vitality (Reid and Taylor 2010), and where processes and systems for their achievement are imagined and built. Supporting (with loving concern) forms of excellent action arising and celebrated at the grassroots is fundamentally a creative craft of practical reason (Lear 2006). Here we are not artist or activist wannabes; we are cultivating art and equity because we must (Welsch 2011).

ADDRESSING BOUNDARIES

But who are *we*? How we know and name ourselves remains a difficult problem. Although US federal agencies have played critical roles in shaping public folklore, this is not top-down work: dispersed activities at the grassroots distinguish the field. Decentralized public folklorists are located at borders – in many senses. Bess Hawes herself, who had so much to do with so many of the people referenced above, worried that there might be better things to do than helping others fill out government forms, even if this sent sorely needed cash to the resource-starved hinterlands (Hawes 2008: 139). Her comment draws attention to disparities in literacies and resources that become visible at critical junctures, to public folklore's sometimes uneasy place where inequalities are visible, and to our accountabilities there. These are shaping dimensions of the work.

Hawes pictures public folklore at borders, places where people rub up against one another (and themselves). She describes herself bridging domains of power and class: rubbing elbows with folk artists and politicians, at dinner parties and rump sessions. She champions fieldwork as an essential craft of connecting with people across widely different contexts (and exults in finding the perfect fieldworker, Dan Sheehy, who later would fill her shoes at the Endowment) (Hawes 2008: 105–106). She points to troubling unarticulated class divisions and to differences in strategy that emerge as chronic schisms further separating people (resistance/assimilation, purism/ creolization). But this one-time Almanac Singer says that folklorists ought to be working where there are problems: the dilemmas faced by every American – attached to a psychic hitching post but bifurcated internally – are divisions that shape the field (Hawes 2008: 118–119).

Others have described public folklore work in terms of bridgework, cultural brokering, mediating, transcontextualizing (Kurin 1997: 18–25; Graves 2005: 149–150; Baron and Spitzer 2007: xvi–xviii, 4; Sheehy 2007: 220; Baron 2010). Discussions of appropriate roles puzzle the same gap between self and community (Shapiro *et al.* 1976; Reagon 1990: 2–3; Long 1991; Robinson 1991; Bambara 1996; Moses and Cobb 2001: 182). The peopling of the field, it has been frequently observed, marked the crossing of social barriers (Whisnant 1983). Many American public folklorists (mostly white, middle-class people, and more men than women in our incomplete histories) first came to the profession through involvement in countercultural movements like the folksong revival (Cantwell 1993: 244–247). Cantwell names this *ethnomimesis,* where boundaries collapse between personal and professional, led by feeling; where transformations happen out of love and desire (Cantwell 1993: 294–300). Or people find themselves bound to "a community of tradition embodied in the people and lifeways... [we have] known since birth but which... [we, like many others], began to discover only after having left it behind" (Lindahl 2010: 252; also Cannon 2000; McCarl 2000). In this era where borders so often mark violence and perpetuate inequality, consider public folklore skills as a humble but powerful way of working against the grain (as Linda Brodkey characterized the radical educator's practice and vernacular sign of quality: Brodkey 1996: 30–51; McCarl 2000). This is anthropology's bricolage and métis-making: means by which we reconstruct pathways forward and back from whatever incomplete resources are at hand and in full view of the communities that constitute and charter us (Lear 2006).

This is laborlore. Archie Green, too, identified boundary-work as a core problem at the heart of folklore. He framed the problem as the human need to address internal divisions, individual and social. Archie surely transgressed (inauthentic) borders (McCarl 2006a: 6–11). So did my generation of public folklorists. With various training, we walk all over the place and talk to everyone. An inclination with familiar antecedents. Jewish peddlers and itinerants like my grandfather and his brothers: poor people who live from the margins, curious young people who play hooky to observe everyday life. I recognize my own history and occupational practice in these details, thanks to the life review work of Kirshenblatt and Kirshenblatt-Gimblett (2007), an exquisite rendering reconstructing a picture of how Jewish people lived, not only how we died. (Also see Hufford *et al.* 1989). Larger struggles and forces may remain murky, in the background, but they surely orient this work, placing us at borders where we make impossible choices, and if we are lucky, learn to cultivate hope.

Fieldwork is rightly celebrated as an occupational craft. Folklorists trained in the mid- to late 1970s faced an era with few academic positions, even as dream jobs emerged in the still-undefined field of public folklore. Many of us were sent into the field as survey workers, charged with uncovering and documenting what mattered to people. Questions immediately presented themselves. Always unfinished and unstable, this creative border-crossing practice remains satisfying and frequently transformational (Hawes 2008: 106; Hawes 2007: 67–70).

The craft deserves more attention. Great fieldworkers (folklorists and organizers) are described as really knowing how to listen, how to make themselves at home, and how to open possibilities (Moses and Cobb 2001: xiv; Payne 1995: xiv, 236–264, 405). More needs to be said. For example: that when people listen well, others have time to explain (some of) what needs to be said. That people tend to hear themselves better when telling a story out loud. That theory and practice are refined in conversation. That conversations have a way of proliferating. That shared stories shine light on alternatives and create change. (And also about the power of reporting back in responsible, ethical manner.) Long-term, intermittent, authentic (feminists recovered these dimensions early): fieldwork acknowledges the time it takes for meanings to flower; dignifies patience, diligence, and humility; embodies real relationships. It honors the importance of emerging significance. Fieldwork may certainly be an extractive and reductive process. But here, I distinguish that important radical tradition where people working together in folk arts and social change create enduring value, transformation, power, radical hope (Lear 2006). Ethical documentation is inherently collaborative and inevitably filled with gaps and divides we feel our way across. Like coalition work, it is risky, and done in view of what is at stake (Long 1991; Robinson 1991; Reagon 1990: 2–3; Moses and Cobb 2001: 182). Folklore is best when it is practiced with a full and loving heart addressing the problems of how we live together: perhaps our most radical vision (Welsch 2011). Consider Archie's words:

> We must touch issues of cultural pluralism at every place they erupt, every place in the polity where there's a wound, every place where people rub each other on matters of identity, or race, or region, or occupation. Folklorists need to consider a deskilled workforce, a closed textile mill, a fire in a chicken plant, a conflict between Hasidic Jews and Blacks, a conflict on an Indian reservation over a nuclear plant. Each place of human tension, that's where a folklorist ought to be. That's our goal. Public folklore has to move into these areas, and it will only move if young academic folklorists are challenged by these problems. ... By dealing with issues of cultural pluralism, national identity, rurality, occupational skill, and ethnicity we may move ahead. If folklorists are not advocates for these issues, then they have little to do. Day-to-day tasks reduce to rubble. (Green 1993: 10)

> You don't really defend a society that is divided internally and filled with tension, not just in economic but in non-economic areas such as religion, region, and gender without cultural workers. Academic folklorists must train students to meet the demands of the next century, of a post-Cold War era. If trained folklorists lack the skill, drive, and creativity to engage in guerrilla warfare, then it will be done by other people. And those others may not be conventional types, such as anthropologists, economists, or sociologists. In every other period in American life, when there was a crisis – over slavery, the frontier, or the Depression – people arose, whether they were called abolitionists, conservationists, or New Dealers, and responded to the challenge. ... Will cultural work continue? ... Of course, advocates will come to the surface. Whether or not we will part of the process, that's the big question. (Green 1993: 12, reproduced by permission of the family of David Shuldiner (Anne Schick) and by permission of Archie Green)

If such motivating feelings drive generative and participatory arts, then the field may be imagined as centrally concerned with community cultural health. Groundbreaking publicly engaged work in legal and medical areas addresses the cultural dimensions of disease, violence, and well-being (O'Connor 1994; Westerman 1994; Payne 1995; Briggs and Mantini-Briggs 2003; Goldstein 2004). These scholars show that beliefs and values (including our own) are generative: orienting how we behave, act, heal one another, and seek justice. Excellences of character – distinct and particular – emerge here as well, as reputations are collectively reconstituted.

Stories of change describe pivotal movement across divides. The field has collectively chronicled tales of visits and first encounters; narratives of origin, conversion, and transformation; often without adequately contextualizing them as moral at core (and requiring appropriate ethical response). Here is folklore's stock in trade, the convention of margin and crossroads where people change and where such shifts defeat the tyrannies of (unjust) divides. We know now to fill in the wider contexts (Danticat 2010: 1–20). Taken seriously, this work teaches us how to get well in worrisome times, how to build power (Bambara 1996: 235; Lear 2006).

Transformation narratives chart territories of struggle and pinpoint moments when people come into a new consciousness of their place in a collectivity. Recognizable, memorable, and powerful, they are indicators that something important is going on. Bernice Johnson Reagon (activist, musician, folklorist, critical theorist) tells a paradigmatic transformation narrative. Reagon came into the voice and power that she has – she came into herself, she became the *who* she is now – when she was working with other freedom movement workers in Albany, Georgia, in 1961. She describes being raised in a tradition of African American congregational singing. And in Albany, in the middle of formative movement action, people said, "Bernice, give us a song." She began the song that goes: "Over my head, I see trouble in the air…" She looked around at beloved people courageously gathered in the face of certain danger, standing up for freedom, singing a familiar song together. At that moment she realized what the tradition offered. She changed the word "trouble" to "freedom," and it was profoundly transformative for her and for the gathered company. *The assembled voices, and her own, clearly sounded different.* They sounded different because people *were* different through courageous action. Reagon's creative political act restructured the frame within which they were all acting. Deepening ownership of this tradition, it unleashed power. Activists explain that "[h]istory demonstrates that taking responsibility for one's own life, one's own learning, can change a person" (Moses and Cobb 2001: 188). Reagon demonstrates how people can create (and feel) power and can change the terms: of voice, song, history, and struggle; of who we feel ourselves to be (Reagon 1991). Citing Sojourner Truth, Harriet Tubman and Bessie Jones, she writes, "I come into my life and my singing as a woman who had the best models – singing mothers who were fighters, whose lives taught me another way to be in this world (Reagon 2001: 141).

I hear this as a story that deserves to be retold (and reenacted). In it the generative power of people listening to one another and acting together is revolutionary. Closing the gap between appearance and reality, universalizing system and freedom, liberates. Here, folk arts are a way for people to take their own life experiences seriously, to close divides, to feel a way to develop their own power: "really a set of challenges by ourselves, and our communities, to ourselves" (Moses and Cobb 2001: 125; also Beck 1997: 124–125; Cantu in Peterson 1996: 26). This narrative goes to the heart of public folklore practice: what it can aspire to do, and how it can work. Notions of "gatherings" (Western Folklife Center website) and "visiting" in humble ways enact this power: embracing reassemblage, celebrating regatherings of the exiled. Living, working, writing beyond ourselves.

HISTORIES AND CONTEXTS

Public folklore emerged in the United States as a barely discernible current among rising waves and movements of social change and social consequence (but note the general absence of folklore and folklorists from footnotes and bibliographies of sister efforts such as public history, applied and public anthropology, and community arts: Atlas and Korza 2005; Community Arts Network, Appalshop). Nevertheless, the discipline of folklore has persistently yielded critical insights related to democratic cultural participation. It has moved demonstrably out of US universities and into public life since the 1960s. It is to that trajectory that I turn now.

Folklorists writing about the field (largely to one another) regarding US practice and disciplinary history have charted terrain with different names: applied folklore, public sector folklore, public folklore, folklore-in-use (Green 2007; Collins 1980). Essays debating and defending the various terms reflect intellectual lineage and internal border skirmishes, placing work with public consequence at the center of the field, finding antecedents in late nineteenth-century ethnographic work, arguing for the significance of negotiated understandings, or for attention to impacts and social issues related to folklore (Sweterlitsch 1971; Collins 1980; Feintuch 1988; Hufford 1994; Green 2001; Baron and Spitzer 2007; Baron 2008). Many of these frameworks represent various strategies of justifying and recontextualizing – indeed, a continuing need to legitimate work outside the academy, which continued to diminish these efforts. A parallel fate has befallen the notion of folklore in general. I argue for an alternative approach to definition and naming: tracking action, keeping an eye on the liberatory power of folklore in critical junctures.

There is context to consider. I still don't know much about the chilling effect of the 1950s Communist witch hunts on folklore in the United States, but see Price (2004) and Davis (2010) on some of the stories they never told us in graduate school about anthropologists and folklorists who were silenced. Not much has been written about the 1970s and 1980s in many American folklore graduate programs, buffeted by the "Culture Wars" – what Mary Louise Pratt describes as "a fatal collision between two historical processes: on the one hand, the arrival on university faculties of the 'children of the '60s' and, on the other, the arrival at the White House of Ronald Reagan along with a dogmatic political right hungry for power" (Pratt 2001: 30). Consider again the oral tradition. The era was characterized by racism: Jerry Davis recalls Richard Dorson telling a racist joke at a Berkeley folklore gathering, and his own vociferous rejection (Davis 1996: 117, 121–123). Sexism: only one folklore faculty member was convicted of sexual assault, I believe, but it is widely known that abuse goes extravagantly underreported. And certain classism: poor people (i.e., a certain version of folk) were becoming déclassé (although books on or by working-class academics did not come out until the 1990s). Many of us in graduate school earlier felt closeted from ourselves as well as others. Ambivalence about poverty and poor people was evidenced by the wholesale abandonment of attention to issues and populations of historic interest to the field, while the general academic drift to postmodernism silenced or co-opted work in laborlore and immigration rights (but see McCarl 2000, 2006a, 2006b). There was the reactionary legacy of Richard Dorson's cold-war politics, his attempt to institutionalize a marginal field, and his antipathy to public folklore (and left-leaning brethren). The notion that public folklore debased the pure coin of scholarship was a considerable burden to productive work, and carried its own unexamined class assumptions and double standards: subordinating sympathy, practice, vernacular politics and poetics, and social good.

This dirty laundry (occupational folklore) is relevant here because it directs attention both to generally oppressive structures and to the liberation movements engaging so many of our peers. In folklore, radicalism seemed closeted. Entering the academy in the 1970s meant that you were expected to leave homegrown identities at the door. In subtle and obvious ways, those who come into folklore as some kind of other – people of color, people from working-class backgrounds, women – continue to learn that professional identities require submersion of primary subjectivities and divide us against ourselves. This is a sure strategy to diminish worth (and self-knowledge), foster internalized oppression, and breed distrust about the legitimacy of working papers. How much does it also impede the field's attention to inequalities or engagement with social issues? How much do these divisions lessen our capacity to treat as equals people who enter the field as subjects, sources, partners, mentors?

Conditions change as unruly subjects challenge aspects of canonical/orthodox thought. Critical race scholar and lawyer Patricia Williams writes that she does not consider herself either remarkable or a troublemaker; in challenging bias, she merely shares "the insights of women, of people of color, of a certain degree of powerlessness" in places where such perspectives are rarely present. Displaced and divided, we have the obligation and capacity to bring wider perspectives to bear. Remembering where we come from, we bring others with us, in conversation and action (Williams 1995: 93). These are among the lessons taught by activist folklore – from Bernice Johnson Reagon, Jerry Davis, Worth Long and others.

Bess Hawes reminds us that this is both lost opportunity and blind spot: a historical accident often repeated. Recalling the complementary missions during the years of discipline-based programs at NEA, of "Expansion Arts" and "Folk Arts," she observes that each tended to those local groups that no one else could manage to fund; one tended to focus on who did work, and the other tended to focus on what they did (Hawes 2008: 143–144). This separation between agent and genre has weakened both camps. Who do we count as allies? What lineages do we follow and why? What do various forms allow and constrain? Where do we feel history as chartering vision, where as oppressive structure? How do we equitably unite disparate efforts?

Radically pluralist and anti-subordination politics animate these examples; they are distinguishing features of the stance Archie Green adopted and that I value. To further elaborate the work that others have distinguished as folklore's public responsibility, I borrow from Mari Matsuda and Patricia Williams in critical race studies where lawyers of color have used folklore and people's own formulations of their experience to shape legal critique and analysis. Progressive philosophers and anthropologists have done a great deal over the last 30 years to offer politically engaged tools, sharp ethnographic lenses, and skill in limning neo-liberal disasters (Lear 2006; Alvarez 2005; Scott 2009; Reid and Taylor 2010). Historians have offered back stories and rationale (Payne 1995; Tchen 2007); so have journalists (Klein 2007). Working in the tradition of great regionalists, "provincial intellectuals" have steadfastly democratized public senses of place (Leary 1998: xv–30, 33–110, 500–502; Noyes 2008: 39). Performance theory (in which many of my generation trained) deserves attention for useful tools: from Bakhtin, Prague School theorists, Russian formalists, semioticians, structuralists, sociolinguists, pragmatists (Hymes 1988; Baron and Spitzer 2007: viii–ix). Using them as recipes for action, public folklorist practice pushes all of these skills in new directions. Dell Hymes' radical formula is extended in vital community arts, where we are able not only to remember, report, repeat, or perform, but also to enact, transform, and regenerate. A reflexive, politically engaged (anarchist) history linking various threads of such state-resisting work would be helpful. Scott's work on hill people of Southeast Asia provides detail and theory for such an effort (Scott 2009). More work needs to be done here, with folk arts as central concern.

Diana N'Diaye and Deirdre Bibby (1991) and others place this labor in international contexts with references to world gatherings of African diaspora workers which have continued to model practice, linking the efforts of cultural workers located in widely diverse contexts. Gustavo Esteva and Madhu Suri Prakash (1998) coined the term "grassroots postmodernism" to describe the whole range of human rights, environmental justice, cultural equity, and land claim efforts initiated by indigenous and non-industrialized people; the cultural dimensions remain too little understood here, as well. Grace Lee Boggs and others have observed that a different theory of change underlies this approach, whereby local actions change the larger system through countless interconnections, rather than through accumulating mass or forcing system change. These frameworks provide a wider context for the dispersed and locally-centered work of public folklorists. Call it grassroots public interest folklore, community cultural development.

Public interest folklore is, at its best, work in community. Older words like *communal* and *collective* have fallen, unfortunately, into disuse in folklore studies. What they offer is an angle on the formative nature of enduring vision and a long view. Collective creation is accountable to carefully tended emerging and unfinished notions of human rights and responsibilities. I sketch it as radical regenerative public health practice: matters of ethics and spirit and of tending diverse excellences and authenticities.

In her foreword to Betsy Peterson's *Report on the Folk and Traditional Arts in the United States*, Jane Alexander quotes Wendell Berry's description of cultural democracy: "it would begin in work and love," he says, describing a community dance, turning towards folk arts as an example. "People at work in their communities three generations old would know that their bodies renewed, time and again, the movements of other bodies, living and dead, known and loved, remembered and loved" (1996: 5). There are, of course, countless ways to frame the public interest folklore effort, equally large and compelling; this view pictures community cultural health as a main aim of folklore, and as a central feature of freedom dream and liberation struggle. It follows that cultural health and vital folklore require resisting state-making machineries, and that folk arts chronicle and advance aspects of this labor. I have noted that James Scott describes state-resisting peoples: these include maroon communities constituted by peoples' political choices (2009). The public interest folklore I am imagining places us as widely dispersed members of just such communities, working to cultivate and detoxify the ground and soil of culture. Here, folklore is an enduring, renewable resource, a constituting mechanism, necessary to community life – cultural diversity taken seriously. It follows that we are accountable to one another. And there is plenty of work to be done.

REFERENCES

Abrahams, Roger. 1970. "Creativity, Individuality and the Traditional Singer." *Studies in the Literary Imagination* 3(1): 5–36.

Alliance for California Traditional Arts. www.actaonline.org (accessed October 16, 2011).

Alvarez, Maribel. 2005. *There's Nothing Informal About It: Participatory Arts Within the Cultural Ecology of Silicon Valley.* San José, CA: Cultural Initiatives Silicon Valley.

Appalshop. www.appalshop.org (accessed October 16, 2011).

Asian Americans United. www.aaunited.org (accessed October 16, 2011).

Atlas, Caron, and Pam Korza, Eds. 2005. *Critical Perspectives: Writings on Art and Civil Dialogue.* Washington, DC: Americans for the Arts.

Bambara, Toni Cade. 1996. *Deep Sightings and Rescue Missions.* Toni Morrison, Ed.

Preface by Tony Morrison. New York: Pantheon.

Baron, Robert. 1999. "Theorizing Public Folklore Practice: Documentation, Representation and Everyday Competencies." *Journal of Folklore Research* 36(2/3): 185–201.

Baron, Robert. 2008. "American Public Folklore: History, Issues, Challenges." *Indian Folklore Research Journal* 5(8): 65–86.

Baron, Robert. 2010. "Sins of Objectification? Agency, Mediation, and Community Cultural Self-Determination in Public Folklore and Cultural Tourism Programming." *Journal of American Folklore* 123(487): 63–91.

Baron, Robert and Nicholas R. Spitzer, Eds. 2007 [1992]. *Public Folklore*. Washington, DC: Smithsonian Institution Press.

Bauman, Richard, *et al.* 1992. *Reflections on the Folklife Festival: An Ethnography of Participant Experience*. Special Publications 2. Bloomington: Indiana University, Folklore Institute.

Beck, Jane. 1997. "Taking Stock." *Journal of American Folklore* 110(436): 123–139.

Briggs, Charles and Clara Mantini-Briggs. 2003. *Stories in the Time of Cholera: Racial Profiling During a Medical Nightmare*. Berkeley: University of California Press.

Brodkey, Linda. 1996. *Writing Permitted in Designated Areas Only*. Minneapolis: University of Minnesota Press.

Camp, Charles. 1983. "Developing a State Folklife Program" in Richard M. Dorson, Ed. *Handbook of American Folklore*. Bloomington: Indiana University Press, pp. 518–524.

Cannon, Hal. 2000. "Blue Shadows on Human Drama: The Western Songscape" in Polly Stewart, Steve Siporin, C.W. Sullivan III, and Suzi Jones, Eds. *Worldviews and the American West: The Life of Place Itself*. Logan: Utah State University Press, pp. 31–33.

Cantwell, Robert. 1993. *Ethnomimesis: Folklife and the Representation of Culture*. Chapel Hill: University of North Carolina Press.

Cantwell, Robert. 2001. "Foreword: In Good Spirits" in Archie Green, Ed. *Torching the Fink Books and Other Essays on Vernacular Culture*. Chapel Hill: University of North Carolina Press, pp. vii–xxvii.

Cocke, Dudley. 2002. "Art in a Democracy." www.communityarts.net (accessed October 16, 2011).

Collins, Camilla, Ed. 1980. *Folklore and the Public Sector*. Special issue. *Kentucky Folklore Record* 26(1–2): 2–83.

Community Arts Network. http://wayback.archive-it.org/2077/20100906194747/http://www.communityarts.net/ (accessed October 16, 2011).

Danticat, Edwidge. 2010. *Create Dangerously: The Immigrant Artist at Work*. Princeton: Princeton University Press.

Davis, Gerald L. 1989. "Foreword: An Appreciation" in Roland Freeman. *The Arabbers of Baltimore*. Centreville, MD: Tidewater Publications, pp. vii–viii.

Davis, Gerald L. 1996. "'Somewhere over the Rainbow …': Judy Garland in Neverland." *Journal of American Folklore* 109(432): 115–128.

Davis, Gerald L. 2007 [1992]. "'So Correct for the Photograph:' 'Fixing' the Ineffable, Ineluctable African American" in Robert Baron and Nicholas R. Spitzer, Eds. *Public Folklore*. Washington, DC: Smithsonian Institution Press, pp. 105–118.

Davis, Susan G. 2010. "Ben Botkin's FBI File." *Journal of American Folklore* 123(487): 3–30.

Diamond, Heather A. 2008. *American Aloha: Cultural Tourism and the Negotiation of Tradition*. Honolulu: University of Hawai'i Press.

Esteva, Gustavo and Madhu Suri Prakash. 1998. *Grassroots Post-Modernism: Remaking the Soil of Cultures*. London and NY: Zed Books.

Feintuch, Burt, Ed. 1988. *The Conservation of Culture: Folklorists and the Public Sector*. Lexington: University Press of Kentucky.

Freeman, Roland L. 1989. *The Arabbers of Baltimore*. Centreville, MD: Tidewater Publishers.

Freeman, Roland L. 2006. *A Tribute to Worth Long. Still on the Case: A Pioneer's Continuing Commitment*. Washington, DC: Smithsonian Center for Folklife and Cultural

Heritage and the Group for Cultural Documentation.

Fund for Folk Culture. https://scholarworks. iu.edu/dspace/handle/2022/3850 (accessed October 16, 2011).

Goldstein, Diane E. 2004. *Once Upon a Virus: AIDS Legends and Vernacular Risk Perception.* Logan: Utah State University Press.

Graves, James Bau. 2005. *Cultural Democracy: The Arts, Community and the Public Purpose.* Urbana: University of Illinois Press.

Green, Archie. 1993. "Conversations With: Archie Green" in David Shuldiner, Ed. *Folklore in Use* 1: 5–14.

Green, Archie. 2001. *Torching the Fink Books and Other Essays on Vernacular Culture.* Chapel Hill: University of North Carolina Press.

Green, Archie. 2007 [1992]. "Public Folklore's Name: A Partisan's Notes" in Robert Baron and Nicholas R. Spitzer, Eds. *Public Folklore.* Washington, DC: Smithsonian Institution Press, pp. 49–63.

Haring, Lee, Ed. 2008. "Special Issue: Grand Theory." *Journal of Folklore Research* 45(1): 1–105.

Hasan-Rokem, Galit. 2007. "Dialogue as Ethical Conduct: The Folk Festival That Was Not" in Bente Gullveig Alver, Tove Ingebørg Fjell, and Ørjar Øyen, Eds. *Research Ethics in Studies of Culture and Social Life. FF Communications* 292. Helsinki: Academia Scientarum Fennica, pp. 192–208.

Hawes, Bess Lomax. 2007 [1992]. "Happy Birthday, Dear American Folklore Society: Reflections on the Work and Mission of Folklorists" in Robert Baron and Nicholas R. Spitzer, Eds. *Public Folklore.* Washington, DC: Smithsonian Institution Press, pp. 65–73.

Hawes, Bess Lomax. 2008. *Sing it Pretty: A Memoir.* Urbana: University of Illinois Press.

Hufford, Mary. 1994. *Conserving Culture: A New Discourse on Heritage.* Urbana: University of Illinois Press.

Hawes, Bess Lomax, Marjorie Hunt, and Steven Zeitlin. 1987. *The Grand Generation: Memory, Mastery, Legacy.*

Washington, DC: Smithsonian Institution Traveling Exhibition Service and Office of Folklife Programs.

Hymes, Dell. 1988. "Preservation of Indian Lore in Oregon" in Burt Feintuch, Ed. *The Conservation of Culture: Folklorists and the Public Sector.* Lexington: University Press of Kentucky, pp. 264–268.

Ivey, Bill. 2008. *Arts, Inc. How Greed and Neglect Have Destroyed Our Cultural Rights.* Berkeley: University of California Press.

Jones, Michael Owen, Ed. 1994. *Putting Folklore to Use.* Lexington: University Press of Kentucky.

Kelley, Robin D.G. 2002. *Freedom Dreams: The Black Radical Imagination.* Boston: Beacon Press.

Kirshenblatt, Mayer and Barbara Kirshenblatt-Gimblett. 2007. *They Called Me Mayer July: Memories of Jewish Life in Poland Before the Holocaust.* Berkeley: University of California Press/Judah L. Magnes Museum.

Klein, Naomi. 2007. *The Shock Doctrine: The Rise of Disaster Capitalism.* New York: Henry Holt.

Kodish, Debora. 2011. "Envisioning Folklore Activism." *Journal of American Folklore* 124(491): 31–60.

Kurin, Richard. 1997. *Reflections of a Culture Broker: A View from the Smithsonian.* Washington: Smithsonian Institution Press.

Lear, Jonathan. 2006. *Radical Hope: Ethics in the Face of Cultural Devastation.* Cambridge: Harvard University Press.

Leary, James P., Ed. 1998. *Wisconsin Folklore.* Madison: University of Wisconsin Press.

Lindahl, Carl. 2010. "Leonard Roberts, The Farmer-Lewis-Muncy Family, and the Magic Circle of the Mountain Märchen." *Journal of American Folklore* 123(489): 251–275.

Long, Worth. 1991. "Cultural Organizing and Participatory Research" in Diana Baird N'Diaye and Deirdre L. Bibby, Eds. *The Arts of Black Folk.* New York: Schomburg Center for Research in Black Culture, pp. 28–35.

MacDowell, Marsha and LuAnne G. Kozma, Ed. 2008. *Folk Arts in Education: A Resource Handbook II.* East Lansing:

Michigan State University. www.folkarts ineducation.org (accessed October 16, 2011).

Matsuda, Mari. 1996. *Where Is Your Body? And Other Essays on Race, Gender and the Law.* Boston: Beacon Press.

McCarl, Robert. 2000. "Visible Landscapes/Invisible People: Negotiating the Power of Representation in a Mining Community" in Polly Stewart, Steve Siporin, C.W. Sullivan III, and Suzi Jones, Eds. *Worldviews and the American West: The Life of Place Itself.* Logan: Utah State University Press, pp. 221–226.

McCarl, Robert. 2006a. "Introduction." Special issue. *Western Folklore* 65(1–2): 5–11.

McCarl, Robert. 2006b. "Foreword: Lessons of Work and Workers." *Western Folklore* 65(1–2): 13–29.

McDowell, John and Moira Smith, Eds. 2004. *Advocacy Issues in Folklore.* Special issue. *Journal of Folklore Research* 41(2/3): 103–294.

Mills, Margaret. 2008. "What('s) Theory?" in Lee Haring, Ed. *Grand Theory.* Special issue. *Journal of Folklore Research* 45(1): 19–28.

Moses, Robert and Charles E. Cobb, Jr. 2001. *Radical Equations: Civil Rights from Mississippi to the Algebra Project.* Boston: Beacon Press.

Mulcahy, Joanne B. 2010. *Remedios: The Healing Life of Eva Castellanoz.* San Antonio: Trinity University Press.

Narayan, Kirin. 2008. "'Or in Other Words': Recasting Grand Theory" in Lee Haring, Ed. *Grand Theory.* Special issue, *Journal of Folklore Research* 45(1): 83–90.

National Endowment for the Arts, www.nea. gov (accessed October 16, 2011). See National Heritage Fellowships Twenty-Fifth Anniversary 1982–2007, http://www.nea. gov/honors/heritage/fellows/ (accessed October 16, 2011) and Lifetime Honors: NEA National Heritage Fellowships (1982–2010) http://www.nea.gov/honors/ heritage/index.html (accessed October 16, 2011).

N'Diaye, Diana Baird, and Deirdre L. Bibby, Eds. 1991. *The Arts of Black Folk.* New York: Schomburg Center for Research in Black Culture.

Noyes, Dorothy. 2008. "Humble Theory" in Lee Haring, Ed. *Grand Theory.* Special issue. *Journal of Folklore Research* 45(1): 37–43.

O'Connor, Bonnie Blair. 1994. *Healing Traditions: Alternative Medicine and the Health Professions.* Philadelphia: University of Pennsylvania Press.

Oring, Elliott. 2004. "Folklore and Advocacy" in John McDowell and Moira Smith, Eds. *Advocacy Issues in Folklore.* Special issue. *Journal of Folklore Research* 41(2/3): 259–267.

Payne, Charles M. 1995. *I've Got the Light of Freedom: The Organizing Tradition and the Mississippi Freedom Struggle.* Berkeley: University of California Press.

Peterson, Elizabeth. 1996. *The Changing Faces of Tradition: A Report on the Folk and Traditional Arts in the United States.* Research Division Report 38. Washington, DC: National Endowment for the Arts.

Philadelphia Folklore Project. www.folklore-project.org (accessed October 16, 2011).

Pratt, Mary Louise. 2001. "I, Rigoberta Menchú and the 'Culture Wars.'" in Arturo Arias, Ed. *The Rigoberta Menchú Controversy.* Minneapolis: University of Minnesota Press, pp. 29–48.

Price, David H. 2004. *Threatening Anthropology: McCarthyism and the FBI's Surveillance of Activist Anthropologists.* Durham, NC: Duke University Press.

Price, Richard and Sally Price. 1994. *On the Mall: Presenting Maroon Tradition-Bearers at the 1992 FAF.* Special Publications 4. Bloomington: Indiana University, Folklore Institute.

Reagon, Bernice Johnson. 1990. "Foreword: Nurturing Resistance" in Mark O'Brien and Craig Little, Eds. *Reimagining America: The Arts of Social Change.* Philadelphia: New Society Publishers, pp. 1–8.

Reagon, Bernice Johnson. 1991. "Interview with Bernice Reagon" in Clayborne Carson et al., Eds. *The Eyes on the Prize Civil Rights Reader.* New York: Penguin, pp. 143–145.

Reagon, Bernice Johnson. 2001. *If You Don't Go, Don't Hinder Me: The African*

American Sacred Song Tradition. Lincoln: University of Nebraska Press (The Abraham Lincoln Lecture Series).

Reid, Herbert and Betsy Taylor. 2010. *Recovering the Commons: Democracy, Place, and Global Justice.* Urbana: University of Illinois Press.

Roberts, John. 2000. "African-American Folklore in a Discourse of Folkness" in Barbara L. Hampton, Ed. *Through African-Centered Prisms.* Special issue. *New York Folklore* 18(1–4): 73–89.

Robinson, Beverly. 1991. "Mind-Builders Project" in Diana Baird N'Diaye and Deirdre L. Bibby, Eds. *The Arts of Black Folk.* New York: Schomburg Center for Research in Black Culture, pp. 59–66.

Scott, James C. 2009. *The Art of Not Being Governed: An Anarchist History of Upland South Asia.* New Haven: Yale University Press.

Shapiro, Linn, Rosie Lee Hooks, and Bernice Johnson Reagon, Eds. 1976. *Black People and Their Culture: Selected Writings from the African Diaspora.* Washington, DC: Smithsonian Institution.

Sheehy, Dan. 1992. "A Few Notions about Philosophy and Strategy in Applied Ethnomusicology." *Ethnomusicology* 36(3): 323–336.

Sheehy, Dan. 2007 [1992]. "Crossover Dreams: The Folklorist and the Folk Arrival" in Robert Baron and Nicholas R. Spitzer, Eds. *Public Folklore.* Washington, DC: Smithsonian Institution Press, pp. 217–229.

Shuldiner, David, Ed. 1993–1995. *Folklore in Use: Applications in the Real World.* Enfield Lock, UK: Hisarlik Press.

Siporin, Steve. 1992. *American Folk Masters: The National Heritage Fellows.* New York: Harry N. Abrams in association with Museum of International Folk Art.

Smithsonian Center for Folklife and Cultural Heritage. www.folklife.si.edu (accessed October 16, 2011).

Smithsonian Folklife Festival. 1967–2010. Washington, DC: Smithsonian Institution Center for Folklife and Cultural Heritage (Program books).

Sommers, Laurie Kay, Ed. 1994. *Michigan on the Mall.* Special issue. *Folklore in Use:*

Applications in the Real World 2(2): 153–279.

Spitzer, Nick. 2007 [1992]. "Cultural Conversation: Metaphors and Methods in Public Folklore" in Robert Baron and Nicholas R. Spitzer, Eds. *Public Folklore.* Washington, DC: Smithsonian Institution Press, pp. 77–103.

Stewart, Polly, Steve Siporin, C.W. Sullivan III, and Suzi Jones, Eds. 2000. *Worldviews and the American West: The Life of Place Itself.* Logan: Utah State University Press.

Sweterlitsch, Dick, Ed. 1971. *Papers on Applied Folklore. Folklore Forum.* Bibliographic and Special Studies 8. Bloomington: Indiana University, Folklore Institute.

Tchen, Jack (John Kuo Wei). 2007. "Thirty Years and Counting: A Context for Building a Shared Cross-Cultural Commons." *Community Arts Network.* Essay prepared for symposium "Sustaining Voices from the Battlefield: Community Grounded Cultural Arts Organizations @ 30," a conference convened by the Caribbean Cultural Center/African Diaspora Institute at Tisch School of the Arts, New York University, June 8–9, 2007, http://www.communityarts.net/readingroom/archivefiles/2007/11/30_years_and_co.php (accessed October 16, 2011).

Wells, Patricia Atkinson, Ed. 2006. *Working for and with the Folk: Public Folklore in the Twenty-First Century.* Special issue. *Journal of American Folklore* 119(471): 3–128.

Welsch, Roger. 2011. "Confessions of a Wannabe: When the Prime Directive Misfires." *Journal of American Folklore* 124(491): 19–30.

Westerman, William. 1994. "Cultural Barriers to Justice in Greater Philadelphia: Background, Bias and the Law." *Working Papers of the Philadelphia Folklore Project* 9: 1–65, http://www.folkloreproject.org/folkarts/resources/index.php (accessed October 16, 2011).

Westerman, William. 2006. "Wild Grasses and New Arks: Transformative Potential in Applied and Public Folklore." *Journal of American Folklore* 119(471): 110–128.

Western Folklife Center. www.westernfolklife. org (accessed October 16, 2011).

Whisnant, David E. 1983.   *All That Is Native and Fine: The Politics of Culture in an American Region.* Chapel Hill: University of North Carolina Press.

Williams, Patricia. 1995.   *The Rooster's Egg: On the Persistence of Prejudice.* Cambridge, MA: Harvard University Press.

CHAPTER 31

THE INSTITUTIONALIZATION OF FOLKLORE

Bjarne Rogan

Folklore as a scholarly discipline is a political as well as an intellectual enterprise. A discussion of its institutionalization must take into account both aspects. Formal organizational units like societies and commissions, archives and museums, university chairs and journals result from the discipline's relationship to society and the authorities. They represent acknowledgment as an academic discipline and a place in the wider framework of cultural policies defined by the state (Honko 1989). Disciplines are thus political projects, whether as a part of relatively innocent identity politics or nation-building processes or as tools for totalitarian or colonial regimes, as outgrowths of cultural-political ideologies or even intelligence strategies (Viires 1991; Dow and Lixfeld 1994; Dracklé *et al.* 2003; Nas and de Groot 2009). This is valid for all disciplines, but one is tempted to say especially so for folklore.

But disciplines are first and foremost intellectual projects. Institutionalization shows how a scholarly field constitutes and delimits itself in relation to neighboring disciplines, and the hierarchy of "mother" discipline and sub-disciplines, its denomination, its epistemological and theoretical basis. The latter may be termed its "interior" history, and the political and societal aspects its "exterior" history (Lebovics 2009). There are, however, close links between the intellectual basis, external political steering, and the rise and fall of institutions. The institutions proper are the meeting point between the internal and the external histories.

Drawing on people's own wealth of knowledge and practices, folklore has an especially great propagandistic value, as is evident in a number of the chapters in Part

A Companion to Folklore, First Edition. Edited by Regina F. Bendix and Galit Hasan-Rokem.
© 2012 John Wiley & Sons, Ltd. Published 2012 John Wiley & Sons, Ltd.

Two, "Location," in this volume. The cases of the Soviet Union (Oinas 1961; Viires 1991; Panchenko in this volume) and the Third Reich are well known (1933–1945) (Jeggle 1988; Lixfeld 1991; Bendix in this volume). After the Spanish Civil War (1936–1939), the fascist Franco regime feared the consequences of ethnographic and folkloristic research so much that all central researchers were forced to leave the country, until a hesitant standardization process started in the 1950s. The fall of the fascist Salazar regime in Portugal in 1974 led to profound changes in the theoretical as well as the institutional contexts of the discipline (Gómez-Tabanera 1967; Carós and Muñoz 1991; Cardeira da Silva 1991).

Language hegemonies must also be taken into account, as political events have brought about changes to knowledge regimes. The replacement after World War II of German by English as a scholarly lingua franca in Northern Europe, and by Russian in Eastern and parts of Central Europe, and likewise after 1989 the replacement of Russian by English, has had a considerable impact on how the folkloristic and ethnological heritage is regarded and how curricula have changed (Mursic 2003).

The chapter begins with general outlines regarding the history of the field's institutionalization. The name of the field is one aspect thereof (Fenton 1993). Another inescapable issue is the changing relationships between the constituent sub-disciplines: folklore or folkloristics, (European) ethnology and (social or cultural) anthropology. A constant pitfall is the fact that these three academic traditions are alternately regarded as independent disciplines and sometimes as specialized fields of one single discipline, with names further differentiated depending on time and place (Vermeulen and Roldan 1995). I will then turn to the institutions on the national level, focusing on specific cases

The challenge is how to present the outcomes of institutions. Frances Gilmore, after having tried to draw the landscape of folklorists and folkloristic institutions in one single country, Mexico, concludes (1961b): "This outline of the present state of folklore in Mexico reveals a complicated picture, one that is overorganized, interorganized, and replete with overlapping personnel. Yet it makes apparent a concern with folklore in many related disciplines, a concern which results in extensive collecting, archiving, publishing, and teaching." This is no less true for folklore worldwide.

INSTITUTIONALIZATION AND ITS COUNTERFORCES

A History of Growth and Progress?

Folklore – a term that refers to both subject matter and a scholarly discipline – has for more than a century found itself at the crossroads of the humanities and the social sciences, with roots in literature studies and national philologies, as well as in geography, anthropology, and biology, with a retrospective glance to the past as well as a keen eye on the present. To some the term covers only popular belief or only folk literature, relying on the etymology: the lore of the folk. For others, the discipline straddles mental, material, and social culture. Spanning different scholarly traditions is a situation that has profoundly marked folklore's institutional history.

Collecting oral literature was for several centuries the concern of solitary, individual amateurs or scholars. In the Romantic period, learned societies were formed to celebrate and salvage old traditions, and the first few courses were taught by academics from various disciplines. A later phenomenon was the fashion for material remnants of the people, in its earliest form a quest for antiquities by some scholars and travelers of the Enlightenment and the Romantic period. However, "institutionalization" can hardly be said to apply to these early practices, in either sense of the term discussed above.

As of the late nineteenth century, ethnographic and folk-life museums served as catalysts for the scholarly (and political) interest in material folk culture. In the wake of the museums came the public tradition archives, particularly in the realm of narrative, song, and belief. Of crucial importance to the development of these archives were the national philologies, especially dialectology. In the Germanic tradition, philology even played an important role for material culture studies, in the *Wörter und Sachen* tradition of the early twentieth century. And finally came university institutes, academies, and chairs. A relatively forgotten history is how physical anthropology, closely entangled with ethnography, established a strong academic position from the latter part of the nineteenth century. We are now well into the era of folklore as an institutionalized discipline, but it still took some decades before scholarly interest in the social aspects of the lives of ordinary people was added. Instrumental in this development were the closely related burgeoning disciplines of sociology and social anthropology.

"Institutionalization" is not a linear and progressive movement. There are cases of (sub) disciplines that split and merge, disappear, and revive, and there are those rare but decisive moments when a discipline turns its back on its own project and enters a new paradigm, as happened in some countries when ethnography shifted to social anthropology in the 1920s or when ethnology became involved in culture analysis in the 1970s (Bausinger 1971; Segalen 2005; Löfgren 2008; Conn 2010). There are other (interconnected) factors that have affected or have even been counterproductive to the institutionalization of folklore; one is a myopic regional or national bias, another the dominant role of the amateurs. During the twentieth century, the scholarly study of oral traditions and material culture changed its "institutional home" from the archives and museums to the universities.

Finally, two other factors counteracting institutionalization have been discussed by the Danish ethnologist Bjarne Stoklund (1969–1971), namely narrow specialization and the risk of being swallowed up by the social sciences. He claimed that there was a remarkable tendency in the discipline to choose a specialized topic and to cultivate it intensively. Specialization threatened to pull the field apart. On the other hand, there were those who saw the glue to stick the discipline together in the aims and methodologies of the social sciences. The challenge of ethnology was to learn as much as possible from other disciplines, without being swallowed up. Whereas Stoklund in the 1960s warned against too close flirtation a with sociology and social anthropology, many folklorists experienced a corresponding temptation from (British) cultural studies in the 1990s. In the 2000s the siren for many is the cultural history movement. A recent international movement like the International Society of Cultural History (ISCH) has attracted many folklorists.

The Lore of the Folk or a Broad, Unified Discipline?
When the English antiquarian John William Thoms coined the phrase "folklore" in 1846, he could hardly have foreseen how much debate his proposal would cause. He

defined folklore as the traditional beliefs, customs, superstitions, legends ballads, and so on, current among the common people. Thoms's focus was on popular culture that had been transmitted from the past. Åke Hultkranz stated that this conception of folklore (1960), was responsible for the subsequent controversies about the concept, the many divergent definitions up to the present time, and "the dubious relations between *ethnology* and folklore." The internal relationship between folklore, ethnology, and anthropology, as well as the question of unity, hierarchy and subordination, remained "rather confused" (1960: 140).

The 1950s and 1960s represented a culmination of the controversies between defenders of a purist conception of folklore and proponents of a unified discipline of ethnology. The question of a common designation for sub-disciplines had been voiced from time to time in international forums. This had been an important issue at the meetings of the *Commission Internationale des Arts et Traditions Populaires* (CIAP) in Arnhem and Amsterdam in 1955, where the Portuguese ethnologist Jorge Dias compared the situation with that of medicine. In the same way a urologist or a cardiologist was also a doctor, everyone should call himself an ethnologist, even if his specialty was that of "a folklorist, *Volkskundler*, musicologist, dialectologist, ethnographer, ethnologist or anthropologist" (Dias 1956).

It was recommended in 1955 that the international name of the whole discipline should be *ethnology*, with the qualification *regional* or *national* when it was necessary to distinguish between (Western) peoples with a written history from those without. But many objected to defining the studies of material culture, folklore, and social life as branches of one and the same discipline, as well as to accepting it as a regional variant of anthropology. There was heavy opposition from the scholars of oral literature, and at the time few German-speaking scholars were willing to let go of the dichotomy *Volkskunde – Völkerkunde*. At the CIAP/SIEF congress in Athens in 1964 the division of the disciplines was cemented in the name of the new society – *La Société Internationale d'Ethnologie et de Folklore* (SIEF) (Rogan 2008a, b). These debates found a parallel in the ongoing controversies in the United States between literary and anthropological folklorists, a division that has now been largely overcome (Zumwalt 1988). This was not so in all European countries, however, as the cast-iron name of SIEF indicates, and judging by the contributions in this volume, the different traditions of folklore-related research assert themselves differently depending on both time and place.

The situation has not been less confused since 1960. The broad research tradition, spanning categories of oral, material, and social culture, is usually called *(European) ethnology*, in continental Europe today but *folklore* in the United States. But this statement requires instant qualification.

In Russia and Eastern Europe *ethnografija* or ethnography has almost invariably been the denomination for this broad field of study since the late 1920s. Former designations were replaced by ethnography almost everywhere. Since the 1990s this term has been replaced by *ethnology* or *social anthropology*. Institutionally they normally form sections within departments of history in humanities faculties (Gellner 1980; Viires 1991; Bondarenko and Korotayev 2003; Ciubrinskas 2008). In the Eastern European context the term *anthropology* equates physical anthropology, as was also the case in several West European countries in the late nineteenth and early twentieth centuries.

In the German-speaking countries *Volkskunde* – a term translated by *folklore* in English and French – covers the three fields. Since the late 1960s, many universities have replaced *Volkskunde* by other terms (*Ethnologie, (Kultur)Anthropologie* or *empirischer Kulturwissenschaft*) (Dracklé 2003; Bendix and Eggeling 2004; see Bendix in this volume).

Folklore has often been used as an overall term in Southern Europe, as was also the case in France until the end of World War II. The term appears in the name of several Southern European journals. A scholar such as van Gennep, for example, included material culture in the term, and a museum founder like G.H. Rivière tried to impose the term *folklore* for the whole field of study on Central and Northern Europe (Rogan 2008c). Due to wartime collaboration, the term folklore was abandoned in France after 1945 and replaced by *ethnologie* (Cuisinier and Segalen 1986; Lebovics 2009), or as the title of a recent anthology on French ethnology between 1930 and 1945: *Du folklore à l'ethnologie* (Christophe *et al.* 2009; see also Segalen 2005).

Arts et traditions populaires has been an alternative expression in Southern Europe, and mainly appears in the names of congresses, associations, commissions, journals and museums. When the League of Nations established the 1928 Prague Congress, the term *arts populaires* (covering material and spiritual folk culture) was chosen, which lived on in the name of the subsequent organization, the CIAP, until 1964 (Rogan 2007). This term was used in France for the names of the national commission, the national department of museum administration, and the national museum – *Le Musée National des Arts et Traditions Populaires* (1937–2008; see Cuisinier and Segalen 1986; Segalen 2005; Bromberger 2009). The corresponding national Italian museum (planned in 1911 but inaugurated in 1956), also covering the whole field – *il campo delle materie demoetnoantropologiche* bears the name *Museo delle Arti e Tradizioni Populari*. In Greece, the term *laographia* includes material, psychological, and social aspects of traditional life (Spyridakis 1967).

The terms *ethnology* and *anthropology* are normally taken to cover the three fields. In most of the Nordic countries there has long been a disciplinary and institutional divide between the study of oral and mental culture – called *folkeminnegransking* or *folkloristikk*, and material and social culture – called *folkelivsgranskning* or *etnologi*. In Sweden, the two have been institutionally together, since the 1960s as *etnologi*. In Norway, they converged in the 2000s and emerged as *kulturhistorie* (Oslo) or *kulturvitenskap* (Bergen).

The term *European ethnology* was introduced in the 1950s by the Swede Sigurd Erixon (1955) as an overall term, but with no great success. The term found its place, however, in the names of several institutes, and lives on in the subtitle of the longest-living general international journal, *Ethnologia Europaea – A Journal of European Ethnology*.

The American and European use and contexts of the terms (folklore, ethnology, and anthropology) cannot be directly equated, among other things because of the much stronger cultural-historical orientation of some of the terms in Europe (Hultkrantz 1952, 1967a,b; Leser 1967). See Zumwalt (1988) for the periodically strained relationship between the "literary" and the "anthropological" folklorists in the United States. Today *folklore* covers all fields, according to the web page of the American Folklore Society, as the study of "what people believe, do, know, make and say."

The Domestic or The Exotic?

A peculiarity of German-speaking Europe is the conceptual differentiation between ethnology of the "exotic" and the "domestic." Studies of the national population (*Volkskunde*) and of distant cultures (*Völkerkunde*) developed both epistemologically and institutionally along different paths. This model has firmly cemented research as well as faculty and department structures in areas under German-Austrian influence, like parts of Central Europe and the Nordic countries. In the latter, the study of distant or exotic cultures came under the aegis of ethnography, later anthropology, whereas the two institutionally separate disciplines *folkloristikk* and *etnologi* embraced the national and European cultures. The study of the exotic belonged to the social sciences and the study of the domestic to the humanities, a distinction that is now attenuated.

In France and Southern Europe, an epistemological divide of this type hardly existed. Even if *ethnographie* and *folklore* in pre-World War II France focused on different geographic areas, the areas were presented side by side in the ethnographic museum at Trocadéro. They were treated in the same way by the national journal *Revue du folklore français et colonial* (1932–1939) and they shared the national *Société du folklore français et colonial* (Cuisinier and Segalen 1986).

In general the Latin countries seem to have adhered to this tradition, to the extent that an anthropology of the thematically exotic has existed. In Portugal, the nationalistically oriented ethnography and folklore of the first half of the twentieth century were replaced after World War II by an ethnology that studied both Portugal and the colonies. The era of modern ethnology/anthropology was inaugurated by Jorge Dias (1907–1973), who published profusely both on national topics and the indigenous populations of colonial Africa. Present-day university studies of anthropology include national as well as extra-European cultures (Dias 1967; Bonte and Izard 1992; Cordeiro and Alfonso 2003).

Italy represents a more complicated case. What may be considered the Italian "mainstream" anthropology today has a threefold origin: *demologia* – the more than century-old study of the national culture; *etnologia* – the study of extra-European cultures; and *antropologia culturale* – a "new" discipline from the 1960s, influenced by American cultural anthropology and focusing on complex societies and especially on Italy. The Italian academic landscape has been marked by controversies between these three disciplines (and physical anthropology), but the national studies – *demologia* and *antropologia culturale* – have now more or less merged, and the conflicting relationship between the latter and the *etnologia* of the exotic has acquiesced. The term *antropologia* is now commonly used to designate this largely unified field, but the memories of a rather chaotic situation can still be evoked in the term officially adopted by the ministry: the "demo-ethno-anthropological disciplines" (Viazzo 2003).

To underscore the varying European anthropological landscape, Greece may serve as a final example of Mediterranean complexity. Anthropology in Greece is more or less synonymous with anthropology "at home," whether one refers to the more than century-old vernacular folklore tradition or to the social anthropological tradition since the 1950s, that is, the American and British anthropologists studying the country. This invasion seems to have contributed heavily to the country's inability to establish an anthropological tradition of its own (Panopoulos 2003). The problem of being the object rather than the subject of anthropological investigation has been faced by all the Southern European countries (Schippers 1995), but not in the same intensity as in Greece.

The *etnografija* in Russia in the Soviet period comprised in principle the study of both local and distant cultures, but in practice the field covered was mainly the domestic one, namely historical study of traditional rural folk culture and urban workers' culture (Bromley 1974b; Gellner 1980). "Armchair studies," based on literature, were undertaken for exotic cultures, but fieldwork was allowed only to research the different *ethnies* or populations within the Soviet Empire. Fieldwork methodology in the Soviet Union differed from its Western equivalent and was undertaken as part of ethnographic expeditions with large groups of scholars and students, as this was the only way of keeping political control of the individuals participating. The Western idea of a solitary fieldworker spending long periods of time among the locals appeared "completely inconceivable" (Bondarenko and Korotayev 2003). There is much variation as to what extent both the near and the distant are included in current Russian ethnology or anthropology. The study of the domestic, of regional and national cultures, still seems to dominate (Mucha 2003; Budil 2003; Mihailescu 2003).

As in the case of Italy (above), there seems to be a tendency towards convergence in some countries (Waldis 2003). On the other hand, nationalistic revivals in Eastern Europe tend to strengthen the study of the local and the national, arguing for the preservation and revival of traditional culture, or, as reported from Slovakia, aimed explicitly at "reawakening Slovak ethnicity and identity" (Bitusikova 2003). History tends to repeat itself.

Internationalist Endeavors

"By its very nature the study of folklore requires an international breadth of vision," stated Richard Dorson, as "[the] materials of folklore transcend all barriers of language and culture, traversing continents and spanning oceans in vast leaps and drifting across borders in easy stages" (1961: 287). Access to the materials across (linguistic) borders and the need for comparison was the earliest motivation for international cooperation, starting with the congresses of folklore/anthropology on the eve of the twentieth century (the First International Folk-lore Congress in Paris in 1889, and the second in London in 1891).

The dream of an international archive organization, nourished by several folklorists in the interwar years, was never realized. Carl Wilhelm von Sydow, head of the archive in Lund (see below), led a restless fight for an international archive for folktale research to make accessible texts preserved in different national archives, especially folk tales, translated into a world language (Rogan 2007). Only on a Nordic level, and much later, an international institute was established, *Nordisk Institut for Folkloristik* (NIF 1959–1997), first situated in Copenhagen and later in Turku. During its 39 years of existence, it developed into a very active center for oral culture research, with an impact far beyond the Nordic countries. There were no endeavors among the ethnologists to create permanent institutes, but an International Secretariat for Research on Agricultural Implements, with a library and archives, was established in Copenhagen in 1954 (Lerche 1979). The secretariat published the scholarly journal *Tools and Tillage* up to 1995.

If permanent institutions were not too easy to establish, organizations and looser networks were more successful. An early initiative, stemming from the "historical-geographic school" within folklore, was the Folklore Fellows (FF), started in 1907 by Kaarle Krohn (Helsinki), C.W. von Sydow (Lund), and Axel Olrik (Copenhagen). The FF grew quickly to form an international movement, with regional FF-societies in around 15 countries, but this expansion came to an end with World War I. The FF came to function primarily as an editorial group for the publication series *Folklore Fellows Communications*, published by the Finnish Academy of Science and Letters, a series that published around 300 scholarly monographs. The series was predominantly Nordic, but with contributions from some scholars from outside Scandinavia. The focus was on oral traditions and literature, but the scope was also widened to include comparative religion and cultural anthropology. In 1990, the FF was revived through the launching of the Folklore Fellows Network (FFN), with an open membership policy and worldwide recruitment (Honko 1991).

Whereas the FFN covers all forms of folkloristics and organizes small workshops and the FF Summer Schools, the International Society for Folk Narrative Research (ISFNR) specializes in folk-narrative studies and organizes world congresses. The idea of the ISFNR was introduced by the German Kurt Ranke in 1959 (Kiel) but was formally inaugurated in Antwerp in 1962. ISFNR has developed from a European/American organization to a worldwide one, since the mid-1990s organizing congresses in Asia and Africa as well as in Europe. The scholarly journal *Fabula* (1958–) became the official journal of the society in 1998. Another thematically specialized organization with a worldwide basis is the International Folk Music Council (IFMC, 1947–), reorganized in 1981 into the International Council for Traditional Music (ICTM), with its *Yearbook for Traditional Music*.

All the above-mentioned organizations are thematically specialized. In the interwar years several *general* ethnological organizations were created. Two of these the International Association of European Ethnology and Folklore (IAEEF), launched by the Swede Sigurd Erixon (1935–) and the *Congrès International de Folklore* (CIFL) led by the Frenchman Georges Henri Rivière (1937–) did not survive World War II (Rogan 2008b, c). CIAP (1928–1964), reorganized as SIEF (1964–, see above), is still active. CIAP/SIEF is mainly a congress organization, whereas most of the scholarly work takes place through its thematic commissions or working groups. CIAP's most important commissions were on cartography and bibliography (*Internationale Volkskundliche Bibliographie*/IVB). Today, SIEF has active working groups on religion, food research, *bildlore*, the ritual year, ethnocartography, historical approaches to cultural analysis, cultural heritage and property, place wisdom, and ballads. The latter organized its fortieth conference in 2010, whereas some groups are quite recent.

The oldest of the anthropological organizations is the International Congress for Anthropological and Ethnological Sciences (ICAES, 1934–), which used to offer sessions for folklore/ethnology (until 1955). After World War II it was reorganized by the International Union of Anthropological and Ethnological Sciences (IUAES, 1948–), an umbrella organization with around 25 thematic commissions, organizing worldwide congresses (Nas and Jijiao 2009). The European Association of Social Anthropology (EASA) was founded in 1989 to serve the interests of anthropologists qualified in, or working in, Europe – but with a worldwide scope, publishing *Social Anthropology/Anthropologie Sociale* (Archetti 2003).

International scholarly journals were regarded as important tools for international cooperation. Specialized journals (e.g., *Fabula* and *Tools and Tillage*, above) seem to have been easier to launch than general journals. A few ephemeral ones were started in the interwar years (Rogan 2008c). Even an organization like CIAP/SIEF has not managed to establish a journal, with the exception of the three issues of *LAOS* (1951–1955). The longest-living one, *Ethnologia Europaea* (1967–), was launched in opposition to SIEF (Rogan 2008b). An important addition in recent years is the *Anthropological Yearbook of European Cultures* (1990), relaunched in 2008 as the *Anthropological Journal of European Cultures* (AJEC). As the title goes, AJEC has a sharp focus on Europe – as a geopolitical entity as well as a cultural construction.

In spite of the international aspects of the field, acknowledged by most folklorists if not by all, the emerging paradox of folklore is that it has developed most energetically along national lines. Or as stated by Dorson (1961: 287):

> [… The] galvanic force behind concerted, subsidized, and firmly organized folklore studies is the force of nationalism. Folklore has served national interests of various sorts: the anxious pride of the small country seeking its cultural identity; the *hubris* of the racist state, glorying in the solidarity of the *Herrenvolk*; the aspirations of an emergent nation, hoping to crystallize its myths; the ideology of the socialist state, extolling the creative powers of the anonymous masses. […] Today the well-equipped political state possesses its accredited historical records, its approved and national literature, and its classified folklore archives.

These "accredited," "approved," and "classified" institutions are the topics for the rest of this chapter.

National Institutions

Societies

The societies, the oldest and most numerous institutions of folklore, vary widely in size, scope, and membership policies. During the twentieth century most countries have had one or more national societies. There is also a dense network of local societies, as well as societies on all levels covering subfields of folklore. The membership is sometimes restricted to professionals, but many societies are open for amateurs. Indeed, many societies were founded by laymen, offering initial arenas also for applied folklore.

As forums for debate and exchange, defending professional interests and disseminating knowledge about the discipline, the societies have normally given high priority to the publication of scholarly journals, newsletters, and monograph series. In some countries in Eastern Europe the national society is the most important publisher of ethnological publications. The oldest "cluster" of societies is in Great Britain and may serve as an example. The Ethnological Society of London was established in London in 1843, as a breakaway faction from an even older society for the protection of aborigines. The earliest members of this scholarly society were military officers, civil servants, and clergy interested in folklore across the Empire as well as in the British countryside. From the 1860s, a group of young career scientists, among them Edward B. Tylor, joined the society. In 1863 many of the latter broke away and established the

Anthropological Society of London. The two societies co-existed until merging in 1871 into *the* Royal Anthropological Institute of Great Britain and Ireland (RAI). The RAI is not only the world's longest established anthropological society, but it is probably also the most inclusive, embracing all types of anthropology: biological, evolutionary, social, cultural, visual, medical anthropology, as well as neighboring disciplines like human genetics, archeology, and linguistics. Its membership, which is not restricted to the UK, includes professional, university-trained anthropologists and students and as well as other interested scholars, and its scope embraces theoretical as well as applied and social aspects of anthropology.

The same broad approach has been pursued in the RAI's publication activities. The quarterly *Journal of the Royal Anthropological Institute* (1995–), formerly *Man* (1901–1994), provides a forum for "anthropology as a whole." The bimonthly *Anthropology Today* (1985–), formerly *RAIN* (1974–1984), provides an outlet for anthropological analyses of public and topical issues. *The Anthropological Index Online* (1997–) is a bibliographic service for students of anthropology worldwide.

As a direct reaction to these broad, multidisciplinary perspectives and the open membership policy, a much more exclusive society was established in 1946, the Association of Social Anthropologists (ASA). Most of the stellar names of British social anthropology were among its founding members. ASA's policy was to promote social anthropology as a university and research discipline, and in general to secure its interests and the professional status of the social anthropologists (Firth 1986; Mills 2003). In the first years, membership was by invitation, but over the years criteria for membership have become steadily more inclusive, and now include the whole Commonwealth. In recent years, the ASA has established a closer working relationship with the RAI.

A direct offspring from the RAI was the Scottish Anthropological and Folklore Society, set up in 1922 in Edinburg as a local RAI branch for its Scottish fellows. It developed into an independent anthropological society in the early 1930s and was reestablished with "Folklore" in its name in 1936. In 1937 it organized a Scandinavian-British congress for the International Association for European Ethnology and Folklore (Rogan 2008c). The Scottish society had been under attack from the RAI because of the alleged Nazi sympathies of some members. The membership began to dwindle in the 1950s and the society was wound up in the early 1960s.

An early contender to the RAI was the Folk-Lore Society (FLS), founded in 1878 and still active today. Once more the central founding father was Edward B. Tylor, England's first professor of anthropology. His studies on the savage mind were instrumental for an anthropological theory of folklore. As Richard Dorson has put it: "The formation of the Folk-Lore Society in 1878, with 'savage' folklorists as key organizers, marked the triumph of ethnology over comparative mythology" (1968: 201). In its first 20 years the FLS was dominated by a group of anthropological folklorists looking for survivals, with a high level of scholarship and a long series of studies published. In 1891, the FLS arranged the Second International Folk-Lore Congress in London, an event which is regarded as the high-water mark of the British folklore movement. Its present journal *Folklore* (earlier *Folk-Lore*) has appeared uninterruptedly since 1890.

The activities of the FLS and the general interest in folklore in England fell dramatically after 1918. Richard Dorson observed the decline of the movement simply by scanning the reduced volumes of *Folk-Lore* after 1918, seeing "how the lean years followed the fat ones" (1968: 440). The reason why folklore never gained academic acceptance in England is complex. After World War I, it was the sister-discipline anthropology that won the place in academia. After World War II, the study of oral traditions also met competition from material and social culture studies, such as the founding of the Ulster Folklife Society in 1960 (with its annual publication *Ulster Folklife*, 1955–) and the Society for Folk Life Research in 1961 (with its journal *Folk Life*, 1963–), with strongholds at the Welsh Folk Museum and the Ulster Folk Museum (Peate 1963). The lack of interest of traditional folklore studies in England has been related to the independence of Ireland (1922). With the founding of the Folklore of Ireland Society in 1927 and the journal *Béaloideas*, edited by Séamus Ó Duilearga, a movement began that resulted in both a very active folklore commission (1935–1971, see below) and a university department (1971–) in Dublin.

A look at the United Kingdom reveals another striking feature, notably strong "applied folklore" societies. At a time when the academic study of folklore receded, some amateur movements flourished more than ever. With reference to the folk music movement, Dorson compared the Tylorian period with what followed as: survival gave way to revival, and performance overtook study (1968).

A good example of "revival and performance" is the English Folk Dance and Song Society (EFDSS), formed in 1932 by the merger of two older organizations, the Folk-Song Society (1898–) and the English Folk Dance Society (1911–), under the leadership of Cecil Sharp and Maud Karpeles. From the outset, collecting and preservation of songs and dances were the primary concerns of the societies, but promotion and popularization became important additional activities. After 1945, the EFDSS adopted a "folk dancing for all" policy, strongly influenced by the United States. From the 1950s onward, they arranged folk song and dance festivals. Many of the activities have continued outside the EFDSS, in affiliated clubs and organizations, and the society still has 4,000 members (www.efdss.org).

There are a number of important national societies. Among the giants are the American Folklore Society (AFS) with well over 2,000 members, founded in 1888 (with its French-Canadian branch from 1892/1917) and publishing the *Journal of American Folklore*, and the American Anthropological Association (AAA), founded in 1905. With its 10,000 members it is the world's largest society of this type. Its main publication is the *American Anthropologist* (1888–).

In German-speaking countries, the national societies are divided between the national and the exotic. In Germany the *Deutsche Gesellschaft für Volkskunde* (1964–), a continuation of the *Verband der Vereine für Volkskunde* (1904–1964), covers the national aspect, while the *Deutsche Gesellschaft für Völkerkunde* (1929–, with earlier predecessors) covers the exotic. Switzerland has its venerable *Schweizerische Gesellschaft für Volkskunde* (1896–) for the vernacular and the *Schweizerische Gesellschaft für Anthropologie und Ethnologie* (1920–1970) for the exotic. In the 1960s, this society was felt to be outdated, mainly because of its references to traditional German *Völkerkunde*, and under the influence of British and French social anthropology it was replaced in 1971 by the *Schweizerische Ethnologische Gesellschaft* (Waldis 2003). Austria has two ethnological societies, the *Verein für Volkskunde* (1894), which is closely associated with the activities of the national *Volkskunde* museum and open for amateurs as well as professionals, and the *Österreichischer Fachverband für Volkskunde* (1958–), with membership restricted to professionals. The Austrian anthropological society, the *Verein Freunde der Völkerkunde,* founded in the late 1930s (the first Austrian anthropological society was founded 1870), is closely associated with the national anthropological museum and with membership open to all. The above-mentioned societies are all national in scope. In addition there are many local and regional societies as well as transnational ones for the Alpine area (Beitl 1961; Schindler 1992).

National societies also flourish in Southern and Eastern Europ, and some are even older than those mentioned above. The first society in Italy was founded in 1870, and its Greek counterpart was founded in 1908. In all these countries there is a range of regional and local ones. On the eve of the twenty-first century, Greece had more than 30 folklore societies, often combining interests with history, archeology and literature, maintaining local archives or small museums and publishing amateur journals (Loukatos 1991). In Eastern Europe, membership of national societies has sometimes been a necessity for researchers, for political reasons but also because the national society was the most important publisher of ethnological publications. After the fall of the Iron Curtain, there was a tendency to establish separate societies for ethnology and anthropology. In Romania, with societies dating from 1875, two separate societies were established in the 1990s (Mihailescu 2003). The Hungarian Ethnographic Society, founded in 1889, established a section for anthropology in the mid-1990s.

Italy offers another case of changing policies. At a time when physical anthropology was the dominant branch of the discipline, the insertion of "ethnology" in 1870 in the name of the first Italian society, *Società Italiana di Antropologia e di Etnologia,* was a strategic action by its founder P. Mantegazza, to gain acceptance for the study of culture. The founding in 1910 of a new society, *Società di Etnografia Italiana,* was an effort to keep the broad spectrum of the anthropological sciences together, even though it ceased to function in the early 1930s as the result of a split. In an improved climate, the three disciplines joined together again in 1991 to form the national *Associazione Italiana per le Scienze Etno-Anthropologiche* (AISEA) (Viazzo 2003).

It is difficult to overview the flourishing of societies past and present. An instructive case is the situation in France. Sixteen ethnological-anthropological societies decided in 2009 to gather in a federation, the *Association Française d'Ethnologie et d'Anthropologie* (AFEA). This umbrella organization includes societies like the Société d'ethnologie, the Société d'ethnologie française, the Société française d'ethnomusicologie, the EthnoArt, the ASPRAS (Association pour la recherche en anthropologie sociale), the AMADES (Anthropologie médicale appliquée au développement et la santé), the AFA (Association française d'anthropologie), the ACAJ (Association des chercheurs en anthropologie du droit), in addition to a series of regional societies (www.asso-afea.fr).

Committees

Between 1928 and the 1960s national committees were established in many countries. A seminal event in the history of folklore was the Prague Congress in 1928 on folk art, when the international organization CIAP was founded (Rogan 2007). Its mentor, the League of Nations, required a membership system based on national committees. The function of these committees was to organize folk art research and promote the revitalization of folklore. Already in 1929, 27 national committees for folklore were established, most of them in Europe and some in South American and Asian countries. The system did not function well, however, partly because of folklore's lack of an national academic basis.

One of the few occasions when the committees were actively summoned was in 1932–1933, when the International Labor Organization (ILO), one of the League's sub-organizations, wanted to make use of them in a campaign for the better use of the workers' leisure time. Unemployment and shorter working hours had created a leisure time "problem" that political authorities wanted to see remedied by a folk art revival. The national folklore committees were invited to put together a plan, but the idea faced opposition from the folklorists and the committees, thus creating a tense situation between a political body wanting to guide research and the researchers who found this policy totally unacceptable. Both parties came out losers; the committees became even more peripheral and ILO had to shelve its 300-page report on the topic (Rogan 2007).

After World War II CIAP's new mentor UNESCO required a return to the system of national committees. In the 1950s, national committees were established in around 50 countries worldwide, many of them in South America, but once again with no great success. Few, if any, turned out viable institutions, in contrast to other organizations that had the same structure, like ICOM and IUSAE. This difference may be due to CIAP's wish to be regarded as a scholarly organization, against ICOM's role as an organization for more general cultural politics. The replacement in 1964 of the CIAP Commission by the SIEF society – with individual membership – meant an end to the system of national committees.

Archives, Commissions, and Institutes

The major research endeavors of folklorists from the late nineteenth century to the mid-twentieth century were collections of verbal art and surveys for folk atlas projects. Both yielded vast amounts of data which in turn gave rise to the need for archives and institutions to house them. This was the case especially for Northern and Eastern parts of Europe, and less so in Southern Europe. These institutions could be regional or national. Some are independent, some are associated, or work closely with universities or academies, some with museums or national societies. They represent a heterogeneous group, but what they have in common is collecting data mainly by questionnaires, local collectors, and informants, and sometimes via wide-ranging fieldwork campaigns. Furthermore, they have research libraries and permanent staff, who carry out research, classification, and archiving (see also Harvilahti, this volume).

From Eastern and Northern Europe, especially Germany and the Nordic countries, archives have spread to Ireland and Scotland, to the United States and from the 1940s to Central and South America (Thompson 1961; Gilmore 1961b; Yoder 1991; Pernet 2007; Corrêa Maia 2009). If any single archive outside Europe should be mentioned, it is the Archive of Folk Culture (AFC, 1928–) at the American Folklife Center (1976–), in Washington, DC. The AFC is America's first national archive of traditional life and covers popular culture not only from all over the United States but from most corners of the world, keeping the world's largest collection of its kind, especially of folk music.

The collecting of folkloristic material depended for a long time on the efforts of individuals. Even in Germany, the cradle of folklore collecting and with its present cluster of archives and commissions, this was so during most of the nineteenth century. Collectors like the Grimm brothers, Wilhelm Mannhardt, or Johannes Bolte had little or no institutional support (Boberg 1953). The earliest folkloristic archives seem to have been established in Eastern Europe. The Finnish Literature Society was founded in 1831, and one of its first tasks was to support Elias Lönnrot collecting oral poetry, which led to the publication of the Kalevala in 1835. The folklore archive of the society has been in continuous activity since the 1830s, and is considered to be one of the largest in the world (Honko 1998).

Another early eastern archive was the Department of Ethnography in St Petersburg, established in 1845 as a section of the Russian Geographical Society. It distributed questionnaires to all districts of the Russian Empire and started publishing an ethnographic volume series from 1853 (Bromley 1974b; Bondarenko and Korotayev 2003). In the early period of the communist regime, various ethnographic commissions and committees, later in the form of institutes, were set up as a corollary to "Lenin's national policy and the need for radical changes in the life and culture of the formerly backward peoples" of the USSR (Bromley 1974b: 18). From the end of the 1930s, a network of ethnographic research institutes were organized, and in the postwar period there were institutes connected to the academies in all the republics of the Russian federation. The names and the organization of the folklore institutions have changed several times, but the two important institutions in the Soviet Union after World War II were the Folklore Committee under the Academy of Sciences in Leningrad and the Gorkij Institute in Moscow (Oinas 1961).

The Nordic countries have focused on folk-life archive institutions, which had their heyday in the first two-thirds of the twentieth century. Both Denmark and Norway established central national archives; the *Dansk Folkemindesamling* (1904–) became an independent state institution in 1917 (Christiansen 2004) and Norway got its *Norsk Folkeminnesamling* in 1914, now at the University of Oslo. Both were based on older collections. In Norway, a strong concern for the dissemination of the collected material back to the informants led to the founding of a folklore society, *Norsk Folkemindelag* (1920–), with the publishing of the material as one of its main tasks. The material and folk-life aspects of popular culture were taken care of by the archives of the national museums in Copenhagen, Helsinki, and Stockholm. The latter – the *Nordiska Museet* – also maintain considerable archives of oral materials. In Norway, the folk-life archive *Norsk Etnologisk Gransking* (NEG, 1946–) was modeled on these two, as an independent state institution that has cohabitated for periods with the national open-air *Norsk Folkemuseum* and for periods with the University of Oslo (Moestue 1996).

Sweden – considered the vanguard of the folk-life archive movement – chose a decentralized model. In the 1870s, a series of local societies were started for the collecting and archiving of dialects and folklore, and these private societies developed into four regional archives for dialects, place names, and folklore, based on the German model of combined archives. The four archives, situated in Uppsala, Lund, Gothenburg and (later) Umeå, have been reorganized several times, but they now form one single national institute with distributed archives (SOFI or *Språk och folkminneinstitutet*).

The best known of these, the ULMA in Uppsala (1914–, with a separate section for folklore from 1928) played a major role not only in Sweden, but also abroad, largely because of its pioneering work on the classification of folklore and folk-life material in the 1930s and 1940s, undertaken by Åke Campbell (Lilja 1996; Bringéus 2008). ULMA's classificatory scheme was adopted by other national archives, for example, the Irish Folklore Commission and the School of Scottish Studies. Due to their classificatory concerns and comparative approach, the national folkloristic archives were active promoters of international cooperation in the 1930s.

The ULMA also held a central position as the main archive for the national Swedish atlas of folk culture, together with the Lund archive (LUF) (Bringéus 2006, 2008). The atlas, which received its inspiration from Germany, was a central concern for many European archives from the early 1930s until the 1960s. In Denmark and Norway, the idea of charting popular culture in atlases never got under way. Plans for a common Nordic atlas were never put into practice, and at the time when the last volume of the Swedish atlas was published (1976), criticism of this project as well as of archive material and practices in general had long been voiced and grew in the following years.

The Irish Folklore Commission (1935–1971) in Dublin grew quickly due to an encouraging political context. The country's recent independence from the United Kingdom was propitious for the construction of a national identity. The gaelicization policies of the Irish State could build on the rich Gaelic and other folklore as well as dedicated researchers like S. Ó Duilearga and S. Ó Súilleabháin. The Irish success was all the more conspicuous as the folklore institutions in England became steadily more fragmented, or as Archer Taylor (1961: 294) stated: "the English [...] seem to have returned to a markedly antiquarian approach to the subject." In stark contrast to England, the archives in Dublin represent one of the largest and most sustained collections of oral material. In addition to its full-time and part-time collectors, schoolchildren from all over Ireland collected traditions from their homes, a campaign that in little more than a year (1937–1938) resulted in half a million manuscript pages. Collectors swarmed over the country with wax-cylinder recording machines (Ó Danachair 1951; Ó Súilleabháin 1963; Almqvist 1977–1979; Ciosáin 2004). Influenced by Swedish archive pioneers, the Irish Commission also conducted material culture surveys. Since 1971, the archives have been held at University College Dublin.

In southern Europe, there are archives like the *Centro de Estudos de Etnologia Peninsular* in Porto (Portugal), established between 1945 and 49 (Dias 1967) and its counterpart in Madrid (Spain), established in 1947 but with larger, older collections (Gilmore 1961a). In Athens the Hellenic Center of Laography was established in 1918 at the Academy of Sciences (Spyridakis 1967; Loukatos 1991).

France holds an intermediate position in-between, with numerous collecting bodies and fervent collecting campaigns in the 1930s and 1940s. The French case illustrates how both left-wing and right-wing movements embraced folklore for political reasons. In 1935 Lucien Febvre began a wide-ranging investigation of rural life, based on questionnaires and organized through the *Commission des recherches collectives*. This archive was amalgamated with those of the *Musée des Arts et Traditions Populaires* in 1938 (Müller 2009). The same year the French radical leftist Popular Front government, established a *Commission nationale des arts et traditions populaires,* which was also channeled to the museum. Shortly afterwards, and with the connivance of the collaborative, Nazi-friendly Vichy government, the museum organized vast collecting campaigns on French rural life, under the leadership of G.H. Rivière (Chiva 1987; Faure 1989; Bromberger 1987 and 2009; Denis 2009).

An effort to establish a French atlas of folk culture based on these investigations was, however, fruitless, and except for a much later book series on vernacular architecture and furniture, very little of this voluminous archive material has actually been published or used for research purposes.

In contrast to France, archives and research endeavors leading to a need for archives in the German-speaking countries have to a large degree developed within a university context (cf. Bendix in this volume). Most of the German archives are part of university institutes, the regional ones as well as the *Zentralarchiv der deutschen Volkserzählung* in Marburg (Becker 1990) and the concluded project *Atlas der deutschen Volkskunde*, with its main depository at the institute in Bonn. The *Enzyclopädie des Märchens*, initiated in the late 1950s, is associated with the Göttingen Academy of Sciences (Zender 1967). Only a few are independent research institutions such as the *Deutsches Volkliedsarchiv* in Freiburg, founded in 1914 and since 1953 an independent research entity within the state of Baden-Württemberg (Brednich 1968). In Austria, where folk-song documentation began in 1904 with imperial support, each of the nine *Länder* maintains its own Volksliedwerk since 1974 and the federal institution, the *Österreichisches Volksliedwerk*, loosely coordinates their endeavors.

The heterogeneity of the European institutional landscape becomes evident if we look at the Netherlands, geographically situated between Germany (with university-based archives) and France (with museum-based archives). Although there had been some teaching of folklore at university level earlier, the institutionalization of folklore in the Netherlands began after 1934, when the Dutch Academy of Sciences established a commission – *Volkskunde Kommissie*, later the *Volkskundebureau*, affiliated to the dialect commission and the later commission of onomastics. These three commissions merged in 1948 and were renamed the Meertens Institute in 1979, after its postwar director Pieter J. Meertens. The Nazi sympathies of the chairman of the commission during World War II seriously tainted the image of folklore studies and for decades after the war, it remained outside the universities. The *Volkskundebureau* kept a low profile and focused on documentation (Margry and Roodenburg 2007). While deploring the unfavorable position of folklore in Dutch universities, Meertens himself described his institution as "the centre of folkloristic research in the Netherlands" (Meertens s. a. [1951]; Bernet Kempers 1967). The well-respected, present-day Meertens Institute has been the most important institution of European ethnology in the Netherlands since the war, though ethnology (in contrast to anthropology) still does not have a very strong presence in Dutch universities.

But the archives have not escaped criticism. A main task after the war for most of the national archives and commissions was to gather material for atlases of folk culture. In the Dutch case, the *Volkskundebureau* worked on an atlas in collaboration with its Belgian counterpart. From 1959 and through the 1960s, only four issues of this atlas were published, and the project and its results have been harshly criticized (Margry and Roodenburg 2007). Criticism, delayed or stopped publications are common in many countries. The criticism concerns questions regarding cartography and the processing and the interpretation of data, but it also touches on general practices and policies. Sweden is also a case in point. Here, archives flourished from about 1920 until the mid-1960s. The political authorities took responsibility for supporting the salvaging of a vanishing cultural heritage, and the collecting took place in close cooperation with the universities. During this period most PhD theses in Sweden were based on material from the archives, and much cutting-edge research took place in this setting. The archives were of vital importance for folklore and ethnology, for source materials and more generally for forming of cohorts of researchers, as long as folklore and ethnology were synonymous with the historical study of traditional culture (Skott 2009).

This situation changed in the 1970s. Many young researchers turned their backs on the past and consequently to the archives. The 1970s and 1980s represented a turn towards contemporary studies inspired by sociology and social anthropology, accompanied by a well-founded critical attitude to cartography and atlas work, but also by a surprisingly harsh ideological criticism of older archive materials and practices. Formerly regarded as the home institution of folklore, the archives now became its scapegoat and the target of criticism that harmed a whole discipline (Skott 2009; Wolf-Knuts 2009; Bringéus 2008). Beginning with a broad critique of "bourgeois" collectors and archivists (Frykman 1979) and followed by more penetrating but still ideologically tinged analyses of archive practices (i.e., Lilja 1996), the effect on archives was devastating (Skott 2009). Archival practice was considered undemocratic: conservative and nationalistically-minded archivists had sought to freeze an image of an innocent, idealized, and non-existent past; conflict-ridden themes were evaded or censured; the coherence of the cultures documented disappeared in classification systems that, furthermore, concealed uncomfortable or dark sides of the past. As a consequence of such criticism, a generation of researchers ignored the archives.

Skott argues that this stance was as much the result of ideological convictions as was the founding archivists' initiative. During a time of industrialization and modernization, the traditional archives were a political issue for radicals, liberals, and conservatives alike. The involvement and support of Swedish politicians indicated that the archive movement can be seen in the light of the Social Democrats' project of constructing the welfare state – perhaps not unlike the large-scale collection efforts after the Great Depression initiated by the American Works Progress Administration. Furthermore, the collecting was regional, anti-nationalistic, and internationalist as much as it was nationalistic. Thus, some 30 years after the initial archive critique, Skott's research places both the period of archive founding and the era of critique in context, showing among other issues also that field informants and folklore recorders were socially much closer to one another than has been claimed.

Criticism of archives and commissions was part and parcel of a general debate concerning the discipline's theory and epistemology. In Sweden, the traditional archives once played a more important role than in most countries. Consequently the critics responded more emphatically. But archives as well as museums are vulnerable institutions. Their function is or was to remind people how society once was, and a repository on which to build the discipline's research. Don Yoder's characterization of these institutions as the basic unit of research in Europe (1991) is certainly valid for the past. The discussion of archives within the context of reflexive disciplinary historiography will likely lead to further engagement with both the institutions and the materials housed in them.

Museums

If the first institutional home for the study of oral traditions was the archive, the museum took on this role for the study of material culture. The *raison d'être* of the ethnological or folk museum was to be a repository for the material remnants of popular culture in its preindustrial phase for the sake of documentation and display. The same rationale lay behind the ethnographic or anthropological museum, with a view to indigenous and exotic cultures. As well as documentation and display, the museum has been the cradle of research in fields like ethnology and anthropology, as well as archeology and natural history. This is as valid for Europe as it is for North and South America (Conn 2010; Corrêa Maia 2009).

Most anthropological collections started as departments within larger natural history museums. A well-known case is the *Musée National d'Historie Naturelle* in Paris (1625–), with its anthropological department *Le Musée de l'Homme* (1932–2003), whose collections have now ended up in the anthropological art museum Branly (Paris, 2006) and in the ethnological *Musée des Civilisations de l'Europe et de la Méditerranée* (Marseilles, inauguration planned for 2013). In France, as well as in most other European countries, these departments or museums have been of crucial importance to the development of anthropology in an early phase.

The situation was similar in the United States, where anthropological collections were established before university departments of anthropology. Most, if not all, of these were part of or affiliated to universities and the majority of the American universities established museums where anthropology formed at least a part of the collections. These museums served as a basis for academic teaching and the formation of the first generation of scientifically trained anthropologists (Darnell 1998; Conn 2010).

Museums and the discipline of anthropology remained on good terms during the first quarter of the twentieth century in the United States. During the following decades, the relationship became more strained, and by the mid-twentieth century the divide was a reality. New theoretical approaches left many cultural and social anthropologists indifferent to objects and museum work.

A similar development took place in Europe where an even more radical break took place between the ethnographic museums and academic anthropology in some countries. The first setback for museums came from England in the early 1920s. Museums, whose main asset was classification and display of material remnants, could not cope with the transition to functionalist and structural-functionalist approaches. The advent of structuralism as of the 1950s also did not map well on to museum practice as cognitive structures and kinship do not lend themselves easily to museum displays. Observations in the field took precedence over objects in the magazines (Johannesen 2008; Eriksen 2009).

Postcolonial criticism in the last quarter of the twentieth century, coupled with the crisis of representation, disputed ownership of collections and ethnographic authority have further challenged museums (Stocking 1985; Clifford 1988; Shelton 2006; Conn 2010). Among the strategies chosen to address new ways of thinking about exhibiting cultures are collaboration with representatives of indigenous groups, a switch of status from anthropology museum to art museum, or repatriation of disputed objects (in North America fostered by the NAGPRA legislation). The criticism and deconstruction of museums by self-reflective anthropologists have contributed in some places to a blend of anthropology, art, and cultural history.

Folk-life and open-air museums were established, in contrast to the relatively restricted number of archives, in amazing numbers. Thousands of institutions calling themselves open-air museums are spread all over Europe, with a high density in parts of Northern and Central Europe. Norway alone, with less than 5 million inhabitants, had close to 600 such institutions before a restructuring of the museums took place in the early 2000s. As with archives, identity politics played a major role in their establishment. The majority of them are small, local institutions without scholarly ambitions, but the national museums and some of the regional ones played an important role for the development of folk-life studies up to the 1970s (Stigum 1956; Rivière 1956). Where ethnology came late if at all to the universities, they were particularly crucial for the field, such as in the Dutch *Niederlands Openluchtmuseum* in Arnhem (1912–), and the Welsh Folk Museum in Cardiff (1946–) and the Ulster Folk and Transport Museum in Belfast (1964–). These museums received strong impulses from Scandinavian folk-life studies and they were modeled on the Skansen open-air museum (Owen 1975; Fenton 1986; de Jong 2007). Given the high number of these museums and the importance of size for their impact on the discipline, only two will be compared below: the national museums in Stockholm and Paris.

The *Nordiska Museet* (1873–) with its open-air section Skansen (1891–) was the earliest and foremost of the Nordic national museums. The idea of open-air museums has been adopted by many countries, and the name "Skansen" has become a generic name for an open-air museum in some languages. The Swedish open-air museum has been called "a visionary idea that conquered the world" (Rentzhog 2007; Stoklund 2003) The founder of the Welsh Folk Museum (1946), Iorwerth Peate, was no less enthusiastic: "[...] the Welsh Folk Museum represents the first British attempt to create a national folk museum on the scale of the great Scandinavian museums. The Scandinavian museums have already illustrated the contribution which such museums can make to civilization" (1951: 176).

The Nordiska Museet for ethnology had a similar impact as did Skansen. In the last quarter of the nineteenth century, when the common principles for collecting and display in ethnographic and archeological museums were still typology and evolution, the founder of the museum, Artur Hazelius, was more interested in distribution and context than in evolution. His concern was not only saving the vanishing peasant culture, but also to document it. He wanted to visualize the whole country in its preindustrial state, appropriate an immaterial and symbolic unity like the nation, and his tool was a comparative cultural-geographical method, parallel to the historical-geographical method developed for oral literature by Finnish researchers (cf. Harvilahti in this volume). His favorite mode of display was diorama-like settings. Regarding the objects as source material for comparative research, Hazelius, as an early diffusionist, collected in series and variants.

Its role as a research institution was strengthened in 1919, when the *Nordiska Museet* established the first chair of "Nordic and comparative folk-life research" through a donation. Extensive collecting campaigns were organized from the 1920s. From 1934 the chair was shared with the University of Stockholm, and an Ethnological research department was established at the museum in 1942 (Hellspong 1993a; Erixon 1955). Sigurd Erixon, probably the most influential ethnologist on the European scene for decades, occupied the chair from 1934 to 1955, and his impact on European museums and on folk-life research in general can hardly be overestimated. There was a strong focus on material culture studies, in their spatial, temporal, and social dimensions, on culture zones and processes. The methodology was aimed toward cartography and atlases, developed in collaboration with the Germans, and the museum became the leading center in Scandinavia for the development of European ethnology. Scandinavian and especially Swedish ethnology came to be regarded as synonymous with this cultural-historical-geographical approach.

Ethnology as a university subject saw an enormous expansion in the 1970s, but much as with archival repositories, young ethnologists lost interest in the field's historical-geographical approach and in material culture. They argued for a study of the contemporary and multicultural society, for the use of concepts from sociology and social anthropology, and for fieldwork and participant observation instead of collecting objects and traditions (Löfgren 2008). Neither the *Nordiska* nor the other museums were prepared for this change, and a serious schism began. It took almost two decades before the museums were back on track again. This confrontation with earlier theories and practices was harder in Sweden than in the other Nordic countries as was the debate on the archives, probably because folk-life studies had held an extraordinarily strong position in Sweden. A parallel confrontation can be seen in Germany from the late 1960s, but here the "*Abschied vom Volksleben*" included a settlement with the wartime history of *Volkskunde* (cf. Bendix in this volume).

France experienced a similar development, but the consequences for the equivalent folk museum were far more destructive. The *Musée National des Arts et Traditions Populaires* (MNATP) evolved out of the *Musée de l'Homme* in 1937. Through this operation, the study of the national culture was separated from the exotic and acquired its first institutional home in France. Some of the most comprehensive collecting campaigns were launched from this museum, covering the material culture and traditions of preindustrial France. As ethnology was not yet a university discipline, most of French ethnology until the 1970s stemmed from the activities in and around this museum, led by its founder Georges Henri Rivière from 1937 to 1968 (Segalen 1986, 2005). Rivière's museology gave preeminence to the objects, their typology and their context. The link between the development of French ethnology and museums was thus inextricably bound up with an interest in material culture. Rivière had to renounce his dream of creating an open-air museum on the model of Skansen, but the first 30 years of the museum were largely a success story. However, French ethnology was exposed to similar impulses and challenges as in Sweden. Young scholars found the old collections and the museum's documenting practices outdated. The public stopped coming, and by 1980 the museum started to decline, culminating in its closure in 2006 and the transfer of its collections from Paris to Marseilles (Segalen 2005).

Why did the two national museums MNATP and *Nordiska museet* fare so differently? Martine Segalen has pointed to a number of structural issues that made the divide between the museum and modern university-based ethnology insurmountable in Paris (2007). Researchers tended to use the museum's campaigns as a training ground before leaving for "real" fieldwork overseas. When the museum obtained from the French research council a research centre within its walls, the *Centre d'ethnologie française* (Cef), it was filled by sociologists and social anthropologists who tended to follow the research interests germane to their disciplines but not those of the museum. The Cef staff was allowed to grow as large as the museum's curator staff, whose focus was on care of the collections and exhibitions. Furthermore, the deep reverence for the *beaux-arts* within the national museum administration allowed less space for popular culture (Guibal 1992).

Two other elements served as the last nails in the coffin of this national ethnological museum. During the 1980s the Ministry of Culture established another ethnological institution that drew heavily on public budgets and human resources, the *Mission du Patrimonie*. This research and documentation unit, a rival to MNATP and Cef, also published its own journal, *Terrain*. Around 1980, Rivière himself proposed another type of institution, the eco-museum. This variety of the open-air museum in the form of a locality with all the units in situ, was established in every region and almost every department of France during the last two decades of the twentieth century. The eco-museum was a response to the "new museology," focusing on the societal and political contexts of museums. The Mission thus challenged the MNATP's documentation and research tasks. The eco-museums, their cultural program and public outreach policy were all contenders for the same budget. When the MNATP closed the doors in 2006, its intention was to rise from the ashes in Marseilles, as the *Musée des Civilisations de l'Europe et de la Méditerranée* (Colardelle 2002; Rogan 2003b), a plan currently unfulfilled.

Some of the big regional museums in France have faced the challenges with far better results. The most successful story is that of the *Musée dauphinois* in Grenoble, established in 1906, rejuvenated by Rivière in the 1960s, and later converted into an ethnological museum that responds to a contemporary, multicultural society (Guibal 1999).

What happened to the *Nordiska museet*, when Swedish ethnologists began turning their back on material culture and folk-life museums from the 1970s? There were fewer problems than in Paris, but the challenge was the same. How can folk-life museums cope with contemporary culture? How can they record and know what to collect, in times of mass production and mass consumption? How can the museum keep track with the development of a discipline like ethnology? Facing a similar crisis, the answer in Sweden was a national organization for museums of cultural history, named SAMDOK, with *Nordiska museet* as the main force. It began in 1977 and counts around 80 satellite museums today. Motivated by the goal to move the museums' focus away from the old agrarian society towards the rapidly changing industrial society, SAMDOK broadened the task to a general documentation of contemporary everyday life. Over the years it has developed into a forum for scholarly discussions of contemporary society and culture, reflections on cultural heritage as a product of collecting and museum policy, acknowledging that museums do not only collect but also create memory and meaning through the process of defining and preserving heritage (Fägerborg 2007; Silvén 2007). After 30 years of existence SAMDOK launched a corresponding international network, *Collectingnet*, which has developed into an international ICOM committee (COMCOL 2010–).

In terms of an institutionalization sequence, ethnographic museums as well as folk-life museums started out as the institutional home of their respective (sub)disciplines, but over time they have tended to drift apart. Museums have had to adapt to society's expectations in far more immediate ways than university disciplines. Where research was once the guiding light, authorities have put steadily more weight on heritage management, education and outreach – sometimes approaching entertainment (Eriksen 2009).

Chairs and Universities

The cultural and political mission of the discipline has remained with the museum, and research has become the task of the university. This is the overall pattern, even if there are exceptions. In some countries, especially in Eastern Europe, research primarily takes place in academies (without teaching duties), whereas the universities are mainly teaching institutions (Zender 1967; Mihailescu 2003; Bituskova 2003).

A protracted weak university basis has marked the discipline profoundly in many countries. Much collecting and dissemination has been performed by dedicated persons without academic training in folklore studies, their main bases being the local folklore society, the local museum, and the local journal (Cardeira da Silva 1991; Chiva 1991). Coming to terms with the role of the amateur or lay scholar is a process to be observed throughout the twentieth century in most countries. In Poland the name of the discipline was changed from *ludoznawstwo* (*lud* = folk) to ethnography/ ethnology in the universities, as the former was associated with the activities of amateur collectors and amateur research (Jasiewicz and Slattery 1995). In an article on "The problem of local studies" (1933) Lucien Febvre, whose journal *Annales* explored many of the fields covered by folklore and folk-life studies, starts by praising "the hard and meritorious work [...] of our local erudites." Then he adds: "It is but too true that one can far too often observe a painful divide between the tiny handful of professional people in the universities and the scholarly institutions of historical studies, and on the other hand the quite high number of persons [...] who engage passionately in the study of the past, but without advice, without general knowledge, without sufficient reading. The work, the methods, the results obtained by the aforementioned are ignored by the latter, to an almost incredible degree. [...] The fact is that this is a serious problem. [...] Everything is description; nothing is explanation" (Febvre 1933: 304–305, author's translation). A generation later, the Portuguese Jorge Dias complained of the amateurs' "excessive love of what is regional and particular": "This state of affairs is even worsened by the fact that in many countries there is no university tradition in the field of regional ethnology. All the research is in the hands of small groups of interested amateurs, who – although very often meritorious persons – are normally opposed to a superior organization, where they fear they may lose the state of personal prestige which they have conquered in their home setting" (Dias quoted in Rogan 2008b).

At the same time Pieter Meertens deplored that "In the Netherlands the study of folklore was greatly hampered by its unfavorable position in the curricula of the universities. The place it occupies there is indeed a poor one. [... The] study of folklore has for the greater part been left to amateurs [...]" (Meertens s.a./1951). Half a century later his compatriots give a similar verdict, describing the history of the discipline until the 1990s as "one of a few scholars and numerous amateurs, of a limited interest in research and heavy emphasis on documentation and popularization" (Margry and Roodenburg 2007b: 261).

How can we explain the field's varying foothold in universities and the inversely proportional impact of amateurs? One factor is colonialism. Colonial powers required cultural information from their distant colonies, and anthropology thus gained university status. The study of the national popular culture was relegated to a place outside the universities. The most conspicuous case is England, once the nation with the largest number of collectors of exotic folklore. Up to World War I, when England was a stronghold of folkloristic collecting and research, the term *folklore* comprised the study of "the uncivilized and half civilized populations of the colonies as well as that of the uneducated at home" (Dorson 1968). But only the study of extra-European cultures became established in the universities. A contributing factor was the diffusionist paradigm embraced by folklorists which poorly matched the theoretical interest of 1930s social anthropology (Owen 1975). Thus anthropologists actively opposed folklore as a discipline in England (Rogan 2008c) with the result that England has remained without any designated chair in folklore. The British situation has been described as a core and periphery problem: nothing in the centre but some small institutions on the fringes – in Wales, Scotland, and Northern Ireland (Kockel 2008; Fenton 1986, 1990, 1993).

Other mechanisms are at play in small nations, apprehensive of their neighbors, or young nations in search of a history and identity. Ireland offers a good example (cf. Ó Giolláin in this volume), the Nordic countries another. Politically, economically, and culturally the Nordic countries emerged as small and weak nations after the Napoleonic wars. They established chairs in folklore before the end of the nineteenth century. The traditions of the rural, uneducated populations were seen as the heritage of the nation and became an important ideological building block. Their oral traditions and material culture were considered *national* rather than universal, and from this point of view it was the duty of the state to support the academic study of popular culture – with university chairs, in addition to museums and archives (Christiansen 2004; Löfgren 2008).

The late nineteenth century saw several appointments to chairs of anthropology (Paris, Rome, Oxford, New York, etc.), as well as to chairs of philology where folklore was taught as a subject. But the first appointment to a university chair in folklore was that of Kaarle Krohn in 1890, who had been a lecturer in Finnish and comparative folklore in Helsinki since 1888. In Oslo, Moltke Moe was appointed to a chair in new/dialectal Norwegian philology with folklore in 1885, which became a folklore chair in 1899. In Copenhagen, Axel Olrik became a lecturer in folklore in 1897 and professor in 1913. Full positions came a little later in Sweden, with Carl Wilhelm von Sydow, who had been a lecturer in Nordic and comparative folklore at Lund since 1910 and was appointed to a combined chair of Nordic ethnology in 1946. In Central Europe, Eduard Hoffmann-Krayer was appointed professor in Volkskunde in Basel in 1900. John Meier taught Volkskunde in Freiburg as professor of German philology as of 1899 and received a full Volkskunde chair in 1912 (Boberg 1953).

After World War I, there was a new series of appointments, including chairs in Eastern Europe. When Estonia gained independence in 1918, a chair of Estonian studies was established at Tartu University (Viires 1991). Lithuania followed suit in 1924 with a program of folklore at the University of Vilnius (Ciubrinskas 2008). Poland had a chair of ethnology and anthropology since 1913 in Lwow, but with independence in 1918, new chairs were very soon created in Poznan, Cracow, Vilnius, and Warsaw (Jasiewicz and Slattery 1995). In what would become Yugoslavia, chairs were established in Skopje in 1921 and in Zagreb in 1924, in addition to an older chair in Belgrade (Filipovic s.a./1951). Between 1933 and 1935 chairs were instituted in Berlin, Heidelberg, Leipzig and Tübingen, and others were instituted in the following years (Jeggle 1988).

As this enumeration shows, the early institutionalization of folklore, then as a field with an emphasis on oral literature, in the form of university posts, took place in

Northern, Eastern, and Central Europe. Their establishment can be related in small nations, to periods of newly won independence, or to other political-ideological movements. Southern Europe, with the exception of Italy, did not develop thus. The same was the case for folk-life studies. In Sweden, the chair of ethnology was established as a research position in 1919, but with the arrival of Sigurd Erixon, regular courses were taught as of 1934. Oslo obtained a chair in 1940 and Copenhagen in 1959/60. A series of combined chairs (*Volkskunde*) came about in the late 1940s, mostly in the same parts of Europe as mentioned above.

Symptomatically, it was the prime motivator of Scandinavian ethnology, Sigurd Erixon, who wanted to promote ethnology as a university discipline. But in order to act, systematic information about the complex world of university departments was necessary. On three occasions, Erixon launched broad inquiries. The first was on the occasion of The International Congress of European and Western Ethnology, which he arranged in Stockholm in 1951. Erixon had asked representatives from each country for reports on the development and status of the discipline, to be published in the proceedings. But these reports (SE 8: 77) were so heterogeneous that he refrained from publishing them. The next inquiry was based on a questionnaire, the results of which were published in CIAP's journal *Laos* in 1955 (Erixon 1955). The third survey, which took place in the mid-1960s, was published as a series of short articles in the first issue of the international journal *Ethnologia Europaea*. Both journals were edited by Erixon himself.

The 1955 survey was incomplete with regard to Eastern Europe, but East Germany, Bulgaria, and Hungary as well as Yugoslavia are included. In 35 departments, with around 40 professors/lecturers and 15 full time university teachers, folklore or ethnology was taught as an independent subject. In 15 departments, with a similar number of academic staff, folklore did not enjoy an independent position but was taught collaterally with other subjects. In total there were around 50 universities teaching folklore and folk-life studies in Europe in the early 1950s, in addition to an unknown number behind the Iron Curtain.

A line of division in Erixon's statistics was whether the subject comprised both material and mental culture, or whether the two were taught separately. Finland, Denmark, and Norway belonged to the latter group, together with East German universities and Budapest. The other Hungarian universities (Debrecen and Szeged) taught "the whole subject," as was the case for the rest of Europe. The overall pattern was that separate chairs belonged to the north and east, and combined chairs to the rest of Europe. Germany was the "big brother." The GDR and FRG together had 19 university departments. Nine of these taught *Volkskunde* as an separate subject: East Berlin, Bonn, Frankfurt, Göttingen, Hamburg, Kiel, Leipzig, Marburg and Münster. Ten offered degrees in *Volkskunde* within the framework of another subject (*Germanistik* or *Deutsche Philologie*): West Berlin, Erlangen, Freiburg, Cologne, Mainz, Munich, Rostock, Stuttgart, Tübingen and Würzburg. The survey enumerates some research institutions to be founded without the obligation to teach, mostly archives and commissions (e.g., Greifswald, Belfast, Dublin, Edinburgh, Porto, Madrid).

As an institution builder, it is probable that Erixon needed this overview of his efforts to create a better international organization – he worked hard to re-establish CIAP in the 1950s – and more generally to promote European ethnology as an academic discipline. After the breakdown of CIAP in 1964 (Rogan 2008a, b), Erixon organized a series of conferences with a view to create a new international organization for European ethnology. He launched the third inquiry on the status of university teaching, research, and publishing, and the third International Conference on European Ethnology, held in Norway (Utstein) in 1967, decided to carry out and publish the investigation. Erixon used this endeavor to build strong alliances among European ethnologists. But Erixon's co-editor, the French-Hungarian Géza de Rohan-Csermak, was quite explicit on how this was motivated (Rohan-Csermak 1967). He presented the inquiry as a crusade against the amateurism that dominated so much of the field:

> The destiny of European ethnology depends directly on the state of its teaching in the universities. If the education of the young ethnologists does not conform to a full and well-organized academic program, we cannot expect a satisfactory quality of their later research. No nation should leave the discovery and the study of the most characteristic part of its heritage, that of its cultures, to the hazardous and improvised activities of the amateurs. Ethnology has a claim, in the faculties of the humanities, to a position like that of history, archeology, geography, sociology, linguistics and philosophy. Not because we are pretentious, but in order to fulfill a scholarly task that is perhaps more urgent than that of any other discipline of culture. (1967: 243, translation by the author)

The inquiry was based on a loosely organized questionnaire and the findings were published in full length (*Ethnologia Europaea* 1967: 1, 243–323). Europe had 68 chairs in European ethnology/*Volkskunde*/folklore (junior teaching posts not included). The European countries were more or less the same as in the 1955 inquiry, but then the Soviet Union featured with three chairs. Not surprisingly, Germany maintained its lead with 15 chairs (13 in West Germany and two in East Germany), spread over 17 departments (Zender 1967). Finland and Poland ranked high on the list, with seven chairs each, followed by Hungary with four. The UK was at the bottom with its sole chair in Northern Ireland. Leeds University ran a folk-life course as part of English studies (Thompson 1967; Sanderson 1967), but this was closed down in response to spending cuts imposed by the Conservative government in the 1980s. The North American contributor, Paul Leser, had some problems with transferring the concept of European ethnology to the American academic landscape, but 24 chairs had been founded and a cohort of literary folklorists, anthropologists specializing in Europe, and members of the newly acknowledged discipline American Folk Culture had been appointed to them (Leser 1967). The Mexican contributor drew the contours of a rich but complex structure of interrelated disciplines, themes and courses, admitting that he was not able to give any concise, comparable information about chairs and staff – a clear echo of Frances Gilmore's report on Mexican folklore a few years earlier (1961b).

The impact of this movement to consolidate the discipline dwindled when the octogenarian Erixon died. The paradigmatic shift that took place when many of the young generation turned their back on traditional folk-life studies and Erixonian ethnology may have been a contributing factor as well. The student explosion, visible also in Sweden, may have necessitated concentration on internal affairs as well (Löfgren 1993; Hellspong 1993a).

A new investigation was organized in the latter half of the 1990s through the initiative of the European Association of Social Anthropologists (EASA). A series of reports from different European countries was to achieve an overview of the teaching of anthropology in Europe. The effort resulted in the anthology *Learning Fields* (Dracklé *et al.* 2003), an informative survey of the institutional development on the national level. In spite of its subtitle, *Educational Histories of European Social Anthropology*, the field covered in most of the chapters is the intertwined picture of folklore, ethnology, and anthropology. Given a European setting, it could hardly have been otherwise. The editors pointed to four different "mindscapes" or supranational ensembles of European anthropological scholarship, characterized roughly by academic affinities, mutual linguistic comprehension and exchange networks.

According to this division, the *Northwestern* variety is centered on British (social) anthropology and to a lesser degree on American cultural anthropology, with English as a predominant *lingua franca*. Countries mentioned in this cluster are the United Kingdom, the Netherlands, Norway and Denmark. The Nordic countries should be added with a strong, separate tradition of national folklore and material culture studies, with a clear historical profile and with German as the lingua franca until World War II. The Central European ensemble, including Switzerland, Austria, Germany, Poland, the Czech Republic, Slovakia, Slovenia and Hungary, has largely been influenced by German-speaking academic traditions. In these countries, anthropology has been closely associated with the historical sciences and with geography, rather than with sociology. It is also important to note that for most central European countries there has been a focus of interest on national or European topics, with *Volkskunde* or ethnography as common denominations. German has been the lingua franca, but sometimes Russian has been used instead. However, a widespread use of national languages to some extent limited scholarly communication.

Southern European anthropologists, France included, also continue to use their respective national languages for publishing. Researchers from this geographical area often do fieldwork both at home and in extra-European settings. The *Eastern European* ensemble has until recently been strongly dominated by Russian ethnographic research, based on area studies and historic studies of "nationalities" and ethnic groups, and with a predilection for material culture studies. Strict political control over academia in the past has hindered the development of anthropology as an autonomous discipline, while the subsequent economic difficulties have posed prolonged problems for its institutionalization.

Quo Vadis, Ethnologia Europaea?

In the history of European ethnology, Sweden has held a special position, both as a model and as a barometer for the course of events. So it may be worthwhile looking at Swedish ethnology at the beginning of the twenty-first century. In 2008, the Swedish higher educational authorities commissioned a teaching and research assessment exercise for ethnology (*Högskoleverkets rapport* 2008: 46R). European ethnology, including folklore as a sub-discipline, is currently taught in five universities and two colleges. The outcome of the exercise was not evident beforehand, as the number of ethnology students has fallen considerably for some years. In 2007, the total number of full time students was just below 500. Around 70 teachers were working at these institutions (50 of them having a PhD), and 50 PhD-students were actively pursuing doctoral programs. The fall in student numbers was partly explained by new educational programs within the field of culture. These programs which included urban studies, international migration and ethnic relations, service management, several variants of cultural studies and cultural analysis, museology, themes related to tourism, consumption, IT, as well as participation in the education of schoolteachers were often taught by ethnologists.

This situation forced the committee to reflect upon the expansionist character of modern ethnology and whether this should be considered an asset or a problem. According to the committee, ethnology offered an interesting example of the ongoing changes in academia, showing how "an old humanistic discipline has become a dynamic discipline affecting a series of other areas, areas which not long ago were virgin fields." The report ends with questions that in the course of the history sketched in this chapter appear timeless: "What happens when a humanistic discipline breaks barriers in its way?" "What will be the consequences of this centrifugal force on the subject itself?"

REFERENCES

Actes du Congrès International d'Ethnologie Régionale. 1956. Arnhem: Rijksmuseum.

Almqvist, Bo. 1977–1979. "The Irish Folklore Commission. Achievement and Legacy." *Béaloideas* 45–47, 6–26.

Archetti, Eduardo. 2003. "Ten Years of 'Social Anthropology/Antropologie Sociale.' Ambiguities and Contradictions." *Social Anthropology* 11(1): 103–112.

Bausinger, Hermann. 1971. *Volkskunde: von der Altertumsforschung zur Kulturanalyse.* Berlin: Carl Habel.

Becker, Siegfried. 1990. "Zur Geschichte und Perspektive der Erzählforschung. Ein Bericht über Bestand und Aufgaben des Zentralarchivs der Deutschen Volkserzählung." *Zeitschrift für Volkskunde* 86: 203–215.

Beitl, Klaus. 1961. "Folklore Studies in Austria, 1945–1965. An Activities Report." *Journal of American Folklore* 74(294): 216–235.

Bendix, Regina and Tatjana Eggeling, Eds. 2004. "Namen und was sie bedeuten." *Beiträge zur Volkskunde Niedersachsen* 19. Göttingen: Schmerse.

Bituskova, Alexandra. 2003. "Teaching and Learning Anthropology in a New National Context: the Slovak Case" in Dorle Dracklé, Dorle, Iain R. Edgar, and Thomas Schippers, Eds. *Learning Fields* I: *Educational Histories of European Social Anthropology.* New York, Oxford: Berghahn Books, pp. 69–81.

Boberg, Inger M. 1953. *Folkemindeforskningens historie i Mellem- og Nordeuropa.* København: Einar Munksgaards Forlag.

Bondarenko, Dimitri M. and Andrey V. Koratayev. 2003. "In Search of a New Academic Profile: Teaching Anthropology in Contemporary Russia" in Dorle Dracklé, Dorle, Iain R. Edgar, and Thomas Schippers, Eds. *Learning Fields* I: *Educational Histories of European Social Anthropology.* New York, Oxford: Berghahn Books, pp. 230–246.

Bonte, Pierre and Michel Izard, Eds. 1992. *Dictionnaire de l'ethnologie et de l'anthropologie.* Paris: PUF.

Brednich, Rolf W. 1968. "'Das Deutsche Volkliedsarchiv' in Freiburg im Breisgau and German Folksong Research." *Journal of the Folklore Institute* 5: 198–211.

Bringéus, Nils-Arvid. 2006. *Carl Wilhelm von Sydow som folklorist.* Uppsala: Kungl. Gustav Adolfs Akademien för svensk folkkultur.

Bringéus, Nils-Arvid. 2008. *Åke Campbell som etnolog.* Uppsala: Kungl. Gustav Adolfs Akademien för svensk folkkultur.

Bromberger, Christian. 1987. "Du grand au petit. Variations des échelles et des objets d'analyse dans l'historie récente de l'ethnologie de la France" in Isac Chiva and Utz Jeggle, Eds. *Ethnologies en miroir. La France et les pays de langue allemande*. Paris: Éditions de la MSH, pp. 67–94.

Bromberger, Christian. 2009. "Introduction: L'ethnologie de la France, du Front Populaire à la Libération: entre continuités et ruptures" in Jacqueline Christophe, Denis-Michel Boëll [Boell - Umlaut on e] and Régis Meyran, Eds. *Du folklore à l'ethnologie*. Paris: Éditions de la maison des sciences de l'homme, pp. 1–10.

Bromley, Yuri, Ed. 1974a. *Soviet Ethnology and Anthropology Today*. The Hague: Mouton.

Bromley, Yuri. 1974b. "Ethnographical Studies in the USSR, 1965–1969" in Yuri Bromley, Ed. *Soviet Ethnology and Anthropology Today*. The Hague: Mouton, pp. 15–30.

Budil, Ivo. 2003. "Teaching and Learning Anthropology in the Czech Republic" in Dorle Dracklé, Dorle, Iain R. Edgar, and Thomas Schippers, Eds. *Learning Fields* I: *Educational Histories of European Social Anthropology*. New York, Oxford: Berghahn Books, pp. 94–101.

Cardeira da Silva, Maria dos Anjos. 1991. "L'ethnologie et ses revues au Portugal" in Jean-Pierre Piniès, Ed. *Au miroir des revues – Ethnologie de l'Europe du Sud*. Carcassonne: Garae Hesiode, pp. 153–156.

Carós, Joan Prat and Joan Josep Pujadas Muñoz. 1991. "Nouvelles Perspectives" in Jean-Pierre Piniès, Ed. *Au miroir des revues – Ethnolgie de l'Europe du Sud*. Carcassonne: Garae Hesiode, pp. 139–142.

Chiva, Isac. 1987. "Entre livre et musée. Emergence d'une ethnologie de la France" in Isac Chiva and Utz Jeggle, Eds. *Ethnologies en miroir. La France et les pays de langue allemande*. Paris: Éditions de la MSH, pp. 9–33.

Chiva, Isac. 1991. "Les revues ethnologiques en Europe: richesses et paradoxes" in Jean-Pierre Piniès, Ed. *Au miroir des revues – Ethnologie de l'Europe*

du sud. Carcassonne: Garae Hésiode, pp. 201–209.

Chiva, Isac and Utz Jeggle, Eds. 1987. *Ethnologies en miroir. La France et les pays de langue allemande*. Paris: Éditions de la MSH (German edition: *Deutsche Volkskunde, französische Ethnologie*).

Christiansen, Palle Ove. 2004. "En kulturinstitutions plads i samfundet. Om Dansk Folkemindesamlings forhold til arkivmaterialet, formidlingen, forskningen og sin egen samtid gjennem 100 år." *Fortid og Nutid. Tidsskrift for kulturhistorie og lokalhistorie* 4/2004: 21–41.

Christophe, Jacqueline, Denis-Michel Boël and Régis Meyran, Eds. 2009. *Du folklore à l'ethnologie*. Paris: Éditions de la maison des sciences de l'homme.

Ciosáin, Niall O. 2004. "Approaching a Folklore Archive: The Irish Folklore Commission and the Memory of the Great Famine." *Folklore* 115: 222–232.

Ciubrinskas, Vytis. 2008. "Challenges to the Discipline: Lithuanian Ethnology between Scolarship and Identity Politics" in Máiréad Nic Craith, Ulrich Kockel, and Reinhard Johler, Eds. *Everyday Culture in Europe. Approaches and Methodologies*. Progress in European Ethnology. Aldershot: Ashgate, pp. 101–117.

Clifford, James. 1988. *The Predicament of Culture. Twentieth-Century Ethnography, Literature and Art*. Cambridge, MA: Harward University Press.

Colardelle, Michel. 2002. *Réinventer un musée. Le musée des civilisations de l'Europe et de la Méditerranée à Marseille. Projet scientifique et culturel*. Paris: Réunion des musées nationaux/Seuil.

Conn, Steven. 2010. *Do Museums Still Need Objects?* Philadelphia: University of Pennsylvania Press.

Cordeiro, Graça Índias and Ana Isabel Afonso. 2003. "Cultural and Social Anthropology in the Portuguese University: Dilemmas of Teaching and Practice" in Dorle Dracklé, Dorle, Iain R. Edgar, and Thomas Schippers, Eds. *Learning Fields* I: *Educational Histories of European Social Anthropology*. New York, Oxford: Berghahn Books, pp. 169–180.

Corrêa Maia, Marilene. 2009. "Les œuvres d'art populaires brésiliens au musée du folklore Edson-Carneiro: entre terrain, musée et marché" (Thèse de doctorat), Université Paris X-Nanterre.

Cuisinier, Jean and Martine Segalen. 1986. *Ethnologie de la France*. Paris: PUF.

Darnell, Regna 1998. *And Along Came Boas. Continuity and Revolution in Americanist Anthropology*. Amsterdam/ Philadelphia: John Benjamins Publishing Company.

Dias, Jorge. 1956. "The Quintessence of the Problem: Nomenclature and Subject-matter in Folklore" in *Actes du Congrès International d'Ethnologie Régionale*. Arnhem: Rijksmuseum, pp. 1–14.

Dias, Jorge. 1967. "The Academic Position of European Ethnology in Portugal." *Ethnologia Europaea* I: 300–301.

Denis, Marie-Noëlle. 2009. "L'enquête d'archtecture rurale (1940–1968), une étape dans la construction de l'ethnologie française" in Jacqueline Christophe, Denis-Michel Boëll and Régis Meyran, Eds. *Du folklore à l'ethnologie*. Paris: Éditions de la maison des sciences de l'homme, pp. 49–61.

Dorson, Richard M. 1961. "Introduction by the editor (Folklore Research Around the World: A North American Point of View)." *Journal of American Folklore* 74(294): 287–290.

Dorson, Richard M. 1968 [1999]. *The British Folklorists. A History*. London and New York: Routledge.

Dow, James R. and Hannjost Lixfeld, Eds. 1994. *The Nazification of an Academic Discipline. German Volkskunde in the Third Reich*. Folklore Studies in Translation. Bloomington: Indiana University Press.

Dracklé, Dorle. 2003. "Farewell to Humboldt? Teaching and Learning Anthropology in Germany" in Dorle Dracklé, Iain R. Edgar, and Thomas Schippers, Eds. *Learning Fields* I: *Educational Histories of European Social Anthropology*. New York, Oxford: Berghahn Books, pp. 56–68.

Dracklé, Dorle, Iain R. Edgar, and Thomas Schippers. 2003. *Learning Fields* I: *Educational Histories of European Social Anthropology*. New York, Oxford: Berghahn Books.

Eriksen, Anne. 2009. *Museum. En kulturhistorie*. Oslo: Pax.

Erixon, Sigurd. 1955. "The Position of Regional European Ethnology and Folklore at the European Universities. An International Inquiry." *Laos* III: 108–144.

Fägerborg, Eva. 2007. "A Network for Developing Collecting and Research." *Samtid and museer* 2/2007. See also http://www.nordiskamuseet.se/upload/documents/322.pdf (accessed October 16, 2011).

Faure, Christian. 1989. *Le Projet culturel de Vichy: folklore et révolution nationale, 1940–1944*. Lyon: Presses Universitaires de Lyon.

Febvre, Lucien. 1933. "Le problème des études locales." *Annales d'histoire économique et sociale* 5: 304–308.

Fenton, Alexander. 1986. "The Position of Ethnology in Britain. Academic and Museum Activity." *Ethnos* 10: 17–39.

Fenton, Alexander. 1990. "Phases of Ethnology in Britain. With Special Reference to Scotland." *Ethnologia Europaea* XX(2): 177–188.

Fenton, Alexander. 1993. "Folklore and Ethnology: Past, Present and Future in British Universities." *Folklore* 104: 4–12.

Firth, Raymond. 1986. "The Founding and Early History of the ASA." *The Annals of the ASA* 7: 4–9.

Frykman, Jonas. 1979. "Ideologikritik av arkivsystem." *Norveg* 22: 231–342.

Gellner, Ernest. Ed. 1980. *Soviet and Western Anthropology*. London: Duckworth.

Gilmore, Frances. 1961a. "Folklore Study in Spain." *Journal of American Folklore* 74(294): 336–343.

Gilmore, Frances. 1961b. "Organization of Folklore Study in Mexico." *Journal of American Folklore* 74(294): 383–390.

Gómez-Tabanera, José Manuel. 1967. "Situation universitaire de l'ethnologie en Espagne." *Ethnologia Europaea* I: 264–267.

Guibal, Jean. 1992. "Quel avenir pour le musée des Atp? Entretien avec Jean Guibal." *Le Débat* 70: 158–164.

Guibal, Jean. 1999. "La diversité des cultures au Musée Dauphinois de Grenoble" in Emilia Vaillant and Germain Viatte, Eds. *Le Musée et les Cultures du Monde, Actes de la table ronde des 9 et 10 décembre 1998.* Paris: Cahiers de l'École Nationale du Patrimoine, pp. 257–259.

Hellspong, Mats, Ed. 1993a. *Lusthusporten. En forskningsinstitution och dess framväxt 1918–1993.* Stockholm: Nordiska Museet.

Hellspong, Mats. 1993b. "Studentexplosion och nya organisationsformer. Lusthusporten på Mats Rehnbergs tid 1969–1981. in Hellspong, Mads, Ed. *Lusthusporten. En forskningsinstitution och dess framväxt 1918–1993.* Stockholm: Nordiska Museet, pp. 108–132.

Honko, Lauri. 1989. "Nationalism and Internationalism in Folklore Research." *NIF News* 2–3: 16–20.

Honko, Lauri. 1991. "Introduction." *Folklore Fellows Network* 1–2 (April): 1–3.

Honko, Lauri. 1998. "Institutional Profiles." *Folklore Fellows Network* 15 (April): 1–2.

Hultkrantz, Åke. 1952. "American 'Anthropology' and European 'Ethnology.' A Sketch and a Program." *Laos* II: 99–106.

Hultkrantz, Åke. 1960. *International Dictionary of Regional European Ethnology and Folklore.* Vol. I. *General Ethnological Concepts.* Copenhagen: Rosenkilde and Bagger.

Hultkrantz, Åke. 1967a. "Some Remarks on Contemporary Ethnological Thought." *Ethnologia Europaea* I: 38–44.

Hultkrantz, Åke. 1967b. "Historical Approaches in American Ethnology. A Research Survey." *Ethnologia Europaea* I: 96–116.

Jasiewicz, Zbigniew and David Slattery. 1995. "Ethnography and Anthropology: The Case of Polish Ethnology" in Han F. Vermeulen and Arturo Alvadan Roldan, Eds. *Fieldwork and Footnotes: Studies in the History of European Anthropology.* London: Routledge, pp. 184–201.

Jeggle, Utz. 1988. "L'ethnologie de l'Allemagne sous le régime nazi. Un regard sur la Volkskunde deux generations après." *Ethnologie Française* XVIII(2): 114–119.

Johannesen, Anders. 2008. "Eventyr og vitenskap. Oppdagelsesreisen som kunnskapspraksis." *Tidsskrift for kulturforskning* 4/2008. 62–84.

de Jong, Adriaan. 2007. *Die Dirigentender Erinnerung. Musealisierung and Nationalisierung der Volkskultur in den Niederlanden 1815–1940.* Münster: Waxmann.

Kockel, Ulrich. 2008. "Turning the World Upside Down: Towards a European Ethnology in (and of) England" in Máiréad Nic Craith, Ulrich Kockel, and Reinhard Johler, Eds. *Everyday Culture in Europe. Approaches and Methodologies.* Progress in European Ethnology. Aldershot: Ashgate, pp. 149–164.

Lebovics, Herman. 2009. "Les sciences divisées, l'humanité partagée" in Jacqueline Christophe, Denis-Michel Boëll, and Régis Meyran, Eds. *Du folklore à l'ethnologie.* Paris: Éditions de la maison des sciences de l'homme, pp. 13–20.

Lerche, Grit. 1979. "International Secretariat for Research on the History of Agricultural Implements 1954–1979." *Ethnologia Scandinavica:* 163–165.

Leser, Paul. 1967. "The Academic Position of European Ethnology in North America." *Ethnologia Europaea* I: 320–322.

Lilja, Agneta. 1996. "Föreställningen om den ideala uppteckningen. En studie av idé och praktik vid traditionssamlande arkiv – ett exempel från Uppsala 1914–1945." *Akad. avh. i etnologi* 75: 31–37.

Lixfeld, Hannjost. 1991. "The Deutsche Forschungsgemeinschaft and the Umbrella Organizations of German 'Volkskunde' during the Third Reich." *Asian Folklore Studies* 50: 95–116.

Loukatos, Demetrios. 1991. "Regard sur les études folkloriqus en Grèce" in Jean-Pierre Piniès, Ed. *Au miroir des revues – Ethnologie de l'Europe du Sud.* Carcassonne: Garae Hesiode, pp. 181–188.

Löfgren, Orvar. 1993. "På John Granlunds tid. Lusthusporten 1955–1969" in: Mads Hellspong, Ed. 1993. *Lusthusporten. En forskningsinstitution och dess framväxt 1918–1993.* Stockholm: Nordiska Museet, pp. 74–107.

Löfgren, Orvar. 2008. "When is Small Beautiful? The Transformation of Swedish Ethnology" in Máiréad Nic Craith, Ulrich Kockel, and Reinhard Johler, Eds. *Everyday Culture in Europe. Approaches and Methodologies*. Progress in European Ethnology. Aldershot: Ashgate, pp. 119–132.

Margry, Peter Jan and Herman Roodenburg. 2007. "A History of Dutch Ethnology in 10½ Pages" in Peter Jan Margry and Herman Roodenburg, Eds. *Reframing Dutch Culture. Between Otherness and Authenticity*. Progress in European Ethnology. Aldershot: Ashgate, pp. 261–271.

Mihailescu, Vintila. 2003. "The Legacies of a 'Nation–Building Ethnology' in Romania" In Dorle Dracklé, Iain R. Edgar, and Thomas Schippers, Eds. *Learning Fields I: Educational Histories of European Social Anthropology*. New York, Oxford; Berghahn Books, pp. 208–219.

Moestue, Anne. 1996. *Spørre og grave i 50 år*. Norsk etnologisk granskings 50–års jubileum. Oslo: NEG.

Mucha, Janusz. 2003. "Teaching Anthropology in Post-1989 Poland" in Dorle Dracklé, Iain R. Edgar, and Thomas Schippers, Eds. *Learning Fields I: Educational Histories of European Social Anthropology*. New York, Oxford: Berghahn Books, pp. 83–93.

Müller, Bertrand. 2009. "Écrire le folklore: les réponses aux enquêtes de la Commission des recherches collectives de 'l'Encyclopédie française'" in Jacqueline Christophe, Denis-Michel Boëll, and Régis Meyran, Eds. *Du folklore à l'ethnologie*. Paris: Éditions de la maison des sciences de l'homme, pp. 29–48.

Mursic, Rajko. 2003. "Teaching Anthropology in Slovenia: 'Small' Languages – Chaos in the Field?" in Dorle Dracklé, Iain R. Edgar, and Thomas Schippers, Eds. *Learning Fields I: Educational Histories of European Social Anthropology*. New York, Oxford: Berghahn Books, pp. 113–125.

Nas, Peter J.M. and Marlies de Groot. 2009. "The IUAES from Past to Present" in Peter J.M. Nas and Zhang Jijiao, Eds. *Anthropology Now*. China: Intellectual Property Rights House, pp. 417–454.

Nas, Peter J.M. and Zhang Jijiao, Eds. 2009. *Anthropology Now*. China: Intellectual Property Rights House.

Nic Craith, Máiréad, Ulrich Kockel, and Reinhard Johler, Eds. *Everyday Culture in Europe. Approaches and Methodologies*. Progress in European Ethnology. Aldershot: Ashgate.

Ó Danachair, Caoimhín. 1951. "Irish Folk Narrative on Sound Records." *Laos* I: 180–186.

Ó Súilleabháin, Seán. 1963. The Irish Folklore Commission. *Acta Ethnographica*, Academiae Scientarium Hungaricae XIII(fasc. 1–4): 97–98.

Oinas, Felix J. 1961. "Folklore Activities in Russia." *Journal of American Folklore* 74(294): 262–370.

Owen, Trefor M. 1975. "Some Trends in Regional Ethnology in Britain." *Ethnologia Europaea*, 8(1): 56–62.

Panopoulos, Panayotis. 2003. "Between Self and Others: The Academic Establishment of Greek Anthropology" in Dorle Dracklé, Iain R. Edgar, and Thomas Schippers, Eds. *Learning Fields I: Educational Histories of European Social Anthropology*. New York, Oxford: Berghahn Books, pp. 193–205.

Peate, Iorwerth C. 1951. "The Welsh Folk Museum and its Development." *Laos* I: 169–179.

Peate, Iorwerth C. 1963. "The Society for Folk Life Studies." *Folk Life*: 1: 3–4.

Rentzhog, Sten. 2007. *Open Air Museums: The History and Future of a Visionary Idea*. Stockholm: Carlssons.

Rivière, Georges Henri. 1956. "Les musées de folklore en tant qu'instituts de science culturelle" in *Actes du Congrès International d'Ethnologie Régionale*. Arnhem: Rijskmuseum, pp. 72–78.

Rogan, Bjarne. 2003b. "The Emerging Museums of Europe." *Ethnologia Europaea* 33(1): 51–60.

Rogan, Bjarne. 2007. "Folk Art and Politics in Inter-War Europe: An Early Debate on Applied Ethnology." *Folk Life* 45: 7–23.

Rogan, Bjarne. 2008a. "From CIAP to SIEF: Visions for a Discipline or Power Struggle?"

in Máiréad Nic Craith, Ulrich Kockel, and Reinhard Johler, Eds. *Everyday Culture in Europe. Approaches and Methodologies.* Progress in European Ethnology. Aldershot: Ashgate, pp. 19–63.

Rogan, Bjarne. 2008b. "The Troubled Past of European Ethnology. SIEF and International Cooperation from Prague to Derry." *Ethnologia Europaea* 38(1): 66–78.

Rogan, Bjarne. 2008c. "From Rivals to Partners on the Interwar European Scene – Sigurd Erixon, Georges Henri Rivière and the International Debate on European Ethnology in the 1930s." *Arv. Nordic Yearbook of Folklore* 64: 61–100.

Rohan-Csermak, Géza de. 1967. "Introduction (to the 1967 inquiry on the teaching of European ethnology)." *Ethnologia Europaea* I: 243–244.

Sanderson, Stewart F. "The University Teaching in European Ethnology in the United Kingdom." *Ethnologia Europaea* I: 304–305.

Schindler, Margot. 1992. "Volkskundliche Gesellschaften in Österreich." *Volkskunde Institutionen in Österreich. Veröffentlichungen des Österreichischen Museums für Volkskunde* B(XXVI): 61–75.

Schippers, Thomas. 1995. "A History of Paradoxes: Anthropologies of Europe" in Han F. Vermeulen and Arturo Alvarez Roldán, Eds. *Fieldwork and Footnotes: Studies in the History of European Anthropology.* London: Routledge, pp. 234–246.

Segalen, Martine. 1986. "Current Trends in French Ethnology." *Ethnologia Europaea* XVI(1): 3–24.

Segalen, Martine. 2001. "Les études européanistes" in Martine Ségalen, Ed. *Ethnologie. Concepts et aires culturelles.* Paris: Armand Colin, pp. 253–271.

Segalen, Martine. 2005. *Vie d'un musée 1937–2005.* Paris: Stock.

Silvén, Eva. 2007. "Reflecting Collecting." *Samtid and museer* 2: 4–5. See also http://www.nordiskamuseet.se/upload/documents/322.pdf (accessed October 16, 2011).

Skott, Fredrik. 2009. *Folkets minnen. Traditionsinsamling i idé och praktik 1919–1964.* Göteborg: Institutet för språk och folkminnen.

Spyridakis, Georges. 1967. "Situation universitaire de la laographie en Grèce." *Ethnologia Europaea* 1: 277.

Stigum, Hilmar. 1956. "Volkskundliche Museen als Institut für Kulturforschung" in *Actes du Congrès International d'Ethnologie Régionale.* Arnhem: Rijksmuseum, pp. 62–71.

Stocking, George W., Ed. 1985. *Objects and Others. Essays on Museums and Material Culture.* Madison: University of Wisconsin Press.

Stoklund, Bjarne. 1969–1971. "Europeisk etnologi mellem Scylla og Charybdis." *Fortid og Nutid. Tidsskrift for kulturhistorie og lokalhistorie* XXIV: 659–670.

Stoklund, Bjarne. 2003. "Between Scenography and Science. Early Folkmuseums and their Pioneers." *Ethnologia Europaea* 33(1): 21–36.

Taylor, Archer. 1961. "Characteristics of German Folklore Studies." *Journal of American Folklore* 74(294): 293–301.

Thompson, George B. 1967. "The Academic Position of Ethnology in Northern Ireland." *Ethnologia Europaea* I: 285–287.

Thompson, Stith. 1961. "Visits to South American Folklorists." *Journal of American Folklore* 74(294): 390–397.

Vermeulen, Han F. and Arturo Alvarez Roldán. 1995. "Introduction. The History of in Anthropology" in Vermeulen and Roldan, Eds. *Fieldwork and Footnotes: Studies in the History of European Anthropology.* London: Routledge, pp. 1–16.

Viazzo, Pier Paolo. 2003. "Teaching and Learning Anthropology in Italy: Institutional Development and Pedagogic Challenges" in Dorle Dracklé, Iain R. Edgar, and Thomas Schippers, Eds. *Learning Fields* I: *Educational Histories of European Social Anthropology.* New York, Oxford: Berghahn Books, pp. 181–192.

Viires, Ants. 1991. "The Development of Estonian Ethnography during the 20th Century." *Journal of Baltic Studies* XXII(2): 123–132.

Viires, Ants. 1994. "Utforskandet av den etniska folkkulturen." *NordNytt. Nordisk tidsskrift for folklivsforskning* 56: 5–12.

Waldis, Barbara. 2003. "Rethinking Local and Global: New Perspectives among Swiss Anthropologists" in Dorle Dracklé, Iain R. Edgar, and Thomas Schippers, Eds. *Learning Fields* I: *Educational Histories of European Social Anthropology*. New York, Oxford: Berghahn Books, pp. 139–154.

Wolf-Knuts, Ulrika. 2009. "In Defence of a Generation of Folklorists." *Arv* 65: 155–157.

Yoder, Don. 1991. *Discovering American Folklife. Studies in Ethnic, Religious and Regional Culture*. Ann Arbor, London: UMI Research Press.

Zender, Mathias. 1967. "Volkskunde an den Universitäten der Bundesrepublik Deutschland." *Ethnologia Europaea* 1: 251–253.

Zumwalt, Rosemary Lévy. 1988. *American Folklore Scholarship. A Dialogue of Dissent*. Bloomington and Indianapolis: Indiana University Press.

FURTHER READING

Aleksejev, V. 1974. "Fifty Years of Studies in Anthropological Composition of Population in the USSR" in Yuri Bromley, Ed. *Soviet Ethnology and Anthropology Today*. The Hague: Mouton, pp. 31–50.

Bernet Kempers, A.J. 1967. "Volkskunde und Universität in den Niederlanden." *Ethnologia Europaea* 1: 278–279.

Bockhorn, Olaf. 1992. "Volkskunde an österreichischen Universitäten" in *Volkskunde Institutionen in Österreich. Veröffentlichungen des Österreichischen Museums für Volkskunde* B (XXVI): 9–19.

Cohen, Claudine. 1980. "La Collection 'Travaux et Mémoires de l'Institut d'Ethnologie.' Cinquante ans d'ethnologie française." *Objets et Mondes* 20(fascicule 2): 75–82.

Erixon, Sigurd, Greta Arwidsson, and Harald Hvarfner, Eds. 1970. *The Possibilities of Charting Modern Life*. Oxford, New York: Pergamon Press.

Fillitz, Thomas 2003. "From the Dictate of Theories to Discourses on Theories – Teaching and Learning Social Anthropology in Vienna" in Dorle Dracklé, Iain R. Edgar, and Thomas Schippers, Eds. *Learning Fields* I: *Educational Histories of European Social Anthropology*. New York, Oxford: Berghahn Books, pp. 102–112.

Meladze, Nana. 2003. "The Past, Present and Uncertain Future of Georgian Ethnography" in Dorle Dracklé, Iain R. Edgar, and Thomas Schippers, Eds. *Learning Fields* I: *Educational Histories of European Social Anthropology*. New York, Oxford: Berghahn Books, pp. 220–229.

Mills, David. 2003. "Teaching the 'Uncomfortable Science.' Social Anthropology in British Universities" in Dorle Dracklé, Iain R. Edgar, and Thomas Schippers, Eds. *Learning Fields* I: *Educational Histories of European Social Anthropology*. New York, Oxford: Berghahn Books, pp. 8–22.

Rogan, Bjarne. 2003a. "Towards a Post-colonial and Post-national Museum. The Transformation of a French Museum Landscape." *Ethnologia Europaea* 33(1): 37–50.

Shelton, Alan Anthony. 2006. "Museums and Museum Displays" in Christopher Tilley, Webb Keane, Susanne Küchler, Mike Rowlands, and Patricia Spyer, Eds. *Handbook of Material Culture*. London: Sage, pp. 480–499.

ARCHIVAL SOURCES

Dias, Jorge s. a. 1951. Bericht über die ethnologische Forschung in Portugal. SE 8:77.

Filipovic, Milenko S. s. a. 1951. Entwicklung und heutiger Stand der Ethnologie in der föderativen Republik Jugoslawien. SE 8:77.

Meertens, Pieter J. s. a. 1951. The State of Folklore in the Netherlands. SE 8:77.

SE 8:77. Nordiska Museets arkiv, Sigurd Erixons samlingar, box 8:77.

INDEX

References to individual pieces of music, narrative etc. are entered by title followed by the country or culture of origin, for example "Fire on the Mountain" (United States).

A Companion to Folklore, First Edition. Edited by Regina F. Bendix and Galit Hasan-Rokem.
© 2012 John Wiley & Sons, Ltd. Published 2012 John Wiley & Sons, Ltd.